BUILDING AND ENGINEERING CONTRACTS

AUSTRALIA
The Law Book Company
Sydney

CANADA
The Carswell Company
Toronto, Ontario

INDIA
N. M. Tripathi Private Ltd
Bombay

Eastern Law House Private Ltd
Calcutta

M.P.P. House
Bangalore

Universal Book Traders
Delhi

ISRAEL
Steimatzky's Agency Ltd
Tel Aviv

PAKISTAN
Pakistan Law House
Karachi

Hudson's

BUILDING
AND ENGINEERING
CONTRACTS

Including the Duties and Liabilities of
ARCHITECTS, ENGINEERS AND SURVEYORS

TENTH EDITION

BY

I. N. DUNCAN WALLACE, M.A. OXON.
of the Middle Temple, Barrister-at-Law

LONDON
SWEET & MAXWELL
1970

First Edition	(1891)	By Alfred Hudson.			
Second Edition	(1895)	,,	,,	,,	
Third Edition	(1906)	,,	,,	,,	
Fourth Edition	(1914)	,,	,,	,,	
Fifth Edition	(1926)	By Alfred Hudson, K.C.			
Sixth Edition	(1933)	By Lawrence Mead.			
Seventh Edition	(1946)	,,	,,	,,	
Eighth Edition	(1959)	By E. J. Rimmer, Q.C., and I. N. Duncan Wallace.			
Second Impression	*(1960)*				
Ninth Edition	(1965)	By I. N. Duncan Wallace.			
Tenth Edition	(1970)	,,	,,	,,	,,
Second Impression	*(1974)*	,,	,,	,,	,,
Third Impression	*(1976)*	,,	,,	,,	,,
Fourth Impression	*(1977)*	,,	,,	,,	,,
Fifth Impression	*(1978)*	,,	,,	,,	,,
Sixth Impression	*(1980)*	,,	,,	,,	,,
Seventh Impression	*(1983)*	,,	,,	,,	,,
Eighth Impression	*(1984)*	,,	,,	,,	,,
Ninth Impression	*(1986)*	,,	,,	,,	,,
Tenth Impression	*(1989)*	,,	,,	,,	,,
Eleventh Impression	*(1991)*	,,	,,	,,	,,

Published by
Sweet & Maxwell Limited now of
South Quay Plaza, 183 Marsh Wall,
London E14 9FT and printed in
Great Britain

SBN 421 13210 8

GENERAL INTRODUCTION AND PREFACE

THIS tenth edition of *Hudson* is longer by one hundred and eighty-four pages, an increase in content of over a quarter, which for an already fairly comprehensive textbook, and after a lapse of only five years since its predecessor, is perhaps a little exceptional. Partly, this is due to quite new sections in Chapter 1 on the English Misrepresentation and Occupiers' Liability Acts; to a new section in Chapter 3 on " package-deal " or " industrialised-building " contracts, and the many references elsewhere in the book to the difficulties and anomalies these are producing in the absence of a proper form of contract for such situations; to a substantial revision and increase of the section on architects' and engineers' duties and other new material in Chapter 2 (including sections on copyright and on ownership of plans and documents and on consultant and associate architects and structural engineers), which means that the one hundred and fifteen pages of this chapter are virtually a separate textbook on the law relating to architects, engineers and quantity surveyors and their contracts of employment and remuneration; to a further increase in the section on practice and procedure in arbitrations in Chapter 18, which seems to fulfil a widely-felt need and is not, so far as I am aware, available in any other legal textbook; to new material in Chapter 9 on the economics of building contracts and the kind of damage suffered by a contractor when an employer's breach delays the work as a whole, and to a further section in the same chapter on the effects of inflation on the damages recoverable by an employer as a result of a contractor's breach; to a short treatment of *force majeure* and Act of God in Chapter 5, and a considerable increase in the section on Indemnities and Insurance in the same chapter; and to the need to deal in many parts of the text with the now rapidly spreading use in building projects of consultants such as structural engineers, often achieved by the highly unsatisfactory method of nominating sub-contractors to perform the services in question as well as to do the work or supply the materials involved—in effect a " sub-package-deal " situation.

But this is not the whole explanation. Since the last edition there have been two building cases dealing with the implied term of suitability—*i.e.*, the contractor's design obligation—which are of

v

immense importance in the wider field of contracts for work and materials generally, quite apart from their special impact in the field of building contracts. These two cases, namely the decision of Diplock L.J., as also upheld by the Court of Appeal, in *Hancock* v. *Brazier (Anerley) Ltd.* (1966),[1] and the decision of the House of Lords in *Young & Marten Ltd.* v. *McManus Childs Ltd.* (1969),[2] are to be unreservedly welcomed as greatly clarifying this vitally important obligation in its application to such contracts, and as finally and successfully harmonising the law in this field with that in the related field of contracts for the sale of goods. Two further closely related decisions of the House of Lords, namely *Gloucestershire County Council* v. *Richardson* (1969)[3] and *Bickerton* v. *N.W. Metropolitan Hospital Board* (1970),[4] in the rather more specialised field of the liability of the main contractor for the work of nominated sub-contractors and suppliers can, however, only be described as cases of the utmost difficulty, the implications and uncertainties of which, in an area of vital and everyday commercial importance, will in my view inevitably trouble the appellate courts and legal advisers in this country until they have been further clarified and explained.

The effect of these four cases, and the analysis and comment which I believe they call for, is that the treatment in Chapter 5 of the obligations of the contractor as to the design and quality of work and materials on the one hand, and of the employer as to the nomination of sub-contractors on the other, have occupied a further very substantial amount of additional text, so that the treatment of the implied terms of quality and suitability in contracts for work and materials in that chapter, particularly where sub-contracting is involved, is probably more detailed and lengthy than in any other textbook in this or other fields. The growth of specialisation, and hence of sub-contracting, in modern industrialised societies makes this one of the most important developing parts of modern contract law.

The two last-mentioned cases would in my view raise a difficulty for any textbook writer, but particularly so if the textbook is designed, as is *Hudson*, for use in Commonwealth and South African jurisdictions. They are, of course, binding in England but not outside England; and the policy I have adopted is to indicate

---

[1] [1966] 2 All E.R. 1 (Diplock L.J.); *ibid.* 901 (C.A.).
[2] [1969] 1 A.C. 454.
[3] [1969] 1 A.C. 480.
[4] [1970] 1 W.L.R. 607.

the difficulties; to state as carefully as possible the extent to which they are binding, until reconsidered, in England; and to indicate where and why it may seem advisable for other jurisdictions, after consideration, not to follow them.[5] In the same way I have not hesitated to indicate decisions outside England which seem wrong in principle, or out of line with the English cases or the practicalities of the parties' situation—*e.g.*, the decision of the Appellate Division of the Supreme Court of South Africa in *Kollberg* v. *Cape Town Municipality* (1967),[6] of the Court of Appeal of New Zealand in *Major* v. *Greenfield* (1965),[7] and of the High Court of Australia in *Florida Hotels Ltd.* v. *Mayo* (1965).[8]

The law on building and engineering contracts can derive immense benefit from this process of international comparison, partly because the practical situation and needs of the parties are much the same in all such contracts, partly because, even outside the Commonwealth, the English language is so often used in international contracts, and partly because the actual forms of contracts are modelled so closely upon each other and upon English forms. Furthermore, in a field where judges are not infrequently unfamiliar with the way in which a building or engineering project is operated and administered, and in which the forms of contract are a compound of archaic legal language and sheer bad draftsmanship, the likelihood of decisions which are anomalous and difficult is increased. This possibility in England is certainly not lessened by the practice in the High Court, in those few cases which reach it after penetrating or avoiding the net of arbitration, of almost invariably remitting such cases for trial by an Official Referee, notwithstanding that they often involve considerably larger sums of money, on a *per diem* basis of judicial time, than a very large proportion of the usual business of the High Court, and notwithstanding that important points of law may be involved which will govern or affect literally thousands of other commercial transactions using similar or identical forms of contract. In consequence, it must be said that a large proportion of the English judiciary have, with some notable exceptions, little or no previous experience in building contracts or situations when called on to deal with the small residue of litigation, nearly always difficult, which does reach them, and the Official Referees in England are

---

[5] See Chap. 5, pp. 304, 335–336.
[6] 1967 (3) S.A. 472; Chap. 18, pp. 821–822.
[7] [1965] N.Z.L.R. 1035; Chap. 7, p. 445.
[8] (1965) 113 C.L.R. 588; Chap. 1, pp. 74–75; Chap. 2, p. 153.

inevitably more experienced in the realities of building-contract situations than the High Court judges. As an example, apart altogether from the difficulties of law involved in the case, it is difficult for this writer at least to feel that the learned Official Referee's views of the secondary facts in *Gloucestershire County Council* v. *Richardson* were not to be preferred to those of a unanimous (on this point) Court of Appeal and House of Lords.[9] This familiarity with the commercial situation on which a contract is designed to operate is in my view an essential prerequisite, at least under English rules of evidence, for the correct interpretation of a badly drafted or ambiguous contract, and the absence of such judicial knowledge is the greatest single cause of " difficult " decisions in the courts.

Perhaps two heresies could be mentioned which lie at the root of nearly all the modern difficult decisions. The first is the not unforgivable impression that the architect or engineer is the " captain of the ship," and that if things go wrong or unexpected events occur it is his duty to assume command and issue fresh instructions to the contractor, and indeed that it is his duty to detect and rectify defective work of the contractor. Contractors have not been slow to appreciate the potential financial advantage to themselves of this view, and have sedulously sought in recent years to encourage its adoption by the courts in seeking to elevate any such duty into one owed to them by the employer. Such a view is in fact wholly inconsistent with a hundred years of building cases and the basic commercial reality of the inclusive price for a building project and, if accepted, would turn the employer into the contractor's insurer, robbing the contract price of all certainty; but the contrary view was unfortunately treated as so self-evident by the courts in the past (and indeed by contractors themselves when presenting claims) that it found little or no overt expression in the judgments or indeed in *Hudson*, except in more extreme cases which led, for example, to claims by contractors that the contract had been frustrated. I have accordingly re-emphasised the law and authorities on this vitally important aspect wherever relevant in the text.[10] The second heresy is the equally forgivable first impression that the system of nomination of sub-contractors owes its origin to the need of the employer to control the *quality* of the work in question; when in fact the need may more often be to secure a *competitive price* for

---

[9] See Chap. 8, pp. 527–528.
[10] See *e.g.* Chap 1, pp. 68–70; Chap. 2, pp. 139–141, 153–155; Chap. 5, pp. 324–325; Chap. 8, pp. 524–530; Chap. 9, pp. 582–583.

it within the practical exigencies of main-contractor tendering. I have felt it necessary, in the light of recent decisions, to explain and emphasise this for the first time in *Hudson*.[11]

To add to the list of difficult cases, another decision which, if correct, is potentially disastrous to the underlying commercial realities of all building and engineering contracts, as at present drafted, is that of Megarry J. in *Twickenham Gardens Developments* v. *Hounslow B.C.* (1970), where he held that a contractor whose employment had been determined under a clause in the contract had an irrevocable right, in the form of an irrevocable contractual licence, to remain on the site, and could not be removed by injunction pending the trial of the issue whether the contractual termination was justified or not. This case is, however, under appeal to the Court of Appeal; and Megarry J.'s judgment was given while *Hudson* was in a late stage of proofs, so in consequence, while the decision has been noted, the relevant text has as yet not been altered.

It is in fact fascinating and rewarding to see the process of cross-reference between jurisdictions at work—see for instance the English cases on the invalidation of liquidated damages clauses, followed by the Court of Appeal of British Colombia in *Perini Pacific Ltd.* v. *Greater Vancouver Sewerage* (1966),[12] the excellent summary of the English cases on the status and duties of certifiers by Banks J. in *Kollberg* v. *Cape Town Municipality* (1966),[13] and the meticulous (and in my view best available) definition of completion in building and engineering contracts, not so clearly expressed in the House of Lords in *City of Westminster* v. *Jarvis* (1970),[14] given by the trial judge and adopted by the Supreme Court of Victoria in *Morgan* v. *S. and S. Construction Ltd.* (1967).[15] By far the best modern case on the remuneration of quantity surveyors on a total remeasurement of work, and of the relationship between scales and reasonable remuneration, is a decision of the Court of Appeal of Jamaica in *Kelly* v. *Northshore Development* (1963).[16] Again, the cases of *McKone* v. *Johnson* (1966)[17] in New South Wales, and the decision of the Supreme Court of Canada in *Steel Company of Canada Ltd.* v. *Willand Management Ltd.*

[11] See Chap. 15, p. 757.
[12] (1966) 57 D.L.R. (2d) 307.
[13] 1966 (3) S.A. 471.
[14] [1970] 1 W.L.R. 637.
[15] [1967] V.R. 147 (Australia).
[16] (1963) 5 W.I.R. 379.
[17] [1966] 2 N.S.W.R. 471.

(1966) [18] are of invaluable assistance in illustrating a contractor's design liabilities; the decision of the Ontario Court of Appeal in *Tannenbaum Meadows Ltd.* v. *Wright Winston Ltd.*[19] raises on its facts the first clear example of an acceptance by a building owner of defective or incomplete work which would render him liable to pay the contract price less any relevant set-off; and the decision of the Court of Appeal of British Columbia in *Imperial Glass Ltd.* v. *Consolidated Supplies Ltd.* (1960) [20] is a fascinating case on the law of mistake. But these are only a few of the interesting and valuable decisions from the Commonwealth and South African jurisdictions reported or included since the last edition of this book.

The two cases of *Hoffman* v. *Meyer* [21] and *Sandy* v. *Yukon Construction Ltd.*[22] in which Ogilvie-Thompson J. in South Africa and the Supreme Court of Alberta refused to follow (in my view rightly) two different decisions of the Court of Appeal in England, and the outstandingly useful decisions of Richmond J. in New Zealand in *Hatrick* v. *Nelson Carlton Construction,*[23] of the Court of Appeal of South Africa in *Concrete Construction Ltd.* v. *Keidan,*[24] of the High Court of Australia in *Carr* v. *J. A. Berriman Ltd.*[25] and of the High Court of Queensland in *Voli* v. *Inglewood Shire Council* [26] have previously been mentioned in the Preface to the Ninth Edition.

This book is not intended solely for lawyers—indeed the majority of its readers are probably involved in the industry itself in one capacity or another. In consequence, in the interests of readability and clarity, there is an element of repetition of various points where different subjects are dealt with. The cross-referencing by way of footnote is now, however, very substantial (there were very few footnotes prior to the Eighth Edition). Furthermore, the book is as concerned to inform lawyers and others of the factual background of building and engineering contracts as it is to explain and set out the law itself since, as already stated, I regard the two as mutually interdependent and essential for the true interpretation of building and engineering contracts, particularly in the light of their usually indifferent draftsmanship.

[18] [1966] S.C.R. 746 (Canada).
[19] (1965) 49 D.L.R. (2d) 386.
[20] (1960) 22 D.L.R. (2d) 759.
[21] 1956 (2) S.A. 752.
[22] (1961) 26 D.L.R. (2d) 254.
[23] [1964] N.Z.L.R. 72.
[24] 1955 (4) S.A. 315.
[25] [1953] A.L.J. 273.
[26] (1963) 56 Q.L.R. 256.

I cannot end this already long Preface without a reference to the unsatisfactory character of the standard forms at present in use in England. The policy and traditional inherited draftsmanship of these forms appeared to me to be so defective at so many points that in the Ninth Edition I felt it necessary in the public interest to bring the more glaring instances of this fully into the open, both in the text of *Hudson* at all relevant points and in the Preface, where I dealt with the matter at some length. I have subsequently developed these criticisms in much greater detail in the introduction and text of my Commentary on the Standard Forms published in 1969. It is reassuring to have received formidable judicial support: " The difficulties arise solely because of the unnecessarily amorphous and tortuous provisions of the R.I.B.A. contract; those difficulties have for a number of years been known to exist and if, as was stated at the Bar, no relevant amendments have been made in the latest edition of the contract, the position reflects no credit on the R.I.B.A. . . . I return to my earlier criticism of the form of contract and emphasise that it seems lamentable that such a form used to govern so many and such important activities throughout the country, should be so deviously drafted with what in parts can only be a calculated lack of forthright clarity. The time has now come for the whole to be completely redrafted so that laymen— contractors and building owners alike—can understand what are their own duties and obligations and what are those of the architect." [27] " It was a new form: it was the 1963 edition and it had predecessors, so that one would suppose that experience would have produced a practical workable form dealing with all the matters shown to be material for the purposes of employers and the main contractors and sub-contractors who would be concerned with the working out of the contract. Unfortunately for this Court, it has produced problems which have given this Court, as well as other Courts in the past, difficulties of interpretation which defy the experienced intelligence of the counsel concerned with these matters and even more the efforts of the Courts concerned, to give a reasonable and clear meaning to the terms of the contract. It is an extraordinary thing that nowhere in the elaborate contract and conditions is there a clear and positive provision requiring the architect to nominate sub-contractors. . . . It is only as a matter of inference that the necessity of such nomination can be dis-

[27] *Per* Sachs L.J. in *Bickerton* v. *N.W. Metropolitan Hospital Board* [1967] 1 All E.R. 977 at pp. 979, 989.

covered." [28]   " Paragraph (g) is highly anomalous, and would appear to have been included in this form of contract without any regard to the manifest injustice and, indeed, absurdity implicit in it. It is, in my view, unjust and absurd because . . . it leaves the employers to bear the loss caused by a delay for which they are in no way to blame and allows the party at fault . . . to escape from the liability which they would otherwise justly have to bear." [29] " It is indeed curious that in this form of contract issued by the R.I.B.A. and approved by members of many other bodies one should find a provision under which a sub-contractor can benefit from its own default." [30]   " Such an illogical consequence suggests that the condition which creates it has been inserted and drafted without any clear appreciation of its purpose or scope . . . a serious reflection on the clause; indeed I cannot believe that the professional body, realising how defective this clause is, will allow it to remain in its present form." [31]   " The form of this contract has been much criticised during the course of the argument—and not without justification. Indeed, if a prize were to be offered for the form of a building contract which contained the most one-sided, obscurely and ineptly drafted clauses in the United Kingdom, the claim of this contract could hardly be ignored, even if the R.I.B.A. form of contract was amongst the competitors." [32]

In spite of these stinging criticisms, there is as yet no sign of reform of the R.I.B.A. forms. Criticisms of the policy of the R.I.B.A. forms will be found in the text in the more important instances, e.g., on the grounds stipulated for the contractor's right to forfeiture generally [33] and the ground of force majeure in particular,[34] on the right to an extension of time for sub-contractor's delays,[35] and on the finality of the final certificate.[36] But there are many further grounds of criticism inevitably not noticed in an overall work on building contracts, which are developed in detail in my commentary on the Standard Forms.

It is, in my view, not only important in the public interest that

---

[28] Per Danckwerts L.J., ibid. at p. 996.
[29] Per Salmon L.J. in Jarvis v. Westminster Corporation (C.A.) [1969] 1 W.L.R. 1448 at p. 1458.
[30] Per Viscount Dilhorne, ibid. (H.L.) [1970] 1 W.L.R. 637 at p. 645.
[31] Per Lord Wilberforce, ibid. at pp. 649, 650.
[32] Per Salmon L.J. in Peak Construction Ltd. v. McKinney Foundations Ltd. (C.A.), July 1, 1970.
[33] e.g. at pp. 343 and 682.
[34] At p. 350.
[35] At p. 651.
[36] At pp. 489–492.

these matters should be ventilated (since only specialist practitioners are likely to appreciate the practical consequences of and policy underlying what are often indirect and complicated details of draftsmanship) but it is also important that those studying this subject should appreciate that the startling results that English cases so often produce today are usually the consequence of forms of contract expressly designed, as a result of commercial pressures which the R.I.B.A. appears to be powerless to resist, to avoid the results which would follow if a reasonable balance of interest between the parties was to be the overriding factor, or (which really is the same thing) if ordinary rules of construction and of the implication of terms were to apply. The last conclusion that any observer outside England should reach is that the English standard forms are calculated to produce a fair or just balance between the parties. As a result of the publicity accorded to the latest judicial decisions and pronouncements in England, and in the light of the fact that all the judicial criticisms quoted above relate to matters noticed and commented upon in *Hudson* during its last two editions over a number of years, it seems to me that the stage has now been reached where architects and others recommending the R.I.B.A. standard forms to their clients in unmodified form should be held liable for professional negligence if damage or loss to the employer ensues, and I have included a special short section in Chapter 2, in the context of the architect's duties to the employer, giving the reasons for this view.[37]

The preceding comments relate to the R.I.B.A. forms. The standard engineering contract in England, the I.C.E. form, is open to criticism less in regard to its deliberate policies than to the appalling uncertainty and confusion of its language. Unfortunately, this lack of clarity is present in undiminished degree in the crucial parts of the contract regulating the legal effect to be given in the bills of quantities, with the result that, notwithstanding that engineering work is of its nature and to the knowledge of the parties inherently far more uncertain and unpredictable than building work, massive claims for additional payment are constantly being advanced by contractors wherever the quantities differ *in either direction* from those billed, even where specific attention to the likelihood of this occurring is made in the specification or by billing the items of work concerned as provisional quantities in the bills. This lack of clarity in the contract is coupled with an apparent

---

[37] pp. 146–148. See also pp. 141–142.

constitutional inability of engineering arbitrators, even of the greatest distinction, to apply the contract strictly and disallow unmerited claims, whether of this kind or under the important clause 12 provision permitting claims for unforeseeable unfavourable conditions.[38] It must be said that a situation is developing in England where, on major engineering works, reputable and efficient contractors who make an accurate assessment of the various contingencies affecting a project, and price accordingly, have little prospect of being successful when tendering, while inefficient or rash contractors secure a disproportionate amount of work and constantly arbitrate unmerited claims, sometimes virtually as a matter of commercial policy. The result is that in engineering contracts, notwithstanding that the work has not been varied and that no breach of contract is alleged, the contract price no longer, as a practical matter, appears to carry any certainty. While this may be excellent from the point of view of the legal practitioners likely to be involved in such litigation, there is little doubt that the public interest would be far better served by a clearer form of contract and by a judicial attitude of arbitrators unaffected by their apparently irrepressible instincts for compromise; since an employer will always prefer to know the true extent of his commitments beforehand rather than undertake an apparent commitment at an unrealistic price and only ascertain the true extent of the price after the expense, inconvenience, loss of professional time, and uncertainties of arbitration or litigation have either been incurred, or discounted in the form of some equally unsatisfactory compromise settlement. The remedies for this state of affairs lie in a new form of contract provided by the Institution of Civil Engineers with the emphasis on clarity, and with a change of attitude by engineering arbitrators; far from being an advantage or fair to the contracting side, the present situation is desperately unfair to the experienced and efficient contractor and benefits only the less efficient and least scrupulous.

The law is here stated as at March 1970 in England. A number of judgments in England occurring or reported since that date and which are of the greatest importance have, wherever possible, been noticed at least by reference up till July 1970. I hope some indulgence will be permitted in regard to recent Commonwealth and South African decisions; and as stated in previous prefaces, I am always grateful to hear from practitioners and others, whether inside or outside England, of any interesting decisions which might

[38] See for comments on this attitude pp. 502, 569, 856 and 868.

merit inclusion in future editions. I also welcome and am most grateful for notification by any legal practitioner anywhere of any interesting unreported cases, which it has always been the policy of this work, since the original Volume II of the Fourth Edition, to incorporate in the text or as illustrations.

I am indebted to my colleague in Chambers, Mr. Nicholas Harington, for the preparation of the index.

I. N. DUNCAN WALLACE.

September 1970.

CONTENTS

TABLE OF CASES

(Pages in **heavy** type refer to illustrations in which the facts of the case are set out.)

TABLE OF STATUTES

lxiii

TABLE OF REFERENCES
TO
R.I.B.A. CONTRACT FORM CONDITIONS
(*1963 (Private) Edition*)

TABLE OF REFERENCES
TO
R.I.B.A. CONTRACT FORM CONDITIONS
(*Pre-1963 Editions*)

(References are to the 1939 (1957 Revised) Edition,
except where otherwise stated)

TABLE OF REFERENCES
TO
I.C.E. CONTRACT FORM CONDITIONS

(4th Edition, 1955)

lxviii

CHAPTER 1

GENERAL PRINCIPLES OF LAW

INTRODUCTION

A BUILDING or engineering contract may be defined, for the purposes of this book, as an agreement under which a person, in this book called variously the builder or contractor, undertakes for reward to carry out for another person, variously referred to as the building owner or employer, works of a building or civil engineering character. In the typical case, the work will be carried out upon the land of the employer or building owner, though in some special cases obligations to build may arise by contract where this is not so—*e.g.* under building leases, and contracts for the sale of land with a house in the course of erection upon it.[1]

At the present time, the majority of the more substantial building and engineering projects in the United Kingdom are designed by a professional adviser of the employer, and are usually supervised and administered on the employer's behalf by this adviser during the currency of the work. This relatively sophisticated arrangement has important legal consequences, since in general the employer places far less reliance under such a contract upon the skill or judgment of the contractor in relation to the design of the work or choice of materials or their suitability for their purpose, and this will have an important effect on the terms to be implied in the contract and on the interpretation of its express terms.[2] The standard forms of contract recommended by the various bodies in the industry in the United Kingdom have, for many years, only contemplated this type of arrangement, and make express provision for the employer's adviser to carry out important administrative and other functions under the terms of the contract. As a result much, though not all, of the more modern law on building and engineering contracts has grown up around this now traditional arrangement, and it is perhaps advisable to point out that the present tendency to return to the older, more primitive arrangement, whereby the contractor not only carries out but also designs the work, generally known as the " package deal,"

---

[1] See *post*, Chap. 5, pp. 279, 281, 289–290.
[2] See particularly *post*, Chap. 5, pp. 278 *et seq.*

means that the body of law applicable to the traditional arrangement may need considerable modification.

The most commonly used standard forms in the United Kingdom are, in the building industry, those generally known as " the R.I.B.A. forms," which are issued " under the sanction of " the Royal Institute of British Architects and a number of other bodies including the National Federation of Building Trades Employers, the associated " F.A.S.S." form of sub-contract issued under the sanction of the National Federation and of the Federation of Associations of Specialists and Sub-Contractors, and, in the civil engineering industry, the conditions usually known as " the I.C.E. Conditions " issued by the Institute of Civil Engineers, also under the sanction of the contracting side of the industry. There is some misunderstanding of the provenance of these forms, which are negotiated by the contractors' representatives with the Institutions concerned, and which therefore represent the outcome of conflicting commercial pressures and interests. Notwithstanding that the policy and wording of the forms are coming under increasing (and deserved) judicial criticism [3] in the United Kingdom, there is still a tendency to treat the forms as emanating from the employer. or his representatives and, particularly since the method of placing contracts by tender requires an initial stipulation of the contractual provisions by the employer, to apply the *contra proferentem* rule of construction against the employer when seeking to resolve their many ambiguities and discrepancies.[4] In fact very considerable direct and indirect pressure is brought to bear on all employers to use those forms by the contracting sides of the industries, and it is submitted that it is unrealistic to apply any such rule to the interpretation of the forms.

In regard to " package deal " contracts, no standard form is available in the United Kingdom at present, and attempts to use modified or existing standard forms in such situations are likely to create serious difficulties. An indication of some of the respects in which these contracts are likely to differ from the traditional arrangement is given in Chapter 3.[5] It must be said that the advocates of

[3] See *e.g.* by Sachs, Danckwerts and Edmund Davies L.JJ., in *Bickerton Ltd.* v. *N.W. Metropolitan Hospital Board* [1969] 1 All E.R. 977 at pp. 979, 991 and 996, by Salmon and Edmund Davies L.JJ. in *Jarvis* v. *Westminster Corporation* [1969] 1 W.L.R. 1448 at p. 1458, by Viscount Dilhorne in *East Ham B.C.* v. *Bernard Sunley* [1966] A.C. 406 at p. 423, and by Mocatta J. in *A.M.F. International* v. *Magnet Bowling* [1968] 1 W.L.R. 1028 at p. 1054.
[4] See *e.g. per* Edmund Davies L.J. in *Jarvis* v. *Westminster Corporation* [1969] 1 W.L.R. 1448 at p. 1456.
[5] *Post,* pp. 207 *et seq.*

these new arrangements appear to be largely unaware of the serious conflict of interest between employer and contractor, inherent in such contracts, in regard to design, or for the need, in order to combat it, of the most rigorous contractual protection for the employer in that regard. Furthermore, such contracts, by reason of the virtual impossibility of devising methods for genuinely comparing tenders, present problems of cost evaluation which are almost beyond resolution, in spite of efforts, by interested parties, to assert the contrary. In general, in the United Kingdom the experience obtained with this type of arrangement has to date been an unhappy one, and has been exacerbated by the absence of any readily available form of contract, and by the refusal of the contracting side of industry to depart substantially from the traditional forms of contract in a " package deal " or " industrialised building " situation, or to give the necessary long-term warranties, suitably bonded, as to the design of their work.

The contracts of employment of the architects, engineers or quantity surveyors who, under the traditional arrangements, generally advise the employer in the preparation and supervision of building contracts, are dealt with in Chapter 2. These contracts are much more rarely contained in formal written documents than the building contracts themselves. Another class of contracts with which this book is necessarily concerned are the numerous sub-contracts, whether for supply of materials only or for the carrying out of work, which every building or engineering contractor is, in practice, likely to make. Special problems peculiar to these are dealt with specifically in Chapter 15.

For the benefit of those readers of this book who are not legally qualified, it is proposed in the present chapter to give an account of the general principles of law relating to the formation of contractual obligations, with special regard to rules which may be relevant in considering the disputes likely to occur in practice between parties to a building and engineering contract. Sections on tortious and ex-contractual liability are also included.

More detailed treatment of many of the matters discussed in this chapter and their particular application to building and engineering contracts will be found in later chapters, particularly Chapter 3, Tenders and Estimates, Chapter 5, Performance, Chapter 8, Variations, Chapter 9, Price and Damages, and Chapter 10, Time for Performance. The discharge of contracts by frustration, breach or illegality is only incidentally noticed in this chapter, and is dealt with more fully in Chapter 5. Chapter 5 is, indeed, the main residual chapter in which the basic obligations of building contracts, including most of the important implied terms, completion and substantial performance, and certain important but detailed subjects, such as limitation of actions, insurance and indemnities, are discussed.

SECTION 1. CLASSIFICATION OF CONTRACTS

The traditional classification of contracts divides them into two types, contracts made by deed, known as contracts under seal, and simple contracts.

Undertakings contained in contracts under seal depend for their validity solely upon the form of the contract and not upon the existence of an agreement between the parties or upon the presence of consideration. Damages for breach of an undertaking given by one party (the covenantor) to another (the covenantee) and embodied in a deed may be recovered by the covenantee against the covenantor, notwithstanding that the covenantee gives no undertaking in return (or that the undertaking which he gives is void).

A simple contract does not, in general, require to be in any particular form. It may be oral, or in writing, or partly oral and partly in writing. The undertaking or promise forming part of a simple contract is enforceable beoause it forms part of an agreement between the parties and is supported by consideration; that is to say, it is given in return for some promise or conduct by the other party to the contract, which is either a detriment to that party or is a benefit to the party giving the promise to be enforced.

If the formalities necessary for the proper execution of a deed are not observed, a contract under seal is not enforceable as such. If it is a building contract, however, it will almost invariably be enforceable as a simple contract, since all the necessary elements of a simple contract will be present. Although, historically, legal obligation arising by covenant under seal is older than obligation arising under simple contract, the latter now forms the basis of the law of contract and is therefore more conveniently considered first.

In the employer's interest, building contracts should invariably be under seal, since by virtue of section 2 of the Limitation Act 1939 this automatically extends the period of limitation from six to twelve years from the date of a breach of contract, and since defective work by a builder is frequently not discovered on completion, or within the six-year period.

Section 2. Formation of a Simple Contract

(1) Elements of a Simple Contract

A simple contract is constituted by an offer made by one party and accepted by the other. The resulting agreement is, however, only enforceable as a contract if the promises it comprises are supported by consideration. If a builder were to offer to build a house without payment, even though the offer were expressly accepted, no enforceable contract would result, since there would be no consideration, or *quid pro quo*, for the promise to build the house—otherwise if the promise were contained in a deed. An accepted offer to do building work may, of course, make no mention of price, as for instance in small jobbing contracts or repair works, but this does not mean that consideration is not present and wherever the offer is made and accepted in circumstances in which an intention to pay and be paid can be inferred, the law implies a promise to pay a reasonable price for the work. Cases can arise in practice, however, where it may be difficult to decide whether a promise to pay will be implied, and some examples of these are given in the subsection on Consideration.[6]

(2) Offer

An offer must be something which invites, and is intended by the offeror to invite, acceptance, and must be sufficiently definite to be capable of resulting in a contract if accepted. There is, however, no requirement that the word " offer " must be used and an offer is no less an offer because some other word such as " estimate " or " quotation " or even " order " or " acceptance " is used.[7] Thus a main contractor will frequently place his " order " " accepting " the quotation which a nominated sub-contractor has previously supplied in reply to an invitation from the architect, but generally, since the original quotation was not given to him, the " order " will only rank as an offer by the main contractor, until accepted by acknowledgment or by conduct, for instance by the sub-contractor starting work.[8] An offer is to be distinguished from a mere invitation to treat.

" In cases in which you offer to negotiate, or you issue advertisements that you have got a stock of books to sell, or houses to let . . .

---

[6] *Infra*, subs. (8), pp. 17–19. See also *post*, Chap. 2, pp. 179–180.

[7] *Crowshaw* v. *Pritchard* (1899) 16 T.L.R. 45.

[8] See *Davies & Co. Shopfitters* v. *William Old* (1969) 67 L.G.R. 395, *infra*, p. 12.

there is no offer to be bound by any contract. Such advertisements
are offers to negotiate—offers to receive offers—offers to chaffer, as I
think some learned judge in one of the cases has said." [9]

An invitation to tender given by a prospective employer to
building contractors is a mere invitation to negotiate with the
persons who reply, and not an offer to make a contract with the
contractor whose tender is the lowest, or with any contractor at all.
It is usual for such an invitation to state that the employer does not
bind himself to accept the lowest or any tender, though such a reservation is an excess of caution, for advertising for or inviting tenders
is a mere attempt to ascertain whether an offer can be obtained
within such a margin as the employer is willing to accept.[10]   Invitations to tender in building and engineering contracts are invariably,
and necessarily, expressly drafted, however, to obtain firm offers
capable of immediate binding acceptance if the employer is so
minded.

A simple advertisement, announcing that it is intended to hold
an auction sale, constitutes no contract between the advertiser and
the highest bidder that the goods shall be sold to him, nor between
the advertiser and any intending purchaser that the goods shall be
put up for sale at all.[11]   To advertise, however, that goods will be sold
" without reserve " or to the highest bidder does constitute a
binding obligation upon the advertiser to sell, and to sell to the
highest bidder.[12] " A vendor who offers property for sale by auction
on the terms of printed conditions can be made liable to a member
of the public who accepts the offer if those conditions be violated." [13]

Furthermore, if a sale of property by auction is advertised by a
person who has no intention of selling, an action will lie against
him in tort for deceit by a person who, in reliance upon the truth
of the advertisement, incurs expense in inspecting and valuing the
property.[14]   It is submitted later in this work [15] that a person who
issues fraudulent invitations to tender would be similarly liable to
a contractor who incurred expense in submitting a tender.   The
contractor's remedy would not, however, be founded upon any
contract, but would arise in tort from the fraudulent representation.

[9] *Carlill* v. *Carbolic Smoke Ball Co.* [1893] 1 Q.B. 256 at p. 268, *per* Bowen L.J.
[10] See *post*, Chap. 3, pp. 216 *et seq.*, Tenders and Estimates, where this subject is more
     fully discussed.
[11] *Harris* v. *Nickerson* (1873) L.R. 8 Q.B. 286.
[12] *Warlow* v. *Harrison* (1859) 1 E. & E. 309; *Johnston* v. *Boyes* [1899] 2 Ch. 73.
[13] *Ibid.* at p. 77, *per* Cozens-Hardy J.
[14] *Richardson* v. *Silvester* (1873) L.R. 9 Q.B. 34.
[15] See *post*, Chap. 3, p. 229.

On the other hand, when an employer invites an architect to prepare plans for the erection of a building, and the architect does so, there will usually be a binding contract and the employer will have to pay for the architect's services even if he does not use the plans. Further, in certain circumstances this may be so even if the architect knows that he is in competition with other architects and that only one of their plans will be used.[16]

If, however, a request for tenders expressly states that the lowest tender will be accepted, it will, if sufficiently definite in other respects, constitute a true offer, so as to produce a concluded contract between the employer and the lowest tenderer. But more usually, it is the tender submitted in response to an invitation to submit tenders which is the offer and which, if accepted by the employer, will result in a binding contract. In every case the exact circumstances and language used must be carefully examined.

ILLUSTRATIONS

(1) The defendants issued a circular stating that they were instructed to offer certain goods for sale by tender. The plaintiff sent in a tender which was the highest, but the defendant refused to sell his goods to him. *Held*, that the circular was a mere proclamation that the defendants were ready to negotiate for the sale of the goods: *Spencer* v. *Harding* (1870).[17]

(2) H. telegraphed to F.: " Will you sell us Bumper Hall Pen ? Telegraph lowest cash price." F. telegraphed in reply: " Lowest price for Bumper Hall Pen £900." H. telegraphed: " We agree to buy Bumper Hall Pen for the sum of £900 asked by you." *Held*, that F.'s telegram was a mere statement of the lowest price and not an offer to sell capable of being accepted by H. so as to constitute a contract: *Harvey* v. *Facey* (1893).[18]

(3) B. advertised a public-house for sale under conditions providing that the highest bidder should be the purchaser and should pay an immediate deposit of 10 per cent. J. made the highest bid, but could not pay the deposit in cash, but only by cheque, and B. refused to sell to J. *Held*, that had J. been able to pay the deposit in cash, B. would have been bound to sell the property to him: *Johnston* v. *Boyes* (1899).[19]

(4) P. wrote to C.: " Estimate—Our estimate to carry out the . . . alterations to the above premises according to the drawings and specifications amounts to £1,230." C. replied accepting the estimate. *Held*, that the estimate was an offer accepted by C.'s letter; that there

[16] *Landless* v. *Wilson* (1880) 8 R. (Ct. of Sess.) 289 and see *post*, Chap. 2, pp. 180–182.
[17] L.R. 5 C.P. 561.
[18] [1893] A.C. 552.
[19] [1899] 2 Ch. 73.

was no custom that a letter in the form of an estimate was not to be treated as an offer and that such a custom would be contrary to law: *Crowshaw* v. *Pritchard* (1899).[20]

(3) Withdrawal of an Offer

An offer may be accepted at any time after it has been made, unless before it is accepted—

(a) it is expressly withdrawn: or

(b) it is rejected: or

(c) it is revoked by a counter-offer: or

(d) it lapses by effluxion of time.

The withdrawal of an offer takes effect from the time when it comes to the notice of the offeree; a mere uncommunicated change of mind by the offeror has no effect. If a withdrawal is posted, it takes effect, not from the time of posting, as does an acceptance, where this method of acceptance is contemplated,[21] but from the time of its receipt by the offeree.[22] " Both legal principle and practical convenience require that a person who has accepted an offer not known to him to have been revoked, shall be in a position safely to act upon the footing that the offer and acceptance constitute a contract binding on both parties." [23] It does not appear to be necessary that the offeror should himself communicate his withdrawal to the offeree; it is enough if the offeree in fact learns of the withdrawal from some other reliable source.[24]

An offeror may undertake to keep his offer open for a certain period. Upon the expiry of this period the offer lapses and can no longer be accepted. The offer can, however, be withdrawn at any time, notwithstanding that the period has not expired, unless the undertaking to keep the offer open was given for valuable consideration, so that there exists a separate contract in the nature of an option.[25] It would also appear that an offer expressed to remain open for a certain period, if made under seal, is irrevocable, since no consideration is necessary to support it.

If the offeree does not accept the offer as it stands, but either rejects it or purports to accept it with the addition or subtraction of some term, the offer lapses and is not thereafter capable of acceptance, unless renewed by the offeror.[26] A distinction must, however,

---

[20] Hudson's B.C., 4th ed., Vol. 2, p. 274.
[21] See *infra*, p. 11.
[22] *Byrne* v. *Van Tienhoven* (1880) 5 C.P.D. 344.
[23] *Ibid.* at p. 348, *per* Lindley J.
[24] *Dickinson* v. *Dodds* (1876) 2 Ch.D. 463; *Cartwright* v. *Hoogstoel* (1911) 105 L.T. 628.
[25] *Dickinson* v. *Dodds, supra.*
[26] *Hyde* v. *Wrench* (1840) 3 Beav. 334.

be made between a counter-offer and a mere request for information, which does not amount to a rejection of the original offer.[27]

An offer lapses after a reasonable time and cannot thereafter be accepted. What is a reasonable time is to be determined in the light of all the circumstances.[28]

ILLUSTRATIONS

(1) The defendant offered to buy a house from the plaintiff and to give the plaintiff six weeks for a definite answer. *Held*, that the defendant might retract the offer at any time before acceptance, although the six weeks had not expired: *Routledge* v. *Grant* (1828).[29]

(2) The defendant offered to sell his farm to the plaintiff for £1,000: the plaintiff in reply offered to pay £950, which the defendant refused. The plaintiff then wrote to the defendant agreeing to pay £1,000, to which the defendant made no reply. *Held*, the plaintiff by making an offer of £950 had rejected the defendant's offer of £1,000 and could not thereafter revive and accept it: *Hyde* v. *Wrench* (1840).[30]

(3) By letter dated October 1, the defendants wrote from Cardiff to the plaintiffs in New York offering to sell certain goods. The plaintiffs received the letter on October 11 and accepted the offer by telegram on the same day. On October 8 the defendants posted a letter to the plaintiffs, which reached them on the 20th, withdrawing their offer. *Held*, that the withdrawal of the offer by the letter of the 8th was ineffective, a binding contract having been concluded on the 11th by the sending of the telegram when the plaintiffs had no reason to think that the offer of the 1st had been withdrawn: *Byrne* v. *Van Tienhoven* (1880).[31]

(4) After discussions, an excavation sub-contractor asked the main contractor to confirm an agreed special definition of rock in writing, and at the same time submitted his own prices in writing. It was known to both parties that the employer had previously made difficulties about the definition. The main contractor did not confirm the definition in writing, but purported to accept the quotation, sending a standard form of sub-contract for the purpose. The sub-contractor withdrew and refused to proceed since he no longer wanted the contract. The main contractor argued that there was a concluded contract, including the agreed definition of rock. *Held*, by the Ontario Court of Appeal (McGillivray J.A. dissenting), that the confirmation in writing was a condition and not a mere incident

---

[27] See *Stevenson* v. *McLean* (1880) 5 Q.B.D. 346. See also the dissenting judgment of McGillivray J.A. in *Pigott Structures Ltd.* v. *Keillor Construction Co.* (1965) 50 D.L.R. (2d) 97 (Canada).

[28] *Metropolitan Asylums Board (Managers)* v. *Kingham and Sons* (1890) 6 T.L.R. 217; *Ramsgate Hotel Co.* v. *Montefiore* (1866) L.R. 1 Ex. 109. See also *post*, Chap. 3, p. 225, where the matter is further discussed.

[29] 4 Bing. 656.

[30] 3 Beav. 334.

[31] 5 C.P.D. 344.

of the agreement, and till it was given there was no agreement and
the sub-contractor could withdraw: *Pigott Structures Ltd.* v. *Keillor
Construction Co.* (1965).[32]

(4) Death of Offeror or Offeree

There is some doubt whether an offer can be accepted after the
death of the offeror, but it is clear that an offeree cannot accept after
he has knowledge of the offeror's death.[33] If, however, he has no
such knowledge at the time of accepting, then it would appear that
a distinction is made between those contracts where the acceptance
of the offer and the offeree's performance are one and the same act
(commonly called " unilateral " or " executed " contracts) and those
contracts (known as " multilateral " or " executory " contracts)
which are formed by the exchange of promises to be performed by
both parties in the future. In the case of unilateral contracts an
offeree who without knowing of the offeror's death does the act
requested of him by the offer—*e.g.* advances money to a person in
reliance upon a surety's standing offer to guarantee its repayment—
makes a valid acceptance and can bring an action upon the contract
against the offeror's personal representatives.[34] Multilateral contracts cannot, it seems, be formed after the death of the offeror,
whether or not the offeree knows of the death. Certainly this must
be the case if the personality of the offeror is an important element
in the contract, *e.g.* where the contract is with an architect for the
preparation of plans.

The effect of the death of the offeree was considered in a dictum
by Warrington L.J. in *Reynolds* v. *Atherton* (1921) [35]: ". . . the offer
having been made to a living person who ceases to be a living person
before the offer is accepted, there is no longer an offer at all. The
offer is not intended to be made to a dead person or his executors,
and the offer ceases to be an offer capable of acceptance." [36]

ILLUSTRATION

J. L. agreed to guarantee " the regular payment of the remaining balance " of H. L.'s account with B. B. continued to give credit
to H. L. after the death of J. L. and without notice of this fact.
Held, that B. could enforce the guarantee against J. L.'s executors
in respect of credit given to H. L. after J. L.'s death: *Bradbury* v.
Morgan (1862).[37]

[32] 50 D.L.R. (2d) 97 (Canada).
[33] *Coulthart* v. *Clementson* (1879) 5 Q.B.D. 42.
[34] *Bradbury* v. *Morgan* (1862) 31 L.J.Ex. 462. See also *post*, Chap. 17, p. 814,
for effect of death on contracts of guarantee.
[35] 125 L.T. 690 at p. 695.
[36] See also *Kennedy* v. *Thomassen* [1929] 1 Ch. 426.
[37] 31 L.J.Ex. 462.

(5) Acceptance

The acceptance of an offer must be unequivocal and must be communicated to the offeror if it is to result in a concluded contract. A conditional acceptance which fails to comply with the requirements of the offer is not a valid acceptance.[38] An acceptance may, however, be made either expressly by words or writing, or impliedly by conduct, always provided that the acceptance corresponds to the mode of acceptance contemplated by the offer. Thus if a householder asks a builder to call and do certain repairs and the builder does so, there is a good contract, the builder having accepted the householder's offer by doing the repairs as asked. Conduct will also, it is submitted, amount to acceptance if no other reasonable inference can be drawn from the conduct in question. This is most important in the field of building contracts, because even in major projects it is not uncommon for a builder or sub-contractor to commence work when all terms have been negotiated and agreed but no formal acceptance has been recorded. In such a case both the employer (by standing by and giving up possession) and the builder (by doing work) will, it is submitted, be evidencing their acceptance of the contract terms.[39]

An offeror cannot, however, impose a contract upon the offeree by a provision that the offeree's silence shall be taken as an acceptance.[40]

Where an acceptance is made by post, the rule is as stated by Lord Herschell in *Henthorn* v. *Fraser* (1892) [41]: " Where the circumstances are such that it must have been within the contemplation of the parties that, according to the ordinary usages of mankind, the post might be used as a means of communicating the acceptance of an offer, the acceptance is complete as soon as it is posted."

ILLUSTRATIONS

(1) After some negotiation for the sale of a horse, A wrote to B " If I hear no more about him, I consider the horse is mine at £30 15s." B made no reply, but when selling his farm instructed the auctioneer to reserve the horse. The auctioneer by mistake sold the horse. *Held*, that A had no right to impose a contract upon B by providing that B's silence should be his acceptance; that although

---

[38] For incomplete agreement where the parties are not *ad idem*, see *post*, Chap. 3, pp. 223–224.

[39] See also *Trollope & Colls Ltd.* v. *Atomic Power Constructions* [1963] 1 W.L.R. 333, *post*, Chap. 3, pp. 224–225.

[40] *Felthouse* v. *Bindley* (1862) 11 C.B.(N.S.) 869.

[41] [1892] 2 Ch. 27 at p. 33.

B in his own mind intended to accept A's offer, he had done nothing to communicate this intention to A and there was no binding contract: *Felthouse* v. *Bindley* (1862).[42]

(2) M. Co. sent a draft agreement for the sale of coals to B., who made certain minor alterations, inserted the name of the arbitrator, wrote " approved," and signed the agreement. B. returned the agreement to the M. Co.'s agent who put it away without further action. M. Co. then ordered and B. supplied coal in accordance with the terms of the agreement. *Held*, that the parties had by their conduct in the ordering and supplying of coal concluded a valid contract in the terms of the draft agreement as altered by B.: *Brogden* v. *Metropolitan Ry.* (1877).[43]

(3) An architect invited and accepted the tender of a nominated sub-contractor. The main contractor placed an order with a term on the back (for no payment of the sub-contractor until the main contractor was himself paid) which conflicted with the earlier documentation. The nominated sub-contractor started work. *Held*, by Blain J., that the architect was not the agent of the main contractor, so that the order of the main contractor constituted a counter-offer which had been accepted by the sub-contractor's starting work: *Davies & Co. Shopfitters Ltd.* v. *William Old* (1969).[44]

In the case of building contracts it is very common for the tender or offer of the contractor to be accepted at some considerably later date, often after changes in the work or modifications in the tender provisions or designs have been discussed and agreed. It is indeed common for contracts to be exchanged and signed some considerable period after work has commenced. While it is usually clearly the parties' intention that the accepted contract should apply retrospectively to work already done, the parties frequently do not expressly say so, or take account of changes in the work occurring since the original tender (by altering the price and contract drawings or specifications for instance), but rely on provisions in the contract for ordering and valuing variations or otherwise dealing with changes such as changes in wage-rates or cost of materials, notwithstanding that these provisions, not unnaturally, are designed to operate after and not before the contract is made. Wherever possible the law will either imply a term for retrospective operation of the contract provisions or construe the final acceptance as applying the contract provisions retrospectively to changes in the work agreed and undertaken prior to contract in anticipation of ultimate acceptance.[45]

[42] 11 C.B.(N.S.) 869.
[43] 2 App.Cas. 666.
[44] 67 L.G.R. 395.
[45] See *Trollope & Colls Ltd.* v. *Atomic Power Constructions* [1963] 1 W.L.R. 333, *post*, Chap. 3, pp. 224–225.

(6) Agreements to Agree and Vagueness

An agreement is not enforceable as a contract if it is in effect " an agreement to agree," that is, an agreement which postulates the need for further agreement between the parties before the terms of their bargain can be finally known, nor if it is so vague as to be incapable of a definite meaning. The courts will not make the bargain for the parties, nor speculate as to their intention, however probable. " It is a necessary requirement that an agreement, in order to be binding, must be sufficiently definite to enable the court to give it a practical meaning. Its terms must be so definite, or capable of being made definite without further agreement of the parties, that the promises and performances to be rendered by each party are reasonably certain." [46] As already mentioned, however, mere absence of an agreement as to price will not be an obstacle if the remaining terms or circumstances show an intention to pay and be paid.[47]

Moreover, in the case of commercial contracts, the courts are loth to hold that there is no binding contract, particularly if the parties have partially performed their promises as if their agreement was binding. " In commercial documents connected with dealings in a trade with which the parties are familiar the court is very willing, if satisfied that the parties thought that they made a binding contract, to imply terms and, in particular, terms as to the method of carrying out the contract, which it would be impossible to supply in other kinds of contract." [48] " The object of the law of contract is to facilitate the transactions of commercial men and not to create obstacles in the way of solving practical problems." [49]

Phrases such as " subject to war clause," [50] " to be had on hire-purchase terms," [51] " subject to force majeure conditions," [52] have been considered too vague and the agreements of which they formed part have been held not to be binding contracts. In each case the phrase was capable of more than one meaning and the court was therefore unable to say that the parties had ever agreed any one of the meanings, or that there was ever a *consensus ad idem*. On the

---

[46] *Scammell v. Ouston* [1941] A.C. 251 at p. 268, *per* Lord Wright.
[47] *Supra*, p. 5, and see *Foley v. Classique Coaches, infra*, pp. 14–15, and subsection (8) *infra*, pp. 17 *et seq.*
[48] *Scammell v. Ouston* [1941] A.C. 251 at p. 255, *per* Lord Maugham. See also *Edwards v. Skyways Ltd.* [1964] 1 W.L.R. 349, *infra*, p. 20, for a similar approach.
[49] *Per* Lord Guthrie in *R. & J. Dempster Ltd. v. Motherwell Bridge and Engineering*, 1964 S.C. 308 (Scotland).
[50] *Bishop and Baxter Ltd. v. Anglo-Eastern Trading Co. Ltd.* [1944] K.B. 12.
[51] *Scammell v. Ouston, supra.*
[52] *British Electrical Industries Ltd. v. Patley Pressings Ltd.* [1953] 1 W.L.R. 280.

other hand, the phrase " usual covenants " in agreements between
a prospective landlord and tenant has been held to be enforceable.[53]

In accordance with the normal rules of construction, however,
extrinsic evidence may be received in order to resolve an ambiguity
in a contract or to identify a particular term which the contract may
incorporate by reference: if this can be done, the contract will not
fail for uncertainty.[54]

Further, if the court concludes that some vague expression used
by the parties is in fact wholly meaningless, the expression will be
disregarded, and, provided that the agreement is sufficiently definite
in other respects, there will be a binding contract.

" In my opinion a distinction must be drawn between a clause
which is meaningless, and a clause which is yet to be agreed. A
clause which is meaningless can often be ignored, whilst still leaving
the contract good: whereas a clause which has yet to be agreed may
mean that there is no contract at all, because the parties have not
agreed on all the essential terms." [55]

Though an expression regarded as meaningless can be disregarded, however, the essential terms necessary to make the
contract commercially workable must have been agreed, and this
includes not merely the terms which the parties themselves regarded
as required to bring a contract into existence, but those which,
even though they did not realise it, were essential for this purpose.[56]

The question whether or not words used in a contract point to
the necessity of further agreement so as to vitiate the whole contract,
is ultimately a question which depends upon all the circumstances
of the particular case.

ILLUSTRATIONS

(1) O. agreed to purchase a motor-van from S. but stipulated
that a certain proportion of the price should be " had on hire-purchase terms over a period of two years." *Held*, that since there were
several types of hire-purchase agreement, there was no *consensus
ad idem* and no concluded contract: *Scammell* v. *Ouston* (1941).[57]

(2) The defendants agreed to purchase from the plaintiff all the
petrol required by them for running their business as motor-coach
proprietors " at a price to be agreed between the parties in writing
from time to time." The agreement contained an arbitration clause.
For three years the defendants bought all their petrol from the

---

[53] *Hampshire* v. *Wickens* (1878) 7 Ch.D. 555; *Flexman* v. *Corbett* [1930] 1 Ch. 672.
[54] See *Shamrock S.S. Co. Ltd.* v. *Storey* (1899) 81 L.T. 413.
[55] *Nicolene Ltd.* v. *Simmonds* [1953] 1 Q.B. 543 at p. 551, *per* Denning L.J.
[56] *Nicolene Ltd.* v. *Simmonds* [1953] 1 Q.B. 543; *Trollope & Colls Ltd.* v. *Atomic Power
Constructions* [1963] 1 W.L.R. 333, *post*, Chap. 3, pp. 224–225, *per* Megaw J.
[57] [1941] A.C. 251.

plaintiff, but a dispute arose and the defendants claimed there was no binding contract. *Held*, that a term could be implied in the contract that the petrol should be sold at a reasonable price, that if any dispute arose as to the price it was to be determined by arbitration, and that accordingly there was a binding contract: *Foley* v. *Classique Coaches Ltd.* (1934).[58]

(3) A charterparty provided that the *Crossbill* should proceed to Grimsby and load coal " in the usual manner according to the custom of the place . . . the loading time to be 36 running hours on terms of usual colliery guarantee." A strike of coal miners resulted in congestion of shipping at the port and the *Crossbill* did not get under the coal tip until ten days after arrival at the port: thereafter there was no delay in loading. In an action for demurrage by the shipowners, *held*, that the term " usual colliery guarantee " meant that form of guarantee which was in general use at Grimsby: that the evidence showed that there were three forms commonly used at Grimsby all of which provided that time did not run until the ship was under the tip and accordingly the charterers were not liable for demurrage: *Shamrock SS. Co. Ltd.* v. *Storey* (1899).[59]

(4) An agreement for the sale of a quantity of reinforcing steel bars was subject to " the usual conditions of acceptance." *Held*, there being no " usual conditions of acceptance," the condition was meaningless and could be ignored, and that the contract was complete and enforceable: *Nicolene Ltd.* v. *Simmonds* (1953).[60]

(5) A contract to grant a lease which was non-assignable contained the words " The lease shall contain such other covenants and conditions as shall be reasonably required by (the plaintiffs)." The defendants entered and paid rent under the agreement, but refused to accept a prohibition against " underletting or parting with possession of the premises or any part thereof." *Held*, by the Court of Appeal, the contract was not so vague as to be unenforceable, the proposed covenant went beyond the meaning of non-assignability, and the requirement was unreasonable. *Sweet & Maxwell Ltd.* v. *Universal News Services Ltd.* (1964).[61]

(6) An agreement was concluded between steel suppliers and consumers for delivery of agreed tonnages of steel over a three-year period, on what was called an " open order " basis, " the prices to be mutually settled at a later and appropriate date." There was evidence that the steel was in short supply, and that price was a a secondary matter. *Held*, the agreement could be enforced: *R. & J. Dempster Ltd.* v. *Motherwell Bridge and Engineering* (1964).[62]

In spite of the obvious anxiety of the courts to rescue contracts lacking clarity, these decisions show that, in building contracts, such expressions as " subject to the usual rise and fall clause " (there being many types of such clause), or " payment by monthly certificates

---

[58] [1934] 2 K.B. 1.
[59] 81 L.T. 413.
[60] [1953] 1 Q.B. 543.
[61] [1964] 2 Q.B. 699.
[62] 1964 S.C. 308 (Scotland).

subject to usual retentions " (there being many possible percentages of retention), or " joinery to be a P-C item " (if there are no contractual provisions governing P-C items), endanger the whole agreement, unless it is possible by extrinsic evidence to resolve the ambiguity, or the clause is so vague as to be meaningless, or relates to a matter not essential to the contract so that it remains fully workable in the commercial sense.

(7) Agreements " subject to contract "

The acceptance of an offer is sometimes stated to be " subject to a proper contract " or " subject to a formal contract." " It is a question of construction whether the execution of the further contract is a condition or term of the bargain or whether it is a mere expression of the desire of the parties as to the manner in which the transaction already agreed to will in fact go through. In the former case there is no enforceable contract either because the condition is unfulfilled or because the law does not recognise a contract to enter into a contract." [63]   In building contracts, all the necessary terms are usually contained in existing documents at the tender stage, as, for instance, where the tender embodies or makes specific reference to the form of contract and general conditions, so that the use of an expression such as " subject to a formal contract " may have the effect of preventing a contract coming into being despite actual agreement on all its terms. The effect of the words " subject to a proper contract " was considered by the Court of Appeal in *Chillingworth* v. *Esche* (1924) [64] where many earlier cases are referred to, and the use of the shorter expression " subject to contract " has now become a commonplace in the law of conveyancing, where questions of title and other matters often cannot be gone into at the time of reaching agreement on price. While it is not uncommon to find that tender documents in building contracts refer to the preparation of a later, formal contract, the very different circumstances in which the words are used, including the fact that all terms have usually been agreed and sometimes work has commenced, should lead, it is submitted, to a less strict view of their meaning and a greater readiness to hold that an effective contract has been concluded. Another expression not uncommonly

[63] *Per* Parker J. in *Hatzfeldt-Wildenburg* v. *Alexander* [1912] 1 Ch. 284 at p. 289. See also the closely analogous case of *Pigott Structures Ltd.* v. *Keillor Construction Co.* (1965) 50 D.L.R. (2d) 97, illustrated *supra*, pp. 9–10.
[64] [1924] 1 Ch. 97.

found in contracts of sale which may be associated with building work is " subject to survey."[65]

Where a later contract is in fact executed, however, it is usually presumed to supersede all previous agreements.[66]

(8) Consideration

A promise not under seal is unenforceable unless supported by consideration. The House of Lords in *Dunlop* v. *Selfridge* (1915) [67] adopted the following definition of consideration: " An act or forbearance of one party, or the promise thereof, is the price for which the promise of the other is bought, and the promise thus given for value is enforceable." [68]

This rule has important practical and legal consequences. In the first place, a third person who has not given consideration (a stranger to the consideration) cannot sue upon the promise, even though he may be a party to the agreement, if the consideration has been given by some other party. For example, a sub-contractor may undertake to carry out work on the building owner's land, and may then agree upon the work and the price with the building owner or his architect. But, if it is agreed that the person who places the order with him (*i.e.* who promises to pay for the work) is to be the main contractor, then the building owner (who has not given any consideration) cannot sue, for instance, for damages on the sub-contract. Looked at in reverse, the building owner cannot be sued for the price, even though the sub-contractor has, by doing the work or promising to do it, furnished ample consideration, because there is no promise by the building owner on which the sub-contractor can sue.[69] So in all cases where a builder has carried out or undertaken work, he must be able to establish the employer's promise, express or implied, to pay for the work. Where there is no express promise, a promise to pay will usually be implied, but there may be cases where, despite the carrying out of work, no promise to pay will be implied.

---

[65] See *post*, Chap. 3, pp. 217–223, where the subject of these and other similar conditions is considered in greater detail.

[66] See *post*, Section 8, Collateral Agreements.

[67] [1915] A.C. 847 at p. 855.

[68] *Pollock on Contracts*, 8th ed., p. 175.

[69] See *post*, Chap. 15, Sub-contracts. See, for a typical case, *Concrete Construction Ltd.* v. *Keidan*, 1955 (4) S.A. 315 *post*, pp. 743–744.

ILLUSTRATIONS

(1) In 1952 a contractor carried out a road contract for a city council. In 1953 the surface deteriorated and the contractor became concerned at the effect on his reputation locally and his prospects of obtaining further work from the council on other contracts. At the time he was owed a balance of $1,800 on the 1952 contract. He then repaired the road, though not requested to do so, and the council did not prevent him from doing so. Later he did not obtain the further work for which he had hoped, and claimed to be paid a reasonable price for the 1953 work. *Held*, by the Court of Appeal of New Brunswick, applying the test [70]—would a reasonable man in the position of the council have believed that the contractor intended to do the work at his own expense ?—that the contractor was not entitled to payment for the work: *City of Moncton* v. *Stephen* (1956).[71]

(2) A council was dissatisfied with the condition of certain work. The contractor asserted that it was not his fault, but the council made it plain that they would not pay when the contractor said he would do the work of repair without prejudice to his making a claim. Certain councillors had told him he would get no more work if he did not do the work of repair. The contractor did the work expressly reserving a claim. *Held*, unless the employer had agreed to the basis of doing the repair work, which it had not, the contractor was not entitled to payment even if his original contentions were correct: *Morton Construction* v. *City of Hamilton Corp.* (1962).[72]

(3) Surveyors agreed to prepare drawings, arrange tenders, obtain consents and settle accounts for alterations to a house on behalf of the defendant, who required it partly to live in and partly to let as lodgings, for a sum of £30. The cost of the work was originally estimated to be £600, but the price quoted by the contractor was £660, plus £400 in the form of P. C. sums for decorations and kitchen equipment. The trial judge held that the agreed fee of £30 was to cover possible extras but not wholly different work. After work had started, more work was ordered, bringing the total to £2,283. The surveyors prepared no specifications or drawings, etc., for this additional work, but supervised it and settled accounts. They did not say anything about an additional fee at the time, but ultimately submitted accounts and sued for an additional 100 guineas based on professional scale fees. *Held*, by the Court of Appeal, in the absence of any new promise to pay reasonable remuneration, the surveyors could recover nothing. In the present case the parties had never discharged their original agreement. The defendant, who was a woman, had never heard of scales, and the surveyors were professionals. It was a hard case, but as between the parties it was better that the surveyors should suffer the hardship: *Gilbert & Partners* v. *Knight* (1968).[73]

---

[70] For the test, see *Anson on Contract*, 20th ed., p. 26, and *Pollock on Contracts*, 13th ed., p. 9.   [71] (1956) 5 D.L.R. (2d) 722 (Canada).

[72] [1962] O.R. 154. Distinguish the Privy Council decision in *Molloy* v. *Liebe* (1910) 81 L.T. 616 (P.C.) illustrated *post*, Chap. 8, Section 2, p. 541, and cp. *Peter Kiewit & Sons* v. *Eakins Construction Ltd.*, Can.Sup.Ct., *post*, p. 543.

[73] 112 S.J. 155. See, for a contrary case, the decision of the Court of Appeal of Jamaica in *Kelly & Partners* v. *Northshore Development Co. Ltd.* (1963) 5 W.I.R. 379 (West Indies) illustrated *post*, Chap. 2, pp. 191–192.

Similar problems arise where preparatory work is done in the expectation of payment, if a contract is awarded, out of the profits of the contract. It is a question of degree, depending on the extent and nature of the work done, whether a promise to pay for work of this nature can be implied if the contract is not, in fact, awarded.[74] The problem can also arise in relation to variations in the contract work, which a builder may carry out in circumstances where no express request or promise by the building owner to pay can be shown, either because he did not know of the variation or, while knowing of it, did not realise that a change of price was likely to be involved.[75] It is for this reason (among others) that variation clauses are included in nearly all building contracts under which the employer agrees to be bound by an architect's instruction, usually in writing, if the result is in fact a variation of the contract work, whatever his own state of knowledge may be.[76]

An act or forbearance done in the past may be the *motive* for the giving of a promise, but it is not a good *consideration* to support the promise, for " past consideration is no consideration." [77]   Thus, if a builder in response to the employer's request erects a house on the employer's land without a price being agreed, and after completion the employer promises to pay him £4,000, the builder cannot enforce the promise to pay £4,000.   He can, however, recover a reasonable sum for erecting the house, relying upon the employer's promise to pay to be implied from his original request to the builder to erect the house.   Moreover the employer's offer of £4,000 would usually be some evidence against the employer of what was a reasonable sum.

There is no requirement of law that consideration should be adequate, or that the person giving the promise should receive a fair or reasonable return for the promise: the slightest action or forbearance by the promisee can be sufficient consideration.[78]   In normal commercial contracts, however, if the consideration is obviously so inadequate as to be derisory, the burden of establishing the contract is correspondingly the greater.   Nevertheless there is no principle of law which will relieve a party from a foolish or disastrous bargain once its terms are clearly established.

---

[74] See *post*, Chap. 3, pp. 230–231, for cases of preparatory work done by contractors, and *post*, Chap. 2, pp. 179–182, for work done by architects.
[75] For a suggested test in this situation, see the passage from *Re Chittick & Taylor* (1954) 12 W.W.R. 653 (Canada), quoted *post*, Chap. 8, p. 544.
[76] See *post*, Chap. 8, pp. 506–507.
[77] See *Roscorla* v. *Thomas* (1842) 3 Q.B. 234.
[78] See *Thomas* v. *Thomas* (1842) 2 Q.B. 851.

(9) Intention to create Legal Relations

In addition to the presence of consideration (though the two things will in the great majority of cases go together) there must be an intention (as always in English law, objectively and not subjectively assessed) to create a legally binding obligation. This will nearly always be ascertained from the general surrounding circumstances of the transaction in question, including, for example, whether it is of a commercial or domestic nature.

ILLUSTRATION

Representatives of an airline which was reducing its staff agreed with the pilots' union that redundant pilots would be given " an *ex gratia* payment approximating to " the total of contributions previously made by the airline to the pilots' pension fund. Consideration was admitted to be present. *Held* by Megaw J., (a) the onus of showing no intention to create legal relations, in the case of an agreement regulating business affairs, was a heavy one and the use of the words " *ex gratia* " as part of a promise to pay simply indicated that no pre-existing liability was present, and were not inconsistent with the intention and (b) the words " approximating to " were not too vague to be enforceable, and in the circumstances connoted the rounding off downwards to the nearest round figure of the sums involved: *Edwards* v. *Skyways Ltd.* (1964).[79]

SECTION 3. CONTRACTS UNDER SEAL

(1) Generally

A contract under seal (sometimes called a specialty) is a contract made by deed, that is to say, a contract in writing sealed and delivered by the parties to it. Where an individual is a party to a contract under seal, his signature is also necessary. A corporation, however, has no signature, and the affixing of its seal is a sufficient execution of the deed.

It is perfectly possible for a building contract to be in writing sealed by one party but only signed by the other. In such a case, although the undertakings of the party sealing the contract claim their validity from that fact, those of the other party are binding by reason of such consideration as may exist.

There are few practical differences between a valid contract under seal and a valid simple contract which is in writing, so far as their construction, performance and enforcement are concerned. Perhaps the most important is that by virtue of the Limitation Act 1939 a

---

[79] [1964] 1 W.L.R. 349.

right of action on a contract under seal is, in general, barred twelve years after its accrual, whereas a right of action on a simple contract, whether in writing or oral, is similarly barred after the lapse of only six years. From the employer's point of view, it is most desirable that the contract should be under seal, since, in the absence of any contractual provisions cutting down his right to do so, he will be able to recover damages for any defect in the work which he may discover within the longer period.

A second difference, though of considerably less importance in practice, relates to the recitals which are commonly found in legally drafted conveyances and other formal contracts, though not usually in building or engineering contracts. In a sealed contract, statements of fact contained in the recitals (as opposed to the body of the deed) operate by way of estoppel against the parties to the contract in any action or proceeding based upon the contract itself. Thus if the recitals to a building contract under seal were to recite that the contractor had examined the site and satisfied himself as to the accuracy of the site levels and dimensions shown upon the contract drawings, the contractor could not in any subsequent action upon the contract deny that he had done either of those things. Whether a recital in a deed is intended as an admission by both parties or by only one of them is a question of construction. In the example quoted, the admissions would be binding upon the contractor but not upon the employer also. Similar statements contained in a simple written contract would not, however, give rise to any estoppel, though they would be some evidence of the truth of the facts stated. A third difference is that a promise under seal but not supported by consideration cannot be specifically enforced [80] and the covenantee is left to his remedy in damages.

(2) Contracts with Local Authorities

A natural person can enter into contracts under seal or into simple contracts, but the basic rule of the common law is that a corporation, which is an artificial legal person, " can only contract under seal, for the proper legal mode of authenticating the act of a corporation is by means of its seal." [81] Many statutory exceptions to this rule existed; for example, trading companies incorporated under the

---

[80] For the limited availability of specific performance in building contracts, see *post,* Chap. 5, pp. 371–375.

[81] *Per* Lord Coleridge C.J. in *Austin* v. *Guardians of Bethnal Green* (1874) L.R. 9 C.P. 91.

Companies Acts could validly enter into simple contracts.[82]   But no statutory exception existed in the case of local authorities, with the result that a considerable body of case law grew up to deal with the anomalies and difficulties to which the rule gave rise in practice, and four pages of text in the eighth edition of this work were devoted to this subject.   This is no longer necessary, since by the Corporate Bodies' Contracts Act 1960 any person acting under the authority of a corporation, whether express or implied, can validly enter into a contract on their behalf, whether orally or in writing.   Though the Act does not apply to companies under the Companies Acts, the Companies Acts contain provisions having a similar effect.

The legal difficulties which can arise in relation to contracts made with corporations or companies can now only be concerned with the extent of the authority of persons purporting to make contracts on their behalf, and (to a considerably lesser extent in practice) the operation of the doctrine of *ultra vires* which, if the subject-matter of the contract is outside the purposes for which the corporation was formed or the powers conferred upon it, may have the effect of invalidating the contract.   These matters are considered *post*, Chapter 4, Special Parties.

SECTION 4.   VARIATION OF CONTRACTS

A simple contract may be validly varied by the subsequent agreement of the parties, so long as there is consideration to support the variation agreement.   If, at the time when the variation agreement is made, obligations remain partly unperformed under the original contract by both parties, there will usually be consideration for the new agreement.   If, however, one party to the contract has wholly performed his obligations, and thereafter agrees without advantage to himself or detriment to the other party to forgo some part of the performance of the outstanding obligations of the other party, there will be no consideration to support his agreement to do so.   The variation agreement will therefore be unenforceable if not under seal and the original contract requiring full performance will remain.   However, consideration may be present in such a case if some bona fide dispute exists and a claim is given up in return for the promise to accept less.   These agreements are often referred to

---

[82] See s. 32 of the Companies Act 1948.

by lawyers as " accord and satisfaction." [83] But the consideration must be real, in the sense of a bona fide claim however wrongly based in law or fact.

ILLUSTRATION

An employer told decorators that unless they agreed to accept a sum substantially less than the amount of their account, she would pay them nothing at all. They signed a written document agreeing to accept the reduced payment in full satisfaction of their claim. Later they sued for the full amount. *Held,* by the Court of Appeal, there was no true accord, because the plaintiffs had acted as a result of a threat which was without any justification, and there was no consideration present: *D. & C. Builders Ltd.* v. *Rees* (1966).[84]

A party to a contract who has promised to forgo full performance by the other and who is later held not to be permitted in law to complain of the breach, is sometimes said to have waived performance, or to be estopped from alleging the breach. Neither the doctrines of estoppel nor waiver (on which a short subsection is included [85]) really make any inroad, however, upon the requirement of consideration stated above in the context of variation of contracts, since a waiver is not permanently binding unless supported by consideration, and a party cannot successfully raise an estoppel unless he can show that he has acted to his detriment on the faith of the statement or conduct complained of. The only principle which does represent an inroad on the requirement is the rule that where full performance of a contract has been waived either notice or a clear indication of an intention once more to insist upon full performance should be given, so as to place the other party in the same position as before.[86]

A simple written contract may be varied by a subsequent oral agreement, just as a simple oral contract can equally be varied by a subsequent written agreement. A simple contract can also be varied by a deed under seal (in such a case there is, of course, no necessity for any consideration to support the variation).

At common law a contract under seal could only be varied under seal.[87] In equity, however, it could be varied by a simple contract either written or oral.[88] By virtue of section 44 of the Supreme Court of Judicature (Consolidation) Act 1925, the equitable rule now

---

[83] The subject of release from contractual obligations in this way is dealt with further, *post*, Chap. 5, Section 3.

[84] [1966] 2 Q.B. 617.

[85] *Post*, pp. 58–61.

[86] *Birmingham & District Land Co.* v. *L.N.W.R.* (1888) 40 Ch.D. 268. See *post*, p. 60.

[87] *Kaye* v. *Waghorn* (1809) 1 Taunt. 428.

[88] *Steeds* v. *Steeds* (1889) ?2 Q.B.D. 537.

prevails, with the result that a contract under seal can in general be varied in the same ways and subject to the same restrictions as a simple contract.

None of the foregoing discussion, which relates to changes or variations made in the provisions of a contract (including, if necessary, the description of work undertaken) is, however, applicable to variations of the work ordered under the express power to order variations very commonly found in building contracts.[89] If the work is varied in accordance with this power, no change in the terms of the contract is involved, and the variation order need only comply with the requirements of the contract in order to be valid. If, however, an architect agrees with the contractor to vary the contract in some respect which is outside his express powers under the contract, as for example, if he agrees with the contractor that the maintenance period shall be altered from six to four months, then the agreement will be unenforceable (quite apart from any question of his authority to make it),[90] unless supported by consideration.

SECTION 5. VOID AND VOIDABLE CONTRACTS

(1) Generally

Notwithstanding the fact that an agreement may have been reached which satisfies the legal requirements as to the form and manner of its conclusion, in certain circumstances such an agreement will be unenforceable as a contract because it is either void or voidable. If a contract is void, there is in law no contract at all. If a contract is voidable, there is a contract valid until such time as one of the parties takes steps to have it set aside; however, the right to have it set aside may be lost by delay, or by conduct affirming the contract, or by some innocent stranger to the contract acquiring rights or title to property under it. Thus, where there is a contract for the sale of goods which is void, no title to the goods passes from the seller to the buyer and accordingly the buyer cannot, in general, pass any title in the goods to a third party, from whom they can be recovered. If, however, such a contract is only voidable, then title to the goods does pass and only reverts when the contract is avoided. If, before steps are taken to avoid the contract, the buyer resells the goods, he passes a good title to a purchaser without notice of the defect of title, and it is then too late to avoid the original contract.

---

[89] See *post*, Chap. 8.
[90] As to which see *post*, Chap. 2, pp. 106–111.

The commonest categories of void contracts are contracts affected by mistake and illegality, and the majority of voidable contracts arise as a consequence of misrepresentation. Illegality, which may affect a contract in being as well as its formation, is considered in Chapter 5.[91] In this chapter it is proposed to consider shortly the law relating to mistake and misrepresentation.

(2) Mistake

(a) Of fact

Mistake as to fact, but not as to a general proposition of law, may prevent the formation of contract by robbing an apparent agreement of the reality of consent. " If mistake operates at all, it operates so as to negative or in some cases to nullify consent." [92] A mistake which merely goes to the motive or purpose of one of the parties cannot prevent the formation of a contract. For example, an employer who, in the mistaken belief that the subsoil of the site has insufficient bearing capability for the building he desires to erect, signs a contract for piles to be driven, cannot avoid the contract for mistake when he discovers his error, whether he does so before or after the work has begun. Equally, a party who signs a contract under a misapprehension as to the true meaning of its provisions or in ignorance of those provisions, cannot set up his mistake as a defence to an action upon the contract.[93] If mistake is to operate at all, there must be an element of mutuality in the mistake, either in the sense that both parties were under a common mistake at the time of making their agreement, or that one party was mistaken to the knowledge of the other. The only exception to this is in certain rather rare cases of mistake where the parties, unknown to each other, mean something different by their contract.[94]

Until the decision of the Court of Appeal in *Solle* v. *Butcher* (1950),[95] it would have seemed a safe statement of the law to say that operative mistake (as opposed to misrepresentation) always rendered a contract void *ab initio*, and not voidable. In that case, however, Denning L.J. (as he then was) expressed a contrary view, and the court in fact set aside the lease in question on terms, a remedy hardly applicable to a contract void *ab initio*. The question

---

[91] *Post*, pp. 361–367.
[92] *Per* Lord Atkin, in *Bell* v. *Lever Bros. Ltd.* [1932] A.C. at p. 217.
[93] *L'Estrange* v. *Graucob* [1934] 2 K.B. 394.
[94] See (d) *infra*.
[95] [1950] 1 K.B. 671.

must therefore be regarded as open, but Lord Denning M.R.'s view
also appears to have been accepted in a case of unilateral mistake
by the Court of Appeal of British Columbia.[96] However, unilateral
mistake known to the other party may be in a different category and
derive its remedies from the law of fraud rather than true mistake.
The recent case of *Magee* v. *Pennine Insurance*[97] suggests that the
law as to the exact nature of common mistake is in a state of confusion
at the present moment in the United Kingdom.

Mistake of fact may also enable a party to recover sums paid by
him, but this has nothing to do with the avoidance of contract, and
forms part of the law of quasi-contract.[97a]

(b) Common mistake

If at the time of contracting both parties were under a common
mistake as to " the existence of the subject-matter " of their contract,
the contract will generally be void. Thus where at the time when a
contract was made for assignment of a life insurance policy the
assured was already, unbeknown to the parties, dead, the contract
was held void.[98] If at the time when a contract for the repair and
alteration of a building was signed, the building had already been
destroyed by fire, such a contract would also be void. (If, however,
the building, though standing at the time of the contract, was
subsequently destroyed by fire without the fault of either party and
before the works had begun, there would be a valid contract, though
it might be discharged on the ground of frustration.) [99]

A common mistake not relating to " the existence of the subject-
matter," but only to its " quality," no matter how fundamental, is
not, it would seem, sufficient to render the contract void. " Once a
contract has been made, that is to say, once the parties, whatever
their inmost states of mind, have to all outward appearance agreed
with sufficient certainty in the same terms on the same subject-matter,
then the contract is good unless and until it is set aside for failure
of consideration, or for fraud, or upon some equitable ground.
Neither party can rely on his own mistake to say it was a nullity
from the beginning, no matter that it was a mistake which to his

---

[96] *Imperial Glass Ltd.* v. *Consolidated Supplies Ltd.* (1960) 22 D.L.R. (2d) 759 (Canada),
illustrated *infra*, p. 30.
[97] [1969] 2 Q.B. 507, illustrated *infra*, p. 31.
[97a] See *post*. Section 10, p. 61.
[98] *Scott* v. *Coulson* [1903] 2 Ch. 249.
[99] See *Taylor* v. *Caldwell* (1863) 3 B. & S. 826 and Chap. 5, pp. 348 *et seq.*, *infra*, on
Frustration.

mind was fundamental, and no matter that the other party knew
that he was under a mistake. *A fortiori*, if the other party did not
know of the mistake, but shared it." [1]

(c) Unilateral mistake

Where the mistake of one party is known to the other at the time
of agreement, the mistake need not, as in common mistake, relate
to the essential subject-matter of the contract.   In such a case,
provided the mistaken party is mistaken as to a fundamental term of
the contract, the other party will not be permitted to rebut the mistaken party's plea that the parties were never *ad idem*, and the contract will be void (or perhaps only voidable, see *supra*).   But the
mistake must be a mistake as to a term of the contract,[2] and not as
to some extraneous matter merely affecting motive.[3]   If one party
enters into an agreement under a mistake which is not only known
to but has been induced by the other party, the case is, of course,
even stronger.

Where the mistake does not relate to a term of the contract, and
has not been induced by the other party, although such a contract
is not void, the courts may nevertheless refuse to order specific
performance of it if the party serving upon it " snapped at an offer
which he must have perfectly well known to be made by mistake," [4]
and in such a case the party will be left to his remedy at law for
damages.

Cases illustrative of these principles have chiefly been concerned
with mistaken identity.   Thus if A, posing as B, makes an offer which
C accepts in the belief that it comes from B, the contract is void
provided always that the identity of B was material and that B in
fact existed.[5]   In such a case A is also, of course, guilty of a fraudulent misrepresentation as to his identity, so that the contract is in
any event voidable,[6] but, as has been pointed out, if an innocent
third party has acquired rights under a contract the defrauded party

---

[1] *Solle* v. *Butcher* [1950] 1 K.B. 671 at p. 691, *per* Denning L.J.   See also *Bell* v.
Lever Bros. [1932] A.C. 1.   *Cf. Nicholson & Venn* v. *Smith-Marriott* (1947) 177 L.T.
189.

[2] As *e.g.* in the *Imperial Glass* case, *infra*, p. 30.

[3] *Smith* v. *Hughes* (1871) L.R. 6 Q.B. 597; *Metcalfe Realty Co.* v. *Elite Interiors Ltd.*
[1966] 2 O.R. 433 (Canada).

[4] *Tamplin* v. *James* (1880) 15 Ch.D. 221; *Webster* v. *Cecil* (1861) 30 Beav. 62.

[5] *Cundy* v. *Lindsay* (1878) 3 App.Cas. 459; *Kings Norton Metal Company* v. *Edridge*
(1897) 14 T.L.R. 58; *Phillips* v. *Brooks* [1919] 2 K.B. 243.

[6] See *infra*, p. 47 *et seq.*

will be bound by the contract unless it was wholly void, so the distinction between mistake or misrepresentation may be vital.

There is an analogous situation in which there is also no contract, but it is not a true illustration of operative mistake. If A makes an offer to B which is received and accepted by C, there is no contract, simply because C cannot accept an offer which has not been made to him.[7] Thus if a builder submits a tender to X, a private person, the tender cannot be accepted so as to form a binding contract by the X Co. Ltd. (If, however, after receipt of the purported acceptance by the X Co. Ltd., the builder begins work, he may by his conduct have accepted the counter-offer to work for the company, and there will then be a valid contract between himself and the company.)

(d) Mistake not known to the other party

A further class of mistake which can frequently arise in practice occurs where each party to the contract unwittingly attaches a different meaning to the agreement, or a particular term of it. In the vast majority of cases, the courts will apply the usual objective tests of construction to the language used and conduct of the parties when making the agreement, and if it was understood by one of the parties in a sense conforming to that construction, will uphold the contract accordingly.[8] But in a rare class of case, the parties may, through no fault on either side, mean something different by the contract which they have apparently made, and if the objective test of construction assists neither party, the contract will be avoided. The classical example of this type of mistake is to be found in the case of *Raffles* v. *Wichelhaus* (1864),[9] illustrated below.

(e) Non est factum

Finally, under the heading of mistake which prevents the formation of contract, there is the defence of *non est factum*. If a party signs a written contract under a mistake as to its essential nature, he can subsequently deny that it was " his deed " in law, with the result that the contract will not be binding upon him.[10] A mistaken belief merely as to the contents of the contract is not sufficient.[11]

---

[7] *Boulton* v. *Jones* (1857) 2 H. & N. 564.
[8] This is so even where one party informs the other of the interpretation he places upon the contract before the contract is signed. The true construction of the agreement will still prevail—see *Boot* v. *L.C.C.* [1959] 1 W.L.R. 1069, *infra*, p. 34.
[9] 2 H. & C. 906.
[10] *Thoroughgood's Case* (1584) 2 Co.Rep. 9.
[11] *Blay* v. *Pollard* [1930] 1 K.B. 628.

If a builder were to sign a contract under the belief that it was for the building of one house whereas in truth it was for the building of two houses, the plea of *non est factum* would not be available to him. If, however, he signed a contract which he believed to be for the construction of a house whereas in truth it was for the purchase of a house, then the contract would not be binding upon him. This rule, in the very rare cases in which it can be applied, affords some mitigation of the principle stated in *L'Estrange* v. *Graucob* (1934).[12]

ILLUSTRATIONS

(1) The defendant, having a set-off against B., ordered goods from him. The plaintiff having, unknown to the defendant, taken over B.'s business, supplied the goods ordered. *Held*, that there was no contract of sale for the goods between the plaintiff and defendant: *Boulton* v. *Jones* (1857).[13]

(2) A commercial contract provided for the sale of cotton by A to B " ex *Peerless* from Bombay." In fact, two ships named *Peerless* sailed from Bombay, one in October and the other in December. The buyer proved he meant the October vessel, while the seller meant the December one. *Held*, the contract was void: *Raffles* v. *Wichelhaus* (1864).[14]

(3) The plaintiff sold a quantity of oats to the defendant knowing that the defendant erroneously believed them to be old oats and that he would not have bought them had he not believed them to be old. But the plaintiff had not induced the defendant's mistaken belief by any representation, neither did the term " old " form part of the description of the oats sold. *Held*, that the contract was not void for mistake: *Smith* v. *Hughes* (1871).[15]

(4) The defendant signed a deed believing it to be a transfer to the real owner of an interest held by himself as nominee. Actually it was a mortgage under which the defendant acknowledged receipt of £1,000 and agreed to repay it with interest. The mortgage was later transferred to the plaintiff, who was innocent of the deception. *Held*, the defendant was not bound by the deed: *Howatson* v. *Webb* (1907).[16]

(5) The defendant signed a document which he knew to relate to a dissolution of partnership, but which contained certain terms of which he was not aware and to which he would have objected had he known of them. *Held*, that he was bound by the document and could not raise the defence of *non est factum*: *Blay* v. *Pollard* (1930).[17]

---

[12] *Infra.* See, however, the strict limitations on the rule enunciated in *Gallie* v. *Lee* [1969] 2 Ch. 17, illustrated *infra*.
[13] H. & N. 564.
[14] 2 H. & C. 906.
[15] L.R. 6 Q.B. 597.
[16] [1908] 1 Ch. 537.
[17] [1930] 1 K.B. 628.

(6) The plaintiffs employed the defendant as managing director of one of their subsidiary companies upon a five-year agreement. Before the agreement expired the defendant became redundant and the plaintiffs agreed to pay him compensation for loss of office. Subsequently the plaintiffs discovered that the defendant had committed breaches of his agreement for which he could have been dismissed without compensation. *Held*, that there was no common mistake which rendered the agreement to pay compensation void: *Bell* v. *Lever Bros.* (1932).[18]

(7) The plaintiff signed a printed sales agreement for the purchase of a slot machine. In small print at the foot of the agreement it was provided that any express or implied condition, statement or warranty was excluded. The machine failed to work and the plaintiff brought an action alleging, *inter alia*, that she knew nothing of the exclusion. *Held*, that the plaintiff having signed the agreement without having been induced to do so by fraud or misrepresentation was bound by the exclusion clause, whether or not she knew of its existence when she signed the agreement: *L'Estrange* v. *Graucob* (1934).[19]

(8) The defendant leased a flat to the plaintiff at £250 a year. Both parties, who were in business as estate agents, believed that the premises were not controlled under the Rent Acts, on the ground that they were of different identity from a letting of the property in 1938 at £140 a year. Subsequently it transpired that the 1938 letting had established a standard rent of £140 and the premises were controlled. After the lease was executed, the plaintiff sued for repayment of excess rent paid by him. *Held*, by the Court of Appeal (Jenkins L.J. dissenting on the ground that the mistake was a mistake of law) that the lease should be set aside, on the defendant undertaking, after serving the necessary notices to permit the standard rent to be raised to £250, to grant a new lease at that rental to the plaintiff: *Solle* v. *Butcher* (1950).[20]

(9) A quoted to B in terms which showed that he had made an error in computing his price. B entered into a binding contract with C in regard to the same subject-matter on receipt of A's quotation, without noticing the error. B later noticed the error, but accepted A's quotation without informing A of the mistake. *Held*, by the Court of Appeal of British Columbia, that it does not necessarily follow that an offeree comes under a duty to reveal knowledge or awareness of a mistake by the offeror or that failure to do so gives ground for rescission, unless the circumstances are such as to support an inference of fraud in concealing awareness of the mistake. There were no grounds for setting aside the contract on its particular facts: *Imperial Glass Ltd.* v. *Consolidated Supplies Ltd.* (1960).[21]

(10) A wrestling promoter paid licence fees over a four-year period on a daily and not annual basis, in the mistaken belief, shared by the

---

[18] [1932] A.C. 161.
[19] [1934] 2 K.B. 394.
[20] [1950] 1 K.B. 671.
[21] (1960) 22 D.L.R. (2d) 759 (Canada). See also *Alampi* v. *Swartz* (1964) 43 D.L.R. (2d) 11 (Canada).

licensing inspector, that the relevant by-laws so provided. On discovering the mistake, he claimed sums for over-payment of fees. *Held*, by the Supreme Court of Canada, he was entitled to recover: *Jacobs* v. *City of Regina* (1964).[22]

(11) A vendor sold a house " subject to the existing tenancy thereof." Both vendor and purchaser thought there was an existing statutory tenancy affecting the house. The occupant left the house four months later, and it transpired that the statutory tenants, whose son he was, had died some time previously in circumstances which made it doubtful if he had any statutory tenancy at all. The value with vacant possession was £2,250 and subject to a tenancy was £850. The purchaser sued for specific performance. *Held*, there was a common mistake as to a fundamental matter, even on the footing that it had been open to the occupant to claim a statutory tenancy, and there was equitable jurisdiction to set aside the sale: *Grist* v. *Bailey* (1967).[23]

(12) A condition of a contract for the sale of land was that it included " fourteen acres of tobacco-growing quota." Both parties were mistaken as to this. *Held*, on the facts this was a false and fundamental assumption going to the root of the contract, which was accordingly void *ab initio*: *R.* v. *Ontario Tobacco Growers Marketing Board, ex p. Grigg* (1965).[24]

(13) In 1961 M made certain mis-statements when applying for an insurance policy on a car, to the effect that he himself had a provisional licence, and that his son of eighteen would also drive the car. In fact he had no licence, and the car was intended for the exclusive use of the son. The policy was renewed from year to year, and transferred to a new car, when in 1965 the son had an accident which damaged the car, and the father's claim for the damage was compromised by agreement at a certain figure. A few days later the insurance company discovered the true state of affairs, and sought to avoid the agreement. *Held* by Lord Denning M.R., following *Solle* v. *Butcher*, that the contract was not void at law but was voidable in equity, by Fenton Atkinson L.J., that the contract was void for a common mistake in a fundamental and vital matter, and *per* Winn L.J. (dissenting), that the case was indistinguishable from *Bell* v. *Lever Bros.*, and the mistake did not relate to the subject-matter of the contract, but only to the rights of the parties: *Magee* v. *Pennine Insurance* (1969).[24a]

(14) A widow of 78 knew that her favourite nephew wished to raise money on the house in which she lived, and signed a document which she could not read, being without her glasses, on being told by a business associate of the nephew, in the nephew's presence, that it was a gift of the house to the nephew. In fact it was a purported sale to the business associate, who then mortaged the house to a building society. On a claim by the mortgagees for possession, the widow pleaded *non est factum*. *Held*, by Russell and Salmon L.JJ., that the character and class and legal consequences of the document

[22] 1964 S.C.R. 326 (Canada).
[23] [1967] Ch. 532.
[24] [1965] 2 O.R. 411 (Canada).
[24a] [1969] 2 Q.B. 507.

she intended to sign were not so different from the reality, in spite of its being in favour of a different person, as to found a plea of *non est factum*; by Lord Denning M.R., that, not having required the document to be read to her, she was estopped by her conduct from saying, as against the building society who had advanced money in good faith, that it was not her deed: *Gallie* v. *Lee* (1969).[24b]

It may perhaps be noted that the views of Lord Denning M.R., as expressed in *Solle* v. *Butcher*, *Magee* v. *Pennine Insurance* and *Gallie* v. *Lee*, appear to diverge from the earlier law and also from other judicial opinion at the present time, in that mistake in general appears to be regarded by him as rendering the contract voidable only. The distinction is, of course, of the greatest practical importance where third persons are involved, and final clarification of the position by the House of Lords is very much to be desired.

(3) Rectification

Mistake which prevents the formation of a contract is to be distinguished from mistake in the written expression of the agreement between the parties. In the latter case the mistake does not invalidate the contract, but may entitle one of the parties to have the written contract rectified by the court so as to make it accord with the true agreement of the parties. Nevertheless it is convenient here to consider the scope of the remedy of rectification.

If parties enter into an agreement, but there is an error in the reduction of the agreement into writing, so that the written contract fails to express accurately the common intent of the parties, whether by misstatement, omission or by the inclusion of provisions contrary to that intent, then the court will correct the written contract so as to make it conform to the common intent. If, of course, the parties agree that the written contract is erroneous, they can rectify it without reference to the court. It is only when one party seeks to adhere to the existing wording of the contract that proceedings for rectification become necessary. It is not, however, necessary that there should have been a previous agreement on all matters before the execution of the written document which is sought to be rectified. It is sufficient if there was prior agreement on the point upon which rectification is sought.[25] " It is sufficient to find a common continuing intention in regard to a particular provision or aspect of

---

[24b] [1969] 2 Ch. 17.
[25] *Shipley U.D.C.* v. *Bradford Corporation* [1936] Ch. 375, 598; *Crane* v. *Hegeman-Harris Inc.* [1939] 1 All E.R. 662; *Carlton Contractors* v. *Bexley Corporation* (1960) 60 L.G.R. 331. *Earl* v. *Hector Whaling* [1961] 1 Lloyd's List Rep. 459, *Joscelyne* v. *Nissen* [1970] 2 W.L.R. 509, C.A.

the agreement. If one finds that, in regard to a particular point, the parties were in agreement up to the moment when they executed their formal instrument, and the formal instrument does not conform with that common agreement, then the court has jurisdiction to rectify, although it may be that there was, until the formal instrument was executed, no concluded and binding contract between the parties." [26] The prior agreement may be oral only, and it is immaterial that the contract itself is required to be under seal.[27]

On the other hand, a plaintiff seeking rectification undertakes a heavy burden in establishing, against the contention of the defendant, not only that there has been a mistake, but that there was a clear common agreement which the unrectified contract does not express. In effect, this means that the plaintiff must be able to specify precisely the alterations which he desires the court to make to the written documents, though it is not necessary to prove a prior agreement as to the exact form of words. Furthermore, the evidence must be such as to leave no fair or reasonable doubt that the written document does not embody the final intention of the parties. " The court can only act if it is satisfied beyond all reasonable doubt that the instrument does not represent their common intention and is further satisfied as to what their common intention was. For let it be clear that it is not sufficient to show that the written instrument does not show their common intention, unless positively also one can show what their common intention was." [28] Thus there can be no rectification if the defendant never knew of or accepted what is said to be the common intention [29] (in other words, a case of simple unilateral mistake). The written contract may not express accurately the plaintiffs' intention or expectation, but if, in the absence of fraud or misrepresentation by the defendant, it does reflect the defendants' intention, the contract cannot be rectified.[30]

We have seen that in evolving the doctrine of mistake the law has been more willing, for readily intelligible reasons, to avoid a contract where a unilateral mistake known to the other party can be established, than in the case of a common mistake, where a mistake of a more fundamental character is required. On principle,

---

[26] *Crane's* case, *supra*, at p. 664, *per* Simonds J.
[27] *Shipley U.D.C.* v. *Bradford Corporation; Carlton Contractors* v. *Bexley Corpn.*, *supra*.
[28] *Crane's* case [1939] 1 All E.R. 662 at p. 664, *per* Simonds J.
[29] *Fowler* v. *Scottish Equitable Life Insurance Society* (1858) 28 L.J.Ch. 228.
[30] See *e.g. Royston U.D.C.* v. *Royston Builders Ltd.* (1961) 177 E.G. 589, illustrated *post,* p. 215.

therefore, it was submitted in the eighth edition of this work that the remedy of rectification should be available in appropriate circumstances if a unilateral mistake known to the other party could be shown, rather than a common mistake, and this has now been established beyond doubt. If the parties are agreed, but the formal contract fails to express the common intention by reason of a mistake of one of the parties of which the other is aware, and he keeps silent and then seeks to rely on the formal contract, he will not be permitted to resist a claim for rectification by alleging the absence of common intent.[31] " Two things seem quite plain: that the defendants cannot be heard to say in this court as a defence to an equitable claim to rectification that they misapprehended their own document . . . still less can they be heard to say that they did not misapprehend it, but sought to gain an advantage over the plaintiffs by getting past the plaintiffs, without their being made aware of it, a change in the obligation. . . ." [32] In such a case there is common agreement, which the defendant cannot escape by proof of his own sharp practice in failing to disclose the mistake and his own change of intent to the plaintiff.[33] It is perhaps unnecessary to emphasise, however, that the parties must have been in agreement —it is not enough that, without any prior agreement, one party knows that the other is mistaken as to a term or its meaning. The following case is not one of rectification, but illustrates the principle.

ILLUSTRATION

A local authority decided to alter the fluctuations clause in its contract so as to exclude from its operation payments under the holidays-with-pay scheme. It accordingly wrote to contractors (including the plaintiff) notifying them of the change in the wording and of its purpose and intended effect. Later the contractor entered into a contract with the authority which used the new form of wording, and at the end of the work claimed that the wording still entitled him to increases in the cost of the holidays-with-pay stamps. The local authority sought to rely on their letter in support of the construction of the words for which they were contending. *Held,* by Lord Somervell in the Court of Appeal (approved on this point in the House of Lords), that the letter could not be received in evidence: *Boot & Sons Ltd.* v. *L.C.C.* (1959).[34]

---

[31] *Monaghan County Council* v. *Vaughan* [1948] I.R. 306; *George Cohen & Sons Ltd.* v. *Docks Executive* (1950) 84 Ll.L.R. 97; *A. Roberts & Co. Ltd.* v. *Leicestershire C.C.* [1961] 1 Ch. 555, illustrated *infra,* pp. 37–38; and see *McMillan* v. *Chapman.* (1953) 2 D.L.R. (2d) 671 (Canada).

[32] *Cohen's* case (1950) 84 Ll.L.R. 97, at p. 111, *per* Evershed M.R.

[33] See *e.g. McMillan* v. *Chapman* (1953) 2 D.L.R. (2d) 671 (Canada).

[34] [1959] 1 W.L.R. 1069. See also *Royston U.D.C.* v. *Royston Builders Ltd.* (1961) 177 E.G. 589, *post* p. 215.

In the *George Cohen* case rectification was ordered of a document proffered by the defendants. Whilst relief upon a defective instrument is more readily awarded against the party who prepared or proffered it, nevertheless the plaintiff can, in a proper case, obtain rectification of his own document.[35]

There have also been cases between vendor and purchaser in which the defendant has known of and sought to take advantage of a slip made by the plaintiff in drawing up a lease or other conveyance and, notwithstanding that the mistake has been unilateral, the defendant has been put to his election either to have the deed rectified or to have it set aside.[36] The basis of these decisions has been doubted but it should be remembered that they were decided before it was established that rectification was available in cases of unilateral mistake known to the other party.

If rectification of a written contract is granted, then the contract is to be treated as rectified *ab initio* and not merely as from the date of the order of the court. Thus the defendant may be successfully sued for a breach of the contract committed before rectification, notwithstanding that it was no breach by the terms of the unrectified contract.

Rectification in the sense discussed in this chapter depends upon differences between agreements made prior to the contract and the final terms of the contract itself. The word " rectification " is sometimes used by the draughtsmen of building and engineering contracts in a quite different and misleading sense, namely, to describe the process of resolving, under the terms of the contract, discrepancies between the drawings, specification or bills of quantities, or arithmetical inaccuracies in the bills of quantities.[37] Sometimes errors in the bills or in arithmetic may result in an accepted contract sum differing from the correctly calculated total of the prices in the bills. In general such difficulties can, it is submitted, only be resolved by giving effect to any relevant provisions of the contract governing the correction of errors and the adjustment of the contract price according to the ordinary rules of construction, and not by resort to the legal remedy of rectification, since it can very rarely, it is submitted, be shown that the pre-contract common intention of the parties was that the contract price should be the true arithmetical total of the prices in the bills, or that it should be a

---

[35] *Collett* v. *Morrison* (1851) 9 Hare 162; *Jadis* v. *Porte* (1915) 8 W.W.R. 768 (Canada).
[36] *Garrard* v. *Frankel* (1862) 30 Beav. 445; *Paget* v. *Marshall* (1884) 28 Ch.D. 255.
[37] See *e.g.* clause 10 of the pre-1963 R.I.B.A. Standard form with quantities, clause 12 of the 1963 R.I.B.A. Standard forms, and clause 6 of the 1955 I.C.E. form.

sum corrected to take account of some other error in the bills, unless this can be established by the terms of the contract documents themselves.[38] It has already been noted that the law of unilateral mistake will not avail a party seeking to set aside such a contract unless the mistake is (subjectively) known to the other party. Furthermore, the mistake would have to relate to an important and major element in the contract price, it is submitted, and even then relief might not be granted if the other party had, without fault, altered his position on the strength of the contract.[39]

In fact most modern building and engineering contracts contain express provisions designed to ensure that the tendered price (which may well have determined the selection of the contractor and the decision to proceed with the project) should prevail over any pricing errors of the contractor concealed within it.[40]

ILLUSTRATIONS

(1) A contractor verbally stipulated at the time of tendering that a provision conferring finality upon the surveyor's decisions should not be insisted upon, and this was agreed to. The surveyor refused to certify the amount to which the contractor claimed to be entitled, and the employers relied on the absence of a certificate. *Held*, as the contractor had entered into the contract on the understanding that the certificates would not be binding, he was entitled to have the contract rectified: *Simpson* v. *Metcalf* (1854).[41]

(2) The defendants contracted to build an exhibition building for X. By the contract the contract price was divided into two parts: (a) the actual cost of labour and materials; (b) a fixed fee of £140,000. It was a term of the contract that X's maximum liability should be £1,209,250 and that any " over-run " should be borne by the defendants. The fee of £140,000 was divided as to £70,000 for expenses and overheads and £70,000 for job-profit, but subject to the over-run. The defendants employed the plaintiff as architect for the works under a supplemental written agreement which provided that he should be paid a minimum fee of £13,000 and " such further amount (not exceeding £20,000 in all) as shall be equal to two equal seventh parts of the amount which the company (the defendants) shall under the terms of the building agreement receive and retain in respect of the fixed fee of £140,000 payable thereunder to the company." A dispute arose as to whether the two-sevenths was to be calculated with or without deduction of the over-run from the fixed fee of £140,000. *Held*, that, on the true construction of the supplemental agreement, the plaintiff was entitled to two-sevenths without prior

[38] For a discussion of this topic with particular reference to the standard forms of contract, see *post*, Chap. 8, pp. 520–521.
[39] See *supra*, pp. 25–32, and the case of *Imperial Glass Ltd.* v. *Consolidated Supplies Ltd.* there illustrated.
[40] See *e.g.* clause 13 of the 1963 R.I.B.A. Conditions.
[41] 24 L.T.(o.s.) 139.

deduction of over-run, but since on the evidence the plaintiff had prior to the execution of the agreement at all times accepted that his fee should be subject to prior deduction of over-run, the agreement would be rectified: *Crane* v. *Hegeman-Harris Co. Inc.* (1939).[42]

(3) The plaintiffs advertised inviting tenders for the demolition of a workhouse. The advertisement did not make it clear whether it was intended that the contractor should be paid or make payments for the work, but the specifications showed that it was intended that he should offer to make payments in his tender, as the materials were valuable. The defendant noticed the ambiguity and took legal advice on the meaning of the specification, and then tendered as follows: " Tender for demolition of Clones Workhouse according to specifications, £1,200." The plaintiffs accepted this tender, and a formal contract was later executed providing clearly for payment by the plaintiffs to the defendant. *Held*, the plaintiffs by their advertisement and the defendant by his tender had both in fact intended to contract for payment by the defendant to the plaintiffs. The defendant had attempted to take advantage of the plaintiff's error and his conduct was dishonest and approximated to fraud, and the contract could be rectified: *Monaghan C. C.* v. *Vaughan* (1948).[43]

(4) The plaintiffs and defendants, in negotiation for the renewal of the plaintiffs' existing lease of warehouse premises, agreed that the new lease should be prepared by the defendants' solicitor and that " terms and conditions in the present lease to be embodied in the new lease where applicable." The old lease contained a covenant by the defendants to keep the quay walls bounding the demised premises in repair, but in the defendants' solicitor's draft this covenant was omitted. This omission was not pointed out to the plaintiffs by the defendants nor did the plaintiffs discover it until after the lease had been executed. *Held*, that the new lease should be rectified by the insertion of the defendants' former covenants to repair the quay walls: *George Cohen & Sons Ltd.* v. *Docks Executive* (1950).[44]

(5) A contractors' revised tender specified a period of completion of 18 months. The county architect and his assistant decided that the period should be 30 months, and caused the clerk's department to draw up formal contract documents accordingly, which meant that the same month but a different year was shown as the date for completion. The contractors were then informed by letter that their tender had been accepted, without being told of the intention to change the date of completion. Later the contract documents were sent to the contractors, who sealed and returned them, without noticing the change in the date. Before the council sealed the contract themselves, two meetings were held between the assistant county architect and the contractors, at each of which the contractors referred to their plans to complete in 18 months and produced a progress schedule on this basis. The council finally executed the contract without the contractors ever being specifically informed of the changed date. On a claim for rectification by the contractors, the council objected that to ground rectification there must be either a common

[42] [1939] 1 All E.R. 662.
[43] [1948] I.R. 306.
[44] 84 Ll.L.R. 97.

mistake or dishonest conduct by the defendant. *Held*, by Pennycuick J., that a party is entitled to rectification of a contract if he can prove that he believed a particular term to be included in a contract and that the other party concluded the contract with the omission or variation of the term, in the knowledge that the first party believed it to be included, and that, on the facts of the case, the contractors were entitled to rectification: *A. Roberts & Co. Ltd.* v. *Leicestershire C. C.* (1961).[45]

Where there is a manifest error or omission on the face of a written contract, the court will correct the error or supply the omission, but this is done as a matter of construction and without extrinsic evidence, and not as a matter of rectification. Thus where the condition of a bond stated that it should be void if the debtor whose debt was being guaranteed did " not " pay, the court read the bond without " not," which was manifestly inserted in error.[46]

Finally, a difficult question can arise whether an arbitrator has jurisdiction to rectify the contract out of which his jurisdiction springs.[47]

(4) Innocent misrepresentation

(a) Effect of the Misrepresentation Act 1967

Since the last edition of this work the Misrepresentation Act 1967 has effected far-reaching and welcome changes in the law relating to innocent misrepresentation. These may be summarised as follows:

(i) Innocent misrepresentations made without reasonable grounds for belief in their truth now confer a right to damages in addition to the pre-existing right to rescind the contract (which, as will be seen, was, and is, hedged about with a number of restrictions which severely limit its availability in practice)—see section 2 (1) of the Act.

(ii) One important restriction on the right to rescission has been removed in all cases (rescission not available if contract has been " executed ")—see section 1 (*b*) of the Act.

(iii) A second possible restriction on rescission (representation itself a term of the contract) has also been removed—see section 1 (*a*).

---

[45] [1961] 1 Ch. 555. See also *Carlton Contractors* case illustrated *post*, pp. 110–111, and *Royston U.D.C.* case, illustrated *post*, p. 215.
[46] *Wilson* v. *Wilson* (1854) 5 H.L.C. 40, 67. See also *Annamunthodo* v. *Oilfield Workers T.U.* [1961] A.C. 945.
[47] This is dealt with *post*, Chap. 18, Arbitration, pp. 837–838.

(iv) In all cases a defendant may avoid rescission if the court or an arbitrator deem it equitable to declare the contract as subsisting, and award damages in lieu of rescission— see section 2 (2).

(v) Clauses excluding or restricting liability for misrepresentations are to be of no effect unless deemed by the court or an arbitrator to be fair and reasonable—see section 3.

The potential importance of this Act in the field of building, and even more of civil engineering contracts, cannot be overstressed. Rescission, practically never available to contractors previously, because of the restriction now perhaps removed by section 1 (*b*) of the Act (see discussion *infra*, pp. 44–45), affords a remedy far more effective than damages to a builder who finds that, for reasons unconnected with the representation, he has underestimated on his pricing of the contract. The search for a means of invoking the remedy is likely to fasten upon the descriptions of the state of the site and the accounts of pre-contract investigations which employers' advisers frequently insert in the tender documents for the assistance of contractors, while at the same time expressly disclaiming responsibility for such statements. It may even include representations said to arise by inference from quantities or provisional quantities or other indications in the bills, drawings or specifications—*e.g.* of the extent of rock in excavations, of soft or made-up ground, or existing foundations requiring to be broken out, of wet conditions necessitating sheet-piling or well-pointing, or other contingent difficulties which are almost invariably contractor's risks in building and civil engineering contracts—see *post*, Chapter 5, sections 1 (*c*), 2 (2) and 3 (3), and see also subsection (6) *infra*, pp. 48–49.

It must remain a matter of speculation how the courts and arbitrators will apply the " fair and reasonable " exception to section 3 of the Act when faced with this type of claim; no doubt an important consideration would be that if, in building and civil engineering cases, disclaimers of liability by employers for such matters were widely held to be invalidated by the Act, the tendency would be for employers and their advisers to avoid giving any assistance at all to tendering contractors for fear of rendering the contract liable to be set aside. The exercise of the discretion to award damages under section 2 (2) whenever rescission is claimed might also do much to check abuse of the Act. It is submitted that in general the uncertainties with which building and civil engineering work are associated are well understood by the industries concerned and are accepted as contractors' risks. Furthermore the financial background to such contracts generally means that the parties are aware that, apart from such adjustments as the contracts permit, a firm price which will not be exceeded is commercially essential from the employer's point of view. In addition, in many engineering contracts specific financial protection is given to the contractors in respect of risks which are not reasonably foreseeable (see *post*, Chapter 9, section 1 (*c*)). All these factors should militate against too rigorous an application of the Act to representations said to arise from the terms of the contract documents.

The form of the Act is such, however, that the great bulk of the law relating to innocent misrepresentation remains relevant and the remainder of this subsection is devoted to a summary of the law on the subject with references to the provisions of the Act where these have the effect of modifying the pre-existing rules.

(b) The law as modified by the Act of 1967

If one party to a contract is induced to enter into it by a material misrepresentation of fact made by the other party, then, subject to the matters mentioned below, the contract is voidable at the option of the party misled, whether the representation is innocent or fraudulent, but where the representation is innocent, damages cannot be recovered unless it is also a term of the contract,[48] or, if not, unless the representor up to the time of the contract being made, did not believe, or did not have reasonable grounds for believing, that the facts represented were true.[49]

" Properly speaking a representation is a statement or assertion made by one party to the other, before or at the time of contracting, of some matter or circumstance relating to it. Though it is sometimes contained in the written instrument, it is not an integral part of the contract: and consequently the contract is not broken if the representation proves to be incorrect. A question may, however, arise whether a descriptive statement in the written instrument is a mere representation, or whether it is a substantive part of the contract. This is a question of construction which the court . . .

---

[48] For a recent possible inroad upon this rule, however, see *post*, pp. 64–67 where the case of *Hedley, Byrne & Co. Ltd.* v. *Heller* [1964] A.C. 441 is discussed. In certain parts of Canada, too, it would seem that the law is different—see the decision of the Privy Council in *W. I. Bishop Ltd.* v. *J. Maclaren Co.* [1937] 2 D.L.R. 625 (Canada), based on s. 1053 of the Civil Code of Ontario.

[49] Misrepresentation Act 1967, s. 2 (1).

must determine." [50]   A representation is thus to be distinguished
from a statement of fact the truth of which is warranted by one of
the parties so as to make it a term of the contract, and the breach
of which will found an action for damages.   The distinction is
neatly shown in the following case:

ILLUSTRATION

A dealer taking a car in part exchange was shown the car and asked
its date of manufacture.   The owner said it was a 1948 model, it
being so described in the log-book, and it was so described in the
part exchange contract.   Unknown to the owner, the log-book had
been forged by a previous owner, and the car was, in fact, much older.
Held, the statement was a mere representation only and not a warranty
or term of the contract: *Oscar Chess Ltd.* v. *Williams* (1957).[51]

The remedy for misrepresentation is usually termed rescission,
though the term is also used[52] in the very different case where a party
elects to treat a breach of a fundamental term of a contract by
the other party as a repudiation bringing the contract to an end,
whereupon his own obligations cease and he is also entitled to
damages.[53]   The party misled by an innocent misrepresentation
which is not a term of the contract cannot, subject to section 2 (1)
of the Act of 1967, sue for damages, but can either, if that is sufficient
for his needs, declare his intention no longer to be bound by the
contract, or, if not, sue for rescission, if he requires the assistance
of the court to be restored to his position before the contract.
Rescission in this more limited sense means setting the contract aside
and restoring the parties to their position before the contract was
concluded.

Where a statement which induces a contract is also a term of
the contract, it was regarded as doubtful whether it might, if so
desired, be relied upon as a representation so as to obtain rescission,
or whether it could only be relied upon as a term of the contract so
as to obtain damages.[54]   (The right to treat the contract as at an end
as well as to sue for damages in the case of breach of a term of a
contract only arises if the term is of a sufficiently fundamental
character or, to use the legal terminology, is a " condition " as
opposed to a " warranty," or if the conduct of the party in breach

---

[50] *Per* Williams J. in *Behn* v. *Burness* (1862) 1 B. & S. 877.
[51] [1957] 1 W.L.R. 370.
[52] See, for instance, the language of the Law Lords in *Heyman* v. *Darwins* [1942]
A.C. 356.
[53] As to this, see *post*, Chap. 5, pp. 340–347.
[54] *Leaf* v. *International Galleries* [1950] 2 K.B. 86, *infra*, p. 46.

evinces an intention no longer to be bound by the contract.) [55]
The doubt referred to has now been effectively disposed of by
section 1 (a) of the Act of 1967, which permits rescission notwithstanding that the misrepresentation is a term of the contract, *if
otherwise the party concerned would be so entitled without alleging
fraud.* This would appear to mean that the exact contractual status
of the term in question is now irrelevant, but that the term must
have induced the representee to enter into the contract, which in
many cases in practice may prove to be a major obstacle in the way
of a party seeking rescission. Other requirements before rescission
can be obtained are as follows:

First, there must be a positive misrepresentation: a mere failure
by one party to make a disclosure of material facts to the other is
insufficient (except in the class of contracts which are *uberrimae fidei*,
into which building contracts do not fall).[56] Nevertheless a half-
truth will be treated as an untruth if its effect is to mislead.[57]
Further, if a representation which is true when made becomes false
during further negotiations and before the contract is concluded, this
fact must be disclosed or it will be treated as misrepresentation.[58]

Secondly, the representation must be one of an existing or past
fact. An innocent representation which is a mere expression of
opinion, or a promise as to future conduct, is not sufficient. Neither
is a representation as to a general proposition of law. A representation as to private right, which is in a sense mixed fact and law,
is, however, regarded as a representation of fact.[59] So, too, is a
promise or opinion if given fraudulently,[60] and in certain circumstances a statement of opinion will carry an implied representation
that reasonable grounds for the opinion exist.[61]

Thirdly, the representation must be made with the intention that
it should be acted upon by the other party.[62]

Fourthly, the representation must have induced the contract. If
the party seeking to set aside the contract did not know of the
representation, or did not rely on it, or knew it to be untrue, he will

---

[55] For the discharge of contracts by breach, see *post,* Chap. 5, pp. 340–347.
[56] *Keates* v. *Lord Cadogan* (1851) 10 C.B. 591.
[57] *Dimmock* v. *Hallett* (1866) 2 Ch.App. 21.
[58] *Davies* v. *London Marine Insurance Co.* (1878) 8 Ch.D. 469, *infra,* p. 46; *With* v.
O'Flanagan [1936] Ch. 575.
[59] *Cooper* v. *Phibbs* (1867) L.R. 2 H.L. 149; *Solle* v. *Butcher* [1950] 1 K.B. 671.
[60] See *Edgington* v. *Fitzmaurice* (1885) 29 Ch.D. 459 at p. 483, *per* Bowen L.J.
[61] *Smith* v. *Land & House Property Corporation* (1884) 28 Ch.D. 7; *Brown* v. *Raphael*
[1958] Ch. 636.
[62] *Peek* v. *Gurney* (1873) L.R. 6 H.L. 377.

not be entitled to relief.[63]   On the other hand " if it is proved that
the defendant, with a view to induce the plaintiff to enter into a
contract, made a statement to the plaintiff of such a nature as would
be likely to induce a person to enter into a contract, and it is proved
that the plaintiff did enter into the contract, it is a fair inference
that he was induced to do so by the statement." [64]

Fifthly, a party seeking rescission must act promptly after discovering the untruth of the representation.   If he thereafter affirms
the contract either by conduct or words his option to rescind will
be lost.[65]   Thus a builder who began work on the site after learning
of the untruth of the misrepresentation would no longer be entitled
to rescind the contract, just as a building owner who had been
misled, but permitted the builder to begin work on the site after
discovery of the untruth, would also thereby have elected to affirm
the contract.   Furthermore, where the misrepresentation is innocent
its untruth must also be discovered within a reasonable time or the
remedy of rescission may be lost.[66]

Sixthly, no innocent third party must have acquired rights for
value under the contract before steps are taken to avoid it.[67]   This
principle is, however, chiefly applicable in practice to contracts for
the sale of goods, and is unlikely to affect building contracts.

Seventhly and finally, a contract cannot be rescinded unless the
parties can be restored to substantially the same position as existed
before the contract was concluded.   It was sometimes said that the
test was whether the contract could be regarded as " executed " or
" executory," but the validity of this distinction may be doubted.[68]
Rescission involves the restoration of benefits received under the
contract, and if this is not in substance possible by reason of acts
in which the party misled has himself participated, rescission may
not be ordered.

ILLUSTRATION

Contractors completed a contract for a branch railway.   Two
years afterwards they claimed rescission of the contract on the ground
of innocent misrepresentation of the railway company's engineer as
to the nature of the strata through which the railway passed.   *Held*,

---

[63] *Arkwright* v. *Newbold* (1881) 17 Ch.D. 324.
[64] *Per* Lord Blackburn in *Smith* v. *Chadwick* (1884) 9 App.Cas. 187 at p. 196, *infra*,
p. 46.
[65] *Clough* v. *L.N.W.Ry.* (1871) L.R. 7 Ex. 26. See also *Wallbridge* v. *W. H. Moore Ltd.*
(1964) 48 W.W.R. 321 (Canada).
[66] *Leaf* v. *International Galleries* [1950] 2 K.B. 86.
[67] *Babcock* v. *Lawson* (1880) 5 Q.B.D. 284.
[68] See for an example of a case which was neither executed nor executory, *Senanayake*
v. *Cheng* [1966] A.C. 63, illustrated *infra*, p. 46.

that the claim failed on the ground that the contractors, by completing the contract with full knowledge of the facts, had rendered
restitutio in integrum impossible: *Glasgow and South Western Ry.* v.
Boyd (1915).[69]

The circumstances in which rescission will be refused for this
reason have not been rigidly defined, but it would appear that the
courts will, by ordering financial allowances to be made, grant
rescission in some cases where complete restitution is strictly impossible, particularly if the misrepresentation was fraudulently made.[70]
" A court . . . can take account of profits and make allowance for
determination. And the practice has always been for a court . . .
to give this relief whenever, by the exercise of its powers, it can do
what is practically just, though it cannot restore the parties precisely
to the state they were in before the contract " [71]: " The court must
fix its eyes on the goal of doing ' what is practically just.' How that
goal may be reached must depend on the circumstances of the case,
but the court will be more drastic in exercising its discretionary
powers in a case of fraud than in a case of innocent misrepresentation. . . . In the case of fraud the court will exercise its jurisdiction
to the full in order, if possible, to prevent the defendant from
enjoying the benefit of his fraud at the expense of the innocent
plaintiff." [72]

Certain authorities suggest that in the case of innocent misrepresentation rescission cannot be ordered after the execution of any
formal instrument transferring property under the contract.[73] The
correctness of these decisions has, however, been doubted.[74]

The difficulty of defining exactly this seventh requirement makes
it correspondingly difficult to assess accurately the effect of section
1 (*b*) of the Act of 1967, which provides that a party shall be entitled
to rescission, *if otherwise entitled without alleging fraud,* notwithstanding that the contract has been performed. The exact result of
the Act must await judicial interpretation, but it is submitted that
the effect is that the mere fact of performance of the contract is not
to be a bar to rescission, though this seems to have been a position

---

[69] [1915] A.C. 526.
[70] *Erlanger* v. *New Sombrero Phosphate Co.* (1878) 3 App.Cas. 1218; *Hulton* v. *Hulton*
[1917] 1 K.B. 813.
[71] *Per* Lord Blackburn in *Erlanger's* case at p. 1278.
[72] *Per* Lord Wright in *Spence* v. *Crawford* [1939] 3 All E.R. 271 at p. 288.
[73] *Seddon* v. *N. E. Salt Co.* [1905] 1 Ch. 326; *Angel* v. *Jay* [1911] 1 K.B. 666. See also
Schonekess v. *Bach* (1968) 62 W.W.R. 673 (Canada).
[74] See *per* Scrutton L.J. in *Bell* v. *Lever Bros.* [1931] 1 K.B. 557 at p. 588; *Solle* v.
Butcher [1950] 1 K.B. 671 at pp. 695, 703; *Leaf* v. *International Galleries* [1950] 2
K.B. 86 at pp. 90, 91; and H. A. Hammelmann in (1939) 55 L.Q.R. at pp. 95–96.

already reached by the courts in a number of cases. Where, however, rescission would be difficult or impractical to bring about, and would previously have been refused on that ground, it seems at least possible that the Act effects no change in the law.

In granting rescission the courts have no power to grant damages, and this would seem to remain the position, unless section 2 (1) of the Act (no reasonable ground for belief in the truth of the facts misrepresented) applies, in which case it would seem that damages can be awarded in addition to rescission. On the other hand, damages can now be awarded as an *alternative* to rescission in all cases at the instance of the defendant, and the contract declared to be subsisting, if it seems equitable to do so having regard to the nature of the misrepresentation and the loss likely to be inflicted on either party if rescission were granted or refused. Nevertheless, as part of the order for rescission and for the purpose of doing what is practically just, the court could grant, under the pre-1967 law, a successful plaintiff a right of financial indemnity against the defendant in respect of " all obligations necessarily entered into under the contract." [75] This right of indemnity is narrower than the right to damages. [76]

In considering these rules, it should be remembered that most of the decisions upon rescission for misrepresentation have been concerned with contracts for the sale of property of one kind or another, rather than with building contracts. There is no reason to doubt, however, that in an appropriate case under the pre-1967 law rescission of a building contract could be obtained before the execution of permanent works on the site had begun. Once, however, building is substantially under way, strict restitution may be difficult, if not impossible, to bring about. The property in the partially erected building will have passed to the owner of the soil in accordance with the maxim *quic quid plantatur solo, solo cedit,* [77] and it is impracticable, if not impossible, to dismantle the building and restore its constituent materials to their former condition. This makes it particularly important in building cases to determine the exact ambit of section 1 (*b*) of the Act of 1967, since rescission may be a very attractive remedy to a builder who comes to the conclusion that his contract prices were underestimated, but who is not in a position to invoke section 2 (1) of the Act and claim damages.

[75] *Newbigging* v. *Adam* (1886) 34 Ch.D. 582, *per* Bowen L.J.
[76] *Whittington* v. *Seale-Hayne* (1900) 82 L.T. 49, *infra.*
[77] See *post*, Chap. 12, p. 655.

ILLUSTRATIONS

(1) A company ordered the arrest of their agent in the belief that he had committed a felony. Friends of the agent, knowing of the order, offered to deposit money with the company as security for the deficiency for which the agent might be liable if the company refrained from having the agent arrested. The company was then advised that no felony had been committed and cancelled its order for arrest, but accepted the friends' offer of money without disclosing the changed circumstances. *Held*, that the contract should be rescinded for misrepresentation: *Davies* v. *London Marine Insurance Co.* (1878).[78]

(2) The prospectus of a company in which the plaintiff had bought shares contained the false statement that a certain important person was on the board of directors. The plaintiff, however, admitted that he had not been influenced by this representation in reaching his decision to buy the shares. *Held*, that the contract for the purchase of the shares could not be rescinded: *Smith* v. *Chadwick* (1884).[79]

(3) The plaintiffs, who were poultry farmers, were induced to take a lease of premises from the defendant on the faith of an innocent representation that they were sanitary. In fact the water supply was poisoned and killed the poultry, and the plaintiffs were compelled by the local authority to renew the insanitary drains. *Held*, in ordering rescission of the lease, that the plaintiffs were entitled to an indemnity from the defendant against the cost of renewing the drains and against the rates paid, as they were obliged by the lease both to pay rates and repair the premises, but not against their financial loss in the death of the poultry, since they were under no obligation to keep poultry on the premises: *Whittington* v. *Seale-Hayne* (1900).[80]

(4) The plaintiff purchased an oil painting from the defendants on the faith of an innocent representation that it was an original Constable. Five years later he discovered that it was not an original Constable and immediately sought rescission of the contract. *Held*, that assuming the remedy of rescission to be open to a buyer of goods after they had been accepted, the plaintiff was not entitled to have the contract rescinded, as he had not brought proceedings within a reasonable time: *Leaf* v. *International Galleries* (1950).[81]

(5) A new partner was induced to join a firm of stockbrokers and invest $20,000 in it by representations that it was " a gold mine." She began to act as partner on April 20, 1959, and later, while temporarily in charge of the firm, saw its books for the first time. She called a meeting of partners on June 30, 1959, and on the day following demanded her money back. On July 29, she brought an action for return of the money, alleging innocent misrepresentation. *Held*, by the Privy Council, on the facts the agreement contemplated a continuing contractual relationship and could not yet be properly regarded as executed, *restitutio in integrum* was possible, there had been no election affirming the contract or unreasonable delay, and rescission should be granted: *Senanayake* v. *Cheng* (1966).[82]

[78] 8 Ch.D. 469.
[79] 9 App.Cas. 187.
[80] 82 L.T. 45.
[81] [1950] 2 K.B. 86.
[82] [1966] A.C. 63.

(5) Fraudulent Misrepresentation

A misrepresentation is fraudulent if the representor either knows it to be untrue or is reckless as to whether it be true or false.[83] Any other misrepresentation is innocent. A misrepresentation is, moreover, innocent no matter how negligently it is made.[84] Negligence itself, however gross, is not fraud, though it may be evidence from which the court will be prepared to infer fraud in the form of recklessness. The difference between one who makes a recklessly fraudulent misrepresentation and one who makes a negligently innocent misrepresentation is that the former has no positive belief in the truth of his representation, whereas the latter has. The distinction is clear in principle, and a party seeking to establish fraud undertakes a very heavy burden of proof.

A person who by his fraudulent misrepresentation causes another to enter into a contract and thereby to suffer loss, commits the tort of deceit and is liable to that other in damages for the loss he occasions. An action for damages for fraudulent misrepresentation is not an action upon the contract which it induces, but a right of action given by the general law of tort arising out of the relationship of the parties, and entirely separate from the remedy of rescission.

As has been stated above, a party who discovers the truth of a misrepresentation which induced him to contract then has an option either to affirm the contract or, if the conditions as to the availability of rescission are satisfied, to sue for rescission. If by word or conduct he affirms the contract, the election is final and there can be no subsequent claim for rescission. Where, however, the misrepresentation is fraudulent, the affirmation which bars rescission does not in any way bar the action for damages for deceit. Moreover, rescission and damages for fraud are not alternative but cumulative remedies, so that it is possible to seek both rescission of a contract induced by a fraudulent misrepresentation and damages in respect of the deceit.[85] (This now also seems to be possible in the case of innocent representations made without reasonable grounds under s. 2 (1) of the Act of 1967.)

A successful plaintiff in an action for deceit is entitled, subject to the usual rules as to remoteness, to recover such financial loss as

---

[83] *Derry* v. *Peek* (1889) 14 App.Cas. 337.
[84] See, however, the effect now of s. 2 (1) of the Misrepresentation Act 1967 on representations made without reasonable grounds for belief in their truth.
[85] *Attwood* v. *Small* (1838) 6 Cl. & F. 232, 444, *per* Lord Brougham; *Newbigging* v. *Adam* (1886) 34 Ch.D. 523, 592, *per* Bowen L.J.

he has incurred by acting upon the misrepresentation.[86] Thus if a builder who is induced by the building owner's fraudulent misrepresentation that the site levels are as shown on the contract drawings, incurs increased costs in constructing the building upon the actual levels, the additional cost will be recoverable as damages.

It should perhaps be emphasised that the duty in fraud almost invariably arises between the representor and the representee. Thus, a builder who suffers damage due to a fraudulent representation by the architect to the employer that the work has not been practically completed has no cause of action because the representation was not intended to be acted on by him (the builder).[87]

(6) Exclusion of Liability for Misrepresentation

It is quite common in standard forms of contract to provide that the contractor shall be deemed to have satisfied himself as to all matters affecting his tender and that all warranties and representations by the employer and his agents are excluded. Until the Act of 1967, it was perfectly possible by such clauses to exclude the contractor from his remedy for an innocent misrepresentation, but in the absence of specific wording, they would not be construed as applying to a fraudulent misrepresentation.[88] It was theoretically possible to exclude remedies arising from fraudulent misrepresentations by express provision in explicit terms, but for obvious reasons these were rarely encountered in practice.[89]

ILLUSTRATIONS

(1) Contract plans showed a wall nine feet below ordnance datum. There was a provision in the contract that the contractors must not rely upon any representation made in the plans, but must ascertain the facts for themselves. *Held*, on the facts, the representation was fraudulent, and the provision was only intended to give protection against honest mistakes: *Pearson & Son Ltd.* v. *Dublin Corporation* (1907).[90]

(2) A specification for waterworks stated that the city did not possess complete information as to the location or occurrence of various existing structures, and disclaimed responsibility for the accuracy or completeness of the drawings. The tenderer was to visit the site and not make any claim because of errors in the documents.

---

[86] See *Doyle* v. *Olby* [1969] 2 Q.B. 158.
[87] *Larkins* v. *Chelmer Holdings* [1965] Qd.R. 68 (Australia).
[88] *Pearson & Son, Ltd.* v. *Dublin Corporation* [1907] A.C. 351.
[89] *Cf. Tullis* v. *Jacson* [1892] 3 Ch. 441, referred to *post*, Chap. 7, p. 455. See, however, *per* Scutton L.J. in *Czarnikow* v. *Roth Schmidt* [1922] 2 K.B. 478, 488.
[90] [1907] A.C. 351, illustrated more fully *post*, p. 175.

In fact there were certain man-made under-water obstructions not disclosed in the drawings and not actually known to the responsible municipal officers, though there were documents in the city archives showing the obstructions. *Held*, there was no misrepresentation. The plans and specification were not misleading and the contract laid no duty on the city to give more information than it did [91]: *Atlas Construction Co. Ltd.* v. *City of Montreal* (1954).[92]

The above cases now need to be read in the light of section 3 of the Act of 1967, which prohibits clauses excluding or restricting liability for misrepresentation (whether fraudulent or innocent), subject to a discretion to permit the clause to be relied on if this appears fair and reasonable in all the circumstances, and the provisional and speculative comments on the possible exercise of this discretion in the case of representations as to the state of the site or difficulties likely to be encountered in subsection 4 (*a*), *supra*.

It has been held that if one party seeks to incorporate into a contract standard conditions which include clauses exempting him from what would otherwise be his legal liabilities, and misrepresents the effect of those conditions to the other party, he will not be entitled to rely upon such exemption.[93] "Any behaviour by words or conduct is sufficient to be a misrepresentation if it is such as to mislead the other party about the existence or extent of the exemption. If it conveys a false impression, that is enough." [94] This principle, if correct, may have an important application in those contracts created by exchanges of letters, which have conditions printed at the foot or on the back, but its application to the more comprehensive formal building contracts is perhaps doubtful.

SECTION 6.   IMPLIED TERMS

(1) General Principles

The express terms in a contract are unlikely, except in the most meticulously and comprehensively drafted contracts, to be the final measure of the obligations of the parties. It has already been seen that, where work is carried out at the request of the building owner, and no price is mentioned between the parties, then the law will imply a term that a reasonable price should be paid for it. This,

[91] For the absence of any such general duty on the employer, see *post*, pp. 231–232, 267 *et seq*, 316–317, and 348 *et seq*.
[92] [1954] 4 D.L.R. (2d) 124 (Canada), distinguishing *W. I. Bishop Ltd.* v. *J. Maclaren Co.* [1937] 2 D.L.R. 625 (Canada).   See also *Bottoms* v. *York Corporation*, *post*, Chap. 5, p. 270.
[93] *Curtis* v. *Chemical Cleaning Co.* [1951] 1 K.B. 805.
[94] *Per* Denning L.J., *ibid.* at p. 308.

of course, is only likely to occur in an unusually informal, and probably not very substantial, building contract. But many other terms can be and are implied in all contracts, and an important part of the specialised law of contract in any particular field consists of the terms which the courts will usually imply in contracts in that field.

A term will only be implied if it is essential to do so in order to give the contract what has been called " business efficacy." [95] This means that the courts will not imply terms merely to make the contract more reasonable in its consequences. They will only imply a term if, without it, the contract would be commercially unworkable. Nor will the courts make a contract for the parties, so that if any reasonable doubt exists as to the unexpressed intention of the parties on an aspect of their bargain which is not wholly unimportant, no term relating to it will be implied, and if it is a matter essential to the business efficacy of the contract, no binding contract can come into existence.[96]

The most important limitation of all is to be found in the rule that no term will be implied that is inconsistent with or contrary to, or so as to vary, the express terms of the contract. On the other hand, implied terms " are for the most part founded on the presumed intention of the parties, and ought certainly to be founded on reason, and with a just regard to the interests of the party who is supposed to give the warranty, as well as of the party to whom it is supposed to be given." [97]

Accordingly, all the circumstances and background and all the express terms of a contract must be carefully examined before a term can be implied, and it follows that every case must be determined in the light of its own particular facts, and that decided cases can only be a guide, and not the final arbiter, as to the terms to be implied in other similar contracts, though the courts do in fact evolve and formulate implied terms designed to apply to broad classes of transaction in the absence of express indications to the contrary.

(2) Application to Building and Engineering Contracts

With the above warning in mind, some of the more important terms usually implied in building contracts may be mentioned. Thus, in the absence of express descriptions, there will usually be

---

[95] See, e.g. The Moorcock (1889) 14 P.D. 64 at p. 68, per Bowen L.J.; Reigate v. Union Manufacturing Co. [1918] 1 K.B. 592 at p. 605, per Scrutton L.J.
[96] See ante, pp. 13–16 and the judgments in Nicolene Ltd. v. Simonds [1953] 1 Q.B. 543.
[97] Readhead v. Midland Ry. (1869) L.R. 4 Q.B. 379, 392.

implied terms that materials and workmanship shall be of a proper standard or quality.[98]

Where the employer does not employ an architect or other adviser, so that he is relying on the skill and judgment of the contractor, and the latter provides the design or specification, there is an implied term not only that the work will be carried out in a proper and workmanlike manner and with proper materials, but also that the work, when completed, will be fit for its purpose (for instance, in the case of a dwelling-house, fit for human habitation).[99]

But no such term for fitness will be implied if what the contractor undertakes is to build a house in accordance with the employer's plans and specification, *a fortiori* if also to the satisfaction of the employer's architect or engineer. In the case of a house sought by a purchaser, the maxim *caveat emptor* applies, and no undertaking as to its quality or suitability will be implied on the part of the vendor. But in the case of a sale of a house in the course of erection, if the vendor is undertaking to complete it for the purchaser according to the vendor's plans or specification, the same term as in the case of a house built to the contractor's design will be implied.[1]

On the other hand, where (as almost invariably is the case) the contract is an entire contract in the legal sense,[2] so that the contractor not only undertakes to carry out *but also to complete* the work in accordance with the employer's designs or specification, there is no room for any implied undertaking by the employer that completion in accordance with the design or specification is possible or practicable. Accordingly the contractor will have to pay damages if he cannot complete, or will be unable to recover extra payment for additional work necessary to achieve completion.[3]

Where a building owner's architect is given power under the contract to decide matters between the contractor and employer in his capacity as a certifier under the contract, there is an implied term that the employer will not interfere with the free and independent exercise of that function by his architect.[4]

In general, there is no implied right to receive payment on

[98] See *post*, Chap. 5, pp. 273–278, 295–306.
[99] See *post*, Chap. 5, pp. 273–294.
[1] See *post*, Chap. 5, pp. 278–281, 289–291, and see *per* Lord Denning M.R. in *Hancock* v. *Brazier (Anerley) Ltd.* [1966] 1 W.L.R. 1317.
[2] See *post*, Chap. 5, pp. 243 *et seq.*
[3] See *post*, Chap. 5, pp. 262–273; Chap. 8, pp. 507–530.
[4] See *post*, Chap. 7, pp. 458–465, 472–473.

account, or by instalments, of the price before completion (one difficulty would be to know what instalments and what periods to include in such an implied term) where a contractor (as is usually the case) on the true construction of his agreement undertakes to carry out and complete a defined work, and it will make no difference that the contract may contain provisions for adjusting the price or varying the work.[5]

If the contract date for completion has passed, an implied obligation to complete within a reasonable time will be substituted. In addition, an obligation to carry out the work with reasonable diligence and due expedition, throughout the period of construction, will also be implied, consistent with the contract period (if any).[6]

Again, drawings and information to enable the work to be carried out must be made available by the architect within a reasonable time, but no more precise definition of this most important implied obligation which may be generally applied can probably be given, and the obligation needs to be assessed in any particular case in the light of a number of possibly relevant considerations.[7]

Architects have no general ostensible authority to bind their employers in contract,[8] and no *implied* authority under a building contract to vary the work in any way.[9] Even under their express authority, in the vast majority of cases at the present day, architects have no authority to commit the employer to pay for compliance with their instructions if on a true view of the contract the work in question, whatever the architect may have thought, is included in the contractor's price and not a variation.[10]

These are but a small number of the propositions in relation to building and engineering contracts which are founded on the principles of the implication of terms, and are all dealt with in greater detail elsewhere in this book.

SECTION 7. CUSTOM AND TRADE USAGE

(1) Generally

It is possible for trade customs, more correctly in law called trade usages, to form part of the terms of a contract, although not expressly

---

[5] See *post*, Chap. 5, pp. 242–262.
[6] See *post*, Chap. 5, pp. 314–315; Chap. 10, pp. 609, 611–612.
[7] See *post*, Chap. 2, pp. 135–139 and Chap. 5, pp. 322–326.
[8] See *post*, Chap. 2, pp. 106–111.
[9] See also *post*, Chap. 8, pp. 506–507.
[10] See *post*, Chap. 8, pp. 523-524.

incorporated in the written or oral agreement of the parties. The incorporation of trade usages is, however, subject to certain principles of law which render such incorporation rarer than laymen engaged in the trade frequently suppose or would wish.

A trade usage consists of a particular course of dealing or line of conduct generally adopted by persons engaged in a particular trade—dealing or conduct which has become so notorious that where persons contract in that trade, they are assumed in law to have intended to be bound by such dealing or conduct, except in so far as they have by the terms of their contract expressly or impliedly excluded it. To be a valid trade usage, capable of forming part of the bargain between the parties, a usage must satisfy four conditions.

First, it must be notorious, that is to say, so well known in the trade that persons who make contracts of a kind to be effected by such usage must be taken to have intended that such usage should form part of their contracts.[11] Notoriety is a matter of evidence.

Secondly, the usage must be certain: it must have the same degree of certainty as any other contractual term. The issue of certainty is an issue of law. Thus, for example, it would be of no avail to prove a widely recognised practice in the building trade for the building owner to retain a proportion of the contract price for a period after completion, if it were not also possible to prove a certain proportion and a certain period of equally wide recognition.

Thirdly, the usage must be reasonable: what is reasonable is a question of law. A usage cannot be reasonable unless it is fair and proper and such as honest and right-minded men would adopt. A usage which is of general convenience to all parties engaged in the trade will not usually be regarded as unreasonable.

Fourthly, the usage must not be contrary to law: a usage which sanctioned conduct which was illegal would be void.

(2) Incorporation of Usage

If a usage satisfies the above conditions, then the express terms of a contract in the trade to which the usage applies are to be regarded as expressing what is peculiar to the bargain between the parties, while the usage supplies what is usual and unexpressed. The usage is just as much a part of the bargain between the parties

---

[11] The usage must be general, and not confined to a particular market or locality— *Re Goetz, ex p. the Trustee* [1898] 1 Q.B. 787.

as the express agreement. " The custom, when proved, is to be considered as part of the agreement: and if the agreement be in writing, though the custom is not written, it is to be treated exactly as if that unwritten customary clause had been written out at length." [12] It is, however, always possible for the parties by the terms of their contract to exclude the operation of a trade usage, either expressly or impliedly. "An alleged custom can only be incorporated into a contract if there is nothing in the express or necessarily implied terms of the contract to prevent such inclusion and, further, a custom will only be imported into a contract where it can be so imported consistently with the tenor of the document as a whole." [13]

It is important in this context to distinguish between trade usages and those provisions which are common to the standard forms of contract which are now commonly used in the building industry. There is, of course, no custom in the building industry that any standard form of contract should be used, nor do the specific provisions of such standard forms, whether as to retention funds, interim payment, fluctuations, variations or other matters, afford any evidence of trade usage. The widespread use of standard forms of contract merely shows that a large number of builders and building owners choose to contract in the same terms. Indeed, an agreement requiring the members of the Building Trade Employers' Federation not to tender for contracts of over £8,000 without using a form of contract employing bills of quantities has been held contrary to the public interest under the Restrictive Trade Practices Act of 1956,[14] so that reliance upon the standard forms as evidence of custom would appear to be doubly misguided. Moreover the standard forms are themselves subject to fairly frequent revision, and are in many respects open to severe criticism on grounds of policy and obscurity.[15]

Trade usage is a variable thing in the sense that a trade usage, once recognised by law, does not necessarily remain a trade usage for ever thereafter. Since it must be established that it is notorious, if a trade practice falls into disuse, it loses its notoriety and ceases to be a valid usage. The illustrations quoted below are not therefore authority that the practices there recognised as trade usages are

---

[12] *Per* Lord Blackburn in *Tucker* v. *Linger* (1883) 8 App.Cas. 508, 511.
[13] *Per* Jenkins L.J. in *London Export Corporation Ltd.* v. *Jubilee Coffee Roasting Co. Ltd.* [1958] 1 W.L.R. 661 at p. 675.
[14] *Re Birmingham Association of B.T.E.'s Agreement* [1963] 1 W.L.R. 484.
[15] See *supra*, Chap. 1, Introduction, p. 2.

still trade usages.[16]   Just as trade usages may lapse, new practices may become valid trade usages.   For example, it may be that the consequences of the " P.C. sum " or " Provisional Sum " are now sufficiently notorious and certain for some meaning and effect to be given to those expressions in a contract, although they are not explained or defined expressly.[17]

(3) Admissibility of Evidence of Trade Usage

It is a general principle of English law that oral evidence is not admissible to contradict, vary, add to or detract from the terms of any written document, including a written contract.   To this principle there are numbers of exceptions, one of which is that oral evidence is admissible to establish a trade usage to be annexed to the written contract, but as has been noted above, such usage must be consistent with the terms and tenor of the written contract.[18]

ILLUSTRATIONS

(1) The plaintiff, a quantity surveyor, was employed by an architect to prepare bills of quantities on which builders were to tender. The specification on which the builder tendered provided: " To provide copies of quantities and plans 25 guineas to be paid to the surveyor out of the first certificate." The defendant's tender was accepted, but he failed to pay the plaintiff out of the moneys received under the first certificate. It was established by evidence that there was a recognised practice that in the event of a tender being accepted the successful builder was liable for the quantity surveyor's fees, but if no tender was accepted then the building owner was liable. *Held*, that the usage was reasonable and valid and that the plaintiff was entitled to recover his fees from the defendant: *North* v. *Bassett* (1892).[19]

(2) The plaintiff employed the defendant, an architect, to design alterations for certain houses and supervise the work. This the defendant did for an agreed remuneration of 5 per cent. on the contract price of the work, and the defendant was paid on completion of the work. The defendant then refused to hand over the plans of the alterations, claiming that, by usage, the property in the plans

---

[16] In particular that relating to the responsibility for quantity surveyors' fees—see *post*, Chap. 2, pp. 193–197; and the cases of *Moon* v. *Witney Union* (1837) 3 Bing.N.C. 814; *Antisell* v. *Doyle* [1899] 2 Ir.R. 275; *Birdseye* v. *Dover Harbour Commissioners* (1881) Hudson's B.C., 4th ed., Vol. 2, p. 76, *post*, pp. 113–114.

[17] See *post*, pp. 204–205 and pp. 758–760. In *Schofield* v. *Scarborough Corporation* (1958) 172 E.G. 809, the Court of Appeal appear to have been ready in principle to imply a term in an incomplete contract for a part of the work to be priced as a " P.C. sum," but the report is not at all easy to follow.

[18] *Hutton* v. *Warren* (1836) 1 M. & W. 466, 475; *Humphrey* v. *Dale* (1875) 7 Ex.B. 66.

[19] [1892] 1 Q.B. 333. The usage probably does not exist at the present day. See *post*, Chap. 2, pp. 113–114, 193–197, for a discussion of this topic.

remained vested in the architect. *Held,* that the usage, if it existed, was unreasonable and therefore void: *Gibbon* v. *Pease* (1905).[20]

(3) In a case where an architect had work done on his own house in excess of the licensed amount, it was admitted to be the universal practice for architects to do everything necessary for the purpose of obtaining a building licence for the work: *Strongman* v. *Sincock* (1955).[21]

(4) An arbitration in accordance with trade rules provided for a right of appeal from the decision of the umpire to a board of appeal. The rules provided that the umpire should not be a member of the board of appeal. In accordance with their practice of some fifty years the board, having heard the appeal, invited the umpire to remain behind with them whilst they considered their decision, despite the protest of all of the parties to the reference. *Held,* that the practice was repugnant to the provisions of the rules, and as such was not a trade usage but merely a long-established irregularity, and that the board's award should be set aside: *London Export Corporation Ltd.* v. *Jubilee Coffee Roasting Co. Ltd.* (1958).[22]

(5) Under the then R.I.B.A. standard form of contract a builder expressly undertook to comply with the by-laws. *Held,* by the Court of Appeal, that he was liable to the employer for the cost of bringing the work done into conformity with by-law requirements, notwithstanding the custom that the architect was responsible for seeing to this: *Townsend (Builders) Ltd.* v. *Cinema News* (1959).[23]

SECTION 8.   COLLATERAL AGREEMENTS

It has already been stated that a contract may be partly oral and partly in writing, or that it may be concluded by separate documents or statements indicating offer and acceptance, from which of course it follows that not all the terms of a written contract need necessarily be found in any one document. The course of negotiations may produce agreement on successive terms until ultimately a point of time is reached at which the contract is finally concluded. Such an agreement may be concluded notwithstanding that the parties' intention from the beginning was to enter into a formal contract, and that in the event no such document was ever signed at all.[24] It is, therefore, perfectly possible, at some time prior to the final conclusion of the contract, to agree on some of its terms either orally or in other written documents or letters, and these other agreements will form part of and supplement the remainder of the contract documents.

---

[20] [1905] 1 K.B. 810.   See *post,* Chap. 2, pp. 189–191.
[21] [1955] 2 Q.B. 525.   Illustrated more fully, *post,* pp. 366–367.
[22] [1958] 1 W.L.R. 661.
[23] [1959] 1 W.L.R. 119.   Illustrated more fully, *post,* pp. 143 and 367.
[24] See *Trollope & Colls Ltd.* v. *Atomic Power Constructions Ltd.* [1963] 1 W.L.R. 333, *post,* Chap. 3, pp. 224–225.

Where, however, the parties have signed what purports to be a complete contract document, the perhaps excessive preoccupation of English law with the written or printed word raises a very strong presumption that this is intended to supersede previous agreements during the negotiating period. " It appears to me that the result is that this case is an illustration of a broad principle of law which is perfectly well known and is constantly acted upon, namely, that where a preliminary contract of any description, whether verbal or written, is intended to be superseded by and is in fact superseded by one of a superior character, then the later contract—the superior contract—prevails, and the stipulations in the earlier one can no longer be relied upon." [25] The party putting forward an earlier collateral agreement therefore undertakes a heavy burden of proof, since the courts generally presume (in spite, it must be said, of a disappointing tendency to the contrary in real life) that the parties will normally take the more logical course of amending their main agreement rather than rely on relatively less formal collateral agreements. Thus it has been said, "But such collateral contracts must from their very nature be rare . . . the more natural and usual way of carrying this out would be by so modifying the main contract and not by executing a concurrent and collateral contract. Such collateral contracts, the sole effect of which is to vary or add to the terms of the principal contract, are therefore viewed with suspicion by the law. They must be proved strictly. Not only the terms of such contracts but the existence of an *animus contrahendi* on the part of all the parties to them must be clearly shown. Any laxity on these points would enable parties to escape from the full performance of the obligations of contracts unquestionably entered into by them and more especially would have the effect of lessening the authority of written contracts by making it possible to vary them by suggesting the existence of verbal collateral agreements relating to the same subject matter."[26]

Where an agreement is inconsistent with or varies or contradicts a later more formal agreement, this presumption hardens into a rule of evidence which actually prevents evidence being given of the earlier agreement, and therefore deprives it of any effect. In such a case, provided the very stringent requirements can be satisfied, rectification of the contract is the only remedy available to the person seeking to set up the previously agreed term.[27]

[25] *Per* Wills J. in *Greswolde-Williams* v. *Barneby* (1901) 83 L.T. 708 at p. 711.
[26] *Per* Lord Moulton in *Heilbut Symons & Co.* v. *Buckleton* [1913] A.C. 30 at p. 47.
[27] See *ante*, pp. 32–38. *Cf. Boot* v. *L.C.C.*, illustrated *supra*, Sect. 5, p. 34.

Contractors frequently seek to qualify their tenders or negotiate some mitigation or alteration of the contract conditions but the contract documents are often nevertheless signed without alteration. It goes without saying that positive agreement—not mere requests, statements or contentions which are ignored [28]—must be shown in order to overcome the presumption that the later document supersedes earlier discussions, negotiations or agreements.

SECTION 9. ESTOPPEL AND WAIVER

(1) Estoppel

Estoppel by representation is a rule of evidence which prevents a plaintiff from alleging a fact necessary to his claim if he has previously, by word or conduct, represented the contrary to the defendant. It is therefore a defence, not a cause of action (though the rule may also prevent a defendant raising a defence otherwise available to him). To be successful, the party raising the estoppel must be able to show that he has acted upon the representation to his detriment. In addition, the representation must be positive and clear, and intended to be acted upon. It is a rule that can be invoked far more seldom than many laymen (and indeed legal pleaders) would appear to suppose, usually because the element of detriment cannot be established.[29]

ILLUSTRATIONS

(1) A contractor alleged that during negotiations it had been agreed that increases in the cost of all materials, and not merely those in the basic price list, should be payable under the fluctuations clause. The employers relied on the contract as signed, which said that only increases in listed materials were payable. The contractor relied on the fact that during the currency of the contract the employers had paid the sums claimed by the contractor on interim certificates for increases in unlisted materials. *Held*, by Ashworth J., that the employers were not estopped by reason of their making the payments from later contending that the sums had not been due: *Royston U.D.C.* v. *Royston Builders Ltd.* (1961).[30]

(2) A city council's engineer's representative accepted substandard hardcore beneath blocks of dwellings being constructed by a contractor, and 11 out of 17 blocks were certified as complete. At this stage the representative was replaced and the new representative, who was more exacting than his predecessor, refused to certify

---

[28] See *e.g. Royston U.D.C.* v. *Royston Builders Ltd.* (1961) 177 E.G. 589, illustrated on this point, *post*, Chap. 3, p. 215; *Boot & Sons* v. *L.C.C.* [1959] 1 W.L.R. 1069, *ante*, p. 34.
[29] See *e.g. Purity Dairy* v. *Collinson* (1966) 57 W.W.R. (Canada). For the so-called rule of equitable or promissory estoppel, see *infra* under Waiver.
[30] 177 E.G. 589 (Ashworth J.).

completion of the remaining six notwithstanding that they were completed to the same standard as those previously certified and the
hardcore for them had been laid during the time of his predecessor.
Held, by the Privy Council, that while on the true construction of the
contract the council could not complain of the certified blocks, they
were not estopped from contending that the uncertified blocks did not
conform with the contract, and damages could be recovered, subject
only to their being limited, in accordance with the duty to mitigate,
to the cost of rectification had the hardcore been condemned at the
time of laying: *Ata Ul Haq* v. *City Council of Nairobi* (1959).[31]

Contractors frequently contend that an employer is estopped
from claiming damages for defective work on the ground that the
work was previously seen, or that the defects could have been
detected, by the architect or clerk of works, or on the ground that
earlier rights under the contract (*e.g.* to condemn work while under
construction, or when certifying practical completion, or when
carrying out satisfactory reinstatement of defects at the end of the
defects liability period) have not been exercised. There is no substance in any of these contentions, unless perhaps in a very special
case the architect's attention is specifically drawn to a suspected
defect for a ruling and he acts or gives instructions in such a way
that the contractor suffers a real detriment.[32] The only way in which
the employer will usually lose his right to complain is if there is some
certificate which, by the terms of the contract, is conclusive as to the
quality or sufficiency of the work.[32a]

(2) Waiver

Waiver occurs where a party to a contract expressly or by conduct
intimates to the other that he will forgo or dispense with a right
which he enjoys under the contract. If consideration is present, no
problem arises since the case in reality is one of variation of the
contract rather than waiver, and the new arrangement can be
enforced by either party.

Where consideration is not present, the true case of waiver, it is
difficult to see any clear distinction from the case of estoppel,
except that in the case of estoppel traditionally the representation
must be one of fact, whereas in the case of waiver it is usually one
of intention.

[31] 1959 P.C. Appeal No. 48 (unreported). This case must be regarded as doubtful
    authority on the duty to mitigate, however,—see the next following paragraph.
[32] See *post*, Chap. 6, pp. 385–388.
[32a] See *post*, Chap. 7, and see also *post*, Chap. 6, pp. 383–385.

ILLUSTRATION

A quantity surveyor was engaged to prepare a specification of war damage repairs and to supervise the work. After preparing the specification but before work started, he became a director of the builders. He informed the owners, who allowed him to continue and supervise on their behalf. *Held,* by the Court of Appeal, although he had committed a fundamental breach warranting instant dismissal, the breach had been waived by his employers and he was entitled to payment of his fees in full: *Hall* v. *Wembley Electrical Appliances* (1947).[33]

The important rule of waiver, from the practical point of view in building cases, is the equitable rule most clearly enunciated by Bowen L.J. in *Birmingham and District Land Co.* v. *L.N.W.Ry.*,[34] that a voluntary concession or waiver cannot be withdrawn so as to render the other party liable for the past acts or omissions done or made on the faith of the waiver, and that time should, if the facts warrant it, be allowed to enable a party once more called upon to fulfil the contract to be placed in the same position as before. Usually this will mean that reasonable notice should be given,[35] but express notice is not strictly necessary and any act showing clearly that the concession is withdrawn will be sufficient,[36] provided that time is available to the other party to restore his position if that is necessary. It is an essential requirement of this rule, however, that the other party should have altered his position and only if restoration of the position becomes impossible will the promise become permanently final and binding.[37]

The main situations in which the doctrine of waiver is likely to be of importance in building and engineering contracts occur when rights of forfeiture arising upon some non-continuing breach or event are not exercised reasonably promptly by the employer, so that the builder irrevocably alters his position by continuing with the work and the right is accordingly lost.[38] On analysis these restrictions, which are equitable in origin, on rights of forfeiture or analogous rights, may not be true cases of waiver.

The fact that an employer may sometimes lose his right to complain of defects in the work after entering into occupation is frequently referred to as an example of waiver or estoppel. As already

[33] [1947] 2 All E.R. 630. See for a further example *Re Elliott, post,* p. 453.
[34] (1888) 40 Ch.D. 286.
[35] See *Charles Rickards Ltd.* v. *Oppenhaim* [1950] 1 K.B. 616.
[36] See *Tool Metal Manufacturing Co. Ltd.* v. *Tungsten Electric Co. Ltd.* [1955] 1 W.L.R. 761, where mere delivery of a counterclaim in legal proceedings was held sufficient.
[37] *Ajayi* v. *R. T. Briscoe (Nigeria) Ltd.* [1964] 1 W.L.R. 1326. See also *Ives Investments* v. *High* [1967] 2 Q.B. 379.
[38] See *post,* Chap. 13, pp. 697–700.

noted,[39] this is quite incorrect and can only come about as a result of express provisions in the contract, usually in relation to the binding effect of certificates given by the architect or engineer.

SECTION 10.   LIABILITY APART FROM CONTRACT

(1) Quasi-Contract and Quantum Meruit

Quasi-contract is a term used by lawyers to denote a miscellaneous series of situations in which a plaintiff can sue a defendant for moneys due although no contract between the parties exists.

It is not proposed to attempt a complete statement of this subject but merely to indicate very shortly certain types of quasi-contractual liability which may arise in the practical context of building and engineering contracts.

First, money paid under a mistake of fact can be recovered under this heading. This applies to nearly all cases of overpayment. So in a case where a building owner's interim payments (or indeed final payment) exceed the value of the work done, the excess can be recovered in quasi-contract, whether or not the contract contains any provision for repayment, since the money was paid under a mistake as to the value of the work done. (Contractual provisions may, however, render a final certificate, for instance, conclusive as to the value of work done, and this may defeat the remedy.[40]) Unlike mistake which avoids a contract,[41] a mistake of this kind can be a unilateral mistake unknown to the other party, and it would seem to be on principle sufficient if the mistake related to some matter which if true would render the mistaken party liable to make the payment.

Secondly, money received by the defendant to the plaintiff's use can be recovered. Building contracts not infrequently contain provisions that include in the sums payable by the employer to the builder under the terms of the contract money intended for onward transmission to a third person. A very common example is payment for nominated sub-contractors or suppliers of the builder. In the case of this latter example the sub-contractor or supplier will be able to sue the builder on the sub-contract, and need not rely on this particular head of quasi-contract. But in some cases there is no

---

[39] *Supra*, Estoppel, p. 59.
[40] See *post*, Chap. 7.
[41] See *ante*, pp. 25 *et seq.*

contractual connection between the builder and the person entitled to the money. Thus the pre-1963 standard R.I.B.A. forms of contract contained optional clauses for payment of the quantity surveyor by the contractor. In such a case, a builder who has actually received sums representing the quantity surveyor's fees will be liable to the quantity surveyor in quasi-contract.[42]

There are various other heads of quasi-contract enabling money paid or received to be recovered, but they are not likely to arise in practice in building contracts. They include money paid by the plaintiff to the defendant's use, money paid on a consideration which has wholly failed, and money paid under void contracts. But the last and by far the most important class of quasi-contractual remedy from the point of view of building contracts is that of *quantum meruit*.

Quantum meruit is a right to be paid a reasonable remuneration for work done. It has already been pointed out that where work is done at the request of the defendant and the price is not fixed by agreement the law will imply a term for payment of reasonable remuneration.[43] This, however, is a purely contractual situation, though the expression *quantum meruit* is frequently applied to it.

The same principle operates if work is done on the basis that if a certain condition is satisfied it will not be charged for, but that condition does not in fact eventuate.[44]

True *quantum meruit* arises in a number of situations where for one reason or another no contract exists. Thus reasonable remuneration can be recovered for work done under a void contract, *e.g.* a contract voided by mistake,[45] or by the operation of the doctrine of frustration,[46] or which may have failed by reason of some technicality, such as absence of seal, or which, in the circumstances which have happened, can no longer be reasonably applied to the work done by the plaintiff [47]; these being cases where the law may have set an apparent contract aside or declared it unenforceable, but where the work was nevertheless done in circumstances where it was intended to be paid for. Very importantly, *quantum meruit*

---

[42] See, *e.g.* the county court case of *Payne* v. *Wheeldon* (1954) 104 L.J. 844.

[43] See *ante*, pp. 5, 49.

[44] See the " preparatory work " cases, *post*, Chap. 3, pp. 230–231.

[45] As to which see *ante*, pp. 25 *et seq.*

[46] See *post*, Chap. 5, pp. 348 *et seq.*

[47] See *e.g. Kilby* v. *Northshore Development* (1963) 5 W.I.R. 379, *post*, pp. 191–192, (quantity surveyor's fees)—and *Parkinson* v. *Commissioners of Works* [1949] 2 K.B. 632, *post*, Chap. 8, pp. 550–551. But see *supra*, Section 2 (8) and the case of *Gilbert & Partners* v. *Knight* (1968) 112 S.J. 155 there referred to.

is also available as an alternative remedy to damages to a party who has done work before accepting a fundamental breach by the other as discharging the contract.[48] This may be of great practical importance in building cases, since if the contract rates turn out to have been highly uneconomical a builder who is in a position to prove a fundamental breach by the employer and thus to treat the contract as at an end may find reasonable remuneration for the work done by him a considerably more valuable remedy than damages.[49] In cases where a party is in breach of contract but is held nevertheless entitled to sue for work done under it, the term *quantum meruit* is sometimes applied to the sums awarded,[50] but it is apparent that this is erroneous, since what the contractor is really entitled to in such a case (under the doctrine of substantial performance)[51] is the contract remuneration less the damages occasioned by his breach.

In cases where a contract has been avoided in one of these ways or discharged by breach, the contract rates are not, of course, applicable to the work sued for on a *quantum meruit*, though they may be some evidence of what reasonable remuneration for the work should be.

(2) Liability under the Law of Tort

(a) Generally

Tortious liability is a liability to pay damages which arises not out of contract, but from a wrongful act. Typical examples are the liability of a negligent motorist (the tort of negligence), or of a newspaper proprietor for defamatory matter in his paper (the tort of libel). It has already been seen that one tort (that of deceit) is highly relevant in considering the law of contract, as the liability to pay damages for a fraudulent misrepresentation arises independently of contract. The importance of this is that a person who has suffered damage as a result of a fraudulent misrepresentation made to him can sue for damages notwithstanding that he is not in contractual relations with the representor, or may not have himself given consideration. So a builder who suffers damage as the result of a misstatement fraudulently made to him by the architect, or an employer who has suffered damage as a result of a sub-contractor's similar misstatement, can sue and recover damages

---

[48] *Lodder* v. *Slowey* [1904] A.C. 442.
[49] See *post*, Chap. 9, pp. 601–602.
[50] See *e.g. Alkok* v. *Grymek* (1968) 67 D.L.R. (2d) 718.
[51] See *post*, Chap. 5, pp. 245 *et seq.*

notwithstanding the absence of any contract between representor and representee. In this section it is proposed to examine shortly the law of tort under three heads affecting building contracts, namely, first, part of the tort of negligence under which it has recently been held that in certain circumstances damagés can be obtained for the financial consequences of negligent statements, second, the general liability in negligence, nuisance or trespass of employers, architects and contractors to third persons suffering damage to property or person as a result of building or civil engineering operations, and, third, the special duty of care of occupiers of property now defined by the Occupier's Liability Act of 1957.

(b) The principle in Hedley Byrne v. Heller

It has already been stated [52] that until the Misrepresentation Act of 1967 no liability to pay damages could arise from an innocent misrepresentation made between contracting parties unless it was also a term of a contract. This had also appeared to be the law for many years in a wider class of cases where misstatements were made to a person who was not necessarily a contracting party, since the much criticised decision of the House of Lords in *Derry* v. *Peek* (1889).[53] This case appeared to lay down that no duty of care existed (apart from contract) in the making of statements, however seriously given and for whatever purpose, which resulted solely in indirect financial loss (as opposed to direct physical damage to person or property). So a negligent false statement resulting only in such loss, in the absence of a contractual duty of care or fraud, was not actionable.[54] (For many years English law has permitted the recovery of consequential financial loss where a duty is owed and breach of it results in physical damage to person or property. Any negligent statements in this sense have always been actionable, as for instance an incorrect diagnosis and prescription for treatment made by a doctor to his patient, or wrong advice given by a harbourmaster to a ship as to the position of a sandbank.[55])

It is now clear as a result of the decision of the House of Lords in *Hedley Byrne* v. *Heller* (1964) [56] that this is not the law, and that

---

[52] *Ante*, pp. 40, 45.
[53] 14 App.Cas. 337.
[54] *Le Lievre* v. *Gould* [1893] 1 Q.B. 491.
[55] See also *Halsbury's Laws of England*, 3rd ed. Vol. 28, p. 8, and the *Rhosina* (1884) 10 P.D. 24 at p. 29, affirmed at p. 131. See also *Anderson Ltd.* v. *Rhodes Ltd.* [1967] 2 All E.R. 850.
[56] [1964] A.C. 465. See also *Anderson Ltd.* v. *Rhodes Ltd.* [1967] 2 All E.R. 850.

circumstances can exist where an innocent but negligent misstatement which results only in such indirect financial loss does give rise to liability, notwithstanding the absence of any contractual relationship between the representor and representee. It is not sufficient, it should be noted, that the statement is inaccurate or false. It must also be established that the person making the statement was careless or negligent in making it, and owed a duty to the person to whom it was made.

It is of crucial importance to determine in what kinds of circumstances this duty of care will be held to exist, but it is too early to attempt any clear definition of the situations in which the principle of this case will be applied. From the judgments it would appear that the duty of care exists when a party seeking information from a party possessed of special skill or knowledge trusts him to exercise due care, and that party knew or ought to have known that reliance was being placed on his skill and judgment. The facts of the case give little assistance in the context of building and engineering, since they relate to an inquiry from bankers as to the financial standing of their clients. It is also clear from the decision itself that an express disclaimer of responsibility for the accuracy of the statement will serve to exclude the liability.

The basis of the duty was variously expressed (for instance, by Lord Pearce, as depending upon the gravity of the inquiry and the importance and influence attached to the answer and, by Lord Devlin, upon the voluntary acceptance of responsibility either generally where a general relationship between the parties is created or specifically in relation to a particular transaction).

Although Lord Pearce's approach appears to have been in the forefront of the reasoning in an important subsequent case,[57] Lord Devlin's more general approach receives some support from an *earlier* (but unreported) decision of the Court of Appeal. In the eighth edition of this work, reference was made to the case of *Townsend Ltd.* v. *Cinema News*[58] where the Court of Appeal had apparently held an architect liable *to a builder* in damages for failure to secure by-law approval of the work, and complaint was made that the official law reports of the case did not even see fit to mention this fact, while no law report even gave the reasons for this, at first sight revolutionary, decision. In the ninth edition it was pointed out

---

[57] *Anderson Ltd.* v. *Rhodes Ltd.* [1967] 2 All E.R. 850.
[58] [1959] 1 W.L.R. 119, illustrated *post*, pp. 143 and 367.

that the reasoning of the Court of Appeal somewhat startlingly anticipated, on Lord Devlin's view, the reasoning of the House of Lords in *Hedley Byrne* v. *Heller*. In *Townsend's* case an architect had told a builder he would be responsible for issuing the necessary notices to obtain by-law approval. The following is an extract from the transcript of the Court of Appeal's judgment delivered by Lord Evershed M.R.: " The responsibility of Wilkie [the architect] to Townsend [the builder] rests, it seems to me, quite plainly in the circumstance that Wilkie, even if there were no consideration as between Wilkie and Townsend, was a professional man acting gratuitously and owing a duty accordingly to Townsend. The matter is sufficiently stated in *Halsbury's Laws of England*, 2nd ed., Vol. 23, p. 586 [59]: ' Where a person skilled in a particular matter gratuitously undertakes to do something involving the exercise of skill he must do it to the best of his skill, which must be such as a person skilled in such matters may reasonably be expected to possess.' The duty pervaded the whole relationship from first to last. I say that in order to reject the suggestion of Mr. Gardam based on the proposition that a man, even though he promises to act gratuitously, cannot be compelled to act at all: it is only if he does act that the duty of care comes in. So it was suggested that, in so far as Wilkie never sent a notice at all he must be treated as though he never acted at all. But that, I think, when you look at the whole story, is quite untenable. Wilkie was acting throughout as the architect; and I have already read the letter at page 24 of December 4, which of course was the day, or roughly the day, on which Wilkie should have sent the notice to the local authority."

The exact *ratio decidendi* of *Hedley Byrne* v. *Heller* must await clarification by the courts, but its possible importance in building cases can be indicated by reference to the following common situations:

(a) An architect inquires of specialist sub-contractors whether a material or process furnished by them will be suitable for incorporation in his proposed design. On the faith of careless statements by them, he selects their material or process, an order is placed by the main contractor, and the material or process fails in its purpose. Can the architect, if sued for negligence by the employer, or the employer who has to order new work in substitution or suffers delay in obtaining

[59] See now, 3rd ed., Vol. 28, p. 8.

possession, sue for damages? [60] (Note that section 2 (1) of the Misrepresentation Act 1967 cannot assist the architect or employer, since that Act applies, it is submitted, only to contracting parties.)

(b) A contractor undertakes that his work will conform with the by-laws (*cf.* clause 4 of the 1963 R.I.B.A. standard form of contract). The architect supplies him with plans of the work and expressly (or perhaps thereby impliedly by custom [61]) indicates that he is satisfied that the design complies with the by-laws. The builder later has to demolish and rebuild at his own expense. Can he sue the architect for his loss?

(c) An engineering contractor makes specific inquiries as to subsoil conditions from the consultant engineers before tendering. He is carelessly given inaccurate information which misleads him. If the contractor cannot recover the additional expense under the contract,[62] can he recover damages under this head from the consultants or the employers?

(d) Specialist sub-contractors are requested to design their part of the work (for instance the manufacturers of the structural steel frame of a building). They prepare and put forward such a design to an architect after being informed of the loading requirements. The contractor places his order with them. The design fails. Can they be sued for the employer's or architect's loss (as opposed to the main contractor's)?

It is unfortunately not possible to do more than state these problems and await the development and application of the *Hedley Byrne* principle by the courts.

(c) Liability to third persons for physical damage

A discussion on this topic may not be considered entirely relevant to a book on building contracts, but some indication of the law may be useful to readers of this book who are not legally qualified, and a full understanding of the indemnity and insurance provisions in building contracts [63] which are designed to redistribute or regulate

---

[60] See *post*, Chap. 15, pp. 742–746; and the cases there referred to of *Shanklin Pier* v. *Detel Products* [1951] 2 K.B. 854, and *Wells* v. *Buckland* [1965] 2 Q.B. 170, which may offer a contractual outlet for the employer.

[61] See *ante*, pp. 52 *et seq.*

[62] See *post*, pp. 232, 267–268, 316–317 and 349.

[63] As to which, see *post*, Chap. 5, pp. 306–313.

the burden, as between the parties to the contract and their insurers, of the claims made by third persons against them arising out of the building operations, is not possible without some knowledge of the liabilities involved.

It is perhaps unnecessary to point out that a contractor will be liable in negligence to persons injured, and in negligence, nuisance or trespass to persons suffering damage to their property, as a result of his building operations. In the case of damage to adjoining property, this liability is likely to be the strict one of nuisance, or even of trespass, and actual lack of care or negligence in the usual sense need not be present. In addition, many building or engineering operations may attract the even stricter liability under the rule in *Rylands* v. *Fletcher* (1868).[64] Wherever a contractor is liable to a third person in this way, the building owner may also be vicariously liable for the builder's acts or omissions, or, perhaps more correctly, will be a joint tortfeasor.[65] By virtue of the Law Reform (Married Women and Tortfeasors) Act 1935, the court is empowered, as between one or more tortfeasors, to apportion the liability and order contribution in respect of a joint tort, but this does not affect the injured party, who can recover his whole loss from any tortfeasor responsible. The Act, however, does not permit the court to override any express agreement between the tortfeasors indemnifying one or the other in respect of the plaintiff's claim,[66] and it in fact is a commonplace of building contracts to find such indemnities—very often in the form of cross-indemnities between the parties depending on the nature of the claim involved.[67]

In addition to the employer, the architect or engineer may also be held liable in tort, in cases where the damage can be shown to result from his permanent design or from his control of the building operation,[68] but considerable misunderstanding appears to exist as to the extent of an architect's or engineer's control over the contractor's operations. In general not only is it neither the function nor interest of the architect to intervene in or control the contractor's day-to-day operations, but on the contrary the contractor has the right to carry out the work in whatever manner he chooses in the

---

[64] L.R. 3 H.L. 330. See, *e.g. Hoare* v. *McAlpine* [1923] 1 Ch. 167, illustrated *infra*.
[65] For a discussion of the very difficult topic of the liability of employers for the acts of independent contractors, see *Salmond on Torts*, 13th ed., p. 152.
[66] See s. 6 (1) (c) of the Act.
[67] See *e.g.* clause 18 of the 1963 R.I.B.A. standard form and clause 22 of the 1955 I.C.E. standard form.
[68] See *Clay* v. *A. J. Crump Ltd.* [1964] 1 Q.B. 533, illustrated *infra*.

absence of express provisions to the contrary.[69]   The architect's function is generally limited to providing the necessary instructions and drawings so as to show the final result required, and to intervene if bad *permanent* work is being constructed. The specification may, of course, expressly impose requirements for particular work processes—*e.g.* of the periods for curing concrete before striking formwork, or temperatures at which concreting is forbidden, the number of passes of specified rollers to achieve compaction of hard surfaces, and so on, and may even provide for inspection by the architect's or engineer's representative at certain stages.   These requirements are not only often expressed to be minimum require- ments but are, of course, almost always inserted in the contract exclusively for the protection of the employers' interest in the quality of the final permanent work, and it is submitted that the architect owes no duty of care to third persons during the course of construc- tion in this regard, except to the extent that strict compliance with positive instructions given by him, as to a method of working, can be shown to be the effective cause of injury or damage to a third person. If the architect gives any instruction which can be safely complied with if full precautions are taken, he cannot, it is submitted, be liable without some further positive intervention on his part. Equally, while an architect can in principle be liable in tort for a failure of his permanent design during construction, this will only be the case, it is submitted, if the failure is due to a fault inherent in the permanent design and not to the contractors' failure to protect or support the work by whatever means may be necessary during construction.   In considering these matters it should be borne in mind that the contractor's supervisory staff are continuously on the site or in touch with the site personnel, whereas the architect's visits are of a periodical character; that the contractor as their employer is able to give direct instructions to site personnel while the architect is not; that the possibility of conflicting instructions is not acceptable for practical purposes; and that an architect, if he intervenes by giving positive instructions as to methods of working, at once exposes the employer to a financial claim on the ground that the instruction is not necessary and so amounts to a variation.

On occasions the courts appear to have leaned somewhat far in holding the architect liable for matters which are more properly the contractors' responsibility,[70] but, fortunately, passages in the

---

[69] See *Clayton* v. *Woodman & Son (Builders) Ltd.* [1962] 2 Q.B. 533, illustrated *infra.*
[70] See *e.g.* the decision of the High Court of Australia in *Florida Hotels* v. *Mayo* (1965) 113 C.L.R. 588, illustrated *infra.*

judgments in three cases in the United Kingdom have done much to clarify the position, it is submitted entirely correctly.[71] This subject is considered further, *post*, Chapters 2,[72] 5,[72a] 6,[73] 8 [74] and 9.[74a]

The two following passages from the judgment of Pearson L.J. (as he then was) in *Clayton* v. *Woodman* (1962) are, it is submitted, an entirely correct analysis and statement of the position. The case is particularly important because it concerned the then current R.I.B.A. form of contract (not, it is submitted, different in any of these respects from the later post-1963 forms):

" It is quite plain, in my view, both as a general proposition and under the particular contract in this case,[75] that the builder, as employer, has the responsibility at common law to provide a safe system of work, . . . so that everything is as safe for the workmen as it reasonably can be. It is important that that responsibility of the builder should not be overlaid or confused by any doubt as to where his province begins or some other person's province ends in that respect. The architect, on the other hand, is engaged as the agent of the owner for whom the building is being erected, and his function is to make sure that in the end, when the work has been completed, the owner will have a building properly constructed in accordance with the contract . . . and any supplementary instructions which the architect may have given. The architect does not undertake (as I understand the position) to advise the builder as to what safety precautions should be taken or, in particular, as to how he should carry out his building operations. It is the function and the right of the builder to carry out his own building operations as he thinks fit. . . . "[76]

" It might be suggested that the fault of the architect was in not advising the builder, through his existing representative on the site, . . . as to how the work required by the specification should be executed. If he had done so, the architect would have been stepping out of his own province and into the province of the builder. It is not right to require anyone to do that, and it is not in the interests of the builder's workpeople that there should be a confusion of function as between the builder on the one hand and the architect

---

[71] *Clayton* v. *Woodman* [1962] 2 Q.B. 533 (Salmon J.); [1962] 1 W.L.R. 585 (C.A.); *East Ham B.C.* v. *Bernard Sunley* [1966] A.C. 406 and *A.M.F. (International)* v. *Magnet Bowling Ltd.* [1968] 1 W.L.R. 1028 (Mocatta J.).
[72] *Post*, pp. 139–141, 153–155.   [72a] *Post*, pp. 324–325.
[73] *Post*, pp. 385–388.
[74] *Post*, pp. 524–530.   [74a] *Post*, pp. 582–583.
[75] The 1957 (revised) R.I.B.A. form.
[76] *Per* Pearson L.J., *Clayton* v. *Woodman* [1962] 1 W.L.R. 533 at p. 593.

on the other. I would hold that it was plainly not the architect's duty to do that . . . it might be suggested that the architect should have given a warning to the builder's workmen . . . as to how the work should be done or that there was some risk involved in doing it in a particular way. But there, also, it seems to me that he would be stepping out of his own province and entering that of the builder. He was entitled to assume that the work would be carried out properly, that the builder knew his own business and would properly perform his own operations."[77]

So far damage resulting from the building or engineering operations themselves has been considered. Another aspect of tortious responsibility arises, however, after the building or works are complete and handed over to the employer, if at some later date third parties are injured or property damaged as a result of a dangerous state of the building or works due to the negligence of those who built or designed them.

English law was at first reluctant to concede any such duty in the absence of contract.[78] But following the decision of the House of Lords in *Donoghue* v. *Stevenson* (1932)[79] the absence of a contractual relationship was no longer an objection in principle. The law, however, remained subject to the unattractive doctrine—*caveat emptor* or lessee—that a purchaser or lessee of an existing or completed house or other property could not complain of any defect in the property, and this meant that in practice many persons injured as a result of such defects were defeated by the immunity so conferred.[80]

It now seems clear that this immunity of the vendor or lessor of a completed building does not extend to his contractor,[81] or his architect,[82] and that the duty is " to use reasonable care to prevent damage to persons whom he may reasonably expect to be affected by his work." [83] It will be seen from the following illustrations that the liability of employer, contractor, and architect or engineer to third persons is now governed by ordinary principles of negligence,

[77] *Ibid.* at p. 595.
[78] *Winterbottom* v. *Wright* (1842) 10 M. & W. 109; *Earl* v. *Lubbock* [1905] 1 K.B. 253; *Malone* v. *Laskey* [1907] 2 K.B. 141; *Ball* v. *L.C.C.* [1949] 2 K.B. 159.
[79] [1932] A.C. 562.
[80] *Otto* v. *Bolton* [1936] 2 K.B. 46, following *Bottomley* v. *Bannister* [1932] 1 K.B. 458 and *Cavalier* v. *Pope* [1906] A.C. 428. And see *Ball* v. *L.C.C.* [1949] 2 K.B. 159.
[81] *Billings* v. *Riden* [1958] A.C. 240; *Gallagher* v. *McDowell Ltd.* [1961] N.I. 26 (Northern Ireland).
[82] *Voli* v. *Inglewood Shire Council* (1963) 56 Q.L.R. 256 (Queensland).
[83] *Billings* v. *Riden, infra.*

untrammelled by any special difficulties arising from completion or non-completion of the building, save only that the now limited immunity as between vendor and purchaser or lessor and lessee remains in those rather special cases to defeat the plaintiffs' claim.[83a]

ILLUSTRATIONS

(1) Contractors drove a large number of piles into the soil while preparing the site for a large building in the heart of the city, and the heavy vibration caused serious damage to an old house belonging to the plaintiffs, who were compelled to demolish a large part of it under a dangerous structure notice. The contractors contended that the building was exceptionally old and frail, and that this action did not therefore constitute a nuisance since a normal building would not have suffered damage. *Held*, even if the building was in such an unusually frail state that nuisance could not be established, the defendants were absolutely liable for the damage done by them under the rule in *Rylands* v. *Fletcher* (1868)[84]: *Hoare* v. *MacAlpine* (1923).[85]

(2) A fireman attending a fire in the first defendants' factory premises was electrocuted and killed. The cause of his electrocution was:

(i) that obsolete tumbler switches, which were in fact the main switches, had been left on, although the firemen had switched off all the other switches so that no current should have been in the part of the building affected by the fire;

(ii) two wires had been transposed so that although all the switches except the main switches were off, current was still flowing in that part of the building. The second defendants or their predecessors had done work in the building in 1930, 1946 and 1950, and the transposing of the wires was due to the negligence of some employee of the second defendants on a previous occasion which it was impossible to identify. The fault was one which might have been found if a proper test had been carried out after work was done. The second defendants had not pointed out to the first defendants, who were the occupiers of the factory, that the main switches were obsolete. It was negligent of the first defendant's manager not to know where the main switch was.

Held, the first defendants were 10 per cent. to blame and the second defendants 90 per cent. to blame, and both were liable in damages for the death of the fireman: *Hartley* v. *Mayoh & Co. and the N.W. Electricity Board* (1954).[86]

(3) Contractors working on occupied premises obstructed the access to the premises, so that visitors to the premises had to make a short diversion onto the adjoining premises in order to reach those

[83a] For a further special exception (abstraction of water) see *Langbrook Properties* v. *Surrey C.C.* [1970] 1 W.L.R. 161
[84] L.R. 3 H.L. 330 (whereby an occupier of land is strictly liable if he brings anything inherently dangerous upon it which escapes and does damage).
[85] [1923] 1 Ch. 167.   [86] [1954] 1 Q.B. 383.

on which the contractor was working. The adjoining premises were in an unfit and dangerous condition and the plaintiff fell and was injured there while on her way home after visiting the occupiers of the premises. *Held*, by the House of Lords, the fact that the contractor was not in contractual relations with the defendant was irrelevant, the duty owed by the contractor was not the same as the duty of his employer (whose duty as a licensor, for instance, might be of limited scope and avoided by proving knowledge of the danger, or warning) and notwithstanding that the plaintiff was aware of the dangerous condition of the adjoining premises the contractor was liable for failure to use reasonable care to prevent danger to persons who might be expected lawfully to visit the house. *Per* Lord Keith, a contractor is not normally liable for a danger not of his own creation on adjacent property, with which he has no right to interfere, but if, as here, he does not provide a reasonably safe approach to a house he may be liable if a person, attempting to enter or leave the house, is precipitated into the danger on the adjacent property: *Billings* v. *Riden* (1958).[87]

(4) Builders negligently plugged a hole in a wooden floor. The defect was not noticed by the employer, who subsequently let the house to the plaintiff's husband. The plaintiff was injured when the heel of her shoe went through the hole. *Held*, by the Court of Appeal of Northern Ireland, that the immunity in relation to real property established by *Cavalier* v. *Pope* (1906) and *Otto* v. *Bolton* (1936) only applied to vendors or landlords of property, and that the builders owed a duty in tort to all lawful users of the house they had constructed: *Gallagher* v. *McDowell Ltd.* (1961).[88]

(5) An architect administering the current R.I.B.A. form of contract was advised by an experienced bricklayer that it would be better to pull down an existing wall (which it was intended to use in the works if it was sufficiently strong) because it would be difficult to cut a chase in it to take a concrete floor. The architect satisfied himself that the wall was adequate for its intended function, and decided not to change the original intention. The bricklayer was injured when the work was carried out without support being arranged for the wall. The contractor was required by the specification to provide all necessary shoring and support. *Held*, by the Court of Appeal, the architect did not in the circumstances owe any duty to the workman. To do more whether by advice or warning would be to step out of his own province into that of the builder. Had he ordered the work to be carried out without supports that would have been a different situation, but all he had done, as he was entitled to do, was to refuse to alter the contract: *Clayton* v. *Woodman & Son (Builders) Ltd.* (1962).[89]

---

[87] [1958] A.C. 240. See also the remarkable facts (contractor damaging cable in road liable to factory owner affected by loss of electricity) in *S.C.M. (U.K.) Ltd.* v. *W. J. Whittall & Son Ltd.*, 1970, C.A.

[88] [1961] N.I. 26 (Northern Ireland).

[89] [1962] 2 Q.B. 533. (Salmon J.) [1962] 1 W.L.R. 585 (C.A.). The judgments of both Salmon J. and of the Court of Appeal are of the greatest importance in regard to the principles involved and should be borne in mind when considering the case of *Clay* v. *Crump*, *infra*. See the discussions *post*, Chap. 2, pp. 139–141, 153–155, Chap. 5, pp. 324–325, Chap. 6, pp. 385–388 and Chap. 8, pp. 524–530.

(6) The plaintiff attended a meeting at a public hall, and was injured when the stage collapsed. He sued both the architect and the owners of the hall, who had hired it out to the association giving the meeting. The design of the floor-joists and stage was defective. Under the architect's contract of employment all his plans and specifications were subject to the inspection and approval of the employers' public works department. *Held,* by the High Court of Queensland, that (1) the architect was independently liable in tort for failing to design a stage capable of bearing the number of people likely to assemble there, (2) nothing in the contract of employment of the architect could affect his liability to third persons, and (3) the owners were also vicariously liable for the architect's negligence, the immunity of landlords (if there was indeed a letting) not extending to persons letting out property for public purposes: *Voli* v. *Inglewood Shire Council* (1963).[90]

(7) Prior to entry on the site by the main contractors, an architect, after a telephone discussion with the demolition contractors who had cleared the site, approved of their leaving an existing wall standing on the site without support in a dangerous condition. The architect had accepted the opinion of the demolition contractors that it was safe, and though he subsequently visited the site and had an opportunity to do so, did not in fact examine the wall carefully. The building contractors did not do so either, but assumed that the architect had satisfied himself about its safety. A workman of the building contractors was injured when the wall collapsed. *Held,* by the Court of Appeal, the architect, the demolition contractors and the building contractors were all liable to the workman: *Clay* v. *A. J. Crump Ltd.* (1964).[91]

(8) An architect was employed under R.A.I.A. terms (similar to those of the R.I.B.A.), which included " periodical supervision and inspection as may be necessary to ensure the works generally are executed in accordance with the contract; constant supervision does not form part of the duties undertaken. . . ." The building owner in fact employed no main contractor, and used his own foreman and leading hands to supervise the work, which included a concrete swimming pool, in conjunction with the architect. The architect visited twice a week, including a Friday at a time when the reinforcement for the concrete aprons of the pool was not yet fixed. After the visit, the mesh reinforcement was placed longitudinally instead of transversely. By the next visit the concrete had been poured. When the formwork was struck, the concrete collapsed due to this cause and injured a workman. The building owner when sued joined the architect as a third party. *Held,* by the High Court of Australia (Windeyer J. dissenting), that the architect's obligation was to inspect formwork and reinforcement before pouring and not to assume that the foreman would postpone pouring of concrete till the next inspection. He should have given clear and express instructions to the foreman that concrete should not be poured until the architect had been notified and had inspected: *Florida Hotels Ltd.* v. *Mayo* (1965).[92]

[90] 56 Q.L.R. 256 (Queensland).
[91] [1964] 1 Q.B. 533.
[92] 113 C.L.R. 588 (Australia).

(Note: Without knowing what evidence was before the court, this decision cannot be legitimately criticised, but the facts as reported certainly would appear to carry the supervisory function of the architect as far as it can possibly go. While Barwick C.J. seems to have thought that the architect was also directly liable in tort to the plaintiff, it is plain, however, that the decision is in terms concerned only with the extent of the duty of supervision owed by the architect to the employer. Furthermore, although the judgments expressly refute any distinction based on the fact that the building owner was the direct employer of the men on the site and had engaged no main contractor, it is obvious that such a special situation must call for a greater degree of care by the architect. The important limits to the architect's area of responsibility as defined in *Clayton's* case also do not appear to have been present in the court's mind.)

(9) Holiday camp proprietors P had a building and maintenance subsidiary which employed N, " labour-only " contractors, to fix joists and boards on a roof to receive the felt of A, specialist roofing contractors. One of the " labour-only " employees left a hole in the roof unguarded before going to lunch, and an employee of the roofers fell from the roof and was injured. He sued P's subsidiary, his own employers A, and N. No special arrangements about safety had been made by anyone. *Held*, by the Court of Appeal, that as P was employing two small contractors who were to work in proximity and one of whom was " labour only, " P had assumed the duty of co-ordinating the work and was under a duty to see that reasonable safety precautions were taken. P, N and A were all liable, and as between each other were each one-third liable: *McArdle* v. *Andmac Roofing* (1967).[93]

(d) Liability under the Occupiers' Liability Act 1957

This Act was passed to unify and clarify the many subtle refinements of liability which the courts had evolved as between various categories of persons entering premises in the control of another. The Act now deals with only two categories of persons, namely, occupiers and visitors, and imposes on the occupier a single all-embracing liability, namely, " to take such care as in all the circumstances of the case is reasonable to see that the visitor will be reasonably safe in using the premises for the purposes for which he is invited or permitted by the occupier to be there " (s. 2 (2)).

At the outset a number of points should be noted, *viz.*:

(i) the Act imposes a duty to avoid damage to property as well as personal injuries, except possibly in regard to certain cases of theft, and includes any consequential financial damage,[94]

[93] 111 S.J. 37.
[94] See s. 1 (3) (*b*), and *Workington Harbour Board* v. *Towerfield Owners* [1951] A.C. 112, and *A.M.F. International Ltd.* v. *Magnet Bowling Ltd.* [1968] 1 W.L.R. 1028, *per* Mocatta J. at p. 1050, and see also s. 5 (1) of the Act.

(ii) a building contractor can be an occupier under the Act.[95] Furthermore, multiple occupancies are possible (that is to say, more than one person can be an occupier of the same premises at the same time),[96]

(iii) the liability under the Act can be restricted or removed by contract,[97] but such restrictions cannot operate against strangers to the contract,[98]

(iv) the Act probably does not apply to damage done by positive building operations or other activities on premises, but only by the *state* of the premises, in spite of the words " things done or omitted to be done " in section 1 (1).[99] Damage due to such active operations would presumably fall within the ordinary tort of negligence on the well-known *Donoghue* v. *Stevenson* principle, however,[99a] and in the *A.M.F.* case Mocatta J. held that premises under construction and in an unsafe state due to negligent protection of the work were covered by the Act.

It cannot be said that the Act has as yet been invoked very often in regard to the duties *inter se* of the more usual parties to a building project, but the following comments on various typical situations may be useful:

(i) *As between employer and contractor*

An employer normally parts with temporary possession of the site under what is in effect a revocable licence, under which the main contractor has a high degree of every-day control of the site.[1] In general an employer only impliedly warrants to do nothing positive to impede or obstruct the contractor.[2] If the employer is occupier, and the contractor a visitor (they can, of course, both be occupiers under the Act simultaneously *vis-à-vis* third persons),[3] then it is clear that the Act imposes a quite new obligation on the employer, and only an express term in the contract can restrict or avoid it. Furthermore,

---

[95] *Savory* v. *Holland & Hannen & Cubitts* [1964] 1 W.L.R. 1158.
[96] *Wheat* v. *Lacon* [1966] A.C. 552; *A.M.F. International Ltd.* v. *Magnet Bowling Ltd.*, *infra*; *Fisher* v. *C.H.T. Ltd.* [1966] 2 Q.B. 475.
[97] s. 2 (1) of the Act.
[98] s. 2 (2) of the Act.
[99] See s. 1 (2); Cambridge L.J., April 1957, pp. 39, 40, and May 17, 1957, p. 308.
[99a] See *supra*, sub-section (c).
[1] See *post*, Chap. 13, p. 681.
[2] See *post*, Chap. 5, 317 *et seq.*
[3] See the cases illustrated *infra*.

clause 3 (1) of the Act would appear to prevent any such exclusion or restriction operating in the employer's favour against
strangers to the contract, such as employees of the main contractor, or sub-contractors. In this context section 2 (3) (*b*),
" An occupier may expect that a person in the exercise of his
calling will appreciate and guard against any special risks
ordinarily incident to it, so far as the occupier leaves him free
to do so," needs to be borne in mind. In addition, the Act only
creates a duty to avoid damage to person or property, it is
submitted (see the words " reasonably safe in using the premises " in s. 2 (2)), so that it will not assist the contractor if
some default of the employer has rendered his work more
difficult or expensive.

(ii) *As between the main contractor and sub-contractor*

Here there certainly seems to be little in the Act which is
inconsistent with the terms normally to be implied in the more
usual sub-contracts where the main contractor is on the site
simultaneously and beyond any doubt, as between these parties,
in overall control of it. The same considerations as are adumbrated in (i) above would appear to apply to certain early types
of sub-contract where the main contractor may not yet be
effectively present on the site himself—for instance in the case
of sub-contractors for clearance of the site or for excavation,
or for the erection of the steel or concrete frame of the building.

(iii) *As between non-contracting parties*

(*e.g.* main contractor and other contractors of the employer,[4]
or as between sub-contractor and employer).   Here the Act
clearly can be vital, since it affords a potential remedy not otherwise available, and furthermore one which cannot by definition
be excluded or restricted. The potential liability of the employer
and main contractor as joint occupiers [4] to such third parties
and also to a far wider class of third parties, such as adjoining
owners or occupiers and the employees of all persons engaged
on the site, renders it doubly important that an effective
indemnity clause is present in the contract between building
owner and main contractor, so as to redistribute the burden of
such claims effectively according to whatever policy is deemed
to be appropriate.   As will be seen [5] the *A.M.F.* decision, if

---

[4] See *e.g.* the *A.M.F. International Ltd.* case.
[5] *Post*, Chap. 5, pp. 306–310.

correct, means that the indemnity clause in the R.I.B.A. forms is totally ineffective in all cases where joint liability, whether under the Act or otherwise, and in whatever proportions, is held to exist as between main contractor and employer on the one hand to some third person on the other.

Before referring to the small number of cases decided under the Act, it may be desirable to emphasise that a finding of " occupancy " under the Act does not necessarily connote liability, and that the nature of the occupancy will be of vital importance in determining whether or not there has been breach of the duty of care. Thus an employer out of possession for a three-year period, for instance, will generally be far less likely to be found to be in breach of duty than the main contractor in effective control of the site, even apart from the vitally important section 4 (*b*) of the Act, which provides that " where damage is caused to a visitor by a danger due to the faulty execution of any work of construction, maintenance or repair by an independent contractor employed by the occupier, the occupier is not without more to be liable if in all the circumstances he has acted reasonably in entrusting the work to an independent contractor and has taken such steps as he reasonably ought in order to satisfy himself that the contractor was competent and that the work had been properly done." This subsection resolves doubt as to the law prior to the Act and the extent to which the occupier's duty was absolute, in the sense that it could not be discharged by delegation to an independent contractor.[6]

Finally, it should perhaps be explained for the benefit of non-legal readers that the Law Reform (Married Women and Tortfeasors) Act of 1935 made it possible for the courts to allocate, as between persons jointly responsible in tort for identical damage, a division of the liability in any proportion that might seem appropriate, so as to enable the one to recover a proportionate contribution (or even a complete indemnity) from the other. Thus tortfeasor A can be found liable to third party X because he did not sufficiently supervise or guard against the carelessness or act of tortfeasor B, which was the primary cause of X's accident or damage, and while both A and B will be separately liable to X for the whole of his damage, A may be entitled to recover a large proportion of the total, or a complete indemnity, from B.

---

[6] See *e.g. Thomson* v. *Cremin* [1956] 1 W.L.R. 103; *Waddle* v. *Wallsend* [1952] 2 Lloyd's Rep. 105, 130; *Green* v. *Fibreglass Ltd.* [1958] 2 Q.B. 245; and *Lyons* v. *Nicholls* [1958] N.Z.L.R. 409 (New Zealand).

ILLUSTRATIONS

(1) Shot-firer sub-contractors, called in to help in blasting rock on a landing site, sent a skilled man to do the blasting, the main contractors providing any further men who were necessary. *Held*, by the Court of Appeal, the main contractors owed the skilled man a duty as occupiers under the Act: *Savory* v. *Holland & Hannen & Cubitts* (1964).[7]

(2) Main contractors in control of a building structure sub-contracted the repairing of roof members and trusses, and in addition ordered the necessary scaffolding and staging for working platforms from competent scaffolders. The roofing sub-contractors' employees made and moved the staging and working platform without any sufficiently experienced supervision. *Held*, the main contractors were not in occupation or control of the staging, and accordingly were not liable under the Act to an injured employee of the sub-contractors: *Kearney* v. *Eric Waller Ltd.* (1967).[8]

(3) A were the owners of a club, and licensed the running of its restaurant to B. B arranged a contract for the redecoration of the restaurant, but used his own electricians. One of the decorators' plasterers was injured by live electric wires. A had the right to go through the restaurant, controlled the door to the whole premises, and had a permanent maintenance man on the premises who took an interest in the work. *Held*, both A and B were occupiers under the Act of 1957: *Fisher* v. *C.H.T. Ltd.* (1966).[9]

(4) M, building owners, entered into a (1957) R.I.B.A. contract with T, contractors, for the construction of a bowling alley at Barnsley. M also entered into a separate direct contract with A for the sale and installation of the bowling lanes and machinery in the building, and A in due course entered under clause 23 of the building contract and commenced work at a stage when the roof was on, but guttering and external surface drainage were incomplete, and external doorways were unfinished. A's work was separated from the rest of the work inside the building by a polythene screen. After an exceptionally heavy rainstorm, surface water flooded into the building through one of the doorways, which was protected by a plank and some polythene, damaging much of A's work beyond repair. A completed the work, and brought an action (*inter alia*) against both M and T under the Occupiers' Liability Act. It was found that relatively simple precautions by T would have prevented the ingress of water during construction, that T was in a better position than anyone else to note and assess the risk, but that M, who had received an express assurance from T that the building would be ready for A, did not, via their own salaried architect, make any specific inquiry from the private architects (whom they had employed under a special arrangement as the named architects under the building contract, with the salaried architect described as a " consultant ") as to whether the premises were fit and ready for A's work to begin. The private architects had themselves made no attempt to satisfy themselves as to the state of the building. *Held*, by Mocatta J., (a) that M was an

[7] [1964] 1 W.L.R. 1158.
[8] [1967] 1 Q.B. 29.
[9] [1966] 2 Q.B. 475.

occupier under the Act, and on the facts had not brought himself within section 2 (4) (*b*) of the Act so that he was liable to A; (b) that (in spite of T's arguments that it was M who had invited A into the premises, that he, T, had only permitted A to enter, that A's work was physically separated from T's, and that T was working under the supervision and control of M's architects) T was nevertheless also an occupier and liable to A[10]; (c) that the Act applied to damage to property as well as personal injuries, and included consequential damages as well as direct physical damages; and (d) that, as between M and T, M was liable as a joint tortfeasor for 40 per cent. and T for 60 per cent. of the damage; but (e) that T was liable in damages to M for the whole of the claim against M since M was in breach of a number of provisions in the bills requiring him to protect the works during construction [11]: *A.M.F. International Ltd.* v. *Magnet Bowling Ltd. and G. Percy Trentham Ltd.* (1968).[12]

(e) Claims by employer in tort

So far the possible liability of the parties to a building contract towards outsiders in tort has been considered, and also their possible liability to each other in tort, either under the *Hedley Byrne* principle or under the Occupiers' Liability Act 1957.

One possible area of tort, however, which could be most important in building contracts, and which should perhaps be briefly mentioned, is the liability in tort of manufacturers of products for general use under the principle in *Donoghue* v. *Stevenson* (1932).[13] It frequently happens at the present day that manufacturers develop and market new products and techniques for use in the building and civil engineering industries and apply all the pressures of modern selling techniques to secure their adoption by architects and employers. It is often forgotten that traditional building materials and methods have evolved painfully by empirical processes and by trial and error. A very substantial proportion of these non-traditional products are insufficiently developed and tested, notwithstanding their provenance from manufacturers who are household names, and prove wholly unsuitable in use after relatively short periods.

The *Donoghue* v. *Stevenson* principle almost certainly applies to physical damage to property as well as to personal injuries, and in such cases no serious problem arises provided lack of care can be established. Furthermore, in such cases of physical damage consequential financial damage (*e.g.* loss of profits or earnings) are

---

[10] *Wheat* v. *Lacon* [1966] A.C. 552 applied.
[11] *Mowbray* v. *Merryweather* [1895] 2 Q.B. 640 applied.
[12] [1968] 1 W.L.R. 1028.
[13] *Donoghue* v. *Stevenson* [1932] A.C. 562.

awarded under the ordinary rules of remoteness. But, in negligence damage is " the gist of the action " (*i.e.* initial liability depends upon the exact nature and foreseeability of the damage) and the law does not yet appear to have conceded a general liability in negligence in cases where there is no physical damage to person or property, but the damage is financial only,[14] save only on the basis of the *Hedley Byrne* principle, which would not appear to apply to mere representations in brochures or advertisements. Thus it has been said, " I see great difficulty in extending to an ultimate consumer a right to sue the manufacturer in tort in respect of goods which create no peril or accident but simply result in sub-standard work under a contract which is unknown to the original manufacturer."[15] This can be a most serious matter in building contracts, since such materials and techniques are nearly always made the subject of P.C. or provisional sum items in the main contract for nominated sub-contractors or suppliers, and great, if not insuperable, difficulties may be encountered in seeking to impose liability on the main contractor for the unsuitability of the goods or work in question.[16] It is to be hoped that the law of tort can be developed in the near future at least to cover cases where goods are manufactured and marketed for a specific purpose, and where it is clear from the outset that, if they are in fact unsuitable for that purpose, then financial damage of a certain kind will inevitably be suffered by the user, and also that in a great number of cases the damage will take the form of the necessity to replace the defective work or materials. Such a liability in fact would not seem to go as far as that imposed on retailers by section 14 of the Sale of Goods Act, and as already pointed out, it is an incident of building and civil engineering contracts (and indeed of many other major contracts for the erection and construction of plant, ships and so on) that the employer may not have a direct contractual link with a merchant or supplier, such as most consumers will have in the case of a simple sale of consumer goods.

---

[14] *Weller & Co.* v. *Foot and Mouth Disease Research Institute* [1966] 1 Q.B. 569. (Widgery J.), *Margarine Union* v. *Cambay Prince S.S. Co. Ltd.* [1969] 1 Q.B. 219 (Roskill J.). But see *S.C.M. (U.K.) Ltd.* v. *W. J. Whittall & Son Ltd.*, 1970 (Thesiger J.) currently under appeal to C.A.

[15] *Per* Lord Pearce, *Young & Marten Ltd.* v. *MacManus Childs Ltd.* [1969] 1 A.C. 454.

[16] See *post*, Chap. 5, pp. 277–278, 281–282, 294–305; Chap. 15, pp. 747–749, 761–765.

CHAPTER 2

ARCHITECTS, ENGINEERS AND SURVEYORS

SECTION 1. NEED FOR EMPLOYMENT

IN some cases a building contract may be constituted without the employer engaging any professional adviser to guide him. Numerous small building contracts are placed by an employer for the repair and maintenance of structures, and even for the construction of buildings, for which the employer relies upon the contractor to guide him as to what should be done. Only in exceptional cases are large building and engineering contracts likely to be placed by an employer with a contractor upon designs and specifications prepared by or on behalf of the contractor without any professional advice being taken by the employer on his own behalf, though, under the "package-deal" or "industrialised building" arrangements now being advocated in certain quarters in the United Kingdom, this protection is usually limited to consultative advice concerned with design co-ordination between employer and contractor at the tender or negotiating stage, and administrative supervision of the contract with particular reference to interim valuation and, to a lesser degree, quality control. The unsatisfactory nature of these arrangements, as at present conducted in the United Kingdom, has already been referred to,[1] and it is doubtful if adequate protection in regard to design and cost is afforded thereby to the employer.

Under the traditional arrangements, which still obtain in the United Kingdom, in the great majority of cases, where substantial building or engineering works are projected, the employer, before he enters into a contract at all, will seek professional advice upon the design of the works and also upon the preparation of the contract under which they are to be carried out. The professional advice available to the employer in building cases in this respect is normally that of an architect, structural engineer or quantity surveyor, and very frequently a combination of all three under the overall control of the architect, or sometimes of a chartered surveyor. These persons may either practise independently or under

---

[1] Referred to *ante* Chap. 1, Introduction, pp. 2–3. See also *post*, Chap. 3, pp. 207–210.

the direct employment of the employer. But even in cases where the employer has a staff professionally competent to advise him, he may often choose to employ independent advisers on projects of importance.

In the civil engineering industry, the employer will usually only look to the consulting engineer, whose firms normally undertake all ancillary professional services such as quantity surveying and the preparation of Bills of Quantities.

The advice sought by the employer from his architect or engineer may, in the first instance, be concerned solely with the practicability and suitability of the works which the employer may be minded to construct, necessitating nothing more than a report, though this will usually also involve the preparation of preliminary drawings and estimates of the project together with sketch designs of the works to be carried out. With modern large buildings this may involve the intervention of the structural engineer, employed either directly by the building owner, or indirectly by the architect. Many architect's firms in fact now include partners with structural engineering qualifications. Only when the employer is satisfied that he wishes the project to proceed and all necessary statutory consents have been obtained is he likely to require drawings and specifications or Bills of Quantities (which under the standard forms of building contract in the United Kingdom include the specification) to be prepared and a building contract to be offered for tender or otherwise placed with a contractor. It is usually the practice in the United Kingdom for the contract drawings in the building industry to be of a fairly general character, their primary purpose being to enable prices to be obtained, and the standard forms all contemplate the issue, after the contract is signed, of further drawings and details—called in the industry working drawings—whether or not the work is varied. The more usual practice, even in well-regulated contracts, is for complete one-eighth inch scale architectural drawings to be available at the tender stage, but it is extremely rare to find engineering drawings (*e.g.* for reinforcement steel in concrete buildings) available at this stage, and the evolution of these drawings can often involve substantial modification of the architect's contract drawings. In addition one-quarter inch or one-half inch details of points of difficulty may or may not (usually not) be available at the tender stage and will be needed before the relevant work can proceed. It is fair to say that this state of affairs may be due to unwise pressure from employers for an early start of work once the successful tenderer is selected. In the civil engineering industry on contracts of any magnitude or complexity there is usually, by reason of the greater uncertainty of the work, an even greater divergence between the quantity and degree of detail of the working drawings and the original contract drawings. Usually the architect or engineer will also be required by his employer to supervise the execution of the works and to certify the payments due to the contractor; and to enable him to do so effectively the building contract almost invariably defines his powers and obligations in some detail. But it should not be forgotten that the building contract is made between the employer and the contractor, while the duties owed by the architect to the employer will depend upon his contract, express or implied, with the employer, often concluded a considerable time before the building contract is let or its terms and conditions necessarily known. It is with these contracts of employment of the professional advisers of the employer that this chapter is concerned, in particular those of the architect, engineer and quantity surveyor. Since the position of the architect, engineer or surveyor under his contract with the employer has such an important effect on the subject-matter of the building or engineering contract, it may be helpful to examine that position in some detail as a preliminary to consideration of building contracts generally.

SECTION 2. DEFINITIONS AND QUALIFICATIONS

(1) Architects

An architect is a person who is skilled in the art of building and who is competent to design buildings and to supervise their erection. He must not only be well versed in building techniques and be able to prepare plans, sections, elevations and specifications, but he must also have the ability to supervise the carrying out of the work and to administer the contract between the employer and the contractor. A major part of an architect's activities are concerned with the preparation of contracts, the obtaining and recommending for acceptance of estimates from builders, the selection of specialist contractors, the inspection of work carried out, the solution of difficulties encountered during the course of erecting the building, the notification to the contractor of defective work, the issue of certificates under the terms of the contract and the settlement of disputes between the employer and the contractor. Thus it will be seen that although it is a primary and vital function of the architect to create new ideas in structural design and to set down those ideas on a drawing-board, his duties extend far into other fields of technical knowledge and business management. Moreover, while he remains primarily responsible to the employer for all matters of design, modern techniques of construction and specialised building products and processes in fact demand expertise and skill for which he will inevitably not always be personally qualified. The employment of outside consultants, and often the very unsatisfactory (from the legal point of view if the employer's interest is to be properly protected) device of delegating important design functions to specialist sub-contractors and suppliers, are therefore a frequent accompaniment of many major building projects but, as will be seen, the architect is the " captain of the ship " and will be the person to whom the employer will normally look if a design failure occurs.

The Architects' Registration Tribunal have formulated a definition which was cited by the Divisional Court in *R.* v. *Architects' Registration Tribunal, ex p. Jaggar* (1945) [2]: " An architect is one who possesses, with due regard to aesthetic as well as practical considerations, adequate skill and knowledge to enable him (i) to originate, (ii) to design and plan, (iii) to arrange for and supervise the erection of such buildings or other works calling for skill in design and planning as he might in the course of his business reasonably be asked to carry out or in respect of which he offers his services as a specialist."

Of course, the architect does not merely design and supervise the erection of buildings, but also gives prospective building owners preliminary advice on the type of building to be erected and the cost of erection. Since it is obvious that a design is wasted which will only produce a building costing considerably more than the employer's resources or the sums allocated by him to the project, the architect must possess the knowledge required for estimating the cost at current prices of buildings or other works which he may design, so that the cost of carrying out his designs will come within a reasonable distance of the employer's requirements in so far as these have been made known to him. [3]

On most major projects the architect in the United Kingdom collaborates with quantity surveyors, whose function it is to prepare the Bills of Quantities upon which contractors will be asked to tender if a form of contract using Bills of Quantities is decided upon, and who will also carry out all the work of valuation for purposes of

[2] [1945] 2 All E.R. 131.
[3] See *post*, pp. 144–146.

interim and final payment (though actual certification is carried out by the architect, to whom the quantity surveyors will refer all matters of principle or disputed items, while making their recommendations on pure matters of valuation or of adjustment of the contract sum for, for example, variations, fluctuations and adjustment of P.C. and provisional sums). The commonest consultants encountered in practice are structural engineers (foundation design and steel and reinforced or precast concrete frames and structures) and heating engineers (heating and ventilation), and in civil engineering contracts, mechanical or electrical engineers (for plant and machinery) and soil mechanics experts.

The use of the name " Architect " is restricted by the Architects Registration Acts 1931 and 1938. No one may practise or carry on business under any name, style or title containing the word " Architect " unless he is a person registered by the Architects' Registration Council.[4] A person may, however, use the designation " Naval Architect," " Landscape Architect " or " Golf Course Architect " without any such registration.[5] The validity of any building contract in customary form is unaffected by the prohibition against the use of the word " Architect " by unregistered persons,[6] although it would appear that an unregistered person who describes himself as an architect when preparing a building contract is contravening the statute. (There are, however, certain exceptions to the requirement of registration in the case of employees of local authorities.) It is also possible for a body corporate, firm or partnership to carry on business under the style or title of " Architect," provided that certain conditions are fulfilled as to the business being under the control and management of a registered architect.[7] The offence under the Act, however, involves the actual use of the word " Architect."

ILLUSTRATION

On the appellants' notepaper appeared their names and under each name the letters " Dipl. Ing. Arch." *Held*, by the Divisional Court, that the appellants were not practising and carrying on business under a name, style or title containing the word " architect," as that word was not used: *Jacobowicz* v. *Wicks* (1956).[8]

Registration is carried out by the Architects' Registration Council, a body composed of representatives of certain government

---

[4] s. 1 of 1938 Act.
[5] *Ibid.*
[6] *Ibid.*
[7] 1931 Act, s. 17, and 1938 Act, s. 1 (3).
[8] [1956] Crim.L.R. 697.

departments and of architectural, engineering and building interests throughout the United Kingdom. The procedure is that an Admission Committee, constituted in accordance with the Third Schedule to the 1931 Act, considers each application for registration and reports thereon to the Council, who register the applicant if they are satisfied on a report of the Admission Committee that the applicant is an architect member of the Royal Academy or the Royal Scottish Academy or that the applicant has passed any examination in architecture which is for the time being recognised by the Council, or that the application was made before the first day of August, 1940, and that at the time of the passing of the 1938 Act [9] the applicant was practising as an architect in the United Kingdom or that the applicant possesses the prescribed qualifications.[10] The phrase " practising as an architect " was considered in *R.* v. *Architects' Registration Tribunal, ex p. Jaggar* (1945).[11] Regulations dealing with qualifications and other matters have been made and are available from the Council. Annual copies of the register can be bought from the Council.

Where an applicant applies under the 1938 Act for registration and his application is refused he has a right of appeal to a specially constituted Tribunal of Appeal.[12]

The Council have power under the 1931 Act to remove from the register the name of any person convicted of a criminal offence or found guilty by the Council's Discipline Committee of conduct disgraceful to him in his capacity as an architect. " Criminal offence " includes disobedience to a by-law.[13] Any person aggrieved by the removal of his name from the register or by a determination that he be disqualified for registration during any period has a right of appeal to the High Court.[14] The court has power to decide, upon the hearing of such an appeal, whether the appellant was guilty of disgraceful conduct, and has the same powers as the Court of Appeal on appeal from a judge of first instance.[15]

The majority of architects, in addition to being registered, also belong to one of the professional institutions, of which the most important is the Royal Institute of British Architects. The R.I.B.A. publishes a code of conduct of its own for its members, the ultimate

[9] July 29, 1938.
[10] 1931 Act, s. 6.
[11] [1945] 2 All E.R. 131.
[12] 1938 Act, s. 2.
[13] *Mellor* v. *Denham* (1880) 5 Q.B.D. 467.
[14] 1931 Act, s. 9.
[15] *Hughes* v. *Architects' Registration Council* [1957] 2 Q.B. 550, *infra.*

sanction for which is presumably the power to expel a member, but such expulsion would not affect the individual's right to practise as an architect once admitted to the register. The Registration Council also publishes a broadly similar code for the guidance of the profession, in the form of a series of principles and examples under those principles, and also publishes concise reports of its decisions to the profession. This code is clearly most desirable as giving the profession an indication of the sort of conduct of which the Council is likely to disapprove in proceedings for removal of an architect from the register, but it cannot be regarded as a con-clusive determination of what is or is not disgraceful conduct, since the statute does not delegate to the Council the power to make rules for the conduct of the profession or to enforce them, and since the only offence for which an architect can be removed from the register is disgraceful conduct in his capacity as an architect. It seems clear that it is not sufficient merely to prove a breach of the code, whether of the R.I.B.A. or of the council, and indeed this follows from the reasoning and judgments in the case below. Since, however, evidence would no doubt in most cases be available to the effect that the great majority of members of the profession faithfully follow the code, then if in any case an architect obtained some advantage over his fellows by deliberately breaking the code that would be some evidence at least of disgraceful conduct.[16]

ILLUSTRATION

An architect was in practice as an architect and estate agent since 1922. He became registered under the Act of 1931 in 1934. In 1936 the Registration Council published the first Code of Professional Conduct, which prohibited the practising of an estate agent's business by architects, but resolved not to take action against architects so practising at the time of their registration. In 1949 the Council amended their code, withdrawing the 1936 concession as from January 1, 1956. The architect discussed his position with the registrar of the Council in 1955, but continued to practise after January 1, 1956. The Council disqualified him from practice for two years. *Held*, by the Divisonal Court, that, in the particular case of this architect, practising as an estate agent did not amount to disgraceful conduct. *Per* Devlin J.: " It is not of itself disgraceful to disagree with a majority view and to act accordingly. It is only if a man has bound himself in honour to accept that view and to act according to the code that a deliberate breach of the code for his own profit can be called disgraceful ": *Hughes* v. *Architects' Registration Council* (1957).[17]

[16] See *per* Devlin J. in *Hughes'* case at pp. 561–562.
[17] [1957] 2 Q.B. 550.

The Acts also set up a board of architectural education composed of representatives of various schools of architecture and other institutions, associations, professional and trade organisations concerned with architecture. This board has the duty of advising the Registration Council upon examinations and also of itself holding examinations.[18]

(2) Engineers

The word " engineer " is a loose term equally applicable to the engine maker, engine driver and the engineer employed in the design and supervision of constructional works. In this book the expression " engineer " is used in the latter sense, and is more fully, perhaps, described as a " civil engineer." This expression has been defined as one who professes knowledge of the design and construction of works such as bridges, docks, harbours, canals, railways, roads, embankments, water, drainage and gas works, and factories.[19]

This definition is, in the light of modern building knowledge, too restricted, and the civil engineer is now widely concerned also with the design of the foundations and structures of buildings as well as the heating, ventilating, electrical and other modern services. In this connection he is often called in to advise and collaborate with the architect.[19a]

The Institution of Civil Engineers describes the profession of civil engineer as " the art of directing the great sources of power in nature for the use and convenience of man." In fact, the basic characteristic of classical civil engineering work (as opposed to civil engineering work associated with the structures of buildings) is that (with the exception of certain special superstructures such as bridges and dams) the great majority of the work is concerned with construction at or below ground or water level. By comparison with building work, therefore, the work is in general more attended by unexpected risks and hazards affecting the commercial profitability of the work.

The engineer's function in relation to design and supervision is similar to that of the architect. Unlike an architect, however, he may on occasions design not only the works in their final form, but also the temporary works ancillary to their construction. Thus where a complex engineering project will clearly require temporary works to

---

[18] 1931 Act, s. 5 (2).   [19] O. Masselin, *Responsibilité des Architects*, 1879, s. 38.
[19a] For structural engineers, see *infra* subs. (6), pp. 97–98, and for consultants generally see further *infra*, pp. 129–132.

be constructed before the main work can be carried out, such as a coffer dam at the entrance to a proposed dry dock or outfall, or temporary diversions of existing roads to maintain traffic flow during major new road works, the engineers will often themselves design such temporary works and include them as part of the contract. Even where an engineer does not actually design temporary works, some engineering contracts, including the I.C.E. Conditions, tend to confer rather more powers on the engineer to intervene in the contractor's methods of working,[20] which may give rise to difficulties in deciding precisely what is included in the contract price,[21] and might conceivably have the effect of extending his own or the employer's liability in tort to third persons suffering injuries or damage as a consequence of the work being carried out.[22]

There are many special classes of civil engineers: *e.g.* mining engineers, whose profession it is to plan and superintend mining operations, electrical engineers, heating engineers and sanitary engineers; and as industrial progress continues, new sub-divisions of specialisation are constantly arising.

Unlike the profession of architect, there is no restriction upon persons styling themselves " engineers " or " civil engineers." Practising civil engineers are, however, usually members of one of the professional bodies, of which the Institution of Civil Engineers is the most important. Membership of this institution is only granted upon obtaining certain professional qualifications. The nature of this institution was discussed in *Institution of Civil Engineers* v. *I.R.C.* (1932).[23] It should perhaps be mentioned that a very high proportion of civil engineering contractors' supervisory staff are qualified civil engineers, and that a far greater degree of movement and " cross-fertilisation " between the two sides of the industry occurs than in the case of the building industry, although a growing number of qualified architects are now to be found on the staffs of the larger national building contractors. Civil engineers in private practice are usually known as " consulting engineers."

---

[20] See *e.g.* clauses 6, 8, 13, 14, 35, 36 (1) and 46 of the I.C.E. Conditions.

[21] See *post*, pp. 529–530, and the case of *Neodox Ltd.* v. *Swinton and Pendlebury B.C.* (1958) there referred to. See, however, clause 6 of the 1955 I.C.E. standard form, which makes provision for payment.

[22] See *ante*, pp. 68–75 and *infra*, where the extent of the architect's duty to third persons suffering damage from building operations under his supervision is considered.

[23] [1932] 1 K.B. 149 (C.A.).

(3) " Consultant " or " Associate " Architects or Engineers

It is by no means uncommon for Hospital Boards, New Towns and other statutory corporations, and for some local authorities or substantial companies with their own architectural or civil engineering departments, nevertheless, to employ " private " or " project " firms of architects or engineers to act on their behalf in relation to specific projects. These individual firms are nearly always the architects or engineers named as such in the contracts of which they are in charge, but it is not uncommon to find in the contract documents the name of the permanent salaried architect or engineer of the employer described as the " consultant " or " associate " architect or engineer in charge, and wording such as " under the direction and overall control of " suggesting that their status is superior to that of the named architect or engineer.

These expressions may gratify the individuals involved, and may reflect the fact that, as with an ordinary employer, the architect will receive his instructions from the person concerned as the employer's agent, but they will rarely accord with reality as between the contractor and the employer, since they are nearly always used when the real burden and responsibility of the task of designing and supervising the contract work is to be discharged by the private " named " firm. The practice is in the highest degree unwise because it can only have the effect of affording the independent firm an argument for repudiating their own professional responsibility in the event of design or other failures of administration. It can also cause serious misunderstanding and legal and practical difficulties in the administration of the contract in the event of the " consultant " or " associate " dealing directly with the construction in any way, since one very important purpose of most building contracts is to avoid this very confusion and provide for one person only, that is to say the named architect to whom the contractor can look for instructions and with whom he can deal. In fact the vast majority of such " consultants " or " associates " are no more than the employer's representatives for the purposes of communicating his wishes and requirements to the independent architects in a rather more informed way than a technically unqualified employer or representative might do, but their interposition *vis-à-vis* the contractor offends against the basic rule that the employer should always avoid dealing directly with the builder, and only do so through the architect named in the contract.

An example of the dangers for the employer of this practice is to be seen in the case of *A.M.F. International Ltd.* v. *Magnet Bowling Ltd.* (1968)[24] where the employer was, largely for this reason, held unable to rely on section 2 (4) (*b*) of the Occupiers' Liability Act 1957 (which would have afforded him a defence had he employed his private architects in the normal way without seeking to place them under some undefined control by his own salaried architect) so as to avoid liability under that Act to a specialist contractor whose work had been damaged by the main contractor's failure properly to protect the works.

The expression " consultant " is, of course, used in this discussion in a sense different from genuine consultants in charge of a specialist part of a project, or the title " consulting engineer " which is often used by civil engineers in effective charge of an engineering project in the usual way.

(4) Professional Assistants and Clerks of Works

In contracts of any magnitude it is obviously necessary for architects or engineers to delegate a part of their functions, in particular with regard to the supervision and administration of the contract. Engineering contracts, by reason of their magnitude, the fact that many firms of civil engineers are centrally located in London rather than in the area of a specific project, and indeed that many engineering works are carried out abroad, frequently contain specific recognition of this fact in the contract documents, in that provision is made for the delegation of duties to a resident engineer, who in major contracts is usually a fully qualified engineer. The resident engineer is usually found by the consulting engineers either by advertisement or sometimes, in very important contracts, from their own staff. In the majority of cases he is employed and paid by the employer under the contract, and when this is so, he has been held to be a servant and not independent contractor.[25] In building contracts, while the use of qualified architectural assistants, who are permanent employees of the architect's firm, is widespread in larger contracts, it is unusual to find their status in any way regulated by the contract documents, and they normally function merely as agents of the architect, though without any power *vis-à-vis* the contractor to discharge or carry out his many quasi-judicial duties under the contract.[26] Resident engineers, on the other hand, frequently are so empowered

---

[24] [1968] 1 W.L.R. 1028, illustrated *ante*, Chap. 1, pp. 79–80.
[25] *Morren* v. *Swinton and Pendlebury B.C.* [1965] 1 W.L.R. 576.
[26] See *post*, Chap. 7, pp. 484 *et seq.*

in a greater or less degree by the contract documents, usually by reason of a provision permitting delegation of the engineer's powers.[27]

Clerks of works are usually employed for a specific project, in most cases on the recommendation of the architect, though it is not unusual for building owners with their own building departments or organisations to put forward one of their own employees. They are almost invariably employed and paid for by the building owner. (Clause 1. 18 of the 1966 R.I.B.A. scales provides that the clerk of works shall be nominated or approved by the architect, and be under his direction and control, but shall be appointed and paid by the client or alternatively employed by the architect who shall be reimbursed for his wages.) Their use is more common in building than in engineering contracts, and their position is frequently regulated by the contract documents in building contracts, while only very rarely is this so in the case of engineering contracts. Their qualifications may vary from those of a retired tradesman or foreman to a fully qualified architect or engineer, but in general their position is considerably inferior to that of a resident engineer, and the extent of their authority much more rigorously circumscribed by the contract documents—thus, under the pre-1963 R.I.B.A. form of contract the clerk of works was only the employer's agent for the purpose of inspection (clause 8), though under clause 1 verbal directions of the clerk of works, if confirmed in writing to the architect and not dissented from, might attain the status of an architect's instruction under that form of contract. This last power has been circumscribed to the point of extinction (probably unintentionally) by clause 10 of the 1963 Standard Form.

The clerk of works, though usually, as stated, employed and paid by the employer, is intended to assist the architect in the discharge of his duties of supervision and control of the work, and, since he is likely to be the only person permanently present on the site, his work is of the utmost importance, particularly in the light of the remarkable efforts which the R.I.B.A. standard forms of contract have progressively made since 1957 to widen and extend the binding effect of the final certificate, thereby often effectively depriving the building owner of any right to complain of defective work once the final certificate has been issued.[28] Nevertheless an architect employed

---

[27] See clause 2 of the 1955 I.C.E. standard form.
[28] See clause 24 (g) of the 1957 form, and clause 30 (7) of the 1963 form, and the discussion *infra*, pp. 121, 168–169, and *post*, pp. 489–492.

to supervise a project remains in the last resort personally responsible for seeing that the work is properly carried out, and cannot evade responsibility for matters which he should have seen to for himself by delegating or leaving them to the clerk of works.

ILLUSTRATION

A clerk of works fraudulently permitted a floor to be laid differently from the method specified and without the precautions against damp provided for in the contract. The architect failed to see that this part of his design was adhered to. *Held*, the architect was personally responsible for the damage arising from dry-rot in the floor: *Leicester Board of Guardians* v. *Trollope* (1911).[29]

On the other hand, an architect only visits a site at periodic intervals, so that clerks of works may be in a position to see many things which the architect would miss. Provided an architect gives proper instructions to a clerk of works, it is submitted that it would be wrong to impose liability on an architect for acts or omissions of the clerk of works in regard to matters which the architect on his own weekly or other visits might not have reasonably been expected to see to for himself. In other words, the presence of a clerk of works who is not an employee of the architect should not in principle either reduce or add to the architect's personal responsibility, it is submitted, although no doubt it would be a factor in deciding on the frequency with which the architect ought reasonably to visit the site. Any other view would mean that on the one hand a part of the architect's duty to his employer was being discharged by a person of infinitely less professional competence, and on the other that the architect was being required to give an absolute guarantee of the competence and diligence of the clerk of works. The same principles will apply, it is submitted, to the engineers' responsibility for the acts of the resident engineer where the latter is not an employee of the engineers' firm or on loan to the employer from them, as often happens in very important contracts (depending on the facts, different considerations might apply in such cases).

Even a resident engineer will have no authority to order variations unless specifically so empowered by the contract, and no purported delegation of the power by the engineer will be effective so as to bind employer or contractor unless the contract so permits. Where the

---

[29] Hudson's B.C., 4th ed., Vol. 2, p. 419. (For this case illustrated more fully, and for other cases on clerks of works and delegation of duties generally, see *post*, Section 6, pp. 149–152.)

contract requires or permits a resident engineer to exercise an independent judgment between the contractor and the employer the same rules apply as in the case of the engineer himself.[30]

By a contract for the erection of engineering works in Brazil, a resident engineer was to be appointed to superintend the work by the chief engineer, who was in England. The contractor suffered damage as the result of honest mistakes made by the resident engineer in refusing to pass materials submitted to him for approval under a provision to that effect in the contract. The contractor sued the employers. *Held*, the resident engineer was not a mere servant or agent of the employers, but was in an independent position, and the employers were not liable for the mistakes, which were made without any interference by the company: *De Morgan Snell & Co.* v. *Rio de Janeiro Flour Mills* (1892).[31]

Equally, approval by the resident engineer will not be taken as satisfying a provision requiring the approval of the engineer.

A contract provided that buildings should only be erected after approval of the specification in writing by the company's principal engineer. Plans were sent in for approval, but the resident engineer failed to submit them to the principal engineer, and himself told the builder that he might proceed. *Held*, the resident engineer's approval did not bind the company: *Att.-Gen.* v. *Briggs* (1855).[32]

It goes without saying that if architects and engineers have no authority to commit their employers under the terms of building and civil engineering contracts, see *infra* section 4 (2), then it is even more the case that persons of inferior status such as resident engineers and clerks of works cannot, by their acts or omissions, prevent an employer from exercising his full remedies against the contractor, for example for defective work, or in resisting claims for variations if these are not justified on a true view of the contract documents.[33]

(5) Quantity Surveyors

The word surveyor covers a wide field. On the one hand it is a word used under the Public Health Acts to embrace the chief officer of a local authority in charge of the construction of public utility

---

[30] For these rules see *post* pp. 159–169, and Chapter 7 " Approval and Certificates," pp. 416 *et seq.*
[31] Hudson's B.C., 4th ed., Vol. 2, p. 185.
[32] 1 Jur.(N.S.) 1084. More fully illustrated, *post* pp. 484 *et seq.*
[33] See also *post*, Chap. 6, pp. 385–388 and Chap. 8, pp. 523–524.

work, who is now usually a civil engineer, and, at the other extreme
a surveyor and valuer of land in private practice.

The quantity surveyor's function is highly specialised and has
received judicial interpretation as being that of a person " whose
business consists in taking out in detail the measurements and
quantities from plans prepared by an architect for the purpose of
enabling builders to calculate the amounts for which they would
execute the plans." [34] (This definition is somewhat archaic and, as
will be seen,[35] was given at a time when the quantity surveyor's
status was very different, and his employers were in reality the general
body of tendering contractors on a particular project.) From these
measurements and quantities, and also from the specification, which
the architect should produce but as to which some architects place
an excessive reliance on the quantity surveyor, what is called a bill
or bills of quantities are prepared. This is a detailed schedule of the
quantities and items of work which it is anticipated will be carried
out. The contractor tenders upon this document by inserting
alongside each item a rate for each unit of measurement used by
the quantity surveyor, together with the total grossed-up amount to
be charged for carrying out the whole quantity of that item shown
in the bill. Other services performed by the quantity surveyor at
the preparatory stage of building contracts include making estimates
of the cost of the works, preparing schedules to be priced by tenderers
where no sufficient drawings or information are available from which
to prepare a bill of quantities (usually referred to as Schedules of
Prices or Rates), and assisting in the negotiating and obtaining of
quotations for work to be carried out by specialists. During the
performance of the works the quantity surveyor performs important
further services which enormously lighten the burden of work on
architects in the administration of the contract. These include the
preparation of detailed recommendations to the architect of the
value of work done for the purpose of interim certificates (for which
purpose periodical valuation-inspections on the site have to be made
and examinations of sub-contractor's accounts and architect's variation orders), and the detailed preparation of the final account,
including any necessary remeasurement of the contract work in
contracts using bills, the adjustment of all P.C. and provisional
sums, the valuation of variations and financial claims permitted by
the contract, and the calculation of sums due under the fluctuations

[34] *Taylor* v. *Hall* (1870) 4 I.R.C.L. *per* Morris J. at p. 476.
[35] *Infra*, Section 10, pp. 193 *et seq.*

clauses. The principles of measurement by which bills of quantities are prepared are the subject of a standard code in each industry, and it is essential under most modern building and engineering contracts that these codes should be strictly followed, as they are usually expressly incorporated by reference.[36]

Quantity surveyors usually function independently, but it is not unusual to find firms of architects who have amongst their partners or staff qualified quantity surveyors able to prepare bills of quantities for works for which they are engaged as architects. Most firms of civil engineers employ their own staff to prepare bills of quantities for the civil engineering works for which they are engaged and do not employ outside quantity surveyors. In addition many substantial contractors in both industries employ qualified quantity surveyors for estimating purposes.

There is no prohibition against the use of the style or title of " Surveyor " or " Quantity Surveyor." The Royal Institution of Chartered Surveyors, however, hold examinations in the various branches of surveying, and persons with the necessary practical experience who have passed the requisite examinations can style themselves Associates or Fellows of the Royal Institution of Chartered Surveyors. In *R.I.C.S.* v. *Shepheard* (1947),[37] an injunction was obtained restraining a defendant from styling himself a Chartered Quantity Surveyor when not admitted to the Royal Institution of Chartered Surveyors. The Institute of Quantity Surveyors is also a body which examines and trains quantity surveyors. Both the Royal Institution of Chartered Surveyors and the Institute of Quantity Surveyors fix a scale of fees and prescribe a code of professional conduct for their members.

Qualified quantity surveyors are in general extremely highly skilled, and in the United Kingdom both they and chartered building surveyors are likely to be at least as well qualified, in matters of technical building construction, as are architects.

(6) Structural Engineers

This is a comparatively new profession evolved largely from the engineering needs of modern buildings which depart from the traditional structure based on load-bearing walls, and from the use of materials like steel, reinforced concrete, and precast and stressed

---

[36] See clause 12 of the 1963 R.I.B.A. form, and clause 57 of the 1955 I.C.E. form, and for the possible legal consequences see *post*, Chap. 8, pp. 516 *et seq.*
[37] *Estates Gazette.* May 31, 1947, p. 370.

concrete. Their presence is accordingly essential in almost all large modern buildings.[37a]

Their presence in a modern contract can come about in four ways; namely, as direct professional consultants of the building owner working in collaboration with the architect; as professional consultants called in by the architect and employed by him; as members or employees of the architect or his firm; and finally as specialist sub-contractors for the supply or supply and erection of the necessary structural steel, reinforcement steel or reinforced or pre-cast concrete, as the case may be. This latter arrangement, which seems to be increasing, is extremely unsatisfactory: (a) because the design fees are concealed from the employer within the price; (b) because competitive tendering on a fair basis between the specialist who has designed, and the others who have not, is difficult to arrange, and leads to undesirable trade practices between the tendering specialists; (c) because the same conflict of commercial interest, leading to under-design, is present as in the case of " package-deal " contracts[38]; (d) because the law finds it difficult to import " suitability " obligations into a contract under the control of an architect[39]; (e) because it is doubtful if a nomination of a sub-contractor to carry out design functions is valid under the standard forms of contract[40]; (f) because it is rare to find that any or any adequate guarantee of suitability is obtained from the specialist for the benefit of the employer, and (g) because appalling complications can arise between the main contractor and the employer if the specialist sub-contractor defaults on those parts of his obligations which form part of the architect's duties—e.g. to supply information, such as reinforcement drawings or bending schedules, in time to permit the main contractor to carry out his work. In fact it is clear that the architect will not avoid his design responsibility by entering into or recommending such an arrangement.[41]

SECTION 3. CONTRACT OF EMPLOYMENT

(1) Generally

The employment of an architect, engineer or quantity surveyor for services in relation to the design and execution of constructional

[37a] See also infra, pp. 129–132.
[38] See ante, Chap. 1, pp. 2–3; post, Chap. 3, pp. 207–210.
[39] See post, Chap. 5, pp. 277–278, 281–282.
[40] See infra, pp. 129–131, post, Chap. 15, p. 764.
[41] See Moresk v. Hicks [1966] 2 Lloyd's Rep. 338, infra, p. 131.

works arises from his appointment by the building owner or by someone authorised on his behalf to make the appointment. The terms of the appointment govern the rights and obligations of the parties and may contemplate a whole-time officer, or a professional adviser for a particular building project or for a particular period of time. Permanent appointments are usually carefully defined in a formal agreement entered into between the parties, but the appointment of independent advisers either for a particular building project or for a period of time are often made in a less formal manner, usually by exchange of letters with or without incorporation by reference of the R.I.B.A. terms of engagement or of R.I.B.A. scales of fees (these are in fact one document, but it may be an important question whether the terms of the incorporation by reference are intended only to apply to the amount of remuneration or whether these conditions of engagement as a whole, including the arbitration clause, are intended).

(2) Form of Appointment

By virtue of the Corporate Bodies' Contracts Act 1960 and section 32 of the Companies Act 1948, no particular form, whether of seal or writing, is required for the appointment of independent advisers, whatever the legal status of the employer.

In the employer's interest, however, the contract relating to any major project should be under seal, so as to obtain the benefit of the longer period of limitation of twelve years should there be any breach of duty resulting, for instance, in defects in the work not discovered at the time of completion.

(3) Conditions of Appointment

Since he is a professional man, and in law an independent contractor, an architect or engineer in private practice is entitled to be left free, in the absence of express provision to the contrary, to carry out the duties necessary to achieve the purpose for which he has been appointed in the way which seems best to him. While he is entitled to be left undisturbed in matters of the day-to-day discharge of his duties, however, he is not entitled to dictate to his employer on matters which come within the latter's legitimate sphere of decision (and indeed is, in such matters, bound to consult the employer, it is submitted, before committing him in any way).[42]

---

[42] See *post*, p. 155, as to variations.

ILLUSTRATION

An architect was employed to prepare sketch designs to the employer's approval, prepare working drawings, and supervise the works in connection with a fountain, ornamental feature, and surrounding area. The employer approved the design of the fountain, but disapproved that of the ornamental feature and surrounding area, and commenced to construct the surrounding area without architectural assistance in a manner different from the architect's design, and proposed to do the same with the ornamental feature. The architect sought to obtain an injunction, arguing that there was an implied term that the respondent could not use only a part of the architect's plans or depart from them without his approval, or alternatively that the employer's action amounted to a breach of copyright. *Held*, neither contention was valid, and the employers were entitled to make such use of the architect's services as they saw fit, provided proper remuneration was paid: *Bennett* v. *Capetown Foreshore Board* (1960).[43]

On the other hand, the building owner is entitled to a professional standard of skill in the discharge of all the duties necessary until the purpose of the appointment has been achieved. A mere request to act as architect or engineer in relation to a project, without specifying at the outset the services required of the architect or engineer, may lead to doubt or dispute as to what are the respective rights and duties of the parties, and it is desirable that, whenever possible, and particularly where more than one type of adviser is employed on the same project, the conditions of appointment should be formulated in greater detail.

In fact, various institutions and associations representing architects, engineers and quantity surveyors issue scales of fees which also set out the conditions of engagement of their members. The best known of these are those issued by the Royal Institute of British Architects, the Royal Institution of Chartered Surveyors and the Association of Consulting Engineers. Each of these fixes fees based upon a percentage of the estimated and ultimate total cost of the works and, in addition, sets out certain of the conditions of employment which, if the scales are adopted, can also be made applicable. One or other of these scales is frequently, by an exchange of letters or by a more formal agreement, made the basis of the agreement between the building owner and his advisers, and when this is done then the conditions set out in the scale may also become applicable to the appointment; but these documents are concerned primarily with protecting the interests of the members of the association

---

[43] 1960 (4) S.A. 439 (South Africa). See also *Rutledge* v. *Farnham Local Board of Health* (1861) 2 F. & F. 406, illustrated, *post*, Section 9 (2), p. 187.

concerned, and on several occasions it has been held by the courts that they are not binding upon the employer unless it can be clearly shown that they have been incorporated into the agreement with him.[44]   Moreover, these documents do not deal with many questions which may arise during the employment or, even when incorporated in the agreement made between the building owner and his professional adviser, may leave for further implementation or agreement a number of matters of importance, including:

(i) What other consultants, designers or specialists are to be employed in addition to the architect, engineer or other adviser appointed.

(ii) Whether an independent quantity surveyor is to be employed and if so for what services.

(iii) The position in the event of retirement, death or incapacity of the architect or engineer.

(iv) The use and ownership of drawings and designs prepared by the architect or engineer (copyright is dealt with).

(v) The authority of the architect to negotiate or contract with contractors and sub-contractors.

(vi) The architect's or engineer's powers to vary the work and bind the building owner once the contract has been made.

(vii) The duration of the appointment.

(4) Duration and Termination of the Appointment

Unless there is agreement to the contrary, an appointment in explicit terms for a particular project cannot be determined until the purpose for which the appointment was made has been achieved.[45]   It is not unusual for the contract of employment to contain provisions dividing the duties to be performed by the architect in accordance with various stages of progress of the contemplated project, and to give either party, in effect, the power of termination at the end of the various stages.   An outstanding example is the Conditions of Engagement contained in the Scale of Professional Charges of the R.I.B.A.   Indeed, this arrangement recognises the reality of the transaction between the parties, since even if nothing specific were said when an architect was first employed to get out plans and advise on a project, it would not necessarily follow that the employer

---

[44] See pp. 182–185, 188 and 191, *infra*.
[45] *Thomas* v. *Hammersmith B.C.* [1938] 3 All E.R. 203, *post*, p. 186.

required his services in letting the contract, if there was to be one, or in the supervision of the work. In fact, in the absence of express provision, an architect engaged informally on a particular project will usually owe his employment to a series of informal appointments rather than one appointment covering the whole project from start to finish. In general, until the time that the decision is taken to prepare contract documents with a view to obtaining a tender, the project is frequently of a tentative or exploratory character and the architect is likely to be employed almost on a day-to-day basis. At that stage the employer is certainly authorising, for the first time, substantial expenditure and, usually, the engagement of other persons, such as the quantity surveyor. But not until tenders are received, and the employer is in a position to know what his financial commitments are likely to be and to make arrangements for finance, that is to say at the time of the decision to accept the tender and place or " let " the contract, has the point of no return, and therefore of a possible anticipatory breach by the employer of the architect's contract of employment, really arrived. But in the event of clear agreement as to the purpose of the appointment any termination of the employment before the purpose of the appointment has been achieved would amount to a breach of contract. In *Thomas* v. *Hammersmith B.C.* (1938) [46] Slessor L.J. said: " . . . I think it helpful first to consider what would have been the agreement between the parties if the appointment had been *simpliciter* to act as architect for the erection of the new town hall without any provision as to scale of charges, and if the council had then, before the work was completed, without cause other than their mere volition, terminated the agreement. In such case, I entertain no doubt that the architect would have been entitled to reasonable remuneration for the work which he had already done, and also to damages for the loss of remuneration which he had been prevented from earning until the work was finished. Although the contract in this assumed form would contain no express term to this effect, I think that it would be implied that the council, having employed the plaintiff to build their town hall, agreed with him that they would not prevent him from doing the work and so prevent him from earning his remuneration." [47]

An architect or engineer may be employed to advise only, or to make drawings, plans or designs only, or to supervise only, or to

---

[46] [1938] 3 All E.R. 203.
[47] See also the discussion *post*, Section 9 (2), pp. 185–186.

advise, design, make plans, and supervise. In the last alternative the duties of an architect or engineer as generally carried out in the United Kingdom are as follows:

(1) To advise and consult with the employer (not as a lawyer) as to any limitation which may exist as to the use of the land to be built on, either (*inter alia*) by planning legislation, restrictive covenants or the rights of adjoining owners or the public over the land, or by statutes and by-laws affecting the works to be executed.

(2) To examine the site, subsoil, and surroundings.

(3) To consult with and advise the employer as to the proposed work.

(4) To prepare sketch plans and a specification, having regard to all the conditions known to exist, and to submit them to the employer for approval, with an estimate of the probable cost, if requested.

(5) To elaborate and, if necessary, modify or amend the sketch plans, and then, if so instructed, to prepare drawings and a specification of the work to be carried out as a first step in the preparation of contract documents.

(6) To consult with and advise the employer as to the form of contract to be used (including whether or not to use bills of quantities) and as to the necessity or otherwise of employing a quantity surveyor (engineers usually do not employ an independent quantity surveyor) to prepare bills and carry out the usual valuation services during the currency of the contract.

(7) To bring the contract documents to their final state before inviting tenders, with or without the assistance of quantity surveyors and structural engineers, including the obtaining of detailed quotations from and arrangement of delivery dates with any nominated sub-contractors or suppliers whose work may have to be ready or available at an early stage of the main contractor's work.

(8) To advise the employer as to tenders received and the selection of the main contractor, and to arrange starting dates and the contract period if this has not already been done.

(9) After work has started, to supply the builder with copies of the contract drawings and specification, and any further drawings, details or instructions which may be necessary for the work, including work to be done by nominated sub-contractors, to make any further nominations which may be necessary, and to advise the

employer if any variation of the work becomes necessary or desirable.[47a]

(10) To supervise the work, making sure in the employer's interest that the contract is complied with in every respect, to value, with or without the assistance of a quantity surveyor, the work both for purposes of interim payment and final payment, and generally to administer the contract so that full effect is given to all its provisions.

(11) To act as certifier on such matters as the terms of the contract may require, up to and including the final certificate—for instance, on questions of extension of time, on practical completion, on payment direct of sub-contractors, and on various claims for additional expense which the contractor may be entitled to make under the terms of the contract. (In the discharge of some of these latter certifying duties required of him under the contract, sometimes referred to as quasi-judicial or quasi-arbitral, the architect or engineer may not owe a duty of care or skill to his employer, but the exact definition of this immunity requires, it is submitted, more care and consideration than it has so far received from the courts.[48])

An architect may sometimes be asked to take over from another architect in the middle of a project, either because of death or retirement, or because the employer is dissatisfied. As will be seen [49] this does not, under the terms of most building contracts, create any formal or legal difficulties in the administration of the contract.

(5) Death, Bankruptcy or Inability to Act of the Architect or Engineer

In the case of a personal appointment (as distinct from the appointment of a firm) of an architect or engineer, that person's death will terminate the contract, as it is clearly one for personal services.[50] This may cause inconvenience to the building owner in relation to the right to use drawings and specifications, unless before the death, e.g. in the contract of engagement, express agreement has been reached either as to ownership or right of user.

In the event of the bankruptcy of the architect or engineer, and in the absence of express provisions in the contract of appointment, the contract will not be determined. If the architect is ready to

---

[47a] See post, p. 155.　　　　　　　　　　　　　[48] See post, pp. 161–169.
[49] Post, Chap. 7, Section 6 (5), pp. 485 et seq.
[50] See post, Chap. 14, "Assignment," p. 738. For the right to payment, see post, pp. 255 et seq. and Stubbs v. Holywell Ry. (1867) L.R. 2 Ex. 311 there illustrated. See also post, pp. 185 et seq.

perform his contract, the trustee will be able to insist on the performance by the building owner of his part of the contract, and if the contract is performed by the architect the trustee may then sue the building owner for the contractual remuneration.[51]

The trustee of a bankrupt architect or engineer cannot insist on performing by another architect or engineer the contract which the bankrupt had undertaken: by reason of the personal nature of the contract of appointment, the benefit of the contract does not pass to the trustee in bankruptcy.[52]

Should the architect or engineer who has been personally appointed be unable to act through serious illness, imprisonment or some other permanent cause, then the contract of employment may be frustrated and the rights of the parties governed by the Law Reform (Frustrated Contracts) Act 1943.

Changes in the identity of the partners of a firm have the effect of dissolving the partnership, and in the absence of an express or implied novation—e.g. by the employer continuing to make use of the firm's services when the circumstance of the change of partner is known or communicated to him—the employer's rights will be restricted to the partners of the firm as it existed at the time of the appointment.

(6) Death or Bankruptcy of Building Owner

As a general rule a contract of employment only determines upon the death of the employer if the personality of the employer is sufficiently material to the contract, or where personal considerations are the foundation of the contract.[53] It is submitted that the personality of the building owner could theoretically be of material importance in certain contracts of appointment of an architect, i.e. in rare cases where the architect is engaged to design work which will satisfy the taste or special aesthetic requirements of the building owner. But in most cases, the rights and liabilities would pass to the personal representatives.

Bankruptcy of the employer will not by itself determine the contract of employment but it will justify the architect or engineer in refusing to perform any subsequent services unless he receives some security or assurance that his fees will be paid, whatever the contract might have said as to payment.[54] Once, however, reasonable

[51] See post, Chap. 16, " Bankruptcy and Liquidation," pp. 775–796.
[52] Compare Knight v. Burgess (1864) 33 L.J.Ch. 727, post, Chap. 14, p. 719.
[53] Farrow v. Wilson (1869) L.R. 4 C.P. 744; Graves v. Cohen (1930) 46 T.L.R. 121.
[54] See Re Sneezum ex p. Davis (1876) 3 Ch.D. 463, C.A., post, Chap. 16, pp. 782–783.

security is given, the architect or engineer will be bound to continue his services under the appointment.

SECTION 4. AUTHORITY OF THE ARCHITECT AND ENGINEER

(1) Generally

When an architect or engineer is first employed on any project his services will be mainly of an advisory nature, and not until he has prepared the drawings and been instructed to proceed with the works by his employer, will he have any authority or even opportunity to act as agent for the building owner.

Once this stage of advising the building owner and the preparation of drawings has passed, the conduct of the building or engineering project will, from the building owner's point of view, be in the hands of the architect or engineer, and the question may arise as to what extent the architect or engineer has authority to bind his employer. When the building owner enters into a written contract with a contractor the authority conferred upon the architect or engineer to vary the contract *work* will usually be set out expressly. It remains important, however, to determine the extent to which the architect, when carrying out his many duties on behalf of the employer, can, in the absence of express terms, commit or bind the employer *vis-à-vis* the contractor, and also the extent to which he can commit the employer to third parties, such as sub-contractors, quantity surveyors and consultants. No problem, of course, exists in a case where the employer specifically instructs the architect to contract on his behalf. The following discussion is concerned with the *implied* or *ostensible* authority of the architect arising out of his appointment as such, and the extent to which, without express authority, he can bind his employer in relation to the contractor and third parties.

(2) As to Waiver of Contractual Requirements of Building Contract

An architect or engineer produces the design and specification to which the contractor has to work, and administers a contract under which he is constantly having to decide whether the work done by the contractor is acceptable, and is constantly having to deal with claims and contentions of the contractor, many of which he may provisionally accept or allow, or decide finally in his own mind in the contractor's favour. It cannot be too strongly emphasised that the architect or engineer, unless there is a contractual provision giving his opinion, decision or certificate finality, has no authority whatever to waive strict compliance with the contract or to bind the employer, and in fact in the United Kingdom, in the vast majority of cases, the only contractual provisions which can have this effect are those relating to the final certificate in building contracts (which even in the current R.I.B.A. forms have certain qualifications and are open to arbitration in certain circumstances) and the maintenance certificate in the I.C.E. Conditions (which have an express saving in favour of claims by the employer). Furthermore, even provisions purporting to confer finality can be interpreted as merely giving an additional protection to the employer, and not as binding him,[55] and the vast majority of arbitration clauses show the clearest intention to permit a review of nearly every opinion, decision or certificate of the architect or engineer.[56] This general inability of the architect to commit the employer in the building contract has a number of consequences including, for instance:

(a) there is no implication that completion of the work by the architect's design is practicable or possible, so that the contractor must do everything necessary to complete without additional payment, and an attempt by the architect to help the contractor out of such a difficulty by ordering the extra work as a variation would in no way bind the employer, provided that the work would have been necessary in any event [57];

(b) acceptance of work by the architect, or his presence and standing by at some earlier time during construction, or on práctical completion, or at the end of the defects liability period, do not prevent the employer in the absence of a binding certificate or approval from suing for damages for defective work at any time during the period of limitation, notwithstanding that by reasonable diligence on the part of the architect the defects could have been discovered earlier and repaired at far less cost [58];

(c) claims approved by the architect on interim certificate can be disallowed at any time subsequently and in no way

[55] See *Billyack* v. *Leyland* [1968] 1 W.L.R. 471, *post*, Chap. 7, pp. 432–433.
[56] See also the short discussion in Subsection (7), *infra*, pp. 120–121.
[57] See *post*, Chap. 5, pp. 267 *et seq.*, 349 *et seq.*; Chap. 8, p. 508. See also assurances given by an architect as to the meaning of bills of quantities, and the case of *Scrivener* v. *Pask* (1866) L.R. 1 C.P. 715, referred to *infra*, subs. (3), p. 109.
[58] See *post*, Chap. 6, pp. 385–388.

bind the employer even if he has paid them in full at the time [59];

(d) the fact that the architect orders work explicitly as a variation under the relevant provisions of the contract for ordering varied work in no way binds the employer if, on a true view of the contract, the work in question is included in the original contract obligation;

(e) the granting of extensions of time by the architect in no way binds the employer, nor do his decisions as to the date of practical completion.

(3) As to Contracts or Variations

An architect or engineer in private practice has no implied authority to make a contract with the contractor binding on his employer, or to vary or depart from a concluded contract.[60] His duty when supervising a contract is to see that it is faithfully fulfilled according to its terms; but it may, of course, be varied by the parties themselves, or by the architect or engineer under specific authority given him in that behalf, whether under the express terms of the building contract, as in the case of a variations clause (which in fact is a clause permitting variation of the contract *work* and not of the contractual provisions as such) or on direct instructions from the employer.

ILLUSTRATIONS

(1) A agreed to build a house for B according to certain plans. B sued A for non-performance of the agreement. A then set up that he deviated from the plans by the authority of B's architect. *Held,* that this was no answer, as no authority was shown on the part of the architect to bind B by any deviation from the plans: *Cooper* v. *Langdon* (1841).[61]

(2) A contracting company went into liquidation. The architect, with the employer's agreement, arranged for the work to be carried on by an individual director of the company. He then made arrangements with the employer's bank for payments to be made in future to the director and to any nominated sub-contractors who might be named in future certificates. Later he gave flooring specialists instructions to lay certain floors, and purported to pledge the employer's credit for that purpose. *Held,* that the employer, not having

---

[59] See *post,* Chap. 7, pp. 492 *et seq.* and see the case of *Royston U.D.C.* v. *Royston Builders Ltd.* (1961) 177 E.G. 589, *ante,* Chap. 1, p. 58.

[60] Hence the need for the express authority of the variation clause—see *post,* pp. 506–507. See also *Ashwell & Nesbitt* v. *Allen* (1912) Hudson's B.C., 4th ed., Vol. 2, p. 462, illustrated *post,* p. 410.

[61] 9 M. & W. 60, 67.

approved or ratified this last arrangement, could not be liable to the specialists: *Vigers, Sons & Co. Ltd.* v. *Swindell* (1939).[62]

Again, an architect has no implied authority to make agreements with adjoining owners as to the method of carrying out building operations which will affect the rights of his employer.

ILLUSTRATION

The plaintiffs had leased for building purposes part of some land of the defendants on which stood old buildings. Their architect arranged with the defendants that certain timbers and stanchions should remain and be built onto the plaintiffs' new building, the agreed plans of which showed windows in the wall in which the timbers, etc., were built. This made the wall a party wall under the London Building Act 1894 and the local authority required the windows to be blocked up. *Held*, that the architect had no authority to make such an agreement, and the defendants were ordered to remove their beams and joists: *Frederick Betts Ltd.* v. *Pickfords Ltd.* (1906).[63]

So an architect who provided a builder with quantities and assured him that they were correct was held to have no power to bind his employer and accordingly the latter was not liable to the builder for errors in the quantities.[64]

Again, in a case where a local authority engaged a surveyor in private practice to assist the architect with the valuations necessary for interim payments under the contract, the Court of Appeal held that, even if certain acts of the surveyor amounted to acts of obstruction in the issue of a certificate, the local authority were not responsible in law for the acts of the surveyor.[65]

It is, however, important to determine the exact legal and practical limitations of the rule. In the first place, an employer who by some conduct or statement has misled a contractor into thinking that the architect has full authority may well be held either actually to have authorised the architect to contract on his behalf or, if not, to have clothed him with ostensible authority to contract. This, or course, would depend upon the particular facts, but does not detract from the general principle that an architect, even if instructed to obtain tenders, has no ostensible authority to conclude a contract, and strong facts would be needed to rebut the presumption.

---

[62] [1939] 3 All E.R. 590. See also *Randell* v. *Trimen* (1856) 18 C.B. 786 (architect ordering stone for a building), *infra*, section 5 (2), pp. 122–123.
[63] [1906] 2 Ch. 87.
[64] *Scrivener* v. *Pask* (1866) L.R. 1 C.P. 715, illustrated, *post*, Chap. 8, pp. 511–512.
[65] *R. B. Burden Ltd.* v. *Swansea Corporation* [1957] 1 W.L.R. 1167, when the House of Lords, however, held that the acts were not as a fact acts of obstruction.

Secondly, an employer who knows what his architect has done and stands by and allows the work ordered to be carried out, will be held to have ratified the contract made by the architect, or to have impliedly promised to pay a reasonable price for the work.[66]

Thirdly, it seems right that a different view should be taken in the case of full-time, salaried architects and engineers, in particular those of local authorities. In the case of the latter, it is customary for negotiation on points requiring alteration or clarification to take place with the selected tenderer, prior to the signing of the contract, and also for matters of qualification, clarification or alteration to be discussed with some or all of the tenderers before the successful contractor has been chosen. Such negotiations are nearly always conducted with the local authority's architects', engineers' or surveyors' departments and their officers, and indeed it is now usual for the contract documents to be prepared in the technical departments of a local authority and only to be forwarded to the legal, or clerk's, department immediately prior to formal execution of the agreement, where sometimes a short formal document under seal is prepared which adds nothing to the terms already agreed. It has already been seen [67] how knowledge by the county architect and his assistant (not of the clerk) of the contractor's mistake entitled the latter to rectification of the contract. Clearly this is because a corporation can only be expected to have knowledge by some official or servant. While it is the case that the standing orders of local authorities require important contracts to be made by the clerk or delegated to particular committees or officials, the provisos to section 266 of the Local Government Act 1933 and section 160 (2) of the London Government Act 1939 absolve outside persons from the necessity for inquiring whether the standing orders have been complied with. In any event, the fact is that the vast majority of all important negotiations by contractors with local authorities are conducted with their technical departments, the heads of which are highly qualified and salaried officials, and it would now seem that these officials do have ostensible authority to contract.

ILLUSTRATION

A local authority's borough surveyor and quantity surveyor, at a meeting with the contractor before signature of the contract at

---

[66] See, for a good example, the county court case of *Williams and Williams* v. *Coatsworth* (1955) 105 L.J. 124; and see *Re Chittick and Taylor* (1954) 12 W.W.R. (Canada) at p. 655; quoted *post*, Chap. 8, p. 544.

[67] *A. Roberts & Co. Ltd.* v. *Leicestershire C. C.* [1961] Ch. 555, illustrated *ante*, Chap. 1, pp. 37–38.

which he pointed out certain errors in the contract documents, orally agreed to vary the contract obligations, and the agreement was confirmed by the contractor by letter.   The contract as signed did not contain the agreed variations.   *Held*, by Ungoed-Thomas J. that the borough surveyor had both actual and ostensible authority to negotiate and agree the terms of the contract with the contractor, and that the contract should be rectified: *Carlton Contractors* v. *Bexley Corporation* (1962).[68]

An important field in which an architect may be concerned to make contracts in connection with a building project is that of nominated sub-contractors, where it frequently occurs that he will conduct the preliminary negotiations, including the invitations to tender to, and acceptance of tenders or quotations from, these sub-contractors, in many cases at a time when the main contract has not yet been let or the main contractor selected.   The true view in such cases is that the architect is obtaining contractual offers on behalf of whatever main contractor will ultimately be selected, or the existing main contractor. In the " early " cases the architect may well need to give provisional or other orders to the sub-contractor in order to secure appropriate completion or delivery dates, and in the event of the project falling through is likely, by virtue of the foregoing rules, to find himself personally liable unless he has obtained express authority from the employer first and then given some sort of conditional guarantee on the employer's behalf to the sub-contractor in return for the latter embarking on work before an effective order from the main contractor has been obtained.[69]   Furthermore in conducting the negotiations with the sub-contractor, while it is submitted that the architect is in fact doing so on behalf of the main contractor,[70] or whatever main contractor will subsequently be appointed, he has no implied authority actually to contract on behalf of the main contractor.[71]

(4) As to Taking out Bills of Quantities

An architect or engineer may take out and prepare a bill of quantities himself or he may decide to employ an independent firm of quantity surveyors to do so.   In the former case the question may arise as to whether or not he may charge the employer fees in addition to fees for his architectural or engineering services, and in the latter case whether he has authority to bind the employer to pay the fees of the independent firm.   In engineering contracts it is usual for engineers

[68] (1962) 60 L.G.R. 331.
[69] See *post*, pp. 743–745.   See also for an analogous case, *Young* v. *Smith*, *post*, p. 194.
[70] See *post*, Chap. 15, pp. 743–744.
[71] See *Davies & Co. Shopfitters Ltd.* v. *William Old* (1969) 67 L.G.R. 395, illustrated *ante*, Chap. 1, p. 12, and see *post*, Chap. 15, pp. 744–745.

to take out their own quantities (which in general are far shorter and simpler documents than the bills in building contracts, which are extremely refined and complicated analyses of the work to be done) and the fee which they agree with the building owner usually expressly includes such services. In the absence of an express term, it is submitted that it would be unnecessary in engineering cases to imply any promise to pay extra fees for taking out quantities, or an authority to employ an independent firm of quantity surveyors to do so.

In the case of architects the fees of an architect do not normally include the services of a quantity surveyor, and the courts held in *Moon* v. *Witney Union Guardians* (1837) [72] and *Waghorn* v. *Wimbledon Local Board* (1877) [73] that the preparation of bills of quantities was not part of the function of an architect and that he might employ a quantity surveyor to take out quantities at the building owner's expense. These decisions support the view that if he were to take out quantities himself which were obviously necessary for the tenders which the building owner had instructed him to obtain, he would be entitled to be paid fees additional to any agreed at the time of the appointment for normal architect's services. In the event of the R.I.B.A. scale being adopted no difficulty arises, as the charges for quantity surveyors' services rendered by the architect are expressly charges the architect can make in addition to the architectural fees.

Moon's and *Waghorn's* cases were decided, however, at a time when the quantity surveyor's function and status were different from those at the present day, in that he formed a necessary part of the machinery for obtaining tenders, and his services were regarded as being given primarily to the tendering contractors and only secondarily to the employer. [74] Under this system, an instruction to obtain tenders was therefore tantamount to an instruction to employ a quantity surveyor. Today it is perfectly possible to obtain tenders without employing an independent quantity surveyor (*i.e.* by way of a contract where quantities do not form part) since tendering contractors now invariably employ full-time estimators with quantity surveyors' qualifications and are therefore capable of pricing complicated work using their own resources. These cases cannot, it is submitted, be regarded any longer as authority for the proposition that an architect has implied or ostensible authority to

[72] 3 Bing.N.C. 814, illustrated *infra*, p. 114.
[73] Hudson's B.C., 4th ed., Vol. 2, p. 52, illustrated *infra*, p. 114.
[74] See *post*, pp. 193 *et seq.*

employ a quantity surveyor on the building owner's behalf, so that the employer will be bound contractually to the quantity surveyor. But on the other hand it is submitted that, at least where the building owner has some actual or reasonably imputed knowledge of the practice in the industry, if he approves a general project for works and gives instructions to the architect to proceed with the obtaining of tenders *on a bill of quantities basis*, then the latter will, unless by the appointment he has himself undertaken the duty, have a sufficient express authority to employ a quantity surveyor on the building owner's behalf, so as to make the building owner liable for the fees of the quantity surveyor for preparing the bills of quantities upon which the tenders are to be invited.[75] In any event, even if not directly liable to the quantity surveyor, the employer in such circumstances should, it is submitted, be liable to pay the architect reasonable additional fees for the quantity surveyor's services provided that the terms of the architect's contract of employment do not expressly exclude such a payment—*e.g.* by agreement on a lump sum fee for the whole project. On the other hand, no such authority will be inferred before the building owner has approved plans and given instructions to proceed.[76]

In the *Moon* and *Waghorn* cases (*infra*), the employers were in fact local authorities to whom knowledge of the details of letting contracts might well be imputed. But it is suggested that where private individuals are concerned, the courts would be slow to impute such knowledge, even if the use of bills of quantities was mentioned. In considering the cases, it should be borne in mind that the question whether the architect has authority to bind the employer in this way may be quite separate from the question whether the architect may charge additionally to his own fees for quantity surveyor's services, though normally the two questions will go hand in hand.[77]

ILLUSTRATIONS

(1) K., an architect, was employed by the Guardians of W. to make plans for a workhouse. L., the clerk to the Guardians, advertised for tenders. K. then wrote to L. desiring him to show tenderers the following instructions: "The builders . . . are informed that the quantities are now being taken out for their use. . . . The successful competitor will have to defray the expenses of taking out the quantities, the charge for which will be stated at the foot of the

[75] *Waghorn* v. *Wimbledon Local Board* (1877) 2 Hudson's B.C., 4th ed., p. 52, *infra*.
[76] *Knox and Rob* v. *Scottish Garden Suburb Co.*, 1913 S.C. 872.
[77] In addition to the cases illustrated below, *see post*, pp. 193 *et seq*.

bill of quantities when delivered." Quantities were taken out by the plaintiff M., at the request of K. The Guardians quarrelled with K. and refused to go on with the work, and so the builders never tendered. K. sent in his account for £113 8s. 8d. and appended thereto M.'s charges, £65. The Guardians settled with K. They had never heard of M. until K.'s account was delivered. M. sued the Guardians for his charges and obtained a verdict, the jury finding that a usage was proved for architects to have their quantities made out by surveyors, and that such usage was beneficial. The defendants appealed on the ground that there was no privity of contract, that the usage was not binding on the defendants; and that it had not been sufficiently proved; the court rejected these contentions, *per* Parke B.: " I think it perfectly clear that there is sufficient in the circumstances of this case to raise an implied contract on the part of the defendants to pay for the services of the plaintiff. K. had authority to proceed in the usual way; and, according to the practice in building contracts, the quantities are made out by a surveyor, and paid for by the successful competitor for the work proposed; is it then to be said that where by the act of the defendants there can be no successful competitor the plaintiff is to receive nothing for his services? ": *Moon* v. *Witney Union* (1837).[78]

(2) A burial board instructed R., their salaried surveyor, to prepare plans and procure tenders for the erection of a building. When R. had prepared the plans he instructed the plaintiff, a quantity surveyor, to take out the quantities, and advertised for tenders, but because these were too high, none was accepted. The quantity surveyor sued the board, who set up that they had never authorised R. to employ him. Manisty J. *held*, " that as they (the building owners) had instructed him (the architect) to procure tenders, and as tenders could not be made without quantities, they had impliedly authorised him to get the quantities taken out ": *Waghorn* v. *Wimbledon Local Board* (1877).[79]

(3) D. employed B., an architect, to prepare plans for certain houses, the cost of which was not to exceed £6,500. B. employed A. to take out the quantities. Tenders were invited, but the lowest was £7,500 and none was accepted. A. brought an action against D. for his charges. The jury found that the employment of A. was not within the scope of B.'s authority; that D. had not sanctioned the employment; that there was no custom authorising the employment irrespective of consent; and that B. had no authority to employ A. for a contract exceeding £6,000. *Held*, that the alleged custom was not, as regards Ireland, one of which the court must take notice as a rule of law, and (O'Brien C.J. dissenting), that there had been no misdirection. *Held*, by O'Brien C.J., that the question whether D. had authorised B. to get tenders should have been left to the jury, for if D. authorised B. to get tenders, that impliedly authorised him to have the quantities taken out: *Antisell* v. *Doyle* (1899).[80]

[78] 3 Bing.N.C. 814.
[79] Hudson's B.C., 4th ed., Vol. 2, p. 52; and see *Gwyther* v. *Gaze* (1875) Hudson's B.C., 4th ed., Vol. 2, p. 34; and *Bayley* v. *Wilkins* (1849) 7 C.B. 886.
[80] [1899] 2 Ir.R. 275 and see *Young* v. *Smith*, illustrated *post*, p. 194.

Antisell's case shows, it is submitted, that the customary form of arrangement for employing quantity surveyors was already changing by that date.[81]

It is suggested that for practical purposes there are two quite separate problems raised by cases of this kind, namely, first, whether an express authority may be inferred so as to bind the employer to pay the quantity surveyor's fees, and secondly whether these fees, whoever may be liable for them, are or are not included in the agreed remuneration of the architect.

It is submitted that where the contract is to be in measured form, *i.e.* requiring bills of quantities, and this is known to the employer, and the architect is authorised to proceed and obtain tenders, an *express* authority may be inferred.[82]   And in the absence of special circumstances or provisions in the contract of employment, the fees will not be included in the architect's remuneration.

Even under the old practice there was, apparently, nothing to prevent an employer expressly limiting the architect's authority by a condition that the architect should not in obtaining tenders commit him to any expense, which suggests that the old cases were, despite some of the language used, cases based on express and not ostensible authority.

ILLUSTRATION

A club committee invited designs for a new club-house, and accepted those submitted by a certain architect. He employed R. to take out the quantities. As the plans proved too expensive to carry out, the work was abandoned. R. sued the committee for his fees, but they proved that they had only authorised the architect to procure tenders, provided that he did not pledge them to pay for them. R. was nonsuited: *Richardson* v. *Beale* (1867).[83]

It may happen, as in *Antisell* v. *Doyle, supra,* that the architect's instructions to obtain tenders, from which his authority to employ a quantity surveyor may be implied, are limited to obtaining tenders not exceeding a certain price. If this is so, it would seem that the architect cannot saddle the building owner with the expense of reducing the quantities for the purpose of rectifying his own mistake in having prepared designs entailing excessive cost. The building owner may, however, become liable to the quantity surveyor by knowledge of his employment for this purpose, or by ratification

---

[81] See also *post,* p. 193, Section 10, Liability for Quantity Surveyor's Fees.

[82] *Waghorn's* case, *supra.* But see the possible limitations of this decision in the case of private building owners suggested *supra,* p. 113.

[83] *The Times,* June 29, 1867.

or tacit assent, though in such a case he may well have a remedy in damages against the architect.

ILLUSTRATION

C. employed A., an architect, to make plans for the building of the S. Theatre. A., in the usual way, employed E., a quantity surveyor, to take out the quantities, which he did, and C., the employer, paid £342 for them. The architect's estimate was between £12,000 and £13,000, but no tender was obtained under £18,000. C. was dissatisfied with the tenders. A. employed E. to reduce his quantities, which he did, and his charge for so doing was £132. C. dismissed the architect, and when sued by E. disputed the liability. The jury, on a question put by the judge as to whether there was actual authority from C. to get the estimates reduced, found that there was, and gave a verdict for E. C. moved to set aside the verdict, and urged that it was the business of A., who had made plans the execution of which would prove far too expensive, to cut them down. However, the court, although not agreeing with the verdict, declined to disturb it, Lord Coleridge C.J. observing: " The recollection of the parties was at variance as to the fact of the alleged authority, but C. did not positively deny that he knew the quantities were being reduced, and ratification or tacit assent would be equivalent to precedent authority ": *Evans* v. *Carte* (1881).[84]

A building owner may at the present day find himself under considerable pressure from various directions to employ quantity surveyors or to use contracts in the bills of quantities form; indeed the Federation of Building Trade Employers actively discourage their members from tendering for work over a certain value (currently £8,000) without bills of quantities prepared by the employer. A trade agreement to this effect has been held not to be in the public interest under the terms of Restrictive Trade Practices Act 1956,[85] and it is quite certain, it is submitted, that mere size or value of a project is no evidence whatever of the need for bills of quantities or quantity surveyors so as to raise any inference of authority by the employer in the context of the preceding discussion.

(5) As to Measurement and Valuation of Variations

Once the building contract has been let the architect may be expressly authorised by a building owner to employ a quantity surveyor for the purpose of measurement and valuation so as to enable him to issue the necessary interim certificates, and to value variations or deviations in the works and make the necessary adjustments to the contract sum for P.C. and provisional sum items, or for claims permitted by the contract, or under the terms of fluctuations clauses,

---

[84] Hudson's B.C., 4th ed., Vol. 2, p. 78.
[85] *Re Birmingham Association of B.T.E.'s Agreement* [1963] 1 W.L.R. 484.

so as to enable the final certificate to be given.   In such a case the quantity surveyor's remuneration will obviously be at the cost of the building owner. A custom or usage of the building trade has in the past been put forward and on occasion accepted by juries, that in works of magnitude the architect has, by custom or by the scope of his agency, implied authority to call in to his assistance a quantity surveyor for the performance of this work, for whose services the employer is liable to pay.[86]

With reference to this custom Denman J. in *Plimsaul* v. *Kilmorey* (*Lord*) (1884) [87] said: " With respect to the general usage, of which evidence had been offered (and in respect of which it was intimated there were other witnesses to call), I think a jury would hesitate to establish it.   There are good grounds for considering it unreasonable as applied to circumstances such as were presented in this case, and it would often prejudice a building owner." Manisty J. in *Birdseye* v. *Dover Harbour Commissioners* (1881) [88] said: " The evidence of a direct contract to employ the plaintiff was not so satisfactory as perhaps the jury might desire. But the great question was whether they thought the custom set up had been proved, *viz.* whether in a work of this magnitude (about £4,000) the architect or contractor had a right to call in to his assistance a quantity surveyor whose services the employers were to pay for."

ILLUSTRATIONS

(1) The plaintiff, a quantity surveyor, sued for £76 5s. for fees for measuring up work, relying on an employment by the defendants' architect, and on a custom in the building trade that when a contractor did work the architect had a right to call in the assistance of a quantity surveyor to measure up, who should be paid by the employer. The defendants denied the employment and denied the custom, and said that it did not apply to this case. The plaintiff had been employed to measure and ascertain the final account. Several architects and surveyors were called for the plaintiff, who spoke to the custom of the building trade that in any large matter—say, over £2,000—an architect was entitled to call in a quantity surveyor, to be paid by the employer. Manisty J. left the custom to be decided by the jury, and they found for the plaintiff: *Birdseye* v. *Dover Harbour Commissioners* (1881).[89]

(2) The defendant employed V., an architect, to direct alterations in the St. James's Theatre, of which the defendant was the owner. V. retained the plaintiff to measure up all the work which had been

[86] See, *e.g. Birdseye* v. *Dover Harbour Commissioners* (1881) Hudson's B.C., 4th ed., Vol. 2, p. 76; *Beattie* v. *Gilroy* (1882) 10 R. (Ct. of Sess.) 226; *Plimsaul* v. *Kilmorey* (*Lord*) (1884) 1 T.L.R. 48, all illustrated *infra*.
[87] 1 T.L.R. 48, illustrated *infra*.
[88] Hudson's B.C., 4th ed., Vol. 2, p. 76.
[89] *Ibid.*

done, for the purpose of a final settlement of account with the
defendant, and the plaintiff now sued the defendant for £187, the
amount of his charges, at the usual rate of 2½ per cent. upon the value
of the work executed and certified by him. V. had appended the
plaintiff's charges to the builder's account and forwarded it to the
defendant. The plaintiff contended that by a general usage or custom
of the building trade an architect is authorised to employ a quantity
surveyor to measure up the work that had been executed and certified
by him, that his commission is charged in the builder's account,
and that on payment to the builder the amount is handed by the
latter to the surveyor, and evidence was called to prove such custom.
But the defendant showed that there had been disputes between
himself and V. and that he had told V. that he had intended to have
the work measured by an independent surveyor, and that V. had
suggested that it would be well that his surveyor, the plaintiff, should
go on the works with the surveyor appointed by the defendant.
Held, by Denman J., that the custom would not be reasonable to
apply in the present case, and that it was evident that V. employed
the plaintiff as his own surveyor: *Plimsaul* v. *Kilmorey (Lord)* (1884).[90]

While in *Birdseye's* case Manisty J. felt obliged to leave the matter
to the jury, Denman J. was clearly of a contrary opinion, and it is
submitted that at the present time no such custom exists. The
standard R.I.B.A. forms of contract, whether or not Bills are used,
all make explicit provision for a quantity surveyor, and the R.I.B.A.
conditions of employment of architects also deal with the position
expressly. No difficulty arises in the latter case, but if the R.I.B.A.
terms of employment do not apply, though a standard form of
contract is recommended by the architect and accepted by the
employer, it will not follow in every case, it is submitted, that the
employer is thereby expressly authorising the employment of surveyors
or additional remuneration for the architect. This must depend on
the degree of knowledge of the terms of the building contract possessed by the employer in question and of the practice of the industry
if contracts with bills of quantities have been used. On any view,
it is clear that, if the building contract contemplates that it is the
architect who will measure up, he can have no express authority
thereby to employ a quantity surveyor to perform that duty or to
charge fees additional to the agreed figure for doing so. (It would
follow, however, that proof of a custom to that effect would constitute the architect ostensible agent whatever his actual authority.)
In cases where the architect himself does this work, his authority
(in the absence of any express provision in the building contract
that a quantity surveyor shall perform such service) is inevitably
implied, in most building contracts, from the fact of the architect

[90] 1 T.L.R. 48.

being required to certify payment to the builder, which he could not do without measurement. As has been said, whether the architect has a right to charge the building owner for this measuring up must depend upon the terms of his employment by the building owner, but he cannot charge the building contractor for doing so, despite certain attempts made in the past.

ILLUSTRATIONS

(1) After certain building work was done the builder presented an account for extras. The contract provided that any additions or deductions should be ascertained and valued in accordance with a schedule of prices. The architect measured up, and included in the builder's certificate his charges for measuring. The building owner paid the builder the amount of the certificate less this amount. The architect sued the builder for these fees. *Held*, that it was in the interest of the building owner, and not of the builder, that these measurements were taken, and that without special employment no action for these fees was maintainable against the builder: *Beattie* v. *Gilroy* (1882).[91]

(2) An architect sued a builder for $2\frac{1}{2}$ per cent. commission for measuring up alterations and additions in a contract for building the Half Moon Tavern, entered into between the builder and P., the owner of the tavern. The plaintiff had been employed by P. and by the contract had power to order alterations. The builder was paid by certificates. The plaintiff ordered and measured alterations, and the $2\frac{1}{2}$ per cent. commission was added to each certificate as it was given. Payment was made by P. on these certificates, but subsequently P. became bankrupt, and a balance of £116 remained due from him to the builder on the contract. The contract was silent as to who was to pay the commission, and the plaintiff contended that it was really due for service rendered to the defendant, and also alleged a general custom of the profession that the charge should be paid by the builder. Lopes J. intimated his opinion that the plaintiff could not recover unless he could show that the commission was in the hands of the builder, in addition to what was due to him on the whole contract.[92] Judgment was given for the defendant: *Locke* v. *Morter* (1885).[93]

Neither can the builder maintain an action against the architect for a careless or wrong-headed measurement, in the absence of fraud.[94]

(6) As to Employment of Engineering or other Consultants

An architect or engineer has no implied authority to employ engineering or other consultants, so as either to render the employer liable

[91] 10 R. (Ct. of Sess.) 226.
[92] When the fee could be claimed in quasi-contract; see *ante*, Chap. 1, p. 62.
[93] 2 T.L.R. 121.
[94] See *post*, Chap. 7, p. 457, and the cases of *Stevenson* v. *Watson* (1879) 4 C.P.D. 148, and *Ludbrook* v. *Barrett* (1877) 46 L.J.Q.B. 798, there referred to.

for their fees or entitle the architect to additional payment in respect of the fees. In complex works it is often necessary for such consultants to be brought in early at the design stage, but as the design is essentially the duty of the architect or engineer [95] such consultants are, in effect, carrying out part of the architect's or engineer's duty. In such cases the architect or engineer, and not the employer, is liable for the consultant's fees unless such consultant's employment has been expressly authorised. Thus it has been said that an architect, in a case involving a reinforced concrete structure, " had three courses open to him if he was not able to design the whole of the work himself. One was to refuse the job; one was to ask the building owner to employ a structural engineer on this part of the work; and one was, while retaining responsibility for the design, himself to seek the advice and assistance of a structural engineer, paying for the service out of his own pocket, but with the satisfaction of knowing that if the advice given was wrong the engineer would owe him the same duty as he owed the employer." [96]

Under the conditions of engagement contained in the R.I.B.A. Scale of Professional Charges it is stated: " The employment of consultants shall be at the architect's discretion in agreement with the client and the payment of their fees shall be a matter of arrangement between the architect and the client." [96a]

It is perhaps possible that, in very large and technical or industrial projects, the court might be asked, on the analogy of *Waghorn's* case [97] to infer an express authority, by virtue of the employers' instructions to put such a project out to tender, to employ consultants for site investigation or design. It is doubtful if such an argument would be successful, and architects and engineers should as a matter of prudence always obtain express approval before incurring such expenditure, unless they are prepared to meet it themselves out of their own remuneration.

(7) Express Powers under Building and Engineering Contracts

Building and engineering contracts themselves expressly confer various powers on the architect or engineer, the exercise of which may be binding on the employer, and sometimes on both parties. [98] In so far as such powers are expressed to be subject to review by an arbitrator (and, therefore, if necessary, by the courts in ordinary

[95] See *infra*, pp. 129–131.
[96] *Per* Sir Walker Carter O.R. in *Moresk* v. *Hicks* [1966] 2 Lloyd's Rep. 338.
[96a] See also *infra*, pp. 129–132.   [97] See *ante*, p. 114.
[98] See also the discussion *supra*, subs. (2), pp. 106 *et seq.*

litigation [99]) they do not merit discussion in the present context. The most important of all, that to order variations, provided that the formalities laid down by the contract are complied with, is, however, binding on the employer, in that he cannot in any circumstances thereafter dispute the architect's authority to give the relevant instruction. But whether or not such an instruction in fact involves a variation is, under the terms of the great majority of contracts, subject to review by an arbitrator or the courts.

The latest (post-1963) R.I.B.A. standard forms of building contract, however, continuing and extending still further the policy commenced in the 1957 edition, have endeavoured to ensure that the architect's final certificate should, in the absence of prior notice of arbitration, be conclusive and binding on both parties over a very wide range of matters as to which the architect is given powers under the contract (which now include, for instance, a remarkable provision making the architect judge in his own cause by enabling him to certify additional sums as payable to the contractor by reason of late delivery of instructions and details [1]). The standard form of engineering contract does not appear to adopt this policy [2] which, as pointed out in Chapter 7, is in practice grossly prejudicial to the interests of the employer and of great benefit to contractors.[3]

(8) Effect of Restrictions as between Employer and Architect

Restrictions both express or implied may well exist as between the architect and the building owner as to the occasions upon which the powers expressly conferred upon the architect in the building contract may be exercised—for instance, that substantial variations are not to be ordered without prior consultation with and approval by the building owner. These will not affect the contractor or any other third party, provided, in the case of the contractor, that the architect acts strictly within the terms of the express authority conferred by the building contract, except, perhaps, in the unlikely event that the builder has full knowledge of all the circumstances, where he might possibly be estopped from relying on the contractual provisions.

---

[99] See *post*, Chap. 7, pp. 447–448.
[1] See clause 24.
[2] See, however, the very obscure and difficult clauses 62 and 63 of that contract, which appear only to have the effect of preventing the contractor from advancing further claims after the maintenance certificate.
[3] See *post*, Chap. 7, pp. 489–491.

SECTION 5. RIGHTS OF CONTRACTOR WHEN ARCHITECT OR
ENGINEER EXCEEDS AUTHORITY

(1) Warranty of Authority

While an architect's or engineer's implied authority to bind his
employer in contract is, as has been seen, extremely limited, he may
nevertheless be himself liable to the contractor for breach of warranty
of authority if he exceeds his actual authority, and the contractor
suffers damage as a result. This liability flows from the general rule
of law that a person who, even in good faith, purports to contract
as agent for another with a third party impliedly warrants to such
third party that he has authority from his principal to make the
contract.[4] But the warranty must be relied upon, and if in fact
the contractor knows of the architect's want of authority, that will
be a good defence to an action of this kind.[5] Also, on general
principles, an architect may render himself personally liable where
he makes a contract in his own name without naming his principals
or expressly excluding his liability,[6] though this is unlikely to occur
in practice in building contracts.

(2) Measure of Damages for Breach of Warranty

The damages recoverable for breach of warranty of authority
are the loss which the contractor has sustained as the natural and
probable consequence of the absence of authority. Thus, where in
building contracts there has been a warranty of this kind, the contractor's damages will normally include the costs incurred in reasonably bringing an action upon the contract against the principal in
addition to his remuneration and loss of profit on any uncompleted
work. If there is any doubt as to the agent's authority the contractor,
before suing the alleged principal, should give notice to the agent
that he will hold him responsible for the costs of the action, if the
event proves that the agent had no authority.

ILLUSTRATIONS

(1) T., an architect, ordered stone from R. for a building which
was being constructed under his superintendence. T. had no authority
to do this. R. brought an action against the building owner, which
was unsuccessful. *Held*, that R. was entitled to recover as against

---

[4] *Randell* v. *Trimen* (1856) 18 C.B. 786; *Collen* v. *Wright* (1857) 8 E. & B. 647; *Firbank's
Executors* v. *Humphreys* (1886) 18 Q.B.D. 54; *Yonge* v. *Toynbee* [1910] 1 K.B. 215.
[5] *Halbot* v. *Lens* [1901] 1 Ch. 344.
[6] *Beigtheil and Young* v. *Stewart* (1900) 16 T.L.R. 177.

T. the value of the stone and also the costs incurred and paid in the action against the building owners: *Randall* v. *Trimen* (1856).[7]

(2) An action was instituted by a contractor against the supposed principal to enforce a contract made by the alleged agent. The contractor gave the agent notice that he would proceed with the action at the agent's expense, if the agent did not give him notice not to proceed, and that, if the action was dismissed on the ground of want of authority to contract, or if the agent gave him notice not to proceed, he would bring an action against the agent for damages. The agent did not give the contractor notice not to proceed, and the action was dismissed on the ground of such want of authority. It was held that the contractor might, in an action against the agent on the implied warranty of authority, recover as part of his damages his costs of the action against the supposed principal: *Collen* v. *Wright* (1857).[8]

SECTION 6. DUTIES AND LIABILITIES OF ARCHITECTS AND ENGINEERS TO EMPLOYER

(1) Generally

The duty of architects and engineers to third persons in tort has already been briefly discussed.[9] But the duty owed by an architect or engineer to his employer arises in contract and not in tort.[10] One important result of this is that for purposes of limitation,[11] time begins to run at the date of the breach [12] and not, as in the tort of negligence, from the date at which the damage occurs.[13] As has been seen—Section 3, *supra*—the contract of employment may be informal, or may be in writing without defining the duties expressly. This Section attempts to set out the duties which will normally

---

[7] 18 C.B. 786.

[8] 26 L.J.Q.B. 147; 27 L.J.Q.B. 215.

[9] See *ante*, Chap. 1, pp. 67 *et seq.*

[10] *Steljes* v. *Ingram* (1903) 19 T.L.R. 534. *Bagot* v. *Stevens Scanlan & Co.* [1966] 1 Q.B. 197. It seems that an architect may be held liable if he gratuitously undertakes a professional obligation—see *Townsends (Builders) Ltd* v. *Cinema News Ltd.* [1959] 1 W.L.R 119, where an architect appears to have been held liable *to a builder* for failure to give notice to a local authority, pursuant to certain by-law regulations. (In this case the architect was also held liable to the employer.) The exact basis of the liability to the builder does not appear from the report, but is indicated *ante*, Chap. 1, p. 66, in the discussion of the principle of *Hedley Byrne* v. *Heller* (1964), under which architects may find their field of liability to third persons widened in the future.

[11] As to which see *post*, Chap. 5, pp. 368 *et seq.*

[12] However, it would seem that where one party is relying upon the other in a confidential relationship (as client and architect, for instance), the Courts will interpret section 26 of the Limitation Act 1939 (concealment of cause of action by fraud) somewhat generously—see *Clark* v. *Woor* [1965] 1 W.L.R. 650 (a case of builder and employer), illustrated, *post*, Chap. 5, p. 370.

[13] *Bagot* v. *Stevens Scanlan & Co.* [1966] 1 Q.B. 197.

be implied from the fact of employment in the absence of any express term to the contrary.

Generally, an employer under a building or engineering contract will have four main interests which he employs his professional adviser to secure, *viz.*:

(i) a design which is skilful, effective to achieve his purpose within any financial limitations he may impose or make known, and comprehensive, in the sense that no necessary and foreseeable work is omitted;

(ii) the obtaining of a competitive price for the work from a competent contractor, and the placing of the contract accordingly on terms which afford reasonable protection to the employer's interest both in regard to price and the quality of the work;

(iii) efficient supervision to ensure that the works as carried out conform in detail to the design; and

(iv) efficient administration of the contract so as to achieve speedy and economical completion of the project.

In so far as any act or omission of the architect or engineer prejudices any of these interests, he will be failing in his obligations and may, if the breach of duty is clear, be responsible to his employer for any damage which he may suffer.

The exact degree of care owed by persons holding themselves out as specially qualified in a particular trade or profession and rendering services for reward has been somewhat variously expressed by different judges. It is a question of fact which " appears to us to rest upon this further inquiry, *viz.*: whether other persons exercising the same profession or calling, and being men of experience and skill therein, would or would not have come to the same conclusion as the defendant." [14]

Thus in a medical case it was said:

" It is not enough, to make the defendant liable, that some medical men, of far greater experience or ability, might have used a greater degree of skill, nor that even he might possibly have used some greater degree of care. The question is whether there has been a want of competent care and skill to such an extent as to lead to the bad result." [15]

---

[14] *Per* Tindal C.J. in *Chapman* v. *Walton* (1833) 10 Bing. 57 at p. 63.
[15] *Per* Erle C.J. in *Rich* v. *Pierpont* (1862) 3 F. & F. 35.

Of architects as such it has been said:

" As architect, he is in the same position as any other professional or skilled person, and whether it be in the preparation of plans and specifications, or the doing of any other professional work for reward, is responsible if he omits to do it with an ordinary and reasonable degree of care and skill." [16]

" As regards matters in which the plaintiff (an architect) was employed merely as agent for the building owner, he was to protect his interests adversely to the builder, and the plaintiff would be liable to an action by his employer if he acted negligently in such matters." [17]

The architect " is bound to do his best for his employer, and to look sharply after the builder whilst the work is going on, and it is his duty in that capacity to form an opinion as to what his employer is entitled while the works are being executed." [18]

Largely as a result of the present systems of negotiating the standard forms, in which the interests of the employer or consumer tend to be under-represented, there has been over the last thirty or forty years a progressive increase in the number of risks transferred from the contractor's to the employer's shoulders. Thus apart from extension of time provisions (which are expressed to operate in the case of many matters, such as weather, availability of materials and labour, and delays by nominated sub-contractors or suppliers, over which the employer can be regarded as having no responsibility or control), direct financial burdens, for instance, rises in costs of materials or labour, the cost of meeting unforeseen unfavourable physical conditions or artificial obstructions,[19] and liability for damage to adjoining property in the absence of negligence by the contractor, have been transferred to the employer. An architect or engineer recommending contracts in such a form is, it is suggested, under a heavy responsibility to see that all that is humanly possible is done at the planning stage to reduce such risks to a minimum.

Furthermore, the fact that under the post-1963 R.I.B.A. forms of contract an employer loses all further right to complain of work done in breach of contract upon the issue of the final certificate, unless *before the final certificate* he has issued notice of arbitration,

---

[16] *Per* Osler J.A. in *Badgley* v. *Dickson* (1886) 13 A.R. 494 at p. 500, illustrated *post*, p. 162.

[17] *Per* A. L. Smith M.R. in *Chambers* v. *Goldthorpe* [1901] 1 K.B. 624 at p. 634.

[18] See *per* Mathew L.J. in *Cross* v. *Leeds Corporation* (1902) 2 Hudson's B.C., 4th ed., p. 339 at p. 343.

[19] In engineering contracts.

and that the only important exception to this relates to defects which " reasonable inspection or examination at any reasonable time during the carrying out of the works or before the issue of the certificate would not have disclosed " [20] can only mean, it is submitted, a drastic revision in the degree of supervision which architects who recommend this form to their clients have hitherto afforded in practice.[21]

On the other hand, as in the case of all professional men, the breach of duty must be clear and self-evident. To show that better methods might have been used is not of necessity to show that the methods employed were so unprofessional or unskilled as to amount to negligence.[22] And, in the case of the administration of building contracts, where the contract is susceptible of two different meanings, it would seem that if an architect acts honestly but erroneously upon one construction he will not be liable for so doing.[23]

If a building owner is considering proceeding against an architect for negligence, one of the first tactical problems which usually faces him is that in many cases he may wish to proceed against the contractor as well, either because the contractor may seem also to be in breach (as in cases of supervisory negligence) or because his breach is an alternative possibility, or likely to be pleaded by way of defence. The obtaining of a single tribunal to hear the tripartite dispute at one hearing, which is a normal part of High Court procedure, may be difficult to achieve, since one or both of the two contracts may contain an arbitration clause, and because without agreement the same arbitrator cannot necessarily be obtained and cannot hold one hearing to resolve both disputes.[24]

Building and engineering disputes in the High Court involving any complication are at the present day, whatever the sums of money involved, usually referred to Official Referees, and while allegations of professional negligence were usually not so referred,[25] because there was no right of appeal on fact from an Official Referee, recent changes in the rules have been made specifically permitting such appeals in cases of professional negligence.[26] So a claim for

---

[20] Clause 30 (7) (*b*), 1963 R.I.B.A. form.
[21] See *infra*, subs. (j) Supervision, p. 152.
[22] See, *e.g. Armitage* v. *Palmer* (1960) 175 E.G. 315, C.A. (Advice on rights of light).
[23] See *Ireland* v. *Livingstone* (1871) L.R. 5 H.L. 395; *Bulmer* v. *Gilman* (1842) 4 M. & G. 108; and the difficult case of *Cotton* v. *Wallis* [1955] 1 W.L.R. 1168, *infra*, pp. 155–156, of which this may be the best explanation.
[24] See *post*, Chap. 18, pp. 844–846.
[25] *Osenton* v. *Johnston* [1942] A.C. 130.
[26] See Ord. 58, r. 5.

professional negligence against an engineer for £500,000 estimated to take some weeks to try has been so referred.[27] This tendency is unfortunate, because even in long building cases the sums involved on a *per diem* basis are often substantially greater than in other classes of case which are tried without question by High Court judges, with the result that it must be said that in England the High Court Bench is often seriously handicapped by lack of experience of the factual background of building contracts and disputes when such cases do come before them. Furthermore building disputes almost invariably involve difficult questions of construction of the contracts used, which are notoriously diffuse and imprecise, which also makes trial by a judge desirable.

The list of duties of architects and engineers in the next following subsection is not intended to be exhaustive, and any set of circumstances should be tested in the light of the interests of the employer set out above.[28]

(2) Duties in Detail

(a) Design

The word " design " in this context includes the specifications, whether or not incorporated in bills of quantities, as well as plans and drawings. The architect or engineer will normally be given a free hand in this part of his duties, but building owners may press their own ideas upon him as to materials to be used or plans to be followed. Where the employer's suggestions or wishes are likely to lead to an unsatisfactory result, the architect's duty will be discharged if he gives a sufficient warning, it is suggested. So, where an architect is specifically instructed to use a new method of construction, its failure may be consistent with a proper degree of care on his part.

ILLUSTRATION

A building owner employed an architect to plan and superintend the erection of model lodging-houses after the latest improvements, and instructed him to put in a new patent concrete roofing which was much cheaper than lead or slate. The roofing proved a failure, and the building owner sued the architect for negligence. Erle J. charged the jury that, although failure in an ordinary building was evidence of want of competent skill, yet if out of the ordinary course an architect was employed in some novel thing in which he had no experience, and which had not the test of experience, failure might be consistent with skill: *Turner* v. *Garland and Christopher* (1853).[29]

Where a project involves new techniques of construction, the architect or engineer is, it is suggested, under a special duty to take

[27] *Scarborough R.D.C.* v. *Moore* (1968) 112 S.J. 986.
[28] At p. 124. [29] Hudson's B.C., 4th ed., Vol. 2, p. 1.

the best advice available upon the use of such new techniques, and to advise his employer of any potential risks; and where the selection of the technique is the architect's, the onus of justifying his action will be correspondingly heavier, since nearly all building and civil engineering techniques are empirical in origin and have evolved gradually by experience and trial and error, and non-traditional methods are notoriously susceptible to unexpected difficulties and failure. It goes without saying that in normal circumstances an architect or engineer will not be automatically relieved from liability for his plans or design by obtaining his employer's approval of them, if the defect of design complained of is one of construction or of a technical character. On the other hand approval of the aesthetic aspect of a design would obviously normally discharge the architect of personal liability. A more doubtful area of liability may arise if the design defect affects the commercial value or purpose of the design. So an architect was held not liable to experienced developers because houses constructed to his design did not have downstairs lavatories.[30]

But if, for instance, by reason of the known facts relating to soil conditions there is only one really foolproof type of scheme, and another which is considerably more economical but involves an element of risk, it is the adviser's duty, it is suggested, to acquaint his employer of the position and leave the decision to him,[31] and in that event approval of the less safe course would clearly negative liability.

If an error in the design is discovered at an early stage, the building owner should normally, as part of the duty to mitigate damage, give the architect or engineer an opportunity to correct it. Thus in *Columbus Co.* v. *Clowes* (1903)[32] Wright J. said: " It seems to me that the most the plaintiffs can get is the reasonable cost of making the plans good. But then comes the difficulty. The defendant himself would have made the plans good without any charge. Indeed he would have been bound to do so. If, however, the plaintiffs had called in another architect, he would in all probability have insisted on commencing the plans *de novo*, and would have refused to make any use of the defendant's plans. But would that have been a reasonable course to pursue? I do not think it would."

The above remarks would not, however, apply if the design was

---

[30] *Worbuoys* v. *Acme Investments* (1969) 210 E.G. 335.
[31] See *City of Brantford* v. *Kemp and Wallace-Carruthers Ltd.* (1960) 23 D.L.R. (2d) 640 (Canada).
[32] [1903] 1 K.B. 244 at p. 247.

quite useless or the defect such as could reasonably be expected to destroy any further confidence in the professional adviser. In that event the building owner would be entitled to treat the contract of employment as repudiated.[33]

The measure of damage for breach of the design obligation will obviously differ widely according to the nature of the breach; it may be nominal if the error can be rectified simply at an early stage, it may be for loss of value or loss of commercial profitability in the case of a non-structural suitability breach, and will usually be the cost of repair in the case of structural breaches.[34]

For further examples of design failures by architects and engineers, see also subsection (b), Examination of Site, *infra*.

A problem of the utmost importance in relation to design is emerging as the result of certain modern tendencies in the organisation of the building and engineering industry in the United Kingdom. The growth of specialisation and the complexities of modern buildings and their contents have meant that in many cases an architect is bound to employ consultants, since he will lack the necessary skill himself.[34a] Furthermore, the specialist sub-contractors who carry out work or supply articles for incorporation in the work are more expert in design in their own field than the architect or engineer in general charge of the project can hope to be. Quite apart from obvious examples, such as the machinery which is often installed in engineering contracts, and heating and ventilation and electrical services, there are many processes which are now a normal part of modern building and engineering techniques, yet which fall into this category. They include, for example, the structural frames of large buildings whether in steel, reinforced concrete, or pre-stressed concrete, specialist piling and foundation work, roofing work of many different kinds, specialist floor finishes, and so on. In some cases consultants practising in these fields either do not exist at all, or are so few in number as to be beyond the practical reach of the ordinary employer or his professional advisers, except in the case of the most massive projects where the expense of employing them could be justified.

In these circumstances a substantial proportion of the technical design of a project can be (and often is) delegated in reality (though quite often not in appearance) to a specialist sub-contractor, who under the present system in the U.K. is usually nominated by the architect or engineer under a power reserved in the contract. Such

---

[33] For discharge by breach, see *post*, Chap. 5, pp. 340 *et seq.*
[34] See the analogous case of damages for defective work, *post*, Chap. 9, pp. 585 *et seq.*
[34a] See also *supra*, pp. 119–120, for his authority to engage consultants.

a sub-contractor of the main contractor, far from receiving plans and details of his work from the architect or engineer, may give a quotation without any detailed drawings or specification, and be required (not usually in any express part of his sub-contract) to supply working or shop-drawings to an architect or engineer for " approval." This approval can often be little more than an act of co-ordination designed to see that the specially designed work will not clash with the architecturally designed part of the project, rather than any genuine technical check upon the efficiency of the design so submitted. A major example can be found in the structures of large buildings, which sometimes are designed by structural engineers advising the architect, but which increasingly frequently are being designed by the sub-contractor supplying and erecting the frame of the building.[35]

It will be seen that, under the traditional arrangement, architects and engineers are responsible to the employer for the design and suitability of the works for their intended purpose, whereas the contractor is only responsible for bringing the works to completion according to the design.[36] The situation under discussion may, however, mean that in respect of the sub-contracted work the employer may have a remedy for an unsatisfactory design against the contractor for breach of contract, in that the terms of the nominated sub-contract in question may show expressly that the sub-contractor (and hence the main contractor) was thereby undertaking a design responsibility.[37] It is submitted that in principle the architect should remain liable to the employer in such a case.[37a] While every case must depend on the exact facts, it is suggested that the fact that the sub-contractor may, as part of the obligations of his sub-contract, have accepted an *express* responsibility for design, and that in accordance with most provisions for nomination of sub-contractors the main contractor is accordingly deemed to have contracted with the employer in identical terms, and accordingly the latter may have a concurrent remedy against the contractor, will usually be irrelevant to the question of the architect's liability. Just as, it is suggested, the scheme of a building contract is to place responsibility for its

[35] See the discussion as to the serious abuses and unsatisfactory nature of this type of arrangement in the case of structural engineers, *supra*, Section 2 (6), p. 98.

[36] *Post*, Chap. 5, pp. 267 *et seq.*, 273 *et seq.*

[37] As to the suggested basis of this liability of the sub-contractor, see *post*, Chap. 15, pp. 761 *et seq.*, where the difficulties of any *implied* liability are also explained. See also *post*, Chap. 5, pp. 277–278, 281–282.

[37a] This is particularly so where his fees are based on a percentage of total cost inclusive of the work in question.

execution, despite a multiplicity of sub-contractors, on one set of shoulders, namely the main contractor's, so too the responsibility for design is also placed on one set of shoulders, namely those of the employer's architect or engineer, and if the architect, however prudently or inevitably, chooses to delegate part of his duties, whether to consultants or specialist sub-contractors, he will remain responsible for their negligence to the employer. In the great majority of cases, however, nothing is said, either in the main contract or in the specialist sub-contract documentation, about any design function which may have been undertaken by the sub-contractor. It seems beyond doubt that in such a case an architect could not divest himself of his design responsibility in this way, and it has been so held.

ILLUSTRATION

A building failed after two years because of the defective design of its reinforced concrete frame, in that the purlins were of inadequate strength and the portal frames were not tied together at knee or ground level. The employer sued his architect, who pleaded an implied term of his contract of employment that he should be entitled to delegate specialist design tasks to qualified specialist sub-contractors. The architect had invited a firm of nominated sub-contractors,[38] with directors having engineering qualifications, to prepare the drawings and construct the frame, and then submit a price for the work to be done, and had approved the drawings and caused a sub-contract to be placed with an appropriate specification. *Held*, by Sir Walker Carter O.R., there was no implied right to delegate the duty of design, and no implied authority for the architect to employ the sub-contractor to design the building: *Moresk* v. *Hicks* (1966).[39]

To the extent, however, that the employer himself chose to employ consultants, or was to order provision to be made in the main contract for matters connected with design, such as a soil survey, to be sub-contracted to specialists, he might not appear to be relying on the architect's skill or judgment, and different considerations would prevail. In a case where an architect or engineer has himself called in a consultant, he will normally himself have a right of recourse, if sued, against the consultant for damages,[40] but in other cases (and in particular that of specialist sub-contractors) there will be no remedy available to the architect or engineer (unless he can successfully invoke the principle of *Hedley Byrne* v. *Heller* (1964) previously discussed in Chapter 1).

[38] The pleadings indicate that it was a case of nominated sub-contractors, though the language in the judgment suggests direct contracting.
[39] [1966] 2 Lloyd's Rep. 338.
[40] See the part of the judgment in the *Moresk* case quoted *supra*, Section 4 (6), p. 120.

In deciding whether an architect or engineer is liable for the negligence of others, such as consultants employed by him or sub-contractors selected by him, it is submitted that it will not avail an architect to show that he selected a reputable and sufficiently qualified person to do the work, and was guilty of no personal negligence in doing so. If an architect undertakes to design a building for reward, it is submitted that he undertakes that the various parts of the project will be properly designed with the necessary skill and care required for those parts of the work, whether the skill demanded is a strictly architectural skill or not.[41] To this extent he guarantees the professional competence of those whom he chooses to delegate his function, but this need be no hardship in the case of his own consultants, against whom he will have recourse in the event of a design failure. In the case of sub-contractors he will be in a difficulty, and in his own as well as his employer's interest should obtain express guarantees of the suitability of the work and its design from the sub-contractor in favour of the employer and of himself.[42]

Finally, reference should perhaps be made to the current (1966) R.I.B.A. Conditions of Engagement, which by clauses 1. 12 and 1. 24 provide for the possibility of employing consultants by agreement, and would seem to suggest that, whoever is their paymaster, the consultants will be solely responsible for " the *detailed* design and supervision of the work entrusted to them." Further by clause 1. 13 the architect may recommend specialist sub-contractors to design and execute any part of the work, and that he shall be " responsible for the *direction and integration* of their design, and for general supervision, but that nominated sub-contractors shall be *solely responsible for the detailed design* entrusted to them." The exact meaning of these provisions, where incorporated into the contract of employment, may be expected to occupy the time of the courts for many years if they remained unaltered and, without advice as to the obtaining of warranties to protect the employer, may constitute a serious threat to the employer's reasonable interest.

(b) Examination of site

A necessary preliminary to a successful constructional design must, in nearly all cases, be a sufficient examination of the site with a view to determining the area available for the proposed

---

[41] See the quotation from the *Moresk* case, *supra*, Section 4 (6), p. 120.
[42] See the suggestions of the Court of Appeal to this effect, made in a somewhat different context in *Bickerton and Sons* v. *N.W. Metropolitan Hospital Board* [1969] 1 All E.R. 977.

works, and the nature of the subsoil with a view to deciding upon the correct design for foundations or methods of underground working. In the case of an architect employed to build a house, he will also require to inspect the foundations during the progress of the works, particularly at the time when the excavation is completed, and before foundation concrete is poured. The by-laws of local authorities invariably require the approval of the local building inspector before the foundations are laid, and most building contracts require the contractor to obtain such approval and construct sound foundations, as well as to comply with all by-law requirements,[43] but this will not affect the responsibility of the architect to his employer for this very important aspect of supervision, in which failure can give rise to disastrous results.[44] Equally, it is suggested, where an architect is instructed to build on old foundations, he must employ reasonable tests of the soundness of the walls and stability of the underlying structures.

The architect or engineer is not bound to make a personal examination,[45] but will employ others to do so at his peril if he adopts incorrect information furnished to him by others.

ILLUSTRATIONS

(1) An engineer was employed to build a bridge. The employer, who had previously employed A to ascertain by boring the nature of the soil, requested him to inform the engineer of the result, which he did. The engineer did not examine the soil for himself. The foundation gave way. The engineer failed to recover his remuneration: *Moneypenny* v. *Hartland* (1826).[45a]

(2) A company employed C. as architect to make plans and to have quantities taken out, and paid £200 to C. and £200 to the quantity surveyor. C. did not measure the site; but, acting on information from an unauthorised person, made plans on the assumption that the site was smaller than it was. C. made borings to ascertain the necessary depth for the foundations. Later the error in the plans was discovered, on which the company brought an action against C. for the return of the money paid him, as the consideration had wholly failed, or in the alternative for damages for negligence. *Held*, that the consideration had not wholly failed. *Held*, also, that the company were entitled to nominal damages for the error in the plans (as they had suffered no loss thereby), and to £40, the amount of the cost of adapting the quantities to a correct plan: *Columbus Co.* v. *Clowes* (1903).[46]

---

[43] See *infra*, p. 142, and *post*, Chap. 5, pp. 293–294.
[44] *Cf.* the position under French law as applied in *Brown* v. *Laurie* (1854) 1 L.C.R. 343 (Canada); affirmed 5 L.C.R. 65. *Cf.* also the *Voli* case, *ante*, p. 74.
[45] See *post*, subs. (j) Supervision.
[45a] 2 C. & P. 378. But see *supra*, pp. 92–95.
[46] [1903] 1 K.B. 244.

Bearing in mind, however, that the architect's duty is relative, namely to show reasonable professional skill, and not absolute, in the sense of a guarantee of the works, and that building inspectors and district surveyors may be highly qualified and have unrivalled local knowledge and experience, it would, it is suggested, be difficult to establish liability in relation to foundations if the evidence showed that the architect had, after a full consideration of all the facts, reached a similar view to that of a sufficiently qualified and experienced district surveyor or building inspector. Generally speaking, however, the latter's function is limited to approval of the actual depth and state of excavations rather than to a critical analysis of the architect's design itself, and there may well be relevant matters known to the architect and not to the building inspector about this. In this particular field, it is not unusual to find that specialist consultants may be called in to advise on the design of foundations or to make surveys and reports on the soil conditions. Where this is the case it will certainly be in the interests of the architect, and very probably of the building owner as well, if they are employed directly by the latter.[47]

In engineering contracts, which are generally more concerned with subsoil conditions than building contracts, the engineer's responsibility is a heavy one, the heavier, and not the lighter, it is submitted, because of the existence of clause 12 of the 1955 I.C.E. standard form, where this is used.[48] It is remarkable that projects of the greatest importance in this field usually appear to be carried out with little or no thorough site or geological survey and a totally inadequate number of boreholes, and yet tendering contractors are in practice required to price the work, which must depend to a great extent upon an accurate assessment of the site conditions, in a period of time permitting nothing but the most cursory visual examination of the site.[48a] One reason why litigation against engineers by their employers in this context is comparatively rare may be the difficulty of proving damage resulting from the breach of duty, since it can usually be shown that if the unfavourable conditions had been discovered beforehand the contract price would inevitably have been greater.[49]

[47] See the discussion *supra*, pp. 131–132.
[48] This entitles contractors to extra payment for unfavourable physical conditions or artificial obstructions which could not have been reasonably foreseen. See *post*, pp. 569–570.
[48a] See also *post*, p. 226.   [49] *Cf. Columbus Co.* v. *Clowes, supra.*

(c) Delivery of drawings and instructions in time

In the absence of any express term, the obligation to supply drawings and information must be to do so in reasonable time, which of course begs the question, what is a reasonable time for this purpose? This is one of the commonest causes of disputes between contractors and employers. The practice of architects and engineers in the United Kingdom of supplying relatively generalised drawings for pricing purposes at the time of the contract and of supplementing them with detailed or working drawings after the contract, has already been referred to,[50] and obviously contains the seeds of possible disturbance and disruption of the contractor's programme. There is, perhaps inevitably, a lack of legal authority on the exact nature of the architect's or engineer's duty in this regard, no doubt because in the vast majority of cases if a contractor can show that he has in fact been held up for lack of information, he will be awarded damages without more ado, and because even if a point of time at which information should theoretically be available could be shown to have passed, it would not avail the contractor if he had not suffered damage thereby. The inquiry in any particular case almost invariably becomes one of fact, therefore, and the precise identification of the point of time at which the contractor needed the information, which is usually necessary to establish the quantum of his damage, is also a question of fact which cannot be of assistance in other cases on different facts. Under the R.I.B.A. standard forms of contract, the duty was expressed before 1963 as a duty to furnish the contractor " within a reasonable time . . . with such further drawings as are reasonably necessary to enable him to carry out all Architect's Instructions and with any further details which in the opinion of the architect are necessary for the execution of any part of the work," [51] and in the post-1963 forms " as and when from time to time may be necessary . . . with such drawings or details as are reasonably necessary either to explain and amplify the Contract drawings or to enable (him) to carry out and complete the works. . . . " [52] Again, by clause 8 of the 1955 I.C.E. form, the engineer is empowered to issue " from time to time during the progress of the works such further drawings and instructions as shall be necessary for the purpose of the proper and adequate execution . . . of the

---

[50] *Ante,* pp. 83–84.
[51] Clause 2.
[52] Clause 3 (4).

works." [53] It is not, therefore, possible to define this duty with any precision, but it is submitted that the duty needs to be assessed in the light of the following criteria (among others):

(a) by far the most important of all, the contractor's actual progress at the time (as opposed to any contractual or other programmes [53a] or contract periods);

(b) the need of the contractor for a reasonable advance knowledge of the work for pre-planning purposes on his part, which obviously will vary considerably according to the subject-matter of the information in question;

(c) whether or not the information relates to a variation, and if so the extent to which the variation in question is capable of absorption into the contractor's overall programme;

(d) any agreed or indicated programmes showing the intended order of working;

(e) requests or notice by the contractor.[54]

It is submitted that, unless an act or requirement of the employers or some circumstances quite outside the architect's control make it impossible, an architect must, as a matter of business efficacy, impliedly undertake to his employer that he will give instructions in time so as to comply with the express or implied requirements of the building contract (which it should be remembered he will normally have recommended to the employer in the first place) and so avoid any claim whether for damages or under the provisions of that contract against the employer—in other words that, subject to the exceptions mentioned, the times for giving instructions under the building contract and in the architect's contract of employment are identical.

Pleaders generally attempt to express the duty in terms of economic and expeditious progress by the contractor. This was rejected in the following unreported case:

ILLUSTRATION

In an engineering contract the contractors alleged an implied term that all necessary instructions and details should be given to the contractor " in sufficient time to enable the contractors to execute and complete the works in an economic and expeditious manner and/or in sufficient time to prevent the contractors being delayed

[53] See also cl. 7 (1) of I.C.E. conditions which requires notice from contractor.
[53a] For the often attempted misuse of programmes for this purpose see *post*, p. 603.
[54] See also *post*, Chap. 5, pp. 322–326 and 329, where this subject is more fully discussed in the context of the position as between employer and contractor.

in such execution and completion." *Held*, by Diplock J., that it was clear from the terms of the contract that instructions would be given from time to time in the course of the contract, and that what was a reasonable time did not depend solely on the convenience and financial interests of the contractors. Reasonableness had also to be regarded from the point of view of the engineer and his staff and of the employers themselves. Other relevant matters affecting reasonableness would be the order in which the works were to be carried out approved by the engineer, whether requests for particular details had been made by the contractors, whether the details related to variations or to the original works, and also the contract period. This list was not exhaustive, and what was a reasonable time was a question of fact having regard to all the circumstances of the case: *Neodox Ltd.* v. *Swinton and Pendlebury B.C.* (1958).[55]

In this context attention should be drawn to a new and remarkable provision in the post-1963 R.I.B.A. standard forms [56] under which, on application by the contractor, the architect is required to ascertain the amount of any loss or expense in which the contractor may have been involved by not receiving in due time necessary instructions, drawings or details from the architect, and to certify the same (on interim certificate if necessary). It would seem that, by virtue of clause 30 (7), notice of arbitration before the final certificate (or within fourteen days in the case of the contractor) is necessary to prevent the architect's decision in what must often be his own cause being binding and conclusive on the employer (but not the contractor [57]).

It is perhaps unnecessary to point out the uncertainty of the contract price if standard forms of contract are used which not only specifically recognise that the contract drawings and information are insufficient for the work to be carried out, but (in the case of the R.I.B.A. form) actually contemplate that drawings and information, though applied for in writing, are nevertheless likely to be issued at a time which will involve the contractor in loss or expense for which, in addition to obtaining an extension of time, he will be reimbursed as a matter of valuation by the architect or surveyor on interim certificate. The justification for such a clause perhaps is that it removes from the many uncertainties and contingencies for which the builder must estimate the standard of administrative efficiency of the particular architect involved in the

---

[55] Q.B.D. (unreported. Diplock J.). See further, *post*, pp. 322–326, and for a different view, the dicta of Wright J. in *Wells* v. *Army and Navy Co-operative Society* (1902) there referred to.

[56] Clause 24.

[57] Clause 24 is expressed to be without prejudice to other remedies, which leaves the contractor free to claim damages, whatever the architect's decision.

contract, thereby enabling a keener price to be tendered, though the clause may have been inserted in the standard forms to cover cases where the employer's acts or omissions are the cause of the late information. Whatever the reasons for the clause, the contract is so worded that it seems clear that the clause, with its special rights on interim payment, is in addition to, and not in substitution for, the ordinary right to sue for damages for breach of contract.[57a]

Difficult questions of fact can arise as to the time by which the contractor is entitled to expect information from the architect or engineer to enable orders to be placed with nominated sub-contractors and suppliers.[58] It is clear that an employer will usually have discharged his obligation if the information is made available in time to permit the sub-contractor to quote delivery or completion dates consistent with the contractor's programme or progress. But shortages or lengthened delivery dates have a habit of occurring very suddenly in industry, and the first that the parties may know of any difficulty may be when the sub-contractor, on being asked to quote or receiving an order, announces that he cannot supply or do the work in the required time. It does not necessarily follow in such a case, it is submitted, that there has been any breach of duty by the architect. Relevant facts in determining what was a reasonable time for such information to be given would include, it is suggested (a) whether the goods and services concerned were well known in the industry to be in short supply or the subject of long delivery dates, (b) whether the availability of the goods, by their nature, ought to be expected to fall within the contractor's knowledge (for example reinforcement steel, or bricks), (c) whether in the light of both the above, he had made any request for the information, (d) whether, on the other hand, the matter was peculiarly within the employer's sphere (for example complicated pipes and specials requiring to be specially made for the contract) and if so whether reasonable inquiries and assurances as to availability had been made and obtained by the architect or engineer in good time. In the modern standard forms the contractor has a right to refuse to place an order with a nominated sub-contractor if satisfactory dates cannot be obtained, and should he not exercise this right this may possibly raise an estoppel or waiver and dispose of his right to recover damages. In extreme cases, the position may be such that the architect has in practice to place an order and give information well in advance before the main contract is let in order

[57a] See *post*, Chap. 5, p. 323.
[58] See also the discussion *post*, Chap. 5, pp. 329 *et seq.*

to secure delivery dates consistent with the contract period, though it is the general practice of many architects and engineers to make use of the P.C. and provisional sum provisions of the standard forms which provide, however anomalously, for such work to be carried out by sub-contractors appointed under a power to nominate *after* the contract is let.[59] In this the standard forms, and not the architects, are at fault, since there are substantial advantages to sub-contracting (in eliminating cross-claims against the employer by contractor or specialist) from the employer's point of view.

Finally, it is perhaps desirable to indicate the precise nature of the instructions which a contractor is entitled to require from an architect or engineer. In general, unless the contract expressly stipulates to the contrary, the contractor is entitled to choose his own methods of working; the corollary of this is that the contractor is not entitled, when faced with difficulties, to demand or require instructions as to how to overcome them.[60] The architect's duty is merely to stipulate the final permanent result required, and if this has already been done, he is under no further duty to assist, and if inclined or requested to do so should be careful to adopt a permissive attitude rather than to give mandatory instructions. Contractors in difficulties frequently demand instructions and threaten to discontinue working unless told what to do. This attitude has no legal justification, and even if instructions are given they will not entitle a contractor to extra payment unless the contractor is in a position to show that he wished to take another and cheaper course of action which would have been effective to produce the required final result.

ILLUSTRATION

A contractor constructing a sewer was passing underneath a road in heading when his workings broke into a leaky old sewer whose approximate position was shown on the plans. It was a very wet time of year, the old sewer was in fact carrying water, and his workings were flooded. An emergency meeting with the engineer was held, at which the contractor asked for instructions and it was agreed to proceed to a position off the site where its location was known and stank the old sewer, then to sink a manhole further along the line of the new sewer and work back to the road, while completing the crossing of the road in open cut. The contractor asked about payment and was told " I'm not talking to you about money. The inquest will come later." *Held*, by Paull J., this was no more than a

---

[59] See *post*, Chap. 15, pp. 758 *et seq.*

[60] See the discussion *ante*, Chap. 1, pp. 68–70, and important case, *Clayton* v. *Woodman & Son (Builders)* [1962] 2 Q.B. 533 there referred to, and see also the fuller discussion *infra*, subs. (k), pp. 153–155, and *post*, Chap. 8, pp. 524–530 and Chap. 9, pp. 582–583.

joint decision about the best way to deal with the situation. The engineer was not bound to give any instructions and the contractor was not entitled to extra payment: *Pearce (C. J.) & Co.* v. *Hereford B.C.* (1968).[61]

Thus in *Kingston-upon-Hull Corp.* v. *Harding* (1892),[62] where contractors' sureties argued that they were released by a jury's finding that there had been a failure properly to supervise which had led to skimping of the work (in a very strong Victorian contract where the engineer had power to order the removal of defective work, all the work was to be carried out and executed under his superintendence and to his satisfaction, and his decision as to the manner of working was to be final and conclusive), Lord Esher M.R. said " The question is, what is the meaning of the provision as to superintendence by the plaintiffs' engineer? It was contended that the meaning really was that the corporation was to direct in what manner the work should be done. When one considers the position of the corporation and the contractors and what the latter have to do, I think it is obvious that that was not the meaning. The corporation never meant to undertake to direct in what manner the work should be done, nor did the contractors agree to submit to their directions. They were to do the work as they thought fit, and in the manner which their experience taught them was the best. The meaning of the provision was only that the corporation should have a right to observe and see how the work from time to time was being done . . . it was merely an option given to the corporation whether they would superintend or not."[63] It is submitted that this passage reflects a completely correct appreciation of the situation and rights of the parties under such terms.

The effect of this is that, if an architect or engineer sees the contractor using or proposing to use a method of working which he considers potentially unsafe or likely to fail in its intention, his duty to the employer will require him to balance the advantage to the employer of the method he himself prefers against the fact that by intervening and giving an instruction he will expose the employer to a claim for a variation, if the contractor can show that his own method would have been equally efficacious (unless, of course, the contract expressly prescribes the method of working or provides, as for instance some specifications do in engineering contracts, that

[61] 66 L.G.R. 647.
[62] 2 Q.B. 494, illustrated *post*, p. 388.
[63] *Ibid.* at pp. 502–503.

the contractor's price is to include for any one of various methods
to be chosen at the discretion of the engineer).[64]

(d) Special duties in regard to nominations

The preceding subsection has considered the question of the
time for effecting a nomination of a sub-contractor or supplier,
but it is submitted that certain anomalies in the system of nomination
have now become so serious and notorious that positive action is
now called for by the architect in more important nominations if
he is to discharge his duty to his client and obtain reasonable protection of his interests. The anomalies arise

(a) when the architect or engineer nominates a sub-contractor
or supplier whose price includes for design services which
would otherwise need to be performed by a consultant,[65]

(b) where a non-traditional manufactured product is selected,
or a sub-contractor or supplier is nominated, whose
products or techniques are so specialist in character that
the architect is not in a position himself to ascertain
their suitability for their purpose either before or during
construction,[66] and

(c) in accordance with the decision of the House of Lords in
Bickerton v. *N. W. Metropolitan Hospital Board* (1970),[67]
when a nominated supplier or sub-contractor repudiates
his obligations under the sub-contract and refuses to complete work which is likely to affect the contractor's general
progress seriously if suddenly discontinued.

It is submitted that an architect advising a private client in fact
fails in his duty if he recommends the standard forms for use by his
client without alteration or does not, in the above cases,

(i) in the case of (a) above, take special care to see that the
sub-contractor's price is genuinely competitive, and also
specifically inform the employer that the price includes a
design element;

(ii) in all cases, obtain formal undertakings from the sub-contractor to the employer as to the suitability of the work
or goods in question, expressed to be in consideration of

---

[64] See *post*, Chap. 8, pp. 529–530, and the *Neodox* case there illustrated.
[65] See *supra*, pp. 129–132, and the *Moresk* case there referred to.
[66] See *e.g.* the catastrophic result for the employer in *Gloucestershire C.C.* v. *Richardson*
[1969] A.C. 480, *post*, Chap. 8, pp. 527–528, and see *ante*, Chap. 1, Section 10, p. 61.
[67] [1970] 1 W.L.R. 607.

the sub-contract being awarded to the sub-contractor, and also for the performance of all obligations under the sub-contract;

(iii) in the case of non-traditional products, obtain an express warranty of suitability from the manufacturer or a substantial merchant or supplier for the benefit of the employer before deciding to use them;

(iv) ensure that the terms of nominated sub-contractors' or suppliers' quotations include no exemption clauses restricting liability for delay or defective work; and

(v) ensure that appropriate warranties identical with those of the sub-contractor or supplier are inserted into the main contract.[68]

It remains to be seen whether the courts will apply and approve the duties suggested in this subsection, or on the other hand take the view that they exact too high a standard of care. There can be no doubt, however, as to the gravity of the potential consequences for the employer if, in the present state of the law, the steps here advocated are not in fact taken.

(e) Knowledge of legislation, building regulations, by-laws, and rights of adjoining owners

It is obvious that a building or project designed without regard to any relevant public legislation, by-laws, or the rights of adjoining owners may, while structurally a well-planned design, be quite useless to the employer, since the work may be prohibited, or if carried out may expose him to fines, demolition orders, or litigation. An architect or engineer will therefore require to have a reasonable working knowledge of the law relating to these matters, and also of the requirements as to service of notices on local or other authorities or adjoining owners and deposit or submission of plans for planning approval or by-law consent.

Despite the fact that the standard forms contain express undertakings by contractors that their work will comply with all relevant by-laws and statutory provisions, it has already been seen [69] that in two decisions the courts have recognised that it is the practice in the industry for architects to assume responsibility for the substance and formalities of compliance with the by-laws.

---

[68] See further on this, *post*, Chap. 5, pp. 334–335, and Chap. 15, pp. 749 and 761 *et seq.*
[69] *Ante*, Chap. 1, p. 56.

ILLUSTRATION

By-laws forbade the construction of a W.C. entered from a room used for human habitation, unless used exclusively with a bedroom or dressing-room, and also required the service of notices before work commenced. The builder constructed two bathrooms containing toilets in accordance with the design of the architect. At the time the builder knew of the by-law, but the plans showed the adjoining rooms as bedrooms or dressing-rooms, and not till the work was far advanced could he know that the work would, in fact, infringe the by-law. The contract was in the then standard R.I.B.A. form, by clause 3 of which the builder expressly undertook to comply with all by-laws and requirements as to notices. After the work was finished, the architect did serve a notice on the local authority, who condemned the work, but allowed it to remain unaltered on the undertaking of the building owner to cure the defects, when his wife gave up occupation, by erecting a partition within the bathroom. *Held*, by the Court of Appeal, (i) that the employer was entitled to recover from the builder as damages for breach of clause 3 the cost of building the partition, notwithstanding the custom in building operations that the architect was responsible for seeing that work complied with the by-laws, but (ii) that the architect, having informed the builder in correspondence that he would be responsible for serving all necessary notices, was liable *in tort* to the builder for the lateness of the notice, and must indemnify the builder against the employer's claim: *Townsend Ltd.* v. *Cinema News* (1959).[70]

A word of caution should perhaps be given in regard to this custom or practice. While it is no doubt perfectly correct that by-laws affecting the superstructure of the building are the special responsibility of the architect *vis-à-vis* his client, there are certain matters where, by virtue of his daily presence on the site, the initial onus is undoubtedly on the builder. Thus, old drains or special ground conditions encountered during excavations often require immediate action and consultation with the local authority, and it is normal for such matters to be taken up immediately by the builder with the sanitary or building inspector, though the architect may be informed or become involved later.

An architect should also inquire of his employer whether there are any restrictions affecting the land to be built upon, or its use for the purpose of the proposed building or work, and he should consider and advise the building owner as to any interference with right to light and air, or to support of adjoining buildings.[71]

---

[70] [1959] 1 W.L.R. 119. *N.B.:* This case is further illustrated *post*, Chap. 5, p. 367, on the question of illegality. The basis of the decision against the architect (unreported) is explained further *ante*, Chap. 1, p. 66. Clearly the architect could have had no defence to an action by the building owner for negligence.

[71] For a case on the duty to advise on rights of light see *Armitage* v. *Palmer* (1960) 175 E.G. 315. See also *Wethered* v. *French* (1967) 203 E.G. 431.

If an architect designs or constructs work without proper reference to the rights of adjoining owners (except under specific instructions from his employer, or unless he has called the employer's attention to the effect of the work on the apparent rights of adjoining owners) he may render himself liable for negligence.

On the other hand the obligations of an architect as to legal knowledge will not be of the same standard as those of a legal adviser, and will be correspondingly lightened or removed if the employer takes legal advice or has legal advisers available in relation to the contemplated project. Of ecclesiastical surveyors, Jervis C.J. said that they " could not be expected to supply minute and accurate knowledge of the law, but we think under the circumstances they might probably be required to know the general rules applicable to the valuation of ecclesiastical property," [72] and no doubt a similar standard would be applied to architects in regard, for instance, to planning and by-law requirements.

(f) Excess of cost over estimates

In the earliest stages of the employment of his architect or engineer, the employer will in practice usually indicate or impose limitations on the cost of the proposed project. Even if no mention of this is made, it is suggested that an architect must design works capable of being carried out at a reasonable cost having regard to their scope and function. There will, therefore, in most cases be an express or implied condition of the employment that the project should be capable of being completed within a stipulated or reasonable cost, and an architect or engineer will be liable in negligence if, in fact, the excess of cost is sufficient to show want of care or skill on his part. Thus, in *Moneypenny* v. *Hartland* (1826) [73] Best C.J. said: " A man should not estimate a work at a price at which he would not contract for it; for if he does, he deceives his employer. . . . If a surveyor delivers an estimate greatly below the sum at which a work can be done, and thereby induces a private person to undertake what he would not otherwise do, then I think he is not entitled to recover."

ILLUSTRATIONS

(1) The architect estimated from a sketch plan that a building would cost £1,545. Some modifications were made by the building owner; but the lowest tender received was £2,056. The building owner declined to accept it, and refused to carry out the plans. The

---

[72] *Jenkins* v. *Betham* (1855) 15 C.B. 168.
[73] 2 C. & P. 378, illustrated *ante* p. 133.

architect then offered to make reductions, and subsequently applied for remuneration and, being refused, brought an action. Cockburn C.J. said to the jury: " These are the questions for you: (1) whether it was an express condition that the works shown on the revised plan should be capable of being executed for the estimated sums? If not, then (2) whether there is an implied condition in such cases that the work shall be capable of being done for a sum reasonably near to the estimated sum? If so, then (3) do you think that the plaintiff's estimate was so reasonably sufficient as that the defendant ought to have employed him? ": *Nelson* v. *Spooner* (1861).[74]

(2) F. was instructed to prepare designs for a building not to exceed in cost £4,000. He prepared plans, and tenders were invited; the lowest tender was £6,000. *Held*, that F. was not entitled to recover his remuneration for the work done: *Flannagan* v. *Mate* (1876).[75]

(3) An architect estimated that a school building he had designed would cost $110,000. He knew the estimate was for the purpose of preparing a by-law to raise the necessary funds. The lowest tender was for $157,800. He then eliminated forty per cent. of the cubic content of the school, and said the remainder could be carried out within the limit. The lowest tender was $132,900. *Held*, by the Court of Appeal of British Columbia, that he had been negligent, and was properly dismissed and liable to pay damages: *Savage* v. *Board of School Trustees* (1951).[76]

Where, however, an architect has obtained tenders which are substantially in excess of the express or implied limitation, he should normally, it is suggested, be given an opportunity of obtaining further tenders (without expense to the employer) unless it is obvious that no tender is likely to satisfy the limitation, or the breach is so serious as to justify the client in treating the contract as repudiated.[77] Whether any proposed modifications or omissions of the architect to get down to the price are reasonable or not may be a difficult question of fact.[78]

Clearly the measure of damage for breach of this duty may often not be very great, since in general an employer will have lost little but a delay in his project coming to fruition. In cases where the excess over estimate is not appreciated until work is completed—as for example in a " cost-plus " contract, or where variations have been ordered the cost of which has been underestimated, the measure of damage is likely to be nominal or difficult to assess since against the

---

[74] 2 F. & F. 613.
[75] 2 Vict. L.R.(Law) 157.
[76] 3 D.L.R. (2d) 39 (Canada).
[77] For an analogous case, see *per* Wright J. in *Columbus Co.* v. *Clowes* [1903] 1 K.B. 244 at p. 247, quoted *supra*, p. 128.
[78] See for a comparable case, *Evans* v. *Carte* (1881) Hudson's B.C., 4th ed., Vol. 2, p. 78, *ante*, p. 116.

higher price the employer has had to pay, work done, to a corresponding value, has been carried out.[79]

(g) Preparation of quantities

If undertaken by the architect or engineer, the liability will be the same as that of the quantity surveyor.[80]

(h) Recommending builders

An architect does not guarantee the solvency or capacity of the builder, but it may be that it is his duty to make reasonable inquiries as to the solvency and capabilities of the builder if he, rather than the building owner, is responsible either directly or indirectly for the selection of the builder chosen to carry out the work, particularly in an area in which he is accustomed to practice and may be expected to have local knowledge: *Cf. Heys* v. *Tindal* (1860) [81] where a jury held that the employment of a house agent to let property imported an obligation to take reasonable steps to ascertain the tenant's solvency.

(i) Recommending form of contract

The time must be rapidly approaching when architects or legal advisers recommending the use without modification of some of the forms of contract in general use at present in the United Kingdom (in particular the R.I.B.A. forms) must be in serious danger of an action for professional negligence. A number of the provisions of the contractor's determination clause (clause 26, R.I.B.A. Conditions) are so self-evidently utterly inimical to the employer's reasonable interest, and so devoid of any commercial or moral justification, and the examples of the use to which they can be put are becoming so notorious, that it can, it is submitted, no longer be consistent with professional competence or duty to recommend such a form of contract without drawing attention to its worst features. These may be listed, it is suggested, as

   (a) determination with attendant severe remedies for non-payment of the amount in a certificate without any saving for bona fide counterclaims or defences by the employer, or even of sums which the contract expressly permits to be deducted by the employer when making payment (clause 26 (1) (a));

[79] See the analogous case of *Wilkes* v. *Thingoe R.D.C. infra,* p. 156.
[80] See *infra,* pp. 172 *et seq.*
[81] 30 L.J.Q.B. 362.

(b) determination with attendant severe remedies for suspension of one month due to *force majeure* (clause 26 (1) (c) (i)) [82];

(c) determination with attendant severe remedies for suspension of three months, due to insured risks (clause 26 (1) (c) (ii)) ;

(d) extension of time for unjustified delays by nominated sub-contractors and suppliers (clause 23 (g)), [83] stigmatised as " unjust and absurd " by Salmon L.J. [84] ;

(e) finality of final certificate in respect of defective work which a reasonable examination at any reasonable time during the carrying out of the works might not have disclosed (unless accompanied by full-time daily supervision by the architect) (clause 30 (7)) [85];

(f) the long delay inherent in the employer's remedies upon a determination by him (clause 25 (3) and (4)) and

(g) the dangers to the employer, with no compensating advantage, in the greatly expanded list of insured risks.

Furthermore, the R.I.B.A. forms are so obscure that a number of claims are possible due to its lack of clarity in dealing with important and well-known practical problems. " The difficulties arise solely from the unnecessarily amorphous and tortious provisions of the R.I.B.A. contract: those difficulties have for a number of years been known to exist; and if, as was stated at the Bar, no relevant amendments have been made even in the latest edition of the contract, the position reflects no credit on the R.I.B.A. . . . I return to the criticism made earlier of the form of contract and emphasise that it seems to me lamentable that such a form, used to govern so many and such important activities throughout the country, should be so deviously drafted with what in parts can only be a calculated lack of forthright clarity. The time has now come for the whole to be completely redrafted so that laymen—contractors and building owners alike—can understand what are their own duties and obligations and what are those of the architect. At present that is not possible." [86] The provisions as to extension of time have also attracted the severest judicial criticism, [87] and it is suggested that the

---

[82] Criticised *post*, Chap. 5, p. 350. [83] Criticised *post*, Chap. 11, pp. 680–682.
[84] *Jarvis* v. *Westminster Corporation* [1969] 1 W.L.R. 1448 at p. 1458.
[85] Criticised *post*, Chap. 7, pp. 489–492.
[86] *Per* Sachs L.J. in *Bickerton and Son* v. *N. W. Metropolitan Regional Hospital Board* [1968] 1 All E.R. 977 at p. 979 and 989. See also *per* Danckwerts L.J. at p. 991.
[87] See *Jarvis* v. *Westminster Corporation* [1969] 1 W.L.R. 1448, C.A., and see also this case in the H.L. [1970] 1 W.L.R. 637.

provisions of clause 12 (1) and (2) in both the bill and Specification forms are also open to strong criticism from the point of view of policy [87a] and obscurity.

Architects must, it is submitted, familiarise themselves with the basic provisions of any contract they recommend, and, while not lawyers, should with reasonable interest and competence be able to know at least as much, and probably more, than a non-specialist solicitor in ordinary private practice, as to the consequences and effect of the standard form recommended by their own professional body.

(j) Supervision

Obviously, an architect or engineer must properly supervise the works and inspect them sufficiently frequently to ensure that the materials and workmanship conform to the contractual requirements.

ILLUSTRATION

An architect was employed by the plaintiff on the usual terms to plan and supervise the building of a house costing £996. The house was completed and the architect's fees paid. The plaintiff went to live in the house, and soon after dry-rot was observed. The plaintiff then had the cement floor of the offices taken up, and discovered that the bottoming of the floor had not been executed according to contract, but consisted to a large extent of miscellaneous rubbish. The architect visited the building about once a week, but he never inspected the bottoming of the floor before the cement was laid down, and without inspecting it gave orders to the plasterer to proceed with the work on the floor. *Held,* that his duties were to give reasonable supervision, and that that meant such supervision as would enable him to certify that the work of the contractors had been excuted according to contract, and that having failed to give such supervision he was liable in damages to his employer on account of work which he had passed, but which in fact did not conform to the contract: *Jameson* v. *Simon* (1899).[88]

In the above case, the Lord Justice Clerk said: " There may, of course, be many things which the architect cannot be expected to observe while they are being done—minute matters that nothing but daily or even hourly watching could keep a check upon. But as regards so substantial and important a matter as the bottoming of a cement floor of considerable area, such as this is shown by the plans to have been, I cannot hold that he is not chargeable with negligence if he fails before the bottoming is hid from view by the

---

[87a] See *M. J. Gleeson (Contractors) Ltd.* v. *Hillingdon B.C.* (1970) 215 E.G. 165 (Mocatta J.) currently under appeal to H.L.

[88] 1 F. (Ct. of Sess.) 1211. See *Leicester Board of Guardians* v. *Trollope* (1911) 75 J.P. 197; Hudson's B.C., 4th ed., Vol. 2, p. 419; illustrated *post*, p. 151 and *ante*, p. 94.

cement to make sure that unsuitable rubbish of a kind that will rot when covered up with wet cement has not been thrown in in quantities as bottoming contrary to the specification."

And Lord Trayner said: " Admittedly, the duty of the defender was to give reasonable supervision, and I think that means such supervision as would enable him to certify that the work had been executed according to contract, which he had to certify before the tradesmen could call for payment of the sums due under the contracts." [89]

The normal practice of architects (though it may legitimately, it is suggested, vary considerably according to the nature of the contract, the distance of the site from the architect's place of business, and the confidence reposed in the contractor) is to visit a site for which they are responsible about once a week. In larger contracts, the architect may arrange for an assistant architect from his own firm to be present on occasions when he himself is not, and perhaps somewhat more frequently than he would visit himself, and a clerk of the works,[90] usually paid and employed by the employer, may be present on the site either full time or for a varying number of days each week. Engineering contracts of any size usually have a full-time resident engineer, sometimes from the firm of the engineer in charge of the contract, usually on terms that the employer pays a proportion or all of his salary, or sometimes separately engaged for the project and directly employed by the employer.[91] Thus it will be seen that the architect's or engineer's personal supervision of any contract of substance is usually supplemented by that of other subordinate persons. From the legal point of view it is submitted that architects and engineers will usually be fully responsible to the employer for their own employees' mistakes or errors, but in general will not be responsible for errors by persons paid and employed by the employer, such as clerks of works and resident engineers separately engaged, unless the matter was of a kind that they should have seen or dealt with themselves but chose instead to leave to the subordinate in question, or unless they failed to give proper instructions to the subordinate.[92] The rather special case of employees " seconded " to the employer probably needs to be considered on its special facts in each case, including any agreed terms of the arrangement. Thus in the task of supervision the architect or engineer, though he may be assisted by professional assistants or

[89] (1899) 1 F. (Ct. of Sess.) 1211 at p. 1222.
[90] See *supra*, pp. 92 *et seq.* for a discussion of the status of these persons.
[91] See *supra*, pp. 92, 94–95.   [92] See the suggested principle, *supra*, p. 94.

clerks of works or both,[93] cannot escape responsibility, except perhaps in the smallest matters of detail, by delegation (unless the contract of employment expressly so provides). He may make use of assistants, provided he retains control of the work and does not cease to exercise his own supervision and judgment. So it has been said [94]:

"If an architect is entrusted with the general direction and superintendence of the work, his duties could not be performed if he were expected to go over individually every matter in detail, and if his certificate were to be held bad by a court of law because he has not himself gone into every detail." And again: "Where a man employs an agent, relying upon his peculiar aptitude for the work entrusted to him, it is not competent to that person to delegate the trust to another, but where the act to be done is of such a nature that it is perfectly indifferent whether it is done by A or B, and the person originally entrusted remains liable to the principal, by whomsoever the thing may be done, the maxim *delegata potestas non potest delegari* does not apply." [95]

This distinction between the act (which can be delegated) and the responsibility (which cannot) is well illustrated by the duty of measurement, which need not normally be carried out personally by an architect or surveyor.

ILLUSTRATIONS

(1) On a reference to two surveyors to settle the terms of a mining lease, one of the surveyors did not go down into the mine, but founded his valuation on the report of a competent agent whom he had sent to inspect it and upon his own knowledge of the neighbourhood. *Held,* that this fact did not render the award bad: *Eads* v. *Williams* (1854).[96]

(2) A building contract stipulated that the work should be measured when finished, and priced at the schedule rates, or in strict accordance therewith, the contractor to pay half the expenses of the measurements and schedule. An action was brought for the price of the work. In his judgment Lord Deas said: "The measurement was made, it seems, by sworn measurers or skilled persons in their employment. It is not understood that in every instance the sworn measurer, who may be the head of an extensive business, goes himself to the ground, in place of sending a skilled assistant to report to him the details, he adopting the result if it appears to him satisfactory and accepting the responsibility": *Kirkwood* v. *Morrison* (1877).[97]

---

[93] See *ante*, pp. 92 *et seq.*
[94] *Per* Grove J. in *Clemence* v. *Clarke* (1880) Hudson's B.C., 4th ed., Vol. 2 at p. 58.
[95] *Per* Williams J. in *Hemming* v. *Hale* (1859) 7 C.B.(N.S.) 487 at p. 498.
[96] 24 L.J.Ch. 531 (C.A.). See also *Caledonian Ry.* v. *Lockhart* (1860) 3 Macq. 808.
[97] 5 R. (Ct. of Sess.) 79, 82. See also *Clemence* v. *Clarke. post,* Chap. 7, p. 466.

The following cases illustrate the principle that a matter of such importance that the architect should see to it for himself cannot be delegated to a subordinate. They do not, it is submitted, prevent an architect saying " This matter could not have been seen by me on my normal periodic visits, though no doubt it must have been seen by the clerk of works, who failed to report it to me."

ILLUSTRATIONS

(1) S., an engineer, was employed to superintend work to be executed for a local board. The local board made a claim against S. for negligence. S. set up (*inter alia*) that the local board had appointed a clerk of the works who was not reliable, and that S. remonstrated against the appointment, and that S. was not responsible for errors of the clerk of the works. The Official Referee found that if S. relied on the clerk of the works, he was liable, as S. knew that the clerk of the works was not reliable: *Saunders* v. *Broadstairs Local Board* (1890).[98]

(2) B. employed L. as architect to superintend the rebuilding of premises after a fire. B. appointed C. clerk of the works. C. thought that certain beams did not require to be replaced, and L. adopted C.'s view without inspecting them. The beams turned out to be insufficient. Cave J. charged the jury that the question whether new beams were required was one for the architect and not for the clerk of the works, and that the responsibility was on L. if he adopted C's view without inspecting them: *Lee* v. *Bateman (Lord)* (1893).[99]

(3) Under a building contract the architect's duty was to supervise the work. The clerk of the works, for corrupt purposes of his own, permitted the builder to deviate from the design, by laying the ground floor without the necessary precautions against damp, and assisted in concealing the deviation, and the architect, relying upon the clerk of the works, failed to detect the deviation and to have it rectified. As a result of such deviation dry-rot set in. The architect pleaded that the employers had appointed an unfit and improper clerk of works, and that the damage was due to the negligence and fraud of the employer's servant, or alternatively that the employers were bound to employ a fit and proper clerk of works. *Held*, by Channell J., that, while personally not greatly, if at all, in default, the architect was liable in damages to the employer for negligence: *Leicester Board of Guardians* v. *Trollope* (1911).[1]

The following passage from the judgment of Channell J. in the *Leicester* case is, it is submitted, an example of the correct approach to this problem. " I think there is no difficulty in seeing what are the respective functions and duties of an architect and of a clerk of the works . . . the clerk of the works has to see to matters of detail, . . . the architect is not expected to do so . . . the architect is responsible

---

[98] Hudson's B.C., 4th ed., Vol. 2, p. 164.

[99] *The Times*, October 31.

[1] 75 J.P. 197; Hudson's B.C., 4th ed., Vol. 2, p. 419. (*Cf.* the architect's responsibility in tort when relying on the opinions of others, *ante*, Chap. 1, p. 74, and the case of *Clay* v. *A. J. Crump Ltd.* [1964] 1 Q.B. 533, there illustrated.)

to see that his design is carried out. That fairly indicates what the respective duties of each are, but it leaves one in each case to say whether the matter complained of is a matter of detail or a matter of seeing whether the design is complied with. . . . Here a protection was devised and it was an essential part of the design. Now the architects admitted that they took no steps to find out whether that was carried out, or whether it was not. It is not a case in which they enquired even of the clerk of works, in which they pointed out to the clerk of works. . . . It is a very large area of building. . . . If in this case the architect had taken steps to see that the first block of buildings was done all right, and then in the next block he had left it to the clerk of works with instructions to see that it was done in the second block in the same way . . . I should then have had some doubt whether he would have been liable. . . . "

It will be noted from the language of the judges in *Jameson* v. *Simon* [2] that the terms of the contract between the employer and contractor are, at the very least, a relevant factor in determining the extent of the duty of supervision. This must be all the more true in the vast majority of cases where the architect himself recommends the contract in question to his employer.

The terms of the post-1963 R.I.B.A. standard forms, under which the final certificate of the architect finally debars the employer from complaining of defects in the work unless notice of arbitration is given before the certificate, have already been commented on in detail.[3] It is submitted that the degree of supervision usually (and quite reasonably) afforded by architects is wholly inadequate to give the employer reasonable protection of his interests in the light of the virtual removal of his common law protection in regard to defective work effected by this clause, and that the only inference can be that an architect recommending a contract in this form is implicitly undertaking to give a degree of supervision which will to some extent at least compensate for the loss of these rights and afford the employer reasonable protection. By reason of clause 30 (7) (*b*) [4] it is submitted that only full time supervision of the most painstaking character can achieve this degree of protection.

If an employer succeeds in establishing a breach of the duty to supervise, so that defective work escapes attention, it is legally quite irrelevant that the employer may in addition to his action for professional negligence also have a right of action against the builder.

---

[2] *Supra*, pp. 148–149.
[3] *Ante*, pp. 125–126. See also *post*, Chap. 7, pp. 489–492.
[4] Set out *ante*, p. 126. See also *post*, p. 490.

The employer may choose to proceed against either or both, and secure judgment for the whole sum in each case, notwithstanding that the measure of damage, namely the cost of repair, may be identical. Nor, in spite of constant efforts by contractors to allege that employers or their architects in effect owe the contractor a duty to detect defective work at the earliest possible stage, will either defendant have any right of contribution from the other, there being no contractual link between them.

There is no doubt that there is a tendency at the present day for the courts to demand a standard of care from architects in detecting defective work which, particularly in major contracts, seems somewhat unrealistic. An architect may have many other important problems demanding attention and decision when visiting a site, and may well, it is suggested, decide to rely on the builder to do his work properly on that occasion while dealing with the problems.[5] The view that he should make a thorough examination of every part of the building in a large contract on each site visit seems somewhat perfectionist. Thus in Australia it seems to have been thought that the architect owes a duty to his employer to be present whenever concrete is poured so as to ensure that reinforcement is properly placed.

ILLUSTRATION

An architect was visiting twice a week. He visited on a Friday when formwork for the concrete apron of a swimming pool was in position but steel not yet fixed. After he left, the reinforcement was wrongly fixed, and concrete poured on the Friday and Saturday, and an accident occurred just before his next visit when the formwork was struck and the concrete collapsed. *Held*, by the High Court of Australia, that the architect was liable to his employer for sums recovered from the employer by an injured workman: *Florida Hotels Ltd.* v. *Mayo* (1965).[6]

It is also essential to realise that the architect's duty of supervision is owed to the employer and not to the contractor. The first and incorrect reaction of many lawyers is often to treat the architect as if he was primarily responsible for everything done on the site.

ILLUSTRATION

A bowling alley under construction was flooded due to lack of temporary precautions by the builder in protecting the works from storm-water, with the result that expensive fittings and machinery

---

[5] See *per* Lord Upjohn in *East Ham B.C.* v. *Bernard Sunley Ltd.* [1966] A.C. 406.
[6] 113 C.L.R. 588 (Australia). See the fuller illustration and the rather special facts and criticism of this case, *ante*, Chap. 1, pp. 74–75.

being installed by another contractor of the employers were ruined, and the employer had to pay damages to the other contractor. The employer sued the main contractor for breach of various provisions in the bills requiring the contractor to protect all work and materials and divert all storm-water, etc. The employer and main contractor had been held liable to the other contractor in tort in proportions of 40 per cent. and 60 per cent. respectively, the employer's part of the responsibility arising from the failure of his full-time salaried architect to draw the named (private) architect's attention to the necessity for safeguarding the building when the other contractor arrived to instal his machinery and fittings. The main contractor relied on the presence and knowledge of the situation of the architects at all times, and their failure to give any instructions. *Held*, by Mocatta J., following *Clayton* v. *Woodman & Son*,[7] that the employers were entitled to recover in full from the main contractor: *A.M.F. (International) Ltd.* v. *Magnet Bowling Ltd.* (1968).[8]

Thus Mocatta J. said of *Clayton's* case: " That case, in both courts, further establishes that an architect has no right to instruct a builder how his work is to be done or the safety precautions to be taken. It is the function and right of the builder to carry out his own building operations as he thinks fit. The architect, on the other hand, is engaged as the agent of the owner for whom the building is being erected, and his function is, *inter alia*, to make sure that in the end, when the work has been completed, the owner will have a building properly constructed in accordance with the contract and any supplementary instructions which the architect may have given." [9] And Salmon J. said in *Clayton's* case: " Mr. Lyell submitted that the [architects] had no right to instruct the [builders] as to either the manner in which the work was to be done or the safety precautions to be taken. He contended that the form of specification and contract make it plain that it is for the [builders] to decide what safety precautions are necessary and to make provision for them in the tender. He further submitted that there is no contractual nexus between the architects and the builders, and that the law imposes no duty on the architect to advise the builders and their servants about their safety. So far as the law is concerned, [the architect] would be within his rights were he to stand by and without protest or warning watch the plaintiff doing something which the architect knew to be highly dangerous. Still less could the architect be liable if, through lack of care or knowledge, he failed to appreciate the risks involved in the plaintiffs' acts. I agree substantially with all those submissions." [10]

---

[7] [1962] 2 Q.B. 533, *ante*, Chap. 1, p. 73.
[8] [1968] 1 W.L.R. 1028, also illustrated *ante*, Chap. 1, pp. 79–80. See also *Pearce* v. *Hereford B.C., supra*, pp. 139–140.   [9] [1968] 1 W.L.R. 1028 at p. 1046.
[10] [1962] 2 Q.B. 533 at p. 539. And see also the judgments in the C.A. [1962] 1 W.L.R. 585, and *ante*, pp. 70–71.

The above cases and language are, it is respectfully submitted, entirely correct statements and of great importance. While concerned primarily with questions of methods and safety of working, exactly the same principles apply in the case of the detection of defective work during supervision. No duty in this regard is owed to the builder, who will be responsible for the cost of repair however late in the day, subject to the period of limitation and the possible binding effect of a final certificate, the defect is discovered, and notwithstanding that it might have been easily detected and swiftly and cheaply repaired at the time the defective work was done.[11]

(k) Administration of contract

The terms of the building contract require an architect to take a number of actions in all of which, with the possible exception of his strictly certifying functions, he will owe a duty of care to the employer. There is a dearth of authority on these various duties. For example, the exact nature of an architect's duty to his employer in ordering variations under a power in the contract has not been considered by the courts. It is suggested there is a duty to consult the employer beforehand, in all but trivial or emergency matters, so as to obtain his prior approval of the variation and its probable cost.[12]

It has already been pointed out [13] that an architect or engineer will not be liable if, in the course of administering the contract vis-à-vis the builder, he honestly adopts one of two possible constructions in interpreting the contractual obligations of the parties. It is suggested that this may be the underlying reason for the otherwise difficult decision illustrated below.

ILLUSTRATION

The defendant entered into a contract with a builder for the construction of a house at a price of £1,910, the plaintiff being nominated as the architect. The contract provided by Clause 1: " The contractor shall carry out and complete the works in accordance with this contract in every respect with the directions and to the reasonable satisfaction of the architect." By Clause 12: " Any defects, shrinkage or other faults which shall appear within the defects liability period stated in the appendix to these conditions and shall be due to materials and workmanship not in accordance with this contract . . . shall within a reasonable time after receipt of the architect's written instructions in that behalf be made good by

---

[11] See ante, Chap. 1, pp. 68–70, supra, pp. 139–141; post, Chap. 6, pp. 385–388; Chap. 8, pp. 524–530; and Chap. 9, pp. 582–583, and the further passages from the A.M.F. and East Ham cases there cited, and the Kingston-upon-Hull case there illustrated.

[12] See the case of Gordon v. Miller (1838) 1 D. (Ct. of Sess.) 832, illustrated infra, subs. (4), p. 162. [13] Supra, pp. 126, 144.

the contractor." The specification under the contract provided that the whole of the materials and workmanship were to be the best of their kind and to the full satisfaction of the architect. At the end of the defects liability period (six months) the plaintiff issued a final certificate. Some two years after the completion of the house the plaintiff sued the defendant for his fees and expenses. The defendant counterclaimed for damages, alleging that the plaintiff had not exercised due skill and care in supervising the work and in ensuring that the house was constructed with proper materials and good workmanship. On the counterclaim the county court judge found that there was a certain amount of inferior material and scamped workmanship but, taking into account the fact that the house was being built down to a price, he held that a certain tolerance must be expected and that the plaintiff had not failed in his duty, although another architect might have required a higher standard; and he gave judgment for the plaintiff in the counterclaim. *Held*, by the Court of Appeal (Denning L.J. dissenting), that the judge was right in taking the view that there must be some tolerance in building down to a price; the question of the adequacy of the work, provided that the architect used his skill and acted reasonably, was one for the county court judge; no case of professional negligence had been made out and consequently the appeal must be dismissed: *Cotton* v. *Wallis* (1955).[14]

For further examples of administrative duties of the architect, see the cases collected *infra*, subsection (4), Negligence in Certifying.

(l) Comprehensive design

An architect will, it is submitted, be failing in his duty if, without warning his employer, he omits from the work (whether deliberately or by negligence) work indispensably necessary for completion of the project, which will have to be added by way of variation.

ILLUSTRATION

An architect let contracts for a number of houses for a local authority and made provision for a smaller number of cookers than there were houses. There were other similar omissions in the bills. *Held*, by Casswell O.R., he was liable to his employers, who, had they known of the true cost of completion, would have effected savings elsewhere: *Wilkes* v. *Thingoe R.D.C.* (1954).[15] (Note: It may not be easy in such cases to determine the measure of damage, if any.)

(m) Surveys

Apart from their employment in building contracts, architects or engineers (and indeed quantity surveyors) may be employed to make surveys, valuations and reports.[16] Skill in valuation has always been

---

[14] [1955] 1 W.L.R. 1168. (For the effect of this case on the position between the employer and the contractor, see *post*, Chap. 5, p. 306.)
[15] Unreported.
[16] *Cf. Parsons* v. *Way and Waller* (1952), illustrated *infra*, p. 157.

difficult to assess by evidence, and while a wide disparity between values may be some evidence of negligence, attention in negligence cases is more likely to be focused upon the method or principle of valuation adopted. In surveys, the test of reasonable skill is easier to apply.

ILLUSTRATIONS

(1) Ecclesiastical surveyors were employed, one for one party and one for the other, to value dilapidations. The valuers for the rector met the valuer for the executrix of the late incumbent, and valued the dilapidations at too small a sum, having, through ignorance, valued as between incoming and outgoing tenant, instead of as between incoming and outgoing incumbent. *Held*, that they were liable for negligence in the exercise of their profession: *Jenkins* v. *Betham* (1855).[18]

(2) Trustees invested money on the mortgage of a brickfield. They acted upon the report of a competent valuer, bona fide, but without any inquiry of their own. The security failed. *Held*, that the trustees were entitled to rely upon the valuer on the pure question of valuation, but should have examined the basis on which the report was made, *i.e.* whether the concern was valued as a going concern or otherwise, and were not entitled to substitute the valuer's judgment for their own judgment as trustees: *Learoyd* v. *Whiteley* (1887).[19]

(3) M. was employed to value a mineral water factory and three licensed houses. His methods might have been better, but there was no evidence of any absolute rule as to the proper methods of valuation in such a case, and the methods adopted were such as a man of position, honestly endeavouring to do his duty, might fairly adopt. *Held*, that M. was not guilty of negligence: *Love* v. *Mack* (1905).[20]

(4) The plaintiff's employers engaged the defendants to survey a house which he was interested in purchasing. The defendants submitted a report to the plaintiff informing him that there was nothing seriously wrong with the house, that about £150 to £200 would be required to be spent on it above the usual decorative repairs, and that the price asked for was a fair one. Relying upon this report, the plaintiff paid a 10 per cent. deposit, signed a contract, and agreed upon the date for completion. A building society then made several inspections and refused to make any advance upon the property. Having received an adverse report from a second surveyor, the plaintiff decided it would be imprudent to complete and so forfeited his deposit. In an action against the defendants for negligence, Lynskey J. held them liable for the amount of the forfeited deposit: *Parsons* v. *Way and Waller* (1952).[21]

---

[18] 15 C.B. 168.
[19] 12 App.Cas. 727.
[20] 92 L.T. 345.
[21] [1952] C.P.L. 417.

The measure of damage for a negligent survey is usually, in a case where a purchaser buys on the faith of a report, the difference in value between the property, if it had been in the reported condition, and the value had the true condition been known. In the great majority of cases this will be the same as the cost of repair, but not always, depending on the facts.

ILLUSTRATIONS

(1) In an action for damages arising from a negligent survey, the proper measure of damage is the amount of money which will put the plaintiff into as good a position as if the surveying contract had been properly fulfilled. The plaintiff, on the faith of a surveyor's report, paid, in 1952, £25,000 for a house and 137 acres of land. On entering into possession it was discovered that the surveyor had been negligent in failing to notice that the timbers of the house were rotten. To carry out the necessary repairs would have cost £7,000 at 1952 prices,[22] but the court found that the actual value of the property in 1952 was £21,000. *Held*, by the Court of Appeal, the proper measure of damage was the difference between the value of the property in its assumed good condition (£25,000) in 1952 and its value in the bad condition (£21,000), which should have been reported to the plaintiff, and he was therefore entitled to recover £4,000: *Philips* v. *Ward* (1956).[23]

(2) An insurance company lent money on the faith of a negligent surveyor's report. *Held*, by Devlin J., the measure of damage was not the full difference between the value in the reported condition and its actual condition, as the company still had the standing and covenant of the borrower available to them: *Eagle Star Insurance Company Ltd.* v. *Gale and Power* (1955).[24]

(3) A negligent survey failed to reveal damp in the basement of a house, which the purchasers then bought for £13,500. *Held*, by Lawton J., applying *Philips* v. *Ward*, that the measure of damage was the difference of value, and that in this case the difference was the same as the cost of repair, namely £550: *Freeman* v. *Marshall* (1966).[25]

(4) A purchaser bought a house on the faith of a negligent survey which did not disclose dry rot. On discovery of the dry rot, the purchaser decided to sell the house without repairing it. The purchaser's own valuer witness considered that a rather high price had originally been paid for the house, but that the sale price was a fair one having regard to the condition of the premises. *Held*, by

---

[22] The plaintiff had not, however, carried out the repairs. This fact appears to have escaped attention when the case has been used to argue that damages for cost of repair should not exceed the cost at the date of the breach—see *post*, p. 590 and the *East Ham* case there referred to.

[23] [1956] 1 W.L.R. 471. See also *Stewart* v. *Brechin*, 1959 S.C. 306 (Scotland), and *Hood* v. *Shaw* (1960) 176 E.G. 1291, where Paull J. awarded cost of removal during repairs while allowing difference in value as the main measure of damage.

[24] [1955] J.P.L. 679.

[25] 200 E.G. 777.

Paull J., accepting the purchaser's evidence, that the purchaser was entitled to the difference between the purchase price less £200, and the selling price: *Hardy* v. *Warmsley-Lewis* (1967).[26]

(3) Quasi-Judicial Duties

An architect or engineer is primarily employed by the building owner and as such is his agent; but by virtue of specific provisions in many building and engineering contracts he may be required to settle certain matters between the parties to the contract, usually by way of a certificate,[27] or by a decision as a preliminary to or condition of arbitration.[28] In such cases it may be that the sense of the contract requires the architect or engineer to act judicially rather than as agent of one party, and his position is then generally referred to as quasi-judicial or quasi-arbitral, to distinguish it from that of an arbitrator in the strict sense, which is generally not the intention of the contract.[29]

In consequence, the architect or engineer may find that, in connection with the same contract, he has a dual function:

    (i) as agent of the building owner; and
    (ii) as a quasi-judge or quasi-arbitrator.

Where an architect or an engineer is acting in this capacity to determine or value some issue between two or more parties, he is not liable to either party for want of skill, ignorance of law, or negligence *when acting in that capacity*.[30] Nor is there any warranty by the employer that he will be skilful.[31]

Many architects and engineers misunderstand and exaggerate the effect of this somewhat peculiar status, and appear to consider that it confers upon them an element of discretion which enables them to give effect to their own opinions or notions of fairness as between the parties without too particular a regard to the letter of the contract. Quite apart from the fact that their decisions as certifiers are, by the terms of most contracts, open to review by an arbitrator[32] and hence by the courts,[33] and that such review will be

---

[26] 203 E.G. 1039.

[27] See Chap. 7, *post.*

[28] See clause 66 of the I.C.E. conditions, *post,* Chap. 18, pp. 820–821.

[29] For a full discussion of the distinction, see *post,* Chap. 7, pp. 416–418, 435–437, 450, and 499 *et seq.* See also Chap. 18, pp. 825 *et seq.*

[30] Provided, it is suggested, that a dispute has been formulated prior to the decision— see *infra,* subsection (4).

[31] See, *e.g. De Morgan Snell* v. *Rio de Janeiro Flour Mills, ante,* p. 95.

[32] See *post,* Chap. 7, pp. 435 *et seq.*

[33] See *post,* Chap. 7, p. 447.

quite objective and without regard to any question of discretion, it is simply not the case that provisions making use of a certifier as a piece of convenient administrative machinery mean that it is thereby desired to give him any discretion, and even provisions making express reference to his satisfaction or approval are not drafted in the expectation or desire that he should apply any standard other than that required by the contract provisions. The duty of the certifier is to apply the provisions of the contract exactly and strictly to the situation upon which he is required to give his decision, and any evidence showing that he has taken any extraneous or irrelevant matter into consideration will deprive his certificate of validity.[34]

It is not necessary that the person acting in this capacity should be, in the strict sense of the term, an arbitrator.[35]   For convenience, because the expression is familiar in the context of building contracts and to distinguish this function from that of an arbitrator in the full sense, it is generally described in this work as the function of " the certifier." The status of the certifier and the effect, as between the parties to a building contract, of his decisions are fully discussed later in this book.[36]   The present chapter is concerned with the narrower aspect of the duties he may owe in that capacity to his employer. In considering the older cases, confusion will be avoided if it is remembered that the certifier is frequently described loosely as an arbitrator, though in fact this is quite inaccurate.[37]   Thus, in *Pappa* v. *Rose* (1871) [38] Brett J. held that a broker (without being an arbitrator) " was a person filling a position which brought him within an exception well known to the law of England, *viz.*, that a person who is appointed and is acting as an arbitrator to determine a matter of difference between two or more persons does not enter into an implied promise to bring to the performance of the duty entrusted to him a due and reasonable amount of skill and knowledge." [39]

Certifiers are called quasi-arbitrators because, although not arbitrators in the full sense and not bound to follow the procedure of arbitration as provided for by the Arbitration Act 1950, they are in a similar (though not identical) position to an arbitrator in

---

[34] See, *e.g. Panamena Europa Navegacion* v. *Leyland* [1947] A.C. 428, and the other cases cited *post*, Chap. 7, pp. 467 *et seq.*

[35] *Pappa* v. *Rose* (1871) L.R. 7 C.P. 32; *Finnegan* v. *Allen* [1943] K.B. 425.

[36] *Post*, Chap. 7, Approval and Certificates.

[37] See *post*, Chap. 7.

[38] L.R. 7 C.P. 32 at p. 39.

[39] See also the language used in the leading case on collusion of *Hickman & Co.* v. *Roberts* [1913] A.C. 229, illustrated and discussed *post*, pp. 462 *et seq.*

regard to the impartiality and disinterest required of them,[41] and because unless there is an overriding arbitration clause (as there usually is in modern contracts) [42] their decisions may be conclusive and binding on the parties.

(4) Negligence in Certifying

There is little doubt that, in his capacity as certifier, in so far as he is determining a dispute formulated between the parties, the architect owes no duty of skill or care to his employer (or, for that matter, the contractor). The reason clearly is that a potential liability of this kind would interfere with the free and unfettered exercise of his judgment when performing his function as certifier. Thus, in *Chambers* v. *Goldthorpe* (1961) [43] Smith M.R. said: " The question raised is whether, in ascertaining and certifying the amount payable by the defendant to the contractor, the plaintiff was in the position of an arbitrator between the building owner and the contractor, or merely in the position of an agent for the building owner. If he were merely in the latter position, he would be clearly liable for negligence; but if he were in the position of an arbitrator then, beyond all doubt, the building owner could not sue him for negligence." The rule has been adopted from the law of arbitration,[44] where the necessity for such a rule is obvious, as no award of an arbitrator would be final if any aggrieved party was free to bring proceedings against him for negligence, in which the evidence might in many cases amount to a rehearing of the arbitration. Furthermore in the case of certifiers, only one party (the employer) is in contractual relations with the certifier and therefore in a position to bring proceedings for negligence against him. No contractor could reasonably be expected to agree to a certifier being free to reach binding decisions affecting his interest in such a one-sided situation.

Difficult questions may, however, arise from the fact that although, in his capacity as certifier, the architect or engineer is not liable to the employer for negligence, his function in this capacity may tend to be closely associated in practice with his functions of supervision and administrative control of the contract, so that it is essential to determine in which capacity the alleged negligence occurred. This distinction does not seem to have been present in the minds of the courts in every case.

---

[41] *Hickman & Co.* v. *Roberts* [1913] A.C. 229, *post*, Chap. 7, pp. 451 *et seq.* (It may be noted that in this case the certifier was also referred to as an arbitrator.)

[42] See *post*, Chap. 7, Section 4.

[43] [1901] 1 K.B. 624 at p. 633.

[44] See the passage from *Pappa* v. *Rose*, cited *supra*.

ILLUSTRATIONS

(1) G. contracted with McK. to have three miles of road made, and employed M., an overseer of roads, to make a specification of the work to be inserted in the contract, and to superintend the making of the road, for £8. During the execution of the contract, M. authorised deviations from the specification. Upon completion G. sued M. for damages for authorising or permitting the deviations and certifying that the works were executed according to the specification. The jury returned a verdict of £50, which was upheld on appeal: *Gordon* v. *Miller* (1838).[45]

(2) A. engaged B. to build a house for him in accordance with certain plans. B. was to be paid on certificates from J. (A.'s architect). J. certified, and A. paid B. A. brought an action against J., alleging that the house was not built in accordance with the contract. Fitz-gerald B. charged the jury that J. would be responsible if they should find that the giving of the certificate arose from his negligence and want of caution in his duty of superintending the work, and that there was incumbent on J. the duty of skilled superintendence. The jury found a verdict for the plaintiff: *Armstrong* v. *Jones* (1869).[46]

(3) The plaintiff sued for services as architect in planning and superintending the erection of the defendant's house. The plaintiff's duties included the certification of payments to the contractors in certain fixed proportions of the value of the work done. In consequence of the plaintiff's failure to perform his duty in this respect, a large amount was overpaid on the carpenter's and joiner's contract, and on the failure of these contractors the defendant was compelled to have the work finished by others at a much higher price, and thereby the defendant wholly lost the amount which he had overpaid to the failing contractors on the plaintiff's certificates, which ought not to have been given. *Held*, that the defendant might deduct his loss from the plaintiff's claim: *Irving* v. *Morrison* (1877).[47]

(4) The plaintiff, an architect, sued the employer for fees and commission. The employer denied liability, and counterclaimed on the ground that, by the plaintiff's negligence and want of care and skill, the contract had been done in a defective and inferior manner. The plaintiff contended that by the building contract he, the plaintiff, was made authorised judge of the quality of the materials used and time and manner of executing works, and so occupied the position of arbitrator, and as such, having approved and certified so as to entitle the contractor to be paid, no action would lie against himself. *Held*, that plaintiff was employed as a skilled professional person to perform services for reward, and that he was not released from his usual liabilities thereunder because under another contract between his employer and the builder he might, as arbitrator, have determined between them as to the performance of that contract in a manner which assumed that he had properly performed his own, and that the defence and counterclaim were good: *Badgley* v. *Dickson* (1886).[48]

[45] 1 D. (Ct. of Sess.) 832.
[46] Hudson's B.C., 4th ed., Vol. 2, p. 6.
[47] 27 Up.Can.C.P. 242. See also *Burns* v. *Furby*, *post*, p. 487.
[48] 5 A.R. 494 (Canada). See also *Young* v. *Ballarat Commissioners* (1878) 4 Vict.L.R. 306.

(5) A building contract expressly disclaimed the accuracy of the bills (which had been provided by the architect to the builder), but provided that the architect should have power to measure the works and adjust the same. The builders, in addition to suing the employer, sued the architect, alleging negligence and a warranty that the quantities were correct. *Held*, since the architects were given power to remeasure, they were in a quasi-judicial position and could not be sued in negligence or for breach of warranty and were not liable except for dishonesty: *Young* v. *Blake* (1887).[49] (Note: This case is an example of the old practice whereby the successful contractor paid the person preparing the bills (see section 4 (*d*) *supra*), and could well have been decided on the grounds of no privity of contract.)

(6) An architect was employed to design and superintend the erection of a house, and by the terms of the contract, the architect's decision in all matters between the builder and the building owner was to be final. The architect gave a final certificate and brought an action for his fees. The building owner counterclaimed for negligence by the architect in the supervision of the work. The architect, in his defence to the counterclaim, alleged that he had taken the defects into consideration in certifying the final amount due, and had deducted a sum in respect thereof. The jury found for the building owner on the counterclaim. *Held*, that the certificate of the architect, in a dispute between the building owner and the builder, allowing deductions in respect of matters previously complained of, is only a final decision as between the building owner and the builder, and not as between the building owner and the architect, and that the building owner was entitled to recover damages for the negligence in supervision, notwithstanding the certificate: *Rogers* v. *James* (1891).[50]

(7) G. employed C. as architect to supervise the erection of houses by a contractor. The contract provided: (8) that any authority given by the architect for an alteration or addition in or to the works was not to vitiate the contract, but all additions were to be measured and valued and certified for by the architect, and (20) that " A certificate of the architect or an award of the referee hereinafter referred to, as the case may be, showing the final balance due or payable to the contractor, is to be conclusive evidence of the works having been duly completed, and that the contractor is entitled to receive payment of the final balance." Clause 22 provided for arbitration in case of disputes. The architect gave his final certificate before any dispute had arisen, and brought an action to recover his fees. G. counterclaimed for negligence, consisting of the negligent measuring up of work done by the contractor, and permitting him to include in his accounts sums to which he was not entitled, and certifying such accounts. *Held*, by A. L. Smith M.R. and Collins L.J. (Romer L.J. dissenting) and distinguishing *Rogers* v. *James* (1891) on the ground that the architect (as he was not in the present case) was there sued for negligence in not properly supervising the work, and further that no question of his quasi-arbitral function was there

---

[49] Hudson's B.C., 4th ed., Vol. 2, p. 110.

[50] Hudson's B.C., 4th ed., Vol. 2, p. 172; see also *Saunders* v. *Broadstairs Local Board* (1890) Hudson's B.C., 4th ed., Vol. 2, p. 164, and *Leicester Guardians* v. *Trollope* (1911), *ibid.* p. 419 for similar cases where architects were held liable after granting binding final certificates.

raised, that the negligence of the architect alleged was in the exercise of his functions under clauses under which he was to act impartially towards the building owner and the contractor, and that he occupied the position of an arbitrator and was not liable to an action by the building owner for negligence in the exercise of those functions: *Chambers* v. *Goldthorpe*; *Restell* v. *Nye* (1901).[51]

(8) Under a contract for the sale of shares in a private company, the price was to be fixed by the defendant, who was to value them according to certain rules, his decision to be binding. A copy of the agreement was sent to the defendant by solicitors acting for both parties, requesting him to value the shares in accordance with the agreement. The defendant's valuation did not follow the agreed rules. *Held* by the Court of Appeal, that a person brought in by the parties to a contract to fix a term on which they cannot agree is not liable to be sued for damages in the absence of bad faith, since he is a quasi-arbitrator enjoying the same protection as an arbitrator: *Finnegan* v. *Allen* (1943).[52]

(9) Cl. 25 of a building contract provided, in identical terms to Cl. 24 of the then R.I.B.A. standard form, that the final certificate should be conclusive evidence of the sufficiency of the works.[53] The arbitration clause differed in that only the contractor was given an unqualified right to go to arbitration. The building owner sued the architect for damages, alleging that the architect negligently certified at a time when the work was not complete and defects had not been made good as required by the contract, and he had accordingly been obliged to pay more than the work was worth. *Held*, on a point of law, and not following *Chambers* v. *Goldthorpe* (1901), that it was a valid cause of action if an architect was negligent in and about the issuing of a certificate: *Hoffman* v. *Meyer* (1956).[54]

It is obviously important to attempt to reconcile the above cases, and to determine the exact extent of the principle applied in *Chambers* v. *Goldthorpe* (1901). In that case, the building contract provided that a certificate of the architect showing the final balance due or payable to the contractor was to be conclusive evidence of the works having been duly completed and that the contractor was to be entitled to receive payment of the final balance. The contract also contained the complicated arbitration clause the construction of which had been the subject of the decisions in *Lloyd Bros.* v. *Milward* (1895)[55] and *Clemence* v. *Clark* (1879).[56] These cases held that if there was no dispute formulated between the parties prior to the final

---

[51] [1901] 1 K.B. 624.
[52] [1943] 1 K.B. 425. It is suggested that as between the parties the valuation might not have been binding, however, under the principle of *Panamena etc.* v. *Leyland* [1947] A.C. 428, *post*, Chap. 7, pp. 466–469, and 476–478.
[53] Compare the wording set out fully in *Windsor R.D.C.* v. *Otterway & Try*, *post*, Chap. 7, p. 442.
[54] 1956 (2) S.A. 752 (South Africa).
[55] Hudson's B.C., 4th ed., Vol. 2, p. 454. See *post*, Chap. 7, pp. 438–439.
[56] Hudson's B.C., 4th ed., Vol. 2, p. 207. See *post*, Chap. 7, pp. 443 and 466.

certificate of the architect the certificate should be conclusive, whereas in other cases the disputes could be settled by the referee.

Both A. L. Smith M.R. and Collins L.J. were clearly influenced by the finality which these two decisions had attributed to the architect's certificate. The former [58] said: " Unless there is a dispute, and a reference under clause 22 before the architect certifies, the certificate of the architect with regard to the amount which the building owner has to pay the builder under clause 20 is final."

Collins L.J. said: " What, then, is the position of an architect who, under a contract such as that here in question, has to give a certificate which is to be final and binding, not only on his employer, but also on the other party to the contract? " [59]

In these circumstances, the majority of the court held that in certifying under this clause the architect owed a duty of impartiality to both parties, and consequently that his negligent acceptance of excessive measurements which were used in calculating the amount due on final certificate gave no remedy to his employer.

The case has been subsequently commented upon. Thus, in *Wisbech R.D.C.* v. *Ward* (1927) [60] Sankey J., in holding an architect liable in negligence in regard to the issue of an interim certificate, said: " Although it is probably right to say that in giving a final certificate the architect acts in a quasi-judicial character unless there is some express clause in the contract to contradict it, it cannot, I think, be asserted that in giving an interim certificate he is so acting." [61]

This decision of Sankey J. was reversed by the Court of Appeal, who found that the architect had not been negligent. But of *Chambers* v. *Goldthorpe* (1901) Atkin L.J. said: " I am not aware of any case which has extended that doctrine (that of *Chambers* v. *Goldthorpe*) to the granting of interim certificates and I do not desire to express any opinion about it except to say that it is obvious that that case would have to be very carefully considered before we came to a conclusion in favour of the plaintiffs (the employer) supposing that negligence were otherwise proved." [62] The case was also mentioned *obiter* by Lord Radcliffe in *Burden* v. *Swansea Corporation* (1957). [63]

[58] [1901] 1 K.B. 624 at p. 635.
[59] *Ibid.* at p. 638.
[60] [1927] 2 K.B. 556.
[61] *Ibid.* at p. 565.
[62] [1928] 2 K.B. at p. 23.
[63] [1957] 1 W.L.R. 1167 at p. 1172.

As indicated above, *Chambers* v. *Goldthorpe* (1901) has not been followed in South Africa. In *Hoffman* v. *Meyer* (1952) [64] a building owner who had contracted with the builder in terms similar to the then R.I.B.A. form of contract [65] was held to have a valid cause of action against the architect for damages sustained by him consequent upon his being obliged, by the terms of his contract with the contractor, to pay out on a final certificate which, as a result of the architect's negligent supervision, had been issued by the architect for an amount greater than that to which the contractor was entitled. In the course of his judgment, Ogilvie Thompson J. said: " . . . if in fact the architect negligently issues a final certificate under clause 25 (f) for an amount which is in excess of the amount to which the contractor is entitled, the building owner must nevertheless pay that amount. On the view taken in *Chambers* v. *Goldthorpe* (1901) . . . and not overlooking the circumstance that that decision has stood in England for more than fifty years, it appears to me to be highly artificial to hold that, in issuing a final certificate under a clause like 25 (f) in the instant case, the architect is in the position of a quasi-arbitrator to the extent of his being relieved from responsibility to his employer for the consequences of his proved negligence in issuing such a certificate. The views expressed by Romer L.J. in his dissenting judgment in *Chambers* v. *Goldthorpe* (1901) commend themselves to me as being preferable to those expressed by A. L. Smith M.R. and Collins L.J. The architect has no privity of contract with the contractor. He is liable to and is remunerated by the building owner, and it is on the latter's behalf that he, in return for remuneration, exercises his expert skill in supervising the erection of the building. The architect is admittedly liable to the building owner for negligence in such supervision. Although clause 25 (g) serves to underline the distinction between interim and final certificates, no good reason would, with the greatest respect, appear to me to exist for absolving the architect from negligence when he comes to issue a final certificate." Nor has *Chambers* v. *Goldthorpe* (1901) escaped criticism by textbook writers. Thus, Beven on Negligence, [66] commenting on *Chambers* v. *Goldthorpe* (1901), said: " Apart from authority there appears no reason why the contract made between the builder and the building owner should vary the independent contract between architect and building owner. The supposition that a judge is entitled to be negligent without possibility of pecuniary harm to

---

[64] 1956 (2) S.A. 752, illustrated *supra*.
[65] Subject to certain important differences in the arbitration clause.
[66] As cited in Hudson's B.C., 4th ed., Vol. 2, p. 1337.

himself is perhaps more a prejudice than a reason, and it is not immediately apparent why it should override his own contract made previously to entering on his judicial office, not to be negligent."

In the Canadian case of *Badgley* v. *Dickson* (1886),[67] it was held that although an architect employed for reward by the owner to superintend the construction of a house may, as between the owner and the contractor by the terms of their own agreement, be in the position of an arbitrator, and his decision between them be unimpeachable except for fraud or dishonesty, yet as between himself and the owner he is answerable for either negligence or unskilfulness in the performance of his duty as an architect.   Osler J.A. said: " In the case before us the action and counterclaim are based upon a distinct contract, by which the plaintiff was employed as a skilled professional person to perform certain services for reward, and he is not, in my opinion, absolved from the usual obligations attaching to such a contract merely because under another contract between his employer and the builder he may, as arbitrator, have determined between them as to the performance of that contract in a manner which assumes that he has properly performed his own."

It is tempting to suggest that the decision in *Chambers* v. *Goldthorpe* (1901) turned upon the binding effect of the certificate in that case, but it is difficult to see in principle why a certificate open to review on arbitration should be in a different case, since the parties clearly intend that even in such a case the certifier shall act impartially, and frequently a certificate open to review is given conditional finality—compare the engineer's function under the arbitration clause in the I.C.E. form of contract.   That this is the correct view (that the position of independence does not necessarily only arise in cases where the decision is by the terms of the contract binding) was recently maintained (it is submitted correctly) in New Zealand by Richmond J.,[68] after a most remarkable and penetrating analysis of the collusion cases.[69]

It is suggested that the immunity of the certifier can at most only be necessary as a matter of business efficacy where he is giving a decision on a dispute formulated before him, either between

---

[67] 13 A.R. 494, *supra*.

[68] In *Hatrick (N.Z.) Ltd.* v. *Nelson Carlton Construction* [1964] N.Z. 72.

[69] See *post*, Chap. 7, pp. 463–464.   The decision of the Appellate Division of the Supreme Court of South Africa in *Kolberg* v. *Cape Town Municipality*, 1967 (3) S.A. 472, denying (in a different context) quasi-judicial status to an engineer giving a decision under a clause similar to clause 66 of the I.C.E. conditions, appears to be out of line with the authorities elsewhere and is criticised *post*, Chap. 7, p. 464, and Chap. 18, pp. 821–822.

himself as agent of the employer and the builder, or between the building owner and the builder.[70] So, if in fact a dispute had arisen as to the measurements in *Chambers* v. *Goldthorpe* (1901), his decision would have been protected from any allegation of negligence. Where, however, an architect accepts measurements submitted by a builder, without investigation, it is hard to see in what respect he can be said to be acting judicially when issuing a certificate based on those measurements. Applying this suggested test to defects in the work, it is suggested that unnoticed defects could not form the basis of any judicial act, whereas known or suspected defects which had been considered by the certifier and valued or ruled upon by him might attract the immunity. Whatever the true view, it is clear, it is submitted, that the decision will not normally prevent an action brought against an engineer or architect where the negligence pleaded is that of faulty supervision.[71] But the case, which stands virtually alone, merits a complete review by the courts.

It is perhaps unnecessary to emphasise the injustice and practical difficulties to which such an immunity can give rise, since an employer will, in the absence of an overriding arbitration clause, be deprived of his remedy for defective work against both the contractor and the architect or engineer, if the reasoning of the decision is correct.

Until recently, this extreme position was unlikely to arise in modern times, because under most standard forms of contract the arbitrator was given power to review even the final certificate of the architect or engineer.[72] Under the 1957 revised edition of the R.I.B.A. form of contract, however, clause 24 [73] was reworded so as to confer beyond any possible doubt binding force upon this certificate in relation to many matters unless notice of arbitration is given prior to its being issued; in addition the grounds of exception were very considerably narrowed. This has restored the urgency of a review of the *Chambers* v. *Goldthorpe* principle. An immunity expressed in wide terms on the authority of that case could not, it is suggested, have been the intention of the contract of employment of the architect (on this point it is difficult to disapprove of the reasoning in the passage from Ogilvie Thompson J.'s judgment quoted *supra*).

[70] See *per* Ogilvie Thompson J. in *Hoffman* v. *Meyer*, 1956 (2) S.A. 752 at p. 758. This judgment contains the clearest and most up-to-date discussion of this subject.

[71] *Saunders* v. *Broadstairs Local Board* (1890), *Rogers* v. *James* (1891), and *Leicester Guardians* v. *Trollope* (1911), Hudson's B.C., 4th ed., Vol. 2, pp. 164, 172 and 419 respectively.

[72] See *post*, Chap. 7, pp. 435 *et seq.*, and the decision in *Windsor R.D.C.* v. *Otterway & Try* [1954] 1 W.L.R. 1494, in fact overruled in *East Ham Corporation* v. *Sunley* [1966] A.C. 406.   [73] See *post*, Chap. 7, pp. 489–492.

The post-1963 R.I.B.A. standard forms have carried the matter still further, since the range of matters over which the architect's final certificate may become binding has been widened (to include, somewhat surprisingly, decisions by the architect as to whether or not he has furnished the contractor with information and drawings on time) although in this instance the certificate will bind the employer and not the contractor.[74] In any event, the provision is far more prejudicial to the employer than to the contractor.[74a]

If the limitation on the effect of *Chambers* v. *Goldthorpe* (1901) put forward above is accepted as correct, however, the employer will at least have a remedy against his architect in the case of unnoticed defective work, and a considerable increase in litigation against architects can be expected as an indirect result of these changes in the standard form since on any view, it is submitted, that case cannot apply to defects which the architect ought to have detected during the currency of the work, where the breach will have no connection with the issue of the final certificate.

SECTION 7. DUTIES AND LIABILITIES OF QUANTITY SURVEYORS
(1) Bills of Quantities Defined

It has become increasingly the practice in the U.K. for substantial projects to be let on a "measured contract" basis, with bills of quantities describing in detail every item of the works to be done forming part of the contract documents.[75]

Bills of quantities normally devote a separate bill to each trade necessary for the erection of a building or the construction of works. For instance, there are usually separate bills for excavation work, for concreting, bricklaying, joinery, paving, tiling, ironmongery, painting, and so on. Generally, also, there is a bill for what are called preliminary items such as general foreman, site huts, insurances, special liabilities under the contract, water, and other items which are applicable to all trades. Preliminary items frequently give rise to difficulty when valuing variations.[76] Some bills, particularly in engineering works, are, however, subdivided with reference to different sections of the works rather than separate trades.

---

[74] This is the clear result of the combined effect of clause 24 and clause 30 (7).
[74a] See *post*, Chap. 7, pp. 489 *et seq*, where the clause is considered more fully.
[75] See *post*, Chap. 8, pp. 509 *et seq*. where the evolution of this type of contract is considered.
[76] See *post*, Chap. 8, p. 555, note 44, and see p. 556.

Bills of quantities in engineering contracts are in general far less detailed, since the processes involved, while more massive, are generally less complex, and since the rates are frequently of a "composite" character—as, for instance, a single lineal-yard rate for excavating, supplying laying and jointing pipes, and backfilling including restoration of the surface.

A bill of quantities is usually divided into columns. As prepared by the quantity surveyor the left-hand columns indicate the quantities and units of measurement which it is anticipated by the quantity surveyor will have to be carried out. Wherever possible these are calculated from or " taken off " the drawings, and may be expected to be very accurate, but some items, such as quantities for taking out soft or unsuitable ground, or for excavation in rock, can in the light of the information available at the tender stage, only be estimates and provisional in character. Then follows a column in which is described, in varying degrees of detail, the item of work to which the quantities apply. The quantity surveyor then leaves two blank columns, in the first of which the contractor inserts his price or rate for each unit of measurement and in the second of which the contractor grosses up the total amount to be charged for the quantities contemplated by the quantity surveyor at the price or rate inserted by the contractor. The exact nature of the work in the bills cannot usually be fully understood or defined without reference to the specification, which describes the work processes and quality of material required in much greater detail by comparison with the " shorthand " descriptions in the bills. In the R.I.B.A. forms the specification is included in the bills of quantities themselves, usually in the form of lengthy preambles to the bills as a whole and also to the individual bills, as well as in the verbal descriptions of items or groups of items.

The amounts to be charged alongside all the various items are then collected into a summary for each bill, these summaries in turn being collected into a grand summary for the whole of the work.

Bills of quantities may, depending on the terms of the contract, serve a number of functions:

(i) they indicate with some precision to tendering contractors the amount and nature of the work they will have to carry out,

(ii) they indicate to persons examining the tender on behalf of the employer the make-up of the tender,

(iii) in measured contracts they are the exact measure of the work undertaken for the contract price, which is adjusted once the work is complete and the actual quantities known,

(iv) they form the basis of valuing variations in the work (a variation being something different from a mere discrepancy between billed and actual quantities arising from errors or inaccurate estimates of the quantities in the bills, which will be adjusted under the special provisions relating to the bills),

(v) in the R.I.B.A. standard forms of measured contract, they are the specification of the work.[77]

Quantities are attractive to builders in the United Kingdom because they greatly reduce the burden and expense of tendering and because, in practice, builders are asked to tender for far more work than they can expect to get; because, in practice, they are usually afforded far too little time to tender; and, less worthily perhaps, because over- or under-estimates (or failure to comply with the standard methods of measurement) which can be detected in the bills at the tender stage, and known or probable variations of the work at that time, can be taken advantage of when pricing, so as to present the employer with an apparently attractive price which in reality will require to be adjusted upwards, while undetected errors will in any event be adjusted. Reference has already been made to the efforts made by trade agreements of the building contractors to secure the universal adoption of measured contracts with bills for all work of more than a certain value.[78]

The employment of quantity surveyors is attractive to architects because they enormously reduce the administrative work of the architect both at the tender stage and during the currency of the contract.

It is not unusual, however, for smaller projects to be tendered for without bills, and there is little doubt that the use of bills of quantities on many projects may have the effect of increasing the total cost. Thus the R.I.B.A. has a standard form of contract available for such works (which however contemplates the employment of a surveyor for valuing variations and interim payments and settling accounts), which is commonly but misleadingly referred to as a "lump sum" contract, and which in this book is referred to as the specification form of contract, or the form without quantities.

[77] As a result of clause 3 (3) of the Forms with Quantities.
[78] *Ante*, Chap. 1, p. 54.

(2) Preparation of Bills and Other Duties

In theory, the quantity surveyor should receive complete drawings and a specification from the architect before he can start to prepare bills. Once he has done so, he takes off the quantities of work from the drawings and prepares the bills, leaving the rate and total columns blank for the tendering contractors. Under the standard R.I.B.A. form there is no specification named as such, and an important aspect of the work with this contract is the drafting of the preambles to the various bills and of the individual items in the bills, which must supplant and embody the architect's specification.

It is obvious that bills which descended to every last minutiae of building or engineering processes would be impossibly long (apart from placing a superhuman burden on the memory and imagination of the quantity surveyor), and accordingly standard methods of measurement are usually incorporated by reference.[79] The purpose of these is to introduce uniformity into the practice of describing work in bills and to make clear what processes are, and what processes are not, deemed to be included in the items of work which are billed, since every item of work, however detailed, is on analysis a composite item. This is effected by recommending that certain processes should be separately described in the bills for pricing purposes, and that others should not be (in which event they will need to be included in some larger composite item). If standard methods are not used, carefully drafted statements in the preambles to the bills or elsewhere should make quite clear the ancillary processes and contingent risks and expenditure deemed to be included in the items actually billed and priced. Failure to make this clear, or to comply meticulously with the standard methods if incorporated, may expose the employer to claims for additional payment on the ground that some necessary ancillary process or the cost of some contingency was not included in the work priced in the bills.[80]

In order to prepare bills, therefore, the surveyor must be a master of the standard methods of measurement, and familiar in every respect with the scheme of the contract of which the bills are to form part, as well as possessing a thorough knowledge of building or engineering design and of traditional, as well as the latest, constructional methods so that he can understand and interpret in detail the drawings and specification furnished by the architect, and calculate correctly therefrom the measurements and items of

[79] See *post*, Chap. 5, pp. 264–267; Chap. 8, pp. 515–520.
[80] See *post*, Chap. 8, pp. 515 *et seq.*

work involved.   The work is therefore extremely demanding both in detail and in knowledge of principle, and calls for the highest degree of professional skill.   It would be quite wrong to regard the practising quantity surveyor as in any way of lesser professional status or competence than the architects or engineers who are formally in charge of the administration of the contracts with which he is concerned.

When the priced bills of quantities are received together with the tenders, the quantity surveyor often has the duty of checking over the priced bills in order to see whether there are any arithmetical or other errors.   If there were a substantial error, for example, in addition, it might mean that the amount payable on a measurement basis would be substantially different (in either direction) from the amount tendered,[81] depending on the exact wording of the contractual provisions relating to remeasurement or the adjustment of the contract sum to take account of differences between the actual and billed quantities.   In fact the building and civil engineering standard forms would appear to produce different answers in this situation.[82]

As the work proceeds the quantity surveyor may have the duty of measuring up and calculating the value of the work carried out and advising the architect or engineer so that he may issue interim certificates in favour of the contractor.   He also has the duty of valuing, for the purposes of addition to or deduction from the contract sum, the omissions or additions in the work.   The quantity surveyor may also be expected to calculate any fluctuations in the contract price arising from alterations in material prices or labour rates under the terms of any relevant fluctuations clause.   Further, under the post-1963 R.I.B.A. standard forms the handling and calculation of various claims by the contractor for additional expense under the provisions of the contract can be delegated to him by the architect.[83]

There is a dearth of authority upon the standard of skill or care owed by a quantity surveyor to his employer.   Since, however, his task involves very large numbers of arithmetical calculations, it seems that an occasional slip or error may be insufficient to sustain an allegation of professional negligence against him.

[81] See *ante*, Chap. 1, pp. 35–36, where the application of the rules of rectification to this situation is considered; and *post*, Chap. 8, pp. 520–521.
[82] R.I.B.A. Forms, clause 13; I.C.E. conditions, clauses 55 and 56.
[83] See, *e.g.* clauses 11 (6) and 24 (1).   See also *supra*, p. 150, and *Clemence* v. *Clarke*, *post*, p. 466.

ILLUSTRATION

A school board employed a quantity surveyor for measuring up buildings of a value of £12,000, which had been completed. They brought an action against the quantity surveyor for (*inter alia*) negligence in making two clerical errors in the calculations, whereby the board had overpaid two sums of £118 and £15. *Held*, that as the quantity surveyor had employed a competent skilled clerk who had carried out hundreds of intricate calculations correctly, the quantity surveyor was not liable for these two errors: *London School Board* v. *Northcroft* (1889).[84]

SECTION 8. FRAUD AND BRIBERY

(1) Fraud

In general, there is no contractual relationship between the architect or engineer, as such, and the contractor. The architect's duties arise in contract and not in tort,[85] and consequently he owes no duty to the contractor in relation to the preparation of plans or quantities, or the measuring up of the work, any more than in relation to his duties of design and superintendence of the work. (Under the old practice as to taking out bills of quantities, an architect who did so and was paid by the builder by virtue of a provision in the building contract requiring the builder to do so, was held liable in principle to the builder for misleading errors in the quantities,[86] but the underlying basis of this situation no longer obtains in practice, and even where provision is made for payment of the quantity surveyor out of moneys paid to the contractor this is no longer sufficient, it is submitted, to place them in contractual relations with each other.)[87]

The liability for fraud (*i.e.* for deliberately or recklessly false representations or conduct[88]) is, however, a liability in tort, and an architect or engineer guilty of fraud in the discharge of his duties will be liable, apart from contract, to either party to the building contract if they have thereby suffered damage. Furthermore, the

---

[84] Hudson's B.C., 4th ed., Vol. 2, p. 147. (Perhaps a less sympathetic view would be taken today when vicarious responsibility is a more familiar concept.)

[85] *Steljes* v. *Ingram* (1903) 19 T.L.R. 534; *Bagot* v. *Stevens Scanlan* [1966] 1 Q.B. 197; and see section 6 (1), p. 123 *ante*. See, however, the possible liability in tort for innocent misrepresentations under the rule in *Hedley Byrne* v. *Heller*, discussed *ante*, Chap. 1, pp. 64 *et seq.*, and *Townsends Ltd.* v. *Cinema News Ltd.* [1959] 1 W.L.R. 119, illustrated *supra*, p. 143.

[86] *Bolt* v. *Thomas* (1859) Hudson's B.C., 4th ed., Vol. 2, p. 3, *post*, p. 196.

[87] See *ante*, pp. 111 *et seq.*; the case of *Locke* v. *Morter* (1885) 2 T.L.R. 121, *ante* p. 119; and the discussion, *post*, pp. 193 *et seq.*

[88] See *ante*, Chap. 1, pp. 47–48.

immunity which an architect or engineer may enjoy as a certifier [89] only applies if he is honest, and fraud or dishonest collusion by him when certifying will render him liable in tort to either party. [90] Liability in fraud depends upon representation by word or deed *to the plaintiff*, however, so that dishonest conduct by the architect not involving a false representation to the aggrieved party and intended to be acted on by him will not give a cause of action. So a fraudulent representation by an architect to a building owner that the work was not yet practically complete was held not to give a cause of action to the contractor. [91] It is no defence that the architect may have been acting as agent: " All persons directly concerned in the commission of a fraud are to be treated as principals. No party can be permitted to excuse himself on the ground that he acted as agent or as the servant of another; and the reason is plain—for this contract of agency or service cannot impose any obligation on the agent or servant to commit or assist in the committing of fraud." [92] In so far as the architect may be acting within the scope of his agency for the employer (*i.e.* in all aspects of the building contract, save his quasi-judicial duties) the employer will, on general principles, be liable for the fraud of his agent. [93] Thus, an employer has been held liable for the fraudulent misrepresentation of his architect in inviting tenders. [94]

(2) Bribes and Secret Commissions

This subject, in so far as the purpose of the bribe is to procure acceptance of a tender, is dealt with later. [95] The general principle is well stated by James L.J. in *Panama & South Pacific Telegraph Co.* v. *India Rubber Co.* (1875). [96]

" Any surreptitious dealing between one principal and the agent of the other principal is a fraud on such other principal cognisable by the court. . . . The defrauded principal, if he come in time, is entitled at his option, to have the contract rescinded or, if he elects not to have it rescinded, to have such other adequate

---

[89] See *supra*, pp. 161 *et seq.*
[90] See also *post*, Chap. 7, pp. 455–458.
[91] *Larkins* v. *Chelmer Holdings Pty.* [1965] Qd. R. 68 (Australia).
[92] *Per* Lord Westbury in *Cullen* v. *Thompson's Trustees* (1862) 4 Macq. (H.L.Sc.) 424 at pp. 432–433.
[93] *Lloyd* v. *Grace, Smith & Co.* [1912] A.C. 716; *Uxbridge Permanent Benefit Building Society* v. *Pickard* [1939] 2 K.B. 248; *Morris* v. *C. W. Martin & Sons Ltd.* [1966] 1 Q.B. 716.
[94] *Pearson* v. *Dublin Corporation* [1907] A.C. 351, illustrated *post*, Chap. 3, p. 231.
[95] *Post*, Chap. 3, pp. 232–233.
[96] L.R. 10 Ch. 515 at p. 526.

relief as the court may think right to give him." Whenever a secret commission or bribe is given to an agent, whether directly in connection with the particular transaction or in such relation to it as to affect it, the consideration is corrupt and the transaction invalidated so far as the principal is concerned. The presumption that the bribe influenced the agent's action is irrefutable, and the actual consequences will not be inquired into.[97] All such sums are treated as money had and received to the use of the principal, for which the agent is accountable.

ILLUSTRATIONS

(1) An architect employed by a building owner to superintend a house being built by a contractor, made an arrangement with the contractor that he, the contractor, should pay him £20. The building owner, when he knew it, dismissed the architect, and the architect sued him for his fees. *Held*, confirming the judgment of the court below, that an architect cannot at the same time be employed in the interests both of the building owner and the builder and receive pay from both, and as it was proved that the architect had covenanted with the builder to receive pay from him, *held*, further, that it was a violation of the contract sufficient to discharge the building owner from liability to pay the architect anything: *Tahrland* v. *Rodier* (1866).[98]

(2) M. authorised T. as his broker to negotiate for the purchase of a ship on the basis of an offer of £9,000. T. was to buy the ship as cheaply as she could be got. The vendor employed as his broker one S. and promised S. any excess over £8,500 which he might be able to obtain. S. arranged with T., without M.'s knowledge, that T. should share the excess. T. bought the ship on M.'s behalf for £9,250, and received £225 as his share of such excess. M., discovering this, sued T. for the £225. *Held*, that he could recover this as money had and received to his use: *Morison* v. *Thompson* (1874).[99]

(3) The V. Co. contracted to pay a commission to H. for superintending repairs to be executed by them on ships belonging to the S.E.R. Co. H. was in a position of trust in relation to the S.E.R. Co. The jury found as a fact that, though the contract was calculated to bias H.'s mind, it had not in fact done so. *Held*, that H. could not maintain an action for the commission, as, even although H. had not been induced to act corruptly, the consideration for the contract was corrupt: *Harrington* v. *Victoria Graving Dock Co.* (1878).[1]

But a profit is not a secret profit in this sense if the employer knows or ought to know that a profit will be received, even though he may not be aware of its actual extent.

---

[97] *Shipway* v. *Broadwood* [1899] 1 Q.B. 369; *Hovenden & Sons* v. *Millhoff* (1900) 83 L.T. 41.
[98] 16 L.C.Rep. 473.
[99] L.R. 9 Q.B. 480.
[1] 3 Q.B.D. 549.

ILLUSTRATIONS

(1) A contractor for railway works employed, through the medium of an agent, a sub-contractor, who allowed the agent a commission upon the contract. The contractor filed a bill against the sub-contractor and agent, alleging collusion with regard to the commission. The claim was dismissed with costs as against the sub-contractor, but without costs against the agent, the court considering that the plaintiff could not have been ignorant of the practice of allowing commission at the time that he approved the sub-contract: *Holden* v. *Webber* (1860).[2]

(2) Factory owners employed a surveyor to prepare a specification of war damage repairs and supervise the work. After preparing the specification but before work started, the surveyor became a director of the company doing the work, and so informed the owners, who nevertheless allowed him to continue in the work of supervision. *Held*, by the Court of Appeal, although the surveyor had committed a fundamental breach entitling the employers to dismiss him instantly, they had waived the breach, and must accordingly pay for his fees: *Thornton Hall* v. *Wembley Electrical Appliances* (1947).[3]

The courts will decline to accept evidence of any custom or usage on the part of agents to receive commission from persons other than their employers. Thus Lord Russell of Killowen said in *Bulfield* v. *Fournier* (1894)[4]: " If [the pocketing of discounts and commissions was a common practice] it was the more reason for juries to say that it was a bad and dishonest practice, and one which they must stamp out."

The above cases are not all closely connected with building contracts, but the principles are clear. An architect, engineer or surveyor should have no financial dealings of any kind with a contractor without the knowledge of his employer. Any practice whereby the architect's fees, or the fees for measuring up or acting as a surveyor, are included in or appended to the builder's account, should be rigorously avoided, unless the employer's attention is expressly drawn to the fact, since otherwise the architect has a personal interest in securing payment to the builders which may conflict with his duty to the employer to check the builder's account and resist any unjustified claim.

Receipt by the architect, engineer or surveyor of any secret commission whether from the contractor or from suppliers of materials or sub-contractors would warrant instant dismissal, recovery of the commission as money had and received, and release of the employer from any liability to pay him for his services.

---

[2] 29 Beav. 117. See also *London School Board* v. *Northcroft* (1889), illustrated *infra*, subsection (9), p. 192.
[3] [1947] 2 All E.R. 630. See also *Re Elliott, post,* Chap. 7, p. 453.
[4] 11 T.L.R. 62.

SECTION 9.   REMUNERATION OF ARCHITECTS, ENGINEERS
AND QUANTITY SURVEYORS

(1) For Completed Services

(a) By special contract

If there is a contract between the employer and the architect, engineer or quantity surveyor containing specific terms as to payment, those terms, unless varied, regulate the professional man's right to payments.   Any such contract may be made orally or in writing. A professional man already engaged on agreed terms should be careful, if events occur which justify him in increasing his fees, to obtain the agreement of his client.   The courts will be slow in such a case to treat the existing agreement as no longer applying and so discharging the concluded agreement and permitting the recovery of the additional fees in *quantum meruit*.[5]

It is quite usual for the professional man to agree with his employer that the scale of professional charges of one of the professional bodies should be applicable to his employment, *e.g.* the scale of professional charges issued by the R.I.B.A.   But if this is to be the basis of payment, a clear record should be made of the fact either in a form of agreement or in an exchange of correspondence. Specific agreements as to remuneration (and the scales themselves) frequently relate remuneration to a percentage on the cost of the works, and it is advisable in such cases to provide clearly as to what is or is not included in the expression " cost."   Extrinsic evidence will be admitted if the expression is ambiguous.

ILLUSTRATION

An engineer, in addition to certain percentages for designing and supervising the work, was entitled to " a further $1\frac{1}{2}$ per cent. on the estimate of £35,000 in the event of my being able to reduce the total cost of the works below £30,000."   The cost of the work itself was below £30,000, but with the fees of the engineer plus the cost of the land came to over £43,000.   *Held*, extrinsic evidence should be permitted to show that " the estimate of £35,000 " was an estimate of cost including fees and cost of land, and that, the " total cost of the works" being clearly co-extensive, the engineer was not entitled to the $1\frac{1}{2}$ per cent.: *Bank of New Zealand* v. *Simpson* (1900).[6]

It is sometimes assumed that if an architect proceeds with work for the building owner without mentioning the question of

---

[5] See the decision of the Court of Appeal in *Gilbert & Partners* v. *Knight* [1968] 2 All E.R. 248, illustrated *ante*, Chap. 1, p. 18.   See, however, for a contrary case, *Kelly & Partners* v. *Northshore Development* (1963) 5 W.I.R. 379 (Court of Appeal of Jamaica), *post*, p. 192.

[6] [1900] A.C. 182.

remuneration he will be entitled to, and in case of dispute the courts will award him, remuneration based upon a scale of professional charges. This is a mistaken view. The courts have frequently expressed antipathy towards professional scales of every kind, and have reiterated by their decisions that if the building owner is not made aware of the scale of fees which the architect seeks to apply, and does not agree to pay those fees, then the courts are entitled to inquire whether such fees are in all the circumstances reasonable for the particular services which have been performed.[7] Indeed they have indicated that the principle of assessing remuneration as a percentage of the cost of the works is not one which the courts will approve unless there is clear agreement between the parties that such assessment shall be made.[8] It seems possible, however, that the hostility of the courts to scale fees may be gradually diminishing,[9] and it cannot be claimed that the law on this subject is entirely clear.

(b) Implication of reasonable remuneration

Even if there is no express reference by the parties to the question of remuneration, the normal inference, except in cases of work done on approval,[10] will be that an architect or engineer, like other professional men, does not intend and cannot be expected to give his services for nothing, and the employer will be held, by the fact of employment, to have bound himself to pay a reasonable reward for the services to be rendered.[11]

In certain exceptional circumstances, however, the courts might hold that services rendered with only the possibility or hope of remuneration in view gave no right of action. The test to be applied, *viz.* whether a reasonable man in the position of the employer would have believed that the person doing the work intended to do it at his own expense, has already been referred to in the context of building work itself.[12] The commonest occasions when the test may need to be applied will usually, in the case of architects, be at

---

[7] *Debenham* v. *King's College, Cambridge* (1884) 1 T.L.R. 170; *Wilkie* v. *Scottish Aviation Ltd.*, 1956 S.C. 198.

[8] See *infra*, pp. 183–184.

[9] See *e.g. Graham & Baldwin* v. *Taylor Son & Davis* (1965) 109 S.J. 793, *infra*, p. 185, the passage quoted from *Wilkie* v. *Scottish Aviation Ltd.*, 1956 S.C. 198, *infra*, p. 185, and the decision of the Court of Appeal of Jamaica in *Kelly & Partners* v. *Northshore Development Ltd.* (1963) 5 W.I.R. 379, *infra*, subs. (9), pp. 191–192.

[10] See *infra*, subsections (c) and (d).

[11] *Manson* v. *Baillie* (1855) 2 Macq. 80; *Moffatt* v. *Laurie* (1855) 15 C.B. 583, 593; *Landless* v. *Wilson* (1880) 8 R. (Ct. of Sess.) 289; *Ex p. Birkenshaw, re Allison* [1904] 2 K.B. 327.

[12] See *ante*, Chap. 1, p. 18. See also *post*, Chap. 3, pp. 229–231.

the earliest or sketch-plan or outline planning consent stage of his activities, where very little work indeed can produce startling claims on an " abandoned work " basis. The latter of the two old cases illustrated below probably illustrates the more modern view in such situations, but an important factor will, it is suggested, be the nature of the services carried out, where the conduct of or language used by the parties is ambiguous.

ILLUSTRATIONS

(1) W. was engaged in going backwards and forwards on the business of a committee, who passed a resolution that " any service to be rendered by W. shall be taken into consideration, and such remuneration be made as shall be deemed right." W. brought an action for reasonable remuneration. *Held*, that the resolution imported that the committee were to judge whether any or what recompense was right, and that the plaintiff was rightly nonsuited: *Taylor* v. *Brewer* (1813).[13]

(2) B. made a parol contract with a public board to perform certain work and labour for whatever " recompense the board might allow as right and proper." *Held*, that an action lay to recover a reasonable recompense, although the board tendered what they considered right and proper: *Bird* v. *McGaheg* (1849).[14]

(c) Work done on approval and probationary drawings

Where work is done on approval, or is in the nature of a proposal, sketch, or design submitted for approval (or " probationary draw-ings," as they were called in *Moffatt* v. *Dickson, infra*) or with the intention of interesting the client in a project which he may be only tentatively considering, the architect may have no claim unless the design is actually approved or used. Such designs are in the nature of offers, or tenders, leading up to a possible contract, but for which there is no obligation to accept or pay.[15] It is not unusual " for architects to send in plans for public buildings taking the chance of being paid for their labour, or not, as they may be adopted or rejected ": *per* Maule J. in *Moffatt* v. *Laurie* (1855).[16] It is suggested that this practice is at the present day less common than formerly.

ILLUSTRATIONS

(1) M., an architect, agreed to examine the site of a proposed asylum and prepare " probationary drawings " for the approval of the committee of visitors, and he also agreed to prepare all other drawings, etc., required to be submitted to the Commissioners in

[13] 1 M. & S. 290. See also *Roberts* v. *Smith* (1859) 4 H. & N. 315.
[14] 2 C. & K. 707.
[15] For the rare cases where remuneration can be obtained by tenderers, see *post*, Chap. 3, pp. 229–231.
[16] 15 C.B. 583 at p. 587.

Lunacy pursuant to the statute, and subsequently to prepare the whole of the working drawings, estimates and specification for the asylum, for which the committee agreed to pay him £437 10s. M. prepared three sets of plans for approval, all of which were rejected, and finally the committee refused to proceed further. *Held*, that " probationary drawings " meant drawings to be approved by the committee for submission to the Commissioners and that as none had been approved, M. was not entitled to recover any remuneration: *Moffatt* v. *Dickson* (1853).[17] [Note: It cannot be certain that this case would be followed today. See, for instance, the analogous cases of work done by contractors in the preparation of tenders for building work in *Lacey* (*William*) v. *Davis* (1957) [18] and *Sinclair* v. *Logan* (1961).[19]]

(2) A, an architect, and B, a building owner, agreed that A should lay out lands for building and make surveys. A was to make no charge for this, but, in the event of the land being disposed of for building purposes, was to be appointed architect for B. A made the surveys. B died, and his executors put it out of their power to dispose of the land for building purposes. *Held*, that there was no implied contract not to dispose of the land otherwise than for building purposes: *Moffatt* v. *Laurie* (1855).[20]

(d) Competition drawings

Where plans or designs are submitted in competition, the same difficulties are likely to arise as in the case of probationary drawings and work done when preparing tenders for work and labour. The test is whether, objectively regarded, the circumstances at the time or which in the event occurred were such as to raise a presumption that the work was intended to be paid for. Obviously the terms of any invitation or purported acceptance will be highly relevant, but so too will be the general background of the transaction.[21]

ILLUSTRATION

Letters were addressed on behalf of the congregation of a church to the plaintiff and three other architects, inviting them to submit plans for a building not to exceed $32,000. If the plans were rejected, the competitor was to receive only $50. All were rejected except the plaintiff's, though his was found not to be in accordance with the conditions. The plaintiff sued upon a *quantum meruit* and obtained judgment for 1 per cent. of the limited price: *Hopkins* v. *Thompson* (1867).[22]

If the plans and estimates are used at all, even if not for the building, the employer must pay for them, unless some express condition excluding liability is inserted in the contract.

[17] 13 C.B. 543.
[18] [1957] 1 W.L.R. 932, *post*, Chap. 3, p. 230.
[19] 1961 S.L.T. (Sh.Ct.) 10, *post*, Chap. 3, p. 230.
[20] 15 C.B. 583.
[21] See also *ante*, Chap. 1, Section 2 (8), p. 18, and *post*, Chap. 3, pp. 280–282.
[22] 3 L.C.J. 36 (Canada).

ILLUSTRATION

A building owner was sued for the cost of preparing plans. The defence was that they were merely on approbation, and that payment was only to be made if they were used. It was true that they had not been used for building, but the building owner used the plans for the purpose of showing intending purchasers of the land how the land could be developed. *Held*, that the building owner must pay the architect: *Landless* v. *Wilson* (1880).[23]

In the above case Lord Shand said: " I think it right to say that if I had been of opinion that the case was one of a competition of plans between the two architects, and the defendant had afterwards thought fit not to build at all, I should have had great difficulty in holding that he would have been entitled to say to the competitors, ' You shall be paid nothing for the plans and labour you have bestowed . . . upon me.' My impression is that each of them would have been entitled to receive a *quantum meruit*."

(e) Amount of reasonable remuneration

In the case of *Brewer* v. *Chamberlain* (1949)[24] Birkett J. indicated the considerations to be applied in determining the reasonable remuneration to be paid to an architect for services which included the preparation of design and sketch drawings for a building project. Although he was considering the amount to be paid to the architect on a *quantum meruit* for partial services under clause 2 (e) of the R.I.B.A. Scale of Professional Charges, his observations were equally applicable to services rendered by an architect or engineer without any express agreement as to the amount of remuneration. The architect claimed to have his remuneration based upon a percentage of the estimated cost of works which had been abandoned, while the building owner claimed that the fees should be determined on a time basis of seven guineas a day. Birkett J. rejected both of these contentions on the ground that neither basis of calculation was appropriate in the circumstances. He rejected the building owner's contention, for the reason that it was impossible to measure on a time basis the value of services of architectural inspiration which solve a problem of how to deal with a particular situation. On the other hand, he rejected the basis of calculating the remuneration on a percentage basis of estimated cost because, as he said, he had to take into consideration other factors including:

[23] 8 R. (Ct. of Sess.) 289. *Cf.* also the cases *post*, Chap. 3, pp. 230–232.
[24] May 13, 1949 (unreported).

(a) the difficulties to be encountered and the merits of over-
     coming them;

(b) the experience and standing of the particular architect
     employed;

(c) the nature of the work done and what it entailed in drawings,
     interviews and correspondence.

When an architect is suing upon a *quantum meruit*, evidence can
be adduced of the nature and extent of his skill to show what the
value of his services is.[25] Where reasonable remuneration has
to be given, it is clear that the services of a famous or specially
skilled man would be valued more highly than those of a less qualified
person, and that the employer must be presumed to have had in
view the special qualifications of the famous man when he employed him. It is not relevant in such cases to prove that the employer could have got another man at a cheaper rate, as he in fact
selected this particular man.

ILLUSTRATION

An agent was employed under a special contract to superintend
the construction of a dry-dock, but died before the work was quite
finished. His executors sued for the value of his services. *Per* Balcom
J.: " It would be palpably unjust to disregard the stipulated value
of the testator's services; for it is evident that he was employed in
consequence of his integrity and capacity for the services required;
and to allow the defendant now to reduce the value of such service,
by proof of the sum for which he could have employed another
person to perform the same services, in whom he might or might not
have had confidence, would enable him, according to the first decision
of the referee, to gain more than $20,000 by the testator's death ":
Clark v. *Gilbert* (1863).[26]

The courts have not been entirely consistent in resisting attempts
to equate professional scales of charges with reasonable remuneration.[27] So in *Upsdell* v. *Stewart* (1794)[28] Lord Kenyon, in a case
where a surveyor employed to settle the builder's accounts sought
to charge a percentage on total cost, said: " As to the custom offered
to be proved, the course of robbery on Bagshot Heath might as well
be proved in a court of justice." And in *Burr* v. *Ridout* (1893)[29]
Lord Coleridge said of the scale that a commission upon expenditure

[25] *Bird* v. *McGaheg* (1849) 2 C. & K. 707 (N.P.), *supra*.
[26] 26 N.Y. 279.
[27] See *Att.-Gen.* v. *Drapers Co.* (1869) L.R. 9 Eq. 69; *Brocklebank* v. *Lancashire &*
     Yorkshire Ry. (1887) 3 T.L.R. 575; and *Buckland & Garrard* v. *Pawson & Co.* (1890)
     6 T.L.R. 421.
[28] Peake N.P. 255, *infra*, p. 188.
[29] *The Times*, February 22.

incurred was open to the gravest possible objection, and that the scale was an unjustifiable attempt by the Institute to increase professional emolument, and did not bind the employer unless he agreed to be bound by it. He gave a similar ruling in *Farthing* v. *Tomkins* (1893).[30] Further criticism of the attempted use of scales by quantity surveyors as a basis of reasonable remuneration for giving evidence was made by Lord Coleridge C.J. in *Drew* v. *Josolyne* (1888),[31] where he said that he " never would sanction the supposed rule that surveyors in such cases were to be paid for their evidence, not with reference to the work done, but by a percentage on the sum in dispute." [32]

ILLUSTRATIONS

(1) The plaintiff, an architect, sued for 4 per cent. as the customary charge for drawing plans and specification, and superintending the completion of a building. The court (Lower Canada) said: " I know of no right in architects, or in any other body of men, be they medical men, lawyers or others, to make tariffs for themselves. Mere proof that a charge of the sum in question is usual is wholly insufficient. It is, moreover, an unjust rule to establish, even in favour of the architects themselves, for it might happen that 4 per cent. was an utterly inadequate remuneration in certain cases ": *Fottner* v. *Joseph* (1859).[33]

(2) A prepared plans for an hotel at B's request, under instructions that the cost was not to exceed £8,000. The cost of the building planned would have been £12,000. The contractor required security, which B was not prepared to give, and finally the project was abandoned. *Held*, that A could not recover the Institute scale of 3 per cent. for the plans, but only his fair charges for the work actually done in the plans, drawings and specifications: *Farthing* v. *Tomkins* (1893).[34]

It is suggested that where the percentage can fairly be seen to reflect a large amount of miscellaneous administrative and other work which would be difficult to itemise (as, for instance, in the supervision and administration of a contract) a scale percentage may not be an unreasonable approach, whereas it seems irrational to apply a scale to a relatively clearly defined and easily itemised service (such as a report or a drawing or series of drawings) where estimates of time and personnel involved can easily be made.

---

[30] 9 T.L.R. 566, *supra*. See also *Debenham* v. *King's College, Cambridge* (1884) 1 Cab. & El. 438.

[31] 4 T.L.R. 717. For a modern Scottish case on this, see *Wilkie* v. *Scottish Aviation Ltd.*, 1956 S.C. 198.

[32] See also *per* Younger J. in *Faraday* v. *Tamworth Union* (1916) 86 L.J.Ch. 436 at p. 439.

[33] 3 L.C.J. 233; S.C. 5 L.C.J. 226.

[34] 9 T.L.R. 566. (A would seem to have been negligent, however—*ante*, pp. 144. *et seq.*—and his claim might have been resisted on that ground.)

It is submitted that the following extract from the headnote of a Scottish case is a correct statement of the law: " in the absence of express agreement regarding his remuneration, the pursuer was entitled to remuneration at the customary rate if he could prove the evidence of a custom which was reasonable, certain and notorious; that if no such custom were established it would be for the court to fix a reasonable remuneration; that accordingly if the schedule were shown to be the basis in practice on which the profession operated, the court, while entitled to take it into account, would not be bound rigidly to apply it unless satisfied that the resulting fee was reasonable in the circumstances." [35]

ILLUSTRATION

Developers had had an application for planning permission refused. An architect by his sole efforts, based on personal inspiration, resolved the differences between his clients (who were the developers' surveyors) and the planning authority, and put forward a scheme which obtained approval. The estimated cost of the project was £460,000 and the successful application earned fees for the surveyors totalling £30,000. The land had also appreciated in value. The architect claimed £4,600, based on the provision for *quantum meruit* " not exceeding one sixth of [6 per cent.] of the cost of the works " in the R.I.B.A. scales. *Held*, by Browne J., following *Brewer* v. *Chamberlain* (1949) [36] that the scale, whether or not incorporated, was some evidence of what was reasonable; the factors to be taken into account were: that the architect had achieved the result wanted; the surveyor's fees of £30,000 but not the increase in the value of the land; the high qualifications and experience of the architect; the considerable architectural merit of the scheme; the size and value of the building work relative to the percentage basis; and since inspiration based on experience was the decisive factor, the time taken was less important than otherwise would be the case. The problem for the court was difficult, and the maximum of £4,600 was only a yardstick. £2,100 would be awarded: *Graham & Baldwin* v. *Taylor, Son & Davis* (1965).[37]

(2) For Uncompleted Services

When a contract of employment between the building owner and the architect has been partly performed, and there is a refusal or failure on the part of the building owner to complete the employment,[38] the architect can sue for all sums due at the time of the breach and for the profits lost by reason of the breach, not exceeding the amount specified in the contract, or, under the principle in *Lodder*

[35] See *Wilkie* v. *Scottish Aviation Ltd.*, 1956 S.C. 198 (Scotland).
[36] K.B.D., May 13, 1949, Birkett J. (unreported).
[37] 109 S.J. 793. See also *Kelly* v. *Northshore Development, infra*, pp. 191–192.
[38] See the discussion *ante*, Section 3 (4), pp. 101 *et seq.*

v. *Slowey* (1904),[39] may treat the contract as at an end and sue upon a *quantum meruit.*

The contract may, however, and often does, contemplate that the employer may abandon the project and terminate the architect's services at certain stages.[38] In such cases the contract usually sets out the basis of the architect's remuneration for partial services or abandoned work.

ILLUSTRATION

In June 1933, the defendant council resolved to appoint the plaintiff architect in connection with its scheme for the erection of a town hall, and to pay his fees in accordance with the R.I.B.A. scale, which was to be inclusive of all incidental fees and services. This was accepted by the plaintiff. A fee for partial services was provided for by clause 5: " If the project or part of it be abandoned, or if the services of the architect cease or are dispensed with before a contract is entered into or order given, the charges in respect of the works abandoned or for which the architect was employed (as the case may be) are as follows: (*a*) for taking client's instructions, preparing sketch design and making approximate estimate of cost by cubic measurement or otherwise, one-fourth of the percentage on the estimated cost of such works; (*b*) for taking client's instructions, preparing sketch design, making approximate estimate of cost by cubic measurement or otherwise, and preparing drawings and particulars sufficient to enable quantities to be prepared or a tender obtained, two-thirds of the percentage of the estimated cost of such works." In September 1935, the council decided to abandon the scheme and to terminate the plaintiff's agreement. At that time he had on their express instructions done all the work set out in clause 5 (*a*) and a substantial part of the additional work set out in clause 5 (*b*). In an action against the council the plaintiff contended that, having employed him on the subject-matter of clause 5 (*b*), they could not exercise their power of abandoning the project or terminating his employment at the end of the work contemplated in clause 5 (*a*), and accordingly were obliged to permit him to complete his work and earn his fee under clause 5 (*b*) or pay damages for breach of contract in preventing him from so doing. *Held*, that the defendants, having instructed the plaintiff to proceed with the work in clause 5 (*b*), had lost their right of terminating his employment at the end of the work in clause 5 (*a*), and were therefore under an obligation to allow him to earn the fee for the work in clause 5 (*b*), and, having broken their contract, they were liable to pay him for the work actually done in respect of the latter and damages: *Thomas* v. *Hammersmith Borough Council* (1938).[40]

Provided, however, that the agreed remuneration is paid, the architect can have no complaint if he is not in fact permitted to complete the project.

[39] [1904] A.C. 442; see *ante*, Chap. 1, pp. 62–63 and *post*, Chap. 9, p. 602.
[40] 82 S.J. 583. See also *Stubbs* v. *Holywell Ry., post*, Chap. 5, p. 256.

ILLUSTRATION

A contract was made by a board of health to employ an engineer about works and pay him £500 during two years, he undertaking to do his best in order to complete the works within that period. *Held*, that the board was not liable for refusing to allow him to carry on the works beyond that time, although the delay was caused by their fault or default, they paying him the whole £500: *Rutledge* v. *Farnham Local Board of Health* (1861).[41]

(3) By whom Remuneration Payable

The architect can only look to the person who employs him for payment of his services, unless he can prove an agreement with himself by some other person to meet his fees, or can frame an action in quasi-contract for money had and received as where, under the old practice, an architect's or surveyor's fees were sometimes paid to the builder under the terms of the building contract for onward transmission by him.

ILLUSTRATION

A building owner employed L., an architect, to superintend certain building works, and the contract was silent as to who was to pay L.'s commission. In an action by L. against the builder for this commission, *held*, that he could not succeed unless the builder had first received the commission from the building owner in addition to what was due to him upon the contract: *Locke* v. *Morter* (1885).[43]

(4) Services Outside Building Contracts

Other services, besides the preparation of plans for building and engineering contracts and the supervision of the work, are performed by engineers, architects and surveyors, such as making valuations, surveys and measurements, attending in court and before arbitrators to give evidence, etc. In this class of work also the courts have refused to recognise any other basis of remuneration than that of reasonableness, unless previous agreement has been reached, but detailed consideration of this subject is not within the scope of the present work.[44]

---

[41] 2 F. & F. 406. See also the South African case of *Bennett* v. *Capetown Foreshore Board*, illustrated *ante* p. 100.

[43] 2 T.L.R. 121. For an example of the latter, see *Payne* v. *Wheeldon* (1954) 104 L.J. 844 (county court).

[44] See *Att.-Gen.* v. *Drapers Co.* (1869) L.R. 9 Eq. 69; *Debenham* v. *King's College, Cambridge* (1884) 1 T.L.R. 170; *Brocklebank* v. *L. & Y. Ry.* (1887) 3 T.L.R. 575; *Drew* v. *Josolyne* (1888) 4 T.L.R. 717; *Faraday* v. *Tamworth Union* (1916) 86 L.J.Ch. 439. *Wilkie* v. *Scottish Aviation Ltd.*, 1956 S.C. 198 (Scotland).

(5) Charges for Settling Builders' Accounts

An architect or surveyor is sometimes specially employed to look over and settle the amount of builders' or sub-contractors' accounts. In such cases, in the absence of special agreement or proof of custom, he is not entitled to charge a percentage on the amount, but only a reasonable payment for the services he has rendered.[45]

ILLUSTRATION

A surveyor claimed £34, being 5 per cent. on all money charged by and allowed to the different tradesmen in a building work. He had done nothing more than measure the work and settle the bills, not being at all employed in building the house. *Held*, that the plaintiff was entitled to a reasonable compensation for his labour, but he must not estimate that by the money laid out by the defendant in finishing his building—*per* Lord Kenyon, " As to the custom offered to be proved, the course of robbery on Bagshot Heath might as well be proved in a court of justice ": *Upsdell* v. *Stewart* (1794).[46]

It is submitted that no such custom exists at the present day, or would be held to be reasonable if it did, particularly since there could be no certainty as to the percentage in question.[47]   A percentage might be supported in evidence as being reasonable, however.[48]

(6) When the Right to Payment Arises

On general principles, when an architect contracts to perform an entire work, as, for instance, to prepare drawings and superintend the whole work for a certain sum, whether fixed on the basis of a commission on the outlay or otherwise, his charges are not recoverable until the whole work is complete, unless provision is made for payment by instalments.   In the view of the long-term nature of architects' work, it would seem reasonable to imply a term for reasonable payments on account, but there is as yet little authority in the general law of contract on this topic.[49]   The R.I.B.A. scale of charges, as already pointed out, makes provision for payment by instalments.

(7) Retention of Plans and Documents

When an engineer, architect or surveyor is employed to perform a specific work, such as to prepare plans or make a survey, he is entitled to be paid for his plans or survey as soon as he has done

---

[45] For a modern case on quantity surveyor's remuneration for adjustment of variations during the course of the work, see *Kelly's* case, *infra*, subs. (9), p. 192.

[46] (1794) Peake N.P. 255.

[47] See *ante*, Chap. 1, p. 53.

[48] See subsection (9), *infra*.   See also *supra*, p. 184.

[49] As to entire contracts, see *post*, pp. 243 *et seq.*; for the absence of any implication of payment by instalments or on account, and a possible exception, see *post*, Chap. 5, pp. 255 *et seq.*

the work and given the employer a reasonable opportunity of inspecting and ascertaining its correctness, and he has a lien upon and may retain the plans until he is so paid.

An architect or surveyor, by demanding more than a reasonable price and refusing to deliver his plans except upon payment of the excessive price, does not preclude himself from subsequently suing for and recovering a reasonable price. He may maintain an action and retain his lien notwithstanding.[50] But upon payment of the architect's charges he must deliver up his plans, unless it has been stipulated that they are not to become the property of the employer. Architects frequently take advantage of this in contracts which have run into trouble, where the employer and his advisers may need to see the documentation and correspondence before deciding against whom they should pursue a claim. A valuable remedy in this situation is that afforded by R.S.C., Ord. 50, r. 8, by virtue of which, on payment of the fees demanded into court to abide the result of the litigation, the architect's lien is discharged and he is bound to surrender the documents. Apart from plans or drawings actually made by the architect, the principle is the same in the case of all maps, plans and other documents relating to the contract collected by him in the course of his employment.[51]

ILLUSTRATIONS

(1) The defendants employed the plaintiff (a surveyor) to survey a parish and then to put down the results of his survey, first in the books provided for him by the defendants, and afterwards on paper to be provided by them for him in the shape of a map or plan. He made a plan, and wrote, saying that he would deliver it on payment of his charges. The defendants inspected the plan. The defendants refused to pay, and the plaintiff retained the plan, and sued for and recovered his charges: *Hughes* v. *Lenny* (1839).[52]

(2) B. employed D. as a land agent, and paid him by commission. In the course of D.'s employment he made memoranda relating to the estate, maps, plans and calculations, etc. D. was discharged from his employment. *Held*, that D. must give up all documents relating to the estate made or collected by him in the course of his employment: *Beresford (Lady)* v. *Driver* (1852).[53]

(8) Ownership and Copyright of Plans and Documents

There is no custom or any general or binding usage to the effect that the plans belong to the architect and not to his employer.[54]

---

[50] *Hughes* v. *Lenny* (1839) 5 M. & W. 183.
[51] See also subsection (8), *infra*.
[52] 5 M. & W. 183.
[53] 22 L.J.Ch. 407.
[54] *Gibbon* v. *Pease* [1905] 1 K.B. 810; *Ebdy* v. *McGowan* (1870) Hudson's B.C., 4th ed., Vol. 2, p. 9; *Moffat* v. *Scott* (1863) 8 L.C.J. 310 (Canada).

While the position of plans presents little difficulty, it may not be easy to decide the ownership of the very large number of miscellaneous documents and correspondence which normally come into existence during the course of the architect's administration of a building contract. It is suggested that the test is whether a document comes into existence or is obtained by the architect as a part of the discharge of his function as agent of the employer for which he is paid.

Thus it is submitted that letters written to the contractor in relation to the contract, correspondence with quantity surveyors or clerks of works appointed under the contract, local and planning authorities, consultants of all kinds, and all other correspondence arising in the administration of the contract satisfy the test and are the property of the employer.[55] On the other hand, personal memoranda or communications between members of his own staff or firm, and calculations and private notes used by them, will remain his property.[56] In cases where a site supervisory organisation is maintained, it is submitted that correspondence passing between the site and the architect's or engineer's office, such as between engineer and resident engineer, or between architect and architect's assistant on site, will be the property of the employer even if the correspondents are in fact employees of the same firm.

So far as copyright is concerned, in the absence of express provision in the contract of employment, the copyright in all plans and drawings remains with the architect. Independently of this copyright, the architect has a copyright in the artistic character or design of *the building itself* (but not of any process or method of construction),[57] so that, for example, if the employer commissions an extension or addition matching the external appearance or internal layout of an existing building, there will be a breach of the copyright in that building owned by its original architect, even if his plans are long lost and not used for the extension or addition.[58] This does not, however, mean that the original architect has any right to be employed on later work, or that his damages for breach of copyright have any connection with the profit he would have earned had he been engaged on the later project.[59] The damages will be based on

---

[55] See *Beresford's* case, *supra.*
[56] See A. L. Smith J.'s judgment in *London School Board* v. *Northcroft* (1889) Hudson's B.C., 4th ed., Vol. 2, p. 147; illustrated *infra*, p. 192.
[57] Copyright Act 1911, s. 35 (1).
[58] *Meikle* v. *Maufe* [1941] 3 All E.R. 144.
[59] *Ibid.*

a reasonable licence fee. Furthermore, the Copyright Act of 1911 expressly prevents any injunction or other remedy issuing to interfere with the physical construction of a building in breach of this latter copyright, once work on it has commenced.[60]

(9) Remuneration of Quantity Surveyors

In practice, whether or not there has been express agreement, quantity surveyors usually submit their accounts for preparing bills of quantities by reference to a percentage calculated on the contract price.[61] In *Gwyther* v. *Gaze* (1875) [62] Quain J., after a conflict of evidence, assessed the remuneration at $1\frac{1}{2}$ per cent., but this was a jury case, and each side was putting forward a percentage. It is submitted that on the principles previously discussed [63] evidence might in theory be received to show a reasonable percentage for true quantity surveyor's work in preparing bills, but it should be remembered that, since the date of the above case, the practice of inserting P.C. or provisional lump sums in bills of quantities has greatly increased both in frequency and extent, and that this inevitably has the effect of greatly reducing the labours of the quantity surveyor, which are virtually nominal in relation to such items.[64]

It is suggested that where, for example, 60 per cent. of the contract price is billed in this way (which nowadays is by no means uncommon) a building owner would be justified in demanding a considerable reduction in the scale percentages, and that an architect with authority to employ a quantity surveyor on his behalf should be slow to agree to remuneration based on the full percentages on total cost for these services.

However, there seems little doubt that modern courts will use scales at least as a yardstick when assessing reasonable remuneration.[65]

ILLUSTRATION

Quantity surveyors' remuneration for adjustment of variations during the course of the work were to be $2\frac{1}{2}$ per cent. on the value of measured additions and $1\frac{1}{2}$ per cent. on measured omissions (excluding omissions not involving the exercise of professional skill). The

---

[60] Copyright Act 1911, s. 9 (1).
[61] Compare the attempt to set up a custom in regard to fees for settling the builder's account, *supra*, subsection (5).
[62] Hudson's B.C., 4th ed., Vol. 2, p. 34, illustrated *post*, p. 196.
[63] *Ante*, Section 9 (1) (*e*), pp. 182–184.
[64] For a discussion of these items see *post*, Chap. 3, pp. 205–206, and Chap. 15, pp. 758–761.
[65] Compare the cases on architect's remuneration, *supra*, subsection (1).

contract sum was £46,000 and the final cost £68,000, but so many variations had been ordered that the quantity surveyors were, as a practical necessity, obliged to remeasure the whole work. The employer contended, and the trial judge awarded, that they should be paid 2½ per cent. on the excess of £22,000. The quantity surveyors contended that they should be paid 2½ per cent. on the whole £68,000, the contract sum being treated as an omission involving no professional skill; alternatively they claimed *quantum meruit*. *Held*, by the Court of Appeal of Jamaica, that since the contract did not contemplate such a large number of variations the provision could not be applied in this different situation; the surveyors were entitled to reasonable remuneration and the trial judge was wrong in only giving a percentage on the excess, since this ignored the fact that the actual variations greatly exceeded the net excess, and would mean, for example, that the surveyors would obtain nothing if after a great many variations the final result was the same as the contract sum. A reasonable basis would be to apply the provision for preparation of bills of quantities, namely 2½ per cent. on the first £20,000 and 2 per cent. on the balance: *Kelly (C.T.R.) & Partners* v. *Northshore Development Co. Ltd.* (1963).[66]

The quantity surveyor usually charges for lithographing his quantities, employing and paying his own lithographer, in which case he may retain any cash discount obtained by him, but must not accept anything in the nature of a commission from such lithographer, nor retain any trade discount.[67]

The charges for lithography are sometimes, however, included in the contract as part of the builder's tender.[68]

ILLUSTRATION

The L. School Board employed N., as a quantity surveyor and measurer, on buildings of the value of £12,000, which had been completed and measured up. The board brought an action in detinue against N. for the return of certain papers of calculations and memoranda and in money had and received in respect of £74 charged by N. for lithography. *Held*, (1) that the measuring up having been done, the board had no right to the memoranda; (2) as to a sum of 15 per cent. paid by the lithographers to N., that though N. being the board's agent, the payment of any commission to N. was illegal and improper, yet, as it was agreed that N. should employ his own lithographer, he might retain this, which was really discount for cash: *London School Board* v. *Northcroft* (1889).[69]

---

[66] (1963) 5 W.I.R. 379 (West Indies). Contrast *Gilbert & Partners* v. *Knight* (1968) 112 S.J. 155, illustrated *ante*, Chap. 1, p. 18. See also *supra*, p. 178.

[67] *London School Board* v. *Northcroft* (1889) Hudson's B.C., 4th ed., Vol. 2, p. 147; *Hippisley* v. *Knee Brothers* [1905] 1 K.B. 1.

[68] See, in addition to the case illustrated, *Campbell* v. *Blyton* (1893) Hudson's B.C., 4th ed., Vol. 2, p. 234.

[69] Hudson's B.C., 4th ed., Vol. 2, p. 147.

SECTION 10.   LIABILITY FOR QUANTITY SURVEYOR'S FEES

(1) Liability for Preparing Bills

At first sight this problem would not appear to present any difficulty, and the normal assumption would be that the building owner is the employer of the quantity surveyor.   Historically, however, quantity surveyors were first employed jointly by the tendering builders to take out quantities, on the basis that payment would be made by the builder ultimately selected to carry out the work.

Probably because it was more convenient for the architect to discuss his design with the quantity surveyor at an earlier stage, it later became the practice for the architect himself to engage the quantity surveyor to prepare the bills, on the basis that payment for this service would be made by the successful tenderer, and to insert a provision into the building contract to that effect.   Consistently with this, it was not unusual to find a provision in the contract with the builder for payment to him of these fees, usually under a provisional sum.   The R.I.B.A. forms of contract had, until 1963, an optional clause for this method of payment via the builder.   It is clear from *Moon* v. *Witney Union* (1837) [70] that this practice was established as early as 1837.   It is important to appreciate that at this time bills did not form part of the contract,[71] but were merely the application of the correct first-stage technique for pricing work, serving as a guide for this purpose for all tenderers.   Because only one person took off the quantities, this part of the cost of tendering was reduced to nothing in the case of the unsuccessful tenderers.   At this time, therefore, the work was primarily for the benefit of the builders, and only secondarily of the employer (who might expect to receive tenders somewhat lower than would be the case if builders had to recover on successful tenders the surveyor's charges incurred by them on their other unsuccessful tenders).   It is therefore not surprising that in the older cases the courts took the view that, by reason of the provision in the building contract for payment of the surveyor by the builder, a contractual relationship between builder and quantity surveyor came into being, and the surveyor could accordingly sue the builder for his fees in contract.[72]   So too in cases where the architect himself prepared the bills, and

---

[70] *Ante*, pp. 113–114.
[71] See *post*, Chap. 8, pp. 509 *et seq.*
[72] *North* v. *Bassett* [1892] 1 Q.B. 333, *infra*, p. 197.

the term for payment was to be found in the building contract, a contractual relationship was accepted by the courts.[73]

A difficulty, however, arose where, for one reason or another, the project was abandoned and no contract was ever let. In these circumstances, of course, the surveyor sought to recover his fees from the building owner, and the courts overcame this difficulty by holding that there was a " conditional " contract which, once the contract was let, replaced the original engagement of the surveyor, and made the builder responsible to him. So, Tindal C.J. in *Moon* v. *Witney Union* (1837) [74] said: " It appears that the custom is beneficial to the parties concerned; that if builders are not assisted by surveyors they send in tenders which lead to loss and inconvenience from a mistake in the quantities. . . . L. (the defendant's attorney) gave out that the successful competitor should defray the expense of taking out the quantities. If this was to be so, what was to be the result if by the act of the defendants there was no successful competitor because there was no competitor at all? In such a case the defendants must be liable for the amount of a charge which they have authorised their builder to incur. . . . This is a conditional contract—a contract under which it was arranged that the expenses of making out the quantities should be paid by the successful competitor (if any); but, if by the act of the defendants there should be no competitor, then, that work which was ordered by their authority should be paid for by them."

And Field J. in *Young* v. *Smith* (1880) [75] said: " What is the contract made with the quantity surveyor? . . . The contract is not a contract for payment, it is a contract that ' I will go on regularly in course to obtain a contractor who by his contract shall not only contract that he will build the house, but shall also enter into an implied contract with you (the quantity surveyor) that if I will add to the sum mentioned in the contract the sum due to him, he (the builder) will pay you.' That is the conditional contract; therefore, if things take their ordinary course, that contract will be completed by the course of conduct."

This case was carried to the Court of Appeal, and came before Bramwell, Baggallay and Brett L.JJ. and the decision of Field J. was upheld. No question of the liability of the quantity surveyor for inaccuracies was in issue or was discussed, but it is plain that the courts had not appreciated that this somewhat ingenious theory,

[73] *Bolt* v. *Thomas* (1859) Hudson's B.C., 4th ed., Vol. 2, p. 3, *infra*, p. 196.
[74] 3 Bing.N.C. 814, at p. 818.
[75] Hudson's B.C., 4th ed., Vol. 2, p. 70, *infra*, pp. 196–197.

which surmounted any difficulties as to remuneration, created a major difficulty of a different kind. To whom, during the various stages of this conditional arrangement, did the quantity surveyor owe his professional duty of skill and care? In particular, could he be liable *to the builder* for inaccuracies in the bills? In *Bolt* v. *Thomas* (1859) [76] Byles J. was prepared to hold in principle that he could, but in *Priestley* v. *Stone* (1888) [77] the Court of Appeal recoiled from such a conclusion, and in doing so expressed grave doubts as to the validity of the customary practice upon which the legal position had previously been based. Despite the fact that *North* v. *Bassett* [78] was decided in 1892, it seems clear that by the end of the century the customary usage was in decline [79] and the decision at least can be fully justified on the basis of an action for money had and received.

In spite of the absence of modern authority, it cannot be seriously doubted that, in the United Kingdom at least, the quantity surveyor is today employed by the building owner, or by his architect acting under the express or implied authority of the building owner.[80] The bills today are almost invariably a contract document [81] and have to be meticulously prepared [82] to protect the employer's interests in many respects and (under the standard forms of building contract) to embody in detail the architect's specification of the work. Indeed, it would be wholly wrong and inconsistent with the quantity surveyor's employment, it is submitted, for him to have any contractual or financial relationship with the builder.[83]

Until 1963 the R.I.B.A. standard forms contained an optional clause whereby the builder was responsible for paying the quantity surveyor's fees out of the money certified to him.[84] This and similar provisions in other contracts represent the last vestiges of the old practice which in the past proved so troublesome to the courts, and in the absence of express provision should be regarded as mere administrative machinery for the payment of the surveyor's fees having no bearing on the contractual rights or duties of the quantity

---

[76] Hudson's B.C., 4th ed., Vol. 2, p. 3, *infra*.
[77] 4 T.L.R. 730, *infra* p. 197. See also *Scrivener* v. *Pask* (1866) L.R. 1 C.P. 715, illustrated *post*, Chap. 8, pp. 511–512.
[78] *Infra*.
[79] *Antisell* v. *Doyle* [1899] 2 I.R. 275, *ante*, p. 114.
[80] See *ante*, pp. 112 *et seq.*
[81] See *post*, Chap. 8, pp. 509 *et seq.*
[82] See *post*, p. 519.
[83] See *ante*, pp. 175–177; and the case of *Thornton Hall* v. *Wembley Electrical Appliances Ltd.* [1947] 2 All E.R. 630 there referred to.
[84] Clause 10.

surveyor. Where, however, a builder has actually been paid the amount of the surveyor's fees under such an arrangement, the surveyor will have an action in quasi-contract for money had and received.[85]

ILLUSTRATIONS

(1) *Moon* v. *Witney Union* (1837).[86]

(2) The plaintiff, a builder, sued the defendant, an architect, for supplying inaccurate quantities. The defendant had advertised for tenders, stating that plans could be seen and quantities would be furnished. The plaintiff obtained a bill of quantities, headed by a statement that the quantities were to be paid for by the successful competitor. From this bill the plaintiff calculated his tender, which was accepted, and according to the plaintiff's evidence, which was contradicted by the defendant, the latter expressly stated to the plaintiff that he was responsible to him for the quantities. Byles J., summing up, directed the jury that the defendant had stipulated that the plaintiff should pay him for the calculation of the quantities, and, having been paid by him, that he was liable to compensate him if the bill was not reasonably accurate: *Bolt* v. *Thomas* (1859).[87]

(3) The defendant, wishing to erect a warehouse, dwellinghouse and shop, instructed S., an architect, to prepare plans, and S. instructed the plaintiff to take out quantities. Three tenders were sent in, but none was accepted. It was proved that it was usual for an architect who prepared plans to employ a surveyor to take out quantities, but that if no tender was accepted, the employer paid him. The warehouse was subsequently erected, mainly after S.'s plans, by a builder who was not one of those who tendered on, and who had not seen, the plaintiff's quantities. The defendant's case was that the architect had only a limited authority, and that he was told that the defendant had engaged a builder and that there was no necessity to take out quantities so as to enable the builder to tender. Quain J. left it to the jury to say whether the architect's authority was limited in the way stated by the defendant, and told them that if it was not so limited the defendant was liable to pay the plaintiff a reasonable remuneration for taking out quantities, and the plaintiff obtained a verdict: *Gwyther* v. *Gaze* (1875).[88]

(4) The defendant's architect, with his knowledge, engaged the plaintiff to take out quantities; tenders were sent in, and the plaintiff's charges were included in the summary. A tender was accepted, the defendant having seen the summary, and the work began. The defendant requested the architect not to include the plaintiff's charges in the earlier certificates in order to keep them moderate. After certificates had been granted to the extent of £1,100 the builder failed, and the defendant took the work into his own hands. The plaintiff applied to the builder for his charges, and on being told that they had not been included in any certificate, sued the defendant on the ground that the defendant had by design prevented him from obtaining his

---

[85] See *e.g.* the county court case of *Payne* v. *Wheeldon* (1954) 104 L.J. 844.
[86] For the facts of this case, see *ante*, pp. 113–114.
[87] Hudson's B.C., 4th ed., Vol. 2, p. 3.
[88] Hudson's B.C., 4th ed., Vol. 2, p. 34.

charges in the usual way. Field J. nonsuited the plaintiff, saying that the defendant had been guilty of no default, and the Court of Appeal approved his decision: *Young* v. *Smith* (1880).[89]

(5) An architect employed a quantity surveyor to take out quantities from his plans. The quantities were prepared and lithographed. The builders brought an action alleging that the surveyor had in breach of duty prepared an inaccurate bill of quantities and that they had suffered damage. *Held*, by the Court of Appeal, there was no privity of contract between the quantity surveyors and the builder. *Per* Lindley L.J., the custom relied on as to privity between builders and quantity surveyors was not proved, and even if proved, would probably be held to be unreasonable: *Priestley* v. *Stone* (1888).[90]

(6) The plaintiff, a quantity surveyor, was employed by an architect to take out the quantities for a building about to be erected; the defendant, a builder, tendered for the work upon the basis of a specification containing the following clause: " To provide for copies of quantities and plans twenty-five guineas to be paid to the surveyor (naming the plaintiff) out of the first certificate." The defendant's tender was accepted, and he received the first instalment of the price of his work from the building owner. In an action by the plaintiff against the builder to recover the twenty-five guineas according to the specification, evidence was given that by the usage of the building trade the builder whose tender was accepted was liable to the quantity surveyor for the amount due for the quantities, but that if no tender was accepted the building owner or architect was liable. *Held*, that the usage was reasonable and valid, and that there was evidence of a contract with the plaintiff upon which he was entitled to recover: *North* v. *Bassett* (1892).[91]

(2) Liability for Measuring up

If the old practice no longer obtains as to preparing bills, it must obviously be the more true of the quantity surveyor's duties involved in valuing the builder's work for interim certificates and in measuring and valuing the work on completion. Despite the decision in *Birdseye* v. *Dover Harbour Commissioners*[92] in 1881, the cases of *Beattie* v. *Gilroy* (1882), *Plimsaul* v. *Kilmorey* (*Lord*) (1884) and *Locke* v. *Morter* (1885)[93] show that any customary practice to this effect did not persist for long.

---

[89] Hudson's B.C., 4th ed., Vol. 2, p. 70.
[90] 4 T.L.R. 730. See also *Scrivener* v. *Pask* (1866) L.R. 1 C.P. 715, illustrated pp. 511–512.
[91] [1892] 1 Q.B. 333. But see *Antisell* v. *Doyle* (1899), *ante*, p. 114.
[92] *Ante*, p. 117.
[93] These are illustrated *ante*, pp. 117–118, 119.

CHAPTER 3

TENDERS AND ESTIMATES

SECTION 1. TYPES OF TENDER DOCUMENTS

(1) Generally

THE normal preliminary to the conclusion of a building or engineering contract is an invitation by the employer to one or more contractors to tender a price at which they are willing to carry out the works required by him. In practice the invitation is usually made on his behalf by the employer's architect or engineer, if he has employed one, and the latter will require express authority for this purpose if he is to charge fees for this service, since mere instructions to prepare plans and estimates of cost will not authorise the obtaining of tenders.[1]

In the United Kingdom, where works of any magnitude are involved, the invitation usually describes the work required to be carried out and specifies the period of time for its execution, though the period may be left open for the contractors to stipulate, or for negotiation when the successful tenderer has been selected. In this type of contract, the architect or engineer of the employer designs the proposed works beforehand, and prepares drawings and a specification or bills of quantities for inclusion in the tender documents, and either identifies by reference (usually to a standard form of contract) or includes in the tender documents specifically drafted conditions of contract regulating the entire contractual position between the parties, and defining in detail the contractual obligations which the tenderer will be required to assume in the carrying out and maintenance of the works.

But this is not universal. The employer may choose to dispense with professional assistance. Thus much of the repair and decoration of buildings and the simpler forms of new construction are tendered for by builders using descriptions, drawings or specifications prepared by themselves. Furthermore even in large projects it has already been noted [2] that work is beginning to be placed under

[1] See *ante*, Chap. 2, pp. 101 *et seq.*
[2] *Ante*, Chap. 1, pp. 2–3; Chap. 2, p. 82.

" package deal " or " industrialised building " contracts whereby
the contractors employ their own architects or engineers to design
the project, or a substantial part of it, and prepare the drawings, and
expressly or impliedly accept responsibility for its design.   No
standard form of contract for such an arrangement exists in either
industry, however, and the anomalies and dangers of using such
arrangements, due largely to the basic conflict of interest between
employer and contractor in regard to design which such arrangements
permit, unless adequate contractual protection for the employer
and certain consequential rights for the builder are available, appear
not to be understood by those responsible for advocating their use.
Subsection (2) (e) below gives some indication of the sort of problems
that need to be dealt with by those concerned with drafting such
contracts.

In addition, it sometimes happens that the employer wishes to
obtain tenders before the full extent of the work is known, or his
advisers have had time to design the work.   In such a case, only a
general description of the work can be given, and a form of tender
to suit the circumstances should be adopted.[3]   But far too often
this is not done, probably because of the absence of any standard
form available for this situation, and the contract is let with one
of the current very detailed standard forms, but with only a vestigial
bill of quantities or specification.   This is a situation in which
the lack of precision in defining the work is an invitation to contractors to make claims based upon alleged variations or delay
in supplying information (notwithstanding that in tendering they
could have been under no illusions as to the position) and in which
the apparent bulk and complication of the documents may conceal
from the employer the facts not only that the work is virtually unplanned but also that the tender price bears little or no relation to
the price he may ultimately have to pay, even if no special claims
are made.[4]   In 1967 the R.I.B.A. published a "fixed fee" form of
cost-plus contract, but it is difficult to see precisely with what sort
of situation the contract is designed to deal, and the fee in fact
appears to be subject to increase in circumstances which are quite
undefined.[4a]

The following broad categories of contractual arrangement
where an employer uses a professional adviser, and which have
come before the courts in the last century, may be useful before

---

[3] See *infra*, subs. (3), pp. 210 *et seq.*
[4] See *infra*, p. 210.
[4a] See particularly clause 3.

considering the tender documents likely to be in use at the present day:

(1) Contracts using drawings and a specification only, where the terms of the contractor's express undertaking to complete the particular project, as described elsewhere in the contract documents in general terms, were taken to prevail over the technical documents, and if there was, by inadvertence or otherwise, a failure to show all the necessary work in precise terms in the documents, the contractor was nevertheless bound to do the whole of the necessary work for the agreed contract price. In such a case the specification and drawings were regarded as a minimum, and not a final and definitive, statement of the work undertaken for the contract price.[5] Smaller less formal jobbing contracts frequently fall into this category at the present day—for instance an informal contract to supply and fit a door may or may not, on its true construction, include an obligation to supply hinges, a door handle and lock or other " furniture," notwithstanding that the contract is silent on the point, for the agreed price.

(2) Contracts using a specification and drawings, and possibly bills of quantities, where the specification and drawings were held to be the definitive description of the contract work, and any bills of quantities, if they existed, only a guide for pricing to the tendering contractors. In such cases the bills did not " form part of the contract " in legal terms, and no adjustment to the price was made if the quantities in the bills turned out to be incorrect.[6] These contracts became known as " fixed price " or " lump sum " contracts. Although the use of bills in this way is today virtually unknown, this type of contract with a specification but without bills is exemplified by the current R.I.B.A. standard forms without quantities.

(3) Contracts using bills of quantities, with or without a specification, where the quantities were held to be the exact measure of the work undertaken by the builder for the price quoted, although the builder remained liable to complete all the work shown on the drawings or specification, with the result that either party might claim to remeasure the work and if necessary recalculate the contract price at the end of

[5] See, e.g. Williams v. Fitzmaurice (1858) 3 H. & N. 844, post, Chap. 5, pp. 265–266.
[6] See post, pp. 509 et seq.

the works, whether or not variations had been ordered.[7]
This type of contract is exemplified at the present day by the
R.I.B.A. standard forms with quantities, and by the I.C.E.
Conditions. They were sometimes described in the past as
contracts " for measure and value " or even as " schedule
contracts," and the only real difference is that, the work to
be done being usually known with some precision beforehand,
the contract at the present day contains an overall contract
price or sum calculated by grossing up all the prices and
quantities in the bills, notwithstanding that this price is,
by definition, subject to readjustment if the actual quantities
differ.

(4)   Contracts using schedules of rates or prices, with or without
drawings or a specification.   These may be used for the
purpose of valuing the whole work where the total amount
of work to be done is not known at the time of contracting,
so that there will usually be no quantities given, or only very
approximate quantities, and accordingly the contract will
not contain a calculated contract sum as in the bill contracts.
If the quantities of work are known at that time, and described
in the documents, there is little legal or practical difference
between these contracts and contracts with quantities in
the modern form.   Schedules of rates are also found, however, in contracts without quantities for the limited purpose
of valuing variations and sometimes, as in the case of
the R.I.B.A. specification forms, the contract somewhat
imprudently leaves them to be prepared at a later stage after
the contract is let.

It may also assist if an indication is given of some of the expressions used to describe these various contractual arrangements,
and possible sources of confusion. " Fixed price contract " may
mean a contract using a specification only but not bills of quantities,
or where any bills of quantities do not form part of the contract, so
that the price is fixed and does not vary if there are errors in the
quantities in the bills. It may also mean a contract (with or without
bills) which has no fluctuations clause. " Lump sum " contract may
mean a fixed price contract in the first of the above senses, or it may
be used in its legal sense to mean an entire contract in which the law
will not imply any term for stage payments (a contract using bills
would also be a lump sum contract in this sense), and in which the

---

[7] See *post*, Chap. 8, pp. 509 *et seq.*

obligation to complete is, subject to the doctrine of substantial performance, unqualified in the legal sense.[8] " Variation " or " variation of price clause " may mean a clause enabling the work, and consequently the contract sum, to be varied, or a fluctuations clause enabling the contract sum to be adjusted for rises or falls in the cost of labour or materials. To avoid confusion, in this book contracts are usually referred to as being in the bill or specification form, or with or without quantities, " lump sum " is used, if at all, in its legal sense, and "variation clauses" and "fluctuations clauses" are so described in the two opposing senses referred to.

(2) Where Extent of Work is Known at Time of Contract

(a) Drawings

The drawings used for the purpose of tender (from which any bills of quantities which may exist will have been prepared) must, as a minimum requirement in the more usual types of contract referred to above, be in sufficient detail to represent a true and complete description for pricing purposes of the works to be undertaken by the contractor, when read in conjunction with any specification which may exist. The contract drawings in the United Kingdom are very rarely sufficient in number or detail to enable the work to be carried out, and the standard forms of contract in both industries find it necessary to confer power on the architect or engineer to issue further drawings and details (usually referred to as " work ing drawings ") after the contract has been placed and during the period of construction.[9] Whether such everyday instructions involve an alteration of the original design and hence of the contract price under a variation clause [10] may be a difficult question of fact, but is a not infrequent cause of dispute. Whether they arrive in time to avoid delay and disturbance of the contractor's programme is, however, one of the commonest causes of building and engineering disputes.[11]

(b) Bills of quantities

Where they exist, these are usually of the greatest importance to tenderers, since in almost all cases [12] they form part of the contract and constitute the exact measure of the work undertaken by the builder for the contract price, though not of his obligation to complete.

[8] See *post*, Chap. 5, Section 1.
[9] See the fuller discussion *ante*, pp. 83–84.
[10] See Chap. 8, pp. 507–508.
[11] See *ante*, Chap. 2, pp. 135 *et seq.*; *post*, Chap. 5, pp. 322 *et seq.*
[12] See *post*, Chap. 8, pp. 509 *et seq.*

Apart from this function, they usually serve, under the terms of the contract, as the basis for valuation of variations, and in addition they provide, at the building owner's expense, a common basis for the comparison and analysis by him of competing tenders, and, once priced, an estimate of the total cost of the work. The bills are prepared with the object of giving a full description of every item of work or expense entailed in the contemplated project, and the quantities of each item to be deduced from or measured off the drawings.

Bills prepared in accordance with the R.I.B.A. standard forms will need to comprehend within their own pages the specification of the work and materials, since under those forms any document actually entitled a specification is denied legal force. If prepared in accordance with the standard method of measurement, they will also contain lists of many of the general obligations of the contractor and of the services which he will have to provide in order to carry out the works, including, for instance, supervision, watching, provision of water, lighting and power, safety measures, temporary hutting, and so on, and a tabulation of the general conditions of contract clause by clause so that tenderers may have the opportunity of pricing them separately if they wish. These items are often referred to as " preliminary " items, perhaps because they usually occur first in the bills before the items of actual work are set out, though a number of items in them (but not all) do refer to initial or preliminary expenditure by the contractor and needed for the contract as a whole, and they may originally have been thought of as " preliminary " in this sense. Well-drawn bills usually provide that failure to price any item merely means that the cost of that item is included or concealed in the prices to be found elsewhere in the bills, but it is submitted that this would in any event be implied as a matter of business efficacy. Well-drawn bills should also provide that the rates and prices in the bills should include for every item of work or service or expense contingently or actually necessary for the carrying out of the work described in the bills, whether specifically mentioned or not. Otherwise there is a risk that provisions in the contract incorporating a standard method of measurement and dealing with errors in the bills may have the effect of exposing the employer to claims based on the omission of items in the bills which the standard method requires to be separately stated,[13] but which it was at all times obvious would have to be carried out.

In engineering works, bills of quantities do not usually incorporate

[13] See *post*, Chap. 8, pp. 515 *et seq*.

the specification, which is provided in a separate document, and the items of work set out in the bills frequently refer back to this document for a description of each item.[14]

In bills of quantities (particularly in those for building contracts) it is becoming increasingly common to find a large number of items marked " P.C." (prime cost) or " Provisional sum," which are priced on behalf of the employer before the bills go out to the contractors for tender. These terms have so far defied legal definition.[15] The origin of the word " provisional " in the expression " provisional sum " is a corruption of the expression " Provide the sum of £— " in old specifications—*i.e.* it is a *provided* sum,[16] rather than an indication of provisional or contingent *work*. The reasons sometimes advanced for dealing with work in this way are, first, that the work may be provisional in character at the time of contract, either because the work may not be carried out at all, or because an element of choice by the employer or his architect is involved, and, secondly, that in relation to some specialist sub-contracted work, the work may not have been designed or may be difficult to price [16a] at the date of the contract. In fact, by a curious confusion of these two quite different considerations, the two terms, which by themselves appear to have little legal significance, are invariably used as part of the contractual machinery relating to nomination or selection of specialist sub-contractors.[17] There is, in fact, no reason why nominated sub-contractors' work should be provisional in character, any more than the builder's or his own sub-contractors' work. Examples of genuine provisional work arise, for instance, where the architect has in mind the possibility of using an alternative method of construction to that shown on the drawings or itemised in the bills, in which case he may include a provisional sum for the alternative work; or of having to increase or change the quantity of a part of the works (*e.g.* foundations); or of encountering an unknown quantity, *e.g.* of rock or " soft spots." In these cases he may insert a nominal quantity, marking the item " Provisional." These latter, however, are cases of *provisional quantities*, not of a provisional *sum*, and do not attract the sub-contracting machinery in the contract. There is, of course, no necessary connection between such genuinely

---

[14] *Cf.* the Standard Method of Measurement of Civil Engineering Quantities.
[15] See *post*, Chap. 15, pp. 758 *et seq.*
[16] See *per* Romer L.J. in *Leslie & Co.* v. *Metropolitan Asylums District* (1903) 1 L.G.R. at p. 868, and the discussion *post*, Chap. 15, p. 758.
[16a] The importance of the pricing difficulty as a reason for the system has perhaps been underestimated—see *post*, Chap. 15, pp. 757–766.
[17] For a discussion of this subject, see *post*, Chap. 15, pp. 756 *et seq.*

provisional items or quantities and sub-contracting, nominated or otherwise. Most contracts make provision for the substitution of the amount of sub-contractors' accounts, or, in the case of work done by the main contractor, a valuation or accepted estimate of the work, for the P.C. or provisional sum. Where no such provision exists it may, it is suggested, be possible at the present day to establish by evidence a usage to this effect. The 1963 Standard Method of Measurement (Fifth Edition) has in the case of building contracts sensibly recommended the use of the term " Provisional sum " (in the absence of express contractual definition) for work or costs not clearly foreseen, defined or detailed at the time of tender (*i.e.* genuine provisional work), and the use of the term "prime cost sum " for work or services to be carried out by nominated sub-contractors, statutory authorities or public undertakings, or for materials or goods supplied by a nominated supplier (*i.e.* in all cases work which definitely will be done, but will be done, or in the case of materials supplied, by persons other than the contractor and selected by the employer).[18] It is to be hoped that all persons in the industry, including those drafting contracts, will adopt this entirely useful and logical definition and bear the important underlying distinction in mind. Regrettably, there is no explicit incorporation of the distinction in the post-1963 R.I.B.A. standard forms,[19] and only in certain parts of the contract do the expressions appear to be used with the standard method definition in mind.

(c) Specifications

As has been seen, in the normal instance where work has been professionally designed prior to the contract on behalf of the employer, and its content is known with a comparative degree of certainty, a contractor may be required to tender on bills of quantities, which in that event may or may not embody the specification,[20] and in addition to providing a basis for re-calculation (or " re-measurement ") of the contract sum are also the basis of valuation of variations. It is, however, quite common to let such contracts, particularly the less substantial ones, such as a contract for a single dwelling-house, not on a measured basis with bills of quantities, but under what is somewhat misleadingly called a " lump sum " or " fixed price " contract, where the contract sum is not subject to re-calculation unless there have been variations in the work. In this

[18] Rule A7.   Later rules, however, blur the distinction.
[19] Certainly there is none in the post-1963 specification forms.
[20] Not under the standard I.C.E. form.

book, these latter are usually referred to as contracts in the specification form, or without quantities, and in such cases the builder's contract price includes for all the work described in the specification and shown on the drawings, and any schedule of rates, bills of quantities or similar documents, however described, exist solely for the purpose of valuing variations.

The use of the expression " lump sum " is misleading and should be avoided, because this term has been used by lawyers and judges to distinguish what are in law " entire " contracts from others,[21] and most measured contracts with quantities are in fact in the same legal category. The use of the expression " fixed price " is misleading, because the prices in specification contracts are subject to adjustment in various ways apart from remeasurement, and because the expression is often used to describe contracts containing no fluctuations clause.[22]

(d) Schedules of rates or prices

There are three quite different categories of tender document which may be called by this name. First, contracts in the " lump sum "[23] or specification form will need a document to introduce some certainty into the valuation of any variations which may be ordered. Such a document usually bears a superficial resemblance to a bill of quantities, but the important differences are that while unit items and prices are inserted for all likely work processes, actual quantities, and therefore the grossed up totals of the prices, are absent. These documents are used, by virtue of express provisions in the contract, to value such variations as may be ordered and constitute, in effect, an offer by the builder to carry out such variations of the work as the employer may require on the basis that the contract sum will be adjusted (whether by omission or addition) in accordance with the prices in the schedule. Because variations by way of omission may obviously involve quite different financial implications, from the point of view of the profitability of the work as a whole to the contractor, it is not unusual to find a saving clause in the contractual provisions for valuation, whereby an allowance can be made for this factor.[24]

Secondly, schedules of rates or prices may be used as the definitive contract document in order to value the whole of the work carried out by the contractor. As such, they represent his tender offer, and

---

[21] See *post*, Chap. 5, pp. 243 *et seq.*; Chap. 9, pp. 563–564.   [22] See *supra*, pp. 201–202
[23] (In the non-legal sense.)   [24] See *post*, Chap. 8, p. 557.

a contract in this form is appropriate where the nature or full extent of the contract work is so vague or difficult to foresee (perhaps for very good reasons) at the time that it is desired to start work, that a contract using bills or a precise specification is not practicable.[25] This type of contract is considered below in subsection (3).

Thirdly, schedules or lists of prices or rates may be found forming part of the contract documents which exist purely to give effect to what are often loosely called " variation of price " or " rise and fall " clauses in contracts.   These clauses (in particular to distinguish them from clauses for the valuation of variations and other clauses varying the contract price) are better described, as they are in the R.I.B.A. standard form, as fluctuations clauses.   In the engineering standard form there is no such clause, but a standard printed clause (specifically called a " Variation of price clause ") is available and frequently inserted into the contract documents for this purpose.   All such clauses are in this book described as fluctuations clauses.[26]   The prices in the lists or schedules which are necessary for the operation of these clauses are not prices of items of work, but of materials and sometimes of labour or wage rates (depending on the terms of the fluctuations clause), and are used as a base from which to calculate increases or decreases in the prices or wages actually paid by the contractor during the currency of the work. They are frequently called "basic price lists," particularly in the case of materials.

(e) " Package deal " or " industrialised building " contracts

Before considering, in subsection (3) below, contracts where the extent of the work is uncertain, it may be useful to indicate the general background, and type of contractual provisions, which are required for this type of contract.

In these contracts the essential feature is that the employer does not employ professional staff to produce the design of the building or project which he requires.   Either by negotiation, or by outline specification to tendering contractors, the employer makes known his requirements and the contractor produces the design, in the form of drawings, a specification and sometimes schedules of rates to cover possible variations.   Bills are not usually used in such contracts.   In some cases the project is of a "mixed package-deal" character, with external works and foundations under the design control of the employer in the usual way, possibly with Bills of

---

[25] See *supra*, p. 199.
[26] For these, see *post*, Chap. 9, pp. 566–569.

Quantities, but the superstructure provided under an "industrialised building" design of the contractors.

The justification for this system advanced by its advocates is that in theory it avoids duplication and the expense of design staff, and enables the contractor, with his specialised knowledge of his own techniques, to design so as to produce maximum economy, and therefore a keener price, in a way that an architect or engineer without knowledge of his techniques would not.

In fact employers usually endeavour to have professional advisers available to ensure that their own interest in the design is safeguarded, but the simple fact that in general it takes longer to check and understand the design of another person than it does to design *de novo*, means that, unless the employer is prepared to pay heavily for design-vetting services, which would defeat the whole purpose of the exercise (even assuming that full access to factory techniques and specialised processes is available) the design protection afforded by his own advisers is bound to be superficial at best. Employers frequently employ quantity surveyors as well, to impose some sort of check on the reasonableness of the contractor's prices. It is to be doubted if, in the absence of truly competitive tendering (which tenders invited on a package-deal basis cannot provide) that any effective check on cost can be provided by such advisers.

In those cases where a contractor supplies his own design (as in the cases evolved in the analogous field of houses sold in the course of erection) there is an implied warranty of suitability for the required purpose, similar to that under section 14 of the Sale of Goods Act.[27] This warranty is absolute, and independent of fault. For some reason, contractors putting forward package-deal contracts at present appear to be unwilling to give such warranties, and in particular, to clothe them in the form of an indemnity so as to allow them to operate over a reasonable period having some relationship to the life of the building—it is of no interest to an employer paying for a building required to last for sixty years that a suitable warranty expires at the end of the period of limitation. Essential requirements of a package-deal contract are:

(a) A warranty of suitability, absolute and independent of fault, expressed to be available for a substantial period of time, but excepting normal replacement and maintenance of parts of the building which might reasonably be expected to have a limited life.

---

[27] See *post*, pp. 273 *et seq.*, and *per* Denning M.R. in *Hancock* v. *Brazier (Anerley) Ltd.* [1966] 1 W.L.R. 1317.

(b) The bonding of this obligation by a substantial surety.

(c) A right of the contractor to object, after giving notice, to any variation ordered by the employer which might prejudice his suitability obligation, but subject to safeguards to prevent frivolous objection.

(d) Where " mixed package-deal " contracts are involved, a warranty by the contractor extending to the employer's work as well as the contractor's, subject to safeguards enabling the contractor to object at the time to the design or suitability of the employer's work.

(e) In industrial building cases, a totally different system of interim payment, since valuation of work done and materials on site which is the normal basis in traditional contracts cannot be applied where much of the work done is off the site and no method of checking costings is available.

(f) A right of the contractor to be permitted to vary the work, if necessary for purposes of suitability and safety, subject to financial and other safeguards for the employer.

(g) A list of any parts of the work intended to be excepted from the contractor's suitability obligation, including any work or goods of nominated suppliers or sub-contractors which it is thought appropriate to exclude from it.

(h) A definition of the precise status and rights of the employer's architect (if any) engaged in supervising the work, and in regard to the remedying of defects.

Probably enough has been said to show that there is hardly a provision of the traditional form of contract which does not require radical rethinking and revision in order to safeguard the interests of both parties and provide a viable commercial document. At the present day in the United Kingdom the standard forms are frequently used in these situations with greater or less, or no modification, often with the employer's architect named as the architect in charge of the project, and with the preambles to the articles of the standard forms, which refer to the drawings and specification as having been prepared by or under the direction of the employer's architect, unaltered. It remains to be seen what the courts will make of such wholly inappropriate contract documents in cases of design failure.

It should perhaps be added that the history of these contracts in the United Kingdom has not been a happy one, and against some advantage in speed of construction no advantage in economy and serious disadvantages in quality have been the usual experience.

(3) Where Extent of Work Uncertain

It will be apparent from the foregoing that the more usual methods of letting contracts on a measured or lump-sum basis are only practicable if the works have been designed in sufficient detail to enable them to be defined and priced by the builder (subject to the inroads effected upon this principle by the use or abuse of P.C. or provisional sums or items for work which is not genuinely provisional). But it frequently happens that an employer may not know at the time he requires tenders precisely what work he will wish the contractor to do. He may also wish, for financial or other reasons, to commence part of the works before a stage of design of the remainder has been reached which would permit the preparation of drawings or bills of quantities. To meet such situations, various methods of obtaining tenders have been evolved, the commonest of which entail the carrying out of work either at unit prices contained in a schedule of prices or rates, or at cost plus a percentage profit.

The use of such a contract, however, clearly involves an admission that no precise design of the works exists at the time of contracting, and for this reason, perhaps, professional advisers appear to be reluctant to recommend such a contract to their employers, and in practice it seems common, particularly in engineering contracts, where even in a well-planned project the bills of quantities are likely to be relatively short and uncomplicated documents, to use the traditional type of contract and a set of drawings of varying degrees of precision, and rely on the power to vary the work contained in the contract. If the drawings and bills appear to be precise on their face and no specific warning is given, this practice is grossly misleading, quite possibly to the employer and certainly to the contractor. If the drawings are very general and the bills contain many provisional items and quantities, the contractor may not be misled, but the employer quite possibly may be. Whatever the actual position, such a contract is likely to be a fertile source of dispute, and substantial claims by the contractor, whether or not the latter was under any real illusion as to the character of the project at the time of tendering, are a probable result. It may be a matter for consideration, if proper pre-planning of projects is not always possible, whether a separate standard form of contract, drafted with a view to eliminating the possibility of these claims, should not be available to the contracting parties, particularly in the engineering industry. (Since the preceding sentence in the ninth edition, the R.I.B.A. published in March 1967 a fixed fee cost plus form of contract. This is closely modelled on the traditional post-1963 standard forms, and the exact type of situation at which it is aimed is not clear, since at a number of points it prohibits changes in " the nature and scope of the works " being ordered by the employer, which suggests that the contract is intended for cases where the intended work is known with reasonable certainty at the time of contracting.)

(a) Contracts employing schedules of prices

There are, in the United Kingdom, schedules of prices prepared by certain Crown departments which define in detail units of work and show a price fixed by the authority against each unit. The contractor may be invited to tender for whatever works he may be ordered to carry out during a given period at the prices in the particular schedule, plus or minus a tendered percentage.

Schedules of prices may also be prepared by the employer's professional advisers designed for the particular project and containing all the units of work which it is expected may be required to be undertaken. These are usually, but not invariably, priced by the contractor, and occasionally may even be used when the full extent of the work is known, but, more usually, the obligation of the builder will be to carry out whatever work he may be ordered to do at the prices in the schedule, rather than to carry out a fully designed project at those prices.

As already indicated, these types of contract require to be distinguished from contracts without quantities where schedules of rates may be required solely for the purpose of valuing variations.

In these forms of tender it is not necessary for any clear or defined project to be determined upon before the invitation to tender. The documents may indicate the scope of the works in general terms and perhaps in some cases the limits of each operation, but their main purpose will be to identify the schedule in question and to define by general conditions of contract or otherwise the obligations and liabilities of the tenderer and the terms of payment. It is essential that the descriptions of work in each item should be complete and make clear all ancillary processes and general obligations which are included in the prices in the schedule.

(b) Contracts on a cost plus basis

The invitation to tender in these cases will describe the work, to the extent that this is possible, and indicate any drawings available at the date of the tender. The contractor will be required to quote the percentage or fixed fee to be added to cost. The general conditions of contract will also require to be stated.

In this type of contract it is essential to have a clear and comprehensive definition of the term " cost," and precise methods of pricing those services which by their nature are not capable of precise costing (*e.g.* provision of plant, tools, transport, supervision and overheads). The contract should also make specific provision as to trade and other discounts obtainable by the contractor on materials and sub-contractors' accounts.[28] The R.I.B.A. in March 1967 published a standard form of cost plus fixed fee contract.[29]

SECTION 2. INCORPORATION OF DOCUMENTS

Whatever types of contract documents are used, the question may arise whether a particular document has been successfully incorporated into, or forms part of, the concluded agreement between the parties. The modern forms of contract specifically list the documents intended to form part of the contract, and make provision for their signature by the parties. This is clearly a prudent course, but all that in fact is necessary is a reference to or identification of the document in question in some part of the contract documents themselves, and an indication of the extent to which the document is intended to govern or control the contractual rights of the parties.

ILLUSTRATIONS

(1) If an order refers to a specification, as if B. engages to do work in conformity to drawings and a specification, the offer incorporates the drawings and specification, and if the specification mentions a time for completion, and the offer is accepted, completion to time is a part of the contract: *Wimhurst* v. *Deeley* (1845).[30]

(2) The fluctuations clause (25A) of a contract in the pre-1963 R.I.B.A. standard form provided for adjustment of the contract sum to take account of differences between the market price current at the date of tender, and the market price paid by the contractor, of any of the materials or goods " specified in the list attached to the bills of quantities." The list never was attached to the bills of quantities, but was simply filed with the contract documents. *Held*, by

---

[28] See *post*, Chap. 15, p. 760.
[29] See *supra*, subs. (3) (a), p. 211.
[30] 2 C.B. 253.

Ashworth J., the failure actually to attach the list to the bills did not deprive it of its legal force: *Royston U.D.C.* v. *Royston Builders Ltd.* (1961).[31]

On the other hand, merely because the document is referred to for one purpose, and may be incorporated to that extent, it does not follow that the whole of the document will be incorporated. Moreover, the intention to incorporate must be sufficiently clear and the provision sought to be incorporated sufficiently certain.[32]

ILLUSTRATIONS

(1) Tender documents provided: " The successful contractor, if any, may be required to enter into the usual form of agreement published by the R.I.B.A. or other form of agreement required by the War Damage Commission." The successful tenderer was not in fact required to sign any form of contract, and sued for fluctuations under clause 25A of the R.I.B.A. form. *Held*, the tender could not be construed as incorporating the R.I.B.A. form of contract and the claim must fail: *Moore* v. *Shawcross* (1954).[33]

(2) A letter accompanying the contractors' form of tender stated " Our tender is subject to adequate supplies of material and labour being available as and when required to carry out the work within the time specified." The remainder of the letter contained references to the working of the fluctuations clause in the contract. The appendix to the form of tender referred to this letter in relation to the fluctuations clause only. The later formal contract between the parties referred to " the said tender " but not to the accompanying letter. *Held*, that while the parts of the letter relating to the fluctuations clause might have been incorporated by the reference in the appendix to the form of tender, as a part of " the said tender," the sentence relating to supplies of material and labour was not so incorporated: *Davis Contractors Ltd.* v. *Fareham U.D.C.* (1956).[34]

(3) A specification, under a sub-heading "Basis of tender," provided that, notwithstanding information in the specification or tender drawings, the contractor should take responsibility for supply, erection *and efficient operation* of the project for the period of maintenance. The tender required the contractor to design the project and submit drawings etc. to the employer's consulting engineer for approval. A formal contract was also contemplated. Between acceptance of tender and formal agreement drawings were agreed for (*inter alia*) the foundations. The agreement was in a form similar to the R.I.B.A. forms, under which the contractor undertook to "execute and complete the work shown upon the drawings and described by or referred to in the specification." *Held* by the High Court of Australia, that the employer could not rely on the words in the

---

[31] 177 E.G. 589.

[32] In addition to the cases cited below, see the case of *Re Fulham B.C. and the National Electric Construction Co. Ltd.* (1905) 74 J.P. 55, illustrated *post*, Chap. 9, Section 2, p. 593, a most interesting example of limited incorporation.

[33] [1954] J.P.L. 431.

[34] [1956] A.C. 696 (see *per* Lord Radcliffe at pp. 725–726). See also *Smith & Montgomery* v. *Johnson* (1954) 1 D.L.R. (2d) 342 (Canada), illustrated *post*, p. 328.

specification when the foundations proved unsuitable, since they did not describe the works and so were not incorporated: *Cable (1956) Ltd.* v. *Hutcherson Ltd.* (1969).[34a]

Sub-contracts, particularly when informally concluded by quotation and order, frequently attempt to incorporate the provisions of the main contract in vague and general language. Unless they are sufficiently explicit, these efforts may fail.[35]

If contract documents purport to be complete, other documents may in certain circumstances amount to or evidence collateral agreements which will have legal force, but it has already been seen [36] that the onus assumed by a party seeking to set up a collateral agreement in the face of a contract which purports to be complete is a heavy one. It is a commonplace that each party during the negotiating stage of a contract may put forward terms for suggested acceptance, but the presumption, once they purport to sign a set of contract documents, is that all such prior contentions or even agreements have been superseded. It has already been seen [37] that a letter prior to the contract from an employer giving his reasons for a change he had caused to have made in the wording of the fluctuation clause, and stating what it meant, was rejected even as evidence of the meaning of the clause.

It is, of course, perfectly possible for the contract documents themselves to limit or control the extent to which any documents may have contractual force, or modify or affect other documents. Where, as in the case of the R.I.B.A. forms,[38] this purports to give priority to the printed standard form over the documents specially prepared for or coming into existence as part of the contract, this can cause grave injustice and anomalies, and defeat the obvious common intention of the parties.[38a]

In both the R.I.B.A. and civil engineering standard forms the formal contract as well as the general conditions are contained in a single document, while the civil engineering form includes in addition the form of surety bond to be entered into. A tender incorporating one of these forms may (provided there has been prior insertion of all necessary details in the various appendices to

---

[34a] (1969) 43 A.L.V.R. 321.

[35] See *post* Chap. 15, pp. 767 *et seq.*, and the cases there set out.

[36] *Ante*, Chap. 1, pp. 56–57.

[37] *Boot* v. *L.C.C.* [1959] 1 W.L.R. 1069, *ante*, Chap. 1, p. 34.

[38] *Cf.* clauses 2 and 10 of the pre-1963 R.I.B.A. form of contract, and clause 12 of the post-1963 forms.

[38a] See *M. J. Gleeson (Contractors) Ltd.* v. *Hillingdon B.C.* (1970) 215 E.G. 165, currently under appeal to H.L.

the forms) be capable of binding acceptance, since all terms will have been agreed and the parties be completely *ad idem*,[39] so far as price and the work to be carried out is concerned, and although there may be arguments while the contract is still in an executory stage that, depending on the wording, a formal contract is a pre-condition of a binding contract,[40] if work then actually starts the presumption of a concluded contract must, it is submitted, become irresistible.[41]

Assuming that a document agreed upon and intended to be incorporated in a formal contract is not in fact incorporated, then, if the failure to do so is due to a common mistake or a mistake of one party known to the other, the remedy of rectification may be available.[42]

But there must be either full agreement, or a mistaken belief (known to the other party) that the documents contain an agreed term, before rectification will be granted. It is not sufficient to inform a representative of the other party, who neither assents nor dissents, that a particular term will be required.

ILLUSTRATION

Before signing a contract a director of the contractors informed the surveyor of the council that, notwithstanding that certain materials and prices only were contained in a list attached to the bills of quantities, for the purposes of the fluctuations clause 25A in the standard pre-1963 R.I.B.A. form, his company would in fact require the clause to operate on all materials whether in the list or not. The surveyor did not repudiate or assent to this intimation, but the contract documents were signed without alteration. During the work the contractors claimed the increases, which were paid by the council on interim certificate. *Held*, by Ashworth J., (1) there was no agreement to vary the contract as signed by the parties, and (2) the payments inadvertently made by the council would not estop them from subsequently contending that they were not due under the contract, since there was neither a representation nor action upon the representation sufficient to found an estoppel: *Royston U.D.C. v. Royston Builders Ltd.* (1961).[43]

---

[39] See *infra*, pp. 223 *et seq.*, and *ante*, Chap. 1, pp. 11 *et seq.*

[40] See *infra*, Section 3 (2) (a) (i), pp. 217 *et seq.*

[41] See the case of *Trollope & Colls* v. *Atomic Power Construction Ltd.* [1963] 1 W.L.R. 333, *infra*, p. 219.

[42] See *ante*, Chap. 1, pp. 32 *et seq.*

[43] 177 E.G. 589. See *ante*, Chap. 1, p. 58, for estoppel, and contrast the cases of *Roberts* v. *Leicestershire C.C.* [1961] 1 Ch. 555, *ante*, pp. 37–38, and *Carlton Contractors* v. *Bexley Corporation* (1962) 60 L.G.R. 331, *ante*, Chap. 2, Section 4 (3), pp. 110–111. See also a very comparable case, *Tharsis Sulphur & Copper Co.* v. *McElroy* (1878) 3 App.Cas. 1040, illustrated *post*, Chap. 8, Section 2, pp. 537–538.

SECTION 3.　ACCEPTANCE OF TENDER

(1) Legal Effect of Tender

In normal circumstances the purpose of an invitation to tender is to obtain from the builder a firm offer capable of acceptance and hence of conversion into a binding contract. The principles of offer and acceptance have been already discussed [44] and it follows that in the usual case there is no obligation on the employer to accept the lowest or any tender.[45] Many tenders contain an express exclusion of the obligation to accept the lowest or any tender, but this is not necessary. On the other hand, an invitation to tender could be so expressed as to impose such an obligation and would be supported by consideration.[46] But no such obligation can be implied, nor will an architect have any implied authority to accept the lowest or any tender, though he might, of course, have express authority to do so.[47]

Whether an offer is capable of acceptance or is merely an expression of willingness to bargain, or of the possible terms on which a bargain can be arranged, is a question of construction in which the line of demarcation can in some cases be very fine. This is not usually a difficulty in the case of tenders for building contracts, since it is generally known that the purpose of the invitation to tender is to obtain a firm offer, and that any tender which sought to depart from this understanding would not be seriously considered by the employer.

There are, however, rare cases, usually in the context of contracts for the supply of materials or the doing of an indefinite amount of work, where acceptance in general terms will not create a binding contract, which will only occur as and when actual orders are placed for distinct and definite goods or work.[48]

(2) Whether Acceptance creates Contract

When the employer accepts a builder's tender, and the fact is notified to the builder, the parties usually consider themselves bound, and frequently work is commenced by the builder on this assumption. But there are at least three reasons which occur frequently in practice

---

[44] *Ante*, Chap. 1, Formation, pp. 5 *et seq.*
[45] *Ante*, p. 6. For cases where the invitation to tender is fraudulent, in that the employer has no intention of letting a contract to the person invited to tender, see *infra*, pp. 229–230.
[46] See, *e.g. per* Willes J. in *Spencer* v. *Harding* (1870) L.R. 5 C.P. 561 at p. 563.
[47] See *Pauling* v. *Pontifex* (1852) 20 L.T.(o.s.) 126 and *ante*, Chap. 2, pp. 108 *et seq.*
[48] These cases are dealt with *infra*, pp. 228–229.

why this may not be so, and in consequence the builder's entitlement, if he has carried out work, may only be to a reasonable price for it (he may, of course, be glad to be paid on a *quantum meruit* if the contract prices prove uneconomical).[49]   A binding contract may not come into existence

(a) because it is expressed to be subject to some overriding condition;

(b) because the parties are not *ad idem* as to all the terms of the contract; or

(c) because the tender, by passage of time, may no longer be capable of acceptance.

(a) Tender subject to condition

(i) **Condition as to a formal contract.** The condition which most often arises in practice is due to the expectation of the parties that a formal contract will be signed at a later stage, which frequently finds verbal expression in the tender documents.[50]   It is then a question of construction of the language used whether the execution of the further contract is a condition of the offer or invitation, or whether it is a mere expression of desire or intention that a formal contract should be drawn up embodying the transaction already agreed upon.[51]

In considering the cases below, it should be remembered that words cannot be construed in isolation from their surrounding circumstances, and that those circumstances in a contract for the sale of land or the grant of a lease (where questions of title can rarely be considered in detail by parties who may be in agreement on all other terms) are very different from those in building contracts, where the parties are frequently, under the modern practice in preparing tender documents, *ad idem* on all possible terms when acceptance of the tender takes place. In *Rossdale* v. *Denny* (1921),[52] where the conveyancing cases were fully considered, Lord Sterndale M.R., commenting on the fact that the trial judge had noted that in all but two cases where the words " subject to a formal contract " had been used they had prevented a contract coming into existence, said [53]: " I am far from saying that there may not be an unconditional

[49] See also the general discussion *ante*, Chap. 1, pp. 11–17.
[50] Thus by the Form of Tender in the standard I.C.E. form of contract it is provided " Unless and until a formal agreement is prepared and executed this tender, together with your written acceptance thereof, shall constitute a binding contract between us."
[51] See also the short discussion *ante*, Chap. 1, pp. 16–17.
[52] [1921] 1 Ch. 57.
[53] *Ibid.* at p. 66.

offer and acceptance of a binding contract although the letters may contain the words ' subject to a formal contract,' but certainly those words do point in the direction of the offer or acceptance being conditional." It is suggested that, particularly where the contract documents show that there has otherwise been agreement in the degree of detail normally associated with building and engineering contracts (as exemplified, for instance, by the standard forms), these words will, in a building or engineering context, fail to prevent a contract coming into being. In addition, if one party in such a situation commences work with the acquiescence of the other, it is submitted that this will amount to a mutual waiver by both parties of any such condition.

One reservation should perhaps be made. If the reference is to a formal contract *under seal*, the position might be different. It has already been pointed out that from an employer's point of view it is most desirable, if not essential, that building or engineering contracts should be under seal, since this will have the effect of extending the limitation period for defective work from six to twelve years. It is submitted that a refusal by a contractor, in the face of an express requirement of this kind, to enter into a contract under seal would be a repudiation of the contract and justify an employer in rescinding the contract notwithstanding that work had started. This consideration may affect the question whether the requirement is a condition precedent to liability in such a case, although a possible view is that there is still a binding contract, one of the terms of which is an obligation to enter into a formal contract under seal. The matter cannot, however, be regarded as free from doubt.

ILLUSTRATIONS

(1) Guardians of the poor of Hull issued an advertisement inviting tenders for the supply of meat for three months, which stated that sealed tenders were to be sent to the clerk of the corporation, and that all contractors would have to sign a written contract after acceptance of tender. *Held*, acceptance of the tender did not form a binding contract, as a written contract was to be executed: *Kingston-upon-Hull (Governor, etc.)* v. *Petch* (1854).[54]

(2) The plaintiff's employer, being desirous of making certain alterations in his premises, sent bills of quantities through his architect, H., to several builders inviting them to send in tenders stating the amount at which they would be willing to execute the work. The defendant sent in a tender in these terms: " I hereby agree to execute complete, within the space of twenty-six weeks from the day of receiving instructions to commence, the whole of the work required to be done in alterations and additions to the above premises, with

[54] 10 Exch. 610.

the best materials, in strict accordance with the plans and specifications, and to the entire satisfaction of the architect for the sum of
£4,193." The plaintiff's architect thereupon wrote to the defendant:
" I am instructed by my client L. to accept your tender of £4,193
for works as above referred to. The contract will be prepared by
Messrs. U. and C., Mr. L.'s solicitors, and I have no doubt it will
be ready for signature in the course of a few days." The defendant
afterwards found that he had made a mistake in his tender, and
thereupon purported to withdraw it. *Held*, by the Court of Appeal,
that though the later contract might have contained further terms—
such as provisions for interim payment—the parties had nevertheless
concluded a binding contract: *Lewis* v. *Brass* (1877).[55]

(3) A term of a local authority's advertisement for tenders for a
sewerage works was that the tenderer should obtain sureties and
execute a contract under seal for due performance of the works.
The plaintiff's tender was accepted by a letter to which the seal of the
council had been attached in accordance with a resolution of the
council, but the tenderer never executed a contract under seal. *Held*,
the acceptance of the tender did not conclude a contract between the
parties: *Bozson* v. *Altrincham U.D.C.* (1903).[56] (Note: There were
other grounds for this decision.) [57]

(4) The plaintiff sent to the defendant's agent a written offer
for certain leaseholds, stating that the offer was " subject to a formal
contract to embody such reasonable provisions as my solicitors
may approve, and to the lease containing no unusual provisions or
covenants." The agent replied on the same day that he was instructed
to accept the offer, and that he would take steps to get the vendor's
solicitors to prepare the formal contract. *Held*, that the offer was
conditional only, and that there was no binding contract: *Rossdale*
v. *Denny* (1921).[58]

(5) Considerable changes in the work were notified to tendering
sub-contractors after they had submitted their price in February
1959. In June 1959 they were asked by letter to start work in the
following terms: " We have to inform you that it is our intention to
enter into a contract with you for (the works). As soon as matters
outstanding between us are settled we will enter into a contract
agreement with you, and in the meantime please accept this letter
as an instruction to proceed with the work necessary to permit you
to meet the agreed programme." By April 1960 all the terms of the
contract had been agreed between the parties, but no contract was
ever actually signed. The sub-contractors contended there was no
contract in being, and sought remuneration on the basis of a *quantum
meruit*. *Held*, by Megaw J., that there was a binding contract:
Trollope & Colls Ltd. v. *Atomic Power Construction Ltd.* (1963).[59]

[55] 3 Q.B.D. 667 (C.A.).
[56] 67 J.P. 397 (see the fuller note on this case, *infra*, p. 224).
[57] See *infra*, p. 224.
[58] [1921] 1 Ch. 57. The case of *Sweet & Maxwell Ltd.* v. *Universal News Services Ltd.*
[1964] 2 Q.B. 699, *ante*, Chap. 1, Section 2 (6) p. 15, shows that the wording was
not too vague to be enforced had the words " subject to formal contract " not been
present.
[59] [1963] 1 W.L.R. 333, further illustrated *infra*, pp. 224–225.

(6) An excavation sub-contractor orally agreed a definition of rock with the main contractor, and requested the latter to confirm it in writing. He then sent in a quotation. The main contractor accepted the quotation without mentioning the rock definition. The sub-contractor decided he wished to withdraw his offer. *Held*, by the Ontario Court of Appeal (McGillivray J.A. dissenting), that the confirmation in writing was a condition precedent, and he was entitled to do so: *Pigott Structures* v. *Keillor Construction* (1965).[60]

(ii) Conditions as to approval or permission. Words similar to " subject to contract " have, therefore, normally been construed, at least in other fields, as imposing a condition precedent to the creation of any contractual bond between the parties. Apart from such stipulations, however, the parties may often seek to attach some other condition to the tender or invitation to tender or acceptance. For instance, it is not unusual for an acceptance by a local authority to be given " subject to loan sanction " or " subject to the approval of the Ministry of ——." In such cases it is a question of construction whether the stipulation is a condition precedent to a contract coming into being, or a condition subsequent—that is to say whether the parties are not bound at all, or whether they are bound, subject to their contractual obligations being cancelled in the event of the condition occurring or not occurring. The practical difference is that in the one case withdrawal in the absence of any binding option is possible by either party at any time before the condition occurs, whereas in the other the parties can be held to their bargain and no withdrawal will be effective.[61] Since a contractor is entitled to have his tender accepted within a reasonable time,[62] it may be that the expected length of time before the conditional event may affect the question whether the acceptance is subject to a condition precedent or subsequent.

Where permission or approval is expressed to be necessary, there is an implied term that the party seeking approval or permission will exercise reasonable diligence to obtain it.[63] If at the time of the contract the other party does not know that the permission or approval is necessary, but the party needing it does, there is an

---

[60] 50 D.L.R. (2d) 97 (Canada). See the fuller illustration of this case, *ante*, Chap. 1, pp. 9–10.

[61] *Cf.* the case of *Churchward* v. *R.* (1865) L.R. 1 Q.B. 173, referred to *post*, p. 238, where the effect of a provision for payment out of parliamentary funds was considered.

[62] *Infra*, pp. 225 *et seq.*

[63] *Compagnie Algerienne, etc.* v. *Katana Societa, etc.* [1960] 2 Q.B. 115. However, an obligation to use best endeavours does not impart a duty to appeal from an adverse planning decision; see *Hargreaves* v. *Lynch* [1969] 1 W.L.R. 215. See also for planning permission *Batten* v. *White* (1960) 12 P. & C.R. 66.

implied term that it will in fact be obtained within a reasonable time [64] and consequently no room for the doctrine of frustration.

(iii) **Other conditions.** Attempts by contractors to qualify their tenders, which are frequently informally phrased, often in documents attached to or contemporaneous with the tender documents, may give rise to considerable difficulty of interpretation. Thus a condition may be intended to affect or cancel the contract as a whole (and hence be relevant to the present discussion), or merely to qualify the prices, or some of them, in the contract, or some particular obligations of the builder or employer. So in the case of *Davis Contractors Ltd.* v. *Fareham U.D.C.* (1956) [65] the contractors, in a letter accompanying their tender, stated " Our tender is subject to adequate supplies of material and labour being available as and when required to carry out the work within the time specified." This letter, which also included statements relating to the fluctuations clause in the contract, was referred to in an appendix to the tender which itself related to the fluctuations clause. The House of Lords (which held that the letter was not, so far as this sentence was concerned, incorporated in the later formal contract concluded by the parties) pointed out the extreme difficulty of defining its precise content and effect, had it formed part of the contract,[66] and there was considerable judicial conflict as to this in the courts below, where it had been held to be a part of the contract. It will be readily seen that such a condition might have been intended to qualify either (a) the builder's obligation to carry out the works at all or (b) the builder's prices or (c) the liability of the builder under the contractual provisions relating to the time of completion. The Court of Appeal in the *Davis Contractors* case held that it referred to the time of completion only. But in a later case where rather similar wording was used a different view was taken.

ILLUSTRATION

A covering letter from contractors stated: " In offering our tender we have made the following assumptions:

(1) Labour. Labour is reported to be available in Yeovil and from all the inquiries made providing the present circumstances are maintained there should be sufficient quantity of men available for the work. We have accordingly allowed for the daily transport costs of labour from Yeovil and for no other importation. Our tender is based upon the assumption of continuous availability of a sufficient

---

[64] *Ibid.* See also *Sethia (1944) Ltd.* v. *Partabmull Rameshwar* [1951] 2 All E.R. 352n (H.L.).

[65] [1956] A.C. 696, illustrated *post*, Chap. 5, p. 358.

[66] *Ibid. per* Simonds L.C. at p. 713.

quantity of suitable workmen to enable the work to be completed in the time which we have stated.

(2) Material. We have assumed the availability of all necessary materials for both permanent and temporary works and of all facilities required enabling the work to be completed in the time stated. We would particularly draw attention to the current difficulty in delivery of special iron fittings.

(3) Earthworks. Our excavation sub-contractors' prices which are fundamental to our offer are based upon the use of tractor-drawn plant and assume that in the case of the main fill for the dam the borrow pits selected by the engineers will be in suitable positions for the use of such plant.

(4) Diversion Works. We assume that the whole of the excavation for the culvert would be carried out in open cut with battered sides and have taken the appropriate excavation item in the Bill to be measured on this basis."

The contract was in the I.C.E. standard form slightly amended and with the liquidated damages clause deleted. As a result of the covering letter, the tender figure was revised upwards from approximately £358,000 to £401,000; £20,000 being allocated to the diversion works, £15,000 to cut-off trench, and a provisional sum of £5,000 being inserted for transport of labour, but the letter was, nevertheless, expressly incorporated in the contract. *Held, per* Danckwerts L.J., distinguishing the view of the Court of Appeal in *Davis Contractors* v. *Fareham U.D.C.* (1956) that if any of the matters the subject of the letter turned out otherwise than as assumed so as to cause extra cost to the claimants, then the claimants should receive reasonable remuneration therefor: *Holland & Hannen & Cubitts Ltd.* v. *Yeovil R.D.C.* (1964).[67]

(Note: This is, even on its very special facts, a most difficult case. Danckwerts L.J. considered that important factors enabling him to distinguish the *Davis Contractors* case were the failure in that case expressly to incorporate the letter, and the fact that in the present case the deletion of the liquidated damages clause, while it might leave the employer to his common law right to damages for delay, meant that delay was a less compelling matter to the parties. No weight appears to have been given to the extraordinary difficulty of giving precise effect in financial terms to the letter, to the fact that the parties in at least two respects appear to have altered the contract price to take account of matters in the letter, or to the very wide scope of possible financial claims under the terms of the letter. On the other hand this was, unlike the *Davis Contractors* case, an engineering contract, where the power to grant an extension of time was in completely general terms (see clause 44), whereas in the R.I.B.A. form and in the *Davis Contractors* case the grounds for an extension of time were far more precisely defined and did not include shortages of labour or materials.)

A condition attached to invitations to tender by the employer [68] and frequently found in practice, especially with local authorities,

---

[67] Q.B.D. Special Paper (unreported).
[68] Compare the Form of Tender in the I.C.E. Conditions, and clause 10 of those Conditions.

imposes an obligation on the tenderer to provide sureties, in the event of his tender being accepted, for due execution of the contractor's obligations under the contract. In such a case the tender documents should contain the form of surety bond required and the amount of the bond. Failure to inform the tenderer of the precise form required may lead to deadlock at the time the bond is required, and may afford an opportunity for the contractor to withdraw from his tender should he desire to do so for other reasons, since it can be contended that the parties are not *ad idem* as to a material term of the contract.[69] (Such a term is fundamental and failure to comply with it will justify the other party in treating the contract as repudiated.) [70]

A phrase commonly found in contracts for sale of land or ships is "subject to survey." Thus phrases such as "subject to surveyor's report,"[70a] "subject to a satisfactory survey,"[70b] and "subject to satisfactory running trials"[70c] have been held to prevent a contract coming into being and to have conferred an absolute right to reject on the purchaser for any or no reason.

(b) Parties not ad idem

Before a contract can be concluded, the parties must be agreed as to all its terms. The law does not recognise an "agreement to agree" and failure to agree on any term will prevent the contract as a whole from coming into existence.[71] The difficulty which usually arises in practice, however, is that offer and counter-offer or acceptance may not be in identical terms—thus a person purporting to accept a contract may at the same time seek to introduce a new term. The question is whether a stage has been reached where agreement between both parties is complete. In building contracts conduct such as starting work or permitting it to be done can be very important as showing acceptance by the contractor or employer.

ILLUSTRATIONS

(1) The D. guardians advertised for tenders for stone. T. tendered, and his tender was accepted. A form of contract was sent to T. who signed it after having added a term. The guardians wrote to T., saying that they had erased the additional term. The same day T. wrote that he

---

[69] See *infra*, p. 224, and *Bozson* v. *Altrincham U.D.C.* (1903) 67 J.P. 397, there illustrated.

[70] See *Swartz & Son (Ppty) Ltd.* v. *Wolmaransstad Town Council*, 1960 (2) S.A. 1 (South Africa), *post*, Chap. 17, p. 798.

[70a] *Marks* v. *Board* (1930) 46 T.L.R. 424.

[70b] *Astra Trust Ltd.* v. *Adams* [1969] 1 W.L.R. 81.

[70c] *John Howard (Northern) Ltd.* v. *Knight Ltd.* [1969] 1 Lloyd's Rep. 364.

[71] See also the discussion *ante*, Chap. 1, pp. 13 *et seq.*

had put the order in hand. Four days later the guardians affixed their seal to the contract. *Held*, that as T. had assented to the alteration made by the guardians, there was mutuality between the parties at the time the seal was affixed, and the contract was binding: *Dartford Union* v. *Trickett* (1889).[72]

(2) Section 174 of the Public Health Act 1875 required urban district councils to enter into contracts under seal where the consideration was in excess of £50, and stipulated that the contracts should state the time for performance of the works. The tender documents required the contractor to obtain sureties for due performance and to execute jointly with them a contract under seal for due performance of the works. The documents made no mention of the time of commencement, and did not identify the sureties. The clerk to the council, following a resolution of the council, accepted the tender by letter, to which he affixed the seal of the council. The contractor attended with his sureties for signature of the formal contract, but for various reasons no contract was in fact signed. *Held*, the tender left two matters for further agreement, namely, the time for commencement of the works and the selection of sureties, and there was accordingly no binding contract: *Bozson* v. *Altrincham U.D.C.* (1903).[73]

(Note: The judgments in this case appear to depend upon the failure to agree these two terms, upon non-compliance with the statute (now repealed), and upon the tender requirement for entry into a formal contract. It is not entirely clear to what extent the court considered these were independent reasons for holding that there was no contract, but it is submitted that all three were valid and independent grounds for the decision.)

In building and engineering contracts a complicating factor is that negotiations between the parties frequently take place in the general framework of contract documents incorporating a contract in the standard form, and often in practice continue for a substantial period after work has commenced, whereas the standard forms assume and are drafted on the basis of complete agreement between the parties before work commences. The negotiations may lead to apparent agreement, but the parties may fail to realise that there may be difficulties in applying the wording of the contract conditions to work done prior to the final agreement. In such a case the courts will do all that they can to give effect to the parties' intention, either by implication of terms in the contract or by construing the final acceptance as having retrospective effect.

ILLUSTRATION

Sub-contractors tendered their price in February 1959 on contract conditions which included a power to vary the work and a fluctuations clause. Considerable changes were made in the work after the date of the tender, necessitating amendment of the drawings, specifi-

---

[72] 59 L.T. 754. Compare the decision of Blain J. in *Davies & Co. Shopfitters Ltd.* v. *William Old* (1969) 113 S.J. 262, *post*, Chap. 15, pp. 744–745.
[73] 67 J.P. 397.

cation, and bills of quantities, and in June 1959 the sub-contractors were asked to start work by a " letter of intent." [74] By April 1960 all the conditions of the contract had been agreed between the parties but no contract was actually signed. Both parties from the outset had intended to make a legally binding contract. The contractors contended that, no contract having been signed, they were entitled to be paid on a *quantum meruit* and not at the tender prices. They pointed out that no amendment of the original tender price had been made, notwithstanding the changes in the work, and that the conditions of contract made no provision for valuing variations made before the contract was concluded. *Held*, by Megaw J., that (1) contractual conditions could not become binding piecemeal, and no binding contract therefore existed before April 1960, (2) there must have been a continuing intention up till that date by both parties to make a contract, (3) the parties must have agreed at that date not only on all terms which they regarded as required to bring the contract into existence, but also on any terms which, even though they did not realise it, were essential if the contract was to be commercially workable, (4) there must be some clear indication of acceptance by the offeree. On the facts (2) and (4) had been satisfied. As to (3) it was necessary, for the contract to be commercially workable, that its provisions for adjustment of the tender price should apply retrospectively to the changes which had occurred between the tender and April 1960. The parties having acted in the course of negotiations on the understanding and in anticipation that a contract, once made, would govern what had been done meanwhile, there was an effective contract in April 1960, either because a term would be implied that the variations clauses should apply retrospectively, or because the ultimate acceptance of the tender (which itself contemplated variations) applied to and embraced the changes requested and agreed in anticipation of ultimate acceptance: *Trollope & Colls Ltd.* v. *Atomic Power Construction Ltd.* (1963). [75]

(c) Acceptance within reasonable time

Unless withdrawn, an offer or tender remains in force until it is accepted or lapses by effluxion of time.

Acceptance (or ratification of any unauthorised or informal acceptance if this is necessary) must take place within a reasonable time. [76] If the contract specifies a date of commencement, acceptance after that date would usually be too late, particularly, it is suggested, in building and engineering contracts where the contractor would need considerable notice to prepare a site and plant organisation and labour force.

ILLUSTRATION

A board advertised for tenders for the supply of goods as from September 30. K. tendered. On September 22 the board passed a resolution that K.'s tender be accepted, and that the board's seal

---

[74] For its terms, see *supra*, p. 219.
[75] [1963] 1 W.L.R. 333.
[76] *Murray* v. *Rennie* (1897) 24 R. (Ct. of Sess.) 965; *Ramsgate Hotel Co.* v. *Montefiore* (1866) L.R. 1 Ex. 107.

should be affixed. On the same day the clerk to the board (who was not an authorised agent for this purpose) wrote to K. informing him that his tender was accepted. On September 24 K. withdrew his tender. On October 6 the board resolved that K. should be held to his offer. The seal was not, in fact, affixed till after October 6. *Held,* that as the ratification of the acceptance by the clerk was not within a reasonable time and was after the date fixed for performance to commence, it was too late: *Metropolitan Asylums Board* v. *Kingham* (1890).[77]

Where, however, the contractor has in fact commenced work in the expectation of a contract being entered into (an extremely common state of affairs in building and engineering contracts), an acceptance after the date for commencement will be valid[78] since this requirement will have been waived.

The practice of local and other government authorities and statutory corporations in accepting tenders at the present day leaves much to be desired. The tendency to put contracts out to tender (particularly in engineering contracts) in a relatively unplanned state, and to allow contractors a wholly insufficient period for making a careful investigation of the site and of any other technical problems involved, has already been mentioned.[79] This is accompanied, para-doxically often in the same cases, by precipitate acceptance of the tenders and orders to commence work before a start is really practical (usually in order to obtain loan sanction within a particular account-ing year), and by a lengthy period (usually because possession of the whole of the site has not been arranged in advance and other diffi-culties due to lack of pre-planning, such as difficulties with ground conditions, and lack of information in regard to foundations, foundation concrete, and column bases, have emerged) during which the whole project hangs fire after the commencement date. Many large contracts let by private property developers suffer from similar deficiencies of administration, which can be grossly unfair to the contractor and make pre-planning on his part impossible, perhaps turning a potentially profitable contract into a loss.

From the legal point of view, the subject of time for acceptance is closely allied to the subject of time for commencement, since it makes little difference to a contractor, for example, if he is infor-mally told that he is the successful tenderer but does not receive formal acceptance for a long period, or if conditional acceptance of

[77] 6 T.L.R. 217. (If in time, the ratification would have been valid and binding notwithstanding the prior withdrawal of the offer; see *infra*, p. 228.)

[78] See *e.g. Trollope & Colls Ltd.* v. *Atomic Power Construction Ltd.* [1963] 1 W.L.R. 333, *supra.*

[79] *Ante*, p. 134.

his tender has to await fulfilment of the condition for a lengthy period, or if his tender is promptly accepted but he does not receive an order to commence for a long period.[79a] The ideal arrangement is a contract put out to tender with a stated and realistic date for starting work, sufficiently distant in time to enable all parties to plan and be ready for an effective start when the date arrives. Employers are usually responsible for the pressure to advance the date.

The R.I.B.A. standard forms have blank dates for insertion in their appendices showing the date for possession. This introduces a sensible degree of certainty into the position, provided the documents go out to tender with the date inserted. If the documents go out to tender in blank, it is submitted that a vital term has not been agreed upon, since the liability for liquidated damages for delay under these forms hinges upon this date, and the contractor cannot be bound by any purported acceptance on behalf of the employer. Should he, however, notify his agreement to the acceptance of his tender by starting work, then he will either have accepted the date put forward in the acceptance, or if none was, the obligation on the parties will be, it is suggested, to afford possession and to start work within a reasonable time, usually, of course, his actual date of starting.

The I.C.E. standard form is considerably less satisfactory, since here the contractor is obliged to commence work within fourteen days of receiving the order in writing to do so from the engineer. In this case the tender can be accepted and the contractor kept waiting for as long as the implication of a term of reasonable time will allow. The only really satisfactory arrangement, to avoid disputes of the greatest difficulty and consequence, is for all tenders to state the date for commencement or possession of the work, but if this is not possible contractors should qualify their tenders by imposing time limits for the notification of acceptance or the date of commencement, or both.

In considering what is a reasonable time for these purposes the nature of the work and the period in which the contract is to be completed may be particularly relevant, since the costs of both building and civil engineering works are likely to be substantially affected by the weather and duration of daylight. So, for instance, a tender in the spring for work which, if accepted at once, would be completed before the winter, would not be likely to be held open

[79a] As to this, see *post*, p. 317.

for acceptance in the autumn or even mid-summer. Similar considerations will apply to coast defence or sea outfall work likely to be affected by spring tides or seasonal weather. Another relevant factor may be the presence or absence of a fluctuations clause. Most important of all, perhaps, is the size of the plant and labour force and site organisation which the contractor will have to organise and provide.

(3) Withdrawal of Tender

An offer may be withdrawn by notice at any time before acceptance,[80] unless it is supported by consideration and amounts to an option. Where the offer is made in such circumstances that acceptance by post is within the contemplation of the parties, the date of posting is the date of acceptance, and a withdrawal of the offer not received prior to the posting will be inoperative.[81]

An unauthorised acceptance by an agent can be subsequently ratified, and, if so, this will create a binding contract notwithstanding that an attempt may have been made to withdraw the offer before the ratification.[82]

(4) Tender for such Work as Employer may Order

When an offer to supply certain goods or do particular work has been accepted, both parties are normally bound, the one to do the work and the other to permit its execution. But in rare cases tenders may not be of this kind, particularly tenders by sub-contractors and suppliers. In such cases it is sometimes a difficult question of construction whether the employer is bound by his initial general acceptance of the tender, or whether his liability arises only as and when he specifically orders work done or goods to be supplied under the tender.

ILLUSTRATIONS

(1) A railway advertised for tenders for the supply of stores. W. tendered to supply at a fixed price, " in such quantities as the company's storekeeper might order from time to time." W.'s tender was accepted. *Held*, that there was a sufficient consideration for W.'s promise to supply the goods, although there was no contract binding on the railway to order any: *Great Northern Ry.* v. *Witham* (1873).[83]

---

[80] *Routledge* v. *Grant* (1828) 4 Bing. 653. See further *ante*, p. 9.
[81] *Byrne* v. *Van Tienhoven* (1880) 5 C.P.D. 344. See the more detailed discussion of these topics, *ante*, Chap. 1, Section 2, pp. 8–10.
[82] *Bolton* v. *Lambert* (1889) 41 Ch.D. 295. See also *Metropolitan Asylums Board* v. *Kingham* (1890) 6 T.L.R. 217, *supra*.
[83] L.R. 9 C.P. 16.

(2) The Admiralty accepted a tender for 2,000,000 tons, or as much as might be required, of stone for a breakwater. After a small quantity had been supplied they gave notice that no more would be required. *Held*, by the House of Lords, that they were not liable in damages for breach of contract: *Stewards* v. *Admiralty* (1901).[84]

(3) The defendants were under contract to construct a dock for the Wellington Harbour Board. The plaintiffs contracted to supply them with " all gravel and sand required by and in accordance with the specifications " for the contract " which shall from time to time be ordered or required by the employer," and the defendants undertook to order all the necessary gravel and sand from the plaintiffs. The designs for the docks proved impracticable, and the defendants were released from their contract with the Board. The plaintiffs sued for the amount of the profits that they would have obtained on supplying the quantities of gravel and sand that would have been required if the work had been carried out. *Held*, by the Court of Appeal of New Zealand (Williams J. dissenting), affirming the decision of Stuart C.J., that the defendants need only order what they required, and that the action failed: *Pitcaithly & Co.* v. *McLean & Son* (1911).[85]

These cases require to be distinguished from tenders to complete work though the actual quantities or extent may not be known—*e.g.*, to carry out a particular engineering or building project in accordance with a schedule of rates.[86] Here the obligation and right of the contractor is to do the whole work (subject to any power of the employer to order omissions)[87] and the parties will be bound on acceptance notwithstanding that the extent of the work may then be unknown.

SECTION 4. LIABILITY APART FROM CONTRACT

(1) Cost of Tendering

The costs of tendering or estimating for a substantial building project may be extremely heavy, since it will involve the employment of surveyors and estimating staff in making the necessary estimates and attending at the site of the works and examining the drawings. In general, however, this is an expense undertaken by the builder in the hope of obtaining the contract, and should he fail to do so the employer will not be liable to him for the expense involved.

If, however, it can be shown that the employer has no intention of letting the contract to the person invited to tender, or to one of a number so invited, the invitation is clearly fraudulent and an action

---

[84] 18 T.L.R. 131 (H.L.); reversing 17 T.L.R. 111.
[85] 31 N.Z.L.R. 648.
[86] *Ante*, pp. 210 *et seq.*, and *post*, Chap. 8, pp. 521 *et seq.*
[87] As to which see *post*, Chap. 8, p. 557.

will, it is submitted, lie to recover such expenses by way of damages.[88]

Even in the absence of fraud, however, a builder may render services falling outside the normal work performed gratuitously when asked to submit a tender. He may render such services in the expectation of receiving a contract, and not intend to receive payment for them additional to his profit on the contract. But if, objectively regarded, these services are rendered in the expectation (not a mere hope) of payment, in suitable cases the law will imply a promise to pay reasonable remuneration for the services.

ILLUSTRATIONS

(1) Builders submitted an estimate for the reconstruction of war damaged premises, and though no binding contract was concluded, were led to believe they would receive the contract. In this belief they prepared, between January 1951 and June 1952 at the request of the owner's surveyors, calculations for timber and steel requirements, an estimate for notional reconstruction of the premises to enable the " permissible amount " to be negotiated with the War Damage Commission, and a revised estimate, together with bills of quantities, in accordance with a new specification. Later they prepared a new estimate following amendments to the plans made by the owner, and varied this estimate from time to time as further alterations were proposed by the owner. The owner ultimately sold the property with the benefit of an agreed War Damage claim, and there was evidence that the services performed by the builders had been of considerable value to him. Fraud was not alleged. *Held*, the work carried out by the builders fell outside the normal work gratuitously performed by a builder asked to submit a tender, and was done in the belief, common to both parties, that the builders would receive the contract for rebuilding the premises. In the circumstances a promise to pay reasonable remuneration for the services would be implied: *William Lacey (Hounslow) Ltd.* v. *Davis* (1957).[89]

(2) A joiner made a number of drawings and obtained all necessary permissions in relation to certain work of alterations in premises, on the basis that he would not charge for them additionally to the price of the work itself. After considerable delay it eventually became clear that the order for the work would not be placed. *Held*, he was entitled to payment on a *quantum meruit*: *Sinclair* v. *Logan* (1961).[90]

The basis of these decisions is clearly that of the presumed intention of the parties. A tenderer in competition knows that he will not be paid if he is unsuccessful, and expects to recover the cost of unsuccessful tenders out of his margins on accepted work. An individual not in open competition with others may go to the trouble of giving estimates gratuitously, but will usually not go

---

[88] *Cf. Richardson* v. *Silvester* (1873) L.R. 9 Q.B. 34, referred to *ante*, Chap. 1, p. 6, where in the case of a vendor advertising a property for sale by auction a plea to this effect was held to give a good cause of action.

[89] [1957] 1 W.L.R. 932.

[90] 1961 S.L.T.(Sh.Ct.) 10 (Scotland).

any further except on the understanding that he will receive payment for his work out of his margins on that particular work, which will be priced accordingly. Adopting the objective standards of the English law of contract in deciding on which side of the line a case falls, it will be the nature of the work done, and whether it is of a kind usually performed gratuitously, which will be the deciding factor. This is the obverse of the test formulated in *Anson on Contracts* and Pollock, *Contracts*, already set out in the analogous case of *City of Moncton* v. *Stephen* (1956),[91] *i.e.* would a reasonable man in the position of the defendant have thought that the plaintiff intended to act without payment? In another analogous Scottish case, *Landless* v. *Wilson* (1880),[92] the decision appears to have been based on the unjust enrichment of the defendant.[93]

(2) Misrepresentation

An employer will also be liable in damages for any fraudulent misrepresentations made by himself or his agent in inviting tenders, and any provision requiring the contractor to ascertain matters for himself or offering inspection of documents or other sources of information from which the truth could be ascertained, will not avail to protect him where the misrepresentation is fraudulent.

ILLUSTRATION

Contractors tendered on plans which showed a wall existing nine feet below ordnance datum. The contract contained a provision that the contractors must not rely upon any representation made in the plans, but must ascertain the facts for themselves. The wall did not extend to the depth shown, and after completing the contract (under an arrangement that such completion should be without prejudice to their claims) the contractors brought an action for deceit. There was evidence that the representation in the plan was fraudulent. *Held*, that the provision gave protection against honest mistakes, but none against fraud by the employer or his agent: it might well be part of the fraud, being inserted in the hope that no tests would be made: *Pearson & Son Ltd.* v. *Dublin Corporation* (1907).[94]

In such a case, in addition to his right to damages, the innocent party may elect to treat the contract as rescinded, but his right will be lost if he continues to act under the contract after discovering the misrepresentation.[95]

[91] (1956) 5 D.L.R. (2d) 722 (Canada), *ante*, Chap. 1, pp. 18–19. See also *ante*, pp. 180 *et seq.*   [92] 8 R. (Ct. of Sess.) 289, *ante*, Chap. 2, pp. 179–182.
[93] In *Lacey's* case also the defendant sold the building with the benefit of the permission and plans.
[94] [1907] A.C. 351. See also *Atlas Construction Ltd.* v. *City of Montreal* (1954) 4 D.L.R. (2d) 124, illustrated *ante*, Chap. 1, p. 49.
[95] See, *e.g. Sharpley* v. *Louth and East Coast Ry.* (1876) 2 Ch.D. 663; *Selway* v. *Fogg* (1839) 5 M. & W. 83; and *Ormes* v. *Beadel* (1861) 30 L.J.Ch. 1.

In cases of innocent misrepresentation, the only remedy prior to the Misrepresentation Act 1967 [96] of the party aggrieved was rescission of any contract entered into as a result of the representation, and this right, too, was lost by acting under the contract with knowledge.[97]

Indeed, the right to rescission in cases of innocent misrepresentation could be lost merely because the contract had been executed or partly executed, so that *restitutio in integrum* was impossible, even though the misrepresentation might not have been discovered.[98]

For these reasons, innocent misrepresentations in the contract documents were seldom likely to be a practical factor in building contracts. Either a representation was a term of the contract, in which case the remedy of damages was available to the contractor, or the truth of the misrepresentation was unlikely to be found out until it was too late for rescission to be available. Furthermore, in important matters, such as the state of the site, it is almost universal to find express exclusions of liability for the accuracy of information in the contract documents,[99] and there is certainly no implied obligation on the employer's part in these matters, so that prior to 1967 the scope for invoking the doctrine in building contracts was extremely limited (the most likely representations to arise in building contracts being, of course, on the part of the employer as to the nature of the site, availability of possession, availability of access roads, availability of facilities, and other matters affecting the difficulty and expense of carrying out the contract work).

The Misrepresentation Act has introduced considerable possibilities in this context, since it confers a right of damages for innocent misrepresentations for which there is no reasonable justification, has removed the bar on rescission after a contract is partly executed, and has imposed a test of reasonableness on clauses excluding liability for misrepresentations.[1]

(3) Bribery and Secret Commissions

If a contractor obtains acceptance of his tender by offering a commission to the employer's architect or other agent, the employer

---

[96] Discussed fully *ante*, Chap. 1, pp. 38 *et seq.*

[97] See *Glasgow & S.W. Ry.* v. *Boyd* [1915] A.C. 526, illustrated *ante*, pp. 43–44.

[98] *Angel* v. *Jay* [1911] 1 K.B. 666 (but see criticisms of this doctrine by Scrutton L.J. in *Lever Bros.* v. *Bell* [1931] 1 K.B. at p. 538 and Denning L.J. in *Solle* v. *Butcher* [1950] 1 K.B. at p. 695).

[99] See, *e.g.* the case of *Atlas Construction Ltd.* v. *City of Montreal* (1954) 4 D.L.R. (2d) 124, illustrated *ante*, Chap. 1, p. 49. See also *post*, pp. 267–269.

[1] For misrepresentation generally, and the effect of this Act, see *ante*, Chap. 1, pp. 38 *et seq.*, and for warranties as to the state of the site, see *post*, Chap. 5, pp. 316–317.

can either repudiate the contract, or treat it as subsisting. In either event he can recover the bribe from his agent, and in addition damages both from the agent and the contractor.

ILLUSTRATION

An employer invited tenders, and the person tendering, with a view of obtaining a recommendation from the agent of the employer, offered him a commission, and in order to recoup himself for such a commission inserted in his tender a sum in excess of the market price by the amount of commission. Thereupon the agent advised the employer to accept the tender. *Held,* that this was a gross fraud giving a right to the employer to recover both damages from the contractor and the commission from the agent: *Salford Corporation v. Lever* (1891).[2]

So strict is the rule, that a party who wrongfully terminates a contract may subsequently justify the termination if the contract, unknown to him at the time of termination, had been brought about in fraud of him in this way.[3]

On the other hand, the right of the employer to receive the secret commission is the right of a creditor, and not of a beneficiary under a trust, so that he will not be able to follow the proceeds of the commission as he could in the case of trust money.[4] Nor can he compel his agent to enforce an improper contract for receipt of commission, so as to obtain it for himself, his right of recovery being limited to any moneys actually received by the agent.[5]

SECTION 5.   COLLUSIVE TENDERING

The frequently heavy cost of tendering sometimes leads contractors to put forward tenders which are not genuine, in the sense that, rather than refuse to make a tender when invited to do so, the contractor tenders a price higher than that "taken" from another contractor who does desire to obtain the contract, thus avoiding expense and leading the employer to believe that he has had genuine competitive tenders for the work. This practice of "taking a price" was considered by the Monopolies Commission under the Monopolies and Restrictive Practices Act of 1948 and found to be against the public interest, but no order was made under the Act, so no legal consequences appeared to follow at that time. On the authority of *Mogul Steamship Co. v. McGregor Gow*

[2] [1891] 1 Q.B. 168. See also *Re North Australian Territory Co.* [1892] 1 Ch. 322.

[3] *Alexander* v. *Webber* [1922] 1 K.B. 642, applying *Panama & South Pacific Telegraph Co.* v. *India Rubber Co.* (1875) L.R. 10 Ch. 515.

[4] *Lister* v. *Stubbs* (1890) 45 Ch.D. 1.

[5] *Powell* v. *Evans-Jones & Co.* [1905] 1 K.B. 11. (For cases of bribery and secret commissions not involving acceptance of the tender, see *ante,* pp. 175–177.)

& Co. (1892),[6] *Sorrell* v. *Smith* (1925) [7] and *Crofter Hand-Woven Harris Tweed Co.* v. *Veitch* (1942) [8] it would seem that combinations not to tender, if made with the object of protecting and extending the business of the parties, do not amount to actionable conspiracies, and would afford an employer no remedy as between himself and a contractor whose tender he had accepted. Thus, after an early conflict of judicial authority, it seems clear that an agreement between two or more persons not to bid against each other, or to deal with profits accruing to the successful bidder, was not unlawful.

ILLUSTRATIONS

(1) Tenders for the supply of stone having been invited by a corporation, it was agreed between A, B, C and D that B should not tender, that C and D should tender above A's price, that A should purchase certain quantities of stone from B, C and D, and that B, C and D should not supply the corporation with stone during 1875. B in breach of the agreement sent in a contract which was accepted. *Held*, that a bill would lie by A to restrain B from supplying the corporation with stone directly or indirectly during 1875: *Jones* v. *North* (1875).[9]

(2) At a sale by a public auction of surplus property belonging to the Ministry of Munitions, the plaintiff and the defendant agreed, in order to avoid competition, that the defendant alone should bid for certain goods and the goods if purchased should be divided equally between them. *Held*, by Banks and Atkin L.JJ. (Scrutton L.J. dissenting), that the agreement was not illegal: *Rawlings* v. *General Trading Co.* (1921).[10]

A small inroad on this doctrine was made by section 1 of the Auctions (Bidding Agreements) Act 1927, which made certain agreements in relation to sales of goods by auction an offence, but the Act does not apply to tendering for building contracts, or even to sales of land by auction.

Collusive agreements in regard to tenders are now, however, registrable in the United Kingdom under the Restrictive Practices Act 1956, and are accordingly void, unless so registered, as being against the public interest.[11] Furthermore the Act of 1968 has introduced sanctions for failure to register such agreements. It is not, however, clear to what extent the employer in a contract so obtained could avoid it or have any other remedy against the successful tenderer.

---

[6] [1892] A.C. 25.   [7] [1925] A.C. 700.   [8] [1942] A.C. 435.   [9] L.R. 19 Eq. 426.
[10] [1921] 1 K.B. 635. See also *Galton* v. *Emuss* (1844) 13 L.J.Ch. 388; *Re Carew's Estate* (1858) 26 Beav. 187; *Heffer* v. *Martin* (1867) 36 L.J.Ch. 372; and *Cohen* v. *Roche* [1927] 1 K.B. 169; *Levi* v. *Levi* (1833) 6 C. & P. 239; a decision to the contrary was disapproved in *Rawlings* v. *General Trading Co.* [1921] 1 K.B. 636.
[11] See the injunctions granted by Mocatta J. in the R. P. Court, July 31, 1970, in the case of electrical contractors.

CHAPTER 4

SPECIAL PARTIES

SECTION 1. GENERALLY

BY their nature, a large number of building and engineering contracts are carried out for employers with special legal personality, such as departments of State, Crown corporations, non-trading corporations, and local authorities. While in the vast majority of instances no complication is likely to arise thereby, theoretical legal problems do exist arising, first, from the extent of the power of such special parties to contract, secondly, from the extent of the authority of their servants or agents to contract on their behalf, and thirdly, from any special formal requirements affecting contracts undertaken by them. In addition, in the case of the Crown and Crown corporations, certain procedural complications in the conduct of litigation arise under the Crown Proceedings Act 1947.

(1) The Crown Defined

" The Crown " is a somewhat loose expression. It consists, among other things, of the Departments or Ministries of State (many of whom are corporations sole by statute, as *e.g.* the Minister of Public Building and Works) and also of corporations which, whether expressly by their statutes or charters, or impliedly as servants or agents of the Crown by reason of the degree of control exercised by the Crown through its Ministries over the performance of their duties, enjoy Crown status. Many modern statutory corporations are likely to be substantial employers under building contracts, *e.g.* the Central Electricity Generating Board, the various Hospital, Gas and Coal Boards, regional and national, and British Railways and the B.R.S. In modern instances such as these Crown status will usually depend upon the statute setting up the corporation and is not usually conferred thereby, *e.g.* new towns, regional hospital boards, boards of governors of teaching hospitals and hospital management committees under sections 12 and 13 (2) of the National Health Service Act 1946 and the National Parks Commission under the National Parks and Access to the Countryside Act 1949, while the indirect control of the Minister, *e.g.* by appointment of the members of the corporation, will not by itself attract Crown status.

(2) Non-trading Corporations and Necessity for Seal

In the absence of express provision, non-trading corporations, whether incorporated by charter or statutory in origin, and whether enjoying Crown status or not, could only contract under their seal.[1] This rule has now been abolished by the Corporate Bodies' Contracts Act 1960.[2]

(3) Doctrine of Ultra Vires

Furthermore, under the doctrine of *ultra vires*, no corporation, whether enjoying Crown status or not, and indeed no agent or Minister of the Crown acting under statutory or other powers, can validly contract if the subject-matter of the contract is beyond the scope of the constitution of the corporation or of the powers in question.[3] In the case of companies and corporations, the scope of the constitution can be determined, in theory, by examining the statute, charter or memorandum and articles of the body concerned. In the case of the Crown, the extent of its servant's power will depend upon any relevant statutory provisions, or, in the case of the higher officers of State, their inherent constitutional power. In the case of corporations (but not the Crown) the officers of the corporation may be liable on an implied warranty of authority in respect of an *ultra vires* contract.[4]

SECTION 2.   THE CROWN

Apart from Crown corporations, the chief contracting departments of the Government are the Service Ministries, and the Ministry of Public Building and Works.[5]

As the principle is that the Crown is only bound by its proper agent acting within the scope of his authority, it is in law the duty of a contractor with a government department to inquire whether the person proposing to contract on behalf of the Government has any necessary authority and is acting within its scope.

ILLUSTRATIONS

(1) A contractor engaged by contract under seal with the Minister of Public Works of the Dominion of Canada to complete for a lump sum of $78,000 a deep sea wharf, agreeably to plans and

---

[1] *Austin* v. *Guardians of Bethnal Green* (1874) L.R. 9 C.P. 91; *Phelps* v. *Upton Snodsbury Highway Board* (1885) 1 T.L.R. 425.

[2] See *ante*, Chap. 1, pp. 21–22.

[3] *Ashbury Railway Carriage & Iron Co.* v. *Riche* (1875) L.R. 7 H.L. 653; *Sinclair* v. *Brougham* [1914] A.C. 398.

[4] See subsections (2) and (4), *infra*.

[5] For their constitutional authority and powers, see Halsbury's *Laws*, 3rd ed., Vol. 7, pp. 395, 400, 419, 425 and 426.

specifications, and to such directions as should be given by the engineer in charge during the progress of the work. By the 7th clause of the contract no extra work could be performed unless ordered in writing by the engineer in charge before the execution of the work. By letters the Minister of Public Works authorised the contractor to make certain additions to the wharf. The contractor sued for the price of these additions. *Held*, that he could not recover: *O'Brien* v. *The Queen* (1880).[6]

(2) Contractors made a contract with the Crown, represented by the Minister of Public Works for Canada, to construct a bridge for a lump sum. After completion a final certificate was given by the engineer, and its amount was paid. The contractors subsequently made a claim for the value of work alleged to have been done, but not included in the final certificate, which work they alleged was caused by alterations ordered by the chief engineer of so radical a nature as to create a new contract. *Held*, that the engineer had no power to make any such new contract binding on the Crown: *R.* v. *Starrs* (1889).[7]

In practice, however, it is not easy to see how the authority of agents of the Crown can be ascertained and defined by the subject, and this is the more unfortunate in that it is doubtful to what extent the ordinary principles of the law of agency apply as between the Crown, its agents, and persons contracting with them. Thus an agent of the Crown contracting as such cannot be sued personally on a contract made by him, unless an intention that he should be personally liable can be inferred from the circumstances.[8] Nor can a public servant acting on behalf of the Crown be liable for breach of any implied warranty of authority to contract.[9] In certain cases, however, officers of a court, *e.g.* receivers or managers appointed by the courts, or a clerk of the court, may be held personally liable if they do not exclude their personal liability.[10]

In certain very special cases, virtually unknown today, Parliament might fix a particular sum to be expended for a particular purpose, and for contracts to be placed before Parliament. In such a case it may be unsafe for a contractor, relying on departmental assurances, to expend additional sums on extras on the chance of a supplementary vote [11] and, even assuming that such a contract is validly made by a person having authority to contract on behalf of the Crown, it is still open to Parliament to refuse to find the funds

[6] 4 Can.S.C. 529 (Henry J. dissenting).
[7] 17 Can.S.C. 118.
[8] *Palmer* v. *Hutchinson* (1881) 6 App.Cas. 619; *Samuel Brothers Ltd.* v. *Whetherley* [1907] 1 K.B. 709.
[9] *Dunn* v. *Macdonald* [1897] 1 Q.B. 401, 555.
[10] *Auty* v. *Hutchinson* (1848) 6 C.B. 266; *Burt, Boulton and Hayward* v. *Bull* [1895] 1 Q.B. 276.
[11] *Wood* v. *R.* (1877) 7 Can.S.C.R. 634.

for the contract. Usually the contract provided that the consideration was payable out of funds provided by Parliament. In such an
event, the provision of the funds was a condition precedent, and no
action for damages would lie if Parliament refused to ratify the
contract.[12]

By section 1 of the Crown Proceedings Act 1947, the Crown can
now be sued in contract as of right, and no longer enjoys the procedurally privileged position which it occupied prior to that Act.
Under section 17 of the Act, a list of authorised departments is
published from time to time by the Treasury, and is available at
H.M. Stationery Office,[13] and civil proceedings against the Crown are
to be instituted against the appropriate department, and service to
be effected against the person whose name and address are shown in
the list as solicitor for that department. In case of doubt, proceedings should be instituted against the Attorney-General, who has
power to apply, as has any other department, for substitution of
another department as defendant. By section 25, provision is made
for the satisfaction of orders or judgments made against the Crown,
and by section 27 attachment of moneys payable by the Crown can
be effected, so that a creditor of a builder can obtain an order
under that section in any case where he could obtain attachment of
moneys due under a contract under the general law, in the same
way as if the Crown was a normal employer.[14]

Under Order 77, r. 3, of the Rules of the Supreme Court, indorse-
ments of writs against the Crown must show the circumstances in
which it is alleged that the liability of the Crown has arisen and the
departments and officers of the Crown concerned.

SECTION 3. LOCAL AUTHORITIES

(1) Authority to Contract

By far the majority of public building contracts in the United
Kingdom are concluded by local authorities. Their contracts need
no longer be under seal.[15]

By section 266 of the Local Government Act 1933 all contracts
made by local authorities are required to be made in accordance
with standing orders, but the proviso to this section absolves
persons entering into contracts with local authorities from the

---

[12] *Churchward* v. *R.* (1865) L.R. 1 Q.B. 173.
[13] See the *Annual Practice*, Vol. 2, notes to the Crown Proceedings Act 1947, s. 17;
   Current Law Year Book, 1957, § 2789.
[14] See *post*, Chap. 14, Assignment, pp. 735 *et seq.*
[15] Corporate Bodies (Contracts) Act 1960, *ante*, Chap. 1, pp. 21–22.

necessity of inquiring whether the standing orders have been complied with, and gives full effect to such contracts despite any omission in this respect. The section contemplates that the power to contract may be delegated to a committee of the local authority, in accordance with section 85 (1) of the Local Government Act 1933. Even where no delegation has taken place, a contract purported to be made by a committee can be validly ratified by the council of the local authority.[16] The importance of this section at the present day is that standing orders cannot be relied upon by a local authority to show that an agent purporting to contract on their behalf did not have ostensible authority to do so. It has already been seen that (contrary to the rule with private architects and their clients) a borough surveyor has been held to have both actual and ostensible authority to contract on behalf of a local authority.[17] The officers of local authorities usually concerned in negotiating and concluding building contracts have already been described.[18]

(2) Public Authorities' Protection

A special period of limitation of one year was formerly prescribed by section 21 of the Limitation Act 1939 in respect of acts done in pursuance of any Act of Parliament or any public duty or authority.

The exact application of this section was a matter of the greatest difficulty, and it was always a matter of doubt to what extent it would apply to an action for breach of contract arising out of a building contract, particularly for the construction of houses under post-war legislation. Happily, this difficulty is now academic, as the section in question was repealed by section 1 of the Law Reform (Limitation of Actions) Act of 1954, and the normal periods of limitation, namely, twelve years from the breach in the case of contracts under seal, and six years in the case of simple contracts, now apply against local authorities as against other legal persons.[19]

SECTION 4. TRADING CORPORATIONS

These may owe their existence to charter or special statutes, but in the overwhelming majority of cases are incorporated under the Companies Acts. In neither case need their trading contracts be under seal. The doctrine of *ultra vires*, however, applies to such

---

[16] *Kidderminster Corporation* v. *Hardwick* (1873) L.R. 9 Ex. 13.
[17] See *Carlton Contractors* v. *Bexley Corporation* (1962) 60 L.G.R. 331, *ante*, Chap. 2, pp. 110–111.
[18] *Ante*, Chap. 2, p. 110.
[19] For limitation, see *post*, Chap. 5, pp. 368–370.

corporations,[20] and for this reason the memorandum of association of a trading company almost invariably sets out its objects in the widest terms so as to give it the greatest possible freedom of contract.

Unlike the case of the Crown, the officers of the company may be liable upon an implied warranty of authority, but under the rule in *Royal British Bank* v. *Turquand* (1856),[21] a contractor dealing with officers of a company is taken to have notice of everything contained in the articles of association, which among other things will define the powers of directors and others to bind the company by entering into contracts.[22] It should perhaps be particularly noted that, unless expressly authorised, the secretary of a company has no power to contract or even to make representations on its behalf.[23] This subject is exhaustively treated in the various standard works on company law.

[20] See *supra*, p. 236.
[21] 6 E. & B. 327.
[22] Contrast the position under s. 266 of the Local Government Act 1933, *supra*, pp. 238–239, when dealing with local authorities.
[23] *Bell* v. *L.N.W.Ry.* (1852) 15 Beav. 548.

CHAPTER 5

PERFORMANCE

IN this chapter, it is proposed to discuss a number of the obligations of the parties associated with the performance of the work of a building or engineering contract, and also the various ways in which the parties may be discharged from their liability for further performance, including frustration, discharge by breach, illegality, and (not strictly a case of discharge) limitation. There is also a section on insurance and indemnities. Much of this chapter is concerned with matters which, though of the most fundamental importance, are regulated more by general principles of law or by the implication of terms than by any explicit express terms in the more usual types of contract. Certain particular subjects associated with performance, however, such as maintenance and defects,[1] time for completion and liquidated damages [2] and payment of the price [3] are dealt with later in this book in chapters devoted exclusively to them, as well as matters such as variations, approval and certificates, assignment, sub-contractors, ownership of materials and plant, and forfeiture and determination, the common link being that all these latter subjects tend to be the subject of fairly detailed express provision in most contracts.

SECTION 1. OBLIGATIONS OF THE CONTRACTOR

(1) The Obligation to Complete

Most formal building or engineering contracts contain an initial express obligation of the contractor in some such words as to "carry out and complete the works in accordance with the contract." This is in fact a dual obligation, with an important consequential effect in regard to the running of the limitation period for defective work,[3a] but otherwise it is doubtful if it adds anything to what the law would in any event imply in any entire contract however informally concluded.

---

[1] *Post*, Chap. 6.
[2] *Post*, Chaps. 10 and 11.
[3] *Post*, Chap. 9.
[3a] See *infra*, p. 368.

This most fundamental obligation of the contractor receives surprisingly little treatment in the express provisions of building contracts. What is called " substantial completion " [4] or " practical completion " [5] is usually required under the scheme of most contracts to start the maintenance period running and secure the release of the first half of the retention moneys, though the phrase is not in general defined. [6] But in addition, nearly all contracts contain an express or implied undertaking by the contractor to complete the whole of the project in question, upon which will depend the right to payment of the full contract price, whether in the form of the retention moneys and any general balance due in the case of contracts where there has previously been interim payment, or, in less sophisticated contracts, the whole contract price itself. The vast majority of building contracts, sophisticated or simple, for the construction of a block of flats or a garden shed, will be construed as contracts of this kind, that is to say, entire contracts in the legal sense; if so, the absence of an express undertaking to complete is irrelevant—a contract which is entire is a contract where the law if necessary implies that one party's obligation must be fully performed before the other party's obligation (usually of course to pay the price) arises. It has already been stated [7] that most measured or " schedule " contracts, with or without bills of quantities, are entire contracts. [8] Thus a contract to build a house in accordance with a schedule of rates, with no estimated quantities or grossed-up contract sum, and perhaps no drawings or specification yet in existence, remains nevertheless a contract to build and complete a house. Half-way through building it the builder cannot, in the absence of breach of contract by the employer, stop work and sue for the value of work done to date, or for half the price. It is vitally important, therefore, to decide the exact nature of this legal obligation to complete, since upon it will depend the vital matter of the contractor's entitlement to the contract price. The subject needs to be considered first in relation to entire contracts, and secondly, in relation to contracts which are not entire. This topic and the qualifications upon the strictest application of the rule which have been effected by what is known as the doctrine of substantial performance, have given rise to considerable legal controversy and

---

[4] Clause 48 of the I.C.E. standard form.
[5] Clause 15 of the 1963 R.I.B.A. standard form.
[6] See *infra*, p. 258.
[7] *Ante*, Chap. 3, pp. 201, 206. See also *post*, Chap. 9, pp. 563–564.
[8] See *Ibmac Ltd.* v. *Marshall Ltd.* (1968) 208 E.G. 851, *infra*, p. 253.

though it is of the greatest practical importance, the discussion in the following pages will primarily be of interest to legally qualified readers.

It should be remembered that, if the contract requires completion to be certified by the architect or engineer, as is very often the case, different principles may apply, and the following discussion may not be relevant. Sometimes in such cases the final certificate may bind both parties (unless there is an arbitration clause) and the actual degree of physical completion of the work will in such a case not be of importance. In some contracts, too, clauses conditional upon completion (such as, for instance, the time periods in certain defects clauses) [9] and which are usually conditioned upon the date of certified completion and not any other date, may also be binding on the parties.[10] By virtue of the presence of wide-ranging arbitration clauses, however, many contracts at the present day are in a form [10a] which ensures that disputes as to completion will be decided on their merits, and the following discussion will accordingly be fully relevant.

(a) Entire contracts

(i) *Completion of contract as a whole.* In a very large number of contracts in everyday life, the entire fulfilment of the promise made by one party is a condition precedent to the right to call for fulfilment of any part of the promise made by the other. So if a contract of sale stipulates for payment in advance, the payment must be made in full before delivery can be called for. Partial payment (unless permitted by the contract) will not do. Equally, if the contract requires delivery of the goods before the price is payable, there must, if it is an entire contract and not a severable one, be a complete delivery of goods, conforming in all respects with the contract requirements, before payment becomes due. A well-known example is furnished by the old case of *Cutter* v. *Powell* (1795),[11] in which the defendant agreed with a sailor at Jamaica in the following terms: " Ten days after the ship *Governor Pary* . . . arrives at Liverpool I promise to pay to Mr. T. Cutter the sum of thirty guineas, provided he proceeds, continues and does his duty as second mate in the said ship from here to the port of Liverpool . . . "; the sailor having done

---

[9] See *post*, Chap. 6, pp. 392 *et seq.*

[10] See *e.g. McCarthy* v. *Visser* (1905) 22 Cape of Good Hope Rep. 122, and the case of *Cunliffe* v. *Hampton Wick Local Board* (1893) 9 T.L.R. 378; Hudson's B.C., 4th ed. Vol. 2, p. 250, illustrated *post*, Chap. 6, p. 393.

[10a] See, however, the discussion and criticism of Clause 35 (7) of the R.I.B.A. Conditions, *post*, Chap. 7, pp. 490–491.

[11] 6 T.R. 320; 2 Sm.L.C. 1. See, however, *Stubbs'* case, *post*, p. 256.

his duty until his death on board before the completion of the voyage, the plaintiff, who was the sailor's personal representative, was held not to be entitled to recover a proportionate or any part of the agreed remuneration.

The essence of a building contract is a promise by the contractor to carry out work and supply materials in consideration of a promise by the building owner to pay for it. In most contracts for major works the contractor is given an express right to payment by instalments on account of the contract price as the works proceed, and so to that extent no question of an entire contract arises. But the rules as to entire contracts will still apply to the last instalment, or to any general balance due, or to any individual instalment if the work is abandoned or brought to an end before the instalment is completely earned.[12] Furthermore, in many smaller contracts the question whether the contractor is bound to complete the works in their entirety before becoming entitled to any payment on account is of vital practical importance. Where entire performance is a condition precedent to payment, the builder, in order to recover his price, must either prove entire performance or else an acceptance of the works by the building owner amounting to a waiver of the condition.[13] In contracts for the sale of goods the buyer must either accept or reject the goods and a failure to reject within a reasonable time will be regarded as an acceptance. The buyer cannot keep the goods without paying for them; if he accepts them, he must pay the price subject to any cross claim for damages for breach of contract. But a building owner who merely allows works erected on his land to remain there does not impliedly accept them.[14] Thus where the contract is entire, the owner may get the benefit of valuable works not entirely completed by the builder without having to pay for them. Nor can a builder who has not fully completed the work, through no fault of the employer, overcome his difficulty by ignoring the contract and sue on a *quantum meruit* for the work he has done.[15] It should perhaps be mentioned that the rigours of this rule are often considerably reduced because, in a large number of cases where there is not entire performance, the employer will decide to sue the builder for damages for breach of contract. If he does, he will

---

[12] See *infra*, pp. 255 *et seq.* See also *Eshelby* v. *Federated European Bank* [1932] 1 K.B. 423 (whether guarantor liable where instalments not fully earned), *infra*, pp. 251–252.
[13] See *e.g. Tannenbaum Meadows Ltd.* v. *Wright-Winston Ltd.* (1965) 49 D.L.R. (2d) 386 *infra*, p. 252. See also *post*, Chap. 6, pp. 376 *et seq.*
[14] See *post*, Chap. 6, pp. 377 *et seq.*
[15] *Munro* v. *Butt* (1858) 8 E. & B. 738.

usually, depending on how he computes his damages and the nature of the breach, have to give credit for what he would have had to pay had the contract been properly performed.[16] But in a case where the employer decides not to sue [17] he may derive considerable advantage from the foregoing rules, which are, however, an essential and necessary sanction to discourage the deliberate breaking or abandonment of contracts which would be absent if in such cases the builder was entitled to demand partial payment notwithstanding his own breach.

Unlike contracts for the sale of goods, therefore, the consequence of a rigid application of the rule can work considerable hardship and anomalies in the case of contracts for services, as in *Cutter* v. *Powell, supra,* or for work done and materials supplied, such as a building contract, since whenever it is not possible to sever or apportion the price and the performance (*i.e.* whenever it is a " lump sum " or entire contract) [18] a builder can nearly complete a project, or complete it while leaving some defects in it, and the employer can avoid payment unless there are express provisions for interim payment. The great majority of building contracts in the traditional form consist of an undertaking to complete the work for a contract price either ascertained (in the case of a specification form of contract without quantities) or ascertainable (in the case of a measurement contract with quantities or schedules of rates) and are therefore " lump sum " or entire contracts, save only to the extent that they may contain express provisions for interim or stage payment. Except in very rare cases the courts will not imply a term for interim or stage payments.[19]

To overcome the difficulties of this rule, the courts have evolved (much earlier than the case of *Dakin & Co.* v. *Lee* (1916) [20] which is usually credited with its inception) the doctrine of substantial performance. Under this, provided the plaintiff can show that he has "substantially performed" his obligations, he can sue for the price, giving credit for any deficiencies which may exist in his work.

It was stated in the seventh edition of this book that contracts for a lump sum [18] ascertained and specified were usually entire. If this

[16] See *post,* Chap. 9, p. 585.
[17] See for a good example *Ibmac Ltd.* v. *Marshall Ltd.* (1968) 208 E.G. 851, *infra,* p. 253.
[18] " Lump sum " in this context should not be confused with the use of the expression in contradistinction to " measured " contracts—as to which see *ante,* Chap. 3, pp. 201 and 206, and *post,* Chap. 9, pp. 563–564.
[19] See *infra,* pp. 260 *et seq.*
[20] [1916] 1 K.B. 566. See the older cases illustrated, *infra,* p. 251.

meant that a builder who substantially performs his obligations under such a contract cannot recover, the statement was too wide— see *per* Denning L.J. in *Hoenig* v. *Isaacs* (1952),[21] where he said:

" It was a lump sum contract, but that does not mean that entire performance was a condition precedent to payment. Where a contract provides for a specific sum to be paid on completion of specified work, the courts lean against a construction of the contract which would deprive the contractor of any payment at all simply because there are some defects or omissions."

That case, and *Dakin* v. *Lee* (1916),[22] followed several considerably earlier decisions to the same effect [23] and may at first sight appear to conflict with the reasoning in certain of the cases on entire contracts. Thus in *Sumpter* v. *Hedges* (1898) [24] A. L. Smith L.J. said: " The law is that where there is a contract to do work for a lump sum, until the work is completed the price of it cannot be recovered."

But the decision in *Sumpter* v. *Hedges* (1898) was clearly right, because the plaintiff abandoned the work when little more than half-done and repudiated his contract. It was, therefore, immaterial whether in fact the contract was an entire contract in the strict sense or merely a contract in which substantial performance was required. Indeed, in considering the previous cases of this kind where a plaintiff was unsuccessful, one must always bear in mind that the *ratio decidendi* may be (i) that the contract which on its true construction called for a particularly strict degree of performance [25] was an entire contract, or (ii) that substantial performance was permissible, but the plaintiff did not achieve substantial performance, or (iii) that the plaintiff repudiated the contract before any right to payment accrued.

As Blackburn J. said, however, in *Appleby* v. *Myers* (1867) [26]: " . . . there is nothing to render it either illegal or absurd in the workman to agree to complete the whole, and to be paid when the whole is complete, and not till then. . . . " If a builder does enter into an entire contract in the strict sense, and fails to complete the work, he can neither claim a *quantum meruit* for what he has done nor maintain a suit in equity for an account or other equitable relief. Nor does the fact that parts of the specified sum are ascribed

[21] [1952] 2 All E.R. 176 at p. 180.
[22] [1916] 1 K.B. 566.
[23] See *infra*, p. 251.
[24] [1898] 1 Q.B. 673 at p. 674, illustrated, *infra*, p. 248.
[25] See *e.g. Eshelby* v. *Federated European Bank Ltd.* [1932] 1 K.B. 254 and 423, and *Morgan* v. *S. & S. Construction Property Ltd.* [1967] V.R. 149 (Australia), *infra*, pp. 251, 253.
[26] L.R. 2 C.P. 651 at p. 660.

to different parts of the works (as, for instance, in a bill of quantities) necessarily result in the contract being severable, so that payment may be recovered for such parts as are complete.

In the foregoing judgments, the use of the expression " lump sum " is used in the legal sense to refer to contracts to do work for a definite sum of money or a sum to be ascertained which cannot be severed and exactly the same considerations will apply to contracts using bills, called in this book "measured contracts" or contracts "with quantities," or to measurement contracts based on schedules of rates (provided they relate to an identifiable project, as opposed to mere " jobbing " or day-to-day contracts), as to contracts in the specification form without quantities (which are frequently loosely referred to as " lump sum " contracts [27]). The following are examples of cases where the distinction between entire and severable contracts was considered. In addition to the cases illustrated below, those under Section 3, Impossibility and Frustration,[28] should also be considered.

ILLUSTRATIONS

(1) The plaintiff brought an action on a contract for building a house to recover the balance of the sum therein agreed on, the principal part of the price having been paid. It was proved that the plaintiff had omitted to put into the building certain joists and other materials of the given description and measure. *Held*, the plaintiff, not having performed the agreement he had proved, could not recover either on the contract, deducting the difference in value, or upon a *quantum valebat*: *Ellis* v. *Hamlen* (1810).[29]

(2) The plaintiff undertook to build a mill and, if it did not answer, to build another, and the defendant agreed to pay a specific sum. *Held*, that the plaintiff could not recover unless he proved either that the mill answered or that the defendant had accepted it: *Davis* v. *Nichols* (1814).[30]

(3) The plaintiff undertook to repair and make perfect three chandeliers for £10 and did repair them in part but did not make them perfect. *Held*, the plaintiff not having performed his part of the contract could not in an action of *assumpsit* recover for the value of the work done and materials supplied: *Sinclair* v. *Bowles* (1829).[31]

(4) A Bros. entered into an agreement with B to erect upon premises in his possession a steam-engine and machinery. The contract consisted of a specification containing ten distinct parts, under each of which were particular descriptions of the work to be done in connection with each respectively and the prices to be charged for the same, and concluded with the words " We offer

[27] See *ante*, Chap. 3, pp. 201, 206, and *post*, Chap. 9, pp. 563–564.
[28] *Infra*, pp. 348 *et seq.* See also the cases of *Maryon* v. *Carter* and *Kingdom* v. *Cox* illustrated *post*, pp. 610–611.   [29] 3 Taunt. 52.
[30] 2 Chit.(K.B.) 320.
[31] 9 B. & C. 92. See also *Pontifex* v. *Wilkinson* (1845), illustrated *post*, Section 3, p. 343.

to make and erect the whole of the machinery of the best materials
and workmanship of their respective kinds, and to put it to work,
for the sums above named respectively, and to keep the whole in
order under fair wear and tear for two years from the date of completion. All brickwork, carpenters' and masons' work, and materials,
are to be provided for us; but the drawings and general instruction
required for them to work will be provided by us subject to the
architect's approval." The total cost of the works would have
amounted to £459. During the course of the works, when items 1–8
had been partially completed and some of the materials for the other
items were on the premises, the premises were destroyed by an
accidental fire. B had made use of a tank erected by A Bros.
A Bros. brought an action to recover £419 for work done and
materials supplied. *Held*, A Bros. having contracted to do an entire
work for a specific sum could recover nothing unless the work was
done or it could be shown that it was the defendant's fault that the
work was incomplete, or that there was something to justify the
conclusion that the parties had entered into a fresh contract: *Appleby*
v. *Myers* (1867).[32]

(5) S. contracted with H. to build two houses and stables for
£565. S. did part of the work worth £333 and received part payment.
S. then told H. that he had no money and could not go on with the
work and abandoned the contract. H. completed the work making
use of materials which S. had left upon the land. In an action by
S. the county court judge gave him judgment for the value of these
materials, but nothing in respect of the work he had done on the
buildings. S. appealed. *Held*, S. having abandoned the original
contract could not recover on it, there were no circumstances from
which a fresh contract to pay for the work done could be inferred,
and therefore S. could not recover for the work done as upon a
quantum meruit: *Sumpter* v. *Hedges* (1898).[33]

(6) The ship *L.* having stranded, the owner instructed the master
to contract for her repair, limiting the price to £6,000 and limiting
the work to the repair of damage by stranding. The master contracted
with F. to do the work for a lump sum. The contract provided
that further work should be paid for at schedule rates. F. did not
carry out the specified repairs but alleged that he had with the
master's authority done the equivalent or better. *Held*, that the
contract was an entire one and not having performed it in its entirety,
F. could not recover the lump sum: *Forman* v. *The Liddesdale*
(1900).[34]

(7) A contractor agreed to supply wallpaper at a certain price,
and labour to fix it at a price per hour. The paper was delivered,
but before the work was complete the building was destroyed by
fire. There was no term in the contract fixing the time of payment,
or that it should be only after completion. *Held*, that this was
distinguishable from *Appleby* v. *Myers* (1867),[35] and that the contract
was not entire, and that therefore the contractor could recover the

[32] L.R. 2 C.P. 651 (for the contract, see L.R. 1 C.P. 615).
[33] [1898] 1 Q.B. 673.
[34] [1900] A.C. 190.
[35] *Supra*.

value of the materials actually worked into the house before the fire, and the value of the labour thereon expended: *Wyett* v. *Smith* (1908).[36] (This New Zealand case contains a careful consideration of and was based upon the English authorities.)

In *Appleby* v. *Myers* (1867), though the price was sub-divided into ten parts, the contract was held to be entire. As stated, contracts to do work for a sum to be ascertained, *e.g.* in accordance with a schedule of prices or bills of quantities, will usually be entire contracts if such appears to be the intention of the parties. The following are examples of cases on each side of the borderline.

ILLUSTRATIONS

(1) W. agreed to make a pavement of about 1,500 sq. yds in three rooms of D.'s laundry to the satisfaction of P. to be paid for at so much per square yard on completion. D. objected to the quality of the work while it was being carried out, nor was the work done to P.'s satisfaction and D. would not allow W. to do the last 200 sq. yds. D. entered into occupation of the laundry but refused to pay. The Official Referee found that in 2 rooms the floor was defective, but not so bad that it would need to be taken up, and gave judgment for the plaintiff, W., for £139. D. appealed. *Held*, there was no evidence that D. had waived the performance of the special contract, which had not been performed; that there was no evidence of a fresh contract to pay for the work as it was done, and, therefore, the plaintiff could not recover: *Whitaker* v. *Dunn* (1887).[37]

(2) A defendant counterclaimed for the value of work done by the defendant for the plaintiffs in boring an artesian well. The contract was to sink the well at 75 cents per foot and to supply pipe at 31 cents per foot. The defendant bored to 160 feet without finding water and then, having encountered an impediment through no fault of his, abandoned the work. *Held* by the Ontario Court of Appeal: there was no term in the contract that the defendant should not be paid unless he found water and that he was, therefore, entitled to be paid for what he had done: *Barrie Gas Co.* v. *Sullivan* (1880).[38]

It is probably a question of semantics whether contracts which may be substantially performed are part of the general class of entire contracts, and the doctrine is a mitigation in certain situations of the rules normally applicable to such contracts,[39] or whether contracts capable of substantial performance should properly not be regarded as entire contracts at all.[40] It is suggested that the true view is that, in the absence of contrary indications in the contract,

[36] 28 N.Z.L.R. 79.
[37] 3 T.L.R. 602.
[38] 5 A.R. 110 (Canada).
[39] See Cheshire and Fifoot, *Law of Contract*, 4th ed., pp. 443–444.
[40] See *e.g.* the language of Denning L.J. in *Hoenig* v. *Isaacs* [1952] 2 All E.R. 176 at p. 180.

substantial performance will be treated as sufficient performance of any entire contract, and, again, in the absence of an express or implied intention to the contrary, that a contract to do a specified work for a specified sum or for a sum to be ascertained is entire in the sense only that substantial performance is a condition precedent to payment.

A question which may be of practical importance arises if a contract is abandoned at a time when substantial performance would otherwise have been regarded as achieved. There are observations both in *H. Dakin & Co. Ltd.* v. *Lee* (1916) and *Hoenig* v. *Isaacs* (1952) [41] stressing the point that the builder cannot recover if he abandons the contract. It may be that the true view is that substantial performance cannot be established if the plaintiff's breaches are fundamental (*i.e.* such as to justify the other party as treating the contract as repudiated),[42] and abandonment would, of course, come into this category, and the repudiation has in fact been accepted and not waived. But it would seem logically immaterial whether the builder merely fails to complete or actually refuses to complete in accordance with the contract, though there might well be policy considerations for refusing to apply the doctrine in such a case. What amounts to substantial performance is a question of degree in each case, and little guidance can be obtained from the decided cases, but the modern trend is undoubtedly to lean against depriving a party not deliberately in breach and who has conferred a substantial benefit on the other of any reward for his work.

It is suggested that certain contractual obligations (as, for instance, the obligation to put right all visible defects, upon which the right to retention monies depends) can of their nature only be substantially performed by a comparatively meticulous discharge of the obligation, whereas others (as, for instance, the general obligation to build and complete a dwelling-house for a price) will be sufficiently performed if a habitable house is produced notwithstanding that it may contain defects requiring repair. Again, where the work undertaken includes the obligation to produce an effective or suitable result[42a] any defect rendering the result unsuitable or ineffective will mean that substantial performance has not been achieved. In every case it is the nature of the main or principal obligation of the contractor against which

---

[41] *Supra.*
[42] As to which see *post*, pp. 340 *et seq.* See also the cases of *Tannenbaum Meadows Ltd.* v. *Wright-Winston Ltd.* (1965) 49 D.L.R. (2d) 386 (Canada), and decision of the Court of Appeal in *Ibmac Ltd.* v. *Marshall Ltd.* (1968) 208 E.G. 851, *infra.*
[42a] This is by no means always the case in building and engineering contracts.

the actual performance needs to be measured. The following cases illustrate the evolution of the doctrine of substantial performance.

ILLUSTRATIONS

(1) The plaintiff proved a contract to build a booth on Bath race ground for 20 guineas, 5 guineas to be paid in advance, and to take back the materials after the races. The plaintiff erected the booth to stipulated dimensions but it fell down in the middle of the races. *Held*, that the plaintiff might recover the balance of 15 guineas though a cross action might be brought against him for building the booth improperly: *Broom* v. *Davis* (1794).[43]

(2) T. contracted to slate buildings for P. according to a specification and at prices therein mentioned. The work was not according to the specification. *Held*, that T. could not recover the whole of the agreed price nor according to the actual value of the work, but the amount of the contract price, subject to a deduction of the amount that it would have cost to alter the work so as to make it correspond with the specification: *Thornton* v. *Place* (1832).[44]

(3) The plaintiff contracted to supply and erect a warm air apparatus. *Held*, that if the jury thought it was substantially performed in the main, though not quite so complete as it might be under the contract, and could be made good at a reasonable rate, the plaintiff might recover the price, less the cost of completion: *Cutler* v. *Close* (1832).[45]

(4) A contract for building work of an approximate value of $20,000 contained a clause that in the event of failure in providing labour or materials the building owners might, after three days' notice, enter and complete, deducting the cost from the contract sum. The architect served notice under this clause in respect of defects totalling $150. *Held*, the contract had been substantially performed, but even if not, the invocation of the clause entitled the contractor to sue for the contract sum less the deduction: *Watts* v. *McLeay* (1911).[46]

(5) The plaintiffs orally agreed with the defendant to do works of repair contained in a specification at the defendant's house for £264. The Official Referee found that the concrete used to underpin the house was not of the proper depth and was badly mixed; that certain joists had not been bolted at the top in accordance with the specification; that solid columns four inches in diameter had been supplied in place of five-inch hollow columns. *Held*, that the defects and omissions amounted only to a negligent performance of the contract and not to an abandonment of the contract or a refusal by the plaintiffs to perform it, and that the plaintiffs were entitled to recover the sum of £264 less the amount necessary to make the work accord with the specification: *Dakin (H.) & Co. Ltd.* v. *Lee* (1916).[47]

(6) A surety guaranteed four equal instalments of £375, due under a small building contract on named dates " subject to the works

[43] 7 East 480n.
[44] 1 Moo. & Rob. 218.
[45] 5 C. & P. 377.
[46] 19 W.L.R. 916 (Canada).
[47] [1916] 1 K.B. 566.

being duly executed." The first instalment was not paid, and it was held that £88 worth of work needed to be done for it to be " duly executed." *Held*, by the Divisional Court and Court of Appeal, that whether or not the builder could have maintained an action for the £375 less the £88, the liability of the surety only arose on full completion: *Eshelby* v. *Federated European Bank Ltd.* (1932).[48]

(7) H. was employed by I. to decorate and provide furniture for I.'s flat for £750, the terms of payment being " net cash, as the work proceeds, and balance on completion." I. paid £400 on account, occupied the flat and used the furniture but refused to pay the balance on the ground that the work was defective. The Official Referee found that a wardrobe door needed replacing, that a bookshelf would have to be remade and that a bookcase would need alteration, and that the cost of remedying these defects would be £55 18s. 2d., but that the work had been substantially completed and he gave judgment for H. for the balance less £55 18s. 2d. *Held*, by the Court of Appeal, (1) in an action on a contract for work and labour and articles supplied for a lump sum payable on completion the defendant could not repudiate liability on the ground that the work, though substantially performed, was in some respects not in accordance with the contract; (2) there was evidence on which the Official Referee could find that the contract had been substantially performed and that the appeal must, therefore, be dismissed; (3) even if entire performance in every respect was a condition precedent to payment under the contract, in taking the benefit of the work by using the defective furniture the defendant had waived the condition and must pay the contract price subject to the appropriate deductions: *Hoenig* v. *Isaacs* (1952).[49]

(8) A agreed with B to build a sewer and pumping station to serve both A's and B's properties, subject to an agreed contribution to the cost by B. Owing to a change in the municipality's plans, the pumping station became unnecessary, as the joint sewer was now to be carried to a new and larger treatment plant. A built the sewer but not the pumping station. B joined his own sewer to A's, as planned, and constructed a pumping main as a temporary measure. *Held*, by the Ontario Court of Appeal, while B might have accepted A's action, which amounted to a repudiation, and built his own complete sewer, he had not in fact done so, but had chosen to take the benefit of A's work. He was therefore liable to pay the agreed sum to A, less the cost of the pumping main. *Per* McLennan J., the reasoning in *Hoenig* v. *Isaacs* (1952) was based on acceptance; in *Sumpter* v. *Hedges* (1898) acceptance could not be inferred: *Tannenbaum Meadows Ltd.* v. *Wright-Winston Ltd.* (1965).[50]

(9) By clause 6 of a contract between vendor/builders and purchasers, the latter were required to apply for loan finance " immediately upon completion of the work," and by clause 3 to pay the price of the house within 120 days of " the completion of the work," which by clause 9 was to be notified in writing to them by the vendors. They were to enter into occupation within seven

[48] [1932] 1 K.B. 254, 423.
[49] [1952] 2 All E.R. 176. The latter finding (3) could not, it is suggested, apply to building contracts, see *post*, Chap. 6, pp. 376 *et seq.*
[50] (1965) 49 D.L.R. (2d) 386 (Canada).

days of this notice. There was a "maintenance and upholding" clause, independent of fault, in respect of defects appearing within a ninety-day period. In default of payment of the price, the purchasers were liable to transfer the house back to the vendors at a fixed price. The vendors did not give an actual notice in writing but informed the purchasers that the house would be complete on a certain date. The owners refused to enter, alleging defects, and ultimately the vendors claimed delivery of the title deeds of the land. The trial judge found that there were defects costing about £150–£250 to remedy which a reasonable building owner might object to. The judge held that " completion " in this contract meant, apart from merely trivial defects, " the reaching of a stage of construction at which the house is ready for occupation in all ways relevant to the contract and is free from known omissions or defects." *Held*, by the Full Court of the Supreme Court of Victoria, that the proper view was that until the work to be done had been carried out in accordance with the contract, except for departures from the contract which were either latent or undiscovered or merely trivial, it would not be " completed." *Held*, also that there was no room for the doctrine of substantial performance in considering provisions like clause 6: *Morgan* v. *S. & S. Construction Ltd.* (1967).[51]

(10) Roadworks contractors quoted £1,494 to developers for a road, stating that it included an item of 5 per cent. for contingencies. They suggested preparing full bills of quantities and rates to enable the work to be measured on completion. Bills were forwarded and the developers accepted " your quotation of £1,494 for the above roadworks as specified." The contractors had not foreseen surface water difficulties, as the site was at the bottom of a steep hill. When these arose, they blamed the developers and abandoned the work, saying they would not return till the developers put the site into a satisfactory state. The developers attempted to improve the state of the site, but the contractors did not return and ultimately the developers determined the contract. In a letter they said that if the contractors did not resume work, and if they completed by other contractors for less than £1,494, they would pay the difference to the contractors. They in fact paid £934 to get the work done by the other contractors. The contractor sued for £1,085 for work done. The trial judge found for the developers on all points—that they were not in breach, that the contractor had abandoned the work without justification, and that the work done was not worth £1,085. He awarded the developers £545 (£1,494 less £934). *Held*, by the Court of Appeal, on his findings the trial judge's award was wrong. Whether or not this was a contract for measurement or a fixed sum, it was an entire contract (9th edition of Hudson cited). The contract had neither been completed nor substantially performed, and the contractors therefore had no ground for any claim at all: *Ibmac Ltd.* v. *Marshall Ltd.* (1968).[52]

[Note: The above case is an excellent example of the correct principle operating in practice. There was, of course, no consideration present for the developers' promise to pay the difference in price, nor was

---

[51] [1967] V.R. 149 (Australia). See also the judgments of the House of Lords in *Jarvis* v. *Westminster Corporation* [1970] 1 W.L.R. 637.

[52] (1968) 208 E.G. 851.

this pleaded or claimed. In fact the judgments show that the developers indicated their willingness to pay £474, but there was no legal
obligation to do so.]

Where the contract is one in which substantial performance
is a condition precedent to payment, the position of the builder
who does not achieve substantial performance is the same as that
of the builder who does not entirely complete an entire contract
in the strict sense.

" On any lump sum contract, if the work is not substantially
performed and there has been a failure of performance which
goes to the root of it, as for instance where the work has only been
half done, or is entirely different in kind from that contracted for,
then no action will lie for the lump sum. The contractor can then
only succeed in getting paid for what he has done if it was the
employer's fault that the work was incomplete, or there was something to justify the conclusion that the parties have entered into a
fresh contract, or the failure of performance is due to impossibility
or frustration." [53]

Denning L.J. in *Hoenig* v. *Isaacs* (1952) [54] suggested *obiter* that
contracts such as building contracts, which provide for retention
money to be payable on completion, might be of the kind requiring
entire performance in the strict sense—presumably in relation to the
last instalments of retention money as opposed to interim payments
under the contract. There would seem to be considerable force in
this view, since under most contracts retention monies are intended
as security for the final repair of all defects visible on completion,[55]
and to allow recovery of the retention monies (as opposed to the
remainder of any general balance due) while visible defects still
needed repair, and the builder was refusing or failing to remedy
them, would be to defeat their purpose.

It should not be forgotten that a builder's difficulty under the
doctrine of entire contracts may be resolved if the employer re-enters
under a provision in the contract regulating the state of accounts

---

[53] *Per* Denning L.J. in *Hoenig* v. *Isaacs* [1952] 2 All E.R. 176 at p. 182, and see *Appleby*
v. *Myers*, L.R. 2 C.P. 651 at p. 660; *Sumpter* v. *Hedges* [1898] 1 Q.B. 673; and
s. 1 (3) of the Law Reform (Frustrated Contracts) Act 1943.
　　(N.B. The learned judge's reference to " impossibility " must be to *supervening*
impossibility equivalent to frustration, since normally the fact that substantial
performance was impossible would not entitle the contractor to recover the value
of the work which he had done.)

[54] See *infra*, p. 259.

[55] See *infra*, pp. 258 *et seq.*, where this topic is further discussed.

between the parties in that event.[56]　And, further, as already stated, where an employer brings a claim for damages and has been relieved by the contractor's failure or breach from the necessity of paying for all or a part of the work under the rules as to entire contracts, he will nevertheless, in calculating his damages, have to give credit for the balance which he would have had to pay had the contractor completed the work properly.[57]　The doctrine is likely to be of practical importance where, as in the *Ibmac* case, *supra*, the employer has no interest in pursuing a claim for damages, or where the advantage to be gained by the doctrine outweighs the amount of damages which would be recoverable.

(ii) *Completion for purpose of interim payment.*　As already explained, while completion of the whole work may be necessary to obtain payment of any general balance or final instalments under a building contract, the vast majority of building contracts make specific provision for stage or interim payment, and in some rare cases it may be that a term for this might be implied.

(A) *Express terms for payment by instalments.*　As most major works are carried out under contracts providing for payments to be made as the work proceeds, it is important to consider the position of a contractor who fails to complete the works as a whole under such a contract.　Where the contractor has become entitled to an instalment payment, he will not normally forfeit his right to such payment by a subsequent abandonment or repudiation of the contract, but will be entitled to sue for any unpaid instalment, if he has satisfied the conditions for it to become due, subject, of course, to the employer's right to counterclaim for damages for breach of contract.　In *Taylor* v. *Laird* (1856)[58] the plaintiff undertook to serve as a commander of a vessel at pay of £50 per month but wrongfully abandoned the contract after eight months having been paid for seven only.　The court held that the plaintiff was entitled to recover £50 for the eighth month, Pollock C.B. saying[59]: " There (*i.e.* in the contract) ' per month ' means each month or monthly and gives a cause of action as each month accrues which once vested is not subsequently lost or divested by the plaintiff's desertion or abandonment of his contract."

---

[56] See *Watts* v. *McLeay* (1911) 19 W.L.R. 916 (Canada), *supra*, p. 251. See also *e.g.* Clause 25 (3) (d) of the post-1963 R.I.B.A. standard forms and Clause 63 (3) of the 1955 I.C.E. form.

[57] *Post*, Chap. 9, pp. 585 *et seq.*

[58] 25 L.J.Ex. 329.

[59] At p. 334.

The following passage in *Salmond & Winfield on the Law of Contract* [60] was quoted with approval in the two Australian cases cited in the Illustrations below.

" Every obligation which has accrued due between the parties before the rescission of the contract, and which so creates a then existing cause of action, remains unaffected by the rescission and can still be enforced. It makes no difference in this respect whether such accrued obligation and existing cause of action is one in favour of the party rescinding the contract or is one in favour of the other party." [61]

ILLUSTRATIONS

(1) A company entered into a contract with a colonial government to make and keep up 340 miles of railway in consideration of receiving for each five miles, as and when completed, a grant of land and a thirty-five-year subsidy. Only eighty-five miles were completed. *Held*, the contract was severable, and that as each five miles was completed the title to land and subsidy accrued, and that the subsidy was payable, but subject to a counterclaim for non-completion of the whole railway: *Newfoundland Government* v. *Newfoundland Ry.* (1888). [62]

[Note: This case illustrates very well the possibility of the contract as a whole being an entire contract notwithstanding express provision for instalment payments.]

(2) The plaintiffs agreed to remove two spans from a wrecked bridge in a river for $25,000—$5,000 when one span was removed from the channel, another $5,000 when it was put ashore, and the balance on completion. The work was to be done if possible that season, but the contractors were to have the right to complete during the next season if necessary. They removed one span from the channel and put it ashore, but never completed the work even in the course of the next season. *Held*, that they were entitled to the $10,000: *Collins Bay Co.* v. *New York & Ottawa Ry.* (1902). [63]

(3) The defendants employed S. as a consulting engineer for fifteen months at a salary of £500, to be paid by five equal quarterly instalments. S. worked for three quarters and was paid one instalment only. Shortly afterwards he died and his personal representative brought an action to recover the two unpaid instalments. *Held*, although S.'s death had dissolved the contract, the plaintiff was entitled to recover the two instalments which had accrued due because the right of action for them had vested in S. before his death: *Stubbs* v. *The Holywell Ry.* (1867). [64]

(4) The plaintiff agreed with the defendant to erect forty-three miles of vermin-proof fencing at £37 per mile. The defendant was to provide the materials. The plaintiff was to receive 75 per cent.

[60] 1927 ed. at p. 286.
[61] " Rescind " in this context means the right of the innocent party to treat the contract as at an end. See *post*, pp. 340 *et seq.*
[62] 13 App.Cas. 199.
[63] 32 Can.S.C.R. 216 (Canada).
[64] L.R. 2 Ex. 311.

on each five miles of completed fence subject to the certificate of the inspector. The defendant failed to provide materials but the plaintiff started the work and erected eleven miles of fence and then wrongly abandoned the work. *Held*, (i) the plaintiff was entitled to damages for the defendant's breach in failing to provide materials, (ii) the plaintiff was entitled to 75 per cent. of the price of ten miles of fencing if he had the certificate, (iii) the defendant would be entitled to damages for breach of contract: *Ettridge* v. *Vermin Board of the District of Murat Bay* (1928).[65]

(5) Contractors agreed to deepen and make certain dams at so much per cubic foot. Time payments were to be made not oftener than once a month and not to exceed 75 per cent. of the value of the work done. The contractors proceeded with the work and were paid £343 on account and then wrongfully abandoned the work. At the date of the abandonment 75 per cent. of the value of work done but not paid for was £128. *Held*, immediately before the abandonment of the work the contractors had a cause of action to recover 75 per cent. of the price for the work done in respect of which nothing had been paid and, therefore, were entitled to judgment for £128: *McLachlan* v. *Nourse* (1928).[66]

There are two qualifications to the general principle illustrated by the above cases: first, the issue of a certificate may be a condition precedent to an instalment becoming due and, secondly, there may be a determination clause in the contract which, if exercised by the employer, will expressly deprive the contractor of an accrued right to an instalment. As to the first, if a certificate is a condition precedent to an instalment becoming due and no certificate has been given before the abandonment of the contract, the contractor will have no vested right of action upon which to sue.[67] As regards the second, most of the common forms of contract in use do in fact contain a clause under which, upon the power of forfeiture being exercised, no further payment has to be made by the employer until the completion of the works.[68]

The effect of the rules as to entire performance also requires to be considered in relation to the individual instalments or the retention money usually due upon "practical" or "substantial" completion under the express terms of building and engineering contracts. Under the usual scheme of building contracts, it is necessary to distinguish between three kinds of instalment, namely: (a) true interim instalments during the course of the work; (b) the

[65] [1928] S.A.S.R. 124 (Australia).
[66] [1928] S.A.S.R. 230 (Australia).
[67] For this subject, and the various exceptions to the rule, see *post*, pp. 492 *et seq.*, where it is suggested that in the standard forms at the present day the certificate is not a condition precedent.
[68] *Cf.* Clause 25 (3) (*d*) of the post-1963 R.I.B.A. forms and Clause 63 (3) of the 1955 I.C.E. form.

instalment in which the first half of the retention money is released; and (c) the instalment in which the second half of the retention moneys is released.

The first retention instalment, which signals the commencement of the "defects liability" or "maintenance" period (and in nearly all contracts the end of any liability of the contractor to pay liquidated damages for delay in completion), is usually expressly conditioned upon "practical" [69] or "substantial" [70] completion. Since the maintenance provisions contemplate that there may be defects needing to be put right during the maintenance period, and the liquidated damages provisions contemplate that the employer's damage due to delay in completion has come to an end, it seems clear that completion for the purpose of this instalment means a sufficient degree of completion to permit occupation and use of the works by the employer and the departure of the contractor from the site, but not a complete and perfect discharge of every last contractual liability of the contractor with regard to the quality or finish of the work. It is submitted that the following definition, framed for a somewhat unusual type of contract, cannot in fact be bettered for traditional building and engineering contracts, namely, "apart from merely trivial defects, a stage of construction at which [the house] is ready for occupation in all ways relevant to the contract and is free from known omissions or defects." [71] "It follows that a practical completion certificate can be issued when, owing to latent defects, the works do not fulfil the contract requirements, and that under the contract works can be completed despite the presence of such defects. Completion under the contract is not postponed until defects which became apparent only after the work had been finished, have been remedied." [71a] These definitions are of great importance in showing that the subsequent discovery of defects, however serious, will not affect practical completion and its express purpose under most contracts of bringing the liquidated damages liability to an end and starting the maintenance period running.

In most building contracts this practical or substantial completion is in fact that contemplated by the contractor's basic express or implied obligation to carry out and complete the work. There is usually no further unqualified physical obligation on the contractor,

[69] Clause 15 of the post-1963 R.I.B.A. standard forms.
[70] Clause 48 of the 1955 I.C.E. standard form. See also Chap. 11, pp. 637 et seq.
[71] Per the trial judge in Morgan v. S. & S. Construction Ltd. [1967] V.R. 149 (Australia), illustrated supra, pp. 252–253.
[71a] Per Viscount Dilhorne in City of Westminster v. Jarvis [1970] 1 W.L.R. at p. 647.

save only the conditional and usually rigorously circumscribed duty to return and remedy defects under the terms of the defects clause. Accordingly the latest date of breach for defective work for purposes of limitation will usually be practical completion,[71b] unless the defect qualifies under the defects clause. Furthermore the risk of damage to the works will usually pass from the contractor to the employer at this date[71b] (in other words, the contractor's duty to complete has now been discharged).

The second retention instalment is in most contracts conditional upon the making good of defects or the expiry of the maintenance period, whichever is the later.[72] In contracts of this kind, where there has been " practical " or " substantial " completion at an earlier stage, and where the second instalment is clearly retention money, i.e. a portion of the value of the work retained as security to cover the making good of defects and insufficiencies not immediately apparent, it may well be that completion of the work or of the making good of defects will be required in a relatively strict sense in order to render the second instalment (and any general balance which under the terms of the contract may not be due till that time) payable. Thus Denning L.J. said in *Hoenig* v. *Isaacs* (1952) [73]: " In the present case the contract provided for ' net cash, as the work proceeds, and balance on completion.' If the balance could be regarded as retention money then it might well be that the contractor ought to have done all the work correctly, without defects or omissions, in order to be entitled to the balance."

These observations were, however, *obiter*, and it is possible to conceive of very large sums being retained on this strict view against comparatively trivial defects. If, however, Denning L.J.'s view is correct, and the making good of defects is made a condition precedent to the payment of a final instalment of retention money, those defects which may be required to be put right under the contract must be entirely made good, subject to the *de minimis* rule, before the final instalment is payable.[74] It is submitted that this is in fact the true view, and its justification, as for the whole doctrine of entire contracts, is the necessary provision of an effective sanction against deliberate breach or abandonment of the contract before it is fully performed.

[71b] See *infra*, p. 272.
[72] Clause 30 (4) (c) of the post-1963 standard R.I.B.A. forms; Clause 60 (2) of the 1955 I.C.E. form.
[73] [1952] 2 All E.R. 176 at p. 181.
[74] For the suggested principle in these cases, see *supra*, pp. 249, 250.

As regards true interim instalments, completion of work is only rarely made the condition of the instalment in the United Kingdom—as, for instance, where fixed proportions of the price become payable on certain stages of the work being reached, or where money becomes due when work to a certain value has been done. In fact it is a great pity that these latter methods of interim payment are not adopted by the standard forms, since they offer the employer a far more effective protection against dilatory contractors, and also reduce the expense of interim valuation. More usually, however, payment is made dependent upon the passage of a period of time, coupled with a valuation of work done up to that time. In the latter class of case there is, of course, no connection between the completion of work and the right to payment of an instalment, and therefore no room or need for the application of the doctrine of substantial performance.

As in the case of the obligation to complete the contract as a whole, it should be remembered that where an employer brings a claim for damages for the failure of the contractor to perform the contract, and has been relieved by that failure under the foregoing rules from having to pay some proportion of the value of the work done, e.g. the retention money due on practical completion and/or the making good of defects, he will nevertheless have to give credit for the balance which he would have had to pay if the contractor had duly performed the contract in assessing his damages.[75]

(B) *Implied terms for payment by instalments.* It does seem that, despite the general rule, there may be some contracts for work and services in which, from the nature of the work as a whole, it is necessary to imply a term for stage or periodical payment, or for reasonable payments on account of the work at reasonable intervals, even though there may also be a contractual obligation to complete the whole work. Thus Blackburn J. said in *Appleby* v. *Myers* (1867)[76]: " Generally, and in the absence of something to show a contrary intention, the bricklayer or tailor or shipwright is to be paid for the work and materials he has done and provided although the whole work is not complete." This remark seems to envisage a type of contract under which the consideration is apportionable and accrues due as the work proceeds, so that at any time the contractor can claim a *quantum meruit* for what he has done.

[75] See *post*, Chap. 9, p. 585.
[76] L.R. 2 C.P. 651 at p. 660.

Phillimore J. made somewhat similar observations in *The Tergeste* (1903) [77]:

" The law follows good sense and business, as shown by the case of *Roberts* v. *Havelock*. A man who contracts to do a long costly piece of work, does not contract, unless he expressly says so, that he will do all the work, standing out of pocket until he is paid at the end . . . and if . . . payment is not made, then the shipwright or other artificer is entitled to review his work, and say: ' I have done work worth so much, true I have contracted to do other work but it is not reasonable that I should do it, as I have not been paid; and in respect of work I have done I claim payment.' "

In a contract of this kind it is a necessary corollary that the contractor will be entitled to treat the contract as repudiated and cease work if there is a refusal to make the interim payment.[78]

It may be, however, that these observations refer to cases where the contract as a whole is not entire; that is to say the consideration or work itself is regarded as severable into different parts, as well as the price—in other words a new contract is regarded as coming into being for each part of the work, as when, for example, a workman is hired by the day to work on some task, but is free to cease work at the end of any one day if he wishes to do so.

It is now so common, if not almost universal, for work in the United Kingdom of any substance to be paid for monthly on an interim basis, that it may in appropriate circumstances be necessary to imply a term for reasonable payments on account. Such circumstances might include, it is suggested, the large size or amount of the work undertaken, the fact that it was likely to last for a considerable time, the financial standing of the contractor, the degree of informality of the contract arrangements, and the exact terms of any provision as to price (including particularly any failure to specify a price). Where, however, contractual arrangements of a fair degree of precision are used, a definite price is agreed, and the contractor's undertaking is to complete a specific described project, it will be correspondingly more difficult to imply any such term.

ILLUSTRATION

The defendant's ship put into Milford Haven damaged and the plaintiff was employed and undertook to put her into thorough repair. No price appeared to be agreed upon. Disputes arose and

[77] [1903] P. at p. 34.
[78] See in addition the cases and discussion on this aspect of the matter, *post*, Section 3 (1), pp. 342–343, and in particular the two early cases of *Rees* v. *Lines* (1837) 8 C.P. 126; and *Pontifex* v. *Wilkinson* (1845) 2 C.B. 349.

the plaintiff was called upon to put the vessel into a fit state to continue her voyage which he refused to do unless he was paid for work already done. He sued for work done and the ship was detained unfinished. *Held*, that there was no specific contract to complete the work and make no demand for payment until completion, but that there was only a general employment in the same way as shipwrights are ordinarily employed and that the plaintiff could recover though repairs were incomplete: *Roberts* v. *Havelock* (1832).[79]

(b) Contracts which are not entire

Two cases where contracts for work associated with building and engineering have been held not to be entire have already been illustrated.[80] Furthermore, it has already been seen that there may be tenders apparently accepted which are no more than unenforceable agreements to do such work as the employer may order from time to time.[81] In addition, as has been stated in the immediately preceding sub-section, terms for interim payment may be expressly or impliedly part of a building contract, notwithstanding that completion of the entire work is also obligatory on the contractor.

It is certainly possible to conceive of a fairly substantial contract, *e.g.* a running contract to carry out repairs to a large building or block of properties under which the right to payment would accrue *pari passu* with the execution of the work, but it is submitted that a relatively clear understanding from the nature of the work, or relatively clear words, in the case of a clearly definable project, showing that the work was to be of a daily or periodical character only, would be required to justify the contractor ceasing work on a mere failure to pay on demand, for example, unless the failure was so persistent or flagrant as ordinarily to amount to a repudiation of the contract.[82] But if a contract is severable in this sense, then it is obvious that the rules of entire performance do not apply to the contract as a whole (even if it be such) but only as to the severable parts.

(c) Extent of work included in obligation to complete

The amount and character of the work which a contractor must do to earn his price depends upon the construction of the particular contract, and consideration of the problems of entire completion and substantial performance cannot be of much assistance unless the exact extent of the work included in the contract and covered by the price is understood.

---

[79] 3 B. & Ad. 404.
[80] *Barrie Gas Co.* v. *Sullivan* (1880) 5 A.R. 110, *supra*, p. 249; and *Wyett* v. *Smith* (1906) 28 N.Z. 79, *supra*, pp. 248–249.
[81] See for this type of contract, *ante*, Chap. 3, Section 3 (4), pp. 228–229.
[82] See *infra*, Section 3, pp. 340 *et seq.* on this subject.

In modern contracts, whether with or without quantities, the tendency is for the work as described in the technical documents—namely, the specification and bills of quantities—to be stipulated as the exact measure of the work undertaken by the contractor for the contract price tendered by him (although in contracts using bills his obligation to complete may well extend to different quantities from those shown in the bills, but if so the price will be recalculated), so that any departure from the technical documents is likely to be treated as a variation and valued accordingly. The problems affecting modern contracts in this context generally arise upon the exact interpretation of the bills or specification, or from the need to reconcile any conflict between these documents and the drawings. This, however, is only the case because of the specific wording of modern contracts, requiring remeasurement or recalculation or adjustment of the price to take account of errors in the bills or drawings; but in less formally concluded or differently worded contracts it may remain a most difficult question to determine the exact extent of the builder's obligation. Broadly speaking there are two main difficulties, namely, whether descriptive words or expressions relating to the work in other parts of the contract should prevail over descriptions in the technical documents that omit specifically to describe a part of the work, so that, for instance, an omission to mention or detail work in the technical documents can be supplemented by descriptions of the work elsewhere, and, secondly, whether work not described in, or originally expected by, the contract documents, but which in the event is found to be necessary in order to achieve completion of the described work, is or is not included in the builder's general obligation to complete the work for the contract price.

It should be borne in mind that bills of quantities were used for many years before the courts could be persuaded to regard them as the definitive measure of the builder's work, as opposed to their original function as a mere guide to tendering contractors. Indications of this have already been seen in Chapter 2.[83] Cases dealing with the liability of the builder where the quantities were incorrect, so that larger quantities or work than those shown in the bills had to be done to comply with the drawings or specification, are dealt with in Chapter 8, Variations, *post*, where the history of the development of the legal function of bills can be seen, and are not considered in the present chapter under the present heading. Here it is proposed to consider those cases where whole items of work not shown

[83] *Ante*, pp. 112 and 193.

in the technical documents (as opposed to differing quantities) may be necessary either (1) by implication or in order that the work as a whole should comply with requirements elsewhere in the contract documents, or (2) to achieve completion of the described work in the face of practical difficulties or for other technical reasons. These two types of undescribed work can be conveniently described as on the one hand indispensably necessary and on the other contingently necessary work.

The determination of the exact extent of the builder's obligation in these cases is, of course, not only relevant to questions of completion but also, in the vast majority of cases where there is power to vary the work, to the question whether or not work in these two categories can be regarded as a variation so as to justify additional payment.[84]

(i) **Indispensably necessary work expressly or impliedly included.** Modern contracts usually deal very explicitly with the contractual effect of drawings, specifications or bills and of their effect upon each other.[85] But it does not necessarily follow, merely because the parties to a building contract use drawings, specifications or bills as part of the contract documents to describe the work, that these technical documents will automatically prevail over other terms or provisions in the contract,[86] if, notwithstanding an omission to describe or refer to some part of the work in the technical documents, the more generalised descriptions or obligations of the builder to be derived from the contract documentation as a whole can be interpreted as requiring that part of the work to be done as well as the specifically described parts. Furthermore, no description, however meticulous, will descend to every detail of building processes, so that it is a cardinal principle of construction, it is submitted, that, in the absence of an expressed contrary intention, an obligation to do described work imports an obligation to do all the necessary ancillary work or processes, whether described or not, which are needed to produce the described work. Thus, to take a simple example, an obligation to construct fair-faced concrete imports an obligation to carry out all the necessary formwork to achieve that result.[86a] In addition to the

---

[84] See for a detailed discussion of this, *post*, Chap. 8, pp. 507 *et seq.*

[85] *Cf.* clauses 1, 6 and 55 of the 1955 I.C.E. standard form, and clause 12 of the post-1963 R.I.B.A. standard forms.

[86] In addition to the cases illustrated here, see the cases of *Bryant and Son* v. *Birmingham Hospital Saturday Fund* [1938] 1 All E.R. 503 and *Farr* v. *Ministry of Transport* (1965) (unreported) illustrated *post*, Chap. 8, pp. 518, 519–520.

[86a] Again, a simple jobbing contract to supply and fit a new door may or may not include an obligation to supply hinges or other door furniture. See also *ante*, Chap. 3, Section 1, pp. 199–201, where the various categories of contract are described.

cases cited below, which are primarily concerned with rather substantial elements of work not specifically described in the technical
documents, reference should also be made to the further discussion
and cases, *post*, Chapter 8, Variations, Section 1, where in particular
the interpretation of modern contracts using bills of quantities is
considered.

ILLUSTRATIONS

(1) A contractor agreed " to execute work connected with the
new pond at H. conformably to specification drawn for the execution
of the work " by a civil engineer for the sum of £23 14s. 0d. The
specification contemplated that sufficient materials would be excavated
from the site, but in fact additional materials had to be brought from
elsewhere. *Held*, that the contractor could not claim more than the
contract price, and could recover nothing extra for these additional
materials: *Weatherstone* v. *Robertson* (1852).[87]

(2) The plaintiff, a joiner, undertook to build a house in accordance with the defendant's plans. The plaintiff [88] prepared a specification which described the timber to be used in the house, specified
the floor joists in detail, but made no mention of the flooring itself.
A memorandum at the foot read as follows:— " The whole of the
materials mentioned or otherwise in the foregoing must be provided
by the contractor." The plaintiff further agreed " to do and perform
all the works of every kind mentioned and contained in the foregoing
specification, according in every respect to the drawings furnished
or to be furnished . . . for the sum of £1,100. The house to be completed and dry and fit for occupation by August 1, 1858." The
plaintiff prepared flooring for some of the rooms and left it on the
premises and placed other floor boards in an adjoining field. He then
refused to do further work unless paid extra for the floors, on the
ground that they were not part of his contract, and four days later
quit the premises. *Held*, it was by inadvertence that no mention
was made of flooring in the specification and it was the intention of
the contract that the plaintiff was to supply it. *Per* Pollock C.B.[89]:
" I had some doubt whether the specification was not to be regarded
as the contract between the parties; but upon the whole facts being
disclosed it appears to me that no person can entertain any reasonable doubt that it was intended that the plaintiff should provide the
flooring as well as the other materials requisite for the building and
that it was merely by inadvertence that no mention of flooring was
made in the specification . . . it is clearly to be inferred from the
language of the specification that the plaintiff was to do the flooring
for he was to provide the whole of the materials necessary for the
completion of the work; and unless it can be supposed that a house
is habitable without any flooring it must be inferred that the flooring
was to be supplied by him." *Per* Channell B.[90]: " The contract was
that the *house* should be completed and fit for occupation by the
1st August 1958, not that the *works* thereinbefore mentioned should

[87] I. Stuart Milne & Peddie (Sc.) 333.
[88] *Not* the defendant, as stated in the headnote of this case.
[89] 3 H. & N. 844, at p. 851.
[90] At p. 852.

be completed by that day. I think that, looking at the terms of the contract, it would not be reasonable to read it as if it excluded all work not specifically mentioned." : *Williams* v. *Fitzmaurice* (1858).[91]

(3) The plaintiffs, having tendered upon a specification prepared by the defendant's engineer, undertook to perform all the works necessary for the perfect execution and completion of a railway in Brazil for the defendants for a lump sum. When the railway was partially completed it was discovered that the proposed mode of conveying the traffic up and down a mountain was wholly inadequate. The engineer prepared new plans and required the plaintiffs to construct the railway according to those plans, which they did, so that excavation of earthworks exceeding the quantity specified by two million cubic yards was necessary. *Held*, the plaintiffs could not recover the excess as an extra. *Per* James L.J.: "What they had contracted to do for a lump sum was to make the line from terminus to terminus complete, and both these items seem to me on the face of them entirely included in the contract. They are not in any sense of the word extra works ": *Sharpe* v. *San Paulo Ry.* (1873).[92]
[Note: This case turned on its own special documentation. It is not to be supposed that the documentation of most modern contracts in the U.K. would bring about this result. Nevertheless, the principle itself is clear.]

(4) Verbal descriptions in a contract for the construction of a cast-iron outlet pipe by the sea described the work in several places in the contract as extending *to low water*. The plan of the work also showed the pipe extending to the low water-mark, but a sectional drawing showed it as extending 279 feet further into the sea. The contractor was required to insert prices in a bill of quantities and there were provisions for measurement of the work at the rates in the bills. The quantities in the bills corresponded with the length of pipe shown in the sectional drawing, but the contractor's rates were uniform throughout. The engineer required the pipe to be carried out for the full length below low-water. *Held*, the prices in the bills were on a true construction of the contract only for work above low-water mark, and the contractor was entitled to a reasonable price for this work, since there was no price in the contract for it: *Re Walton-on-the-Naze U.D.C. and Moran* (1905).[93]
[Note: In this case it will be seen that the various verbal descriptions prevailed over a sectional drawing and the quantities taken off that drawing.]

In modern contracts using bills and incorporating standard methods of measurement it is sometimes possible for a contractor to base a claim for extra payment, notwithstanding that there has been no variation of the work, on the ground that, contrary to the

---

[91] 3 H. & N. 844. (This case is an example of the second category of contract referred to *ante*, Chap. 3, pp. 199–201.)
[92] L.R. 8 Ch.App. 597.   See also *Re Nuttall and Lynton and Barnstaple Ry.* (1899), illustrated *infra*, p. 271.
[93] Hudson's B.C., 4th ed. Vol. 2, p. 376.

requirements of the standard method, certain items of work have not been separately described or set out in the bills. This subject is dealt with in Chapter 8.[94]

Whether the description of the work in some other part of the contract over-rides or supplements any technical document may well, it is submitted, depend on the identity of the party preparing the technical document.[95] A contractor who prepares such a document and omits expressly to describe obviously necessary work will do so at his peril. On the other hand an employer, particularly one employing a professional adviser, cannot complain unduly if his own technical documents are taken at their face value or, in a case of genuine doubt or conflict, construed against him under the *contra proferentem* rule.

(ii) **Work contingently necessary to achieve completion.** It not infrequently occurs in practice, particularly in engineering contracts, that unexpected difficulties may be encountered which may not only necessitate a change from the expected method of working, but in extreme cases may mean that completion of the work in accordance with the original design is impossible. In addition, damage to the works while under construction may occur as the result of some unforeseen event or act of a third party which needs to be made good if the works are to be brought to completion. Most contracts contain express provisions making such risks or contingencies the responsibility of the contractor, in the form of, for example, express disclaimers as to the state of the site and physical conditions or dangers generally, and also of provisions for the protection of the work during construction, though it should perhaps be mentioned that under the standard I.C.E. form of contract the contractor only undertakes to complete the work " save in so far as it is legally or physically impossible," [96] is not liable to protect the works against damage due "*solely* to the engineer's design," [97] and furthermore under that contract he is entitled to be paid for additional work due to certain matters which could not have been reasonably foreseen by an experienced contractor.[98] But in most contracts, even in the absence of an express disclaimer, an employer who uses a professional adviser does not warrant that completion according to his adviser's

---

[94] *Post*, pp. 515 *et seq.*
[95] *Cf.* the position in regard to the contractor's obligations in regard to the design or suitability of the works, *infra*, pp. 278 *et seq.*
[96] Clause 13 of the 1955 I.C.E. standard form.
[97] Clause 20 (2) of the 1955 I.C.E. conditions.
[98] *Ibid.* clause 12. For detailed discussion, see *post*, Chap. 9, pp. 569–570.

plans or design is practicable,[99] and even in the absence of express provisions for the protection of the works, the risk in regard to the safety of the works remains with the contractor until they have been re-occupied by the employer, and accordingly a contractor who (as is almost invariably the case) expressly or impliedly undertakes to complete the work or project according to the contract drawings and design thereby impliedly warrants that he can do so, and if he cannot will be liable in damages. In consequence, any additional work necessary to achieve completion must be carried out by him at his own expense if he is to discharge his liability under the contract. So too any work of reinstatement or repair if the works have been damaged by some external cause. The only possible qualification, as to which there is at present no authority, is the extent to which these liabilities should (if at all) be modified in the case, not of original contract work, but of variations in the work called for by the employer under a power in the contract. The contractor has not, at the time of contracting, any possibility of assessing the practicability of such work. Usually no financial difficulty arises in such cases where difficulties are surmounted, because the cost of doing so may be recovered under the provisions for valuation of variations. But does an unqualified obligation to complete exist in the case of work which the contractor could not foresee at the time of contracting? It is tentatively suggested that the obligation does extend to variations, such as extra work, which can be shown to be similar in all respects to the contract work, but may well not extend to variations which are different in character or location. However, a builder undertaking such work without protest would be accepting the liabilities and, it is submitted, estopped from subsequently seeking to repudiate them. In any event, all these liabilities should be carefully distinguished from questions as to the contractor's responsibility for the suitability of the work or the adequacy of its design once it has been completed. These questions are dealt with later [1] and raise quite different considerations. Not only does an employer not impliedly warrant the practicability of his or his adviser's design, but it is extremely rare to find that an employer gives any express warranty as to the physical state of the site or of the subsoil,[1] and indeed most contracts contain express exclusions of liability for any reports or information which may have been made available

---

[99] Nor indeed, that he is competent in any way, e.g. in making decisions as to the contractor's method of working; see the case of *Neodox Ltd.* v. *Swinton and Pendlebury B.C.* (1958) unreported, illustrated *post*, Chap. 8, pp. 529–530.

[1] *Infra*, (2), Obligations as to Design.   [1a] See also *infra*, pp. 316–317.

to the contractor, whether in the contract documents or otherwise. The possible effects of the Misrepresentation Act 1967 on these has already been considered.[2]

In addition to the cases cited below, reference should also be made to Section 3, *infra*, Impossibility and Frustration, and the cases there cited.

ILLUSTRATIONS

(1) The plaintiff contracted with the defendants to take down an old bridge and to build a new one. Plans and specifications prepared by the defendants' engineer were furnished to him and he was required to obey the directions of the engineer. The descriptions given were not guaranteed. Part of the plan consisted of the use of caissons to enable the work to be done despite the tide. The caissons proved to be useless and the plan of the work had to be altered so that it was done when the tide permitted. Much delay and extra expense were caused to the plaintiff. The plaintiff alleged that there was an implied warranty by the defendants that the bridge could be built according to the plans and specifications, without tide work, and in a manner comparatively inexpensive, and that the caissons would resist the pressure of water during the construction of the bridge. The plaintiff claimed damages for breach of that warranty. *Held*, no such warranty was to be implied: *Thorn* v. *London Corporation* (1876).[3]

(2) Contractors agreed with a company to furnish and erect all the iron and general work required for a works for a lump sum. The contract provided that the contractors should not be entitled to make an alteration in the specified works without a written order of the company's engineer. The contractors found that they were unable to make certain girders owing to the thinness of the metal specified and their liability to twist. With the oral consent of the engineer the contractors made the girders of thicker metal. *Held*, the contractor took the risk of being able to make the girders of the specified dimensions and, there being no order in writing by the engineer for the girders to be made of thicker metal, the contractors could not recover the extra cost. " When, as in this case, the contractors say ' We cannot do the work as we have promised to do it unless you permit us to make it thicker than we undertook to make it ' and the engineer on behalf of the company says ' I will not object to your making it thicker if you cannot do it otherwise,' I think there is nothing in that to imply that there was to be payment for that additional thickness ": *Tharsis Sulphur & Copper Co.* v. *McElroy & Sons* (1878).[4]

(3) A contractor undertook to build a sea-wall for a Local Board. The Board under a Local Act was also empowered to construct and maintain groynes. Old groynes were present at the site of the works. The design of the work was such that the wall could clearly not be built unless it was protected against the tidal scour of shingle

---

[2] See *ante*, Chap. 1, pp. 38 *et seq.*; Chap. 3, p. 232; and *post*, Section 2, Obligations of the Employer. See also *Trade Indemnity* v. *Workington* [1937] A.C. 1.

[3] 1 App.Cas. 120.

[4] 3 App.Cas. 1040, *per* Lord Blackburn at p. 1054.

by adequate groynes. By the terms of the contract the contractor
accepted the risk of accidents and damage by seas, winds, or any
other cause, and the tender was to include for completing and
upholding the works for six months after completion, no additional
payment being made for work fairly to be inferred from the specification or drawings or which might become necessary in the execution
of the works. During the work the contractor advised the Board
that the old groynes were inadequate and that they should build
new ones, and the Board put new groynes out to tender, but delayed
placing any contract for them. As a result, the shingle on the beach
was washed away and a storm destroyed the partly built wall, which
the contractor refused to repair without payment on being called
on to do so. *Held,* by the House of Lords, that in the absence of any
provision that the Board should make groynes or maintain the
existing groynes, the obligation of the contractor was, within the
principle of *Thorn's* case, to do everything necessary to complete,
and the contractor was accordingly liable in damages to the Board:
Jackson v. *Eastbourne Local Board* (1886).[5]

(4) B contracted to execute sewerage works for York Corporation
in the vicinity of the River Ouse. He had planned to use poling
boards for his excavations, but the soil turned out to be of a muddy
and spongy character necessitating the driving of timber runners
and the rendering of the entire excavation watertight before brickwork could be laid. No boreholes had been sunk by either party,
but the Corporation had had reports prior to signing the contract
that B's price was such that he was certain to lose money in the type
of ground to be expected. B asked the engineer to authorise payment
for the extra works as a variation, and on this being refused abandoned the work, and sued for the value of work done. *Held,* as there
was no express guarantee or representation as to the nature of the
soil, B was not entitled to abandon the contract on discovering the
nature of the soil or because the engineer refused to give written
orders entitling him to extra payment in consequence of the unforeseen difficulties in executing the works, and accordingly could recover
nothing for the work done by him: *Bottoms* v. *York Corporation* (1892).[6]

(5) M. entered into a contract with Workington Corporation to
construct a system of sewers. Part of the work, which involved
tunnelling, turned out to be impracticable without additional precautions because of water in the soil. M. suggested certain modifications, which the engineer refused to pay for, and then threw up
the contract, suing the Corporation for £7,000 alleged to be due
for work so far done. The engineer had not certified any part of this
sum, but M. contended that the Corporation was in breach of contract
in that the specification amounted to a warranty that the ground was
dry. *Held,* that had there been any such statement it would have
only amounted to a representation and not to a warranty,[7] but there
was in fact no such representation, M. was not entitled to throw up
the contract and could not recover in the absence of a certificate:
McDonald v. *Workington Corporation* (1893).[8]

[5] Hudson's B.C., 4th ed. Vol. 2, p. 81.
[6] Hudson's B.C., 4th ed., Vol. 2, p. 208.
[7] For the distinction see *ante,* Chap. 1, p. 41.
[8] (1893) 9 T.L.R. 230; Hudson's B.C., 4th ed. Vol. 2, p. 228.

(6) N. contracted to build a railway, including " earthworks," for an ascertained price. A bill of quantities was supplied to him which said: " These quantities are not guaranteed as correct, and are furnished merely for the convenience of contractors." The specification provided that the contractor was to " satisfy himself of the nature of the soil . . . of all probable contingencies, and generally of all matters which would in any way influence the tender for the contract," and he was to take upon himself all the risk and responsibility of the due and complete execution of the works. N. claimed to be paid extra for quantities of excavation in excess of that set out in the quantities and drawings, and for the cost of removing rock which could only be removed by blasting. *Held*, that N. was not entitled to recover anything extra for the additional quantity of excavation or for the necessary blasting operations: *Re Nuttall and Lynton and Barnstaple Ry.* (1899).[9]

(7) A contractor was constructing a sewer in heading underneath a road crossing under the terms of the 1955 I.C.E. Conditions. The approximate position of an ancient sewer was shown on the plans which also traversed the road at an angle diagonal to and crossing the contractor's line. Its depth was not known. The contractor's heading collapsed and was flooded when it passed under the old sewer, which was about ten feet from its plotted position, due to the fact that at the time weather conditions were extremely bad, the old sewer was carrying a considerable quantity of water, and the plaintiff's workings had either disturbed or actually breached the under-side of the old sewer. The contractor was obliged, on receipt of agreed instructions from the engineer, to stank off the old sewer at a point some distance from the site of his own works, sink a shaft at the far side of the road, and work back in open cut before being able to complete the crossing. *Held*, by Paull J., in the absence of a claim under clause 12 of the I.C.E. Conditions (which on the facts would not have succeeded) the contractor could not recover. Clause 20 of the I.C.E. Conditions could not assist the contractor, since the damage was not due to the engineer's design of the works within the terms of that clause: *Pearce* v. *Hereford Corporation* (1968).[10]

(8) A contract for the conversion of a shop and living accommodation for £4,000 contained the words " provide everything necessary for the proper execution and completion of the works in accordance with the specification " and " allow for covering up and protecting the works during frosty and inclement weather or from damage from any other cause and reinstating any work so damaged." A day before completion and occupation of the shop, which was virtually finished (though the living accommodation was not finished), and at a time when £3,250 out of £4,000 had been paid, vandals broke into the shop and did damage to the extent of £450. The owner's surveyors instructed the contractors to make good the damage at

---

[9] Hudson's B.C., 4th ed. Vol. 2, p. 279; 82 L.T. 17. See also the case of *Bryant and Son* v. *Birmingham Hospital Saturday Fund* [1938] 1 All E.R. 503, *post*, Chap. 8, p. 518, when additional payment for rock was obtained by invoking the provisions of the incorporated standard method of measurement. For the cases on additional quantities, see *post*, Chap. 8, pp. 509 *et seq.*

[10] (1968) 66 L.G.R. 647.

the earliest possible moment. *Held*, by Nield J., the contract was entire and must be completed before payment was due. The work in the present case had to be done before full payment was due, and the contractors could not recover: *Charon (Finchley) Ltd.* v. *Singer Sewing Machine Ltd.* (1968).[11]

It is important to realise that in most, but not all,[12] building and engineering contracts, any obligation of the contractor after practical or substantial completion to put right defects free of charge is limited to defects due to the contractor's breaches of contract. In the majority of cases, therefore, the obligations to do contingent work for the contract price discussed in this subsection are limited to matters arising before practical or substantial completion prior to the employer entering into occupation.[12a] Having brought the works to practical completion, the implied obligations here referred to will have been discharged, and the risk will have passed to the employer. Consistently with this, the contractor's obligation to insure the works, if any, is, under the majority of contracts, terminated at practical completion.[13] A class of contracts where the liability after completion is of a " maintenance and upholding " character independent of fault,[12] may, however, have the effect of continuing the contingent work obligations until the expiry of the relevant period, depending on its ·wording. In such a case the obligation to complete will continue until the end of the later period.

Before leaving this subject, it may be desirable to consider the main contractor's obligation to complete in relation to the work of nominated specialist sub-contractors. While there is little difficulty in construing the main contractor's express undertaking to complete in accordance with the employer's or architect's design as an unqualified one, can the same be said for the highly specialist work of nominated sub-contractors, the design of which may often either not be specified at all or known to the main contractor at the time of signature of the main contract,[14] and which in any case is probably in a specialised field outside the main contractor's competence? Where, as in most modern contracts, there is a power for the contractor to object to the appointment of a sub-contractor who will not enter into comparable obligations to those

---

[11] (1968) 207 E.G. 140.

[12] *Post*, Chap. 6, pp. 389 *et seq.*

[12a] See also the discussion *supra*, p. 268.

[13] Clause 20A, post-1963 R.I.B.A. forms, Clause 20 (1) (not explicit but clear by implication) 1955 I.C.E. Conditions.

[14] *Cf.* the comment *supra*, p. 268, in relation to work ordered under a power to vary.

of the main contractor,[15] there is, it is submitted, no difficulty in so construing the obligation, at least in relation to the sub-contract work itself, since the main contractor in the event of inability to complete the sub-contract work will have his contractual remedy against the sub-contractor if and when himself sued or penalised by the employer.   It is further submitted that there is an implied term of the contract that the employer will not nominate a sub-contractor or supplier whose work or contracts are in any way inconsistent with the main contractor's obligations: " The plaintiffs clearly could not be compelled to enter into a [sub-] contract which did not adequately protect them,"[16] and, if so, it is submitted that no distinction exists between cases where there is an express right of objection and the implied right of objection inherent in the implied term referred to. If therefore, on receipt of a nomination, a contractor accepts it without demur, and particularly bearing in mind that he is usually better equipped than the employer to decide whether or not the sub-contract will place his own obligation to complete under the main contract in jeopardy, it is suggested that the contractor will be estopped from subsequently asserting that he is not bound to complete, and there is no need to qualify the nature of his obligation.

This matter is more fully discussed *infra*, Section 2,[17] and *post*, Chapter 15,[18] but the whole of the law on this subject must now be regarded as in doubt following the decision of the House of Lords in *Bickerton* v. *N.W. Metropolitan Hospital Board*.[19]

(2) Obligations as to Design and Quality of Materials and Work

So far, the contractor's obligation to bring the work to completion has been considered, and it has been seen that an employer does not in any way warrant the practicability of his architect's or engineer's design, and that the contractor's obligation to bring the works to completion by whatever means may be necessary is, in the absence of express terms, unaffected by the architect's production of the initial design. It is now proposed to deal with obligations which may continue after completion in regard to the work done by the contractor. In so far as there is a clear breach of an express term describing the work to be done, no problem arises other than that

---

[15] See clause 59 (1) of the 1955 I.C.E. standard form, and clause 27 (a) of the post-1963 R.I.B.A. standard forms.

[16] *Per* Romer L.J. in *Leslie* v. *Metropolitan Asylums District* (1903) 1 L.G.R. at p. 868, illustrated *post*, Chap. 15, p. 750.

[17] At pp. 329 *et seq.*

[18] At pp. 761 *et seq.*

[19] [1970] 1 W.L.R. 607, illustrated and discussed *infra*, Section 2, pp. 333 *et seq.*

created by the possible binding effect of a final certificate. The present subsection is concerned with implied obligations, or the interpretation of express warranties, as to quality, and it is now proposed to consider the subject under three heads, namely, design, materials and workmanship. In fact it should be appreciated that, in the senses in which they are often used, these expressions may overlap to a considerable extent. Thus design is wide enough to include (and include correctly) not merely structural calculations and the dimensions, shape and location of the work, but the choice of particular materials for particular functions and, similarly, the choice of particular work processes. In other words, in sophisticated contracts the design includes the specification as well as the drawings. The concept of workmanship as it is often used may really mean design in one of the senses indicated above, as when a carpenter decides to use non-corrosive nails or screws in an exposed position or where a long life is demanded of his work, or a butt joint where a mortise and tenon is necessary, or where a plasterer decides that an extra coat is needed on a particular surface to give an even finish, or a tiler lays tiles to falls to take off stormwater, or a bricklayer chooses a particular mix for his mortar. Again, materials may be said to be of poor quality when what is meant is that they have been chosen for the wrong purpose, as common bricks for facing bricks, or iron cramps for zinc. All these are, on close analysis, cases of design, because they involve the element of deliberate choice as suitable for their purpose, but are frequently not so referred to because the finer details of construction, even in sophisticated contracts, and in less formal contracts a great deal of important design, may be left to the " good building practice " of the tradesmen or contractor concerned, for which the word " workmanship " is commonly used. In this subsection the word " design " is used in the sense of the suitability for its intended purpose of the final permanent work, in so far as that may result from the intentions of those conceiving and planning the work, whoever they may be.

It is submitted that a contractor undertaking to do work and supply materials impliedly undertakes:

(a) to do the work undertaken with care and skill or, as sometimes expressed, in a workmanlike manner;

(b) to use materials of good quality. In the case of materials described expressly this will mean good of their expressed kind. (In the case of goods not described, or not described in sufficient detail, it is submitted that there will be reliance on the contractor to that extent, and the warranty in (c) below will apply);

(c) that both the work and materials will be reasonably fit for the purpose for which they are required, unless the circumstances of the contract are such as to exclude any such obligation (this obligation is additional to that in (a) and (b), and only becomes relevant, for practical purposes, if the contractor has fulfilled his obligations under (a) and (b)).[20]

The first two obligations (a) and (b) correspond to the warranty of merchantability, and that under (c) to the warranty of suitability, under section 14 of the Sale of Goods Act 1893. The obligation under (c) is here called the " design " obligation and extends, it is submitted, to all defects of planning or conception of the building or project in question including, as stated, the selection of all materials and work processes. The purpose for which the work or materials are required must, it is submitted, be considered in the light of the reasonable life of the building or project, or of the relevant part of it if the part can reasonably be expected to have a shorter life than that of the main structure.

In rare cases the circumstances of the contract may serve to exclude the warranties in (a) and (b),[21] as well as the warranty in (c).

It is now certain that the obligation to use good materials is absolute and independent of fault.[22] Defects in a large number of the "materials" used by contractors may in fact be due to the careless *work* of a sub-contractor, but to one working off the site rather than upon it, *e.g.* in the manufacture of items such as windows, doors and joinery, and pre-cast concrete units, and even bricks; so to that extent the contractor's implied obligation is, on close analysis, only a warranty that someone else's work, whether or not in contractual relations with him, has also been carefully and skilfully done.[23] But in the last resort, the warranty is indeed absolute in every sense, as in the case of a material which contains a latent defect which no one could have detected or avoided before making use of it,

---

[20] See the statements of Lord Denning M.R. and du Parcq L.J. cited *infra*, paragraph (a), p. 279, and the cases cited under (a) and (b) *infra*.

[21] *Myers* v. *Brent Cross Service Co.* [1934] 1 K.B. 46; *Gloucestershire C.C.* v. *Richardson* [1969] 1 A.C. 480, *infra*, pp. 297, 298–300.

[22] *Hancock* v. *Brazier (Anerley) Ltd.* [1966] 1 W.L.R. 1317 (Diplock L.J.) and [1966] 2 All E.R. 901; *Young & Marten* v. *McManus Childs Ltd.* [1969] 1 A.C. 454.

[23] Compare the facts in the case of *Gloucestershire C.C.* v. *Richardson* [1969] 1 A.C. 480, *infra*, p. 298.

whether for sub-manufacturing purposes or in the building itself. It will not avail the contractor that he obtained the material from a reputable source, and took all possible steps to test and examine it.[24]

Until recently, it was an open question whether the liability under (c) was absolute or qualified by a concept of care and skill. This is likely to be of the highest importance in the case of "package deal" contracts. It is now clear that, contrary to what was suggested in the Ninth Edition of this work, this obligation is, in the light of the reasoning of the House of Lords in *Young & Marten Ltd.* v. *McManus Childs* (1969),[25] absolute also.[26]

The extremely important cases of *Hancock* and *Young & Marten* have resolved many difficulties, but for the purpose of building contracts the vital problem, which still requires the most careful attention in every case, is to decide what circumstances are sufficient to exclude the design/suitability warranty in (c), or the work and materials warranties in (a) and (b). The *Young & Marten* case, which related to a possible exclusion of the materials obligation (b), shows that, in the case of that obligation (and, therefore it is submitted, the workmanship obligation in (a) as well) even if the employer relies exclusively on his own judgment in selecting a material or source of supply or work, that by itself will not prevent the obligation from being implied. Something more will be needed in the case of these two obligations. On the other hand, it is reasonably clear that if the employer relies upon his architect or engineer for the design of the project, then in a case where the defect in the work complained of is due to the architect's or engineer's specific design requirements the employer cannot be said to be relying on the contractor's skill and judgment, and the suitability warranty in (c) above will be excluded. But, as already stated, the architect's or engineer's design requirements, even in sophisticated contracts, may be silent on a large number of detailed matters, and, if so, it is submitted there are no circumstances requiring the exclusion of the suitability warranty if the complaint relates to such a matter,[27] since an architect owes no duty to the contractor during the course of supervision to detect the latter's defective work or to indicate his requirements early or at any other stage of the work.[28] On the other hand, in

---

[24] See *Hancock's* case, *per* Diplock L.J., and see the *Young & Marten* case.

[25] [1969] 1 A.C. 454. See also *per* Diplock L.J. in *Hancock's* case, *infra*.

[26] See *infra*, pp. 290–291.

[27] See *e.g. Cammell Laird* v. *Manganese Bronze and Brass* [1934] A.C. 402.

[28] See *post*, Chap. 6, pp. 385–388, and the cases of *East Ham B.C.* v. *Sunley* [1966] A.C. 406 and *AMF International Ltd.* v. *Magnet Bowling* [1968] 1 W.L.R. 1028 there cited.

" package deal " contracts,[29] where the work is designed by the contractor, it is submitted that, notwithstanding that the employer may employ architects or engineers to check and make recommendations on the contractor's designs, and whatever nomenclature may be used in the contracts to describe the status or function of such architects or engineers, the realities of the relationship and the practical impossibility already mentioned of making a thorough check of a contractor's designs [30] mean that in such cases the implied terms enumerated above will all obtain without exclusion or modification.[30a]

The cases which present most difficulty, and which have troubled the courts most seriously, are those where the employer has nominated or selected a sub-contractor or supplier for work or materials, often but by no means always of a specialist character, and usually under the well-known provisions for nomination of sub-contractors or suppliers to be found in building and engineering contracts. Do such nominations show that the employer is not relying on the skill and judgment of the contractor, and so avoid the suitability warranty (c), or are they inconsistent with the work and materials warranties (a) and (b)? It is submitted that, in spite of difficulties created by the reasoning in two of the judgments in the House of Lords in the difficult case of *Gloucestershire County Council* v. *Richardson*, the mere fact of selection of a source of work or materials, however specialist in character, either in the original contract documents [30] or by virtue of the exercise of a power of nomination, are not circumstances sufficient to exclude the warranties in (a) or (b) (in the case of nominations this is particularly indicated by the express provisions in most nomination clauses stating that the nominees are declared to be sub-contractors or suppliers of the contractor).[31] On the other hand, since the design element of the sub-contract work, in so far as it is expressly stated or described in the sub-contract documentation, is by virtue of the nomination merely a delegation of the architect's design function,[32] then if the matter complained of is due to the specific requirement of the sub-contract, as *e.g.* the general unsuitability of the product or work process involved, or a design specifically provided for in the sub-contract drawings or specification, the suitability warranty in (c) will be excluded; *aliter* if,

---

[29] See *ante*, Chap. 3, pp. 198–199, 207–210, and see also Chap. 1, pp. 2–3.
[30] See the *Young & Marten* case.
[30a] But see, for a difficult borderline case, *Cable (1956) Ltd.* v. *Hutcherson Ltd.* (1969) 43 A.L.J.R. 321 (Australia), *infra*, p. 288.
[31] See the discerning judgment of Lord Pearson in *Gloucestershire C.C.* v. *Richardson* [1969] 1 A.C. 480 at p. 512.
[32] See the case of *Moresk* v. *Hicks* [1966] 2 Lloyd's Rep. 338.

as in the case of the main contractor's own work, the sub-contract documentation leaves some matter generally undescribed and therefore to the skill and judgment of the sub-contractor, and hence of the main contractor. The dividing line in such cases may not always be easy to establish, but the principle is, it is submitted, clear. Thus if, for example, the nominated sub-contractor for the reinforced concrete frame of a building were to choose a mix of concrete with inadequate compressive strength for the loads to be expected, and the sub-contract specification was silent on the composition of the mix, the implication of a term of suitability would not be avoided by the facts (a) that the architect was responsible for the overall design of the project or (b) that the work was being carried out by a nominated sub-contractor. Nor, it is submitted, will the specialist character of the sub-contract work prevent implied requirements of the necessary specialist skill by the main contractor, notwithstanding that he has not the skill himself, since by placing the order with a nominated specialist on terms that the specialist shall become his own sub-contractor or supplier, the contractor thereby himself adopts and assumes, it is submitted, the same obligations in the main contract as the specialist in the sub-contract.[32a] One area of special difficulty may arise if, as is often the case, a sub-contract specification in fact emanates from the specialist and not from the architect or engineer.[33] It will be seen, however, that the House of Lords has held that a nomination of a sub-contractor on terms limiting the supplier's liability, where there is no express right to reject the nomination, may displace the implied terms.[34]

In the light of the above discussion it is now proposed to examine the cases under the three heads referred to, but in reverse order.

(a) Design and suitability

As will be appreciated from the foregoing discussion, the cases on this subject are, in the majority of instances, though not all, likely to arise where an architect or engineer is not engaged by the employer.[34a] Apart from the relatively new development of the "package deal" contract, the only class of more important building or engineering contracts which has satisfied this requirement in the United Kingdom in modern times has been that

---

[32a] See *post*, Chap. 15, pp. 761 *et seq*.

[33] See *infra*, pp. 281–282.

[34] *Gloucestershire C.C.* v. *Richardson* [1969] 1 A.C. 480, *infra*, pp. 298–300.

[34a] Or such cases are likely to arise where, despite his presence and overall control over the design, it has not condescended to deal with some matter in detail, which has been to that extent left to the skill and judgment of the contractor.

for the sale of houses to be erected or in the course of erection by private developers. The design obligation in contracts of work and materials has, therefore, tended to evolve, wherever the rule of *caveat emptor* in the case of sales of completed houses could be avoided by the courts, from cases where the employer's requirement is almost invariably a dwelling-house, or from fields outside the building and civil engineering industry altogether. Making allowance for the special situation of the contract before him, therefore, the following statement of Lord Denning M.R. may be taken as authoritative and of general application: "It is clear from *Lawrence* v. *Cassell* and *Miller* v. *Cannon Hill Estates* that where a purchaser buys a house from a builder who contracts to build it there is a threefold implication: that the builder will do the work in a good and workmanlike manner, that he will supply good and proper materials, and that the house will be reasonably fit for human habitation." [35] Further, the following statement of Lord Justice du Parcq has been accepted as correct by all the judges in the House of Lords in the *Young & Marten* case: "A person contracting to do work and supply materials warrants that the materials which he uses will be of good quality and reasonably fit for the purpose for which he is using them, unless the circumstances of the contract are such as to exclude any such warranty."

As already stated, a liability for design on the part of the contractor may arise, notwithstanding the presence of an architect or engineer in charge of the design of the work, by reason of his implied obligation to carry out the work with sound workmanship and materials. This means that wherever the contract is silent on these matters (usually, of course, in the relatively small and less important processes of building) a design responsibility of the contractor will arise. Thus, if a contract, while requiring reinforced concrete, does not specify the mix of concrete to be used, the contractor will be expected to select and provide a mix suitable for the intended function of the concrete in question. If the reinforcement is not, or not sufficiently, detailed, adequate reinforcement must be provided. Again, if the carpentry details of a roof are not shown, the design, for instance, of the roof trusses, or the methods of nailing, must be reasonably skilful. However, the more important matters of design and selection of materials are likely to be expressly stipulated for in the contract documents, and the effect of the warranty is that the builder who carries out the described work with the described quality of materials

[35] *Hancock* v. *Brazier (Anerley) Ltd.* [1966] 1 W.L.R. 1317, see *infra*.

and workmanship warrants, if he and not some agent of the employer has provided the design or made the choice, that the final result will itself prove satisfactory. This situation is, of course, closely analogous to that covered, in the field of sale of goods, by section 14 (1) of the Sale of Goods Act 1893, which provides as follows:

" Where the buyer, expressly or by implication, makes known to the seller the particular purpose for which the goods are required, so as to show that the buyer relies on the seller's skill or judgment, and the goods are of a description which it is in the course of the seller's business to supply (whether he be the manufacturer or not), there is an implied condition that the goods shall be reasonably fit for such purpose, provided that in the case of a contract for the sale of a specified article under its patent or other trade name, there is no implied condition as to its fitness for any particular purpose." The House of Lords in the *Young & Marten* case[36] have now finally made it clear that the Sale of Goods Act merely restated the existing law, and that that law, as evolved by the judges, had applied the identical principles in the case of contracts for work and materials as in contracts for sale of goods.

So in one of the earliest cases it has been said: "Where a person is employed in a work of skill the employer buys both his labour and his judgment; he ought not to undertake the work if it cannot succeed and he should know whether it will or not; of course it is otherwise if the party employing him choose to supersede the workman's judgment by his own."[37] The following Australian dictum is, it is submitted, an entirely correct statement of the principle: "Unlike a warranty of good workmanship, a warranty that the work will answer the purpose for which it is intended is not implied in every contract for work. The essential element for the implication of such a term is that the employer should be relying, to the knowledge of the contractor, upon the contractor's skill and judgment and not upon his own or those of his agents." [37a]

It follows that for any such term to be implied in a building or engineering contract, the employer must be relying, to the knowledge of the contractor, upon the latter's skill and judgment and not upon his own or those of his agent. This reliance need not, however,

---

[36] *Young & Marten Ltd* v. *McManus Childs Ltd.* [1969] 1 A.C. 454.

[37] *Per* Bayley J. in *Duncan* v. *Blundell* (1820) 3 Stark. 6.

[37a] *Corben* v. *Hayes*, April 27, 1964, Full Court of New South Wales, unreported, cited by Sugerman J.A. in *McKone* v. *Johnson* [1966] 2 N.S.W.R. 471, illustrated *infra*.

be exclusive, provided it is substantial.[38] This latter proposition
can be most important in building contracts, because it not infrequently happens that the employer or architect consults a contractor
or specialist sub-contractor before drawing up some part of the
specification or design for incorporation in the documents, and in
many cases may be wholly or almost wholly relying on the contractor
or sub-contractor when doing so.[39] Whether or not this will avail
the employer as against the main contractor, if he has relied on a
specialist sub-contractor in drawing up the sub-contract specifications, or has even had it prepared by the specialist sub-contractor
(both of which unfortunately occur frequently in practice) seems an
open question—see *infra.*

For reasons already stated, in the case of dwelling-houses sold to
purchasers while in the course of erection the courts have applied
the concept of fitness for its purpose to a dwelling-house, and have
emerged with a ready-made obligation to provide a house "fit for
human habitation."[40] As legal short-hand this may be perfectly
satisfactory, but it may tend to over-simplify the exact nature of the
term to be implied in every case, and may not always be a reliable
guide as to when the term should be implied. Thus, errors of design
or in choice of materials may produce unsightly or unwanted defects
or results which may not affect the fitness of the house for habitation,
though they may affect its value or amenities. There seems no
reason why such defects should be outside the responsibility of the
seller or the builder.[41]

As stated above, in the case of much specialist work, often
carried out by nominated sub-contractors, there seems in principle
no reason why, depending on the facts, the specialist should not
impliedly warrant the suitability of his product to the the main contractor, despite the presence of an architect or engineer of the employer and despite the approval of plans or details by the adviser
concerned, in those cases where only the specialist has the knowledge
or experience to be able to know with exactitude its suitability for
the intended requirements of the employer. A case where this must
as a fact be so, for example, is in the case of manufactured goods
supplied by nominated suppliers for incorporation in the works, as,

---

[38] See *Cammell Laird Ltd.* v. *Manganese, Bronze & Brass Co. Ltd.* [1934] A.C. 402
and *Att.-Gen. of Canada* v. *Laminated Structures* (1961) 28 D.L.R. (2d) 92, *infra.*
[39] See for a discussion of the dangers and abuses of this practice, *ante*, Chap. 2, pp. 98,
129–131.
[40] *Miller* v. *Cannon Hill Estates* [1931] 2 K.B. 113; *Perry* v. *Sharon Development Co.
Ltd.* [1937] 4 All E.R. 390; *Jennings* v. *Tavener* [1955] 1 W.L.R. 932.
[41] See *per* Diplock L.J. in *Hancock* v. *Brazier (Anerley) Ltd., infra,* pp. 297–298.

for instance, the pipes, valves or specials required for a waterworks contract. Is the employer to lose all rights if the machinery in question is unsuitable, because of the accident of the interposition of the main contractor? But there are many less extreme cases, such as roofing work and structural steel, where a design responsibility by the sub-contractor (and hence of the main contractor under the terms of most modern main contracts) might be implied to give the whole arrangement between the parties business efficacy.[42] So too, cases where, for example, specialist heating contractors are engaged without a heating consultant being called in to advise the employer. As already stated, the answer to this question must turn upon the effect to be given to the nomination provisions when they state that the specialist concerned is to be a sub-contractor of the main contractor. Thus of nomination provisions identical with the 1963 R.I.B.A. forms it has been said: " If that form of words used in clause 21 has the effect (as I think it must) of imposing on the contractor responsibility for the quality of work done by nominated sub-contractors, the very similar form of words used in clause 22 would naturally have the similar effect of imposing on the contractor responsibility for the quality of materials supplied by nominated suppliers." [43]

As in the case of all implied terms, it is dangerous, it is submitted, for lawyers to attempt to lay down too rigidly the occasions for and exact content of implied terms. There are many possible situations in the modern building and engineering industries where a design responsibility, though rarely an absolute one, can be implied on the part of the person carrying out the work. But every case will depend upon its special facts. As a broad generalisation, if plans and specifications are supplied to a builder to work to, *a fortiori* if the building owner employs an architect, the contractor will not normally have to do more than carry out the work according to the plans and specification in a workmanlike manner and using proper materials, though he may well be fully aware of the purpose for which the work is required, and may even shrewdly suspect that it will not fulfil that purpose satisfactorily.

As Lord Esher said in *Hall* v. *Burke* (1886) [44]: " There were two well-known kinds of contract—first, a customer might ask a manufacturer to make a machine according to a given plan, or according to

---

[42] See the fuller discussion, *post*, Chap. 15, pp. 761 *et seq.*
[43] *Per* Lord Pearson in *Gloucestershire C.C.* v. *Richardson* [1969] 1 A.C. 480 at p. 512.
[44] 3 T.L.R. at p. 165.   See also *per* Lord Wright in *Cammell Laird Ltd.* v. *Manganese Bronze & Brass Ltd.* (1934) 50 T.L.R. at p. 357.

a plan supplied by the customer; in that case the manufacturer would only have to make the machine according to the plan, and in a workmanlike manner. Secondly, a customer might ask the manufacturer to make a machine for a particular purpose, not supplying any plan, but leaving it to him to make it for that purpose; in that case, unless the contrary was expressly stated in the contract, the manufacturer would have to make a machine fit for that purpose. There might be a third kind of contract, where both parties said that they would jointly endeavour to make a machine that would do its business, when there would be no warranty that it would effect its purpose."[44a] This dictum, of the greatest value, inevitably could not envisage possible situations and liabilities of parties under modern contracts where many techniques or products are necessarily beyond the technical capacities of the employer's advisers, and where the situation may further be complicated by the nomination procedures.

Again, as a broad generalisation, if the builder himself designs or selects materials for the work, either because he provides the whole design or because a part of the design is left to his judgment and choice, there will be an implied term that the work and materials will be suitable for their purpose, but each case needs to be carefully considered on its facts, and in the case, criticised below, of *Lynch* v. *Thorne* (1956), the Court of Appeal appears to have held that, even where the specification and plans are supplied by the builder, there is no room for any implication of fitness for its purpose, if the specification is clear and explicit as to the particular work the subject of complaint, and the work has been carried out in accordance with the specification.

But between these two extremes there exists at the present day a wide range of possibilities of shared responsibility. The cases below are concerned with what appear to be design or suitability failures. As it happens, three vitally important modern cases on the possible exclusion of the implied terms, and a number of older ones, have involved questions of the obligation of good quality in respect of materials, and these cases, under paragraph (b) below,[45] are in principle equally applicable to questions of design and suitability.

ILLUSTRATIONS

(1) The plaintiff by the defendant's order erected a stove in a shop and laid a tube under the floor for the purpose of carrying off the smoke. The scheme failed entirely, and the stove could

---

[44a] See for a startlingly similar situation, the *Cable* (1956) *Ltd.* case illustrated *infra*, p. 288.   [45] *Infra*, p. 295.

not be used. *Held*, the plaintiff could not recover: *Duncan* v. *Blundell* (1820).[46]

(2) The plaintiff employed the defendant as a workman to put up a new kitchen range with an old boiler behind. Hot water could not be got from the boiler, the flues not being efficient. The defendant said the space was not large enough to make the flues effective. The plaintiff replied that if he had known this he would not have had the work done at all. *Held*, the defendant was under a duty to advise the plaintiff that the work could not be done, and the plaintiff was entitled to recover from him in an action for fitting up the range in an improper and unworkmanlike manner: *Pearce* v. *Tucker* (1862).[47]

(3) The plaintiffs contracted with the defendants to construct a waterworks for a lump sum in accordance with specifications and bills of quantities. The water was to be raised by a windmill, as to which the contract provided: " The contractors will be required to obtain the windmill tower and pump from Messrs. X, windmill engineers, for which a sum of £127 has been included in the quantities. This sum does not include profit to the contractors, and they must add to it any charges they may think proper. They must be carefully fixed and their continuous satisfactory working during the period of maintenance must be guaranteed by the contractors." Item 16 of the bills contained a prime cost sum of £127 10s. for a (described in detail) " Canadian Imperial " windmill. The windmill supplied proved useless for its purpose the moment it was installed, and the defendants called on the plaintiffs during construction and before work was completed to supply an efficient windmill but the plaintiffs refused to do so and the defendants thereupon gave them notice determining the contract, and completed themselves using an entirely different type of windmill. The plaintiffs sued the defendants for the work done and materials supplied. *Held*, that since the defendants had insisted upon a specified windmill being supplied by a specified firm, the plaintiffs were not responsible for the defects which made it inefficient and were entitled to recover on a *quantum meruit. Per* Lawrance J.: " Was the plaintiffs' contract to make the mill answer its purpose; or was it a contract to do the work in accordance with the specification and plans? . . . It was no part of their contract to guarantee in any way that it would be efficient." *Held*, also, that the maintenance clause never applied, since the maintenance period had not started, but even if this were not so, it would not apply if the mill was incapable of doing its work properly. *Bowers Bros.* v. *Chapel-en-le-Frith R.D.C.* (1911).[48]

(4) The specification of a contract required all bricks used to be sound, hard, square, well-burnt bricks free from lime or other impurities or other extraneous matter, fine cracks or other defects, and from an approved yard. It was also provided that the whole of the work was to be done in a thoroughly workmanlike manner with the best materials. The architect ordered certain named stock bricks to be used for underground manholes, and approved samples of the

[46] 3 Stark. 6.
[47] 3 F. & F. 136.
[48] 9 L.G.R. 339, 663; 75 J.P. 122, 321. A new trial was, however, ordered for some unexplained reason by the C.A. (But many building contracts contain express warranties not limited to the builder's own work, see *infra*, pp. 291–293.)

bricks. Bricks equal to the sample were used, but owing to underground water and the nature of the bricks, the manholes were not watertight and were condemned by the engineer. *Held*, by Phillimore J., as the bricks conformed to the specification, no complaint could be made against the contractor who was entitled to be paid for his work: *Adcock's Trustee* v. *Bridge R.D.C.* (1911).[49]

(5) Specialist manufacturers of ships' propellers undertook to make them in accordance with drawings of the shipbuilder for use in two particular ships. The drawings specified the thicknesses of the blades along their medial lines, but as to the rest of the dimensions provided merely that the edges " were to be brought up to fine lines." In one of the two ships, the propeller, though it complied with the dimensions shown on the drawings within the permitted tolerances, made a noise when in use which resulted in the ship failing to receive the required Lloyd's classification. *Held*, by the House of Lords, that on the facts the shipbuilders relied on the manufacturers' skill and judgment in relation to the final finishing and shaping of the propellers; that the source of the trouble lay in the region of the matters left to the manufacturers' skill and judgment, and that there was, therefore, a breach of the implied condition of reasonable fitness for its purpose under section 14 of the Sale of Goods Act 1893: *Cammell Laird* v. *Manganese, Bronze & Brass Ltd.* (1934).[50]

(6) A builder prepared plans and a specification for a house to be built on doubtful ground, using a concrete raft. After the house had been built and occupied, the raft cracked, and the only remedy was to use a pier-and-beam system costing more than the original price of the house. *Held*, following *Miller* v. *Cannon Hill Estates* (1931)[51] and *Lawrence* v. *Cassel* (1930),[52] that there was an implied warranty that the house should be reasonably fit for the purpose for which it was required, and the builder was liable: *Cooke* v. *Rowe* (1950).[53]

(7) A building owner was informed by the builder that the specified roofing would not be obtainable for some time, and the builder recommended " Cornish Tiles," a type of concrete tile. The owner told him to " go ahead with Cornish tiles." *Held*, following *Cammell Laird* v. *Manganese, Bronze & Brass Co. Ltd.* (1934)[54] and *G. H. Myers & Co.* v. *Brent Cross Service Co.* (1934),[55] that there was an implied condition as to the quality and fitness of the roofing, and since the evidence showed that the owner relied on the builder's skill and judgment, it was immaterial that the goods were ordered by their trade name: *Martin* v. *McNamara* (1951).[56]

(8) A car owner took his car to motor repairers for repairs to his brakes. He suggested that the relining of the drums, which was a specialist part of the work which he knew was not undertaken by the repairers themselves, should be done by a named firm, from whom

49 75 J.P. 241.
50 [1934] A.C. 402.
51 [1931] 2 K.B. 113.
52 [1930] 2 K.B. 83.
53 [1950] N.Z. 410 (New Zealand).
54 [1934] A.C. 402.
55 [1934] 1 K.B. 46 *infra*, p. 297.
56 [1951] Q.S.R. 225 (Queensland).

the repairers obtained a quotation. The owner and the repairers thought it too high, and the repairers suggested another firm who normally did work for them. This firm's quotation was accepted, but the type of liner which was fitted was not, in fact, suitable for the car in question, and, as a result, the owner had an accident. *Held*, by Sellers J., following *G. H. Myers* v. *Brent Cross Service Co.* (1934),[57] that an absolute warranty of fitness for the intended purpose of the work can be implied in a contract for work done and materials supplied, if the work is of a kind which the contractor holds himself out to perform either by himself or his sub-contractors. The contractor is liable for defective work on the part of his sub-contractor even if the customer consents to the work being done by that particular sub-contractor, unless the customer, without placing reliance on the skill and judgment of the repairer, selects a particular sub-contractor by whom the work is to be done: *Stewart* v. *Reavell's Garage* (1952).[58]

(Note: The language and reasoning of this case should not be treated as suggesting that a main contractor will not be liable for a nominated sub-contractor's lack of skill. This was not a building case. Most building and engineering contracts provide that nominated sub-contractors are " deemed to be " or " declared to be " sub-contractors of the main contractor, and give a main contractor the right to object to the appointment of a sub-contractor on any reasonable ground. Sellers J. was in fact the dissenting judge in the Court of Appeal in *Gloucestershire C.C.* v. *Richardson* (1969) and there considered a main contractor liable for a nominated supplier's bad workmanship notwithstanding the absence of any express right of objection. It is submitted that the main contractor's responsibility for such work must, as a matter of business efficacy, be identical with that for his own work.[59])

(9) A house was purchased from a builder when certain matters still needed to be attended to, but these were all later completed satisfactorily. The agreement of sale contained the words " the purchaser acknowledges that he has inspected the property and that he purchases the same solely in reliance on his own judgment and not on any representation or warranty made by the vendor." *Held*, (i) that the implied term was twofold, namely (a) that the work remaining to be performed would be carried out in a proper and workmanlike manner and with proper materials (if no materials were specified) and (b) that the dwelling-house, when completed, must, as a whole, be fit for human habitation, but (ii) that the clause quoted was sufficient to exclude any implied term: *McKey* v. *Rorison* (1953).[60]

(10) A house was sold which was still not complete. The house was built in close proximity to an elm tree, the roots of which removed moisture from the subsoil, causing subsidence which subsequently damaged the foundations and structure of the house. *Held*, following

---

[57] [1934] 1 K.B. 46. Illustrated *infra*, p. 297.
[58] [1952] 2 Q.B. 545.
[59] See *supra*, pp. 281–282 and also the comment *infra*, p. 302 on the *Gloucestershire County Council* case and *post*, Chap. 15, pp. 761 *et seq*.
[60] [1953] N.Z.L.R. 498 (New Zealand). See also *Kent* v. *Saltdean Estate Co.* (1964) 114 L.J. 555, *post*, Chap. 6, p. 398, for another case where the express terms prevailed over the implied terms in the case of a house in the course of erection.

Miller v. *Cannon Hill Estates* (1931),[61] that the vendor was liable: *Jennings* v. *Taverer* (1955).[62]

(11) A builder sold a house in the course of erection, undertaking to complete it in accordance with plans and specifications annexed to the agreement of sale. After the purchaser had taken possession, it appeared that a specified 9 inch brick wall would not keep out driving rain, and the evidence was that a wall of this thickness in that position would be unlikely to keep out the weather. The county court judge found as a fact that the purchaser had throughout relied on the builder's skill and judgment, and found for the purchaser. *Held*, by the Court of Appeal, the express term of the contract specifying the type of wall was inconsistent with the condition usually to be implied of fitness for human habitation, and as the defendant had exactly complied with the specification using sound materials and good workmanship, he was not liable: *Lynch* v. *Thorne* (1956).[63]

N.B.—It is submitted that this decision of the Court of Appeal cannot, with the greatest respect, be right. Its effect, of course, is to avoid the responsibility of the builder, provided he takes steps to see that the proposed work is accurately described in sufficient detail in the specification or drawings he prepares or puts forward. Moreover, it is hard to see, by analogy with contracts for the sale of goods, why a description of what an expert might know to be defective or unsuitable should remove liability in a situation in which, by definition, the buyer or employer is relying on the seller's or builder's skill and judgment. Is a chemist, asked to make up a prescription for a particular complaint, to escape liability if he provides a prescription useless for this purpose but affixes a label to the bottle accurately describing the ingredients? Nor, it is suggested, is an implied term that a 9 inch brick wall will be fit for habitation inconsistent with the express obligation to build a 9 inch brick wall. The Court of Appeal appears to have disregarded the provenance of the specification and drawings implicit in the county court judge's finding of fact, a vital factor, it is submitted. For a case of an express term where the Supreme Court of Canada, has, it is submitted, approached the matter in the correct way, see *Steel Co. of Canada* v. *Willand Management Ltd.* (1966).[64]

(12) A contractor quoted £320 for labour and materials to the owner of a block of flats, describing in his quotation the work necessary to provide a 3 inch vermiculite concrete roof upon and above an existing flat roof surrounded by a low parapet wall. The contractor knew that the existing roof was leaking, and that that was the reason for his own work. The additional thickness of the superimposed roof had the effect of reducing the depth to which water could accumulate on the roof during heavy rain before it rose above the level of the flashing along the parapet wall. The flashings ought accordingly to have been raised or the capacity of the available outlets increased. Water flooded into the building during heavy rain. There were also other factors of the design which resulted in minor leaks or staining, apart from the flooding. *Held*, by the Court of

---

[61] [1931] 2 K.B. 113.
[62] [1955] 1 W.L.R. 932.
[63] [1956] 1 W.L.R. 303. See also the criticism, *infra*, p. 289.
[64] [1966] S.C.R. 746 (Canada), illustrated *infra*, pp. 292–293.

Appeal of New South Wales, upholding the trial judge, that the roof should have provided for the chance of the rain which occurred, which though heavy was not abnormal, and the contractor was liable for the cost of eliminating by the most reasonable method the two deficiencies in the roof. *Duncan* v. *Blundell* (1820) and *Corben* v. *Hayes* (1964) [65] applied, *Lynch* v. *Thorne* (1956) distinguished: *McKone* v. *Johnson* (1966). [66]

(13) A contractor tendered for the design, supply and erection of a storage hopper, on the basis of a specification and drawings prepared by the employer's engineer. None of the engineer's drawings related to the foundations. The specification required the contractor to supply and instal concrete foundations. It further provided that tenderers, irrespective of the information on the specification and drawings, should take responsibility for the supply and erection and efficent operation of the project for twelve months after acceptance of the work. The contractor supplied drawings of foundations, to which the engineer required amendments to be made; the tender was accepted, and a final set of drawings, supplied by the contractor but amended and approved by the engineer, emerged, including a ring-beam type of foundation. A formal agreement, in a form very similar to the R.I.B.A. forms, was then entered into whereby the contractor undertook to "execute and complete the work shown upon the contract drawings and described by or referred to in the said specification and conditions." Near the end of the work it transpired that the foundations would be adequate for the hopper until completion, but that once filled there would be subsidence due to the nature of the subsoil, and that a piled foundation was necessary. The contractor refused to do the piling work without additional payment, and was dismissed. *Held* by the High Court of Australia, that although the contractor had supplied the design in the first place, and notwithstanding the wording of the specification, the contractor had promised no more than to carry out the specified work in a workmanlike manner. *Cable (1956) Ltd.* v. *Hutcherson Ltd.* (1969). [66a]

[Note: This was obviously a difficult borderline case in what was clearly a " package-deal " situation, with preliminary drawings and an outline specification only supplied originally by the employer. As so often is the case, however, an inappropriate traditional form of contract was ultimately used by the parties, and this clearly weighed very heavily with the Court, together with the degree of control over the drawings in fact exercised by the engineer.]

The foregoing cases show clearly that, as expressly stated in the recent decision of the House of Lords in *Young & Marten* v. *McManus Childs* (1969)[67] the courts have assimilated the position in contracts for work and materials with that under section 14 (1) of the Sale of Goods Act. As a result, a contractor will be liable under an implied

[65] *Corben* v. *Hayes*, April 27, 1964, Full Court of New South Wales, unreported. See *supra*, p. 280.   [66] [1966] 2 N.S.W.R. 471.
[66a] (1969) 43 A.L.J.R. 321 (Australia). Contrast the *Steel Co. of Canada* case, illustrated *infra*, pp. 292–293.   [67] [1969] 1 A.C. 454, *infra*, p. 298.

term for suitability or design whenever it can be shown that there was substantial reliance on his skill and knowledge in that regard. " Unlike a warranty of good workmanship, a warranty that the work will answer the purpose for which it is intended is not implied in every contract for work. The essential element for the implication of such a term is that the employer should be relying, to the knowledge of the contractor, upon the contractor's skill and judgment and not upon his own or those of his agents." [65] It has already been suggested that, while the identity of the person putting forward the plans or specification is probably a most important factor, it is not necessarily conclusive. Careful analysis shows, it is submitted, that the question of suitability can only become relevant when a builder can show compliance with all the express requirements of the specification or drawings—if he cannot, he is beyond any doubt in breach of contract. It is precisely this point that the Court of Appeal appear to have failed to appreciate in *Lynch* v. *Thorne* (1956).[68] Indeed, as already stated, a design or suitability obligation is only relevant or necessary if the contractor has not only complied with every express obligation, but has also used good materials of the described kind and done his work carefully in accordance with his other two implied obligations. Failure in any of these respects will render him liable to the employer without recourse to a design or suitability obligation.

A word should perhaps be added on the subject of the obligation in sales of uncompleted houses. The position here may seem somewhat unreal, in that developers of property frequently complete dwellings for all practical purposes, but deliberately leave certain minor matters such as decorations, or sanitary fittings, and sometimes floors, uncompleted to await the purchaser's choice.[69] The courts, in their desire to escape from the rule of *caveat emptor*, which prevents the implication of any warranty of fitness for habitation upon the purchase of a new house from a builder if the house is completed at the time of the contract of sale,[70] have been able to justify a refusal to apply the rule of *caveat emptor* by finding that at the time of sale the house was " in the course of erection," [71] and frequently apply the implied term as to habitability to houses which

---

[68] *Supra.*

[69] See *Perry* v. *Sharon Development Co. Ltd.* [1937] 4 All E.R. 390; where a house with certain decorations incomplete, and without water-taps, baths or grates was held to be in the course of erection.

[70] See *e.g. Hoskins* v. *Woodham* [1938] 1 All E.R. 692.

[71] *Miller* v. *Cannon Hill Estates Ltd.* [1931] 2 K.B. 113; *Perry* v. *Sharon Development Co. Ltd.* [1937] 4 All E.R. 390; *Jennings* v. *Tavener* [1955] 1 W.L.R. 932.

are virtually completed at the time of sale.[72] Furthermore, while it might at first sight seem logical that the warranty of fitness should extend only to the work uncompleted at the time of sale, this difficulty has been brushed aside, and, once a building has been held to be in the course of erection, the warranty has been applied to the whole building including work already done.[73] It is submitted that this strict view is in fact right in principle. The reason why the " house in the course of erection " test was applied, it may be surmised, was that this was an almost invariably accurate way of identifying a commercial or business sale by someone engaged in the business of building and selling houses, on whom the purchaser would for that reason rely, as opposed to an ordinary owner-occupier selling his home. On this view the factual analogy to section 14 of the Sale of Goods Act is close, and the precise degree of lack of completion at the time of the sale irrelevant. The position is now established by modern authority.[74] The definition of the implied term as an absolute warranty of " habitability " has already been criticised in this chapter as being too narrow.[75]

In the last edition of this book it was suggested that the implied terms as to materials and suitability might not, in the case of sales of houses in the course of erection and in building and engineering contracts without professional advisers, be absolute and independent of fault, unlike the case of contracts for sale of goods. For example, it was suggested that a builder might not absolutely guarantee the foundations of a house against differential settlement of the sub-soil, but only undertake to design and construct the foundations using all reasonable skill and care. In the light of recent authority this would appear to be wrong. On further consideration it is clear that the liabilities must be absolute, since otherwise contractors could, by using reputable sub-contractors or sources of supply, escape responsibility, and in consequence over a wide area of the work in both the building and civil engineering industries a virtual immunity for bad or unskilful work would exist. It was further suggested that the duty on a seller of a house in the course of erection might be stricter than that in the case of an ordinary builder in a contract

---

[72] See the conflict of judicial opinion on the facts in *McKey* v. *Rorison, supra.*

[73] See *e.g. Henderson* v. *Raymond Massey* (1963) 46 W.W.R. 100 (Canada). See, however, the criticisms of this by Scrutton L.J. in *Lawrence* v. *Cassell* [1930] 2 K.B. at p. 89, and by Romer L.J. in *Perry* v. *Sharon Development Co. Ltd.* [1937] 4 All E.R. 390 at p. 395.

[74] *Hancock* v. *Brazier (Anerley) Ltd.* [1966] 2 All E.R. 901, illustrated *infra*, pp. 297–298, and *post*, Chap. 6, p. 399.

[75] *Supra*, p. 281. See also *Hancock's* case.

without an architect, but this too seems wrong. " Under our principles of jurisprudence, apart from a so far scarcely charted sea of the law of tort in this area, the practical business effect and just solution to this type of breach of contract is that each vendor or contractor of labour and materials should warrant his supply of materials against patent or latent defects so that by the well known chain of third party procedures the ultimate culprit, the manufacturer, may be made liable for his defective manufacture." [76] " So I cannot see any logical distinction between the obligations which ought in general to be implied with regard to quality and fitness between a sale of goods and a contract for work and materials. Indeed, for my part I think, as a matter of common sense and justice, one who contracts to do work and supply materials ought to be under at least as high, if not a higher, degree of obligation with regard to the goods he supplies and the work that he does than a seller who may be a mere middleman or wholesaler. Greer L.J. took this view in the Court of Appeal in *Cammell Laird* v. *Manganese Bronze and Brass*." [77]

The importance of this in " package-deal " contracts is considerable, since it means that the contractor will not be able to escape liability by showing that he designed the project according to the best accepted standards of architectural or engineering knowledge, if in fact his design turns out to be unsuitable.

Hitherto the subject of design and suitability has been considered solely in the light of the possible implied obligations. There is, of course, nothing to prevent express undertakings as to design or suitability being given, and where this occurs they will usually prevail, notwithstanding compliance in all other respects with the contract requirements.

So a contractor will sometimes expressly undertake to carry out work which will perform a certain duty or function, in conformity with plans and specifications, and it turns out that the works constructed in accordance with the plans and specifications will not perform that duty or function. It would appear that generally the express obligation to construct a work capable of carrying out the duty in question overrides the obligation to comply with the plans and specifications, and the contractor will be liable for the failure of the work notwithstanding that it is carried out in accordance

---

[76] *Per* Lord Upjohn in *Young & Marten Ltd.* v. *McManus Childs Ltd.* [1969] 1 A.C. at p. 475.
[77] *Ibid.* at pp. 473–474.

with the plans and specifications.[78] Nor will he be entitled to
extra payment for amending the work so that it will perform the
stipulated duty. Such undertakings will, however, be construed in
cases of doubt in the light of the degree of reliance being placed
on the contractor's skill and judgment, as in the case of the implied
obligation.

ILLUSTRATIONS

(1) The defender asked the pursuer to quote prices at which he
would supply tanks to certain specifications, each to stand a head
pressure of sixty feet of water. The pursuer quoted lump sums for
each tank totalling £25 12s. 0d., but found that in order to make the
tanks capable of standing the required pressure it was necessary to
strengthen them by adding stays which were not contained in the
specifications. The defender refused to pay the extra cost. *Held*, the
pursuer could not recover: *Wilson* v. *Wallace* (1859).[79]

(2) Merchants ordered from a shipbuilder a ship to be built
according to a specification which contained the stipulation " To
carry 1800 tons dead weight." The contract provided that the
shipbuilder was to make a model for the merchants' approval. The
shipbuilder made a model which the merchants approved and subsequently built a ship according to the model. The ship as built
would not carry the weight. *Held*, the shipbuilder had not fulfilled
the contract and was liable in damages: *Gillespie & Co.* v. *Howden &
Co.* (1885).[80]

(3) The defendant contracted to cast cylinders according to a
specification and plans, the cylinders to stand a pressure of 25 cwt.
to the square inch. It turned out that if the cylinders were cast
according to the specification there would be an unavoidable defect.
Held, that the defendant had contracted to supply sound cylinders
and that as he had not done so although he had adhered to the plans,
he was liable in damages: *Hydraulic Co.* v. *Spencer* (1886).[81]

(4) A highly qualified roofing contractor was asked by the
employer's representatives for his advice as to the best method of
constructing a particular steel sheet roof. A substance called
" Curadex," of which the contractor had experience, was discussed
as an adhesive to bond insulating material to the steel sheet, and though
the contractor expressed a preference for hot asphalt for sloping
roofs, he indicated that he was prepared to use it for the roof if the
employer wished. The employer then prepared contract documents
specifying " Curadex or approved equal " and the contractor duly
tendered. The contract required the contractor to furnish a written
five-year guarantee " that all above work specified will remain
weather-tight and that all material and workmanship employed are
first class and without defect," which the contractor duly gave. The

---

[78] The preceding sentences of this paragraph were cited by the Supreme Court of
Canada in *Steel Co. of Canada* v. *Willand Management Ltd.* [1966] S.C.R. 746,
illustrated *infra*.
[79] 21 D. (Ct. of Sess.) 507.
[80] 22 S.L.R. 527.
[81] 2 T.L.R. 554.

roof failed because in high winds the " Curadex," which had been properly applied, was not capable of maintaining adhesion between the materials in question.   The Ontario Court of Appeal had held that the contractor was not guaranteeing the employer's specification, but merely the freedom of the materials and workmanship from defects resulting in the roof not being watertight.   *Held*, by the Supreme Court of Canada, that the words " work above specified " in the guarantee included the " Curadex," notwithstanding that it had been selected by the owners, and further that the words " first class and without defect " referred (*inter alia*) to the purpose or intended use of the work: *Steel Co. of Canada Ltd.* v. *Willand Management Ltd.* (1966).[82]

The last of the above cases is of considerable interest, and with respect, eminently right.   The last edition of this book, commenting on the decision in the Ontario Court of Appeal, stated that any such case must turn on its particular facts and the degree of reliance in fact placed upon the contractor's skill.   If the roof specification was of a highly specialist character, it was submitted that the decision might well have been the other way, since it was not uncommon for architects or engineers to put up preliminary designs of highly specialist work for approval by the specialist, requiring the latter to give a guarantee or to indicate his approval of the design, or even requiring him to provide working drawings for approval by the architect or engineer, with an opportunity, if desired, to depart from the original design on which the work was priced.[82a]   In such circumstances it has already been submitted[83] that a term warranting the design might well be implied—*a fortiori*, of course, an express term would not be cut down in its application, as in the above case, where the guarantee was expressed in terms approximating very closely, if not for all practical purposes exactly, with the implied terms as to work, materials and suitability.

Before passing from the subject of express undertakings, it may be advisable to point out that, under the modern standard forms of contract, the contractor expressly undertakes to comply with all statutory provisions affecting the work, including by-laws.[84] While under the R.I.B.A. form (but not under the I.C.E. form) such compliance may entitle the contractor to extra payment, failure to comply will be a breach of contract, notwithstanding the usual practice whereby the employer's architect assumes responsibility for

[82] [1966] S.C.R. 746 (Canada).
[82a] The Supreme Court of Canada appears to have arrived independently at the same conclusion.
[83] *Supra*, pp. 281–282.
[84] *Cf.* clause 4 of the 1963 R.I.B.A. conditions, and clause 26 of the 1955 I.C.E. conditions.

by-law compliance.[85] Many by-laws in fact impose design requirements upon the work, usually from the point of view of structural
safety or public health, and in consequence an express provision
similar to those used in the standard forms may well impose an
express and perhaps unintended design liability upon the contractor,
notwithstanding that the architect may also be liable to the employer
if the works fail to comply with a by-law requirement as to design
or suitability.

It should also perhaps be mentioned that in many building and
engineering contracts the contractor's undertaking is to carry out
and complete the work, not only in accordance with the contract,
but also to the satisfaction of the engineer or architect. It is submitted that, unless the circumstances are such as to impose an
express or implied contractual obligation on the contractor as to
design or suitability, it would not be a bona fide exercise of the
power to express dissatisfaction if this was done on grounds of
suitability or design, and accordingly an architect could not in
such circumstances impose a design or suitability requirement
indirectly in this way.[86]

Finally, it has already been noted that problems of the greatest
complexity and difficulty in this field arise where sub-contractors or
suppliers are nominated or sources of supply prescribed by the
contract documents. Architects and quantity surveyors who are
fully abreast of their subject would do well to include in the contract
documents express provisions warranting the quality of all work
and materials in the contract, including (expressly) all nominated
or " approved source ", work, and in the case of important sub-
contracts where the employer's advisers have been obliged to leave
the design element to a specialist sub-contractor, an express suitability undertaking both in the main contract documents and in the
sub-contract documents. There is no hardship in this, since a sub-
contractor who will not give it should never be nominated, and the
main contractor will have a comparable undertaking against the
sub-contractor to protect his own interest.[87]

The cases under the next paragraph (b) of this subsection are of
great importance, and should also be considered in relation to the
design and suitability obligation.

[85] See the case of *Townsend's Ltd.* v. *Cinema News* [1959] 1 W.L.R. 119, illustrated
post, p. 367, and the discussion *ante* Chap. 2, pp. 142–143.
[86] See the judgment of Lord Wright in *Cammell Laird* v. *Manganese, Bronze & Brass*
[1934] A.C. 402, the case of *Panamena, etc.* v. *Leyland* [1947] A.C. 428, and the
discussion *post*, Chap. 7, pp. 419–420, 433–434 and 476–478.
[87] See the discussion, *ante*, Chap. 2, Section 6 (d), pp. 141–142.

(b) Materials

Building and engineering contracts usually define with some precision in the specification or bills the materials to be used by the contractor. The selection of materials for use on a building project is one element of the design of that project, and it has already been seen that there will, in the appropriate circumstances, be an implied warranty on the part of the contractor, corresponding to the warranty of suitability in section 14 (1) of the Sale of Goods Act 1893, as to the suitability or effectiveness of the final work completed using the described materials, and of the described materials themselves.[88] It has been submitted that this warranty of suitability is absolute and independent of fault, as in the case of the Sale of Goods Act warranty.[89] The basic warranty in regard to materials, however, corresponding to the warranty of merchantability under the Sale of Goods Act, is that they shall be of good quality, that is to say good of their kind as described, and this warranty is not displaced by the stipulation of a branded product or of the source of supply in the original contract documents [90] or, it is submitted (if the views expressed *infra* as to the effect of the *Gloucestershire C.C.* case [91] are correct) if the supplier is nominated under a provision in the contract. Beyond any doubt this basic warranty is independent of fault.[92] It has also been explained that the implied warranty of suitability of materials will not necessarily be displaced if an architect or other adviser is engaged by the employer, or in a case where there has been a nomination by the architect or engineer under a provision in the contract, if their design requirements are silent as to the particular matter in question.[93] Undoubtedly, however, as a general rule the contractor's obligation will not extend beyond supplying a material of good quality conforming to the express description of it in the contract documents, if the description is precise and the choice of the material is indeed the architect's or engineer's.[94]

Where the contract is silent as to the materials to be used (and as already explained, this may mean partially silent), it is submitted that, to give the contract business efficacy, both warranties must be implied. " I think the true view is that a person contracting to do work and supply materials warrants that the materials which he uses

---

[88] *Supra*, pp. 278 *et seq.*
[89] *Supra*, pp. 290–291.
[90] See the *Young & Marten* case, *infra.*
[91] *Infra*, pp. 300 *et seq.*
[92] *Myers* case, *ibid.*; *Hancock's* case; *Young & Marten's* case.
[93] *Supra*, p. 293.
[94] See *e.g.* the case of *Adcock's Trustee* v. *Bridge R.D.C.*, illustrated *supra*, pp. 284–285.

will be of good quality and reasonably fit for the purpose for which he is using them, unless the circumstances of the contract are such as to exclude any such warranty." [95]

" I do not hesitate to say that I am clearly of opinion, as a general proposition of law, that where one man engages with another to supply him with a particular article or thing, to be applied to a certain use or purpose, in consideration of a pecuniary payment, he enters into an implied contract that the article or thing shall be reasonably fit for the purpose for which it is to be used and to which it is to be applied." [96]

As was pointed out by du Parcq J. in *G. H. Myers & Co.* v. *Brent Cross Service Co.* (1934) [97] the remarks of Kelly C.B. in the passage quoted referred to a contract for work and labour and not to a contract for the sale of goods.[98] It is now clear from the *Young & Marten* case that there is no distinction or difference between the principles to be applied in the case of contracts for the sale of goods and contracts for work and materials. " The cases which preceded and crystallised in the Sale of Goods Act 1893, do not, as far as conditions or warranties are concerned, seem to show any clear consciousness of a difference in principle between a sale of goods and a contract for labour and materials." [99]

Where materials are the subject of a nominated sub-contract or supply provision, it is submitted that both the language of such provisions and business efficacy require an implied warranty of quality in terms identical to those applicable to the main contractor's own materials, since it is usual for the main contract specifically to declare such suppliers or sub-contractors to be suppliers of the contractor,[1] or to be " deemed to be sub-contractors employed by the contractor," [2] and without any such implied terms such a supplier could default on his obligations as to quality with impunity.[3] Several cases involving sub-contractor suppliers of materials have already been illustrated under paragraph (a) above [4] in addition to those below.

---

[95] *Per* du Parcq J., in *G. H. Myers & Co.* v. *Brent Cross Service Co.* [1934] 1 K.B. 46 at p. 55, approved by all judges in the House of Lords in the *Young & Marten* case.
[96] *Per* Kelly C.B. in *Francis* v. *Cockerell* (1870) L.R. 5 Q.B. 501 at p. 503.
[97] [1934] 1 K.B. 46.
[98] See also *Samuels* v. *Davis* [1943] K.B. 526.
[99] *Per* Lord Pearce in the *Young & Marten* case, and see the extracts from the judgment of Lord Upjohn, quoted *supra*, p. 291.
[1] *Cf.* clause 28 of the post-1963 R.I.B.A. standard forms.
[2] *Cf.* clause 59 of the 1955 I.C.E. standard form.
[3] *Supra*, pp. 277–278. See also Chap. 15, pp. 761 *et seq.*
[4] *Supra*, pp. 283 *et seq.*

ILLUSTRATIONS

(1) A connecting-rod fitted in a car by motor repairers broke and damaged the engine, due to a latent defect. The repairers had bought the rod from the makers of the car and could not by reasonable care and skill have discovered the defect. *Held*, by the Divisional Court, the implied warranty in a contract for work done and materials supplied as to the fitness of the materials was not less than that implied in a contract for sale of goods—namely, an absolute warranty of fitness. The warranty could only be excluded if the plaintiff did not rely on the defendant's skill and judgment: *Myers* v. *Brent Cross Service Co.* (1934).[5]
[Note: On analysis of the facts, and despite the language used, this case clearly involves the warranty of quality and not the design/ suitability warranty, so that reliance on the defendant was irrelevant.]

(2) Roofing contractors undertook to supply a wooden frame to support the roof of a building. One of the roof trusses was made of faulty material, and failed. *Held*, in such a contract there was an implied condition of fitness of the materials analogous to, if not identical with, the condition of fitness implied in a sale of goods, unless the contractor or purchaser does not rely on the supplier's skill and judgment for the quality and fitness of materials used. The reliance is a question of fact and may be shown by implication from the circumstance or even by mere communication of the purpose for which the materials are required, and the implied conditions may arise where the reliance is substantial but not exclusive: *Att.-Gen. of Canada* v. *Laminated Structures Ltd.* (1961).[6]
[Note: In this case also the court seems to have become confused between suitability of the roof or materials for their purpose, and the basic obligation to use good materials in constructing it.]

(3) A builder sold a house in the course of erection. By clause 9 of the contract he undertook to erect, build and complete it in accordance with the plan and specification in a proper and workmanlike manner. The plans showed hardcore under four-inch site concrete, but there was no detailed specification of the hardcore. Through no fault of the builder, the hardcore contained sulphates which ultimately expanded and cracked the floor. *Held*, by Diplock L.J. (after considering various contractual provisions and arguments of law concerned with the conveyance and deciding that they did not cut down the obligation under clause 9), [7] (a) that the obligation under clause 9 applied to work done before the contract was entered into, as well as subsequent work, (b) that there was no substantial difference between the formulation of a warranty of materials suitable and fit and proper for their purpose and work carried out in a proper efficient and workmanlike manner, and the alternative formulation that the house should be habitable and fit to live in, (c) that the effect of clause 9, together with the implications arising from the nature of the contract itself, was that the obligation in regard to hardcore was not merely that it should be selected with skill and judgment, but that it should be fit, proper and suitable for

---

[5] [1934] 1 K.B. 46.
[6] 28 D.L.R. (2d) 92 (Canada).
[7] See the case further illustrated on these points, *post*, Chap. 6, p. 399.

its purpose, and (d) that the liability was absolute in the sense of being independent of fault. *Held*, by the Court of Appeal, that in such a case there is a threefold obligation—to do the work in a good and workmanlike manner, to supply good and proper materials, and to provide a house reasonably fit for human habitation: *Hancock v. Brazier (Anerley) Ltd.* (1966).[8]

[Note: It will be noticed that the language used above by Diplock L.J. suggests, as in the *Myers* case, a breach of the suitability obligation but, though it does not affect the importance of or principles laid down by this case, it would seem that the breach was also a breach of the basic " good quality " obligation, since the hardcore contained a serious latent defect, unless it could be said that for other purposes the hardcore might have been of satisfactory quality. The case is an excellent example of a specification which was (not unnaturally) partially silent, *i.e.* the exact quality of hardcore was not specified, so hardcore suitable for laying under concrete had to be provided. While on the facts before him, Diplock L.J's finding (b) above is unexceptionable, the situation would have been quite different had the precise kind of hardcore stipulated and supplied been the cause of the later defects. In that case there would only have been a breach of the suitability warranty.[8a]]

(4) M, developer-main contractors, by their representative (who was experienced in roofing and tiling work) requested an estimate from sub-contractors Y to supply and fix a high-grade type of tile known as a " Somerset 13 " for the houses on their estate. They relied entirely on their own skill in the choice of the tile. These tiles were made by only one manufacturer (B). Y obtained and fixed the tiles through their own sub-sub-contractor Z, who purchased the tiles from B. This particular batch of tiles contained a defect which could not be detected. When sued by the various house purchasers, M joined Y as third parties. Y could not join Z, because in his case the limitation period had expired, so the issue was between M and Y. Y argued that as both material and ultimate supplier were chosen by the developers, there was no warranty as to fitness or quality, only a warranty of skill and care, and that the position was different from that under the Sale of Goods Act. *Held*, by the House of Lords, while reliance on their own judgment by the developers was sufficient to displace any warranty of suitability, no further effect should be given to their selection of the goods and source of supply, and this did not displace the warranty of merchantability or good quality, so that M was entitled to recover from Y. The justification, as in the case of sale of goods, was the desirability of a chain of responsibility under which, if proper terms were obtained by sub-suppliers, the person ultimately responsible would be made liable. *Young & Marten Ltd.* v. *McManus Childs* (1969).[9]

(5) An R.I.B.A. contract in the 1957 (revised) form contained a

---

[8] [1966] 2 All E.R. 1 (Diplock L.J.), *ibid.* 901 (C.A.). See also *Billyack* v. *Leyland* [1968] 1 W.L.R. 471 (Edmund Davies L.J.), illustrated *post*, Chap. 7, Section 3, pp. 432–433.
[8a] See *supra*, p. 289, where it is pointed out that the design/suitability warranty only becomes relevant if the materials and workmanship warranties have been duly performed.
[9] [1969] 1 A.C. 454.

P.C. sum for the " supply only " of pre-cast pre-stressed concrete columns. Clause 21 of that contract gave the main contractor a right to object on any reasonable grounds to the nomination of a sub-contractor, and also on the ground that the sub-contractor would not indemnify him against the same obligations in respect of the sub-contract as those for which the contractor was liable under the main contract. No similar right was given under clause 22 in the case of nominated suppliers. The architect nominated suppliers of the columns. The supplier's terms of trading, which were incorporated into the original quotation, excluded liability for defective columns beyond their replacement free of charge. When the columns began to be erected, serious cracks were observed, and the clerk of works orally instructed the contractors to suspend work on the frame till the cause was discovered. The contractor admitted he would have stopped work in any event. He confirmed the instruction in writing to the architect, however, saying that a delay would be caused and recorded, and the latter acknowledged the letter without comment. The contractors found other work to do, but finally wrote saying that all work was now held up, and shortly after asked for confirmation that damages would be paid. Without any warning, the contractors purported to determine the contract some five weeks later under clause 20, which entitled them to do so if the work was delayed for a month by (*inter alia*): (a) architect's instructions and (b) late receipt of instructions. At the time, the architect was still awaiting a report from consultants he had called in. Subsequently it transpired that the defects in the columns were due to an incorrect and unsuitable mix with excessive quantities of calcium chloride. The contractor conceded that, if he was in breach of contract himself, his determination would not be valid. It was accepted that there was a breach of the warranty of good quality, if it was to be implied. The issue was solely, therefore, whether or not the contractor was in breach, and this in turn depended on whether the implied term was displaced or not. *Held*, (a) by Lord Pearce, that the contrast between clauses 21 and 22 showed an intention to exclude the warranty, and the particular circumstance of the architect nominating a supplier who limited his liability fortified this view; (b) by Lord Upjohn, that the contrast between clauses 21 and 22 did not exclude the warranty, but the restriction on liability by the supplier did; (c) by Lord Wilberforce,[10] that the imposition on the contractor of special conditions in the sub-contract restricting his right of recourse and the absence of a right to object under clause 22 were strongly against the implication of the warranty. By virtue of the special terms of the contract and of the circumstances of the sub-contract, no warranty should be implied; (d) by Lord Pearson (dissenting), that the contrast between clauses 21 and 22 did not point to exclusion of the warranty, and that on the contrary the words " declared to be suppliers to the main contractor " in clause 22 had a similar effect to the words " declared to be sub-contractors employed by the contractor " in clause 21; further the restriction of liability in the sub-contract did not prevent the implication of a warranty of quality similarly restricted in the main contract,

---

[10] The effect of his judgment is set out at greater length, because the head-note of the report does not, it is submitted, accurately state its effect in attributing its basis exclusively to the contrast between clauses 21 and 22.

so the main contractor was in breach of contract: *Gloucestershire C.C.* v. *Richardson* (1969).[11]

The last of the above cases is, on examination, extraordinarily difficult to assess, and poses many more questions than it answers. Lord Reid gave no reasons. The consequence seems to be that two judgments were clear that the contrast between clauses 21 and 22 did not displace the warranty (Lords Upjohn and Pearson), one was clear that it did (Lord Pearce), and one that a combination of the language of clauses 21 and 22 and the conduct of the parties displaced it (Lord Wilberforce). On the other hand three of the judgments held that the sub-contract exclusion displaced or contributed to displacing the warranty, and one that it merely restricted the warranty. It is essential to attempt to dissect the reasoning, because so many vitally important questions remain open, as *e.g.*:

    (a) If a main contract contains no express right of objection for *any* class of nominated sub-contract (*i.e.* there is no "contrast") does a restriction on liability in a sub-contract or similar conduct by itself displace the warranty?

    (b) If a contract contains no express right of objection, is an unrestricted sub-contract subject to the warranty?

    (c) If there is a " contrast " (*i.e.* an *inapplicable* right of objection) but an unrestricted sub-contract, is the warranty displaced?

    (d) If a contract contains a single right of objection to all nominated sub-contracts (*cf.* the I.C.E. Conditions) or an *applicable* right in " contrast " cases, and there is a restricted sub-contract, is the warranty displaced?

    (e) What is the effect of the decision, forgetting all questions of some express right of the contractor to determine, on the contractor's obligation to complete the work? Is the employer warranting good quality work or materials by the sub-contractor to the main contractor, and is the main contractor released from his obligation to reinstate and complete if the work or materials are defective?

It is submitted with all possible respect that the reasoning of Lord Pearce and (if and to the extent that his judgment depends upon it) Lord Wilberforce, based exclusively upon the absence of a right to object, is open to question, for the following reasons:

    (a) It means, in the case of an unrestricted sub-contract, that

---

[11] [1969] 1 A.C. 480.

not withstanding the full potential right of recourse by the main contractor against the sub-contractor and the undoubted implication of the terms in question in the sub-contract, and so an unbroken potential chain of liability, the employer will be unable to imply the same term in the main contract, which seems repugnant to the whole concept of an implication in absolute terms independent of fault,[12a] as well as to common sense and social need.

(b) The " contrast " argument and the indications given in the judgments of apparent differences between sub-contracts for work, and supply-only contracts for goods, is itself open to doubt

(i) because it is frequently the merest accident which of two such clauses will apply to particular work. On the very facts of the *Gloucestershire County Council* case, specialist sub-contractors of pre-cast pre-stressed concrete often quote alternative prices on either a " supply only " or " supply and erect " basis, or may require or refuse to quote on one or other basis depending on the commitments of their erection organisation or the geographical location of the site. It would no doubt astonish them to be told of their immunity for defective work in manufacturing their units, if nominated on a supply-only basis under the pre-1963 standard forms, as opposed to a supply and erect basis. Furthermore, many " supply only " items, as in the present case, are items of building work as opposed to goods; the only difference being that they are done off the site by the sub-contractor (and hence are "supply only") rather than upon it.

(ii) because it is submitted (as stated at pages 236–237 and 239 of the Ninth Edition of this work, not apparently cited to the House of Lords, though other passages were), that there is an implied term that an employer will not nominate a sub-contractor whose terms are inconsistent with the main contractor's obligations, *in other words an identical implied right to object in respect of nominated suppliers already existed—*" The (contractors) clearly could not be compelled to enter into a (sub-) contract which did not adequately protect them " [13] and " If the terms of

---

[12a] See *supra*, pp. 290-291.
[13] *Per* Romer L.J. in *Leslie* v. *Metropolitan Asylums District Managers* (1901) 1 L.G.R. 862, 868 (not cited to H. of L. in *Gloucestershire*). See also *infra*, Sect. 2, p. 329.

those (sub-) contracts prove insufficient to properly protect the (contractors), that is their fault or misfortune and they cannot hold the (employers) liable in any way."[14]

(iii) because the wording of the R.I.B.A. forms is notoriously illogical and subject to anomalies [15] and the interpretation of some special intention to eliminate implied or residual rights which the main contractor might have under clause 22 from the fact that care was taken to spell those rights out expressly in clause 21, is not justified, and attributes an expertise in the law not elsewhere visible in the traditional draftsmanship of the contract—see *e.g.* the prohibition on " assignments and sub-letting " in clause 17 of the Conditions. No doubt the right was specially referred to in clause 21 because of the generally greater importance, from the point of view of potential disruption of the contractor's programme, of " work " sub-contracts as opposed to " goods " sub-contracts. If the intention was to prohibit a right of rejection under clause 22, why not say so expressly?

(iv) because if due weight is not to be given to the words " declared to be suppliers to the main contractor " in clause 22 (see Lord Pearson), there seems no reason why the immunity should not apply *even to breaches of the express (as well as the implied) terms of the sub-contracts.*

It is submitted that on this point the views of Lord Upjohn (whose judgments in both the *Young & Marten* and the *Gloucestershire County Council* cases are of great clarity and force) and Lord Pearson (and also of Sellers L.J. who dissented in the Court of Appeal) are to be preferred over that of Lord Pearce and (if indeed held by him) Lord Wilberforce. On the second ground advanced in the judgments (the restriction of liability in the sub-contract) there are in fact also formidable contrary arguments, it is submitted, as follows:

    (a) if there is, as submitted, a breach by the employer in nominating an " inconsistent " sub-contract, it may well have been waived by the contractor's placing the order without protest;

    (b) it by no means follows, as seems to have been thought, that in " supply only " contracts the architect will seek to control

---

[14] *Ibid.* at p. 869.

[15] See *e.g.* the strictures of the Court of Appeal in *Bickerton* v. *N.W. Metropolitan Hospital Board* and in *Jarvis* v. *Westminster Corporation, post.*

the terms of those contracts. He may, and frequently does, after comparing current price lists with the employer of a number of products, such as tiles, sanitary ware, plumbing fittings etc., simply inform the contractor of the kind required, leaving him to order them from his own suppliers in the usual way. Moreover, terms which restrict liability in the vast majority of cases simply escape the attention of both architect and main contractor, being contained in " Terms of Trading " on the back of quotations. Indeed, there is no evidence from the reports that this was not so in the *Gloucestershire County Council* case. In these circumstances it would seem reasonable that the contractor, who is after all the contracting party with the sub-contractor and who, depending on the nature of an inconsistent term, may know better whether it is inconsistent with his programme and intentions than the architect, should bear the loss, rather than the employer, whose architect is likely to be concerned far more with technical matters of specification and price than with other contractual terms when inviting quotations from specialists. The suggestion in some judgments that the restrictions may be put forward by sub-contractors with a corresponding price advantage, while no doubt a theoretical possibility, particularly in cases where the goods in question are of extremely small value relative to the possible consequences if they fail, is generally not a commercial reality, in the United Kingdom at any rate.

(c) In the instant case, had there been liability to the employer, the main contractor would have had an irrefutable claim for breach of the warranty of quality (and perhaps of workmanship) against the suppliers, though limited by the restriction to the free replacement of the defective columns. It is difficult to see why an identical term could not be implied in the main contract by virtue of the " deemed to be a supplier to the main contractor " provision in clause 22 of the Conditions (see *per* Lord Pearson).

(d) No real consideration seems to have been given to the consequences. Forgetting all questions of an express power of the contractor to determine, what is to happen to the contractor's obligation to complete the work if he is not liable for defects in nominated supplier's work? Does this mean that the employer warrants due performance by the supplier to the main contractor, and undertakes to order repair work as a variation, or is liable in damages, if completion becomes impossible or more costly or expensive for the contractor?

The problems created by this decision in the United Kingdom will be somewhat mitigated by the fact that the current standard forms in both industries now confer a right of objection in respect of all nominated sub-contractors of every kind, though a major difficulty may well arise on the wording of the R.I.B.A. forms which provides that " the Architect shall not nominate any person as a sub-contractor/supplier . . . (save where the Architect and Contractor shall otherwise agree) . . . who will not enter into a sub-contract/contract of sale which provides. . . ." (Clauses 27 (a) and 28 (b).) This wording, expressed as a contractual obligation of the employer (compare also Clause 59 of the I.C.E. Conditions) may entitle main contractors to claim, as damages for breach of the obligation, the difference between the sums payable by them to the employer under the implied warranty and the restricted sums recoverable by them under the sub-contract, unless the main contractor is held to have waived the breach by entering into the sub-contract without protest. But the problems will remain in other jurisdictions, or wherever forms of contract are used without any express right of objection. It is submitted that, until reconsideration has been given to the decision in England, it must be treated (in England) as authority for the narrow proposition that, where a "contrast" in rights of objection points to an intention to deny any right of rejection, express or implied, in the particular case; and where the nomination in question controls the terms of the sub-contract in question and has the effect of imposing a limitation or restriction on liability in the sub-contract; that restriction may, depending on its nature, displace altogether the " merchantability " implied terms of workmanship and materials, *a fortiori* the " suitability " implied term. In other jurisdictions, it is submitted that subjective (and not constructive) knowledge of the restriction in the sub-contract by the nominating employer or architect should be the *minimum* requirement of conduct to displace the implied term, coupled with a *clear* exclusion in the main contract of any right, implied or otherwise, to object. This would mean that the employer's nomination would be a clear breach of contract, and furthermore one which would not be waived by the main contractor placing an order with the sub-contractor without protest, and the employer could not then complain of the consequences which might follow.

(c) Workmanship

In the absence of any special term or direction in the contract specifying the manner in which work is to be done, there is an implied condition in all contracts for work and labour that the work will be carried out with care and skill, or as it is sometimes expressed, in a good and workmanlike manner.[16] As in the case of the materials obligation in (b) *supra*, this corresponds to the "merchantability" obligation in section 14 (2) of the Sale of Goods Act 1893. It has already been pointed out that this obligation may involve, in matters of detail not specifically dealt with by the contract documents, a design responsibility,[17] since in such cases there is to that extent reliance on the contractors, and accordingly the obligation is the suitability obligation corresponding to section 14 (1) of the Sale of Goods Act, which is dealt with under paragraph (a), Design and Suitability, *supra*, and not the "merchantability" obligation in section 14 (2). In cases where the work is sufficiently described, however, it amounts to no more than a warranty that reasonable skill and care has been used in carrying out the described work.

The foregoing remarks and cases in paragraph (b), Materials, *supra*,[18] in relation to the main contractor's responsibility for the quality of materials supplied by nominated sub-contractors or suppliers, and the circumstances in which the implied terms may be displaced, apply equally, it is suggested, to his responsibility for the standard of workmanship shown by such sub-contractors. Indeed the dividing line between materials and workmanship may often be finer than is commonly supposed. Thus in the *Gloucestershire County Council* case, *supra*, a supply-only sub-contract for pre-cast pre-stressed concrete columns which had excessive calcium chloride in the mix and so lacked compressive strength would no doubt have been regarded as a case of bad workmanship had the work been done on and not off the site. Business efficacy and the express provisions to be found in most contracts relating to nominated sub-contractors require, it is submitted, a responsibility for workmanship similar to that for the main contractor's own work whenever possible in order that the necessary chain of responsibility may be established.[18a]

[16] *Duncan* v. *Blundell* (1820) 3 Stark. 6; *Pearce* v. *Tucker* (1862) 3 F. & F. 136, illustrated *supra*, pp. 283–284 and *cf. Harmer* v. *Cornelius* (1858) 5 C.B.(N.S.) 236.

[17] *Supra*, pp. 274, 276, 279.

[18] *Supra*, pp. 296 *et seq.*

[18a] See the discussion *supra*, pp. 300 *et seq.*, and see *per* Lord Upjohn, *supra*, p. 291.

In the difficult case of *Cotton* v. *Wallis* (1955),[19] the Court of Appeal (Denning L.J. dissenting) held that where under the then R.I.B.A. form of contract the builder undertook that the materials and workmanship should be " the best of their respective kinds and to the full satisfaction of the surveyor," the architect was not negligent in passing work admittedly not of the best quality, as the low price of the building was a material factor in determining whether the work could be properly passed to his reasonable satisfaction in accordance with the contract. Apart from the obvious difficulties of this decision, it may be doubted whether it lays down any principle bearing upon the rights *inter se* of the contractor and the building owner.[20]

(3) Indemnities and Insurance

While not necessarily obligations of the contractor, since cross-indemnities by the employer in favour of the contractor are sometimes given (see *e.g.* clause 22 (2) of the I.C.E. Conditions), it is proposed to deal shortly with the subjects of indemnity and insurance in this part of this section.

The performance of all building and engineering operations involves an element of risk. An accident may result in damage to the works themselves, or lead to claims in tort for damage to property by third persons such as adjoining occupiers, or for personal injuries by workmen, neighbours or passers-by. It has already been pointed out [21] that, while it by no means follows that an employer will always be vicariously liable in tort for the acts of the contractor, there is, nevertheless, a very real possibility that the employer may find himself sued by third persons as a result of damage being done by the contractor, on the ground that he or the architect owed a duty of care in contract or tort to the injured person or his property, or was at least partly to blame with the contractor in tort to injured persons or adjoining occupiers.

Building and engineering contracts accordingly commonly contain provisions whereby one party to the contract gives the other an indemnity in the event of a claim being made against that other party by some third person.[22] Unfortunately, the draftsmen

---

[19] [1955] 1 W.L.R. 1168.
[20] See the attempted explanation of this case, *ante*, Chap. 2, pp. 155–156.
[21] *Ante*, Chap. 1, p. 68.
[22] See, *e.g.* clause 18 of the 1963 R.I.B.A. standard form, and clause 22 of the 1955 I.C.E. standard form. These clauses are not infrequently worded sufficiently widely to enable the employer to rely on them where *the works themselves* have been damaged. *Cf.* Clause 18 of the 1963 R.I.B.A. standard forms.

of most building and engineering contracts appear not to have appreciated that in many cases a joint responsibility to third persons might be established, and that pursuant to the Law Reform (Miscellaneous Provisions) Act of 1934 an apportionment of responsibility between the tortfeasors for purposes of contribution *inter se* might be made. As a result, the indemnity provisions only appear to contemplate cases-where one party or the other is solely responsible for the claim being made. Instead of interpreting such provisions on the basis of ascertaining the party effectively to blame for an accident or claim, however, the courts appear to be in the process of creating a complicated body of case law stemming from exclusion clauses in charterparties, under which the indemnity provisions become unenforceable even where the intention of the parties is plain and the party effectively to blame for the claim is easily ascertainable.

On the other hand, it is not unusual to find express provisions under which the contractor undertakes to protect the works themselves during construction and to reinstate them free of charge in the event of any damage occurring from whatever cause.[23] Indeed, by virtue of the express undertaking to complete (and in some contracts to maintain for a fixed period after completion) the contractor would be liable to carry out his work again free of charge in the event of some accidental damage occurring before completion even in the absence of any express provision for protection of the work.[24] So the employer will usually have a "parallel" remedy for breach of contract where the works themselves have been damaged. Furthermore, wherever a breach of contract can be established from which the claim by a third party can be shown to arise within the ordinary laws of remoteness of damage, then the amount paid to the injured third party can be recovered from the party in breach as damages, notwithstanding that a "parallel" indemnity clause is, by virtue of the foregoing case law, unenforceable.[25]

ILLUSTRATIONS

(1) S, by their agents, left an oil drum with dangerous vapour inside in the vicinity of the workings of WH, who was constructing a tank for S at their refinery, while WH's men were away over the

---

[23] See, *e.g.* clause 20 of the 1955 I.C.E. form.
[24] See, *e.g.* the reasoning in *Appleby* v. *Myers* (1867) L.R. 2 C.P. 651, illustrated *post*, p. 355, and see full discussion *ante*, Sect. 1 (2), pp. 267–268. This sentence was cited by Nield J. in *Charon* v. *Singer Sewing Machine Ltd.* (1968) 207 E.G. 140, illustrated *supra*, subs. (1), pp. 271–272.
[25] *Mowbray* v. *Merryweather* [1895] 2 Q.B. 640; *The Kate* [1935] P. 100; *Sims* v *Foster Wheeler* [1966] 1 W.L.R. 769; *A.M.F. (International) Ltd.* v. *Magnet Bowling* [1968] 1 W.L.R. 1028. See also *Hadley* v. *Droitwich Construction Co.* [1968] 1 W.L.R. 37.

weekend. W, one of WH's workmen, was killed because there was an earthing fault on his welding machine which normally would have had no serious consequences but, in the situation created by S's agents, caused an explosion. W's widow brought an action. S was held 80 per cent. and WH 20 per cent. responsible. S sought to recover his own share from WH under an indemnity clause in their contract, which indemnified S against claims for personal injuries arising out of the operations undertaken by WH in pursuance of the contract. *Held*, by the Court of Appeal, that indemnity clauses should not be construed so as to include the consequences of the negligence of the party to whom the indemnity was given, unless those consequences were expressly covered, or impliedly covered because there was no other subject-matter but negligence by that party on which the indemnity could operate [26]: *Walters* v. *Whessoe Ltd. and Shell Ltd.* (1960).[27]

(2) A workman was injured by faulty staging provided by a sub-sub-contractor C, and sued C and the main contractor A. It was held that the main contractor A should have inspected C's staging and was also liable. A was adjudged 25 per cent. responsible and C 75 per cent. A then joined his sub-contractor B in respect of his share, on the basis of an implied term in the sub-contract to provide sound scaffolding and alternatively on an express indemnity. For unspecified reasons the claim on the indemnity was not proceeded with. *Held*, by the Court of Appeal, applying *Mowbray* v. *Merryweather*,[28] the implied term did apply, and the contractual right to damages against B was not affected by the separate liability in tort of A to the plaintiff, so that A could recover from B in respect of his own liability to the plaintiff: *Sims* v. *Foster Wheeler* [1966].[29]

(3) An engineering sub-contract between A, the main contractor, and B, the sub-contractor, in fact incorporated the I.C.E. main contract Conditions. An employee of A was injured in an accident caused by a missing cover (provided by B) over a hole dug by B. A was held partly to blame and liable to the plaintiff for failure to note B's omission and require a replacement. Clause 22 (2) of the Conditions provided that A should indemnify B for any act or neglect done or committed during the currency of the contract by A, his servants or agents. *Held* by Chapman J., clause 22 was intended to apply only to cases where one party or the other was solely liable, and so could afford B no defence, and *Sims* v. *Foster Wheeler* [29] was authority for saying that B was liable to A in respect of A's liability to the plaintiff, as damages for breach of B's contractual duty to fence and protect the works under clause 19 of the Conditions: *Kenney* v. *Copper Pipe Services Co.* (1968).[30]

(4) Building owners M and main contractors T were held liable under the Occupiers' Liability Act as to 40 per cent. and 60 per cent. respectively to another contractor of the building owner, A, whose machinery and equipment had been damaged when a building under

[26] See *Travers* v. *Cooper* [1915] 1 K.B. 73; *Rutter* v. *Palmer* [1922] 2 K.B. 87; *Alderslade* v. *Hendon Laundry* [1945] K.B. 189; *Canada Steamship Lines* v. *R.* [1952] A.C. 192.
[27] Unreported, November 18, 1960 (C.A.).
[28] [1895] 2 Q.B. 640, *post*, p. 593.
[29] [1966] 1 W.L.R. 769.
[30] 112 S.J. 47.

construction was flooded in a heavy storm.[31]   M were liable because, by their architects, they had failed to make sure that T had got the building into a fit state to receive A's machinery on the date for delivery, as T had promised to do.   The contract between M and T was in the R.I.B.A. (1957) revised form with quantities.   By clause 14 (b) of the Conditions, T indemnified M against damage to property arising out of the works, " provided always that the same is due to any negligence omission or default of [T]."   Further, by items in the bills, T contracted with M to divert storm water to channels and drains, to protect all work and materials from injury by weather, to cover up and protect work, and to prevent water accumulating on the site.   M sought to recover from T in respect of their share of their liability to A (a) under the indemnity clause and (b) as damages for breach of the provisions in the bills of quantities.   *Held*, by Mocatta J., following *Walters* v. *Whessoe and Shell Ltd.* (1960), *Canada Steamship Lines* v. *R.* (1952) [32] and *Alderslade* v. *Hendon Laundry* (1945),[33] that as M had also been negligent, and as there were other claims than negligence on which the clause could operate, they could not recover under the terms of the indemnity clause but, following *Mowbray* v. *Merryweather* (1895),[34] M were entitled to recover their loss from T in full as damages for breach of the provisions in the bills of quantities: *A.M.F. International Ltd.* v. *Magnet Bowling and G. P. Turtham Ltd.* (1968).[35]

If this last decision is correct, the indemnity clauses in the standard forms and the vast majority of building contracts are largely worthless.   The *Walters* case presents no difficulty, because there Shell, who were seeking to operate the indemnity clause, were themselves 80 per cent. (and effectively) responsible for the accident.   But to seek to operate the rule in cases where a partial liability in negligence, however small, arises from failure to oversee and detect the primary and effective negligence or fault of the party giving the indemnity seems to be carrying canons of construction (derived originally from exclusion clauses, and not indemnity clauses, in a totally different field of commerce) to a point where they defeat not only the intentions of the parties but also, quite obviously, of the legal draftsmen they have employed.   Not only is the result inconsistent with the obvious intention of the R.I.B.A. clause (now clause 18 (b)) but it is also, it is submitted, inconsistent with the general principle of building contracts that the architect owes no duty *to the contractor* when supervising the contract to advise him on methods of working, or to detect his breaches of contract,[36] as was

[31] For the facts more fully set out, see the case illustrated *ante*, Chap. 1, pp. 79–80.
[32] *Supra*, p. 308.
[33] [1945] K.B. 189.
[34] *Post*, Chap. 9, p. 593.   Contrast the *Westcott* case, *infra*, pp. 312–313.
[35] [1968] 1 W.L.R. 1028.
[36] *Ante*, Chap. 1, pp. 68–70; Chap. 2, pp. 139–141; and *post*, Chap. 6, pp. 385–388.

indeed stated very clearly by Mocatta J. in the above case. It is submitted that this subject needs reconsideration by the courts. It is not only of vital importance to reconcile the *Mowbray* v. *Merryweather* and *Alderslade* principles in securing a reasonable interpretation and application of the indemnity clauses in building and civil engineering contracts, but it also frequently arises in practice in the industry because plant, such as a crane, is frequently hired for building and other work, with or without a driver, on special terms as to the incidence, as between the parties, of faulty driving or maintenance of the plant.

ILLUSTRATION

A clause in a contract for the hire of a crane provided that the driver was to be regarded as the servant of the hirer, and that the hirer was to be responsible for all claims arising in connection with the operation of the plant. *Held*, by the House of Lords, that the *Alderslade* principle did not apply to this provision, and it could be given effect, notwithstanding that the owner of the crane was partially liable to the third party: *White* v. *Tarmac Civil Engineering* (1967).[37]
[Note: a full indemnity clause apparently existed in this case, but was not proceeded with, and *Walters* v. *Whessoe and Shell Ltd.* (1960) was apparently cited, presumably in that connection.]

A further complication which should perhaps be noted in this context is section 1 (1) of the Law Reform (Contributory Negligence) Act of 1945 which, if it applies to claims in contract as well as in tort, may have the effect of reducing the amount of a plaintiff's claim under an indemnity clause in a case where he himself has been at fault—see *Mayne on Damages*, 12th edition, p. 359. It also seems possible that this section may validate indemnity clauses which otherwise would be defeated by the *Walters* principle as interpreted in the *A.M.F. International* case. At the moment there is no authority on this.

It is, in addition, common to find insurance provisions in building and engineering contracts designed (a) to protect the employer from claims by third persons, whether or not these claims fall into a category in respect of which he is entitled to an indemnity from the contractor and (b) to insure the works themselves (and hence, indirectly, the contractor) against accidental damage of one kind or another, including particularly damage by fire. The insurance and indemnity clauses frequently interact upon each other and careful consideration of both may be necessary in order properly to interpret either clause.

---

[37] [1967] 1 W.L.R. 1508. See also *Hadley* v. *Droitwich Construction Co.* [1968] 1 W.L.R. 37.

(1) Clause 14 (*b*) of the 1952 edition of the R.I.B.A. form of contract provided that the contractor should be liable for, and indemnify the employer against, damage to property arising out of the works provided it was due to the negligence of the contractor and *subject also as regards loss or damage by fire to the provisions of clause* 15. Clause 15 (*b*) provided that the works should be at the sole risk of the employer as regards loss or damage by fire, and that the employer should maintain a policy of insurance against that risk. Fire broke out on the employer's premises due to the negligence of the contractors, and the employer sued for the cost of repair under clause 14 (*b*). *Held*, on its true construction clause 14 (*b*) must be read subject to clause 15 (*b*), and consequently the risk of damage by fire due to the contractor's negligence was the employer's, and the contractor was not liable: *Archdale* (*James*) *& Co. Ltd.* v. *Comservices Ltd.* (1954).[38]

(2) By clause 18 of a painting and repairing contract, the contractors indemnified the employer against loss, etc. " provided always that such damage is caused by the negligence of the contractor, his servants . . . or any circumstances within the contractor's control." By clause 19 the works were to be at the sole risk of the employer as regards loss or damage by fire and the employer was to pay the contractor for any materials lost or damaged by the fire. The works were damaged by fire caused by the negligence of the contractor's workmen. *Held*, by Sellers J., clause 19 was not intended to be an exception cutting down the effect of clause 18, and accordingly the contractor was liable: *Buckinghamshire C.C.* v. *J. Lovell & Son Ltd.* (1956).[39]

Insurance taken out in the name of one party only may fail in its intention if the risk in question is one in respect of which the insured party enjoys an indemnity from the other party to the building contract, since the insurance company will be subrogated to the insured person's rights, and will be able to recover under the indemnity from the other party to the contract. In all such cases it is necessary for the party giving the indemnity to make certain that the policy should be in joint names if his own interest is to be protected. In the absence of clear words a contractual requirement for insurance is unlikely to be construed as requiring more than insurance of the interest of the person taking out the insurance.

By clause 14 of the current R.I.B.A. form of contract, the contractor undertook to indemnify the employer against claims in respect of damage to property arising out of the works, provided it was due to the negligence or default of the contractor or his subcontractors. By clause 15, he was required, without prejudice to this liability, to effect or cause any sub-contractor to effect such insurances

---

[38] [1954] 1 W.L.R. 459.
[39] [1956] J.P.L. 196.

as might be specifically required by the bills of quantities. The bills contained a provision as follows: " The contractor is to insure or make payments in connection with the following: . . . (*b*) Insurance of adjoining properties against subsidence or collapse." Without negligence on the part of the contractor or his sub-contractors, bored piles sunk by specialist sub-contractors damaged adjoining properties. The contractor, under a third party policy, was insured against this risk, but the adjoining owners sued, not the contractor, but the building owner, under the terms of party-wall awards previously made in their favour. In an action against the contractor, the building owner contended that he was in breach in failing to take out an insurance policy for the employer's benefit. *Held*, by the Court of Appeal, over-ruling Gorman J., that the contractor's obligation, on the true construction of the bills, was only to insure himself, and not the building owner: *Gold* v. *Patman and Fotheringham* (1958).[40]

There seems to be a tendency to construe protection and indemnity clauses in the light of similar clauses in shipping cases. As already noted, it may be doubted if this always accords with the intention of the parties in building and engineering contracts or of the draftsmen of those contracts.

ILLUSTRATIONS

(1) The plaintiffs agreed to construct a destroyer wharf for the defendants. The contract provided that the superintending officer (S.O.) might order variations, additions and omissions to the work, and that the contract sum should be increased by the amount of any additional expense incurred in complying with the S.O.'s instructions. The contract also provided that the plaintiffs should be responsible for and should make good any loss or damage to the works arising from any cause whatsoever. A vessel belonging to the defendants was negligently navigated and collided with and damaged the works, the S.O. instructed the plaintiffs to repair the damage, and the plaintiffs did so at an extra expense of £2,038 12s. 5d. *Held*, applying the shipping case of *Travers* v. *Cooper*,[41] the words " any cause whatsoever " included negligent navigation of a ship by the defendant's servant, and the plaintiffs were accordingly liable under the contract to make good the damage and could not claim extras for complying with the S.O.'s instruction: *A. E. Farr Ltd.* v. *Admiralty* (1953).[42]

(2) A sub-contract contained the following indemnity clause: " the sub-contractor shall indemnify (the main contractor) and the employer and adequately insure against all employers' liability and third party risks arising out of the work." An accident occurred to a workman of a sub-sub-contractor, caused by the main contractor negligently leaving a hole on the site uncovered. *Held*, by the Court of Appeal (Harman L.J. dissenting), that the indemnity included all third party risks, not merely those caused by the sub-contractor for

40 [1958] 1 W.L.R. 697.
41 [1915] 1 K.B. 73.
42 [1953] 1 W.L.R. 965.

which the main contractor might be vicariously liable, and the main contractor was accordingly entitled to an indemnity from the sub-contractor: *Westcott* v. *J. H. Jenner (Plasterers) Ltd.* (1962).[43]

The preceding cases in this section serve to show the need for the utmost precision in drafting indemnity and insurance clauses. In both it is essential to define with extreme care the exact risk to be guarded against. In insurance provisions it is desirable to remember that insurance companies not infrequently impose upper limits on claims for any one accident, or may require an excess payment, and that insurance in joint names may be needed to give the protection required by the contract.

(4) Notices before Claims

Building and engineering contracts frequently contain provisions requiring a contractor to give notice within a reasonable time of events occurring which he considers may entitle him to claim additional payment under the terms of the contract. Since the purpose of such provisions is to enable the employer to consider the position and its financial consequences, and by cancelling or authorising a variation, for example, he may be in a position to reduce his possible financial commitment if the claim is justified, and since special attention to contemporary records may be essential either to refute or regulate the amount of the claim with precision, there is no doubt that in most cases the courts will be ready to interpret these obligations of the contractor as conditions precedent to a claim and failure to give the notice may deprive the contractor of all remedy. Thus notice under clause 40 (1) of the I.C.E. Conditions (suspension of work), for example, is obviously a condition precedent.[44] The I.C.E. Conditions has particularly difficult provisions as to notices in clause 52, which is the clause for valuation of variations, and as to a " decision " of the engineer in clause 66, which may have the effect of barring a claim if an appeal is not made from the decision within a fixed period. The very important clause 12 of the I.C.E. Conditions (unfavourable physical conditions) also has stringent but difficult provisions for notices. The cases on clause 52 are set out *post*, Chapter 8, on clause 12 *post*, Chapter 9 and on clause 66 *post*, Chapter 18. The R.I.B.A. forms of contract are far less stringent in this respect and there is virtually no important claim *of the contractor* under those conditions which can be said to be clearly barred

---

[43] 106 S.J. 281. (Contrast the cases *supra*, pp. 307–309.)
[44] *Crosby* v. *Portland U.D.C.*, Q.B., November 8, 1967, Donaldson J., unreported.

by the wording of the contract, though there are a number of references to notices, and certainly some financial claims under the
contract will be barred by the not very stringent requirement that
notice of arbitration should be given within fourteen days after the
final certificate.[44a] This, however, is far more likely to prejudice
the employer than the contractor.[44b] In consequence no cases have
yet been decided on these forms.

The following case, however, is relevant to any financial claim
made under the I.C.E. Conditions.

ILLUSTRATION

A contractor brought a claim for unfavourable physical conditions due to the scouring action of the sea. The arbitrator rejected
the claim under clause 12 of the conditions because the necessary
notices had not been served. Clause 52 (4) of the conditions required
monthly notices and vouchers of claims, but contained a proviso
as follows: " Provided always that the engineer shall be entitled to
authorise payment to be made for any work notwithstanding the
contractor's failure to comply with this condition if the contractor
has at the earliest practicable opportunity notified the engineer that
he intends to make a claim for such work." The arbitrator considered he was entitled to make a partial award under this proviso.
Held, by Sachs J.: clause 52 (4) was concerned with machinery only
and could not possibly admit of such an interpretation. In addition,
there were two possible views of clause 52 (4): one narrower view
that it dealt only with the machinery for claims under clause 51,
that is to say, for variations, and the other that it provided machinery for payments under any clause of the contract, either for work
done or for damages for breach. The narrower interpretation was
probably the right one: Blackford & Sons (Calne) v. Christchurch
Corporation (1962).[45]

(5) Obligation as to Progress

In the absence of express provision, a contractor must complete
within a reasonable time. In addition to the express provisions for
completion by a stated date, the standard forms contain express
provisions that the contractor " shall . . . regularly and diligently
proceed with the [works] " [46] and " shall proceed with the [works]
with due expedition and without delay," [47] but even in the absence
of such provisions it is submitted that there must, as a matter of
business efficacy, be an implied term that the contractor will proceed
with reasonable diligence and maintain reasonable progress. As

---

[44a] See Clause 30 (7) of the R.I.B.A. forms. [44b] See post, Chap. 7, pp. 489 et seq.
[45] (1962) 60 L.G.R. 214. See also on sub-clause (2) of this clause Tersons Ltd. v.
Stevenage Development Corporation, post, Chap. 8, pp. 535–536.
[46] Clause 21 (1), post-1963 R.I.B.A. forms.
[47] Clause 41, I.C.E. Conditions.

in the case of the obligation to complete within a reasonable time, this may not be a fundamental term or condition, mere breach of which will entitle the employer to treat the contract as repudiated; but failure to proceed expeditiously after reasonable notice will, it is submitted, evince an intention no longer to be bound and so justify the employer in treating the contract as at an end.[48]

SECTION 2. OBLIGATIONS OF THE EMPLOYER

The obligations of an employer under a building contract are clearly not limited to paying for the work, though in many contracts this is the only express obligation cast upon the employer. The possible obligations of the building owner apart from payment may be summarised under the following heads:

    (i) to give possession of the site;

    (ii) to appoint an architect, surveyor or engineer;

    (iii) to supply instructions as to the carrying out of the work;

    (iv) not to interfere with the progress of the work;

    (v) to nominate specialist sub-contractors and suppliers;

    (vi) to carry out works or supply materials for the use of the contractor;

    (vii) to permit the contractor to carry out the whole of the work.

The obligation to pay for the work and the other obligations of building owners will be dealt with seriatim.

(1) Payment

We have seen that the obligation of the employer to pay for the work does not arise in the case of entire contracts until the whole of the work is entirely performed, subject to the mitigating effect of the doctrine of substantial performance, whereas in the rare instances of contracts of general employment payment becomes due *pari passu* with the execution of the work. An obligation to pay by instalments or on account at specified stages or intervals will usually only arise from the express terms of the contract, but such arrangements are common in building contracts. It remains to be considered whether a failure to make payment when due amounts to a repudiation of the contract, and this is dealt with in Section 3, Discharge from Further Performance.[48a] The different types of price in building and engineering contracts are considered *post*, Chapter 9.

---

[48] This subject is dealt with in more detail, *post*, pp. 608–612.

[48a] *Infra*, pp. 342 *et seq.*

(2) Giving Possession of the Site

This may conveniently be considered under two heads, namely, the state of the site, and the extent and time of possession.

(a) State of the site

The only duty that the employer will usually owe to a contractor in this regard will be in tort under the Occupiers' Liability Act of 1957, although in special cases, such as contracts for the conversion of premises or for doing work in premises, uncleared sites, and sub-contracts, the employer or, in the case of sub-contracts, the main contractor, may be under an express or implied contractual duty to have the site ready for the contractor or sub-contractor.[49]

The duty in tort under the Act of 1957 has been fully discussed,[50] and it should be appreciated that this is a duty as to the *safety* of the premises, in relation to damage to property or personal injuries, and is not a duty in respect of an indirect financial loss, such as more difficult or costly work occasioned by the state of the site or sub-soil.

In general, therefore, the employer owes no duty to the contractor to do work to render the site easier to work upon,[51] or to conduct surveys or sink boreholes or make other investigations, notwithstanding that the reality of the situation may be that, on engineering contracts in particular, a lengthy survey may in fact be necessary before the project can be properly designed or its cost estimated, and notwithstanding that the system of tendering may only permit tendering contractors a very short period in which to price and tender.[52] The employer may suspect or know that the contractor has underestimated the difficulties, but is under no duty to warn him[53] and, in the absence of fraud, will not be liable even for a representation as to the state of the site, though under the Misrepresentation Act 1967 damages can now be awarded for such an innocent misrepresentation, if there were no reasonable grounds for believing it to be true. The effect of this Act is potentially important

---

[49] See *e.g. A.M.F. (International) Ltd.* v. *Magnet Bowling Ltd.* [1968] 1 W.L.R. 1028, at p. 1040, for the contractual terms in that case, and for the implied term. See also the case of *Carr* v. *A. J. Berriman Ltd.*, illustrated *infra*, Section (b), p. 319.

[50] *Ante*, Chap. 1, pp. 75 *et seq.*

[51] See *e.g.* the facts in the case of *Ibmac* v. *Marshall* (1968) 208 E.G. 851, *supra*, p. 253, and see *Jackson* v. *Eastbourne Local Board* (1886), illustrated *supra*, pp. 269–270.

[52] See *ante*, Chap. 2, Section 6 (b), p. 134; Chap. 3, pp. 226–227.

[53] See *e.g.* the case of *Bottoms* v. *Yorkshire Corporation*, illustrated *supra*, Section 1 (1), p. 270, and see also *Atlas Construction Co. Ltd.* v. *City of Montreal*, *ante*, Chap. 1, Section 5, pp. 48–49.

in building and engineering contracts, as fully explained in Chapter 1, *ante*, since contractors, particularly in engineering contracts, naturally expect to be given all the information available as to the geological and physical conditions of the site. It should perhaps be emphasised that the Act only applies to representations made *before* the contract is entered into, which (having regard to the habit in both industries of signing formal contracts often long after work has commenced) can be expected to produce difficult problems as to the application of the Act. As pointed out in Chapter 1, contracts almost invariably contain express exclusions of responsibility for information given, and these are now caught by the " fair and reasonable " test in section 3 of the Act. There are a wide variety of possible situations at the tendering stage in building and civil engineering contracts, and the reasonableness or fairness of such clauses must, it is submitted, depend on the facts in each case.

(b) Extent and time of possession

The degree of possession or access which must be afforded by an employer must obviously vary with the nature of the work (which might, for instance, in an extreme case be for repairs or reinstatement of existing premises while still occupied) or other circumstances (as in sub-contracts, when the work often must take place alongside and subject to interference by other trades or the main contractor's own work). But in the case of a new project the main contractor will normally be entitled to exclusive possession of the entire site in the absence of express stipulation to the contrary.[54] One common express exception is to be found in the terms normally found permitting the presence on the site of other contractors employed by the building owner [55]; another is a provision commonly found permitting the employer to engage other contractors to do a part of the contract work if the contractor refuses to comply with any relevant instructions of the architect.[56]

" I think the contract clearly involves that the building owner shall be in a position to hand over the whole site to the builder immediately upon the making of the contract. I think that there is an implied undertaking on the part of the building owner, who has contracted for the buildings to be placed by the plaintiff on

---

[54] The right is in legal terms a mere licence, however—see *post*, Chap. 13, pp. 681, 712–714, but see also the decision of Megarry J. in *Twickenham Garden Developments* v. *Hounslow B.C.* (1970), currently under appeal to C.A.
[55] Clause 29, post-1963 R.I.B.A. forms; clause 31, I.C.E. Conditions.
[56] Clause 2 (1), R.I.B.A. forms; clause 39 (2), I.C.E. Conditions.

his land, that he will hand over the land for the purpose of allowing the plaintiff to do that which he has bound himself to do." [57]

Since a sufficient degree of possession of the site is clearly a necessary pre-condition of the contractor's performance of his obligations, there must be an implied term that the site will be handed over to the contractor within a reasonable time of signing the contract [58] (though in the I.C.E. Conditions the engineer is given an apparently free hand to give the order to commence work), and, in most cases, it is submitted, a sufficient degree of uninterrupted and exclusive possession to permit the contractor to carry out his work unimpeded and in the manner of his choice. This must particularly be so when a date for completion is specified in the contract documents.

" If in the contract one finds the time limited within which the builder is to do the work, that means, not only that he is to do it within that time, but it means also that he is to have that time within which to do it." [59]

ILLUSTRATIONS

(1) The plaintiffs, having contracted with the defendants to make drainage works, sued the defendants for damages for having wrongfully prevented them from completing the works, and on a *quantum meruit* for works already completed. The defendants set up in answer to the first claim a forfeiture for insufficiency in progress and to the second that the work was only to be paid for on a certificate of completion. The plaintiffs replied that the insufficient progress was occasioned by the default of the defendants in not providing land for the works in accordance with an express term in the contract. *Held*, on demurrer, the provision of the land was a condition precedent to be fulfilled by the defendants, and that the defendants' demurrers were bad: *Arterial Drainage Co.* v. *Rathangan Drainage Board* (1880). [60]

(2) The plaintiffs agreed to pull down fifteen houses belonging to the defendant and build in their place twelve houses constructed in a single block within six months of the date of the contract. There was a clause in the contract that the brickwork was to be carried up simultaneously all round. The plaintiffs agreed to a postponement of a fortnight of the commencement and date of completion of the work. The defendant did not give the plaintiffs possession of any of the site until long after the fortnight had elapsed, and then gave possession piecemeal so that the plaintiffs did not get possession of the last house to be demolished until one month before the date for completion.

---

[57] *Per* Collins L.J. in *Freeman* v. *Hensler* (1900) 64 J.P. 260; Hudson's B.C., 4th ed., Vol. 2, 292 at p. 296.

[58] See *e.g. Roberts* v. *Bury Commissioners* (1870) L.R. 5 C.P. 310 at pp. 320 and 325.

[59] *Per* Vaughan Williams L.J. in *Wells* v. *Army & Navy Co-operative Society* (1902) 86 L.T. 764; Hudson's B.C., 4th ed., Vol. 2, at p. 354.

[60] 6 L.R.Ir. 513.

A summer contract was thus turned into a winter contract and the plaintiffs sued for damages for breach of contract. *Held*, it was an implied term of the contract that the defendant should give possession of the whole site to the plaintiffs within a reasonable time and that a reasonable time did not in the circumstances extend beyond the fortnight agreed and that the plaintiffs were entitled to recover: *Freeman* v. *Hensler* (1900).[61]

(3) By a building contract dated May 3, 1950, the employer undertook to excavate over the site to certain levels and hand over possession of the site to the contractor on May 29, 1950. He failed to do either by May 29. The contractor telephoned about once a week up to the middle of July asking when the site would be clear. In July he learnt that certain sub-contract work would be omitted from his contract and carried out by a contractor of the employer's. The contractor refused to go on with the contract, alleging that the delay in possession and omission of work were two fundamental breaches of contract entitling him to treat the contract as repudiated. *Held*, both breaches had been established. On the facts, a failure to remedy the breach after the due date might continue for so long and in such circumstances as to evince, notwithstanding the absence of any notice by the contractor, an intention not to be bound by the contract, and therefore amount to a repudiation: *Carr* v. *J. A. Berriman Pty. Ltd.* (1953).[62]

In the case of sub-contracts, or cases where the contract contemplates that other contractors of the employer will be on the site at the same time, however, it is obvious that, depending on the facts, different considerations may apply. Cases of this kind are illustrated *infra*, subsection (7).[62a]

Where a contract stipulates that possession is to be given to the builder, du Parcq L.J. was of the opinion that the owner has no general right to come upon the premises after possession has been given,[63] but it is submitted that " possession " in such a context must be construed as subject to an implied right of access for the owner or persons authorised by him for purposes of inspection and also, of course, for the architect or engineer or other consultants for all purposes necessary for the supervision and administration of the contract.[64] Where nothing is said regarding possession, the implication is certainly not necessarily that exclusive possession should be given, but the contractor must clearly be allowed such use of the site as he requires for the purpose of carrying out the work in the way which he thinks best. The common express obligation of the main contractor to assume responsibility for the

---

[61] 64 J.P. 260; Hudson's B.C., 4th ed., Vol. 2, p. 292 (C.A.). Contrast the *Pigott* and *Swanson* cases, *infra*, pp. 338–339.

[62] (1953) 27 A.L.J. 273 (Australia).   [62a] pp. 337–339.

[63] *Nabarro* v. *Cope & Co.* [1938] 4 All E.R. 565.

[64] Express rights are reserved in the standard forms—see clause 7 of the 1963 R.I.B.A. forms (for the architect) and clause 37 of the 1955 I.C.E. form (for the engineer).

safety of the works during construction requires, it is suggested, a high degree of effective control of the site, and the very important limits, often not sufficiently appreciated by lawyers, on the architect's or engineer's control over methods of working,[65] reinforce this view. If, therefore, it is intended that the premises should remain occupied by the building owner, his servants or agents, or that other contractors should have access for special works, the contract should make express provision for these contingencies.[66] Further, the contractor is prima facie entitled to possession of the whole of the site until completion or practical completion and the employer is not, in the absence of an express right, entitled to take possession of parts of the works before the completion of the whole.[67]

(3) Appointing an Architect, Engineer or Surveyor

Where work is to be done under the direction or to the satisfaction of a skilled person to be appointed by the employer, the appointment of that person is usually a condition precedent, unless waived, to the contractor's obligation to carry out the work.

ILLUSTRATIONS

(1) The plaintiff let premises to the defendant and the defendant covenanted to spend £100 in substantial and beneficial improvements of and additions to the said premises and in the repairs thereof under the direction or with the approbation of some competent surveyor to be named by or on behalf of the plaintiff. The plaintiff sued the defendant for breach of this covenant. The defendant demurred that it was not alleged that the plaintiff had ever named or was willing to name or had offered to name a surveyor according to the covenant. *Held*, the appointment of a surveyor was a preliminary step and until that step was taken the defendant could not fulfil his part of the contract and that, therefore, the appointment of a surveyor was a condition precedent to the defendant's liability and the plaintiff must fail: *Coombe* v. *Green* (1843).[68]

(2) The defendant covenanted to complete certain houses under the direction and to the satisfaction of the surveyor of the lessor or his assigns. No surveyor was ever appointed. The defendant did not complete the houses. The plaintiff, who was the assignee of the lessor, sought to recover possession of the premises relying on a clause in the lease giving a right of repossession for breach of covenant. *Held*, no surveyor having been appointed, no direction could be given or satisfaction expressed and there was, therefore, no breach of the condition: *Hunt* v. *Bishop* (1853).[69]

[65] See *ante*, Chap. 1, pp. 68–70; Chap. 2, pp. 139–141, 153–155, and *post*, Chap. 6, pp. 385–388.
[66] The standard forms do, for the latter contingency.
[67] See also subs. (5), *infra*, pp. 326 *et seq.*, and clause 16 of the 1963 R.I.B.A. forms, which only contemplates partial repossession by agreement.
[68] 11 M. & W. 480.
[69] 8 Ex. 675.

Where, however, the employer merely reserves to himself or a third party a liberty to superintend, it is not a condition precedent to the contractor's obligation that actual superintendence should be furnished.

ILLUSTRATION

The defendant covenanted in a deed that she would within eighteen months from the date of the indenture erect certain buildings, the whole of which were to be left to the superintendence of the plaintiff and his son. The breach alleged was that, though the eighteen months had expired, the defendant had not erected the buildings. *Held,* that the declaration was good, although it contained no averment that the plaintiff was ready and willing to superintend the erection of the buildings; that the covenant to erect the buildings was an absolute covenant, and the clause respecting the superintendence merely granted a liberty to the parties to superintend, but did not impose any duty so as to make the superintendence a condition precedent or concurrent: *Jones* v. *Cannock* (1850).[70]

The above are, however, old cases, more in the nature of building leases than building contracts, and much turned upon whether or not it was a condition precedent to obtain the satisfaction in question. Modern building contracts contain arbitration clauses which usually enable the full merits of disputed opinions to be investigated, and this very considerably reduces the importance of the certifier. It is not uncommon for private developers, and others, to let building contracts to associated companies without an architect, and to use the R.I.B.A. forms for the purpose without any architect being named. The practice is, of course, extremely unwise, but if work commences the courts are likely to do their best to apply the contract, particularly if the contract documentation makes it clear that no architect is to be appointed. Failure to appoint an architect will also obviously be waived if work continues for any length of time and other methods of effecting interim payment, for example, have been adopted.

In most modern contracts the architect or engineer is often expressly defined in the contract documents as "X or such other person as may be nominated by" the employer,[71] or the employer's "architect or engineer appointed from time to time." [72] In such cases, or where the architect or engineer is by its terms an essential part of the administrative machinery of the contract—as for instance in issuing certificates for interim payment or as to completion of the work to his satisfaction—it is submitted that if the architect or

---

[70] 5 Ex. 713. See also *Kingston-upon-Hull Corporation* v. *Harding, post,* p. 388.
[71] *Cf.* article 3 of the 1963 R.I.B.A. standard forms.
[72] *Cf.* clause 1 of the 1955 I.C.E. standard form.

engineer dies or becomes seriously ill or is dismissed during the
progress of the works, the employer is impliedly bound to appoint
another within a reasonable time,[73] and a refusal to do so, unless
waived, would be a breach going to the root of the contract, since
the contract is unworkable in the absence of an architect or engineer.
Where there is no such express term, however, an architect who has
been dismissed may remain the only effective certifier under the
contract.[74]

(4) Supplying Instructions as to the Carrying Out of the Work

What is a reasonable or proper time for instructions has already
been discussed in considerable detail in the context of the architect's or engineer's duty in this respect.[75] As already pointed out,
ante, Chapter 2, Section 6, the architect's duty to his employer is,
in the absence of some special need or intervention of the employer,
likely to be conditioned by and co-terminous with the employer's
duty to the contractor in this regard under the building contract, so
that it is not proposed to develop the subject further in this subsection. The basic position is that, even apart from any question
of variations, it frequently happens that the drawings and other
documents forming part of the contract do not provide sufficient
information for the contractor to carry out the works, and that
detailed drawings have to be issued from time to time for this
purpose. If the architect or engineer fails to issue such detailed
drawings at the proper time he will, as the building owner's agent,
commit a breach of contract for which the owner will be liable in
damages to the contractor.

" The contractor, also, from the nature of the works, could not
begin his work until the commissioners and their architect had
supplied plans and set out the land, and given the necessary particulars; and, therefore, in the absence of any express stipulation on
the subject, there would be implied a contract on the part of the
commissioners to do their part within a reasonable time; and, if they
broke that implied contract, the contractor would have a cause of
action against them for any damages he might sustain . . . "[76]

The express term as to the time of instructions in the R.I.B.A.

---

[73] *Cf. Kellett* v. *Mayor of Stockport*, illustrated *post*, Chap. 7, Section 6, p. 488.
[74] See *post*, Chap. 7, pp. 484 *et seq.*
[75] *Ante*, Chap. 2, pp. 135 *et seq.*; and see unreported case of *Neodox Ltd* v. *Swinton
and Pendlebury B.C.* (1958) Q.B.D. there illustrated.
[76] *Per* Blackburn and Mellor JJ. in *Roberts* v. *Bury Commissioners* (1870) L.R. 5 C.P.
310 at pp. 325-326.

form of contract is " as and when from time to time may be necessary " [77] and in the I.C.E. form " from time to time during the progress
of the works." [78]   In the *Neodox* case,[79] a definition based exclusively on the contractor's requirements was expressly rejected by
Diplock J., but a different view has been expressed in an earlier
case: . . . " The plaintiffs " (who were the builders) " must within
reasonable limits be allowed to decide for themselves at what time
they are to be supplied with details." [80]

It is not easy to say whether the term that would normally be
implied, in the absence of express provisions, would be that details
should be supplied on request only.[81]   It is submitted that in circumstances where it is obvious that the contractor requires the
details at a particular time the employer would be bound to ensure
that they were supplied at that time without any request, but otherwise the contractor could not claim damages unless he had requested details which had not been duly provided, but which the
architect had no reason to suppose were needed immediately.[81a]

The 1963 edition of the R.I.B.A. standard forms contains a new
and highly complicated definition of the time for instructions which
is related to the contract date for completion, in a clause designed
to secure additional payment to the contractor in the event of
instructions arriving late.[82]   It seems that this clause, and the
elaborate machinery of notices set up under it, is not intended to
supplant the common law right to damages for breach of contract
if instructions are received late.[83]

The supplying of instructions to enable nominated sub-contractor's work to be ordered in due time is dealt with *infra*, subsection (6), and in greater detail *ante*, Chapter 2, pp. 138–139.

A special problem exists if an architect or engineer chooses to
delegate his own design function (that is to say, the drawings or
choice of specification necessary for the carrying out of the main
contractor's final permanent work) to a person who is, or later
becomes, a nominated sub-contractor or supplier, with or without
express provisions in the main contract or sub-contract that the design function (for example the provision of reinforcement drawings

---

[77] Clause 3 (4), post-1963 R.I.B.A. forms.
[78] Clause 8, 1955 ed.   [79] Illustrated *ante*, Chap. 2, pp. 136–137.
[80] *Per* Wright J., *Wells* v. *Army & Navy Co-operative Society* (1902) 86 L.T. 764;
     Hudson's B.C., 4th ed., Vol. 2, 346 at p. 352.
[81] *Cf. Stevens* v. *Taylor* (1860) 2 F. & F. 419.
[81a] For a list of the suggested criteria, see *ante*, Chap. 2, p. 136. For the abuse of
     " programmes " for this purpose, see *post*, p. 603.
[82] Clause 24 (1) (*a*).   [83] Clause 24 (2).

and bending schedules) shall be carried out as part of the sub-contract. This unsatisfactory practice has already been discussed,[84] and it has been seen that an architect cannot escape his professional responsibility to the employer in this way, particularly because of the conflict of commercial interest in regard to design between a nominated sub-contractor and the employer.[85] It is submitted that where this occurs, and the sub-contractor fails to discharge his duties properly, *e.g.* by failing to supply the necessary information to the contractor in time, the employer will be liable to the main contractor, notwithstanding the general rule that employers are not liable to contractors for the defaults of their nominated sub-contractors,[86] because under the terms of nearly all contracts the power to nominate a sub-contractor extends to the doing of work or supply of materials, but not to the discharge of the architect's or engineer's function of providing the design.

In addition to details of the work, the contractor will frequently require instructions upon other matters, such as the depth to which the ground is to be excavated for foundations [86a] and the same principles will apply as in the issue of details. But the important limits on the architect's (and hence his employer's) duty *to the contractor* in regard to the latter's methods of working [87] should be borne in mind. Contractors faced with difficulties or unexpected contingent expenditure necessary to achieve completion [88] frequently seek to persuade architects or engineers to give instructions in these situations as a first step to presenting a financial claim for an alleged " variation." [89] Thus contractors will argue that the words " such drawings or details as are reasonably necessary . . . to enable the contractor to carry out and complete the works in accordance with these conditions " in clause 3 (3) or (4) of the post-1963 standard forms, entitle them to be given instructions when an unexpected difficulty occurs. Similarly, where the difficulties arise in the course

---

[84] *Ante*, Chap. 2, pp. 98, 129–131; *supra*, Section 1 (2), pp. 277–278, 281–282.
[85] See the case of *Moresk* v. *Hicks*, *ante*, Chap. 2, p. 131.
[86] See *post*, Chap. 15, pp. 750 *et seq.*, and the leading case *Leslie* v. *Metropolitan Asylums District Managers* there referred to.
[86a] Where this is left by the contract to later decision, as where the drawings are not dimensioned and the quantities are marked " provisional ".
[87] *Ante*, Chap. 1, pp. 68–70, and Chap. 2, pp. 139–141, and the important case of *Clayton* v. *Woodman* [1962] 2 Q.B. 533 (Salmon J.) and [1962] 1 W.L.R. 585 (C.A.) there referred to. See also *post*, pp. 385–388, in relation to the remedying of defective work and *post*, pp. 524 *et seq.* and pp. 582–583, for a further discussion.
[88] *Supra*, Section 1, pp. 267 *et seq.*
[89] Compare the cases of *Charon* v. *Finchley* and *Pearce* v. *Hereford B.C.*, *supra*, pp. 271–272, and see *post*, Chap. 8, pp. 524–530 and the case of *Kirk & Kirk* v. *Croydon Corporation* there illustrated.

of nominated sub-contractors' work they will seek to rely on provisions such as clauses 11 (3) and 27 of the current R.I.B.A. forms, which provide that P.C. or provisional sums are to be expended in accordance with the architect's instructions. These particular provisions mean no more, it is submitted, than that an effective nomination giving full details of the work to be done must take place and not that there is any continuing duty to supplement or alter previous instructions as and when difficulties, however unexpected, may occur.[89a] All such clauses need to be construed in the light of the fact that the architect's duty is only to supply such information as will indicate the permanent final result required by the employer, and not to assist the contractor in a difficulty by devising methods of work or ordering variations for this purpose in cases where the contractor's obligation to complete according to the existing design is unqualified.

On the other hand, while not bound to do so, it may be in an employer's interest to give instructions when a contractor is in a difficulty, or in the face of unexpected conditions, particularly if the difficulty or conditions are such as to throw doubt on the long-term suitability of the work after completion. Thus an employer is entitled, for example, to do nothing if ground conditions make completion hazardous or costly; but if they will result in a completed building likely to fail after completion (when the contractor will usually no longer be responsible), he will have an overwhelming interest, for example, to alter the design of the foundations, which may also have the effect of extricating the contractor from a costly or uneconomical situation.[90] Nor is a contractor entitled to expect detection of his own defective work at an early or any stage of the work, or instructions to remove and replace it, when to do so might be comparatively inexpensive.[91]

ILLUSTRATIONS

(1) The defendant agreed on November 28 to supply the plaintiff with 150 tons of iron girders according to drawings to be provided by the plaintiff's architect. The plaintiff provided some drawings and ordered fourteen tons of girders but on March 4, no further drawings having been provided, the defendant wrote declining to proceed with the contract. Thereupon the plaintiff's solicitors on March 13 sent further plans and ordered a further fifty tons of girders and asked for delivery of the fourteen tons. The defendant

---

[89a] But see, in regard to P.C. and provisional sums, the decision of the House of Lords in *Bickerton* v. *N.W. Metropolitan Hospital Board* [1970] 1 W.L.R. 607, illustrated and discussed *infra*, subs. (6), pp. 333 *et seq.*

[90] See *post*, Chap. 8, p. 524.

[91] See *ante*, Chap. 2, pp. 153–155, and *post*, Chap. 6, pp. 385–388.

refused to supply any girders and the plaintiff brought an action for damages. The jury found that the drawings were not delivered within a reasonable time. *Held*, the contract was entire; and that as the plaintiff had failed to furnish drawings for the whole 150 tons within a reasonable time, he could not maintain an action for non-delivery of the girders: *Kingdom* v. *Cox* (1848).[92]

(2) During a contract for carrying out alterations and additions to a dwelling house, the contractor was delayed (*inter alia*) by the non-supply of drawings, details and information. The works were to be completed by a certain day but the contract provided that if the contractor should be delayed by reason (*inter alia*) of his not having received in due time necessary instructions from the architect for which he should have applied in writing, the architect should make a fair and reasonable extension of time for completion. In an arbitration the contractors claimed damages for loss suffered by reason of the delay. The employer counterclaimed penalties for non-completion by the due date. The arbitrator extended the time for completion to the date of actual completion pursuant to the power in the contract. The award was stated in the form of a special case. *Held*, the contractors were entitled to damages for delay occasioned by the non-supply of drawings, details and information, in addition to the extension of the time for completion: the counterclaim was dismissed. *Re Trollope & Colls Ltd.* v. *Singer* (1913).[93]

(3) A specification omitted all mention of many necessary items— fireplaces, tiles, kitchen fitments, wardrobes, garden walls, cupboards, etc. An arbitrator found that both parties had expected to give and receive instructions for such items. *Held*, by Blain J., there was an implied term for sufficient instructions. The employer had failed to give instructions until after practical completion, and the contractor was, on the facts, entitled to rescind the contract: *S. J. & M. M. Price Ltd.* v. *Milner* (1968).[94]

The above case, though somewhat inadequately reported, is of some interest in that it is submitted that under most sophisticated contracts variations cannot be ordered after practical completion in the absence of express provision, unless of course the contractor is willing to carry them out.[94a] If it were otherwise, the employer could use the power to vary to change the contract into a "two-visit" project.

(5) Not to Interfere with the Progress of the Work

In the absence of express stipulation,[95] a building owner has no right to dictate the order in which the works will be carried out, and if he interferes with the progress of the works by refusing to allow the contractor to carry out the works in the order of his

---

[92] 5 C.B. 522.   [93] Hudson's B.C., 4th ed., Vol. 1, p. 849.
[94] (1968) 206 E.G. 313.
[94a] See also *post*, Chap. 8, pp. 551–552 and the case of *Russell* v. *Sa da Bandeira* there illustrated.   [95] See *post*, Chap. 8, pp. 529–530.

choice, the contractor will be entitled to damages for breach of contract,[96] or possibly, depending on the terms of the variation clause, to extra payment on that ground. A difficult question often arises as to whether a power to order extras or alterations must be exercised at such a time as not to affect the economic or systematic execution of the works. Normally, of course, the ordering of extras or alterations under a stipulation conferring power to vary the works is not a breach of contract: " Authorised extras and additions are, of course (being authorised and being contemplated by the contract), no breach of contract, and it is not a breach of contract by the employer to order something extra. . . . " [97] While a court would lean against an interpretation which prevented the building owner varying the work at any stage, there is, it is submitted, room for an implication that extras and alterations will be ordered at a reasonable stage in relation to the works as a whole, particularly if the provisions for payment for extras or alterations are such as to preclude the contractor from recovering the loss he suffers from the interference with the economic or systematic execution of the works in addition to the value of the work done. Whether, however, such a term can be implied in contracts similar to the modern standard forms is more doubtful, since both of these set up machinery whereby variations can be valued to take account of circumstances rendering the billed or scheduled rates for similar work inappropriate, and which presumably include among such circumstances the lateness of the relevant instruction.[98]

Whether or not the employer undertakes that the works will not be interfered with by third persons will depend upon the exact circumstances and the nature of the interference, and there are also express provisions commonly permitting their presence on the site,[99] and sometimes provisions in the bills or specification requiring the contractor to include in his price for dislocation and disturbance due to other contractors. Other express provisions, such as indemnity

---

[96] The exact meaning in this context of clause 14 of the 1955 I.C.E. standard form, under which the engineer is given power to approve the contractor's programme, is not by any means clear. Its purpose is, in all probability, it is suggested, to indicate to the engineer the *order* in which drawings and information will be required. See also for the limitations on the architect's power to control methods of working, *ante*, pp. 68–70, 139–141, 153–155 and *post*, pp. 524–530.

[97] *Per* Channell J., *Trollope & Colls* v. *Singer* (1913) Hudson's B.C., 4th ed., Vol. 1, 848 at p. 858.

[98] See clause 11 (6) of the post-1963 R.I.B.A. forms and clause 52 (1) of the 1955 I.C.E. form.

[99] See, *e.g.* clause 31 of the 1955 I.C.E. standard form, and clause 29 of the 1963 R.I.B.A. form (other contractors of employer).

clauses, may also have an effect in this situation.[1] In general, however, an employer will be liable to the contractor if other contractors of the employer disturb the contractor in his work in circumstances which he could not reasonably have foreseen at the time of tendering.[1a]

ILLUSTRATIONS

(1) When the work of rebuilding part of a bridge for a highway authority was nearly complete, a surfaceman in the employment of the authority, with the consent of one of the contractor's workmen, but without the contractor's knowledge, prematurely removed the wooden supports under the arch, in consequence of which the bridge fell. The contractor brought an action against the authority for the contract price less the estimated cost of the work not yet done at the time of the accident. *Held*, the work having been done according to contract and the contractor not having caused the accident by any fault on his part, he was entitled to recover: *Richardson* v. *Dumfriesshire Road Trustees* (1890).[2]

(2) The plaintiff contracted to erect a school upon a site provided by the defendants. The only access was from an adjoining road. The owner of the soil of the road made an *unfounded* claim that the road was not a public highway and delayed the building operations by two months. The plaintiff sued the defendants for damages occasioned by this delay. *Held*, that the defendants were not liable for the wrongful interference of a third party: *Porter* v. *Tottenham Urban District Council* (1915).[3]

(3) Tunnelling sub-contractors undertook " the execution of the work . . . according to the dimensions and specifications as set forth in the contract between " the main contractors and the employers. By the specification in the main contract the employer reserved the right to stop the excavation and require the contractor to complete the sewer and backfilling up to such point as the engineer might direct before proceeding further with the excavation, and the contractor should not thereby become entitled to demand any allowance or compensation. The engineer exercised this power, with the result that the sub-contractors' work had to stop. They claimed damages, and the main contractor contended that the main contract specification was incorporated, but that even if it was not, there was no express term obliging the main contractor to permit the sub-contractors to do the work. *Held*, the specification was not incorporated for the purpose of the clause in question, and in the absence of an express term there was an implied term that the main contractor should permit the sub-contractors to proceed in a reasonable manner without any undue or unreasonable delay or suspension of their operations, and the main contractor was accordingly liable in damages: *Smith and Montgomery* v. *Johnson Bros.* (1954).[4]

---

[1] See the case of *Farr* (*A. E.*) v. *Admiralty*, illustrated and commented on, *supra*, p. 312.

[1a] See *infra* Subsection (7) where the subject of other contractors is specifically dealt with.

[2] 17 Ct. of Sess.Cas. (4th Series) 805 (Scotland).

[3] [1915] 1 K.B. 776.

[4] 1 D.L.R. (2d) 392 (Canada). *Cf. Neodox* case, *post*, pp. 529–530.

Where, however, the interference takes the form of justified action by third parties due to the employer not having an effective title to the land, or power to carry out the works in question, it is submitted that there will be a breach either of this obligation or of the possession obligation, *supra*, subsection (2).

(6) Nomination of Specialist Sub-contractors and Suppliers

Where work is to be done by sub-contractors or suppliers nominated by or on behalf of the employer, it is submitted that there must be an implied term that the architect or engineer will select or nominate the supplier or sub-contractor, and take the necessary preliminary steps by way of obtaining tenders and quotations, in sufficient time to enable the main contractor to fulfil his obligations as to time and carry out his work economically and expeditiously. In addition there must also, it is submitted, be an implied term that the employer will nominate a supplier or sub-contractor willing to enter into a sub-contract in a form consistent with the obligations of the main contract,[5] although the standard forms now contain express powers of objection, or prohibitions on such a nomination [6]—see *e.g. per* Romer L.J. in the leading case on the subject: "The [contractors] clearly could not be compelled to enter into a [sub-] contract which did not adequately protect them" and "If the terms of those [sub-] contracts prove insufficient to properly protect the [contractors], that is their fault or misfortune and they cannot hold the [employers] liable in any way." [7] On the other hand, the contractor, by placing an order with a sub-contractor, without protest, particularly where there is an express right to object, may well be held to have waived any breach of this term, or be estopped from alleging it.

As previously pointed out, the architect or engineer may rely on nominated specialists to prepare drawings and details of sub-contracted work. In such a case the architect must, it is submitted, act in sufficient time to enable the sub-contractor not only to be engaged, but also to provide the main contractor with all necessary

[5] This point was neither considered nor argued in the House of Lords in *Gloucestershire C.C.* v. *Richardson* [1969] 1 A.C. 480, commented on *supra*, pp. 300–301. These words were in the Ninth Edition.

[6] Post-1963 R.I.B.A. forms, clauses 27 (a) and 28 (b), I.C.E. Conditions, clause 59 (1) (a).

[7] In *Leslie* v. *Metropolitan Asylums District Managers* (1901) 1 L.G.R. 862, at pp. 868, 869.

drawings and information for the work to be done and completed within the contract period (or a reasonable time if no period is applicable). On the other hand, it is not necessary as a matter of business efficacy for the employer to warrant that nominated sub-contractors will honour their promised delivery or starting and completion dates and, provided these are satisfactory, he will not be liable for their subsequent delays in doing work or delivering goods,[8] since in such an event the main contractor will have his remedy against the sub-contractor. *Aliter*, however, as submitted and explained *supra*,[8a] in the case of design duties for which he and the employer will remain liable whatever rights the main contractor may have against the sub-contractor under the terms of the sub-contract.

ILLUSTRATIONS

(1) The plaintiffs agreed with the defendants to build a hospital, including chimney stacks and heating apparatus, in two years. The contract provided for the stacks and heating apparatus to be done by specialists, and the architect, having negotiated a price per stack with the specialists, instructed the plaintiffs to send formal orders to the specialists, which the plaintiffs did. The plaintiffs suffered loss as a result of delay by the specialists and sued the defendants for damages alleging that there was an obligation on the defendants to see that the work was done by the specialists and sub-contractors within a reasonable time. *Held*, that the plaintiffs and not the defendants had made the contract with the specialists and that the defendants were not liable to the plaintiffs for the delay by the specialists: *Leslie & Co.* v. *The Managers of the Metropolitan Asylums District* (1901).[9]

(2) The plaintiff contracted to do certain works for the defendants for a lump sum. The contract provided that the engineering and other specialists' work was to be done by named firms, who were to be paid by the plaintiff. The plaintiff was not to be liable for delay caused by the specialists or for defective plant supplied by them unless he was guilty of contributory negligence. The specialists caused delay in the execution of the works which caused damage to the plaintiff. The plaintiff sued the defendants for this damage alleging that there was an implied promise by the defendants that the delivery of the machinery should not be unreasonably delayed or that the delivery and fixing should be made and done at such reasonable times during the erection of the buildings as would enable the plaintiff to complete the same within the time fixed by the contract or within a reasonable time thereafter. *Held*, there was no such implied promise and there being no contract between the defendants and the specialists the defendants were not liable for the delay: *Mitchell* v. *Guildford Union* (1903).[10]

[8] See also *post*, Chap. 15, pp. 749 *et seq.*
[8a] *Supra*, p. 324.
[9] 1 L.G.R. 862, illustrated more fully *post*, Chap. 15, p. 750.
[10] 1 L.G.R. 857.

In practice most difficult problems can arise in this field.[11]   The employer may nominate a supplier immediately following signature of the main contract, and even at this early date it may be found that the supplier cannot deliver in time to permit completion within the contract period.   The goods in question may have been notoriously subject to long delivery dates, or on the other hand the difficulty in supply may have been quite unexpected.   The employer may have nominated in what would normally be ample time, but an unforeseen change in the supply position may have rendered satisfactory delivery impossible.   Are these nominations in breach of contract?   At least where the supply position is well known in the industry, should not the contractor be taken to know as much or more about this than the employer, if he signs a contract with an impossible contract period having regard to the delivery position, or if he omits to warn the employer or request early nomination and details?   Or should he in such a case be entitled to suppose that the employer has already made arrangements before the main contract has gone out to tender which will enable quite exceptional dates to be obtained?   Is there any distinction between mechanical goods, like machinery or pipes and specials, which are intended to be incorporated in the works in many engineering contracts as part of a later or secondary stage of the work peculiarly under the employer's design or control, and which in times of inflation or steel shortage may be on very long delivery, and on the other hand goods connected with the strictly civil engineering, or in building contracts the structural, part of the contract work, such as structural steelwork or bricks?

The above examples show how difficult it may be to define in precise terms the timing of the employer's obligation to nominate and make information available.   It is submitted with some diffidence that the duty is to make information available so that supplies can be ordered within a reasonable time, and that in deciding what is a reasonable time, regard should be had

(a)   to the general state of knowledge in the industry as to the delivery position of the goods in question,

(b)   any special knowledge the employer may be expected to have of the delivery position or manufacturing period of the goods in question (for instance in relation to unusual materials or goods specially chosen or manufactured for the contract works),

[11] See also the discussion *ante*, Chap. 2, pp. 129–131.

(c) any requests for details or warnings from the contractor in a matter of which he has special knowledge,

(d) the contractor's programme, if known,

(e) the contract period,

(f) the contractor's actual progress on site.

If the architect or engineer has delayed unreasonably in the light of the above considerations, and a satisfactory delivery or completion date cannot be obtained in consequence, there will be a breach of contract. But if the employer or architect nominates a sub-contractor ready to promise delivery or completion by a satisfactory date, he will not, it is submitted, be liable for any subsequent default. But the promise must be legally binding and any qualification or exclusion of legal liability by the sub-contractor would, it is submitted, entitle the contractor to reject the nomination.[12]

As already indicated in subsection (5) *supra*, the architect is under no further duty, in regard to information, any more than in the case of the contractor's own work, once he has provided a sufficiently detailed specification or drawings of the sub-contract work and made an effective nomination. Thereafter he is under no further duty, should unexpected difficulties arise, to supplement or alter the original instructions, and express terms in the contract requiring instructions in regard to the expenditure of P.C. and provisional sums mean no more than that an effective nomination with a sufficiently detailed description of the final permanent result required by the employer needs to be made.

A further problem which arises in relation to nominated sub-contractors occurs when through death, liquidation, bankruptcy or repudiation, the sub-contractor is no longer able or willing to continue and complete his work. In this situation it is frequently contended by main contractors that the employer is bound to nominate a further sub-contractor in substitution for the original one, which by virtue of the provisions as to payment for sub-contracted work in the main contract will usually mean that the new sub-contractor's price (which in practice may often be higher than the original sub-contractor's) will be substituted for the appropriate P.C. or provisional sum in the main contract. The opposing contention of the employer will be that the main contractor is in

---

[12] This sentence was in the Ninth Edition. The proposition was not in fact argued before or considered by the House of Lords in the case of *Gloucestershire C.C.* v. *Richardson* [1969] 1 A.C. 480, commented on *supra*, pp. 300 *et seq*.

breach of contract by failing to complete with the nominated sub-contractor, and that it is his duty to mitigate the loss by arranging for the work to be completed by any means available. On this view the contractor is entitled to be paid the amount of the original sub-contractor's price for the completed work, whatever the actual cost to the contractor of completing it. It must, however, also follow from this view that the employer loses the right of control over the identity of the persons completing the work.

The answer to this problem must be found in the exact words of the provisions in the main contract empowering the employer to nominate and providing for the appropriate adjustment of the contract sum in the settlement of accounts with the main contractor. Where these provisions are ambiguous it is submitted that business efficacy does not require the implication of a term compelling the employer to renominate, particularly in cases where, as in the standard forms, the main contractor is given wide powers to object to a nomination but has not exercised them. If no such term is implied, the contractor can recover as damages from the original sub-contractor the difference between the original and the later sub-contractor's price, whereas if such a term is to be implied the result must be that a nominated sub-contractor, provided he acts in good time, can repudiate his contract with impunity, since the main contractor will have suffered no damage as a result.

However, the House of Lords has now held that a duty to renominate does arise in these circumstances in the case of the current (post-1963) R.I.B.A. standard forms.

ILLUSTRATION

Nominated heating sub-contractors under the post-1963 R.I.B.A. forms of main contract went into voluntary liquidation before starting work, and the liquidator refused to carry on with the sub-contract. The main contractor did the work by his own heating division on a without prejudice basis, contending that the employer was bound to nominate a second sub-contractor and pay the main contractor the amount of the second sub-contractor's account, while the employer contended that there was no duty to renominate, or to pay more for the work than the amount of the original sub-contractor's account. suitably adjusted, if necessary, for variations. *Held*, by the House of Lords (over-ruling H.H. Sir Walker Carter, Q.C., O.R., in *K. Cross* v. *East Riding County Council* (1966) (unreported) and the Court of Appeal of Northern Ireland in *Reilly Ltd.* v. *City of Belfast* (1968) (unreported) that the words "such [P.C.] sums shall be expended in favour of such persons as the Architect shall instruct" in clause 27 (a) of the R.I.B.A. standard forms must be interpreted as referring to the sums due under the relevant sub-contracts, and not the P.C. sums themselves, and that

by virtue of these words there was a duty on the employer to make a
second nomination when the first sub-contractor repudiated. *Per*
Lord Reid: "The main contractor has neither the right nor the duty
to do prime cost work himself when the nominated sub-contract
drops out, any more than he had before the sub-contract was
nominated. . . ." *Per* Lord Hodson, Clause 17 (a) should be construed as requiring nomination "when necessary." *Per* Lord Dilhorne "[The purpose of clause 27] . . . is to provide that prime
cost work can only and shall only be carried out by persons nominated by the Architect." *Bickerton* v. *N.W. Metropolitan Regional
Hospital Board* (1970).[13]

The reasoning on which *Bickerton's* case appears to be based
means that repudiations of every kind (not merely those involving
abandonment of the work) by nominated sub-contractors or suppliers will now give rise to the duty to renominate, and hence transfer
the burden of the sub-contractor's breach from his own shoulders
onto those of the employer, at least so far as the employer's losses
are concerned. Thus, in spite of references by Lord Dilhorne to
the main contractor being liable in damages to the employer for
defective work by a nominated sub-contractor, this would now only
seem to apply in practice where the defects are discovered after the
work is completed—where the defects are discovered while the main
contract work is going on, or during the defects liability period, a
sub-contractor by abandoning work or refusing to return and remedy
the defects will bring into being the duty to renominate. Indeed it
is difficult to conceive of any breach by a nominated sub-contractor
which cannot be rapidly turned by him into a repudiation of the sub-
contract, as a matter of deliberate policy in order to obtain the financial
relief which will be afforded by the consequential duty of the employer to renominate. Furthermore, employers may frequently find
themselves, by virtue of the accounting provisions in the R.I.B.A.
forms, paying the main contractor twice for the defective work
carried out by the first sub-contractor but later remedied by his
successor.

Furthermore, if the solution propounded by the Court of Appeal
to deal with these anomalies (the obtaining of direct warranties
from nominated sub-contractors in favour of the employer as a
standard practice) is generally adopted, it will only be a matter of
time before it is contended by main contractors that, in the light
of the practice, not only does business efficacy no longer require *any*
implied terms of workmanship, quality or suitability in nominated
work or goods, but that *the employer* should now be regarded as

[13] [1970] 1 W.L.R. 607.

impliedly *warranting to the main contractor* due performance by the nominated sub-contractor of all his undertakings and obligations.

It is not too much to say that, unless and until the R.I.B.A. standard forms are altered, the entire system of nomination under those forms has been subverted by this decision, and the employer, to the extent that those forms are used without amendment, no longer has any effective contractual protection in regard to the price, completion date, or described or implied quality of all nominated work and goods in the contract.

The decision is, of course, binding in England, unless and until reconsidered by the House of Lords, in regard to this particular form of contract, but it is submitted that in other jurisdictions, even where similar wording is used, the decision should not be followed without the most careful consideration being given to the following points relevant to the reasoning in the House of Lords:

(a)   that the meaning ascribed to the expression "such [P.C.] sums shall be expended in favour of such persons as the Architect shall instruct" may only be "draftsman's jargon" for the process of a completed or perfected nomination, *viz*: nomination, provision of detailed description of work, order by main contractor without taking objection, and acceptance of order by the sub-contractor.

(b)   that a duty of the employer to give instructions "when necessary," or from time to time as difficulties or impossibilities arise, is inconsistent with the nature of the instructions that a contractor is entitled to expect in relation to his own work, and the absolute nature of a contractor's overall obligation to complete.[13a]

(c)   that there is no difficulty in the concept of an involuntary breach of an absolute obligation which is independent of fault, such as on this reasoning would arise in the main contract immediately a nominated sub-contractor repudiated. Similar breaches (*e.g.* in regard to the quality or kind of a particular described material which is unobtainable at the time it is required) are a commonplace of building and indeed other contracts, and do not give rise to any duty of the employer to give fresh instructions in such an event. Nor is it relevant to say that in such an event a contractor has "no right or duty" to offer a substitute by

[13a] As to which see *supra*, pp. 267–269, 324–325, and see *ante*, Chap. 2, pp. 139–141.

way of substantial, though imperfect, performance in order to earn the contract price.

(d) that the words "are hereby declared to be sub-contractors employed by the Contractor," ignored in the judgments, have a meaning wider than a mere denial of privity between the employer and sub-contractor, and mean that, since the sub-contractor is to be the main contractor's agent, the main contractor assumes towards the employer obligations identical with those of the sub-contractor, including the obligation to complete, and not merely the obligation to do work of the stipulated quality.[13b]

(e) that the consequence of the contrary view, namely that the sub-contractor who has committed a serious breach of any kind can substantially reduce his own liability by deliberately repudiating the sub-contract, is so subversive of the whole object of nomination that only the plainest possible express words could be permitted to bring this about.[13c]

(f) that the view that it could not have been contemplated by the parties that the employer should lose his right to control the identity of the second nominated sub-contractor in the event of a repudiation by the first overlooks one of the most important objects of the system of nomination. In the majority of cases the sub-contractor, just like the main contractor, is selected because of his price, rather than because of his personality and reputation. A duty to re-nominate means that the employer is deprived of what may to him have been his primary object both in describing the work in question as a P.C. or provisional sum item and in making the particular nomination—namely obtaining the most competitive price possible for specialist work or goods which the main contractor himself would have had difficulty in pricing in the ordinary way in the main contract.[13d]

It should perhaps be added that the *Bickerton* decision turned on the particular meaning attributed by the House of Lords to clause 27 of the post-1963 Standard Forms. Apart from the fact that

[13b] See *post*, Chap. 15, pp. 756 *et seq.*, and see *per* Lord Pearson in *Gloucestershire C.C.* v. *Richardson*, quoted *supra*, p. 282.

[13c] Contrast the House of Lord's reasoning in the immediately succeeding case before the same Law Lords, of *Jarvis & Sons* v. *Westminster Corp.* [1970] 1 W.L.R. 637.

[13d] See *post*, Chap. 15, pp. 757–758, 766.

the judgments recommend early attention to the draftsmanship of the contract in this context, the case cannot, it is submitted, be treated as authority upon other differently worded nomination provisions, including in particular the I.C.E. Conditions currently in use in the United Kingdom.

(7) Carrying out Works or Supplying Materials for the Use of the Contractor

Where the contract contemplates that the employer will, by himself or other contractors, do work or supply materials in connection with the contract works, he will usually, but not invariably, be liable for damage suffered by the contractor as a result of his failure to do the works or supply the materials at the proper time. The exact circumstances of each case must be carefully examined to see whether the implication of such a term is required. Obviously different considerations might apply where contractors or sub-contractors were expected by their contract to co-ordinate their work with other trades,[14] or where an employer undertook to assist in obtaining materials which the contractor was originally bound to supply but which he had difficulty in obtaining. Furthermore, the mere fact that the employer contracts directly with a supplier does not in all cases mean that he undertakes responsibility to the builder for the supplier's due performance of his obligations, particularly where the direct contract is contemplated by the building contract. This will undoubtedly usually be the case, but all the circumstances must be looked at.

ILLUSTRATIONS

(1) The plaintiff agreed to build a railway for the defendants and complete it by June 1, 1840, and to suffer a deduction from the contract price of £300 per day if he did not. The defendants agreed to provide the rails and chairs necessary for completing the permanent way by instalments on certain dates. The plaintiff did not complete the railway until twenty-four days after June 1, 1840, and the defendants claimed to deduct £7,500. The defendants had failed to provide the rails and chairs necessary to enable the plaintiff to complete the railway by June 1, 1840. *Held*, the plaintiff was entitled to bring his action against them for breach of contract in which it would be open to the jury to give full redress for all the damages (including the deductions if caused by the defendants' neglect) which the plaintiff had suffered: *MacIntosh* v. *Midland Counties Ry.* (1845).[15]

---

[14] *e.g. Swanson Construction* v. *Government of Manitoba* (1963) 40 D.L.R. (2d) 162 (Canada), *infra*, p. 358, and *Duncanson* v. *Scottish Investment Co. post*, p. 607.
[15] 14 M. & W. 548.

(2) The plaintiff contracted to do the carpenter's work on the defendant's house according to plans prepared by the defendant's architect by November 2, 1864. The stonework was let to other contractors, and in consequence of their delay the plaintiff was delayed and had to do his work in winter at much greater cost. The plaintiff brought an action to recover the extra cost. The defendant pleaded that the plaintiff knew that the stonework was to be done by other contractors, and therefore that he (the defendant) had not undertaken to proceed with the stonework so as to enable the plaintiff to perform his contract within the specified time. *Held*, the plea showed no defence as the defendant must be treated as having impliedly undertaken to do what was necessary to enable the plaintiff to proceed with his contract, and the fact that the defendant had employed others, against whom the plaintiff could have no remedy, made no difference: *Yates* v. *Law* (1866).[16]

(3) In May 1878 the plaintiff agreed with the defendants to do certain dredging in the Mersey by October 1, 1878, subject to an extension of time should staging on the site to be dredged not be removed in time to enable the plaintiff to complete by the day named. The staging was not removed until September 1879. The plaintiff claimed damages in respect of this delay. *Held*, that there was an implied contract that the removal of the staging would not be unreasonably delayed and that the plaintiff was entitled to damages: *Lawson* v. *Wallasey Local Board* (1883).[17]

(4) The plaintiffs agreed to build a memorial arch and two lodges at the entrance to a park for the defendants for a lump sum by a certain day. It was provided by the contract that the defendants, who had previously with the consent of the plaintiffs negotiated for the supply of the stone for the works, should pay the suppliers of the stone and deduct the amount to be paid from the contract sum. By reason of delays in the delivery of the stone the plaintiffs suffered damage which they sought to recover from the defendants. *Held*, there was no implied obligation on the employers to supply the stone. At the highest, they were only obliged to hold the benefit of the contract with the suppliers for the plaintiffs, and accordingly were not liable to them: *W. H. Gaze & Sons Ltd.* v. *Corporation of Port Talbot* (1929).[18]

(5) A plastering sub-contract contained no provisions as to the time of carrying out the work, other than that it was to be carried out in accordance with the main contractor's requirements. The main contract had been entered into at a time of steel shortage and the main contractor had undertaken to do the work as fast as possible as and when steel was available, but leaving out plumbing, heating and ventilation and providing temporary heating in the buildings during construction only. The main contractor started work in 1956 and in September told the sub-contractor that his work would soon be required. Later he told him, without objection, that his work would not be required until the following spring. During the winter of

---

[16] 25 Up.Can.Q.B. 562. Compare this case with *Swanson Construction* v. *Government of Manitoba* (1963) 40 D.L.R. (2d) 162 (Canada) illustrated *infra*, p. 339. See also *Duncanson* v. *Scottish Investment* (1915), illustrated *post*, p. 607.

[17] 11 Q.B.D. 229.

[18] 93 J.P. 89.

1956 the main contractor did not provide heating as required, which slowed down the work generally. The plasterers visited the site in March 1957 for an inspection, and made no protest until April 1957, when they were required to start work, which they refused to do except on the basis of extra payment. *Held,* on the facts, there was no implied term that work should start on any particular date. Even though the failure to provide temporary heating during the winter of 1956 might have been a breach of a term of the main contract to proceed as expeditiously as possible, it did not go to the root of the sub-contract or constitute repudiation: *Pigott Construction* v. *W. J. Crowe Ltd.* (1961).[19]

(6) A contract for the concrete deck and sidewalks of a bridge in Canada provided that it was expected that the erection of structural steel would not be completed before August 15, 1959, that the deck contractor was expected to proceed with his work prior to completion of steel erection and should co-operate to this end with the steel contractor, that the contract was expected to be completed in the summer, and that no payment would be made for any heating which might be necessary. The steel erector did not, in fact, leave the site till October 1959, and as a result the deck contractor could not complete that year and a summer contract (in Canada) became a winter one. *Held,* in view of the express provisions, no term could be implied affording the deck contractor exclusive possession after August 15: *Swanson Construction* v. *Government of Manitoba* (1963).[20]

(8) To Permit the Contractor to Carry out the Whole of the Work

It is self-evident that the building owner must permit the contractor to carry out the whole of the work, and that if he prevents the contractor from so doing, the contractor will have a remedy either on a *quantum meruit* for what he has done or by way of damages.

ILLUSTRATION

The S. Co. agreed to supply to T. A. & Co. " the whole steel " required for the Forth Bridge less 12,000 tons of plates subject to certain conditions. The conditions contained a clause: " The estimated quantity of steel we understand to be 30,000 tons more or less." The S. Co. claimed to be entitled to supply the whole of the steel required. T. A. & Co. contended that " 30,000 tons more or less " meant with a margin for waste five per cent. more or less of 30,000 tons. *Held,* the S. Co. were entitled to provide the whole of the steel required for the bridge: *Tancred Arrol & Co.* v. *The Steel Company of Scotland Ltd.* (1890).[21]

The point arises, however, in a more subtle way where there is a variation clause in the contract empowering the employer to omit work, and the employer attempts to omit work under that clause because he wishes the work to be carried out by someone else than

[19] 27 D.L.R. (2d) 258 (Canada).
[20] 40 D.L.R. (2d) 162 (Canada). Affirmed (1964) 44 D.L.R. (2d) 632.
[21] 15 App.Cas. 125.

the contractor. Under the terms of most contracts, an employer who exercises a power to omit work must genuinely require the work not to be done at all, and cannot exercise such a power with a view to having the work carried out by someone else.[22] Thus in the absence of express provision or the contractor's agreement, it is submitted that work to be done by the main contractor could not be omitted and the same work by a nominated sub-contractor substituted under a power to vary the work.[23]

SECTION 3. DISCHARGE FROM FURTHER PERFORMANCE

(1) Repudiation

It remains to be considered how the parties to a contract can be discharged from their obligations under it. Obvious examples needing little further comment are full performance and mutual release. But the commonest form of discharge prior to complete performance of the contract, and a common source of litigation, arises upon repudiation of the contract by one of the parties. This subject is further considered at some length *post*, Chapter 13, Section 1 (2).

Repudiation is an act or omission of a party which can fairly be regarded as evincing an intention by that party no longer to be bound by the terms of the contract. So a party may repudiate a contract before the time for performance arrives by communicating a renunciation of it to the other party.[24] Such conduct is sometimes called an anticipatory breach. The position then arising is thus described by Cockburn C.J. in *Frost* v. *Knight* (1872).[25]

" The promisee, if he pleases, may treat the notice of intention as inoperative, and await the time when the contract is to be executed, and then hold the other party responsible for all the consequences of non-performance; but in that case he keeps the contract alive for the benefit of the other party as well as his own; he remains subject to all his own obligations and liabilities under it, and enables the other party not only to complete the contract, if so advised, notwithstanding his previous repudiation of it, but also to take

[22] See *post*, Chap. 8, p. 533, and the cases there illustrated of *Gallagher* v. *Hirsch* (1899) N.Y. 45 App.Div. 467 (New York), 61 N.Y.Supp. 607, and *Carr* v. *A. J. Berriman Pty. Ltd.* (1953) 27 A.L.J. 273 (Australia).
[23] The current standard forms would not appear to permit this.
[24] *Hochster* v. *De La Tour* (1853) 2 E. & B. 678.
[25] L.R. 7 Ex. at p. 112.

advantage of any supervening circumstance which would justify him in declining to complete it. On the other hand, the promisee may, if he thinks proper, treat the repudiation of the other party as a wrongful putting an end to the contract, and may at once bring his action as on a breach of it; and in such action he will be entitled to such damages as would have arisen from the non-performance of the contract at the appointed time, subject, however, to abatement in respect of any circumstances which may have afforded him the means of mitigating his loss." (The final act of ending the contract by accepting the other party's repudiation is known as rescinding the contract or rescission, the same term also being used [25a] when a contract is ended following a misrepresentation by the other party.) Sooner or later, however, the innocent party will usually be obliged in his own interests to rescind, if the other party persists in his breach, though there are cases where this is not so (as *e.g.* an employer who, notwithstanding that a contractor is persistently refusing to comply with a particular contractual obligation, prefers to allow the contractor to complete the work and sue for or deduct damages at the end of the contract). See further the comment on the leading case of *Heyman* v. *Darwins* (1942).[26]

Equally a party may repudiate a contract by disabling himself from performing it either before the time for performance has arrived or when the contract has been partly performed. For instance, a building owner who engaged a builder and then sold the proposed site of the building to a third party without any stipulation regarding the building contract would be guilty of repudiation.[27] The most common cases of repudiation arise, however, during the course of the contract. This can either take the form of an explicit renunciation communicated to the other party, or breach of a term which is regarded as fundamental, so that the breach by itself evinces the necessary intention no longer to be bound [28] (or perhaps is regarded as of so serious a character that the only appropriate remedy is, in addition to the right to damages, to release the other party from further performance). Terms of this character are usually called conditions, as opposed to mere warranties (for which the available remedy is the right to damages only). Breach of terms not fundamental (*i.e.* mere warranties) may, however, if persisted in for

---

[25a] See *ante*, Chap. 1, pp. 38 *et seq.*
[26] *Infra*, pp. 346–347.
[27] *Cf. King* v. *Allen (David) & Sons Billposting Ltd.* [1916] 2 A.C. 54, where a billposting site was alienated after the grant of a licence to post bills thereon.
[28] *Rhymney Ry.* v. *Brecon & Merthyr Tydfil Ry.* (1900) 69 L.J.Ch. 813.

considerable periods or after notice to discontinue the breach, evince an intention no longer to be bound by the contract and so justify rescission. The law is, however, now clear that a single breach of one such stipulation does not necessarily carry with it even an implication of an intention to repudiate the whole contract.[29] Thus where a contractor abandons the work, or the building owner prevents him from proceeding with it at all, e.g. by wrongfully exercising a power of forfeiture, there is a clear case of repudiation, but not if the contractor is dilatory or the owner fails to pay one instalment of the contract price. Nor is a contractor justified in abandoning a contract if the employer has delayed payment for work done on other contracts by the same contractor.[30]

The general principle in regard to sale of goods is stated in *Freeth* v. *Burr* (1874) [31]:

" The principle to be applied in these cases is whether the non-delivery or the non-payment amounts to an abandonment of the contract or a refusal to perform it on the part of the person making the default."

The tendency has been to hold that mere non-payment of an instalment due in respect of goods does not constitute a repudiation,[32] while a general refusal to pay instalments on the due date will do so.[33] Lord Blackburn said in the *Mersey Steel & Iron Co.* case [34] in regard to a failure to pay one instalment:

" So far from the respondents saying that when the iron was brought in future they would not pay for it, they were always anxious to get it. . . . There was a statement that for reasons which they thought sufficient they were not willing to pay for the iron at present, and if that statement had been an absolute refusal to pay . . . I will not say it might not have been evidence to go to the jury for them to say whether it would not amount to a refusal to go on with the contract, for a man might reasonably so consider it. But there is nothing of that kind here. . . . "

These principles clearly apply, it is submitted, to building contracts. An employer who, on the advice of his architect or engineer or for any other reason, honestly contends that the contractor has not earned, and refuses to pay, the sums claimed for interim

---

[29] *Cornwall* v. *Henson* [1900] 2 Ch. 298 at p. 303.
[30] *Small & Sons* v. *Middlesex Real Estate Ltd.* [1921] W.N. 245.
[31] L.R. 9 C.P. 208.
[32] *Mersey Steel & Iron Co.* v. *Naylor Benzon & Co.* (1884) 9 App.Cas. 434.
[33] *Withers* v. *Reynolds* (1831) 1 L.J.K.B. 30.
[34] At p. 443.

payment will not, even if he is in the wrong, thereby be held to repudiate the contract, particularly since under the arbitration clauses in both the R.I.B.A. and I.C.E. forms of contract claims by the contractor of this kind can be arbitrated before the end of the contract.[35] Under the R.I.B.A. standard forms, however, the builder has a right to determine the contract if the employer does not pay any sums actually certified by the architect after receipt of written notice to do so.[36] This provision is open to grave criticism in that not only does it not recognise that the employer might have bona fide reasons for not paying on a certificate, but the contract actually entitles him not to do so in certain cases, as *e.g.* the deduction of liquidated damages, yet this too does not appear to be recognised in the determination clause.

Whether or not acts or words amount to a renunciation or abandonment of the contract may be a difficult question of fact. " It must be shown that the party to the contract made quite plain his own intention not to be bound by it." [37]

ILLUSTRATIONS

(1) R. agreed for a lump sum to build a house for L. R. asked for an advance. L. said he would never pay a farthing. R. brought an action against L. alleging that L.'s statement amounted to an abandonment of the contract. *Held*, that nothing was due from L. at the time of L.'s statement, and his statement did not amount to an abandonment of the contract: *Rees* v. *Lines* (1837).[38]

(2) P. agreed to manufacture and fix a copper necessary for fitting up a brewery, nothing being said about time or mode of payment. When part of the work was done, P. refused to complete without security, which W. refused to give. P. brought an action against W. for not permitting him to proceed with the work and for payment for what he had done. It was left to the jury to say upon the evidence which party was at fault in causing the contract not to be carried into effect. The jury having found for W., it was held on a motion for a new trial that there was no misdirection: *Pontifex* v. *Wilkinson* (1845).[39]

(3) Defendant agreed with plaintiff for erection of a house on defendant's land. While the plaintiff was engaged on the work, he alleged that unnecessary delay had been caused by the defendant. The defendant then said: " If you won't go on with your work, go away." *Held*, that this did not amount to a repudiation and the plaintiff was not entitled to rescind the agreement: *Clayton* v. *McConnell* (1888).[40]

---

[35] See *post*, Chap. 18, pp. 857–858. See also *post*, Chap. 7, pp. 494–496.

[36] See clause 26 (1) of the post-1963 forms.

[37] *Per* Lord Atkin, *Spettabile, etc.* v. *Northumberland Shipbuilding Co.* (1919) 121 L.T. 628 at p. 634.

[38] 8 C. & P. 126.   [39] 2 C.B. 349.   [40] 15 A.R. 500 (Canada).

(4) F. contracted to pull down some houses for W. within 42 days, and was to pay so much a working day by way of liquidated damages for delay. F. delayed beyond the fixed time, and on being asked if he could complete in one, two or three months said that he could not say. There was no other evidence of renunciation or abandonment of the work by the builder. W. entered after thirteen days and refused to let F. complete. *Held*, that the termination was wrongful. If W. wished to treat F.'s reply as an abandonment of the contract, he should so have informed him at once and not waited thirteen days and then acted without warning: *Felton* v. *Wharrie* (1906).[41]

(5) Employers gave three days' notice under a forfeiture clause entitling them to the possession of plant and materials without vitiating the contract upon the voluntary liquidation of the contractor. Before the three days had expired they entered on the site and took certain measures in relation to the plant, including stencilling their name on it and controlling the movement of vehicles. *Held*, by Elwes J., their premature action under the forfeiture notice did not *ipso facto* amount to repudiation, and on the facts the employers had not by their conduct shown an intention to repudiate the contract: *Earth and General Contracts Ltd.* v. *Manchester Corp.* (1958).[42]

(6) A prospective lessee under a contract to grant a lease entered into possession and paid rent. It had been agreed that the lease should be non-assignable, but the landlords required the lessee to agree to a prohibition against underletting or parting with possession of any part of the premises. The lessee refused by letter to accept the prohibition and this was treated as a repudiation by the landlords. *Held*, by the Court of Appeal, the requirement was more than the landlords were entitled to under the contract, but even if the lessee had not been entitled to refuse the proposed covenant, an erroneous but bona fide view of the construction of the agreement would not amount to a repudiation of it: *Sweet & Maxwell Ltd.* v. *Universal News Services* (1964).[42a]

What is a term sufficiently fundamental to rank as a condition justifying rescission will depend upon the particular facts of each case. Thus the provision of a surety bond required " forthwith on the acceptance of his tender " was held to be a fundamental term, breach of which justified the other party in treating the contract as repudiated.[43] Again, in a case where information was not available for a large number of matters not covered by the specification by the time the remainder had been completed, this was held to

---

[41] Hudson's B.C., 4th ed. Vol. 2, p. 398, and see *post*, Chap. 13, Forfeiture, where this case is discussed.

[42] 108 L.J. 665. See also *Hawthorne* v. *Newcastle, etc. Ry.* (1840) 3 Q.B. 734, illustrated *post*, pp. 663–664.

[42a] [1964] 2 Q.B. 699. See, however, the decision of the Supreme Court of Canada in *Peter Kiewit & Sons* v. *Eakins Construction Ltd.*, *post*, Chap. 8, p. 543.

[43] *Swartz & Son (Pty.) Ltd.* v. *Wolmaranstadt Town Council*, 1960 (2) S.A. 1.

justify rescission by the builder.[44]   On the other hand, a term which made proof of payment in full of all sub-contractors a condition precedent to interim payment of the main contractor, was held not to justify a rescission by the employer.[45]   Breaches of terms not in themselves fundamental may evince an intention not to be bound if persisted in for long periods, or after receipt of notice or if wilful or deliberate in character.

ILLUSTRATION

An employer, in circumstances already illustrated,[46] had by the month of July, despite numerous requests by the contractor, failed to excavate over the site to certain levels and hand over possession, which he was contractually bound to do by the end of May.   Under the terms of the contract the employer was to provide certain structural steel which the contractor was required to fabricate. The latter had made arrangements to do so.   In July the architect informed the contractor that the employer had made his own arrangements for the fabrication of the steel, and that this work should be omitted from the contract.   The contractor then refused to carry on with the contract.   *Held*, that as to possession, failure to remedy the breach after the due date might continue for so long and in such circumstances as to evince an intention not to be bound, notwithstanding the absence of any notices from the other party, and therefore amount to a repudiation.   Furthermore, the breach involved in omitting the fabrication, which was deliberate, was a further indication that the employer did not regard himself as bound by the contract: *Carr* v. *J. A. Berriman (Pty.) Ltd.* (1953).[47]

The exercise of the right to treat the contract as repudiated must be unqualified and made within a reasonable time.[48]   The contract must not have been affirmed in any way,[49] or the rights of third parties have intervened, or the other party have altered his position on the basis that the contract still subsisted.[50] If not so exercised, the remedy of damages is still available.[51]   Where, however, the fundamental breach is a continuing one, the right to rescind can be exercised at any time while the breach continues, and a renunciation not withdrawn may be evidence of a continuing refusal to perform the

---

[44] *S. J. & M. M. Price Ltd.* v. *Milner* (1968) 206 E.G. 313, illustrated *supra*, Section 2, p. 326.

[45] *Alkok* v. *Grymek* (1968) 67 D.L.R. (2d) 718 (Canada).   [46] *Supra*, p. 319.

[47] (1953) 27 A.L.J. 273 (Australia).

[48] See, *e.g. Felton* v. *Wharrie, supra.* See also *post* for the discussion of a closely allied subject, Chap. 13, pp. 697–700.

[49] See, for a good example where advantage was taken of the work done by the party in breach, so that the latter was entitled to sue, *Tannenbaum Meadows Ltd.* v. *Wright & Winston Ltd.* (1965) 49 D.L.R. (2d) 386, illustrated *supra*, Section 1, p. 252.

[50] *Marsden* v. *Sambell* (1880) 43 L.T. 120, illustrated *post*, Chap. 13, Section 1, p. 699.

[51] *Bentsen* v. *Taylor Sons & Co.* [1893] 2 Q.B. 274.

contract.[52] Furthermore, mere delay in acceptance of repudiation will not be a bar unless there has been an alteration of position to his detriment by the other party.[52a]

The necessity as a matter of prudence for a clear election to be communicated to the other party cannot be over-emphasised. Thus in a case where a contractor wrongly (as it was held) stopped work, and negotiations followed but broke down on the terms upon which he should return, the Supreme Court of Canada divided three to two as to which party had in the event finally repudiated, on the ground that a particular inconclusive meeting might have amounted to a withdrawal of a previous written intimation of an election to treat the contract as repudiated.[53] Again, in the case of *Pigott Construction Ltd.* v. *W. J. Crowe Ltd.* (1961),[54] where plastering sub-contractors were kept waiting till April of the following year before being asked to start work, visits of inspection to the site made in March without protest were held to be an election not to treat the contract as repudiated by delays during the previous winter.

It has been seen that notices may be of importance in turning acts which might not otherwise be a repudiation into a repudiation if persisted in subsequent to the notices.[55] This is of particular importance in relation to contractual obligations to do some act by a particular time or date.[56]

The exact nature of the right to treat a contract as repudiated was considered by the House of Lords in *Heyman* v. *Darwins* (1942).[57] It was there stated that, just as in the case of anticipatory breach, in the case of a breach while the contract was partly performed, a party could either accept the repudiation and sue for damages, or could treat the contract as subsisting and continue to call for performance,[58] though this latter right was not usually a useful remedy unless the contract was of a kind which could be specifically enforced.[59] Rescission, or acceptance of the repudiation, only

---

[52] See *Ripley* v. *McClure* (1849) 4 Ex. 345.
[52a] *Allen* v. *Robles* [1969] 1 W.L.R. 1193, following *Clough* v. *L.N.W.R.* (1871) L.R. 7 Ex. Ch. 26.
[53] *Kamlee Construction Ltd.* v. *Town of Oakville* (1961) 26 D.L.R. (2d) 166 (Canada). See also *post*, pp. 687 *et seq.*, 697–700, and *cf. Marsden* v. *Sambell* (1880) 43 L.T. 120, *post*, p. 699. See also *Verona Construction Ltd.* v. *Frank Ross Construction Ltd.* [1961] S.C.R. 195 (Canada).
[54] Illustrated *ante*, pp. 338–339.
[55] See *supra*, pp. 341–342, and *post*, pp. 604–605, 611–613.
[56] See the more detailed discussion, Chap. 10, *post*, Time for Performance.
[57] [1942] A.C. 356.
[58] See *supra*, p. 341, for occasions when it may pay a party, in practical terms, to rely on damages and not repudiate.
[59] Most building contracts are not, see *infra*, pp. 371 *et seq.*

means that the party invoking the remedy is thereafter relieved of any obligation to perform it further. It does not bring the contract to an end in any theoretical sense, and provisions in the contract— for instance regulating the state of accounts between the parties, controlling damages, or providing for the handling of disputes by arbitration or otherwise—continue to have effect.[60]

A most important result of an accepted repudiation in building and engineering contracts is that the rescinding party, if he has done work for which he is entitled to be paid, may at his option sue in *quantum meruit* for the reasonable value of any work done by him as an alternative to the right to damages.[61] This may be of considerable practical importance to a contractor who has elected to treat a contract as repudiated by the employer, if he has carried out a considerable amount of work prior to the breach and if he considers that his contract prices were serious underestimates of his actual costs because, as will be seen, his damages for breach of contract in such a case are inevitably calculated with reference to the sums which he would have received if the contract had not been broken.[62]

(2) Release

Parties to a contract can be discharged from further performance by a mutual release or by entering into a fresh agreement in substitution therefor.[63]

Where the second agreement is express, it is a question of construction as to how far, if at all, the original agreement is discharged or varied thereby. The second agreement may be inferred from the acts of the parties, but there must be something to justify the conclusion that the parties have entered into a fresh contract.[64] For example, barring some provision giving an architect's decision on variations finality (such provisions are rare at the present day), agreement by architect or employer to pay for work as a variation of the contract will not be enforceable, if on a true view of the contract the work in question was not a variation, since there will be no consideration for the employer's promise.[65] Again, a release

---

[60] *Heyman* v. *Darwins* [1942] A.C. 356. See *e.g.* at pp. 374, 379, 397–399.

[61] *Lodder* v. *Slowey* [1904] A.C. 442.

[62] See *post*, Chap. 9, p. 585.

[63] See *ante*, pp. 22–24, as to how far an agreement under seal or in writing can be varied or discharged by a subsequent written or parol agreement.

[64] *Per* Blackburn J. in *Appleby* v. *Myers* (1867) L.R. 2 C.P. 651 at p. 661, and see *Munro* v. *Butt* (1858) 8 E. & B. 738, and *Whitaker* v. *Dunn* (1887) 3 T.L.R. 602. See also *Hunt* v. *S.E. Ry.* (1875) L.J. 45 C.P. 87, and *Courtnay* v. *Waterford and Central Ireland Ry.* (1878) 4 L.R.Ir. 11.

[65] *Post*, Chap. 8, pp. 523–524; *ante*, Chap. 2, pp. 106–108.

of the employer from his obligation to pay the price is also a theoretical possibility but, as in the case already mentioned, there must be consideration present.

The only consideration which is likely to be present in such cases is the forgoing of some claim. Thus in the first of the two examples given, a contractor demanding £10,000 for a previously agreed variation, but who agrees to accept £5,000 in settlement, will be able to sue for the £5,000 notwithstanding that it is subsequently held that there never was a variation at all. A surrender of a bona fide, even though wrong, claim for more in return for payment of less is good consideration. So too, in the second of the above examples, an agreement by the builder to accept less than the contract price will be enforceable notwithstanding that it was in consideration of some honestly held claim by the employer which later is held to have no validity. These agreements are usually referred to by lawyers as " accord and satisfaction." But there must be an honest, even if invalid, claim to found the necessary consideration.

ILLUSTRATION

An employer told small builders who she knew were pressed for money that unless they accepted a sum considerably less than the sum in their account, she would not pay them at all. They gave a receipt acknowledging that the payment was in full settlement of their account. Subsequently they decided to bring an action for the balance. *Held*, by the Court of Appeal, a mere threat not to pay at all could not be a good accord and satisfaction: *D. & C. Builders Ltd.* v. *Rees* (1965).[66]

(3) Impossibility and Frustration

Frustration is the legal term for a doctrine whereby in certain circumstances a contract is held no longer binding on the parties. In the event of frustration, the financial position between the parties is governed by sections 1 and 2 of the Law Reform (Frustrated Contracts) Act 1943, which can be summarised in very broad terms as giving the court a discretion to award reasonable sums for work done or benefits conferred by the parties to the contract—in other words, for practical purposes the contract rates cease to be applicable in the event of frustration, and the obligation to complete ceases.

Frustration can arise in a number of ways. Although it has sometimes been said to arise by reason of facts unknown to the parties but existing at the time of the contract, it is more probable that such situations are governed, and the contract will be avoided if at all, by the very stringent requirements of the law of mistake,

[66] [1966] 2 Q.B. 617.

which in cases of common mistake must relate to what is usually described as the fundamental subject-matter of the contract.[67]

In the context of building and engineering contracts, frustration will normally arise by reason of some supervening event, such as destruction of the entire site (not the works on the site) by fire or flood so that a resumption of the project is impossible, or the passage of legislation rendering the work illegal. It is important to appreciate that, as will be seen when the basis of the doctrine is considered below, the supervening event must be so unexpected and beyond the contemplation of the parties, even as a possibility, that neither party can be said to have accepted the risk of the event taking place when contracting.

It is precisely for this reason that frustration can only very rarely come about in building and engineering contracts, since their performance is, as a matter of reasonable foresight, hedged about with many uncertainties and far more likely to be prevented by physical difficulties than in the case of other types of contract. In general the contractor is taken to have assumed the risk of the many uncertainties and difficulties associated with work in his field. Thus it has already been seen [68] that the difficulty of the work is not in general a valid excuse for non-performance of a contract to execute it, nor is a contractor entitled to abandon work which proves unexpectedly onerous. A building owner does not impliedly warrant that the plans or methods specified by him or his agent are practicable,[69] and a contractor who undertakes to carry out work in accordance with plans and a specification must do it or pay damages. Thus a person may be liable in damages for failing to do something which was at the time of his contract impossible. " Certainly if he does in direct terms enter into a contract to perform an impossibility, subject to a penalty, he will not be excused because it is an impossibility." [70]   " Where there is a positive contract to do a thing, not in itself unlawful, the contractor must perform it or pay damages for not doing it, although in consequence of unforeseen accidents, the performance of his contract has become unexpectedly burdensome, or even impossible." [71]

The test is whether the party charged expressly or impliedly

---

[67] *Bell* v. *Lever Bros. Ltd.* [1932] A.C. 161 at p. 217, *per* Lord Atkin; and see *ante*, Chap. 1, pp. 25 *et seq.*

[68] *Ante*, pp. 267 *et seq.* The cases illustrated there should be borne in mind as well as the cases illustrated *infra* in this subsection.

[69] See also *ante*, Chap. 2, p. 107, and *supra*, pp. 267–268, 316–317.

[70] *Per* Hannen J. in *Jones* v. *St. John's College* (1870) L.R. 6 Q.B. 115.

[71] *Per* Blackburn J. in *Taylor* v. *Caldwell* (1863) 3 B. & S. at p. 833.

warrants the possibility of doing that which he contracted to do.[72]
It should be pointed out that in the I.C.E.standard form of contract [73]
the contractor only contracts to carry out the work " save in so
far as it is legally or physically impossible," and his express obligation
to reinstate damage to the works during construction (which is a
very different obligation from the obligation to complete the works)
is subject to a number of specially excepted risks, including " causes
solely due to the engineer's design of the works." [74] These provisions may be criticised for the obscurity which they create in relation
to the contractor's obligation to complete, but under the R.I.B.A.
forms it would seem that the R.I.B.A. have (in so far as they may
be regarded as the custodian of the employer's interests) agreed
that in nearly all cases of frustration the contractor should have the
same rights as if the employer had wrongfully repudiated the contract,
since the contractor is given the right to determine the contract
(with attendant rights to seize goods and materials even though paid
for by the employer, and to recover loss of profit on the remaining
work) should the work be suspended (*for one month*) by "*force
majeure*." [75] The policy of this clause, once it is understood,
can only be described as incredible, and is unlikely to be found in
any other contract anywhere in the world, whatever may be the
individual or collective bargaining power of contractors in other
countries. It would be interesting to see what justification for it
could be put forward by an architect or legal adviser sued for negligence who had recommended such a contract to the employer.

Damages for breach of a contract to do something which is
impossible may in some situations be nominal only. Thus the breach
of a contract to construct a building which, if constructed, would be
so unstable that it would inevitably fall down would not result in any
loss to the building owner. On the other hand, substantial damages
would flow from the breach of a contract to erect a structure which
would be perfectly sound when erected, but which could not be
erected by the methods specified, *e.g.* a bridge or dock requiring
preliminary or temporary works different from those envisaged in
the contract. In addition to the cases illustrated below, those
illustrated in Section 1 (1), The Obligation to Complete, should also
be considered in this context.[76]

[72] *Hills* v. *Sughrue* (1846) 15 M. & W. 253; *Clifford (Lord)* v. *Watts* (1870) L.R. 5 C.P.
577.
[73] Clause 13 of the 1955 edition.
[74] Clause 20 of the 1955 edition.
[75] Clause 26 (1) (c) (i). For the meaning of the expression, see *infra*, pp. 359–360.
[76] *Supra*, pp. 267 *et seq.*

ILLUSTRATIONS

(1) A contract provided that " the contractors shall and will duly execute and complete the works hereby contracted for, with such alterations, additions, deductions, or deviations respectively as shall be respectively directed by every and any such alteration order, in the same manner and subject to the same conditions, stipulations, and provisions, to all intents and purposes as if such alteration, addition, deduction, or deviation directed by any such order had been originally comprised in the works of the contract, and in the specification hereunder written, and the plans, elevations and sections so signed as aforesaid. And, further, that the periods for completing all such alterations or extra works shall not exceed the period limited by these presents for the completion of the works hereby contracted for, unless an extension of time also be allowed by order, specifying the limit of extension, signed by the clerk of works and bursar, within twenty-one days after the delivery of the alteration order." The defendants averred that the plaintiff ordered alterations and additions, etc. which it was impossible to execute within the time. *Held*, on demurrer, that the contractors were bound to do the work, including alterations, within the time, although it might involve an impossibility: *Jones* v. *St. John's College, Oxford* (1870).[77]

(2) A main contract contained a provision [78] whereby the engineer reserved the right to stop the excavation and require the contractor to complete the trench and backfill with the excavation. The main contractor had entered into a sub-contract with tunnelling sub-contractors, and these latter through no fault of their own had their work suspended when the engineer exercised this power. They sued the main contractor for damages, but he contended that the engineer's instruction was an event which frustrated the contract. *Held*, there was an implied term in the sub-contract that the main contractor should permit the sub-contractors to proceed in a reasonable manner without any undue or unreasonable delay or suspension of their obligations, and that the impossibility of completing the sub-contract work was not a natural or legal one such as might give rise to frustration but was merely a relative impossibility arising out of the main contractor's own agreement with the employers, and it was their fault if in the sub-contract the main contractors ran the risk of undertaking to perform an impossibility: *Smith & Montgomery* v. *Johnson Bros.* (1954).[79]

The foundation of the doctrine of frustration has been much debated and the best view appears to be that it is not dependent upon the implication of any term into the contract, but rather upon

[77] L.R. 6 Q.B. 115. The *ratio decidendi* of this case depended upon the finality expressly conferred upon the decision of the bursar as to extension of time—see *post*, Chap. 11, p. 628, where the case is illustrated more fully, but it illustrates that there is nothing intrinsically unusual or legally offensive in undertaking a task not in fact capable of being performed.

[78] Set out more fully *ante*, p. 328.

[79] 1 D.L.R. (2d) 392 (High Court of Ontario).

the true construction of the contract as it stands.[80] The doctrine was stated in its simplest terms by Lord Radcliffe in the *Davis Contractors* case [81] as follows:

" Frustration occurs whenever the law recognises that without default of either party a contractual obligation has become incapable of being performed because the circumstances in which performance is called for would render it a thing radically different from that which was undertaken by the contract. *Non haec in foedera veni.* It was not this that I promised to do.

" There is, however, no uncertainty as to the materials upon which the court must proceed. ' The data for decision are, on the one hand, the terms and construction of the contract, read in the light of the then existing circumstances, and on the other hand the events which have occurred.' [82] In the nature of things there is often no room for any elaborate inquiry. The court must act upon a general impression of what its rule requires. It is for that reason that special importance is necessarily attached to the occurrence of any unexpected event that, as it were, changes the face of things. But even so, it is not hardship or inconvenience or material loss itself which calls the principle of frustration into play. There must be as well such a change in the significance of the obligation that the thing undertaken would, if performed, be a different thing from that contracted for."

Put in another way, the test is whether the risk of what happened was a risk taken by one of the parties to the contract.

The doctrine has been explained in an earlier case: " upon the ground that there was an implied term in the contract which entitled (the parties) to be absolved. Sometimes it is put that performance has become impossible and that the party concerned did not promise to perform an impossibility. Sometimes it is put that the partners contemplated a certain state of things which fall out otherwise. In most of the cases it is said that there was an implied condition in the contract which operated to release the parties from performing it, and in all of them I think that was at bottom the principle upon which the court proceeded. It is in my opinion the true principle, for no court has an absolving power, but it can infer from the nature of the contract and the surrounding circumstances

---

[80] *Davis Contractors* v. *Fareham U.D.C.* [1956] A.C. 696, *per* Lord Reid at p. 720.
[81] *Ibid.* at p. 729.
[82] *Denny, Mott and Dickson Ltd.* v. *James B. Fraser & Co. Ltd.* [1944] A.C. 265, *per* Lord Wright at pp. 274–275.

that a condition which is not expressed was a foundation on which the parties contracted." [83]

The cases illustrated below show that the destruction by fire of the place where the work is to be done can be a frustrating event, if the effect is that the contract can never thereafter be performed, in the sense of producing the permanent result originally intended, but in general the destruction by fire, storm or other natural agencies of that which is being built before it is completed is a risk assumed by the builder, and the builder will remain under an obligation to complete the work by doing it over again: hence the fire insurance provisions in most modern forms of contract. [84] An indefinite stoppage of work pursuant to a government order coupled with a compulsory sale of plant has been held sufficient to cause frustration. [85] On the other hand the *Davis Contractors* case [86] decided that where, owing to an unexpected lack of labour, a contract took twenty-two months instead of eight, but there was never any actual interruption of work, the contract was not frustrated. In the light of this decision of the House of Lords it would appear impossible to sustain a *quantum meruit* claim based on frustration where the work was never stopped but merely proceeded much more slowly than was expected, or where the cost to the contractor of completing the project has increased, however astronomically.

A *quantum meruit* claim succeeded in *Bush* v. *Whitehaven Trustees* (1888), [87] but in the *Davis Contractors* case [88] the House of Lords indicated disapproval of the *ratio decidendi* of *Bush's* case. If a contract is frustrated and subsequently the work is started up again or proceeded with under protest, then, in the absence of any express agreement, the contractor would on general principles be entitled to payment for the work done after the frustration on a *quantum meruit*. (The Act of 1943 would not apply in such a case.) It was not clear before 1943, however, that a contractor could recover on a *quantum meruit* in respect of work done *before* the frustration. At common law the loss fell where it lay, and a contractor was entitled to any progress payments already made or due

---

[83] *Per* Earl Loreburn in *Tamplin S.S.* v. *Anglo-Mexican Petroleum Products Co.* [1916] 2 A.C. 397 at pp. 403 and 404.

[84] See also the maintenance provisions in some contracts, *post*, Chap. 6, pp. 389 *et seq.*, which may have the effect of keeping the work at the contractor's risk for a fixed period after completion.

[85] *Metropolitan Water Board* v. *Dick, Kerr & Co.* [1918] A.C. 119, illustrated *infra*, p. 357.

[86] *Infra.*

[87] Hudson's B.C., 4th ed., Vol. 2, p. 122.

[88] *Infra.*

to him before the frustrating event, but could recover no more, although the value of the work done might exceed the progress payments. Now the position is governed by the Law Reform (Frustrated Contracts) Act 1943, which makes all sums paid recoverable but gives a court or arbitrator a discretion to allow a party to retain or recover all sums paid or payable before discharge up to the amount of the expenses incurred by him. In addition, where one party has received a valuable benefit before the time of discharge (*e.g.* by the construction of works on his land), there is recoverable by the other party such sum not exceeding the value of the benefit to the first party as is considered just. There are also savings for provisions of the contract intended to operate in circumstances amounting to frustration, and for treating a contract as severable where a part has been performed and can properly be severed from the remainder.

Where the frustration results from deliberate delay by one of the parties with the intention that frustration shall take place, that party will not be relieved from liability under the contract, even though the state of affairs brought about by the delay might otherwise have amounted to frustration.[89] When frustration occurs, it avoids the contract itself and discharges both parties automatically. In this situation a plaintiff suing upon the contract can only succeed if he can show that the event which would otherwise have frustrated the contract was due to the defendant's default. It is for the plaintiff who seeks to avoid the legal result of an otherwise frustrating event to establish that the destruction of the subject-matter of the contract was due to the neglect or default of the defendant.[90] In addition to the cases illustrated below, those illustrated in Section 1 (1), The Obligation to Complete, should also be considered.[91]

ILLUSTRATIONS

(1) P. undertook to build a bridge for a company and to keep it in repair. During the period of maintenance the bridge was swept away by an extraordinary flood. *Held*, that P. was not released from his obligation under the contract, and must rebuild the bridge: *Brecknock Navigation Co.* v. *Pritchard* (1796).[92]

(2) A contract was made to erect hustings for a certain sum on receiving the wood back again. The mob carried the wood away.

---

[89] *Mertens* v. *Home Freeholds Co.* [1921] 2 K.B. 526.
[90] See *per* Lord Simon L.C. in *Joseph Constantine Steamship Line Ltd.* v. *Imperial Smelting Corporation Ltd.* [1942] A.C. 154.
[91] *Supra*, pp. 267 *et seq.*
[92] 6 T.R. 750.

Held, that the employer was bound to return or pay for the wood: *Fuller* v. *Pattrick* (1849).[93]

(3) A covenanted with B to build a bridge, both parties treating it as certain that a stream would be diverted. The stream was not diverted, and the bridge was not built. *Held*, that no action would lie for not building it: *Rashleigh* v. *South Eastern Railway* (1851).[94]

(4) In an action on a policy of insurance against fire, which contained a condition by which the society reserved to itself the right of reinstatement in preference to the payment of claims, the defendants pleaded that, having elected to reinstate the insured premises, they were proceeding with the reinstatement thereof, when, by order of the Commissioners of Sewers, lawfully acting in that behalf, the premises were taken down as being in a dangerous condition, such a condition not being caused by the fire; and that if the said premises had not so been taken down, they would have proceeded with the reinstatement, and would have restored them to the condition they were in before the fire. *Held*, on demurrer, *per* Lord Campbell C.J., Crompton and Hill JJ. that the plea was bad on the ground that performance in the preferred way was merely impossible and not illegal; and that as the defendants could not reinstate they must pay damages: *Brown* v. *Royal Insurance Society* (1859).[95]

(5) The plaintiff contracted with the defendant to erect certain machinery upon buildings and premises of the defendant, and in his occupation, for a specified sum, and to keep the whole in order, fair wear and tear excepted, for two years. When the machinery was only partly erected a fire accidentally broke out in the buildings, and, without any fault of either party, destroyed the whole of the buildings and the machinery then erected thereon. *Held*, reversing the decision of the Court of Common Pleas, that as the premises were entirely destroyed without the fault of either, both were excused and neither had a cause of action, though if the accidental fire had left the defendant's premises untouched and only injured the part of the works which the plaintiff had already finished, he must have done that part over again in order to complete; but that as it was, the plaintiff was not entitled to recover anything in respect of any portion of the machinery which had been erected and destroyed, as the whole work contracted to be done by him had not been completed: *Appleby* v. *Myers* (1867).[96]

(6) The defendant contracted to make, supply and instal new boilers in a ship, and to make alterations in the existing machinery to receive the boilers. The price was to be £5,800, payable as to £2,000 when the boilers were plated, £2,000 when the work was ready for fixing on board, and the balance on completion. One instalment of £2,000 had been paid, and the work was ready for fixing, when the ship was lost at sea. Subsequently the plaintiffs paid the further £2,000 at a time when they, but not the defendant,

---

[93] 18 L.J.Q.B. 236.
[94] (1851) 10 C.B. 612.
[95] 28 L.J.Q.B. 275.
[96] L.R. 2 C.P. 651. See also the fuller illustration *ante*, pp. 247–248. The financial result might now, of course, be different under the Act of 1943.

knew of the loss of the ship. The plaintiffs claimed delivery of the boilers and machinery, or, alternatively, to recover back the £4,000 as upon a consideration that had wholly failed. *Held*, the contract was entire and indivisible, and that the parties were released from further performance by the loss of the ship. On its true construction, the property in the materials was not to pass till fixing in the ship. Consequently the plaintiffs could not recover the materials, nor could the consideration be said to have failed so as to entitle them to recover the £4,000: *Anglo-Egyptian Navigation Co.* v. *Rennie* (1875).[97]

[Note—This case was taken to the Exchequer Chamber [98] which seems to have been disposed to differ from the Court of Common Pleas on the first point, but decided nothing and referred the dispute to arbitration. The decision of the Court below is therefore of doubtful authority, but it is submitted that in so far as it decides that the instalments paid to the contractors could not be recovered back, it would appear to be correct within the rule laid down in *Appleby* v. *Myers* (1867).[99]]

(7) J. entered into a contract to erect a sea-wall for the E. Local Board. The local board were bound by a special Act of Parliament to protect the adjacent shore from the action of the winds and the seas. By the action of the sea the shingle was swept away and the wall fell. *Held*, that J. took the risk of interference with the work while in progress by the action of the winds and seas, and there was no implied covenant on the part of the board that the seashore on which the works were to be executed should remain in the same state as at the date of the contract: *Jackson* v. *Eastbourne Local Board* (1886).[1]

(8) A had been contractor with a colonial government for the construction of works, but the government was dissatisfied, and had taken the works out of A's hands. A believed that the restoration of the contract might be effected, and agreed with B that B should complete the work and receive 90 per cent. of the profits, the agreement reciting that A had agreed to take B into his service for the purpose of completing the contract. B was aware of the loss of the contract, but believed he could obtain its restoration. The government refused to restore the contract. B brought an action claiming damages for breach of contract to take him into A's service, and for moneys expended on the work. *Held*, that as from circumstances known to and in the contemplation of both parties at the date of the agreement, it was and continued to be beyond the power of A to carry out the work, no agreement would be implied on the part of A to supply B with the work to do: *McKenna* v. *McNamee* (1887).[2]

(9) A contractor tendered in June to lay certain water mains and divert certain streams in Cumberland within four months, on the understanding that work would commence at once. In fact he was

---

[97] L.R. 10 C.P. 271.

[98] L.R. 10 C.P. 571.

[99] *Supra.*

[1] Hudson's B.C., 4th ed. Vol. 2, p. 81. See the fuller illustration *ante* pp. 269–270.

[2] 15 Can.S.C. 311. *Cf. Compagnie Algerienne* v. *Katana Societa etc.* [1960] 2 Q.B. 115 and *Sethia (1944) Ltd.* v. *Rameshwar* [1951] 2 All E.R. 352n. (H.L.) referred to *ante*, Chap. 3, Section 3 (2), p. 220.

not given full possession of the site till October, and the contract became a winter one. Express terms in the contract provided that in the event of delay in giving possession the contractor should not be entitled to any increased allowances of money or time, except only to the extent that he might be allowed an extension of time by the engineer. *Held,* the circumstances contemplated by the contract had so changed that the contract ceased to be applicable and the contractor was entitled to be paid on a *quantum meruit: Bush* v. *Whitehaven Trustees* (1888).[3]

[N.B.—This case was expressly disapproved by the House of Lords in the *Davis Contractors'* case (*infra*) and it can be assumed it would now be decided in the opposite sense against the contractor.]

(10) The defendants, who had undertaken to erect a house for a fixed sum, engaged the plaintiffs as sub-contractors to do the plumbing and tinsmithing work for 500 dollars. Before the completion of the plaintiffs' contract the building was destroyed by fire without fault on the part of the plaintiffs, the defendants or the building owner. Although they had done work to the value of 488 dollars before the fire, the plaintiffs did not allege that they had substantially completed their contract, but brought an action on a *quantum meruit.* *Held,* following *Appleby* v. *Myers* (1867),[4] that the house having been destroyed without any fault of the parties or the building owner, it was a misfortune equally affecting both plaintiffs and defendants, and excusing each from further performance of the contract, but giving a cause of action to neither, and the plaintiffs could not recover: *King et al.* v. *Low et al.* (1901).[5]

(11) The defendant contractors, in July 1914, entered into a contract to construct for the plaintiffs at an agreed price certain reservoirs, and by condition 32 of the contract the whole of the works were to be completed and delivered up within a period of six years from the engineer's written order to commence. The engineer had power, under the same condition, to extend the time if in his opinion the contractors were unduly delayed or impeded by reason (*inter alia*) of any " difficulties, impediments, obstructions oppositions . . . whatsoever and howsoever occasioned." The works were commenced in July 1914, and a substantial amount of work had been done when the work was stopped by the Minister of Munitions in February 1916, and the contractors' plant and materials sold and removed under the Minister's direction. The plaintiffs claimed a declaration that the contract was still in existence and that the defendants were bound to perform it. *Held,* that condition 32 did not cover the case in which the interruption was of such a character and duration as vitally and fundamentally to change the conditions of the contract, and could not possibly have been in the contemplation of the parties when the contract was made, and the defendants were entitled to treat the contract as at an end: *Metropolitan Water Board* v. *Dick, Kerr & Co. Ltd.* (1918).[6]

---

[3] Hudson's B.C., 4th ed. Vol. 2, p. 122. For cases of extra work ordered where the contract was held no longer to apply, see *post,* Chap. 8, Section 2, pp. 548 *et seq.*
[4] L.R. 2 C.P. 660.
[5] 3 Ont.L.R. 234 (C.A.).
[6] [1918] A.C. 119.

(12) Plans for certain building work were passed on July 10, 1916. On July 14, an order was made by the Minister of Munitions that after July 20, no one should commence or carry on building work without a licence. On July 21, the contractor applied for a licence and worked fairly well until August 12, when he deliberately slowed down work with the object of ensuring that the licence was refused so that he could put an end to the contract. While under notice from the architect to proceed with due diligence, it was intimated that the licence had been refused. *Held*, by the Court of Appeal, that a plaintiff cannot take advantage of circumstances as frustrating the contract if he has himself brought those circumstances about, and the damages payable by the contractor must be the higher cost of completing the work after the order was cancelled: *Mertens* v. *Home Freeholds Co.* (1921).[7]

(13) D. entered into a contract to build seventy-eight houses for F. within a period of eight months. D. attached to its form of tender a letter stating that it was subject to adequate supplies of labour being available as and when required. Owing to unexpected circumstances, and without fault of either party, adequate supplies of labour were not available and D. took twenty-two months to complete and incurred extra expense owing to the prolongation of the contract period. D. contended: (1) that the contract price was conditional upon adequate supplies of labour being available by virtue of the letter attached to the tender, (2) that the contract had been frustrated, and (3) that in either event D. was entitled to recover on a *quantum meruit*. *Held*, (1) that the letter was not incorporated in the contract, (2) that the contract had not been frustrated but had merely been rendered more onerous than had been expected, and D. took the risk of lack of labour: *Davis Contractors Ltd.* v. *Fareham Urban District Council* (1956).[8]

(14) A contract for the deck of a bridge in Canada [9] stated that the work was expected to be completed in the summer, and that no payment would be made for any heating which might be necessary. The deck contractor was to proceed with his work prior to completion of steel erection, which would not be completed before August 15. The steel erector did not in fact leave till October, and the deck contractor's contract became a winter one. *Held*, following the *Davis Contractors'* case, delays on building contracts were not abnormal circumstances, and the contract could not be said to be frustrated: *Swanson Construction* v. *Government of Manitoba* (1963).[10]

It is perhaps desirable, particularly because express terms are often found in building contracts using the expressions, to deal with the two concepts of " act of God " and "*force majeure*."

An act of God is a circumstance " which no human foresight can provide against, and of which human prudence is not bound to

---

[7] [1921] 2 K.B. 526.
[8] [1956] A.C. 696.
[9] Set out more fully, *ante*, p. 339.
[10] 40 D.L.R. (2d) 162 (Canada). See also the *Smith and Montgomery* case, *supra*, p. 351.

recognise the possibility." [11] The exact relevance of the concept when not the subject of an express term is not entirely clear. It is usually considered as a sufficient defence, if established, to cases of " strict " or " absolute " liability in the law of tort, such as claims in nuisance, and under the rule in *Rylands* v. *Fletcher*, or for breach of statutory duty. In contract, it would seem that it may absolve a person from the performance of an obligation, or of part of an obligation, and has been so held in principle by the Court of Appeal of East Africa.[12] However, to be successful the plea must show that the event was due *exclusively* to natural causes of so extraordinary a nature that it could not reasonably have been foreseen and the results of which occurrence could not have been avoided by any action which could reasonably have been taken by the person setting up the plea.[13] Examples which might qualify in the United Kingdom might be an earthquake, or floods from the breaching of sea defences due to an exceptional combination of wind and tide. Rainfall has been so held in the United Kingdom,[14] but the qualification as to the impossibility of avoiding the results is important, and Mocatta J. held that a fall of rain at Barnsley of at least 2·7 inches in one hour, which on the meteorological evidence was likely to occur at any one place in the United Kingdom once in 800 years, was not an act of God.[15]

Force majeure is an expression taken originally from the Code Napoléon. It covers a wider class of events than act of God, including man-made events such as strikes or wars, but it must be beyond the control of the person alleging it, and must be construed in the light of the general background and terms of the contract in question, so that differing decisions may be reached in different contracts.[16]

The expression has not received judicial interpretation in a case of a building contract.

ILLUSTRATIONS

(1) A liquidated damages clause in a shipbuilding contract contained an exception for *force majeure* and/or strikes at the building yard or machinery workshops or at steelworks supplying the ship

---

[11] *Per* Lord Westbury, in *Tennent* v. *Earl of Glasgow* (1864) 2 Macph.(H.L.) 22.
[12] *Ryde* v. *Bushell* 1967 E.A. 817.
[13] *Ibid.*
[14] *Nichols* v. *Marsland* (1876) 2 Ex.D. 1, C.A., but see *Greenock Corporation* v. *Caledonian Ry.* [1917] A.C. 556 and *Sedleigh-Denfield* v. *O'Callaghan* [1940] A.C. 880.
[15] *AMF (International) Ltd.* v. *Magnet Bowling* [1968] 1 W.L.R. 1028 (the evidence not reported on this point).
[16] *Lebeaupin* v. *Crispin* [1920] 2 K.B. 714.

or at sub-contractors' works. *Held*, by Bailhache J., the universal coal strike of 1912, and a breakdown of machinery, but not bad weather, constituted *force majeure*: *Matsoukis* v. *Priestman* (1915).[17]

(2) The appellants were liable to penalty for failing to supply electricity, but subject to inevitable accident or *force majeure*. Two of the appellants' workmen had refused to do the work necessary to maintain the supply. The appellants contended that had they dismissed the men it would probably have resulted in all their employees terminating their engagements. *Held*, by the Court of Appeal, *force majeure* applied only to physical or material constraint, and although it applied to strikes actually proceeding, it did not apply to fear, however reasonable, of the consequences of threatened action. *Per* Bankes L.J., " The appellants yielded to a threat, and so failed to persist in an attempt to do the work which might have been successful ": *Hackney B.C.* v. *Doré* (1922).[18]

(4) Death or Illness of a Party

Where a contract is not " personal " in character, the death of a party merely has the effect of transferring its benefit and burden to the executors or administrators,[19] while the illness of a party will afford no excuse, since it is always open to the party concerned to arrange for vicarious performance of his liabilities.

While it has somewhat readily been assumed in the past that building contracts are not personal in character in this special sense, it is suggested [20] that this is in fact not invariably so, and that in certain building and engineering contracts, at any rate, the personality of the builder may be of vital importance to the employer. In the case of contracts of employment of architects and engineers their personality will normally be essential to the contract.[21]

In personal contracts the effect of the death of the party whose personality is involved [22] is to dissolve the contract from the date of death, so that, while it is null and void as to the future, any rights accrued due at the date of death, whether to payment or otherwise, enure to or are enforceable against the estate.[23] The same result will come about in the case of illness or disability of sufficient gravity to prevent further performance of the contract.

[17] [1915] 1 K.B. 681.
[18] [1922] 1 K.B. 431.
[19] See Chap. 14, Assignment, *post*, pp. 738–739.
[20] See Chap. 14, Assignment, *post*, pp. 717–718.
[21] See Chap. 16, *post*, pp. 793–794.
[22] But not the other party; see *Philipps* v. *Alhambra Palace Co.* [1901] 1 K.B. 59, *post*, p. 739.
[23] See *Stubbs* v. *Holywell Ry.* (1867) L.R. 2 Ex. 311, *post*, Chap. 14, p. 738, where the position is more fully discussed.

ILLUSTRATIONS

(1) An apprenticeship deed contained a covenant, absolute in terms, that the apprentice would remain with and serve his master for a certain term. *Held*, that the covenant was subject to an implied condition that the apprentice should continue in a state of ability to perform his contract, and that permanent illness, arising after the making of the deed, was an answer to an action by the master for breach of the covenant: *Boast* v. *Firth* (1868).[24]

(2) The plaintiff contracted with the defendant's wife (as her agent) that she should play at a concert on a specified day. On the day she was too ill to perform. In an action against the husband for damages for breach of the contract, the court held that the incapacity of the wife consequent upon her illness excused him, the contract not being absolute but conditional, and being one which could not be performed by a deputy: *Robinson* v. *Davison* (1871).[25]

(3) In an action against the sureties of a cess-collector, on a bond for the due performance of his duties, the defendants pleaded that, immediately after the delivery of the warrant to the collector, and before he had collected any money, he became insane, and that the defendants were thereby discharged. *Held*, on demurrer, that the plea was good: *Grove* v. *Johnstone* (1889).[26]

Whether an illness is sufficiently grave to have this frustrating effect upon a personal contract is a question of fact which must be decided in the light of all the circumstances. There does not appear to be any direct authority on building and engineering contracts. It is submitted that the personality of a small local builder may be vital to a building contract where the quality of the workmanship is of relatively great importance—as in the case of a private dwelling-house. On the other hand, very many modern contracts are made with limited companies where questions of death and illness cannot arise, and where the effects of a liquidation are governed by the Companies Act.[27] The personality of the employer cannot, it is submitted, be of any relevance in this context.

(5) Illegality

A building contract, like any other contract, if it is affected by illegality when it is made, is void *ab initio* and unenforceable. Thus neither party is ever under any obligation to perform such a contract and the question of a party being discharged from performance does not arise. Where, however, it is the performance or further performance of a lawful contract which becomes illegal, the contract

[24] L.R. 4 C.P. 1.
[25] L.R. 6 Ex. 269.
[26] 24 L.R.Ir. 352.
[27] See *post*, Chap. 16.

will either be frustrated or at the least the parties will be discharged from further performance until such performance again becomes lawful. It is therefore convenient to deal with the whole topic of illegality in this chapter.

A contract made in disobedience to a statute or statutory regulation is plainly illegal and it matters not whether the contract is expressly declared to be void, or whether the making of the contract is merely subject to a penalty. " Every contract made for or about any matter or thing which is prohibited and made unlawful by statute is a void contract, though the statute itself does not mention that it shall be so, but only inflicts a penalty on the offender, because a penalty implies a prohibition though there are no prohibiting words in the statute." [28]

A contract involving the commission of a criminal offence at common law would also be plainly illegal, and the doctrine extends to contracts for immoral purposes or contrary to public policy. " Nor can any distinction be made between an illegal or immoral purpose; the rule which is applicable to the matter is, *ex turpi causa non oritur actio*, and whether it is an immoral or illegal purpose in which the plaintiff has participated, it comes equally within the terms of that maxim and the effect is the same; no cause of action can arise out of one or other." [29]

As already indicated, however, the contract may not be illegal in itself or tainted with illegality but the performance of it without some further authority or licence may be illegal. This situation has arisen in regard to building contracts at times when the carrying out of works in excess of a certain limit of cost without a licence has been prohibited by regulations. Here, unless the parties intended at the time the contract was made to do work without a licence or in excess of the licensed amount without obtaining a further licence, the contract itself would not be illegal, and the value of work done within the limit prescribed by the regulations or, where there was an actual licence, within the licensed amount, is recoverable.[30] Another example of this kind of case arises from the by-law control (now effected by the Building Regulations in nearly all instances), exercised in the interest of public safety and health, which governs nearly all building operations in the United Kingdom. By-laws or building regulations generally require the submission of all plans of proposed work for approval by the by-law authority, and prohibit the carrying

---

[28] *Per* Holt C.J. in *Bartlett* v. *Vinor* (1692) Carth. 251, 252.
[29] *Per* Pollock C.B. in *Pearce* v. *Brooks* (1866) L.R. 1 Ex. 213 at p. 217.
[30] *Frank W. Clifford Ltd.* v. *Garth* [1956] 1 W.L.R. 570.

out of work without such approval. Illegality of this kind may be visible on the face of the original contract—as where the contract drawings or specification plainly infringe the provisions of an applicable by-law—or may only supervene at a later stage when detailed drawings are issued or the purpose of the work becomes clear [31] or because failure to serve notices and secure approval occurs at a later stage. In spite of the fact that it is the invariable custom for architects and engineers to assume responsibility for seeing that at least the original design of the work complies with the by-laws,[32] the modern standard forms contain express undertakings by the contractor to do everything necessary to secure compliance with the by-laws,[33] including, if necessary, to vary the work.[34] As already explained, however, in a number of respects the builder may of necessity be in closer touch with the local authority than the architect during the progress of construction when day-to-day problems may arise.[35]

Lastly, the further performance of a contract may become illegal by supervening illegality, as when emergency legislation is brought into force. The effect of such supervening illegality will in general be to frustrate the contract, unless it is an event for which provision has been made in the contract.[36]

Where a contract is void for illegality, or after the time when further performance of a valid contract becomes illegal, nothing done under it can found any rights; instalments paid under it are irrecoverable and work done under it can found no claim for payment. In general, the test as to whether a demand connected with an illegal transaction is capable of being enforced is whether the plaintiff requires to set up and rely upon such transaction in order to establish his case.

This rule flows from the principles laid down by Fry L.J. in *Kearley v. Thomson* (1890) [37]:

" As a general rule where the plaintiff cannot get at the money which he seeks to recover without showing the illegal contract, he cannot succeed. In such a case the usual rule is *potior est conditio defendentis.*"

[31] *Cf. Townsends Ltd.* v. *Cinema News* [1959] 1 W.L.R. 119, *infra.*
[32] See the cases illustrated *infra.* See also *ante*, Chap. 1, p. 56.
[33] See clause 4 (1) of the 1963 R.I.B.A. standard form, and clause 26 of the 1955 I.C.E. standard form.
[34] See the R.I.B.A. forms, clause 4; I.C.E. Conditions, clause 26.
[35] See *ante*, Chap. 2, p. 143, *supra*, Section 1 (2), pp. 293–294.
[36] *Cf. Metropolitan Water Board* v. *Dick, Kerr & Co. Ltd.* [1918] A.C. 119, illustrated at p. 357, *ante.*
[37] 24 Q.B.D. 742.

Thus, where the plaintiff's goods are being detained by the defendant without any claim of right, the plaintiff's right to the goods will be enforced notwithstanding that they originally came into the defendant's possession as a result of an illegal hiring agreement,[38] since the plaintiff need only allege his ownership and the wrongful detention in order to found his claim.

It is no ground for resisting the application of the general rule that the defendant is gaining an unfair advantage. In *Holman* v. *Johnson* (1775) [39] Lord Mansfield said:

" The objection that a contract is immoral or illegal as between plaintiff and defendant sounds at all times very ill in the mouth of the defendant. It is not for his sake, however, that the objection is ever allowed; but it is founded in general principles of policy which the defendant has the advantage of, contrary to the real justice, as between him and the plaintiff by accident, if I may so say. The principle of public policy is this: *Ex dolo malo non oritur actio*. No court will lend its aid to a man who founds his cause of action upon an immoral or illegal act."

Thus a builder cannot recover the value of work done in excess of the limit permitted by licences issued under Defence Regulations.[40] A " licence " will generally be construed as a written licence, but the question whether a licence granted retrospectively is valid is a matter of the construction of the particular regulation,[41] as is the question of circumstances in which work done in excess of the amount of the licence can be covered by the licence-free limit.[42] It has been held that architects' fees were not included in the " cost " of the work for the purpose of Regulation 56A of the Defence (General) Regulations 1939,[43] and that the person at whose expense the work is carried out need not be named in the licence.[44] Where legal and illegal work has been done, a building owner who has paid instalments generally under the contract and has not consented to their appropriation by the builder to illegal

[38] *Bowmakers Ltd.* v. *Barnet Instruments Ltd.* [1945] 1 K.B. 65 (C.A.).
[39] (1775) 1 Cowp. 341 at p. 343.
[40] *Brightman & Co. Ltd.* v. *Tate* [1919] 1 K.B. 463; *Bostel Bros.* v. *Hurlock* [1949] 1 K.B. 74.
[41] See *Jackson Stansfield & Sons* v. *Butterworth* [1948] 2 All E.R. 558; *Howell* v. *Falmouth Boat Co.* [1951] A.C. 837.
[42] *J. Dennis & Co. Ltd.* v. *Munn* [1949] 2 K.B. 332; *Muir* v. *James* [1953] 1 Q.B. 454; *Brewer St. Investments Ltd.* v. *Barclays Woollen Co. Ltd.* [1954] 1 Q.B. 428.
[43] *Young* v. *Buckles* [1952] 1 K.B. 220.
[44] *Woolfe* v. *Wexler* [1951] 2 K.B. 154.

work is entitled to appropriate to the cost of the legal work instalments paid before any licence had been granted.[45]

In an action to recover damages for refusal by the defendant to accept goods sold to him, it is immaterial that the plaintiff was induced by a misrepresentation of the defendant to believe that the transaction was lawful, whereas it was in fact unlawful,[46] but if the misrepresentation were fraudulent, the plaintiff would be entitled to recover damages for fraud. It also appears that if the representation amounts to a warranty which is not fulfilled, the plaintiff, provided he had not been culpably negligent in not discovering the illegality, could recover damages for breach of the warranty which induced him to do the illegal acts.[47] Further, lack of reasonable grounds for belief in the truth of an innocent misrepresentation will now give a right to damages under section 2 of the Misrepresentation Act 1967.[48]

If the plaintiff's case discloses that the transaction on which his claim is based is illegal, the court cannot ignore the illegality even if the point is not raised by the defendant,[49] but if the transaction is not prima facie illegal, then the court will not entertain any question of illegality unless it is properly raised in the pleadings.[50]

ILLUSTRATIONS

(1) The Act 17 Geo. 3, c. 42 (now repealed by 19 & 20 Vict. c. 64), required bricks for sale to be of certain dimensions, and imposed a penalty for the breach of that regulation to protect the buyer against the fraud of the seller. It was held that the seller could not recover the value of bricks sold under the statutory size: *Law* v. *Hodson* (1809).[51]

(2) A tenant of a house employed S. to rebuild a party wall, without reference to the Fires Prevention (Metropolis) Act 1774. *Held*, that the builder was entitled to payment without observing the requisites prescribed by the Act for obtaining payment: *Stuart* v. *Smith* (1816).[52]

(3) It is unlawful to lease a building in a manner forbidden by a Building Act: *Gas Light and Coke Co.* v. *Turner* (1840).[53]

(4) A contract to erect a wooden structure contravening the provisions of the Metropolitan Building Act, 1855, was illegal, and the builder could not enforce it: *Stevens* v. *Gourley* (1859).[54]

[45] *A. Smith & Son (Bognor Regis) Ltd.* v. *Walker* [1952] 2 Q.B. 319.
[46] *Re Mahmoud and Ispahani* [1921] 2 K.B. 716.
[47] *Strongman (1945) Ltd.* v. *Sincock* [1955] 2 Q.B. 525, *infra*.
[48] *Ante*, Chap. 1, pp. 38 *et seq*.
[49] *Gedge* v. *Royal Exchange Assurance Corporation* [1900] 2 Q.B. 214.
[50] *North Western Salt Co. Ltd.* v. *Electrolytic Alkali Co. Ltd.* [1914] A.C. 461.
[51] 11 East 300.   [52] 7 Taunt. 158.
[53] 6 Bing.N.C. 324 (Ex.Ch.).   [54] 7 C.B.(N.S.) 99.

(5) A contract by a surveyor of highways to perform work or supply materials in violation of the Highway Act 1835, s. 46, is unlawful, and the justices have no power even to allow payment under it: *Barton* v. *Piggott* (1874).[55]

(6) The plaintiffs contracted to do certain work for the defendants. A licence was necessary under the Defence of the Realm Regulations, and was obtained for work not exceeding £1,350. The plaintiffs did work of the value of £2,671 and had been paid £1,500. *Held*, that they could not recover the balance: *Brightman & Co. Ltd.* v. *Tate* (1919).[56]

(7) B. did work for H. to an amount of £98 in excess of the limit of cost prescribed by two building licences. *Held*, that work done in excess of the cost prescribed by a building licence issued under the relevant Defence Regulation was work done without a licence and thereby prima facie unlawful. As B. could not establish any of the defences set out in the Regulation which would entitle him to be acquitted, he could not recover the amount of £98.

Held, further, that if the cost of work for which a licence is issued includes the cost of providing and fixing a given article, it is not permissible to disregard the cost of the article: *Bostel Bros.* v. *Hurlock* (1949).[57]

(8) Before any licence had been granted S. carried out, under a contract with W. providing for demolition and construction, certain demolition work for which a licence was required under Defence Regulations, and W. paid two instalments. The receipts but not the payments referred in terms to the unlicensed work. Later licences for construction work were granted. *Held*, in an action for the balance due in respect of both legal and illegal work, W. had paid the first two instalments generally under the contract and had not consented to their appropriation to the illegal work and he was therefore entitled to appropriate them to the lawful work done under the contract: *A. Smith & Son (Bognor Regis) Ltd.* v. *Walker* (1952).[58]

(9) The defendant, an architect-owner, contracted with the plaintiff builders for work at his premises and promised orally that he would obtain all the licences necessary under Defence Regulations. He did not do so and work considerably in excess of the licensed amount was carried out.

Held, (i) the builders could not recover the balance under the contract, since the doing of the relevant work was illegal;

    (ii) the architect's promise amounted to a collateral warranty that he would obtain a supplementary licence or stop the work, if he could not obtain it;

    (iii) that in the absence of culpable negligence on the part of the builders in relation to a supplementary licence a civil action for damages for breach of warranty would lie;

[55] L.R. 10 Q.B. 86.
[56] [1919] 1 K.B. 463.
[57] [1949] 1 K.B. 74.
[58] [1952] 2 Q.B. 319.

(iv) the builders had not been culpably negligent in relying upon the architect to get a supplementary licence, since it was admitted to be the universal practice for the architect to obtain the necessary licences: *Strongman (1945) Ltd.* v. *Sincock* (1955).[59]

(10) By-laws forbad the construction of a water-closet entered from a room used for human habitation, unless used exclusively with a bedroom or dressing-room, and also required the service of notices with reference to such work before its commencement. A builder constructed two bathrooms containing toilets in accordance with the design of an architect. At the time of the contract the plans showed the adjoining rooms as bedrooms or dressing-rooms, and not till the work was far advanced was the builder in a position to know that the work would in fact infringe the by-law. The architect had informed the builder in correspondence that he (the architect) would be responsible for serving all necessary notices.[60] The contract was in the then standard R.I.B.A. form, by clause 3 of which the builder expressly undertook to comply with all by-laws and before making any variations necessitated thereby to apply to the architect for instructions. After the work was finished the architect served a notice out of time on the local authority, who then condemned the work in the bathrooms, but allowed it to remain unaltered on the undertaking of the building owner to cure the defects, when his wife gave up occupation, by erecting a partition within the bathroom. *Held*, by the Court of Appeal, (1) that the contract was on its face a lawful one, and that as the local authority had allowed the works to remain it could not be said that, at the date of their compromise with the owner, the work was illegal work, and consequently the builder could recover the price of the work, but (2) that the owner was entitled to recover from the builder as damages for breach of clause 3 the cost of rebuilding the bathroom so as to conform with the by-laws notwithstanding the practice in building operations for the architect to see that work complied with the by-laws [61]: *Townsends Ltd.* v. *Cinema News* (1959).[62]

(11) An error in the contract design of a building meant that it contravened the by-laws. The building contract in terms required compliance with the by-laws. The building collapsed during construction, and the employer sued the builders and his engineering consultant for breach of their contracts. *Held*, by the Ontario Court of Appeal, since the work could have been altered under the terms of the contract so as to comply with the by-law, and since there was no intention to violate the by-law and the illegality was unknown to the employers, the contracts were not illegal. *Held* also, bondsmen with the drawings annexed to their bond were also liable: *One Hundred Simcoe Street* v. *Frank Burger Contractors Ltd.* (1968).[63]

---

[59] [1955] 2 Q.B. 525.
[60] This fact *ex rel.* D. H. Gardam, Q.C.
[61] For the finding as between builder and architect, see *ante*, Chap. 2, p. 143. For the practice, see *supra*, Section 1 (2), pp. 293–294 and *ante*, Chap. 2, p. 143.
[62] [1959] 1 W.L.R. 119.
[63] [1968] 1 Ont.L.R. 452 (Canada).

(6) Limitation of Actions

Though not strictly a form of discharge from the obligation to perform a contractual obligation, it is proposed to discuss at this point the principle of limitation of actions, whereby the right to a legal remedy, such as a claim for money due under a contract or for damages for its breach, is extinguished by the passage of time. The law on this subject is governed in England by section 2 of the Limitation Act 1939, which provides that the right to bring an action founded on a simple contract is extinguished six years after the date on which *the cause of action* [63a] accrued, and in the case of contracts under seal, twelve years. An action will be in time if the writ is issued (not necessarily served), or if notice of arbitration is given, within the relevant period.

For this reason alone, it is in the interest of the employer that all building and engineering contracts should be under seal, since this will keep alive his right to sue for undiscovered defects in the work for the longer period. [64]

Either party to a contract who has delayed bringing an action until a critical time will therefore search for the latest possible date upon which he can establish that the breach of contract occurred. This may not always be easy to determine. In the case of payment by the employer, the date on which payment is due is usually fairly precisely defined by the contract. In the case of breaches of a continuing nature, the latest date of the breach can be taken—for instance it is suggested that a contractor alleging late instructions by the employer can rely upon the last moment of time before the instructions were finally supplied, though the contrary is undoubtedly very arguable. Equally, an employer alleging defective work can rely upon the latest possible breach—namely, the express obligation to complete the works in accordance with the contract—which, in most cases, depending on the language of the contract, will be on practical or substantial completion at the time that the employer reoccupies the site, since under most defects clauses [65] a contractor is only liable after this date to put right free of charge defects which are due to breach of contract, which shows that there is no intention to prolong the basic obligation to complete beyond the date. But in the quite separate case of a defect which is required to be put right

---

[63a] Not the damage, which might well be a juster rule. See *infra*, p. 370.

[64] Unless he has already forfeited the right under some express provision in the contract, such as clause 30 (7) of the 1963 R.I.B.A. standard forms.

[65] As *e.g.* in the R.I.B.A. forms and I.C.E. Conditions.

within the defects or maintenance period (usually, under the terms of most contracts, a defect which " appears " within the period [66]) then the expiry of the maintenance period will be the relevant date or, more correctly, in modern contracts, within a reasonable time of being called on to remedy the defects by the architect at the end of the period.   Indeed, in such cases it would seem that, depending on the wording, if the architect or engineer did not notice the defect and act under the defects clause, the employer will be left with the " substantial completion " date from which the breach will run, since the contractor's obligation is usually only to remedy defects of which he is notified.   On the other hand " maintenance and uphold-ing " clauses in the more archaic form inherited from leases,[67] which require reinstatement of defects independent of fault, may have the effect of postponing the completion obligation till the end of the maintenance period, which will then be the last date on which the cause of action could accrue.   It is true that in the Canadian case of *McBride* v. *Vasher* (1951),[68] the Ontario Court of Appeal held that, by virtue of the obligation to complete, the breach, in the case of defect-ive work, arises on assumption of possession of the premises as re-gards defects discoverable on inspection, but in respect of matters not then discoverable only when the defect was discovered, but this latter ruling appears to have been a decision under the law of limitation applicable to Ontario [69] and does not accord with the law of England when a date later than that of accrual of the cause of action can only be relied on if there has been fraudulent concealment of the cause of action.[70]   It appears, however, that where no architect is involved and a builder departs from the drawings or specification without informing the employer, the Courts in England will not be slow to find fraudulent concealment.[71]   (The adjective in this context has been held not to be synonymous with the meaning of the word " fraudulent " in other branches of the law.[72])   It is not necessary that the fraudulent concealment should be subsequent to the right of action, and the manner of the breach may itself amount to fraudu-

---

[66] See *post*, Chap. 6, pp. 388–389.
[67] See Chap. 6, *post*, pp. 388 *et seq.*
[68] 2 D.L.R. (2d) 274.
[69] Limitation Act R.S.O. 1937 C. 118.
[70] Limitation Act 1939, s. 26.
[71] See *e.g. Clark* v. *Woor* [1965] 1 W.L.R. 650.
[72] See *Beaman* v. *A.R.T.S. Ltd.* [1949] 1 K.B. 550.

lent concealment [73]—clearly an important factor in cases of defective work done by a contractor.

A builder undertook to construct a bungalow and garage without an architect to advise the owner. The materials and workmanship were to be the best of their respective kinds, and the specification provided: " facing bricks to be multi-coloured Dorking." At the date of the contract the builder knew there were delays in deliveries of Dorkings, and he ordered " best Ockleys " from his suppliers without telling the owners. The builder had drawn up the specification, and knew there would be no supervision, the drawings having been produced in his spare time by the person introducing the builder to the employer. Some eight years after completion the bricks began to flake and it was then discovered that they were Ockleys, and that between 20 and 25 per cent. of them were seconds or rejects. The builder was an experienced bricklayer and knew that the bricks were not good but bad Ockleys. *Held*, by Lawton J., the building owner could not have discovered the breach with reasonable diligence before 1961 and, following *Beaman* v. *A.R.T.S. Ltd.*,[72] in all the circumstances the cause of action had been concealed by fraud within section 26 (1) of the Limitation Act 1939: *Clark* v. *Woor* (1965).[74]

[Note: Though from the point of view of giving a liberal effect to clause 26 *Clark's* and *Beaman's* cases are to be welcomed, it must be admitted that they involve violence to the language of the section.]

By an historical anomaly, in the tort of negligence the cause of action does not arise until there has been damage, and consequently it can be of material benefit to a plaintiff to rely on this cause of action rather than breach of contract if the original breach of duty went undetected.[75] This cannot avail parties to building or engineering contracts, or to the contracts between architects and engineers and their employers, since their only relationship is one of contract,[76] but it may become relevant if one or other of the parties to the employer, contractor and architect or engineer relationship is able to sue the other in tort within the principle of the case of *Hedley Byrne* v. *Heller* (1964).[77]

In the case of architects and engineers employed to design and supervise a contract, great difficulty is likely to be experienced on any particular facts in deciding whether these duties are of a con tinuing character, and if so at what stage the last breach occurs.

---

[73] *Ibid.*
[74] [1965] 1 W.L.R. 650.
[75] See the attempt to invoke tortious liability for this reason in the case of architect's negligence, *ante*, Chap. 2, p. 123. Contrast Halsbury's *Laws*, Vol. 24, p. 223.
[76] See *ante*, Chap. 2, p. 123.
[77] *Ante*, Chap. 1, pp. 51–53.

Section 4.　Specific Performance

(1) Generally

Specific performance is in essence an order by the court requiring a party to carry out a legally binding contractual obligation. The remedy of specific performance is only permitted by the courts in the comparatively rare cases where damages will not be an adequate recompense to a wronged party. The source of this remedy, and the vast majority of the examples of its application, are to be found in the field of sale of land, where a vendor in breach of his obligations can be compelled to convey the land to the purchaser. The ultimate sanction for the remedy is committal for contempt. There are very few instances of the remedy being granted to a party in a situation similar to a building or engineering contract,[78] as opposed to building leases.[78a]

This is because the court does not normally grant decrees of specific performance in the case of contracts that involve personal services, trust, or skill, or in cases where it would not be able adequately to supervise performance, if it should order it.

" Now, it is settled that, as a general rule, the court will not compel the building of houses." [79]

Nor will the court compel the building of ships.[80]

ILLUSTRATIONS

(1) A railway company agreed that a firm of contractors should work the line and keep the engines and rolling stock in repair for a certain remuneration. *Held*, that no decree of specific performance of the agreement could be granted, nor its breach be restrained by injunction: *Johnson* v. *Shrewsbury and Birmingham Railway* (1853).[81]

(2) W. agreed to construct a railway in accordance with a specification to be prepared by the company's engineer, and to give a bond for due performance. W. refused to carry out the agreement. The railway claimed specific performance of the contract and execution of the bond. *Held*, that the contract was of such a nature that the court could not, consistently with public convenience, decree specific performance, and that the execution of the bond would be a piecemeal performance of the contract which the court would not decree: *South Wales Railway* v. *Wythes* (1854).[82]

---

[78] See the further discussion of this subject, *post*, Chap. 13, Section 3, pp. 712 *et seq*.
[78a] As to which see *infra*, pp. 374 *et seq*.
[79] *Per* Sir J. Mellish L.J. in *Wilkinson* v. *Clements* (1872) L.R. 8 Ch. 96.
[80] *Merchants' Trading Co.* v. *Banner* (1871) L.R. 12 Eq. 18.
[81] 22 L.J.Ch. 921.
[82] 24 L.J.Ch. 87.

(3) The directors of a railway company entered into a written agreement to give the plaintiff " a contract for the construction of the line for the sum of £55,000, subject to a specification of the works on the line included in the said sum, to be agreed upon between the plaintiff and the engineer of the company, in case of dispute the matter to be referred to an arbitrator." On the faith of this the plaintiff entered into subsidiary contracts for the supply of materials, etc. The company, however, delayed the commencement of their works and then gave the contract to J. The plaintiff sued for specific performance of the company's agreement to employ him as contractor. *Held,* on demurrer, that the agreement was of such a nature that specific performance of it could not be decreed: *Greenhill* v. *Isle of Wight Railway* (1871).[83]

(4) A preliminary building agreement was entered into, whereby S. agreed to let plots to W., who was to build on them. S. was to advance 75 per cent. of the actual cost of each house as soon as the houses were roofed in. *Held,* specific performance could not be decreed: *Wood* v. *Silcock* (1884).[84]

(5) By an agreement S. provided the land, and a company contracted to complete a road thereon to the satisfaction of the public authority according to a plan and specification, and to do everything necessary in order that the road might be declared by such authority a public highway. The road was made substantially according to the plan and specification, but the authority refused to declare it a public highway or to take it over, on the ground that they were not entitled to do so until it was flagged and lighted. The specification provided for gravel paths, and did not provide for lighting at all. S. brought an action claiming specific performance of the agreement, and damages. *Held,* that the court could not decree specific performance of the agreement, the specification being what it was, and, as no damage was proved by S., the action was dismissed with costs: *Saunders* v. *Brading Harbour Improvement Co.* (1885).[85]

In the case, however, of *Moseley* v. *Virgin* (1796),[86] Loughborough L.C. said:

" If the transaction and agreement is in its nature defined, perhaps there would not be much difficulty to decree specific performance; but if it is loose and undefined, and it is not expressed distinctly what the building is, so that the court could describe it as a subject for the report of the master, the jurisdiction could not apply."

In *Brace* v. *Wehnert* (1856),[87] Romilly M.R. seemed to be of the like opinion, although in that case no decree was granted because the court had no means of ascertaining the plan according to which

83 23 L.T. 885.
84 50 L.T. 251.
85 [1885] W.N. 36.
86 3 Ves. 184.
87 25 Beav. 348; 27 L.J.Ch. 572.

the house was agreed to be built. In the case of *Hepburn* v. *Leather* (1884) [88] specific performance of a contract to build a wall was decreed. Further discussion of this subject will be found *post*, Chapter 13, Section 3.[89]

But an exception to the rule is undoubtedly recognised in cases (somewhat similar to a building lease) where the plaintiff has parted with land to the defendant under a contract, whereby the defendant's obligation to build upon it arises. In the case of contracts for building and engineering work upon the employer's own property, the employer can, upon a breach of the contract, himself complete, and recover damages: whereas if the owner has parted with possession of the land, it may be impossible for him to do the work himself, or be compensated in damages, or for the damages to be ascertained.[90]

ILLUSTRATIONS

(1) An agreement was entered into between the railway company and G., part of whose land had been taken by the company, whereby G. undertook to withdraw a petition to Parliament against the company's Bill, and the company undertook to construct, on G.'s land, a siding of specified length for his use. *Held*, that this agreement could be specifically enforced: *Greene* v. *West Cheshire Railway* (1871).[91]

(2) An urban sanitary authority, in pursuance of a scheme of street improvement, sold to E. land abutting on a street, and E. agreed to erect buildings thereon within a certain time. Subsequently, in consideration of further time, E. bound himself to erect certain special buildings. *Held*, that this case came within the exception to the general rule, and specific performance of the building contract would be decreed: *Wolverhampton Corporation* v. *Emmons* (1901).[92]

(3) D. sold certain land to C. for building development and covenanted to make certain roads and lay certain sewers, drains and mains on land retained by him, which he failed to do. It was argued that, as D. had not obtained possession of the land retained by virtue of the contract of sale, but was in possession of that land under his own title, he could not be ordered to perform his obligation. *Held*, that in the circumstances an order for specific performance constituted the only adequate remedy, and should be granted: *Carpenters Estates Ltd.* v. *Davies* (1940).[93]

In all cases where specific performance is desired the contract must be quite definite and clear as to what is to be performed.

[88] 50 L.T. 660.
[89] See pp. 712 *et seq.*
[90] *Wolverhampton Corporation* v. *Emmons* [1901] 1 Q.B. 515, *infra*; *Carpenters Estates Ltd.* v. *Davies* [1940] Ch. 160, 162, *infra*.
[91] L.R. 13 Eq. 44.
[92] [1901] 1 Q.B. 515 (C.A.).
[93] [1940] Ch. 160.

ILLUSTRATIONS

(1) The defendant covenanted in a lease to pull down and rebuild the premises, and to do for that purpose such work as the landlord's surveyor should direct and approve to the value of £600. This covenant was not performed, and the plaintiff sought a decree of specific performance. *Held*, that the case was distinguishable from *Wolverhampton Corporation* v. *Emmons, supra*, because here there were no agreed plans, and that the covenant was not sufficiently specific for the decree to be granted: *Rushbrook* v. *O'Sullivan* (1908).[94]

(2) P. agreed in writing with O. that he would build certain houses on certain land in consideration of O. taking a transfer of the unexpired term of a lease thereof at a certain rent. It was further agreed that O.'s wishes should be consulted in building, and that a formal contract should be drawn up by a named solicitor. This contract was never drawn up, but possession was given and P. altered the buildings at O.'s request. *Held*, that specific performance could be decreed, and that the court could have regard to the conduct of the parties in dealing with the property in considering whether the agreement was sufficiently clear in intention: *Oxford* v. *Provand* (1868).[95]

(3) A municipal corporation agreed to let to C., for a term of years, land to be stumped out by a committee and himself at his expense. The corporation did not stump out the land, and C. did so himself, took possession, erected a concrete terrace in the manner referred to in the minutes of agreement, and paid rent. *Held*, that C. so acted with the acquiescence of the corporation, and was entitled to a decree of specific performance. The court took into consideration what had been done in coming to a conclusion as to whether the agreement was sufficiently certain in intent: *Crook* v. *Corporation of Seaford* (1870).[96]

(4) Brick manufacturers excavated claypits, and as a result slips occurred which were damaging adjoining land. A mandatory injunction was granted " that defendants do take all necessary steps to restore the support to plaintiff's land ": *Morris* v. *Redland Bricks* (1967).[97]

(2) Decrees in the Case of Agreements for Building Leases

In the ordinary case of a building lease, where a person agrees to take a lease of land and erect premises thereon, a decree of specific performance will issue.

ILLUSTRATIONS

(1) The Corporation of London agreed to grant a lease of premises to the defendant when he should have rebuilt the house thereon to

[94] [1908] 1 Ir.R. 232; and see *Waring & Gillow Ltd.* v. *Thompson* (1912) 29 T.L.R. 154; *Stimson* v. *Gray* [1929] 1 Ch. 629.
[95] L.R. 2 P.C. 135.
[96] L.R. 10 Eq. 678.
[97] [1967] 1 W.L.R. 967. See the further discussion of the whole subject, *post*, Chap. 13, Section 3, pp. 712 *et seq.*

the satisfaction of their architect.   The defendant entered into possession, but neither paid rent nor commenced rebuilding.   The corporation sought a decree of specific performance, and the defendant
demurred on the ground that the contract to build to the satisfaction
of a third party could not be specifically enforced.   The corporation
waived the satisfaction requirement, and the demurrer was overruled: *Mayor of London* v. *Southgate* (1869).[98]

(2) R. took a lease of land and covenanted to erect seven houses
thereon.   The minerals were reserved to the owner with power
to destroy the surface.   R. also at the same date acquired a lease of
the minerals from the owner with full surface rights.   The houses
in the street in question were not all of the same size.   M., the landlord,
sought a decree of specific performance of R.'s covenant to build.
Held, that upon the construction of the lease, the covenant was not
destroyed by the power reserved to the mineral owner to destroy
the surface, that damages assessed upon the principle of *Ebbetts* v.
Conquest (1895) [99] would afford no adequate remedy, that the
houses to be erected were sufficiently defined for the purpose, and
that specific performance should be decreed: *Molyneux* v. *Richard*
(1906).[1]

---

[98] 38 L.J.Ch. 141.
[99] [1895] 2 Ch. 377.
 [1] [1906] 1 Ch. 34.

CHAPTER 6

ACCEPTANCE AND DEFECTS

SECTION 1. ACCEPTANCE

(1) Generally

IT has already been seen that where a person undertakes to sell goods or do work for a price, and the obligation is entire, complete performance of the contract is necessary before the right to be paid can arise; and that to prevent the manifest injustice that the rule can cause if a substantial benefit is conferred upon the employer although complete performance has not taken place, the courts have evolved, in the case of contracts for the sale of goods, the theory of acceptance, and in the case of contracts for work and labour, the doctrine of substantial performance.[1]

In the case of sale of goods, acceptance (which can easily be inferred from receipt and use of the goods concerned, or from failure to reject or to give notice of rejection within a reasonable time after delivery) has the same effect as substantial performance, in that the buyer becomes legally liable to pay for the goods, subject to his right to claim damages for any breach of contract which may have occurred. But precisely because, it is submitted, acceptance can only rarely be inferred where work or labour takes place upon the employer's land, since work, whether well or badly done, becomes automatically the property of the employer as soon as the materials have been fixed or attached to the employer's land or buildings,[2] it has been necessary in such cases to evolve the very different basis of substantial performance in order to achieve the desired result. In previous editions of this work acceptance was treated as a doctrine applicable to building contracts, but there are almost no cases which, on analysis, lend support to this view, and ample authority to the contrary, though, as will be seen, certain unusual facts can undoubtedly show acceptance, as where a building owner who could take an alternative course of action chooses instead to make use of the contractor's work.[3] Moreover, it is

---

[1] See *ante*, Chap. 5, pp. 245 *et seq.*
[2] *Infra*, subsection (2); *post*, Chap. 12, Section 1.
[3] See the *Tannenbaum* case, *infra*, p. 379.

difficult to conceive of a situation where acceptance could be reasonably inferred from acts of the employer where there would not also be substantial performance, though again this can in fact happen in an unusual case.[3]   Acceptance is sometimes discussed in the context of building contracts in a sense having still more drastic consequences, since it is frequently contended by contractors that there is some general theory whereby acceptance of the work by the employer has the effect of depriving him altogether of his right to claim damages at some later time for defective or incomplete work.   It is sufficient to say that even in the case of the sale of goods no such rule has ever existed, and that the common law right of the employer to sue for damages for any breach of contract, including the right to recover for defects in the work, can only be lost as a result of some express provision in the contract, or by operation of the doctrines of waiver or estoppel which, it will be remembered, require either consideration, or a clear representation intended to be acted upon and accompanied by an alteration of the other party's position to his detriment.[4]   It will be seldom that facts could arise in practice, it is submitted, which would found such a waiver or estoppel.[5]

(2) Acceptance not Implied by Occupation

In considering what amounts to acceptance there must be borne in mind the difference between a building contract and a contract for the sale of or work done to a chattel.   In the case of goods sold and delivered acceptance can be shown from the retention of the goods; the buyer, if dissatisfied, is bound to reject or give notice of rejection, and, if he does not, he is bound to pay for the goods subject to any claim which he may have for damages for breach of warranty.   Thus, in a contract to manufacture furniture, acceptance can be shown by using the furniture.[6]   It is otherwise when work is done on land.   A building owner does not accept work merely by resuming occupation or continuing in possession of the land on which the work has been carried out.

ILLUSTRATIONS

(1) M. agreed with B. to complete two houses to the satisfaction of B.'s surveyor by January 21, 1856, time being of the essence of the contract, for £240.   On January 26, 1856, M. claimed that the

---

[4] See *ante*, Chap. 1, p. 59; Chap. 2, pp. 153–155, and *infra*, pp. 385–388.
[5] See *infra*, subs. (5), pp. 383–385.
[6] *Hoenig* v. *Isaacs* [1952] 2 All E.R. 176, *ante*, Chap. 5, pp. 245 *et seq.*—where the doctrine of substantial performance is fully discussed.

houses were complete, but the surveyor said they were not and M. never obtained his certificate. B. took possession of the houses and enjoyed the fruits of the work. M. sued for the £240 under the agreement, alternatively on a *quantum meruit* for the labour and goods supplied. *Held*, M. could not recover on either count, not having performed the contract and there being no evidence of a fresh contract to pay for what was done: *Munro* v. *Butt* (1858).[7]

(2) W. entered into a contract to build and seat a church. The architect objected to the materials and workmanship of the pews as they were being put in, but on completion they were occupied. *Held*, that this did not constitute acceptance of the work: *Wood* v. *Stringer* (1890).[8]

Other cases which illustrate the same principle are *Sumpter* v. *Hedges* (1898) [9] and *Whitaker* v. *Dunn* (1887).[10]

In *Munro* v. *Butt* (*supra*) Lord Campbell C.J. said: " Now admitting that in the case of an independent chattel, a piece of furniture for example, to be made under a special contract and some term, which in itself amounted to a condition precedent, being un-performed, if the party for whom it was made had yet accepted it, an action might upon obvious grounds be maintained, either on a special contract with a dispensation of the conditions alleged or on an implied contract to pay for it according to its value; it does not seem to us that there are any grounds from which the same conclusion can possibly follow in respect of a building to be erected or repairs done, or alterations made, to a building on a man's own land, from the mere fact of his taking possession. Indeed, the term, ' taking possession ' is scarcely a correct one. The owner of the land is never out of possession while the work is being done. But, using the term in a popular sense, what is he under the supposed circumstances to do? The contractor leaves an unfinished or ill-constructed building on his land; he cannot without expensive, it may be tedious, litigation compel him to complete it according to the terms of his contract; what has been done may show his inability to complete it properly; the building may be very imperfect, or in-convenient, or the repairs very unsound, yet it may be essential to the owner to occupy the residence, if it be only to pull down and replace all that has been done before. How then does mere posses-sion raise any inference of a waiver of the conditions precedent of the special contract or of the entering into of a new one? If, indeed, the defendant had done anything coupled with taking possession

[7] 8 E. & B. 738.
[8] 20 Ont.Rep. 148 (Canada).
[9] [1898] 1 Q.B. 673, *ante*, Chap. 5, p. 248.
[10] 3 T.L.R. 602, *ante*, Chap. 5, p. 249.

which had prevented the performance of the special contract, as if he had forbidden the surveyor from entering to inspect the work, or if, the failure in complete performance being very slight, the defendant had used any language or done any act from which acquiescence on his part might have been reasonably inferred, the case would have been very different." [11] (The last sentence of the above quotation may suggest a theory of acceptance, but it is clear from the two illustrations given that these would either be a breach of contract by the employer, or the prevention principle might be invoked, in the first case, and there was substantial performance in the second.)

However, in some unusual circumstances acceptance may be inferred where there may be no substantial performance, and may have the same legal consequences.

ILLUSTRATION

A had built a sewer, but no pumping station as agreed, which was to serve both A's and B's land under a contract between A and B. B constructed a pumping main as a temporary measure, and then connected up his own sewers to the one built by A. *Held,* by the Ontario Court of Appeal, while A's conduct might have amounted to a repudiation if accepted, B, by accepting the benefit of A's work, was liable to pay the agreed sum less the cost of the pumping station: *Tannenbaum Meadows Ltd.* v. *Wright Winston Ltd.* (1965).[12]

(3) Acceptance, Payment or Judgment no Bar to Claim for Damages

Even though a building owner may have accepted the work so that a liability to pay the price of it arises,[13] that will not (in the absence of a provision in the contract making the acceptance binding on the employer [14]) prevent the building owner from showing that the work is incomplete or badly done; he may either counterclaim or set off damages in an action by the builder, or he may pay or suffer judgment to be obtained against him for the full price and later bring a separate action for his damages, or he may set up the defects in diminution of the price by way of defence to an action by the builder and later bring a separate action for any special damage which he may suffer by reason of the breaches of contract. The reason why payment of the price for the work in full is no

[11] *Munro* v. *Butt* (1858) 8 E. & B. 738.
[12] 49 D.L.R. (2d) 386 (Canada). Illustrated more fully, *ante,* Chap. 5, p. 252.
[13] In the rare cases where this can occur, see *supra.*
[14] See *infra.*

bar to a subsequent action by the building owner for his damages was well put by Hannen J. in *Davis* v. *Hedges* (1871) [15]: " The hypothesis is, that the plaintiff " (*i.e.* the contractor) " suing for the price is in default. The conditions on which he can bring his action are usually simple and immediate. The warranted chattel has been delivered or the work contracted for has been done, and the right to bring an action for the price, unless there is some stipulation to the contrary, arises. On the other hand the extent to which the breach of warranty or breach of contract may afford a defence is usually uncertain; it may take some time to ascertain to what amount the value of the article or work is diminished by the plaintiff's default. It is unreasonable, therefore, that he should be able to fix the time at which the money value of his default shall be ascertained. In many cases the extent to which the value of the works may be diminished by defects in their execution may be altogether incapable of discovery until some time after the day of payment has arrived."

ILLUSTRATIONS

(1) S. built a ship for M. which was not in accordance with the specification. S. sued M. for the balance of the price and M. set up the breach of contract in diminution of the price. S. recovered a smaller sum than the balance. Later M. sued S. for the special damage arising from the loss of the use of the ship while she was being repaired. S. demurred, setting up an alleged estoppel founded on the former action. *Held*, M. could recover damages: *Mondel* v. *Steel* (1841).[16]

(2) To an action against B for unskilfully erecting a kitchen range in A's house, B pleaded that A ought not to be admitted to allege that B did not use due skill in constructing the range because, after the supposed grievance, B commenced an action against A for work and labour in constructing the range and for the price thereof, and that A pleaded payment of money into court, which B took out of court in full satisfaction. *Held*, that the plea did not amount to an estoppel, and afforded no answer to the action: *Rigg* v. *Burbidge* (1846).[17]

(3) D. employed H. to do certain building work. When the work was completed H. brought an action against D. for the contract price, and recovered the whole amount. D. then brought an action against H. for the improper performance of the work, and for not performing the work in accordance with the specification. *Held*, that although D. might have used the causes of action for which he claimed in reduction of the claim in the former action, yet he was not bound to do so, but might maintain a separate action for them: *Davis* v. *Hedges* (1871).[18]

[15] L.R. 6 Q.B. 687, 690.
[17] 15 L.J.Ex. 309.

[16] 8 M. & W. 858.
[18] L.R. 6 Q.B. 687.

(4) The plaintiff contracted to build a shed for the defendants to be completed to the satisfaction of the defendants' engineer and to be paid 90 per cent. on completion and 10 per cent. six months after completion. The 90 per cent. was paid in February before completion in the anticipation that the work would be complete at the end of the month. Work was still being done in June and was never completed to the satisfaction of the engineer. The plaintiffs refused to do certain remedial work in October and defendants had it done by another contractor. The plaintiff sued for the 10 per cent. It was agreed at the trial that if there was evidence to go to the jury of the plaintiff's right to recover he should recover £84 10s., but that if the court was of opinion that the defendants were entitled to go into the amount of defective work, the verdict should be reduced to £50. *Held*, the payment of 90 per cent. did not create an estoppel, and the defendants might go into the amount of defective work. The plaintiff recovered £50: *Moss* v. *L. & N.W. Railway* (1875).[19]

(5) A shop-owner purchased blinds to be supplied and erected at the front of her shop. When sued for the price, she pleaded that the blinds had been badly erected so that they did not protect the windows from the sun, and were not up to specification in that they had faded. The plaintiff contended that, not having rejected the goods, the defendant was liable for the price. *Held*, this was not a mere contract for the sale of goods, but was for work and labour as well, and acceptance could not be inferred from the mere fact that the blinds had not been returned. Accordingly there was a good defence to the claim for the price: *Sacher* v. *African Canvas & Jute Industries* (1952).[20]

Just as payment of the price in full does not (in the absence of any express stipulation to the contrary) prevent the building owner complaining of defects, nor does payment on account or by instalments on interim certificates issued under the contract. Such certificates are for the benefit of the contractor to enable him to obtain payment on account and are not, unless it is expressly so provided, evidence or conclusive as to the satisfactory performance of the work.

ILLUSTRATION

The plaintiff built an entrance lodge and chapels for the defendants, whose architect, although he frequently complained of the mode of execution, allowed the work to proceed and issued certificates for instalments of the price on account. The architect refused to issue a final certificate until certain work had been taken down and re-executed. The plaintiff sued for the balance of the price and contended that the architect had certified his satisfaction and that to withhold the final certificate was a fraud on the plaintiff. *Held*, there was no evidence that the architect had a corrupt or malicious motive, he had not disqualified himself from refusing a certificate of

[19] 22 W.R. 532.
[20] 1952 (3) S.A. 31 (South Africa).

sufficient performance, and the plaintiff could not recover: *Cooper* v. *Uttoxeter Burial Board* (1865).[21]

Mere lapse of time does not, subject to the Limitation Act 1939 and subject to any express provisions in the contract,[22] debar a building owner from complaining of defective work, although the effect of it may, of course, make it more difficult to prove that any damage which may appear was caused by defective work; but if that is proved, liability must follow.

ILLUSTRATION

M. employed G. to do certain plumbing work. Four years later certain pipes gave way and there was a flood. M. was found liable to her tenant for the damage caused by the flood and sued G. for the amount of damages and costs she had been ordered to pay. It was proved that the cause of the flood was defective work by G. G. pleaded that no tradesman could be expected to guarantee his work four years after. *Held*, M. should recover the amount claimed: *McIntyre* v. *Gallagher* (1883).[23]

Unless the work is to be done to the building owner's approval, and there is evidence that it has been given, his knowledge of defects at the time when the work was done does not prevent him from later complaining of the defects.[24]

(4) Defects where Work is Done to the Approval
of the Employers

In the comparatively rare case where work is to be done to the approval of the building owner (as opposed to some third person, such as his architect), the general rule in building cases is that the covenant to obtain approval overrides any other stipulation describing the work, and once approval has been expressed the building owner is liable for the whole price and is debarred from complaining of defective work, unless there is an arbitration clause in the contract in sufficiently wide terms.[25]

---

[21] 11 L.T. 565. For the effect of interim payments on other claims, see *Royston U.D.C.* v. *Royston Builders Ltd.* (1961) 177 E.G. 589, *ante*, Chap. 1, p. 58, and see also *post*, Chap. 7, pp. 492 *et seq.* For certificates which may be conclusive as to defects, see *infra*, subss. (4) and (5).

[22] See, *e.g. Marsden U.D.C.* v. *Sharp* (1931) 48 T.L.R. 23, illustrated but doubted, *infra* p. 398.

[23] 11 R.(Ct. of Sess.) 64.

[24] See, *e.g. Whitaker* v. *Dunn* (1887) 3 T.L.R. 602, *ante*, Chap. 5, p. 249 and see *ante*, Chap. 1, Section 9, p. 59; Chap. 2, Section 2, pp. 153–155, and subs. (6), *infra*.

[25] See *post*, Chap. 7, pp. 412 *et seq.*, where the subject is much more fully discussed. See in addition *Bruens* v. *Smith*, 1951 (1) S.A. 67, illustrated at pp. 429–430.

ILLUSTRATIONS

(1) Work was agreed to be done using the best materials and also to the satisfaction of the architect and of the employer, and the architect was to certify; and it was provided that, notwithstanding the certificate of the architect, the employer might recover for defects discovered within twelve months. The architect certified, and the employer expressed satisfaction by paying under the certificate; defects were discovered after twelve months; no fraud by the architect was alleged. The employer brought an action against the builder for damages for inferior materials. *Held*, that the employer could not, after certificate given, and expression of satisfaction by himself, sue for defective work after the expiry of the twelve months: *Bateman (Lord)* v. *Thompson* (1875).[26]

(2) A building contract provided that all work should be done to the satisfaction of the building owner, who was satisfied and paid for the work. Later he sought to recover damages for defects. *Held*, this expression of satisfaction freed the builder from all further liability: *Gorfinkel* v. *Januarie* (1954).[27]

(This does not always mean that, conversely, the building owner's approval is a condition precedent. In such a case, even though the building owner may not have expressed his satisfaction, the contractor may be able to recover the price of the work if the building owner ought reasonably to have been satisfied, except where the work is to be done to the taste and convenience of the building owner.[28])

Whether payment by a building owner for work which was to be done to his approval amounts to an expression of that approval must, it is submitted, be a question of fact in each case. Thus payment could hardly be said to show approval of the work in a case where it is insisted upon as a condition for the handing over of the keys of a newly constructed house, or where the payment is merely a payment on account for the convenience of the contractor. But payment following a certificate of satisfaction by the architect has been held to be an expression of satisfaction by the building owner.[29]

(5) Defects where Work is Done to the Approval of a Third Person

In the more usual case where work is agreed to be executed to the approval of a third person, *e.g.* the architect, engineer or surveyor of the building owner, the general rule in building contracts is that the contractor cannot, in the absence of a sufficiently wide

---

[26] Hudson's B.C., 4th ed. Vol. 2, p. 36.
[27] (1) S.A. 88 (South Africa), and see cases cited, *post*, Chap. 7, Approval and Certificates, pp. 416 and 425 *et seq*.
[28] See *post*, Chap. 7, Approval and Certificates, pp. 412 *et seq*.
[29] *Bateman (Lord)* v. *Thompson, supra.*

arbitration clause,[30] recover payment for the works until such approval has been obtained,[30a] unless he can show that the approval is dishonestly withheld. Conversely, if the architect has in fact approved the work in question, no complaint as to defects, whether latent or patent, can usually be made by the building owner, so that from this point of view the effect is the same as the satisfaction of the building owner.[31] Where, however, the third person is not employed by the building owner, such as an independent person like a Lloyd's surveyor or a local authority's building inspector, it is possible that the courts will be less likely to treat the satisfaction or approval, if given, as binding on the employer, but rather as an additional protection for him. This latter qualification is very important, because in builder-developer contracts (*i.e.* where there is no architect) or in " package-deal " contracts, references to local authority approval are frequently inserted in the specification prepared by the builder-developer for the purpose of the contract of sale.[32] One purchaser in Canada even appears to have sought to argue that in these circumstances the local authority might owe him a duty of care.[33]

Building and engineering contracts not infrequently contain express provisions for materials or samples to be submitted for approval before the relevant work is carried out. Usually these provisions relate to materials. In such a case, provided the materials actually used by the contractor conform to the observable characteristics of the sample, or, in a case of simple approval, the ultimate cause of the trouble is not due to some hidden defect, it will not be open to the employer subsequently to contend that the characteristics of the material or sample apparent on inspection do not in fact comply with any other provisions of the contract. For instance, if a specification required timber to be reasonably free from knots, and all timber to be approved by the architect before incorporation in the works, and if the architect approved samples containing knots in no greater numbers than the timber finally used, it would not, it is submitted, be possible later to criticise the timber on that ground, and this apart entirely from any question of waiver or estoppel. In such a case the term for approval is clearly intended

---

[30] But nearly all modern contracts contain such clauses.
[30a] Such approval is usually required to be given in the form of a certificate.
[31] See *post*, Chap. 7, pp. 425 *et seq.*, where this subject, and the possible exceptions to and qualifications upon these rules are fully discussed.
[32] See the important recent case of *Billyack* v. *Leyland* [1968] 1 W.L.R. 471, *post*, Chap. 7, pp. 432–433.
[33] *Neabel* v. *Town of Ingersoll* [1967] O.R. 343 (Canada).

to override any other description of the work or materials, unless there is some express indication to the contrary, and subject always to the possible effect of an arbitration clause.

Bricks for an engineering contract were required to be sound, hard, square, well-burnt bricks free from lime or other extraneous matter, fire cracks or other defects and from an approved yard. The whole of the works were to be done in a thoroughly workmanlike manner with the best materials and to the satisfaction of the engineer. Samples of stock bricks to be used for manholes were approved by the engineer, but underground conditions were unexpectedly wet and the bricks failed to keep out water, and the engineer refused to accept the work. The bricks used did not contain any hidden defect, but were ordinary stock bricks conforming to the sample. There was an applicable arbitration clause. *Held*, by Phillimore J., that the contractor was not in breach of contract, and could not be called on to replace the bricks free of charge: *Adcock's Trustee v. Bridge R.D.C.* (1911).[34]

It is clear, however, that approval will not bind the employer if the defect is a concealed one not apparent on inspection. " I think, therefore, that if the bricks were equal to sample, and to the apparent sample—I do not mean if the sample actually had a number of concealed cracks—the defendants would be bound by the acceptance of that particular sample of brick." [35]   Furthermore, the remarks in *Adcock's* case were made where there was an express description.

(6) Defects which could have been Previously Detected

In the vast majority of contracts power is given to the architect to order the contractor to re-execute defective work or to remove inferior materials during the progress of the works. The power will also be implied, it is submitted, whenever work is expressed to be done under the direction or to the satisfaction of the architect or engineer. (It should be remembered that building contracts, by virtue of the incorporation of the work into the employer's land, are not like other contracts for work and materials, such as a contract to make furniture, where no doubt there is no breach in regard to defective work until delivery. A building owner does not have to stand by, it is submitted, and permit defective work or materials to be incorporated into the fabric of his building.) It has been

[34] 75 J.P. 241.
[35] *Per* Phillimore J., *ibid.*

suggested that where the work has been examined by the architect and not condemned, this power is no longer exercisable, but that the employer in such a case will still be able to rely on a clause requiring the contractor to make good defects which appear within the maintenance period and which result from the work or materials not being in accordance with the contract at his own cost.[36] This view, however, if it means that an architect who does not notice a defect on inspection cannot condemn it at a later stage of construction, is wrong both on principle and (now) on authority, unless what is referred to are facts sufficient to ground an estoppel or waiver.[37] Nor is such a power to order the removal of work intended as a substitute for or to replace the employer's ordinary right to damages for defective work.[38] It should also be remembered that under the scheme of most building and engineering contracts the architect or engineer has to certify practical or substantial completion before the employer enters into occupation. At this stage, too, there is obviously power to withhold the certificate if unremedied defects are present. Finally there is the special power, usually limited to defects which appear within a fixed period after practical completion and which are due to breach of contract, to require defective work to be put right at that stage.[39]

It is frequently sought to be contended on behalf of contractors who have carried out defective work that the employer has waived or is estopped from claiming damages by reason of the fact that the breaches of contract were visible during the course of the architect's or clerk of work's usual visits to the site while supervising the work, but that no disapproval was then expressed. This is tantamount to alleging that the architect or clerk of works has been employed to supervise for the protection of the builder rather than the employer, and indeed, if correct, would mean that an employer would legally be better protected in regard to defective work if he abstained from employing an architect. It is clear, it is submitted, that no estoppel or waiver could arise unless some matter was expressly brought to an architect's attention by the builder and he was expressly asked for and gave his approval. Even in such a case the estoppel would only, it is submitted, operate in relation to an apparent characteristic of the doubtful work or

---

[36] See the remarks of Phillimore J. in *Adcock's Trustee* v. *Bridge R.D.C.*, *supra*, at p. 245.

[37] See *infra*, p. 387.

[38] See *infra*, p. 396, where a similar view expressed in regard to ordinary defects clauses has now been confirmed by the courts.

[39] See *infra*, pp. 388 *et seq.*

materials, and not to some concealed defect of which the architect was unaware at the time of expressing his approval.[40]

" I have already cited [41] from *Clayton* v. *Woodman & Son Ltd.*[42] the general proposition that an architect has no right to instruct a builder how his work is to be done or the safety precautions to be taken. Moreover, in general an architect owes no duty to a builder to tell him promptly during the course of construction, even as regards permanent work, when he is going wrong; he may, if he wishes, leave that to the final stages notwithstanding that the correction of a fault then may be much more costly to the builder than had his error been pointed out earlier; see Hudson (1965) Ninth edition, pages 280–281, and *East Ham Corporation* v. *Bernard Sunley.*" [43]

" It seems to me most unlikely that the parties to the contract contemplated that the builder should be excused for faulty work at an early stage merely because the architect failed to carry out some examination which would have disclosed the defect. Even if the architect . . . was in clear breach of his duty to his client, the building owner, I can see no reason why this should enable the builder to avoid liability for his defective work; the architect owes no duty to the builder. . . . " [44]

" I cannot see why [the builder] should be allowed to escape from the ordinary consequences of his negligence when discovered years later, a consequence which would undoubtedly flow if the building owner had not appointed an architect for his, the building owner's, protection." [45]

" It seems to me unreasonable . . . to let [the contractors] shelter behind the architect's failure to detect faults in the course of his visits during the progress of the work. The architect's duty is to the employers and not to the contractors. . . . Prima facie the contractors should be and remain liable for their own breaches of contract, and should not have a general release from liability in respect of all breaches which the architect should have detected but failed to detect throughout the currency of that contract." [46]

[40] This paragraph in the ninth edition was cited by Mocatta J. in *AMF International Ltd.* v. *Magnet Bowling* [1968] 1 W.L.R. 1028 in the passage next quoted in the text above. See also *infra*, pp. 399–400 for a possible effect on damages, and *post*, Chap. 8, pp. 524–530 and Chap. 9, pp. 582–583 for a further discussion.

[41] For this important passage, see *ante*, Chap. 2, p. 154.

[42] [1962] 1 W.L.R. 585, *ante*, Chap. 1, p. 73.

[43] The *AMF* case, at p. 1053, *per* Mocatta J.

[44] *Per* Lord Upjohn in *East Ham B.C.* v. *Sunley* [1966] A.C. 406.

[45] *Per* Lord Upjohn, *ibid.*   [46] *Per* Lord Pearson, *ibid.*

A contract provided that the engineer might order the removal of suspect work, that the works should be conducted and completed under the superintendence and to the satisfaction of the engineer, that his decision as to the manner in which work was to be executed was to be final and binding, and that he should give a final certificate after the works had been executed and maintained to his satisfaction. The jury found that there was an omission on the part of the employer properly to superintend the work, which led to its being scamped fraudulently. Sureties of the contractors averred that there was a duty of the employer to supervise, and that since it had not been exercised they should be released. *Held,* by the Court of Appeal, the power was in the nature of an option given to the employer whether he should superintend or not. The fact that he did not exercise the option did not relieve the contractors from the obligation to do the work properly. Nor could the final certificate, having been obtained by fraud, release the sureties. *Per* Lord Esher M.R.: " The meaning of the provision was only that the corporation should have a right to observe and see how the work from time to time was being done. If that be the true view, it was merely an option given to the corporation whether they would superintend or not. Therefore . . . the fact that they did not exercise that option did not relieve the contractors from the obligation to do the work properly. . . ." *Kingston-upon-Hull Corporation* v. *Harding* (1892).[47]

SECTION 2. DEFECTS

(1) Types of Defects Clause

The great majority of building and engineering contracts contain a clause which requires the contractor, on being called on to do so, to rectify all defects which may appear during a fixed period after completion of the work and entry into occupation by the employer.[48] This period is usually called the maintenance or defects liability period, and it is usual, as in the case of the standard forms, but not universal, for the contractor to be paid for this work if the defects are not due to breach of contract. It is also usual for the payment provisions of the contract to release one-half of the retention moneys at the beginning of this period and the other half at the end, after the defects have been put right, when the final certificate usually (but not immediately under the post-1963 R.I.B.A. standard forms) is required to be given. Contracts frequently also contain express provisions whereby the employer is entitled to bring another contractor onto the site to do work which the contractor has failed to carry out when called on to do so, or to determine the contract.

---

[47] [1892] 2 Q.B. 494. See also *Jones* v. *Cannock* (1850) 5 Ex. 713, *ante*, p. 321.
[48] *Cf.* clause 15 of the 1963 R.I.B.A. standard form and clause 49 of the 1955 I.C.E. form.

It should be made clear that the word " defects " in this context includes any breach of contract affecting the quality of the work, whether structural on the one hand or merely decorative on the other, and whether due to faulty material or workmanship, or even design, if the latter is part of the contractor's obligation, Indeed, in modern clauses where the contractor is entitled to be paid extra if the defect is not due to breach of contract, the wording gives an indication that design errors of the architect are intended to be covered. But in nearly all the cases the defect, whatever its cause, must be a defect which " appears " within the maintenance period. Defects which " appear " after the period has expired are not within the ambit of the clause. On analysis, the word " defect " in this particular context may often mean the *symptom* rather than the *cause*, which may often be difficult or impossible to establish until work has been demolished, removed or uncovered, or special investigations carried out.[48a]

Despite the similarity of many modern clauses, there are in fact different types of wording which can be used which may have most important consequences, particularly if a form of contract is used in which the contractor's obligation arises independently of any fault on his part, so that he is not entitled to extra payment even though he has not been at fault. Thus wording of this kind may have the result (a) of starting the limitation period for defective work generally (not the special defects obligation) running from a date later than practical or substantial completion, from which it normally runs,[49] or (b) of prolonging the period during which the works remain at the risk of the contractor, which likewise also usually ends at practical or substantial completion.[50] If, as in the modern standard forms, however, the contractor is entitled to extra payment for defects not due to breach of contract by him, the exact form of wording may not be of great importance. But in " absolute " cases the wording may need to be carefully considered. The possible types have been described as, first, that the contractor shall *rectify all defects* appearing within a certain period (the usual modern form); secondly, that he should *repair* the works as necessary during the period; and, thirdly, that he should *maintain and uphold* the works for the period.[51]

[48a] See the case of *Cunliffe* v. *Hampton Wick Local Board*, illustrated *infra*, subsection (2), p. 393.
[49] *Ante*, Chap. 5, p. 272.
[50] *Ante*, Chap. 5, p. 268.
[51] *Roux* v. *Colonial Government*, *infra*.

The precise obligation of the contractor under a defects clause depends upon the construction of the clause in each case and it may be that all three types of liability may be embodied in one clause. An important consideration may be whether the obligation arises only on receipt of notice or instructions from the architect or engineer or whether the obligation is unconditional. Generally, however, a *defects* clause would seem to be less burdensome than a repairing clause because whereas in the former the contractor's liability, even if " absolute," usually only extends to reinstating an actual defect, and the word " defect " hardly seems appropriate to include damage done to the works by some external factor, in the latter the contractor may be called upon to rebuild the structure if it is accidentally destroyed, as by fire or tempest. As stated, under the general law the contractor will usually be under this obligation until the work has been practically or substantially completed and handed over,[52] but a clause of this type may extend the obligation beyond the completion date for the period stated in the clause.

It would seem that a repairing clause imposes upon a contractor much the same obligation as is imposed by a repairing covenant in a lease; that is, he will be obliged to keep the structure in that condition in which it would be found had it been managed by a reasonable owner, having regard to its age and the locality and class of person likely to occupy it at the time when the obligation to repair began.[53] The I.C.E. conditions which adopt the wording of a repair obligation (albeit " non-absolute ") have a " fair wear and tear " exception.[54]

Defects clauses of all kinds seldom make any mention of consequential damage. In the seventh edition of this book it was said that if a party who undertook to keep a structure in repair failed to carry out his obligation, he might be liable in damages for loss of rent or profit during the execution of such repairs by the other party, and *Birch* v. *Clifford* (1891) [55] was cited. That, however, was a case where a tenant had failed to repair during the term, so that after the term expired the landlord had to carry out repairs when he might otherwise have let the building or put it to profitable use. It is submitted that it is a different case where a contractor fails to keep in repair a building which is in the possession of a building owner, because in such a case the building owner would in any

[52] See Chap. 5, *ante*, pp. 268, 272.
[53] *Anstruther-Gough-Calthorpe* v. *McOscar* [1924] 1 K.B. 716.
[54] Clause 49 (2).
[55] 8 T.L.R. 103.

event lose the use of the building while the repairs were carried out, so that in an " absolute " case where the builder was not at fault these consequential expenses would not, it is submitted, be payable —*aliter*, of course, if the defects were due to defective work by the builder, when they would be recoverable as damages for that breach. Further, unlike a lessee in possession, a contractor's obligation to repair will usually be subject to his having notice of the lack of repair.[56]

A maintenance and upholding clause, provided the period during which it is operative is limited, would seem to be much the same as a repairing clause; but, in cases where the period is a lengthy one, whereas the replacement of the whole, once it is entirely worn out, is not part of the obligation under a repairing clause,[57] it would seem that such replacement might be part of the obligation in a maintenance and upholding clause; further, the word " maintenance " may include improvements reasonably necessary for the proper use of the structure maintained.[58]

In all cases, however, the language of the particular clause must be carefully considered in order to determine its exact scope, and its effect on the period of limitation for defective work and on the transfer of the risk from contractor to employer.

ILLUSTRATION

In a contract to construct a dam it was provided that payments should be made on account as the work proceeded, that the balance of the contract sum should be paid to the contractor within twelve months after the date of the final certificate of the chief inspector, and that during this period the contractor should make good at his own cost all omissions and defects that might appear and arise subsequent to the issuing of the final certificate. The final certificate was issued in January 1900, and in March the dam collapsed. After twelve months the contractor sued for the balance. *Held*, there are three distinct classes of undertaking which are commonly entered into with regard to retention money; the first being a repairing clause; the second, a clause that the builder shall rectify all defects appearing within a certain period, and the third, a maintaining and upholding clause. This clause was of the second type, and it not being established that the collapse of the dam was due to any defect or omission on the part of the plaintiff, he was entitled to recover: *Roux* v. *Colonial Government* (1901).[59]

[56] See *infra*, pp. 394–395.
[57] See *per* Atkin L.J. in *Anstruther-Gough-Calthorpe* v. *McOscar, supra.*
[58] *Sevenoaks Ry.* v. *London, Chatham & Dover Ry.* (1879) 11 Ch.D. 625.
[59] 18 Cape of Good Hope (S.C.) Rep. 143.

(2) The Maintenance or Defects Liability Period

The period during which the obligation to make good defects, repair or maintain is to have effect is frequently called " the maintenance period " and sometimes the " defects liability " period, which in some contracts are expressed to run from the time when the architect gives his certificate that the works are completed to his satisfaction.[60]   Since, however, the final certificate may be considerably delayed for various reasons and so unreasonably postpone the maintenance period, it is frequently provided that the architect shall certify " practical " or " substantial " completion for the purpose of starting the maintenance period, and that the certificate of final completion or final certificate shall be given at or shortly after the end of that period.[61]   Nearly all contracts in the United Kingdom are of this kind, and in such cases the certificate which starts the period is not usually regarded as a certificate of the architect's satisfaction with the quality of the work, since the certificate usually requires to be given notwithstanding the presence of minor defects which are not inconsistent with entry by the employer into occupation, and merely records freedom from patent defects.[61a] Certain forms of contract used in Australia and New Zealand, however, treat the completion certificate at the *beginning* of the period as the definitive certificate of satisfaction and in these contracts the final certificate appears to have only a minor role from this point of view.[61b]   A part of the retention fund is normally retained as a security for the performance of the contractor's obligation, but a proportion of the fund will usually be released to the contractor at the start of the period.   If the work is divided into several parts and some parts are completed before the others, but there is no provision for stage completion or provision for only one maintenance period, the period will run from the time when the last part is completed or from the date when the architect or engineer certifies that the whole works are complete or practically complete.   (Other rights, such as liquidated damages for delay, or the required date for the final certificate, may also, of course, depend on the date when the period starts to run.)   The exact words of each contract must, however, be carefully considered.

[60] *Cf.* the unreported case of *Ata Ul Haq* v. *City Council of Nairobi* [1959] P.C. Appeal No. 48, illustrated *infra.*

[61] *Cf.* clauses 15 (1) and 30 (6) of the 1963 R.I.B.A. forms and clauses 60 (2) and 62 (1) of the 1955 I.C.E. form.   [61a] See *ante*, Chap. 5, Section 1 (1), p. 258.

[61b] See *e.g.* the cases of *Stratford (Borough of)* v. *Ashman* [1960] N.Z.L.R. 503 and *Major* v. *Greenfield* [1965] N.Z.L.R. 1035, illustrated *post*, Chap. 7, p. 431, as well as the *Ata Ul Haq* case illustrated *infra.*

ILLUSTRATIONS

(1) In a contract for sewers it was provided that the contractor should maintain and keep in order the works during a period of three months from the completion of the same. One part of the works was completed before the rest and an interim certificate was given in respect of that part. Later the whole was finished and the engineer issued a final certificate showing the balance due to the contractor, which under the contract was to be conclusive evidence of the works being fully completed. Within three months of that certificate a defect appeared in the part which had in fact been completed more than three months before. Also, a stoppage in the sewer was discovered within the three months, but the cause was not found until the sewer had been opened up after three months. *Held*:

> (i) the final certificate was the sole evidence of completion and the three-month period ran from the date of that certificate and the contractor was liable to make good the defect, and

> (ii) the contractor was liable to remove and make good the cause of the stoppage: *Cunliffe* v. *Hampton Wick Local Board* (1893).[62]

(2) A contract provided for retention of a proportion of the price as security for making good defects appearing within two months of completion. The work was to be to the satisfaction of the architect, and payment was to be upon his certificate. The architect certified the final balance due, subject to the making good of certain listed defects. These were remedied and the contractor paid. The employer then sued for damages for certain defects which had been apparent during the carrying out of the work, and others appearing after the two months. *Held*, the certificate was binding except in regard to defects appearing within two months of the certificate, and the employer could not recover: *McCarthy* v. *Visser* (1905).[63]

(3) Clause 7 of the contract provided " when the works have been completely executed according to the provisions of the contract and to the satisfaction of the engineer, the date of such completion shall be certified by him and any such date shall be the commencement " of the period of maintenance. There was an obligation to rectify defects during the maintenance period in the usual form. Completion was certified under this clause as to eleven out of seventeen blocks of buildings (there was power to do so) but the certificate was refused as to the remaining six. After the expiry of the maintenance period the employer brought an action alleging defects in all the blocks. *Held*, by the Privy Council, (*a*) a decision under clause 7 was final and binding and not subject to arbitration [64] and, (*b*) it was in effect a certificate that the works were both in accordance with the contract and to the engineer's satisfaction, (*c*) accordingly the only remaining obligation of the contractor in respect of the eleven blocks was to repair such defects within the maintenance period as he might be called upon to do under the defects clause and, no such defects having appeared or been brought to his attention, he was under

---

[62] 9 T.L.R. 378; Hudson's B.C., 4th ed. Vol. 2, p. 250.
[63] 22 Cape of Good Hope Rep. 122 (South Africa).
[61] See the doubts expressed on this point, *post*, Chap. 7, p. 444.

no further liability and was entitled to the full price of the eleven blocks, but (*d*) no certificate having been given in relation to the remaining blocks, the employer was in those cases entitled to damages: *Ata Ul Haq* v. *City Council of Nairobi* (1959).[65]

In many modern contracts the certificate is open to review by an arbitrator, so that it loses its binding quality,[65a] and the employer would therefore be free to sue for damages notwithstanding that he might have lost the right to recall the contractor to put right defects under the defects clause.[66] This is not so in the case of the R.I.B.A. forms, however, under which the final certificate can bind the employer if he does not issue notice of arbitration before it is given.[67] This is criticised in the employer's interest, *post*, Chapter 7.[68]

(3) Nature of Maintenance or Defects Obligation

It is important to understand the precise nature of the maintenance or defects obligation. It is quite different from the employer's right to damages for defective work, under which he will be able to recover the financial cost of putting right work either by himself or another contractor. It involves essentially the right to call for the physical return to the site of the contractor for a limited period after the employer has resumed occupation. Since maintenance work can usually be carried out much more cheaply by the original contractor than by some outside contractor brought in by the building owner, defects clauses in practice confer substantial advantages on both parties to the contract. So the contractor not only has the obligation but also in most cases, it is submitted, the right to make good at his own cost any defects which appear within the maintenance period. Thus if a building owner who discovers such defects has them made good without giving an opportunity to the contractor to do the making good himself (unless, of course, the contract has come to an end prematurely for some reason, such as rescission or a contractual determination), the building owner may not be able to recover the additional cost of doing the work by an outside contractor, if this was greater than the cost at which the repair could have

---

[65] Unreported [1959] P.C. Appeal No. 48. Doubted, *post*, p. 431.
[65a] See *post*, Chap. 7, Section 4, pp. 435 *et seq.*
[66] See *infra*, pp. 396–397.
[67] See clause 30 (7) of the post-1963 forms, and the decision of the House of Lords on the (1950 Revised) R.I.B.A. forms in *East Ham B.C.* v. *Bernard Sunley Ltd.* [1966] A.C. 406.
[68] See pp. 489–492.

been effected by the original contractor, either because the employer
has, under the rules as to mitigation of damages, acted unreasonably
in so doing, or because the difference in cost will be recoverable by
the contractor as damages for breach of contract. There may be
cases, depending on the wording of the contract, where in such
circumstances the employer might lose his right to recover any part
of the cost from the contractor, but most explicit wording would be
required to bring this result about in a building or engineering
contract, it is submitted.[69] The cases below show the law as between
landlord and tenant.

In the absence of express provision, it would appear reasonable
to imply a term that the contractor should be given notice that the
employer has discovered the defects, and intends to stand upon his
rights and insist upon the defects being remedied in accordance with
the contract, since the employer will, by definition, be in occupation.[70]

ILLUSTRATIONS

(1) A built a bridge underneath the plaintiff's railway pursuant
to powers in a special Act of Parliament obtained for that purpose
which also imposed upon him and his successors in title an obligation to maintain the bridge. The defendants were A's successors
in title. The plaintiffs were in possession of the bridge and did
necessary repairs to it without giving any notice to the defendants
of any want of repair. *Held*, the plaintiffs could not recover the
cost of the repairs: *London & S. W. Railway* v. *Flower* (1875).[71]

(2) A lease contained a covenant by the lessor to keep in repair
the main walls, main timbers and roofs of the premises. *Held*, that
the lessee could not sue for non-repair unless the lessor had received
notice of non-repair: *Makin* v. *Watkinson* (1870).[72]

(3) The plaintiff sued the defendant, her landlord, for breach of
covenant to keep the drains in repair. Neither plaintiff nor defendant
knew of the risk of damage before it occurred but the defendant
had the means of knowing. The plaintiff had repairs done without
giving notice to the defendant and then sought to charge him with the
cost. *Held*, not having given notice of the defect she could not
recover. *Per* Brett M.R. " I doubt whether if the landlord had notice,
aliunde, he would be liable ": *Hugall* v. *McLean* (1884).[73]

What will amount to a sufficient notice will depend on the
facts and circumstances of the case; where it is desired that the
contractor should do a particular piece of work the notice should
specifically state it, but where the complaint is that in general the

---

[69] See *London & S.W. Ry.* v. *Flower, infra.*

[70] The R.I.B.A. forms, of course, provide expressly for notice in the form of a schedule
of defects, and the I.C.E. Conditions for written instructions from the engineer.

[71] (1875) 1 C.P.D. 77.   [72] L.R. 6 Ex. 25.

[73] 53 L.T. 94. (N.B. None of these are building cases, however, and the liability to
damages for defective work will usually remain—see *infra*.)

work has been done in a negligent and inefficient manner a general notice might be sufficient.[74]   Likewise, where the effect of the defect can be seen, but the cause is not known, a general notice may be sufficient as in *Cunliffe* v. *Hampton Wick Local Board*,[75] though it may be that, if the clause is of a " non-absolute " kind, the architect or engineer must obviously decide whether or not the defect is due to breach of contract, because of the financial consequences; and since in such a situation the architect must, it is submitted, be under a duty to supply, and the contractor entitled to demand, instructions as to the work to be done if the defect is due to a design failure, it is submitted that he will also be under a duty to take charge of any necessary work of investigation unless or until he is satisfied that there has been a breach of contract by the contractor.

As already stated *supra*, if the contract provides that the work is to be done to the satisfaction of the architect, and in particular if that satisfaction is required to be recorded in a certificate such as a final certificate or certificate of final completion, an employer will not usually be permitted to complain of defective work, once the satisfaction or certificate has been recorded, unless there is an arbitration clause wide enough in scope to permit the matter to be reopened.[76]

Where, however, there is no provision that satisfaction or a certificate shall be conclusive, or where the arbitration clause enables the courts or an arbitrator to deal with the matter on its merits, it may become necessary to decide whether the defects clause is or is not intended as a substitute for the common law right to damages for defective work. In the eighth and ninth editions of this book it was submitted that, where the contract does not provide to the contrary, although the building owner cannot insist upon the contractor making good defects which may appear after the period expires, there is nothing to prevent him bringing an action for damages in respect of defects which arise from breaches of contract by the contractor, and this view has now received the support of modern authority.[77]   It is always a question of construction whether the rights under the maintenance clause are intended to supplant the right to damages at common law altogether. In the absence of express provision the remedies under these clauses are in addition

---

[74] *Pauling* v. *Dover Corporation* (1855) 10 Ex. 753, *per* Parke B.
[75] (1893) 9 T.L.R. 378; Hudson's B.C., 4th ed. Vol. 2, p. 250, illustrated *supra*, p. 393.
[76] See *post*, Chap. 7, Sections 3 and 4.
[77] *Hancock* v. *Brazier* (*Anerley*) *Ltd*. [1966] 2 All E.R. 901 illustrated, *infra* (*per* Diplock L.J.) and at p. 904 (*per* Denning M.R.).

to and not in substitution for the common law rights,[78] and even where the defects have appeared within the period the employer may sue for damages rather than call on the contractor to do the work, subject, in that event, to the employer's damages being limited, for the reasons stated *supra*, to the cost to the contractor of doing the work at that time, rather than the possibly greater cost of bringing in another contractor either then or at a later date.

Although, therefore, a defects liability clause by itself will not usually cut down the normal period of limitation in which the employer may complain of defective work, express terms of the contract providing for the approval of a third person without a sufficiently wide arbitration clause may have this effect, though it is difficult to see why any building or engineering contract drafted in the employer's reasonable interest should contain such a clause if it is not balanced by a corresponding " condition precedent " obligation on the contractor to obtain the certificate (as to which see *post*, Chapter 7). Furthermore, in the case of " developer " contracts (or houses in the course of erection as they are usually termed) where the contracts are frequently couched in the terms of a contract for the sale of land with a defects clause grafted onto it, the rule of " *caviat emptor*," if the house is completed at the time of the sale, or provisions for satisfaction or approval without an arbitration clause, may result in the defects clause being the only and exclusive right available to the purchaser.[78a]

ILLUSTRATIONS

(1) A contract contained a defects clause in the usual form to operate during a maintenance period of four months from completion of the work. The contractor was entitled to be paid the balance due to him four months after the architect's certificate in writing that the works had been completed in accordance with the contract, and the certificate of the final balance due was to be conclusive evidence of the works being duly completed. It was, however, further provided that despite any such certificate the contractor should remain liable for four years after completion for any " fraud, default or wilful deviation " from the contract. Defects appeared within the four years due to slovenly workmanship by the contractor's workmen but not to deliberate "scamping" of the work. *Held*, in the face of the final certificate the contractor was not liable, because it must be shown that deliberate breaches of contract had been

---

[78] See the remarks of Stirling L.J. in *Robins* v. *Goddard* [1905] 1 K.B., at pp. 302 and 303. See also *Johns & Son* v. *Webster & Tonks* [1916] N.Z.L.R. 1020, illustrated *post*, p. 440. See also the cases illustrated *post*, pp. 426–431.

[78a] For the nature of the builder-developer's obligations, see *ante*, Chap. 5, Section 1 (2) (a), pp. 289–290. In addition to the cases below, see *post*, Chap. 9, pp. 580–581.

committed with a view to benefiting the contractor or saving his pocket if the effect of the certificate was to be avoided: *London School Board* v. *Johnson* (1891).[79]

(2) A contract for making roads provided " Should it at any time subsequent to the termination of the period of maintenance up to but not exceeding a period of five years from the date of completion of the works be discovered that the terms of this specification have been violated by the execution of bad, insufficient or inaccurate work, the council shall be at liberty to make good such work and to recover the cost thereof from the contractor." Due to bad concrete some defects were discovered within five years and others after the expiration of five years. *Held*, the plaintiffs could only recover in respect of defects discovered within five years: *Marsden U.D.C* v. *Sharp* (1931).[80]

[Note: This case has always seemed out of line with the general principle and has now (it is respectfully submitted, rightly) been doubted and criticised to the point of extinction by Diplock L.J. in *Hancock's* case, *infra*.[81]]

(3) Clause 5 of the contract for the sale of a bungalow in the course of erection provided that the purchase should be completed on or before the fourteenth day after notification by the vendor of completion of the work in accordance with the contract. By clause 11 the vendors undertook to erect and complete the bungalow by a certain date in a good and workmanlike manner in accordance with plans and a specification, all the work being carried out to the reasonable satisfaction of the purchaser and her surveyor, and if within fourteen days of the notice under clause 5 she or her surveyor were not reasonably satisfied as to its completion, the purchaser was entitled to refuse to complete. By clause 12 the vendors undertook to make good any defects which might become apparent in the bungalow, within three months of the conveyance, due to faulty materials or workmanship. Any dispute as to such defects was to be referred to arbitration, and the clause was to continue with full force and effect notwithstanding the completion of the sale and conveyance. Defects were discovered in the central heating system outside the three months, and the purchaser sued for breach of clause 11. *Held*, by Norman Richards O.R., following *Marsden* v. *Sharp* (1931), that clause 12 was intended to be the exclusive remedy. Even if clause 12 had been absent, he would have held the purchaser barred as she had an opportunity to express dissatisfaction before the conveyance was executed: *Kent* v. *Saltdean Estates* (1964).[82]

[Note: There were special pointers in this case to an intention to bring an end to the general obligation upon the conveyance, including in particular the wording of the arbitration provision, and the reference to the satisfaction of the purchaser and her surveyor. It should not be regarded as applying any principle to be derived from *Marsden's* case. Compare the satisfaction cases, *post*, Chapter 7, Section 3.]

[79] Hudsons' B.C., 4th ed. Vol. 2, p. 176.
[80] 48 T.L.R. 23.
[81] [1966] 2 All E.R. 901.
[82] (1964) 114 L.J. 555. See also *McKey* v. *Rorison* [1953] N.Z.L.R. 498, illustrated *ante*, Chap. 5, Section 1, p. 286, and see further the satisfaction cases, *e.g. Bateman (Lord)* v. *Thompson* and *Bruens* v. *Smith*, illustrated *post*, pp. 426–431, of which this is only a further example.

(4) By clause 9 of a contract for the sale of a house in the course of erection, the developer undertook to erect and complete it in accordance with the plan and specification in a proper and workmanlike manner. The contract further provided (by clause 11) that the developer would make good structural defects discovered within six months of completion and notified to him in writing. The sale was also made subject to the National Conditions of Sale, so far as not inconsistent with the contract conditions. Clause 12 of the National Conditions provided that the purchaser should be deemed to buy with full notice of the actual state of the property and took it as it was. Defects were found after the six months.[83] *Held* by Diplock L.J. (and upheld by the Court of Appeal)

(*a*) applying *Lawrence* v. *Cassel* (1930) that the contract to build did not merge in the conveyance,[83a]

(*b*) that the obligation under clause 9 applied to work done before the contract was entered into as well as subsequent work,

(*c*) that clause 12 of the National Conditions of Sale was wholly inconsistent with clause 9 and should be disregarded,

(*d*) disapproving *Marsden* v. *Sharp* (1931) and distinguishing *Kent* v. *Saltdean Estates* (1964), that in the absence of clear terms the right to have defects made good under clause 11 was an alternative remedy and did not replace the rights under clause 9: *Hancock* v. *Brazier (Anerley) Ltd.* (1966).[84]

The most far-reaching and remarkable clause absolving the contractor from his ordinary common law responsibility for defective work is the clause governing the legal effect of the final certificate in the post-1963 R.I.B.A. standard forms of contract.[85] This clause has already been commented upon in relation to the architect's duty of supervision [86] and is considered in more detail in Chapter 7.[87]

(4) Damages for Defects

Damages for the general obligation to do the work in accordance with the contract, or the special obligation under a defects clause, will usually be equivalent to the cost of repair and (except, it is submitted, in the case of any " absolute " defects obligation, which is not very usual at the present day, where the defect is not a breach of

---

[83] See the fuller illustration on this, *ante*, Chap. 5, pp. 297–298.

[83a] This is another way of describing the survival of the vendor's obligation in spite of the " *caveat emptor* " rule in " house in course of erection " cases.

[84] [1966] 2 All E.R. 901.

[85] Clause 30 (7).

[86] *Ante*, Chap. 2, pp. 126, 152.

[87] *Post*, pp. 489–492.

the general obligation) any necessary consequential damages, such as compensation for loss of use of the building during repairs, in accordance with the ordinary rules of remoteness of damage.

This subject and the qualifications that may need to be made on the general rule, are fully dealt with *post*, Chapter 9. With inflation as rapid as it now is in the United Kingdom, delay by the employer, after discovery of a defect, in effecting the necessary repairs means that the monetary cost increases substantially after even quite short periods. It must be accepted that the law is at present that the cost is calculated as at the time of discovery of the defects, on the basis that the employer then puts the work in hand without unreasonable delay, though this view is criticised as not logical, *post*, Chapter 9. On the other hand, consistent with the dicta quoted above in Section 1, the cost is calculated as at the date of actual discovery, and not as at some earlier date when, with due diligence on the part of the architect or employer, they might or ought to have been discovered.[88]

It is submitted that the rules as to mitigation of damage, or of estoppel or waiver, will only have effect, in the context of the employer's or architect's earlier knowledge, if after actual subjective knowledge of defective work the employer or architect act wholly unreasonably in failing to draw the contractor's attention to it within a reasonable time, and so act that the contractor alters his position to his detriment.[89] But only very unusual facts could bring this about, and delays, for instance, during a period when the cause of a particular symptom is not fully known, will certainly not so qualify. One possible case, where an employer deliberately does not avail himself of his rights under a defects clause, has already been mentioned.[90] Furthermore, it has already been explained that the architect or engineer is under no duty to tell the contractor *how* to remedy a defect or bring the work satisfactorily to its properly completed state (and indeed may expose the employer to financial claims if he seeks to do so),[91] though it has been suggested that after practical completion the architect must under most defects clauses take charge of affairs if defects develop, until such time as he is satisfied that the cause of the defect is a breach of contract by the contractor.[92]

---

[88] *East Ham B.C.* v. *Bernard Sunley* [1966] A.C. 406.
[89] See *supra*, pp. 385–388.
[90] *Supra*, p. 397.
[91] *Ante*, Chap. 2, pp. 139–141; Chap. 5, pp. 324–325; *post*, Chap. 8, pp. 525–526.
[92] *Supra*, p. 396.

CHAPTER 7

APPROVAL AND CERTIFICATES

SECTION 1. APPROVAL OF WORK

(1) Generally

IN building and engineering contracts there are frequently to be found express terms that the work, in addition to its compliance with the contract requirements and descriptions, is to be done to the approval or satisfaction of the architect or engineer, or of the employer, or of some person quite unconnected with the contracting parties, such as the local or by-law authority. Very often in the same clause, but sometimes independently, the contractor is required to be paid on certificates of the architect, and it is common for the final (and sometimes the penultimate) certificates, under which in many contracts the instalments of retention money are released, to be further expressly conditioned upon the work having been carried out and completed in all respects in accordance with the contract to the satisfaction of the architect or engineer, though in the United Kingdom today it is more usual to find the initial release of retention money conditioned on "practical" or "substantial" completion,[1] and in such cases only the final certificate is treated as evidencing satisfaction.[1a] Certificates of this kind are, if given, treated as evidencing the satisfaction of the architect or engineer, notwithstanding that they may only purport to certify the final or other balance due.[1b]

These provisions may relate to the quality, completion or value of the work as a whole. But in addition many other detailed matters, such as whether or not particular work is or is not an " extra " or variation, or how much, if any, extension of time should be awarded to the contractor, may be expressly referred for decision to or made dependent upon the opinion of the architect or engineer, his decision or opinion usually but not necessarily being required to be recorded in a certificate.

[1] Defined *ante*, Chap. 5, pp. 257–259.
[1a] See also the discussion *ante*, Chap. 6, Section 2 (2), p. 392.
[1b] See *infra*, Section 6.

In the great majority of cases the language used by the parties makes it clear that the architect or engineer who is required to express his approval or satisfaction, or decide, or certify, or give his opinion in relation to these matters in this way, is not intended to be an arbitrator in the full sense of the word. Nevertheless, unless the parties make it clear that they wish the certifier's decision or approval to be open to review by an arbitrator or the courts, the language and scheme of the contract frequently make it clear that the certifier's decision or approval, though in the nature of an administrative act rather than the full judicial hearing associated with arbitration, is intended to be binding upon the parties.

Furthermore, consideration of a very large number of the cases in this chapter will show quite clearly that in building contracts the certifier will, more often than not, be required to decide questions of law as well as of fact—for example, a decision as to whether or not work is an extra is a pure question of law involving the true construction of the original contract obligation, before any question of valuation arises. Even questions of valuation, where the contract lays down rules for ascertaining the value of work, varied or otherwise, may involve questions of law. So too, questions of extension of time will involve decisions as to entitlement under the terms of the contract (law), as well as of the amount of the extension (fact). One of the commonest of all certifying provisions (payment) will usually involve the interpretation of many different provisions of the contract as well as of schedules of rates or bills of quantities, and the other commonest provision (satisfaction) may often involve the interpretation of the specification describing the required work. The following recent opinion *obiter* by Ungoed-Thomas J., in a somewhat different field, must therefore, it is respectfully submitted, be treated with the greatest caution, and be regarded as out of line with virtually the entire body of law in this chapter.[1bb]

ILLUSTRATION

The decision of the lessor's surveyor as to the contribution of the lessee to certain identified categories of repair for which the lessor was liable was to be " final and not subject to any challenge in any manner whatsoever." *Held, obiter* by Ungoed-Thomas J., following *Lee* v. *Showman's Guild* (1952) [1c] that even if the question whether a particular repair was within the identified categories was a matter within the surveyor's jurisdiction, the provision was void as being against public policy, since it purported to oust the jurisdiction of the Courts to the extent that it made the surveyor's decision binding

[1bb] See particularly, for example, the " extras " cases, *infra*, pp. 427 *et seq.* and *post*, Chap. 8, pp. 553 *et seq.*   [1c] [1952] 2 Q.B. 329.

on questions of law as opposed to questions of fact: *Re Davstone Estates Ltd.'s Leases* (1969).[1d]

[Note: The wording of the certifying provision in the above case may be compared with " the said certificate shall be conclusive evidence in any proceedings arising out of this contract (whether by arbitration . . . or otherwise) that the Works have been properly carried out and completed in accordance with the terms of this contract *and that any necessary effect has been given to all the terms of this contract which require an adjustment to be made to the Contract Sum. . . .*" (clause 30 (7) of the current R.I.B.A. conditions), and the often still severer wording of many of the Victorian contracts illustrated in this chapter.]

On the other hand, there is undoubtedly a class of case where, if the certifier purports to act outside the terms of his own jurisdiction, his decision will be invalidated or disregarded.[1e] This is because, it is submitted, a certifier will not generally be treated as empowered to decide questions as to the extent of his own jurisdiction, and it may well be that there would be objections of public policy to a certifying provision which was so framed.

The earlier tendency of modern contracts in this century was to move away from the Victorian form of contract, in which the contractor was frequently placed at the mercy of the employer's professional adviser in this way over a wide range of matters; so that by the beginning of the Second World War most matters were subject to review by an arbitrator. But in recent years the R.I.B.A. form (not the I.C.E.) has sought to impose a very severe time limit on the right to go to arbitration and failing arbitration accords binding effect to the final certificate.[2] It can only be supposed that the pressure for this has come from the contracting side of the industry, since the time limit in practice cannot embarrass the contractor, whereas it can gravely prejudice an employer who, after final certificate and when the right to arbitrate has been lost, may discover defective work and wish to sue the contractor for breach of contract.[3]

This chapter is concerned with the extent to which a provision for satisfaction, approval, decision or certificate, when acted on by the architect, engineer or certifier, binds the parties finally and conclusively; the circumstances in which such a stipulated approval or satisfaction or certificate can be dispensed with or disregarded; and an examination of the status and duties of the certifier and of the formalities relating to certificates.

[1d] [1969] 2 Ch. 378. Illustrated more fully *infra*, subs. (2), p. 411.
[1e] See *infra*, Section 6, pp. 476–478.
[2] See clause 30 (7).
[3] See *post*, pp. 489–492.

It is helpful to bear in mind certain broad principles when considering the cases. These are, first, that the intention of the parties to be deduced from the contract will, if its sense is clear, always prevail. Secondly, that there is no magic in the existence of a contractual provision as to a *certificate.*

" It has been argued that there is no provision in this contract for the engineer giving a final certificate. . . . I attach no importance to this argument as I find it expressly stated that the work is to be done to the satisfaction of the engineer. A certificate is only a mode of expressing this satisfaction." [4]

Thirdly, provisions of this kind need to be construed strictly, since they may deprive a party of what would otherwise be his legal rights. Thus a provision for payment to be made on certificate may be interpreted as meaning that the certificate relates to the apparent value of the work, and not to its quality.

" It is not too much to ask that contracting parties who are desirous of giving conclusive effect to a quasi-arbitrator's certificate of liability should express that intention quite clearly." [5]

Indeed, it is usual in contracts of this kind to find both types of provision, *viz.*: a provision requiring the work to be carried out or completed to the satisfaction of the architect (*i.e.* a provision as to the sufficiency or quality of the works), and also a provision for payment of the contractor upon the certificate of the architect or engineer (*i.e.* a provision for ascertainment of the amount due). Accompanied by an undertaking elsewhere in the contract to do work to the architect's satisfaction, the final certificate is usually strong evidence of that satisfaction.[6] The governing principle has been stated in the following terms:

" A contract may be so framed as under ordinary circumstances to take away the jurisdiction of courts of law and courts of equity to determine what is the amount payable under the contract. Wherever, according to the true construction of the contract, the party only agrees to pay what is certified by an engineer, or what is found to be due by an arbitrator, and there is no agreement to pay otherwise—that is to say, in every case where the certificate of the engineer or arbitrator is made a condition precedent to the right to recover, then the court has no right to dispense with that which the parties have made a condition precedent, unless, of course, there has

---

[4] See *per* Grove J. in *Dunaberg, etc. Ry.* v. *Hopkins* (1877) 36 L.T. 733. See also Section 6, *infra*, pp. 480 *et seq.* for further cases on the form of certificates.

[5] *Per* Evatt J. in *Kirsch* v. *Brady* (1937) 58 C.L.R. 36 (Australia).

[6] See Section 6, *infra*, p. 482.

been some conduct on the part of the engineer or the company which may make it inequitable that the condition precedent should be relied upon." [7]

It should also be remembered that in the absence of a specific provision to the contrary a certificate need not be in writing and can be issued orally. [8]

An attempt will be made to set out the law on this subject in Section 3, below, Approval by Third Person. Confusion will be avoided if it is remembered that cases upon the effect of certificates are usually equally authoritative upon questions relating to approval and satisfaction, and vice versa.

As will be seen, the existence of a provision in a contract whereby a builder undertakes to do work to the satisfaction of some other person, or to be paid upon his certificate, will, if it has the binding character referred to, have the most important consequences, since the builder may be unable to recover the price unless he obtains the stipulated approval or certificate, while, on the other hand, if he does obtain it, the employer may be precluded from alleging defective work or other failure to comply with the terms of the contract (as will be seen, however, these two results are not necessarily complementary, though usually they will be so). [9] This is particularly serious in building contracts, since once the work is done it is attached to the soil and becomes the property of the owner, who thereby obtains the benefit of it beyond recall, while the builder cannot mitigate his loss, as in the case of a chattel, by taking it back. It follows from this that such provisions are liable to be particularly strictly construed when the stipulated approval is that not of a third person but of a party to the contract.

It should also be borne in mind that the courts will often attach more importance to the sense of the transaction to be deduced from the whole contract between the parties than to the actual language of a particular provision. " The clearest words of condition must yield to the intention of the parties as visible on the whole instrument." [10]

Finally, warning should be given that nearly all modern forms of contract contain arbitration clauses sufficiently wide in scope to rob the stipulated approval or certificate of the finality which

---

[7] *Per* Mellish L.J. in *Sharpe* v. *San Paulo Ry.* (1873) L.R. 8 Ch.App. 597, at p. 612.

[8] See *Re Hohenzollern Actien-Gesellschaft & City of London Contract Corporation* (1886) 2 T.L.R. 470, and see cases, *post*, p. 479.

[9] An obvious exception is an interim certificate: see *post*, pp. 492 *et seq.*

[10] See *per* Byles J. in *London Gaslight Co.* v. *Vestry of Chelsea* (1860) 2 L.T. 216.

it would otherwise enjoy. The wording of any arbitration clause may be of overwhelming importance in determining whether an approval or certificate is conclusive, and may indeed override provisions which on their face appear to be clear and precise.[11]

(2) Construciion of Stipulations

" In modern times the doctrine of conditions precedent has been considerably relaxed, and there is no disposition in the courts to consider stipulations in that light unless the terms of the contract clearly require it." [12] This early dictum, representing the initial reluctance of the courts to accord finality to decisions of a person employed by one of the parties, and hence not entirely in an impartial position, has not, in the event, exerted much influence on the development of the law relating to such stipulations in building contracts. Such mitigating tendency as there has been has manifested itself in two main directions of somewhat limited effect, namely, in confining any power of approval strictly within any limits to be deduced from the contract, and secondly, in cases where the person whose approval is required is a party to the contract, in implying wherever possible a term as to reasonableness. (This latter rather limited class of cases will be dealt with in the next following section, Approval by Building Owner.)

The following are examples of cases where the courts have, as a matter of construction, narrowed the ambit of the powers conferred by clauses of this kind.[13] It will be seen that they have been particularly reluctant, in the absence of sufficiently explicit language, to confer finality on a certificate or approval so as to bind a party alleging prevention or breach of contract by the other. In addition to the cases illustrated below, the cases collected *infra*, Section 6 (2) should also be considered.[14]

ILLUSTRATIONS

(1) The defendant agreed to buy a sixteen horse-power engine to be erected on his premises, and to pay part of the price on delivery, and that he would, on being satisfied with the work, pay the plaintiff the remainder two months later. The engine installed was not of the specified horse-power. On an action for the price, *held*, that the

---

[11] See, *e.g. East Ham B.C.* v. *Sunley,* illustrated *post*, p. 446; and generally Sect. 4, *post*.
[12] *Per* Vaughan J., *Dallman* v. *King* (1837) 4 Bing.N.C. 105 at p. 110.
[13] In addition to the cases illustrated below, see the important case of *Panamena etc.,* v. *Leyland* [1947] A.C. 428, illustrated *post*, Section 5, p. 468.
[14] *Infra*, p. 480.

seller must allow an abatement of the price for breach of warranty as to horse-power, since the provisions as to satisfaction applied to the work of erection only: *Parsons* v. *Sexton* (1847).[15]

(2) A contract for the construction of a tank for a gas company provided that in case of default the contractor should pay the company such sum as the engineer should adjudge to be reasonable and proper. *Held*, the engineer was a mere valuer or appraiser, that he had no power to say whether the covenants had been broken, and the company must prove positively the fact of any default: *Northampton Gas Light* v. *Parnell* (1855).[16]

(3) R. contracted to make a glue-cutting machine according to drawing, etc., with " strong and sound workmanship to the approval of A." *Held*, that the approval of A was to be as to the strength and workmanship of the apparatus, and not as to its efficiency for cutting glue pieces: *Ripley* v. *Lordon* (1860).[17]

(4) Under a shipbuilding contract, the builder was liable to penalties for delay unless the employer's agent certified that such delay was the result of events beyond the builder's control. Delays occurred due to acts of the employer, but no certificate for the delay was given. *Held*, that as the employer had caused this delay, the builder was not liable for the penalties: *Russell* v. *S. A. da Bandeira* (1862).[18]

(5) A contract provided that, as to " all matters connected with the works, or the execution thereof or the value of the entire work or reductions, or the meaning of the plans or specifications," the award of the architect in writing should be a condition precedent to any proceeding whatever. *Held* (O'Brian J. dissenting) an award was not a condition precedent to an action by the employer against the contractor for leaving the work unfinished: *Mansfield* v. *Doolin* (1869).[19]

(6) An engineering contract contained an extension of time clause under which *it was lawful* for the architect to give an extension of time (*inter alia*) for failure to supply drawings or directions to the contractor in time. There was a separate forfeiture clause empowering the employers to terminate the contract if, in the opinion of the architect, the contractor failed to proceed with due diligence. The contractors sued for wrongful termination, and the employers pleaded that the architect had certified that the contractor had not proceeded with due diligence. The contractors replied that the delay was due to failure to supply plans and drawings and to set out the land. *Held*, on demurrer by the Court of Exchequer Chamber (Kelly C.B., Channell B., Blackburn and Mellor JJ. (Cleasby and Pigott BB. dissenting)), that the architect had no power *under the forfeiture clause* to decide matters of breach of contract

---

[15] 16 L.J.C.P. 181.

[16] 15 C.B. 630. For a decision in a contrary sense see *Richards* v. *May* (1883) 10 Q.B.D. 400 illustrated *post*, Chap. 8, Section 2, p. 554.

[17] 2 L.T. 154.

[18] 13 C.B.(N.S.) 149.

[19] 4 Ir.L.R.(C.L.) 17. [N.B.—This case is perhaps of doubtful authority if applied to any modern contractual provision referring disputes in general terms to a named person.]

or prevention by the employers. While under the extension of time clause he might have power to refuse an extension of time for such matters, this did not enable him to bind the contractor for purposes of the termination clause. *Held* also, *per* Blackburn and Mellor JJ., the language of the extension of time clause being permissive only, a decision under that clause could bind the employer, but not the contractor unless he accepted the extension of time given: *Roberts* v. *Bury Commissioners* (1870).[20]

[Note: It should be noted that on the reasoning of this case, the architect's opinion would have been conclusive and binding on the contractor (in relation to the forfeiture clause) on any matter except prevention or breach of contract by the employer. This case was decided on demurrer (*i.e.* on the basis of hypothetical facts as pleaded). In a contract such as this the contractor would have to prove, not only that delays were caused by the employers' breaches of contract, but that it was these delays which operated on the certifier's mind when he certified (or refused to certify) as he did.][21]

(7) A contract for the construction of a railway contained a clause empowering the company's engineer to terminate the contract upon written notice if in his opinion there were just grounds for believing that it would not be completed in the time and manner specified in the contract. *Held*, that the condition did not empower the engineer to determine conclusively that the delay was not due to the company's acts or omissions as alleged by the contractor: *McDonnell* v. *Canada Southern Railway* (1873).[22]

(8) The plaintiffs contracted to construct certain drainage works for the defendants. The contract stipulated that the work should be finished by a specified date, and that if it should at any time appear to the defendants' engineer that the works were not being carried on with due diligence or with such speed as would ensure their completion in the stipulated time, the defendants might on notice given take the works out of the plaintiffs' hands. The defendants undertook to provide all land permanently necessary for the completion of the works. An action was brought by the plaintiffs for prevention of performance of the contract, to which the defendants pleaded that due diligence had not been exercised and that notice had therefore been given under the contract. The plaintiffs replied that the failure to comply with the requisitions of the notice was due to the defaults of the defendants and their engineer in not providing the land and drawings necessary for the works. *Held*, that the engineer's opinion was not conclusive as to this, and that in fact the delay was due to the defendants' default: *Arterial Drainage Co.* v. *Rathangan Drainage Board* (1880).[23]

(9) A contract for dredging provided that if a temporary staging was not removed in sufficient time to enable the contractor to

[20] L.R. 5 C.P. 310. This case, in so far as the view expressed by Blackburn and Mellor JJ. as to the extension of time clause is concerned, is further considered *post*, Chap. 11, p. 628.
[21] See the case of *Wadey* v. *Mort's Dock & Engineering Co.* [1902] 2 N.S.W.R. 391 (Australia), illustrated *post*, Chap. 13, p. 693.
[22] 33 Up.Can.Q.B. 313.
[23] 6 L.R.Ir. 513.

complete his work within the fixed time, he was to be entitled to such extension of time as the engineer should deem reasonable. If any difference arose between the contractor and the employers " concerning the work contracted for, *or concerning anything in connection with this contract*," such difference was to be referred to the engineer, whose decision was to be final. The work was delayed by non-removal of the staging; the engineer admitted that the contractor was entitled to compensation for the expense thereby occasioned, but could not agree the amount with the contractor. The engineer then certified for a less amount than that claimed. *Held,* that there was an implied contract that the staging should be removed in a reasonable time, for breach of which the contractor was entitled to damages. But *held,* also, that the breach of the implied term was not a matter " concerning anything in connection with the contract," and that the certificate was not, therefore, final or binding: *Lawson* v. *Wallasey Local Board* (1883).[24]

[Note: The court seems to have been influenced in this case by the fact that this was a contract under seal and that the breach was of " an implied but independent contract." It is submitted that it is doubtful if it would be followed today.]

(10) A builder contracted to do work according to plans and specification. The specification provided that the work was to be done to the satisfaction of the architect; there was no power for the architect to order deviations. *Held,* that the architect had no power to sanction deviations from the contract, and that the owner was not bound by a certificate to accept work other than that contracted for: *Ramsay* v. *Brand* (1898).[25]

[Note: Where, however, the architect's certificate as to extras or their value is expressed to be conclusive, the employer cannot object to the certificate on the ground that the extras certified had not been ordered in writing as required by the contract,[26] or were not extras at all.[27]]

(11) A contract provided that the architect might in certain circumstances extend the time of completion, but gave him no express power to deal with the question of the damages which were to be deducted for delay.[27a] The architect issued a final certificate without any apparent deduction for damages. The contractors took a preliminary point of law that the certificate was conclusive evidence that time had been extended. The building owners brought an action to recover damages. *Held,* as the contract did not empower the architect to deal with damages, the certificate was not evidence of any decision by the architect, and the building owners might prove

---

[24] 11 Q.B.D. 229; affirmed on appeal (1883) 48 L.T. 507, the Court of Appeal expressing no opinion as to whether the action could have been stayed.

[25] 25 R. (Ct. of Sess.) 1212.

[26] See, *infra*, pp. 426 *et seq., Clemence* v. *Clarke* (1880) Hudson's B.C., 4th ed. Vol. 2, p. 54, *infra*, p. 466, and *post*, Chap. 8, pp. 553 *et seq.*, and the cases there cited.

[27] *Richards* v. *May* (1883) 10 Q.B.D. 400, illustrated *post*, Chap. 8, p. 554.

[27a] This is also the case in nearly all modern contracts, where the actual monetary calculation or deduction of liquidated damages is for some reason not usually expressed to be the subject of a certificate.

by evidence what the architect had intended to do: *British Thomson-Houston Co. Ltd.* v. *West Brothers* (1903).[28]

(12) Under the terms of a sub-contract the sub-contractors were to be paid upon the certificate of the architect. There was no power to vary the contract. In fact the sub-contractors were instructed to carry out certain unauthorised variations, which they did. The architect issued a certificate for the work as varied. The sub-contractors sued on the certificate, and the contractors alleged that the work under the contract had not been done. *Held*, that the certificate was bad and did not bind the contractors as to the value of the work: *Ashwell and Nesbitt Ltd.* v. *Allen & Co.* (1912).[29]

(13) A building contract provided for payment of 99 per cent. of the contract price upon a certificate of practical completion, and of the remaining balance six months thereafter upon a final certificate for the balance, provided the work had been completed to the satisfaction of the architect. The architect never gave the 99 per cent. practical completion certificate at the time the employers took possession but ultimately gave a final certificate stating the final balance due. The builder sued upon it in the courts, and the employer alleged delay and defective work. The builder argued that the certificate was conclusive. *Held*, by the High Court of Australia, that as the right to sue upon the final certificate did not arise until six months after the certificate of practical completion, and as there was no such certificate, the final certificate could not be relied upon. Even if it could be regarded as a certificate of practical completion, the plaintiff could not recover as he had issued his writ within six months of the certificate. *Kirsch* v. *Brady* (1937).[30]

(14) Clause 29 of a Scottish building contract provided that the final certificate should, subject to the rights of the parties under the arbitration clause, be conclusive evidence of the value of the work and materials. The liquidated damages clause provided that the architect or an arbitrator might award an extension of time. The architect issued a final certificate which made no deduction for liquidated damages, but the employers claimed to withhold liquidated damages. The contractors claimed that the employers were bound by the certificate. *Held*, questions of extension of time and the final certificate itself were expressly subject to review by an arbitrator, but even if they were not, the final certificate was conclusive only as to the value of work done, and the employers could accordingly deduct and retain the liquidated damages: *Port Glasgow Magistrates* v. *Scottish Construction Ltd.* (1960).[31]

(15) Clause 2 of a contract for the sale of a house in the course of erection provided that the owner should pay the contractor the second half of the purchase money " on the issue of the certificate of

---

[28] 19 T.L.R. 493. See also *Peters* v. *Quebec Harbour Commissioners* (1891) 19 S.C.R. 685 (Canada), illustrated *post*, Section 5, p. 467 (deduction of sums arising on measurement), and see also the *Port Glasgow Magistrates Case*, illustration (14) *infra*.

[29] Hudson's B.C., 4th ed., Vol. 2, p. 462; and see *Trade Indemnity Co.* v. *Workington Harbour & Dock Board* [1937] A.C. 1, *per* Lord Atkin at p. 22 (certificate including sums loaned to contractor by employer).

[30] (1937) 58 C.L.R. 36. (This is a difficult case, and should be contrasted with *Borough of Stratford* v. *Ashman* [1960] N.Z.L.R. 503, *infra*, Sect. 4, pp. 444–445).

[31] 1960 S.L.T. 319.

habitation by the local authority, which certificate shall be conclusive evidence of the completion of the said dwelling-house." [32] *Held*, by Edmund Davies L.J., that clause 2 contemplated a certificate designed to regulate the time of payment and was not intended to be a certificate as to the quality of the work: *Billyack* v. *Leyland* (1968). [33]

(16) A lessee covenanted to pay a contribution towards expenses reasonably incurred by the lessor in performing " the covenants on the part of the lessor set forth in clause 3 " of the lease, as certified by the lessor's surveyor. Clause 3 was a covenant rendering the lessor liable for certain described kinds of repair. The surveyor certified, but the lessee wished to contend that the matters in respect of which the surveyor had certified did not fall within clause 3 at all. *Held* by Ungoed-Thomas J., on the true construction of the lease the question whether a particular defect fell within the clause 3 obligation was not intended to be decided by the certifier: *Re Davstone Estates Ltd.'s Leases* (1969). [33a]

Despite some of the above cases there is, however, nothing to prevent a clause being drafted so as to enable a certifier to make binding decisions upon matters involving prevention or breach of contract. This not infrequently occurs in extension of time clauses. [34]

(3) Evidence of Approval

The employer's or architect's approval must be testified in writing, but only if this is required by the provisions of the contract.

ILLUSTRATION

B. agreed to pay M. for building work upon receiving the architect's certificate in writing that the work was done to his satisfaction; the architect checked and approved of M.'s charges and sent them on to B., but gave no certificate that the work had been executed to his approval. *Held*, that under the contract a certificate was a condition precedent to M.'s right to recover, and that what the architect had done did not amount to such a certificate: *Morgan* v. *Birnie* (1833). [35]

(4) Vendor's Approval of Building on Land Sold

Many conveyances and leases contain covenants by the purchaser or lessee to build to the approval of the vendor, lessor or his architect

---

[32] The case is fully illustrated, *infra*, pp. 432–433.

[33] [1968] 1 W.L.R. 471.

[33a] [1969] 2 Ch. 378.

[34] See, *e.g.* the clauses in *Jones* v. *St. John's College* (1870) L.R. 6 Q.B. 115 and *Sattin* v. *Poole* (1901) Hudson's B.C., 4th ed., Vol. 2, p. 306, both illustrated *post*, Chap. 11, pp. 628, 629–630, and in the modern R.I.B.A. standard forms. The I.C.E. extension of time clause is, however, drafted without any such provision, which will frequently have the effect of invalidating the clause—see *post*, Chap. 11, p. 625.

[35] 9 Bing. 672. See *post*, Section 6, p. 482, for the form of the certificate.

on the land sold or leased. This, of course, is a totally different legal situation from that previously discussed, and does not fall within the scope of this work.[36]

SECTION 2. APPROVAL BY BUILDING OWNER

(1) Implication of Reasonableness

Terms of this kind are comparatively rare in modern contracts. As previously indicated, where work has to be done to the approval of a building owner, the courts will generally endeavour to construe the term to mean that the approval cannot be withheld by him unreasonably.[37] Despite certain early dicta, this probably does not depend upon any supposed maxim that " no man shall be judge in his own cause," since, if the objection on the ground of interest is patent on the face of a contract stipulating that the work is to be done to the satisfaction of the building owner, it is hardly possible for the contractor to take such an objection after an expression of dissatisfaction by the owner.

ILLUSTRATION

If A agrees to refer a dispute between himself and B to B himself, he cannot object to the award on the ground that B was judge in his own case: *Matthew* v. *Ollerton* (1672).[38]

With reference to arbitration clauses or agreements, this particular difficulty was removed by section 14 of the Arbitration Act 1934,[39] which permits an application for removal of an arbitrator notwithstanding that the ground of objection was known at the time of the submission to arbitration, but that section does not affect the position where the named person is not an arbitrator,[40] and, as will be seen in the next following section, a person whose satisfaction has to be obtained, whether by certificate or otherwise, is seldom an arbitrator in the proper sense. The true view is that the courts are extremely reluctant to regard the satisfaction of a party as

---

[36] See *Brace* v. *Wehnert* (1856) 27 L.J.Ch. 572; *Goolden* v. *Anstee* (1868) 18 L.T. 898; *Re Northumberland Avenue Hotel Co.* (1887) 56 L.T. 833 (C.A.); and *cf. Att.-Gen.* v. *Briggs* (1855) 1 Jur. 1084, illustrated *infra*, Section 6, p. 485; and *Dallman* v. *King*, illustrated *infra*, pp. 413–414.

[37] In addition to the cases cited in this section, see also the passage from Devlin J.'s judgment in *Minster Trust Ltd.* v. *Traps Tractors Ltd.* [1954] 1 W.L.R. 963, quoted below in Section 3, Approval by Third Person, at pp. 417–418.

[38] 4 Mod. 220.

[39] Now s. 24 of the Act of 1950.

[40] See, *infra*, Section 4, p. 450.

binding if it can be possibly avoided, but that if the wording or sense of the contract is sufficiently explicit then the strict view will still prevail. Thus in a case where a lessee had agreed to expend £200 on repairs to be inspected and approved by the lessor, Tindal C.J. said: " It never could have been intended that he (the lessor) should be allowed capriciously to withhold his approval; that would be a condition going to the destruction of the thing granted, and if so, according to the well-known rule, the thing granted would pass discharged of the condition " [41]; but Cockburn C.J. said in *Stadhard* v. *Lee* (1863) [42]: " We quite agree that stipulations and conditions of this kind should, where the language of the contract admits of it, receive a reasonable construction, as it is to be contended that the party in whose favour such a clause is inserted meant to secure only what is reasonable and just, and we therefore entirely accede to the propriety of the decision in *Dallman* v. *King*. But we are equally clear that, where from the whole tenor of the agreement it appears that, however unreasonable and oppressive a stipulation or condition may be, the one party intended to insist upon and the other to submit to it, a court of justice cannot do otherwise than give effect to the terms which have been agreed upon between the parties."

The courts, therefore, in dealing with stipulations requiring the approval of the owner, will, wherever the construction of the clause will permit of it, imply a qualification of reasonableness and the contractor will be entitled to payment if he has done the work in a manner with which the employer ought in reason to have been satisfied. It should, however, be appreciated that so to hold in fact deprives the term for approval of virtually all force.

Such questions of reasonableness are questions of fact for the decision of the jury, if there is one,[43] and the employer must not (except in the case of matters of mere taste [44]) unreasonably withhold approval when he ought to be satisfied with what has been done, unless an absolute discretion has been expressly and unequivocally reserved to him by the contract.

ILLUSTRATIONS

(1) It was agreed that a lessee should spend £200 in repairs, to be inspected and approved by the lessor, and that the sum should be retained by the lessee out of the first year's rent. *Held*, (1) that

[41] *Dallman* v. *King* (1837) 4 Bing.N.C. 105.
[42] 3 B. & S. 364 at p. 371.
[43] *Burton* v. *Griffiths* (1845) 11 M. & W. 817.
[44] As to which, see *infra*, p. 415.

the lessor's approval was not a condition precedent to the lessee's right to retain out of his rent the sum spent on repairs; (2) that, even if it were, the contract could not mean that the lessor should be allowed capriciously to withhold approval; and the work having been properly done, the condition had been substantially performed: *Dallman* v. *King* (1837).[45]

(2) Where a contract contained a provision that an engine was to be erected to the satisfaction of the purchaser, it was a question for the jury whether the work was such as ought reasonably to have satisfied the defendant: *Parsons* v. *Sexton* (1847).[46]

(3) A policy of insurance provided that, as a condition precedent to payment, proof satisfactory to the directors should be furnished of the death of the insured, together with such further evidence as the directors should think necessary to establish the claim. *Held*, that this meant such evidence as the directors might reasonably require, and not such as they might unreasonably and capriciously require: *Braunstein* v. *Accidental Death Insurance Co.* (1861).[47]

(4) A contract between a builder and a sub-contractor contained a provision that, in the event of the builder being dissatisfied with the sub-contractor's progress, he might take over the work himself and deduct the expense from the contract sum due to the sub-contractor. The sub-contractor contended that his progress was in fact such as should satisfy any reasonable person, and that the builder's dissatisfaction was capricious and unjustified on the facts. *Held*, on the construction of the contract, and taking into account that the builder was probably himself subject to stringent terms, that this contention, even if it could be established, could not, in the absence of fraud, avail the sub-contractor: *Stadhard* v. *Lee* (1863).[48]

[Note: This is an important case, because (apart from the absence of an arbitration clause) its provisions are very similar to those in many modern sub-contracts, such as the F.A.S.S. standard form of sub-contract in England. See the case further commented on and the further quotation from the judgment, *post*, Chapter 13, Section 1 (6).]

(5) Where work is agreed to be done to the satisfaction of the employer, the plaintiff is not entitled to a verdict, unless the jury are satisfied not only that the contract as alleged was entered into, and that the works were executed, but that the defendant, as a reasonable person, ought to have been satisfied with the way in which they were executed: *Smith* v. *Sadler* (1880).[49]

(6) Clause 4 gave the purchaser of a yacht the right to have her surveyed, and clause 5 provided that " if any material defect in the yacht or her machinery shall have been found, the purchaser may give notice to the vendor of his rejection of the yacht. . . . If the

---

[45] 4 Bing.N.C. 105.
[46] 4 C.B. 899, *supra*, pp. 406–407.
[47] 1 B. & S. 782; 31 L.J.Q.B. 17.
[48] 3 B. & S. 364; 32 L.J.Q.B. 75; and see *Tredegar* v. *Harwood* [1929] A.C. 72; and *Shipway (James) & Co.* v. *Wyndham & Albery* (1908) *The Times*, December 1. Digest, Vol. VII, p. 386. See also *Grafton* v. *Eastern Counties Ry.* (1853) 8 Ex. 699 illustrated *post*, p. 422.
[49] 6 Vict.L.R. 5.

vendor shall decline to make good the defect or if the parties fail to agree the amount of the cash allowance either party may . . . cancel this agreement." The arbitration clause was in general terms, but specifically included disputes as to whether the vendor had satisfactorily remedied defects under clause 5. The purchaser notified the seller of defects, which the latter by his surveyors disputed. The purchaser argued that his opinion as to whether there were defects, provided it was honest, was conclusive, and purported to determine the agreement. *Held*, by the Court of Appeal, for the notice to be valid there must in fact be material defects, and whether or not there were such defects was open to arbitration: *Docker* v. *Hyams* (1969).[50]

(2) Disapproval must be Honest

In addition, however, the refusal to approve, whether or not it must be reasonable, must be honest and genuine.[51] If the refusal is fraudulent, the builder is entitled to be paid, since no person can take advantage of his own wrong, or set up, as an answer to an action, the non-performance of a condition when he has himself prevented performance.[52] So the employer must make some trial or inspection; and if without even looking at the work he were to say that he did not approve, such conduct would amount to bad faith. Further, if the employer were not to intimate any disapproval, but remain in possession without protest and when sued for the price simply say that he did not approve, his conduct would be strong evidence of bad faith, though, as has been seen,[53] mere passive occupation of building work will not usually amount to acceptance.

(3) Approval as to Matters of Taste

The implication of reasonableness does not, however, usually apply to matters of taste. When work or labour is agreed to be done to the taste or convenience of the employer, he may exercise his power of rejection to any extent, provided that he does so in good faith, and not dishonestly; since the standard of the taste of the employer, which is essentially subjective, cannot by its nature be supplanted by an objective test such as a test of reasonableness.

ILLUSTRATION

A. undertook to execute an order for a carriage " in a manner which shall meet with B.'s approval not only on the score of

[50] [1969] 1 W.L.R. 1060.
[51] *Andrews* v. *Belfield* (1857) 2 C.B.(N.S.) 779; *Stadhard* v. *Lee, supra.*
[52] See, *e.g. Roberts* v. *Bury Commissioners* (1870) L.R. 5 C.P. 310, 326; and see Section 5, *infra*, Recovery Without Certificate.
[53] *Ante*, Chap. 6, pp. 377–379.

workmanship, but also that of convenience and taste." B. disapproved of the carriage when it was built. *Held*, that he might do
so if he acted bona fide: *Andrews* v. *Belfield* (1857).[54]

(4) Binding Effect of Approval

In those cases where approval is given pursuant to a contractual
provision of this kind, it will generally bind the building owner so as
to prevent him subsequently alleging defective work or other breach
of contract. This subject is more fully discussed in Section 3, below,
Approval by Third Person, where it will be seen that this result is
not necessarily the exact converse of the builder's obligation to
obtain an approval, and will not necessarily always arise though
the builder is under this obligation. Therefore, even in a case
where a term as to reasonableness can be implied, so that absence
of a certificate or approval is not fatal to the builder, the approval
or certificate, once given, may still bind the employer. This will be
the result in the great majority of cases, since obviously the courts
are even more likely to hold a party bound by his own personal
approval, if given, in a case where it can have the effect of barring
the other party's claim if withheld, than in the case of a third person
such as the employer's professional adviser. As will be seen, the
same principle may explain why an employer may be bound by his
own agent's approval but not in the case of a third person owing
him no duty at all, such as a local authority.[54a]

ILLUSTRATION

A building contract provided that all work should be done to
the satisfaction of the building owner. The owner was satisfied,
and paid for the work. Later he sought to recover damages for
defects. *Held*, that the expression of satisfaction freed the builder
from all further liability: *Gorfinkel* v. *Januarie* (1954).[55]

SECTION 3. APPROVAL BY THIRD PERSON

(1) Generally

The great majority of building contracts contain a provision that
the work generally shall be done to the satisfaction of a third person,
usually, of course, the employer's architect or engineer, and in many
cases that payment shall be dependent upon a certificate. The contract may or may not contain express provisions stating that

---

[54] 2 C.B.(N.S.) 779.
[54a] See the *Billyack* case and the comment, *infra*, pp. 432–433.
[55] (1) S.A. 88 (S. Africa). Also *Bruens* v. *Smith*, 1951 (1) S.A. 67, *post*, pp. 429–430.
The whole of this subject is fully dealt with in Section 3, subsection 3, *infra*.

the satisfaction or certificate are to be a condition precedent to the builder's right to sue. In other cases, a particular matter under the contract may be stipulated to depend upon the approval, certificate, or decision of the architect—for example, the valuation of and determination of liability for additions or variations to the work, or extensions of time and the consequential liability to pay liquidated damages. In all cases, as previously indicated, the binding effect of such approval, certificate or decision depends upon the sense of the contract. An indication of the various legal implications that can be drawn from this kind of provision may be seen from the following extract from the judgment of Devlin J. in *Minster Trust Ltd.* v. *Traps Tractors Ltd.* (1954).[56]

" There is no general rule of law prohibiting the influencing of certifiers. Apart from fraud, a duty not to influence can only be imposed by an implication arising from contract. Such implication must, in accordance with settled principles, be both reasonable and necessary, and the contract must be examined to see what it yields in this respect. There is, after all, nothing to prevent a party from requiring that work shall be done to his own satisfaction. He might then choose to act on the recommendation of an agent. If an agent is named in the contract, it may be plain that he is to function only as the *alter ego* of his master, and then his master can tell him what to do. . . . Whether it be the act of the master or the servant there may be a question (again depending on the implication to be drawn from the contract) whether the dissatisfaction must be reasonable, or whether it can be capricious and unreasonable so long as it is conceived in good faith. . . . The tendency in modern cases seems to be to require the dissatisfaction to be reasonable. What has to be ascertained in each case is whether the agent is or is not intended to function independently of the principal. The mere use of the word " certificate " is not decisive. Satisfaction does not necessarily alter its character because it is expressed in the form of a certificate. The main test appears to be whether the certificate is intended to embody a decision that is final and binding on the parties.[57] If it is, it is in effect an award, and it has the attributes of its arbitral character. It cannot be attacked on the ground that it is unreasonable, as the opinion of a party or the certificate of one who is merely an agent probably can. On the other hand, it must be made independently, for independence is the essence of the arbitral

---

[56] [1954] 1 W.L.R. 963 at p. 973.
[57] But not the only test—see *Hatrick* v. *Nelson Carlton Construction* [1964] N.Z.L.R. 72, illustrated *post*, Section 5, pp. 463–464.

function. . . . If a party to a contract is permitted to appoint his agent to act as arbitrator in respect of certain matters under the contract a similar term must be implied; but it is modified by the fact that a man who has to act as arbitrator in respect of some matters, and as servant or agent in respect of others, cannot remain as detached as a pure arbitrator should be.

" There is another distinction between certifiers. If work under a contract has to be completed to the satisfaction of a certifier, it may mean that his duty is merely to see that the requirements of the contract are met, or it may mean that he is entitled to impose a standard of his own. It may be that his standard is that to which the parties submit and that it constitutes the only provision in the contract about quality, or it may be that his standard is an added protection, so that performance under the contract must satisfy both the contract requirements and the certifier. . . . "

It should be said at once that in building contracts the architect or engineer in his certifying capacity does not fall into the first category mentioned by Devlin J. in the above passage, namely, a servant or agent who is the *alter ego* of his master or principal.[58] Further, it should be noted that in referring to the situation in terms of arbitration, as in the above passage, the courts do not always mean that the function of the person expressing satisfaction is that of an arbitrator within the Arbitration Acts, and therefore subject to the control and rights of appeal on points of law conferred by those Acts. Confusion will be avoided if it is remembered that, when dealing with contractual provisions relating to satisfaction, approval or certificates, the courts frequently resort by analogy to the terms of arbitration, and refer to the certifier or other person named as an " arbitrator " but do not mean thereby that he is a " pure " arbitrator in Devlin J.'s words.

In cases where the approval or certificate relates to the quality or completeness of the work as a whole the two basic problems which arise in construing these provisions are, first, whether the builder must obtain the necessary approval or certificate before he can sue for work done, and secondly, whether the employer is bound once the stipulated approval is given, and thereby precluded from alleging that the work was not in accordance with the contract. These two aspects will be dealt with in the separate subsections (2) and (3) below.

[58] *Cf. De Morgan Snell & Co.* v. *Rio de Janeiro Flour Mills* (1892) 8 T.L.R. 292, illustrated *ante*, Chap. 2, p. 95 (a case of a resident engineer).

At first sight these questions may seem to be the exact converse of each other, and obviously it is to be expected that where the courts hold satisfaction, approval or a certificate to be a condition precedent to the right of the builder to sue, they will lean towards holding the employer precluded from alleging defective or insufficient work once the satisfaction, approval or certificate has been obtained. Further, the cases cited in the separate sections below usually proceed upon the assumption that the two questions are identical, and accordingly are often authority for the corresponding proposition in the other section. But in fact it is perfectly possible for the contractual provisions to stipulate for a different conclusion upon the two questions, and in many modern contracts this would in fact happen were the question not rendered academic by reason of the overriding provisions of the arbitration clause.[59]

Nor are these questions exactly the converse of each other, even in the absence of some express special provision of the kind referred to, because an employer may be entitled to allege defective work for either of two reasons; first, that the covenant to obtain satisfaction is, on a true construction of the contract as a whole, not a condition at all and is subordinate to the obligation to do the work in accordance with the contract, or, secondly that even if it is a condition (and accordingly, the builder is not entitled to sue without obtaining it) it is an added protection, and the obligation to carry out the work in accordance with the contract remains unaffected. In fact there are three possible obligations by a builder on which his right to payment may depend:

(a)   to obtain satisfaction, conformity in other respects with the contract being subordinated thereto and not a condition [60];

(b)   to obtain satisfaction and to conform to the contract, both being conditions which the builder must perform [60]; and

(c)   to do the contract work as specified, the satisfaction of the person concerned not being a condition at all (and substantial performance of the contract being possible without it).[61]

In the case of contracts falling into categories (a) or (b) on the one hand, the builder will be unable to recover unless he obtains the required satisfaction, approval or certificate, but not in the case of

---

[59] See, *e.g.* the provision in *Robins* v. *Goddard* [1905] 1 K.B. 294, *infra*, p. 439, and see *e.g.* the terms of the contract in *Miller* v. *L.C.C.* (1934) 50 T.L.R. at p. 483. As to the post-1963 R.I.B.A. forms, see *post*, pp. 489–492.
[60] *Cf. per* Devlin J. *supra*, pp. 417–418.   [61] *Cf. Dallman* v. *King*, *supra*, pp. 413–414.

category (c). On the other hand, in the case of category (a) the employer will be precluded from alleging that the work was not in accordance with the contract if the builder has succeeded in obtaining the required satisfaction, approval or certificate, but not in the other two cases.

It will be seen in the following subsections that the majority of building contracts where the certifier is the architect or engineer of the employer appear to fall into the first of the above categories, but the rule is not universal, and it would now seem that where the person whose satisfaction is referred to has no connection at all with the parties to the contract, the contract may well fall into the second category.[61a] Further it may be advisable to reiterate the warning given earlier that in modern forms of contract the effect of the arbitration clause, if it is or can be invoked, may well be to give the arbitrator powers sufficiently wide to deprive the satisfaction, approval or certificate of any binding effect whatever.[62] In addition, it should be noted that, depending on the wording of the contract, a certificate may be intended to relate to quality only, or the amount due only, or to both.[62a] An obvious example is an interim certificate, which almost invariably does not have any bearing on the quality or sufficiency of the work, but which may be a condition precedent to the builder's right to sue.[63]

(2) Whether Certificate, Satisfaction or Approval a Condition Precedent to Builder's Right to Sue

As previously indicated, there are two possible views, namely, that obtaining the stipulated approval or satisfaction is not a condition of the contract, so that by carrying out the work the builder has substantially performed his obligations, and on the other hand, that the obtaining of the required approval is a condition, so that until it has been obtained the builder has failed to satisfy a fundamental term of the contract, and is thereby disentitled from suing upon it. In most building contracts this latter interpretation is, subject to the terms of the arbitration clause, likely to be the true view, and if the sense of the transaction requires it, it matters not

---

[61a] See *Billyack* v. *Leyland* [1968] 1 W.L.R. 471, commented on *infra*, p. 433.

[62] See Section 4, *infra*, Effect of Arbitration Clause. But see, now, the considerably narrower clauses in the 1957 and 1963 revised editions of the R.I.B.A. form of contract discussed *post*, pp. 489–492 which are seriously disadvantageous to the employer.   [62a] See Section 1 (2), *supra*.

[63] See Section 6, *infra*, pp. 492 *et seq.* where in fact it is suggested that in the standard forms of contract it is not even a condition precedent by virtue of the particular wording of their arbitration clauses.

whether the approval or satisfaction is expressed to be a condition precedent, or required to be evidenced by a certificate, or whether there is no covenant to obtain approval at all, but only a covenant by the employer to pay upon the certificate of his architect. Similar principles apply to provisions relating to questions involving extras to the contract, extension of time, or other detailed matters as opposed to the main work undertaken.[64]

ILLUSTRATIONS

(1) By a building contract, after providing for payment of instalments, it was stipulated that the employer should pay the balance " within two calendar months after receiving the said architect's certificate that the whole of the buildings and works thereby contracted for had been executed and completed to his satisfaction." *Held*, that the production of the architect's certificate was a condition precedent to payment of the balance: *Morgan* v. *Birnie* (1833).[65]

(2) C contracted to execute work according to plans and a specification, and to the satisfaction of B, or any other architect whom the building owners might appoint. *Held*, that there was a valid reference to B, which excluded proof as to the sufficiency of the work: *Chapman* v. *Edinburgh Prison Board* (1844).[66]

(3) A building contract provided that no instalments should be payable unless the plaintiff should deliver to the defendant a certificate signed by the defendant's surveyor that the work was in all respects well and substantially performed. The defendant appointed his own father surveyor. The builder alleged fraud in withholding the certificate, and sued for work done. *Held*, the action was not maintainable without a certificate, and the builder's proper remedy was a separate action for fraud, and not an action on the contract: *Milner* v. *Field* (1850).[67]

(4) A building contract provided that the works should be executed to the satisfaction of the architect; additions and alterations were not to be executed without his order in writing. The architect ordered additions. The builder brought an action against the employer in which he alleged (*inter alia*) that the architect did not ascertain the amount of the additions, and that the balance of the whole account was unpaid. The employer set up that the builder was not entitled to have the amount of the additions ascertained as he had not obtained the certificate of the architect that the work

[61] In addition to the cases illustrated below, see the cases of *Mills* v. *Bayley* (1863) 2 H. & C. 36, *Canty* v. *Clarke* (1878) 44 Up.Can.Q.B. 222, and *Murray* v. *Cohen* (1889) 9 N.S.W.R. (Eq.) 124, all illustrated *post*, Section 6 (5), pp. 486–487, and see also *Miller* v. *L.C.C.*, *supra*, p. 419.   [65] (1833) 9 Bing. 672.

[66] 6 D. (Ct. of Sess.) 1288. (Note: This Scottish case, and the two other Scottish cases of *Muldoon* v. *Pringle* (1882) 9 R. (Ct. of Sess.) 915, and *Ayr Road Trustees* v. *Adams* (1883) 11 R. (Ct. of Sess.) 326, set out in the next Section, proceed upon the basis that the promise to do work to the satisfaction of B, was in effect a submission to arbitration. This, in the sense of arbitration proper, is not, as has been pointed out, the basis of the English cases.)

[67] 5 Ex. 829. (N.B. The latter part of this decision requires considerable modification in the light of subsequent cases. See Section 5, Recovery without Certificates, *infra*.)

had been executed to his satisfaction. *Held*, that the obtaining of the certificate was a condition precedent to having the amount of the additions ascertained: *Glenn* v. *Leith* (1853).[68]

(5) A agreed to supply coke of a certain quality, and to the satisfaction of the company's inspecting officer for the time being. In the case of his not supplying coke of the quality required, and to the satisfaction of the said company's officer, the company might refuse to accept, and buy elsewhere. *Held*, that the satisfaction of the inspector was a condition precedent: *Grafton* v. *Eastern Counties Railway* (1853).[69]

(6) It was provided by clause 11 in a contract that the consulting engineer should have power to make additions to or deductions from the works and that " the value of all such additions, deductions, alterations and deviations should be ascertained and added to or deducted from the amount of the contract price, as the case may require." There was also a clause that any dispute as to the value of additions, alterations, deductions, etc. should from time to time be referred to the consulting engineer, whose decision, valuation or award, interim or final, should be conclusive and binding upon both parties to the contract. *Held*, that the ascertainment of value by the engineer under clause 11 was a condition precedent: *Westwood* v. *The Secretary of State for India* (1863).[70]

(7) A contract empowered the clerk of works to order variations, without any extension of time unless he so ordered. He did order alterations, but gave no extension of time. The builder pleaded that completion within the contract period was impossible by virtue of the alterations. *Held*, even if this were so, he was bound by the terms of the contract to accept the clerk of works' decision: *Jones* v. *St. John's College Oxford* (1870).[71]

(8) A contract provided that " all the accounts relating to this contract between the company and the contractors shall be submitted to and adjusted and settled by the company's engineer-in-chief, and his certificate of the ultimate balance of the account shall be final and conclusive on both parties without any appeal." *Held*, that the certificate of the engineer-in-chief was a condition precedent to the determination of the sum which the company were to pay, and that the contractor could not recover any further payment beyond the amount certified by the engineer-in-chief: *Sharpe* v. *San Paulo Railway* (1873).[72]

(9) A contract provided that " the contractor and the director will be bound to leave all questions or matters of dispute which may arise during the progress of the works or in the settlement of the account to the architect, whose decision shall be final and binding upon all parties. The contractor will be paid on the certificate

[68] 1 Com. Law Rep. 569.
[69] (1853) 8 Ex. 699. See also *Munro* v. *Butt* (1858) 8 E. & B. 738, *ante*, Chap. 6, Section 1, pp. 377–378.
[70] 7 L.T. 736. (N.B. This and cases (8) and (9), *infra*, are cases where the architect's function under the clause in question was very close to, if not actually, that of a true arbitrator.)
[71] L.R. 6 Q.B. 115. Illustrated more fully *post*, Chap. 11, p. 628.
[72] L.R. 8 Ch.App. 597, 605.

of the architect." *Held*, that before the contractor could recover anything from the company, there must be a certificate of the architect as to what was due: *Stevenson* v. *Watson* (1879). [73]

(10) By a written agreement a tenant of a furnished house agreed at the expiration of the tenancy to deliver up possession of the house and the furniture in good order, and in the event of loss, damage, or breakage, to make good or pay for the same, the amount of such payment, if disputed, to be settled by two valuers. *Held*, that the settlement of the amount of the payment by the valuers was a condition precedent to the right of the landlord to bring an action in respect of the dilapidations: *Babbage* v. *Coulburn* (1882). [74]

(11) A building contract provided: "(1) The works shall be completed in all respects . . . on or before the 16th day of December, 1901, to the satisfaction of the surveyor . . . to be testified by a certificate under his hand." "(4) . . . The contractor shall be paid by the council at the rate of 80 per cent. of the value of the work done in each month, and the balance one month after completion of the contract. Provided that the district council shall not be required to pay to the contractor any sum exceeding the value as valued by the said surveyor or other officer of so much of the works as shall have been executed by the contractor during the preceding month." *Held*, that the contract made a certificate by the surveyor that the work had been completed to his satisfaction a condition precedent to the payment of the retention money: *Wallace* v. *Brandon and Byshottles Urban District Council* (1903). [75]

(12) A building contract provided (Clause 26) that "The certificate of the architect is a condition precedent to the contractor's right of action against the employer." It was further provided (Clause 27) that "The architect is to be the sole arbitrator or umpire between the employer and the contractor, and is to determine any question, dispute or difference that may arise either during the progress of the work or in determining the value of any variations that may be made in the work contracted for, and the certificate of the architect's decision upon such question, dispute or difference shall be final and binding between the employer and contractor, and without further appeal whatsoever." The contractor, who had been fully paid by the employer upon every certificate issued by the architect, and had not demanded arbitration under the arbitration clause, sought to recover further payment by bringing an action. *Held*, that in the absence of fraud or collusion or other improper conduct between the employer and the architect, the contractor could not succeed in his action: *Eaglesham* v. *McMaster* (1920). [76]

(13) A term of a main contract incorporated into a sub-contract [76a] provided that payment respecting any work comprised in the sub-contract would not be due until receipt by the main contractor of

[73] 4 C.P.D. 148.   [74] 9 Q.B.D. 235.
[75] Hudson's B.C., 4th ed., Vol. 2, p. 362.
[76] [1920] 2 K.B. 169. (Note: In this case, as it was expressly provided that the certificate of the architect was to be a condition precedent to the contractor's right of action, it was obvious that he could not maintain an action without the certificate: *Scott* v. *Avery* (1856) 5 H.L.C. 811, and see *Lloyd Bros.* v. *Milward*, illustrated *infra*, pp. 438–439. For a fuller discussion of *Eaglesham's* case see *post*, Sect. 7 (3), pp. 503–504.
[76a] For the term in the sub-contract, see *post*, Chap. 15, p. 769.

the architect's certificate relating to the work. Judgment creditors of the sub-contractor sought to garnish the money owed by the main contractor, after the main contract and sub-contract work was complete but before any certificate relating to the sub-contract work had been issued by the architect. *Held*, by the Divisional Court, there was no debt capable of being garnished by the judgment creditor until a certificate was issued: *Dunlop and Ranken Ltd.* v. *Hendall Steel Structures* (1957). [77]

(14) The order from a main contractor to an excavation sub-contractor stated " This order is all based on unit prices. Quantities compiled by the Dept. of Transport engineer in charge of the work and allowed by the Dept. to (the main contractor) will be the final figure in making payments to (the sub-contractor)." The sub-contractor alleged that the engineer had made mistakes in measuring the quantities. *Held*, by the Ontario Court of Appeal, following *Sharpe* v. *Sao Paulo Railway*, that since dishonesty was not imputed, the sub-contractor was bound by the engineer's measurements: *Croft Construction Co.* v. *Terminal Construction Co.* (1960). [78]

The following cases are illustrations of the courts taking an opposite view. [79]

ILLUSTRATIONS

(1) A covenanted to light a town to the satisfaction of B's surveyor, to keep the lamps burning for a certain time with certain burners, and to pay a certain sum on default. B covenanted " if A did well and effectually light the lamps and fulfil all his covenants," to pay A certain prices. *Held*, that the covenant to pay was separate and severable, and that the performance by A of all his covenants was not a condition precedent to his right to recover, by action on B's covenant, the price of gas supplied: *London Gas Light Co.* v. *Chelsea Vestry* (1860). [80]

(2) In a contract for the supply and erection of electric plant it was provided that the contractors were to be paid in three instalments: " the said respective instalments shall be paid within fourteen days after the production of the certificate of the engineer that such instalments are respectively due and payable." An action was brought by the contractors for the unpaid balance of the purchase price without production of the engineer's certificate. *Held*, that the action was competent. *Per* the Lord President: " It is possible to phrase a contract so that the possession of an engineer's certificate should be made a condition precedent to any action whatsoever. All I can say is that that has not been done here ": *Howden & Co. Ltd.* v. *Powell Duffryn Steam Co.* (1912). [81]

---

[77] [1957] 1 W.L.R. 1102. This case is criticised *post*, Section 6 (7), p. 496, on the ground (*inter alia*) that the effect of the arbitration clause (if incorporated, which is not entirely clear) seems to have been overlooked.

[78] 20 D.L.R. (2d) 247 (Canada).

[79] See also *Dallman* v. *King* (1837) 4 Bing.N.C. 105 and the other cases illustrated *supra*, pp. 413–414.

[80] 2 L.T. 217. This is not an easy case to support in principle.

[81] 1912 S.C. (Ct. of Sess.) 920 (Scotland).

[Note: Beyond the simple statement quoted, no considered reasons for the decision are given in this Scottish case. The English authorities do not appear to have been cited to the court, and it can only be said that the decision does not appear to be in line with the English cases. The case was, however, followed in the South African case next illustrated.]

(3) Clause 2 of a building contract provided that the employer would pay the contractor the contract sum of £575 or such other sum as might be payable " at the times and in the manner specified in the conditions." Clause 25 (*a*) of the conditions provided that the contractor should be entitled to a monthly certificate from the architect of the amount due to him from the employer and within three days of issue to payment by the employer. *Held*, following *Howden* v. *Powell Duffryn* (no other cases apparently being cited) that a certificate was not a condition precedent to a right to sue. *Errico* v. *Lotter* (1956). [82]

[Note: This case might be explained on the ground that the sum in fact claimed, namely the balance at the end of the work, could not be the subject of a monthly clause 25 certificate, or alternatively on the ground that there was an overriding arbitration clause. There is no mention of either ground in the judgment, however, and it is difficult to approve of or understand the apparent *ratio decidendi*.]

In addition to the cases cited above as illustrations of the view that a certificate or approval is usually a condition precedent to the builder's right to recover, the cases in Section 4, *infra*, Effect of Arbitration Clause, should also be considered as showing that the parties would have been bound but for the arbitration clause.

(3) Whether Employer Bound by Certificate, Satisfaction or Approval

Here the two possible views are, firstly that the satisfaction, approval or certificate is intended to be the only, or the overriding, requirement as to the sufficiency of the work, or secondly, that this requirement is either not a condition at all, or is an added protection to the employer, so that to recover the builder must satisfy all other contractual provisions defining the work to be done. [83] In the last case, if the employer can show, despite the satisfaction, approval or certificate having been obtained, that the work is nevertheless not in accordance with the contract, then he is not precluded from suing for breach of contract, or from setting up this allegation as a defence to a claim by the builder for the price of the work. It will be seen that, where the person whose satisfaction is required is the

[82] 1956 (4) S.A. 139 (South Africa).
[83] See the passage in the last paragraph of the quotation from Devlin J. set out *supra*, p. 418. For a criticism of this latter interpretation see, however, *infra*, pp. 433–434.

architect or engineer of the employer, the courts in the past have almost invariably adopted the first of these views, and it made no difference in *Harvey's* case,[84] for instance, that the obligation is expressed to be to do work in accordance with the contract " and " to the satisfaction of the architect or engineer.[85] The important recent decision of Edmund Davies L.J. in *Billyack* v. *Leyland* [86] adopted the second view, following *Newton Abbot Development Co. Ltd.* v. *Stockman.*[87] Both these cases involved the satisfaction of local authority officials who were not the agents of either party to the contract, and it is suggested *infra* that this may be (and if so very understandably) the basis of the distinction.

It should also be noted that not only is the employer precluded from disputing sufficiency of the work, but also that in some cases the courts have not permitted him to allege that under the special provisions of the contract the certificate or approval should not have been given, *e.g.* because of the contractor's failure to obtain written authorisations for extras, or to give notice as required.[87a] It cannot be pretended that there has been any great consistency of principle about this, since it has already been seen [87b] that certifiers' decisions will be invalidated in other circumstances where the strict requirements of the contract have not been complied with, and the "extras" cases (where the certifier was in favour of the contractor) seem inconsistent with the modern tendency to invalidate decisions (usually in favour of the employer) unless the certifier has acted strictly within the terms of his contractual jurisdiction.[87c]

ILLUSTRATIONS

(1) The builder agreed to repair certain houses " according to the specification and drawings prepared by A," the works " to be done with the best materials . . . according to the drawings, specifications . . . and to the full satisfaction of the building owner or his architect." There was no provision as to certificates. The architect certified his satisfaction on the completion of the contract. *Held*, that in an action by the builder against the owner for the money agreed to be paid by the latter no evidence could be received from the defendant that the work was not done according to the plans and specifications: *Harvey* v. *Lawrence* (1867).[88]

---

[84] *Infra.*
[85] In addition to the cases illustrated, see the South African case of *McCarthy* v. *Visser* (1905) 22 Cape of Good Hope Rep. 122, illustrated *ante*, Chap. 6, p. 393, and the case of *Burns* v. *Furby* (1885) 4 N.Z.L.R. (Supr.Ct.) 110, illustrated *post*, Section 6 (5), p. 487.
[86] [1968] 1 W.L.R. 471, illustrated *infra*, pp. 432–433.
[87] (1931) 47 T.L.R. 616, illustrated *infra*, p. 432.
[87a] See also *post*, Chap. 8, pp. 553–555 for this subject.
[87b] See *supra*, Section 1 (2), pp. 406 *et seq.*
[87c] See *infra*, Section 5 (5), pp. 466–469. See also pp. 476–479.   [88] 15 L.T. 571.

(2) A building contract provided that extras should be ordered in writing, but no claim should be made for extras without production of the written order, that certain proportionate payments should be made from time to time on the certificate of the architect, whose opinion as to value was to be final, that if any dispute arose as to the meaning of the specification or contract, the architect was to define the meaning, and that his decision as to the nature, quality and quantity of the works executed or to be executed should be final, and also his decision as regards the value of extras. The architect gave a certificate that a certain sum, which included extras, should be paid. *Held*, that the certificate was conclusive, and prevented the question whether or not there was a sufficient order in writing for extras from being raised: *Goodyear* v. *Weymouth Corporation* (1865). [89]

(3) An engineering contract provided that no extra work should be executed without an order in writing; that such extra works should be valued by the engineer, whose decision as to value should be final; that accounts of extras ordered should be sent in within one month; that in default of their being so sent in the employers should not be bound to pay for the extras contained in them; that the engineer should be exclusive judge of the execution of the works and of everything connected with the contract, and that the certificates of the engineer should be binding and conclusive on both parties. The engineer gave a final certificate, which included the price of extras. The employers refused to pay the part of the price relating to such extras. The contractors brought an action on the certificate. The employers set up the defences that the extras had not been ordered in writing, and that the accounts for them had not been sent in within one month. *Held*, on demurrer, that both defences were bad, as the certificate was binding on both parties: *Connor* v. *Belfast Water Commissioners* (1871). [90]

(4) L. contracted to erect a pier for the H. Company. The contract provided that payments should be made on production of the engineer's certificates. The contract further provided that no extra work should be paid for unless L. should produce written orders signed by the engineer and countersigned by the chairman of the company. The engineer was to furnish monthly certificates of the value of the work executed, and L. was to be paid 85 per cent. of these amounts forthwith, and the balance three months after the giving of a certificate of satisfactory completion of the work, provided that, within three months of the giving of such certificate, L. should have delivered to the engineer a full account of all claims which he might have upon the company, and that the engineer should have certified the correctness of the account. The engineer gave his final certificate, in which he certified for extra work which had not in fact been done, and also for extra work which had been done, but for which no signed and countersigned orders had been given. *Held*, that the final certificate precluded the company from raising the point whether particular extras had been done or had been done

[89] 35 L.J.C.P. 12. (Note: This and the following are examples of the type of case where the analogy to arbitration is very close.)
[90] 5 Ir.L.R.(C.L.) 55.

without signed and countersigned orders: *Laidlaw* v. *Hastings Pier Co.* (1874).[91]

(5) Extras were to be paid or allowed for at the price fixed by the building owner's surveyor. The surveyor certified in his final certificate sums in respect of matters which the employer contended were not extras at all. *Held*, the employer was bound by his surveyor's certificate: *Richards* v. *May* (1883).[92]

(6) The builder sued for the price under a contract and for extras, producing a certificate for that amount from the architect. The decision of the architect was by the contract to be final and without appeal. The defence set up was that the architect had by mistake certified for work not done and improperly done; that his certificate included extras for an amount over £10, the orders for which had not been countersigned as required by the contract; and that he had not made sufficient allowances for work not done. *Held*, by A. L. Smith J., that it was not competent for the defendants to go behind or quarrel with the certificate on any of the grounds alleged: *Lapthorne* v. *St. Aubyn* (1885).[93]

(7) The defendant contracted to alter the plaintiff's mansion-house, the work done and materials supplied to be to the satisfaction of the plaintiff and his architect, whose certificate was to be final, but if any defects were discovered within twelve months after the giving of the certificate, such certificate was to be no bar to the action. The stone used was subsequently found defective and not adapted for external use. *Held*, that the covenant to supply good work and materials according to the specification was subordinate to the clause as to the satisfaction of the architect, and that after such certificate no action could be maintained except within the twelve months provided for; and that though it was hard on the plaintiff, yet, if he employed an architect who did not know his business and certified when he ought not to express his satisfaction, he was bound by his architect's mistake in the absence of fraud, which was not here imputed: *Bateman (Lord)* v. *Thompson* (1875).[94]

(8) The defendants contracted with the plaintiff, a railway company, to supply rails of a certain pattern and sample, to be inspected by the engineer. The contract stated that his inspection (which was to be at the manufacturer's works) was not in any way to commit the company to the approval and acceptance of any rails which when delivered should not be strictly in accordance with the drawings and specification. There was also a provision that the entire contract was to be executed in every respect to the satisfaction of the engineer who should have the power of rejecting any rails he might disapprove on any ground whatever, and whose decision on any points of doubt or dispute that might arise in reference to the contract should be final. There was no provision as to certificates. The rails were delivered and found satisfactory by the engineer, and paid for,

---

[91] Hudson's B.C., 4th ed., Vol. 2, p. 13; following and approving *Goodyear* v. *Weymouth Corporation, supra.*

[92] (1883) 10 Q.B.D. 400, illustrated more fully *post*, Chap. 8, p. 554.

[93] 1 Cab. & El. 486; following *Laidlaw* v. *Hastings Pier Co., supra.*

[94] Hudson's B.C., 4th ed., Vol. 2, p. 36 (affd. by C.A.); following *Goodyear* v. *Weymouth Corporation* (1865) 35 L.J.C.P. 12.

but after half of them had been laid it was discovered that they were defective. The employer sued for breach of contract. *Held,* that the company had no right of action, as it was the intention of the parties on the construction of the contract to make the satisfaction of the engineer final, and to take away any subsequent right of action: *Dunaberg Railway* v. *Hopkins* (1877).[95]

(9) A builder agreed to do work to the satisfaction of an inspector. The employer sued the builder for defects. The inspector had failed to inspect, but had given certificates. *Held,* that the employer could not recover from the builder for defects in work done under the eye of the inspector: *Muldoon* v. *Pringle* (1882).[96]

(10) A. contracted to construct a bridge for road trustees. The work was to be done to the satisfaction of one of a firm of engineers. A resident inspector appointed by the engineer was to superintend the work. A. was to maintain the bridge for one year. In fact, the resident inspector was appointed by the trustees, and was subject to their orders. On completion of the bridge, the engineer, on reports of the resident inspector, gave his certificate, and the final instalment of the price was paid. More than a year afterwards the trustees brought an action against A., alleging that the work was not according to contract. *Held,* that the trustees, having taken the appointment of the resident inspector into their own hands, his knowledge was their knowledge, and that the certificate having been given on reports by him, and not on any fraudulent representations by A., the trustees were not entitled to reopen the matter: *Ayr Road Trustees* v. *Adams* (1883).[97]

(11) The whole of the works were to be carried out to the entire satisfaction of the architect. The contractor was entitled to be paid the final balance due at the end of four months after the architect should have given his certificate in writing that the works had been completed according to the contract, and the certificate of the final balance due was to be conclusive evidence of the works being duly completed. Defects appearing within the four months were to be made good. It was further provided that the final certificate should not relieve the contractor from liability for " any fraud, default, or wilful deviation " from the contract until four years from completion. Defects were discovered during the four years due to slovenly workmanship, but not made with the object of benefiting the contractor or saving his pocket. *Held,* the employers were precluded from setting up the defects against the contractor: *London School Board* v. *Johnson* (1891).[98]

(12) A contract provided for a house to be built to the satisfaction of the owner and an inspector of housing. The owner was also entitled to require renewal or replacement of work which was in his opinion defective. Further, the builder undertook to maintain the works for three months after completion. The owner and inspector were satisfied, and a final certificate given. More than three

[95] 36 L.T. 733; following *Goodyear* v. *Weymouth Corporation* (1865) 35 L.J.C.P. 12; and *Bateman (Lord)* v. *Thompson* (1875) Hudson's B.C., 4th ed., Vol. 2, p. 36.
[96] 9 R. (Ct. of Sess.) 915.
[97] 11 R. (Ct. of Sess.) 326.
[98] Hudson's B.C., Vol. 2, p. 176. See also *McCarthy* v. *Visser* (1905) 22 Cape of Good Hope Rep. 122, illustrated *ante,* Chap. 6, p. 393.

months later the owner sued for latent defects. *Held*, following *Bateman* (*Lord*) v. *Thompson, supra*, that the undertaking of the builder to supply good materials and workmanship was subordinated to the satisfaction of the building owner and inspector. The owner's right to require renewal or replacement of defects could only be exercised before the satisfaction was given, and the obligation to maintain was to maintain in the condition existing at the time satisfaction was expressed: *Bruens* v. *Smith* (1951). [99]

(13) By clause 2 of a building contract the contractor undertook to carry out the works as detailed in the specification and drawings in accordance with the contract. By clause 3 the work was to be to the entire satisfaction in all respects of the engineer. Clause 7 provided " when the works have been completely executed according to the provisions of the contract and to the satisfaction of the engineer the date of such completion shall be certified by him, and such date shall be the date of commencement " of the period of maintenance. There was a defects liability clause in usual form operating during the maintenance period, and by clause 16 a provision that no certificate for interim payment should be considered conclusive evidence as to the sufficiency of the works or materials. The clause for interim payments provided for 90 per cent. of the value of work and 95 per cent. on satisfactory completion. There was an arbitration clause which in the event was held not applicable. [1] Completion was certified under clause 7 as to eleven out of seventeen blocks of buildings (as there was power to do). Serious breaches of contract were discovered after the expiry of the maintenance period on the eleven blocks and the engineer's representative refused to certify completion of the remaining six blocks. The employers sued for damages. *Held*, by the Privy Council, after considering the *Bateman* case (1875), [2] the *Newton Abbot* case (1931), [3] *Harvey* v. *Lawrence* (1867) [4] and the *Petrofina* case (1937) [5] (*a*) that little help was to be derived from other contracts decided on different wording, (*b*) that though clause 7 did not contain the words " final and conclusive " the decision of the engineer under that clause was intended to be binding on the parties and hence the matter was not subject to arbitration, (*c*) that a certificate under clause 7, being a certificate that the works had been completed in accordance with the contract and also to the engineer's satisfaction, extinguished any further liability on the part of the contractor save only the obligation of the contractor under the defects liability clause to put right repairs as he might be called upon to do within the maintenance period and (*d*) that no defects having appeared or been brought to the contractor's attention within the maintenance period in respect of eleven blocks, the contractor was entitled to the full price of those blocks, though in the case of the remaining six blocks the employer was entitled to damages: *Ata Ul Haq* v. *City Council of Nairobi* (1959). [6]

---

[99] 1951 (1) S.A. 67 (South Africa).
[1] For the clause, see *infra*, Section 4, p. 444.
[2] *Supra*, p. 428.
[3] *Infra*, p. 432.
[4] *Supra*, p. 426.
[5] *Infra*, p. 432.
[6] [1959] P.C. Appeal No. 48 (unreported).

[Note: This case was criticised in a note in the Ninth Edition, but on reconsideration it may be that it is an example of a type of contract which, while very rare at the present day in the United Kingdom, still appears to be in use in the Commonwealth, in which the definitive certificate of satisfaction is that given at the *beginning* of the maintenance or defects period, and not the final certificate itself, though such an intention seems strange.[6a]　See the next two illustrations.]

(14) A contract provided that the work should be done to the reasonable satisfaction of the architect, and for a certificate of completion to be given when the architect had approved and passed the work as complete, and that from the date of such certificate the contractor was to be liable for maintenance of the works only. The final certificate releasing the retention should not absolve the contractor from his liability for defective work due to fraudulent conduct on his part and which appeared after the period had expired. There was an arbitration clause which it was admitted did not apply. No certificate of completion was in fact ever given, but the architect ultimately gave his final certificate, after discussing certain defects with the contractor which he was told had been rectified, but which he did not check for himself. *Held*, by the Court of Appeal of New Zealand, that on the facts there had been no fraud by the contractor, that the certificate should be treated as the certificate of satisfaction, and that the employer was accordingly bound by the certificate: *Stratford (Borough of)* v. *Ashman* (1960).[7]

(15) By clause 2 of a building contract the contractor, at the time fixed for completion, was to hand the works over to the employer fully completed in every respect to the satisfaction of the architect to be signified by a certificate of completion, and by clause 26 two instalments of retention money became payable one month and three months respectively after this certificate. It was further provided that the certificate on completion should not prevent the architect at any time before the expiry of the period of maintenance and the issue of the final certificate from rejecting defective work or materials. *Held*, by the Court of Appeal of New Zealand, that the relevant certificate of satisfaction was that on completion before the maintenance period began, and that, the arbitration clause not being on its true construction applicable,[7a] the employer was bound by the certificate unless a defect appeared within the relevant period: *Major* v. *Greenfield* (1965).[7b]

The following are examples of the less usual situation where the courts have taken the view that the employer remains free to dispute the quality of the work despite a certificate or approval.

ILLUSTRATIONS

(1) S. contracted to make and deliver to B. certain iron rails of an agreed quality. The rails were, by the contract, to be inspected before delivery by B.'s agent, who could approve and accept such as he should think fit. The rails were so inspected and approved. *Held*,

---

[6a] See *per* Edmund Davies L.J. in *Billyack*, *infra*, p. 433, who similarly doubted it.
[7] [1960] N.Z.L.R. 503.　　　　[7a] Criticised on this point *infra*, Section 4, p. 445.
[7b] [1965] N.Z.L.R. 1035.

that the stipulations were distinct, and that the approval of the agent under the second stipulation was no proof that the first stipulation (as to quality) had been complied with: *Bird* v. *Smith* (1848).[8]

(2) The defendants agreed to build a number of houses for the plaintiffs in accordance with plans and specifications, the work to be to the satisfaction of the local surveyor and sanitary inspector. They were satisfied, and the plaintiffs sold the houses at a profit but the houses were not in fact built in accordance with the specifications. *Held*, that the approval, not being expressed to be final under the contract, was merely an added protection, and the plaintiffs, who had paid compensation to the purchasers, could recover the difference between the actual value of the houses when completed and what it would have been had they been properly built: *Newton Abbot Development Co. Ltd.* v. *Stockman Brothers* (1931).[9]

(3) A charterparty contained a clause that a steamer was to be in every way fitted for a voyage, and another that the captain was bound to keep the tanks always clean. By Clause 27 it was further provided that the steamer was to be clean for the cargo in question to the satisfaction of the charterer's inspector. The inspector's requirements as to cleaning were complied with and he was satisfied. *Held*, that as to cleanliness of the tanks the shipowner's obligation under Clause 27 was superadded to his other obligations as an additional protection to the charterers, and the shipowners were accordingly liable for damaged cargo: *Petrofina S.A. of Brussels* v. *Compagnia Italiana, etc.* (1937).[10]

(4) A developer/contractor sold a house in the course of erection, undertaking by clause 1 of the contract to " build and complete in a workmanlike manner and in accordance with the specification hereto annexed." The specification provided that " excavation, concreting . . . will be carried out in accordance with by-laws of the local authority and to their satisfaction." Clause 2 provided that the owner should pay the contractor the second half of the purchase money " on the issue of the certificate of habitation by the local authority which certificate shall be conclusive evidence of the completion of the said dwelling-house." The local authority issued its certificate of habitation. The foundations had not in fact been properly constructed and infringed the by-laws, and major underpinning work had to be carried out. When sued, the builder pleaded (a) that the certificate under clause 2 was an independent reason why the purchaser was barred from claiming (b) that the provision for satisfaction in the specification overrode the obligation to comply with the by-laws and (c) that the express requirement for conformity with the by-laws negatived any implied term as to the design or suitability of the foundations. *Held*, by Edmund Davies L.J.,[10a] (a) that the clause 2 certificate was a certificate designed to regulate the time of payment and was not intended to be a certificate as to the quality of the work,[10b] (b) that the provision for the local authority's satisfaction was an added protection for the purchaser and that,

---

[8] 12 Q.B. 786.
[9] 47 T.L.R. 616. Criticised *infra*. The case is further criticised (on measure of damage), *post*, Chap. 9, pp. 577–578.   [10] 53 T.L.R. 650.
[10a] Doubting the *Ata Ul Haq* case, *supra*.
[10b] Contrast decision on similar wording in *London School Bd.* v. *Johnson, supra*, p. 429.

following the *Newton Abbot* and *Petrofina* cases, it did not override the express obligation to carry out the work in a workmanlike manner and (c) there was nothing in the contract inconsistent with the three-fold implied undertakings of quality referred to by Denning M.R. in *Hancock* v. *Brazier (Anerley) Ltd.*[11]; *Billyack* v. *Leyland* (1968).[12]

The above cases are examples of the second category referred to in the section " Generally " above,[13] namely cases where the satisfaction or approval is regarded as an added protection to the employer, and compliance with the contract in all respects must also be shown. Although the *Newton Abbot* case (1931) was cited without disapproval as an illustration by Devlin J. in the *Minster Trust* case (1954) [14] in the passage already quoted [15] it is submitted that the case is, in fact, of doubtful authority in building or engineering contracts in the proper sense, where an architect or engineer of the employer is present, and is the person whose certificate or satisfaction is required under the terms of the contract. Thus in his careful judgment in *Billyack's* case (1968), Edmund Davies L.J. said, when distinguishing *Bateman's* case, " but there, as in many of the other cases cited, the architect or other party whose satisfaction was required was himself appointed by the building owner." Apart from the fact that none of the relevant cases appears to have been cited to Roche J. in the *Newton Abbot* case, careful analysis shows that, where the obligation is to do work in accordance with the contract and to the satisfaction of the architect, the choice lies between two constructions, namely (a) the contractor must do the described contract work, and for this purpose the decision of the architect as to what is a sufficient performance of the described contract work is to be binding on both parties (this is the effect where the approval or satisfaction prevails over the contract description of the work); or (b) the contractor must do the contract work, and if the architect honestly but mistakenly requires him to do more he must be prepared to do that as well without extra payment or he will be in breach of contract (this is the effect when the satisfaction or approval is regarded as a superadded protection on the employer). This latter view is not likely, it is submitted, to be the intention of the parties to a conventional building contract. On the other hand, it is well known that a local authority building inspector may demand more than is provided for in the contract—as *e.g.* a greater depth of foundations, or a rolled steel joist where ordinary brickwork or

[11] See *ante*, Chap. 5, p. 279.   [12] [1968] 1 W.L.R. 471.
[13] *Supra*, p. 419.
[14] [1954] 1 W.L.R. 963 at p. 973.
[15] *Supra*, pp. 417–418.

concrete was proposed—and in addition, it is also well known that with vast numbers of houses under his care a local authority official cannot give the personal attention to a project that the architect or engineer may be expected to give. Finally, of course, the architect is the building owner's representative, so that it is, again, not unreasonable to suppose that the parties intended the employer to be bound by his decision in a case where the builder was also agreeing to be bound by it. On this view, the decision in *Billyack's* case appears eminently reasonable and is to be welcomed on social grounds, because purchasers from private developers are frequently misled by references of this kind into thinking that a high standard of work or supervision is being referred to, when in reality the standards applied by local authorities (notwithstanding the reference above to the possibility of more than the contract requirement being demanded) are by definition minimum standards, and the supervision, inevitably limited to visits at certain crucial stages of construction, is unfortunately by no means always foolproof.

Except in this rather special type of case, the "additional protection" view would also appear to be inconsistent with the principle of a number of cases, including particularly *Panamena Europea* v. *Leyland* (1947),[16] referred to in Section 5 *infra*, whereby a certificate is invalidated and disregarded if it can be shown that the certifier took into account some matter extraneous to the contract when making his decision. On the other hand, the following case in the House of Lords, which by reason of its findings is of no direct authority on the point, contains certain dicta of interest on this difficult subject which lend support, it is submitted, to the views expressed above as to the *ratio decidendi* of the *Newton Abbot* and *Billyack* cases.

ILLUSTRATION

Specialist manufacturers of ships' propellers contracted with a *shipbuilder* to make propellers in accordance with the latter's drawings and specification. They also undertook that the propellers should be to the entire satisfaction of the *shipowner's* representative. The House of Lords *held* that there were breaches of an implied term of suitability or workmanship,[17] and of the express term as to satisfaction. *Per* Lord Tomlin and Lord Russell of Killowen, the view of Roche J. at first instance and Scrutton L.J. in the Court of Appeal, that if the article complied with the specification and was of good material and workmanship there was no right in law to disapprove of it on some other ground not in the contract, overlooked the fact that the shipowner was a stranger to the contract with the

---

[16] [1947] A.C. 428, *post*, pp. 468, 476–478.
[17] For the facts, see the case illustrated *ante*, Chap. 5, p. 285.

manufacturers and need not necessarily know its terms.   At least where the shipowner was concerned (as opposed to the shipbuilder) there was no need to limit the satisfaction to matters undertaken by the manufacturer under his contract with the shipbuilder, provided the shipowner acted in good faith and not capriciously. *Per* Lord Wright, the satisfaction could only be withheld on the ground of some failure to comply with the contract and not for any other reason: *Cammell Laird* v. *Manganese Bronze & Brass Ltd.* (1934).[18]

It is suggested that in a building contract, where the certifier is usually named in the contract, has generally prepared the contract documents himself, and is certainly, or ought to be, familiar with its contents, the consensus of judicial opinion in the above case would have been prepared to limit the satisfaction to matters of contractual obligation on the part of the contractor. If so, this is strong support for the former of the two possible constructions [19] in all cases where a conventional architect or engineer is the certifier.

It is also submitted that in conventional building and engineering contracts, where it is customary to describe the contract work in detail and with precision, the former construction is more likely to prevail than in cases where the contract work is not very precisely defined in the contract documents.

In addition to the cases already cited, the appropriate cases in the next section are also by inference authority for the proposition that, were it not for the arbitration clause, the employer would be bound by the stipulated approval or certificate.

Section 4.   Effect of Arbitration Clause

(1) Generally

As previously indicated, the finality which would otherwise attach to a stipulated approval or certificate may in many cases be avoided by the operation of an arbitration clause, and it remains to examine the principles upon which this result may come about.

(2) Distinction between Certifier and Arbitrator

In the first place it is necessary to bear clearly in mind the difference between an arbitrator in the full sense and a certifier. Essentially,

---

[18] [1934] A.C. 402.

[19] See *supra*, p. 433. On the other hand, the cases as to certification of extra work, *ante*, pp. 427 *et seq.*, *post*, Chap. 8, pp. 553 *et seq.*, seem to suggest the certifier has power to disregard or waive contractual requirements, though this is different from imposing an additional requirement of his own, and is criticised *supra*, p. 426, as not being really consistent with principle.

the certifier is performing an administrative rather than a judicial
function. He has been described as a " preventer of disputes "
in contradistinction to an arbitrator, whose function only arises
once a dispute is in existence.[20] He is not under the same obligation to afford the parties or their representatives a full judicial
hearing and receive evidence from them.[21] (The status and duties of
certifiers are defined in Section 9, *infra*.)

Thus each contractual provision must be carefully scrutinised to
see into which category the person named falls. It should be borne in
mind that a certifier does not become an arbitrator merely because
it is provided that he shall " adjudge " what is due,[22] or because
he is stated to be the " exclusive judge " of some matter.[23] If the
word " arbitrator " or " arbitration " is not used, there must be an
inference, and certainly no contrary indication, that what is intended
is a proper hearing of the opposing parties with witnesses and
evidence heard in a manner similar to that of a court of law.

ILLUSTRATION

> The wording of a clause was " If . . . any dispute shall arise . . .
> as to whether the works have been properly executed or completed
> or as to delay in such completion or as to extras to or deviation from
> the works either the owner or the builder may apply to appoint an
> architect to decide the same and such architect *after such investiga-*
> *tions as he may consider proper* may by his certificate in writing
> decide such dispute and declare what payment or deduction is to
> be made . . . and such decision and declaration shall be conclusive
> and binding on both the owner and contractor." *Held*, since there
> was no indication of a judicial hearing, the clause was not an arbitra-
> tion clause: *Pierce* v. *Dyke* (1952).[24]

In most cases it is not difficult to judge whether the intention is
to make a person a full arbitrator, but the situation may be further
complicated by the fact that, as will be seen, some contracts used to
confer both the powers of a certifier and of an arbitrator upon the
same person, very often in different clauses. In modern contracts in
England, however, this is now virtually unknown, since under the
Arbitration Acts, as previously indicated,[25] it has been possible since

---

[20] See, *e.g. Laidlaw* v. *Hastings Pier Co.* (1874) Hudson's B.C., 4th ed., Vol. 2, p. 13,
and *Re Carus-Wilson and Greene* (1886) 18 Q.B.D. 7.

[21] See also the discussion and passage from Devlin J. in the *Minster Trust* case, *supra*,
pp. 417–418.

[22] *Northampton Gaslight Co.* v. *Parnell* (1855) 24 L.J.C.P. 60; 15 C.B. 630.

[23] *Kennedy* v. *Barrow-in-Furness* (*Mayor of*) (1909) Hudson's B.C., 4th ed., Vol. 2,
p. 411.

[24] [1952] 2 W.I.R. 30 (Jamaica). See fuller discussion *post*, Chap. 18, pp. 825–831.

[25] *Supra*, p. 412. See also *infra*, p. 450.

1934 to revoke the appointment of an arbitrator on the ground of an interest known to the parties at the time of making the contract, and this was, in fact, specifically aimed at this type of provision.

Where, therefore, a contract provides for some matter to be dealt with by a certificate or approval, and by virtue of the principles discussed in Section 3, above, such certificate is final between the parties, the question still may arise whether an arbitrator appointed under the contract is bound by any approval or certificate which may have been given or can, by his award, supply the deficiency where the certifier has failed or refused to issue the certificate to which either party claims to be entitled.   In all such cases it is necessary to consider carefully the precise terms of the certificate clause and the arbitration clause, and to decide whether on its true construction the latter was intended to confer the necessary power to override the certifier upon the arbitrator.

At first, in cases where the contract provided in general terms that the arbitrator was to have a wide jurisdiction over all disputes, and indeed even in some cases where it was clear that he had specific jurisdiction over a matter governed by an approval or certificate, the courts appear to have felt considerable difficulty in allowing the merits of the dispute to be finally resolved by an arbitrator in the face of a previous certificate or the absence of one [26] but it is now clear that, once the courts are satisfied that an arbitrator has jurisdiction to go into a matter, they will not, in the absence of a clearly expressed intention, allow his findings to be emasculated by any failure of the parties specifically to make the necessary procedural provisions to enable him to give substantive effect to his decision, or by formal difficulties created by the specific provisions of the contract relating to the original certifier's decisions.[27]

" I read the case of *Brodie* v. *Cardiff Corporation* (1919),[28] where this matter was very fully considered, to mean, in substance, this: where an arbitrator having jurisdiction has to decide that something ought to have been done by the architect or engineer which was not done, if the terms of the reference are wide enough to enable him to

---

[26] See, for instance, the decision of Farwell J. in *Robins* v. *Goddard* [1904] 2 Ch. 261, subsequently overruled by the Court of Appeal, [1905] 1 K.B. 294; the decision of the Court of Appeal in *Brodie* v. *Cardiff Corporation* (1919) overruled by the House of Lords (Lord Sumner dissenting), [1919] A.C. 337; and the passage from the judgment of Greer L.J. in *Prestige* v. *Brettell* (1938) 55 T.L.R. 59, cited *infra*.

[27] See *Brodie* v. *Cardiff Corporation* (1919), *Prestige* v. *Brettell* (1938) and *Neale* v. *Richardson* (1938), *infra*.   See also for this principle *Hatrick* (*N.Z.*) *Ltd.* v. *Nelson Carlton Construction* [1964] N.Z.L.R. 72, illustrated *post*, Section 5, pp. 463–464.

[28] [1919] A.C. 337, *infra*, p. 440.

deal with the matter, he may by that decision himself supply the deficiency, and do that which ought to have been done." [29]

" It is because I am impressed with the effect of the two authorities which have been cited that I am able to agree with the view which has been expressed by my brethren. I cannot read either *Brodie* v. *Cardiff Corporation* (1919) [28] or *Neale* v. *Richardson* (1938) [30] except as expressing the view that in the opinion of the House of Lords in *Brodie* v. *Cardiff Corporation* (1919), and in the opinion of this court in *Neale* v. *Richardson* (1938), [30] an arbitrator to whom a matter is remitted in the form it was in this case, has the power to dispense with the conditions precedent and to order, that, notwithstanding the non-performance of those conditions precedent, a liability may be established on which money may be ordered to be paid. It is because of the decisions in those two cases that I am constrained to concur with the judgments given by my brethren." [31]

The following are examples of cases where the arbitrator was held to be empowered under the arbitration clause to reopen a matter declared by the contract to be dependent upon the architect's certificate, or to disregard the absence of one. While most of the cases deal with certificates and certifiers, it should not be forgotten that provisions for mere approval or satisfaction without any certificate come equally within the principles laid down by the cases. [32]

ILLUSTRATIONS

(1) Certain locomotives and boilers were to be built under the inspection and to the satisfaction and approval of the purchasers' engineer. The purchasers were to pay one-half of the purchase price upon his certificate that the locomotives had been delivered in perfect order. There was an arbitration clause stating simply that all disputes were to be settled by an umpire. The engineer refused to give the certificate or any reason for not doing so. The sellers referred the dispute to arbitration. *Held*, the dispute was within the umpire's jurisdiction under the clause and his award of the price in favour of the sellers should stand: *Re Hohenzollern Actien-Gesellschaft & City of London Contract Corporation* (1886). [33]

(2) Clause 20 of a form of contract provided that the certificate of the architect *or* an award of the referee appointed under the contract showing the final balance due to the contractor should be conclusive evidence of due completion of the works and the contractor's entitlement to receive payment of the final balance. Clause

---

[29] *Per* Slesser L.J. in *Prestige & Co. Ltd.* v. *Brettell* [1938] 4 All E.R. 346; 55 T.L.R. 59 at p. 62.

[30] [1938] 1 All E.R. 753, *infra*, p. 441.

[31] *Per* Greer L.J., 55 T.L.R. 59 at p. 64.

[32] In addition to the cases illustrated below, see the Privy Council decision of *Molloy* v. *Liebe* (1910) 102 L.T. 616, *post*, Chap. 8, p. 541.

[33] Hudson's B.C., 4th ed., Vol. 2, p. 100; 54 L.T.R. 596; 2 T.L.R. 470.

22 (the clause appointing the referee, which was in the form of a proviso) provided that disputes (described in the widest terms including disputes arising from the withholding by the architect of any certificate to which the contractor might be entitled) should be referred to a referee, whose award should be the equivalent of a certificate of the architect. Disputes arose as to whether the works had been duly completed, and as to authorisation of and charges for certain extras. The architect subsequently issued his final certificate, upon which the builder brought an action to recover the sum certified. *Held*, that on the true construction of the two clauses the contract contemplated the issue of certificates by the architect only before disputes had arisen, and by the referee thereafter. Once a dispute arose, the architect's jurisdiction to certify disappeared, so that his certificates had no effect. Since, however, the builder had not obtained an award of the referee his action must fail: *Lloyd Bros.* v. *Milward* (1895).[34]

(3) Clause 30 of a building contract made a certificate of the architect a condition of payment. It further provided that " no certificate shall be considered conclusive evidence as to the sufficiency of any works or materials to which it relates, nor shall it relieve the contractor from his liability to make good all defects as provided by this contract." There was an arbitration clause providing that any dispute as to any matter or thing arising from the contract or its construction should be referred to an arbitrator who should have power to open up, review and revise any certificate, opinion or decision and to determine all matters submitted to him as if no such certificate, opinion, etc., had been given. The architect issued certificates, upon which the contractor sued the building owner. No application was made to stay the action and have it referred to arbitration. The building owner sought to counterclaim alleging defective work outside the maintenance period. *Held*, that even if the last part of clause 30 referred only to the liability to make good defects under the maintenance clause within the maintenance period,[35] the arbitration clause was sufficiently wide to enable an arbitrator to go behind the certificates and consider the employer's counterclaim. Since there was no provision making the award of the arbitrator a condition precedent to bringing an action, the defendant was free to raise his counterclaim in the action, in the absence of any application to refer it to arbitration, and the court could accordingly consider the merits of the counterclaim in the same way that the arbitrator could do: *Robins* v. *Goddard* (1905).[36]

(4) Clause 16 of a contract in the then standard R.I.B.A. form empowered the architect during the progress of the works to order

---

[34] Hudson's B.C., 4th ed., Vol. 2, p. 262. This was a very special type of contract not encountered at the present day in the United Kingdom. The same or similar forms of contract were also considered in *Clemence* v. *Clarke* (1879) Hudson's B.C., Vol. 2, p. 54, illustrated *infra*, p. 443, *Murray* v. *Cohen* (1889) 9 N.S.W.R. (Eq.) 124, illustrated *post*, Section 6 (5), p. 487, *Kirsch* v. *Brady* (1937) 58 C.L.R. 36 (Australia), illustrated *supra*, Section 1, p. 410, and *Grant* v. *Trocadero* (1938) 60 C.L.R. 1, illustrated *post*, Chap. 18, p. 854. See also *Milestone & Sons Ltd.* v. *Yates Brewery Ltd.* [1938] 2 All E.R. 439.

[35] (As Farwell J. had held at first instance.)

[36] [1905] 1 K.B. 294. (See particularly *per* Sterling L.J.)

the removal and replacement of any work not in accordance with the contract. Clause 17 was a defects liability clause in the usual form requiring defects to be made good during the maintenance period. There was an arbitration clause in wide terms, but it expressly excluded clause 16 from its ambit. Defects due to materials used appeared in the work shortly after completion and the architect gave notice to replace them. The contractors contended the employer was bound by the architect's decision under clause 16. *Held*, by Phillimore J., that an arbitrator, or if no arbitrator, the courts, was entitled to review the decision under clause 17. In his opinion clause 16 was intended to apply to matters arising in the immediate course of building requiring executive rather than judicial action, and once a part of the work was finished and the contractor had moved on from it without the architect condemning it, the employer, though he had lost his rights under clause 16, still retained his rights under clause 17: *Adcock's Trustee* v. *Bridge R.D.C.* (1911).[37]

(5) A builder undertook to carry out works " to the entire satis-faction of the architect." The arbitration clause was in wide terms, with a power to open up, revise and review in terms identical with *Robins* v. *Goddard* (1905), and applied to all matters " not otherwise distinctly provided for by any of the foregoing clauses " of the conditions. There was not, as in *Robins'* case, an express provision that no certificate should be considered conclusive evidence as to the sufficiency of the work. The architect certified completion, and the contractor sued in the courts on the final certificate. *Held*, following *Robins* v. *Goddard*, that the employer was free to allege that the work was not in accordance with the contract: *Johns & Son* v. *Webster & Tonks* (1916).[38]

(6) A contract[39] provided that no charges for extra work should be allowed unless ordered in writing by the engineer in a particular form acknowledging it was an extra, and that the employer should not become liable to pay for the same unless an instruction had been given in writing. The arbitration clause was in wide terms, covering (*inter alia*) objections by the contractor to decisions or certificates of the engineer, and provided for arbitration either at the time of a dispute or otherwise at the end of the work at the discretion of the arbitrator. The engineer orally ordered certain work to be done which the contractor contended was extra work, but the engineer disagreed and refused to order it in writing. The contractor carried out the engineer's instructions, under protest, but was prepared to leave the matter to arbitration at the end of the contract. *Held*, by the House of Lords, that the arbitrator had power to award sums for extra work notwithstanding the absence of orders in writing: *Brodie* v. *Cardiff Corporation* (1919).[39a]

(7) A building contract provided that the contractor should be entitled to payment from time to time under certificates to be issued to the contractor by the architect. It also contained a clause that if any dispute should arise as to the construction of the contract or as to the withholding by the architect of any certificate it should

[37] 75 J.P. 241. See the comment on this case *ante*, Chap. 6, Section 1, pp. 385–386.
[38] [1916] N.Z.L.R. 1020 (New Zealand).
[39] This case is more fully illustrated *post*, Chap. 8, pp. 541–543.
[39a] [1919] A.C. 337.

be referred to an arbitrator, who should have power to open up, review and revise any certificate. The contractor claimed that the architect had under-certified, and abandoned the work. The arbitrator, upon a certain construction of the contract, held that there had been no under-certification. *Held,* upon a case stated, that his view on the question of construction was incorrect, that there had been under-certification, and that the arbitrator should have revised the last certificate in such a way as to entitle the contractor to the sums claimed: *F. R. Absalom* v. *G. W. (London) Garden Village Society* (1933).[40]

(8) A building contract provided for payments to be made by the employer to the contractors from time to time during the progress of the work upon certificates to be granted by the architect. There was also an arbitration clause which provided for arbitration by an agreed independent arbitrator in case of any dispute or difference as to any matter or thing arising under the contract (except as to certain matters left to the sole discretion of the architect) or as to the withholding by the architect of any certificate to which the contractors claimed to be entitled. The architect refused to issue a further certificate, and the contractors gave to the employer notice of dispute by a letter which, after setting out that there was an amount of £10,667 due to them which ought to be certified, stated: " We are only concerned with the failure or refusal [of the architect] to issue a certificate, and as in effect there is now a difference or dispute under the contract, we give notice . . . " (to refer such dispute to arbitration). The arbitrator by his award ordered that the employer should pay to the contractors the sum of £7,500. *Held,* that the terms of the contract were sufficiently wide to give the arbitrator jurisdiction to order payment of the sum of money for which in his opinion a certificate ought to have been granted by the architect: *Prestige & Co. Ltd.* v. *Brettell* (1938).[41]

(9) A building contract provided that payments should be made by four equal instalments upon the certificate of the architect. There was an arbitration clause which provided simply that in all cases of dispute arising out of the contract, the decision of the architect should be binding upon the parties. The builder, following the building owner's taking possession, asked the architect for his final certificate for the last instalment, but this was refused, and the architect purported to appoint another architect as arbitrator. This was objected to by the builder, and, following continued refusal by the architect to issue any further certificate, the builder brought an action in the courts, to which the defendant objected that the builder had not obtained a certificate. *Held,* that the arbitration clause was sufficiently wide to empower the architect as arbitrator to determine whether a certificate should have been given, and that since he had refused to act and the defendant had taken no steps to have a new arbitrator appointed under section 5 of the Arbitration Act, the court could assume the powers which the arbitrator would have had and determine whether a certificate should have been given: *Neale* v. *Richardson* (1938).[42]

[40] [1933] A.C. 592.
[41] [1938] 4 All E.R. 346; 55 T.L.R. 59
[42] [1938] 1 All E.R. 753; 54 T.L.R. 539.

(10) Clause 24 (*f*) of the R.I.B.A. standard form of contract [43] provided that the final certificate of the architect should, save in certain circumstances, be conclusive evidence of the sufficiency of the works and materials. The architect issued a final certificate, which was honoured by the employers, but subsequently remeasured the works, and he and the employers then contended that there had been an overpayment of £1,000 upon the final certificate. The contractor, when this sum was claimed by the employers in an arbitration, argued that the final certificate was conclusive, the excepted circumstances not being applicable. *Held,* that Clause 27 of the conditions, which referred all disputes to arbitration and empowered the arbitrator to open up, review and revise any certificate and to determine all matters in dispute as if no such certificate had been given, overrode the express wording of Clause 24 (*f*) and that the arbitrator was accordingly not bound by the certificate: *Windsor R.D.C.* v. *Otterway & Try Ltd.* (1954). [44]

[Note: This case could have been, but was not, decided on the ground that the dispute between the parties did not relate to " the sufficiency of the works."]

(11) A contract for the sale of a yacht permitted the purchaser to give notice of rejection if a survey by the purchaser disclosed material defects, unless the defects were remedied. An arbitration clause in general terms specifically included disputes as to whether the vendor had satisfactorily remedied defects. *Held,* by the Court of Appeal, the clause entitled the arbitrator to decide whether there were any defects at all requiring to be remedied, and the vendor was not bound by the plaintiff's survey or notice in a case where he denied the existence of any defects: *Docker* v. *Hyams* (1969). [45]

The following are examples of cases where a certificate was held to be binding (or its absence fatal) despite the existence of an arbitration clause:

(1) A contract provided that no sum should be considered as due nor any claim be made unless the engineer should certify that the contractors were reasonably entitled thereto. The employer was also given power to determine the contract in certain events, and thereupon the engineer was to fix the amount earned by the contractor, and the value of any tools or materials taken by the employer, and the amount due was to remain in the employer's hands until twelve months after completion of the works, with power to the engineer by his certificate to authorise the deduction of any damage suffered by the employer. There was also an arbitration

[43] 1939 (1950 Revised) Edition.
[44] [1954] 3 All E.R. 721, *per* Devlin J. ([1954] 1 W.L.R. 1494). Disapproved by the House of Lords in the case of *East Ham B.C.* v. *Bernard Sunley Ltd.* [1966] A.C. 406, illustrated *infra*, p. 446. See now, clause 24 (*g*) of the (1957 Revised) and clause 30 (7) of the post-1963 R.I.B.A. form of contract, which, regrettably, fully restores the complicated and difficult position obtaining under the *Lloyd Bros.* v. *Milward* (1895) (illustrated *supra*, p. 438 and *Clemence* v. *Clarke* (1879) (illustrated *infra*, p. 443) arbitration provisions, and see *post*, pp. 489–492, for a discussion of this change.
[45] [1969] 1 W.L.R. 1060.

clause in wide terms for the reference of disputes (including disputes as to any certificate) to the engineer. The employers terminated the contract, and it was conceded that they were entitled to do so. Following the determination, the contractors submitted an account and the engineer appointed a day to proceed with the reference of their claims under the arbitration clause. He amended his notice of this to make it plain that he was acting under the termination clause. The contractors refused to attend, and subsequently filed a bill in equity for an account. *Held*, that in the absence of any certificate of the engineer, or proof that it had been fraudently withheld, their claim must fail. *Per* Lord Chelmsford L.C. " If the parties have provided for the settlement of disputes . . . by . . . arbitration . . . such a stipulation cannot be urged as an answer to either party who prefers to resort to the courts, nor can it deprive the tribunals of the country of their jurisdiction, whatever remedy may be open to the parties against whom proceedings are instituted. But where the contract provides for the determination of the claims and liabilities of the contractors by the judgment of some particular person, this would be incorrectly called . . . arbitration as no dispute can exist in such a case, everything being dependent upon the decision of the individual named, and until he has spoken no right can arise which can be enforced either at law or in equity. I think that (the engineer) stands in this relation to the plaintiffs in this case: *Scott* v. *Corporation of Liverpool* (1858).[46]

(2) A contract contained an arbitration clause in the same form as that in *Lloyd Bros.* v. *Milward* (1895).[47] The architect issued his final certificate, and the contractor brought an action upon it. The employer contended (among other things) that no written order had been given for certain extras. *Held*, the certificate was conclusive, there having been no dispute between the parties at the time it was given: *Clemence* v. *Clarke* (1879).[48]

(3) A contract provided that disputes touching any matter or thing arising out of the contract " unless provided for in the foregoing clauses " should be referred to an arbitrator. A previous clause provided that extra work should be measured and valued and certified for by the architect and the amount added to or deducted from the contract sum. The contractor was dissatisfied with the architect's valuation of the extras and sought to refer the matter to arbitration. *Held*, the dispute was one of the matters excepted from the arbitration clause: *Re Meadows & Kenworthy* (1896).[49]

(4) Clause 26 of a contract provided that the certificate of the architect was to be a condition precedent to the contractor's right of action against the employer, Clause 27 that the *architect* was to be sole arbitrator and determine any dispute that might arise either during the progress of the work or in determining the value of variations, and his certificate of his decision upon such dispute was to be

[46] 28 L.J.Ch. 230.

[47] (1895) Hudson's B.C., Vol. 2, p. 262. Illustrated *supra*, pp. 438–439.

[48] Hudson's B.C., Vol. 2, p. 54, illustrated more fully *post*, p. 466. (But see *per* Latham C.J. in *Kirsch* v. *Brady* (1937) 58 C.L.R. 36, who held *obiter* on a similar clause that had the architect's certificate in that case been valid it would have been open to arbitration.)

[49] Hudson's B.C., Vol. 2, p. 265.

final and binding. The contractor alleged that further sums beyond those certified were due to him. He made no application for arbitration under Clause 27, but brought an action. *Held*, in the absence of the certificate, or of fraud or collusion, the action must fail: *Eaglesham* v. *McMaster* (1920).[50]

(5) Clause 6 of an engineering specification provided that excavations should be timbered with suitable timber or alternative forms of sheeting other than timber as and where necessary to the satisfaction of the engineer. An arbitrator found that the engineer unreasonably required timbering in places where excavation by machine and battering the sides of trenches to a slope was practicable, causing additional expense. The contractor claimed the expense as a variation. *Held*, by Diplock J., that provided his decision was honest the engineer's requirement was conclusive: *Neodox Ltd.* v. *Swinton & Pendlebury B.C.* (1958).[51]

(6) An arbitration clause governed disputes "otherwise than such matters or things hereinbefore left to the decision or determination of the Engineer." The contract had required the Engineer to certify completion of the work to his satisfaction so as to start the maintenance period running.[51a] *Held*, by the Privy Council, that the certificate was intended to be a binding certificate of satisfaction, and consequently was excepted from the arbitration clause: *Ata Ul Haq* v. *City Council of Nairobi* (1959).[51b]

(7) A contract contained a clause attributing finality to the final certificate in terms identical for all practical purposes with that in *Windsor R.D.C.* v. *Otterway & Try* (1954).[51c] The arbitration clause provided, however, that all disputes were to be referred to the *architect*, whose decision was to be binding, except that the *contractor* could, if dissatisfied, refer the dispute to arbitration within fourteen days. The employer's only right to arbitration arose if the architect failed, within fourteen days of being asked to do so, to give a decision. The arbitrator had the same power to open up, review and revise certificates as in the *Windsor* case. The architect gave a final certificate at a time when there was no dispute between the parties. Subsequently the employer sought to dispute the certificate and claimed that he should be entitled to refer his dispute to the architect and, if no decision were given within fourteen days, refer the matter to arbitration. *Held*, distinguishing the *Windsor* case, that the final certificate was conclusive: *Ballantine* v. *Western Hotels (Pty.) Ltd.* (1960).[52]

(8) A contract provided that from the date of the architect's certificate of completion the contractor should be liable for the maintenance of the works only.[52a] The arbitration clause had no

---

[50] [1920] 2 K.B. 169. Criticised *infra*, p. 448. For a discussion of this case, see *post*, Section 7 (3), pp. 503–504.

[51] [1958] Q.B.D. (special paper) Diplock J. (unreported), illustrated more fully *post*, Chap. 8, pp. 529–530.

[51a] See fuller illustration, *supra*, Section 3, p. 430.

[51b] [1959] P.C. Appeal No. 48; illustrated *supra*, p. 430.

[51c] [1954] 1 W.L.R. 1494, *supra*, p. 442.

[52] 1960 (4) S.A. 137 (South Africa).

[52a] See fuller illustration, *supra*, Section 3, p. 431.

" open up, review and revise " formula, and expressly excepted from its ambit certain identified (irrelevant) provisions of the contract, but included all other matters " if not otherwise distinctly provided for by any of the foregoing provisions." *Held*, by the Court of Appeal of New Zealand, that the certificate was intended to be a certificate of satisfaction, and that, it being conceded that the arbitration clause did not apply,[52a] the certificate was binding on the employer: *Borough of Stratford* v. *Ashman* (1960).[53]

(9) A contract for the sale of a house in the course of erection contained a defects clause for a limited period after completion, which was to be to the satisfaction of the purchaser and her surveyor, who were in fact satisfied. Any dispute as to such defects was to be referred to arbitration, and the (arbitration) clause was to continue in full force and effect notwithstanding the completion of the sale and conveyance. *Held*, by Norman Richards O.R., the satisfaction was binding and defects outside the period were not within the scope of the clause and could not be pursued in proceedings before him: *Kent* v. *Saltdean Estate Co. Ltd.* (1964).[54]

(10) A contract provided for a certificate of satisfaction at the commencement of the maintenance period.[54a] The arbitration clause provided that in the event of disputes *between the employer and the architect on his behalf and the contractor* (other than certain identified but inapplicable matters in which the Architect had a full discretion under the Conditions) they should be referred to arbitration. The employer disputed the certificate, alleging defects. *Held*, by the Court of Appeal of New Zealand, following observations of Grove J. in *Clemence* v. *Clarke* [54b] and noting the decision of the English Court of Appeal in *East Ham B.C.* v. *Bernard Sunley*,[54c] that the italicised words in the arbitration clause were not apt to cover a dispute between the employer and his architect where a certificate had been given in such a way that there was no dispute between the architect and contractor, and consequently the arbitration clause did not override the certificate: *Major* v. *Greenfield* (1965).[55]

[Note: It is respectfully submitted that this decision cannot be right. In the *Clemence* case the provision was, " A certificate of the architect or an award of the referee is to be *conclusive evidence* of the works having been duly completed." Similarly, in the *East Ham* case the certificate was to be " *conclusive evidence* as to the sufficiency of the works." No such words were present in the *Major* case. Furthermore, the word " and " in the expression " between the employer and the architect on his behalf " needs to be read as " or," since to read it literally would involve the view that the architect was involved in the arbitration as a party, which would be absurd. Furthermore, the architect might well himself be in dispute with the contractor after giving a certificate if he later found a serious defect. Neither the *Neale*, *Hohenzollern*, or *Brodie* cases appear to have been cited to the Court.]

[52a] The concession seems open to argument.
[53] [1960] N.Z.L.R. 503 (New Zealand).   [54] 114 L.J. 555.
[54a] See fuller illustration, *supra*, Section 3, p. 431.
[54b] (1880) Hudson's B.C., 4th ed., Vol. 2, p. 54.
[54c] [1965] 1 W.L.R. 30.
[55] [1965] N.Z.L.R. 1035.

(11) On completion of a school for a local authority, the architect issued his final certificate under clause 24 (*f*) of the (1950 Revised) R.I.B.A. form of contract (identical with that in *Windsor R.D.C.* v. *Otterway & Try*). By clause 24 (*f*) the final certificate was to be conclusive evidence as to the sufficiency of the works save as regards defects which a reasonable examination would not have disclosed. By clause 27 (the arbitration clause) the arbitrator had full power to open up, review and revise any certificate, etc. of the architect and to decide any matter before him, as if no such certificate had been given. Subsequently to the final certificate, part of the stone facing of the buildings fell, revealing widespread faults in the fixing of the stone to the structure. The arbitrator found that these faults were due to breaches of contract by the contractors, and that while the defects could have been detected on the sort of visits an architect might be expected to make during the carrying out of the work, they could not have been seen at the end of the defects liability period at the time of giving the final certificate. The employers contended (a) that the final certificate was not conclusive, being overridden by the arbitration clause, and (b) that even if it was, the words of the exception referred to an examination at the end of the defects liability period at the time of giving the final certificate, and not during the carrying out of the works. *Held*, by the House of Lords (a) *per* Lords Dilhorne, Grant, Upjohn and Pearson (Lord Cohen dissenting), that the final certificate was final and conclusive in spite of the arbitration clause unless the exception applied (reasoning of Devlin J. in *Windsor* case disapproved), but (b) (Viscount Dilhorne dissenting), the exception referred to an inspection made after the work was complete (*per* the majority, after the defects liability period, *per* Lord Pearson, after practical completion) for the purpose of issuing the final certificate, so that on the facts the exception applied and the contractors were liable for the defects: *East Ham B.C.* v. *Bernard Sunley Ltd.* (1966).[56]

It is suggested that the following principles emerge from the above cases:

(a) An arbitration clause in general terms, *a fortiori* if it empowers the arbitrator to open up, review and revise any opinion or certificate, or specifically mentions disputes arising on the withholding of a certificate, will, in the absence of any provision to the contrary, empower the arbitrator to disregard a certificate or the absence of one.[57]

(b) Once an arbitrator is held to have jurisdiction to hear the merits of a claim, any purely technical or procedural difficulties in the way of giving full practical effect to his decision arising out of the wording of the contract in relation to the certifier and the parties

[56] [1966] A.C. 406.
[57] *Re Hohenzollern* (1886) Hudson's B.C., 4th ed. Vol. 2, p. 100; *Prestige* v. *Brettell* (1938) 55 T.L.R. 59; *Robins* v. *Goddard* [1905] 1 K.B. 294; *Windsor R.D.C.* v. *Otterway* [1954] 3 All E.R. 721; *Brodie* v. *Cardiff Corporation* [1919] A.C. 337; *Neale* v. *Richardson* [1938] 1 All E.R. 753; 54 T.L.R. 539.

are likely to be disregarded, the implication being that all necessary powers have been conferred on the arbitrator to enable him to give full effect to his decision.[58]

(c) On the other hand express words of exclusion in the arbitration clause may make it plain that a particular matter the subject of a certificate or approval is not within the arbitration clause.[59]

(d) There may be cases where, even in the absence of words of exclusion in the arbitration clause, the clause will not prevail over the provision for approval or a certificate. Thus the use of the words " conclusive evidence " in relation to the final certificate may override an arbitration clause, however widely expressed, unless the latter expressly permits the arbitrator to reopen the final certificate.[60] Again some contracts in a very special form may not contemplate any overlap of jurisdiction between certifier and arbitrator, the latter's jurisdiction arising only if a dispute has arisen prior to the certifier having acted,[61] or because, in addition, the right of arbitration was never available at all to the party seeking to dispute the certificate.[62]

(e) In the more usual case where the arbitration clause overrides the certifying clause the plaintiff can normally, if he wishes, proceed by action and, unless the action is stayed, the court will have the same powers of review as the arbitrator.[63] There was undoubtedly a dictum to the contrary by Lord Cohen in the House of Lords and by Salmon L.J. in the Court of Appeal in the *East Ham* case, and Viscount Dilhorne there also expressed the view that *Robins* v. *Goddard* (1905) did not establish or support this proposition. The question was, however, very much on the fringe of the argument and reasoning in that case, and neither *Neale's* nor *Adcock's* cases were cited nor the New Zealand case of *Johns*, which expressly followed *Robins* v. *Goddard* (1905). It is submitted with the greatest respect that these dicta are not consistent with authority.[63] Furthermore, it is submitted that, on principle, (i) to allow contracting

---

[58] *Brodie* v. *Cardiff Corporation*; *Prestige* v. *Brettell, supra.*
[59] *Re Meadows & Kenworthy*; *Borough of Stratford* v. *J. H. Ashman*; *Ata Ul Haq* v. *City Council of Nairobi, supra.*
[60] This appears to be the effect of the House of Lords' decision in the *East Ham* case. Even on this view the *Windsor* decision would have been right, because the dispute was not a dispute as to " the sufficiency of the works " and so not caught by the " conclusive evidence " provisions.
[61] *Lloyd* v. *Milward*; *Clemence* v. *Clarke*; *Ballantine* v. *Western Hotels (Pty.) Ltd., supra.*
[62] *Ballantine's case, supra.*
[63] *Robins* v. *Goddard* [1905] 1 K.B. 294, at p. 321, *per* Stirling L.J.; *Adcock's Trustee* v. *Bridge R.D.C.* (1911) 75 J.P. 241; *Johns* v. *Webster and Tonks* [1916] N.Z.L.R. 1020; *Neale* v. *Richardson* [1938] 1 All E.R. 753 *per* Scott L.J.

parties to clothe an arbitrator with judicial powers which the courts were not also to possess would infringe a basic principle of English law by ousting the jurisdiction of the courts to that extent, (ii) it would be wholly unrealistic to attribute to the parties an intention to restrict the power of the courts to entertain the full merits of a dispute simply because they have, when providing for the tribunal which they contemplate will normally deal with their disputes, taken pains to make clear that that tribunal should have that power—had it indeed been the intention, the clause would at the very least, it is submitted, have been couched in *Scott* v. *Avery* form [64]—and (iii) such a ruling would be catastrophic in its consequences, to no possible advantage, in the many cases where the courts, for good reason, decide to exercise their discretion and refuse a stay for arbitration, or revoke the appointment of an arbitrator so that the matter may be dealt with in the High Court (for instance in multi-partite proceedings [65]).

(f)   This will not be so, however, if the arbitration clause is in the *Scott* v. *Avery* (1856) form, or the construction of the contract is otherwise held to require that, failing a certificate, an award of the arbitrator must be obtained as a condition precedent to an action. In such a case, the plaintiff's action will fail unless he has obtained the certificate or the award. [66]

It is suggested that the wording of the contract in the cases of *Scott* v. *Corporation of Liverpool* (1858) and *Eaglesham* v. *McMaster* (1920) does not really warrant the construction placed upon them by the courts, and that these decisions are out of line with the cases referred to under principle (a) above and should now be considered as decisions upon their own rather special facts.   Had the builder, for example, been able to invoke the Act of 1934 and secure the appointment of an independent arbitrator in *Eaglesham's* case, the decision might well, it is submitted, go the other way today. The reference to the certificate of the arbitrator in that case might also be regarded as showing a *Scott* v. *Avery* (1856) intention. It is submitted that in interpreting doubtful cases, the courts should bear in mind that, at the present day, it is inherently unlikely that either party to a building contract intends or wishes that in the last resort their rights should be finally determined by the particular architect or engineer in charge of the contract.   For reasons which are not clear

---

[64] See for this *post*, Chap. 18, p. 853.
[65] See *post*, Chap. 18, pp. 844–846.
[66] *Eaglesham* v. *McMaster*; *Lloyd Bros.* v. *Milward, supra*.

(except on the part of the contractor), it is, however, the case that in recent years the R.I.B.A. standard forms of contract have been amended and reworded so as to render the final certificate binding on the parties unless notice of arbitration has been given before it has been issued (by the employer) or within a fortnight thereafter (by the contractor).[67]

(g) There is no difference in principle between a case where the certifier is also the arbitrator and a case where he is not.[68] While it may be that in such cases the courts have been more disposed to require an award of the arbitrator to be obtained as a condition precedent to an action,[69] any practical difficulty to which this may have given rise in the past (in the sense that an arbitrator who is also a certifier is unlikely to alter a decision previously given by him as certifier) can now be avoided (so far as the contractor is concerned) by obtaining a revocation of the appointment on the ground of interest and the substitution of a new arbitrator under the powers now contained in the Arbitration Acts.

SECTION 5.   RECOVERY WITHOUT CERTIFICATE

(1) Generally

Apart from the existence of an overriding arbitration clause, or cases of waiver or estoppel, there are certain circumstances in which the necessity of obtaining a binding certificate can be dispensed with, or an existing certificate can be disregarded.   The earlier decisions suggest that these circumstances are limited to cases where there exists an undisclosed interest of the certifier having the effect of disqualifying him, or fraud, or collusion by him with the employer, or conduct of the employer amounting to interference with or prevention of the issue of a certificate.   On certain occasions the courts do appear, however, while formally accepting these categories, to have set aside or disregarded the decision of a certifier when, while not guilty of fraud or collusion in the usually accepted sense of those terms, he has acted in an indiscreet or unimpartial way.   In addition, where it can be shown that the certifier, while

---

[67] See *infra*, Section 6, pp. 489–492, for the practical consequences of this.
[68] See *e.g.* the judgment of Slesser L.J. in *Neale* v. *Richardson* [1938] 1 All E.R. 753 at p. 757.
[69] See *per* Reading C.J. in *Eaglesham* v. *McMaster* [1920] 2 K.B. 169, more fully discussed on this point *post*, Section 7 (3), pp. 503–504.

acting with complete impartiality and good faith, has taken an incorrect view of the considerations which should govern his decision, and has erred in the principles which he applied in reaching it, there now seems little doubt that the presence or absence of the approval or certificate in question will be disregarded, but the reasons for this are not so much the conduct of the certifier, but follow from the true construction of the provision for satisfaction or certification, depending upon whether it falls into the second or third category of these provisions as analysed and explained *supra*, Section 3.[70]

It should be remembered that, while in the case of arbitration statutory powers exist to revoke an arbitrator's appointment and appoint a substitute on the grounds of interest or misconduct (and whether or not the interest was known to the other party at the time of contracting [71]), and also to obtain the opinion of the High Court on a case stated, no such powers exist in the case of a mere certifier, and consequently the courts have no alternative, if they are to do justice between the parties when the interest, misconduct or error of law is of a kind to vitiate the certificate or approval, but to disregard the contractual provisions as to finality altogether and entertain any claim on its merits. Furthermore, if the *ratio decidendi* of *Chambers* v. *Goldthorpe* (1901) [72] is correct, a certifier's function [73] is of a quasi-arbitral character, and consequently he owes no duty to either party to carry it out with reasonable skill or care. This being so, it is obvious that there can be no implied term to that effect in the contract between the employer and the builder. On the other hand, whatever the contractual position of the parties, if the certifier is guilty of fraud or collusion, he renders himself liable to an action in tort at the suit of any party who may have suffered damage as a consequence of any representation made by him to that party [74] in the course of the fraud, in addition to depriving his certificates, approval or decisions of any binding effect as between the employer and the builder. Finally, in considering disqualification and misconduct, particularly on the ground of interest or bias, while the same general principles will apply as in the case of a full arbitrator, considerable allowance requires to be made to take account of the certifier's inevitable administrative functions and duties under the

---

[70] *Supra*, pp. 419 and 433–434.
[71] See s. 24 of the 1950 Act. See also *post*, Chap. 18, pp. 847 *et seq.*
[72] [1901] 1 Q.B. 624. See *ante*, Chap. 2, pp. 161 *et seq.*
[73] But see the need for exact definition of the function for this purpose, *ante*, pp. 164 *et seq.*
[74] Not, however, if made to the other party—see *Larkins* v. *Chelmer Holdings* [1965] Qd.Rep. 68 (Australia).

contract.[75] An attempt will be made in subsection (6) below to discuss and analyse the combined effect of the next four subsections which, in the light of the foregoing general remarks, are intended to classify the main grounds upon which binding certificates can be dispensed with or avoided, since the wording of the cases has sometimes tended to blur what are necessary distinctions.

(2) Disqualification on Ground of Interest

In the first place, an interest will not disqualify if it was known to the complaining party at the time of contracting.[76] This is implicit in all the cases, and is recognised by the specific exception made in the case of arbitration by the Arbitration Acts.[77]

ILLUSTRATIONS

(1) It was objected by contractors that the engineer was disqualified from deciding a question of forfeiture for delay, since their case was that he had caused the delay himself. *Held*, that the parties must have foreseen that in accepting the engineer as arbitrator, they would be bound although he might be a party involved in the dispute at the time of its occurrence: *Trowsdale* v. *Jopp* (1864).[78]

(2) A contract provided that payments were to be made on certificates by the engineer of the company or his assistant resident engineer, and in case of dispute between the contractor and the resident engineer, that the decision of the engineer of the company was to be final. *Held*, that as the contractor had agreed that the company's engineer should be the person who should decide disputes, he could not object to his decisions on the ground of the bias, of which he was aware when he agreed to the stipulation: *Ranger* v. *Great Western Railway* (1854).[79]

Accordingly, before considering the cases on the types of interest which will disqualify a certifier, it is perhaps desirable to define what sort of interest or bias an architect or engineer may properly be expected to have, and which should consequently be in the contemplation of a contractor at the time of entering into a building or engineering contract. It is suggested the following factors should be borne in mind:

[75] See next section, and Section 9 (Status and Duties of Certifier), and see subsection (5) below, Conduct not Amounting to Fraud or Collusion.

[76] See *Matthew* v. *Ollerton, supra*, p. 412; or if it is waived after contract see *Thornton Hall* v. *Wembley Electrical Appliances* [1947] 2 All E.R. 630; *infra*, p. 472, footnote, and illustrated *ante*, Chap. 1, p. 60. See also the discussion on the disqualification of arbitrators *post*, Chap. 18, pp. 847 *et seq.*

[77] s. 24 of the Act of 1950. As to which see *post*, Chap. 18, p. 848. See, however, the case of *Bristol Corporation* v. *Aird, post*, Chap. 18, p. 852, and the discussion *post*, Chap. 18, p. 849.

[78] 2 M. (Ct. of Sess.) 1334; 4 M. (Ct. of Sess.) 31.

[79] 5 H.L.C. 72.

(1) The architect or engineer is employed and paid by the building owner and is in some cases a salaried official;

(2) The architect or engineer, whether a person exercising an
independent calling or not, is the agent of the building owner
(from the date of his ceasing to be a mere designer or
draughtsman), except in so far as he acts as a certifier
or in a quasi-judicial position, or as arbitrator;

(3) The architect or engineer in almost all cases gives an estimate
(generally approximate) of the cost of the work to be done
before the tenders are received;

(4) The building owner consults the architect or engineer as to
the bargain to be made with the contractor, and often
employs him to strike the bargain. In such a case the
architect's or engineer's duty is to make the best bargain he
can for his client;

(5) The architect or engineer, often without consulting the
employer, prepares or recommends the contract under
which his duties are defined and he is constituted valuer,
certifier or quasi-arbitrator, and sometimes arbitrator;

(6) The architect or engineer runs the risk of losing his employment, not being paid his fees, or not being again employed,
if the cost which he originally estimated is greatly exceeded;

(7) The architect or engineer, for the same reasons, naturally
desires to avoid extras, and if there are extras, to keep down
the cost of them;

(8) The architect or engineer is liable to make mistakes or
omissions in the plans and specifications which may involve
increased cost, which for the same reasons as before he
will wish to avoid admitting.

It is not proposed to set out the general principles and cases on
the disqualification of persons exercising a judicial or quasi-judicial
function on the ground of interest, which stem from the case of
Dimes v. *Grand Junction Canal Co.* (1852),[80] but only to set out below
such cases as seem to be particularly relevant to building and
engineering contracts.

ILLUSTRATIONS

(1) In the sale of some land the vendor's arbitrator was, unknown to the vendor, a shareholder in a company materially interested in the success of the undertaking for which the land was bought,

---

[80] 3 H.L.C. 759. These were set out in the editions prior to the ninth edition. See
also *post*, Chap. 18, pp. 847 *et seq.*, and the further cases, pp. 849 *et seq.*

and the umpire, chosen by the vendor's arbitrator from a list furnished by the purchaser's arbitrator, was also, unknown to the vendor, a surveyor employed in some matters by the same company. *Held,* that these were not such objections to either as to afford judicial grounds for setting aside the award, though Knight Bruce V.-C. said: " I think the award has been saved very narrowly indeed." In the same case the purchaser appointed as his arbitrator to settle the price of the land a person who had previously acted as his agent in attempting to negotiate with the vendor, and who had actually offered the vendor a specific price for the land in question. *Held,* that the vendor, having appointed his own arbitrator with knowledge of the disqualification of the purchaser's arbitrator, had waived his rights to object: *Re Elliott, ex p. South Devon Railway.* (1848) [81]

(2) Wide powers of certification under an engineering contract were conferred upon the " Principal Engineer of the Company or his Assistant Resident Engineer." Unbeknown to the contractors, the engineer was a shareholder in the company. *Held,* this did not disqualify him: *Ranger v. G. W. Railway* (1854). [82]

[Note: This decision cannot be applied generally, it is submitted. Consideration of the judgments of Cranworth L.C. and Lord Brougham shows that they proceed upon the fact that in the special circumstances of the case the engineer was a full-time employee of the company, and as such was merely acting as the *alter ego* of the company. [83] " Thus the whole tenor of the contract shows that it was never intended that the engineer should be indifferent between the parties. When it is stipulated that certain questions shall be decided by the engineer appointed by the company, this is, in fact, a stipulation that they shall be decided by this company. . . . The company reserved the decision to itself, acting, however, as from the nature of things it must act, by an agent and that agent was for this purpose the engineer." [84] This would not generally be the view today. The type of shareholding and type of company must be of importance, too, it is suggested. (Compare *Sellar v. Highland Railway, infra.*) [85]]

(3) An architect, unknown to the builder and previous to a contract being signed, gave an assurance to his employer (but declining to bind himself by any guarantee) that the cost of a building would not exceed a certain amount, upon the faith of which the employer embarked on the undertaking. *Held,* that, without alleging fraud, the architect's decision was not binding upon the builder, if there was the smallest speck or circumstance which might unfairly bias his judgment which was unknown to the builder: " and the court might consider itself what was properly due to the builder ": *Kemp v. Rose* (1858). [86]

[81] 12 Jur.(o.s.) 445.
[82] 5 H.L.C. 72.
[83] See *per* Lord Cranworth at p. 89 and see *per* Devlin J. in *Minster Trust Ltd.* v. *Traps Tractors Ltd.* [1954] 1 W.L.R. 963 at p. 973, quoted and commented on *supra,* Section 3, pp. 417–418.
[84] *Per* Lord Chelmsford.
[85] See *infra,* Interest of Certifier, pp. 471–472.
[86] 1 Giff. 258.

(4) An architect sent an employer an estimate of the cost of a proposed building (£15,000) saying, " which I feel sure may be relied upon as a guide to the cost." He then obtained an estimate from a builder for £14,860, and in writing to the employer said " So that you may safely rely upon the £15,000 covering everything, unless you want more done than I have proposed. *Indeed I can now promise it shall not exceed that sum.*" The architect was, by the terms of the contract, arbitrator in case of dispute; and it was provided that this submission might be made a rule of court. *Held,* that the undertaking to the employer having been concealed from the builder, the submission could not be enforced: *Kimberley* v. *Dick* (1871).[87]

(5) A and B, two coal masters, agreed that X (who was the consulting engineer of A), whom failing Y (who was the consulting engineer of B), should have power to prohibit B from working certain coal if he considered that such working was likely to injure a canal used by A. *Held,* that X was not disqualified from acting under the agreement by being employed by A in subsequent litigation between A and B on a different matter: *Addie* v. *Henderson* (1879).[88]

(6) Payments under a contract were to be made on A's certificate. A was a relation of and largely indebted to the employer. Of this the contractor had no knowledge. *Held, per* Armour C.J.O. that these relationships should have been disclosed, and that the certificate clause was of no effect in these circumstances: *Ludlam* v. *Wilson* (1901).[89]

(7) In a dispute between a railway company and the proprietor of certain fishings, each side appointed an arbitrator and the dispute was finally referred to an umpire. It happened that the railway company's arbitrator owned, unbeknown to the other party, a small quanitity of ordinary stock in the company. *Held,* that the umpire's award could not stand: *Sellar* v. *Highland Railway* (1919).[90]

While it is obviously not possible to give any comprehensive definition of the sort of interest that will be held to disqualify, it is suggested that any interest concealed from the contractor which lies outside the factors enumerated above at page 452 will prima facie disqualify, in the absence of special circumstances. Many of the early cases occupy themselves with the architect's or engineer's position as arbitrator (as opposed to certifier) and in such a case it should be remembered that, in so far as they may have been decided upon the basis of the contractor's actual or imputed knowledge at the time of contracting, they are no longer a practical

[87] L.R. 13 Eq. 1.
[88] 7 Ct. of Sess. Cas. (4th Series) (Rettie) 79. (For cases where the arbitrator or certifier had previously expressed an adverse view to the contractor's claim in a dispute; see *Scott* v. *Carluke Corporation* (1879) 6 R. (Ct. of Sess.) 616; *Halliday* v. *Duke of Hamilton's Trustees* (1903) 5 F. (Ct. of Sess.) 800; and *Cross* v. *Leeds Corporation* (1902) Hudson's B.C. Vol. 2, p. 339, in subs. (5), *infra,* at pp. 469–470, Conduct not Amounting to Fraud or Collusion.)
[89] 2 Ont.L.R. 549 (Canada).
[90] 1919 S.C.(H.L.) 19.

difficulty to a contractor in view of the special statutory provision in the Arbitration Acts governing the revocation of an arbitrator's appointment.[91]

(3) Disqualification on Ground of Fraud or Collusion

It has been held that a provision in a contract that no certificate of an architect shall be set aside for any reason, or for any suggestion or charge of fraud, collusion or confederacy, is valid and enforceable provided the contract itself was not fraudulently entered into.[92] But in the absence of an express provision of this kind, a certificate given or refused as a result of fraud or collusion with either party has no effect.   In the next following subsection cases of prevention by the employer will be dealt with separately, but, as appears from the facts of the cases in both subsections, the borderline between these two classes of case may not always be a very distinct one.[93]

ILLUSTRATIONS

(1) An engineering contract provided that the works were to be completed within a given time to the satisfaction of the engineer, and that if the works should not be so done the employers might enter into possession of the contractor's plant and complete the works. The employers covenanted to pay for the works from time to time on the engineer's certificate. All disputes were to be referred to the engineer. The works were not completed within the fixed time, and, some time after, the employers gave notice of their intention to enter under the agreement and complete. The contractor claimed an account of monies due and an injunction stating that he had done all that he had contracted to do, except what the employers had prevented him from doing, that he had not been fully paid for the work which had been done, that the engineer fraudulently and in collusion with the employers withheld certificates, and certified a less amount than was due to the contractor, and requested him not to proceed, and then asked him to go on at a very quick rate. The employers demurred. *Held*, that the demurrers must be dismissed, on the ground that the contractor would be entitled to some relief at the hearing, and that the species of fraud alleged, not being a mere general charge, but an allegation of a fraudulent purpose in doing a particular act, gave jurisdiction to the court, although the contractor had not completed the whole of his work: *Waring* v. *Manchester Railway* (1849).[94]

(2) A builder filed a bill against a company, and also (for the purpose of discovery, and without claiming any relief) against their

[91] s. 24 of the 1950 Act.
[92] *Tullis* v. *Jacson* [1892] 3 Ch. 441. See, however, *per* Scrutton L.J. in *Czarnikow* v. *Roth, Schmidt & Co.* [1922] 2 K.B. 478, and *Redmond* v. *Wynne* (1892) 13 N.S.W.R. 39, where such an agreement was held void as contrary to public policy.
[93] See also subsection (5) below, Conduct not Amounting to Fraud or Collusion.
[94] 18 L.J.Ch. 450.

secretary, and the engineer, alleging that the works which he had undertaken for them had been properly completed, and that notice had been duly given thereof, and that the engineer had refused to give his certificate, and " that he had so refused because he had been desired by the company not to give his certificate, and that in such refusal he had acted under the direction and authority of, and in collusion with, the company." The demurrers for want of equity were overruled. " It appears to me that this is clearly a case in which the plaintiffs cannot obtain what they are entitled to at law, and their inability to do so has arisen from the acts of the defendants or their agents and whether such acts were orginally from any fraudulent motive or not, I think that to use them for the purpose of defeating the plaintiff's remedy would constitute a fraud which this court will not permit them to avail themselves of ": *Macintosh* v. *G. W. Railway* (*No.* 1) (1850). [95]

(3) A builder sued the employer, alleging that he had completed the work to the satisfaction of the architect, and that in breach of contract the architect unfairly and improperly neglected to certify, in collusion with the defendant and by his procurement, by means of which the plaintiff had been unable to obtain payment of a balance due to him. *Held*, that the words " collusion " and " procurement " imported fraud, and that the declaration disclosed a good cause of action: *Batterbury* v. *Vyse* (1863). [96]

(4) A contractor alleged that the engineer had unfairly neglected to sign a final certificate and so neglected in collusion with the employers, and by their procurement. *Held*, that a demurrer to this allegation must fail. It appeared that the employers had passed a resolution that a certificate should be given, and that the engineer professed to comply and gave a document which was useless as a certificate, but expressed his willingness to certify if he were personally released from all responsibility. The contractors applied to the commissioners to dismiss the architect and appoint another who would act according to the contract. This the commissioners refused to do. The jury found that there was collusion. On demurrer: *Held*, that though the engineer refused to give a final certificate, it was open to the jury to find from his acts and conduct that the work had been completed to his satisfaction, but that the contractor could not recover from the employer unless it be alleged and proved that the certificate was refused in collusion with the employer. *Held*, also, that an engineer to whose satisfaction work is to be done, is not an arbitrator but a skilled agent of the employer, and that he owes a duty to the contractor as well as to the employer, and is bound to act fairly towards both parties: *Young* v. *Ballarat Water Commissioners* (1878). [97]

It is immaterial whether fraud occurs prior or subsequent to the making of the contract.

---

[95] 19 L.J.Ch. 374, *per* Lord Cottenham L.C. Despite the language used this was really a case of prevention or interference—*cf.* the case of *Alberta Building Co.* v. *City of Calgary* (1911), *post*, pp. 461–462.

[96] 32 L.J.Ex. 177.

[97] 4 Vict.L.R. 306, 502; 5 Vict.L.R. 503. (The duty referred to is the duty of honesty in the context of the tortious liability for fraud.)

ILLUSTRATIONS

(1) Company A entered into a contract to lay telegraph cables for company B, payment to be upon certificate of X, company B's consultant engineer. Subsequently company A subcontracted a considerable amount of the work to X upon terms that X should be paid as and when payments were received from company B. There was a conflict of evidence as to whether, at the time of the original contract, company A and X were contemplating some such arrangement as they finally made to subcontract the work. *Held*, on either view, the second agreement was a fraud upon company B, who could avoid the contract altogether: *Panama and South Pacific Telegraph Co. v. India Rubber, etc. Co.* (1875). [98]

(2) Contractors deliberately carried out defective work, organising a system of signals when the clerk of works was approaching to inspect the works. As a result the final certificate was given in ignorance of the deficiencies in the work. *Held*, by the Court of Appeal, that not only the contractor but also the sureties of the contractor were liable to the employer, notwithstanding the issue of the final certificate, and notwithstanding the jury's finding that failure to supervise properly had led to the scamping of the work. *Kingston-upon-Hull Corporation v. Harding* (1892). [99]

As previously stated,[1] fraud by the architect renders him liable to an action in tort by the builder (or indeed by the employer) but no action will lie for conduct less than fraud.[2]

ILLUSTRATIONS

(1) A builder brought an action against an architect in which he alleged that the architect, in collusion with the employer, refused to certify satisfaction, and falsely pretended that he was dissatisfied with the work. *Held*, on demurrer, that a good cause of action was disclosed against the architect. In the action special damages were claimed and recovered: *Ludbrook v. Barrett* (1877). [3]

(2) A builder sued an architect for the balance of the contract price, alleging that the architect did not use due care and skill in ascertaining the amounts to be paid by the building owner to the builder, but neglected and refused to ascertain, and did not ascertain, the amount of additions and deductions to be made in the same manner as the quantities had been taken out, and at the same rates as they had been priced. *Held*, that the function of the architect required the exercise of professional judgment, opinion, and skill, and that in the absence of any allegation of fraud or collusion no action would lie against him at the suit of the builder: *Stevenson v. Watson* (1879). [4]

[98] L.R. 10 Ch.App. 515.

[99] [1892] 2 Q.B. 494. See also for a case of fraud between contractor and architect, *Wakefield etc. v. Normanton Local Board* (1881) 44 L.T. 697, illustrated *post*, Chap. 14, Section 5, pp. 733–734.

[1] See *ante*, Chap. 2, pp. 174–175.

[2] See now, however, the possibility of such an action under the principle in *Hedley, Byrne v. Heller, ante*, Chap. 1, pp. 64 *et seq.*

[3] 46 L.J.C.P. 798, approved in *Stevenson v. Watson, supra.*

[4] (1879) 4 C.P.D. 148. See also *Young v. Smith* (1880) Hudson's B.C. 4th ed., Vol. 2, p. 3, and *Priestly v. Stone* (1888) 4 T.L.R. 730, illustrated *ante* Chap. 2, pp. 196–197.

But to found an action in fraud, the plaintiff in that action must prove that a fraudulent misrepresentation by word or conduct was made to him. It will not be sufficient if it is made to someone else (though if this induces the issue or refusal of a certificate it will avoid the effect of the certificate or its absence).

ILLUSTRATION

An architect was alleged to have made a fraudulent representation to a building owner to the effect that the work had not reached practical completion. *Held*, this could not, in accordance with the principles governing the law of deceit, give a cause of action to the builder against the architect: *Larkins* v. *Chelmer Holdings* (1965).[5]

(4) Prevention or Interference by the Employer

Given the quasi-arbitral nature of the certifier's function, it would seem that there must be an implied term that both parties will do nothing to prevent a true and unfettered exercise of his powers when certifying.[6] Consequently, action taken by the employer with a view to influencing the certifier in the exercise of his powers will mean that damages equivalent to the contract price or other resulting loss can be recovered despite any certificate or the absence of one. Some cases suggest that this is an example of the wider principle that prevention by a party to a contract of the performance of a condition by the other disables him from insisting on its performance, other applications of which have been seen previously, *e.g. Roberts* v. *Bury Commissioners* (1870), where Kelly C.B. said: " It is a principle very well established at common law that no person can take advantage of the non-fulfilment of a condition the performance of which has been hindered by himself," [7] and see *per* Ashhurst J. in *Hotham* v. *East India Co.* (1787) [8]: " Where a certificate is a condition precedent and the builder has taken all proper steps to obtain the certificate, but the employers have rendered performance of the condition precedent impossible by the neglect or default of themselves or their agents (which is a question for a jury) the condition precedent is treated as performed (or dispensed with)," and *per* Romilly M.R. in *Bliss* v. *Smith* (1865) [9]: " Courts of equity interfere . . . where there is collusive dealing and concert between the employer and the

---

[5] [1965] Qd. Rep. 68 (Australia).
[6] See the passage from Devlin J.'s judgment in *Minster Trust* v. *Traps Tractors Ltd. ante*, Section 3, pp. 417–418.
[7] L.R. 5 C.P. 310, illustrated at pp. 407–408, *ante*.
[8] 1 T.R. 638, 645.
[9] 34 Beav. at p. 510.

person whom he has appointed architect, for the purpose of injuring the contractor or defeating his claim," and *per* Esher M.R. in *McDonald* v. *Mayor of Workington* (1893) [10]: " I should say myself that if they wickedly and by collusion with the surveyor prevented him giving the certificate, I should treat the case as though he had given it."

Despite the above statements, however, there seems to be some confusion in the cases on the perhaps somewhat academic question as to whether the builder's claim is upon the contract or for damages for its breach—see, *e.g. per* Vaughan Williams L.J. in *Smith* v. *Howden Union* (1890) [11]: " The case of refusal by the engineer ... in collusion with the building owner to grant certificates is spoken of as an exception. It is not, however, really an exception. In such a case the building owner and engineer fraudulently prevent the contractor from ... getting the certificates, and what is recoverable by the contractor in such a case is not really the price, but damages. That the performance of the condition precedent is necessary at law appears from the case of *Clarke* v. *Watson* (1865).[12] The cases in equity ... may contain observations seeming to show that misconduct or fraud of the architect, without collusion of the employer, will entitle the contractor to recover the price without obtaining the certificate required by the contract. But when these cases are looked at nothing of the sort seems at all events involved in the decision...." (Vaughan Williams L.J. then considers *Macintosh* v. *G. W. Railway* (1850) [13] and *Waring* v. *Manchester, etc. Railway* (1849).[14]

In considering the somewhat confusing language in the following cases, it may assist if the following categories of conduct (all likely to lead to the same practical result of disregarding a certificate or its absence) are distinguished, namely:

(a) some act of the employer, such as dismissal of the architect or a wrongful termination of the builder's employment or a suspension of the work or withholding of the site, which indirectly may have the effect of depriving the builder of the opportunity of obtaining the certificate. These may properly be regarded as cases of prevention.

(b) a deliberate putting together of heads by the employer and architect (or indeed of the contractor and architect) in order to

[10] 9 T.L.R. 230; Hudson's B.C., Vol. 2, at p. 232.
[11] 1 Cab. & Ell. 125; illustrated *infra*, pp. 460–461.
[12] 18 C.B.(N.S.) 278.
[13] *Supra*, pp. 455–456.
[14] *Supra*, p. 455.

withhold from the contractor certificates to which he was entitled or to obtain certificates to which he was not entitled—this would properly be regarded as collusion or fraud on the other party.

(c) fraudulent conduct by either party designed to deceive the architect into giving or withholding a certificate contrary to his intention had he known the true facts.

(d) innocent but improper pressure on the architect by either party—this would be breach of an implied term not to exercise improper influence on the certifier.

It should be remembered in considering the judgments in the following cases that " prevention " may be used to describe inter-ference with the architect by the employer (which may not be easy to distinguish from " collusion " or improper pressure) or it may take the form of some other act, such as a wrongful termination of the builder's employment, which indirectly has the effect of depriving the builder of the certificate.

ILLUSTRATIONS

(1) An employer wrongly dismissed a builder, purporting to act under a provision in the contract. In consequence the builder did not have the architect's certificates for the work done by him. *Held*, he could recover the sums due to him by way of damages: *Smith* v. *Gordon* (1880).[15]

(2) In an action by a builder against a building owner under a contract by which the architect's certificate was a condition pre-cedent to payment, the plaintiff alleged that the employer, after the work was completed, complained to the architect of alleged defects therein, and told him that he should not accept his certificate unless they were attended to and remedied. The defendant denied this, and produced evidence to the effect that there had been no communication at all between the defendant and the architect. Watkin Williams J. to the jury: " If you think that the architect, acting upon his judgment, withheld his certificate, you must find a verdict for the defendant. If, however, you are of opinion that the withholding of the certificate was due to the improper interposition of the defendant, and that he prevented the architect from giving his certificate, you must find a verdict for the plaintiff." The jury found a verdict for the plaintiff: *Brunsdon* v. *Beresford* (1883).[16]

(3) A contractor finished the construction of certain sewers, but remained on the site carrying out certain further work under the supervision of the engineer. The contract sum was £2,616, and the builder had been paid £2,318. There was a claim for extras of about £800. The engineer had set out the works very roughly, and left their supervision entirely to a clerk of the works whose reports he

---

[15] 30 Up.Can.C.P. 553. See also *Roberts* v. *Bury Commissioners* (1870) L.R. 5 C.P. 310, *supra*, pp. 407–408, and *Mackay* v. *Dick* (1881) 6 App.Cas. 251.
[16] 1 Cab. & Ell. 125.

adopted, and certified thereon. He was satisfied with the works on completion. Most of the extras had not been ordered in writing, but were certified during the course of the works. Soon after completion, the levels were found to be incorrect, and the engineer refused to issue any further certificates, and condemned the work. The incorrect levels were in fact due to errors in the plans, sections and orders of the engineer. The employers then turned the contractor off the site, and seized a very small quantity of his plant. The contractor brought an action and the Official Referee held that the engineer acted improperly and unfairly, though not to the knowledge of his employers, and refused to exercise his honest judgment upon the question whether any further sum was due to the plaintiff. He also held that the employers' re-entry and seizure was a breach of contract, and gave judgment for the plaintiff for the sums due under the contract. *Held*, by the Divisional Court, that in the absence of collusion with the employers, the contractor's remedy against the employers was for damages for the wrongful re-entry, and not an action for the price upon the contract itself: *Smith* v. *Howden Union* (1890).[17]

(4) P. was employed by a rural council to construct certain works. The contract provided " that the decision of the surveyor with respect to the value, amount, state and condition of any part of the works executed, or of any part thereof altered, omitted or added, and also in respect to any and every question that may arise concerning the construction of this contract, or the said drawings, plans, specification or bill of quantities, or schedule of prices, or the execution of the works hereby contracted for, or in anywise relating thereto, shall be final and without appeal." Disputes arose, and after protracted negotiations the surveyor gave his final certificate. P. brought an action against the council, in which he alleged that the surveyor's final certificate " was not honestly made or given in the exercise of, or in reliance upon, his own judgment, but was made and given by reason of the interference of, and in obedience to, the directions and orders of the council." The evidence showed that the council had asked for the preparation of an account by their surveyor and had instructed him that he should not use a day-work method of computing the value of part of the work but should estimate quantities himself and apply a measured rate, though he had no means of making a measurement. *Held*, that as the council had interfered (though without any fraud on their part) with the surveyor in the exercise of his functions as quasi-arbitrator between the parties, the final certificate was not conclusive and binding on the contractor: *Page* v. *Llandaff and Dinas Powis Rural Council* (1901).[18]

(5) Builders undertook to erect a city hall at Calgary in Canada for $142,000. By a clause in the contract, the City Council were empowered to expel the builders and take possession upon failure to proceed with the work, upon a certificate of the architect to that effect. The Council were unable to raise the whole of the money to pay for the hall. After two years, at a time when they had been

---

[17] Hudson's B.C., 4th ed., Vol. 2, p. 156. It is suggested, p. 472, that there is an implied term that the certifier will be honest. If so, the latter part of this decision is of doubtful authority.

[18] Hudson's B.C., 4th ed., Vol. 2, p. 316.

paid $105,000 under provisions for monthly payment upon certificates, the builders made application for a certificate for a further $7,000 to the architect. The architect did not dispute the correctness of the application, but refused to issue a certificate upon it. After repeated demands, and notice that they would do so, the builders stopped work a fortnight later. The architect then certified failure to proceed, and the Council took possession. *Held*, the architect's refusal of a certificate for payment was, on the facts, due to instructions from the City Treasurer, and not to doubts as to the correctness of the builders' application. He was accordingly actuated by improper motives when bound to act quasi-judicially and impartially, and the builders were not disentitled from suing by the absence of a certificate. Further, the Council, having been given notice of the consequences of failure to pay, were bound to make inquiries before acting upon the architect's certificate of failure to proceed, had failed to do so, and could not rely upon the certificate to justify their entry into possession, which was a breach of contract by them: *Alberta Building Co.* v. *City of Calgary* (1911).[19]

(6) A clause in a building contract provided that in the event of failure or delay in providing labour and materials necessary in the architect's opinion for completion of the work, the owners might, after three days' notice, complete themselves and deduct the cost from the contract sum. The architect served notice under this clause as to defects and omissions totalling approximately $150 on a total contract sum of $20,000. *Held (inter alia)*, that the architect refrained from issuing a final certificate containing a deduction of $150 because he was instructed by the owners and their solicitors, whom he had consulted, not to do so. His duty was, if necessary, to obtain independent legal advice, and the need for a certificate could be dispensed with: *Watts* v. *McLeay* (1911).[20]

(7) An architect, who was being asked for a certificate for £750 by the builder shortly before the work was complete, received a letter from the employers saying that he should on no account issue a certificate till he had received the builder's account for extras. After receiving further letters from the builder, he wrote to the employers stating that he wished to issue a certificate for £600, adding that the builder was entitled to a certificate under the contract. The employers replied as before, and said that they would not meet the certificate. The architect then wrote to the builder stating that he regretted he could not issue a certificate as the employer had instructed him to issue no further certificates until his final certificate, and suggested the builder should meet the employers, since in the face of their instructions he could not issue a certificate, whatever his private opinion. Ultimately, he gave a certificate (not a final certificate) for £400 to the builder, who obtained judgment upon it, and issued a writ for the balance due. Other letters between the employer and architect, not shown to the builder, indicated that the employer was pressing the architect to cut down the builder's claims as much as possible in view of the employer's difficulties. *Held*, that while the architect was not guilty of fraud or collusion, and accepting that his final certificate, when and if it had been issued, would have stated the amount in his opinion properly due, he had

[19] 16 W.L.R. 443 (Canada).   [20] 19 W.L.R. 916 (Canada).

allowed himself to be influenced by the employer in a manner inconsistent with his position as certifier, and the employer was precluded from setting up the absence of a certificate as a defence to the claim: *Hickman* v. *Roberts* (1913).[21]

However, it is clearly natural and to be expected that both parties, and particularly the employer, may in practice make representations to and communicate with the architect or certifier on the subject-matter of his decision. Whether such representations or communications amount to improper interference will depend, it is suggested, upon whether they are of a character which recognises the independence of the certifier and his ultimate responsibility for making an impartial decision. The following case is an excellent example of a type of perfectly proper communication between employer and architect likely to occur in practice and which will not invalidate a certificate. Despite some dicta suggesting that the certifier should afford both parties an opportunity to be heard,[22] and while it may be agreed that a certifier should certainly not refuse to hear a party wishing to be heard, there seems no reason why the certifier should invite representations or encourage meetings for this purpose, or should see or hear both parties at the same time. The degree to which he should be prepared to hear either party will depend upon the matter on which his approval or certificate is required.

ILLUSTRATION

An engineer certified that in his opinion the contractor had failed to make satisfactory progress, and the employer terminated the contract under a provision empowering him to do so. Under the contract the " reasonableness " of the engineer's certificate was subject to arbitration. The parties concurred in the submission of this question, and whether the contractor was entitled to damages for wrongful termination, to arbitration. The arbitrator found that the engineer, on the morning of the day before he certified, took steps to encourage the contractor to carry on with the work, but that after two meetings of about an hour each with the employer, at which the contractor was not present, and at which the employer indicated that he did not wish the contractor to continue and asked if the engineer would give the certificate, he did in fact issue the certificate the following day. The arbitrator further found that on the facts the certificate was reasonable, but that the certificate was a nullity as the engineer had received representations from one side and not from the other, and further held that the contractor was entitled to damages. *Held*, (1) [23] that the fact that the certificate

[21] [1913] A.C. 229. Discussed *post*, pp. 468, 471–473.

[22] See the remarks of Channell J. in *Page* v. *Llandaff R.D.C.* (1901) Hudson's B.C., 4th ed., Vol. 2, p. 239, quoted *infra*, Section 9, pp. 500–501.

[23] After considering the passage from Devlin J.'s judgment in the *Minster Trust* case quoted *supra*, Sect. 3, pp. 417–418, *Hickman* v. *Roberts*, *supra*, and other authorities.

was subject to review did not mean that the certifier was not bound to act with the impartiality and independence required of any other certifier, but (2) that the evidence only showed that during the discussions the engineer might have been of a different opinion from the employer on the advisability of allowing the contractor to complete the work (which was not a matter with which he was concerned as certifier), (3) there was no evidence that he had surrendered his independence or impartiality on the question of the contractor's progress or received representations of a kind likely to bring this about, and in the circumstances there was no obligation to listen to both sides or give the contractor an opportunity to be heard. Accordingly the employer was not in breach of contract: *Hatrick (N.Z.) Ltd.* v. *Nelson Carlton Construction* (1964).[24]

The following case concerns the rather difficult status of the engineer on a preliminary reference under a clause similar to (but not identical with) the I.C.E. arbitration clause, which under the terms of these clauses is an indispensable preliminary reference to arbitration.

ILLUSTRATION

An arbitration clause provided that if any dispute should arise between the council, or the engineer on its behalf, and the contractor, the engineer should determine such dispute by a written decision given to the contractor. The decision was final and binding unless the contractor gave notice within fourteen days. The employer dismissed the contractor for failing to comply with notices requiring him to do the work properly, employed another contractor to complete, and claimed the cost from the contractor, who disputed his liability to pay. Without informing the contractor of his intentions, the engineer forwarded to him a written decision that he was liable for the sum in question unless the decision was disputed within fourteen days. After this period had expired the employers brought an action for the money. *Held*, by the Appellate Division of the Supreme Court of South Africa, that as the engineer's decision was not immediately final, and as he would himself be a party to the dispute, the engineer was neither an arbitrator nor a quasi-arbitrator, and the decision, not having been appealed against in time, was binding on the contractor: *Kollberg* v. *Cape Town Municipality* (1967).[25]

[Note: This case is more fully set out *post* Chapter 18, where it is doubted on a number of grounds. Since the engineer's decision was given conditional finality, it seems remarkable that written representations at least were not asked for from the contractor before the decision was given.]

The following case, which turned upon an express term of the contract, is nevertheless of assistance in this context.

ILLUSTRATION

By Clause 20 (1) of a contract in the standard R.I.B.A. form the contractor was entitled to terminate the contract " if the employer interferes with or obstructs the issue of any . . . certificate." The architect was also the surveyor under the contract, but at a stage when a considerable amount of work had been done the employers, acting on his recommendation, appointed other surveyors. At that stage, owing to the pressure of work on the architect, there was some doubt in the employers' mind as to whether the contractor had not been overpaid on interim certificates. The new surveyor made no proper valuation at all, while substantially reducing the sums claimed by the builder in his recommendation to the architect, who certified accordingly. Shortly afterwards the surveyor discovered he had made a mistake justifying a larger payment to the contractor, but did not inform the architect of this. The contractor then terminated the contract. *Held*, by the House of Lords (Lord Somervell of Harrow dissenting) that since the employers had given no instructions impeding the architect in the performance of his duty of certification, they could not be said to have interfered with or obstructed the issue of the certificate, and the contractor was therefore in breach of contract: *Burden* v. *Swansea Corporation* (1957).[26]

(5) Conduct Not Amounting to Fraud or Collusion

It has been said many times by the courts that in the absence of fraud or collusion the effect of contractual provisions giving finality to a certificate cannot be avoided.

ILLUSTRATIONS

(1) A bill in equity filed by contractors against a corporation and their engineer prayed that the withholding of the certificate might be declared a fraud upon them. It appearing by the evidence that the engineer was able and willing to do all the duties imposed upon him by the contract, and not incapacitated by collusion, corruption or otherwise, and that the contractor had refused or neglected to send in weekly claims and produce books and vouchers as required by the contract, the bill was dismissed with costs: *Scott* v. *Liverpool Corporation* (1858).[27]

(2) A builder brought an action against the building owner, alleging that although all things had been done by the plaintiff to entitle him to a certificate, the owner's surveyor had not given such certificate, but had wrongfully and improperly neglected and refused so to do, and the defendants had not paid the money payable on such certificate. *Held*, bad, on demurrer, as not disclosing any cause of action against the defendants. *Per* Erle C.J.: " If it had been alleged that the defendants had wrongfully colluded with the surveyor to cause the certificate to be withheld, they could not have sheltered themselves under their own wrongful act. But the word ' wrongfully,' as used here, does not intimate anything of that sort ": *Clarke* v. *Watson* (1865).[28]

(3) The engineer of a railway company prepared a specification of a proposed railway, and contractors fixed prices to the several

[26] [1957] 1 W.L.R. 1167.
[27] 28 L.J.Ch. 230.
[28] 18 C.B.(N.S.) 278. Total refusal may afford an escape. See *post*, pp. 475–476.

items in the specification, and offered to construct the railway for a lump sum made up of these prices. The engineer made a mistake in the calculations of the earthwork of two million yards, and it was alleged that he, finding that this involved more expense than he had calculated upon, promised that he would make other alterations, making a corresponding diminution so as to save the contractors from loss. The engineer did not make any other alterations, and certified for the final sum due to the contractors without taking any account of the alleged extra works. No fraud was alleged, but it was argued that this had the effect of fraud. *Held*, that unless the engineer had wilfully made miscalculations in order to deceive the contractors, they could not recover anything for the omission, and then only from the engineer personally, and not from the company. *Held*, also, that if the contractors could not show any dishonesty or any fraud or sinister motive, they were bound by the engineer's certificate: *per* Lord Romilly M.R., *Sharpe* v. *San Paulo Railway* (1873).[29]

(4) A building contract provided for written orders for extras and that " a certificate of the architect or an award of the referee hereinafter referred to, as the case may be, showing the final balance due or payable to the contractors, is to be conclusive evidence of the works having been duly completed, and that the contractors are entitled to receive payment of the final balance." The architect employed a surveyor to measure up the work, and certified for the final balance " as certified by the measuring surveyors to be the final amount due." In an action by the builder to recover the amount certified, the employer set up that written orders had not been given for extras included in the certificate, and that the reference to the " measuring surveyors " made the final certificate bad, as not being an exercise of the skill and judgment of the architect. *Held*, that as no allegation of fraud was made against the architect, the certificate was binding on both parties, and that the architect had not abdicated his duties: *Clemence* v. *Clarke* (1880).[30]

(5) A contract provided for final payment on the architect's certificate of completion to his satisfaction. The contractor refused to remedy certain defects, and the architect refused to certify. The contractor sued the employers and pleaded that the certificate was " wrongfully " withheld. *Held*, that if fraud and collusion had been shown, the absence of the certificate might not have been a bar to the contractor's claim, but to say it was " wrongfully " withheld was no answer to the plea of the absence of the certificate: *Botterill* v. *Ware Guardians* (1886).[31]

However, it would seem that there may be situations other than prevention, fraud or collusion in which the courts will dispense with the certificate.

ILLUSTRATIONS

(1) During the course of a building contract the builder, who had received £1,240 already, requested certificates from the architect,

---

[29] L.R. 8 Ch.App. 605, note (1); and see *De Worms* v. *Mellier* (1873) L.R. 16 Eq. 554.
[30] Hudson's B.C., 8th ed., 227, 241.
[31] 2 T.L.R. 621.

claiming that £2,600 of work had been done, but this was refused, on the ground that the work had not been done in accordance with the contract. As the architect did not give details, the builder asked two of his suppliers to meet the architect in order to find out what his complaint was, which they did, and the architect told them that the work was completed except for some £200 of work, and would be completed in two or three weeks, and gave no further details. The architect then terminated the builder's employment, and the latter instructed two surveyors to visit the site to examine the work. The employers and the architect, though notified of this, refused to have anything to do with it. The architect made no account or memorandum of the state of the work at the time of terminating the builder's employment, and completed the work himself on behalf of the employer. The builder filed a bill in equity against the employer and the architect asking for an account of what was due to him, and the defendants relied on the absence of a certificate. *Held*, that the conduct of the architect had been oppressive and unfair, and, without imputing fraud to either defendants, was not of the discreet, impartial and fair description which it ought to have been, and that the plaintiff was entitled to a decree for payment of the balance due to him under the contract: *Pawley* v. *Turnbull* (1861).[32]

(2) The rules of a tramway company required its servants to sign an agreement that " in case of any breach by the conductor of any of the rules the company may retain all wages due, and that the manager for the time being shall be the sole judge as to a breach, and his certificate binding and conclusive between the parties." The plaintiff was dismissed by the manager and brought an action for wages earned prior to his dismissal. The manager then issued a certificate showing the amount due and declaring the whole to be forfeited. He gave the plaintiff no hearing. *Held*, the certificate was void as the plaintiff had not been heard: *Armstrong* v. *S. London Tramway* (1890).[33]

[Note: It is suggested that in building contracts, the degree to which a certifier should afford the parties an opportunity of making representations may vary according to the terms of the contract and the subject-matter of the certificate.] [34]

(3) Engineers in their final certificate deducted from the contract price a sum to take account of an alleged error in calculating the quantities. *Held*, they had no right to do so under the contract, their certificate was binding as regards any matter within their jurisdiction, but in this respect the certificate should be corrected: *Peters* v. *Quebec Harbour Commrs.* (1891).[35]

(4) The plaintiff agreed to do the work for the defendants to the satisfaction of an engineer, and the defendants agreed to pay the plaintiff upon the certificate of the engineer. The engineer never addressed himself to determine and certify, but wrongfully refused,

[32] 3 Giff. 70, *per* Stuart V.-C. approved on appeal (unreported) by Lord Westbury (see *per* Malins V.-C. in *Panama, etc.* v. *India Rubber* (1875) L.R. 10 Ch.App. 515, at p. 523n.) and explained by Vaughan Williams L.J. as a case of damages in *Smith* v. *Howden Union, supra*, p. 459.

[33] 7 T.L.R. 123.

[34] See the discussion *supra*, p. 463.

[35] 19 S.C.R. 685 (Canada).

or wrongfully and unreasonably delayed, so to determine and certify, and the defendants, who knew of this, took advantage of his refusal and delayed payment. Fraud was not alleged. *Held*, that the plaintiff could recover from the defendants without a certificate: *Kellett* v. *New Mills Urban District Council* (1900).[36]

(5) A contract gave the architect power to extend time, and certify liquidated damages for delay. The architect told both parties that he would not decide the question of damages. *Held*, as he had absolutely refused to act, the court must assess the liquidated damages themselves: *Watts* v. *McLeay* (1911).[37]

(6) *Hickman* v. *Roberts* (1913).[38] (N.B. This case has been summarised above under the heading of " Prevention by the Employer," but consideration of its judgments suggests that it was decided on wider grounds, similar to those adumbrated in *Pawley* v. *Turnbull*, namely, that the certifier's failure to maintain a properly independent and judicial attitude towards his function deprived his certificates of their binding effect.)

(7) A builder was to be paid by instalments on certificates issued by the architect. In case of disputes, the architect was to act as arbitrator. A dispute arose, but the architect refused to act himself or to issue a certificate, and sought to nominate a third person as arbitrator. The employer took no steps to appoint a new arbitrator or to stay an action commenced by the builder. *Held*, since the architect had failed to act as required by the contract, the need for a certificate could be dispensed with and the plaintiff could recover: *Neale* v. *Richardson* (1938).[39]

(8) A contract for the repair of a ship provided that the owners should pay the repairers during the progress of the work on the basis of their expenditure, payment to be effected upon certificates of the owners' surveyor that the work had been satisfactorily carried out, and of the Investigation Branch of the Ministry of War Transport as to the amount due. The certificates were to be final and conclusive. The certificate of cost was issued, but the surveyor took the view that his approval and certification extended beyond the quality of the work to the question whether reasonable economy had been exercised, and refused to give a certificate without certain fuller information by the repairers. On an action by the repairers, *held*, that on the true construction of the contract the surveyor's view was incorrect and the necessity for the surveyor's certificate would be dispensed with: *Panamena Europea* v. *Leyland* (1947).[40]

(9) A contractor undertook to supply gravel and asphalt to be paid for by weight, and possession of an estimate or certificate signed by the employer's engineer was to be a condition precedent to the right of payment. The engineer refused to certify for the materials by weight and used his own methods of calculation in

---

[36] (1900) 4th ed., Vol. 2, p. 298.
[37] 19 W.L.R. 916 (Canada), illustrated more fully, *ante*, p. 462.
[38] [1913] A.C. 229, illustrated *supra*, pp. 462–463.
[39] [1938] 1 All E.R. 753. Illustrated more fully *supra*, p. 441.
[40] [1947] A.C. 428. See the discussion of this case *infra*, pp. 476–478. See also the discussion *supra*, Section 3 and the case of *Cammell Laird* v. *Manganese Bronze & Brass* there illustrated.

arriving at the amounts to be paid. *Held*, the engineer's refusal to certify in accordance with the contract was arbitrary and illegal and an abdication of his function under the contract. The employers had concurred in the position taken by the engineer,[41] and had thus brought themselves within the principle of the *Panamena* case, and the contractor was absolved from the requirement with respect to the certificate: *Corporation of City of Oshawa* v. *Brennan Paving Co. Ltd.* (1955).[42]

On the other hand, in the following cases conduct which no doubt would not have been accepted in a fully independent arbitrator was held not to affect the validity of an award of a named-architect arbitrator, since it arose as a result of the proper discharge of the architect's or engineer's other duties under the contract.[43] The principle in these cases must apply at least as strongly to an architect or engineer who is a mere certifier, notwithstanding that at the present day they are for practical purposes academic in the field of arbitration proper in England by reason of section 24 of the Act of 1950.

ILLUSTRATIONS

(1) Under an engineering contract the engineer was both certifier and arbitrator. A dispute arose as to whether stone or rocky marl had to be provided by the contractor so as to satisfy the provisions of the contract. Correspondence took place between the contractor and the engineer, in which the latter stated his view that the contractor was bound to use stone, and that it was not an extra. The matter was then formally referred to the engineer under the arbitration clause, and on the day appointed for the reference the engineer again wrote to the contractors repeating his former view. On an action by the contractor to restrain the employers from proceeding with the arbitration, *held*, that the final letter on its fair construction, did not indicate that the engineer had made up his mind so as not to be open to change it upon argument, and since his position as engineer meant that he must already have expressed his opinion on the point, he was not disqualified from acting as arbitrator: *Jackson* v. *Barry Railway* (1893).[44]

(2) Under a contract for the execution of waterworks for a local authority the engineer of the authority was also appointed arbitrator. During the course of the works he submitted a report to his employers complaining in strong terms of the way the works had been carried out. *Held*, he was not thereby disqualified from acting as arbitrator: *Scott* v. *Carluke Corporation* (1879).[45]

(3) Under a contract for the construction of a pier the employers' engineer was appointed arbitrator. After completion a question arose as to extras, and the engineer wrote to his employers in answer

---

[41] See the criticism of this part of the reasoning in the *Panamena* case, *infra*, p. 478.
[42] [1955] S.C.R. 76 (Canada). See *post*, p. 478.
[43] See also the case of *Hatrick* v. *Nelson*, illustrated *supra*, pp. 463–464.
[44] [1893] 1 Ch. 238.
[45] 6 R. (Ct. of Sess.) 616.

to a request from them giving detailed reasons why the sums claimed were not in his opinion due. *Held,* he was not thereby disqualified from acting as arbitrator: *Halliday* v. *Duke of Hamilton's Trustees* (1903).[46]

(4) A named arbitrator, who was the city engineer of the Leeds Corporation, wrote a letter in answer to a claim by the contractors against the corporation stating that their claim was outrageous. *Held,* he was not disqualified from acting as arbitrator: *Cross* v. *Leeds Corporation* (1902).[47]

(5) M. contracted to do engineering work for the B. Parochial Board. All matters, claims and obligations whatever arising out of the contract were to be referred to A., who was, in fact, the engineer of the board. A. had, as engineer, complained of some of M.'s work, and had measured the work and brought out as due to M. less than he claimed. *Held,* that A. was not disqualified from acting as arbitrator: *Mackay* v. *Barry Parochial Board* (1883).[48]

The principle underlying these cases is perhaps best expressed in the following passage from the judgment of Bowen L.J. in *Jackson* v. *Barry Railway* (1893).[49]

" The perfectly open judgment, the absence of all previously formed or pronounced views, which in an ordinary arbitrator are natural and to be looked for, neither party to the contract proposed to exact from the arbitrator of their choice. . . . The question is whether the engineer has done anything to unfit himself to act, or render himself incapable of acting, not as an arbitrator without previously formed or even strong views, but as an honest judge of this very special and exceptional kind."[50]

(6) Summary and Discussion of Preceding Subsections

The preceding sections have subdivided the cases in which a certificate can be dispensed with into the following classes, namely (a) " Disqualification by Interest," (b) " Fraud or Collusion," (c) " Prevention by the Employer," and (d) the omnibus class " Conduct Not Amounting to Fraud or Collusion." This was the classification adopted in the preceding editions, and, indeed, generally in works on this subject, and it finds support in the wording of many of the judgments in the cases previously cited. But consideration of the facts of these cases suggests that this classification involves considerable overlapping and confusion, and it is suggested that the following classification is more accurate.

[46] 5 F. (Ct. of Sess.) 800.
[47] Hudson's B.C., 4th ed., Vol. 2, p. 339.
[48] 10 R. (Ct. of Sess.) 1046.
[49] [1893] 1 Ch. 238.
[50] Now s. 24 of the Act of 1950 will enable a new arbitrator (but not a certifier) to be appointed, since the fact that his interest was known to the parties at the time of contracting is no longer a bar to an architect-arbitrator being removed.

(i) A special interest of the certifier not known to a party to the contract.

(ii) Fraud of the architect or engineer, or of either party to the contract, whether at the time of the contract or subsequently, and whether collusive or not.[51]

(iii) Any improper pressure, influence or interference by a party having an effect upon the issue or refusal of a certificate.

(iv) Conduct of the architect or engineer which (consistent with his other duties) falls short of a high standard of fairness, discreetness and impartiality in relation to the issue or refusal of a certificate.

(v) Breach of contract by the employer having the effect of preventing the builder obtaining the certificate.

(vi) Any act or omission of the employer, not being an explicit breach, but necessarily having the effect of preventing a certificate being issued.

(vii) An unreasonable refusal by the certifier to give his consideration to the matter upon which he is required to certify.

(viii) The certifier's taking into consideration matters extraneous to his proper jurisdiction under the contract.

(a) Interest of certifier

Here it should be noted that acts which would be considered collusion or interference by the employer or indiscreet conduct by the architect if they occurred after the contract was signed,[52] tend to be classified under this head if they occur prior to contract being signed. On the other hand, acts occurring subsequent to the contract, *e.g.* an acquisition of shares by the engineer in one of the parties to the contract, may be regarded either as a disqualifying interest, or, it is suggested, as indiscreet conduct within *Hickman* v. *Roberts* (1913).[53]

Cases where the interest is financial, *e.g.* the holding of shares, are always likely to give rise to difficulty, since the chief engineer of, for instance, any really large industrial company might well be

---

[51] For cases of fraud by the contractor in obtaining a certificate, and the effect on third parties, see *Wakefield, etc.* v. *Normanton Local Board* (1881) 44 L.T. 697, *post* pp.733–734 (assignee) and *Kingston-upon-Hull Corporation* v. *Harding* [1892] 2 Q.B. 494 (guarantor) *post*, pp. 807–808.

[52] *e.g.* the request for the assurances as to keeping down final cost in *Kimberley* v. *Dick* and *Kemp* v. *Rose, supra.*

[53] *Infra*, at pp. 473–474.

expected to have a holding of shares in the company.[54] These cases will probably turn upon whether such an interest was to be expected in the circumstances of the particular case,[55] and also, perhaps, on the relative size of the interest and the degree to which it might be affected by the contract and decision in question.

(b) Fraud

The essence of fraud is a deliberate intention to deceive. Notwithstanding the dicta of Vaughan Williams L.J. in *Smith* v. *Howden Union* (1890) *supra*, p. 459, and of Lord Romilly M.R. in *Bliss* v. *Smith* (1865)[56] it is suggested that collusion with the architect or knowledge of his fraud by the other party is not necessary to avoid any certificate affected by fraud of the architect alone, though such fraud may be rare in practice. While there may be no implied term that a certifier will use reasonable skill, it is submitted that the honesty of the architect is probably the basis of the agreement between the parties to abide by his certificates, and may be impliedly warranted by the employer to the contractor.[57] It should be remembered that in the earlier cases there was still a tendency to regard an architect or engineer as a servant or *alter ego* of his employer when certifying,[58] and that his independent status does not appear to have been fully recognised until the decision in *Chambers* v. *Goldthorpe* (1901).[59] While this earlier view continued, the courts were bound to be influenced by the view, which prevailed until the case of *Lloyd* v. *Grace-Smith* (1912),[60] that a master was not vicariously liable for the unauthorised fraudulent acts of his servant. Whatever the true position about this additional liability of the employer to the contractor, the architect will, of course, be personally liable for his fraud to any party injured by a fraudulent misrepresentation made to that party.

(c) Interference with the certifier

It is submitted that fraudulent motive is irrelevant in considering this head, which is sufficiently wide to cover any improper

[54] *Cf. Ranger* v. *G.W.Ry., supra.*

[55] Or knowledge of this interest may constitute waiver. See *Thornton Hall* v. *Wembley Electrical Appliances* [1947] 2 All E.R. 630, where a surveyor employed to supervise work subsequently became managing director of the builders with the knowledge of his employer (illustrated *ante*, Chap. 1, p. 177). See also *Re Elliott, supra*, p. 453.

[56] Quoted *supra* at pp. 458–459.

[57] See *per* Diplock J. in *Neodox Ltd.* v. *Swinton & Pendlebury B.C.* (1958) unreported, *post*, Chap. 8, p. 530.

[58] *Cf.* Lord Chelmsford's judgment in *Ranger* v. *G.W.Ry.* quoted *supra*, p. 453.

[59] [1901] 1 K.B. 624, *ante*, Chap. 2, pp. 164 *et seq.*

[60] [1912] A.C. 716. See also *Morris* v. *G. W. Martin & Sons Ltd.* [1966] 1 Q.B. 716.

interference with the certifier's independence and function by either party. It is, of course, both usual and proper for both parties to make representations, however strongly worded, to the certifier upon any matter or dispute upon which the contract requires him to certify.[61] The dividing line between such representations and pressure of an improper kind is not difficult to discern in practice, and broadly speaking any pressure or action which goes beyond representations confined to the merits of the matter in question, or which does not impliedly recognise the certifier's ultimate right and duty to decide the matter impartially on its merits, will be suspect. "Where a surveyor is put into that position to give a certificate, I do not say that he is an arbitrator, but he is an independent person. His duty is to give the certificate according to his own conscience and according to what he conceives to be the right and truth as to the work done, and for that purpose he has no right to obey any order or any suggestion by these people who are called his masters; for that purpose they are not his masters." [62]

In theory, no doubt, it is necessary to show that the certifier was in fact influenced by the conduct in question, but in practice the courts will not concern themselves unduly with this if the certifier's independence once becomes suspect in this way. Indeed, in *Hickman* v. *Roberts* (1913),[63] Lord Shaw of Dunfermline expressly indicated that he thought that the architect would not have been influenced in any way as to the contents of his final certificate, though he was influenced to the extent of delaying the issue of interim certificates due under the contract.

This exception can be justified on the ground either of an implied term of the contract or the doctrine that a party cannot rely upon a failure to comply with a provision of a contract when he himself has prevented or obstructed the compliance by his own act.

(d) Want of impartiality or indiscreet conduct of the certifier

This head is, of course, closely allied with the preceding one, though the improper conduct of the certifier need not necessarily arise from collusion with or interference by a party to the contract.

It must be realised that a certifier's administrative and supervisory duties and his obligations to his employer mean that in the normal course of events he may well already have given a decision or submitted reports as to some matter in relation to which at some later

[61] *Cf. Hatrick* v. *Nelson*, illustrated *supra*, pp. 463–464.
[62] *Per* Lord Esher M.R. in *McDonald* v. *Mayor of Workington* (1893) 9 T.L.R. 230.
[63] [1913] A.C. at 229. *Supra*, pp. 462–463.

stage he is called upon to certify. Conduct showing previously formed views, however strongly expressed, will not amount to indiscreet conduct unless lack of independence or honesty of belief can be deduced from it.[64]

It must be conceded that this class rested for its authority upon one single case, namely, *Pawley* v. *Turnbull* (1861),[65] until the case of *Hickman* v. *Roberts* (1913), which itself could, on its facts, be explained as depending upon prevention or interference by the employer. Thus in *Panamena* v. *Leyland* (1947),[66] Lord Thankerton said of *Hickman* v. *Roberts*: " It is clear from all the judgments that the ground of disqualification was that Mr. Hobden, the owner's architect, had referred to the owners for instructions and had accepted and acted on their instructions in reference to the matter submitted to him as arbitrator (*sic*) regardless of his own opinion." But it is submitted that a consideration of the judgments shows that it was the conduct of the architect rather than his employers which was the basis of the decision, and leaves little doubt that conduct of a certifier, independent of any act of the employer, which shows lack of a properly independent attitude to his function will deprive his certificates of their effect.

(e) Breach of contract by the employer

If the breach has the effect of depriving the contractor of the opportunity of obtaining the certificate (*e.g.* a wrongful termination) the basis of the contractor's remedy is his claim for damages, which may, where he has completed the work, be co-extensive with the amount to which he would have been entitled upon a certificate, whether interim or final. This class of case therefore differs from the rest in its judicial basis, and involves no true exception to the rules as to finality of certificates. Confusion has arisen, however, because under the classification of " Prevention by the employer," examples of this type of case [67] were cited along with cases of improper interference by the employer with the issue of the certificate by the architect.

(f) Conduct of the employer not amounting to a breach

This class is a further example of prevention by the employer, which obviously does not exclusively consist of the cases of interference with the architect already mentioned. For example, an

---

[64] See Section 9 below, and the cases collected *supra*, pp. 465–466, 469–470.
[65] 3 Giff. 70; 4 L.T. 672.
[66] [1947] A.C. 428 at p. 438.
[67] *e.g. Smith* v. *Howden Union, supra.*

employer might dismiss his architect for good reasons, and not appoint another, or he might appoint another, but the contract might contain no provision for appointing another architect, or the original certifier might be expressly named in the contract in such a way that his substitute would not inherit his powers. Or again, the architect might die, or become insane, or terminate his own employment and the employer fail to appoint another.[68] (In some cases, of course, it may well be that failure by the employer to appoint an architect or a substitute is a breach of contract.[69])

(g) Refusal of the certifier

This, of course, means not a refusal to issue a certificate because none is due on the merits,[70] but refusal or failure by a certifier to give any consideration to the matters upon which such issue will depend.

Whether this could give rise to any remedy was much canvassed in earlier editions of this work. Cases undoubtedly showed that there was no implied covenant by an employer that his architect would certify, see *Kempster* v. *The Bank of Montreal* (1871),[71] and a builder was refused relief in equity upon an unreasonable refusal of an architect to certify in *Moser* v. *S. Magnus and S. Margaret's Churchwardens* (1795),[72] but these cases were really concerned with a refusal of an architect to issue a certificate on the merits. On the other hand there were dicta which suggested that the courts would give relief, *e.g.* " It was said that . . . this clause leaves the contractors wholly at the mercy of the engineer, who is only to determine the amount which they are to receive, and it is urged that he may consult his own supposed convenience and indefinitely postpone his determination . . . if he were to decline to enter upon the question or by any affected delay, or any improper practice of any kind, were to attempt to evade a decision, a court of equity would know how to deal with such a state of things," [73] and "Whether such acts arose originally from any fraudulent motive or not, I think that to use them for the purpose of defeating the plaintiff's remedy would constitute

---

[68] See *per* Phillimore J. in *Kellett* v. *New Mills U.D.C.* (1900) Hudson's B.C., 4th ed. ' Vol. 2, p. 298, *supra.*

[69] See Chap. 5, *ante*, pp. 320 *et seq.* where this is discussed.

[70] Even here, where work is done under protest after refusal to certify it as an extra, the courts have held arbitrators entitled to reopen the matter: *Molloy* v. *Liebe* and *Brodie* v. *Cardiff Corp., post,* Chap. 8, pp. 541–543.

[71] 32 Up.Can.Q.B. 87.

[72] Cited in *Worsley* v. *Wood* (1796) 6 T.R. 710 at 716, and *Mahoney* v. *Le Rennetel* (1892) 13 N.S.W.R. (Equity) 7.

[73] *Per* Lord Chelmsford L.C. in *Scott* v. *Liverpool Corporation* (1858) 28 L.J.Ch. 230.

a fraud, which this court will not permit the defendants to avail themselves of." [74]

The case of *Kellett* v. *New Mills U.D.C.* (1900),[75] undoubtedly went very far in support of the view that absence of a certificate in these circumstances was not fatal, though this case was adversely commented upon by Slesser L.J. in the case of *Neale* v. *Richardson* (1938),[76] where he said:

" I cannot see why in principle the defendant should not be entitled to stand upon her contract and say that she has undertaken to pay when, and only when, the architect gives his final certificate. . . . To say that a person, by relying on his legal rights, has taken advantage of somebody else's failure of duty in a case where there is no suggestion that he has prompted or even acknowledged that breach of duty seems to me to be contrary to principle, and if *Kellett* v. *New Mills Urban District Council* (1900) is to be taken to provide more than another example of collusion, respectfully I find myself unable to follow it." Furthermore, examination of the judgment in *Kellett's* case does suggest that the court was thinking in terms of collusion, though this was hardly applicable to the facts as found and pleaded. However, it is submitted that refusal or utterly unreasonable delay by an architect or engineer in giving his attention to a matter requiring his decision, satisfaction or a certificate must, as a matter of business efficacy, enable the absence of the certificate or lack of satisfaction to be disregarded, the correct basis for this being that a contractual obligation to obtain a certificate or ratification can only be construed as subject to an implied proviso that the architect or engineer is willing or able to do his part.[77] It is suggested that, as stated by Slesser L.J., the "taking advantage" basis for dispensing with a certificate is not correct in principle. As will be seen in paragraph (h) *infra*, this is of considerable importance in considering the exact *ratio decidendi* of the *Panamena* case referred to there.

(h) Wrong matters taken into consideration

It has already been seen (*supra*, Section 1 (2)) that as a matter of construction satisfaction provisions will usually be restrictively

---

[74] *Per* Cottenham L.C. in *Macintosh* v. *Great Western Ry.* (1850) 19 L.J.Ch. 374; and see *Smith* v. *Howden Union* (1890) Hudson's B.C., 4th ed., Vol. 2, p. 156.

[75] Illustrated *supra*, pp. 467–468.

[76] 54 T.L.R. at 541; [1938] 1 All E.R. 753.

[77] See, in addition to *Kellett's* case, *Watts* v. *McLeay* and *Neale* v. *Richardson*, illustrated *supra*, pp. 462 and 468, and *Young* v. *Ballarat Water Commissioners*, illustrated *ante*, p. 456. See also *Swiney* v. *Ballymena Commissioners* (1888) 23 L.R.Ir. 122, illustrated *post*, Chap. 18, Section 2 (2) (c), p. 841.

interpreted, so that a particular matter may be held to be outside the purview of a certifier's decision; and also that in one direction at least (the formal requirements for extra work) there has been a tendency to interpret such provisions generously, so that the certificate will bind the employer notwithstanding a failure by the contractor to comply with the contract (*supra*, Section 3 (3)). The taking of wrong matters into consideration by the certifier is in reality only another facet of the same problem.

Where it can be shown that a person whose approval or certificate is required has misinterpreted his function and taken into account matters which the parties on a true construction of their contract did not intend that he should, it is submitted as a matter of principle that the decision cannot have any validity, since the jurisdiction of the architect or certifier can only arise from the act of the parties as expressed in their contract, and by definition he has exceeded that jurisdiction. This proposition may, however, beg the real question, because it has already been seen[78] that binding provisions for satisfaction can fall into two categories, and that the " additional protection " category (which it has been submitted will not generally be involved when the architect or engineer is the certifier), on analysis must mean that the certifier is free to require something more than the strict contractual requirements, and that the builder must comply in order to obtain payment. There is a difference, perhaps, between requiring a higher standard of work than that called for by a specification, and taking matters totally unconnected with the quality of the work into consideration when required to certify on quality only. Faced with an invalid decision of this kind, the only practical way of achieving a just result between the parties is to disregard the decision in question, and it is suggested that the correct basis for this is that already set out in relation to a certifier's refusal to act, namely, an implied qualification upon the contractual obligation of a party to obtain a certificate or satisfaction in the event which has happened.

This is, it is suggested, the true basis of the important case of *Panamena Europea* v. *Leyland* (1947).[79] Unfortunately the earlier cases on refusal by a certifier adopted "collusion" on the principle

---

[78] *Supra*, Section 3 (3), p. 419.
[79] [1947] A.C. 428. See also *Peters* v. *Quebec Harbour Commissioners* (1891) *ante*, p. 467, the reasoning of the House of Lords in *Cammell Laird* v. *Manganese Bronze and Brass* [1934] A.C. 402, discussed *ante*, Section 3 (3), pp. 433–435, and *Ashwell & Nesbitt* v. *Allen & Co.* (1912) Hudson's B.C., 4th ed., Vol. 2, p. 462, and *British Thomson-Houston* v. *West Brothers* (1903) 19 T.L.R. 493, illustrated *ante*, pp. 409–410. See also *Ramsay* v. *Brand*, illustrated *supra*, p. 409.

that a party may not take advantage of a breach of this kind [80] as the legal basis for the desired result.[81] The House of Lords in the *Panamena* case, while explicitly rejecting " innocent collusion " or indiscreet conduct by the surveyor, appeared to base their decision (a) upon the employer's sharing of the surveyor's incorrect view, and (b) upon the principle that a party may not take advantage of a breach due to his act or default, as enunciated in *Roberts* v. *Bury Commissioners* (1870) and *Hotham* v. *East India Co.* (1787). But the facts as found do not suggest or indicate any interference or prevention by the employer, and in the absence of this element it is difficult to see how the principle of *Roberts* v. *Bury Commissioners* (1870) can be applied to the facts. It is unfortunate that the Supreme Court of Canada in the *Oshawa* case [82] felt constrained to adopt the same language and to give as a reason for their decision that the employer " had concurred in the position taken by the engineer." Provided the employer had done nothing to bring about that position, it is difficult to see why he should be treated as having invalidated the engineer's certificate simply by accepting the contract stipulation that he was bound by it or by its absence, and it is difficult on this aspect to disapprove of the remarks of Slesser L.J. when criticising *Kellett's* case, quoted *supra*.

While, therefore, it is submitted that there is now no doubt that a certificate or approval, or their absence, will be disregarded if a certifier is shown to have had regard to matters wholly outside the parties' intentions as expressed in the contract, the exact basis of the rule certainly cannot be regarded as having been clearly stated by the courts.

SECTION 6. CERTIFICATES

(1) Generally

As has been seen, certificates under building and engineering contracts are of various kinds. The commonest are as follows:

(a) Interim or Progress Certificates, upon which periodical payments or advances to the contractor on account are made.[83]

---

[80] *Cf. Macintosh* v. *G.W.Ry.* (1880) 19 L.J.Ch. 374, *ante*, pp. 455–456, and quoted *supra*, pp. 475–476; *Kellett* v. *New Mills U.D.C.* (1900) 4th ed., Vol. 2, p. 298, *supra*, pp. 467–468.

[81] See *supra*, subs. (4), pp. 458–459.

[82] Illustrated *supra*, pp. 468–469.   [83] See *infra*, pp. 492 *et seq.*

(b) Final Certificates, which frequently are certificates both of satisfaction with the work and of the sum due to the contractor upon his final discharge of his obligations under the contract.[84] Although in some earlier contracts, not usually found at the present day in the United Kingdom, an earlier certificate at the beginning of the maintenance period is the definitive certificate of satisfaction.[84a]

(c) Various other certificates (*e.g.* of practical or substantial completion, upon which the provisions as to payment of retention moneys, maintenance of the works or liquidated damages for delay may depend; or that the contractor is not duly proceeding with the work, upon which a special contractual right of determination by the employer may depend).

As generally understood in building contracts, a certificate is the expression in a definite form of the exercise of the judgment, opinion or skill of the engineer, architect or surveyor in relation to some matter provided for by the terms of the contract. Unless so required by the contract, the certificate need not be in writing.

ILLUSTRATIONS

(1) To a suggestion that " no certificate or written allowance being expressly required, an oral allowance will suffice " Hill J. replied, " Clearly so ": *Coker* v. *Young* (1860).[85]

(2) A building contract stipulated for payment " provided that the architect shall have certified that the whole of the work has been done to his satisfaction." *Held*, that it was not necessary that the architect should certify in writing: *Roberts* v. *Watkins* (1863).[86]

(3) A building contract provided for payment " on the surveyor certifying that the whole of the works are in a complete and satisfactory state." *Held*, that an oral certificate was sufficient: *Elmes* v. *Burgh Market Co.* (1891).[87]

And the fact of a certificate having to be " delivered " would not, it would seem, imply that it had to be in writing. On the other hand, a mere checking of the amounts claimed for work done has been held not to be a certificate of satisfaction where such was required.[88]

---

[84] See *post*, pp. 480–483, 489–492. There is in fact no equivalent of these in the I.C.E. Conditions.

[84a] See *supra*, Section 3 (3), p. 431.

[85] 2 F. & F. 98 at p. 101.

[86] (1863) 14 C.B.(N.S.) 592.

[87] Hudson's B.C., 4th ed. Vol. 2, p. 170; and see *Re Hohenzollern Actien-Gesellschaft* (1886) Hudson's B.C., 4th ed., Vol. 2, p. 100; 2 T.L.R. 470. See also *Meyer* v. *Gilmer, infra.*

[88] *Morgan* v. *Birnie* (1833) 9 Bing. 672, *infra*, p. 482. See, however, *Meyer* v. *Gilmer* (1899) 18 N.Z.L.R. 129, illustrated *infra*, pp. 480–481.

(2) Form and Sufficiency of Certificate

Whether or not a certificate in writing is required, the question whether it is a certificate of the kind required by the contract may give rise to difficulty. In each case it is necessary to consider what kind of certificate is required by the contract and whether the acts or terms of the statement relied upon can constitute such a certificate. In addition to the cases illustrated below, those in Section 1 (2) *supra*, should also be considered.[89]

ILLUSTRATIONS

(1) A building contract provided that upon a certificate of the architect that the work had been completed to his entire satisfaction, the contractor should be paid such a sum as, with any previous payment, would amount to $97\frac{1}{2}$ per cent. upon the contract price, and that upon a further certificate to the same effect, but further stating the final balance due, such balance should be paid within a time named. *Held*, that the two certificates might in principle be combined in one,[90] but as the actual certificate in the present case was qualified, stating that the contractors were entitled to receive a certain sum —the balance, less a sum retained as security for reparation of any defects—such certificate could not be treated as the final certificate entitling the contractors to payment of the final balance: *Walker* v. *Black* (1879).[91]

(2) An architect received the builder's account for extras, placed his own figures in the margin, thus reducing the builder's claim, and at the foot wrote, " Balance due as per conditions, £125," and signed his name thereunder. *Held*, that this did not amount to a certificate: *Goodman* v. *Layborn* (1881).[92]

[Note: The above case seems to be out of line with the *Harman* v. *Scott* cases illustrated *infra*.]

(3) Where there were two clauses in the same contract—one that the builder was not to be paid the balance until two months after the architect had " expressed his satisfaction," the other that the balance was not to be paid till " after " the architect had given his final certificate—the architect wrote expressing his satisfaction in 1883, and in June 1884 gave his final certificate. *Held*, that the meaning of the two clauses was that satisfaction was to be expressed by a final certificate, and an action brought within two months of delivery of the certificate was premature: *Coleman* v. *Gittens* (1884).[93]

(4) The architect wrote at the bottom of the contractor's account " I certify that this account is correct." The contract provided for payment on certificates in writing under the hand of the architect, and for 25 per cent. of the final balance to be retained till forty days after the work was satisfactorily completed and a certificate to that

[89] *Supra*, pp. 406 *et seq.*
[90] Distinguish *Kirsch* v. *Brady* (1937) 58 C.L.R. 36 (Australia), illustrated *supra*, Section 1 (2), p. 410.
[91] 5 Vict.L.R. (Law) 77. (Distinguish *McCarthy* v. *Visser*, *infra*, pp. 482–483.)
[92] Roscoe's *Digest of Building Cases*, 4th ed., App., p. 162 (C.A.).
[93] 1 T.L.R. 8.

effect granted. *Held*, the document was a sufficient certificate for payment of the final balance less the retention, but it was doubtful if it was sufficient for release of the 25 per cent. retention. However, there being no provision that the second certificate should be in writing, and the architect having orally expressed his satisfaction, the contractor was entitled to the whole contract sum: *Meyer* v. *Gilmer* (1899).[94]

(5) A contract provided that on the expiration of three months after completion of the works the architect should issue a " final certificate of the value of the works executed." The architect issued a document stating that the contractor had completed his contract including all work on a certain date, and in a later, second document, called a final account, stated that " the amount due to date " was a certain sum. *Held*, the second document was a valid final certificate: *Portuguese Plastering Contractors* v. *Bytenski* (1956).[95]

(6) A contract required the architect to certify completion to his satisfaction *at the beginning* of the maintenance period. The architect wrote a letter to the contractor on April 26, 1957 " subject to certain amendments not now required to be executed the residence in essence is now complete and under the terms of the contract the maintenance period will commence as from April 11, 1957." Subsequently the architect gave his final certificate at the end of the maintenance period. *Held*, by the Court of Appeal of New Zealand, that the letter was a valid certificate of satisfaction and bound the employer in the absence of notified defects: *Major* v. *Greenfield* (1965).[95a]

Thus the final certificate required by a contract may be one of three kinds, *viz.*:

(a) of satisfaction only;

(b) as to the value of the work or amount due under the contract; or

(c) (the most usual case) as to both of these matters.

If the required certificate is of satisfaction only, no amount need be stated in the certificate, and the amount due, if in dispute, must be determined by the courts or an arbitrator, as the case may be. In such a case, if an amount is stated, it does not bind.

ILLUSTRATION

P. sued for £4,461 19s. 8d., as the balance of the contract price and extras due on building a gaol. The contract provided for payment of the retention money " after the architect shall have certified the completion of the whole work to his satisfaction." The architect made two certificates or reports to the employer declaring his satisfaction with the work, but not mentioning the amount due to P.,

[94] 18 N.Z.L.R. 129.
[95] 1956 (4) S.A. 812.
[95a] [1965] N.Z.L.R. 1035.

and made another certificate to the effect that £59 7s. 2½d. was due on the balance of the contract, and £3,923 for extra work. *Held*, that a certificate of satisfactory completion alone was required, that it was unnecessary to mention the amount due, and that the plaintiff having obtained such certificate was at liberty to prove *aliunde* a different amount due: *Pashby* v. *Birmingham Corporation* (1856).[96]

However, a document showing a final or other amount as due to the contractor, without any reference to satisfaction or any other matter on which the payment in question is conditioned under the contract, will, unless there is some indication to the contrary, impliedly certify satisfaction or whatever other matter is required by the contract. On the other hand, a document showing the final value of extras and omissions only has been held not to certify satisfaction with the works.

ILLUSTRATIONS

(1) In an action by a builder to recover for extras, where the contract stipulated for payment on the architect's written certificate of satisfactory completion, the plaintiff proved that the architect had examined and approved of the builder's charges, and had written to the employer enclosing a document headed: " Final statement of extras and omissions of the carcase of a house for G. B. Esqre., by T. M. builder." *Held*, that this was not a certificate; for the effect of a certificate would be altogether different, applying to the manner in which the work had been done, while the checking of the accounts applied only to the propriety of the charges: *Morgan* v. *Birnie* (1833).[97]

(2) A building contract provided for interim payments, and that the balance of the stipulated price " shall be paid by the proprietor to the contractor within fourteen days from the architect's certificate being given that the works are completed to his satisfaction." The architect gave a certificate in this form: " I hereby certify that Messrs. S. B. are entitled to the sum of £——, being balance of amount due to them on account of contract and extras for your house at S." *Held*, that this was a sufficient certificate under the contract: *Harman* v. *Scott* (1874).[98]

(3) A contract provided for the work to be done to the satisfaction of the architect, for payment on his certificate, and for retention of a proportion of the price as security for the making good of defects appearing within 2 months of completion. The architect certified that a certain sum was due, subject to the contractor putting right a number of listed defects. These were in fact remedied. *Held*, following *Bateman* (*Lord*) v. *Thompson* (where a similar qualified

[96] 18 C.B. 2; and see *Robinson* v. *Owen Sound Corporation* (1888) 16 Ont.Rep. 121.
[97] 9 Bing. 672; and see this case commented on in *Harman* v. *Scott* (1874) 2 Johnst. N.Z.Rep. 407, *infra*. See also *Goodman* v. *Layborn* (1881), illustrated *supra*, p. 480.
[98] 2 Johnst.N.Z.Rep. 407; see also *Clarke* v. *Murray* (1885) 11 Vict.L.R. (Law) 817.

certificate was issued), that this was a valid final certificate once the listed defects had been remedied: *McCarthy* v. *Visser* (1905).[99]

(4) A contract provided that a certain percentage of the purchase price was only to be paid " two months after the date of the certificate of final completion, when the architect shall have certified that the works are completed in terms of the contract and to his satisfaction and that the roofs have proved watertight." The architect gave a certificate reading " final instalment certificate. I hereby certify that the sum of £—— is due to G. Swan & Co. on account of work executed and materials supplied." *Held*, it was a final certificate under the contract and implied satisfaction: *Lowther* v. *Swan* (1915).[1]

(5) Under a contract requiring the definitive certificate of completion to the architect's satisfaction *at the beginning* of the maintenance period, no such certificate was ever given, but ultimately the architect gave a certificate No. 16 for payment, stating " that in accordance with the conditions of the above contract the Progress Payment No. 16 (final) is due to the contractors for the sum of £——." *Held*, by the Court of Appeal of New Zealand, following *Harman* v. *Scott*, that the certificate was a certificate of satisfaction and bound the employer in the absence of notified defects: *Borough of Stratford* v. *Ashman* (1960).[1a]

A provision for payment of the contractor on the certificate of the architect must confer by implication the power to ascertain and decide the amount due and will, in the absence of an arbitration clause or any term to the contrary, enable the certifier to give a binding decision on the various adjustments to the contract sum for which the contract may make provision, *e.g.* under remeasurement, variations or fluctuations clauses. It is submitted that in the absence of express provision no objection can be taken to a certificate on the ground that it does not specify these various adjustments, and a mere statement of the balance due is sufficient as regards the form of the certificate.

A certificate which may satisfy all requirements of form may nevertheless fail to have effect if it is clearly given at the wrong time under the terms of the contract, or some other certificate on which it is itself dependent has or has not been properly issued.[2]

(3) Mistakes in Certificates

A final certificate cannot be attacked because it is based upon erroneous reports of an agent of the employer,[3] or of the certifier.[4]

[99] (1905) 22 Cape of Good Hope Rep. 122 (South Africa).
[1] [1915] T.F.D. 494 (South Africa).
[1a] [1960] N.Z.L.R. 503.
[2] *Kirsch* v. *Brady* (1937) 58 C.L.R. 36 (Australia) illustrated *supra*, Sect. 1 (2), p. 410.
[3] *Ayr Road Trustees* v. *Adams* (1883) 11 R. (Ct. of Sess.) 326.
[4] *Cf. Clemence* v. *Clarke* (1880) illustrated *ante*, p. 466.

(4) Correcting a Mistake in a Certificate

If the effect of the contract is to confer finality upon a certificate, a certificate validly issued cannot, in the absence of a contractual provision to the contrary,[5] or agreement or waiver by the parties, be withdrawn in order to correct mistakes of fact or value in it. Having issued the certificate, the certifier has discharged his function, and unless an arbitration or other clause empowers him to decide a dispute arising upon the certificate, or to amend it, he has no jurisdiction to alter it or issue another.

ILLUSTRATION

A contract to build bridges gave the building owner power to terminate the contract on notice, and pay for work and materials provided up to the date of the notice, on production of the engineer's certificate of the amount due. The building owner exercised the power and the engineer certified as to the value of the work done, but subsequently delivered a second certificate amending the one previously given. *Held*, that the first certificate given was a final certificate and not a progress certificate, and therefore was binding: *McGreevy* v. *Boomer* (1880).[6]

There may be circumstances, however, where if the original certificate can be regarded as a nullity, the subsequent issue of a valid certificate may be effective.

ILLUSTRATION

A local board of health gave notice, under section 69 of the Public Health Act 1848, to the owners of premises fronting two streets to level, pave, etc. and the owners having made default, the board did the work themselves. An apportionment was made by the surveyor of the board, which was held to be a nullity because the surveyor had apportioned the expenses of both streets, instead of each street separately. *Held*, that the surveyor was not *functus officio*, and was, therefore, right in making a fresh apportionment: *Cook* v. *Ipswich Local Board* (1871).[7]

(5) Who is to Give the Certificate

A certificate, in the absence of any provision or implication to the contrary, can only be given by the person or persons designated in the contract (whether by name or description). Some legal persons (*e.g.* a limited company or a local authority) can only act

---

[5] *Cf.* clause 60 (4) of the 1955 I.C.E. standard form.

[6] Supreme Court of Canada (1880) *Cassell's Digest* 73 (Canada). And see *Davey* v. *Gravesend Corp.* (1903) 67 J.P. 127, where it was held *obiter* that an interim certificate once given could not be withdrawn.

[7] L.R. 6 Q.B. 451. This, however, is a very special case depending on statutory, and not contractual, powers.

through agents, but apart from such cases a strict view is likely to be taken of the contractual provisions identifying the certifier, and attempts to delegate this function will not normally be held to satisfy the contractual provisions.

ILLUSTRATIONS

(1) Goods were agreed to be sold at a valuation to be made by A. A's clerk B valued the goods. *Held*, that the purchaser was not bound unless a new agreement to accept B's valuation be proved: *Ess* v. *Truscott* (1837). [8]

(2) Where a certificate of two or more architects is required, a certificate by one of them only will not comply with the terms of the contract: *Lamprell* v. *Billericay Union* (1849). [9]

(3) A railway disposed of land over a tunnel to B., and stipulated that no buildings were to be erected, except in accordance with a specification in writing, to be approved by the principal engineer of the railway. B. submitted plans to the resident engineer, who did not lay them before the principal engineer, but said verbally that the works might proceed. B. began to build. Four months later the principal engineer saw the plans for the first time, and condemned them as dangerous to the tunnel. B. persisted in continuing to build. The railway promoted an information against B. *Held*, that the approval of the resident engineer did not bind the railway, and that there was no such acquiescence as to prevent B. being bound by the contract: *Att.-Gen.* v. *Briggs* (1853). [10]

In many building contracts the certifier is named in the contract as an individual. If a firm is named, it is submitted that a certificate issued by a partner for and on behalf of the firm will satisfy the contractual requirement. Whether or not the employer has express or implied power, *vis-à-vis* the contractor, to dismiss the certifier or appoint another will depend upon the contractual provisions. [11] Where he has no power, he will be bound by the certifier's certificates even after dismissal. [12] Most modern contracts use the " or other for the time being " formula, [13] so no problem will exist. Where the power does exist, the new architect will, as a necessary implication, take over (except in so far as they may have been discharged) the certifying powers of his predecessor. [14] In most modern contracts this will create no problem, firstly because nearly

---

[8] 2 M. & W. 385; 6 L.J.Ex. 144.

[9] 18 L.J.Ex. 283, 285; see also *Marryat* v. *Broderick* (1837) 2 M. & W. 369.

[10] 1 Jur. 1084. But see *De Morgan Snell* v. *Rio de Janeiro Flour Mills, ante,* p. 95.

[11] For the employer's possible obligation to appoint an architect, see *ante,* Chap. 5, Section 2 (3), pp. 320 *et seq.* See also Article 2, R.I.B.A. forms.

[12] *Burns & Kenealy* v. *Furby* (1885) 4 N.Z.L.R. 110, and *Clarke* v. *Murray* (1885) 11 V.L.R. 817 (Victoria).

[13] See *infra.*

[14] See *Kellett* v. *Mayor of Stockport* (1906) 70 J.P. 154, *infra.* See also Article 3, R.I.B.A. forms.

all decisions of the architect are in the last resort open to arbitration on the merits prior to the final certificate, and secondly because nearly all provisions for interim valuation are based on a formula for revaluation of the whole work on the occasion of each interim certificate, less amounts previously certified, so that if the second architect disagrees with the valuations of the first, or is aware, for example, of defective work not known to the first when he gave his earlier certificates, the second architect is in a position to make interim valuations giving effect to his own views. Furthermore, in the case of work defective in his opinion but passed by the earlier architect, it has already been seen [15] that no bar can arise in such a case because on an earlier occasion the defective work could or should have been condemned. Powers to order removal and re-execution of the work can therefore be exercised at any time.[15a]

It is submitted that if the contract contemplates the issue of certificates as a condition of payment then the contractor could require an employer who had taken no steps to do so to appoint a successor upon the death, dismissal or withdrawal of the architect. In most cases, however, he would probably sue without the certificate.[16] In so far as the architect may be appointed an arbitrator in the full sense by the terms of the contract, the Arbitration Acts contain provisions to enable the courts to appoint a new arbitrator in such a situation,[17] but practically no modern contracts in England have constituted the architect an arbitrator in the full sense since the Act of 1934.[18]

ILLUSTRATIONS

(1) M. agreed in writing to empty B.'s mill pool on the terms of being paid fivepence a yard for all mud removed. The agreement provided that the measurement of the mud should be settled by N., and that any dispute which arose should be referred to N. A dispute arose as to whether B. had prevented M. from completing the work by flooding the mill pool, which N. decided in M.'s favour. *Held*, by the court, that M. could revoke N.'s authority as to settlement of disputes, but could not revoke his authority to determine the amount of mud removed: *Mills* v. *Bayley* (1863).[19]

[Note: At the time this case was decided submissions to arbitration in the full sense were revocable. See also the next following cases.]

---

[15] See *ante*, Chap. 6, pp. 385–388.
[15a] See, however, the remarks of Phillimore J. in *Adcock's Trustees* v. *Bridge*, doubted *ante*, Chap. 6, p. 386.
[16] See *Degagne* v. *Chave* (1896) 2 Terr.L.R. 210 (Canada), and Section 5, *supra*.
[17] See s. 24 of the Act of 1950.
[18] See *ante*, pp. 412, 450.
[19] 2 H. & C. 36.

(2) A., a contractor, brought an action for work and labour done. The defendant pleaded (1) that the work was under a contract which provided that the work was to be measured, calculated and determined by the engineer, whose decision should be conclusive, and that the engineer had measured and determined the value of the work, which value the defendant had paid; (2) that the contract provided that the work was to be done to the satisfaction of the engineer, and that the engineer was not, before action, satisfied therewith. A. replied that he had withdrawn the engineer's authority. *Held*, on demurrer, that the first plea was good, as there was not a covenant to refer to arbitration, but one which made ascertainment by the engineer a condition precedent to A.'s right to recover; and that the second plea was good, as the covenant made the satisfaction of the engineer a condition precedent to A.'s right to recover. *Held*, also, that A. could not revoke the engineer's authority: *Canty* v. *Clarke* (1878).[20]

(3) B. and K., in answer to an advertisement by H., an architect, sent in a tender to build a house for F., which was accepted, and then entered into a building agreement which provided (*inter alia*) that the certificate of the architect should be conclusive. F. dismissed the architect, and appointed another whom B. and K. declined to recognise. On completion, they obtained and sued on the first architect's certificate. *Held*, that as neither fraud nor collusion was proved, the architect was architect for the whole work, and the sole judge, and that neither party could dispute his judgment. If the building owner could prove bad workmanship, his remedy was against the architect: *Burns* v. *Furby* (1885).[21]

(4) In the case of a building contract in the same form as that in *Lloyd Bros.* v. *Milward* (1895),[22] the building owner discharged the architect before he had given his final certificate. He nevertheless certified and the builder sought to charge the estate of the building owner, who was a married woman, with the amount of the certificate. She moved to stay proceedings, on the ground that there was a dispute, which must be referred. *Held*, (1) following *Mills* v. *Bayley* (1863),[23] that the architect was the one agreed on between the parties and could not be discharged; (2) that his certificate was conclusive: *Murray* v. *Cohen* (1889).[24]

But where the contract identifies the certifier by description—as for instance, " the engineer for the time being of the employer," or " the engineer in charge of the work,"—or where the certifier is referred to by name, but some such words are added as " or other the engineer of the employer," the person answering the description at the material time is the proper person to certify. What the

---

[20] 44 Up.Can.Q.B. 222; followed in *Robinson* v. *Owen Sound* (1888) 16 Ont.Rep. 121.
[21] 4 N.Z.L.R. (Supr.Ct.) 110; and see *Stevenson* v. *Watson* (1879) 4 C.P.D. 148. See, however, the discussion *ante*, pp. 161 *et seq.* on *Chambers* v. *Goldthorpe* [1901] 1 K.B. 624.
[22] Hudson's B.C. 4th ed., Vol. 2, p. 262, illustrated *ante*, Section 4, pp. 438–439.
[23] 2 H. & C. 36, *supra*.
[24] 9 N.S.W.R. (Eq.) 124.

material time is may occasionally give rise to difficulty, though in most cases it will be the time when the certificate is required to be issued by the contract.

ILLUSTRATIONS

(1) An engineering contract between the W. Railway Co. and T. provided for the reference of disputes to A., if and so long as he should continue to be the company's principal engineer. The W. Railway was amalgamated with another railway, and A., who still continued to be the engineer of the W. portion of the railway, was not the principal engineer of the amalgamated railway. *Held*, that A. remained the proper referee in disputes arising out of the contract: *Wansbeck Railway* v. *Trowsdale* (1866).[25]

(2) S. agreed with the plaintiff in November, 1871, to pay the amount due for certain work previously performed in the construction of a bridge under a contract with another party " under a certificate from the engineer in charge of the said work." In September and October, 1870, M. was in charge of the bridge, and gave certificates for work done and materials supplied by the plaintiff. F. was in charge of the bridge from September, 1871, to a time subsequent to and including the date of the agreement with S. *Held*, that the certificate required must be had from M., the engineer who had charge of the work at the time it was done, and not from F., because the court inferred that the parties had in mind the engineer who prepared the plans and the specifications, who knew what was to be done, " who knew also what had been done, and who, knowing of the delivery of the materials and the work as it went on from day to day, was the person most likely, if not the only one, who was capable of measuring from his own knowledge the inquiries called for by the agreement. . . . Much of the materials and work was evidently of a temporary nature, necessary for the permanent structure which was to follow it, and of a character to be estimated only by a daily eye-witness or one whose duty required his actual supervision of the work. . . . It is impossible to suppose that one having no personal knowledge of the work or means of acquiring it, and whose connection with the structure began long after the services were rendered and material furnished, could have been selected by a person wholly ignorant as to these things to determine not only the quantity of each but the amount due therefor ": *Wangler* v. *Swift* (1882).[26]

(3) A building contract provided that the engineer's certificate should be a condition precedent to payment for all extra work. The engineer was expressed to be " A.B. or other the engineer " of the employer. A.B. died, and the contractor objected that his successor had no jurisdiction to fix the price for the extra work. *Held*, that " or other the engineer " meant the engineer from time to time appointed by the employer, and that where work begun under one engineer had to be continued under his successor, it was the certificate of such successor that was necessary under the contract: *Kellett* v. *Mayor of Stockport* (1906).[27]

[25] L.R. 1 C.P. 269.   [26] 90 N.Y. 38.   [27] 70 J.P. 154.

Although, however, the certifier may not delegate his function, he can delegate the detailed work necessary for the preparation of certificates to competent persons to a considerable extent.[28]

(6) Final Certificates

The form and binding character of these have already been dealt with in detail.[29] It may be of interest to consider the position under the standard forms of contract currently in use.

Under the 1955 I.C.E. form, no specific reference to a final certificate is made, but the second half of the retention money (and by implication the final balance due to the contractor) is payable fourteen days after the expiry of the period of maintenance, provided that defects have been made good.[30] The last certificate in point of time appears to be the maintenance certificate, which is required to state that the works have been completed and maintained to the engineer's satisfaction, and which is not, at least expressly, a certificate for payment.[31] No other certificate is to be deemed to constitute approval of any work or an admission of any matter in respect of which it is issued,[32] but there is no positive provision that it is final and binding, other than a provision that the employer shall not be liable to the contractor in any respect unless the contractor has made a claim in writing before the maintenance certificate.[33] There follows a bewildering provision [34] to the effect that the contractor (and the employer) are to remain liable to each other after the certificate in respect of obligations not performed at the time of the certificate. The arbitration clause is in the widest possible terms, with power to open up, revise and review any certificate.[35] Since no contractor could fail to make a claim in writing before the maintenance certificate unless he was grossly careless, and since the conflicting contractual provisions are so incomprehensible, it is perhaps not surprising that this provision [33] has never received consideration by the courts.

In the case of the R.I.B.A. standard forms,[36] the case of *Windsor*

---

[28] See *ante*, Chap. 2, pp. 150 and 173. See also *Clemence* v. *Clarke*, *supra*, p. 466.
[29] See (2), " Form and Sufficiency of Certificate," *supra*, and Section 3, *ante*.
[30] Clause 60 (2).
[31] Clause 62 (1).
[32] Clause 61.
[33] Clause 62 (2).
[34] Clause 62 (3).
[35] Clause 66.
[36] 1939 Edition, at the time of the *Windsor* case in the (1950 revised) form.

R.D.C. v. *Otterway and Try* (1954),[37] which held that the arbitration clause overrode the provisions of the contract relating to the final certificate, notwithstanding the use of the words " shall be conclusive evidence " in relation to the final certificate in clause 24 (f), had in 1954 brought about a situation where arbitrators felt free to decide all disputes under these forms of contract on their merits. This case was, however, overruled by the Court of Appeal in 1964 and later by the House of Lords in the *East Ham* [38] case. Meanwhile, however, in 1957 the then current edition [39] was reworded, so that unless *prior* notice of arbitration had been given the final certificate was to be conclusive " that the works have been *properly carried out* and completed and *properly* and accurately *measured and valued* in accordance with this contract." The only exception of any material importance was in respect of " defects . . . in the works which reasonable inspection or examination *at any reasonable time during the course of the execution of the works or before the issue of the said certificate* would not have disclosed." (These latter words were far wider than in the (1950 Revised) form, where the words had been " which a reasonable examination would not have disclosed.")

It is difficult to understand the policy underlying this change. In practice the binding nature of the final certificate under this wording could not prejudice the contractor, who if he had any claims was free to give notice of arbitration before the final certificate, that is to say before the end of the maintenance period or the making good of defects, whichever was later.[40] On the other hand it could be devastatingly prejudicial to the employer, since in by far the most important field in respect of which he might require protection or wish to advance a claim, namely defective work, his right to sue for a period of six years or twelve years, depending on whether the contract was under seal or not, was virtually removed,[41] and this in spite of the fact that through no fault of his own or his architect he might be totally unaware of the defects at the time of the final certificate.

In the post-1963 standard forms, the matter has been carried

---

[37] *Supra.*
[38] *East Ham B.C.* v. *Bernard Sunley Ltd.* [1965] 1 W.L.R. 30, [1966] A.C. 406, illustrated *supra*, p. 446.
[39] By clause 24 (*g*).
[40] Furthermore claims for damages (the commonest claims by contractors) do not appear to be governed by the certificate at all.
[41] The practical value to the employer of the exceptions is minimal, being limited for all practical purposes to latent defects in materials.

further still since the contractor (but not the employer) is now permitted to serve notice of arbitration within a limited period after the final certificate [42] and the certificate is now not only expressed to be conclusive, in identical terms, that the work has been properly carried out, but also " *that any necessary effect has been given to all the terms of this Contract which require an adjustment to be made to the Contract Sum.*" [43] These latter terms include a number of possible claims by the contractor—for instance a claim that " direct loss and expense " should be paid to the contractor over and above the contract rates by reason of varied work,[44] or by delay in receiving instructions from the architect [45]—some of which are entirely new in principle in building contracts, since they constitute the architect as judge of matters which hitherto have been regarded as breaches of contract suitable for determination by an arbitrator or the courts (and which in the second of the cases instanced above probably involve questions of the architect's own competence). Yet the employer, unless consulted by the architect upon them, will have no knowledge of these claims before the final certificate, when his opportunity to question the architect's decision, unlike the contractor's, will have been lost. The omission to permit the employer any period for questioning the certificate is little short of astonishing, and calls for a degree of consultation between employer and architect prior to issuing the certificate of which the contractor might be expected to be the first to complain.

It is suggested that this clause must place upon the architect a heavy duty of disclosure to his employer of all matters of possible dispute before issuing his certificate. Furthermore, the effect of the decision in *Chambers* v. *Goldthorpe* (1901) [46] must, it is submitted, require reconsideration in the light of this clause, and a considerable increase in litigation against architects by building owners deprived of their remedies against builders by the existence of a final certificate is to be expected. No employer properly advised should accept the clause in its present form.

The full effect of this clause, and of its impact upon the duties owed by architects to their clients, must await judicial consideration. But, as pointed out earlier in this work,[47] it is suggested that it is

---

[42] Clause 30 (7).
[43] *Ibid.*
[44] Clause 11 (6).
[45] Clause 24 (1) (*a*). This latter claim will in any event survive the certificate, being expressed to be without prejudice to the contractor's other remedies.
[46] Discussed, *ante*, pp. 161 *et seq.*
[47] *Ante*, Chap. 2, p. 152.

bound to increase the burden of supervision of a day to day character which is required of the architect if his clients' interests are to be properly safeguarded, and indeed logically it must call for virtually full-time supervision of the work, having regard to the new and very wide wording of the exception relating to unnoticed defects.

A question often arising in practice relates to the time at which final certificates should be given. This is, of course, the subject of express provision in the standard forms.[48] In the absence of express provision a term must be implied for issue within a reasonable time, and in contracts where the certificate is a condition precedent, it is suggested that refusal to act by the certifier within a reasonable time after notice will enable the certificate to be dispensed with.[49]

(7) Interim Certificates

Provisions for interim or progress certificates are almost invariably inserted in building contracts for the benefit of the builder, to enable him to obtain payments on account during the progress of the work. As a rule, the payments contemplated by such provisions only represent the approximate value (or a proportion of it) of the work done, and possibly also of materials delivered to the site, at the date of payment,[50] and, in the absence of express provision, they are not conclusive or binding on the employer as an expression of satisfaction with the quality of the work or materials.[51] It makes no difference that they are frequently expressed to represent the value of work properly done, since such a qualification is an obvious one in any provision for payment on account, and would probably be implied in any event, even if the concept of value did not involve an element of deduction for work containing a defect requiring to be repaired or reinstated. In addition the whole scheme of the contract, including the powers to order the removal of work exercisable at any time, to withhold the certificate of practical completion, and to order defects to be repaired during the maintenance period, is obviously inconsistent with any such intention. Indeed most provisions for interim payment involve a revaluation of the whole work (not the work done since the last certificate) each time a new

---

[48] Clause 30 (6) of the 1963 R.I.B.A. forms, clause 62 (1) of the 1955 I.C.E. form (maintenance certificate).

[49] See *ante*, Section 5 (6) (g), pp. 475–476.

[50] *Pashby* v. *Birmingham Co.* (1856) 18 C.B. 2.

[51] See, *e.g. Cooper* v. *Uttoxeter Burial Board* (1865) 11 L.T. 565, illustrated *ante*, Chap. 6, pp. 381–382, and *McCarthy* v. *Visser* (1905) 22 Cape of Good Hope Rep. 122, and see the cases collected *post*, Chap. 8, Section 2 (1) (a), pp. 537–538.

certificate is given. Such certificates, then, are usually subject to re-adjustment, not only in the final certificate but also in subsequent interim certificates, though as a matter of pure valuation they may, in the absence of an overriding arbitration clause or a right of the employer to set off the cost of remedying or the value of defective work, be given binding effect until the time for the final certificate, or a subsequent amending interim certificate, has arrived. Thus in *Tharsis Sulphur & Copper Co. v. McElroy* (1878),[52] Lord Cairns L.C. described the certificates in that case as follows:

" The certificates I look upon as simply a statement of a matter of fact, namely, what was the weight and what was the contract price of the materials actually delivered from time to time upon the ground, and the payments made under those certificates were altogether pro-visional, and subject to adjustment or to readjustment at the end of the contract." In the same case, Lord Blackburn said: " They were made out with a view to regulating the advances, and showing how much should be paid on account; not at all as showing how much was to be paid ultimately upon the final account and reckoning."

Again, in *Lamprell* v. *Billericay Union* (1849), Pollock C.B. said[53]:

" When the payments were from time to time made on the certificates of the architect, the obvious meaning of both parties was that . . . they were to be treated as sums paid on account of what-ever the plaintiff might eventually be entitled to recover from the defendants, whether for the original or additional works." Further, the fact that the employer has made payments or allowed claims of one kind or another on interim certificates creates no estoppel and does not bind him when the final account is being drawn up.[54]

According to the terms of the contract, interim certificates may include not only work done but also materials supplied, even though not fixed: see *Pickering* v. *Ilfracombe Railway* (1868),[55] and other cases on vesting.[56] On the other hand, the certificates may be for work done only, as in *Tripp* v. *Armitage* (1839).[57] In some modern long-term contracts they may include the value, or a proportion of it, of plant brought onto the site (for eventual deduction from the

---

[52] 3 App.Cas. 1040, at p. 1045. Illustrated *post*, Chap. 8, pp. 537–538.
[53] 18 L.J.Ex. 282, at p. 305. Illustrated *post*, Chap. 8, p. 537.
[54] See, *e.g. Royston U.D.C.* v. *Royston Builders Ltd.* (1961) 177 E.G. 589, illustrated *ante*, Chap. 1, p. 58.
[55] (1868) L.R. 3 C.P. 235, illustrated *infra*.
[56] *Post*, Chap. 12, pp. 663–668, 674–675.
[57] (1839) 4 M. & W. 687; 8 L.J.Ex. 107, *post*, Chap. 12, pp. 656–657.

contract sum on final account), and the R.I.B.A. conditions now have an optional clause for payment for " off-site " materials or goods.[58]

The meaning of " value " in this context may give rise to difficulty. In the absence of any provision to the contrary, it is suggested that this means the value of the work or materials at the contract rates (or in lump sum contracts, as a proportion of the contract sum), as opposed to the actual cost to the contractor.

ILLUSTRATION

A building contract provided for interim payments of 80 per cent. of the " value of the work done." *Held*, that the " value of the work done " was not the cost to the contractor, but the value of the partial work as measured by the price for the completed work: *Hawkins* v. *Burrell* (1902).[59]

In the absence of an overriding arbitration clause, interim certificates will generally be a condition precedent to the builder's right to sue for payment during the currency of the work [60] while, as already indicated, in no way evidencing satisfaction or approval of the work, so that it is submitted that the employer will generally be entitled to set up defective work or any other breach of contract as a defence when sued upon them, whether or not an overriding arbitration clause is available, though no doubt he will be bound by the certificate to the extent that he will not be able to dispute the valuation element in it. In many cases this may need to be proved in evidence by calling the architect, or other evidence outside the certificate itself, since interim certificates do not usually disclose the various reasons for arriving at the sum in question. But in modern contracts provision is frequently made for disputes arising on such certificates to be referred to arbitration during the currency of the work,[61] and the existence of such a clause will be essential if the builder is to recover more than the amounts certified by the architect during the course of the contract. This is of immense practical importance, and it is to be regretted that the standard forms in both industries in England contain provisions of deplorable obscurity on which there is at present little clear authority.

---

[58] Clause 30 (2A).

[59] N.Y. 69 App.Div. 462.

[60] The case of *Errico* v. *Lotter*, 1956 (4) S.A. 139 which suggests the contrary, has already been criticised *ante*, Section 3, p. 425. See *Dunlop & Ranken Ltd.* v. *Hendall Steel Structures* [1957] 1 W.L.R. 1102, doubted on other grounds, *infra*.

[61] And in the R.I.B.A. forms the contractor is in addition given a right to terminate the contract if there is obstruction or interference by the employer in the issue of a certificate—see *Burden* v. *Swansea Corporation* [1957] 1 W.L.R. 1167 illustrated *ante*, Section 5, pp. 464–465.

ILLUSTRATION

The arbitration clause in the I.C.E. form of contract provided that references to arbitration should not be opened without consent till after completion of the work, " except references as to the withholding by the engineer of any certificate or the withholding of any portion of the retention money under clause 60 hereof to which the contractor claims to be entitled." In clause 60, which provided for interim payments on certificate, there were, as it happened, express powers to " withhold " certificates and the second half of the retention money in certain events (which did not in fact occur). The contractor contended on interim measurement that as a matter of construction of the bills he was entitled to certain additional payments for working space outside the actual retaining walls of the tunnel he was constructing. The engineer certified the work done at the billed rates and refused to include any additional payments. The employer contended that the arbitration could not be opened till the end of the work, since the only matter which could be the subject of an earlier arbitration was the withholding of certificates which was specifically referred to in clause 60 (and which was not applicable to the dispute). *Held*, by Buckley J., that the exception applied to the withholding of any certificate of any kind under the contract, and not merely the particular withholding referred to under clause 60, since the words " under clause 60 " qualified the withholding of retention money and not the certificates, and accordingly the matter could be arbitrated forthwith. *Per* Buckley, J., *obiter*, while a simple difference in valuation or measurement on interim certificate would not constitute the " withholding " of a certificate to which the contractor claimed to be entitled, an adverse decision on a matter of principle, which if incorrect would mean that the contractor was clearly entitled to additional payment, did amount to a withholding of a certificate: *Farr* v. *Ministry of Transport* (1960).[62]

[N.B. As a matter of first impression, it is submitted that, once the verbal obscurity dealt with (it is respectfully submitted perfectly rightly) by Buckley J. has been disposed of, the " withholding of a certificate . . . to which the contractor claims to be entitled " may well in this context include cases where the difference between the contractor and engineer is one of amount only and not of principle, and that the above dicta of Buckley J. should be treated with caution. After all, on a strict view withholding a certificate could be held to mean refusing to give any certificate at all. If the expression is intended to be wider than this, there seems no reason of business efficacy why it should be limited in the way suggested by Buckley J. The matter must be regarded, however, as extremely uncertain.[63] Under the R.I.B.A. forms of contract a dispute whether a certificate " has been improperly withheld or is not in accordance with these conditions " can be referred to arbitration during the carrying out of the works. The conditions (by clause 30) naturally do define the value to be certified on interim certificate, and the question again arises whether a dispute of mere valuation, as opposed to principle, can be arbitrated before the end of the work. The second phrase

[62] [1960] 1 W.L.R. 956.
[63] See a (very) *obiter dictum* of Lord Simonds on this point, in *Burden* v. *Swansea Corporation* [1957] 1 W.L.R. 1167 at p. 1169.

may suggest something wider than the first, and it is possible that the R.I.B.A. wording is therefore somewhat wider than that in the I.C.E. arbitration clause, but again the position is extremely obscure.[64]]

Once granted, an interim certificate at the very least creates a debt due, and the contractor is entitled to immediate payment, subject to any right of the employer to set off or counterclaim, for example, for liquidated damages [65] or defective work.

ILLUSTRATIONS

(1) A railway construction contract contained powers for the engineer to certify for " the extent and value of the works then executed, and the materials then provided for the works." A progress certificate was granted thereunder to the amount of £96,200 for work done and materials supplied. *Held*, that the engineer had power to certify for materials which had not been actually affixed to the line; and that the progress certificate created a debt: *Pickering* v. *Ilfracombe Railway* (1868).[66]

(2) A sub-contract was held to have incorporated the terms of the then R.I.B.A. standard form of contract by virtue of a provision: " Payment by this order is to be made (a) as to the amount (if any) provided for in the main contract for the works in this order; in accordance with the certificates and the terms provided in the said contract." At a time when the main contract work was complete, but no certificate relating to the sub-contract work had been issued by the architect to the main contractor under clause 24 of the main contract (the interim and final valuation clause), judgment creditors of the sub-contractor sought to attach the money owed to him by the main contractor. *Held*, by the Divisional Court, in the absence of a certificate there was no debt capable of being garnished: *Dunlop & Ranken Ltd.* v. *Hendall Steel Structures* (1957).[67]

[Note: From the report of this case it appears that the main contractors had obtained all certificates except the final certificate, for which they had applied. The case is open to criticism in the light of the principles relating to the garnishing of debts [68] and has not been followed in Canada,[69] but in addition the Court of Appeal does not appear to have considered the effect of the arbitration clause in the main contract which, if incorporated, would mean that the contractor or sub-contractor was free to commence proceedings (since the work was finished), whether by arbitration or in the courts, and accordingly there was a debt due despite the absence of the certificate.]

But a contract may be so worded as to avoid this result. Thus in *Tharsis Sulphur & Copper Co.* v. *McElroy* (1878),[70] there was a

---

[64] See also the discussion *post*, Chap. 9, Section 1 (3), p. 574.
[65] *Newfoundland Govt.* v. *Newfoundland Ry.* (1888) 13 App.Cas. 199.
[66] L.R. 3 C.P. 235.
[67] [1957] 1 W.L.R. 1102.
[68] See *post*, Chap. 14, pp. 736–738.
[69] By the Appellate Division of the Supreme Court of Alberta in *Sandy* v. *Yukon Construction Co. Ltd.* (1961) 26 D.L.R. (2d) 254.
[70] (1878) 3 App.Cas. 1040, *supra*.

provision " that no payment shall be held as legally due until this contract is completed, but advances shall nevertheless be made to the amount thereof, under the engineer's certificate." [71]

(8) Final Accounts

The contractor's accounts are the usual prelude in practice to the final certificate being given, but their existence is not recognised in the standard forms of contract, although the 1963 R.I.B.A. forms [72] do require the submission of certain " documents " by the contractor as a condition of the issue of the final certificate by the due date. Apart from this provision, therefore, it would seem that in theory on a strict view the architect, engineer or surveyor under other forms of contract is bound to value the work according to the contract for the purpose of the final certificate, whether or not the contractor submits an account and if necessary without that assistance.[73]

SECTION 7.   EFFECT ON THIRD PERSONS

It goes without saying that certificates or awards of an architect or engineer, or his approval or satisfaction, which are expressed to be final or binding by the contract, will not bind strangers to the contract unless they have themselves contracted to be bound by them, or are claiming in some way through a party to the contract. This can be of particular importance in considering guarantees for the performance of contracts. Equally, while a certificate may bind a party to the contract *vis-à-vis* the other party, it may not bind him against a stranger, or even, in appropriate cases, the certifier himself.[74]   On the other hand, an assignee of a contract is in no better position and is bound in the same way as was his assignor.[75]

In cases of contracts with third parties, it is necessary to consider very carefully whether the third party has agreed in terms which show an intention to be bound by the certifier's decisions.

[71] Note: As to the effect of interim certificates on vesting property, see *post,* Chap. 12, pp. 674–675, as to their effect as orders in writing for extras, see *post,* pp. 528–546, and as to their effect on the release of liquidated damages, see *post,* pp. 635–636. As to whether non-payment amounts to repudiation, see *ante,* pp. 342–343.
[72] Clause 30 (5) (b) and (6).
[73] See, *e.g.* clause 9 of the pre-1963 standard forms.
[74] See, *e.g. Rogers* v. *James* (1891) 56 J.P. 277; 8 T.L.R. 67; *ante,* Chap. 2, p. 163.
[75] See *post,* Chap. 14, pp. 731–734.

ILLUSTRATIONS

(1) The respondent advanced money to the appellant on a guarantee to be repaid " on the completion of six houses, in accordance with the contract between myself and T." (the builder). The houses were to be built to the satisfaction of a surveyor, and payment was to be made upon his certificate. No such certificate had been given. In an action on the guarantee, brought by the respondent against the appellant, the jury found that, as a matter of fact, the houses were completed. *Held* (affirming the judgment of the court below), that the respondent was entitled to recover notwithstanding the absence of the certificate: *Lewis* v. *Hoare* (1881). [76]

(2) A contractor abandoned the work, and the employer, in an interview with a sub-contractor, told him to go on, and that he (the employer) would see him paid. In the original contract the work was to be paid for on a certificate of completion. *Held,* this did not apply to the new contract, which was not assigned, but that the employer had made himself personally liable, and could not insist on the certificate as a condition precedent if the work was done in fact so as to entitle the builder to a certificate: *Petrie* v. *Hunter* (1882). [77]

SECTION 8.   SUMMARY OF THE LAW ON CONCLUSIVENESS OF
SATISFACTION OR CERTIFICATES

It may be helpful to summarise briefly the position as disclosed by the preceding sections of this chapter. In order for the satisfaction or certificate of an architect or engineer to be conclusive and binding on the parties, the following conditions must exist:

(1)   The matter in dispute must be one upon which the contract confers jurisdiction on the architect or engineer to express his satisfaction or certify. [78]

(2)   The contract must on its true construction provide that the certificate or satisfaction is intended to be binding. In most but not necessarily all building contracts this will be the case bilaterally, that is to say both parties will be bound by the certificate. There are, however, cases, apart from the obvious example of interim certificates, where the certificate will only bind unilaterally. [79] But in either case a provision

[76] 44 L.T. 66.
[77] 2 Ont.Rep. 233; following *Lewis* v. *Hoare, supra.*
[78] See, *e.g.,* the cases under Section 1, *supra,* and *Lloyd* v. *Milward* and *Clemence* v. *Clarke, supra,* pp. 438–439 and 443, and the cases referred to in Section 5 (6) (h), *ante,* pp. 476–478.
[79] See Section 3, *supra.*

enabling a party to go behind or question or dispute the decision will destroy the conclusiveness of the satisfaction or certificate, in particular any applicable arbitration clause.[80]

(3) The certificate or satisfaction must be honestly given. It must be given without collusion, interference or undue influence, and the certifier must preserve his independence and not act in a way that suggests that he has lost his independence.[81]

(4) The provisions of the contract must be strictly adhered to, the approval or certificate must be given by the correct person at the correct time, and must not take into account any matters quite outside the stipulated requirements of the contract,[81] though there may be a class of " unilateral " cases where the certifier may impose a stricter standard, *e.g.* of quality, on the party bound than the contract documents expressly require.[81a]

(5) The employer must have done nothing, by breach of contract or otherwise, to prevent the contractor from obtaining the certificate or satisfaction.[81]

Section 9.   Status and Duties of Certifier

(1) Generally

Much of what follows in this section is not of great practical importance if there is an available arbitration clause which permits the decisions or approvals of the architect or certifier to be reviewed. On the other hand if there is no, or no sufficiently wide, arbitration clause, or if the right to arbitration is for some reason lost, as by failure to give notice of arbitration in time, the exact status of and performance of his duties by the certifier may be of critical importance. Much of this subject has already been discussed, Section 5, *supra*, which should be borne in mind when considering the present section.

An architect, in certifying, is not, as has been pointed out, an arbitrator.[82] He has been described as a " preventer of disputes " in

---

[80] See Section 4.
[81] See Section 5, *ante*.
[81a] See the analysis, *supra*, Section 3, pp. 433–434.
[82] *Kennedy* v. *Mayor of Barrow in Furness* (1909) Hudson's B.C., 4th ed., Vol. 2, p. 411.

contradistinction to an arbitrator, whose powers only become operative when a dispute has arisen.[83]   His function is usually referred to
as " quasi-arbitral."

In essence the certifier's function is administrative and only
incidentally judicial, and it may often require to be exercised before
any dispute has arisen or upon matters on which he has already
formed an opinion.   Hence the same obligation to hear and determine disputes in a fully judicial manner without prior interest which
rests upon a full arbitrator is not imposed upon him.   Extracts from
the following judgments on which the courts have commented upon
the position of a certifier may make this distinction clearer.   Thus in
Jackson v. *Barry Railway* (1893),[84] Bowen L.J. said:

" The perfectly open judgment, the absence of all previously
formed or pronounced views, which in an ordinary arbitrator are
natural and to be looked for, neither party to the contract proposed
to exact from the arbitrator of their choice. . . . The question is
whether the engineer has done anything to unfit himself to act, or
render himself incapable of acting, not as an arbitrator without previously formed or even strong views, but as an honest judge of this
very special and exceptional kind."

This judgment has been quoted with strong approval in subsequent cases, in particular in *Hickman Co.* v. *Roberts* (1913).[85]   Again,
in *McDonald* v. *Mayor of Workington* (1893),[86] Lord Esher M.R.
said:

" Where a surveyor is put into that position to give a certificate,
I do not say that he is an arbitrator, but he is an independent person.
His duty is to give the certificate according to his own conscience
and according to what he conceives to be the right and truth as to
the work done, and for that purpose he has no right to obey any
order or any suggestion by these people who are called his masters;
for that purpose they are not his masters."

And in *Page* v. *Llandaff and Dinas Powis R.D.C.* (1901),[87] Channell J. said: " They may each argue their case before him, and it would
be perfectly right for the engineer to give opportunities to either of
them by saying ' Now my view is so and so: what have you to say to
that? ' provided he does it equally to the other person.   There would

---

[83] *Laidlaw* v. *Hastings Pier Co.* (1874) Hudson's B.C., 4th ed., Vol. 2, p. 13, Ex.Ch;
     Re Carus-Wilson and Greene (1886) 18 Q.B.D. 7.
[84] [1893] 1 Ch. 238.
[85] *Supra*, pp. 462–463.
[86] Hudson's B.C., 4th ed., Vol. 2, p. 228.
[87] Hudson's B.C., 4th ed., Vol. 2, p. 316.

be no objections whatever to his doing that, but he must, so far as regards the portions of his duty in which he is deciding between the parties, deal equally with both parties. If he gives opportunities to one, he must give the same opportunities to the other; and although he may listen to arguments which may be addressed to him, he is not to allow his judgment to be influenced by directions given him of the character which would be properly given to him if he were doing some other part of his work; namely, the part in which he is surveyor only and directing the mode in which the work is to be done."

Again, in *Cross* v. *Leeds Corporation* (1902),[88] Mathew L.J. said: "Now it is said that we ought to come to the conclusion that he was unfit to act judicially, because he anticipated the time when he would have to act judicially, without hearing or giving the opportunity of hearing the builder with regard to the matters in dispute; but if you look at the correspondence, it is a perfectly good-tempered correspondence from beginning to end, there is not in the course of it the smallest imputation upon the honour of the engineer, but he took the position when he was appealed to in the matter, ' I have given you your certificates and there they are, and I see no reason now for altering them.' "   In the same case Mathew J. said [89] that the architect is: "Bound to do his best for his employer and to look sharply after the builder whilst the work is going on, and it is his duty in that capacity to form an opinion as to what his employer is entitled while the works are being executed."

Thus there is really only one rule for the guidance of engineers and architects in performing their duties as supervisors of the works and certifiers of money from time to time due to the builder when they may subsequently have to act judicially, whether as final certifiers or arbitrators, and that is that they should act honestly and without any perverse conduct or refusal to deal with the matter at all.   Thus Collins M.R. said in *Cross* v. *Leeds Corporation* (1902) [90]: " A strong man forming an opinion and acting on it, and if need be expressing it does not negative his right, for the reasons I have already pointed out, to act as arbitrator afterwards. You have got to get something more than a strong opinion strongly expressed before you have something equivalent to a refusal to consider the matter on its merits at all."

[88] Hudson's B.C., 4th ed., Vol. 2, at p. 344.
[89] *Ibid.* at p. 343.
[90] Hudson's B.C., 4th ed., Vol. 2, at p. 342.

As the above passages indicate, it is often impossible for an engineer or architect to perform the many duties devolving upon him during the progress of the works without expressing an opinion on matters as to which he may have to adjudicate later as certifier.

Nevertheless, it should be borne in mind by certifiers that their duty to their client requires them to protect his interest. That duty is in no way inconsistent with a duty to act impartially when called upon by the contract to do so, but this does not mean, as some architects and many engineers, whether acting as certifiers or arbitrators, seem to think, that they are free to give way to their own ideas of what is fair in defiance of the strict letter of the contract.[91]   The contract confers no personal discretion whatever upon the certifier,[92] unless it expressly so states, or is in one of the comparatively rare categories (as it has been submitted that in the case of architect and engineer certifiers it will almost invariably not be) where the contract on its true construction requires the satisfaction of the person concerned as an " additional protection " to the employer.[93]   The duty of the certifier is to apply the contract as strictly and impartially as a judge would do, it is submitted, though no doubt the application of the " de minimis " rule might allow him to pass over purely trivial defects in the same way that a judge would do.

Furthermore, the important and useful case of *Hatrick* v. *Nelson* (1964) [94] shows (and indeed the latest R.I.B.A. forms of contract implicitly require) [95] that a close liaison between architect and employer over some of his more important certifying decisions should exist prior to his making them, and of their nature these are not discussions at which the contractor would or should be present.   On the other hand, an opportunity to make representations should be afforded to the contractor wherever possible (see the doubts expressed as to the South African case of *Kollberg* v. *Cape Town Municipality*,[96] *supra*, Section 5, and *post*, Chap. 18).

(Many of the above cases refer to the certifier as " arbitrator," but this is because similar principles also apply where the same person is named as certifier and arbitrator, and the cases in question are dealing with contracts of this type, which are nowadays rare.)

[91] See for further references to this tendency, *post*, Chap. 9, p. 569, and Chap. 18, pp. 856, 868.
[92] See for an example where an engineer arbitrator sought to find one in one of the express provisions of the contract, *supra*, Chap. 5, p. 314, and the case of *Blackford & Sons (Calne) Ltd.* v. *Christchurch Corp.* [1952] 1 Lloyds Rep. 349 there referred to.
[93] *Supra*, Section 3, pp. 419, 433–434; Section 5, pp. 476–477.
[94] [1964] N.Z.L.R. 72, *supra*, Section 5, pp. 463–464.
[95] *Supra*, Section 6 (6), p. 491.
[96] 1967 (3) S.A. 472.   *Supra*, p. 464; *post*, pp. 821–822.

(2) Duty when a Final Certificate has to be Given

The duty of engineers and architects when they have to give a final certificate is to be open, fair and above board in all their dealings with the parties, and they should (depending upon the nature of the subject in respect of which they have to give a final certificate) hear all the parties wish to say, though not in the form of a hearing with both parties present.[97]

(3) Where the Same Person is named as both Certifier and Arbitrator

Various interpretations are in fact possible where a contract names the same person both as certifier and arbitrator. Such contracts are not common at the present day, though they were widespread in England until 1934, when the Arbitration Act of that year made it possible to secure the revocation of such an arbitrator's appointment.[98] But where the person named as the certifier under a building contract is also the arbitrator, this may, depending on the true construction of the contract, mean either

(a) that only disputes other than those covered by certificates should be referred to the arbitrator [98a] or

(b) that before certifying the engineer or architect is under a positive duty to hear the parties first or

(c) that all disputes, whether the subject of a previous certificate or not, may be referred to the arbitrator.

The second of these interpretations appears to have appealed to Lord Reading L.C.J. in the difficult case of *Eaglesham* v. *McMaster* (1920) [99] when he said:

"Clause 27 in my view still leaves clause 26 in operation and makes it necessary that the plaintiff should have a certificate before he can recover, but clause 27 does not leave it to the architect to make his certificate without hearing the parties and adjudicating upon any dispute that may arise between them." In that case the two clauses referred to were as follows:

Clause 26: "The certificate of the architect is a condition precedent to the contractor's right of action against the employer."

[97] See *supra*, Section 5 (4), pp. 463–465, and *supra*, subs. (1).
[98] See now s. 24 of the Act of 1950.
[98a] See the cases of *Lloyd Bros.* v. *Milward* and *Clemence* v. *Clarke*, *ante*, Section 4, pp. 438–439, 443.
[99] [1920] 2 K.B. 169 at p. 174, illustrated *ante*, pp. 443–444.

Clause 27: "The architect is to be the sole arbitrator or umpire between the employer and the contractor, and is to determine any question, dispute or difference that may arise either during the progress of the work or in determining the value of any variations that may be made in the work contracted for, and the certificate of the architect's decision upon such question, dispute or difference shall be final and binding between the employer and contractor and without further appeal whatsoever."

It will be seen, however, that this particular contract was in a very special form, expressly making the certificate of the architect a condition precedent of the contractor's right of action, and providing for the decision under the arbitration clause 27 to be made by certificate, which suggests that the intention may in fact have been to have a " Scott v. Avery " type of arbitration clause [1] with the architect as the arbitrator. In the majority of cases, particularly where the wording of the arbitration clause is perfectly general, the certificate of the certifier's decision ceases to be a condition precedent and the award of the arbitrator is a substitute for it.[2] Where arbitrator and certifier are one and the same person, and the decision may be given by either method, it is suggested that the architect or engineer when issuing his certificate should do nothing to prevent the contractor from subsequently having the benefit of the arbitration clause and of having his claims fully and judicially inquired into, if either party so requires and if no objection is taken under the Act of 1950 to his appointment as arbitrator.

(4) Duties of Certifier to Building Owner

The building owner is naturally entitled to have a high degree of control, consistent with his exact status as a salaried official or as a professional man in private practice, over the services of the engineer or architect for which he is paying, but where the contract with the builder requires the architect to decide matters judicially the employer of necessity ceases to be entitled to control his activities in relation to the matter he is called upon to decide, whether as certifier or arbitrator. The building owner must then leave the engineer or architect to decide impartially, so far as he can do so as the paid agent of one side with possibly previously expressed opinions on the matter in question. While proper and no doubt strong representations can be made to him they must not seek to limit his authority to

[1] See post, Chap. 18, pp. 853 et seq.
[2] See Section 4, supra.

decide, or pass the borderline beyond which they interfere with the free exercise of his function.[3] Moreover, the certifier cannot, it seems, be sued for certifying negligently,[4] though the exact scope of this principle requires, it has been submitted, clarification by the courts. Where the engineer or architect is acting as an arbitrator he must be careful to avoid receiving evidence or representations in the absence of the other party to the dispute, since, when acting in this capacity, there is not the slightest doubt that to do so once he had formally opened the reference, or indeed after receipt of notice of arbitration, would be contrary to natural justice and invalidate his award altogether.[5]

---

[3] See Section 5, *supra,* and the cases of *Hickman* v. *Roberts* [1913] A.C. 229; Hudson's B.C., 4th ed., Vol. 2, p. 426, and *Hatrick* v. *Nelson* [1964] N.Z.L.R. 72 there referred to.

[4] Provided, it is suggested, that a dispute has been formulated before him for his decision—see *Chambers* v. *Goldthorpe* [1901] 1 K.B. 624, discussed *ante,* Chap. 2, pp. 164 *et seq.*

[5] See *Re Camillo Eitzen and Jewson & Sons* (1896) 40 S.J. 438, *Re O'Connor and Whitlaw's Arbitration* (1919) 88 L.J.K.B. 1242, and *London Export Corporation* v. *Jubilee Coffee Roasting Co. Ltd.* [1958] 1 W.L.R. 661.

CHAPTER 8

VARIATIONS

SECTION 1. GENERALLY

(1) Reasons for Variation Clauses

WORKS which are not expressly or impliedly included in the original contract and, therefore, are not included in the contract price, are generally termed variations, whether they represent a change or alteration of the original work, or simply an addition to or omission from it, and may occur without authorisation by the employer or his architect, in which case they will be a breach of contract by the builder, or may be ordered by the employer or his architect. It is perfectly possible for such variations to be ordered, carried out and paid for under a separate agreement between the employer and the contractor, whether made orally or in writing,[1] and quite independently of any provision permitting variations in the contract, unless there is some provision specifically denying any effect to such a separate agreement. In general such provisions are rare at the present day, but they were common in the last century, when they generally took the form of providing that no extra payment of any kind should be made to the contractor unless he obtained an order in writing from the architect or engineer, and sometimes also a certificate as to the sum due for the variation.[2]

The provision usually found in building and engineering contracts under which the employer, or more usually his architect or engineer, is given power to order variations, is inserted in the contract for two important reasons. In the first place it gives the employer the power to require a variation of the work as of right, as opposed to relying on the readiness of the contractor to agree. In the second place, it has already been seen[3] that an architect has no *implied*

---

[1] See *ante*, Chap. 1, pp. 22–24, for the principles; and, for examples, Section 2 (c) (iv), *infra*.

[2] See *e.g.* the cases of *Tharsis Sulphur & Copper Co.* v. *McElroy* and *Brodie* v. *Cardiff Corporation*, and the other cases illustrated *post*, pp. 537–540.

[3] *Ante*, Chap. 2, pp. 106–111. See, however, the case of *Carlton Contractors* v. *Bexley Corporation*, there referred to, in which a local authority's architect was held to have authority to contract.

authority to contract on behalf of his employer.[4] In the absence of such a provision, therefore, the contractor will not be able to recover payment for any additional or varied work which he has done on the architect's instructions unless he can show a separate contract with the employer that he should do it and be paid for it (as for example where the employer knows of the architect's instruction and does not countermand it). Otherwise, not having done the work originally contracted for, he may be unable to recover the contract price and may even be liable in damages for breach of contract in the absence of such a new contract.

Thus, an employer may be liable to pay for varied work because he has expressly or impliedly ordered or authorised or ratified it himself (in which case his liability usually arises independently of the building contract) or because it has been ordered by some person, usually the architect or engineer, pursuant to an express general authority conferred upon him by the terms of the building contract (in which case the liability arises under that contract).[5] In the latter case, any express requirements of form prescribed by the contract will usually have to be complied with in order to render the employer liable [5] (unless of course the employer can also be shown to have authorised the variation ordered by his architect). But in the former case, unless the contract expressly provides to the contrary—e.g. by making an architect's instruction in writing a condition of liability in all cases—form is not usually of importance, and the authorisation or promise to pay can be inferred from mere knowledge of and acquiescence in the proposed variation, provided that it is realised or ought to be realised that a change of price is intended or probable as a consequence of the variation.[6] Failure to comply with requirements of form may not, therefore, be fatal to a builder if he can prove that the employer actually authorised the variation.[5]

(2) Work Included in the Contract

Apart from the problems caused by the extent of the architect's authority under the building contract to order variations, and the effect of any contractual requirements of form, there is little doubt that the most frequent and difficult questions of construction that arise in building and engineering contracts relate to whether particular

---

[4] See *e.g.* the case of *Ashwell & Nesbitt* v. *Allen* (1912) Hudson's B.C., 4th ed., Vol. 2, p. 462, referred to *ante*, Chap. 7, p. 410.

[5] See Section 2, *infra*.

[6] See *e.g. Re Chittick and Taylor* (1954) 12 W.W.R. 653 (Canada), referred to *infra*, p. 544.

items of work are in fact a variation of the work undertaken, either
where the work is meticulously described in a bill of quantities or
specification, or only generally described when the contract is made
upon a more informal basis. In either case it may be a very difficult
question whether work described is intended to include other ancillary work or processes indispensably necessary for the proper
completion of the work described.[7]

In addition, cases where unexpected technical difficulties have
made necessary more or different work from the contract expectation
in order to achieve completion of the contract work have already
been considered in detail. So, though well-drawn contracts will contain express provisions making it plain that all such risks and
contingencies are the obligation of the contractor, the express or
implied undertaking to complete which is a commonplace of most
substantial building or engineering contracts will almost invariably
have a similar if not identical effect.[8]

Both these major questions have already been considered in some
detail, *ante*, Chapter 5, where they arise in identical form when considering the exact nature of the contractor's obligation to complete,
and also discharge by impossibility or frustration. The only difference
is that the present chapter is primarily concerned with the financial
consequences of the principles there stated.

It has been seen that an employer does not generally warrant the
accuracy of the drawings or designs of his architect or engineer,[9] so
that alterations in the work due to this cause, in the absence of express
provision [10] will similarly not entitle the contractor to extra payment.

Whether work described in contract documents such as a specification or bills includes ancillary work is a question of construction
which must often depend upon the circumstances of the parties. Thus
a price quoted by a jobbing builder for supplying new doors for a
house in a small informal contract might be held to include hinges
and door-handles,[11] but if a carefully drawn bill of quantities prepared by the employer's advisers omitted to make any mention of
these items a different view might be taken (apart altogether from

---

[7] See *e.g.* the case of *Williams* v. *Fitzmaurice, ante*, Chap. 5, pp. 265–266.

[8] See *ante*, Chap. 5, pp. 267–273, and the cases there discussed. See also *infra*, subss.
(f) and (g), pp. 524–530, and the other cases there illustrated.

[9] *Ante*, Chap. 2, p. 107; Chap. 5, pp. 267–268, 349 *et seq.*

[10] As *e.g.* clause 24 (i) (c) of the 1963 R.I.B.A. standard forms, clause 12 (2) of the
1963 Forms without quantities, and clause 6 of the 1955 I.C.E. form.

[11] See, *e.g.* the case of *Williams* v. *Fitzmaurice, ante*, Chap. 5, pp. 265–266. But see
also the possible effect of clause 12 (2) of the 1963 R.I.B.A. standard forms without
quantities.

any incorporation of a standard method of measurement [12] which might assist in the interpretation of the description in question). Questions of construction of this kind do not depend upon any distinction between contracts in the bill or specification form. Thus if the description of concrete known, by reference to the drawings or from its location, to be fair-faced, omitted any mention of the necessary formwork, the question of construction would be the same in each case, except for such complications as might arise from the incorporation of standard methods of measurement in a contract using bills of quantities. There is a remarkable lack of authority on this kind of problem. It is suggested that wherever it can reasonably be inferred from the contract description that other undescribed work will be necessary to achieve completion or a satisfactory and effective result within the terms of the contractors' express or implied obligations as to design, workmanship and materials,[13] then in the absence of some indication to the contrary the undescribed work will be included in the price. Every case must, however, depend on its special facts, and under the *contra proferentem* rule much may turn upon which party to the contract put forward the description in question. Normally, it is submitted that both parties to a building or engineering contract may be presumed to intend the contract price to be comprehensive and not subject to adjustment, in the absence of variations or fluctuations or (in the case of forms with quantities on a measured basis) differences between the quantities of the work described in the bills and the same items of work as actually carried out.[14]

(a) Where actual quantities differ from those in bills

A special problem arises in the case of bills of quantities, however, where the ultimate actual quantities necessary to complete the work in accordance with the contract drawings or other description are different from those shown in the bills. It may at first sight surprise the layman that this can happen without there being a variation. This arises, however, because the bills are essentially an estimate which, depending on the particular process involved, can often be extremely accurate, although sometimes they cannot be accurate, of

---

[12] As to which see *infra*, pp. 515 *et seq.*

[13] As to which see *ante*, Chap. 5, Section 1, pp. 273 *et seq.*

[14] See *per* Lords Hodson and Guest in their dissenting judgments in *A. E. Farr* v. *Ministry of Transport* (1965) *infra*, pp. 519–520, a case which, perhaps not surprisingly, appears to have defeated the enthusiasm of the law reporters notwithstanding the stature of its tribunal. See also the judgments of the Court of Appeal in this case.

the different work processes necessary to produce the final permanent result indicated by the drawings as supplemented by the specification. The historical evolution of bills has already been shortly stated in the context of the duties and rights of quantity surveyors, and the liability to pay for their services, and their original function as a mere guide to tendering contractors to assist them in pricing the work, not warranted as accurate by the employer, explained. While bills fulfilled this function, the contractor took the risk of their being inaccurate, and the fact that he might have to carry out marginally greater quantities of work than those billed in order to complete the contract work would not entitle him to claim that there had been a variation. Very often the bills in these contracts were not even mentioned at all, or, if they were, in terms which were construed as not giving them any legal effect. In such cases the courts frequently referred to them as " not forming part of the contract." Later, contracts began to refer to bills in terms which showed that the rates in the bills were to be used for pricing such variations as the employer or his architect might order, and later still in terms which showed an intention that the contract price should be adjusted if, without any actual alteration in the work being ordered, the actual quantities needing to be done differed from those shown in the bills. This latter result could be brought about by a provision empowering the architect or engineer to remeasure and revalue the work at the end of the contract [15] or by a provision that errors in the bills should be treated as a variation and valued accordingly.[16] (" Remeasurement " in this context more often than not only means recalculation, for example, off the working drawings, since the standard method rules very sensibly require measurements wherever possible to be calculated on net plan areas or dimensions as shown on the drawings, so that any " over-work " is usually a contractor's risk or decision and included in his prices. Physical measurement or dimensions taken on site only occur in relation to work not of its nature subject to calculation off drawings as, *e.g.* cubic yardages of unsuitable ground removed to reach a sound base for foundations.) The quantity surveyor was by now usually employed by the building owner, and the practical advantage of such contracts was that tendering contractors did not have to incur expense in checking the accuracy of the quantities when pricing the contract. The courts frequently referred to these as contracts where the bills of quantities " formed part " of the

[15] *Cf.* clause 56 of the 1955 I.C.E. standard form.
[16] *Cf.* clause 12 (2) of the 1963 R.I.B.A. standard form with quantities.

contract, or as contracts for " measure and value," or as " schedule of rates " contracts, on the one hand, as opposed to " lump sum " contracts, where the price was fixed and not subject to recalculation unless actual alterations in the work had been required.[17] Nearly all the contracts at the present day which provide for bills of quantities fall into the former category where the contract is subject to adjustment apart altogether from variations. As will be seen, the courts were somewhat slow and uncertain in recognising these distinctions.[18]

ILLUSTRATIONS

(1) The plaintiff, a builder, signed a tender to build a house for the defendant according to specification and plans for £1,985, the tender being based on quantities calculated by the defendant's surveyor. The plaintiff completed the work and claimed the sum of £1,985 " as per contract," and also claimed a further sum of £142 for work or materials in excess of the quantities calculated by the defendant's surveyor. *Held*, that the plaintiff had adopted the contract and claimed payment under it, and could not therefore at the same time ignore it and recover the further sum of £142: *Coker* v. *Young* (1860).[19]

(2) A builder contracted to build a church for £1,988. Owing to errors in the plans and bills of quantities the work cost him £3,600, including extras, which, however, had not been ordered in writing as provided by the contract. In an action for the extra cost of the work, the builder contended that the errors in the quantities and plans amounted to a fraud on the plaintiff. *Held*, that since there was no evidence of fraud to go to the jury, or of waiver of the condition that extras should be ordered in writing, the claim must fail: *Sherren* v. *Harrison* (1860).[20]

(3) The plaintiff, the defendant, and one P., an architect, entered into a contract whereby the plaintiff agreed to build a house for the defendant in accordance with drawings, a specification and conditions of contract, to the satisfaction of P., in consideration of the sum of £440. P. agreed to inspect and superintend the works, to furnish detail drawings, and to certify the payment of advances and completion of the work. P. had prepared quantities which did not form part of the contract, but which he supplied to the plaintiff and which he assured the plaintiff were correct. The plaintiff paid P. for the quantities and included the sum paid in his tender.[21] The quantities proved to be inaccurate and in the event had to be exceeded. The plaintiff sued for goods sold and delivered, work done and materials supplied, and for damages for breach of a guarantee that the quantities were accurate. *Held*, there was no evidence that P. was the

---

[17] See *e.g.* the language used by Lord Alverstone L.C.J. in *London Steam Stone Saw Mills* v. *Lorden* (1900), illustrated *infra*, p. 513.

[18] In addition to the cases illustrated, see *Re Nuttall and Lynton & Barnstaple Ry.*, (1899) Hudson's B.C., 4th ed., Vol. 2, p. 279, illustrated *ante*, Chap. 5, p. 271.

[19] 2 F. & F. 98.

[20] Hudson's B.C., 4th ed., Vol. 2, p. 5.

[21] For the origins of this practice see *ante*, Chap. 2, pp. 111–113, 193 *et seq.*

defendant's agent or that any guarantee was given by the defendant, and the plaintiff could not recover: *Scrivener* v. *Pask* (1866).[22]

(4) The plaintiff tendered to the defendant to build a mansion shown on rough drawings for £13,690. The defendant's architect had orally given rough quantities to the plaintiff. Subsequently a specification and working drawings were prepared and the plaintiff incautiously agreed to complete the mansion house in accordance with the specification and working drawings for the sum of £13,690. The quantities of work described in the specification and shown on these working drawings were considerably in excess of those originally given by the architect. The contract contained a power enabling the architect to order alterations or omissions and provided that if any difference of cost should be caused by such alterations, a formal order signed by the architect should be sent to the plaintiff and that the plaintiff should not claim any extra except on these conditions. The architect had agreed with the defendant that the total cost of the mansion should not exceed £15,000, but the plaintiff did not know this. Extra works were done under the direction of the architect and the cost of the works exceeded £15,000. The architect refused to certify extra for the work done in excess of the quantities given by him or for the extra work ordered by him. *Held*, the plaintiff was bound by the contract he had entered into and could only recover extra for the extra work ordered and not for the excess due to the inadequate quantities: *Kimberley* v. *Dick* (1871).[23]

(5) J. contracted to construct a railway for a lump sum. On the profile plan it was stated that the best information in possession of the engineer would be found in the schedules " but contractors must understand that these quantities are not guaranteed," and in the " bill of works " it was stated " the quantities herein given as ascertained from the best data obtained are, as far as is known, approximately accurate, but at the same time they are not warranted as accurate and no claim of any kind will be allowed, though they may prove inaccurate." *Held*, that there was no guarantee, express or implied, as to the quantities, nor any misrepresentation respecting them: *Jones* v. *The Queen* (1877).[24]

(6) A firm of architects took out quantities of a house and supplied them to the builders and were paid by them. The builders entered into a contract with the building owner to build the house in accordance with plans and specifications. The contract expressly provided that the quantities were believed to be correct but that if any error or misstatement should be found in them the architect should have power to measure all or any of the works and to adjust the same. The builder sued both the building owner and the architects, alleging against the building owner a warranty that the quantities were the basis of the contract and that in case of error the builders should be paid for work and materials in excess thereof. *Held*: The contract with the building owner did not contain a warranty that

[22] L.R. 1. C.P. 715.
[23] L.R. 13 Eq. 1.
[24] 7 Can. S.C.Rep. 570.

the quantities were correct, and the quantities were not the basis of the contract: *Young* v. *Blake* (1887).[25]

(7) A builder, by an offer appended to a schedule, offered to do the mason work of a proposed tenement " agreeably to plans thereof now shown, and to the extent of this schedule, for the sum of £286 10s. 8½d." The schedule gave the estimated quantities of work required, and the builder inserted the rate at which he proposed to do each item. There was a stipulation that the work was to " be measured when finished, and charged at schedule rates." In calculating the price the builder had made an under-calculation of £30. *Held*, that the contract was on a schedule of rates, and not a contract for a lump sum, and that the builder was entitled to be paid for the work as measured and at his rates: *Jamieson* v. *McInnes* (1887).[26]

(8) An estimate for the delivery, fixing and cleaning down of stone-work for a lump sum contained the words " The bill of quantities to form part of the contract, and all variations to be priced at the rates stated in the bill, and added to or deducted from the lump sum, as the case may be." There were differences from the quantities in the bill, and the employer contended that he was entitled to measure up the whole of the work. *Held*, measurement was only applicable to variations: *London Steam Stone Saw Mills* v. *Lorden* (1900).[27]

(9) B. instructed architect R. to prepare plans and invite tenders for certain works. R. prepared plans and a bill of quantities and invited tenders on them. A contract was entered into by which the builders agreed to execute " the whole of the works required in accordance with the plans and specification for the erection of the new works " for a lump sum. The specification was, in fact, a bill of quantities with rather fuller descriptions than usual. The quantities turned out to be incorrect and less than they should have been. There was some evidence of a custom in the building trade that a builder was entitled to rely on the bill of quantities on which he tendered. *Held*, that the quantities in the margin of the specification were merely an estimate, and no part of the contract at all, and did not amount to a warranty by the owner, and, therefore, that B. was not entitled to anything beyond the lump sum agreed. *Held*, also, that the custom contradicted the contract and could not be maintained: *Re Ford & Co. Ltd. and Bemrose & Sons* (1902).[28]

(10) A building contract contained the following stipulations: " Full power is reserved to make alterations . . . the work will be measured and charged at the schedule rates . . . and all subject to revision and correction by measures, and to any addition or deduction which may be made by the contractor in filling up his offer." W. returned a schedule with the rate at which he offered to do each

---

[25] Hudson's B.C., 4th ed. Vol. 2, p. 110. (It may be doubted whether this case would be decided in the same way today, since the contract appears to be designed to be a " measured " contract, though the court held, in fact, that there was no entitlement to re-measurement, but only a discretion in the architect to permit it. At the date of this case, however, the concept of the " measured " contract had not been clarified by the courts. See the later cases *infra*.)

[26] 15 R. (Ct. of Sess.) 17.

[27] Hudson's B.C., 4th ed., Vol. 2, p. 301 (D.C.).

[28] Hudson's B.C., 4th ed., Vol. 2, p. 324.

item, but made an arithmetical mistake of £151 in one item. Appended to the schedule, W. wrote: " I hereby offer to execute the work . . . in conformity with and to the extent of the foregoing estimate for the sum of £ . . ." (an incorrect total of the items). W. brought an action against the owners for the £151. *Held*, that the contract was not a lump sum contract, but one on a schedule of rates, and that W. was entitled to be paid on a correct calculation at schedule rates: *Wilkie* v. *Hamilton Lodging House Co.* (1902).[29]

(11) A contractor undertook to complete certain works for a sum of £17,000 " according to the plans, invitation to tender, specification and bills of quantities." Other clauses provided that the contractors should supply everything requisite for the execution of the works included in the contract according to the true intent of the drawings, specification and quantities, whether or not particularly described in the specification and shown on the drawings, and for measurement of alterations and additions and valuation of them according to the prices on the bills. There was no express provision for measurement of the works as a whole. *Held*, that if the quantities in the bills were less than those required by the drawings, the contractor was entitled to be paid an appropriate addition to the contract sum, since the quantities were introduced with the contract as a part of the description of the contract work, and if the contractor was required to do more, it was an extra: *Patman and Fotheringham Ltd.* v. *Pilditch* (1904).[30]

(12) Builders agreed to erect and complete two cottages according to plans, specification and quantities for a lump sum. There was in fact no specification, but there was a bill of quantities. There was a mistake in the quantities, and the amount of brickwork necessary to be carried out in order to complete the cottages was short. The builders did not go to the site before tendering, and did not check the quantities before signing the contract. The builders claimed payment for the extra brickwork necessary to complete the cottages beyond the amount taken in the quantities. Judgment was given for the plaintiffs: *Meigh & Green* v. *Stockingford Colliery Co. Ltd.* (1922).[31]

The case of *Patman and Fotheringham Ltd.* v. *Pilditch*, illustrated above, represents the final recognition by the courts that, even where the language used might be not entirely clear, the parties' presumed intention might be that the quantities in the bills should be used for the purpose of recalculation of the contract price. It should be realised that, if bills which have been incorporated into a contract are only intended for the valuation of such variations as may be ordered, there is no need for any quantities to be inserted into the bills at all— merely a sufficient number of rates or prices for the particular work

---

[29] 4 F. (Ct. of Sess.) 951. Distinguish the case of *Gleeson Ltd.* v. *Sleaford U.D.C.*, illustrated *post*, subs. (c), p. 521.

[30] Hudson's B.C., 4th ed., Vol. 2, p. 368, *per* Channell J.

[31] May 25, 1922 (unreported). Sankey J. expressly stated that he followed the decision of Channell J. above.

processes likely to be involved in any varied work called for. Channell J. was clearly (and rightly) influenced in his judgment in the *Patman* case by the fact that, as the bills were clearly identified and referred to in and for the purposes of the variations clause of the contract, there was no need to have the further separate undertaking to complete the work " according to the plans, invitation to tender, specification *and bills of quantities* " unless the bills were to have some additional legal effect beyond the valuation of variations. The case is therefore an important watershed in the interpretation of provisions incorporating bills, despite the failure of the official law reports to record it or the later decision of Sankey J. in *Meigh & Green* v. *Stockingford Colliery Co. Ltd.*[32] which expressly followed it. In most modern contracts it is now usual to find rather more explicit provisions as to the effect of the incorporation of the bills, but the *Patman* case will remain of considerable importance where the incorporation is effected in less precise terms.

(b) Where work is not mentioned at all in bills

It is inevitable that neither bills of quantities nor specifications can descend to every minutest detail in describing the work processes which a contractor will necessarily have to perform in order to complete the billed or described work. For example, it would be unusual in the case of joinery items to find the nailing arrangements described. In addition, more substantial work may not be mentioned, though it can be seen as a matter of clear inference that it will be necessary in order to achieve completion of the billed or described work. The example of shuttering or formwork, where fair-faced concrete is required by the contract, has already been cited. One of the most difficult questions of interpretation in building and engineering contracts is whether the described work includes this necessary ancillary work, and the suggested principles of interpretation have already been stated.[33] This question of interpretation may, where the description in question is in the bills, be further complicated by the express provisions commonly found in modern contracts incorporating standard methods of measurement, particularly if the provision for recalculation of the contract price does not take the form of a provision for remeasurement,[34] but provides that errors or omissions in the bills shall be treated as a variation,[35] since the failure to

---

[32] *Supra.*
[33] *Supra,* p. 509. See also *ante,* Chap. 5, p. 264.
[34] As in the 1955 I.C.E. standard form (clause 56).
[35] As in clause 12 (2) of the 1963 R.I.B.A. standard forms.

conform to the standard method can be said to be the " error or omission " in the bills. Even in the case of the R.I.B.A. specification form *without* quantities, obvious difficulties are created by clause 12 (2), of the form which provides as follows: " Any error in description or in quantity in or omission of items from the contract drawings and/or the *specification* shall not vitiate this contract but shall be corrected and deemed to be a variation (*sic*) required by the architect." The effect of this provision where obviously necessary items, perhaps occasioned by unexpected difficulties in the work, are not specifically mentioned in the specification, does not appear to have been considered, nor indeed is any suggestion made as to how the true contract obligation can be identified—until this has been done, it would be impossible to decide whether the " error " in the documents should produce an addition to or deduction from the contract price.

Standard Methods of Measurement are documents produced with the praiseworthy purpose of securing uniformity of practice in measuring and tendering for building and engineering work. Broadly speaking, they have two functions. The first is to lay down precise rules of physical measurement and as to the dimensions and formulae to be used in calculating quantities. The second is to secure uniformity in the types of process which are to be used as units for pricing work in bills of quantities, and this part of their function consists of making recommendations as to which processes are on the one hand considered too small or imprecise to warrant being priced separately, and which should therefore be included in the larger composite processes of which they form part and which are so described and priced separately, and which processes on the other hand are sufficiently important or susceptible of measurement to warrant separate pricing on their own and not as part of some larger composite process. An example of the first would be a recommendation that rates for excavation should include for removing surplus soil after back-filling, and an example of the second that shuttering or form work should be separately billed and not included in rates for concrete. As will be seen, a failure by the bills, however patent and obvious, to comply with one of these latter recommendations, so that an obviously necessary ancillary process to work which is described in the bills is not separately itemised for pricing as recommended, has led to an ingenious type of claim by contractors for extra payment on the ground that their contract price does not, on the wording of the provisions as to the incorporation of the standard method and as to the effect of the bills, include for the work in question.

In the case of bills of quantities, clause 12 (2) of the R.I.B.A. standard form with quantities provides: " (1) The quality and quantity of the work included in the contract sum shall be deemed to be that which is set out in the contract bills which bills unless otherwise expressly stated *in respect of any specified item or items*[36] shall be deemed to have been prepared in accordance with the principles of the Standard Method of Measurement of Building Works . . . (2) Any error in description or in quantity in or omission of items from the contract bills shall not vitiate this contract but shall be corrected and deemed to be a variation (*sic*) required by the architect." In this case also, it can only be repeated that the effect of the somewhat unnecessarily wide wording of clause 12 (2), in cases where necessary ancillary work has not been mentioned (even in cases of minute detail) or where work necessitated by some risk otherwise the responsibility of the contractor (for instance the practicability of the design from the point of view of completing the work)[37] does not appear to have been considered.

The method by which the I.C.E. Conditions give effect to the bills of quantities is totally different. Clause 55 provides that the quantities in the bills are estimated quantities and not to be taken as the actual and correct quantities to be executed in fulfilment of the contract obligations, and by Clause 56 it is provided: " The engineer shall except as otherwise stated ascertain by admeasurement the value in accordance with the contract of work done in accordance with the contract." The provision in the 1955 I.C.E. standard form as to the incorporation of the standard method of measurement is as follows[38]: " Except where any general or detailed description of the work in the bill of quantities expressly shows to the contrary bills of quantities shall be deemed to have been prepared . . . according to the procedure set forth in the standard method of measurement of civil engineering quantities . . . "

The effect of such provisions for incorporation of standard methods of measurement and the possibility of unmerited claims by the contractor to which they may give rise is illustrated by the following case.

---

[36] The words in italics represent an addition to the pre-1963 wording, and have obviously been inserted at the instance of contractors in order to safeguard and extend as far as possible the opportunity to make claims for additional payment on the principle of *Bryant's* case illustrated *infra*.

[37] See *ante*, Chap. 5, pp. 267 *et seq*.

[38] Clause 57.

ILLUSTRATION

Clause 11 of the 1931 R.I.B.A. standard form provided in terms similar to those of the 1963 form above quoted (with the exception of the reference to a specified item or items quoted in italics above) that the bills unless otherwise stated should be deemed to have been prepared in accordance with the current standard method of measurement. The latter provided as follows: " Where practicable the nature of the soils shall be described and attention shall be drawn to existing boreholes. Excavation in rock shall be given separately." By bill No. 1 the contractor was referred to the site to satisfy himself as to local conditions and to the full nature and extent of the operations and the execution of the contract generally, and no claim on the ground of want of knowledge in such respects or otherwise was to be entertained. The bills referred the contractor to two boreholes, though in fact five had been dug. In two of the five there was evidence of rock, but the contractors only inspected two (which of the five these were was not known). The bills further stated: " Include for removing any natural stone or rock that may be encountered in the excavations." The arbitrator held this latter clause could not be fairly read to indicate blasting and lifting of rock below the surface.[39] There was evidence of rock on other parts of the site and the architect was aware of the fact, but the plans and bills made no mention of it. On a case stated, the employer contended that clause 11 of the R.I.B.A. standard form had not been incorporated into the contract between the parties. *Held*, by Lewis J., that on the facts it was, and counsel for the employer having conceded (in the court's opinion rightly) that if it was, the contractor was entitled to the extra cost of excavating rock, the contractor's claim must succeed: *Bryant & Sons Ltd.* v. *Birmingham Hospital Saturday Fund* (1938).[40]

Furthermore, it would seem that the method of giving effect to bills of quantities in the R.I.B.A. forms, with its reference to " errors in description or in quantity in or *omission of items from* the contract bills " certainly lends more support to this type of claim than the I.C.E. wording though, even so, the provision, if it has the meaning contended for, is a trap which few employers could possibly understand (and it is difficult to believe, intend) on reading the wording of the relevant provisions.

It seems by no means clear why a provision that excavation for rock should be given separately should entitle the contractor to extra payment in cases where there is no positive intention to excavate in rock, and rock is merely a contingent risk which may or may not occur, and it is suggested that the entire principle of this case needs further consideration by the courts.[41] In particular it is suggested

---

[39] This finding was not disputed but seems extremely questionable.
[40] [1938] 1 All E.R. 503, criticised *infra*, p. 520.
[41] See particularly the (dissenting) judgments of Lords Guest and Pearson and of the Court of Appeal in *A. E. Farr Ltd.* v. *Ministry of Transport, infra* pp. 519–520.

that while the incorporation of the standard method is usually wholly effective to incorporate the techniques and formulae for measuring quantities, as to which the contract will usually be wholly silent, in regard to the recommendations as to separate pricing these could only have an effect on the interpretation of the contract obligation where a genuine doubt or ambiguity as to the work to be done existed. Thus where the drawings or bill descriptions made it clear that fair-faced concrete, and consequently form work, was required, for instance, the recommendation of separate pricing for form work in a standard method could not, it is submitted, assist because there would be no ambiguity as to what the contractor had to do; or in other words, the bills of quantities would show on their face or " otherwise state " the contrary intention. It is submitted that far more explicit words than " deemed to have been prepared " would need to be used if the intention was to secure additional payment for the contractor every time the standard method recommendation was not followed.

While there remains any doubt as to the possibility of financial claims of this kind, however, the importance of professional preparation of bills of quantities in meticulous compliance with the standard form is obviously essential in the employer's interest in order to protect him from such claims. Furthermore, the very stringent wording of the italicised part of the 1963 R.I.B.A. standard form may result in express words of a clear but general nature indicating the full extent of the contractor's risks or obligations failing in their purpose if not applied specifically to particular items in the bills. The following case and the remarkable conflict of appellate judicial opinion to which it gave rise, is a further illustration of the difficulties and obscurities which can arise from the use of bills, under the terms of the present standard forms, in ascertaining the exact work undertaken for the contract price.

ILLUSTRATION

By clause 12 (1) of the standard I.C.E. Conditions of Contract the rates and prices in the bill of quantities were to cover all the contractor's obligations under the contract and all matters and things necessary for the proper completion and maintenance of the works. Similar provisions were to be found in the bills of quantities themselves, and in the Standard Method of Measurement (itself incorporated by clause 57 of the Conditions). The bills stated that the price or rate set down against each item was to be considered as the full inclusive price or rate of the finished work described in each item, and also to cover the cost of every description of timbering works executed or used in connection therewith, except those in respect of which specific provision was made by way of separate items. By clause 16 of the bills the measurement of excavation in pit or trench for a structure was, unless otherwise stated, to be the net plan area of the permanent work multiplied by the depth to the authorised bottom, and " any additional excavation which may be required for working space, etc. will be paid for under separate items, the measurement being the sum of the areas of the sides of the excavation." Excavation for the main part of the contract work was billed at ordinary cubic yard rates, but no additional square yard items for working space were included, though two specific items for such additional excavation were included in a part of the bills relating to subsidiary parts of the work. The engineer approved a programme showing an intention to carry out additional working space excavation in the main part of the work. The contractor contended that he should be paid a reasonable extra rate for working space whenever it was reasonable in all the circumstances to excavate outside the planned area. *Held*, by the House of Lords, (Lords Hodson and Guest dissenting), overruling a unanimous Court of Appeal, that on its true construction clause 16 was a promise to pay for whatever working space might be necessary, whether or not described in a special item in the bills. *A. E. Farr Ltd* v. *Ministry of Transport* (1965).[42]

It is submitted that in approaching this problem the important question to ask is whether, on a true view of the bills, and in particular of the associated or " parent " items which *are* described in the bills, there is any reasonable doubt that the items of work in question which are not described are to be carried out as a part of the work in the described items. If this is so, only the clearest possible wording should be permitted, by way of incorporating a standard method, to defeat the obvious expectation and legal presumption that a price quoted for described work includes for all indispensably necessary or contingent work required to bring the described work to completion. Judged by these standards, it is most respectfully submitted that the decisions in the *Bryant* and *Farr* cases were wrong, and that the judgments and reasoning of the Court of Appeal and of Lords Guest and Hodson are to be preferred. Fortunately no statement of principle emerges from the *Farr* case (which did not involve the incorporation of the standard method as part of its *ratio decidendi*, since the language used in the bills in that case was in fact identical with that of the standard method) and the whole matter is still relatively free of authority.

(c) Mistakes of contractor in the bills

The above provisions in the pre-1963 R.I.B.A. standard forms for the correction or rectification of errors in the bills have been held,

---

[42] House of Lords (unreported). See also the case of *Crosby* v. *Portland U.D.C.*, illustrated and discussed *infra*, pp. 522–523.

it is submitted rightly, not to be applicable to mistakes made by the contractor in pricing the bills.[43]

ILLUSTRATION

Contractors, through an oversight, omitted to price a substantial portion of one of the bills of quantities, and consequently tendered a contract sum which was too low. There were rates in other parts of the bills for similar work by which the work could have been measured and valued. *Held,* by Vaisey J., that the contractors could recover nothing for the work in question under the R.I.B.A. provision for rectification of errors in the bills, there being no error or omission *in the bills* (only in the contractor's pricing of them): *M. V. Gleeson Ltd.* v. *Sleaford U.D.C.* (1953).[44]

In the post-1963 R.I.B.A. forms this situation is now expressly governed by clause 13, which also prevents an adjustment of the price in this situation. On the other hand, the totally different method of adjustment of the contract price under clause 56 of the I.C.E. conditions will usually mean, it is submitted, that a mistake of this kind will be corrected when the remeasurement provided for by the contract takes place.[44a]

Where, however, the mistake is common to both parties, or the mistake of one is known to the other, the legal remedy of rectification may of course be available.[45]

(d) Necessary work in contracts at schedule rates

These contracts are very similar in their legal effect to contracts incorporating bills with provisions for remeasurement, since the essence of a schedule contract is an undertaking to complete work for payment based on measurement of the whole work at the scheduled rates. A schedule contract differs in appearance from a bill contract in that quantities need not be and generally are not inserted in the schedule, and in consequence no grossed up overall price for the work is likely to be found in the contract documents. The schedule merely contains descriptions of items of work similar to those in bills, and rates or prices for each item. Some examples of schedule or near-schedule contracts have been illustrated in the context of the development of the bill form of contract.[46] Such contracts may be for a

---

[43] See also now clause 13 of the 1963 standard forms.

[44] [1953] (unreported). See now clause 13 of the post-1963 R.I.B.A. forms which expressly governs the position.

[44a] See *e.g. Jamieson* v. *McInnes* and *Wilkie* v. *Hamilton Lodging House Co.,* illustrated *supra,* pp. 513, 514.

[45] See *ante,* Chap. 1, pp. 32 *et seq.*

[46] *Supra,* pp. 511–514.

defined project, where perhaps the detailed design is not yet available at the time of contracting. In such a case the ordinary obligation to complete the whole will be found in the contract in express or implied form. On the other hand, such contracts may be used for ordering work from time to time, and the completion obligation may be limited to individual " slices " of work as and when they come to be ordered. It is generally not difficult to determine into which category they should be placed.

Subject to measurement, therefore, disputes as to additional quantities will not usually arise under such contracts any more than in the modern form of bill contract. Where, however, necessary or contingent work is not mentioned in the schedule, the same problems of construction will arise in determining whether the items of work described and priced in the schedule do or do not allow for the necessary or contingent work associated with the described work. If the schedule rates do not apply, this will mean that (whether or not there is a variation in the usual sense of a change from the contract intention when the drawings and specification are examined) some different price or rate will need to be agreed, either because of the absence of any fairly applicable rate for the contract work in question, or because the work is a change from the contract work.

ILLUSTRATIONS

(1) M. contracted to construct works including " cast iron outlet pipe *to low water*, as described in the specification and conditions, and set forth on the drawings "; M. also agreed to deliver a copy of the priced bill of quantities on which the tender was based. The general plan of the work showed the outlet pipe extending to low-water mark, but the section showed it as extending 279 feet further into the sea. The length of pipe in the bill of quantities corresponded with the length of pipe shown in the section, but there was no price fixed in the bill of quantities for underwater works. The engineer decided, under a power in the contract, that M. was under an obligation to carry out the work in accordance with the section. M. constructed the work according to the section and claimed to be paid for the work beyond low-water mark at fair and reasonable prices. *Held*, the contract was clearly a schedule of prices contract and, the work done beyond low-water mark not being covered by any price in the schedule of prices, M. was entitled to be paid for it at a fair valuation. He was paid the price he claimed, there being no dispute as to the amount if liability was established. *Re Walton-on-the-Naze Urban District Council & Moran* (1905).[47]

(2) Item 1 in a bill was for excavation in trench not exceeding 5 feet in depth, Item 46 was a small provisional quantity for excavation for depths in excess of 5 feet, and Item 24 was an item for moulding

---

[47] Hudson's B.C., 4th ed., Vol. 2, p. 376, also illustrated and discussed *ante*, p. 266.

laying and jointing pipes which on its true construction was held only to apply to the Item 1 work. In fact there was a considerable amount of work shown on the drawings in excess of 5 feet in depth. The contractor contended that the contract, which was in the I.C.E. form, was a contract for measure and value, and that a new rate must be used for laying etc. below 5 feet. Alternatively, he contended that there was power to fix a new rate under clause 52 of the Conditions. *Held*, by Donaldson J., that there was power to fix a new rate under clause 52. *Crosby* v. *Portland U.D.C.* (1967).[47a]

[Note: The exact facts and terms of the bills are not clear from the judgment in this case. While Donaldson J. undoubtedly appears to have held that clause 52 of the I.C.E. conditions applied to differences in quantities not amounting to a variation, there are in fact serious difficulties about this, not mentioned in the judgment, on the wording of the I.C.E. conditions, and in principle the decision seems to be more easily supported by clause 55 of the conditions and the *Walton-on-the-Naze ratio decidendi*.]

Disputes on schedule contracts usually involve the contention on the part of the contractor that work required to be carried out is not included in the schedule rates as properly construed. The schedule requires to be carefully drafted if disputes of this kind are to be avoided. All possible contingencies should be considered, and the schedule should provide for them. To take a simple instance, a schedule contract for laying a sewer will probably contain several items or composite items, priced per lineal yard according to the depth of the sewer, for excavation; providing, laying, jointing and testing pipes; and backfilling and reinstating. The contract should at some point then provide that the prices for these items include all incidental matters such as timbering, pumping, temporary works of support and protection required where gas and water mains, etc., are crossed, and so on, and the specification should describe with greater detail still the work required within the terms only briefly summarised in the priced items in the schedule. It is no hardship to a contractor to have these risks put upon him if what is included in the schedule rates is made clear to him when tendering. But again, as in the case of contracts with bills of quantities, the basic presumption must be that the prices for described items of work include for all ancillary or contingent work which may be necessary for the completion of the described work.[48]

(e) Promise to pay when contractor already bound

If a contractor is already bound, on the true construction of the contract, to do certain work for the contract price, there will be no

[47a] (1967), unreported (Donaldson J., Q.B.D.).
[48] See *supra*, p. 509 and *ante*, Chap. 5, Section 1, p. 264.

consideration for any promise by the employer to pay for it under the mistaken impression that it is a variation.[49] Equally, in most contracts an instruction by the architect or engineer to execute certain work expressly stating it to be a variation cannot bind the employer to pay for it if, on the true construction of the contract, the work is included in the contract price.[50] The only exception to this would be the comparatively rare case at the present day of a provision in the contract making an order in writing or certificate of the engineer in relation to extra work conclusive and binding on the parties.[51] So if a contractor alleged that work he was ordered to do was an extra and refused to continue without a promise to pay for it, and the employer on that account promised to pay extra for it, he would not be liable on such a promise. James L.J. said of such a promise in *Sharpe* v. *Sao Paulo Ry.*[52]: " It is perfectly *nudum pactum*. It is a totally distinct thing from a claim for payment for actual extra works not included in the contract." [53] The dividing line between this class of case and that in paragraph (f) below is so fine that the illustrative cases there collected should also be considered in the present context.

(f) Instructions to assist contractors in difficulty

A more difficult problem arises, however, if an effective alteration in the permanent work is ordered with a view to assisting the contractor in a difficulty which otherwise it would be his contractual obligation to surmount by whatever methods he chose to adopt and at his own cost—for instance where he was finding difficulty in completing the work in accordance with the contract design, or where unexpected site difficulties arose. In such cases there may be a benefit obtained by the employer as well as the contractor, since delays which might be costly to the employer may be avoided by the alteration, and furthermore the difficulty may throw doubt on the long-term suitability of the permanent work after completion, and hence in the employer's interest may call for a design change which incidentally will assist the contractor.

The cases in fact may raise two somewhat different contentions— in the first place, there may be a real and effective change in the permanent work, but the employer's case is that it was agreed to solely to assist the contractor in a difficulty and not for any interest or

---

[49] See *ante*, Chap. 1, pp. 22–23. [50] *Ante*, Chap. 2, pp. 106–108
[51] See Chap. 7.
[52] L.R. 8 Ch. App. 597 at p. 608.
[53] Compare the analogous case of *D. & C. Builders Ltd.* v. *Rees* [1966] 2 Q.B. 617, illustrated *ante*, Chap.5, Section 3, p. 348.

advantage of the employer; in the second place, the employer may contend that the work concerned was not a variation at all, but only contingent work which on the true construction of the contract was the obligation of the contractor. If the latter (and the dividing line may be a fine one), that will dispose of the matter on the basis of the principles stated in paragraph (e) *supra*.

It is not easy to lay down any general rule if such an order is given when the employer is strictly entitled to rely on the contract and do nothing. But if in a situation such as this an architect or engineer complies with the formal requirements of the contract for variation orders by issuing an instruction in writing, when in reality the contractor is only being given permission to depart from the contract, it is obvious that a dispute over payment is likely to occur in which the true reason for the instruction is likely to be in issue and in which the employer would be bound to contend for some implied term limiting the effect of the variation clause in such circumstances.[54] To avoid doubt, architects or engineers should be careful to use permissive language only when authorising such an alteration, and should expressly disclaim any intention to give an instruction or order in the matter under the terms of the contract variation clause.

It has already been seen that an architect or engineer owes no duty to the contractor in regard to instructions or information other than to give sufficiently clear instructions as to the final permanent result required by the contract, and that in particular the architect or engineer owes no duty to the contractor, in the absence of express provisions in the specification or other technical documents, to prescribe or supervise or control his methods of working.[55] Nor does the architect or engineer owe any duty to the contractor to detect defects at an early stage or, when they have been discovered, to tell the contractor how they should be remedied, once it has been established that they are due to breach of contract by the contractor.[56] Contractors, when faced with unexpected difficulties,[56a] or even with the emergent symptoms of their own or their sub-contractors' defective work, almost invariably seek to obtain formal instructions from the architect, or purport to confirm advice given by him as if it was an instruction, with a view to preparing the ground for a financial claim based on the instruction. A careless acknowledgment of such a letter

[54] See, for instance, the analogous case of the appointment of new sub-contractors in substitution for original sub-contractors who have failed, *ante*, pp. 332 *et seq.*
[55] *Ante*, Chap. 1, pp. 68–70; Chap. 2, pp. 139–141; Chap. 5, pp. 324–325.
[56] *Ante*, Chap. 2, pp. 153–155; Chap. 6, pp. 385–388, 399–400. See also *post*, Chap. 9, pp.582–583.
[56a] See also the cases on the obligation to complete, *ante* Chap. 5, pp. 269–272.

can, under the remarkable policies of the R.I.B.A. forms, have
utterly disastrous consequences for the employer.[57] The following
cases are examples of the difficulties which can arise.

ILLUSTRATIONS

(1) An architect, prior to letting the main contract, which was
in the 1948 R.I.B.A. standard form, arranged with a nominated
supplier of facing bricks for stocks to be held available for delivery
by certain dates. Later the contractor placed his order with the
supplier, being informed by the architect of the arrangements made
for delivery. The supplier defaulted on delivery, and the architect
authorised the contractors, who were unable for this reason to keep
to their planned programme, to build only the inner brick skins of
the walls, leaving the outer skin of facing bricks for completion as
a separate operation, which necessitated re-erection of scaffolding
and an overall delay of four weeks. The builder claimed additional
payment on the ground that the original arrangement for delivery
and the later instructions to build the walls in two stages were
" architect's instructions " involving a variation within clause 1 of
the contract. *Held*, by Sellers J., the original arrangements were
merely part of the nomination, and the later instruction, being the
result of the failure of the supplier to deliver bricks and designed
to assist the builder, was not an instruction for the postponement
of the work within the meaning of clause 1, and consequently the
claim must fail: *Kirk and Kirk Ltd.* v. *Croydon Corporation* (1956).[58]

(2) Contractors undertook to design and carry out pile-driving
work for the foundations of a block of flats for the defendant
council, and that the piles would satisfy certain tests. Conditions
were encountered which rendered it impracticable to carry out
the work in the way which had been contracted for or to satisfy the
tests. The contractors then suggested two other methods of providing the necessary foundations, one which they could carry out themselves, and one involving the engagement of sub-contractors. After
they had submitted prices to him, the defendants' architect wrote,
" we are prepared to accept your proposal that the piles . . . should
be of the bored type in accordance with quotations submitted by
[the sub-contractors]." The contract was in the R.I.B.A. form.
Held, although the contractors would have had no defence to an
action for breach of contract when it became clear that their design
was impracticable, the architect's letter was an architect's instruction
involving a variation in the design or quality of the work within clause
1 of the contract conditions and the contractors were entitled to be
paid for the varied work in accordance with the sub-contractor's
quotation and not at the price originally tendered by them: *Simplex
Concrete Piles Ltd.* v. *St. Pancras Borough Council* (1958).[59]

---

[57] See particularly the *Gloucestershire C.C.* case, illustrated *infra*.

[58] [1956] J.P.L. 585. See also the case of *Tharsis Sulphur & Copper Co.* v. *McElroy*
(1878) 3 App.Cas. 1040, illustrated *infra*, subs. (b) (i), pp. 537–538, and the part of
Lord Blackburn's judgment cited in the illustration *ante*, Chap. 5, Sect. 1, p. 269.

[59] An unreported decision of Pilcher J. Compare, in relation to re-nomination of sub-
contractors, the decision of Lord Goddard L.C.J. in *Rogers* v. *East Suffolk C.C.* (1953)
Q.B.D., R. No. 269 (unreported).

(3) Vandals broke into shop premises, which were being converted, the day before they were due to be completed, and did considerable damage. There was a provision in the specification for protection of the works. The owner's surveyors instructed the contractors to make good the damage at the earliest possible moment. *Held*, by Nield J., the contract was an entire contract which needed to be completed before the contractor was entitled to the price and the contractor was therefore bound to reinstate the damage and could not recover extra payment: *Charon (Finchley)* v. *Singer Sewing Machine Ltd.* (1968).[60]

(4) By clause 13 of the I.C.E. conditions the contractor was required to comply with and adhere strictly to the engineer's instructions and directions on any matter. A contractor driving a sewer in heading under a road ran into an old sewer which collapsed into and flooded his heading. At a meeting on the site with the engineer it was decided to stank off the old sewer at a point off the site, and sink a shaft on the far side of the road and work back to the crossing, which was to be completed in open-cut. The contractor asked about payment, and the engineer replied "I'm not talking to you about money. The inquest will come later." The work done was the only practical way of dealing with the matter, and the contractor admitted he would have done the same thing himself. *Held* by Paull J., what had been done was in nature of a joint decision as to the best way of doing the work. Even if there were instructions under clause 13, they would not create any financial liability for the work, which the contractor was bound to do to complete the contract: *Pearce* v. *Hereford Corporation* (1968).[61]

(5) Clause 20 of the R.I.B.A. (1957 revised) Conditions[62] permitted the contractor to determine the contract if the works were delayed for one month by reason of (*inter alia*) " architects' instructions," and also delay in giving instructions. Cracks appeared in concrete columns supplied by nominated suppliers and erected by the main contractor, and the contractors admitted that they would have stopped work at once in any event. However, the clerk of the works in fact had orally told them to do so. The contractor then wrote to the architect " with reference to the above site, and the instructions to stop all work connected . . . to the perimeter columns we wish to place on record that this will result in delay. . . ." The architect replied by letter " Thank you for your letter of August 21, . . . the contents of which are noted." The contractor's other work finally came to an end on September 23, while investigations as to the cause of the cracking were still proceeding. The contractor wrote a further letter reserving a financial claim but, after the month had expired, terminated the contract without warning on November 8. It subsequently transpired that the cracks in the columns were due to faulty workmanship in their construction, there being excessive quantities of calcium chloride in the mix. The Official Referee held that the oral instructions and letters were not " architect's instructions " under clause 1 of the

---

[60] (1968) 112 S.J. 536, illustrated more fully *ante*, Chap. 5, pp. 271–272.

[61] (1968) 66 L.Q.R. 647.

[62] See the criticism of the policy of this and the present clause, *post*, Chap. 13, p. 682, and further of the present clause *ante*, Chap. 5, pp. 343 and 350.

contract, and that the delay was caused by the defect, and not by the instruction, in any event. The Court of Appeal held that there was an architect's instruction, and (Sellers L.J. dissenting) that and not the defect had caused the delay. *Held*, by the House of Lords, there was an architect's instruction, obedience to which had caused the delay, and the contractor was accordingly entitled to determine the contract: *Gloucestershire C.C.* v. *Richardson* (1969).[63]

[Note: In the above case the report indicates that counsel for the employers conceded that once the cause of the cracks in the columns was discovered the contractors would be entitled to receive instructions from the architect. Neither *Clayton* v. *Woodman* [64] nor *East Ham B.C.* v. *Sunley* [65] appear to have been cited to the House, and it is submitted that this concession was in fact wrong.[66] This view of the law, however, coloured much of the approach to the question whether or not there was an instruction—see *e.g.*, *per* Lord Pearson, who was apparently even prepared to hold that the determination clause would be successfully invoked under its second limb if instructions *necessitated by a breach of contract by the contractor* were delayed. In fact no instructions, it is submitted, are ever owed to a contractor under the terms of building or engineering contracts in respect of his breaches of contract. In particular, there is no *duty* to tell him how to remedy defective work, it is submitted. The true position when the cracks were discovered was, it is submitted, that the employer was, strictly, not bound to take any action at all, and the contractor was, strictly, bound to complete the works, whether or not (as held by the House of Lords, *ante*, Chap. 5) he was in breach of contract in regard to the cracks in the columns. The practical situation was that, on the one hand, the employer had a practical interest to investigate the cause in order (*a*) to consider varying the work if the permanent result after completion would be unsuitable for its purpose in a long-life building if the contractor managed to bring it to completion, or (b) to avoid delays in construction if the building failed during construction, or if remedial work at the expense of the contractor took place later, and also possible claims by third parties; and on the other hand the contractor had an interest since, whether or not he was originally in breach, he would be bound to complete at his own cost if the building failed during construction, and he too would be exposed to claims in tort by third persons. Viewed in this light the exchange of letters between contractor and architect seems difficult to construe as an architect's instruction to cease work, or as other than acquiescence in an inevitable situation, and it is hard not to feel sympathy for the Official Referee's finding of fact, notwithstanding the unanimous views of the Court of Appeal and House of Lords.]

The *Gloucester* case illustrated above is not, of course, strictly a case of variations and on any view is a decision only on its particular

---

[63] [1969] A.C. 480. Illustrated and considered at length on the question whether or not the contractor was in breach of contract, *ante*, Chap. 5, pp. 298–304.

[64] [1962] 2 Q.B. 533 (Salmon J.), [1962] 1 W.L.R. 585 (C.A.), illustrated and referred to *ante*, pp. 68–70, 73, 139–141, 153–155, 324–325, 385–389.

[65] [1966] A.C. 406. See the passages cited therefrom, and also from *A.M.F. International*, *ante*, p. 387.   [66] See also *Kingston-upon-Hull* case, *ante*, p. 388.

facts and correspondence, but it is illustrated to show how easily the courts, who have a tendency to confuse the very wide *powers* which building and engineering contracts undoubtedly confer on architects and engineers with *duties* owed by the employer or his advisers to the contractor, can be persuaded to find that there has been an *instruction*, which is, of course, at least one part of the necessary basis for a variation payment under the terms of these contracts (the other part is, of course, that there should be a variation in fact from the earlier contract intention).

(g) Instructions as to method of working

It has already been shown that the employer or his architect and engineer owe no duty to the contractor regarding the selection of control over the latter's methods of working. It is not uncommon, however, in building contracts, and very common in engineering contracts, to find express provisions giving the architect or engineer power to exercise a degree of control over some specified part of the contractor's methods of working. Such provisions are, of course, intended for the protection of the employer's interest in the quality of the final permanent work, and are not intended to be operated so as necessarily to assist or benefit the contractor. In such a case the correct view may often be that the contractor, in the absence of specific contract prices differing according to the method of work decided upon, accepts whatever method the engineer may decide upon (provided the decision is honest and bona fide) as included in the contract price.

ILLUSTRATION

Clause 10 of an engineering contract provided [67] that the work should be carried out under the direction and to the satisfaction of the engineer. By clause 18 the work was to be executed with the best workmanship and in the best manner to the satisfaction of the engineer. The specification provided that the precise position of trenches would be determined by the engineer as the work proceeded, the trial holes were to be opened ahead of the works and precise distances on plan between new and existing sewers determined as the work proceeded. It also provided by clause 6 of the specification that excavations should be timbered with suitable timber or alternative forms of sheeting other than timber *as and where necessary to the satisfaction of the engineer.* An arbitrator found that the resident engineer unreasonably required timbering in places where excavation by machine and battering the sides of trenches to a slope was practicable, and also unreasonably prohibited the laying of pipes until trenches were excavated for long lengths in bad ground,

[67] *Cf.* clause 13 of the 1955 I.C.E. form.

and that these combined requirements caused the contractor heavy additional expense. The contractors had protested at the time and claimed extra payment, but the engineer had upheld his resident engineer's decision and refused to issue a variation order. *Held*, by Diplock J., clauses 10 and 18 of the conditions and the specification gave the engineer power to determine the method of working; the employers did not warrant his competency or skill, or that his decision should be reasonable, provided he was honest; and that a direction by an engineer intimating the manner in which work was to be carried out in order to satisfy him was neither a breach of contract nor, in the absence of a specific method of carrying out the works being required by the contract, a variation of the work: *Neodox Ltd.* v. *Swinton & Pendlebury B.C.* (1958).[68]

[Note: This case should, it is submitted, be treated with some caution as a decision turning primarily on the special wording of clause 6 of the specification. In the absence of such a special express provision, general provisions like clauses 10 and 18 above do not empower an architect or engineer to do more, it is submitted, than identify defective or potentially defective work and require it to be done again or replaced, and confer no right to interfere with or control the contractor's methods of working from any point of view other than the need to inform him of the final stipulated result required by the contract documents,[69] or to ensure that the work is carried out so as to comply with the contract requirements. If an architect or engineer does step out of his own province into that of the builder [70] in this way by seeking to control the latter's methods of working, and gives an instruction in the absence of some express provision governing the working methods of the contractor, that instruction, if the contractor can prove that he would, left to himself, have done the work differently and still have produced a satisfactory result will, it is submitted, amount to a variation unless some express term in the contract provides to the contrary. Generally speaking, it is submitted that it will not be the sense of a building contract that the contractor will undertake to obey any such instructions free of charge where they do not implement some express provision and are not necessary for the production of a satisfactory result, and a potent factor in support of this will usually be found in the terms of modern arbitration clauses which, whatever express powers of this kind may be conferred on the architect or engineer, will usually provide for a review of his decisions in general terms which would lack all force if bona fide but mistaken instructions did not give rise to liability.]

SECTION 2. THE POWER TO ORDER VARIATIONS

From the preceding section it has been seen that the power to order variations contained in a building or engineering contract needs to be

---

[68] [1958] Q.B.D. (special paper) Diplock J. (unreported).
[69] See *ante*, pp. 68–70, 139–141, 153–155, 324–325, 385–388, 399–400 and the important cases of *Clayton* v. *Woodman* [1962] 2 Q.B. 533; *Kingston-upon-Hull Corporation* v. *Harding* [1892] 2 Q.B. 494 and *A.M.F. International* v. *Magnet Bowling* [1968] 1 W.L.R. 1028 there referred to and quoted.
[70] See the language of Pearson L.J. in *Clayton's* case, illustrated *ante*, p. 73.

carefully considered and construed only in a relatively limited number of situations in practice, namely,

(a) where the work claimed for is in actual fact a variation, in the sense that on a true construction of the contract it is not included in the contract price, and either

(b) where the contractor is unable to show that the employer expressly or impliedly authorised the variation in question, or

(c) where, although the contractor can show the employer's knowledge of or authority for the variation, there is a provision in the contract denying legal effect to any express or implied promise to pay by the employer.

In these cases (which occur relatively seldom in practice) it is necessary to consider whether the contractor can obtain payment by reliance on the variation clause. Such clauses vary greatly. In some of the older cases there was a tendency to construe the range of matters as to which an order might be given somewhat strictly if the language was ambiguous, but it may be doubted whether this would be so at the present day. The following case, for instance, probably turned, at least partly, on the then strict rules of pleading, and it is suggested that virtually any alteration or variation of work can be covered at the present day by a clause giving a power to add or omit work.

ILLUSTRATION

The defendant agreed with His Majesty's Commissioners of Customs to build a certain house, excavate ground, and pile foundations, etc. The contract provided that in case " the commissioners or their successors, or the surveyor by them appointed, should at any times or time order or direct any extra work to be done or executed, or that any part of the work should not be done or executed," then the amount of such work should be added to or deducted from the sum contracted for, as the case might be. The builder, by direction of the surveyor, built the foundations of a customs house without certain piling specified, and filled up some spandrils (that is to say, the V-shaped space on the top of the arches, where they meet) with broken materials instead of with solid brickwork or cross-walls, as specified. In an action on the bond the defendant pleaded that the piling was not possible and that the surveyor had ordered him to vary the work, and that the piling was abandoned. The jury found that the piling could have been done, but that written orders were given to vary the work, but the commissioners applied for judgment *non obstante veredicto. Held*, that no power was given to vary, but that the power was limited to such extra works as might be done, or something which was to be omitted, and that as the defendant had not pleaded that the variation was in the nature of an addition or omission, the Crown was entitled to succeed: *R.* v. *Peto* (1826).[71]

[Note: This decision can also be justified by the view that an architect will generally not have authority to vary work even under an express power to vary, so as to make it practicable, since the contractor is already bound to do whatever is necessary to complete.[72]]

The power to vary in modern contracts is usually extremely wide, however, and difficulties of construction of this nature are not likely to occur frequently in practice.

Where the contract contains a power to order additional work, there is no implied term that, if additions are desired, the employer must necessarily employ the contractor to carry them out.

ILLUSTRATION

An engineering contract provided that the engineer might in his discretion require the contractor to do certain work outside the contract. *Held,* that there was no implied contract that, if the engineer wished this work to be done, the contractor should have the right to do it: *Gilbert Blasting & Dredging Co.* v. *R.* (1901).[73]

On the other hand, the contractor is normally entitled to occupation of the site, so that in the absence of any reservation entitling the owner to send workmen or other contractors on to the site during the progress of the works, the contractor could object to any other person being brought on to the site during this period to execute other work or alterations in the works which he has undertaken. Thus the 1963 standard forms of contract issued by the R.I.B.A. contain the following clause:

" The Contractor shall permit the execution of work not forming part of this contract by artists, tradesmen or others engaged by the Employer. . . ." [74]

The contractor, however, is entitled to perform all the contract work, so that a provision giving to the employer, his architect or engineer a power to make omissions only contemplates genuine omissions, that is, things which are to be entirely omitted from the works. The employer is not, it is submitted, entitled to use the power

---

[71] 1 Y. & J.Ex. 37. *Note*: Moulton L.J., in an unreported case of *Stevens* v. *Mewes & Davis* (1901), June 8 (C.A.), referring to the case of *R.* v. *Peto,* said: " It is no decision as to what the powers of an architect are when there is express power to vary; it was a decision certainly that in the absence of the word ' vary ' you must prove that this change may be fairly considered to be an addition or an omission."

[72] See *ante*, Chap. 2, Section 4 (2) and Chap. 5, Section 1, pp. 267 *et seq.*, and the *Tharsis* case as there illustrated, p. 269.

[73] 7 Can.Ex.R. 221.

[74] Clause 29. *Cf.* clause 31 of the 1955 I.C.E. form.

to omit work from the contract works in order to give it to another contractor to do, whether under a provision similar to the above clause or otherwise.

ILLUSTRATIONS

(1) A building contract gave power to order omissions from the contract without in any way affecting or making void the contract, and provided that there should be a deduction from the contract price by a fair and reasonable valuation. *Held*, that the word " omission " contemplated things to be left out of the contract altogether, not such as were taken out of the contract and given to another contractor: *Gallagher* v. *Hirsch* (1899).[75]

(2) A building contract contained a provision that the architect might in his absolute discretion issue written instructions in regard to the omission of any work. It also provided that no variation should vitiate the contract. Under the terms of the contract the employer was to provide structural steel, which was to be fabricated by the contractor. After a considerable delay in the start of the work due to the fault of the employer, the architect informed the contractor that the employer had made his own arrangements for the structural steel to be supplied and fabricated and that the work of fabrication should be omitted from the contract. The contractor refused to go on with the work, claiming that the employer had broken the contract in two fundamental respects, namely, failure to hand over the site on the due date, and the omission of the work of fabrication. *Held*, both breaches had been established. Apart from the question of handing over the site, the breach involved in omitting the fabrication, which was deliberate, was a further indication that the employer did not regard himself as bound by the contract, and the contractor was entitled to damages for the employer's repudiation: *Carr* v. *J. A. Berriman Pty. Ltd.* (1953).[76]

It is submitted that this principle applies equally where an employer wishes to nominate a sub-contractor or supplier in a case where the work is billed or otherwise described as being carried out by the contractor in the ordinary way. In the absence of express provision (not to be found in the standard forms in England) it is submitted that the employer cannot omit the contractor's work and add it back in nominated form.

The authority of the architect to order extras or other variations may not always need to depend upon a provision in the contract between the builder and the employer. Thus, if a building owner consults with his architect and authorises him to order a variation knowing it to be such, he will be liable to the builder under the general law, whether or not the variation falls within any power to

[75] N.Y. 45 App.Div. 467, N.Y.Supp. 61.607.
[76] 27 A.L.J. 273 (Australia).

order variations under the contract, and whether or not any requirements of form in the contract are complied with [77] (unless there is some express provision making compliance with the prescribed form in all cases a condition of recovery by the builder,[78] and no such provision, it may be pointed out, is to be found in the current R.I.B.A. forms of contract). Nor, it is submitted, does clause 51 (2) of the 1955 I.C.E. forms, which in regard to variations ordered by the engineer provides that " No *such* variation shall be made by the contractor without an order in writing," amount to such a provision.[79] But where the extent of the architect's express authority to order extras or other variations must, in the absence of explicit authority from the employer, depend upon the terms of the building contract, if it is provided in the building contract that in ordering extras the architect shall use a certain form, his authority to order extras would not be validly exercised if that form was not used and the employer would not be bound by the architect's act. Not only has an architect no implied authority to order extra works or other variations,[80] or to promise to pay extra for work under the variation clause which the contractor is already under an obligation to perform for the contract price,[80a] but he cannot without express authority make new contracts for work wholly outside the contract, or certify for payment therefor, or in any other way vary the terms upon which the work is to be done.[81]

(1) Orders in Writing

(a) What are orders in writing

Most contracts provide that the power to order variations must be exercised by the architect in writing.

In determining whether or not any particular document is a written order within the meaning of the contract, it should be remembered that there must, from the nature of the work to be carried out, be constant written and other communications between the builder and the engineer or architect in which the drawings are explained and instructions are given as to the carrying out of the work. It is more than probable that one or more of these communications may contain instructions which are thought to involve extras, and disputes

---

[77] See (3) (*a*), *infra*, and *supra*, pp. 506–507.

[78] See (2) (*c*), *infra*.

[79] See, *e.g.* the provisions in *Myers* v. *Sarl*; *Tharsis Sulphur & Copper Co.* v. *McElroy*; and *Smyth* v. *R.*, illustrated *infra*, (2) (*a*), pp. 537–538.

[80] See, *e.g. Ashwell & Nesbitt* v. *Allen, ante,* Chap. 7, p. 410.

[80a] *Supra*, pp. 523–524.

[81] See Chap. 2, pp. 106–111, and the cases there referred to, and a possible exception in the case of architects who are officers of local authorities.

frequently arise in consequence. For the purpose of avoiding this kind of dispute, contracts sometimes provide that work must be ordered as an extra, or that the order must be given in a prescribed form in order to found a claim upon it, or that the contractor must give notice if he proposes to claim an extra, in order that the matter may be clear. The clause in the I.C.E. form of contract designed for this purpose is particularly complicated and ill-drafted.

ILLUSTRATION

By the second proviso to clause 52 (2) of the I.C.E. form of contract no increase in price or variation of rates under that clause was to be made unless " as soon after the date of the Engineer's order as is practicable, and in the case of extra or additional work before the commencement of the work or as soon thereafter as is practicable " notice in writing was given of the contractor's intention to claim extra payment or a varied rate. Sub-clause (4) of the same clause required the contractor to furnish detailed particulars once a month of " any additional expense to which the contractor may consider himself entitled and of all extra or additional work ordered by the engineer which he has executed during the preceding month, and no claim for any such work will be considered which has not been included in such particulars. Provided always that the engineer shall be entitled to authorise payment to be made for any work notwithstanding the contractor's failure to comply with this condition if the contractor has at the earliest practicable opportunity notified the engineer that he intends to make a claim for such work." There were two contracts between the parties in these terms. Under one contract work started on July 6, 1951. On July 24, the engineers sent a drawing which they required the contractor to follow, and on December 30, 1951, the contractor wrote: " With reference to your letter of July 24, last . . . we shall, as you will appreciate, require reimbursement for the additional work entailed in carrying out your instructions." Under the second contract, the instruction was given on August 15, 1951, the contractors wrote a similar letter on February 6, 1952, and work did not in fact start until March 12, 1952. The contractors never sent in monthly detailed particulars. *Held*, by the Court of Appeal, (1) the notice in the proviso to clause 52 (4) was not, as the employers contended, a notice in relation to work carried out in a particular month, (2) *per* Willmer and Upjohn L.JJ., in any event, clause 52 (4) as a whole was only applicable to the right of the contractor to receive interim payment and not to his ultimate right to receive payment, so that even if the engineer refused to exercise his discretion under the proviso this was not a final bar to the contractor's claim. *Per* Pearson L.J., the first sentence of clause 52 (4) was a very stringent provision against which the proviso gave a discretionary power to alleviate hardship to the engineer or an arbitrator, (3) *per* Willmer L.J., the effect of the proviso to clause 52 (2) was that notice must be served as soon as practicable *or* before the commencement of work in the case of extra work; the word " and " did not mean " and also," so that two notices were not required; (4) that a notice under clause 52 (2) or the proviso to clause 52 (4) need only indicate the intention to make a claim and identify in general terms the additional work to · which the claim would relate when precisely formulated, (5) that the letters satisfied this test, and (6) that there was evidence on which the arbitrator could find that notice was given as soon as was practicable—*per* Willmer L.J., the contractors must be allowed a reasonable time to make up their minds. Being a limited company, the matter was of sufficient importance to require to be considered by the board or management. It was not an easy matter in this case to decide whether the instructions did or did not involve extra work, and study and consideration of the specification was necessary for the purpose: *Tersons Ltd.* v. *Stevenage Development Corporation* (1964).[82]

Where a written order is provided for, prima facie, and in the absence of any special provision, a written order *prior* to the execution of the work is intended. Pollock C.B. in *Lamprell* v. *Billericay Union*[83] said: " The deed when it requires written directions clearly means written directions before the additional works should be done. A subsequent written approval, even if the documents in evidence amount to that, is a very different thing from a previous order to the builders." As a result modern contracts frequently contain provisions for " subsequent sanction in writing " of variations,[84] or for confirmation in writing.[85] Interim certificates, being given after the varied work has started and being also by their nature subject to review on the final certificate,[86] cannot constitute an order in writing, though they might well, it is submitted, constitute " subsequent sanction " in writing[87] if they included on their face sums for the varied work. It has been seen that payment under interim certificates does not in general create an estoppel against the employer in respect of any type of claim by the contractor,[88] and in any event, as already pointed out, even an order in writing will not normally bind the employer if the work is not in fact a variation.

Requirements of form, however, if specified, must be complied with if the employer is to be bound. Thus an unsigned sketch made by an architect's assistant was held not to be a " direction by the architect in writing under his hand".[89] The cases and discussion

[82] [1963] 2 Lloyd's Rep. 333. See also on this clause *Blackford* case, *ante*, p. 314.
[83] (1849) 18 L.J.Ex. 282.
[84] See clause 11 (1) of the 1963 R.I.B.A. form. See *infra*, under heading (b).
[85] See clause 51 (2) of the 1955 I.C.E. form. See *infra*, under heading (b).
[86] See *ante*, Chap. 7, pp. 492 *et seq*.
[87] See pp. 538–539, *infra*.
[88] See the case of *Royston U.D.C.* v. *Royston Builders Ltd.* (1961) 177 E.G. 589, *ante*, Chap. 1, Section 9, p. 58.
[89] *Myers* v. *Sarl* (1860) 3 E. & E. 306; 30 L.J.Q.B. 9, *infra*.

ante, Chapter 7, Section 6 (7), should be considered as well as the cases below.

ILLUSTRATIONS

(1) The plaintiff covenanted by deed with a corporation to do certain special work for the sum of £5,500, and that if their architects Messrs. S. & M. should require any alterations or additions in the progress of the works, the architects should give to the plaintiff written instructions signed by them, and he should not be considered as having authority for the same without such written instructions. The plaintiff did additional works but no written authority or directions were given by the architects for the additional works, except letters, given in evidence, some signed by Mr. S. and the others by Mr. M., written during the progress of the works, in which allusion was incidentally made to some of the additional works in progress, and which contained suggestions as to the mode of executing them, and save also that long after the works were all complete, the architects, on the application of the plaintiff, made a valuation of the additional works, which they estimated at £3,133, and signed a paper stating that to be the amount of their valuation. *Held*, that the meaning of the condition being that a previous written authority should be given by the architects to the plaintiff, the letters written by them did not amount to such previous authority: *Lamprell* v. *Billericay Union* (1848).[90]

(2) In a contract under seal, by which the plaintiff contracted to build for the defendant a house and premises for a certain sum, it was provided that " no alterations or additions should be admitted unless directed by the defendant's architect by writing under his hand." In an action on the contract: *Held*, that sketches and drawings prepared in the office of the architect by his clerks and not signed by him or them were not sufficient written orders under the contract: *Myers* v. *Sarl* (1860).[91]

(3) A contract for the construction of large iron buildings for a lump sum contained a clause, *inter alia*, that no alterations or additions should be made without written order from the employers' engineer, and that no allegation by the contractors of knowledge of, or acquiescence in, such alterations or additions on the part of the employers, their engineers or inspectors, should be accepted or available as equivalent to the certificate of the engineer, or as in any way superseding the necessity of such certificate as the sole warrant for such alterations and additions. During the execution of the contract the contractors alleged that it was impossible to cast certain iron trough girders of a specified weight; and subsequently they were allowed to erect girders of a much heavier weight; and the actual weights were entered in the engineer's certificates issued from time to time authorising interim payments. On the completion of the work the contractor claimed a considerable amount in excess of the contract price for the extra weight of metal supplied. *Held*, reversing the decision of the court below, that the engineer's certificates were not

---

[90] 18 L.J.Ex. 282.
[91] 3 E. & E. 306.

written orders, and that the claim was therefore excluded by the terms of the contract: *Tharsis Sulphur and Copper Co.* v. *McElroy* (1878).[92]

(4) A contract provided that " no extras, additions, deviations, or alterations whatever will be . . . paid for which shall be done without an order in writing." Extra work was in fact included in a progress certificate, but not stated to be extra work. A note, not signed by the engineer, was pinned to this certificate referring to the payment on account of extra work, " to be paid and made right in next certificate," and the voucher for payment showed this amount as paid as a part of the contract price. The amount was never allowed as an extra in any subsequent certificate, and in the final certificate the payment for it was credited to the employer among the general payments under the contract. *Held*, that the engineer had not recognised and authorised the payment as an extra and that it was not recoverable by the contractor: *Smyth* v. *R.* (1884).[93]

(b) Confirmation or subsequent sanction in writing

A builder faced with a verbal instruction by an architect which he considers involves a variation may be placed in a dilemma, since contracts frequently provide that he must obey all instructions of the architect. In practice, too, clerks of works frequently give oral instructions of one kind or another, though their authority under most forms of contract is so restricted that such instructions have no legal force, albeit the architect may condone the practice. To meet the contractor's difficulties in such situations, it is frequently provided that if the architect or clerk of works gives an instruction orally which under the contract the architect has express power to give in writing, the contractor may confirm the instruction in writing to the architect, and if the architect does not then dissent in writing within a specified time the instruction is deemed to be an instruction in writing of the architect, so that the contractor may be paid for any extra work involved.[94] In addition, to avoid injustice where the building owner has benefited from extra work ordered verbally, contracts frequently give to the architect a power subsequently to sanction in writing extra or varied work which has been carried out without an order in writing, and provide that variations so sanctioned shall be measured and valued in the same way as those ordered in writing beforehand.[95] Whereas this power was quite general in the pre-1963 R.I.B.A. forms it is now limited in the current forms[96] to

---

[92] 3 App.Cas. 1040. See also the illustration of this case and the part of Lord Blackburn's judgment cited *ante*, Chap. 5, p. 269.

[93] (1884) 1 N.Z.L.R. 80 (C.A.)

[94] The new provision in the 1963 R.I.B.A. forms relating to confirmation of the clerk of work's instructions is unintentionally self-defeating, and confirmation under this clause has no practical advantage for the contractor—see clause 10.

[95] *Cf.* clause 9 of the pre–1963 R.I.B.A. form of contract.

[96] Clause 11 (1).

variations made by the contractor " otherwise than pursuant to an instruction of the architect," so that it is arguable that under this form the architect has no power to sanction in writing instructions given by him orally, except under the special power contained in clause 2 (3), proviso (b), of the conditions. The post-1963 R.I.B.A. forms are most obscurely drafted on the whole subject of orders in writing, but fortunately contain no prohibition against separate contracts or authorisations with or by the employer. The power of subsequent confirmation in the I.C.E. form is specifically confined to variations ordered orally by the engineer.[97]

An interim certificate specifically authorising payment for varied work does, it is submitted, constitute subsequent sanction or confirmation by the architect or engineer of a variation, though it will not, of course, preclude the employer from arguing that the work was not in fact a variation.

(c) Where an order in writing is a condition precedent to payment for extra work

A contract may be so worded that an order in writing, or written confirmation of an oral order, or written sanction of work done, is a condition precedent to any right to be paid for extras.[98] If so, it will not avail the builder that the employer has actually authorised or ordered the variation in question.[99]

ILLUSTRATIONS

(1) An engineering contract provided that the contractor should not be entitled to claim for extra work without instructions in writing signed by the engineer. *Held,* that an account of the moneys due to the contractor in respect of works done under the contract was a proper subject of a suit in equity, but that a direction for an account of works done under the contract did not authorise an account of extra works done by the contractor with the privity of the employers without written instructions: *Nixon* v. *Taff Railway* (1848).[1]

(2) The plaintiffs agreed by a contract under seal to build two ships for the defendants, and that they should not make any alterations unless on the authority of a letter signed by the secretary of the defendants stating that the court of directors had directed the alterations to be made and specifying the precise amount which the defendants would allow. The defendants required alterations

---

[97] Clause 51 (2) of the 1955 form.
[98] See the cases (3), (4) and (5) illustrated *infra.*
[99] See the cases (1) and (2) *supra.* There are, however, cases to the contrary—see, *e.g. Melville* v. *Carpenter,* illustrated *infra,* p. 547.
[1] 7 Hare 136.

to be made. but there was never any such letter signed by the secretary. The plaintiffs sued at law for the price of the alterations. *Held*, the requirement of the deed that alterations should only be made upon the authority of a letter signed by the secretary of the defendants, etc., could only be discharged by deed and as that had not been done the plaintiffs could not recover at law; whether they had relief in equity was not a matter for the opinion of the court: *The Thames Ironworks Co.* v. *R. M. Steam Packet Co.* (1861).[2]

(3) A contract provided that no charges should be demanded for extras, but any additions which might be made by order in writing of the defendant's agent should be paid for at a price to be previously agreed upon in writing. *Held*, that the plaintiff could not recover for alterations and additions during the performance of the contract, not being able to show written orders for the same: *Russell* v. *Sa da Bandeira* (1862).[3]

(4) The plaintiff sued for extras on a building contract. The contract provided that the plaintiff was not to do any extra work unless upon the authority of the architect in writing, and for a weekly bill to be delivered to the architect at latest during the week following that in which the work was done. The certificate of the architect was to be conclusive evidence of the work having been duly completed. There was an arbitration clause. The plaintiff did not have the written authority of the architect for the extras. *Held*, the plaintiff could not recover for the extras and, that being so, was not entitled to damages for the defendants' refusal to go to arbitration on his claim: *Brunsden* v. *Staines Local Board* (1884).[4]

(5) The plaintiffs erected works for the defendants under a contract which provided: " The contractor shall execute all alterations and additions which shall be ordered by the county surveyor, but if the contractor shall be of the opinion that any such alterations or additions will cause additional expense, he shall not be bound to execute the same without an order in writing signed by the clerk of the county council. . . ." The clerk of works of the defendants verbally instructed the plaintiffs' managing director that a part of the works was to be dressed with a kind of stone more expensive than that specified by the contract. *Held*, that in the absence of any order in writing as provided by the contract, the claim for the increased cost failed: *Taverner & Co. Ltd.* v. *Glamorgan County Council* (1940).[5]

Although an order in writing may be a condition precedent to the contractor's right to recover payment, the existence of a written order is not conclusive evidence against the employer that the work to which it relates is in fact an extra, and the employer may resist payment on the ground that the work is really included in the contract,

---

[2] 13 C.B.(N.S.) 358. (Since 1875 the reference to a discharge by deed no longer obtains.)
[3] 13 C.B.(N.S.) 149.   Illustrated further, *infra* subs. (d), p. 552.
[4] 1 Cab. & E. 272.
[5] 57 T.L.R. 243.

provided always that the decision of the architect is not by the contract made final, as for instance where the architect is required to certify as to extras and there is no overriding arbitration clause.[6]

Notwithstanding a provision preventing recovery without a written order, it has, however, been held that where a contractor requests an order in writing on the ground that an instruction involves a variation, and the architect refuses to give the order in writing, an arbitrator empowered to determine this matter can award payment despite the absence of a written order. It is submitted that the reason is that an arbitration clause in sufficiently wide terms is a clear indication that the requirement of writing must in such a situation yield to the over-riding intention that the matter should be open to review. It is further submitted that in the absence of an arbitration the courts would have the same power of review as the arbitrator.[7]

ILLUSTRATIONS

(1) L. agreed to build a theatre, hotel and other buildings for M. The contract provided that no works beyond those included in the contract would be allowed or paid for without an order in writing from the employer and architect. M. insisted upon certain works being performed and asserted that they were included in the contract. L. said that those works were extras and would be charged as such. M. would not give an order in writing. *Held*, by the P.C., affirming the Supreme Court of Western Australia, that L. could recover the cost of those works upon an implied promise to pay. " As Molloy (the employer) insisted on the works being done, in spite of what the contractor told him, the umpire naturally inferred (and it was for him to draw the inference) that the employer impliedly promised that the works would be paid for either as included in the contract price or, if he were wrong in his view, by extra payment to be assessed by the architect. It is difficult to see how the umpire could have drawn any other inference from the facts as found by him without attributing dishonesty to Molloy ": *Molloy* v. *Liebe* (1910).[8]

(2) A contract for the construction of a reservoir provided that " no extra charges in respect of extra work or works will be allowed . . . unless such works shall have been ordered in writing by the engineer," and also, " It is to be distinctly understood that the corporation shall not become liable to the payment of any charge in respect of any (such) additions, alterations or deviations unless the instruction for the performance of the same shall have been given in writing by the engineer." The contract further stipulated that the

---

[6] See *ante*, Chap. 7, Section 3.

[7] See *ante*, Chap. 7, pp. 447–448, and the cases there referred to.

[8] 102 L.T. 616. Distinguish the case of *Morton Construction* v. *City of Hamilton* [1962] O.R. 154 (Canada) illustrated *ante*, Chap. 1, Section 2 (8), p. 18.

orders in writing should be given in a special form which expressly acknowledged that the work was a variation. The contract contained an arbitration clause which provided that, " In case any dispute or difference shall arise between the corporation, or the engineer on their behalf, and the contractor either during the progress of the works or after the determination, abandonment, or breach of the contract, as to the construction of the contract or as to any matter or thing arising thereunder . . . *or as to any objection by the contractor to any certificate, finding, decision, requisition or opinion of the engineer*, then either party shall forthwith give to the other notice of such dispute or difference, and such dispute or difference shall be referred to the arbitration and final decision of a single arbitrator to be agreed upon by the corporation and the contractor." Either party could require a dispute or difference to be determined forthwith, and the arbitrator was empowered to decide whether to hear it at once, or to await completion of the work.

Disputes arose during the progress of the works as to requirements by the engineer for executing certain portions of the work in a particular manner and with certain materials. The contractor contended that these requirements were extras, for which he was entitled to be paid in addition to the contract price. The engineer refused to give written orders for these items on the ground that in his opinion they were included in the contract. The contractor carried out the work as required by the engineer, and on completion of the contract the matter was referred to arbitration. The arbitrator awarded certain sums to be paid to the contractor in respect of the extras claimed for. *Held* by the House of Lords, that by arrangement between the engineer and the contractor the arbitration had been stood over until the works were completed, and that the arbitrator had power so to award notwithstanding the absence of any orders in writing by the engineer.

Per Lord Finlay L.C.: " The dispute was whether the item was an extra for which an order in writing should be given, and when the parties agreed that the work should be done and that the question should stand over for arbitration, the effect of the contract is that the finding of the arbitrator is to take the place of the order in writing which ought to have been given. Otherwise the postponed arbitration would be entirely useless." *Per* Lord Wrenbury: " I rest my judgment not upon any authority of the arbitrator to waive a condition precedent, or to supply the want of the engineer's order in writing, but upon holding, as I do, that the arbitration clause has remitted it to the arbitrator to determine that work or materials are extras, and that payment is due for them under the contract, notwithstanding that the engineer wrongly, as the arbitrator finds, refused to give an order in writing." *Per* Lord Atkinson: " It would, *a priori*, I think be natural to expect that where the parties by the contract provided an alternative mode of avoiding these embarrassing contingencies and escaping from such an impasse—namely, arbitration— they intended that arbitration should have a reach and operation adequate to solve the matters in dispute, and not an arbitration so restricted in its scope as to be absolutely abortive, leaving the parties to it in a position, for all practical purposes, the same as that which they occupied before it had been held. . . . I entirely concur with Bankes L.J. in thinking that the real dispute between the parties which was referred to the arbitrator, and which his award was to determine finally, was whether or not the contractor should under the circumstances be paid for the work he in fact executed, though no written order had been given for it by the engineer": *Brodie* v. *Cardiff Corporation* (1919).[9]

(3) A pile-driving sub-contract incorporated provisions of the main contract, under which the engineer had power to order variations in writing, his decision as to what constituted a variation being final, and an order in writing being a condition precedent of payment. Just before commencing part of his work the sub-contractor received amended plans requiring him to drive his piles to greater depths. He contended that there was a variation, the engineer contended there was not, and the main contractor stated he could only conform to the engineer's view. The sub-contractor carried out the work under protest and in the British Columbia Court of Appeal was awarded payment for all work done by him on a *quantum meruit* basis. *Held*, by the Supreme Court of Canada (Cartwright J. dissenting), that it was impossible to imply a new contract when both parties were maintaining contrary positions when the work was carried out, and that the proper remedy of the sub-contractor was to refuse performance except on his own interpretation of the sub-contract, and if this was rejected, elect to treat the contract as repudiated: *Peter Kiewit & Sons* v. *Eakins Construction Ltd.* (1960).[10]

[Note: It is difficult not to agree with the vigorous dissenting judgment of Cartwright J. on the point that it was asking too much of a party in a case of doubtful interpretation to risk a wrongful repudiation by ceasing work.[11] Neither *Brodie's* case nor *Molloy* v. *Liebe* appear to have been cited. It is submitted that there is no inherent difficulty in implying a promise to pay reasonable remuneration if wrong, while contending that the contract prices cover the work, and this did not disturb the court in *Molloy* v. *Liebe*. It is suggested that the decision itself was correct on the wording of the very severe variation clause in the main contract, which made the engineer's decision final. If his decision had been open to arbitration, it is submitted that the decision should have gone the other way on the authority of *Brodie's* case.]

(2) Recovery of Payment for Extra Work without an Order in Writing

(a) Where an order in writing is not a condition precedent to payment for extra work

A clause as to orders in writing may be so worded that such orders will not be a condition precedent to the contractor's right to payment,

---

[9] [1919] A.C. 337. Clearly the request and refusal before doing the work are the basis of this and the preceding case.

[10] 22 D.L.R. 465 (Canada).

[11] *Cf.* the analogous cases on repudiation, *ante*, Chap. 5, p. 344, where the courts have held that a party holding to an erroneous but honest view of the contract cannot be regarded as repudiating it. In the present case, however, the contractor could not maintain his view without ceasing work, which would therefore inevitably involve repudiation if he was wrong. See, however, the cases *ante*, Chap. 1, p. 18.

e.g. where a clause provides that the contractor shall execute such alterations as the architect may direct in writing, and does not exclude any claim for work not so ordered.[12] In such a case there is nothing to prevent the employer being liable under the general law on a separate contract express or implied.

ILLUSTRATION

A contract for the erection of a church according to certain plans and specifications provided that if the defendants should at any time desire to make any alterations or additions, the plaintiff should erect the church with such alterations and additions as the defendants or one S. should direct, by writing under his or their hand. Certain extra work was done at the desire of the defendants, though not expressed in writing under their hand. *Held,* that the plaintiff was entitled to recover therefor, for the contract did not provide that no such work was to be allowed or paid for, unless ordered in writing, which would have prevented the plaintiff's recovering, but merely that the plaintiff was bound to execute such extra work as the defendants or S. should direct in writing to be done: *Diamond* v. *McAnnany* (1865).[13]

Such a separate contract can be inferred from any circumstances which show that the employer requested or knew of a variation which was for his benefit and which the builder had been asked to carry out, and which he must as a reasonable person have realised would involve extra expense. Thus in a Canadian case it has been said: " What amounted to instructions from the defendant is dependent on the circumstances relating to each item. If the defendant, without giving definite instructions, knew the plaintiff was doing extra work or supplying extra materials and stood by and approved of what was being done and encouraged the plaintiff to do it, that, in my opinion, amounts to an implied instruction to the plaintiff, and the defendant is liable." [14] The principle is well illustrated in the following case where the employer in such circumstances even became liable to a sub-contractor.

ILLUSTRATION

T. contracted with the defendant to do the plastering for the defendant's house, and thereupon sub-contracted the work to the plaintiff. It appeared that the plastering did not dry fast enough and that the defendant's architect, *in the presence of the*

---

[12] *Cf.* clause 2 of the 1963 R.I.B.A. form of contract.
[13] 16 Up.Can.C.P. 9.
[14] *Re Chittick and Taylor* (1954) 12 W.W.R. 653 (Canada) at p. 655 *per* Egbert J. in the Alberta Supreme Court. See also the county court case of *Williams* v. *Williams and Coatsworth* (1955) 105 L.J. 124.

defendant, requested the plaintiff to gauge it, *i.e.* mix plaster of paris, work which was distinct and totally different from ordinary plastering. Martin B. directed the jury that the first question was whether the architect was the agent of the defendant to order the work and that if he was, the plaintiff being told to do extra work which he was not bound to do, what could he understand but that the defendant was to pay him for it. The plaintiff obtained a verdict: *Wallis* v. *Robinson* (1862).[15]

On the other hand, the employer's mere presence at and interest in the works does not amount to standing by. Knowledge of the true position is clearly essential.

ILLUSTRATION

Road trustees stipulated in a contract with a road contractor that " no additional work should be done with a view of extra payment without a written order of the trustees or their surveyor." The contractor claimed for certain additional cuttings, for which no order in writing was produced, and alleged that the greater part of the trustees " lived in the neighbourhood of the said road, took a great interest in its progress and formation according to the most approved plan, and went frequently along it while it was in the course of execution," and that they had fully assented to the line and levels of the road as finished. *Held*, that the plaintiff could not recover. " I think it impossible to supply the want of a written order by the averment that the road trustees frequently saw the progress of the work, and took an interest in it and must be, therefore, barred from objecting now to the additional works and cuttings claimed, since they did not challenge them at the time. They were not bound to suppose that Brown was working without reference to his contract or was performing extra work, so long as they were aware that he had no written order to do so." *Per* the Lord President (Hope): in *Brown* v. *Lord Rollo* (1831).[16]

It is submitted that where work is undertaken by a contractor at a given price the employer will not, by assenting to or even requesting an alteration from the original plan, render himself liable to pay extra for it, unless he is either expressly informed or must necessarily from the nature of the work be aware that the alteration will increase the expense; and even then the employer will not be liable to pay extra if the circumstances are that the variation is assented to by way of a concession to the contractor, since in such circumstances no promise to pay extra for the altered work could properly be implied.[16a]

ILLUSTRATIONS

(1) L. contracted to do carpenter's work for a lump sum. He then suggested certain alterations to his employer, which were not

---

[15] 3 F. & F. 307.
[16] 10 S. 667 (Ct. of Sess.).
[16a] See also *supra*, Section 1 (2) (*f*), pp. 524 *et seq.*

of such a kind as necessarily to import an increase of expense, and did not tell him that they would increase the expense. The employer assented. *Held,* that the employer was not liable for more than the contract price: *Lovelock* v. *King* (1831).[17]

(2) The plaintiff agreed to build and complete a house to the satisfaction of the defendant or her surveyor for £220. During the course of the work the plaintiff suggested certain alterations to the defendant to which the defendant agreed, but the defendant did not agree to pay extra, nor were the alterations of the sort that unskilled persons would necessarily know would cause an increase of expense or were not included in the specification. Neither the defendant nor her surveyor expressed satisfaction. The plaintiff sued for the balance of an account made out by measure and value, although the defendant had never agreed to pay by measure and value. *Held,* the plaintiff should be non-suited. *Per curiam* on motion for a rule nisi: " It is peculiarly important with respect to additions to the contract price that the employer should be satisfied that they are in respect of matters not included in the specification ": *Johnson* v. *Weston* (1859).[18]

(b) Where there is an arbitration clause

As has already been mentioned, even where an order in writing is a condition precedent to the recovery of payment for extra work, if there is an appropriately worded arbitration clause in the contract, the contractor may be able to recover payment for extra work where the contractor has, before commencing the work, requested and the architect has refused to give an order in writing, and his ruling is disputed by the contractor.[19]

(c) Where it would be a fraud on the contractor to rely on the absence of an order in writing

Even in the case where there is no arbitration clause, and a written order is a condition precedent, if an architect gives an order for work which the contractor considers to be no part of the contract, and refuses therefore to execute it without a written order, but the architect or the employer, while refusing the written order, requests him to carry out the work without prejudice to his right to make a claim for it, it becomes, it is submitted, a question for the court whether the work or materials are within the contract or not, and the employer would be estopped or otherwise prevented from setting up the absence of written orders as a defence to an action by the builder,

---

[17] 1 Moo. & Rob. 60.
[18] 1 F. & F. 693. See also *Tharsis Sulphur & Copper Co.* v. *McElroy* (1878) 3 App.Cas. 1040, illustrated *ante,* pp. 537–538, and *Kirk & Kirk Ltd.* v. *Croydon Corp., ante,* p. 526.
[19] *Brodie* v. *Cardiff Corporation, supra,* pp. 541–543.

as this would plainly be a fraud on the builder and inconsistent with the request made to him.[20]

It is also suggested that where an *employer* (as opposed to his architect) orders varied work orally which he is told or knows will cost extra, the court will imply a promise to pay for that work despite the absence of a written order, especially where any other inference from the facts would be to attribute dishonesty to the employer. It would, it is submitted, be strong evidence of fraud if an employer, desiring alterations or additions to be made by a contractor, and knowing that they would cost more than the contract price, were to request the contractor to do the work and stand by and see the expenditure going on upon the alterations or additions and then, taking the benefit, refuse to pay upon the ground that proper orders had not been obtained.[21] Furthermore, the employer might make it plain he was acting outside the contract altogether in requesting work.[22]

ILLUSTRATION

C. employed M. under a building contract, in which it was stipulated that there should be no charge for extra work, unless it had been specially ordered in writing by the architect employed. C. himself requested M. to do certain work on the building, and desired his men to take their orders from him and not from the architect. *Held*, that for this work M. might recover on the common counts without reference to the contract: *Melville* v. *Carpenter* (1853).[23]

It has been held in America and New Zealand that where a contractor, with the assent of the employer, did extra work verbally ordered by an agent of the employer, a clause requiring orders in writing had been waived.[24] Depending on the circumstances, it is perhaps possible that a builder might succeed in establishing that the employer had waived compliance with the requirements of form, *e.g.* by frequently ordering variations informally.[25]

---

[20] Provided, of course, that the employer was aware of the matter. See, *e.g. Molloy* v. *Liebe*, illustrated *supra*, p. 541.

[21] But see, however, the cases of *Nixon* v. *Taff Vale Ry.* (1848) 7 Hare 136 and *Thames Iron Works Co.* v. *R. M. Steam Packet Co.* (1861) 13 C.B.(N.S.) 358, illustrated *supra*, pp. 539–540.

[22] See also (*d*), *infra*.

[23] 11 Up.Can.Q.B. 128.

[24] *Norwood* v. *Lethrop* (1901) 178 Massachusetts Rep. 208; *Meyer* v. *Gilmer* (1899) 18 N.Z.L.R. 129, illustrated *infra*.

[25] See *Meyer* v. *Gilmer*, *infra*.

(d) Where the extra work is outside the contract

If the extra work which has been ordered is not ordered under a contract the terms of which require that a written order is a condition precedent to payment, then, of course, the absence of the written order will be no bar to payment. Whether the extra ordered is of the character contemplated by the contract and so within the conditions of the contract relating to the power to order extras, or whether on the other hand it is outside the contract,[26] must depend in each case on the nature of the work and the terms of the contract.

ILLUSTRATION

W. agreed to do all carpenter's, joiner's, glazing and tin work in the erection of two houses for B. After the work was executed, B. determined that he would have attics added to the houses, which rendered necessary more wall and additional carpenter's work in windows, doors, etc., and he totally changed the plan as to the back building, erecting large stables as for an inn. *Held*, that this was not extra work done under the contract but work done under a subsequent new agreement, wholly deviating from the former contract, and which could not be in any sense regarded as work done upon the terms thereof, either as to time or mode of payment; otherwise a contract for a cottage might be enlarged into a contract for building a mansion of three times its cost: *Watson* v. *O'Beirne* (1850).[27]

The contract work, therefore, may be so greatly altered that the work actually done cannot be regarded as done under it at all. Thus in *Thorn* v. *London Corporation*[28] Lord Cairns said: " If it is the kind of additional work contemplated by the contract, he (*i.e.* the contractor) must be paid for it and will be paid for it according to the prices regulated by the contract. . . . If the additional or varied work is so peculiar, so unexpected and so different from what any person reckoned or calculated upon, it may not be within the contract at all, and he could either refuse to go on or claim to be paid upon a *quantum meruit*." Again, in *Pepper* v. *Burland*[29] Lord Kenyon said: " If a man contracts to work by a certain plan, and that plan is so entirely abandoned that it is impossible to trace the contract, and to what part of it the work shall be applied, in such a case the workman shall be permitted to charge for the whole work done by measure and value, as if no contract at all had ever been made."

---

[26] An example of this has already been seen in the case of *Melville* v. *Carpenter* (1853) 11 Up.Can.Q.B. 128, illustrated *supra*, p. 547.

[27] 7 Up.Can.Q.B. 345.

[28] (1876) 1 App.Cas. 120 at p. 127; illustrated *ante*, Chap. 5, p. 269.

[29] (1792) 1 Peake N.P. 139.

It is seldom, however, that it is possible to contend that a contract for building or engineering work is so changed as to entitle the contractor to recover payment otherwise than in accordance with the contract, unless and until some stand is taken by the contractor in the matter. The continued execution of the works without protest under the terms of the contract, as, for example, the application for and the receipt of payment from time to time upon the certificate of the engineer or architect, will render it difficult for a contractor to contend that the contract has no application to the work as executed so as to entitle him to payment on a *quantum meruit*. " As regards *quantum meruit* where there are two parties who are under contract, *quantum meruit* must be a new contract, and in order to have a new contract you must get rid of the old contract." [30] Both the standard forms of contract contain express and perhaps somewhat optimistic provisions that no variation ordered under the power to order variations shall " vitiate the contract." [31] It is submitted that such a provision cannot as a matter of business efficacy be taken at its face value, and must be subject to an implied limitation of reasonableness.

It is suggested that, under the terms of most contracts, the power to order extras, although apparently unlimited, must in fact be limited to ordering extras of a certain value and type, and that additional work outside these limits will no longer be governed by the terms of the contract. The project as a whole and, if necessary, the pre-contract correspondence, must be looked at, it is submitted, and a common-sense view taken of the variations ordered. Thus in the case of an ordinary contract for a single dwelling-house, an order for a small outbuilding or garage might be acceptable, but not for, say, a further identical dwelling-house. On the other hand a contract for 300 dwelling-houses for a local authority might not be " vitiated " by an order for a further ten or twenty houses.

In considering the cases below, it should be remembered, however, that in modern contracts using bills or detailed specifications very small or even trivial changes in the work will rank as variations, and in many large contracts, it is not uncommon to find literally hundreds of variations in the final variation account when the final building is in all important respects unchanged from the original intention. Mere numbers of variations, therefore, are no evidence at

---

[30] Per Lord Dunedin in *The Olanda* [1919] 2 K.B. 728, approved by the Court of Appeal in *Gilbert & Partners (A Firm)* v. *Knight* [1968] 2 All E.R. 248, illustrated *ante*, Chap. 1, Section 2 (8), p. 18.

[31] See clause 51 (1) of the 1955 I.C.E. form, and clause 11 (1) of the 1963 R.I.B.A. standard forms.

all of a change in the character of the work unless related to the type of project, and even then are of only minor importance as compared with the subject-matter of the variations.

ILLUSTRATIONS

(1) Two contracts provided for an extension of time for extras ordered in writing. The employer himself required a large number of extras, and at a number of meetings at which he was present his architect orally instructed the builder to do the extra work. On one contract the number of extras was so great that the work as finished bore no resemblance to the work as originally planned. These extras on this contract, and certain quite independent work carried out for the employer on the other, delayed the contracts. Some of the extra work was paid for on interim certificate, and the builder's final account was queried only in relation to a claim for liquidated damages by the employer. In relation to this claim the employer relied on the absence of orders in writing. *Held*, there was evidence on which a jury could hold that the requirement of writing had been waived. *Held*, also, that the requirement of writing could not apply where the number of extras was so great as to totally change the character of the work, and the employer's claim must fail: *Meyer v. Gilmer* (1899).[32]

(2) The plaintiffs agreed to erect a factory according to general conditions, specifications and bills of quantities and drawings for £3,500,000, the work to be completed by January 30, 1939. The defendants had power in their absolute discretion to modify the extent and character of the work or to order alterations and additions, and the plaintiffs had to comply with the architect's instructions in this respect. The bills of quantities stated that it was probable that further work to the value of approximately £500,000 would be ordered on a measured basis. Delay was caused by the act or default of the defendants, but the defendants being anxious that the factory should be completed by January 30, 1939, a deed of variation was entered into whereby it was agreed that the plaintiffs should adopt an uneconomic method of working to bring about completion by that date, and that the sum eventually to be paid to the plaintiffs should not be less than the actual cost to them, as defined, plus a net remuneration of £150,000 and should not be greater than the actual cost to them plus a remuneration of £300,000. There was evidence that the plaintiffs contemplated that the estimated actual cost of the work would be £5,000,000, being £3,500,000, plus the probable extras of £500,000, plus £1,000,000 in respect of uneconomic working, and the minimum and maximum remuneration were based on 3 and 6 per cent. respectively of that estimated cost.

The defendants ordered work to be executed greatly in excess of the amount so contemplated, although not different in character from that covered by the varied contract, so that the work was not completed until a year beyond the time anticipated and the

---

[32] 18 N.Z.L.R. 129 (New Zealand). Compare, in a case involving the quantity surveyor's remuneration for valuing variations in such circumstances, *Kelly* v. *Northshore Development* (1963) 5 W.I.R. 379 (Jamaica), illustrated *ante*, Chap. 2, pp. 191–192.

actual cost to the plaintiffs was £6,683,056. During the course of the work the plaintiffs complained that they were being called on to execute more work than was contemplated by the varied contract. The plaintiffs had been paid £6,683,056, plus £300,000, and claimed extra remuneration in excess of the £300,000. *Held,*

(i) that the basis of the varied contract was that the quantum of work which the defendants were entitled to require was work measured approximately by the sum of £5,000,000; and

(ii) a term must be implied in the varied contract that the defendants should not be entitled to require work materially in excess of that sum;

(iii) work in excess of £5,000,000 having been done by the plaintiffs at the request of the defendants, the plaintiffs were entitled to be paid a reasonable remuneration therefor: *Parkinson (Sir Lindsay) & Co. Ltd.* v. *Commissioners of H.M. Works and Public Buildings* (1949).[33]

But it is submitted that the *Parkinson* case must nevertheless be regarded as one turning very much upon its special facts and particular contract. In the absence of express provision, there is no principle, it is submitted, that agreed fees under " cost-plus-fee " contracts should be raised if cost exceeds estimates. If this were so, it would be impossible for parties to contract on a " fixed " or " target " fee basis. The cost of building work is, in spite of attempts by quantity surveyors and others to suggest the contrary, notoriously difficult to predict with any even reasonable accuracy, and impossible to predict without considerable knowledge of the individual builder's organisation, methods and intentions. In contracts of this nature the contractor must be taken to be far better equipped than the employer or his advisers to gauge the accuracy of any pre-contract estimate of cost. It is submitted that it is changes in the physical quantity or quality of the work which should determine whether a contract remains applicable, rather than departures from earlier estimates of cost, and, in general, differences of cost are not even an indication of differences of work or even of quantities of work. It is on the specification and drawings or other documents describing the intended work that attention should be focused.

In addition, the time when the work is ordered may determine whether it is extra to or outside the contract.[34] If the works are ordered after the contract work is completed, they may on that ground be held to be outside the contract. So, too, differences in their situation or location may affect the position.

---

[33] [1949] 2 K.B. 632. See also the remarks of Lord Kenyon in the old case of *Pepper* v. *Burland*, quoted *supra*, p. 548.

[34] As to whether this may be a breach of contract, see *ante*, Chap. 5, Section 2 (4), p. 326, and the case of *Price Ltd.* v. *Milner* (1968) 206 E.G. 313 there illustrated.

ILLUSTRATIONS

(1) Plasterers were employed under a written contract to do work on the interior of a house and afterwards, during the continuance of that contract, were ordered by parol to execute an entablature outside. *Held*, in an action for the price of the entablature, that this was outside the contract, which need not be produced: *Reid* v. *Batte* (1829).[35]

(2) By a contract R. agreed to construct for S. a warship ready for sea according to Lloyd's regulations, fitted, etc., according to the practice with ships of H.M. Navy under contract with the Admiralty, the contract price to be inclusive, and no charges to be demanded for extras; but additions which might be demanded in writing by S., as an extra or extras, should be paid for at a price to be previously agreed upon in writing. No orders in writing were obtained, but R., in addition to certain alterations and additions carried out during construction without the order in writing, supplied certain articles after the contract was completed, and also £2,000 worth of warlike stores, and stores, masts, duplicate sails, etc., not included by Lloyd's regulations, and not included in Admiralty contracts with private builders, but issued from stores. *Held*, that as to the former, they were entirely separate from the contract, and must be paid for, and that as to the latter, they were supplied upon a new contract, and being accepted must be paid for, but that without an order in writing the cost of the alterations and additions carried out during the construction of the vessel could not be recovered.

Per Erle C.J.: " With respect to such articles as were supplied after the contract was fully completed, it appears to me that they are entirely severed from the contract and from any restriction contained in it, and that those who were authorised to act on the part of the Portuguese Government are subject to the ordinary implications of the law, and must pay for those articles so much as they are worth ": *Russell* v. *Sa da Bandeira* (1862).[36]

If the extra work ordered is outside the contract, it follows that the terms of the contract have no application, and although the production of an order in writing may be a condition precedent to recovery of payment for an extra done under the contract, it is not a condition of payment for extra work which is outside the contract. It is not necessary to produce the contract in evidence to recover payment for that work except, in the event of the defence being raised, to prove that the work in question is outside the contract and payment is to be made for it not at the contract rates but upon a *quantum meruit* or otherwise in accordance with the separate contract or request relied on.

It is, of course, axiomatic that the contractor will be unable to recover payment for work outside the contract if it has not been

---

[35] M. & M. 413.
[36] 13 C.B.(N.S.) 149.

ordered by the employer or by his authorised agent. Thus if a contractor, having agreed to do work with certain materials in a certain way for a stipulated price, puts in materials of a better kind or executes the work in a better way without the request of the employer, he is not at liberty on that account to charge more than the stipulated price.

(e) Where there is a final certificate

In certain older contracts it was provided that an order in writing was a condition precedent to payment for extra or varied work, but at the same time the architect should have power to determine what were extras, and that the architect's final certificate should be conclusive as to the value of the work done.

In such a case if, despite the non-fulfilment of the condition requiring an order in writing, the architect includes in his final certificate the value of extra work executed without such an order in writing the contractor will be entitled to be paid for it and the employer will be precluded, in the absence of fraud, from relying upon the lack of an order in writing. Likewise, if the architect certifies for work which is not an extra or has not been done at all, the employer will have no remedy. The reverse will also be true in such a case—if the architect issues a final certificate and does not include something which the contractor has done and considers should be paid for as an extra, the contractor will be unable to recover additional payment.[37]

ILLUSTRATIONS

(1) Under an entire contract to build a market, it was provided that no deviations should be made without the architect's written authority, that the architect's opinion as to the value thereof should be final, that if any dispute arose as to the meaning of the specifications or contract the architect was to define the meaning, and that his decision as to the nature, quality and quantity of the works executed or to be executed should be final. The architect certified a gross sum for extras, without giving items. The builders brought proceedings in the courts under three heads: (1) the contract price; (2) extras under the contract; (3) additional work independent of the contract. An arbitrator appointed by the court to state a case found that the whole sum claimed was in respect of the work contracted for or connected therewith. *Held*, by the full Court of Common Pleas, the plaintiffs had failed to establish that there was any work independent of the contract and, since the architect was supreme judge as to extras and additions under the contract, both the plaintiffs and the defendants were bound by his certificate, and neither

[37] This subject is also discussed, *ante*, Chap. 7, pp. 426 *et seq.*

party could raise any question of extras not being ordered in writing: *Goodyear* v. *Weymouth Corporation* (1855).[38]

(2) By a contract to build a pier it was provided that any disputes or differences arising upon any matter connected with the contract were to be referred to the engineer, whose certificate was to be final. The engineer, notwithstanding a provision that the contractors should be paid " provided . . . they shall have delivered to the employer a full account in detail of all claims they have on the employer, and the engineer shall have given a certificate, in writing, of the correctness of such claims," certified as extra work work which had never been done at all, and work which, although extra, had not been done on signed or countersigned orders in pursuance of a clause providing that " no additional or extra work shall be paid for unless it has been executed under the authority of such signed and countersigned instructions." *Held*, that the certificate of the engineer precluded the defendants from raising the question whether extras had been done, and that the engineer had power to determine whether a particular work was within the contract or was an extra. " The signature and the countersignature is no doubt a condition precedent to the right of payment, but so is the completion of the work to the satisfaction of the engineer; but so are a variety of other matters all conditions precedent. But all those matters are to be taken into account, the right to which is to be ascertained by certificates, the engineer is to go into all those matters, is to satisfy himself that the conditions precedent to a right to payment have been fulfilled; and he would have neglected his duty if he had certified for any work if any of the stipulations of the contract which he, as the agent of the defendants, was to enforce, had not been complied with by the plaintiffs," *per* Coleridge C.J. *Laidlaw* v. *Hastings Pier Co.* (1874).[39]

(3) A building contract contained the following clause: " All extras or additions, payment for which the contractor shall become entitled to under the said conditions, and all deductions which the building owner shall become entitled to, shall be respectively paid or allowed for at the price which shall be fixed by the surveyor appointed by the building owner." The surveyor, in his final certificate, certified for certain extras and additions, which the defendant, the employer, alleged were not extras and additions. *Held*, that the certificate was conclusive, not only as to prices, but also as to the question whether these matters were extras or not, and that the clause giving him power to value extras, standing alone, impliedly gave him power to determine what were extras: *Richards* v. *May* (1883).[40]

(4) A building contract contained a clause that the decision of the architect with respect to the amount, state and condition of the works actually executed, and also in respect of any and every question that might arise concerning the construction of the present contracts, or the said plans, drawings, elevations, specifications, or the execution of the works thereby contracted for, should be final and without appeal. The contract also contained another

[38] 35 L.J.C.P. 12. See particularly the judgment and reasoning of Willes J.
[39] Hudson's B.C., 4th ed., Vol. 2, p. 13.
[40] 10 Q.B.D. 400.

clause, that the builders were not to vary or deviate from the drawings or specifications, or execute any extra work of any kind whatever, unless upon the authority of the architect, to be sufficiently shown by any order in writing, or by any plans or drawings, expressly given and signed or initialled by him as an extra or variation, or by subsequent written approval similarly signed. In all cases where such deviations or extras exceeded £10, the order was to be, in addition to the above, countersigned by two of the building committee. The architect certified a certain sum as due. *Held*, that the decision of the architect as to extras not properly ordered was conclusive, and that the building owners could not resist payment of any part of this sum on the ground that the architect had, by mistake, certified for work not done and improperly done, and that the architect had not made sufficient allowances for work not done: *Lapthorne* v. *St. Aubyn* (1885).[41]

The above cases are based on the principle that the requirement that the builder should obtain the certificate is the overriding one, and that, the employer having required the determination of liability for extras to be left to the certifier, cannot complain of the latter's decision.[42] While the basis of the principle can be easily accepted, it is not, however, logically easy to reconcile all the cases with these which show that a certifier who takes incorrect matters into account or who acts outside the terms of his authority may render his certificate a nullity.[42a]

In considering any case in which there is an arbitration clause, however, it should be borne in mind that if the arbitration clause is wide enough, the decision of the architect as to what works are or are not extras, and even the conclusiveness of the final certificate, may be open to review by the arbitrator.[43]

SECTION 3. VALUATION OF AND PAYMENT FOR EXTRAS AND VARIATIONS

It is usual for the contract to provide for the measurement and valuation of extras and variations. Thus it is usual to find that the varied work is to be paid for at rates contained in a schedule attached to the contract, if there are no bills of quantities, or in a contract with quantities at the rates or prices contained in the bills of quantities.[44]

[41] 1 Cab. & El. 486, following *Laidlaw* v. *Hastings Pier Co., supra*.
[42] *Ante*, Chap. 7, pp. 419–420.
[42a] *Ante*, Chap. 7, Section 5, p. 477.
[43] See *ante*, Chap. 7, Section 4, for a full discussion of this subject.
[44] In such provisions, the words " rates " or " prices " mean, it is submitted, *all* rates or prices applicable to the varied work, including any preliminary or other items which may be affected by a variation.

In such provisions, the words " rates " or " prices " should include, it is submitted, a proper proportion of the " preliminary " or general items, which are usually found at the beginning of any bills of quantities, or other items of expenditure not referable to any particular part of the work, which are sometimes also found in the summary at the end of bills of quantities, provided that the items in question can be shown to have been affected by a variation. It is not usual to find such items in the schedules of rates in fixed price contracts, in which event the prices in the schedule of rates, which are prepared in these contracts exclusively for the purpose of valuing variations, must be deemed to be inclusive of all such overheads and general expenditure. If there is no appropriate rate in the schedule or in the bills of quantities it is often provided that a rate analogous to the rates contained in the bills, or based on those rates, shall be determined by the architect or the surveyor or the engineer as the case may be. Thus if a contractor has inserted a low price for a particular item of work in the expectation that it would prove to be an unimportant item, it will follow, if more is ordered of that or a similar kind of work, that he will be paid for the extra at the same or a similar low rate. On the other hand, if the contract does not provide how the rates for extra work are to be fixed, or if it is left to the architect, surveyor or engineer to fix a reasonable rate, then the contractor is entitled to have a reasonable rate fixed for the extra or varied work, regardless of the contract rates, though naturally these latter will be prima facie evidence of what is a reasonable rate. In many contracts it is left to the architect or engineer to fix a rate for varied or extra work at his discretion if he does not consider the bill or schedule of rates reasonably applicable to the varied work.[45] Generally speaking the presence of an arbitration clause in general terms will show an intention that his decision should be open to review,[46] but in the absence of such a clause his decisions will usually be binding.[47]

If the contract provides that the varied work shall be valued at contract rates or at rates based upon them, it is sometimes also provided that, if the contractor is put to any unforeseen loss or expense as a result of the variation, the amount of such loss or expense shall be ascertained and paid to him.[48] Such loss or expense may well be occasioned if the variation is ordered late in the day, and in this

[45] See clause 52 (i) of the 1955 I.C.E. form, and clause 11 (4) (b) of the post-1963 R.I.B.A. forms.
[46] See ante, Chap. 7, Section 4, Effect of Arbitration Clause.
[47] Ante, Chap. 7, Section 3.
[48] See clause 1, pre-1963 R.I.B.A. standard form; clauses 11 (6) and 24 (1) of the post-1963 forms, and clause 52 (2) of the 1955 I.C.E. form.

connection it should be remembered that if the contractor is given instructions unreasonably late he may have a co-terminous cause of action for damages for breach of contract.[49]

Where work is omitted a deduction falls to be made from the contract price; depending on the terms of the contract, the amount of the deduction will either be fixed by reference to contract rates or a fair deduction will be made, the same principles applying as with extra work. If work is omitted on the instructions of the architect or engineer leaving only a small amount of other work to be done, it is in principle fairer and more accurate to value the work done at a fair rate having regard to the amount done, rather than to value the work omitted, because the contractor will have had the expense of providing and bringing to the site possibly very expensive equipment the cost of which was spread over the whole of the work originally anticipated, so that the contract rate would not be fairly applicable to the amount of work done. For this reason it is not uncommon to find special provisions entitling the valuer to make an allowance for this element where substantial omissions are ordered.[50]

If the employer by agreement performs some of the work or supplies some of the materials in the contract, the contractor will, of course, have to give credit for these against the contract price. The correct legal basis for these " *contra* items," as they are usually known in the industry, is that they represent a new agreement varying the original contract price and work rather than a separate agreement by the contractor to pay for the goods or services concerned.[51]   So, where the work as a whole is being paid for on a *quantum meruit*, the amount which the contractor is entitled to be paid will be reduced if the employer has provided a service which otherwise the contractor would have had to supply.[52]

It should be remembered, however, that in the absence of agreement the contractor is entitled to do all the work and supply all the materials.[53] If, therefore, the employer himself does work or supplies materials without the consent of the contractor he may be faced with a claim by the contractor for the profit which the contractor might have made had he done the work, or the discount which he might have earned had he supplied the materials, and possibly also a claim for damages for interfering with the progress of the work.

[49] See *ante*, Chap. 5, pp. 322 *et seq.*
[50] See, *e.g.* clause 11 (4) (*d*) of the 1963 R.I.B.A. form and clause 52 (2) of the 1955 I.C.E. form (which applies to additions as well).
[51] *Turner* v. *Diaper* (1841) 2 M. & G. 241; *Newton* v. *Forster* (1844) 12 M. & W. 772.
[52] *Grainger* v. *Raybould* (1840) 9 C. & P. 229.
[53] *Supra*, pp. 532–533.

The value of the variations is normally added to or subtracted from the contract sum (except in the case of those schedule or " measure and value " contracts where there is no contract sum and the whole of the work done is to be valued at the schedule rate or analogous or fair rates).[54] Where, however, the variations ordered are so substantial that it is no longer possible to trace the original contract work, it has been shown[55] that the contractor may in certain rare circumstances be entitled to charge for the work done upon a *quantum meruit*.

In such a case the true position is that the original contract has been abandoned and a new one to pay a reasonable sum for the work done has been substituted. In most cases, however, although there may be very numerous and substantial variations, it is not possible to say that the contract has been entirely abandoned. Nevertheless, where the contract is not a measured contract, a practice is sometimes adopted by quantity surveyors of remeasuring the work done and valuing it all at schedule rates or at analogous or fair rates instead of measuring and valuing only the variations, and the action certainly constitutes an admission (not of course binding on the employer) that in the opinion of the surveyor concerned the contract work has been changed beyond recognition. Where the practice is adopted the terms of payment are in fact varied because the contract is changed from one where the work is done for an ascertainable sum subject to variations to one where the whole of the work done is paid for on a schedule of rates. It follows that unless the architect, surveyor or engineer, as the case may be, has the express authority of the employer to adopt the practice, it should not be done, because the employer would not be bound to accept a final account prepared on that basis without his authority. In practice the difference between the two methods is of great importance because a complete remeasurement is technically extremely difficult, if not impossible, to achieve with any precision once the work is complete and much of it covered up. This is the reason why, even in contracts with quantities, complete physical remeasurement (as opposed to recalculation) is rarely intended by the contract provisions. Furthermore, the prices in the schedule of rates may have been loaded or lightened by the contractor according to his expectation of possible variations, just as in the case of bills of quantities, and bear no relation to his calculation of his overall tender sum.[55a]

---

[54] See *ante*, Chap. 3, pp. 206–207, 210–211, and *supra*, pp. 521–522.
[55] *Supra*, pp. 549–551.
[55a] See also for the practice of measurement *post*, Chap. 9, pp. 563–566.

SECTION 4.   APPROPRIATION OF PAYMENTS TO EXTRAS

Attempts have occasionally been made by contractors, faced with the difficulty that they lacked an essential order in writing for extra work, to obtain payment for it by alleging that, under the legal rules as to appropriation of payments, the work in question had already been paid for by the employer, so that the final balance claimed by the contractor related only to the original contract work and not the extra work.

The legal rules relating to two possible types of appropriation are of relevance in this context, namely, appropriation of payments as between different debts between the same debtor and creditor, and appropriation of payments made on account of work to particular items of work.

The first only arises if there is in fact more than one debt, and there will not be more than one debt if there is not more than one contract. The general rule of law is stated in *Cory Bros. & Co. Ltd.* v. *The Mecca* [56] by Lord Macnaghten as follows:

" When a debtor is making a payment to his creditor he may appropriate the money as he pleases, and the creditor must apply it accordingly. If the debtor does not make any appropriation at the time when he makes the payment the right of application devolves on the creditor. In 1816, when *Clayton's Case* [57] was decided, there seems to have been authority for saying that the creditor was bound to make his election at once according to the rule of the civil law, or at any rate, within a reasonable time, whatever that expression in such a connection may be taken to mean. But it has long been held and it is now quite settled that the creditor has the right of election ' up to the very last moment,' and he is not bound to declare his election in express terms. He may declare it by bringing an action or in any other way which makes his meaning and intention plain."

Once a payment has been appropriated by a creditor, however, the appropriation cannot be varied subsequently without the consent of the debtor. [58]

In the application of this principle to building contracts, therefore, it is first necessary to see whether there is more than one contract. If extras have been ordered under the contract there is but one contract, but if they were ordered separately outside the terms of the

[56] [1897] A.C. 286 at p. 288.
[57] 1 Mer. 585.
[58] *Mahomed Jan* v. *Ganga Bishnu Singh* (1911) L.R. 38 Ind.App. 80, P.L.

contract[59] there will be two contracts and the possibility of appropriation of payments to either the original contract work or the extra
work will arise. Secondly, it must be discovered whether the debtor
made any appropriation, and, as appears from *Lowther* v. *Heaver*[60]
illustrated below, that appropriation need not be expressed and may
be presumed. Thirdly, if there was no appropriation by the debtor,
the intention of the creditor must be ascertained from the evidence.

ILLUSTRATIONS

(1) Sums were paid by a corporation on account of a building
contract, without distinguishing in respect of what works the payments were made. The contract, which was for £5,500, provided
that if the architect should require any alterations or additions in
the progress of the works, the architect should give to the builder
written instructions signed by him, and that the builder should
not be considered as having authority for the same without such
written instructions. The architect certified for £5,500, but, in
fact, payments were made to the amount of £6,300. The builder
brought an action for the balance. No orders had been given for
extra works in writing, in accordance with the contract under seal.
Held, that the builder could only apply the payments to the extra
works on the ground of a new valid contract to pay, and that, inasmuch as the corporation could only be liable under such a contract
if it was under seal,[61] the builder could not apply the payments to
the extras not ordered in writing or recover.

" Suppose, for instance, a contract under seal, whereby a
builder contracts to build a house, and the owner of the land covenants to pay £1,000 as the price of the work, and also to pay for
any extra work authorised in writing by the architect. During the
progress of the works the architect authorises extra work to the
amount of £500, which the builder completes in a proper manner,
and to the satisfaction of the owner of the land, but without any
authority in writing. We will suppose that the owner of the land
pays the builder from time to time £1,200 on account, generally,
and that more than six years after the whole has been completed the
builder brings an action of covenant against the owner for non-
payment of the balance, and the owner pleads payment. In such a
case the argument for the plaintiff here might prevail, but it would
rest wholly on the ground that under the circumstances the owner
of the land must be taken to have entered into a new parol contract
to pay for the extras, independently of his liability under the deed.
There would in such case be two debts due from the owner of the
land—one a debt arising by deed, the other a debt on simple contract,
and in such a case the doctrine of indefinite payments would apply.
. . . But before any such question can arise, it must be plain that
there must be two debts. The doctrine never has been held to
authorise a creditor receiving money on account to apply it towards

---

[59] See *supra*, pp. 548 *et seq.*
[60] (1889) 41 Ch.D. 248.
[61] This requirement is, of course, no longer necessary. See *ante*, Chap. 1, pp. 21–22.

the satisfaction of what does not nor ever did constitute any legal or equitable demand against the party making the payments," *per* Pollock C.B.: *Lamprell* v. *Billericay Union* (1849).[62]

(2) H. agreed to grant R. or his nominee leases of certain plots of land as soon as certain buildings agreed by R. to be erected thereon were roofed in. R. assigned the benefit of the agreement to L. and died. The form of lease contained a proviso for re-entry in the event of non-payment of rent. L. roofed in four houses and sued for specific performance of the agreement to grant him leases of that land. H. alleged that R. was in arrears of rent under the building agreement before the houses were roofed in and refused to grant the leases. An account showed the rent due to be £1,062 and that H. had lent R. £15,157. R. had paid a total of £6,865. H. had appropriated the greater part of that to the loan account and showed a balance of £375 due from R. for rent. *Held*, prima facie R. must be presumed to have appropriated his payments so as to discharge his liability for rent so as to avoid the proviso for re-entry. H. had not given any evidence that R. had not made such an appropriation and so could not himself appropriate any part of the sums paid and had failed to show that any rent was unpaid. L. was entitled to have the leases granted: *Lowther* v. *Heaver* (1889).[63]

Where what is being sought, however, is the appropriation of payments on account to particular items of work, it has been held that no such appropriation can be made by the contractor. Thus where a contractor had done both work which he might lawfully do and work which was illegal, it was held that he could not appropriate the payments on account to the illegal work (in which case they would have been irrecoverable) but must treat them as having been made on account of the work in respect of which he could lawfully claim payment. The same principle would seem to apply to prevent a contractor from appropriating a payment to satisfy a claim for an extra executed under the contract but in respect of which an essential order in writing did not exist.

ILLUSTRATION

The plaintiffs agreed to carry out work to the defendant's house. Before a building licence as required by reg. 56A of the Defence (General) Regulations, 1939, had been obtained the plaintiffs pulled down a wall and rebuilt it. On April 23 and June 11 the defendant paid two sums of £500 to the plaintiffs. On June 11 and 30 the plaintiffs obtained the building licences, authorising an expenditure of £3,200. The value of the unlicensed work was £1,700. The receipts for the two sums of £500 were expressed to be " for demolition of faulty structure " and " on account of work carried out." The plaintiffs claimed that they had appropriated the two payments of £500 to the unlicensed work and might recover further

[62] 18 L.J.Ex. 282; 3 Ex. 283.
[63] 41 Ch.D. 248.

the cost of the work up to £3,200. *Held*, despite the wording on the receipts they were to be treated as payments on account generally of work done under the contract and should be allocated to work in respect of which the plaintiff could lawfully claim and must, therefore, be allocated to the licensed work: *A. Smith & Sons Ltd.* v. *Walker* (1952).[64]

It would seem to follow from the foregoing discussion that appropriation of payments is not a doctrine of any practical importance in the field of building and engineering contracts. While in theory there is nothing to prevent an employer from agreeing to the appropriation of a payment to illegal or extra work, very unusual facts would be needed to bring this about. Thus, it has already been seen that the allowance and payment of claims on interim certificate does not estop the employer from subsequently disputing them.[65]

---

[64] [1952] 2 Q.B. 319. See further for this subject, *ante*, Chap. 5, pp. 361 *et seq.*
[65] See *Royston U.D.C.* v. *Royston Builders Ltd.* (1961) 177 E.G. 589, *ante*, Chap. 1, p. 58, and *Tharsis Sulphur & Copper Co.* v. *McElroy* (1878) 3 App.Cas. 1040, *ante*, pp. 537–538.

CHAPTER 9

PRICE AND DAMAGES

SECTION 1. PRICE

(1) Price Fixed by Contract

THE price to be paid by the employer under a building contract will either be a reasonable price (sometimes described as " cost plus," or from one of the forms of action upon which it depended, as " *quantum meruit* ") or it will be fixed by or ascertainable from the contract. In the absence of certain special circumstances, such as frustration, or a fundamental breach by the employer entitling the contractor to treat the contract as repudiated, or work done under a void or unenforceable contract (of which the commonest example, before the abolition of the requirement of seal for the contracts of certain corporations, was where work had been carried out for such corporations without a contract under seal being entered into [2]), no action upon a *quantum meruit* for a reasonable price can be maintained if an express contract regulating or fixing the price of the work is in existence. It is, however, possible to have fairly detailed express contracts which specifically require payment to be on a " cost-plus " basis,[3] and the R.I.B.A. in March 1967 published a form of contract entitling the contractor to be paid the prime cost (as elaborately defined in a number of schedules) and a fixed additional fee. In fact the definitions of prime cost include important elements of profit to the contractor, and the circumstances in which the fee really will remain fixed are highly obscure, but detailed consideration of this contract is not within the scope of the present book.

Building contracts at the present day tend to fall into two broad categories, namely, those where the extent and design of the work is not fully known at the time of the contract, where a schedule of rates or prices is usually used,[4] and those where the work is sufficiently known, where contracts are usually either in the specification form without quantities (with a schedule of rates only for the purpose of

---

[2] See, *e.g. Lawford* v. *Billericay R.D.C.* [1903] 1 K.B. 772.
[3] See *infra*, pp. 571–572.
[4] See *ante*, Chap. 3, pp. 198–202, 206–207.

valuing variations), or in a form with quantities (where the bills will govern the valuation of the whole of the work). Both types of contract in this latter category are " lump sum " contracts in the legal sense for the purpose of the rules as to entire and substantial performance,[5] *i.e.* they are contracts to carry out and complete defined work for a price ascertained or to be ascertained—though it is not unusual in the industry for contracts without quantities to be referred to as " lump sum " contracts in contradistinction to contracts with quantities. Lump sum contracts in the legal sense, with or without quantities, are by far the most common in practical use, though it is to be regretted that where the work is in reality not precisely defined or planned projects are sometimes put out to tender by consulting engineers and architects using these forms, relying on their powers to vary the work and issue working drawings for the supply of the actual design during the currency of the work, when they would be far better advised to recognise the reality and use a schedule form of contract, thereby avoiding the probability of large claims of uncertain amount by the contractor. Schedule contracts are not infrequently used by the service departments in the U.K., but are only rarely used by other departments of the Crown or by local authorities or statutory corporations.

(a) Adjustment of the price by remeasurement of work

In contracts in the second category without bills of quantities, the price is a firm price, and any schedule of rates or bills of quantities which exist are designed solely for the purpose of placing a value upon the variations, whether by way of omission or addition, which the contract may empower the employer or his architect to order. In such contracts the contract price is, subject to variations, fluctuations, and any other claims which the contract may permit, a firm price. In contracts with bills, either party can require remeasurement of the work, and the price (if grossed up and inserted in the contract documents) is recalculated upon the basis of the measurement of works actually carried out (which as previously explained[6] will in regard to the greater part of the work involve recalculation off drawings rather than physical measurement on the site), using the schedule rates or bills of quantities for the purpose. The evolution of this type of contract, and the difficulty the courts originally felt in giving effect to this intention in the absence of clear wording, has already been described

---

[5] *Ante*, Chap. 3, pp. 201–202; Chap. 5, pp. 245, 247.
[6] *Ante*, Chap. 8, p. 558.

in detail.[7] Every contract must be separately considered to determine into which category it falls, and in doing so it will not be conclusive that the schedule of rates or bills of quantities are so described, or even that the words " lump sum " are used. The key provision will be some term, express or implied, providing for measurement (apart from any question of variations) of the contract work. Such a provision may be expressed only in an oblique form (*cf.* the current R.I.B.A. contract, which by clause 12 provides that any error in quantity in the bills of quantities shall be rectified and treated as a variation [8]), and it may be a matter of some difficulty in informal contracts [9] to determine into which class the contract falls.

The usual practice, even in measured contracts, is for measurement or recalculation to be carried out only if the work has been varied, and then only with specific reference to the variations or in relation to work of inherently uncertain extent, or where the contractor points out an error in the quantities. This is because bills of quantities (which differ from schedules of rates in that quantities have been estimated opposite each item and rate) have usually been professionally prepared from the contract drawings and specification and may be expected to be reasonably accurate. But this does not alter the fact that in a measured contract either party has a right to measure or recalculate the price of the work, whether varied or not. Difficult questions may also arise in measured contracts as to whether work not described in the bills or schedule of rates, but necessary for the contract work to be carried out, is in fact included in the schedule or bill rates or not,[10] and to a lesser extent similar problems can arise under fixed price or lump-sum contracts without quantities. For this reason, well-drawn bills of quantities and specifications will contain a provision to the effect that all work necessary for the carrying out of the work described in the bills shall be deemed to be included in the bill rates or contract sum, as the case may be; but on the other hand modern forms of contract with quantities frequently incorporate by reference the Standard Method of Measurement of Building Works or similar publications, in terms which may possibly have the effect of defeating such an intention, contrary to what must in the vast majority of cases be the true

---

[7] *Ante*, Chap. 8, pp. 509 *et seq.*

[8] See the provision set out *ante*, Chap. 8, p. 516.

[9] See for a good example of a doubtful case, *Ibmac* v. *Marshall* (1968) 208 E.G. 851, illustrated *ante*, Chap. 5, p. 253.

[10] See *ante*, Chap. 5, pp. 262–272; Chap. 8, pp. 515–529.

intention.[11] This possibility is, however, doubted and criticised, *ante* Chapter 8.

Apart from the question of measurement, other common provisions in building and engineering contracts, whether in the lump sum or measured form, may introduce considerable elements of flexibility into the contract price. Apart from the valuation of variations, the most common at the present day, perhaps, are fluctuations clauses, under which alterations in the price of labour and materials between the date of tender and the carrying out of the work are taken into account and added to or deducted from the price. But there are many others, for instance, those dealing with compliance with architect's instructions involving the contractor in loss or expense under certain standard forms of contract, the encountering of adverse physical conditions and artificial obstructions in certain engineering forms of contract, and also, for instance, provisions for deduction of liquidated damages, or for bonus payments in certain events.

(b) Fluctuations clauses

These clauses are variously designed to obtain for the contractor the amount of any increases in his costs, usually of labour or materials or both, which may take place after his tender and before the work is completed. The R.I.B.A. forms contain an optional fluctuations clause.[12] The I.C.E. form contains no such clause, but a standard printed " Variation of Price " clause adapted to the standard form is frequently incorporated in the contract documents in engineering contracts.

In the case of labour, it is not generally difficult to determine with precision the amount of any such increases, since wage rates are controlled by official or statutory bodies within the industry and come into operation on fixed dates. In this case difficulties of interpretation are only likely to arise where there is doubt as to the exact payments likely to be covered by the clauses.

ILLUSTRATION

A fluctuations clause entitled the contractor to be paid increases in cost due to increases in " the rates of wages payable for any labour." *Held*, by the House of Lords, these words were not wide enough to include increases in the cost of stamps purchased by the employer for the credit of his workmen under the holidays with pay scheme for the engineering industry: *Henry Boot* v. *L.C.C.* (1959).[13]

A further difficulty in relation to the cost of labour, as defined by

---

[11] For the effect of incorporation of a standard method, see *ante*, pp. 515–520.
[12] Clause 31, 1963 forms.
[13] [1959] 1 W.L.R. 1069, criticised by A. L. Goodhart, Q.C. (1960) 76 L.Q.R. 62.

fluctuations clauses in building contracts, which has recently arisen in the United Kingdom, is that most of these clauses [14] operate upon the wages payable by the contractor " in accordance with the *rules or decisions* of the National Joint Council of the Building Industry." In order to give advance notice to the industry of such rising costs, the Council has, however, adopted a sensible practice whereby the negotiated increases are to operate from a date some months in the future. Unfortunately, the Council in giving effect to this policy has ignored the wording of these fluctuations clauses and has adopted machinery under which the " decision " is now separated considerably in point of time from the change in " the rule." It is only fair to the Council to say that the R.I.B.A., who might have rapidly modified their fluctuations clauses in the light of the Council's practice, appear to have taken many years to do so. The consequence is that, where the decision precedes, but the change in the rule succeeds, the date of the tender, the fluctuations clause, which was originally drafted on the assumption that the decision and rule are contemporary events, in a vast number of contracts in England has for some years become virtually impossible to apply so as to accord with any intention or presumed intention of the parties.

In relation to materials, it is extremely difficult to draft any fluctuations clause which will operate both fairly and precisely and will not be open to serious abuse which is very difficult for the employer's advisers to control, partly because of the great practical difficulty, particularly with many of the more elementary building materials, of establishing exactly what the price of those materials is at the date of tender against which to compare later actual cost. Furthermore, on many large contracts, contractors may make their own arrangements, outside any available market, for the supply of materials such as sand, hardcore and gravel, and may even have their own quarries or deposits for winning them. Even where this is not so, the concept of a market price often does not really apply, and it is impossible to obtain a realistic price for a material unless the location of the site, quantities needed and time for delivery are known. The method adopted by most contracts is to use the concept of a market price prevailing at the time of tender, and to attempt to avoid the difficulties referred to by providing for the insertion of all materials in respect of which the contractor intends to claim under the fluctuations clause in a list or schedule forming part of the contract documents, usually known as a " basic price list," together with the

---

[14] *Cf.* clause 31 (1) (*a*) (i) of the 1963 R.I.B.A. standard forms.

alleged market price of the material at the date of tender. In the employer's interest it is essential that the prices in such a list should be most carefully checked and agreed before the contract is signed since, if the prices are too low, the employer will be compelled to make substantial additional payments. The task of the architect or surveyor in checking these prices is an unenviable one, since, as already indicated, in many cases no reliable quotation can be obtained by a tendering contractor not yet in a position to give a firm order. Suppliers are often willing to supply quotations freely for token quantities or on a " subject to adjustment of price on delivery " basis at optimistic prices during the tender stage, or at the stage when the basic price list is being compiled, but later, when a firm order is asked for, quote realistic and substantially higher prices. There is also little doubt that the system amounts to an invitation to suppliers to raise their prices since, once armed with a fluctuations clause, the contractor has no interest or incentive to resist the imposition of higher prices by suppliers.

Comparatively recently, contracts without fluctuations clauses (often referred to as " fixed price " contracts, as contracts without quantities are also often described) have become more common, largely at government insistence rather than as a result of any policy decision by those responsible for the standard forms.

One problem which arises not infrequently in regard to fluctuations clauses is whether increases under those clauses are recoverable during the period when the contractor has, in breach of contract, failed to complete on time. It is submitted that this depends upon whether or not there is a liquidated damages clause for delay in completion. If there is not, the increases are not recoverable, because in a generally inflationary world they follow as a direct reasonably foreseeable consequence of the breach, and if due under the contract are recoverable by the employer as damages for the breach. If there is a liquidated damages clause, however, the liquidated damages represent the employer's pre-estimate of *all* his damage resulting from the breach.[14a] The submission made above in relation to the cases where there is no liquidated damages clause is, possibly open to argument, because it should be remembered that fluctuations clauses usually operate (theoretically) in a downward as well as an upward direction, and because the phenomenon of monetary inflation is not necessarily a concept which the courts in England find easy to accept —see the commentary on the *East Ham* case, *infra*, Section 2 (2).

[14a] This view was followed in *Peek Construction* v. *McKinney Foundations* C.A., July 1, 1970.

(c) " Unfavourable conditions " clauses

Many engineering contracts, following the example of the I.C.E. standard forms, contain a provision enabling the contract price to be adjusted upwards if the contractor should meet unfavourable physical conditions or artificial obstructions which an experienced contractor could not reasonably have foreseen.[15] It is easy to understand the reason for such clauses, since engineering contracts generally operate in conditions of greater uncertainty than building contracts (and often with inadequate pre-contract site investigations), but it is not, perhaps sufficiently appreciated that the consequences of such a clause may be rather different from the intention (which is that the employer should have the benefit of lower contract prices, since any contingent element in the tender price to take account of risks which may not eventuate can be reduced or avoided altogether on the basis that, if the risk does eventuate, the contractor can claim under the clause). This would be so if the risk were described in the contract documents, and all tendering contractors informed that, in the event of its materialising, a claim under the clause would be permitted. This does not, however, occur, with the result that some contractors with experience, foreseeing the possibility of an adverse condition, assume that, because of its foreseeability, it will not be allowed as a basis for a clause 12 claim, price accordingly, and fail to obtain the contract; whereas inexperienced, rash or optimistic contractors ignore the risk, price accordingly, and (particularly under the system of public tendering in the United Kingdom) are awarded the contract, and later seek to extricate themselves from this difficulty by arbitration in which the issue is, generally, whether or not the risk was foreseeable. The exceptionally sympathetic attitude of some engineering arbitrators[16] (who, unlike architects, have often passed at least a part of their working lives on " the other side," as contractors) encourages this tendency, which can drive honest and efficient contractors out of business and provokes wholly unmerited litigation. Logically, such clauses contradict the policy on which they are based, since if the risk is truly unforeseeable, it is unlikely that, without such a clause, there would be any material difference in the contract price, and the clause is, therefore, of little or no practical benefit to the employer, while imposing a real risk upon him. It is far preferable in the employer's interest, where a known risk exists, that the cost of dealing

---

[15] *Cf.* clause 12 of the I.C.E. standard forms.
[16] See *e.g.* the case of *Blackford (Calne) Ltd.* v. *Christchurch Corporation* [1962] 1 Lloyd's Rep. 349, illustrated *ante*, Chap. 5, p. 314. See also *post*, pp. 856, 868, and *ante*, p. 502.

with it, by the appropriate methods of working, should be dealt with by provisional items in the bills of quantities, rather than by the use of such clauses. This really does give the employer the benefit of a keener price.

Whatever their policy, such clauses are usually and rightly subject to stringent provisions limiting their operation, particularly in regard to the service of notices by the contractor, so as to enable the employer's advisers to consider the financial and technical position at as early a stage as possible. Failure to comply with these provisions may well defeat a claim based upon such a clause.

> Clause 12 (2) of the 1955 I.C.E. form provided that if the contractor intended to make a claim under that clause for additional payment he should give notice in writing specifying (a) the physical conditions or artificial obstructions encountered, (b) the additional work and additional plant proposed, and (c) the extent of anticipated delay in or interference with the work. The proviso to this clause stated that all work or plant prior to or not specified in such a notice should be deemed to be covered in the contract rates and prices.   By clause 12 (3) it was further provided that if the additional work and plant was sufficiently defined the contractor should submit a quotation for it, and also for the delay and interference if practicable, and in all other cases he should submit with the notice an estimate of the additional cost of the work and plant, and also of the delay and interference. *Held*, by Mocatta J., that a notice which did not comply with the requirements of clause 12 (3) as well as clause 12 (2) was invalid to found a claim, and the courts had jurisdiction where an inadequate notice was served to make a declaration preventing an arbitrator from entertaining a claim: *Monmouth C.C.* v. *Costelloe & Kemple Ltd.* (1964).[17]
>
> [Note: This clause is strangely drafted in that the proviso to clause 12 (2) does not appear in terms to rule out the cost of *delay and interference*, as opposed to additional *work or plant*. On any view there seems some doubt whether clause 12 (3) is a condition precedent as held by Mocatta J.]

(d) When price is due

Price calculated and adjusted in the various ways mentioned above represents, nevertheless, a liquidated debt or demand, though

---

[17] (1964) 63 L.G.R. 131 (the declaration, which also referred to a number of other claims by the contractor, see *post*, Chap. 18, p. 820, was overruled in regard to the other claims by the C.A. and the Council do not appear to have sought to retain the declaration in regard to this claim, but Mocatta J.'s judgment on the points illustrated above was neither argued before nor considered in the C.A. and so remains a valid authority. See also, *Blackford & Son (Calne) Ltd.* v. *Christchurch Corp.* [1962] 1 Lloyd's Rep. 349, illustrated Chap. 5, p. 314, where an arbitrator was held not entitled to ignore such provisions by reason of an " implied " discretion under clause 52 (4) of the 1955 I.C.E. form of contract (for the wording of this provision see the case of *Tersons Ltd.* v. *Stevenage Development Corp.*, illustrated *ante*, Chap. 8, pp. 535–536).

since the amendment of the R.S.C. relating to specially indorsed writs and summary judgments this is no longer of great importance.

In those cases where the ascertainment of the price depends upon ascertainment or certification by the architect or engineer, the debt becomes due upon such event.[18] In other cases, if the contract is an entire contract, the debt becomes due upon completion of the contract, subject to the doctrine of substantial performance.[19]

Provisions for payment by instalments, however, which are, of course, extremely common in building contracts, form an important exception to this rule, and in most cases the instalment will itself be a debt due.[20]

(2) Reasonable Price

As has been indicated, the liability to pay a reasonable price arises either expressly, or impliedly where the contract is either silent as to price, or for one reason or another an existing contract is held not to apply to the work in question. Thus a contract may provide for work to be carried out on a " cost plus " or on a " dayworks " basis without further defining these expressions. While at first sight these words may appear to have a special connotation in valuing building work, consideration will show that, in the absence of more precise description, such as a statement of the percentages to be added for cost plus purposes or identification with a particular Dayworks Schedule, they in fact mean no more than a reasonable price, though the word " dayworks " means a method of pricing work by recording the hours spent on it by the various tradesmen and their hourly wages, and recording also the quantities of any materials and the hours of any plant used. For this reason, it is usually, but not invariably, used when the work is of its nature not capable of assessment on an ordinary pricing basis. Thus instructions to tidy up a site after bad weather, or to provide for lighting or perform some other service will often be given on the basis of the contractor being " paid on dayworks."

In practice, in determining a reasonable price, the courts may act upon evidence calculated upon the cost of labour, plant and materials plus a reasonable percentage for profit, or they may act upon evidence of what reasonable rates or prices for the physical work involved would be. This is a perennial problem in the conduct of building litigation arising out of less formal contracts or disputed variations

[18] See Chap. 7, *supra*, Approval and Certificates, and in particular sections 4 and 6 (7).
[19] See *ante*, Chap. 5, pp. 245 *et seq.*
[20] See *infra*.

and there is no general rule of practice with regard to it. The decision may depend upon the nature and amount of the work involved, or upon whether the work has been actually carried out, or is hypothetical work, *e.g.* in a claim for damages for loss of profit, or upon the nature of the issues raised between the parties, and will be influenced by considerations of convenience from the evidentiary point of view. As stated, some work is, of course, by its nature incapable of accurate measurement by means of rates.

Where the agreement is silent, it should not be forgotten, though it will only rarely be otherwise in the case of building or engineering work, that on well-known general principles a right to reasonable remuneration will only arise where from the circumstances an intention that the work should be paid for can be implied, and there are circumstances where this will not always be so.[21]

An agreement may also be partly silent as to price. The commonest example is a case where varied work has no counterpart in the schedule of rates or bills of quantities, but it may also be the case that the schedule or bills are incomplete and an item of work necessary to the contract work has been omitted therefrom.[22] In the case of variations, the modern standard forms of contract have somewhat vague and imprecise provisions for such a case—*e.g.* the use of rates for varied work " based on " those in the schedule or bills.[23] But in the absence of some clear applicable provision, the value of any part of the work which is to be paid for and is not priced in the contract will have to be assessed on the basis of a reasonable price. This can also happen in certain rather rare cases where the number of variations is so great that the original contract work is in effect totally replaced by a different total *corpus* of work.[24]

Apart from cases where the liability to pay a reasonable price arises expressly or impliedly under the contract, the following are examples of other situations in which such a liability may arise, and form exceptions to the rule, already mentioned, that an action upon a *quantum meruit* will not lie where a contract fixing or regulating the price is in existence:

[21] See for cases to the contrary *ante*, pp. 17–20, 179–182, 230–231.
[22] See, *e.g.* the case of *Walton-on-the-Naze U.D.C.* v. *Moran*, illustrated *ante*, Chap. 8, p. 522.
[23] For valuation of variations, see *ante*, Chap. 8, pp. 555 *et seq.*
[24] See *Sir Lindsay Parkinson Co. Ltd.* v. *Works and Public Buildings Commissioners* [1949] 2 K.B. 632, and the cases illustrated *ante*, Chap. 8, pp. 548–552, where varied work so greatly in excess of the amount contemplated by the contract was ordered that the contract rates were held not to be applicable.

   (i) where the contractor is entitled to treat the contract as repudiated by reason of a fundamental breach of contract of the employer, or conduct by him evincing an intention no longer to be bound [25];

   (ii) where a contract has been frustrated, under section 1 (2) of the Law Reform (Frustrated Contracts) Act of 1943 [26];

   (iii) where the work has been carried out under a void (but not an illegal) contract [27];

   (iv) where work has been carried out under an unenforceable contract.[28]

(A possible fifth exception, namely, a change in the circumstances under which the work was carried out from those contemplated at the time of the contract, as adumbrated in the case of *Bush* v. *Trustees of Port and Town of Whitehaven* (1888),[29] may now be taken to have been overruled by the decision of the House of Lords in *Davis Contractors Ltd.* v. *Fareham U.D.C.* (1956).[30])

(3) Instalments of the Price

It is, of course, an extremely common feature of building and engineering contracts that provision is made for advances on account, or payment by instalments, to be made to the contractor.[31] These may be arranged to become due at certain stages of the work as a fixed proportion of the contract price, or at certain stipulated intervals of time as the value of work done and materials delivered to the site up to that time, or from time to time in amounts of not less than a fixed sum. The standard forms at present all adopt monthly payment of a fixed percentage of the value of the work done and materials brought onto the site, the percentage retained being referred to as retention money, and specific provision being made for its use.

---

[25] *Planché* v. *Colburn* (1831) 8 Bing. 14; *Lodder* v. *Slowey* [1904] A.C. 442. See *infra,* p. 602.

[26] *Ante,* Chap. 5, pp. 348 *et seq.*

[27] See *e.g. Lawford* v. *Billericay R.D.C.* [1903] 1 K.B. 772 (absence of seal), or cases of contracts avoided by mistake, *ante,* Chap. 1.

[28] *Scott* v. *Pattison* [1923] 2 K.B. 723; *James* v. *Kent* [1951] 1 K.B. 551. The commonest class of such contracts in the past were those required to be in writing under the Statute of Frauds. Contracts of guarantee and contracts within s. 140 of the Law of Property Act 1925 are the only contracts in this category likely to be met with in the context of building contracts—see *post,* Chap. 17 for Contracts of Guarantee.

[29] Hudson's B.C., 4th ed. Vol. 2, p. 122.

[30] [1956] A.C. 696. See *ante,* Chap. 5, pp. 353–354.

[31] See for full discussions of this in the context of entire and substantial completion, *ante,* Chap. 5, Section 1, pp. 255–262, and in the context of interim certificates, *ante,* Chap. 7, Section 6 (7), p. 492 *et seq.*

In the absence of express provision, such terms will create a debt
due in respect of each instalment.[32] Where, however, a certificate is
necessary, this may be a condition precedent to the debt coming into
existence [33] unless there is an overriding arbitration clause enabling
an arbitrator to entertain a claim on its merits. Even if there is an
arbitration clause, it has already been pointed out [34] that Buckley J.
suggested *obiter* in the case of *Farr* v. *Ministry of Transport* (1960) [35]
that the terms of the arbitration clause in the standard I.C.E. form of
contract would only enable an arbitrator to consider the merits of a
claim for an interim certificate before the completion of the work if
the dispute related to a point of principle rather than mere valuation,
but this view has been doubted earlier in this book [36] on the wording
of the I.C.E. form of contract before Buckley J., and it has also been
submitted that there is at least as great a doubt in the case of the
arbitration clause in the R.I.B.A. standard forms,[37] where the wording permits an arbitration before completion where the dispute is
" whether or not a certificate has been improperly withheld or is not
in accordance with these conditions," [38] and where, by clause 30 (2)
of the conditions, the amount in an interim certificate shall be " the
total value of the work properly executed . . . less any amount which
may be retained by the Employer . . . " at the relevant date. In
consequence, it is submitted that, on the wording of the standard
forms, interim payments can be claimed without a certificate or in the
face of a certificate, even if the dispute is one of valuation only, and
a debt due will arise once the time for issuing the certificate has
arrived.[39]

Most interim certificates are dependent upon the passing of a
period of time, but where they are dependent upon the work reaching
a certain stage, it has already been suggested [40] that the rules as to
entire performance and substantial performance will apply to work
done to earn any instalment due under such a provision. It is also
submitted that any relevant period of time must completely elapse

---

[32] *Workman, Clarke & Co. Ltd.* v. *Lloyd Brazileno* [1908] 1 K.B. 968; *Taylor* v. *Laird*
(1856) 25 L.J.Ex. 329, *ante*, p. 255.
[33] See the case of *Dunlop & Ranken Ltd.* v. *Hendall Steel Structures* [1957] 1 W.L.R.
1102, discussed on this point *ante*, p. 496. See generally pp. 492–497.
[34] *Ante*, Chap. 7, p. 495.
[35] [1960] 1 W.L.R. 956
[36] *Ante*, Chap. 7, p. 495.
[37] See *per* Viscount Simonds (*obiter*) in *Burden* v. *Swansea Corporation* [1957] 1 W.L.R.
1167 at p. 1169.
[38] Clause 35 (2) of the post-1963 standard forms.
[39] *Ante*, Chap. 7, Section 6 (7).
[40] *Ante*, Chap. 5, pp. 244, 257–260.

before the instalment becomes due, so that a contractor on abandoning work will not be entitled to any part of the last relevant instalment.

Where no provision for payment by instalments exists, no term
to that effect will usually be implied.[41] But, in some cases, it does
seem a possibility that in the case of long and costly work in informally concluded contracts such a term might in certain circumstances
be implied, and in the absence of reasonable payment the contractor
could refuse to continue.[42] However, no body of law on this subject
has as yet emerged.

(4) Interest

This can be an important matter in practice, as final accounts are
frequently settled by architects and engineers long after the work has
been completed, despite provisions in the contract to the contrary.
In the absence of express agreement,[43] or mercantile usage, interest
was not recoverable at common law upon a debt due[44]; and no such
usage has been established in relation to building contracts. Interest
upon judgment debts and awards of arbitrators has, however, been
recoverable for many years by statute—see the Judgment Act 1838,
and the Arbitration Acts [44a]—but in these cases only runs from the
date of the judgment or award.

There are, however, two important exceptions to the general rule.
In the first place, where money has been obtained or retained by
fraud, interest is recoverable as an item of damage.[45] And, secondly,
by section 3 (1) of the Law Reform (Miscellaneous Provisions) Act
of 1934, in any proceedings tried in any court of record for the recovery of debt or damages, the court may, if it thinks fit, order that
there shall be included in the sum for which judgment is given interest
at such rate as it thinks fit on the whole or a part of the debt or
damages for a whole or a part of the period between the date when
the cause of action arose and the date of judgment. This power may
be exercised by an arbitrator.[46]

---

[41] See, *e.g. Appleby* v. *Myers* (1867) L.R. 2 C.P. 651, and *ante*, pp. 243–249.

[42] *Roberts* v. *Havelock* (1832) 3 B. & Ad. 404; *The Tergeste* [1903] P. 26 at p. 34. These
are not, however, building cases. See *ante*, Chap. 5, pp. 260–262.

[43] *Cf*. I.C.E. form of contract, cl. 60 (3).

[44] See *e.g. London, Chatham and Dover Ry.* v. *S.E. Ry.* [1892] 1 Ch. 120 at p. 140, and
[1893] A.C. 429 at pp. 437–438.

[44a] For the power of an arbitrator under section 20 of the Act of 1950 to order a rate in
excess of the 4 per cent. permitted under the Judgment Act, see *per* Donaldson J. in
The Myron [1969] 3 W.L.R. 292.

[45] *Johnson* v. *R.* [1904] A.C. 817; *Barclay* v. *Harris* (1915) 85 L.J.K.B. 115.

[46] *Chandris* v. *Isbrandtsen-Moller Co.* [1951] 1 K.B. 240 at p. 255.

This provision needs to be carefully considered. It will be noticed that the discretion to grant interest only arises " in any proceedings." So, whatever the delay, it would seem that payment or tender of the sum due without any interest before a writ is issued or notice of arbitration given will prevent any claim for interest being entertained. Furthermore, while interest may run from the time when the cause of action arose, this does not necessarily mean, in the case of a contractor's claim for work done, the time when the work was completed, since the contractor's right to sue may only arise upon the issue of a certificate or expression of satisfaction by the architect or engineer. This, of course, will depend upon the exact terms of the contract. It has already been suggested that in cases of refusal by a certifier to exercise his function at all, it may well be possible to dispense with the certificate. But where the contractor is not entitled to sue until he obtains a stipulated certificate or satisfaction, there are obvious difficulties in the way of imposing an obligation express or implied that the certifier shall issue a certificate within a reasonable or stipulated time, for which the employer may be held liable in damages.[47] In nearly all modern contracts, however, there is an overriding arbitration clause which will enable the contractor to sue or give notice of arbitration the moment he is entitled to receive a certificate, and, provided he does take action, the Act of 1934 will be brought into operation and the discretionary entitlement to interest will arise. For some reason, arbitrators (and indeed some judges) often appear to be reluctant to award interest for the full period from the date the cause of action arises. In principle, although there is a complete discretion in the matter, it is submitted that it should be awarded for the full period unless there is some palpable reason to the contrary. The background to most building litigation is a commercial one, and assessments of the risks of that litigation are made by the parties and their advisers with a view to securing their position on costs by sealed offers or payments into court. Such calculations are liable to be confounded if unjudicial awards of interest are made.

The same considerations apply to the rate of interest. Few tribunals appear to award realistic interest, and many appear automatically to award rates of interest below bank rate. This, of course, bears no relation to realistic borrowing rates, which, it is submitted, are the correct ones to apply. This tendency seems only explicable on the basis that judges and others find interest usurious

---

[47] See Chap. 7, Approval and Certificates, *supra*, pp. 450, 475–476.

and ungentlemanly.[48] A more realistic tendency now seems to be
developing in the English Courts, however.[48a]

(5) Bonus and Deductions Provisions

Building contracts (though not the standard forms at present in
force) sometimes contain provisions designed to give the contractor
a financial inducement either to complete the contract to time, or to
complete it economically.

Where time is concerned, such provisions may be found in
association with the liquidated damages clause and extension of time
clauses,[49] and may provide, for instance, that for every week or day
by which actual completion precedes the stipulated date, a certain
sum shall be payable to the contractor by way of bonus. Alternatively, a fixed sum may be payable provided the work is completed
by a stipulated date. To earn bonuses of this type, completion by the
date, or breach of contract by the employer preventing such completion, must be established, and in the latter case the bonus will be
recovered as damages for the breach. It is clear that provisions of
this type will be strictly construed, and the mere existence of circumstances beyond the builder's control delaying completion will not,
in the absence of express provision, assist the builder to obtain the
bonus.

ILLUSTRATIONS

(1) L. contracted to execute certain work within a fixed time,
subject to penalties, and was to have a bonus if the work was completed in time. Sub-contractors named by the architect, but employed
by L., caused delay. *Held*, that L. was not entitled to the bonus:
Leslie v. *Metropolitan Asylums Board* (1901).[50]

(2) B. tendered on January 29, 1903, to do certain alterations
to C.'s restaurant for the sum of £12,395. At an interview on
February 4 between B. and C. the tender was accepted. Simultaneously it was agreed as follows: " That in consideration of B. undertaking to give possession of the basement and ground floor within
nine weeks from the date of commencement C. would pay to B.
the sum of £360 as a bonus." B. began to work on February 11,
1903, but was at once stopped, as C. had not made arrangements
with the occupier of the adjoining house for interfering with a party
wall. B. was unable to resume working until March 3, when a party
wall award was made. Possession of the basement and ground

---

[48] See also the comments on the attitude to successful parties in litigation as possibly
   exemplified by the refusal to award the results of inflation to plaintiffs, *infra*, pp. 590–
   592.
[48a] See *e.g. Pagman & Fratelli* v. *Tradax Export* [1969] 2 Lloyds Rep. 150 and *The Myron*
   [1969] 7 W.L.R. 292.
[49] See *post*, Chap. 11, pp. 647–648, for their possible effect on bonus provisions.
[50] 68 J.P. 86.

floor was not given by B. to C. until May 16. C. paid the £12,395, but refused to pay the £360. *Held*, that there was such a prevention by C. of B. earning the £360 as to entitle B. to damages, and that as no attempt had been made at the trial to quantify the damages, a judgment giving B. £360 as damages must be upheld: *Bywaters* v. *Curnick* (1906).[51]

Draftsmen of such provisions should be careful to deal specifically with the effect of variations ordered under a power in the contract on the contractor's opportunity to earn his bonus, since it does not follow that an extension of time clause will necessarily be construed as extending the bonus date of completion.[52]

Bonus provisions designed to obtain economic completion are usually found in association with a target or estimated figure of final cost, and provisions for remuneration of the contractor based on actual cost. An example of this type of contract is to be seen in the case of *Jones & Lyttle Ltd.* v. *Mackie* (1918).[53] Such provisions may also provide for deductions to be made should actual cost exceed the estimated cost. Surprisingly, such contracts are comparatively rare; and certain complications may arise in calculating the final price, as a result, for instance, of ordering additions and omissions, or the operation of rising costs during the contract, which should be the subject of special provision in the bonus clause. To protect the employer's interest adequately it is obvious that an exceptionally high degree of supervision will be required in contracts of this type, and exceptional care as to the accuracy of the original estimate.

Section 2.   Damages

(1) Generally

In this section it is not proposed to deal with liquidated damages or penalties, which are separately dealt with in Chapter 11. The general principles governing damages for breach of contract, as first enunciated in the leading case of *Hadley* v. *Baxendale* (1854),[54] were fully considered and explained in the judgment of Asquith L.J. in *Victoria*

---

[51] Hudson's B.C., 4th ed., Vol. 2, p. 393; and see *Ware* v. *Lyttelton Harbour Board* (1882) 1 N.Z.L.R.S.C. 191, *post*, Chap. 11, pp. 647–648.

[52] See *Ware* v. *Lyttelton Harbour Board* (1882) 1 N.Z.L.R.S.C. 191, illustrated *post*, Chap. 11, p. 648.

[53] (1918) 2 W.W.R. 82 (Canada), illustrated in Section 2, *Damages, infra*, at p. 602. See also the provisions in *Crane* v. *Hegeman-Harris* [1939] 4 All E.R. 68, illustrated *ante*, Chap. 1, Section 5 (3), pp. 36–37.

[54] 9 Ex. 341.

Laundry (Windsor) Ltd. v. *Newman Industries* (1949),[55] and further refined and explained by the House of Lords in *Czarnikow Ltd.* v. *Koufos* (1969).[55a] Briefly, the injured party is entitled to be indemnified against any loss likely to arise in the usual course of things from the breach, and also such other loss outside the usual course of things as was in the contemplation of the parties at the time of the contract as the likely result of the breach of it. In the latter class of case, the knowledge of the defendant must have been brought home to him in such circumstances that he impliedly undertook to bear any special loss referable to the breach.[56] Various judicial attempts have been made to define the degree of likelihood which is involved—Asquith L.J.'s " on the cards " in the *Victoria Laundry* case has now been discarded, it seems, in favour of a result which is " not unlikely " or " a serious possibility or real danger " or " liable to " occur by the House of Lords in the *Koufos* case. In the sections below these principles will be considered in their application to breaches by the contractor and the employer, respectively. It should be appreciated by legally unqualified readers that a breach of contract may only give rise to nominal damages, and it is only if the application of the above principles shows that effective damages can be recovered that litigation of any sort can be justified. Questions of damages arising out of the contracts of employment of architects and surveyors have already been dealt with in Chapter 2.

(2) Breach by the Contractor

Under the complicated provisions of many building contracts the possible breaches of contract by the contractor are numerous, and in each case the general principles set out above must be applied in order to determine what, if any, damage is recoverable for the breach in question. Typical breaches of the less common kind are, for example, unauthorised sub-contracting, failure to insure as required, failure to give notices, payment of unauthorised wages, and so on, which, depending on the particular circumstances of the case, may or may not cause damage. The commonest breaches causing substantial damage, and hence giving rise to litigation, may be broadly divided into three categories, namely, those involving abandonment or total failure to complete, those involving delay in completion, and those involving defective work.

[55] [1949] 2 K.B. 528.
[55a] [1969] A.C. 350.
[56] *British Columbia Sawmills* v. *Nettleship* (1868) L.R. 3 C.P. 499.

A single breach may, in fact, involve one or more of these factors. Before considering the measure of damage in these cases, it is perhaps advisable to point out that the contract may by its terms contain explicit provisions as to the measure of damage in the event of a breach—the determination clauses with their special codes governing the damages recoverable by the party determining the contract, and the provisions for liquidated damages for delay in completion in the current standard forms of building and engineering contracts are an example. Where these exist, they will be given effect to (unless, in the case of the latter, held to be penalties), and may in certain cases affect or reduce the damages otherwise recoverable,[57] unless (in the case of the former) they are expressed to be without prejudice to any other remedies of the injured party.[58] Thus it is submitted that a liquidated damages clause for delay in completion will usually mean that a contractor completing late will be entitled under a fluctuations clause to increases occurring in the period of delay, since the liquidated damages are the employers' pre-estimate of *all* his damages arising from the delay.[58a] In the case of defective work it should also be remembered that the final certificate may, in the absence of an overriding arbitration clause, bind the employer and prevent him from alleging defective work altogether,[59] and many contracts where no architect is used, particularly private-developer sales (or sales of houses " in the course of erection ") may, depending on their terms, extinguish liability upon the later conveyance under the *caveat emptor* principle.[60] In contracts of this kind, an express remedy for defective work may be made available to the employer of a more limited character than the common law right to damages, either in relation to the period of time during which it may be available, or the character of the defective work itself.[61]

ILLUSTRATIONS

(1) The final certificate in a building contract was to be binding and conclusive, but the contract also provided that no final or other certificate should relieve the contractor from his liability for " any fraud, default or wilful deviation from the contract " until four years after completion. *Held*, the contractor was not liable for defects within the four years caused merely by slovenly workmanship as opposed to deliberate deviations made with a view to

---

[57] See *post*, Chap. 11, Penalties and Liquidated Damages.
[58] See, *e.g.* clause 24 (2) of the post-1963 R.I.B.A. forms.
[58a] This view has now been taken by the Court of Appeal—see *supra*, p. 568.
[59] *Ante*, Chap. 7, Sections 2–4, and *cf.* clause 30 (7) of the 1963 R.I.B.A. standard form, commented on in detail *ante*, Chap. 7, pp. 489–492.
[60] *Ante*, Chap. 5, pp. 289–90; Chap. 6, Section 2, pp. 396–397.
[61] See also the cases, *ante*, Chap. 6, pp. 397–399.

increasing the contractor's profit: *London School Board* v. *Johnson* (1891).[62]

(2) A contractor's employment was terminated under a forfeiture clause in the contract. The employers sought to recover loss of rents on the building and similar items of damage. *Held*, such matters were governed by a provision in the contract for liquidated damages for delay in completion: *Grace* v. *Osler* (1911).[63]

(3) A road-making contract contained a clause " Should it at any time subsequent to . . . the period of maintenance but not exceeding five years from the date of completion of the works be discovered that the terms of this specification have been violated by . . . bad . . . work the council shall be at liberty to make good such work and to recover the cost thereof from the contractor." *Held*, the council could not recover for defects discovered after the five years: *Marsden U.D.C.* v. *Sharp* (1932).[64]

[Note: This case cannot, in the light of the severe (and, it is respectfully submitted, correct) criticisms of Diplock L.J. in *Hancock* v. *Brazier (Anerley) Ltd.* (1966), [65] be regarded as of any authority on its wording, which is insufficient to displace the prima facie right to damages for defective work for the full period of limitation.]

(4) A housing contract for a local authority provided that the contractor should not assign or sub-contract except with their consent and that " compliance with the foregoing conditions is of the essence of this contract and in the event of any non-compliance . . . it shall be lawful for the corporation to adopt either of the following remedies . . . namely firstly the corporation may absolutely determine this contract . . . or secondly the corporation may call upon the contractor to pay in respect of such non-compliance the sum of £100 by way of liquidated and ascertained damages and not by way of penalty." The contractors sub-contracted work in breach of this clause, and the corporation determined under the clause, and completed by other contractors at an extra cost of £21,000, which they sought to recover as damages. *Held*, apart from the express stipulation, the breach would not have entitled the corporation to determine. Under the clause there was no express right to recover the extra cost of completion in the event of determination, and the council's claim must fail: *Feather (Thomas) & Co. (Bradford) Ltd.* v. *Keighley Corporation* (1953).[66]

It is also important for the employer, in considering his remedies against a contractor in breach of contract, to take account of the doctrine of entire contracts and substantial performance (*ante*, Chapter 5). Many building contracts will be entire contracts, though in most cases the full rigour of the rule preventing recovery unless

---

[62] Hudson's B.C., 4th ed., Vol. 2, p. 176.
[63] 19 W.L.R. 109, 326 (Canada).   [64] 48 T.L.R. 23.
[65] [1966] 1 W.L.R. 1317. See *ante*, Chap. 6, Section 2, pp. 398–399.
[66] 52 L.G.R. 30. (Note.—Under the rule in *Hadley* v. *Baxendale* the extra cost of completion could not arise in the usual course of things from this particular breach. The right to recover this cost could therefore only arise under the express provisions of the contract.)

the contract is substantially performed is considerably mitigated by the existence of provisions for interim payment, which create debts due on each payment or instalment. In these latter cases, the rule will only apply to the balance due since the last payment or instalment, where the work is abandoned, or to the retention moneys and any other balance owing, in a case where the work is completed but defective. But it remains true that an employer should weigh carefully the damages recoverable, on the one hand, against the advantage he may derive under the above doctrine from the builder's inability to sue for the balance of the price of the work on the other, since if he decides to sue for damages he will have to give credit for what the work would have cost him if properly completed or performed.[67]

The law as to mitigation should also not be forgotten in this context. Briefly, the injured party must, faced with the fact of a breach by the other party, conduct himself reasonably in dealing with its consequences if he wishes to recover damages. Being the innocent party, his conduct will not be examined in any very severe light, but should he exacerbate the consequences of a breach by his own act or clear neglect, he will not be able to recover the additional cost occasioned thereby as damages. It is submitted, however, that the innocent party is not under any duty to detect breaches by the other party, and is entitled to assume, however imprudently in the commercial sense, that the other party will fulfil his obligations. His duty to mitigate only arises once he actually knows of a breach and is fully aware of its extent. Otherwise it would be open to every contractor accused of defective work to contend that the employer or his architect should have detected it at the earliest possible moment, and an employer employing an architect might find himself in a worse case than an employer without one. Indeed, in so far as his duty of supervision was concerned, the architect would, on this view, be protecting the contractor's interest as much as the employer's.[68]

The foregoing paragraph in the Ninth Edition of this work may be regarded as in all essential respects confirmed by the judgments of the House of Lords in *East Ham B.C.* v. *Sunley*,[69] passages from which, and from the judgment of Mocatta J. in *A.M.F. (International) Ltd.* v. *Magnet Bowling*,[70] are cited *ante*, Chapter 6, Section 2.[71]

---

[67] See *e.g. Mertens* v. *Home Freeholds* [1921] 2 K.B. 526, *infra*, pp. 585–586.

[68] See the case of *East Ham B.C.* v. *Bernard Sunley Ltd.* (1964), illustrated *infra*, pp. 583–584. It is submitted that *Ata Ul Haq* v. *City Council of Nairobi* (1959) P.C., *ante*, pp. 58–59, is of doubtful authority in so far as it is concerned with questions of waiver.

[69] [1966] A.C. 406. Illustrated on Damages, *infra*.   [70] [1968] 1 W.L.R. 1028.

[71] *Ante*, pp. 385–388. See also Chap. 1, pp. 68–70; Chap. 2, pp. 139–141, 153–155; Chap. 5, pp. 324–325; and Chap. 8, pp. 524–530.

Equally, it should not be forgotten that waiver of a breach, or a renunciation of the right to damages, or a liability to pay for the work, will not, in general, and in the absence of express provision,[72] be implied from acceptance of the work by the building owner or his architect, even in the case of patently defective work.[73] For such a result to occur, it would, it is submitted, be necessary to find some fresh consideration moving from the builder, or at least sufficient facts to support an estoppel against the employer's relying on the breach, involving some action of the builder to his detriment based upon conduct or a representation of the employer. For instance, a decision by the architect to deal in a certain way with a defect detected by him, followed by the reinstatement and covering up of the work by the builder on the architect's instructions, would only, in the event of the remedy proving ineffective, and if the first attempt had been wholly unreasonable, prevent the owner from claiming the cost of the original repairs and later reopening, under the doctrine of mitigation of damage. On the other hand, the deliberate acceptance for incorporation in the works of defective materials, after consideration of an apparent defect by the employer or architect, might well estop the owner from complaining of the consequences of that defect (but not some other undetected defect), even in the absence of any express provision in the contract,[74] unless the contractor himself had recommended or urged the use of the materials, notwithstanding the defect. But the facts would, it is suggested, have to be strong, and a substantial detriment to the builder established, before any acceptance could absolve the builder from the consequences of his own breach of contract.

ILLUSTRATION

Builders constructed a school with serious defects in the stone facing. The contract was in the 1956 R.I.B.A. standard form. Some years after the architect's final certificate a stone fell and the employers discovered the defects. The arbitrator found that the defects could have been, but in fact were not, discovered or noticed by the architect during the course of his normal supervision of the work. At the date of the breach (which the parties agreed should for purposes of convenience be treated as the date of completing the work), the cost of repair would have been considerably less, due to rising prices, than it was when the employers finally discovered the defects. *Held*, by Melford Stevenson J., distinguishing *Phillips* v. *Ward* (1956),[75] that

---

[72] See *e.g.* the case of *Adcock's Trustee* v. *Bridge R.D.C.*, illustrated *ante*, p. 385.

[73] *Ante*, Chap. 6, pp. 376–382.

[74] See *e.g. Adcock's* case, *ante*, Chap. 6, p. 385, where there was, however, an express provision in the contract.

[75] [1956] 1 W.L.R. 471, *ante*, p. 158.

since the employers had been guilty of no unreasonable delay once they discovered the defects, they were entitled to the greater cost of the repairs at the time they carried them out. *Held,* by the House of Lords, that the parties must have contemplated that the architect might fail to notice defective work. The cost of repair at the date of discovering the breach was " on the cards " or a " loss liable to result " from the breach within the test formulated by Asquith L.J. in the *Victoria Laundry* case. *Per* Lord Upjohn: "where the cost of reinstatement is the proper measure of damages it necessarily follows as a matter of common sense that in the ordinary case the cost must be assessed at the time when the defect is discovered and put right and it is not suggested here that the building owner unreasonably delayed the work of repair after discovery of the defect. . . . I am at a loss to understand why the negligent builder should be able to limit his liability by reason of the fact that at some earlier stage the architect failed to notice some defective work. . . .": *East Ham B.C.* v. *Bernard Sunley Ltd.* (1966).[76]

Finally, the legal nature of the employer's right to damages against a building contractor where the latter sues for the price of the work was until recently somewhat obscure. It is now clear that it operates as a defence to the claim (technically, as an equitable set-off), which may have an important bearing on costs, since, if it exceeds the amount claimed, the claim will be treated as having failed.[77] It has been held to be a set-off for the purpose of the mutual dealings clause in bankruptcy.[78] It has also been held to be an " equity " binding upon an assignee of the builder.[79] In cases where the builder sues in *quantum meruit,* and there has been defective work, it has been held that the true view is that nothing is payable or due for the defective work, and that, if other work has to be undone to allow repairs of the defective work, that other work should similarly not be charged for.[80] But this may not be the final word upon the subject, since it is not difficult to conceive of cases where the cost of repair or replacement may be greatly in excess of the cost of the defective work not charged for.

It is now proposed to consider the measure of damage in cases of a breach by the contractor under two headings, namely, breaches

---

[76] [1966] A.C. 406. *Cf.* for the same principle on measure of damages the case of *Mertens* v. *Home Freeholds Co.* [1921] 2 K.B. 526, illustrated *infra*, p. 586. See also *Clark* v. *Woor* [1965] 1 W.L.R. 650.

[77] *Hanak* v. *Green* [1958] 2 Q.B. 9. See also the cases on substantial performance illustrated *ante*, Chap. 5, pp. 251–253, *viz. Cutler* v. *Close* (1832) 5 C. & P. 337; *Watts* v. *McLeay* [1911] W.L.R. 916 (Canada); *Dakin* v. *Lee* [1916] 1 K.B. 566, and *Hoenig* v. *Isaacs* [1952] 2 All E.R. 176.

[78] *Post*, Chap. 16.

[79] *Young* v. *Kitchin* (1878) 3 Ex.D. 127, *post*, Chap. 14, p. 725.

[80] *Ogilvie* v. *Cooke & Hannah* [1952] Ont.R. 862 (Canada).

involving (i) defective or incomplete work and (ii) delay and consequential damages.

(a) Defective or incomplete work

In those cases where, in breach of contract, the work has been left incomplete, whether by abandonment, termination, or otherwise, or containing defects, the direct measure of damage will be the difference between the reasonable cost to the employer of repairing the defects or completing the work, together with any sums paid by or due from him under the contract, and the sums which would have been payable by him under the contract if it had been properly carried out.[81] (Where the former does not exceed the latter, only nominal damages would be recoverable, and where the sums due under the contract have been paid in full, as where a contractor has completed and defects or omissions are discovered at some time after final payment, the direct measure is, of course, the reasonable cost of repair *simpliciter*.) Such damages are clearly recoverable within the first branch of the rule in *Hadley* v. *Baxendale, supra,* as likely to arise in the usual course of things from the breach.

ILLUSTRATIONS

(1) B agreed to erect a house for the plaintiff according to plans by a certain day. The defendants were B's sureties. After partly completing, B ceased work, and the plaintiff, after giving notice to the sureties, entered and completed and sued the sureties. *Held*, that the measure of damages was what it cost the plaintiff to complete the house substantially as it was originally intended, and in a reasonable manner, less any amount that would have been due and payable to B by the plaintiff had B completed the house at the time agreed by the terms of his contract: *Hirt* v. *Hahn* (1876).[82]

(2) A contract provided for the installation of pews in a church. Sub-specification timber was used. The contractor sued for the price. *Held*, a reduction in the contract price to take account of the lower value of the timber actually installed was not an adequate measure of the set-off to which the owner was entitled, and sums were allowed for strengthening the pews in addition to the reduced value: *Wood* v. *Stringer* (1890).[83]

(3) A builder agreed in May 1916, to build a house for the plaintiff for a lump sum and to complete the house within a specified time. After starting the work the builder intentionally delayed progress for the purpose of ensuring that the Ministry of Munitions

---

[81] For the measure of damage in cases of termination, see further Chap. 13, *post*, pp. 705, 710–712.

[82] 61 Missouri 496; approved by the Court of Appeal in *Mertens* v. *Home Freeholds Co.* [1921] 2 K.B. 526.

[83] 20 Ont. 148 (Canada).

should refuse a licence for the construction of the house under the Defence of the Realm Regulations, and that he would thereby (as he thought) be released from his contract. The licence was refused, and the work had to be entirely suspended till 1919, when the plaintiff completed the building. *Held,* that the builder could not take advantage of frustration brought about by his own act, and that the proper measure of damages was what it cost the plaintiff to complete the house as soon as the statutory restriction ceased, less any amount which would have been due and payable to the builder if the builder had proceeded with due diligence up to the date when the licence was refused: *Mertens* v. *Home Freeholds Co.* (1921).[84]

(4) A number of houses were built for a development company with inferior cement. They were paid for and resold to purchasers. On complaints by the purchasers, the development company, though not legally bound to do so, carried out repairs to make the houses habitable. *Held,* the company were entitled to recover the difference between the *value* of the houses as they ought to have been when completed and their value in fact: *Newton Abbot Development Co. Ltd.* v. *Stockman Bros.* (1931).[85]

(5) Foundations were laid for certain elevators which did not conform to the requirements of the contract. Some of the defects at least were not repairable. *Held,* the measure of damages was the cost of alterations or repairs necessary to bring about compliance with the contract: *Pearson-Building Ltd.* v. *Pioneer Grain Co. Ltd.* (1933).[86]

(6) In breach of contract the foundations of a house built on a concrete raft failed. The only remedy was to rebuild using a " pier and beam " system, which would cost more than the original house. The owner sued for the cost of the new type of foundation, £2,200, and £500 for depreciation in value. *Held,* that the disparity between the original cost of the house and the new foundations was not a reason for departing from the normal rule, but that from the cost of repair should be deducted a sum to take account of the fact that the new foundations would eliminate all danger of sinking, whereas some sinking on an even plane was expected with the original house, and the damages should be £2,000: *Cooke* v. *Rowe* (1950).[87]

(7) A builder substantially departed from the specification in relation to the foundations of a house, which was consequently unstable. *Held,* the measure of damage was not the difference between the value of the building as erected and the value if erected in accordance with the contract, but the cost, in excess of any amount of the contract price unpaid, of reasonable and necessary work to make it conform to the contract: *Bellgrove* v. *Eldridge* (1954).[88]

---

[84] [1921] 2 K.B. 526, following *Hirt* v. *Hahn, supra.* See for the application of the rule where building costs rise before repairing work is done, the case of *East Ham B.C.* v. *Bernard Sunley Ltd.* illustrated *supra,* pp. 583–584, and discussed in this context *infra,* pp. 591–592.

[85] 47 T.L.R. 616; discussed *infra,* p. 588.

[86] [1933] 1 W.W.R. 179 (Canada).

[87] [1950] N.Z.L.R. 410 (New Zealand).

[88] A.L.R. 929. Vol. 90 C.L.R. 613 (Australia).

(8) Suppliers installed plant in an old mill which was used as a plasticine factory. The plant had a serious defect, and as a result there was a fire which destroyed the mill. The owners built a modern two-floor factory, of similar capacity and floor area but totally different design, in place of the mill, which was a five-floor building. The owners sued the suppliers for breach of contract. The suppliers, relying on *Philips* v. *Ward*,[88a] contended that loss of value was the measure of damage. *Held* by the Court of Appeal, that the owners were entitled to the cost of building the new factory, and not the value of the old mill prior to its destruction, that the new design did no more than replace what had been lost, and that no credit need be given because of the betterment factor of the modern design and materials of the new building: *Harbutt's Plasticine Ltd.* v. *Wayne Tank and Pump Ltd.* (1970).[88b]

However, the cost of completion in an express provision usually means the cost of completing the contract work, not different work.

ILLUSTRATION

S. contracted to construct a tunnel for the city of M. The contract provided that in case of default, the city should be entitled to complete the work at S.'s expense. On S.'s default the city constructed a tunnel which was essentially different in plan and cost of construction from that contemplated by the contract. *Held*, that the city were not entitled to recover damages from S.: *Milwaukee City* v. *Shailer* (1898).[89]

It may be open to a contractor who abandons work which turns out to be unsuitable for its purpose as originally designed to argue in certain cases that the employer has suffered no damage. But this may depend upon the extent of the contractors' liability for design.[90] On the other hand, a contractor who abandoned work which was impossible of completion according to the original design, but which would have been effective once completed, would be liable, it is submitted, for the additional cost of completing using some different method, by virtue of his obligation to complete.[91]

Consideration of the cases illustrated above shows that, in the case of defective work (or work not in accordance with the contract) there are in fact three possible bases of assessing damages, namely, (a) the cost of reinstatement, (b) the difference in cost to the builder of the actual work done and the work specified or (c) the diminution in value of the work due to the breach of contract. There is no doubt

[88a] [1956] 1 W.L.R. 471.
[88b] [1970] 1 Q.B. 447. See also the quotation from Widgery L.J.'s judgment, *infra*, p. 590.
[89] 84 Fed.Rep. 106.
[90] See Chap. 5, pp. 273 *et seq.*
[91] See *ante*, pp. 262 *et seq.*, 267–269.

that, wherever it is reasonable for the employer to insist upon rein-statement, the courts will treat the cost of reinstatement as the measure of damage,[92] and the *Newton Abbot* case [93] (where the owners had parted with the house and were not in any case legally liable to pay for the repairs) appears to be a departure from the pre-vailing rule. On the special facts of that case it may be that the employers were held to be acting reasonably (within the rules for mitigating damage) in paying compensation to purchasers though not legally bound to do so, but to pay more than the diminution in value of the houses and actually repair them may have been considered unreasonable (within the same rules).

The rule is perhaps best summed up in the following quotation from a Canadian judgment:

" It is not a mere matter of difference between the value of the material supplied and that contracted for, or of the work done and that which ought to have been done, or of the house as it stands and that which ought to have been built under the contract. If these were the standards of damages, there would be no point in a man contract-ing for the best materials. The owner of the building is, therefore, entitled to recover such damages as will put him in a position to have the building he contracted for."[94]

It is, however, obvious that in some cases the cost of carrying out work so as to comply with the specification may be very great once the contract work as a whole has been completed. (Even in the case of chattels, however, such as a damaged motor-car, the courts will, rightly, be indulgent to owners who wish to have their property restored at a cost which objectively regarded might seem high.)[95] It is suggested that, in deciding whether to substitute what are usually the lower bases of the difference in value, or the difference in cost to the builder of the actual and specified work, the following factors should be taken into account, *viz.*:

  (a) whether the work actually carried out is reasonably satis-factory for its purpose;

  (b) whether the building owner has carried out or in fact intends to carry out the work of reinstatement;

---

[92] This and the preceding sentence appear to have been approved by Lord Upjohn in *East Ham B.C.* v. *Sunley* [1966] A.C. 406 at p. 445.

[93] *Supra.*

[94] *Per* Wetmore J. in *Allen* v. *Pierce* (1895) 3 Terr.L.R. at p. 323 (Canada).

[95] See Edmund Davies J's decision in *O'Grady* v. *Westminster Scaffolding Ltd.* [1962] 2 Lloyd's Rep. 238.

(c) whether the defect or omission has substantially affected either the market value or the amenity value to the building owner of the works;

(d) whether the cost of reinstatement is wholly disproportionate to the advantages of reinstatement.

It is suggested that if, for the above reasons, cost of reinstatement is rejected as the measure of damage, then the measure should be the difference in cost to the builder,[96] or the diminution in value of the works, whichever is the greater. As to the basis of difference in cost it is clear, it is submitted, that if a builder by breach of contract can save himself a certain sum of money, the direct consequence of such a breach is that the building owner has received a building for the contract price which he could have obtained at the time of tender for the contract price less the sum saved by the contractor's departure from the contract—in other words, a building costing less by that amount. This, it is suggested, is therefore the minimum damage suffered, but evidence can be received to show a greater diminution of value if the defect is such as to cause this in the existing market for buildings of that kind.

" The distinction between those cases in which the measure of damage is the cost of repair of the damaged article, and those in which it is the diminution in value of the article, is not clearly defined. In my opinion each case depends on its own facts, it being remembered, first, that the purpose of the award of damages is to restore the plaintiff to his position before the loss occurred, and secondly, that the plaintiff must act reasonably to mitigate his loss. If the article damaged is a motor car of popular make, the plaintiff cannot charge the defendant with the cost of repair when it is cheaper to buy a similar car on the market. On the other hand, if no substitute for the damaged article is available and no reasonable alternative can be provided, the plaintiff should be entitled to the cost of repair. It was clear in the present case that it was reasonable for the plaintiffs to rebuild their factory, because there was no other way in which they could carry on their business and retain their labour force. The plaintiffs rebuilt their factory to a substantially different design, and if this had involved expenditure beyond the cost of replacing the old, the difference might not have been recoverable, but there is no suggestion of this here. Nor do I accept that the plaintiffs must

---

[96] Where this is greater than diminution in value, it may also be justified, perhaps, by any provision which may exist in the contract for remeasurement, or for valuation of variations.

give credit under the heading of ' betterment ' for the fact that their new factory is modern in design and materials. To do so would be the equivalent of forcing the plaintiffs to invest their money in the modernizing of their plant which might be highly inconvenient for them. Accordingly I agree with the sum allowed by the trial Judge as the cost of replacement." [96a]

At first sight it may seem puzzling that the diminution in value of property is not identical with the cost of repair. There is no doubt that prima facie this is so, but for tax reasons or because of the nature of the plaintiff's interest in the land, which may be of a reversionary character, or because of the character or age of an exist- ing building, this may not be universal. Thus in the *Newton Abbot* case, illustrated above, the plaintiffs' real loss might have been nil had they not felt morally or commercially constrained to make com- pensatory payments to their sub-purchasers. A full discussion of the cases where the cost of repair has been rejected as the measure of damage in the analogous fields of breach of repairing covenants, damage to property by tortfeasors, and negligent reports by archi- tects or surveyors, is contained in the case of *Philips* v. *Ward* (1956).[97]

On the aspect of rising building costs, certain expressions used in *Philips* v. *Ward* may at first sight appear to suggest that a plaintiff is limited to damages calculated *at the date of the breach*, which would mean that, in the context of the very rapid inflation of building costs in this country, an employer would always be out of pocket unless he discovered defective work the moment it had been done. The facts in *Philips* v. *Ward*, however, show that in that case the plaintiff abstained from doing repairs after he had discovered the defects. *Philips* v. *Ward*, certain sale of goods cases, and the cases on the exchange rates applicable to damages awarded by the English courts where the damage has been incurred in foreign currency, were all considered by Melford Stevenson J. and the House of Lords in *East Ham B.C.* v. *Bernard Sunley Ltd.* (1966).[98] The principle that " dam- ages are assessed at the date of the breach " has been enunciated by the courts, particularly in international cases where rates of exchange have altered, when rebutting the argument that damages should be assessed at the date of *judgment*, and does not mean that damages should be assessed at a date earlier than the date on which a breach is

---

[96a] *Per* Widgery L.J. in *Harbutt's Plasticine Ltd.* v. *Wayne Tank & Pump Ltd.* [1970] 1 Q.B. at pp. 472–473.
[97] [1956] 1 W.L.R. 471, illustrated *ante*, Chap. 2, p. 158.
[98] [1966] A.C. 406.

discovered. It is now clear beyond doubt that a plaintiff who has not unreasonably delayed carrying out repairs or completing the work after he becomes aware of the breach will obtain the cost of repair prevailing at the date the repairs are done, whenever that may be.[99]

However, it undoubtedly appears to be the law of England at present that, once he knows of the existence of a breach, a plaintiff will be limited to the cost of repair *at or within a reasonable time of discovery*, so that if he waits unreasonably before carrying out repairs the additional cost due to inflation in the interim period will not be recoverable.

ILLUSTRATION

In 1953 a contractor who had undertaken to supply " multi-coloured Dorking " facing bricks instead used " Ockley " seconds.[1] By 1961 the bricks had flaked and broken down. The plaintiffs, possibly due to lack of funds, waited till 1964 before getting an estimate. *Held* by Lawton J., the damages should be assessed at 1961 prices: *Clark* v. *Woor* (1965).[2]

It is submitted that the law on this point, which may be treated as generally accepted, and underlying the judgments and reasoning in the *East Ham* case, requires reconsideration. There are compelling reasons why in " international " torts and breaches of contract damages are computed in the relevant currency at the date when the plaintiff is aware of his rights and in a position to recoup his loss by repair or repurchase in the market. The change in the currency is an event the parties did not contemplate and not causally connected with the breach.[3] Furthermore, the futures market enables the injured party immediately to safeguard himself against any possible exchange loss, and any other rule would mean that the injured party could " take a view " on currencies with the wrongdoer paying the bill if he was wrong in his view. With the rule as it is, the damage is fixed, and the innocent party can take a view if he wishes, only he suffering or gaining according to whether his view is correct. Precisely the same considerations underlie, it is submitted, the sale of goods cases, where a purchaser who has received defective goods for which there is a market is entitled to the difference in market value as at the date when he knows of the breach and his potential loss. But it is submitted that neither of these lines of cases offers any useful analogy in the case of a steady, foreseeable and seemingly irreversible internal

---

[99] *Mertens* v. *Home Freeholds* [1921] 2 K.B. 526; *East Ham B.C.* v. *Bernard Sunley Ltd.* [1966] A.C. 406.
[1] See the fuller illustration *ante*, Chap. 5, p. 370.
[2] [1965] 1 W.L.R. 650.
[3] See *e.g. Aruna Mills* v. *Dhanrajmal Gobindram* [1968] 1 O.B. 655.

inflation. In times of steady monetary values, a plaintiff can choose the time when, for many different reasons, it suits him to carry out repairs, without suffering loss when he sues for his damages. He may not be in a position to vacate premises. He may, faced with a very heavy repair bill, and with an alternative cheaper but far less satisfactory way of dealing with the defects, wish to establish liability in a disputed case before deciding on the full programme of repair. All these are perfectly foreseeable as a result of a breach, it is submitted, and do not offend against any principle of mitigation of damage. Furthermore it is financially naive, it is submitted, to regard the plaintiff's action as increasing the defendant's loss—the defendant has had the use of the money during the period he has not had to pay the damages, and it is unrealistic to suppose that his assets or income are laid out or regulated in such a way as to remain static in the face of inflation—indeed most builders operate on borrowed working capital, and inflation actually operates to their real advantage in that respect, to which the present rule adds a further advantage by imposing a reduced liability in real terms. It would be interesting, incidentally, to know whether the courts would apply the same rule during a period of deflation, thereby conferring a profit on the employer if he delayed repairs.

It is submitted that the true rule should be that delay should only be a relevant factor in reducing the damage recoverable if it has had the effect of increasing the *real* cost of repair, *i.e.* by increasing the *physical* amount or quality of work to be done. The only reason for the present rule appears to be the generally disapproving attitude of English law towards the successful party in litigation, as exemplified by the rules as to party and party costs, which really benefit the unsuccessful party (whose intransigence has probably led to the litigation and whose interests are amply protected by the rules as to payment into court or sealed offers in arbitrations) at the expense of the successful party. The tendency is similarly evidenced by the reluctance of many tribunals to award interest for the full period or at realistic commercial rates.[4]

A consequential result of defective or incomplete work may be that the employer will suffer damage to his person or property, or be compelled to meet claims for damages to property, or personal injuries, from third persons. Provided that this results from a breach of contract by the contractor, and not as the direct result of doing what he was bound to do under the contract without any default on

---

[4] See the comments *supra*, pp. 576–577.

his part, such loss will be recoverable as damages, subject to the rules as to measure of damage in *Hadley* v. *Baxendale* (1854).[5]

ILLUSTRATIONS

(1) A firm of stevedores were engaged in discharging a ship with apparatus (supplied to them under their contract with the shipowner) which proved defective, and injured one of the workmen. The shipowner was held liable to reimburse the stevedores for compensation paid by them to the workmen under the Employer's Liability Act: *Mowbray* v. *Merryweather* (1895).[6]

(2) A firm of contractors undertook to install electric lighting apparatus in a building " in accordance with the existing rules " of a fire insurance company. Those rules provided for earthing metal tubes, except where such earthing would not be desirable. The contractors did not earth certain pipes, and two men were killed by contact with part of the installation. The employers settled claims by the relatives of these persons, and claimed the sums so expended from the contractors. *Held*, that as the rules of the fire office were framed to prevent fire, and as the earthing would not have been desirable in this case from that point of view, although it would have prevented this accident, the contractors had duly carried out their contract, and therefore were not liable: *Re Fulham Borough Council and the National Electric Construction Co. Ltd.* (1905).[7]

A further consequential result of defective work may be that the employer will be forced to vacate his premises during repairs. In appropriate cases, the costs occasioned by this will also be recoverable as damages.[8]

Hitherto damages for defects have only been considered in the context of the employer-contractor relationship. In the case of sub-contractors, defects in their work will clearly not only require to be repaired, but may also affect the profitability or expense of the main contractor's work,[9] or expose him to liability for liquidated damages or otherwise to the employer. All these are possible heads of damage in such a case.

(b) Delay and consequential loss

The measure of damage in the event of delay will be largely governed by the nature of the works undertaken by the builder or

---

[5] Most contracts contain, however, express provisions, usually known as " indemnity clauses ", regulating liability, as between employer and contractor, to third parties. See, *e.g.* clauses 18 and 19 of the 1963 R.I.B.A. forms of contract, clause 22 of the 1955 I.C.E. form, and the discussion on Indemnities, *ante*, Chap. 5, pp. 306–313. See also, for the possible application of s. 1 of the Law Reform (Contributory Negligence) Act 1945 in cases of contract, Mayne on Damages, 12th ed., p. 359.

[6] [1895] 2 Q.B. 640 (C.A.), followed in *The Kate* [1935] P. 100. For the great importance of these cases in saving defective indemnity clauses, see *ante*, Chap. 5, pp. 308–310.   [7] 70 J.P. 55.

[8] See *infra*, subsection (b).   [9] See, by analogy, subsection (3), *infra*.

contractor. If the works involve a commercial building, such as a factory or shop, it is obvious that delay in completion will affect the profits that the employer is likely to earn from the use of the building. In the case of blocks of flats, it is equally obvious that the employer's profits from his rents are likely to be affected. In the case of a dwelling-house it may not, on the other hand, be obvious that it will be let by the owner and, if the owner wishes to recover loss of profits from letting, he will have to satisfy the requirements of the second branch of the rule in *Hadley* v. *Baxendale* (1854). It is, perhaps, not sufficiently realised that in the cases of factories, shops, flats and other profit-earning buildings, the right to damages arises under the first branch of the rule, as arising naturally and in the usual course of things from the breach. See *e.g. per* Asquith L.J. in *Victoria Laundry (Windsor) Ltd.* v. *Newman Industries* (1949),[10] and the following extract from a judgment of the Privy Council in an earlier case:

" It is clear upon the evidence that both parties knew the purpose for which this factory was designed, namely, the manufacture of Portland Cement for sale. They were both necessarily well aware that the installation of machinery . . . within it was indispensable for this purpose, that the completion of the building was the necessary preliminary of the installation, that delay in the completion of the building necessarily involved the postponement of the latter, and that the loss of use of the machinery which could not be installed would result in the loss of those ordinary profits which might have been reaped upon what, if worked, it would have produced. So that the loss of this profit was at once what fairly might have been considered as arising naturally, that is, according to the ordinary course of things, from the breach of the appellants complained of, and was also such a loss as might reasonably be supposed to have been in the contemplation of the parties at the time they made the contract as the probable result of the breach of it. If so, both the tests laid down in *Hadley* v. *Baxendale* and the cases which have followed it would appear to be satisfied."[11]

Thus in general, under the first branch of the rule in *Hadley* v. *Baxendale*, normal or reasonable profits may be recovered for delay in completion of what are obviously profit-earning building or engineering projects, or a reasonable figure for inconvenience and loss of business. In order to recover special or abnormal profits, the employer will have to satisfy the requirements of the second branch

---

[10] [1949] 2 K.B. 528.
[11] *Per* Lord Atkinson in *Canada Foundry Co. Ltd.* v. *Edmonton Portland Cement Co.* [1918] 3 W.W.R. 866 (P.C.).

of the rule, showing that the particular purpose for which the building was intended was in the contemplation of the parties at the time of contracting. In the case of an apparently ordinary dwelling-house required for personal occupation, damages recoverable within the first branch of the rule would include, it is submitted, the reasonable cost of living accommodation or living elsewhere and storing furniture, etc. if in fact expenses of this kind were incurred, but not rent from lodgers or paying guests, unless this fact was brought to the attention of the builder in some way at the time of contracting. On the other hand delay in the case of a house designed as a boarding-house would come within the first branch of the rule.

ILLUSTRATIONS

(1) Delay occurred due to breach of contract by the builder in the construction of buildings required for the reception and storage of hops, for which purpose they had been designed. *Held*, in an action by an assignee of the builder for the price, that the owner was entitled to set off against moneys due sums representing the loss of rent which would have been obtained during the period of delay: *Young* v. *Kitchin* (1878).[12]

(2) A builder furnished mortar to the keeper of a lodging-house who was building a dormitory to one of his lodging-houses. The local authority condemned the building on the ground that the mortar was bad, and required the owner to pull down and rebuild. *Held*, the owner could recover from the builder the cost of pulling down and rebuilding and also damages for loss of ground-rent: *Smith* v. *Johnson* (1899).[13]

[Note: It must be assumed that the builder supplied the mortar in this case with some knowledge of its purpose. Nor is it clear from the report what the exact nature of the " ground-rent " recoverable was.]

(3) A plasterer was unable to obtain materials and consequently delayed the completion of a lodging-house. *Held*, he was liable in damages for the loss of rent from lodgers occasioned by the delay: *Vogan* v. *Barry* (1908).[14]

(4) A contractor undertook to supply and install a lift described as a passenger lift in the employers' office building. The employers actually intended to use it for carrying merchandise as well, but this was not known to the contractors. *Held*, the employers might recover speculative and contingent damages for loss of business and inconvenience during a period of delay due to the contractor's breach of contract, but not wages and the cost of hiring a hoist and lighting for the carriage of goods: *Steven* v. *Pryce-Jones Ltd.* (1913).[15]

[12] 3 Ex.D. 127.
[13] 15 T.L.R. 179.
[14] 7 W.L.R. 811 (Canada).
[15] 25 W.L.R. 172 (Canada).

(5) Contractors for the erection for a Portland Cement factory caused delay in completion in breach of their contract. *Held*, they were liable for the loss of reasonable profits during the period of delay: *Canada Foundry Co.* v. *Edmonton Portland Cement* (1918).[16]

(3) Breach by the Employer

The measure of damage as a legal problem gives little theoretical difficulty in cases of breach of contract by the employer. It is obvious that builders work for a profit, and, apart from his entitlement to the price, the damage to a builder caused by any breach of contract by the employer will be assessed in the light of its impact upon his profits.

The employers' breaches are of two kinds from the point of view of damages, depending upon whether on the one hand they have the effect of bringing the work to an end, or preventing its starting, in which case the builder will be deprived of the right to his profits upon work never actually carried out, or whether on the other hand they merely reduce his profits upon (or increase the cost of) work done by him. In earlier editions of this work, these were described somewhat inaccurately as cases of prevention and partial prevention.

In the case of prevention, that is to say, where the employer has wrongfully terminated the contract, or has committed a fundamental breach justifying the builder in treating the contract as at an end, and the latter accordingly ceases work, the measure of damages will be the loss of profit which he would otherwise have earned. In the more usual case where the work is partly carried out at the time when the contract is repudiated, the builder will normally be entitled to the value of the work done assessed at the contract rates, plus his profit on the remaining work.[17]

In the case of partial prevention, *i.e.* where the breach by the employer is not fundamental and does not entitle the builder to cease work, or, being fundamental, is not treated as a repudiation by the builder, the measure of the damage is the loss of profit arising from the reduced profitability or added expense of the work carried out and completed by the builder. It is, of course, quite possible for a continuing fundamental breach by the employer first to affect the profitability of work carried out, since the builder may not immediately elect to treat the contract as at an end, and then to give rise to a claim for loss of profit on the uncompleted work when he does so.

---

[16] 3 W.W.R. 866.
[17] For a further discussion of this situation, see *infra*, pp. 601–603.

Reduced profitability or partial prevention can arise from many possible breaches of contract by the employer, such as failure to give uninterrupted or prompt possession of the site—see *e.g. Lawson* v. *Wallasey Local Board* (1882),[18] or drawings, details and information —see *e.g. Trollope & Colls* v. *Singer* (1913)[19]—or interference by other contractors, and so on. This type of damage is by far the commonest in building litigation where contractors are plaintiffs.

At this point it may assist if an indication is given of the types of consequential damage which contractors are likely to or may suffer when a contract is monetarily affected by an employer's breach, the heads of damage (apart from the direct damage immediately suffered on some individual work process, which will obviously vary from case to case) are likely to be as follows:

(a) When delay in completion of the whole project results, a contractor will usually suffer:

(i) a loss owing to the fact that his *off-site overheads*, which will partly be independent of the actual site expenditure or even the period the contract takes to complete (such as head-office rents) and partly may be dependent (such as additional administrative expenditure in relation to a dislocated and longer contract) will have either increased in the latter case, or need to be recovered from a smaller annual turnover than that budgeted for in the former case;

(ii) a *loss of* the *profit-earning capacity* of the particular contract organisation affected, due to its being retained longer on the contract in question without any corresponding increase in the monetary benefit earned and without being free to move elsewhere to earn the profit which it otherwise might do;

(iii) an increase of cost in his running *on-site overheads*, that is to say those elements of cost directly attributable to the contract which are governed by time and which are independent of the amount of work carried out—for instance supervisory costs, costs of permanent plant such as site huts, and certain special plant needed throughout the work;

(iv) in a contract without an applicable fluctuations clause, the inflationary or other *increases in the cost of*

---

[18] 11 Q.B.D. 229, illustrated *ante*, Chap. 5, Section 2, p. 338.
[19] 1 Hudson's B.C., 4th ed., p. 849, illustrated *ante*, Chap. 5, Section 2, p. 326.

labour or materials (less any decreases) which he would
not have incurred but for the delay.
(b) Whether or not delay in completion results, the disturbance
of a contractor's progress or planning may also result in
lower productivity from the contractor's plant or labour.

All these heads of damage can be conveniently discussed under
the following four paragraphs (a) to (d).

(a) " Head Office Overheads " and profit

Off-site overheads are usually known in the industry as " Head
Office Overheads". It is convenient to deal with these together with
profit, because it is the practice of most contractors of any substance
in major contracts, after making their best estimate of the prime cost
of the whole project, to add a single percentage thereto for both the
above items. In bill contracts, the total sum calculated from prime
cost may be distributed across the bill rates, or the contractors may
have built up the tender sum by estimating bill rates for particular
processes, adding the same percentage to cost when calculating
each rate, and in really important contracts two teams of estimators
may each estimate separately by the two methods as a cross-check
before finally producing the tender sum. Other things being equal,
the contractor's loss from an extended contract period must be a
proportionate extension of this percentage of his contract sum,
and the loss calculated in this way is a real loss (provided the true
percentage used can be determined) and is quite independent of
the extent to which his contract prices may have been profitable or
unprofitable, which depends on the accuracy of his estimates of *cost*
on that particular contract and not on the profit percentage (this is
not, of course, the case where an extended contract period is not involved, and the contractor sues for loss of profit *on work which he has
not done*, as where the contract has been wrongly terminated by the
employer. There he must prove that he would have made a profit in
fact—*i.e.* that his contract prices were an accurate estimate, or an
over-estimate, of cost.) The percentage used in the United Kingdom
in pricing for head-office overheads and profit obviously varies from
contractor to contractor, and is usually a closely guarded secret, but
evidence given in litigation on many occasions suggests that it is
usually, in a major contract subject to competitive tender on a
national basis, between 3 per cent. and 7 per cent. of the total prime
cost, including P.C. and provisional sum figures for nominated sub-
contractors. It should be remembered that these percentages, which

may seem small in relation to turnover, in fact represent a return *on capital employed* of several times that percentage per annum (it is, in effect, this very high " gearing " element in the pricing of building and engineering contracts, due to the very high ratio between turnover and capital employed, that means that a very small difference in pricing or estimating may produce very heavy losses or very large profits). Some contractors do consciously apply a breakdown of the percentage as between head-office and profit, but for the purpose of assessing the loss due to delay in completion, the division is not theoretically important. The formula usually used is as follows:

$$\frac{H.O./Profit\ Percentage}{100} \times \frac{Contract\ Sum}{Contract\ Period} \times Period\ of\ delay\ (in\ weeks)$$
$$(e.g.\ in\ weeks)$$

A caveat should, however, be entered in regard to the profit element in the above formula. The formula assumes that the profit budgeted for by the contractor in his prices was in fact capable of being earned by him elsewhere had the contractor been free to leave the delayed contract at the proper time. This itself involves two further assumptions, namely that on average the contractor did not habitually underestimate his costs when pricing, so that the profit percentage was a realistic one at that time, and secondly that there was thereafter no change in the market, so that work of at least the same general level of profitability would have been available to him at the end of the contract period. There is no doubt that satisfactory evidence on these matters is necessary, and the case of *Sunley* v. *Cunard White Star* (1940),[19a] and a number of cases involving the wrongful detention of ships and consequential loss of charterparty profits,[19b] indicate that in the absence of such evidence a contractor who has been delayed will only be entitled to interest on capital employed, and not to loss of profit.[19c]

The following interesting case, it is respectfully submitted, approaches the question of overheads correctly from the point of view of principle, though the method of calculation is not entirely clear and it does not follow the same formula.

ILLUSTRATION

A master, in a case where work had been delayed for 4¾ months and where the contractor's average percentage of overheads to total

---

[19a] Illustrated *infra*, para (b).
[19b] See *e.g.* the decisions of the House of Lords in *The Greta Holme* [1897] A.C. 596; *The Mediana* [1900] A.C. 113; and *The Marpressa* [1907] A.C. 241; and *Mayne and McGregor on Damages*, 12th Ed., 668–673.
[19c] See *Peek Construction Ltd.* v. *McKinney Foundations Ltd.* C.A., 1st July 1970.

turnover over the last two years had been 4·99 per cent. allowed the contractor (a) $3,600, being 4·99 per cent. of the additional direct cost of a particular breach causing delay and (b) $2,802 for overheads during the period of delay. The Court of Appeal of Ontario disallowed (b). *Held,* by the Supreme Court of Canada, during the 4¾-month period overheads were continuing to run, but the contractor was obtaining no revenue from which to defray his overheads and the contractor was entitled to (b): *Shore* v. *Horwitz* (1964).[20]

[Note: The basis of some of the above calculations is not disclosed by the report, but it would seem that the sum in (a) above represented the percentage for overheads on the cost of additional work due to the breach carried out during the period of delay and (b) the loss of contribution to overheads by the original contract work carried out during the delay period.]

(b) Site overheads

These will include items like supervision (including, perhaps, part of the time of a contracts manager as well as a full-time site agent or general foreman), hutting, permanent gantries or hoists, certain types of pumping or dewatering in engineering contracts, and standing time of plant required to be retained on the site. Some of these will not necessarily be present for the whole period of delay. The " standing time" of unproductive plant (which, incidentally, may overlap with the loss of productivity head of damage in (d) below), is frequently claimed by contractors on the basis of hire-rates, which may result in the capital value of a new piece of plant being claimed over a relatively short period of time. Hire-rates may sometimes be adopted by the courts, where satisfied that a loss of profit has occurred, and where evidence of that particular loss exists, but in the absence of evidence of profit opportunity, only depreciation and maintenance may be allowed.

ILLUSTRATION

An excavating machine costing £4,500 when new, and with a life of three years, was delayed by one week under a contract for its transport from Doncaster to Guernsey. While still at Doncaster during the delay, it worked for one day and earned £16. There was very little other evidence before the court. The plaintiffs had originally claimed £577. *Held,* by the Court of Appeal, in the absence of evidence as to actual loss of profit, the damage was depreciation during the period, interest on the money invested, some maintenance and some wages thrown away. Average depreciation when working would be £29 per week. As the machine was idle, £20 per week would be allowed and £10 for interest, maintenance and wages, making £30, less the £16 receipts, for which credit must be given: *Sunley* v. *Cunard White Star* (1940).[21]

[20] [1964] S.C.R. 589 (Canada).
[21] [1940] 1 K.B. 740. See also *Galbraith's Stores* v. *Glasgow Corporation*, 1958 S.L.T. (Sh.Ct.) 47 (Scotland) and see Street, *Principles of Law of Damages*, pp. 206–210.

(c) Rises in cost of materials and labour

These call for little comment, except that it may be a very difficult exercise, for which careful examination of the contractor's likely programme will be required, to decide when materials would have been ordered, or labour engaged, but for the delay.

(d) Loss of productivity

As stated, this may not necessarily be associated with any overall delay. This damage is usually very hard to assess. In many cases where there has been delay, a delaying factor may cause little or no loss under this head, because if the extent and duration of the delay can be forecast with reasonable notice, the contractor can postpone engaging, or reduce, his plant and labour force during the period when the delaying factor is operating, so that they bear a similar ratio to output to that during periods when progress is more rapid. In other cases he may not be able to do this, and in inflationary times a contractor will have good reason not to disperse his labour force once he has organised it, for fear that he will not be able to get it back later. Bonus schemes can also be seriously upset, whether or not there is overall delay. In assessing claims for loss of productivity of plant, such plant, if hired, will be paid for by the contractor at " standing " rates. Plant not in this category should be valued on a depreciation basis and loss of profit should not be allowed upon it in the absence of evidence of an available profitable use elsewhere— see the *Sunley* case, *supra*. It is not unusual, in the absence of any more precise method, to claim this type of loss as an arbitrary percentage on total labour or plant expenditure during the period of dislocation.

(e) General considerations

In cases where the work is partly carried out and the contract is repudiated, a contractor should consider his position carefully before deciding to sue for damages for breach of contract, since it has been held that in such a case he may elect not to sue for damages but instead bring an action in *quantum meruit* for the work done by him. In a case where the contractor's rates are highly profitable it is obviously likely to be the best course to sue for loss of profit. If, on the other hand, the contract rates or price are low or uneconomic,[22] it may well be that a reasonable price for the work done will be more advantageous to him, particularly if a substantial amount of work has been done prior to the employer's repudiation.

[22] It may not, of course, be an easy matter from the evidentiary view to satisfy an arbitrator or the court that the contract rates were uneconomic.

ILLUSTRATION

A guarantor of a building contractor who defaulted was called upon by the employers, a local authority, to complete the works under his guarantee. He engaged another builder to do so, but left the supervision of the contract to the council, who in breach of the contract obstructed the builder in the expeditious carrying out of the works, and then wrongfully seized them. *Held*, that the guarantor had constituted the council his agents, that the builder was entitled to treat the contract as rescinded, and could sue the guarantor in *quantum meruit* for the actual value of the work, labour and materials, instead of bringing an action for damages for breach of contract: *Lodder* v. *Slowey* (1904).[23]

In cases where loss of profit is sought from the employer it is necessary to consider the method of payment and the profitability of the price or rates provided for in the contract in order to determine the amount of profit (if any) which the contractor could have expected to earn.

ILLUSTRATION

Under a building contract the owner was to pay for all labour, material, and other charges from time to time as they became due, and the builder was to be paid a fixed sum, subject to increase or decrease by 20 per cent. of any saving or excess respectively between the actual final cost and an agreed figure of estimated cost. The owner became short of funds and the work ceased. Subsequently he entered into a contract with another builder for the completion of the work. *Held*, the owner had broken his contract, and the measure of damage was the fixed sum payable to the builder, adjusted according to the probable difference between the hypothetical cost of completion and the agreed estimated cost, but less an allowance for the time, labour and expense saved by the builder's being relieved of his obligation to carry out the contract: *Jones & Lyttle Ltd.* v. *Mackie* (1918).[24]

The fact that the element of the profitability of the contractor's rates or prices is such an essential part of any claim by the contractor for damages means that in nearly all such cases the internal documents of the contractor, showing the make-up of his original tender prices, are highly relevant documents which, under the rules of discovery, will have to be disclosed in any litigation, however commercially confidential these documents may be thought to be. This fact frequently does not appear to be appreciated by contractors embarking on litigation.

---

[23] [1904] A.C. 442, and see *Planché* v. *Colburn* (1831) 8 Bing. 14, a case of a contract for literary services.

[24] 2 W.W.R. 82 (Canada). See also *Bywaters* v. *Curnick* (1906) Hudson's B.C., 4th ed. Vol. 2, p. 393, *supra*, pp. 577–578.

In regard to claims based on delay, litigious contractors frequently supply to architects or engineers at an early stage of the work highly optimistic programmes showing completion a considerable time ahead of the contract date. These documents are then used (a) to justify allegations that information or possession has been supplied late by the architect or employer and (b) to increase the alleged period of delay, or to make a delay claim possible where the contract completion date has not in the event been exceeded. The determination of the correct period of delay attributable to an employer's breach is one of the most complicated and difficult issues of fact in building litigation, and cases involving this issue can rarely be tried properly in a short space of time since they involve an examination and analysis of the whole history of the contract.

(f) Express terms

Obviously these may be various, but one expression not infrequently used in some building contracts is " direct damage " or " direct loss and expense." [25]   The word " direct " may often be meaningless, because unless there is some clear contrary indication it may only be construed as meaning the damages recoverable at law according to the ordinary principles of remoteness within the first rule in *Hadley* v. *Baxendale*, which, as has been seen, applies to nearly all building and engineering situations.[26]

ILLUSTRATION

A contract for the provision of main engines limited liability as follows: " nor shall their liability . . . extend to any indirect or consequential damages or claims whatsoever." Shipowners claimed (a) loss of profit during the period of loss of use of the vessel, (b) wages, stores, etc., during the period, (c) fees for superintendence by experts. *Held*, by Atkinson J., as all the above were the direct and natural consequences of the breach, they were recoverable. " What the clause does is to protect the respondents from claims for special damages which would be recoverable only on proof of special circumstances and for damages contributed to by some supervening cause ": *Saint Line* v. *Richardsons Westgarth Ltd.* (1940).[27]

The words " direct loss or damage " in clause 26 (2) of the R.I.B.A. forms were similarly construed by Megaw J. in *Wraight* v. *P.H.T. Holdings.*[28]

---

[25] *Cf.* Clauses 11 (6), 24 (1), 25 (3) (*d*) and 26 (2) (*b*) (vi) of the post-1963 R.I.B.A. forms.
[26] *Supra*, p. 578.
[27] [1940] 2 K.B. 99.
[28] (1968) unreported, Megaw J.

CHAPTER 10

TIME FOR PERFORMANCE

(1) Generally

CONTRACTS of every kind commonly specify a date for the performance of some act. When they do so, it is a question of construction, usually depending on the subject-matter of the promise and the commercial sense of the transaction, whether the obligation is a condition, so that failure to meet the date is a fundamental breach, evincing a presumed intention no longer to be bound, and hence justifying the other party in treating the contract as repudiated—in legal parlance, whether time is of the essence. If time is not of the essence, the injured party has his remedy in damages, but no more. The principle has been well stated in an Australian case, where the obligation under review was that of the employer to make the site available for the contractor to start work by a certain date:

" Where a contract contains a promise to do a particular thing on or before a specified day time may or may not be of the essence. If it is, the promisee is entitled to rescind, but he may elect not to exercise the right and an election will be inferred from any conduct which is consistent with the contract remaining in being. If not of the essence or no longer of the essence because of election, rescission is generally only permitted after giving a notice requiring performance within a specified reasonable time, and after non-compliance with the notice."[1]

The above quotation shows that the courts have evolved the doctrine that time not originally of the essence can be rendered of the essence by notice, and so too where performance by the specified time has been waived. While the theoretical basis for such a rule may not be easy to analyse, there can be no doubt of its practical necessity, since otherwise a defaulting party could treat the original intention of the transaction with contempt, while holding the other party to his obligations, in some cases, depending on the facts, being able to do so at little or no cost to himself if the innocent party has difficulty in proving damage.

The rule is well settled, and though it is only of academic interest it is suggested that the true basis for the rule is that, wherever there

---

[1] *Carr* v. *J. A. Berriman Ppty. Ltd.* (1953) 27 A.L.J. 273 (Australia), illustrated *ante* Chap. 5, p. 319.

is a promise to do an act by a certain date, a failure to do so can continue so long and in such circumstances as to evince an intention no longer to be bound by the contract. Whenever the period and circumstances give rise to any doubt, a notice to complete the promised act within a further reasonable time gives the party concerned an opportunity to show that he does regard himself as bound. If he does not then comply with the notice, he is clearly and beyond any doubt evincing an intention no longer to be bound by the contract, and the other party can elect to treat the contract as repudiated on ordinary general principles.[2]

It follows that in extreme cases even notice will not be required, since the intention no longer to be bound can already be inferred from the conduct of the defaulting party.[3] Thus in the case quoted above it was held that the failure to remedy the breach after the due date continued for so long and in such circumstances that, notwithstanding the absence of notice, the contract had been lawfully determined. Obviously, however, in all cases of delay, and even of total cessation of work, notice by the innocent party is a wise precaution. Notice is clearly also especially necessary wherever there has been election by the innocent party to treat the contract as subsisting after a breach or breaches by the contractor, as will usually happen in practice in building and engineering contracts, where in the vast majority of cases the contractor will already be in breach before the employer decides to take action.[4]

In this chapter it is proposed to consider the above principles in relation to the contractor's obligations under building and engineering contracts to carry out and complete the works with reasonable expedition and within the specified or a reasonable time. Most such contracts contain provisions for liquidated damages and extension of time, which are discussed in the next succeeding chapter, Chapter 11, and also provisions for determination by the employer (usually expressed to be without prejudice to any other rights or remedies and so expressly keeping alive the ordinary common law right to rescind[5]) conditioned upon (among other things) failure of the contractor to

---

[2] As to which see *ante*, Chap. 5, pp. 340 *et seq.*

[3] See *e.g.* the case of *Kingdom* v. *Cox* (1848) 5 C.B. 522, *infra*, subsection (4), p. 611, where no notice is referred to in the report or appears to have been considered necessary, and *Carr's* case illustrated *ante*, pp. 340, and 533.

[4] See *e.g.* the case of *Pigott Construction Ltd.* v. *W. J. Crowe Ltd.* (1961) 27 D.L.R. (2d) 258 (Canada), illustrated *ante*, Chap. 5, Section 2, pp. 338–339 and commented on in this context *ante*, Chap. 5, Section 3 (1), p. 346, and the case of *Felton* v. *Wharrie* (1906) Hudson's B.C., 4th ed., Vol. 2, p. 398, illustrated *infra*, subsection (5) p. 615.

[5] *e.g.* clause 25 (1) of the 1963 R.I.B.A. standard form.

proceed with due expedition. In fact, even if saving words are not used, there seems no reason, in the absence of express wording, to treat such express rights of determination as intended to supplant the common law right to rescind. These express clauses are considered in Chapter 13, Forfeiture and Determination.

(2) Where Time Specified

Most building and engineering contracts expressly specify a date for completion. Whether the contract time is of the essence justifying termination of the contract is discussed in Sections (4) and (5) below. But failure to complete by the due date will expose the builder to a claim for damages which, in the absence of a liquidated damages clause (discussed in Chapter 11, *post*), will fall to be calculated in accordance with the principles set out in the preceding chapter. As will be seen, the specified time is usually not of the essence, and will not in the normal case entitle the employer to treat the contract as repudiated by the builder, or prevent the builder from recovering the price of the work, subject to any counterclaim for damages for the delay.[6]

Where the time is specified, the builder has till the last hour of the day fixed for completion in which to finish the work.[7]

(3) Where No Time Specified, or Specified Time Inapplicable

Where no time for completion is specified, a term for completion within a reasonable time will be implied, and this too will occur where the time fixed for completion has ceased to be applicable and the contractor is continuing work under the contract.[8] The contract time will cease to be applicable for this purpose where there has been agreement to that effect, or waiver, or where the employer has in one way or another prevented completion within the contract time, as, for instance, by ordering extra work or delaying the contractor by some breach of contract.

ILLUSTRATIONS

(1) Contractors, who were bound to pay heavy liquidated damages for failure to complete carpentry work at a brewery within the stipulated time, were prevented from doing so, for a part of the

---

[6] *Lucas* v. *Godwin* (1837) 3 Bing.N.C. 737, illustrated *infra*, p. 610.
[7] *Startup* v. *McDonald* (1843) 6 M. & G. 593.
[8] In addition to the cases illustrated below, see also *Joshua Henshaw & Sons* v. *Rochdale Corporation* [1944] K.B. 381, illustrated *post*, pp. 696–697, and *Electronic Industries* v. *David Jones* (1954) 91 C.L.R. 288 (Australia).

period of their default, by delay in giving them possession and certain delays on the part of the defendants' workmen. *Held,* liquidated damages could not be deducted from their claim for the price of the work: *Holme* v. *Guppy* (1838).[9]

(2) A building owner sought to deduct penalties from the contract sum because the works had not been completed till twelve weeks after the completion date. The contractors replied that, by a subsequent agreement, they had undertaken to carry out certain extra works, that these were mixed up with the original work, that it was thereby impossible to complete the original work to time, and that all the work had been completed within a reasonable time. *Held,* this was a good answer to the claims for penalties: *Thornhill* v. *Neats* (1860).[10]

(3) Both parties to a railway contract continued to work under it after the time limited for completion. *Held,* that work done after the date fixed for completion was done under the terms of the contract, so far as they could properly and reasonably be applied to the new or prolonged contract, on the analogy of holding over on a lease: *McDonnell* v. *Canada Southern Railway* (1873).[11]

(4) A company contracted to supply iron by twelve equal deliveries commencing in January. Between January and November the purchaser requested them to postpone delivery, which they did. In December he asked them to deliver the whole undelivered balance. The company contended that their obligation was only to supply the December delivery. *Held,* they were bound to deliver the balance within a reasonable time and, on the facts, had wrongly repudiated the contract: *Tyers* v. *Rosedale Iron Co.* (1875).[12]

(5) Joiners undertook work on a building where other tradesmen were being employed by the defendants in the following terms: " We offer to execute the work . . . for the sum of £2,128 and undertake to finish our department of the work by April 15 next." The joiners were in fact delayed by plasterers, in whose contract the defendants had omitted to insert a strict provision as to time. *Held,* either there was an implied condition precedent that the joiners should be given possession so as to make completion by the contract date possible, or the defendants, by omitting to bind the plasterers to complete by a fixed date, had prevented the joiners from completing in time, and consequently the latter were entitled to the price of the work: *Duncanson* v. *Scottish Investment Co.* (1915).[13]

(6) Car builders undertook to build a body on a Rolls-Royce chassis supplied by them. The car was to be ready by a specified date (which was held to be of the essence of the contract). After that date the buyer continued to press for delivery, and new dates were promised and accepted by him, but delivery still was not effected, and he eventually gave notice that he would not accept if it was not ready by a certain date. *Held,* completion by the original date had

[9] 3 M. & W. 387.
[10] 8 C.B.(N.S.) 831; see also *Courtnay* v. *Waterford, etc., Ry.* (1878) 4 L.R.Ir. 11.
[11] 33 U.C.Q.B. 313, 320.
[12] L.R. 10 Ex. 195. Compare and distinguish *Kingdom* v. *Cox, infra,* p. 611.
[13] 1915 S.C. 1106.

been waived, but an obligation to complete within a reasonable time was substituted therefor; the date stipulated in the notice was reasonable, and the buyers were entitled to reject the car: *Charles Rickards Ltd.* v. *Oppenheim* (1950).[14]

In so far as the above cases show that the completion date may have ceased to be applicable for purposes of recission by reason of agreement or waiver by the employer, it should not be supposed that acts of the employer which may deprive him of the right to treat the contract as repudiated without further notice will necessarily or even probably mean that he is thereby abrogating, waiving or reducing his right to damages. Thus an employer who treats the contract as subsisting after the completion date may, as a matter of common sense, have every intention of exacting common law or liquidated damages as from the stipulated completion date and not from some later date in the future.[15] Quite different and most unusual conduct would be needed to show that the employer had accepted a new date for this latter purpose,[16] and it will be noted that the cases of agreement or waiver illustrated above are not cases of building contracts and relate to very different situations. Apart from an agreement to suspend the works for one reason or another, it is not easy to conceive of a situation in building or engineering contracts where such an agreement or waiver could arise. In fact, as will be seen from the following subsection, it will only be very rarely that the time of completion will be of the essence in building contracts, unless notice has been given.

Accordingly, the circumstances in which some later reasonable date for completion replaces the contract date in building or engineering contracts are likely to be limited to prevention or breach of contract by the employer or his architect or engineer.

(4) Whether Time of the Essence

This phrase is used to indicate that performance within the stipulated time or a reasonable time is an essential condition of the contract. The legal consequences in a building contract would be that upon expiry of the stipulated (or reasonable) time the employer might treat the contract as repudiated and dismiss the builders, and, conversely, that the builder could not recover for the work done by him if he had not completed to time.[17] In deciding such matters, the courts have

---

[14] [1950] 1 K.B. 616.
[15] See *e.g.* the cases as to liquidated damages, *post*, Chap. 11, Section 2 (4), p. 637.
[16] In most contracts, of course, an express extension of time clause exists for this very purpose—see Chap. 11, *post*, pp. 638 *et seq.*
[17] See *Platt* v. *Parker* (1866) 2 T.L.R. 786, *post*, Chap. 13, Forfeiture.

always had regard to the business reality of the transaction as a whole and, if this does not require such a term, only the clearest express wording will prevail so as to bring about such catastrophic (bearing in mind that, being affixed to the land, building work becomes the property of the employer independently of any act of acceptance by him) and perhaps unintended results. Thus, while the courts have had little difficulty in holding time to be of the essence in contracts for delivery of goods, or for the exercise of options over interests in land, they have taken a contrary view in respect of most contracts for payment of money, and all contracts for the sale of land. A further consideration in the case of building contracts is that, even were time to be of the essence, it would afford a building owner little practical relief against a recalcitrant builder. In most building contracts the contract period is comparatively lengthy, and long before it has expired the owner or his architect will know that the builder is in default on his programme and that completion by the stipulated time is for all practical purposes impossible. Nevertheless, no right to terminate on this ground could arise until the completion date, while the obligation in most building contracts to make interim periodic payments will continue, in spite of the mounting probability of the employer incurring substantial damage. In addition, if he allows the completion date to pass and acquiesces in work continuing under the contract, the employer will be held to have waived compliance with the original date for this particular purpose.

It is for this reason that it is suggested that, as a matter of business efficacy, there must be an implied term in building and engineering contracts that the contractor will proceed with reasonable diligence and expedition.[18] In fact, most contracts, including the standard forms, contain express terms to this effect, and in addition confer express powers to determine upon the builder failing to proceed with the works with due diligence or reasonable expedition.[19]

When, finally, it is remembered that the builder's work on the employer's land cannot be refused or returned (as in the case of chattels) it is not surprising that only in the most exceptional cases will the courts hold time to be of the essence in a genuine building contract. Thus in *Lucas* v. *Godwin* (1837)[20] Tindal C.J. said:

---

[18] *Ante*, Chap. 5, pp. 314–315.

[19] See *post*, pp. 695–697. These powers can be exercised at any time, and whether or not the completion date has passed: *Joshua Henshaw & Sons* v. *Rochdale Corporation* [1944] K.B. 381, illustrated *post*, Chap. 13, pp. 696–697.

[20] 3 Bing.N.C. at p. 744, illustrated *infra*.

" It is not a condition, but a stipulation, for non-observance of which the defendant may be entitled to recover damages; but, even if a condition, it does not go to the essence of the contract, and is no answer to the plaintiff's claim for the work actually done. It never could have been the understanding of the parties, that if the house were not done by the precise day, the plaintiff would have no remuneration; at all events, if so unreasonable an engagement had been entered into, the parties should have expressed their meaning with a precision which could not be mistaken."

Further, the existence of provisions for extension of time and payment of liquidated damages will generally be regarded as inconsistent with an intention that time should be of the essence, and it is suggested that the existence of a forfeiture clause conditioned upon reasonable expedition by the builder might also (depending on the exact wording) be so regarded. Thus in *Lamprell* v. *Billericay Union* (1849) [21] Rolfe B. said:

" Looking to the whole of the deed, we are of opinion that the time of completion was not an essential part of the contract; first, because there is an expressed provision made for a weekly sum to be paid for every week during which the work should be delayed after June 24, 1840; and, secondly, because the deed clearly meant to exempt the plaintiff from the obligation as to the particular day in case he should be prevented by fire or other circumstances satisfactory to the architect; and here, in fact, it is expressly found by the arbitrator that delay was necessarily occasioned by the extra work."

ILLUSTRATIONS

(1) In a contract to purchase a row of houses, then being completed by the plaintiff, the defendant covenanted to pay a further sum of £80 provided that the adjoining houses should be completed, *i.e.* roofed, sashed, paved in front, enclosed with iron railings in front, and occupied by tenants, etc., by April 21, 1829. The foot pavement was not all laid down before April 21 on account, it was alleged, of bad weather. *Held*, that the plaintiff could not recover the £80: *Maryon* v. *Carter* (1830).[22]

(2) A building owner agreed to pay £216 to a builder "ʃon condition of the work being done in a proper and workmanlike manner . . ., and to be completed by October 10, 1836." The work was completed on October 15. *Held*, the delay was no defence to a claim for the price of the work: *Lucas* v. *Godwin* (1837).[23]

[21] 3 Ex. 283
[22] 4 C. & P. 295.
[23] 3 Bing.N.C. 737.

(3) Fabricators undertook at the end of November to supply 150 tons of girders, fifty on or before December 31, fifty on or before January 28, fifty on or before March 31, provided drawings for the first fifty tons were supplied by the purchasers within three days, and for the remainder within three weeks. Some drawings were delivered on December 5, and on December 15 an order for fourteen tons only was placed. On March 13, after the suppliers had repudiated the contract, further drawings were sent and a further order for fifty tons. *Held*, the contract was entire, time was of the essence, the purchasers had failed to supply drawings within a reasonable time, and the suppliers were accordingly not liable in an action for failure to deliver: *Kingdom* v. *Cox* (1848).[24]

(4) A contractor undertook to erect a workhouse, and to complete it by June 24, 1840. There was a power for the architects to order additions, and the work was to be done to their satisfaction. The contractor further undertook to pay liquidated damages of £10 per week if he should fail to complete by June 24, unless hindered by fire or other cause satisfactory to the architects. Final completion was delayed till December 1840 as a consequence of additions ordered by the architects, who were satisfied. *Held*, the time of completion was not an essential part of the contract: *Lamprell* v. *Billericay Union* (1849).[25]

(5) A. agreed to make alterations in a house, and to complete the whole work by June 14; B., in consideration of these conditions, agreed to take the house on June 24 for three years, with the option of a lease for seven, fourteen, or twenty-one years. *Held*, that the completion of the whole work by June 14 was a condition precedent to B.'s liability to take the house on the 24th: *Tidey* v. *Mollett* (1864).[26]

It will be seen that the obligations in the cases set out above where time was held to be of the essence differ in important respects from those of a building or civil engineering contractor. The only rule that can be laid down is that either there must be clear and explicit language in the contract, or the sense of the transaction as a whole must require a provision as to time, whether specified or reasonable, to be of the essence. As has been pointed out above, even where this is the case in a building contract, the practical benefits to the building owner are extremely limited and, for practical purposes, the implication of a *fundamental* term [26a] requiring due diligence by the builder [27] is more essential to the employer in comparatively lengthy contracts for work done such as building contracts, rather than a doctrine which has largely been evolved to suit the requirements of contracts for the sale of land or goods. It is submitted that in most building contracts this term is necessary to give the con-

---

[24] 5 C.B. 522.   [25] 3 Ex. 283.
[26] 16 C.B.(N.S.) 298.
[26a] Or at least a term capable of being enforced by rescission after notice.
[27] Express terms to this effect are, of course, extremely common in building contracts. See *post*, Chap. 13, pp. 695–697.

tract business efficacy, and that where a builder persists in a rate of progress bearing no relation to a specified or reasonable date of completion, and the employer gives him notice requiring a reasonable rate of progress, if he then fails to proceed at a reasonable rate he will be evincing an intention no longer to be bound by the contract and his dismissal would be justified notwithstanding the absence of any express term empowering the employer to determine.   Otherwise, provided the builder does not openly evince an intention no longer to be bound by the contract, for instance by abandonment or protracted suspension, he cannot be dismissed until the completion date, and in the usual case where time is not of the essence, not even then.[29] In very extreme cases, it is possible that notice would not be necessary [30]—though always, of course, a desirable precaution to reduce the possibility of a wrongful determination to a minimum.

The whole subject of determination of contracts by the employer, including the grounds of failure to complete to time or to show reasonable expedition, is dealt with in some detail *post*, Chapter 13, Section 1.

(5) Notice Rendering Time of the Essence

The fact that notice can render time of the essence has already been mentioned.[31]   The rule appears first to have evolved in the case of contracts for the sale of land, where it has been held that, notwithstanding that the stipulated time is not of the essence, time can be rendered of the essence (but only if the other party to the contract has been guilty of delay) by service of notice giving a date for completion.[32] The exact basis of this doctrine may not, at first sight, be easy to understand, since, if time is not of the essence of a contract when it is executed, it is difficult to see how the subsequent unilateral act of one party can alter the position, and indeed this view has been specifically rejected.[33]   The practical necessity for such a rule and what is submitted is the correct basis for it, namely, the evidentiary crystallisation of the defendants' intention no longer to be bound by the contract terms, has already been discussed.[34]   The doctrine has

---

[29] See, *e.g. Felton* v. *Wharrie*, Hudson's B.C., 4th ed., Vol. 2, p. 398, *infra*, p. 615.

[30] See *Carr* v. *J. A. Berriman (Pty.) Ltd.* [1953] A.L.J. 273, illustrated *ante*, Chap. 5, Section 2 (2), p. 319, also p. 533.

[31] *Supra*, Section (1).

[32] *Taylor* v. *Brown* (1839) 9 L.J.Ch. 14. (As to the length of the notice, see *Stickney* v. *Keeble* [1915] A.C. 386.)

[33] *Per* Fry J. in *Green* v. *Sevin* (1879) 13 Ch.D. 589 at p. 599, and see *per* Harman J. in *Smith* v. *Hamilton* [1951] 1 Ch. 174 at p. 181.

[34] *Supra*, pp. 604–605.

been applied to contracts for the sale of goods [35] and to contracts for sale of goods and work done (to a motor-car),[36] and is now of general application.[37] Those cases were, however, cases where the original stipulated time was of the essence, but performance within this time had been waived earlier prior to the final breach. In a building contract the remedy would be of some limited value in such circumstances (*i.e.* after the completion date), but such a notice can, as already pointed out, be of little practical value to a building owner where the builder is seriously delaying the earlier stages of the work.

However, wherever this ground for termination is relied upon, notice should be given, particularly in a case where the completion date has been waived though, as previously indicated, there are certainly extreme cases where the failure is so persistent or flagrant as to evince an intention not to be bound and so constitute repudiation without any notice.[38]

ILLUSTRATION

A demolition contract provided for completion within forty-two days, and liquidated damages for delay. After expiry of the forty-two days, the employer's solicitors asked the contractor when he would finish, whether in one, two or three months. He replied that he could not say. This was on August 16. On August 29, the employer, without warning, terminated the contract. *Held,* if the employer was going to act on the contractor's conduct as evidence of an intention not to be bound, he should have told him so, and not waited for thirteen days before acting: *Felton* v. *Wharrie* (1905).[39]

So, too, in *Lowther* v. *Heaver* (1889),[40] Lindley L.J. appears to have doubted, in relation to a forfeiture clause in a building lease entitling the lessor to re-enter on the undemised plots of the works when not proceeded with for twenty-one days, whether advantage could have been taken of such a clause without reasonable notice. See further *post*, Chapter 13, Section 1 (3).

[35] See *Hartley* v. *Hymans* [1920] 3 K.B. 475.
[36] See *Rickards (Charles) Ltd.* v. *Oppenhaim* [1950] 1 K.B. 616, *supra.*
[37] See *e.g. Carr* v. *J. A. Berriman (Pty.) Ltd.* quoted *supra*, p. 604 and Singleton L.J.'s judgment in *Rickards (Charles) Ltd.* v. *Oppenhaim* [1950] 1 K.B. 616 at p. 628, and the passage in Halsbury's *Laws of England* there referred to.
[38] *Carr* v. *J. A. Berriman (Pty.) Ltd.* [1953] A.L.J. 273 (Australia), illustrated *ante*, Chap. 5, p. 319, Chap. 8, p. 533. *Kingdom* v. *Cox* (1848) 5 C.B. 522 illustrated *supra*, p. 611.
[39] Hudson's B.C., 4th ed. Vol. 2, p. 398 (probably a borderline case). See also the analogous case, where an employer was delaying the contractor's start, of *Pigott Construction Ltd.* v. *W. J. Crowe Ltd.* (1961) 27 D.L.R. (2d) 258 (Canada), illustrated *ante*, Chap. 5, pp. 338–339, and the case of *Carr* v. *J. A. Berriman (Pty.) Ltd.* [1953] A.L.J. 273 (Australia), illustrated *ante*, Chap. 5, p. 319, where notice was held not to be necessary.
[40] 41 Ch.D. 248, illustrated *ante*, Chap. 8, Sect. 4, p. 561.

(6) Reasonable Time

It has been seen that an obligation to complete within a reasonable time sounding in damages arises either because the contract is silent as to time or (apart from some very rare cases of agreement or waiver) because the specified time has ceased to be applicable by reason of some matter for which the employer is responsible. It remains to consider what is a reasonable time. It has been said that where the law implies that a contract shall be performed within a reasonable time, it has " invariably been held to mean that the party upon whom it is incumbent duly fulfils his obligations, notwithstanding protracted delay, so long as such delay is attributable to causes beyond his control and he has neither acted negligently nor unreasonably." [41] It is not a question of what is an " ordinary time " or what are " ordinary circumstances." Reasonableness will be determined in the light of the circumstances as they actually exist at the time.[42]

This is a question of fact and must depend on all the circumstances which might be expected to affect the progress of the works. There are no reported cases directly involving a typical building or engineering contract, but it is suggested that certain questions require to be answered before a reasonable time can be properly assessed.

In the first place, the parties may or may not have contracted with the particular resources and capacity of the particular builder in mind. Thus an employer may have deliberately chosen a small local or jobbing builder, with limited resources of capital, plant and labour, to build his house, in the hope of getting a cheaper or better quality job while sacrificing speedy completion. On the other hand, a builder with limited resources might tender for a large contract in competition with more substantial contractors, and give no indication of his inability to carry out the work as rapidly. In the former case the test might well be subjective, and in the latter objective,[43] it is submitted, notwithstanding some of the language in the *Hick* case, because a party may have expressly or impliedly warranted his ability or capacity to maintain progress in a particular situation or at a particular speed.

Thus, while it may be that most factors beyond the builder's control will excuse him, it is possible that expressly or impliedly the parties will have contracted with a particular factor in mind. Thus, whereas there is little doubt that allowance would be made for delay

[41] *Per* Lord Watson in *Hick* v. *Raymond and Reid* [1893] A.C. 22 at pp. 32, 33.
[42] *Ibid. per* Lord Herschell. See also the discussion on *force majeure* and Act of God, *ante*, Chap. 5, Section 3, pp. 358–360.
[43] See *Attwood* v. *Emery* and *Hydraulic Engineering Co.* v. *McHaffie*, illustrated *infra*.

due to an unexpected strike, it would not, it is suggested, follow that the contractor's inability to obtain sufficient labour in competition with other contractors in the district would necessarily excuse him. In the case of sub-contractors of all kinds, however, whether nominated or otherwise, it is submitted that the tendency of the courts should be not to excuse the main contractor in any case where delay is caused by some act or omission within the sub-contractor's control but for that reason outside the main contractor's direct control, since, in such a case, the contractor will or should have his remedy against the sub-contractor, who in law is the contractor's agent for the purpose of carrying out the works, whether nominated or not.[44] Any tendency to excuse the main contractor would in effect be an invitation to sub-contractors to default on their obligations, and might well result in the employer failing to recover his own loss, whereas the contractor might still be able to recover any loss he personally might have suffered at the hands of the sub-contractor. Again, it may be a question whether the parties contracted with the builder's other commitments in mind. In approaching this question, it should be borne in mind that with the increasing degree of specialist and sub-contracted work in the building industry, the direct responsibilities of the main contractor have become correspondingly limited to the provision of a site-organisation, a non-specialised labour force, and materials and plant, so that in most cases the builder, by entering into the contract, is, in effect, warranting that he has or will have at least these available in sufficient quantity for due performance of his obligations.[45]

ILLUSTRATIONS

(1) A contracted to furnish goods to E " as soon as possible." *Held*, that " as soon as possible " meant as soon as A possibly could, and that A's contract was so far performed if he furnished the goods without unreasonable delay, regard being had to his ability to make them and the orders which he had already in hand, but that the goods must be completed within a reasonable time, using all means available in the trade: *Attwood* v. *Emery* (1856).[46]

(2) Where a contract was to be performed " within a reasonable time ": *Held*, that the reasonableness was to be measured, not by the particular existing staff and appliances of the contractor's business, but by the time which a reasonable diligent manufacturer of the same class as the contractor would take to carry out the contract: *Hydraulic Engineering Co.* v. *McHaffie* (1878).[47]

---

[44] See for the analogous case of quality of work *ante*, pp. 273 *et seq.*, and the passages from *Young and Marten* there referred to at pp. 290–291. See also *post*, pp. 761 *et seq.*
[45] Under an optional clause in the R.I.B.A. form of contract, however, he is entitled to an extension of time even on these grounds—see clause 23 (*j*) of the 1963 forms.
[46] 26 L.J.C.P. 73.   [47] 4 Q.B.D. 670.

(3) A bill of lading did not specify the time for discharge. During the unloading a strike occurred which delayed the ship twenty-five days longer than otherwise would have been the case. *Held,* that the obligation on the consignee was to unload within a reasonable time, and that that obligation was discharged if he unloaded in a reasonable time under the circumstances, assuming that those circumstances, so far as they caused delay, were not caused or contributed to by him: *Hick* v. *Raymond* (1893).[48]

(4) By a charter a cargo was to be " discharged with all reasonable dispatch as customary." The custom at the port was to discharge into railway wagons. Without any negligence on the part of the charterers, but owing to stress of work, and the consequent deficiency in the number of wagons available, the ship was delayed. *Held,* that the charterers, having done their best to procure the appliances that were customarily used for discharging such a ship, and having used them with proper dispatch, were not liable for delay: *Lyle Shipping Co.* v. *Cardiff Corporation* (1900).[49]

(5) Shipbuilders contracted to build and deliver a vessel by a certain date, but the contract provided for an extension of time for delay through certain specified causes " or other circumstances beyond the builders' control." A suitable berth for building the vessel did not become vacant until three months before the date named for completion. The vessel was not completed to time. An arbitrator found that the parties contemplated that the vessel was to be built when a suitable berth became vacant. The vessel until then occupying the berth was delayed in building through causes of the same nature as those specified in the contract. *Held,* that in fixing the time for completion, allowance must be made for the delay in completing the previous vessel: *Re Lockie and Craggs* (1902).[50]

It could happen that, even in a contract with an extension of time clause, the stipulated date for completion might have ceased to be applicable and the contractor's obligation become one to complete within a reasonable time, within the principles stated above.[51] In such an event it might be specially relevant, in considering what circumstances should be taken into account in deciding upon a reasonable time for the work, to consider the circumstances stipulated in the extension-of-time clause as justifying an extension of time, either as indicating circumstances which should be taken into account or possibly as excluding any circumstances not mentioned in the clause.

---

[48] [1893] A.C. 22; followed in *Sims & Co.* v. *Midland Ry.* [1913] 1 K.B. 103.
[49] [1900] 2 Q.B. 638.
[50] 86 L.T. 388.
[51] *Supra,* pp. 606–608.

CHAPTER 11

PENALTIES AND LIQUIDATED DAMAGES

SECTION 1. CONSTRUCTION AND EFFECT OF CLAUSES

(1) Generally

CONTRACTS often contain provisions for the payment of sums of money or the forfeiture of goods or other property in the event of particular specified breaches of the contract. These provisions vary very considerably, but their main characteristic is the intention to secure due performance of contractual obligations, and to regulate beforehand in an agreed and certain manner the rights of the parties, rather than leave them to the less predictable remedies otherwise available, and in particular the assessment of damages for breach of contract.

The simplest provisions of this type are provisions stating in round figures what payments are to be made or what the damages are to be in a certain event. These are classical liquidated damages or penalties provisions, most commonly found in building contracts in relation to the obligation to complete the work within the specified time. But a forfeiture clause making provision for the payment of money or forfeiture of plant or materials in the event of determination on breach of the contract may also fall into the same general category. Clauses of these kinds require to be distinguished from clauses empowering a party to do something upon payment of a sum of money. In such cases, the act is a permitted act, and not a forbidden one, and the sum of money is in the nature of the price for being permitted to do it. Thus if in a farming lease a tenant covenanted not to sell or carry away hay without consent, save upon payment of an increased rent of £10 per ton so carried away and sold, he would have the right to do so, and could not be prevented from doing so by injunction.[1] On the other hand, if a bank employee covenants not to enter the employment of any other bank, and promises to pay £1,000 by way of penalty should he do so, he will not be permitted to enter other employment upon payment of the £1,000, and an injunction will issue.[2]

---

[1] *Woodward* v. *Gyles* (1690) 2 Vernon 119.
[2] *National Provincial Bank* v. *Marshall* (1888) 40 Ch.D. 112.

But in all cases where the act in question is a breach of contract, the law will inquire whether the payment or forfeiture provided for in the contract is a penalty, or liquidated damages. If it is held to be a penalty, the party claiming it will not be permitted to recover the full amount, if his damage has in fact been less, but on the other hand will not be limited to that amount if his damages have been greater.[3] (It is evident, however, that there would be difficulties in the way of a party who had suffered greater damage arguing that a clause inserted for his benefit was in fact a penalty, though a clause which is not a genuine pre-estimate of damage may in some cases be a deliberate limitation imposed by the parties on the amount of possible damage rather than a penalty *in terrorem*.[4]) On the other hand, if it is held to be liquidated damages, the aggrieved party will be entitled to the stipulated sum, whether his real damage be greater, or less, or non-existent.[5]

(2) Distinction between Penalties and Liquidated Damages

The actual description of the sum or payment is of little importance, even if the words " penalty " or " liquidated damages " are used. The distinction between the two, and the tests to be applied, have nowhere been more clearly stated than in the following passage from the judgment of Lord Dunedin in *Dunlop Pneumatic Tyre Co. Ltd.* v. *New Garage & Motor Co. Ltd.* (1915).[6]

> " 1. Though the parties to a contract who use the words ' penalty ' or ' liquidated damages ' may prima facie be supposed to mean what they say, yet the expression used is not conclusive. The court must find out whether the payment stipulated is in truth a penalty or liquidated damages.
>
> " 2. The essence of a penalty is a payment of money stipulated as *in terrorem* of the offending party; the essence of liquidated damages is a genuine covenanted pre-estimate of damage.[7]
>
> " 3. The question whether a sum stipulated is penalty or liquidated damages is a question of construction to be decided

---

[3] For the historical basis of this rule, see *Wall* v. *Rederiaktiebolaget Luggude* [1915] 3 K.B. 66 and *Watts, Watts & Co.* v. *Mitsui Ltd.* [1917] A.C. 227.

[4] See *e.g. Widnes Foundry (1929) Ltd.* v. *Cellulose Acetate Silk* [1931] 2 K.B. 393 affirmed in the House of Lords [1933] A.C. 20, (1933) 48 T.L.R. 595, and illustrated *infra*, p. 623. See also *Feather (Thomas) & Co. (Bradford) Ltd.* v. *Keighley Corporation* (1953) 52 L.G.R. 30 illustrated *ante*, Chap. 9, Section 2 (2), p. 581.

[5] See the *Widnes* case.

[6] [1915] A.C. 79 at p. 86.

[7] *Clydebank Engineering and Shipbuilding Co.* v. *Don Jose Ramos Yzquierdo y Castaneda* [1905] A.C. 6.

upon the terms and inherent circumstances of each particular contract, judged of as at the time of making the contract, not as at the time of the breach.[8]

" 4. To assist this task of construction, various tests have been suggested, which if applicable to the case under consideration may prove helpful, or even conclusive. Such are:

(a) It will be held to be a penalty if the sum stipulated for is extravagant and unconscionable in amount in comparison with the greatest loss that could conceivably be proved to have followed from the breach.[9]

(b) It will be held to be a penalty if the breach consists only in not paying a sum of money, and the sum stipulated is a sum greater than the sum which ought to have been paid.[10] This, though one of the most ancient instances, is truly a corollary to the last test.

(c) There is a presumption (but no more) that it is a penalty when ' a single sum is made payable by way of compensation, on the occurrence of one or more or all of several events, some of which may occasion serious and others but trifling damage.'[11]

(d) It is no obstacle to the sum stipulated being a genuine pre-estimate of damage that the consequences of the breach are such as to make precise pre-estimation almost an impossibility. On the contrary, that is just the situation when it is probable the pre-estimated damage was the true bargain between the parties."[12]

ILLUSTRATIONS

(1) A builder agreed to pay £10 per week for every week after the expiration of the time limited for the doing of certain repairs to a church, until the said work should be completely finished. *Held*, that the £10 a week was in the nature of liquidated damages, as the amount of damage was difficult of ascertainment by a jury, and was therefore properly fixed by the parties beforehand: *Fletcher* v. *Dyche* (1787).[13]

---

[8] *Public Works Commissioner* v. *Hills* [1906] A.C. 368, and *Webster* v. *Bosanquet* [1912] A.C. 394.

[9] Illustration given by Lord Halsbury in *Clydebank* case, *supra*.

[10] *Kemble* v. *Farren* (1829) 6 Bing. 141.

[11] Lord Watson in *Lord Elphinstone* v. *Monkland Iron and Coal Co.* (1886) 11 App.Cas. 332.

[12] *Clydebank* case, *supra*, Lord Halsbury; *Webster* v. *Bosanquet*, *supra*, Lord Mersey. For a modern example, see *Att.-Gen. for British Guiana* v. *Serrao* (1965) 7 W.I.R. 404 (West Indies).

[13] 2 T.R. 32.

(2) An agreement contained a provision that if either of the parties should neglect or refuse to fulfil the said agreement, or any part thereof, or any stipulation therein contained, such party should pay to the other the sum of £1,000, to which sum it was thereby agreed that the damages sustained by any such omission, neglect, or refusal should amount; and which sum was thereby declared by the said parties to be liquidated and ascertained damages, and not a penalty or penal sum, or in the nature thereof. *Held*, that the sum of £1,000 was in the nature of a penalty: *Kemble* v. *Farren* (1829).[14]

(3) In an action for breaking up a road, the defendant gave to the plaintiff a cognovit confessing judgment for £200, with a condition of defeasance if the defendant should reinstate the road by an agreed date in accordance with a plan and with the approval of a surveyor. The road was not completely reinstated by that date, and the plaintiff sued out execution and levied £200 and costs. *Held*, that the £200 was a penalty, and the court referred the question of damages sustained: *Charrington* v. *Laing* (1830).[15]

(4) R. contracted to construct a railway. The contract provided (1) that if, after seven days' notice, R. did not proceed regularly with the works the company might proceed and complete the works themselves, paying for the same out of the money then remaining due to R. on account of the contract. Payments then already made to R. were to be taken as full satisfaction for all works then already done by him. All moneys then due, or which would thereafter have become due to him under the contract, and all the tools and materials on the works, were to become the property of the company. And if the moneys, materials, and tools were insufficient to provide for the completion of the work, R. was to supply the deficiency. (2) That specified sums, increasing every week, should be paid as " penalties " in case of delay. *Held*, that the first provision imposed a penalty on R., but that the second provision provided for liquidated damages, although the word " penalties " was used: *Ranger* v. *G. W. Railway* (1854).[16]

(5) The plaintiff contracted with the defendant to do certain repairs and alterations to a house, to be completed in a specified time, " subject to a penalty of £20 per week that any of the works remain unfinished " after the stipulated periods. *Held*, that the sum of £20 per week was in the nature of liquidated damages, and could be deducted by the defendant without proving the loss he had actually sustained by reason of the delay: *Crux* v. *Aldred* (1866).[17]

(6) A contract provided for the retention of 15 per cent. of the value of the work done, and that in certain events " the unpaid balance of the work shall be forfeited by G. to the use of the said company in the nature of liquidated damages." *Held*, that the forfeiture of the unpaid value was to be considered as a fixed sum for compensation in the nature of liquidated damages: *Geiger* v. *Western Maryland Railway* (1874).[18]

---

[14] 6 Bing. 141.
[15] 3 M. & P. 587.
[16] 5 H.L.C. 72.
[17] 14 W.R. 656.
[18] 41 Md. 4, criticised *infra*, p. 623.

(7) An engineering contract provided for 10 per cent. retention money, which, in case the contractor failed to perform the contract, was to be forfeited to the employers. *Held*, that this was a penalty and not liquidated damages: *Savannah, etc. Railway* v. *Callahan* (1876).[19]

(8) A contract contained a clause providing for £10 per week to be paid in case of non-completion to time, and also a provision that in case the contract should not be in all things duly performed by the contractors, they should pay to the governors £1,000 as liquidated damages. *Held*, that the latter sum was in the nature of a penalty: *Re Newman, ex p. Capper* (1876).[20]

(9) Under a mining lease the lessee covenanted that he would reinstate the lands from time to time, and at the end of the lease, as they were before, or, if not, would pay £100 per acre. He failed to reinstate about thirty acres. An arbitrator found that the actual damage done amounted to £1,375. *Held*, that £100 per acre was an attempt to assess the damages, and not in the nature of a penalty, and that the whole £3,000 must be paid: *Re Mexborough (Earl of) and Wood* (1883).[21]

(10) A contract provided that works should be completed in all respects by a specified date, and that in default of such completion the contractor should forfeit and pay the sum of £100, and £5 for every seven days during which the work should be incomplete after the said date, as and for liquidated damages. *Held*, that as the sums were to be paid on a single event only, they were to be regarded as liquidated damages and not as penalties: *Law* v. *Redditch Local Board* (1892).[22]

(11) A agreed with B to pull down and rebuild a hotel in carcase before December 25, 1896, and to take a lease for eighty years from June 24, 1896, at a peppercorn for the first year, and £1,000 a year afterwards. Clause 2 of the contract provided that in case of failure to complete within the time allowed, the benefit of the agreement and all buildings and materials were to be forfeited. Clause 11 of the agreement gave power of re-entry in case of non-completion to time, or want of proper diligence, etc. A went into possession and pulled down about £200 worth of materials. B re-entered on January 19, 1897, and could only re-let from June 1899, at £900 a year. *Held*, that in the absence of some such express words as " as and for liquidated damages," clauses 2 and 11 could not be construed as depriving B of the right to prove, if he could, actual damages from the defendant's failure to perform the contract: *Marshall* v. *Macintosh* (1898).[23]

(12) W. contracted to supply an electric light installation. The contract provided that the whole of the work except the plant was to be completed by a certain day, subject to a " penalty " for each day of delay, and there was a similar provision as to the plant.

[19] 56 Ga. 331; US.Dig. 1877, p. 156.
[20] 4 Ch.D. 724 (C.A.).
[21] 47 L.T. 516.
[22] [1892] 1 Q.B. 127.
[23] 78 L.T. 750.

Held, that although the word " penalty " was used, the real intention was that the amounts specified should be treated as liquidated damages: *Re White and Another and Arthur* (1901).[24]

(13) A contract for the building of four torpedo-boats provided that " the penalty for later delivery shall be at the rate of £500 per week, for each vessel." The vessels were delivered after the specified time. *Held*, that the sum of £500 per week was liquidated damages and not a penalty: *Clydebank Engineering etc. Co.* v. *Yzquierdo y Castaneda* (1905).[25]

(14) P. agreed to buy ten motor-cars from the B. Co. at prices varying from £320 to £590, which were to be delivered at certain dates. P. deposited £300 with the company, which deposit the company " shall be at liberty to declare to be wholly forfeited " if P. refused to accept delivery and pay for any of the said goods. *Held*, that the fact that the sum in question was to be paid on the breach of any one of a variety of stipulations of different degrees of importance was not conclusive as to its being a penalty; nor was the fact that the sum in question had been deposited at the making of the contract conclusive as to its being liquidated damages, though both these facts formed material elements to be taken in ascertaining the intention of the parties; and that in this case the parties had intended the sum in question to be liquidated damages: *Pye* v. *British Automobile Commercial Syndicate* (1906).[26]

(15) A firm of timber merchants entered into a contract with a landowner whereby they bought certain standing timber under the condition: " The wood to be cleared away by April 1, 1918, under a penalty of 10s. a day until such is done." In April, 1919, the wood not having been completely cleared away, the landowner brought an action against the timber merchants for payment of one year's " penalty " at the agreed rate. *Held*, that although the sum of 10s. was described in the contract as a " penalty," yet as it was *ex facie* a reasonable pre-estimate of loss, and not a mere random figure, and was not averred by the timber merchants to be exorbitant, it must be regarded as liquidated damages and not as a penalty: *Cameron-Head* v. *Cameron* (1919).[27]

(16) A railway construction contract provided that in the event of non-completion by a certain date the contractor should forfeit the retention-moneys under the contract and two other contracts, and also certain necessity money lodged with the railway company's agent " as and for liquidated damages sustained by the defendants for the non-completion." *Held*, the amount of retention-money was indefinite and depended upon the progress of the construction, and could not therefore be a genuine pre-estimate of loss. The company was therefore not entitled to these sums, but only such damage as it might actually have suffered: *Public Works Commissioner* v. *Hills* (1906).[28]

[24] 17 T.L.R. 461.
[25] [1905] A.C. 6.
[26] [1906] 1 K.B. 425.
[27] 1919 S.C. 627.
[28] [1906] A.C. 368.

(17) A contract for delivery and erection of an acetone recovery plant contained a provision, inserted at the request of the purchasers, for payment of a weekly sum of £20 by way of penalty for every week in default. The defendants counterclaimed £5,850 as damages in respect of thirty weeks' delay, and the plaintiffs contended that they were limited in any event to the £600 provided by the contract, which the defendants said was a penalty. *Held*, the provision was one for liquidated damages and bound the parties. *Per* Scrutton L.J.: " I do not decide that a party is always bound by the figure mentioned from recovering a larger sum; it turns upon whether the sum mentioned can be said to be an estimate of the damage to be paid for the breach; but I find great difficulty in saying that an estimate less than the actual loss can ever be a penalty *in terrorem* ": *Widnes Foundry* (1925) *Ltd.* v. *Cellulose Acetate Silk Co. Ltd.* (1931).[29]

With one exception in an American case,[30] the above illustrations show that provisions in building contracts for the forfeiture of retention-moneys, however described, offend against the basic principle and are penalties, since the amount retained, which is principally designed as a security for possible defective work, and consequently increases, quite logically from this point of view, as a greater quantity of work is completed, can bear no reasonable relation to the potential loss to the employer arising on delay in completion or on termination of the contract. On the other hand regular weekly or monthly figures for delay are not open to attack on principle, since they correspond to the reasonable concept of a running loss to the employer while out of occupation, and hence they will only be invalidated if they are wholly unreasonable in amount relative to the value of the completed project to the employer. They are particularly suitable for projects which are not directly commercial in character, such as private houses, libraries, schools, subsidised housing and other public buildings and engineering works, where it may not be possible to prove any loss in the direct commercial sense if completion is delayed, and there are no reported cases in the United Kingdom where liquidated damages for delay in building contracts have been held excessive so as to constitute a penalty. Liquidated damages clauses are not looked on with the same disfavour at the present day, and modern disallowances arise almost entirely in the field of hire-purchase, where Lord Dunedin's principle 4 (c) above is frequently flagrantly violated.[31]

Finally, it is desirable perhaps to emphasise that liquidated damages clauses for delay by definition represent a pre-estimate of

---

[29] [1931] 2 K.B. 393.
[30] *Geiger* v. *Maryland Ry.*, *supra*, but see two further American cases, *post*, p. 704.
[31] See *e.g. E.P. Finance Co. Ltd.* v. *Dooley* [1964] 1 All E.R. 527.

all (not some of) the employer's damages in the event of delay in completion. So it is submitted that if there is a fluctuations clause in the contract, the contractor will be entitled to increases in price under that clause notwithstanding that, but for his culpable delay, the work would have been done at lower prices and so would have cost the employer less.[31a] So too with other clauses, such as variation clauses, where the effect may be the same.

SECTION 2. RELEASE OF LIQUIDATED DAMAGES

(1) Release by Prevention

It has been seen [32] that, for the purpose of treating the contract as repudiated, in the rare cases where time is of the essence, the contract time for completion may cease to be applicable for a variety of reasons, including the ordering of extras or other interference or prevention by the employer. In the case of damages, it is equally obvious that where the reason is some act of the employer or his architect or engineer preventing completion by the due date, it cannot be the intention of the parties [33] that liquidated or other damages should be calculated from that date even if the act, such as ordering extras, is not a breach of contract. Liquidated damages stipulated for at a rate for each day or week of delay in completing the works must begin to run from some definite date. It follows, therefore, that if the date in the contract has for some such reason ceased to be the proper date for the completion of the works, and no contractual provision exists for the substitution of a new date, there is in such a case no date from which liquidated damages can run and the right to liquidated damages will have gone. This, rather than solicitude for the contractor, is the reason for the provision usually known as the extension of time clause. It is essential for the understanding of the cases below to appreciate that the courts, in the nineteenth century, viewed any liquidated damages clause with the greatest suspicion, and were ready to hold that it was invalidated by virtually any event not expressly contemplated by the contract and not within the contractor's sphere of responsibility. On this view, an extension of time clause, which prima facie would appear to be inserted for the benefit of the contractor, might also be regarded as being for the benefit of the employer, since in cases of prevention or breach its function might

---

[31a] Now so decided by the Court of Appeal, *ante*, p. 568.
[32] *Ante*, Chap. 10.
[33] Despite the two quite exceptional cases illustrated below.

be to keep alive a liquidated damages clause which would otherwise have been treated as no longer applicable. For this reason, the extension of time clauses were themselves most strictly construed, and only if a sufficiently explicit intention could be found for them to be operated in the particular circumstances involving prevention or breach by the employer or his architect would they be regarded as saving the liquidated damages clause where such circumstances had occurred.[34]

Thus, unless there is a sufficiently specific clause, it is not open to the employer, where the contract date has ceased to be applicable, to make out a kind of debtor and creditor account allowing so many days or weeks for delay caused by himself, and, after crediting that period to the builder, to seek to charge him with damages at the liquidated rate for the remainder.[35] (" Day " in liquidated damages clauses includes holidays and Sundays, unless " working days " are specifically referred to.[36])

As will be seen in the following cases, even where the contract contains a clause empowering the architect or the employer to award an extension of time, the courts have been reluctant to construe such a clause as giving the architect or employer power to extend the time in circumstances where the delay has in fact been caused by the act of the employer or his agents.[37] In principle, however, there is no objection to this provided the contract is sufficiently explicit.[38]

In considering the cases, which are not all easy to reconcile, it should be realised that many of them were decided on demurrer, and that when the right to liquidated damages disappeared, the right to damages at common law would remain. This latter right would operate, however, as from the ending of a reasonable time for completion, the contract date having gone.[40] In such a case, it remains uncertain whether an employer, having invalidated a liquidated

---

[34] It is noteworthy that clause 43 of the I.C.E. form of contract does not appear to have been drafted with this part of the law in mind, and accordingly, apart from the ordering of extras, which is specifically referred to in this clause, the clause is highly vulnerable. See the *Perini Pacific* case, illustrated *infra*, p. 630.

[35] This was unsuccessfully attempted in *Dodd* v. *Churton, infra*. See also *Perini Pacific* v. *Greater Vancouver Sewerage* (1966) 57 D.L.R. (2d) 307, *infra*.

[36] *Brown* v. *Johnson* (1842) 10 M. & W. 331.

[37] See also *ante*, Chap. 7, pp. 406 *et seq*. and *infra*, Section 3, Extension of Time.

[38] *Cf.* clause 23 (*f*) (late instructions) and 23 (*h*) (other contractors of the employer) in the 1963 R.I.B.A. standard forms. Except in relation to extras, the 1955 I.C.E. form is not sufficiently explicit—see clause 44 and the use of the expression " other special circumstances of any kind whatsoever," and the Note to the *Perini Pacific* case, *infra*, p. 631.

[40] See *ante*, Chap. 10.

damages clause and contract date by his own act of prevention, would be permitted to recover a larger weekly or other sum as unliquidated damages on establishing failure to complete within a reasonable time.[41]

In conclusion it should perhaps be stated that, while the principles are clear, and not difficult for an expert draughtsman to understand, and have been correctly applied by the British Columbia Court of Appeal as recently as 1966,[42] the modern attitude to liquidated damages clauses which satisfy Lord Dunedin's tests is no longer so hostile, and it seems possible that one day the courts may wish to review the whole of this rather complicated subject. On the other hand, an advantage of and perhaps the basic reason for the strict traditional view is that liquidated damages clauses usually confer a power to deduct the damages immediately from monies due to the contractor on interim certificate, and the need for certainty as to the date upon which they become due is inconsistent with a retrospective informal reduction of the period of delay to take account of the acts of the employer.[42a]

ILLUSTRATIONS

(1) Contractors who were bound to pay heavy liquidated damages for failure to complete joinery work at a brewery within the stipulated time of four-and-a-half months were prevented from starting work by the defendant's other workmen. After the conclusion of the evidence, it was agreed that this had caused a delay of four weeks, while the contractors were in default to the extent of one week. *Held*, liquidated damages could not be deducted from the contractor's claim for the price of the work: *Holme* v. *Guppy* (1838).[43]

(2) A contractor undertook to build a railway for a lump sum. By a subsequent contract, on the employers agreeing to pay a further £15,000 and supply certain rails and chairs, he undertook to complete by a certain date, and to pay liquidated damages if he failed to do so. The employers sought to deduct liquidated damages, and the contractor alleged that the delay was due to non-delivery of the promised rails and chairs. *Held*, that the covenant to supply rails and chairs was independent of the covenant to complete, as otherwise non-delivery of one rail or chair would excuse the contractor from performance, and that liquidated damages could be deducted; but that if the contractor had in reality been prevented from completing to time, his remedy was a separate claim for damages for breach of the covenant to deliver, which would include the liquidated damages he had been compelled to pay: *Macintosh* v. *Midland Counties Railway* (1845).[44]

[41] See *supra*, pp. 618, 623.   [42] See the *Perini Pacific* case, *infra*.
[42a] See, in addition to cases illustrated below, *Peak Construction Ltd.* v. *McKinney Foundations Ltd.*, July 1, 1970, C.A., which confirms the law as here stated.
[43] 3 M. & W. 387. (No extension of time clause in this case.)   [44] 14 M. & W. 548.

[Note: The " separate claim " would now be an equitable set-off and available as a defence.[45] But it is submitted that in the light of the other authorities the principle as stated in this case is also not correct, and that in fact no right to liquidated damages could arise once prevention was established.]

(3) A building contract provided for completion by a fixed date, and for liquidated damages of £1 per day for delay in completion. There was a power to order extra work, and the builder was to be allowed so much extra time beyond the completion date as might be necessary to do the additional work. There were thirty-one days' delay, and the employers alleged that nine were due to the extra works, and twenty-two were the fault of the builder. *Held*, on demurrer, that liquidated damages might be deducted for the twenty-two days: *Legge* v. *Harlock* (1848).[46]

(4) A building owner sought to deduct penalties from the contract sum in respect of twelve weeks' delay. The contractors replied that, by a subsequent agreement, they had undertaken to carry out certain extra works, that these were mixed up with the original work, and it was thereby impossible to complete the original work to time, and that all the work had been completed within a reasonable time. *Held*, this was a good answer to the claim for penalties: *Thornhill* v. *Neats* (1860).[47]

(5) A shipbuilding contract provided for liquidated damages for failure to deliver complete by a certain day. If the ship was not so delivered for any cause not under the control of the builders, to be proved to the satisfaction of the owner's agent and certified by him, the liquidated damages were not to be enforced for the number of days specified in the certificate. There was very considerable delay, a substantial proportion of which (six weeks) was due to interference by the owners. *Held*, following *Holme* v. *Guppy*, *supra*, that no liquidated damages might be deducted: *Russell* v. *Sa Da Bandeira* (1862).[48]

[Note: The extension of time clause seems to have been largely ignored in this case, but there is subsequent authority (see *Wells* v. *Army & Navy Co-op. Society*, *infra*) that this clause would not, in the absence of express words, be construed to include acts of the employer within its ambit, so that it would not have saved the liquidated damages clause.]

(6) A building contract authorised the engineer to order alterations and " if by reason thereof he should consider it necessary to extend the time for completion of the work, such extension of time shall be given in writing under his hand, or otherwise the time of completion shall be deemed to be not extended." Extra work was ordered, rendering, so it was alleged, performance within the stipulated time impossible. *Held*, on demurrer and following *Holme* v. *Guppy*, that liquidated damages could not be deducted: *Westwood* v. *Secretary of State for India* (1863).[49]

[45] See *ante*, Chap. 9, p. 584, and *post*, Chap. 14, pp. 725, 731–733.
[46] 12 Q.B. 1015.
[47] 8 C.B.(N.S.) 831; and see *Courtnay* v. *Waterford Ry.* (1878) 4 L.R.Ir. 11.
[48] 13 C.B.(N.S.) 149.
[49] 1 New Rep. 262.

[Note: It is suggested that the extension of time clause in this case should have been given effect to—see *e.g. Sattin* v. *Poole, infra*—and that this case was for this reason wrongly decided.]

(7) An engineering contract contained an extension of time clause under which *it was lawful* for the architect to give an extension of time (*inter alia*) for failure to supply drawings or directions to the contractor in time. There was a separate forfeiture clause empowering the employers to terminate the contract if, in the opinion of the architect, the contractor failed to proceed with due diligence. The contractors sued for wrongful termination, and the employers pleaded that the architect had certified that the contractor had not proceeded with due diligence. The contractors replied that the delay was due to failure to supply plans and drawings and to set out the land. *Held*, on demurrer, by a majority of the Court of Exchequer Chamber, that the architect had no jurisdiction to bind the contractor as to these matters under the forfeiture clause, and (*per* Blackburn and Mellor JJ.) that the extension of time clause, by reason of its permissive language, on its true construction, only enabled the architect to bind his employers, not the contractors, by any extension of time he might give. The latter would only be bound if they applied for and accepted his decision: *Roberts* v. *Bury Commissioners* (1870).[50]

[Note: It should be pointed out that this latter view was not necessary for the decision and was expressed by only two out of six judges. The basis of the decision (which it is submitted was correct) was that the extension of time clause had no connection with the forfeiture clause, and that the architect's opinion under the latter clause could not be binding when prevention by the other party was alleged. The dicta based on the form of wording seem difficult to support, it is submitted.]

(8) A contractor undertook to complete the works on a certain day, with any alterations or additions which might be made, and to pay liquidated damages for failure to complete, the decision of the owner's inspector as to the time within which they should have been executed to be final. The agreement further provided that no extra works should be undertaken without an order signed by the clerk of works, and in the event of any alteration or addition being ordered, the plaintiff should carry out the original works, with such alterations and additions, in the same manner as if they had been originally comprised in the works of the contract, and the period for completing the entire works should not exceed the contract period unless a written extension of time was given. Extras were ordered, and no extension of time was given, though it was alleged that the extras rendered completion by the stipulated date impossible. *Held*, distinguishing *Roberts* v. *Bury Commissioners*, *supra*, that on the true construction of the contract the contractors had undertaken to complete by the stipulated date, whatever extras might be ordered, unless relieved by the decision of the clerk of works as to extension of time, which was to be binding: *Jones* v. *St. John's College* (1870).[51]

[50] L.R. 5 C.P. 310. See *ante*, Chap. 7, pp. 407–408, for this case more fully illustrated and explained.   [51] L.R. 6 Q.B. 115.

(9) A builder undertook to complete the works " with such addition, enlargement or alteration of, and deviation from the said work, if any " by a certain date. The architect was given power to extend the time for completion in proportion to extras or alterations ordered by him. Extras were ordered which the jury found prevented completion to time, but no extension was made. *Held*, distinguishing *Russell* v. *Sa Da Bandeira, supra,* and following *Jones* v. *St. John's College,* that liquidated damages might be deducted: *Tew* v. *Newbold-on-Avon School Board* (1884).[52]

(10) A building contract authorised the ordering of extra work, but contained no extension of time clause. There was a completion date and a provision for liquidated damages. Extras were ordered, which necessarily delayed completion. In an action by the builder for the price, the employer claimed to set off liquidated damages for delay, less a fortnight which he claimed was adequate allowance for the extras. *Held,* following *Westwood* v. *S. of S. for India, Holme* v. *Guppy,* and *Russell* v. *Sa Da Bandeira,* and distinguishing *Jones* v. *St. John's College,* the provision for liquidated damages could no longer be applied: *Dodd* v. *Churton* (1897).[53]

(11) A building contract empowered the architect to award an extension of time if extras ordered by him caused delay. The architect ordered extras, but not in writing, and failed to extend the time. *Held,* under the terms of the contract, orders for extras were required to be in writing, without which the contractor could not recover for their value. The extension of time clause, on its true construction, only applied to extras ordered in accordance with the contract, and the architect accordingly had no power to give an extension of time for improperly ordered extras, and accordingly, the contractor having been prevented from completing by acts of the employer outside the extension of time clause, the liquidated damages clause was gone and liquidated damages could not be deducted: *Murdoch* v. *Luckie* (1897).[54]

(12) An employer ordered extras personally, but not in writing as required by the contract, and in such number and of such a size that the final work bore no resemblance to the work as planned. *Held,* that by their nature the extras were outside the contract and that, as they had prevented completion by the stipulated date, the damages were set at large and liquidated damages could not be deducted: *Meyer* v. *Gilmer* (1899).[55]

(13) A builder undertook (by clause 23) to complete by a certain date subject to the provisions for extension of time contained in the contract. These (clause 24) provided that the architect " shall make a fair and reasonable extension of time " in respect of (*inter alia*) extras or delay in receipt of instructions from the architect. There was considerable delay, and after completion the builders applied for an extension of time. The architect did not reply at

---

[52] 1 C. & E. 260.

[53] [1897] 1 Q.B. 562.

[54] 15 N.Z.L.R. 296.

[55] 18 N.Z.L.R. 129. See *ante,* Chap. 8, Section 2 (2) (d), p. 550, where this case is more fully illustrated.

once, and the builders issued a writ based on the sum of £681 certified by the architect as due, subject to penalties. After issue of the writ, the architect wrote extending the time, but not for the whole of the delay, and certified that £231 was due as liquidated damages. The builders wished to call evidence to show that the delay was due to the ordering of extras, lack of information, and other matters involving breach of contract by the employer. *Held*, distinguishing *Roberts* v. *Bury Commissioners* on the ground that the language of the extension of time clause there was permissive and not mandatory, and also that there was no provision in that case whereby the builder undertook to be bound by the architect's decision as in clause 23 of the present contract, that the evidence was rightly excluded and the liquidated damages certified for must be deducted: *Sattin* v. *Poole* (1901).[56]

(14) Builders undertook to erect buildings for a company within a year, unless delayed by alterations, strikes, sub-contractors " or other causes beyond the contractor's control." By clause 16 the decision of the directors of the company in matters of time was to be final, and liquidated damages were payable if the work was not completed within a time considered reasonable by them. There was one year's delay. The principal cause was sub-contractors, for which the directors were prepared to allow three months. The builders contended that this was insufficient, and also that the delay was due to alterations (*i.e.* within the ambit of clause 16) and also to delay in giving possession and providing plans. *Held*, on the evidence there was substance in all these complaints, and it was impossible to say to what extent each one contributed to the delay, but the words " or other causes beyond the contractor's control " could not include the breaches of contract or other acts of the employers in not giving possession and failing to supply plans and drawings in due time, and consequently liquidated damages could not be deducted: *Wells* v. *Army and Navy, etc., Soc.* (1902).[57]

(15) A contract for the construction of a sewage disposal plant permitted an extension of time for " extras or delays occasioned by strikes, lockouts, *force majeure* or other cause beyond the control of the contractor." Liquidated damages were to be $1,000 *per* day. There was a delay of ninety-nine days, and an extension of time for forty-six days, and the employer accordingly sued for $53,000. The trial judge found that forty-five days' delay had been caused by the employer's delivery of certain machinery in a defective condition requiring considerable repairing work, and that this was a breach of contract by the employer. He accordingly awarded $8,000 liquidated damages. *Held*, by the Court of Appeal of British Columbia, applying *Wells* v. *Army & Navy Society Ltd.*, that on these facts no liquidated damages could be recovered: *Perini Pacific Ltd.* v. *Greater Vancouver Sewerage* (1966).[58]

[56] Hudson's B.C., 4th ed. Vol. 2, p. 306.
[57] 86 L.T. 764; Hudson's B.C., 4th ed. Vol. 2, p. 346, followed by C.A. in *Peak Ltd.* v. *McKinney Foundations Ltd.* July 1, 1970. See also *Gallivan* v. *Killarney U.D.C.* [1912] 2 I.R. 356, illustrated *infra*, Section 3 (3), p. 643.
[58] (1966) 57 D.L.R. (2d) 307 (Canada). There was no appeal to the Supreme Court of Canada from this part of the decision—see [1967] S.C.R. 189. See note on this case *infra*, p. 631. In addition to the cases above, see also *A.B.C. Ltd.* v. *Waltham Holy Cross U.D.C.* [1952] 2 All E.R. 452.

[Note: This case is of the greatest importance in England, because for all practical purposes the extension of time clause was the same as that in the current I.C.E. conditions, which it is submitted will be similarly invalidated if a part of the contractor's total delay can be shown to be due to any act or omission (other than the ordering of extras) of the employer.[58a]]

It is suggested that the effect of the preceding cases is as follows:

(a) that acts of prevention by the employer, whether authorised by or breaches of the contract, will in general set time at large and invalidate any liquidated damages clause, in the absence of an applicable extension of time clause.[59]

(b) that where the act of prevention is a cause of part of the delay but not of the whole, the liquidated damages clause will still be invalidated,[60] unless an applicable extension of time clause exists.[61]

(c) that where there is an extension of time clause, this is regarded as being inserted for the benefit of the employer, since it operates to keep alive the liquidated damages clause in the event of delay being due to an act of the employer or his agents.[62] Where it does not cover the acts of prevention which have in fact occurred, no decision under the clause can bind the builder, or preserve the liquidated damages clause.[63]

(d) that general or ambiguous words in an extension of time clause, such as " any matters beyond the control of the builder " will, for this reason, not be construed to include acts of prevention or breaches of contract by the employer or his architect.[64]

(e) but that where an extension of time clause does clearly cover the delay in question, even if it involves prevention or breach of contract by the employer, the normal sense of the contract,

---

[58a] See clause 44 I.C.E. Conditions. See now also *Peak Construction Ltd.* v. *McKinney Foundations Ltd.*, C.A., July 1, 1970.

[59] *Holme* v. *Guppy*; *Thornhill* v. *Neats*; *Dodd* v. *Churton*; *Wells* v. *Army and Navy Co-op. Society, supra.*

[60] *Holme* v. *Guppy*; *Russell* v. *Sa Da Bandeira*; *Dodd* v. *Churton* and *Wells* v. *Army and Navy, etc.*; *Peak Construction Ltd.* v. *McKinney Foundations Ltd.*

[61] *Legge* v. *Harlock* (1848) 12 Q.B. 1015.

[62] See *post*, Section 3.

[63] *Murdoch* v. *Luckie*; *Meyer* v. *Gilmer*; *Wells* v. *Army and Navy Co-op. Society*; *Peak* v. *McKinney, supra*. See also *Gallivan* v. *Killarney U.D.C.* [1912] 2 I.R. 356, *infra*, Section 3 (3), p. 643. The clause will be equally inoperable in the hands of an arbitrator, it is submitted.

[64] *Wells* v. *Army and Navy Co-op. Society* (1902) Hudson's B.C., 4th ed., Vol. 2, p. 436; *Perini Pacific Ltd.* v. *Greater Vancouver Sewerage* (1966) 57 D.L.R. (2d) 307 (Canada); *Peak* v. *McKinney*; and see *Russell* v. *Sa Da Bandeira* (1862) 13 C.B.(N.S.) 149. This principle does not seem to apply, however, in the somewhat analogous case of forfeiture clauses—see *Wadey's* case, illustrated *post*, Chap. 13, p. 693.

and the law relating to the approval and certificates of quasi-arbitrators [65] will require that, if an extension of time is refused, this will bind the builder,[66] *a fortiori* if some extension has been given, subject to any overriding arbitration clause.[67]

(f) an extension of time clause may, however, fail, and with it the whole of the liquidated damages clause, if it is not exercised within any time permitted by the contract, in certain rare cases where the contract may restrict the time for its exercise.[68]

In the seventh edition of this work language was used which may have suggested that, where an appropriate power to extend time had not been exercised because of the certifier's rejection of the claim, but there was in fact prevention of some kind by the employer, the contract time would in all cases cease to be applicable. The decisions which might be held to support this view are *Roberts* v. *Bury Commissioners* and *Westwood* v. *Secretary of State for India*. The first of these cases was in reality a decision on the forfeiture clause, and not on the admittedly closely allied extension of time clause (which neither party had attempted to invoke). The decision in *Westwood* v. *Secretary of State for India* can only be said to be wrong, since the extension of time clause in that case seems perfectly explicit. The case of *Russell* v. *Sa Da Bandeira*, which ignored the difficulty raised by the extension of time clause, is sufficiently explained in the note to the case above, since on its true construction the extension of time clause was not applicable.[69] Accordingly, it is submitted that matters of prevention or breach of contract can be conclusively determined by the certifier if a sufficiently specific extension of time clause is to be found in the contract, though only, of course, in the context of the employer's right to liquidated damages for delay, and subject always to the possibility of an over-riding arbitration clause giving the arbitrator power to substitute his own decision in the matter.

[65] See *ante*, Chap. 7, Approval and Certificates.
[66] *Jones* v. *St. John's College* (1870) L.R. 6 Q.B. 115; *Tew* v. *Newbold-on-Avon School Board* (1884) 1 C. & E. 260; *Sattin* v. *Poole* (1901) Hudson's B.C., 4th ed., Vol. 2, p. 306.
[67] As to which see Chap. 7, Section 4, *ante*, pp. 435 *et seq.*, and *infra*, Section 3 (2). The foregoing paragraphs (a) to (e) (in the Eighth Edition) appear to have been approved by the Supreme Court of Canada in the *Perini Pacific* case, and in the Ninth Edition by the English C.A. in the *Peak* case.
[68] See *infra*, Section 3, p. 643.
[69] Extension of time clauses generally, the effect of related architect's certificates, and the time for exercise of the power under these clauses, are dealt with, *infra*, Section 3, Extension of Time.

It should perhaps be repeated, before passing from this highly technical subject, that the failure of the liquidated damages clause will not prevent unliquidated damages being obtained for failure to complete within a reasonable time.

(2) Effect of Forfeiture

If the builder, by abandoning the contract or committing a fundamental breach, thereby entitles the employer to treat the contract as repudiated, or if the employer is enabled to operate a forfeiture or determination clause in the contract, the effect of such an event upon the liquidated damages provisions in the contract requires to be considered. In the case of forfeiture or determination clauses, the contract may contain express provisions dealing with the position, and where this is so they will be given effect to,[70] but in the case of a common law rescission on repudiation by the contractor the problem occurs without such assistance.

In the absence of special provision, it is submitted that liquidated damages accrued due prior to the date of rescission or forfeiture or determination will be recoverable, but thereafter the employer will be entitled only to unliquidated damages. (It should, of course, be remembered that in such an event an employer's damages would probably arise under two main heads, namely, damages for delay, and the additional cost, if any, of completion,[71] and it is the first only of these heads which can be affected by a liquidated damages clause.) In support of this view, it is suggested that, since a liquidated damages provision specifically contemplates completion by the builder without his being dismissed, it would be wrong without express provision to apply the clause to completion by another builder.[72] Thus in a case where termination had taken place before any liquidated damages accrued, the court said:

" If the concluding provisions of the re-entry clause had been omitted; if there had been a power simply to re-enter and terminate the contract and the company had exercised that power, then we are of opinion . . . that the council could not afterwards have claimed these liquidated damages as against the contractor. . . . Having elected to dispossess the contractor and taken the performance of the

---

[70] *Baylis* v. *Wellington City* (1886) 4 N.Z.L.R. 84, *infra*. The post-1963 R.I.B.A. forms have now made express provision which appears to substitute ordinary damages for liquidated damages in this event—see clause 25 (3) (*d*).

[71] See *ante*, Chap. 9 Price and Damages, pp. 579–580, 585 *et seq.*

[72] *British Glanzstoff Manufacturing Co. Ltd.* v. *General Accident Insurance Corporation Ltd.*, 1912 S.C. 591; [1913] A.C. 143, *infra*.

contract out of his hands they must have been taken to abandon their right to these damages." [73]

Conversely, as in many forms of contract liquidated damages become due immediately and provision is made for deduction of liquidated damages from moneys due[74]—e.g. on interim certificate —financial rights or obligations may well have accrued by the time of forfeiture, determination or rescission, and it would, to say the least, be highly inconvenient to reopen the whole state of accounts between the parties, as would be the case if the liquidated damages provision was held to have gone for all purposes upon forfeiture.

ILLUSTRATIONS

(1) A contract for work provided (1) that liquidated damages should be paid for each day beyond the day fixed for completion; (2) that in case of breach the employer might take the works out of B.'s (the contractor's) hands, and if the balance of the contract price was not sufficient to pay for completion by a second contractor, B. should pay the difference; and that if the works were not completed by the second contractor in time, in consequence of B.'s default, the employer should give an extension of time, and that B. should pay liquidated damages for the delay caused by such extension. B., after delaying the work about five months, wrote and said that he had decided to proceed no further. *Held*, that B. was liable to pay (1) liquidated damages from the date fixed for completion to the date on which he threw up the work; (2) the sum required to make up the price to the second contractor; (3) liquidated damages for the further delay caused by an extension of time given to the second contractor: *Baylis* v. *Wellington City* (1886).[75]

(2) A building contract gave the employers power to deduct liquidated damages from the retention money. The contract also empowered the employer, in case of undue delay on the part of the contractor, " to terminate the contract, so far as respects the performance of the same under the directions and by means of the contractor, but without thereby affecting in any other respects the liabilities of the said contractor." The contract was terminated under this provision, and W., one of the contractor's sureties, took an assignment of the contract, and agreed with the employers to complete the works in accordance with the original contract. In consequence of delay on the part of the original contractor, W. could not complete in the stipulated time. *Held*, that the words " without thereby affecting in any other respects the liabilities of the said contractor " effectually kept alive the employers' right to deduct liquidated damages from the retention money, and that W. was subject to the contractual liabilities of the original contractor and to the deduction of the liquidated damages: *Re Yeadon Waterworks Co. and Wright* (1895).[76]

---

[73] *Per* Kennedy J. in *Re Yeadon Waterworks Co. and Wright* (1895) 72 L.T. 538 at p. 540.
[74] See *e.g.* clause 22 of the post-1963 R.I.B.A. forms and clause 47 (1) of the 1955 I.C.E. form.
[75] 4 N.Z.L.R. 84
[76] 72 L.T. 538.

(3) A contract for the erection of a gas works provided for liquidated damages of £10 per week, and empowered the employers, if the contractor failed to proceed properly with the work, to enter and complete at the contractor's cost, or to set off such cost against any sums due. The contractor defaulted after the expiry of the contract period, and the employers entered and completed. *Held*, in addition to the cost of completion, the employers were entitled to recover liquidated damages up to the date of termination: *Simpson v. Trim Town Commissioners* (1898).[77]

(4) A contract for the construction of works by a specified date provided for liquidated damages for each week of delay beyond that date. It further provided that the employers might, if the contractor should suspend the works, engage others to complete them. The contractor became bankrupt and suspended the works, and the employers had them completed, but completion was delayed until six weeks after the specified date. The employers claimed from the contractor (*inter alia*) damages in respect of this delay. *Held*, that this claim could not be founded on the liquidated damage clause, which applied only where the contractor himself completed: *British Glanzstoff Manufacturing Co. Ltd.* v. *General Accident, etc., Insurance Corporation Ltd.* (1912).[78]

(3) Effect of Payment without Deduction

A building owner will not, apart from special provisions in the contract, lose the right to liquidated damages by paying the builder moneys otherwise due to him, or by permitting the completion of the work after the due date for completion. But in some forms of contract (now rare) the provision for deduction from moneys due, which is usually framed in a permissive or alternative sense,[79] may be construed to be mandatory and exclusive, and in such an event failure to make the deduction may disentitle the employer from recovering the damages. The language requires to be closely examined.

ILLUSTRATIONS

(1) A building contract provided that in the event of delay the builder should forfeit and pay to the employer £5 weekly, such penalty to be deducted from the amount which might remain owing on the completion of the work. *Held*, the employer had a double remedy, to deduct or recover as a payment: *Duckworth* v. *Alison* (1836).[80]

(2) F. contracted with R. to do the masonry work on buildings which R. was erecting. The work was to be done by April 1. F. did not complete it till July 1. R. allowed F. to go on with the work after April 1, and made payments under the contract. *Held*, that

---

[77] 32 I.L.T. Reports 129 (Ireland).
[78] 1912 S.C. 591: [1913] A.C. 143.
[79] *Cf.* the current R.I.B.A. form of contract.
[80] 1 M. & W. 412.

there was no release or discharge of the stipulation as to time, and that F. was liable in damages to R.: *Ruff* v. *Rinaldo* (1873).[81]

(3) In the event of delay, a contractor undertook to " forfeit and pay to (the employer) £20 a week, to be paid to and retained by the employer . . . for each and every week during which such work shall remain unfinished." Interim payments were made for 14 months after the completion date without retaining any sum for liquidated damages. *Held*, that by this conduct the employers had disentitled themselves from recovering liquidated damages: *Laidlaw* v. *Hastings Pier Co.* (1874).[82]

[Note: The court also found that the architect's unqualified certificates were evidence that he had exercised a power of extension of time in the contractor's favour [82a] and the employers were accordingly bound by them. The finding above, while unanimous, was therefore not strictly necessary to the decision, and there is no indication in the report that *Duckworth* v. *Alison, supra*, or any cases were referred to in this context. In *Baskett* v. *Bendigo Gold Dredging Co.* (1902),[83] the court rightly felt a difficulty about the words " to be paid to . . . the employer " in *Laidlaw's* case, and it is suggested that it is of doubtful authority on this point.]

(4) A contract provided that work should be completed within eight months from the acceptance of the tender, " failing which the sum of £2 for every working day by which such time of eight calendar months shall be exceeded will be deducted from any money due to the contractor by way of liquidated damages, and not in the nature of a penalty." *Held*, following *Laidlaw's* case, *supra*, that if the employers wanted to recover penalties they could only do so by deducting them, and that if moneys were paid without deducting penalties which had accrued, the penalty clause was gone: *Baskett* v. *Bendigo Gold Dredging Co.* (1902).[83]

(5) A contract for building torpedo boats provided that " the penalty for later delivery shall be at the rate of £500 per week for each vessel." Delivery was delayed, but payment was made in full. *Held*, that such payment in full did not bar a claim for the liquidated damages: *Clydebank Engineering, etc., Co.* v. *Yzquierdo y Castaneda* (1905).[84]

(4) Effect of Completion or Re-entry

It is self-evident that completion will bring the right to liquidated damages to an end, but it may be difficult to decide what is completion for this purpose, in particular if the employer enters into possession while the work is partly incomplete, or only retakes possession of part of the work.

There is conflicting authority on this point, and it is suggested that if completion is sufficient to justify the application of the doctrine

[81] 55 N.Y. 664.
[82] Hudson's B.C., 4th ed., Vol. 2, p. 13, further criticised *infra*, p. 642.
[82a] See *infra*, pp. 640 *et seq.*
[83] 21 N.Z.L.R. 166.
[84] [1905] A.C. 6.

of substantial performance, and the employer chooses to re-enter the right to liquidated damages will cease. But it may be a consideration that in certain circumstances, notwithstanding re-entry into possession, the employer may continue to suffer damage, in which case it would seem to be at least arguable that the liquidated damages should continue until the contract is completely performed, and that all that can be inferred from the re-entry is an understandable wish to reduce the loss or inconvenience of the employer rather than a waiver of the right to liquidated damages.

ILLUSTRATIONS

(1) H. contracted to repair T.'s house, under liquidated damages of $25 for each week's delay. There was delay for eight weeks, but T. moved in after three weeks, when the repairs were substantially completed. *Held*, that T. was entitled to set off liquidated damages for eight weeks up to entire completion, as his moving in before the repairs were completed was no waiver of his right to claim for the whole period: *Horton* v. *Tobin* (1887).[85]

(2) In a contract worth $20,000, the employer re-entered at a time when minor defects worth about $200 were still outstanding, and the architect was demanding that they be remedied forthwith. *Held*, the contract had been substantially performed, and liquidated damages ceased to run upon the re-entry: *Watts* v. *McLeay* (1911).[86]

Under the scheme of most modern contracts, liquidated damages come to an end on " practical " or " substantial " completion, but a liability to make good defects survives for a limited period. It is submitted that the most accurate definition to date of the state of completion contemplated by all provisions for completion to time in building and engineering contracts, and whether or not expressly conditioned as " practical " or " substantial " completion, is that adopted by the Full Court of the Supreme Court of Victoria: " the work . . . carried out in accordance with the contract . . . (except for departures from the contract which were either latent or undiscovered or merely trivial "[87]—even though that case did not involve an ordinary building contract.

This definition is important because, when an employer or purchaser enters an apparently satisfactory building on completion, defects may later manifest themselves which, if known at the time, would have justified a refusal to enter, or of the certificate of practical or substantial completion by the architect or engineer. In such a case

[85] 20 Nov.Sc. (8 Russ. & Geld.) 169.
[86] 19 W.L.R. 916 (Canada).
[87] *Morgan* v. *S. & S. Construction (Property) Ltd.* [1967] V.R. 149 (Australia), illustrated *ante*, Chap. 5, pp. 252–253.

it is not possible, it is submitted, for an employer, even in a case where the question of completion is open to dispute on the merits and he is in no way bound by any relevant certificate, to seek to impose liquidated damages retrospectively on the ground that the works were not in fact properly completed at the time of re-entry. It is submitted that the whole scheme of building contracts, including the commencement of the defects liability or maintenance period, (and, for example, the latent defect exception to the binding effect of the R.I.B.A. final certificate)[88] is inconsistent with such an intention (which if correct, would mean that an employer could add a claim for liquidated damages whenever he claimed damages for defective work, and however long after completion the defects were discovered).[88a]

SECTION 3.   EXTENSION OF TIME

(1) Generally

Provision is frequently made in building contracts for the architect or engineer to grant extensions of time for the completion of the work where delay due to certain specified causes has occurred. At first sight such a clause appears to be designed primarily for the benefit of the builder, since its effect, if the clause is operated, will be to reduce his liability to pay liquidated damages in the event of delay. This is certainly so where the delay is due to causes for which the builder would otherwise be responsible—*e.g.* bad weather, or strikes. But as has been seen,[89] such clauses are also of substantial benefit to the employer since, in the absence of an applicable clause of this kind, the liquidated damages provisions will cease to have effect where the delay, or even a part of it, is due to some act or default of the employer or his agents, or any other matter for which he would be responsible. It is for this reason that extension of time clauses have tended to be narrowly construed, so that only specific language in the clause will serve to give the architect or engineer jurisdiction to fix the extension of time for a delay due to some act of the employer or his agents.

The power of granting extensions of time for delays, when acted upon, fixes a new date for completion, and the obligation of the

---

[88] See *ante*, Chap. 7, p. 490.
[88a] See the discussion *ante*, Chap. 5, Section 1 (1), p. 258, and the passage from Viscount Dilhorne's judgment in *Jarvis & Sons* v. *Westminster Corporation* [1970] 1 W.L.R. at p. 647 there referred to. See also the case illustrated *infra*, p. 652.
[89] *Supra*, Release by Prevention, pp. 624 *et seq.*

builder is then to complete by that date. There is, in most contracts,
no reason why subsequent additional extensions of time should not
be granted, and it is not uncommon to provide that the architect
shall have power to extend the time " from time to time and at any
time." However, it is submitted that, on the wording of most contracts, once a stage has been reached when, allowing for all extensions
of time then justified, the works should have been completed,
liquidated damages commence to run and will continue to do so till
completion, and later events which otherwise would have justified an
extension of time can no longer be relied on by the builder to reduce
his liability. It may be that an event which could qualify as an act of
God might suspend or reduce the damages, however.[90]

(2) Whether Decision of Architect Binding

The status of the person nominated to exercise the power, usually, of
course, the architect or engineer, is almost invariably that of the
certifier, namely, quasi-arbitral in character. This means that the
sense of the contract will normally require that his decision, whether
it is to be expressed by written certificate or by word of mouth, is to
bind both parties, and to bind them finally, subject to any overriding
power which may be conferred upon the arbitrator, if there is an
arbitration clause in the contract.[91] In most modern contracts the
power is subject to review in this way.

ILLUSTRATION

 The liquidated damages clause provided that the architect *or
arbitrator* might award an extension of time for certain reasons and
grant a certificate to that effect. The arbitration clause referred all
disputes " except those expressly stipulated to be determined by
the architect or employer " to an arbitrator. The final certificate
was expressed to be conclusive evidence, subject to the rights of the
parties under the arbitration clause, of the value of the works and
materials. The employer was entitled to deduct and retain any
sums due to him out of moneys due to the contractor. The architect
issued a final certificate making no allowance for liquidated damages.
The employers claimed to deduct liquidated damages, but the contractors contended they were bound by the certificate. *Held*, by
Lord Kilbrandon, the extension of time clause was expressly subject
to the decision of the arbitrator, and the final certificate itself was
subject to review by the arbitrator, but even if it were not, it was
conclusive only as to the value of the work, and the employers
could accordingly deduct and retain liquidated damages: *Port
Glasgow Magistrates* v. *Scottish Construction Co. Ltd.* (1960).[92]

[90] See *Ryde* v. *Bushell* [1967] E.A. 817 (East Africa), and *ante*, Chap. 5, pp. 358–360.
[91] The whole of this subject is fully dealt with *ante*, Chap. 7, Approval and Certificates.
[92] 1960 S.L.T. 319 (Scotland).

As is pointed out in Chapter 7, *ante*, there is no reason in theory why a contract should not be framed so as to make a certifier's decision binding upon one party and not the other, but in relation to extension of time provisions the courts would obviously hesitate before so construing the contract. In the difficult case of *Roberts* v. *Bury Commissioners* (1870) [93] (where it was held that the architect had no jurisdiction to decide matters of breach of contract by the employer under a forfeiture and related extensions of time clause so as to bind the contractor) some at least of the judges suggested that had the architect decided the matter in the contractor's favour this would have bound the employer. But normally, it is suggested, the two must go hand in hand,[94] and normally, provided the extension of time clause is so worded as to cover the cause of delay in question, the architect's decision will bind the parties, subject to any arbitration clause.[95]

(3) Effect of Unqualified Certificate

The scheme of most modern contracts does not, for some reason, usually provide for an extension of time or liquidated damages decision to be shown in the final certificate, either expressly or by reduction of the amount certified. Nevertheless, where an architect decides that some liquidated damages must be deducted, the fact of his decision will normally be apparent, either because he will have issued a separate certificate of some kind recording that decision, *e.g.* a certificate that the works ought reasonably to have been completed by a certain date under the terms of the R.I.B.A. forms, or because the contractor will be notified of any deductions from the amounts certified by him in interim or final certificates. But where he has decided to give a full extension of time and make no deduction, his decision may not be so apparent, since any certificates for payment are unlikely to contain any reference to the matter, and, as stated, many modern contracts do not require the decision to be reflected in the payment or final certificates. In a contract where his decision is binding, therefore, the question may well arise whether in the particular circumstances the architect has decided the matter in the contractor's favour, so as to prevent the employer from subsequently claiming to deduct or be paid liquidated damages. The

---

[93] 5 C.P. 310, illustrated *ante*, pp. 407–408; *supra*, p. 628.
[94] See *Jones* v. *St. John's College* (1870) L.R. 6 Q.B. 115, and *Sattin* v. *Poole* (1901), Hudson's B.C., 4th ed., Vol. 2, p. 306, *supra*, pp. 628, 629–630, and *ante*, pp. 416 *et seq.*
[95] See *supra*, pp. 631–632.

commonest situation will be where the architect has, after the delay, certified payment in full without deduction, usually upon final certificate. It has been seen that in those rare forms of contract where the only right consequent upon delay is to deduct liquidated damages (as opposed to a right to sue for and recover the damages) full payment without deduction will deprive the employer of his remedy.[96] But in the more usual case, the employer will have the right either to deduct or sue for the liquidated damages.

Wherever the architect's decision is final, and he has power to extend the time for the matters which have caused delay, and is required to take account, in his certificate for payment of the final balance, of the liquidated damages due from the builder to the building owner, the right to recover liquidated damages will be lost if the architect gives an unqualified final certificate. This, it is submitted, must follow from the fact that, once the architect has issued his final certificate under such a contract, he is *functus officio*[97] (subject, of course, to any power of an arbitrator or the courts to reopen the final certificate on this matter under the provisions of the arbitration clause).[98]

On the other hand, in the more usual case where the architect is not specifically empowered to take the liquidated damages into account in his certificates for payment,[99] the absence of any reference to them in the final certificate obviously cannot affect the substantive position between the parties,[1] and the employer will not be prevented from recovering or deducting them, on proof that the architect had made his decision in the way required by the contract. In each case the contractual provisions must be carefully examined. It may be advisable also to reiterate the warning that most modern contracts contain arbitration clauses sufficiently wide in scope to deprive the architect's certificates of their binding force.[2]

ILLUSTRATIONS

(1) After completion, an employer, without mentioning delay, instructed his architect to issue a certificate for what was due, and

---

[96] See *ante*, Payment with Deduction, p. 635.

[97] See *ante*, Chap. 7, p. 484.

[98] *Supra*, subsection (2).

[99] The architect does not appear to have any such power under clauses 22 and 30 (7) of the 1963 R.I.B.A. forms of contract; and the engineer certainly does not under the 1955 I.C.E. form. Under the pre-1963 R.I.B.A. forms the architect appears to have had power to deduct from the penultimate certificate on practical completion— see the words " subject to clause 17 " in clause 24 (*d*) of the pre-1963 forms.

[1] See, however, *Laidlaw* v. *Hastings Pier Co.*, *infra*.

[2] See, *ante*, Chap. 7, Approval and Certificates, Section 4, Effect of Arbitration Clause, and *supra*, subsection (2).

the architect gave a certificate without deducting liquidated damages. The employer more than once promised to pay on this certificate. The builder tendered evidence of hindrance and waiver by the employer, but the court was of opinion that the question of liquidated damages was in any event concluded by the architect's certificate: *Arnold* v. *Walker* (1859).[3]

(2) A contract provided for liquidated damages for non-completion to be paid to or deducted by the employer from any money due to the contractor, and that the contract period should not be exceeded unless an extension of time was allowed in writing.[4] The inspector certified without making any deduction. *Held*, a certificate was not a condition precedent to recovery of liquidated damages by the employer and the employer could accordingly deduct them from the amount certified: *Jones* v. *St. John's College, Oxford* (1870).[5]

(3) A contract provided that in any dispute the architect's decision should be final. The contract also contained provisions for payment and certification of the final balance after completion, " subject to any deduction for the non-fulfilment of the terms of the agreement." No complaint was made, but on presentation of the final certificate the employers sought to deduct liquidated damages for delay. *Held*, on the wording of the contract they were entitled to do so: *Simpson* v. *Kerr* (1873).[6]

(4) A contract provided that liquidated damages for delay should be forfeited to the employers, and paid to and retained by them, but that the engineer should have power to grant extensions of time in certain circumstances. Long after expiry of the contract date the engineer issued interim certificates from time to time which were paid without deduction. The final certificate likewise took no account of penalties. *Held*, independently of the payments, the certificate was evidence that he had extended the time, and liquidated damages could not be recovered: *Laidlaw* v. *Hastings Pier Co.* (1874).[7]

[Note: Although this was a decision of five judges of the Court of Exchequer Chamber, who appear to have been unanimous, it can only be suggested that the decision cannot be supported on either ground, there being no evidence in the report that the architect had power to take liquidated damages into account in his certificate, and there being no specific provision for retention of damages as an exclusive remedy and indeed an express reference in the contract to payment of the damages.[8]]

(5) A contract empowered the architect to award extensions of time, but made no specific provision for him to deal with liquidated damages in his certificates. There was delay, but he certified without any deduction. The contractors took a preliminary point of law,

---

[3] 1 F. & F. 671.
[4] See the clause in more detail, *supra*, p. 628.
[5] L.R. 6 Q.B. 115. This case is more fully illustrated *supra*, Section 2, p. 628.
[6] 33 Upp.Can.Q.B. 345.
[7] Hudson's B.C., 4th ed., Vol. 2, p. 13.
[8] See also as to payment not being a bar generally, *Royston U.D.C.* v. *Royston Builders Ltd.* (1961) 177 E.G. 589, *ante*, Chap. 1, p. 58.

contending that the certificate was conclusive evidence that time had been extended. *Held*, that while the certificate was very strong evidence that the architect had extended the time, it was not conclusive, and it was open to the employers to prove that he had not in fact determined the matter: *British Thomson-Houston Co. v. West* (1903).[9]

(6) A contract made the engineer's decision final in the event of any dispute. He also had power to order extras, but his power to order extensions of time was expressed to be referable only to strikes or lock-outs. The final certificate included the value of extras, but contained no deduction for penalties or delays arising from the extras. *Held*, that the engineer had no power to determine the question of liquidated damages in respect of delay due to extras, his certificate did not prevent that issue being raised, and as in fact the delay was due to the extras, the provision for liquidated damages was of no effect: *Gallivan v. Killarney U.D.C.* (1912).[10]

(4) Time for Exercise

In practice certifiers often delay reaching a decision on questions of extension of time until a very late stage in the works, or even after actual completion. It remains to consider to what extent this may be permitted by the contract. It has already been suggested that express refusal to deal with extension of time or liquidated damages at all will, as in other matters requiring certification, absolve the party concerned from the necessity of obtaining the certificate or decisions required by the contract.[11] But here the more usual situation of reluctance or procrastination, whether in making an application for an extension by the builder, or in dealing with it by the architect, is involved. Regrettably, the law on this subject appears to have become unnecessarily complicated. It will be remembered that, in those cases where the delay is due to an act or default of the employer or his agents, or some other matter for which he is responsible, liquidated damages provisions cease to have effect if no applicable power to extend the time is to be found in the contract.[12] The same result may possibly occur in such cases, despite the existence of an applicable power, if no action is taken under the clause within any time stipulated by the contract.[13] A distinction should, however, be made between those cases where the architect considers the matter at the appropriate time and decides that no extension of time is warranted, and those cases where an attempt is made, positively or negatively,

[9] 19 T.L.R. 493. See also the *Port Glasgow Magistrates* case, *supra*, p. 639.
[10] [1912] 2 I.R. 356.
[11] See, *e.g. Watts* v. *McLeay* (1911) 19 W.L.R. 916 (Canada); *ante*, Chap. 7, p. 468 and see pp. 475–476.
[12] *Supra*, pp. 624 *et seq.* Section 2 (1), Release by Prevention.
[13] See the comment *supra*, however.

to deal with the question of extension of time after any time prescribed by the contract. It is also possible that the contract may place the onus of applying for an extension of time upon the contractor, so that failure to do so will prevent him from displacing the original time for completion in the contract.

However it seems that where there is power to extend the time for delays caused by the building owner, and such delays have in fact taken place but the power to extend the time has not been exercised due to failure to consider the matter within the time expressly or impliedly limited by the contract, the building owner may have lost the benefit of the clause. The contract time has in such case ceased to be applicable because of the employer's act of prevention, there is no date from which penalties can run because any purported extension of time is given too late, and therefore no liquidated damages can be recovered. This would seem to be yet another example of the severity with which the courts in the past have tended to interpret extension of time clauses in cases of prevention, where the clause is regarded as more for the benefit of the employer than the contractor,[14] and, if possible, is held inapplicable so as to invalidate the liquidated damages clause as a whole. In principle on this very strict view there seems no reason why a purported extension of time that is too late should not have an equally invalidating effect in cases where no element of prevention is present and the cause of delay is clearly a matter otherwise within the contractor's sphere of responsibility, as e.g. bad weather.

There are, it is suggested, three possible constructions of extension of time clauses in so far as the time for exercise of the power is concerned. In the first place, the contract may contemplate that the power should be exercised at once upon the occurrence of the event causing delay. This construction may be appropriate to non-continuing causes of delays, such as the ordering of extras.[15] Secondly, the contract may contemplate that the power should be exercised when the full effect upon the contract programme is known. This is appropriate to continuing causes of delay, such as strikes, withholding of the site, and so on,[16] or to cases, like some extras, where precise estimation is difficult or impossible. Or, thirdly, the contract may contemplate exercise of the power at any time before issue of the final certificate. Since the case of *A.B.C. Ltd.* v. *Waltham Holy Cross*

---

[14] See *ante*, pp. 624 *et seq.*
[15] See *Anderson* v. *Tuapeka County Council* (1900) 19 N.Z.L.R. 1, *infra.*
[16] See *Miller* v. *L.C.C.* (1934) 50 T.L.R. 479, *infra.*

U.D.C. (1952)[17] a decision on the then current R.I.B.A. form of contract, which distinguished *Miller* v. *L.C.C.* (1934)[18] on somewhat slender grounds, it is suggested that this latter interpretation will normally prevail in the absence of clear language to the contrary, particularly as the ambit of most modern extension of time clauses usually comprehends delays due to causes of many different kinds.[19] Even, however, where a contract falls into the second of the above categories, the extension of time need not necessarily be granted before the contract date for completion. If, for example, a strike were to last beyond the contract date, the extent of the delay could not be known, or the necessary extension of time granted, until after the contract time had expired.

ILLUSTRATIONS

(1) A contract provided that " in the event of any alterations . . . being required, the engineer shall allow such an extension of time as he shall think adequate." Extra works were ordered, but no reference was made to extension of time. After the contract completion date, the architect, for the first time, deducted penalties from the sum due on an interim certificate, and thereafter continued to do so. Later still, he ordered further extra works, again without reference to extension of time. The contractors sued to recover the deducted penalties. *Held*, that even if the failure to deduct until the first deduction amounted to an extension of time up to that date, it was too late, since the power should have been exercised at the time of ordering the extras, and the contractors could recover: *Anderson* v. *Tuapeka County Council* (1900).[20]

(2) A contract provided that " it shall be lawful for the engineer . . . to grant from time to time and at any time or times . . . such extension of time for completion . . . and that either prospectively or retrospectively, and to assign such other time or times for completion as to him may appear reasonable." The engineer's decision under this clause was to be final. The contractor completed in July, and in November the engineer granted an extension of time till February, and certified liquidated damages as due accordingly. *Held*, on the construction of the contract as a whole, and having regard to the words " to assign such other time . . . for completion," the contract contemplated exercise of the power within a reasonable time of the cause of delay having ceased to operate, the exercise of the power came too late, and the liquidated damages could not be recovered by the employer: *Miller* v. *London County Council* (1934).[21]

---

[17] [1952] 2 All E.R. 452, *infra.*

[18] *Infra.*

[19] *Cf.* the analogous case of contractual right to determine on the ground of delay, discussed *post*, Chap. 13, pp. 696–697, and the case of *Joshua Henshaw & Sons* v. *Rochdale Corporation* [1944] K.B. 381 there illustrated.

[20] 19 N.Z.L.R. 1. (It is difficult to believe that this case would be decided in this way at the present day.)

[21] 50 T.L.R. 479. Cited by Salmon L.J. in *Peak* v. *McKinney Foundations*, C.A., July 1, 1970, a decision on virtually identical wording.

(3) The then standard form of R.I.B.A. contract provided that " if in the opinion of the architect the works be delayed . . . (for a number of causes) . . . the architect shall make a fair and reasonable extension of time for completion." One month before the completion date the contractors made two applications for an extension of time, based on non-availability of labour and materials, which the architect only formally acknowledged. The work was completed in August, and the architect wrote in December extending the time till May. The building owners claimed liquidated damages from May to August. The contractor took no step to dispute the architect's decision or invoke the arbitration clause, but took a preliminary point of law that the extension was given too late. *Held*, distinguishing *Miller* v. *L.C.C.* (1934) on the ground of the very special wording, " assign such other time or times for completion," in that case, that the power could be exercised at any time: *A.B.C. Ltd.* v. *Waltham Holy Cross U.D.C.* (1952).[22]

In the seventh edition of this work, it was suggested that there might be some distinction between extension of time clauses where the provision was mandatory—" the architect shall . . . "—or permissive.[23] This seems very doubtful. What seems more arguable is that in a contract where, unlike the R.I.B.A. forms, no special certificate [24] is required before the employer is permitted to deduct or claim liquidated damages, it may as a matter of construction be reasonable to require an extension of time decision before the contract completion date has passed, since otherwise there would be uncertainty as to the parties' rights.

It is submitted that in the absence of some such indication to the contrary an extension of time can be awarded at any time. In modern contracts, too, the arbitrator is usually given power to reopen the matter and substitute his own finding; where this is so there would seem to be little point in construing the contract so as to require an early decision on extension of time by the architect.

As previously indicated, once the contractor is in default in that the time for completion, after any proper extensions of time, has passed and liquidated damages have begun to run, later matters which would otherwise have justified a further extension cannot, it is submitted, be used as a basis for reducing the period during which the damages run, save only, perhaps, matters which might qualify as an act of God,[25] and perhaps the ordering of extras.

---

[22] [1952] 2 All E.R. 452. See also *Peak Construction Ltd.* v. *McKinney Foundations Ltd.*, C.A., July 1, 1970.

[23] See the judgments in *Sattin* v. *Poole* (1901) Hudson's B.C., 4th ed., Vol. 2, p. 306, and in *Roberts* v. *Bury Commissioners*, *ante*, pp. 407–408 and *supra*, p. 628.

[24] See *e.g.* clause 23 of the post-1963 forms.

[25] As to which, see *ante*, Chap. 5, pp. 358–360.

(5) Effect on Damages Claimed by Contractor

Where the cause of delay is due to breach of contract by the employer, and there is also an applicable power to extend the time, the exercise of that power will not, in the absence of the clearest possible language, deprive the contractor of his right to damages for the breach.[26] Thus, in *Roberts* v. *Bury Commissioners* (1870)[27] Kelly C.B. said: " It is provided that it shall be lawful for the architect to grant an extension of time, but it is neither said that the architect must give it . . . nor that the contractor must accept whatever extension of time the architect is pleased to give, in full satisfaction of his claim for damages."

Provisions which attempt to achieve this result will be strictly construed against the employer.

ILLUSTRATION

A contract provided by clause 11 that non-delivery of the site, delay in giving the written order to commence, or delivery of plans, drawings, sections " or any other delay from whatever cause alleged against the council or its officials " should not vitiate the contract or entitle the contractor to any allowance in respect of money, time or otherwise other than such extension of time as might be given. The extension of time clause included, among other things, delay due to extras ordered by the employers. *Held, obiter*, by du Parcq J., clause 11 did not include delay due to extras, or interference by other contractors of the employer: *Miller* v. *L.C.C.* (1934).[28]

(6) Effect on Bonus Provisions

Building contracts sometimes contain provisions for the payment of a bonus for completion on or before the stipulated time (see *ante*, Chapter 9, Price and Damages).[29] If there is a bonus for expedition, and a power to extend time, the contract may or may not intend that the bonus should be calculated with reference to any new completion date substituted by the operation of the extension of time clause. No general rule can be laid down, and the answer must depend upon the provisions of the particular contract.

ILLUSTRATION

By a contract it was agreed that " The Board will grant the contractors a bonus of £100 per week for every week or part of

---

[26] See *e.g. Trollope & Colls* v. *Singer* (1913) Hudson's B.C., 4th ed., Vol. 1, p. 849, illustrated *ante*, Chap. 5, Section 2, p. 326, and *Lawson* v. *Wallasey Local Board* (1883) 11 Q.B.D. 229, illustrated *ante*, Chap. 7, pp. 408–409.

[27] (1870) L.R. 5 C.P. 310 at p. 327.

[28] 50 T.L.R. 479.

[29] At pp. 577–578.

a week in which the contract shall be finished within the specified time." The contract was to complete certain specified works and extra works if properly ordered. The plaintiffs completed six weeks before the appointed day, and received £600 bonus. They claimed further bonus in respect of time taken, as they alleged, by extra works. There was an extension of time clause. *Held*, that the clause only applied, in case the engineer should consider that the contractors could not complete within the time, to save the contractors from liquidated damages, and not to give them additional bonuses: *Ware* v. *Lyttelton Harbour Board* (1882).[30]

SECTION 4. SUMMARY OF PRECEDING SECTIONS

In view of the complications and difficulties of past decisions of the English courts on liquidated damages and extension of time clauses —due to an anxiety to avoid the effect of the liquidated damages clause altogether, evidenced by the frequent use of the term " penalty " in relation to such clauses, and perhaps not shared at the present day, when the distinction between liquidated damages and penalties has been finally clarified by the courts[31]—it may be useful if a short summary is attempted of the effect of the preceding two sections and the present state of the law. This is as follows:

(a) Unless an extension of time clause is sufficiently specific a decision under it will not bind the contractor if it can be shown that the delay, or even a part of it, is due to prevention or a breach of contract by the employer, and the liquidated damages clause cannot, in such circumstances, be applied at all.[32]

(b) Even where it is sufficiently specific, a decision under the clause may not bind the contractor in prevention or breach of contract cases,

(i) because on the true construction of the contract the decision is open to review by an arbitrator,[33] or failing an arbitrator, the courts[34] (in this event, however, the liquidated damages clause will usually remain alive to be operated by the arbitrator or the courts);

[30] 1 N.Z.L.R.S.C. 191.
[31] See *ante*, Section 1.
[32] *Holme* v. *Guppy* (1838) 3 M. & W. 387; *Thornhill* v. *Neats* (1860) 8 C.B.(N.S.) 831; *Russell* v. *Sa Da Bandeira* (1862) 13 C.B. (N.S.)149; *Dodd* v. *Churton* [1897] 1 Q.B. 562; *Murdoch* v. *Luckie* (1897) 15 N.Z.L.R. 296; *Wells* v. *Army and Navy Co-op. Society* (1902) Hudson's B.C., 4th ed., Vol. 2, p. 346; *Perini Pacific Ltd.* v. *Greater Vancouver Sewerage* (1966) 57 D.L.R. (2d) 307; *Peak* v. *McKinney Foundations.*
[33] See, perhaps, *Port of Glasgow Magistrates* v. *Scottish Construction Co. Ltd.*, *supra*, p. 639.
[34] See *ante*, Chap. 7, Section 4, pp. 447–448.

(ii) because (only very rarely at the present day) its wording shows that it is intended to bind the employer only and not the contractor [35] (in this event, too, the clause will remain alive); or

(iii) because the decision is made out of time. This too, it is suggested, will only happen if most exceptional wording is used at the present day (but if it is out of time the clause will be invalidated).[36]

(c) A decision under an extension of time clause will usually (subject to arbitration on the merits) bind the employer for all practical purposes, since, if he successfully argues that the extension of time clause is not applicable or the decision out of time, the liquidated damages clause and contract completion date will have gone, and an obligation to complete within a reasonable time substituted with attendant common law damages only.[37] Not surprisingly, therefore, there are no reported cases where the employer has contested an extension of time decision on legal grounds of this kind, though nowadays he will usually be able to contest a decision which he disputes on the merits and secure a new decision from an arbitrator or from the courts under the provisions of the arbitration clause.

(d) However, either party may, depending on the language of the contract, be bound by a final or other certificate in this respect. This, however, can only occur if the certificate is required to deal with or take account of questions of liquidated damages (there is no really clear-cut reported case of such a contract, though there is no particular reason why there should not be), or the certificate is not itself subject to review by an arbitrator (which it usually is at the present day [38]).

(e) In cases where the contract does not provide for the liquidated damages to be dealt with on final certificate or in some other special way, a certificate issued without any qualification or deduction is at best only evidence that the architect has granted a full extension of time, which can be rebutted by evidence to the contrary,[39] but in modern contracts, which make it clear that the matter is to be dealt with outside the payment machinery, not even that. A

---

[35] See *e.g. Roberts* v. *Bury Commissioners* (1870) L.R. 5 C.P. 310, *supra*, p. 628.

[36] *Miller* v. *L.C.C.*, *supra*, p. 645; *Peak* v. *McKinney Foundations*, C.A., July 1, 1970.

[37] See *ante*, Chap. 10, p. 606.

[38] It usually is, see *Port of Glasgow Magistrates* v. *Scottish Construction*, 1960 S.L.T. 319 (Scotland), *supra*, p. 639.

[39] *British Thomson-Houston* v. *West* (1903) 19 T.L.R. 493, *supra*, pp. 642–643.

final certificate under the post-1963 R.I.B.A. forms of contract would not appear to be in the binding category referred to, since by clause 30 (7) the certificate is to be conclusive only " that any necessary effect has been given to all the terms of this contract which require an adjustment to be made to the Contract Sum," and the liquidated damages clause (clause 22) does not appear to " require an adjustment " in the special sense in which this expression is used in this contract.

(f) Wherever the liquidated damages clauses or the extension of time decisions are invalidated for any of the above reasons, an obligation to complete within a reasonable time will be substituted, and the employer will not lose his right to damages at common law, though, depending on the circumstances, it seems at least possible that the employer will not be allowed to recover more than the sum fixed for liquidated damages.[40]

SECTION 5.   POLICY OF LIQUIDATED DAMAGES AND EXTENSION OF TIME CLAUSES

The advantage of a liquidated damages clause is that it can be operated with comparative clarity and certainty in the case of a builder not making satisfactory progress, and that it removes all doubt from what might otherwise be an expensive and complicated enquiry, namely, the amount of damage suffered by the employer as a result of the delay. Properly administered, therefore, such a clause can act as a salutary inducement to the builder to maintain a proper degree of progress. It is particularly useful where the employer's loss is difficult to assess in monetary terms, as e.g. a local authority's late receipt of a public building such as a swimming-pool or school, or of loss-making projects, like subsidised public housing.

The R.I.B.A. standard forms of contract, however, have progressively widened the grounds upon which an extension of time must be given, and by virtue of two of these grounds in particular, no employer in modern conditions can regard the contract completion date as being of very much significance, or accompanied by any real sanction.

The first important ground is that provided for in clause 23 (g) of the 1963 R.I.B.A. forms, namely, delay by nominated sub-contractors or suppliers which the main contractor has taken all practicable steps

---

[40] See *ante*, Section 1.

to avoid or reduce. This means that, however culpable the delay by such a sub-contractor, and whatever its effect on the progress of the works as a whole, the employer loses any right to recover his loss from the main contractor. If it were not for the extension of time clause, the latter could be sued by the employer for liquidated damages and could then pass on the liability to the sub-contractor by suing on the sub-contract. (Ironically for a contract recommended by architects to employers, however, most careful provisions are contained in the main contract ensuring that the main contractor can recover *his own* damages from nominated sub-contractors and that sums so recovered should be for his benefit and not the employer's.[41]) It would be understandable if the extension of time clause was conditioned upon delays by nominated sub-contractors caused by some act or default of the employer, but it is, of course, perfectly general. The clause has been in existence for many years in the United Kingdom, and certainly offers no encouragement to specialist sub-contractors to maintain proper progress in their work. In view of the increasing proportion of building work carried out by such specialists,[42] such a clause must militate most strongly against the prospects of building contracts being carried out by the contract completion date and it is difficult to understand the policy underlying it, which merely prejudices the employer and benefits defaulting sub-contractors.[43] The preceding sentences of this paragraph in the Ninth Edition have now received powerful judicial support— " Paragraph (g) is highly anomalous and would appear to have been included in this form of contract without any regard to the manifest injustice and indeed absurdity implicit in it. It is in my view unjust and absurd because . . . it leaves the employers to bear the loss caused by a delay for which they are in no way to blame and allows the party at fault . . . to escape from the liability which they would otherwise justly have to bear. . . ."[44] "I cannot believe that the professional body, realising how defective this clause is, will allow it to remain in its present form."[44a]

---

[41] Clauses 27 (*a*) (vi), 27 (*b*), and proviso to clause 30 (5) (*c*) of the 1963 forms.

[42] In many cases over 50 per cent. of the work by value.

[43] See the further passage criticising the working of this clause, *post*, Chap. 15, Section 3 (4), p. 766, and cited by Edmund Davies L.J. in *Jarvis Ltd.* v. *Westminster Corporation* [1969] 1 W.L.R. 1448.

[44] *Per* Salmon L.J. in *Jarvis Ltd.* v. *Westminster Corporation* [1969] 1 W.L.R. at p. 1458. See also the criticisms of Edmund Davies L.J. in the C.A., and the further criticisms in the House of Lords [1970] 1 W.L.R. 637.

[44a] *Per* Lord Wilberforce [1970] 1 W.L.R. at p. 650.

Furthermore, a special difficulty arises from the peculiar wording in clause 23 (*g*), namely, " delay *on the part of* nominated sub-contractors or suppliers " (as opposed to delay *caused by* such sub-contractors). What if the sub-contractor is not guilty of delay himself but his bad work or poor co-operation, for instance, delays the main contractor? The following case shows that on this particular wording delays of this kind will only qualify if they lead to delay of the sub-contractor's work itself.

ILLUSTRATION

Nominated sub-contractors were due to complete their piling work by June 20. Towards the end of May a defect became apparent in one pile, No. 43. This was remedied, and the sub-contractors purported to complete on June 20, removing their equipment from the site a few days later. On July 21 a meeting was held to discuss possible shortcomings in the piles, and the sub-contractors were subsequently recalled to the site to examine the piles, a number of which were found to be defective. Replacement piles were then constructed, but the work was not completed till September 29, a delay of three months. The sub-contractors, in proceedings against the employer for a declaration originally commenced by the main contractors, argued that they (the sub-contractors) had been guilty of " delay on their part," so that the main contractor was entitled to an extension of time under clause 23 (*g*), and they (the sub-contractors) would not accordingly be liable to the main contractors for the employer's damage. The employer contended that, since the sub-contractors had completed their work, their subsequent recall and carrying out of remedial work did not amount to delay on their part, and that he was entitled to liquidated damages against the main contractor. *Held*, by the Court of Appeal, over-ruling Donald-son, J., that the sub-contractors had on the facts never completed their work to the satisfaction of the architect until September, so that there was delay by them, and accordingly the main contractor was entitled to an extension of time. *Held*, by the House of Lords, over-ruling the Court of Appeal, that " delay " within the meaning of the clause did not run after there was such completion of the sub-contract works as would enable the main contractor to take over himself, that there had been apparent completion of the sub-contract works, notwithstanding the latent defects, and that the sub-contractor's return subsequently had been to remedy a breach and not to carry out the sub-contract itself. Accordingly there had been no " delay on the part of " the sub-contractor. *Jarvis Ltd.* v. *Westminster Corporation* (1969).[45]

The above case, while it is primarily concerned with the interpretation of clause 23 (*g*) of the post-1963 R.I.B.A. forms, is also of the greatest importance in defining precisely what is meant by " practical " or " substantial " completion in building and engineering contracts.[46]

[45] [1969] 1 W.L.R. 1448.
[46] See *Morgan* v. *S. & S. Construction Property Ltd.* [1967] V.R. 149 (Australia), *ante*, pp. 252–253, and the discussion *ante*, Chap. 5, p. 258, and *supra*, Section 2, p. 637.

The second ground, optional in the R.I.B.A. standard forms,[47] is the inability of the contractor " for reasons beyond his control and which he could not reasonably have foreseen " at the date of the contract, to obtain labour or materials essential for the works. Such a clause is, equally, no encouragement to merchants and suppliers of building materials to honour their obligations as to delivery. With extension of time clauses of this description in common use, it can only be said that the original purpose of the liquidated damages clause has been largely undermined in the building industry. In the engineering industry, the complete generality of the extension of time clause in the standard I.C.E. form " extra or additional work of any kind or other special circumstances of any kind whatsoever " [48] would appear to make the liquidated damages clause in that contract little more than a fruitful source of litigation, should an employer seek to deduct liquidated damages in any but the clearest case of default by the contractor. Furthermore, the clause is in a form which will render it invalid if any act of prevention (other than ordering extras) by the employer can be established, it is submitted.[49]

As a summary of the foregoing views, a properly drafted liquidated damages clause should

(a) explicitly confer a power to extend time in general terms for any breach of contract or prevention by the employer, and in particular terms by reason of variations of the work or delay in issuing instructions or information;

(b) define with precision any other circumstances for which an extension of time is to be granted, and avoid general expressions;

(c) make it clear that the power to extend time is exercisable at any time; and

(d) empower the employer either to deduct damages from any payment or sum certified under the contract, or to recover them from the contractor by way of action or arbitration.

In addition, since the person extending time may inevitably have to be the judge of matters affecting himself, it is at least desirable that his decision should be subject to review by an arbitrator or the courts, and that any provision as to the conclusiveness of the final certificate should avoid bringing questions of liquidated damages within its ambit.

---

[47] Clause 23 (j), 1963 ed.
[48] Clause 44, 1955 ed.
[49] See *supra*, pp. 630–631, and the *Perini Pacific* and *Peak* cases there referred to.

CHAPTER 12

VESTING AND SEIZURE OF
MATERIALS AND PLANT

SECTION 1. OWNERSHIP IN THE ABSENCE OF EXPRESS PROVISION

(1) Generally

MOST building contracts contain express provisions governing the ownership of materials or plant. The effect of these will be considered in Section 2, Express Provisions, below. In the absence of such provisions, questions of ownership fall to be determined on general principles, the most important of which is that the intention of the parties to be deduced from the surrounding circumstances will normally prevail. In considering problems of this kind, it is important to distinguish between materials or fittings on the one hand and plant on the other. Barring certain hybrid or borderline cases, the former are intended for incorporation into the buildings or other works contemplated, whereas the latter, even if attached, will usually require to be removed from the building or site when the work is completed. An obviously important consideration, where a problem of disputed ownership arises, depends upon whether the materials or plant in question have in fact been affixed to the land or buildings of the employer. In the seventh edition of this work many illustrations from shipbuilding contracts were cited, but it is obvious that a shipbuilding contract differs from a building contract in a most vital respect, namely, that the work is not being done upon, nor is it affixed to, the land of the employer, and the shipbuilding cases are consequently usually concerned with two main questions, *viz.*: at what point of time does the general property in the ship as a whole pass to the employer or purchaser, and, secondly, what is included with the ship when the property does pass. In the present edition, shipbuilding examples will only be referred to where it is thought that a proposition of general application is illustrated, and in considering them the essential distinction referred to above should not be forgotten. In the present section it is proposed to consider materials and plant separately, and to deal with cases where no express provision as to the property in them exists. It should be borne in mind that in those

654

cases where the ownership of materials or plant is effectively transferred to the building owner, whether by express provision or otherwise, the transfer is never quite absolute, since it will usually be subject
to a right express or implied for the builder to remove the plant,
or any excess of materials if they have not been used and fixed, on
completion of the work.

(2) Materials

The well-known rule is that the property in all materials and fittings,
once incorporated in or affixed to a building, will pass to the freeholder—*quicquid plantatur solo, solo cedit*. The employer under a
building contract may not necessarily be the freeholder, but may be a
lessee or licensee, or even have no interest in the land at all, as in the
case of a sub-contract. But once the builder has affixed materials,
the property in them passes from him, and at least as against him they
become the absolute property of his employer, whatever the latter's
tenure of or title to the land. The builder has no right to detach them
from the soil or building, even though the building owner may himself be entitled to sever them as against some other person—*e.g.* as
tenant's fixtures. Nor can the builder reclaim them if they have been
subsequently severed from the soil by the building owner or anyone
else. The principle was shortly and clearly stated by Blackburn J. in
Appleby v. *Myers* (1867)[1]: " Materials worked by one into the property of another become part of that property. This is equally true
whether it be fixed or movable property. Bricks built into a wall
become part of the house, thread stitched into a coat which is under
repair, or planks and nails and pitch worked into a ship under repair,
become part of the coat or the ship." The principle is so firm that,
notwithstanding an express provision to the contrary in the contract,
the builder will not be able to take advantage of it as against a third
party entitled to the land.

ILLUSTRATIONS

(1) Bells were hung in a house by the tenant and left there after
the end of his tenancy. *Held*, that the tenant could not maintain
trover for them after the landlord had severed them from the freehold, because they remained fixed to the freehold after the expiration
of the term, and thereby vested in the landlord as part thereof:
Lyde v. *Russell* (1830).[2]

[Note: This case is one of landlord and tenant but would, it is
suggested, be equally applicable to a case of builder and building
owner.]

---

[1] (1867) L.R. 2 C.P. 651 at p. 659.
[2] 1 B. & Ad. 394.

(2) A burial company sold to the plaintiff a right of burial in a plot of ground for £2 10s., thereby apparently passing the freehold; the plaintiff interred a relative therein, and purchased from the defendant company a monument. The monument was erected, but as it was not paid for, the company removed it. *Held*, that they had no right to remove it, but could only sue for the money: *Sims* v. *London Necropolis Co.* (1885).[3]

(3) Contractors undertook to supply materials for the erection of a factory. Condition 9 (e) of the conditions of sale provided that materials erected or otherwise on site remained the contractor's property till paid for. A receiver for debenture holders of the owner sold the freehold to a third party, and the contractors finished their work and rendered their account, but the owner went into liquidation. *Held*, by Plowman J., since the factory was not a movable building, the materials became annexed to the land as part of the freehold. The contractor was therefore an ordinary unsecured creditor: *Re Yorkshire Joinery Co. Ltd.* (*in liquidation*) (1967).[4]

On the other hand, a builder is usually bound by his contract to complete the works, or to keep them in good repair till completion, or to remedy defects, and a consequential right to remove and replace materials for these purposes is clearly necessary to give the contract business efficacy. Thus in *Appleby* v. *Myers* (1867), where the contract was for the installation and maintenance of certain machinery, Blackburn J. said: " We think that the plaintiffs, who were to complete the whole for a fixed sum, and keep it in repair for two years, would have had a perfect right, if they thought that a portion of the engine which they had put up was too slight, to change it and substitute another in their opinion better calculated to keep in good repair during the two years, and that without consulting or asking the leave of the defendant."

Until, however, materials are actually affixed to a building, the property in them will in law remain with the builder, notwithstanding that they may have been approved by the employer or his agent or brought onto the site, unless the agreement between the parties evinces a clear intention to the contrary. All the contractual provisions must be carefully considered, however.

ILLUSTRATIONS

(1) A builder contracted to build an hotel for a specified sum, payment to be by instalments at certain dates. In the event of his becoming bankrupt, the owners were empowered to take possession of " work already done " by him, subject to paying a fair proportion of the contract price to be determined by the architect. The builder became bankrupt. Before the bankruptcy, he had delivered certain

---

[3] 1 T.L.R. 584.
[4] 111 S.J. 701.

wooden sash-frames to the site for inspection and approval by the clerk of works. They were then returned to his workshop to be fitted with iron pulleys after approval, and were there when the act of bankruptcy was committed. They were redelivered to the site three days later, before the fiat of bankruptcy was issued. The trustee of the builder sued the owners for the frames or their value. *Held*, that despite the owner's approval, at the date of the bankruptcy the property in the frames remained in the builder, as they had not been affixed; further, that as they had not been affixed they were not " work already done " by the builder so as to empower the owners to take possession; and that in any event this power, being expressed to arise upon bankruptcy, was on general principles void. " This is not a contract for the sale and purchase of goods as removable chattels; it is a contract to make up materials, and to fix them; and until they are fixed, by the nature of the contract, the property will not pass ": *Tripp* v. *Armitage* (1839).[5]

(2) A sub-contractor undertook to erect two specified storage tanks, to be paid for after completion. When partly finished, a receiver of the main contractor was appointed. The tanks were not fixed to the soil of the employer, but were too heavy to move. *Held*, the property had not passed, and the sub-contractor was entitled to require payment in full from the receiver before completing: *Bellamy* v. *Davey* (1891).[6]

(3) Main contractors for a complete electrical installation costing £1,363 sub-contracted the supply and erection of a storage battery for £286. *Held* by the Court of Appeal, that though the matter was one of the greatest difficulty, on the true construction of the sub-contract it was a contract of sale of the component parts of the battery with a supplemental contract for erection after delivery at the employer's premises, that delivery of the goods to the premises was an unconditional appropriation of goods in a deliverable state, and the property accordingly passed on delivery to the main contractors, notwithstanding that the work of erecting remained to be done: *Pritchett & Gold* v. *Currie* (1916).[7]

(4) Specialist sub-contractors undertook to supply, erect, commission and test sewage disposal plant for a main contractor. The sub-contract was silent as to the ownership of the sewage plant to be supplied by the sub-contractor. The plant was delivered and taken charge of and stored by the main contractor. The sub-contractors admitted that in the majority of their formal sub-contracts there was an express provision transferring the ownership to the main contractor or employer on delivery to the site. *Held*, that, in the absence of express provision, the time when ownership was intended to pass must be determined by having regard to all the terms and circumstances

[5] 4 M. & W. 687, *per* Lord Abinger C.B. at p. 698. See also *Williams* v. *Fitzmaurice*, *infra*, p. 659, and *Sumpter* v. *Hedges* [1898] 1 Q.B. 673, *ante*, p. 248.

[6] [1891] 3 Ch. 540. (The right to payment in advance in such a case depends on the bankruptcy law and does not depend upon the contract—see *post*, Chap. 16, p. 782. See also footnote 7, *infra*.)

[7] [1916] 2 Ch. 515. This case disapproved of the reasoning in *Bellamy* v. *Davey* in so far as it dealt with the position between the sub-contractor and the employer (see *infra*, p. 679), but not on the question of the property passing.

of the particular contract; there was no presumption that ownership should pass either on delivery or on incorporation, but in the present case ownership passed when the plant was incorporated into the main works. Till then the main contractor was merely acting as custodian of such plant and equipment as might have been delivered: *Edward L. Bateman Ltd.* v. *Eric Reed Ltd.* (1960).[8]

Tripp v. *Armitage* (*supra*) was approved in *Seath* v. *Moore* (1886)[9] (a shipbuilding case, but one of the leading cases in this branch of the law) where Lord Watson said: " Materials provided by the builder, and portions of the fabric, whether wholly or partially finished, although intended to be used in the execution of the contract, cannot be regarded as appropriated to the contract or as ' sold ' unless they have been affixed, or in a reasonable sense made part of the corpus "; and Lord Blackburn said [10]: " But it is competent to parties to agree for valuable consideration that a specific article shall be sold, and become the property of the purchaser as soon as it has attained a certain stage: though if it is part of the bargain that more work shall be done on the article after it has reached that stage, it affords a strong prima facie presumption against it being the intention of the parties that the property should then pass. I do not examine the various English authorities cited during the argument. It is, I think, a question of the construction of the contract, in each case, at what stage the property shall pass; and a question of fact, in each case, whether that stage has been reached." Other shipbuilding cases illustrating this principle are *Wood* v. *Bell* (1856),[11] *Baker* v. *Gray* (1856),[12] *Reid* v. *Macbeth and Gray* (1904)[13] and *Re Blyth Shipbuilding and Dry Docks Ltd.* (1926).[14] (These are in fact very strong cases, since the decisions to a large extent override express provisions in the contract which may have been designed to pass the property or the right to possession but which were held not to be sufficiently explicit for this purpose. Thus in *Baker* v. *Gray* the owner was empowered to enter and complete the works " *using* such of the materials " of the builder " as shall be applicable to the purpose." And in *Reid* v. *Macbeth and Gray*, it was provided that " the vessel,

---

[8] 1960 (4) S.A. 151 (Southern Rhodesia). To avoid any confusion, it should be noted that while the subject-matter of this particular case is commonly referred to in the industry as " plant," it is not plant in the sense used in this chapter, being intended for permanent incorporation into the works, and really ranks as " materials " for the purpose of the present sub-section.
[9] (1886) 11 App.Cas. at p. 381.
[10] *Ibid.* at p. 370.
[11] 25 L.J.Q.B. 321.
[12] 25 L.J.C.P. 161.
[13] [1904] A.C. 223.
    [1926] Ch. 494.

as she is constructed . . . and all materials from time to time intended for her, whether in the building-yard, workshop or river or elsewhere shall, immediately as the same proceeds, become the property of the purchaser and shall not be within the ownership, control or disposition of the builders," yet the property in plates intended for the ship, lying at a railway station, which had been passed by a Lloyd's surveyor at the builder's works and marked with the number of the vessel and the position they were to occupy, was held not to have passed. Again in *Re Blyth Shipbuilding, etc. Ltd.* (1926) it was provided that " all materials and things appropriated for " the vessel should become the purchaser's property, but it was held that worked material approved by the purchaser's surveyor did not pass under this clause. And in *Seath* v. *Moore* (1886) itself, a series of contracts for the construction of marine engines, the provision was that " all materials laid down for the purpose of constructing the same shall become, and be held as being, the absolute property of " the purchaser.)

It may be, however, and the language of the judgments in *Baker* v. *Gray* [15] also suggests it, that something less than actual affixing may be sufficient to pass property—*e.g.* actual fitting into the corpus of the building, without the final stage of fixing being completed

ILLUSTRATION

> The plaintiff agreed to build a house complete for the defendant, no mention being made of the flooring. The plaintiff prepared flooring boards, brought them on the premises, and planed and fitted them to certain rooms, but refused to lay them down without extra payment. Other boards were left by him in an adjoining field, not fitted to any particular room. *Held*, first, that the plaintiff was not entitled to recover for the flooring as an extra; and, secondly, that he could not sue for conversion of the flooring boards left by him in the rooms and subsequently used by the defendant for the completion of the building, but that he could do so for the boards left in the field: *Williams* v. *Fitzmaurice* (1858),[16]

There have, on the other hand, been shipbuilding cases where the property in unfixed chattels was held to pass with the ship, but these are rather special cases, involving articles such as rudders, cables, cordage, fishing-gear, charts, instruments, etc.[17] and, by virtue of their subject matter, it is submitted that these are not properly applicable to a building contract, where the essence of the transaction is

[15] *Supra.*

[16] 3 H. & N. 844. See also *Sumpter* v. *Hedges* [1898] 1 Q.B. 673, illustrated *ante*, p. 248.

[17] See *e.g. Woods* v. *Russell* (1822) 5 B. & Ad. 942; *Clarke* v. *Spence* (1836) 4 A & E. 448 and *Goss* v. *Quinton* (1842) 12 L.J.C.P. 173.

the completion of work rather than the sale of the subject-matter of the work.

The shipbuilding cases are further referred to in Section 2.[18] As will be seen, they are not consistent with the leading decisions in those building cases where express provisions exist regulating the ownership or right to use plant and materials.

While a building contract may contain no explicit provision as to the passing of the property in materials, it frequently will expressly provide (often in relation to the calculation of interim payments) that materials shall be paid for either on delivery to the site, or on delivery being certified by the architect or engineer. Where this is so, the property in them will pass to the employer, either on payment or as soon as the condition as to the certificate has been fulfilled.[19] Modern contracts (e.g. Clause 14 of the 1963 R.I.B.A. standard forms) also frequently expressly provide that unfixed materials paid for in this way become the property of the employer upon payment.[20]

(3) Plant

Plant may be defined for this purpose as anything required for carrying out the work but not intended for ultimate incorporation in the land or buildings. The case of unfixed plant gives rise to no difficulty. In the absence of express provision the property will remain throughout in the builder. In many cases, however, plant will be attached, albeit temporarily, to the land or buildings. Familiar examples are huts, hoarding, scaffolding, form-work, hoists and cranes. In every case the intention of the parties to be deduced from the surrounding circumstances must be considered. There is, of course, little difficulty in implying a term that the builder should be at liberty to take away the plant when no longer required, particularly where removal involves no injury to the land or building. But this does not entirely answer the question, in whom is the property while the plant is attached? So-called " tenants' fixtures " are perhaps an analogous example. There is, however, little authority on the subject.

ILLUSTRATIONS

(1) Forty years previously a fender and hatch had been placed by a miller in a mill stream to prevent the escape of water. The banks of the stream and the surrounding land did not belong to

[18] *Infra.*
[19] *Banbury, etc. Ry.* v. *Daniel* (1884) 54 L.J.Ch. 265, *infra*, Section 2 (2), p. 675.
[20] See *infra*, Section 2 (2), pp. 674 *et seq.*

the miller. *Held*, that it was a matter of evidence whether by agreement the hatch did not remain the property of the miller: *Wood* v. *Hewitt* (1846).[21]

(2) A building owner let the hoarding separating the premises from the street to one advertising company, while his builder let it to another. There was a clause in the building agreement " that the hoardings are not to be let for advertising." In an action between the rival advertising companies, *held*, that the hoarding belonged to the builder, and that his tenants had acquired a title, although the builder might, under the express provision of the contract, be liable in damages: *Partington Advertising Co.* v. *Willing & Co.* (1896).[22]

It is suggested that, on the principles which it is submitted emerge from the cases on express provisions [23] some kind of property does pass to the building owner in attached plant—for instance scaffolding or form-work—and that persons claiming the same through the builder might be defeated until at least the time for removal in the normal course of doing the work has arrived. But the question is one of great difficulty and there is no authority on the point.

SECTION 2.   EXPRESS PROVISIONS

(1) Generally

Clauses in building contracts relating to rights over materials and plant are commonly of two kinds, *viz.*: what may be termed " seizure " or " user " clauses, often associated with a clause for forfeiture of the contract as a whole, under which the employer is empowered at his option to take possession or assume ownership of materials and plant and use them to complete the work in certain specified events (usually some default of the builder), and, on the other hand, " vesting " clauses, under which ownership or a right of detention is expressed to pass automatically in certain specified events, often, for instance, upon delivery to the site.

Examination of the cases shows, however, that this common distinction between the clauses is not particularly useful, and indeed is not even accurate. The important distinctions between the clauses are:

(a) that they may be expressed to operate automatically in a certain event on the one hand, or on the other hand they may be

---

[21] 15 L.J.Q.B. 247; 8 Q.B. 913.
[22] 12 T.L.R. 176.
[23] See the discussion at the end of Section 2 (1), *infra*, p. 671.

brought into operation at the employer's option in a certain event, and

(b) that they may purport to transfer ownership, on the one hand, or lesser rights such as possession, a right of use, or a mere right of detention on the other.

The classical vesting clause operates automatically, and transfers ownership. The seizure clause operates at the employer's option, and may often though not necessarily transfer rights less than ownership. But every possible combination of these characteristics can be found in practice.[24]   None of these provisions can, of course, affect *pre-existing* rights of third persons in the plant or materials (though, as has been seen, the fact of incorporation of materials certainly can), and, furthermore, it will be seen that, in so far as such clauses are expressed to take effect on bankruptcy (as opposed to failure to proceed with due diligence or some other ground connected with non-performance of the contract), and are in fact invoked on that ground, they will be void against the trustee or liquidator.[25]

While these clauses may purport to transfer full ownership, or a lesser right, such as the right of possession, or a mere right of detention, even these distinctions are likely to be obscured when the rights concerned are carefully analysed. For instance, a seizure clause may purport to give a mere right to possession and use of materials and plant for a limited period, *i.e.* until completion of the work. Where materials are concerned, however, it is obvious that once they have been used and incorporated under such a clause, the ownership will pass. On the other hand, despite an apparent transfer of absolute ownership under a vesting clause, it will usually, it is submitted, be necessary to imply a term, if the contract is silent upon the point, re-transferring the ownership of plant (and indeed of any surplus materials) on completion to the builder.[26] As will be seen, the necessarily qualified nature of the property or other rights which pass under such clauses has been recognised by the courts.

In addition, both the seizure and vesting types of clause are frequently found in the same contract. Where this is so, they may be treated as complementary to each other, and one may achieve the employer's object where the other may fail. Furthermore, despite the vital distinction between plant and materials, which is obviously of

---

[24] See *infra* (7).

[25] See *e.g. Tripp* v. *Armitage, ante*, pp. 656–657, and see also *post*, Chapter 16, Bankruptcy and Liquidation, pp. 784 *et seq.*

[26] *Cf.* clause 33, I.C.E. Conditions.

great importance in construing these clauses, in many contracts plant and materials are classed together and dealt with by the same provision.

It is important to realise that there is no general rule, and the relevant provisions of every contract must be carefully considered before their legal effect can be determined. But, provided the provisions of the contract are clear, the courts will give effect to the intention to transfer the right to possession or ownership to the building owner. The cases below are, as one would expect, concerned with the rights of third parties in the materials or plant in question, since, as between the parties themselves, their rights and obligations under the contract do not usually depend upon an exact analysis of the nature of the ownership or other rights transferred. In considering the cases, the fact that the property which the contract purports to pass may be of the qualified nature referred to above should not be forgotten. The result may be that a third party claiming through one of the parties to the contract—e.g. an execution creditor or assignee of one of them—may be defeated even though the contract has been effective in transferring the property to the party through whom he claims, by virtue of the fact that the other party may still retain a limited interest of the kind previously described, and the transfer is not therefore absolute. In the cases set out below, numbers (1) and (2) may be regarded as examples of seizure clauses passing a right less than ownership. Number (3) is not strictly a decision on an express provision, and does not apply the English law, but nevertheless illustrates very well the distinction between the rights in plant and materials, and their qualified nature. Numbers (4) to (14) are either vesting cases in the normal sense, or cases where ownership is purported to be transferred.

ILLUSTRATIONS

(1) A railway company entered into a contract with R., a builder, for the construction of a bridge over their railway. The contract provided that if the company's architect considered that R. was not proceeding with proper expedition, the company might, on seven days' notice, use the implements and materials for the time being used by R. in or about the works, and complete themselves, and R. was to pay any additional expenses. It was also provided that the company were to have a lien on the implements and materials on the site of the bridge as security for completion. On July 31, a fiat of bankruptcy issued against R. On that date the company took possession of the implements and materials used by R. On August 1, they gave notice under the contract, and, on August 2, they started to complete the bridge, using some of the materials and detaining the remainder as against the trustee in

bankruptcy. *Held,* the use of the materials prior to expiry of the notice was a conversion, but after expiry the company were entitled to use them, and also to use and detain both materials and plant being used for the work not only on the site of the bridge but also on adjoining land not belonging to the company. *Held,* also, that any lien created by the contract would merge in actual ownership in so far as materials were worked up: *Hawthorn* v. *Newcastle-upon-Tyne & North Shields Railway* (1840).[27]

(2) A building contract provided that if the contractor should fail to proceed, or become bankrupt, the architect might, on two days' notice, appoint others to complete, and seize and retain all materials, plant and implements, and also all materials wholly or partially made up or ready for fixing which were still on the contractor's or employer's premises, and might either proceed with the work or sell the materials and apply the proceeds to the completion of the work, provided the builder had received advances under the contract. Further, that if the contract be put an end to in this way, the contractors might not remove either work, materials, implements, scaffolding or plant, which must be appropriated for the use of whoever might finish the work. The contractors received considerable advances under the contract, including the value of materials, plant and implements on the premises. They then filed a petition for liquidation. Three days afterwards they were given notice under the contract for failing to proceed, and on expiry the employers took possession of all materials and plant. *Held,* following *Hawthorn* v. *Newcastle Railway* (1840) *supra,* that they were entitled to detain them against the trustee: *Re Waugh, ex. p. Dickin* (1876).[28]

(3) A draft contract, which was not executed by the parties, and objected to by the builder in other respects, contained a clause declaring that all materials, articles and others which the builder should bring upon the building owners' premises for the purposes of the work should not be thence removed until the full completion of the contract, but be held as pledged to the building owners for due performance of the work. The builder commenced operations and the employers raised no objection to his doing so without signing a contract. The builder eventually became bankrupt, leaving a crane and various materials on the site. The trustee demanded delivery, which was refused, and the building owners used both plant and materials to complete, and maintained their refusal to deliver after completion. *Held,* the building owners were entitled to use the materials and plant for completion, subject to payment for the materials and the use of the crane, but must deliver up the crane on completion: *Kerr* v. *Dundee Gas Light Co.* (1861).[29]

---

[27] 3 Q.B. 734. The judgment of Denman C.J. in this case proceeds on the basis that there had been a default by the builder. Had the determination been based on the bankruptcy alone it would, it is submitted, have been invalid—see footnote 25, *supra.* For a modern case where premature seizure was held not to be repudiation of the contract, see *Earth and General Contracts Ltd.* v. *Manchester Corporation* (1958) 108 L.J. 665, illustrated *post,* Chap. 13, Section 1 (2), p. 686.

[28] 4 Ch.D. 524.

[29] 23 D.(Ct. of Sess.) 343.

[Note: This Scottish case is not strictly a decision upon the wording of the contract, which was never executed, and turns upon the right of retention in Scottish law, but it is useful in emphasising the distinction between plant and materials and the presumed intentions of the parties.[30]]

(4) Under a contract with a railway company, materials and plant provided by the contractor became the absolute property of the company when placed on the land, and the contractor was to have no property in them, except the right of using them on the land for the purpose of the works, and, on due completion, the right to the return of unused materials and plant, and in the event of their being used by the company on his default, to compensation for their use. There was also provision for monthly payments of 95 per cent. of work executed and materials supplied. *Held*, materials brought onto the site were not so absolutely the property of the company as to be seizable under a judgment against them: *Beeston* v. *Marriott* (1864).[31]

(5) A contract provided by clause 7 that all materials which should have been brought on the premises by the builder for the purpose of erecting the buildings should be considered as immediately attached to and belonging to the premises, and that no part thereof should be removed without the owner's consent, and by clause 8, that in case the builder should fail to proceed with the erection and completion of the houses within the time specified, it should be lawful for the owner to enter and take possession of the land and all bricks and other building materials thereon for his own absolute use and benefit. A judgment creditor of the builder sought to seize certain materials before any action had been taken under clause 8. *Held*, that clause 7 gave the building owner at the least an equitable interest in the materials so as to disentitle the sheriff from seizing them, and further that clause 8 did not in any way qualify the owner's rights under clause 7: *Brown* v. *Bateman* (1867).[32]

(6) A building agreement contained a provision that the lessee builder should not remove any sand or other materials from the premises, and that all materials brought thereon should become the property of the lessors. A judgment creditor of the builder seized the materials. *Held*, following *Brown* v. *Bateman*, that they could not be taken in execution: *Blake* v. *Izard* (1867).[33]

(7) An engineering contract provided that the plant brought by the contractor onto the works was to be deemed the property of the employers for the time being, and was not to be removed during the progress of the works without the written order of the engineer, and, in the case of suspension of the works due to default of the contractor, was to be subject to be used in and about the completion of the works. The works were suspended, the contractor went into liquidation, and the employers having completed the

[30] See the judgment quoted *post*, pp. 670 *et seq.*
[31] 8 L.T. 690. Discussed *infra*, p. 672. Compare also the closely comparable case of *Banbury, etc., Ry.* v. *Daniel*, illustrated *infra*, p. 675.
[32] L.R. 2 C.P. 272.
[33] 16 W.R. 108.

works themselves, the plant was by agreement sold. *Held*, the effect of the above clause was to give the employers a right of use only, and the trustee could not have removed the plant without being liable in damages. But the ownership of the plant remained in the contractor, and the trustee was accordingly entitled to the proceeds of sale. Nor could the employers set off the value of the plant against sums due to them from the contractor by invoking the "mutual dealings" clause in bankruptcy [34]: *Re Winter, ex p. Bolland* (1878).[35]

(8) A building contract contained no vesting clause in the usual sense, but provided that the owner, upon default by the builder for a certain number of days, might re-enter upon the land and expel the builder, and on such re-entry all the materials then in and about the premises should be forfeited to and become the property of the landowner "as and for liquidated damages." The builder became bankrupt, and then defaulted for the requisite number of days, whereupon the owner entered and seized the materials. On a claim by the trustee, *held*, that the builder's interest in the materials was a defeasible one, and the trustee obtained nothing better than the builder had, and accordingly his claim must fail: *Re Garrud, ex p. Newitt* (1881).[36]

(9) A clause in a building lease agreement made between an intended lessor and lessee provided "that all building and other materials brought by the intended lessee upon the land shall, whether affixed to the freehold or not, become the property of the intended lessor." An execution creditor of the intended lessee took certain of the materials in execution. On interpleader, the creditor contended that the contract required registration as creating an equitable interest in chattels.[37] *Held*, that even if an equitable interest of this kind required registration,[37a] which on the authority of *Brown* v. *Bateman* (*supra*) was doubtful, the moment the materials were brought onto the premises the property in the materials had passed in law to the intended lessor. The builder's agreement was at no time an equitable assignment of anything, but a legal contract that, upon the happening of a particular event, the property in law should pass in certain chattels which the event itself would identify without the necessity of any further act on the part of anybody, and which could not be identified before: *Reeves* v. *Barlow* (1884).[38]

(10) A contract for the construction of a school contained a provision (clause 10) that "all plant, work and materials brought to and left upon the ground by the contractor or to his order for the purpose of carrying out the contract, or of forming part of the works, shall be considered the property of the Board, and the same shall not on any account be removed or taken away by the contractor without the express licence of the architect." The clause also provided that the Board should not be in any way

---

[34] As to which see *post*, Chap. 16, p. 781.
[35] 8 Ch.D. 225, discussed *infra*, p. 673; *cf. Kerr* v. *Dundee Gas Light Co. supra*.
[36] 16 Ch.D. 522. No contention that this provision might be a penalty was advanced by the trustee—as to which see *ante*, Chap. 11, Section 1.
[37] *i.e.* as a bill of sale.   [37a] See *infra*, pp. 675–676.
[38] 12 Q.B.D. 436, C.A.: *per* Bowen L.J., applying *Brown* v. *Bateman, supra*, and *Blake* v. *Izard, supra*.

answerable for any loss or damage which might happen to such plant, work or materials. There was no provision for revesting the goods. Finally, by clause 20 it was provided that if the builder should delay performance, the Board after giving notice might enter and take possession, and in that event the plant and materials should be forfeited to the Board. After the builder became bankrupt, the Board gave the necessary notice and took possession of the plant and materials. The trustee contended that, at the time of the bankruptcy, and before the forfeiture was exercised under clause 20, the goods were the property of the Board as true owners by virtue of clause 10, but that they were in the order and disposition of the builder with their consent, and consequently passed to the trustee under the " order and disposition " clause in bankruptcy. *Held,* the language of the agreement was wholly different from that in *Reeves* v. *Barlow (supra).* The opening words of clause 10, when read in connection with the remainder of the clause, and with reference to the purpose and scope of the whole contract, made it clear that it was not intended to vest the materials at once in the building owners. All that the Board had was a contractual right to have the goods remain on their land for use by the builders in the construction of the building. Accordingly, the Board were not the true owners at the time of the bankruptcy, the " order and disposition " clause did not apply, and their subsequent forfeiture under clause 20 was valid and defeated the trustee's claim: *Re Keen, ex p. Collins* (1902).[39]

(11) Under a building lease agreement between intending lessor and lessee, the lessor was empowered to take possession of materials in the event of the lessee's default. It was further provided that all materials brought onto the land were to be deemed to be annexed to the freehold. *Held,* this latter provision passed the property to the lessor, who was the true owner, but they were in the order and disposition of the lessee in such circumstances as to make him the reputed owner, and the trustee of the lessee was accordingly entitled to recover them from a mortgagee of the lessee who had seized them: *Re Weibking, ex p. Ward* (1902).[40]

(12) A contract for the construction of a harbour contained a provision that in case the builder became bankrupt the owners might enter and take possession of the works and complete them, and also provided that " The whole of the plant and materials brought on to the ground by the contractor is to be marked with his initials in legible characters. All such plant and materials shall be considered the property of the company until the engineers shall have certified the completion of the contract." The contractor gave a Bill of Sale on plant and materials to H. Later he became bankrupt, and the company took possession. H. sued them on his Bill of Sale. *Held,* applying *Reeves* v. *Barlow* (1884),[41] and distin-

---

[39] [1902] 1 K.B. 555, discussed *infra,* p. 669. See *post,* pp. 788 *et seq.* for a full discussion of the bankruptcy rules of reputed ownership and their effect on vesting clauses.

[40] [1902] 1 K.B. 713. See also Chap. 16, Bankruptcy and Liquidation, *post,* pp. 788 *et seq.* where the finding in this case that the materials were in the order and disposition of the lessee was not applied in the case of an ordinary building contract—see *Re Fox, ex p. Oundle & Thrapston R.D.C.* [1948] Ch. 407, illustrated *post,* p. 790.

[41] *Supra.*

guishing *Re Keen, ex p. Collins* (1902),[42] on the ground that the words in that contract rendered it plain that no property, as a matter of construction, ever passed, that the plant and materials were vested in the company subject to the condition that when completion was certified the property reverted to the contractor, that the clause was intended as a security for completion of the work, and even though the company had not completed the work or employed another contractor, H. could not recover the materials: *Hart* v. *Porthgain Harbour* (1903).[43]

(13) A building contract provided that "the plant, tools and materials provided by the contractor shall from the time at which they respectively may be brought upon the site . . . and during the construction and until the completion of the said works become and continue the property of the Board, and the contractor shall not remove the same or any part thereof without the consent in writing of the engineer." By other clauses, the contractors were to make good loss or damage to the works or plant by any accident, and were to be advanced 50 per cent. of the value of plant, the advances to be repaid at 5 per cent. per month by deduction from monthly certificates. *Held*, per Bray J., following *Hart* v. *Porthgain Harbour Co.* (1903) and distinguishing *Re Keen, ex p. Collins* (1902), that the property passed to the Board: *Metropolitan Water Board* v. *Dick Kerr & Co.* (1917).[44]

[Note: Bray J.'s decision was overruled on other grounds in the Court of Appeal.]

(14) Under a contract for the construction of certain tunnels in Canada it was provided that "all machinery, tools, plant, materials, equipment, articles and things whatsoever provided by the contractor . . . for the works . . . shall from the time of their being so provided become and until the final completion of the said work shall be the property of His Majesty for the purposes of the said works." The contractors provided at the site a large amount of plant. The local authority raised an assessment on the contractors, under an Act imposing liability upon either the owners or persons in legal possession of assessable personal property. The contractors contended that the Crown were the owners of the property, and that their own interest in it was limited to a licence to use the plant and equipment. *Held*, following *Reeves* v. *Barlow* (1884) and *Hart* v. *Porthgain Harbour Co. Ltd.* (1903)[45] that the Crown were the owners of the property, but that while the delivery on the Crown site was a delivery to the Crown and vested the ownership in the Crown, there was a notional or actual bailment or redelivery of possession to the builders for the purpose of carrying out the building contract, and they were accordingly in legal possession of the property. (The assessment was then held invalid for other reasons): *Bennett and White (Calgary) Ltd.* v. *Municipal District of Sugar City* (1951).[46]

---

[42] *Supra.*
[43] [1903] 1 Ch. 690.
[44] [1917] 2 K.B. 1 at p. 13.
[45] *Supra.*
[46] [1951] A.C. 786.

At first sight it may seem impossible to reconcile all the above cases. In *Bennett and White (Calgary) Ltd.* v. *Sugar City* (1951), the latest case in which this subject was considered, the Privy Council appears to have thought that the distinction between some of the above cases depended upon the use of words such as " considered " or " deemed " in the vesting clauses, as opposed to clauses where the words used were " be and become," [47] and it must be admitted that up to the 8th edition this book lent some support to this view. But in *Hart* v. *Porthgain Harbour* (1903)[48] Farwell J. said: " In my opinion the true construction of the clause ' all such plant and materials shall be considered the property of the company ' is that it vests the property in the materials in the company at law subject to a condition that, when the engineer shall have certified the completion of the contract, the contractor shall be at liberty to remove them " and he felt no difficulty in distinguishing *Re Keen, ex p. Collins* (1902) on the grounds that " there were words in the contract which rendered it plain that no property ever passed." What those words were is shown in the judgment of Bigham J. in *Re Keen, ex p. Collins*, when he said that the vesting clause in this form, if read by itself, was an ambiguous phrase, but " when read in connection with the rest of the same clause and with reference to the whole purpose and scope of the contract " (which included a forfeiture clause as well), " it becomes reasonably clear that it was not intended to vest the materials at once in the building owners."

Quite apart from the cases of *Hart* v. *Porthgain Harbour*, and *Brown* v. *Bateman*, where the word " considered " was used, it is suggested however that a careful examination of the judgments in the remaining cases does not, with the greatest respect, support the Privy Council's view, and that it is in fact a misleading exercise to inquire in each case whether or not " the property passes " upon the use of certain words. Part of the difficulty arises from the fact that the same clauses in nearly all cases govern both plant and materials, when a moment's consideration shows that in most cases the parties will not intend the same consequences to arise in the case of plant and surplus materials on the one hand and incorporated materials on the other. In fact, as already explained, it is only in rare cases that the parties will intend the property to pass in any absolute sense at all. Where this is so, the courts will, of course, give effect to the parties' intention.[49] But in the great majority of cases the transfer is

[47] See *per* Lord Reid at pp. 813 and 814.
[48] [1903] 1 Ch. 690 at p. 694.
[49] See *e.g. Re Garrud, ex p. Newitt* (1881) 16 Ch.D. 522, *supra.*

not absolute, and even where no express provision exists in the contract it is necessary to imply a right to the revesting at least of equipment, plant and surplus materials; and in *Bennett and White (Calgary) Ltd.* v. *Sugar City*, the Privy Council further held that prior to completion the contractors were entitled to legal possession of plant.

By far the most careful discussion of this point is to be found in the judgments in the Scottish case of *Kerr* v. *Dundee Gas Co.* (1861).[50] There the Lord Justice-Clerk said: " Retention is a right of a varying character, which is always measured according to the title on which that possession is held, which is the ground of the right of retention. Now, what was the nature of the defender's title? It was a title arising *ex contractu.* It is in vain to consider to what extent, or in what sense, delivery of these materials into the possession of the defenders made them the property of the defenders. In one sense it did, and in another sense it did not. But in performance of the contract obligation, these materials were delivered, and in my view the right emerging to the defenders was that they were entitled to retain them for those purposes of the contract for which they were brought there, *viz.*: to be worked up into the work contracted to be executed. And, therefore, I come to the conclusion, without any difficulty, that the defenders were entitled to keep these materials, and to use them in building the tank. But on the other hand, they must allow the pursuer the value of these materials; because although they have paid for all the work done, they have not paid for these materials . . . .

" But as regards the other portion . . . representing the value of the plant and tools brought onto the defender's premises, not to be permanently worked up into the work contracted for, but merely to be used temporarily in the execution of the work, it is obvious that there is, in point of fact and legal principle, a plain distinction between this part of the claim and the other. But here there is no longer the same right of retention on the part of the defenders, but a more limited right than they had over the stores and other materials; and it was more limited just in exact correspondence to the purposes for which the plant and tools were brought on the defenders' ground. Their right of retention . . . was necessarily limited to the contract purposes; for the tools were there to be used for the purpose of executing the works contracted for, not to be exhausted in executing the work, as the materials were, but to be used temporarily, and returned (no doubt deteriorated by wear and tear) as soon as the

[50] (1861) 23 **D.** (Ct. of Sess.) **343** at p. 348.

works were executed. . . . And therefore, while they were entitled to retain the crane and other tools to be used in the execution of the contract, on the completion of the contract there arose in the trustee two rights. In the first place, a right to a reasonable consideration for the use of the tools, that being parallel to his right to payment of the value of the materials. But, secondly, there was a right on the part of the trustee to restoration of the plant and tools as they stood at the completion of the works. . . . "

Once the qualified nature of these interests is fully realised, the decisions fall, it is submitted, into a logical pattern. The courts have acted on the basis that these clauses are inserted not merely to enable the contract to be performed, but also to obtain due security for its performance.[51] It will be seen that in every single case (except where the doctrine of reputed ownership in bankruptcy was successfully invoked in *Re Weibking, ex p. Ward* (1902)[52] the courts have prevented materials or plant from being seized or claimed by creditors, trustees, or other third parties before the completion of the work, thus giving effect to this view of the purpose of the clauses. This protection has not been limited to cases where the claim has been made through the builder, but has even been extended to cases where the claim has been through the building owner, and the important residual rights of the builder in the plant and materials would otherwise have been prejudiced.[53] On the other hand, once the work was complete, the purpose for which the property or interest in plant had passed was satisfied, and the builder's trustee or others would be entitled to recover.[54] The case which has, perhaps, given rise to most difficulty, *Re Keen, ex p. Collins* (1902),[55] was a case where the builder's trustee, in order to avoid the effect of a clear-cut forfeiture provision, had to put forward the somewhat paradoxical contention that prior to the forfeiture the goods in question had vested, immediately on delivery to the site, in the building owners under the vesting clause, so that he would be in a position to invoke the reputed ownership provisions in bankruptcy. The court defeated his claim by pointing out that there were other provisions in the contract inconsistent with immediate vesting, and that in effect an apparent vesting clause

[51] See *per* Farwell J. in *Hart* v. *Porthgain Harbour* and *per* Bowen L.J. in *Reeves* v. *Barlow, supra.*
[52] [1902] 1 K.B. 713. For a full discussion of this doctrine, see *post,* Chap. 16, pp. 788 *et seq.*
[53] *Beeston* v. *Marriott* (1864) 8 L.T. 690.
[54] *Re Winter, ex p. Bolland* (1878) 8 Ch.D. 225; *Kerr* v. *Dundee Gas Co.* (1861) 23 D. (Ct. of Sess.) 343.
[55] [1902] 1 K.B. 555.

only gave a contractual right to have the goods remain on the land for use by the builder.[56] Yet within a week of this decision, one of the judges in the case (Wright J.) held that the property *did* pass to the employer in a dispute between the builder's trustee and the holder of a bill of sale given by the builder.[57]

It may be doubted whether, in the normal case, much turns upon whether the property is held to pass, with immediate redelivery of legal possession to the builder [58] and an ultimate implied right to revesting, or whether all that is held to pass is a mere right of user or retention on the site,[59] since it is submitted that the above cases show that only in most exceptional circumstances will the courts permit the rights of third parties, claiming through a party to the contract, to interfere with due completion. In effect, the courts appear to recognise possessory rights, albeit of a qualified or even temporary character, somewhat akin to a lien, which will be binding *in rem* (that is to say, against all the world claiming subsequently) as coming into existence as a result of these provisions. In the case of *Beeston* v. *Marriott* (1864), for instance, it is suggested that an execution creditor of the *lessee* would have had as short shrift as the execution creditor of the lessor, and it may well be that the effect of many of these clauses, whether of the " seizure " or " vesting " type, is to create differing interests in plant and materials which would defeat persons claiming the goods through *either* party. Thus in *Beeston* v. *Marriott*,[60] Stuart V.-C. said: " It is true the contract says that . . . these chattels shall be the absolute property of the company, and that the plaintiff shall have no property in them, but immediately afterwards follow these exceptions qualifying that absolute right of property . . . which the first words of the contract give. . . . The right of using them, the rights, as to some of them, of becoming absolutely possessed of them, and the right to demand compensation . . . if this company shall use them, so qualify the right of the company and give such a right and interest of a legal character to the plaintiff in these chattels, that they cannot be considered the property of the company so as to be taken in execution. They are chattels upon the ground of

[56] *Cf. Re Winter, ex p. Bolland, supra.*

[57] *Re Weibking, ex p. Ward* [1902] 1 K.B. 713, distinguished, in so far as the application of the doctrine of reputed ownership to the facts was concerned, in the case of *Re Fox, ex p. Oundle & Thraptson R.D.C.* [1948] Ch. 407, illustrated *post*, Chap. 16, p. 790.

[58] *Bennett and White (Calgary) Ltd. v. Sugar City* [1951] A.C. 786.

[59] *Hawthorn v. Newcastle Ry.* (1840) 3 Q.B. 734; *Re Waugh, ex p. Dickin* (1876) 4 Ch.D. 524; *Re Keen, ex p. Collins* [1902] 1 K.B. 555; *Re Winter, ex p. Bolland* (1878) 8 Ch.D. 225.

[60] *Supra.*

the company, dedicated to a particular purpose, in which purpose both the plaintiff and defendants are interested as to the use of the chattels, and, as to the surplus, they are ultimately to become the absolute property of the plaintiff. *Chattels in that situation cannot be taken in execution.*" [60a]

And in *Re Winter, ex p. Bolland* (1878),[61] Bacon C.J. said: " This plant might have been protected against execution by this agreement —that it was to be deemed property that was to be left in the hands of the Commissioners for the purposes of the contract—but not with respect to the claims of the creditors if he became bankrupt."

This last remark shows clearly the source of confusion. By virtue of the fact that there must have been an implied right to revesting of the plant concerned in the above case, it was obvious that the trustee was entitled to the proceeds of sale of the plant on completion of the work. The court achieved this result by holding that " the property did not pass " under the clause in question, and the case is cited as an authority for that proposition. But had the claim been by a judgment creditor *of the builder* during the currency of the contract, this statement shows that in the court's view he too would have been defeated, in which event the case would, no doubt, have been cited as authority for the proposition that the property *did* pass under the clause in question.

In the foregoing discussion and illustrations, the shipbuilding cases have been deliberately omitted. As has been previously pointed out, these cases differ on their facts in important respects, since while on a building site it can safely be assumed that all plant and materials have been brought there for the purpose of the employer's work, in a shipbuilder's yard materials and plant are on the shipbuilder's land, and may well be being used for other work. The cases undoubtedly exhibit a divergent tendency in the interpretation of express terms governing the ownership or care of materials, in that the courts appear to be reluctant, even in the face of express provisions, to hold that the property in materials will pass to the purchaser until they have been incorporated in the ship. The cases of *Baker* v. *Gray* (1856),[62] *Seath* v. *Moore* (1886),[63] *Reid* v. *Macbeth and Gray* (1904),[64] and *Re Blyth Shipbuilding and Dry Docks Ltd.* (1926) [65] have already

---

[60a] Compare the decision on closely comparable facts in *Banbury, etc., Ry.* v. *Daniel,* illustrated *infra,* p. 675.
[61] A case where the trustee sued after the work was completed—see *supra,* pp. 665–666.
[62] 25 L.J.C.P. 161.
[63] 11 App.Cas. 350.
[64] [1904] A.C. 223.
[65] [1926] Ch. 494.

been referred to.[66]   On the other hand, in *Re Walker, ex p. Barter* (1884),[67] the property in unfixed goods and materials " bought or ordered for " a ship and her engines was held to pass under a vesting clause, where a wider forfeiture clause failed in its effect by reason of its being exercised on the ground of bankruptcy.   Of these cases, *Baker* v. *Gray* is the only one to be cited at all frequently in building cases, and it has been frequently distinguished.[68] Examination of the judgments of Jervis C.J. and Cresswell J. in *Baker* v. *Gray* shows that, as a matter of construction, while the contract passed the property in the ship, it did not intend to pass the property in the timber until it had been at the least used, if not necessarily actually fastened, in the ship: " Perhaps the parties might have intended that the timber which had been provided for the construction of the ship should be the property of the defendant if the shipbuilder should fail in the performance of his contract, but I do not think . . . the language employed is sufficient to carry out that intention.   I think there is only a provision for the ship becoming the defendant's property; but as to the materials, so long as they remain on the premises and the property of the builder, the defendant has the right to use them, and until they are actually used and put into the corpus of this ship, they remain the property of the builder. . . . It is not necessary to say whether it would be requisite, in order to give the defendant an interest in the materials, that they should be actually *fastened* to the ship."[69]

The shipbuilding cases are, it is submitted, of doubtful authority in construing express terms in ordinary building and engineering contracts, and the leading cases of *Brown* v. *Bateman, Reeves* v. *Barlow* (1884) and *Hart* v. *Porthgain Harbour Co.* (1903) leave little doubt that the courts will give effect to the prime purpose of vesting and seizure clauses alike, namely, the provision of security for the due completion of the works, which may entail defeating the claims of third parties whether made through the employer or the builder, at least until completion of the work.

(2) Effect of Provisions for Payment

Even where no explicit provisions for passing the property in materials or plant exist, there may be provisions in a contract for payments which include the value of materials brought onto the site.   Such

---

[66] *Supra*, pp. 658–659.
[67] (1884) 26 Ch.D. 510, illustrated on the bankruptcy point *post*, Chap. 16, p. 786.
[68] *e.g.* in *Brown* v. *Bateman* (1867) L.R. 2 C.P. 272, *supra*.
[69] (1856) 25 L.J.C.P. 161, *per* Jervis C.J.

provisions will normally pass the property to the building owner upon payment, or if the contract so provides, upon the issue of any relevant certificate.

ILLUSTRATION

A contract entered into between a company and a contractor for the construction of a railway contained a provision that once a month during the construction the engineer of the company should certify the amount due and payable to the contractor according to a scale to be agreed upon between the contractor and the engineer in respect of the value of the works executed and materials delivered, until a certain sum had been certified, and that the amounts certified for should be paid by the company to the contractor within seven days after presentation of the certificate. *Held*, that the property in unused materials delivered by the contractor for the purpose of the construction of the railway which had been comprised in certificates of the engineer, but had not been paid for by the company, passed to the company on the making of the certificates comprising them, and an injunction was granted to restrain the contractor from removing such materials from the land of the company. *Held*, also, that a clause giving the company a lien did not apply to materials which they had paid for, but to materials delivered but not valued or certified for: *Banbury, etc., Railway* v. *Daniel* (1884).[70]

[Note: But see *Beeston* v. *Marriott*, and the commentary thereon *supra*, where there was a provision for monthly payments.]

Modern contracts (*e.g.* clause 14 of the 1963 R.I.B.A. standard forms) frequently provide expressly that unfixed materials paid for in this way become the property of the employer.[71] These provisions are usually only a part of the machinery of interim payment, however, and it is submitted cannot be regarded as outright purchases of the materials, so that surplus materials will ultimately revest in the builder.

(3) Whether Vesting or Seizure Clauses are Bills of Sale

Various attempts have been made from time to time to assert that clauses of this kind in a building contract constitute a bill of sale over the chattels in question, and should be registered. They have been uniformly unsuccessful.[72] Vesting clauses, being in effect contracts whereby chattels vest absolutely in the building owner as part of the

---

[70] 54 L.J.Ch. 265.

[71] *Cf.* the case of *Re Fox, ex p. Oundle & Thrapston R.D.C.* [1948] Ch. 407, illustrated *post*, Chap. 16, p. 790.

[72] See *Brown* v. *Bateman* (1867) L.R. 2 C.P. 272; *Reeves* v. *Barlow* (1884) 12 Q.B.D. 436 and *Re Garrud, ex p. Newitt* (1881) 16 Ch.D. 522.

freehold, and attaching as they do to unspecific and unidentified chattels, have been held to be dissimilar to the assignments and assurances specified in the Bills of Sale Acts, while forfeiture clauses, though admittedly licences to take possession of chattels within section 4 of the Bills of Sale Act 1878, are not intended as security for a debt, but for damages which are or may become due from the builder. On the other hand, an assignment by a builder, as a security for a loan, of his rights under a building agreement, together with all plant and materials on the site, under which the assignee was in certain events entitled to take possession and complete, was held to be a bill of sale of the plant and materials.[73]

(4) Validity of Seizure or Forfeiture

Ordinary vesting clauses, if operative, usually operate to transfer the property on an easily determined event, such as delivery to the site. Provisions for forfeiture or seizure, however, depend upon taking possession by the employer, the right to which is usually conditional upon default by the builder. In such cases, all the matters upon which the power to forfeit or seize is conditioned must be established before the property will be held to pass.

ILLUSTRATION

B entered into a contract with E, of which the material terms were as follows: There was a power of forfeiture in the event of delay or default by B, with power to take the work out of B's hands and use plant and materials, and it was also provided that E might apply any moneys to which B would otherwise be entitled in satisfaction of losses or expenses caused to E by B's default; and further, that the plant and materials which at the time of the delay or default should be in or about the site of the works should thereupon become the absolute property of E and should be valued or sold, and the amount of such valuation or of the proceeds of such sale be credited to B in reduction of the moneys (if any) recoverable from him by E. E took the work out of B's hands, and B brought an action for breach of contract, which was referred. *Held*, that the plant and materials did not become the absolute property of E until it had been established that loss or expense had been occasioned to E, and an interlocutory injunction was awarded to restrain E from removing and selling the materials and plant pending the arbitration: *Garrett* v. *Salisbury Railway* (1866).[74]

(5) Time of Vesting or Seizure

This may be of considerable importance in determining the rights of third persons, and must be gathered from the contract. It may be

[73] *Church* v. *Sage* (1892) 67 L.T. 800.
[74] L.R. 2 Eq. 358.

made to depend on the engineer's opinion or certificate, or upon a default of the builder after notice given by the building owner. As against a trustee or liquidator of the builder, it would seem that, unless, perhaps, there has been disclaimer,[75] the time of vesting or seizure relative to the date of the bankruptcy or liquidation is immaterial, since the trustee will obtain no greater interest than the bankrupt, and if it is a defeasible interest, it matters not that the defeasance follows the bankruptcy,[76] provided that the contract itself was entered into without notice of any act of bankruptcy. But in other cases, the builder's ownership or possession of the property may come to an end before the vesting or seizure has taken place, and this will consequently be fatal to the building owner's rights.

ILLUSTRATION

A building agreement provided that on default by the builder the owner might give notice in writing, and thereafter the builder should not be at liberty to remove plant from the premises, and the building owner should have a lien upon the plant till the notice was complied with. The sheriff seized the goods on behalf of a creditor of the builder. Subsequently the owner served notice in writing. On interpleader, *held*, that the prior possession obtained by the sheriff prevented the notice taking effect: *Byford* v. *Russell* (1907).[77]

As between the parties, a mistakenly premature seizure will have few practical consequences provided that events validating the seizure occur shortly thereafter.[78]

(6) Reputed Ownership

As has been seen, the doctrine of reputed ownership in bankruptcy may, in the case of clauses passing the property, but not a lesser right, defeat the building owner as against the trustee in bankruptcy of the builder. The doctrine has, however, no place in the law of liquidation. For this and other bankruptcy and liquidation aspects of vesting and forfeiture clauses generally, see *post*, Chapter 16.

---

[75] As to which see *post*, Chap. 16, pp. 778 *et seq.*

[76] *Re Garrud, ex p. Newitt* (1881) 16 Ch.D. 522; *Re Keen, ex p. Collins* [1902] 1 K.B. 555 and *Hawthorn* v. *Newcastle Ry.* (1840) 3 Q.B. 734, and for a full discussion see *post*, Chap. 16, pp. 784 *et seq.*

[77] [1907] 2 K.B. 522.

[78] See *e.g. Hawthorn* v. *Newcastle Ry.* (1840) 3 Q.B. 734, illustrated *supra*, pp. 663–664, and *Earth and General Contracts Ltd.* v. *Manchester Corporation* (1958) 108 L.J. 665, illustrated *post*, Chap. 13, Section 1 (2), p. 686.

(7) Ownership of Plant or Materials by Stranger to the Contract

It is perhaps unnecessary to emphasise that no vesting or seizure clause can operate to prejudice existing interests of persons not parties to the contract in the plant or materials. In many cases plant is hired by the builder, or, in the case of large contractors, may be owned by a subsidiary company. This represents a serious practical inroad on the apparent security for due completion which an employer may possess under such clauses.[79]

SECTION 3. LIEN

In the cases in the previous sections of this chapter it will probably have been noticed that the right of the employer or builder over materials and plant is occasionally described, either in the contract or by the courts, as a lien.[80]

In its proper sense, lien means the right of a person in possession to retain the property of another until certain claims have been satisfied. A general lien enables the property to be detained until the general state of account between the parties has been satisfied, a particular lien until charges for work done to the property in question have been met. In both cases the lien arises by operation of law, not by contract. In the case of common law liens, no power of sale exists. In the case of equitable liens (which arise on the sale of land), such a power does exist.

No lien in these senses can arise from the carrying out of building or engineering work. Where a right similar in its characteristics to a lien is created by a contract, express or implied, the contract itself must be examined in every case in order to determine exactly what rights over the property concerned the parties intended to create. There is, however, a tendency, where a contractual right less than ownership is intended to pass, to describe it as a lien if it appears to have characteristics analogous to a lien proper. In most cases the term is used to mean a right of detention less than ownership, in the nature of a pledge or security for due performance. But to determine the exact incidents of the right, the contract itself must be examined.

The use of this expression in the context of building contracts is, therefore, inaccurate and confusing. No lien can arise from a building contract, whether by operation of law or under the terms of the

---

[79] See *post*, Chap. 16, p. 791, where possible escapes from the difficulty are mentioned.
[80] See *e.g. Tripp* v. *Armitage* (1839) 4 M. & W. 687, *ante*, pp. 656–657; *Hawthorn* v. *Newcastle Ry.* (1840) 3 Q.B. 734, *ante*, pp. 663–664; *Banbury, etc. Ry.* v. *Daniel* (1884) 54 L.J.Ch. 265, *ante*, p. 675.

contract. The contract may, however, confer contractual rights over materials or plant having some or all of the characteristics of a lien. The cases where these rights arise have been considered and discussed in the preceding sections of this chapter.

Where goods or materials have not yet been incorporated into the work, so that they remain the property of the original owner, a lien becomes a theoretical possibility, but in practice such goods will usually remain in the physical control of their owner (*i.e.* the builder) so that no question of a lien, which is a right to detain by a person not the owner, can arise. In *Bellamy* v. *Davey* (1891),[81] however, Romer J. apparently held that an unpaid sub-contractor, whose goods were on the site but were too heavy to move, had a lien on the goods as against the building owner, but this part of the case was disapproved by the Court of Appeal in *Pritchett & Gold* v. *Currie* (1916)[82] and in principle seems to have been wrongly decided on this point.

SECTION 4. OLD MATERIALS

In some cases building contracts contain a provision that the contractor shall make use of or be entitled to old and other materials belonging to the employer for the purposes of the work. Furthermore it may, even in the absence of express provision, be an inevitable consequence of carrying out the work that surplus materials will result. In some cases the ownership of those materials may be quite valuable, and questions of some difficulty may arise in arriving at the contract intention. Thus an obligation to excavate foundations would not of itself entitle the builder to appropriate the sand, gravel or other material so won, but an obligation to remove materials without any provision as to their disposal would seem to pass the property therein to the contractor, who would be at liberty to dispose of them as he thought fit.

Whether or not such provisions involve adjustment of the contract price may not always be clear.

ILLUSTRATION

H., a builder, sued for £800, the price payable on completion. The architect had certified completion. The contract contained a clause, " That all old lead to be displaced by new is to become the property of the contractor, who will make a due allowance for

---

[81] [1891] 3 Ch. 540, illustrated *ante*, Section 1, p. 657.
[82] [1916] 2 Ch. 515, illustrated *ante*, Section 1, p. 657.

the same." The employer pleaded a set-off of £38, the value of the old lead. *Held*, that as H. could not prove that he had informed the employer or the architect that in making his estimate he had allowed for the value of the old lead, as he alleged, the set-off was good: *Harvey* v. *Lawrence* (1867).[83]

---

[83] 15 L.T. 571.

CHAPTER 13

FORFEITURE AND DETERMINATION

SECTION 1. THE GENERAL NATURE OF THE POWER TO FORFEIT
OR DETERMINE

IN the absence of express provisions to the contrary, the contractor in ordinary building or engineering contracts for the execution of work upon the land of another has merely a licence to enter upon the land to carry out the work. Notwithstanding that contractually he may be entitled to a considerable degree of exclusive possession of the site for the purpose of carrying out the work,[1] such a licence may be revoked by the employer at any time, and thereafter the contractor's rights to enter upon the site of the works will be lost. The revocation, however, if not legally justified, will render the employer liable to the contractor for damages for breach of contract, but subject to this the contractor has no legally enforceable right to remain in possession of the site against the wishes of the employer.[2] The validity of the foregoing view must now, however, be regarded as in some doubt in England following the decision of Megarry J. in the Chancery Division in *Twickenham Garden Developments Ltd.* v. *Hounslow B.C.* (1970) which is currently, however, under appeal to the Court of Appeal.

Most building and engineering contracts contain an express forfeiture clause empowering the employer, in certain specified events, to determine the contract, or to exercise other rights over the work or property of the contractor, *e.g.* to take possession of the works, and complete them himself. Apart, moreover, from any express power given by the terms of the contract, the employer has the legal right to treat the agreement as having been repudiated, and so to determine it, in cases where the contractor shows an intention not to be bound by it, or has committed a breach of a fundamental term or " condition " (as it is sometimes called in legal terminology, in contradistinction to a " warranty ") of the contract.[3] The principles of

[1] For the implied term and the nature of the contractor's interest, see *ante,* Chap. 5, pp. 317 *et seq.*
[2] See *post,* Section 3 (2) where the subject is more fully discussed.
[3] See *Mersey Steel & Iron Co.* v. *Naylor* (1884) 9 App. Cas. 434, *per* Lord Blackburn.

681

rescission or discharge of a contract on a repudiation in this way have already been considered.[4]

In the same way, the contractor has the legal right to treat the contract as repudiated where the employer has evinced an intention no longer to be bound, or has committed a breach of a fundamental term or condition of the contract. Further, the R.I.B.A. standard forms (but not the I.C.E. form) confer wide express powers of determination on the contractor accompanied by more powerful remedies than those available on a common law determination.[5] In the pre-1963 forms, the grounds upon which this power could be exercised were astonishingly wide,[6] and in many cases were conditioned upon matters for which the employer could not be in any way held morally or physically responsible, such as bad weather and defaults by nominated sub-contractors, and though in the post-1963 forms the grounds have been somewhat curtailed and the more obvious anomalies removed, the possibility of most serious difficulties and injustices remain under the present clause. A typical example of what is possible under such clauses is to be found in the facts of the vitally important recent leading case on the implied terms relating to the work and materials of nominated sub-contractors of *Gloucester C.C.* v. *Richardson*,[7] where a contractor was held entitled to determine a contract without warning because investigations into defects in pre-cast concrete columns (which were subsequently found to be due to poor workmanship by a nominated supplier) had had the effect of delaying his operations by one month. When it is remembered that under the R.I.B.A. conditions such a termination exposes the employer to a claim for loss of profit on the remaining work, to seizure of materials already paid for as security for the sums due to the contractor, and the delay and expenditure involved in trying to re-let a large project in " mid-stream," the policy underlying much of the clause is simply impossible to understand.

(1) Events upon which the Express Power to Forfeit is Usually made Conditional

In modern contracts the commonest contingencies upon which the employer's power to forfeit is made to depend are failure on the part

---

[4] See *ante*, Chap. 5, pp. 340 *et seq.*
[5] Clause 26.
[6] See clause 20 (1) of the 1957 edition.
[7] [1964] A.C. 480.

of the contractor to proceed with the contract works with due diligence, failure to remedy defective work when called upon to do so,
and the contractor's bankruptcy or liquidation.[8] A study of the
earlier cases, however, reveals a great diversity in the definition of the
events, other than bankruptcy, upon the happening of which the
power is conditioned. It is reasonable to suppose that the draftsmen
of these contracts, being more familiar with the terminology of conveyancing and building leases rather than the practical requirements
of building and engineering contracts, tended to concentrate unduly
upon the concept of completion by the contract date rather than the
concept of due expedition or diligence. As will be seen later in this
chapter, the concept of completion by the contract date gives rise to
difficulties and is not well suited to the practical requirements of the
employer in a building contract.[9] All of the following forms of words
have been used:

(1) Not commencing the work: *Mohan* v. *Dundalk, etc. Railway*
    (1880).[10]

(2) Not regularly proceeding with the work for a certain fixed
    period: *Re Garrud, ex p. Newitt* (1881) [11]; *Re Walker, ex p.*
    Barter, ex p. Black (1884).[12]

(3) Not proceeding to the satisfaction of the employer or of the
    architect: *Davies* v. *Swansea Corporation* (1853) [13]; *Stadhard*
    v. *Lee* (1863).[14]

(4) Not proceeding for any reason independent of prevention by
    the employer: *Roach* v. *G.W. Railway* (1841).[15]

(5) Not, in the opinion of the architect, exercising due diligence
    and proceeding with such dispatch as will enable the works to
    be duly completed to time: *Brown* v. *Bateman* (1867) [16];
    Roberts v. *Bury Commissioners* (1870) [17]; *Walker* v. *London*
    and North Western Railway (1876) [18]; *Arterial Drainage Co.*
    v. *Rathangan River Drainage Board* (1880) [19]; *Cork Corpora-*
    tion v. *Rooney* (1881).[20]

---

[8] For a discussion of the law of bankruptcy in this connection and the doubtful
validity of such a power, see *post*, Chap. 16, pp. 784 *et seq.*
[9] See also *ante*, pp. 314–315, 609, and 611.
[10] 6 L.R.Ir. 477.
[11] 16 Ch.D. 522.
[12] 26 Ch.D. 510.
[13] 22 L.J.Ex. 297.
[14] 32 L.J.Q.B. 75.
[15] 10 L.J.Q.B. 89.
[16] L.R. 2 C.P. 272.
[17] L.R. 5 C.P. 310.
[18] 1 C.P.D. 518.
[19] 6 L.R.Ir. 513.
[20] 7 L.R.Ir. 191.

(6) Not completing as stipulated or to time: *Baker* v. *Gray* (1856) [21]; *Marsden* v. *Sambell* (1880),[22] or to the satisfaction of the surveyor: *Hunt* v. *Bishop* (1853).[23]

(7) Not complying with the orders and directions given by the architect or engineer: *Hunt* v. *South Eastern Railway* (1875).[24]

(8) Not complying with the specification, stipulations, conditions or drawings: *Mohan* v. *Dundalk Railway* (1880) [25]; *Stevens* v. *Taylor* (1860).[26]

(9) Being guilty of any default in the fulfilment of the contract: *Garrett* v. *Salisbury, etc. Railway* (1866).[27]

(10) Leaving the works unfinished: *Re Garrud, ex p. Newitt* (1881).[28]

(11) Failing, after due notice, to rectify defective work: *Arterial Drainage Co.* v. *Rathangan River Drainage Board* (1880).[29]

(12) Removing materials from the site: *Marsden* v. *Sambell* (1880).[30]

(13) Not maintaining the works: *Walker* v. *London and North Western Railway* (1876).[31]

[Note: The above cases do not necessarily turn upon the construction of the form of words with which they are cited, but are merely examples of the particular form used.]

Where a contract contains a clause conferring an express power of termination upon the contractor, the conditions upon which the exercise of that power are generally made dependent are failure of the employer to honour interim certificates within a specified period, the interference of the employer with the issuing of an interim certificate, and bankruptcy of the employer.[32] However, it is fair to say that practically no building or engineering contracts other than the more modern R.I.B.A. contracts have ever conferred rights of determination on the contractor, and the foregoing short list is in fact greatly expanded in the post-1963 forms, which permit a large

---

[21] 25 L.J.C.P. 161.
[22] 28 W.R. 952.
[23] 8 Exch. 675.
[24] 45 L.J.Q.B. 87.
[25] 6 L.R.Ir. 477.
[26] 2 F. & F. 419.
[27] L.R. 2 Eq. 358.
[28] 16 Ch.D. 522.
[29] 6 L.R.Ir. 513.
[30] 28 W.R. 952.
[31] 1 C.P.D. 518.
[32] See, however, the considerably wider grounds in clause 25 of the 1963 R.I.B.A. standard forms. As to the validity of provisions conditioned on bankruptcy, see *post*, Chap. 16, Bankruptcy, pp. 784 *et seq.*

number of grave injustices and anomalies, on any reasonable view, to be inflicted on the employer.

(2) Events Justifying the Determination of a Contract under the General Law

The very limited extent to which a failure by the contractor to discharge his obligation to complete to time can justify a common law determination, has clearly been explained, *ante*, Chapter 10, p. 604. The acts or omissions of either of the parties to a building or engineering contract which may justify the other in rescinding or treating the contract as repudiated, and the nature of the available remedies, have also been previously discussed at some length in Section 3 (1), Repudiation, *ante*, Chapter 5. Broadly speaking, they may be either breach of fundamental terms or " conditions " in the contract, or other conduct evincing an intention no longer to be bound.

Breach of a term not fundamental to the contract (sometimes called a " warranty ") may, depending on the facts, evince an intention not to be bound if persisted in for a sufficient period of time. Notice calling on a party to perform his obligation not complied with by the party in default [33] may assist in establishing the necessary intention no longer to be bound, but if the breach is sufficiently persistent, absence of notice may not be crucial.[34] Breach of a term not in itself fundamental may also evince the intention if done deliberately, and with eyes open to the fact that it is a breach.[34] Obvious examples of conduct evincing an intention not to be bound, and so justifying rescission, are abandonment of the works or their suspension without good cause by the contractor. So, too, failure by an employer to hand over the site by the stipulated date, persisted in for two months in spite of requests by the contractor asking when he might be permitted to start, has been held to constitute repudiation, and lack of any specific notice was disregarded.[34] Again, omission of work and its transfer to another contractor, if done deliberately and with eyes open, has been held to amount to repudiation by the employer.[34] (Clearly, however, if the breach was not deliberate, or related only to a small part of the work, a different view might be taken.) On the other hand, failure to allow a sub-contractor to start work during the first season of a contract, where no specific date was

---

[33] See in particular in regard to obligations required to be performed by a stipulated time, *ante*, Chap. 10, pp. 604–605 and 612 *et seq.*

[34] *Carr* v. *J. A. Berriman (Pty.) Ltd.* (1953) 27 A.L.J. (Australia) 273, *ante*, Chaps. 5 and 8, pp. 319 and 533.

mentioned, was held not to amount to repudiation.[35] Failure to pay sums due as interim payment (not, it is submitted, by itself a fundamental term) would, even in the absence of any express provision, clearly entitle the contractor to cease work if persisted in after reasonable notice. In every case, the conduct of the party will be looked at in a realistic light to see if it evinces the necessary intention, and the modern tendency is certainly not to interpret the parties' actions too legalistically. In the words of Atkin L.J., " It must be shown that the party to the contract made quite plain his own intention not to perform the contract." [36]

ILLUSTRATIONS

(1) Employers gave three days' notice under a forfeiture clause entitling them to take possession of plant and materials without vitiating the contract upon the voluntary liquidation of the contractor. Before the three days had expired, they entered on the site and took certain measures in relation to the plant, including stencilling their name on it and controlling the movement of vehicles. *Held,* by Elwes J., premature action under a forfeiture notice did not *ipso facto* amount to repudiation, and on the facts the employers had not by their conduct shown an intention to repudiate the contract: *Earth & General Contracts Ltd.* v. *Manchester Corporation* (1958).[37]

(2) The defendants were in occupation of premises under a contract to grant a lease which was to be non-assignable, and was to contain such covenants and conditions as the plaintiffs might reasonably require. The plaintiffs required the defendants to enter into a lease containing a covenant prohibiting assignment or sub-letting of the premises or any part of them. The defendants refused to do so, and the plaintiffs claimed they had repudiated the contract. *Held,* by the Court of Appeal, the covenant went beyond what had been agreed, and was also unreasonable. But even if the defendants had not been entitled to refuse the proposed covenant, an erroneous but bona fide view not unreasonably held as to the construction of an agreement would not amount to a repudiation of it: *Sweet & Maxwell Ltd.* v. *Universal News Services* (1964).[38]

Examples of contractual terms held to be fundamental or a " condition," breach of which entitles the other party to treat the contract as repudiated, include the failure of the contractor to obtain a surety bond for due performance of the contract,[39] the removal of

---

[35] *Pigott Construction Ltd.* v. *W. J. Crowe Ltd.* (1961) 27 D.L.R. (2d) 258 (Canada), *infra,* pp. 709–710.
[36] (1919) 121 L.T. at p. 634.
[37] (1958) 108 L.J. 665.
[38] [1964] 2 Q.B. 699.
[39] *Swartz & Son (Pty.) Ltd.* v. *Wolmaranstadt Town Council* 1960 (2) S.A. 1 (South Africa).

materials from the site without written permission,[40] but not breach of a term prohibiting assignment or sub-contracting,[41] or failure to finish the works by the contract completion date.[42] Again a requirement by an employer's engineer that the contractor should do work, without extra payment, which the engineer contended incorrectly was part of the original contract work and not a variation, has been held in Canada to be conduct amounting to repudiation if persisted in [43] but the grounds of this decision have already been criticised,[44] and the reasoning of this part of the decision appears to be inconsistent with the *Sweet & Maxwell* case in the English Court of Appeal,[45] which it is submitted is more correct in principle on this point.

It has already been suggested that a term for due expedition must be implied in building and engineering contracts, and that after notice an employer would be entitled to treat the contract as repudiated if the contractor continued his failure to maintain reasonable progress.[46]

It may, however, be noted here that a given event may be both one which justifies the innocent party in treating the contract as repudiated, and also one upon the happening of which an express forfeiture clause may be invoked. In such a case, unless the contract shows an explicit intention that the stipulated remedy should exclude the ordinary remedies, the innocent party may make an election. He may simply treat the contract as repudiated and rely upon the remedies available upon repudiation under the general law, or he may proceed under the forfeiture clause and avail himself of the rights contained therein. Indeed there would seem to be no reason why he should not enforce both sets of remedies simultaneously and cumulatively.

(3) Necessity for Unequivocal Act

A power to determine, whether arising under the general law or an express condition of the contract, must be exercised in an unqualified manner and by some act sufficient to show that the power actually has been exercised, although neither writing nor any other formality

---

[40] *Marsden* v. *Sambell* (1880) 43 L.T. 120, illustrated *infra*, p. 699.
[41] *Feather (Thomas) & Co. (Bradford) Ltd.* v. *Keighley Corporation* (1953) 52 L.G.R. 30, illustrated *ante*, Chap. 9, p. 581.
[42] *Ante*, Chap. 10.
[43] *Peter Kiewit & Sons* v. *Eakins Construction Ltd.* (1960) 22 D.L.R. (2d) 465 (Supreme Court of Canada, Cartwright J. dissenting).
[44] *Ante*, Chap. 8, p. 543, where this case is illustrated.
[45] *Supra*.
[46] *Ante*, Chap. 10, pp. 609, 611–612.

is necessary, unless it is expressly provided for by the contract.[47] If, as is usually the case, the sense of the contract is to confer a discretionary remedy upon one or other of the parties, it makes no difference that the actual wording is that it shall terminate automatically in a certain event. Some act invoking the provision by the party entitled to do so must take place.

ILLUSTRATIONS

(1) A licence by deed to mine, etc. contained a condition that if the licensee neglected to work the mines for a certain time, the indenture and the liberties and licences thereby granted should " cease, determine, and be utterly void and of no effect." *Held*, that the word, " void " in the proviso meant voidable by the grantor, and that in an action against the licensee for trespass it was necessary to show that the grantor, or some person claiming under him, had by some act evinced his intention to avoid the licence: *Roberts* v. *Davey* (1833).[48]

(2) A building contract empowered the building owner to forfeit the contract in case of the builder's bankruptcy. The builder became bankrupt and his trustee completed the work. *Held*, that the trustee must be held to have completed under the original contract, and not a new contract, as the building owner had taken no active steps to forfeit: *Drew* v. *Josolyne* (1887).[49]

[Note: In this case, distinguishing *Tooth* v. *Hallett* (1869),[50] it was held by the court that, although it is not necessary that writing or any particular formality should be used in order to exercise the power, yet it must appear that as a matter of fact the power was actually exercised.]

Thus the R.I.B.A. forms [51] contain a peculiar provision for " automatic " determination of the contract in the event of the contractor's bankruptcy or liquidation, and its possible subsequent " reinstatement " by agreement. Apart from the doubtful validity of the clause as a whole,[52] it is submitted that the above principles apply and that notice would be necessary before such a clause could be invoked to show that the contract had been determined.

Where a previous warning notice of specified duration is expressly required by the contract before notice of termination, the notice should be explicit as to the grounds of dissatisfaction, so that during the time mentioned in the notice the builder may have the opportunity

---

[47] *Drew* v. *Josolyne* (1887) 18 Q.B.D. 590 (C.A.); *Roberts* v. *Davey* (1833) 4 B. & Ad. 664, *infra*.
[48] 4 B. & Ad. 664. See also *Marsden* v. *Sambell* (1880) 28 W.R. 952; 43 L.T. 120, illustrated *infra*, p. 699.
[49] 18 Q.B.D. 590, C.A.
[50] L.R. 4 Ch.App. 242. See *post*, Chap. 14, Assignment, p. 732.
[51] Clause 25 (2), post-1963 forms.
[52] See *post*, Chap. 16, pp. 784 *et seq*.

of removing the cause of objection,[53] if that is the intention of the contract, but the degree of particularity required in the notice must depend on the facts upon which the termination is conditioned.

In *Pauling* v. *Dover Corporation* (1855),[54] Parke B. said: " If the engineer had desired the plaintiff to do some particular act, for example, to pull down some of his work, he ought to give him a notice to that effect, specifying to what extent he wished to have the work pulled down; but here the engineer's objection is that the work is generally performed negligently, and that being so, the engineer is entitled to give a general notice."

ILLUSTRATIONS

(1) A building contract provided that, in case it appeared to the employer or his engineer that the contractor was not proceeding to execute the work properly or with due expedition, they should be at liberty to give notice in writing to the contractor to remedy defects or supply sufficient materials and labour, and that on his failure to comply with such notice within seven days, they might take the works out of his hands. The notice sent to him was: " I give notice to you to supply all proper materials and labour for the due prosecution of the works, and to proceed therewith with due expedition, and further, that if you shall for seven days after giving this notice fail or neglect to comply therewith, I shall, as engineer, and on behalf of the Corporation, take the works wholly out of your hands." *Held*, that this general notice was enough, and that a forfeiture for non-compliance with it was valid: *Pauling* v. *Dover Corporation* (1855).[55]

(2) A building contract provided that in case the works were not carried on with such expedition and with such materials and workmanship as the architect might deem proper, he should be at liberty, with the consent of the employer, to dismiss the contractor after notice. *Held*, that such notice must intimate to the contractor in what respect the architect was dissatisfied with the conduct of the works, and what he required to be done as regarded expedition, material and workmanship, so that during the time mentioned in the notice the contractor might have an opportunity of removing the architect's objections; failing which, and after the expiration of the time mentioned in the notice and not before, the architect might dismiss him: *Smith* v. *Gordon* (1880).[56]

[Note: In so far as the clause in the above case contemplated two quite different classes of breach, the decision is easily explicable; but it is difficult to see how a notice requiring due expedition could be more specific, and it is submitted that a notice based on defective work need do no more than identify the defect and need not specify either the cause or remedy.[56a]]

[53] See *Smith* v. *Gordon, infra.*   [54] 24 L.J.Ex. 128 at p. 129.
[55] 10 Ex. 753.
[56] 30 Up.Can.C.P. 553.
[56a] For the architect's duty to the contractor in relation to defects, see *ante*, Chap. 6, pp. 385–388.

The necessity for a clear and unequivocal act is of particular importance under the general law where the event on which determination may be effected is not regulated by an express term for termination but is conduct by the other party evincing an intention no longer to be bound, or breach of a fundamental term. If situations of this kind result in work under the contract ceasing altogether, the courts have, of necessity, to find that one of the parties was in the wrong, but in cases where the parties continue under protest, it has been seen that repudiation will not easily be inferred merely because an incorrect stand has been taken,[57] and technical difficulties in the way of their raising their original contentions in the courts or before an arbitrator will if possible, be avoided or disregarded.[58] Once work has ceased, failure to make a clear election may result in the party originally in the right being held to have repudiated the contract. Thus, in *Kamlee Construction Ltd.* v. *Town of Oakville*,[59] the Supreme Court of Canada divided by three to two as to which party had repudiated (where the contractor had wrongly suspended work in the first instance, but where negotiations followed as to the terms of his return which finally broke down) on the ground that what occurred at a final inconclusive meeting might have amounted to a withdrawal of a previous written intimation by the employer of his intention to treat the contract as repudiated. Again, in *Pigott Construction Ltd.* v. *W. J. Crowe Ltd.*[60] failure by a sub-contractor to make it plain that it was too late to expect him to start work after many months delay in giving him possession of the site, and other conduct recognising the contract, resulted in his being held to have repudiated by reason of his refusal to start work without extra payment when finally called on to do so.

(4) Forfeiture Clauses in Building Leases

Section 146 (1) of the Law of Property Act 1925 (re-enacting earlier provisions) provides as follows: " A right of re-entry or forfeiture under any proviso or stipulation in a lease for a breach of any covenant or condition in the lease shall not be enforceable by action or otherwise, unless and until the lessor serves on the lessee a notice—

---

[57] *Sweet & Maxwell Ltd.* v. *Universal News Services Ltd.* [1964] 2 Q.B. 699, and *Earth & General Contracts Ltd.* v. *Manchester Corporation* (1958) 108 L.J. 665, *supra*, p. 686.

[58] *Brodie* v. *Cardiff Corporation* [1919] A.C. 337, illustrated *supra*, Chap. 8, pp. 541–543; but see *Peter Kiewit & Sons* v. *Eakins Construction Ltd.* (1960) 22 D.L.R. (2d) 465 (Canada), *ante*, Chap. 8, p. 543.

[59] (1961) 26 D.L.R. (2d) 166 (Canada).

[60] (1961) 27 D.L.R. (2d) 258 (Canada), illustrated *supra*, pp. 338–339; *infra*, pp. 709–710.

(a) specifying the particular breach complained of; and
(b) if the breach is capable of remedy, requiring the lessee to remedy the breach; and
(c) in any case, requiring the lessee to make compensation in money for the breach;

and the lessee fails, within a reasonable time thereafter, to remedy the breach, if it is capable of remedy, and to make reasonable compensation in money, to the satisfaction of the lessor, for the breach."

This section applies to forfeiture clauses contained in agreements for a lease upon terms as to building upon the land (as distinct from ordinary building contracts) and if the lessor purports to exercise a power of forfeiture before he has served the required notice on the lessee, relief will be granted to the lessee when the breaches upon which the lessor sought to rely have been remedied.[61] (The distinction between a building contract and an agreement for a lease with a covenant to build is, that while in the former no provision is made for giving the builder an interest in the land built upon, in the latter it is provided that the builder shall, in certain events, be entitled to a lease with or without an option to purchase the freehold of the land built upon.)

Until the builder has performed his obligations under the building agreement, he is not entitled to specific performance of the agreement to grant a lease or to retain possession of the site as if a lease had been granted. It follows that his right to set up section 146 of the Law of Property Act 1925 with respect to breaches of the building agreement can only apply to attempts to forfeit made by the building owner after the happening of the event which entitles the builder to his lease. Generally, the events so entitling the builder are those which would entitle him to final payment under a building contract. This depends, however, upon the terms of the agreement between the parties, as does also the method, if any, of ascertaining or determining the occurrence of the qualifying events.[62]

(5) Who is to Ascertain Event

How the occurrence of the event upon which a power of forfeiture may be exercised shall be ascertained, and by whom such power may be exercised, are questions which are usually dealt with specifically by the contract; and the special provisions of each contract must be

[61] See *North London Land Co.* v. *Jacques* (1884) 32 W.R. 283.
[62] See *Lowther* v. *Heaver* (1889) 41 Ch.D. 248, *infra,* p. 709; *ante,* p. 561.

referred to in order to ascertain the events in which the power is to arise, *e.g.* insufficient progress. If, however, no method is provided by the contract for ascertaining whether or not the prescribed event has happened upon which the power is exercisable, it must be ascertained, as any other fact is ascertained, by a court or an arbitrator.

ILLUSTRATION

P. covenanted with a gas company to make a tank within three months, and that in case of default he would pay the company such sum as the engineer should adjudge to be reasonable and proper. The company alleged default, and the engineer adjudged a certain sum as reasonable and proper damages. The company then brought an action against P.'s sureties for such sum. *Held*, and admitted, that the engineer was a mere valuer or appraiser, and that it was not referred to him to say whether the covenants were or were not broken, and that the plaintiffs were bound to aver and prove before a jury that in fact there had been a breach by P.: *Northampton Gas Light Co.* v. *Parnell* (1855).[63]

[Note: The above case shows how courts will tend to treat forfeiture or penalty clauses strictly,[64] and also will hesitate to give a third person power to decide questions of breach of contract unless specifically empowered to do so.[64a] In all other cases the courts will tend to give a certifier or other third person the implied power necessary to implement his stated function, as *e.g.* to enable a certifier required to value variations to decide also whether or not there have been variations.[65]]

Usually, however, the contract expressly gives the third person or certifier the right or duty to decide whether or not the event has happened upon which the right to forfeit the contract arises.

When the ascertainment of the event is left to the opinion of a third party whose decision is to be final and who is acting in a quasi-judicial capacity as certifier, it has already been seen that the decision of such person will usually bind the parties, unless there is an overriding arbitration clause.[66] However, even where the certifier's decision is binding, provisions of this kind will not usually, in the absence of explicit words, enable the certifier to decide matters of breach of contract or prevention by the employer,[67] and in cases where the event justifying termination is delay by the contractor, such

---

[63] 15 C.B. 630.
[64] Compare the prevention qualifications on the ambit of liquidated damages clauses, *ante*, Chap. 11, pp. 624 *et seq*.
[64a] See *ante*, Chap. 7, pp. 406 *et seq*.
[65] *Ante*, Chap. 8, pp. 553–555.
[66] See *ante*, Chap. 7, Approval and Certificates.
[67] *Ante*, Chap. 7, Section 1, pp. 406 *et seq*., Chap. 11, Section 2 (1), pp. 624 *et seq*.

an allegation by the contractor against the employer is not uncommon. In such a case, it is not sufficient for the builder, relying on the " prevention " principle illustrated by *Roberts* v. *Bury Commissioners* (1870) [68] merely to allege that the delay was due to an act or omission of the employer. It must be proved that the delay which operated on the certifier's mind was so caused before the finality of his decision can be avoided.

ILLUSTRATION

A contract contained a provision that A, a third person, might terminate the contract if dissatisfied with the rate of progress, and A did so. The contractor sued for damages, alleging that A's dissatisfaction was caused by delay occasioned by the employer. *Held*, that the contractor to establish this must prove that the delay which had caused dissatisfaction was in fact due to the employer: *Wadey* v. *Mort's Dock and Engineering Co.* (1902).[69]

If the powers under a forfeiture clause are expressed to arise in the event of work not being performed or completed under the direction or to the satisfaction or approval of the employer's architect or engineer, the event cannot arise until he has been appointed.[70]

It is, of course, open to the parties to leave the ascertainment of the event to the building owner himself, and not to a third party. When this is done, the building owner may be under a duty to decide reasonably, just as he may have to be reasonable in approving or disapproving work done for him. The terms of the contract may, however, show that the decision of the employer is intended to be final, whether reasonable or unreasonable.[71] " We are satisfied that the intention was that the defendants, if dissatisfied, whether with or without sufficient reason, with the progress of the work, should have absolute and unqualified power ' to put in force the forfeiture,' and therefore, if these terms had been ever so unreasonable, we should have felt bound to give effect to them and to hold that so long as the defendants were acting bona fide under an honest sense of dissatisfaction, although that dissatisfaction might be ill-founded and unreasonable, they were entitled to insist on the condition, and consequently the replication which only alleges that their dissatisfaction was unreasonable and capricious, but which stops short as alleging *mala fides* in the defendants in acting as is stated in the plea, is insufficient. It amounts only to this, that the defendants, who are the principal

---

[68] (1870) L.R. 5 C.P. 310, *ante*, Chap. 7, pp. 407–408, Chap. 11, p. 628.
[69] 2 N.S.W.S.R. 391; affirmed, 22 T.L.R. 61, P.C.
[70] *Hunt* v. *Bishop* (1853) 8 Ex. 675, and cases cited, *ante*, pp. 320–321, and pp. 485–488.
[71] See *ante*, Chap. 7, pp. 412 *et seq.* for a full discussion of this principle.

contractors for a great public work, and who are themselves probably under stringent terms to complete the undertaking with despatch, insist, when employing the plaintiff to do a subordinate portion of the work, that if such work should not progress as rapidly as they may desire, they shall be at liberty to put on more hands and deduct the cost of them from the contract price, still leaving to the plaintiff the benefit of the contract." [72]

ILLUSTRATION

A contract for drainage works provided that S., as sub-contractor, should execute certain works to the satisfaction of L., the main contractor, and of the employers, with a power of for-feiture if the works should not proceed as rapidly and satisfactorily as required by L. or his agents. The forfeiture was enforced, but S. sued L. and set up that the work progressed as satisfactorily as he could reasonably and properly require, and that L. had acted improperly, unreasonably and capriciously in exercising the forfeiture. *Held*, that such a plea was bad, and L. obtained judgment: *Stadhard* v. *Lee* (1863).[73]

In most modern contracts, however, the merits of the exercise of the power of forfeiture are usually within the ambit of the arbitration clause, and hence within the jurisdiction of the courts if the action is not stayed.[74]

(6) Construction of Clause

Normally, clauses will be strictly construed in order to determine whether the operative event has occurred or not.[75] But the courts will not in other respects seek to mitigate the severity of the clause. Thus, it has been held that where there is a right to forfeit on the happening of some event, coupled with a provision that the amount already paid to the contractor shall be considered to be the full value of the work done, the right may be exercised even though the contractor has not become entitled to any payment for work done.

ILLUSTRATION

The plaintiff contracted by deed with a local Board of Health to execute certain works according to a specification, and that the works should be begun, proceeded with, and completed to the satisfaction of the surveyor to the Board. Payment was to be made by instalments upon the certificate of the surveyor. It was also

---

[72] *Per* Cockburn C.J. in *Stadhard* v. *Lee, infra.*
[73] 32 L.J.Q.B. 75.
[74] *Ante*, Chap. 7, Section 4.
[75] See *e.g. Burden* v. *Swansea Corporation* [1957] 1 W.L.R. 1167, where an improper valuation by a surveyor was held not to amount to obstruction or interference by the employer in the issuing of certificates justifying determination by the contractor.

provided that if the plaintiff, from bankruptcy, or any cause whatsoever, should not proceed with the works to the satisfaction of the surveyor, it should be lawful for the Board, after three days' notice, signed by their surveyor, to employ other persons to complete the works; and that the deed should, at the expiration of the said notice, be voidable at the option of the Board, and that the amount already paid to the plaintiff should be considered the full value of the works which should up to that time have been executed, and that the materials on the premises should become the property of the Board without any further payment. *Held*, that this forfeiture clause might be enforced, although the plaintiff had not become entitled to any payment for the work done: *Davies* v. *Swansea Corporation* (1853).[76]

(7) Time when Forfeiture Exercisable

The power to forfeit for delay is often made to arise upon the happening of either or both of two events, *viz.* delay in progress and failure to complete to time. For reasons already explained, in some earlier contracts in particular progress is often expressly defined by reference to the contract date for completion, rather than some standard of reasonable diligence or expedition. In such cases, difficulty may arise when it is sought to enforce the power of forfeiture after the contract date for completion has passed. In the seventh edition of this book the rule was stated as follows:

" In the case of contracts giving a power of forfeiture for not proceeding with the work at the required rate, if the contract date for completion has ceased to be binding, no forfeiture for delay in progress can be made, for there is no period in respect of which speed can be gauged. The clause, therefore, can only be acted upon and enforced in respect of delay when there is a date fixed for completion, and offers no power of forfeiture after that date has passed or has ceased to be applicable."

The case of *Walker* v. *London & North Western Railway* (1876)[77] was cited as authority for this statement, but examination of the dual provision in that case shows that no such general proposition could be justified,[78] and this view was properly criticised as being too broad in *Joshua Henshaw & Sons* v. *Rochdale Corp.* (1944),[79] and the case of *Walker* v. *London & North Western Railway* (1876), the facts of which are set out below, was distinguished.

[76] 22 L.J.Ex. 297.
[77] 1 C.P.D. 518, *infra.*
[78] (This would be a most unusual form at the present day.)
[79] [1944] K.B. 381, *infra.*

ILLUSTRATIONS

(1) The plaintiffs contracted with the defendants to construct a dock, and other works in connection therewith, and the contract provided as follows: " Should the contractor fail to proceed in the execution of the works in the manner and at the rate of progress required by the engineer, or to maintain the said works, as herein-after mentioned, to the satisfaction of the engineer, his contract shall, at the option of the company, but not otherwise, be considered void as far as relates to the works or maintenance remaining to be done, and all sums of money that may be due to the contractor, together with all materials and implements in his possession, and all sums named as penalties for the non-fulfilment of the contract, shall be forfeited to the company, and the amount shall be con-sidered as ascertained damages for breach of contract." The contract also provided that " the whole of the works should be entirely com-pleted on or before August 31, 1873," and that should the works not be completed by the stipulated date, the employer might engage other contractors to complete. The works were not completed by that date. There was no power of extending the time, but by mutual consent the time for completion was disregarded. *Held*, that upon the true construction of the contract the forfeiture clause could not be enforced after the time originally fixed for completion of the works had expired; in such an event the employer's remedy was to employ other contractors: *Walker* v. *L. & N.W. Ry.* (1876).[80]

(2) An engineering contract provided for forfeiture after seven days' notice if the engineer was of opinion that the contractor was not making due progress with the works " sufficient to secure their completion within the specified time." It also gave the engineer power to extend the time. *Held*, that after an extension of time all power to enforce the forfeiture clause was gone, unless a new consent was given to it being applicable to the extended time: *Essenden and Flemington Corporation* v. *Ninnis* (1879).[81]

(3) A building contract contained the following clause: " The contractor shall carry on the work with due diligence and as much expedition as the surveyor shall require and in case the contractor shall fail to do so . . . or if the works of this contract are in the judgment of the surveyor not being carried on in all respects . . . with such progress as would enable them to be efficiently completed at the time . . . specified the same shall be intimated to the con-tractors by the surveyor and in case he refuse to . . . comply with any order he may so receive to that effect . . . then the corporation . . . are hereby authorised, after giving the contractor forty-eight hours' notice in writing, to take the works . . . out of the hands of the contractors." A date for completion was provided by the contract; the surveyor being given a power to certify for an extension. No extension, however, was applied for or granted. Six months after the contract date for completion, the corporation exercised their

---

[80] 1 C.P.D. 518. (Apparently followed by the Divisional Court in *Wood* v. *Tendring Sanitary Authority* (1886) 3 T.L.R. 272.)

[81] 5 Vict.L.R. 236, and see *Mohan* v. *Dundalk etc. Ry.* (1880) 6 L.R.Ir. 477. (For a full discussion of time for completion and extension of time, see *ante*, Chap. 10, Time for Performance, Section (6), pp. 614 *et seq.*, and Chap. 11, Penalties and Liquidated Damages, Section 3, Extension of Time, pp. 638 *et seq.*)

power of forfeiture under the clause. The contractors brought an action for breach of contract against the corporation, contending, on the basis of the passage from this book quoted above, that the clause ceased to have any application after the expiration of the time fixed by the contract for completion. *Held*, that the contract date having passed without any extension, the duty of the contractor was to complete within a reasonable time, and that the wording of the clause in question was such that, with certain necessary modifications, it was as applicable to the fulfilment of the contract within a reasonable time as to its completion on the contract date: *Joshua Henshaw & Sons* v. *Rochdale Corporation* (1944).[82]

The above cases show that a contract may be so worded as to relate the rate of progress expected from the contractor to the contract date for completion, and since forfeiture clauses are always strictly construed, this may place an express right of forfeiture, if conditioned in this way, in jeopardy after the date of completion.[83] The existence of an alternative right more appropriate to the period after the completion date has passed may also imperil a forfeiture clause which is not sufficiently precise in this respect.[84] But a clause in general terms based upon failure to make satisfactory or reasonable progress can obviously be operated either before or after the completion date.[85]

(8) Effect of Waiver and Estoppel

Although the circumstances may have occurred under which the right to forfeit arises by the terms of the contract, the employer may find himself precluded from enforcing the forfeiture, either because he has waived his right, or because he has, by his own actions, rendered it inequitable that he should do so, and is therefore estopped; just as at common law he must accept a repudiation, and may lose the right to rescind by a failure to accept promptly.[86]

Subject to the express wording of the clause, a power of forfeiture must be exercised within a reasonable time after the occurrence of the breach on which the power is conditioned to arise. Otherwise, the breach, unless it is a continuing one, will be deemed to have been waived.[87] (In principle it is clear, it is submitted, that this means

---

[82] [1944] K.B. 381.

[83] See *Barclay* v. *Messenger* (1874) 43 L.J.Ch. 449; *cf. Essenden & Flemington Corporation* v. *Ninnis, supra.*

[84] *Walker* v. *London & North Western Ry., supra.*

[85] *Joshua Henshaw* v. *Rochdale Corporation, supra.* See also *Klimack Construction Ltd.* v. *Belleville* (1951) 4 D.L.R. (2d) 837 (Canada).

[86] *Ante*, Chap. 5, pp. 345–346, a closely allied subject with cases highly relevant to the present discussion.

[87] *Marsden* v. *Sambell* (1880) 28 W.R. 952.

within a reasonable time after the innocent party has learnt of the breach, since no waiver can be imputed if in fact there is no knowledge of what is being waived, and there can be no duty owed by an innocent party to detect the breaches of the guilty party.) Further, failure to complete to time is not, generally, to be regarded as a continuing breach.[88] On the other hand, failure to use due diligence clearly is a continuing breach, and it has been suggested [89] that as a matter of business efficacy there must be an implied term to this effect in most contracts for work and labour, and whether or not such a term is fundamental, notice will serve to crystallise the position and, if there is no improvement, establish the necessary intention no longer to be bound, thereby entitling the employer to treat the contract as repudiated.[90]

If the building owner positively treats the contract as subsisting after the date when the right to forfeit occurs, he will be regarded, *a fortiori*, as having waived his right.[91] However, if the breach is a continuing one, the making of payments to the contractor after the breach does not amount to a waiver.[92] The extent to which mere delay in exercising a right to forfeit will operate as a waiver of that right is a question of fact.[93] A waiver operates once and for all in respect of that particular right of forfeiture to which it relates.[94] Where, however, a fresh right arises, or the breach is a continuing[94a] one, the new or continuing right is unaffected by a previous waiver. The following cases illustrate the difficulties, already referred to, arising out of the conveyancing practice of conditioning forfeiture clauses upon completion by a stipulated date, as opposed to a requirement of due diligence or expedition.

ILLUSTRATIONS

(1) A clause in a building agreement (not amounting to a demise) provided that in case of default in not completing the buildings, on successive dates, the owner should be at liberty to re-enter and seize the materials. Successive defaults had been made

[88] *Platt* v. *Parker* (1886) 2 T.L.R. 786 (C.A.).
[89] *Ante,* Chap. 5, pp. 314–315, and Chap. 10, pp. 609, 611.
[90] Only, however, if he makes his election to do so clear—see *e.g. Pigott Construction Ltd.* v. *W. J. Crowe Ltd.* (1961) 27 D.L.R. (2d) 258, illustrated *ante,* Chap. 5, pp. 338–339 and *infra,* pp. 709–710.
[91] *Walker* v. *North Western Ry.* (1876) 1 C.P.D. 518, *Ex p. Newitt, re Garrud* (1881) 16 Ch.D. 522, C.A., *cf. Joshua Henshaw* v. *Rochdale Corporation* [1944] K.B. 381.
[92] *Cooper* v. *Uttoxeter Burial Board* (1864) 11 L.T. 565, (defective work) illustrated *ante,* pp. 381–382. See also *ante,* pp. 635–636 (liquidated damages).
[93] *Morrison* v. *Universal Marine Insurance Co.* (1873) L.R. 8 Ex. 197; *Marsden* v. *Sambell* (1880) 28 W.R. 952; 43 L.T. 120.
[94] *Platt* v. *Parker, Marsden* v. *Sambell, infra.*
[94a] See also for this whole subject *ante,* Chap. 5, pp. 345–346.

and several periods of indulgence granted, but there had been no waiver of the last default. *Held*, that the owner was entitled to re-enter and seize the materials: *Stevens* v. *Taylor* (1860).[95]

(2) Under a building agreement a builder agreed to complete by June 24. The builder was not to remove any materials delivered on the site, unless he had a written licence. There was also a forfeiture clause in the event of the work not being duly proceeded with. Part of the work was not completed by June 24. The building owner sent an agent on July 5 to prevent the removal of materials, and " to keep an eye " on the houses. The builder removed materials on July 31, under protest from the building owner. The building owner brought an action to restrain the builder from trespassing, alleging that by non-completion on June 24, and possession by the building owner's agent on July 5, the premises and materials had become forfeited. *Held*, (1) that the intervention of the building owner's agent was not an unqualified election to avoid the agreement; (2) that the election must be exercised within a reasonable time, or at all events not after the party against whom it was claimed had been allowed to alter his position on the faith of the continuance of the contract; but (3) that the removal of the materials on July 31 was a fresh breach of the contract, for which the building owner was entitled to forfeiture, as there was no actual rescission by the builder, even assuming that the building owner had earlier refused to recognise the contract as subsisting and given the builder a right to rescind: *Marsden* v. *Sambell* (1880).[96]

(3) An owner went on making advances after the failure of the contractor to complete on a particular day. *Semble*, that this amounted to a waiver of the right of forfeiture: *Re Garrud, ex p. Newitt* (1881).[97]

(4) A builder, under a building agreement, agreed to build certain houses by a certain day, and if they were then not completed, that the building owner might re-enter and take possession. The building owner agreed to make advances, and the builder having failed to complete, the building owner went on making advances after the date of completion. *Held*, that this amounted to a waiver of the right to forfeit: *Platt* v. *Parker* (1886).[98]

(5) F. contracted to build a house for W. by a certain time. The house was not completed to time, but F. was allowed to continue working for two months, when W. took possession. *Held*, that W. had waived the right to forfeit, and that a subsequent forfeiture was wrongful: *Foster* v. *Worthington* (1886).[99]

Where the employer has permitted the rights of third parties to be altered, or the builder to change his position to his prejudice, under the belief that the contract was to be treated as still subsisting,

---

[95] 2 F. & F. 419.

[96] 43 L.T. 120.

[97] 16 Ch.D. 522, illustrated *ante*, Chap. 12, p. 666.

[98] 2 T.L.R. 786 (C.A.).

[99] 58 V.T. 65; U.S.Dig. (1886), p. 125. See also *Felton* v. *Wharrie* (1906) Hudson's B.C. 4th ed., Vol. 2, p. 398, illustrated *ante*, Chap. 10, Section (5), p. 613.

the employer will be estopped from any subsequent exercise of his right. But a positive act of election to continue with the contract, or an alteration of position by the builder, must be affirmatively proved.[99a]

ILLUSTRATION

A broker insured the ship C without disclosing certain information which it was material that the insurers should know. He did this in good faith, believing from inquiries that the information was not true. On October 13, after initialling the slip (the time when the contract was held to be concluded), but before executing the policy, the insurers became possessed of this information. On October 14 or 15 they issued the policy without any protest or notice that they would treat it as void. On October 20, on receiving news of the loss of the ship, they gave the owner notice that they did not consider the policy binding on them. The jury, being directed that the insurers were bound, on discovering the misrepresentations, to elect within a reasonable time whether they would go on with the policy, found that the insurers had not elected to go on with the policy. *Held*, the jury having found that there was no election in fact, and in the absence of evidence that the shipowner had been prejudiced by the insurers not electing earlier to disaffirm the policy, the insurers were not estopped from relying on the invalidity of the policy, and that it was wholly immaterial whether the shipowner understood, or had a right to understand, the conduct of the insurers as an election: *Morrison* v. *Universal Marine Insurance Co.* (1873).[1]

The power of forfeiture cannot be exercised where the employer has caused the default upon which it is agreed that the power shall arise. In such a case the rule of law applies which exonerates one of two contracting parties from the performance of a contract, where the performance of it is prevented or rendered impossible by the wrongful act of the other contracting party.[1a]

SECTION 2.   EFFECT OF EXERCISING A FORFEITURE CLAUSE

(1) Generally

The nature and extent of the rights of a party properly exercising an express power of forfeiture fall to be determined, just as does the accrual of the power to forfeit itself, by the express terms of the contract. The effect of exercising the power may either be to determine the contract altogether, or else to change the rights of the parties in an agreed fashion. The forms of contract in current use generally

---

[99a] See also *Allen* v. *Robles* [1969] 1 W.L.R. 1193, referred to *ante*, Chap. 5, p. 346.

[1] L.R. 8 Ex. 197, Ex.Ch. No doubt the jury's finding of fact may have been doubtful, and the evidence of prejudice might have been obtained, in the above case, but the principle is not affected.

[1a] See *ante*, Chap. 11, pp. 624 *et seq.*, in relation to liquidated damages clauses, and *ante*, Chap. 7, pp. 406 *et seq.*, in regard to certifying clauses.

enable the employers operating the forfeiture clause to take possession of the works and to oust the builder from the site. There may
also be a right to complete the execution of the contract at the
builder's expense, and to use his materials and plant. The operation
of associated vesting and user clauses in respect of materials or plant
has already been discussed.[2]

In the case of a contract determined or rescinded not under an
express power of forfeiture but under the general law, acceptance of
the other party's repudiation does not strictly bring the contract to
an end, though language to this effect is often loosely used by lawyers
and others, but merely releases the rescinding party from further
obligation to perform the contract.[3] So provisions of the contract, if
applicable, will survive and govern the position of the parties, such as
any relevant provisions as to damages, or the ownership of materials
or plant, or an arbitration clause.[3]

(2) The Rights Conferred

Modern determination clauses are relatively simple, generally giving
the employer a discretionary right to re-enter and use all materials
and plant, and providing for the ascertainment of all loss and expense
occasioned him thereby in considerable detail but in terms generally
consistent with the rules for ascertaining the measure of damage on a
rescission under the general law. The earlier cases reveal a considerable variety in the nature of the rights given by building and engineering contracts to the employer under the forfeiture clause, some of
which might, on principles already discussed,[4] be held to be inapplicable as penalties at the present day. The following are typical
examples:

To seize materials
    (1)   To seize the materials and take possession of the whole or
          part of the work already done.[5]
    (2)   To seize the materials and use them.[6]
    (3)   To use up the materials and use the plant on the site to
          complete the works or to have them completed, without
          making payment for the same.[7]

---

[2] See *ante*, Chap. 12, Vesting of Materials and Plant.
[3] See *Heyman* v. *Darwins* [1942] A.C. 356, for a full discussion on this. See also *ante*,
    Chap. 5, pp. 340 *et seq.*
[4] *Ante*, Chap. 11, Section 1.
[5] *Tripp* v. *Armitage* (1893) 4 M. & W. 687.
[6] *Baker* v. *Gray* (1856) 25 L.J.C.P. 161.
[7] *Mohan* v. *Dundalk Ry.* (1880) 6 L.R.Ir. 477.

(4) To use and sell the surplus materials and the plant, after completion of the works, to recoup loss.[8]

(5) To become possessed of the materials absolutely (leaving open the question of damages against the contractor)[9]; or of the materials and plant.[10]

(6) To become possessed of the materials and things on the site absolutely as and for liquidated damages.[11]

(7) To become possessed absolutely of the materials and plant, paying for them the amount fixed by the architect.[12]

To seize money in hand

(1) To keep the money due or accruing due to the builder,[13] either by a condition that " the amount already paid to the builder by the employers shall be considered to be the full value of the works executed by the builder up to the time when such notice shall have expired," [14] or by a condition that " the builders shall not be entitled to claim from the employers any payments whatsoever for any work done or labour or materials provided or used since the accrual of any then preceding instalment." [15]

(2) To forfeit for breach of contract named sums of money as ascertained damages for the non-fulfilment of the contract.[16]

To complete the works

(1) To complete the works or to employ some other person so to do, paying for the same out of any money due to the builder on account of the contract.[17]

(2) To take possession of the works and to pay whatever number of men may be left unpaid by the builder, and to set on more hands and deduct the cost from the contract price.

(3) To procure and pay for all labour and materials out of the money that may then be due or that may become due to the

[8] Garrett v. Salisbury & Dorset Ry. (1866) L.R. 2 Eq. 358.
[9] Davies v. Swansea Corporation (1853) 22 L.J.Ex. 297, illustrated supra, pp. 694–695.
[10] Roach v. Great Western Ry. (1841) 10 L.J.Q.B. 89.
[11] Ex p. Newitt, re Garrud (1881) 16 Ch.D. 522 (C.A.)
[12] Roberts v. Bury Commissioners (1870) L.R. 5 C.P. 310, Ex.Ch.
[13] Roach v. Great Western Ry. (1841) 10 L.J.Q.B. 89.
[14] Davies v. Swansea Corporation (1853) 22 L.J.Ex. 297.
[15] Mohan v. Dundalk Ry. (1880) 6 L.R.Ir. 477.
[16] Walker v. London and North Western Ry. (1876) 1 C.P.D. 518.
[17] Mohan v. Dundalk Ry. (1880) 6 L.R.Ir. 477; Re Walker, ex p. Barter (1884) 26 Ch.D. 510 (C.A.).

contractor, [18] and if the cost to the employers shall exceed the balance in their hands, to recover the excess from the builder.[19]

Agreement void or voidable on re-entry

The agreement upon re-entry to be:

(a) Void absolutely [20];

(b) Void at the option of the employers, without prejudice to any right of action by the employers, against the builder [21];

(c) Void at the option of the employers as far as relates to the works or maintenance remaining to be done.[22]

[Note: The cases cited above do not necessarily turn upon the application of the form of words with which they appear, but are, in each case, examples of contracts in which that form of words was used.]

(3) What Sums are Included in Forfeiture

Forfeiture clauses sometimes contain provisions forfeiting any moneys due to the contractor at the time of the forfeiture. Such clauses may be held to be penalties, and consequently of no effect without actual proof of damage.[23] But where valid, it may be a question exactly what moneys are forfeited under the clause. A power to forfeit retention money as such does not, it would seem, include money due and payable under certificates already given but not paid. Generally, where work has been done but is not yet due for certification at the date of the forfeiture, the contractor will have no right to receive payment for it.[24] The following American cases illustrate the difficulties which may arise, but should not be taken as authority for any general propositions of law.

---

[18] *Stadhard* v. *Lee* (1863) 3 B. & S. 364.

[19] *Walker* v. *London and North Western Ry.* (1876) 1 C.P.D. 518; *Re Walker, ex p. Barter* (1884) 26 Ch.D. 510 (C.A.).

[20] *Tripp* v. *Armitage* (1839) 4 M. & W. 687; *Re Garrud, ex p. Newitt* (1881) 16 Ch.D. 522 (C.A.). Even where the word " void " is used, this usually means no more than " voidable." See *supra*, p. 688.

[21] *Davies* v. *Swansea Corporation* (1853) 22 L.J.Ex. 297.

[22] *Walker* v. *London and North Western Ry.* (1876) 1 C.P.D. 518, *supra*, p. 696.

[23] See *ante*, Chap. 11, Penalties and Liquidated Damages, pp. 618 *et seq.*, and see *Ranger* v. *G.W. Ry.* (1854) 5 H.L.C. 72, *ante*, p. 620. But see *Ex p. Newitt, Re Garrud* (1881) 16 Ch.D. 522, illustrated *ante*, Chap. 12, p. 666 and *Walker* v. *London and North Western Ry.* (1876) 1 C.P.D. 518, illustrated, *supra*, p. 696.

[24] See *ante*, Chap. 5.

ILLUSTRATIONS

(1) An engineering contract provided for 15 per cent. retention money. The employers had power to terminate the contract if they were dissatisfied with the rate of progress, etc. *Held*, that the retention was by way of indemnity and not of forfeiture, and that the contractor was entitled to it subject to any damage sustained by the employers by reason of the default, negligence or misconduct of the contractor: *Philadelphia etc. Railway* v. *Howard* (1851).[25]

(2) An engineering contract provided for payment at the rate of 90 per cent. of the value of the estimated work done, and empowered the engineer, in case the contractor did not observe his contract, to declare the contract at an end, and provided that any sum due to the contractor was then to be forfeited to the employer. *Held*, that this clause only applied to the 10 per cent. retention money, and not to instalments which had been certified for: *Ricker* v. *Fairbanks* (1855).[26]

(3) In a contract for the construction of a railroad there was a condition that upon forfeiture " the unpaid part of the value of the work done " should be " forfeited by the said contractors to the use of the employers " in the nature of liquidated damages at the time of the forfeiture; the employer had in hand the 15 per cent. retention money, and in addition was indebted to the contractors in a certain amount on account of the monthly estimates. *Held*, that the latter amount was not intended to be included in the forfeiture, but only the 15 per cent.: *Geiger* v. *Western Maryland Railway* (1874).[27]

(4) A agreed to do certain work for B, 10 per cent. of the payments to be retained and forfeited in case of A's breach of contract. C contracted with A to do the work on the terms stipulated between A and B. C failed to do the work and A completed it. *Held*, that C could not claim the retention money: *Lara* v. *Greely* (1885).[28]

(5) H. contracted to construct a canal for the Government. The contract provided that a percentage was to be retained as security for the performance of the contract. H. abandoned the contract. *Held*, that H. could not maintain an action for any of the retention money, if the Government had been damnified to a greater extent: *Hennegan* v. *United States* (1883).[29]

In fact, however, most modern forms of forfeiture clause contain reasonably clear provisions regulating the adjustment of accounts between the parties upon forfeiture; and in such cases practical difficulties of this kind are unlikely to arise.

[25] 13 How.(U.S.) 307.
[26] 40 Me. 43.
[27] 41 Md. 4. This and the preceding cases are probably wrong under modern English law in holding retention money not to be a penalty in these circumstances—see *ante*, Chap. 11, p. 623.
[28] 20 Fla. 926; U.S.Dig. (1885) p. 119.
[29] 17 Ct. of Cl. 273; U.S.Dig. (1883), p. 159.

(4) Position of Employer Completing after Forfeiture

Where the employer enters under a forfeiture clause on default by the contractor and completes, and the clause empowers him to deduct the cost of completion from all moneys due from him to the contractor, or to recover the cost of completion from the contractor after giving credit for what would be done under the contract, the employer is not in the position of a mortgagee in possession, all of whose acts are jealously scrutinised,[30] but as against the contractor and those claiming under him, *e.g.* assignees of retention money, the employer, although he may be bound to account to the contractor,[31] is allowed a reasonable discretion in the way in which he completes.[32]

" The contractor cannot, in the absence of fraud or extreme negligence, complain if the work be carried on in an uneconomical manner . . . every allowance should be made in considering the conduct of the employer for the position in which the default of the contractor has placed him." [33]

" It would be wholly inconsistent with the whole spirit and scope of the contract to suppose that contractors might file a bill in this court to have the whole accounts of the contract taken, because through their own default the company were obliged to take possession of the plant, the value of which was not to be ascertained by the engineer".[34]

These statements reflect the basic principle of mitigation of damage—namely that only clearly unreasonable conduct will serve to reduce the damages otherwise recoverable by the innocent party.[35]

Building contracts in the past not infrequently contained provisions forfeiting to the building owner any moneys due to the builder at the time of termination.[36] Whether the building owner is under an obligation to account to the builder after deducting the cost of completing the works must depend upon the particular clause, and also the question whether it can be construed as a provision for liquidated damages.[37] In a case of unliquidated damages, of course, he clearly must do so.[38] Thus, in *Ranger* v. *Great Western Railway*

---

[30] *Fulton* v. *Dornwell* (1885) 4 N.Z.L.R.(S.C.) 207.
[31] *Ranger* v. *G.W. Ry.* (1854) 5 H.L.C. 72.
[32] *Fulton* v. *Dornwell* (1885) 4 N.Z.L.R.(S.C.) 207; *Dillon* v. *Jack* (1903) 23 N.Z.L.R. 547.
[33] *Per* Williams J. in *Fulton* v. *Dornwell, supra.*
[34] *Per* James L.J. in *Sharpe* v. *San Paulo Ry.* (1873) L.R. 8 Ch.App. 597, 610.
[35] See *ante,* Chap. 9, Section 2, p. 582.
[36] *Supra,* p. 702.
[37] See *ante,* Chap. 11.
[38] See *ante,* Chap. 9, Price and Damages, pp. 582, 585 *et seq.,* Chap. 11, Section 2 (2), and *supra,* pp. 703–704.

(1854), *supra,* there was an obligation on the part of the builder to make good any deficiency in the cost of completion, and he was there held to be entitled to an account. But the employer is not obliged to account at all if the forfeiture is held to be in the nature of liquidated damages.

Where the clause provides that the employer shall complete the works after taking possession, it would seem that completion means completion under and subject to the terms of the contract, in so far as they are then applicable, and that the employer would be at liberty to add to, alter or omit parts of the works only if and so far as there was power reserved by the contract to add to or alter or omit. Such a clause may not be apt, therefore, to cover the employer's position where he does not wish to complete the works, and in such a case the employer may need to rely on ordinary damages rather than upon the specific remedies conferred by the clause. It is a criticism of the modern standard forms that they do not make any provision for this possibility by enabling the employer to sue for damages immediately upon determination should he so elect. On either view, he must keep a strict account of any additions, and omissions, so that any sum due from him to the builder, or from the builder to him, may be capable of ascertainment.

It should not be forgotten that, in the absence of express provision, the employer on forfeiture will be entitled to damages assessed under the general law, if the forfeiture is justified under the general law, which will include the additional cost of completion and damage due to delay in completion,[38] and under which no difficulty would arise in taking account of omissions or additions in the work actually done.

Similarly, other heads of damage assessed in this way may be recoverable, despite the omission of the forfeiture clause to provide specifically for them. Thus the pre-1963 R.I.B.A. forms of contract did not, on an employer's determination, while providing for the recovery of the cost of completion from the contractor, make any provision for the recovery of damages for delay in completion. If the determination was based on facts justifying rescission under the general law, it is submitted that, in the absence of any expressed intention to exclude such damages, they would be recoverable in addition to the damages specifically provided for in the determination clause. The 1963 forms [39] have been amended in the employer's interest in

[39] Clause 25 (3) (*d*).

this respect. Whether liquidated damages are recoverable on determination under a forfeiture clause has already been considered.[40]

SECTION 3. WRONGFUL FORFEITURE

(1) When Forfeiture is Wrongful

A power of forfeiture will be wrongfully exercised if one of the events upon which it is conditioned has not occurred. Further, if, by the terms of the contract, notice has to be given to the party in default, allowing a time in which to rectify the default, the power may only be exercised after the expiration of the notice and a failure to rectify the default within the time,[41] unless the employer's action can be rescued by being shown to be justified under the general law. Even if, however, an accepted repudiation can be inferred under the general law, this still may not entirely rescue an improperly exercised forfeiture, since any rights outside the general law specifically provided for in the clause cannot be enforced, though the usual common law consequences will, of course, follow.

Mere action, however, under a forfeiture clause conditioned on progress may not automatically involve a common law repudiation. "It was argued that B. and D. can justify the conversion under the ' user ' clause as arising on the cesser for working for fourteen days, on the ground that the receiver had in fact refused to go on, and that, although the fourteen days had not run out, there was every reason to believe the work would never be recommenced, . . . but B. and D. commenced working on the ship within the fourteen days allowed, and thereby, in our opinion, prevented a resumption of work by the builders or those claiming under them. It was indeed suggested that the receiver had declared his intention of not further prosecuting the work. But even if he had authority so to do, there is no satisfactory evidence of his having communicated to the [employers] any fixed intention on his part not to complete the ship." [42]

Though the common law right to damages confers substantial protection on the innocent party, the most important respect in which it differs from the usual specific remedies in building and engineering contracts is that it confers no right to seize or use plant

---

[40] *Ante*, Chap. 11, Section 2 (2), where this subject is more fully discussed, pp. 633–635.
[41] See *ante*, Section 1, pp. 688–689.
[42] *Per* Fry L.J. in *Re Walker, ex p. Barter* (1884) 26 Ch.D. 510, at p. 520 (C.A.); and see *Frost* v. *Knight* (1872) L.R. 7 Ex. 111.

or materials not the employer's property at the time of the determination.

Since, while the employer is the owner of the site, the contractor has a licence to occupy it, a purported exercise of the power to determine, if it results in the contractor leaving the site, must clearly in nearly all cases evince an intention by the employer no longer to be bound if, whatever the general merits, it transpires that the determination was wrongful and unjustified. In such a case, if the contractor accepts the repudiation and rescinds (which he will clearly do, though he may choose to allow the employer some time for reflection,[43] since the nature of his interest in the land does not entitle him to remain on the site against the will of the employer[44]) the employer will be liable for the possibly heavy damages attendant upon repudiation and cannot, if he discovers his mistake, restore the contract and the *status quo ante* without the agreement of the contractor. On the other hand, acts short of expelling the contractor from the site, giving rise to perhaps small or nominal damage, may, though wrongful, not amount to repudiation by the employer.[45]

The exercise of a power to forfeit may be invalidated either by reason of the fact that none of the events upon which it is conditioned has occurred or, although such an event has happened, that it was caused by the act of the party seeking to exercise it, or his agents,[46] or that the required notice has not been given,[47] or that there has been delay or other conduct recognising the continued existence of the contract after knowledge of the breach, if the breach is not a continuing one. Nor can a wrongful forfeiture be justified by reference to a *subsequent* event which would have justified it.[48] On the analogy of the cases relating to the dismissal of a servant,[49] however, it may be that a forfeiture purportedly made in respect of a breach which has

---

[43] See *ante*, Chap. 5, Section 3, pp. 340–341.

[44] See *supra*, p. 681, but see the *Twickenham* case there referred to.

[45] *Cf.* the wrongful interference with plant in *Earth & General Contracts Ltd.* v. *Manchester Corporation* (1958) 108 L.J. 665, and the refusal to enter into a lease in *Sweet & Maxwell Ltd.* v. *Universal News Services* [1964] 2 Q.B. 699, both illustrated *supra*, p. 686. See also the discussion *ante*, Chap. 5, pp. 340 *et seq.*

[46] See *e.g. Roberts* v. *Bury Commissioners* (1870) L.R. 5 C.P. 310, illustrated *ante*, Chap. 7, pp. 407–408, and Chap. 11, p. 628.

[47] See *e.g. Lowther* v. *Heaver* (1889) 41 Ch.D. 248, *infra*.

[48] *Re Walker, ex p. Barter, ex p. Black* (1884) 26 Ch.D. 510. Except, it would seem, in cases of bribery and fraud. See *ante*, Chap. 3, pp. 232–233, and the case of *Panama etc. Telegraph Co.* v. *India Rubber etc. Co.* (1875) L.R. 10 Ch. 515, illustrated *ante*, Chap. 7, p. 457.

[49] See *e.g. Boston Deep Sea Fishing Co.* v. *Ansell* (1888) 39 Ch.D. 339.

not in fact occurred may be justified by proof of another breach existent at the date of the forfeiture.[50]

ILLUSTRATIONS

(1) Employers determined a contract under a forfeiture clause conditioned upon failure to proceed with the works with due diligence. The contractor pleaded the delay was due to failure by the architect to set out the works and issue drawings in time. *Held*, on demurrer, and despite an architect's certificate in the employer's favour, a good plea in support of the contractor's claim for damages: *Roberts* v. *Bury Commissioners* (1870).[51]

(2) A building lease agreement provided for the granting of leases of individual houses as they were completed. There was a proviso for re-entry on the unleased plots should the rent be in arrear, or if at any time the works were not proceeded with for twenty-one days. *Held, per* Lindley L.J., that it was doubtful if any advantage could be taken of the clause without giving reasonable notice: *Lowther* v. *Heaver* (1889).[52]

(3) An architect fraudulently refused to give a certificate of completion, and the employers then took possession of the site and certain plant. *Held*, that their entry was wrongful; and the employers were liable in damages for the value of the works despite the absence of a certificate, on the ground that they had prevented the builder from completing the works: *Smith* v. *Howden Union* (1890).[53]

(Note: It does not appear from the report of this case whether there was a forfeiture clause or not.)

(4) F. contracted to pull down some houses for W. by a certain time, and was to pay so much a working day by way of liquidated damages for delay. F. delayed beyond the fixed time, and on being asked if he could complete in four months said that he could not say. There was no other evidence of renunciation or abandonment of the work by the builder. W. entered after thirteen days and refused to let F. complete. *Held*, that the termination was wrongful. If W. wished to treat F.'s reply as an abandonment of the contract, he should so have informed him at once and not waited thirteen days and then acted without warning: *Felton* v. *Wharrie* (1906).[54]

(5) Plastering sub-contractors were told in September, 1956 that their work would soon be required. The main contractor later neglected to provide temporary heating (as required by the main contract) which slowed down progress considerably, and later in the year told the sub-contractors that they would not now be required till the following spring. They visited the site in March 1957 for an inspection, and made no protest till April 1957, when they were

---

[50] In *Heyman Constructions Ltd.* v. *Algrephy Ltd.* (February 1966, unreported) Sir Percy Lamb O.R. did so decide.

[51] 5 C.P. 310, illustrated more fully *ante*, pp. 407–408 and 628.

[52] 41 Ch.D. 248 at p. 258, more fully illustrated *ante*, Chap. 8, p. 561, see also *infra*, p. 711.

[53] Hudson's B.C., 4th ed., Vol. 2, p. 156, more fully illustrated *ante*, pp. 460–461.

[54] Hudson's B.C., 4th ed., Vol. 2, p. 398. This was a 42-day contract—see the case illustrated *ante*, Chap. 10, p. 613.

required to start work, but refused to do so unless a new price was
agreed. *Held*, the failure to provide heating and consequential delay
under the main contract, though it might have been a breach of an
implied term in that contract to proceed expeditiously, did not go
to the root of the sub-contract or constitute repudiation. Even if it
did amount to a repudiation, the sub-contractors had not elected
to treat it as such, but had continued to treat the contract as on
foot thereafter, and they were accordingly in breach of contract:
Pigott Construction Ltd. v. *W. J. Crowe Ltd.* (1961).[55]

In the last of the above cases, it will be seen that, had the sub-
contractors continued to work under protest, they might have recovered the equivalent of their new prices by way of damages against
the main contractors. The case underlines the importance in doubtful
cases of minimising the risk of a wrongful rescission or termination
by relying on the right to damages.

If forfeiture by the employer depends upon the quasi-judicial
determination by the architect of facts giving rise to the power, the
exercise of the power by the employer will not be wrongful if the
architect, though mistaken in his determination, has acted honestly
and in a quasi-judicial manner. But the clause conferring jurisdiction
on the architect must be carefully considered, since the courts are
reluctant to construe such a clause as empowering the certifier to
decide whether his employer or he himself has in fact caused the delay
complained of.[56] However, a decision by a certifier on a matter
giving rise to forfeiture can, like other certifier's decisions be disregarded if fraud or collusion or wrongful interference are established,
and in the majority of modern contracts will be subject to review by
an arbitrator, and hence by the courts.[57] In the event of review by an
arbitrator or the courts being permitted, a finding that the forfeiture
was unjustified would inevitably mean that the employer had repudiated the contract by a wrongful forfeiture, it is submitted.

(2) Remedies for Wrongful Forfeiture

Generally, the measure of damages in the case of a wrongful forfeiture falls to be determined by the ordinary common law rules.[58]

" The right of the appellant (the contractor) would be to recover

---

[55] 27 D.L.R. (2d) 258 (Canada), more fully illustrated *ante*, Chap. 5, pp. 338–339. See
also *Tannenbaum Meadows Ltd.* v. *Wright-Winston Ltd.* (1965) 49 D.L.R. (2d) 386,
ante, Chap. 5, p. 252.

[56] See *Roberts* v. *Bury Commissioners* (1870) L.R. 5 C.P. 310; *ante*, Chap. 7, pp. 407–
408, Chap. 11, p. 628, as distinguished in *Sattin* v. *Poole* (1901) Hudson's B.C.,
4th ed., Vol. 2, p. 306, *ante*, pp. 629–630.

[57] These subjects are fully discussed, *ante*, Chap. 7, Sections 4 and 5.

[58] See *ante*, Chap. 9, pp. 578–579, 596 *et seq.*

such amount of damages as would put him in as nearly as possible the same position as if no such wrong had been committed—that is, not as if there had been no contract, but as if he had been allowed to complete the contract without interruption." [59]

ILLUSTRATIONS

(1) P. agreed to build a ship for R., to be paid for by four instalments of £750. P. became bankrupt, and when the ship was nearly finished and all the instalments except the last were paid, R. wrongfully took possession of the ship and prevented completion. *Held*, that the assignees of the bankrupt P. were entitled to the £750 less the cost of what was still required to be done when the defendant took possession: *Woods* v. *Russell* (1822).[60]

(2) The plaintiff had practically completed a sewerage contract and the engineer fraudulently refused to certify. The defendants took possession of the works and certain plant. *Held*, that the plaintiff was entitled to damages for prevention of completion, such damages being what he would have been entitled to if he had completed and the engineer had certified; and judgment was given for the unpaid balance of the contract price, extras properly ordered, extras previously certified, and the value of the plant seized: *Smith* v. *Howden Union* (1890).[61]

But the builder is not restricted to suing for damages for breach of contract. He may, as an alternative, where he has elected to treat the contract as rescinded, sue upon a *quantum meruit*. This will enable him to seek to establish, if he can, that the contract rates were low or uneconomical.

ILLUSTRATION

L. guaranteed the due carrying out by M. of a contract to construct certain works for a borough council. M. made default and the council called upon L. under his guarantee. L. agreed with S. for the completion of the works by S. by a contract which provided that S. should be bound by the conditions of M.'s contract. L. left the supervision of the contract to the council, who prevented S. from proceeding with the expedition contracted for, and wrongfully seized the works. *Held*, that L. had made the council his agent, that, as the delay was caused by their acts, the re-entry could not be justified, and that S. was entitled to treat the contract as determined and sue for a *quantum meruit*, the measure of which was the actual value of the work, labour and materials, instead of bringing an action for damages for breach of contract: *Lodder* v. *Slowey* (1904).[62]

[59] *Per* Lord Cranworth in *Ranger* v. *G.W. Ry.* (1854) 5 H.L.C. at p. 72.
[60] 5 B. & Ald. 942.
[61] Hudson's B.C., 4th ed., Vol. 12, p. 156. (*Cf. Smith* v. *Gordon* (1880) 30 Up.Can.C.P. 552.)
[62] [1904] A.C. 442. [For a further discussion, see *ante*, Chap. 9, Price and Damages, pp. 601–602.]

Forfeiture under express provisions in the contract frequently involves seizure or use of plant. Where the forfeiture turns out to be wrongful, the builder will naturally be entitled to damages for any plant seized by the employer.

No injunction will ordinarily be granted to restrain the exercise of the powers given by a forfeiture clause, for the contractor can be amply compensated in damages if the forfeiture is wrongful, whereas if the contractor were allowed to continue the work, the court could not specifically enforce the contract, nor compel the due completion of his obligations.[63] (The foregoing view, and the remainder of this chapter, must be regarded as open to doubt in the light of the important recent decision of Megarry J. in the Chancery Division in the case of *Twickenham Garden Developments Ltd.* v. *Hounslow B.C.* (1970). This case is, however, currently under appeal to the Court of Appeal, and no useful comment can be made upon it until it is finally decided by the Court of Appeal or House of Lords.)

" To suppose, in a case like this, where, if the company are wrong, ample compensation in damages may be obtained by the contractor, that the company are to have a person forced on them to perform these works whom they reasonably or unreasonably object to (whereas there would be no reciprocity if the wrong were on the other side) for the purpose of compelling the performance of the works, is more than I am able to do." [64]

" The court cannot enforce specific performance of the works; it cannot look after the acts and conduct of the plaintiff, nor say how far he does or does not depart from what is right in executing the works or professing to execute them. If he is, or shall be wronged by his exclusion from the works, and by the act of the company in executing the works themselves, that will be a case for damages to be assessed and given, either in this court or in a court of law; but it is not a case for specific performance, or relief analogous to specific performance, which to proceed to grant an injunction on this part of the prayer of the bill would necessarily amount to." [65]

In the case of a ship-repairing contract, which provided that if the repairers failed to do the work the owners should be at liberty to enter the shipbuilder's yard and do the work, it was held by Lord Romilly M.R. that the court could not decree specific performance of the

---

[63] See also the discussion of this subject *ante*, Chap. 5, pp. 371 *et seq.*
[64] *Per* Knight Bruce L.J. in *Garrett* v. *Banstead and Epsom Downs Ry.* (1864) 12 L.T. 654. See also *Jennings* v. *Brighton Sewers Board* (1872) 4 De G.J. & S. 735n.
[65] *Per* Knight Bruce L.J. in *Munro* v. *Wyvenhoe, etc. Ry.* (1865) 12 L.T. 655.

contract, and would therefore not restrain the builder's trustee in bankruptcy from selling the dock in which the ship lay.[66]

But in the following case, where the court considered that the forfeiture clause and the arbitration clause should be read together, an interim injunction was granted restraining the employers pending the arbitration.

ILLUSTRATION

F. contracted with the corporation of H. to sink wells. By clause 2 of the contract it was provided that if any difficulty or dispute should arise between the council or the engineer and the contractor as to the mode of carrying out the work or the interpretation of the contract or otherwise in relation thereto, the same should be referred to arbitration. Clause 10 empowered the corporation to dismiss F. from the works, if in the judgment of the engineer the work was improperly conducted, or sufficient dispatch was not used. Under this latter clause the corporation dismissed F. from the works. F. moved for an injunction to restrain the corporation from doing this. Held, by Farwell J., the dispute was within the arbitration clause and there was an implied term that the employer would not act on the clause once the matter had been properly referred to arbitration until the decision of the arbitrator had been given. An injunction was granted until judgment or further order, or until the arbitrators should have held the judgment of the engineer correct: Foster and Dicksee v. Hastings Corporation (1903).[67]

[Note: This case was decided on an interlocutory application as a matter of urgency and, in so far as it relates to the granting of an injunction, may not be of general application. Farwell J. clearly doubted the bona fides of the engineer and was influenced by the fact that the employers had purported to act without any previous complaint.]

In certain cases a building owner will be restrained from using or selling materials or plant seized by him, where the loss sustained by him upon a forfeiture has not been ascertained, but this is, of course, an entirely different situation involving the contractor's and not the employer's property.

ILLUSTRATION

Employers took the works out of a contractor's hands and completed them. By the terms of the contract the employers might sell the contractor's plant and apply the money in or towards the satisfaction of losses and expenses. Held, that they could not do so until it was proved that losses and expenses had been sustained. An injunction was granted to restrain the employers from removing and selling the plant pending an arbitration: Garrett v. Salisbury and Dorset Railway (1866).[68]

[66] Merchants Trading Co. v. Banner (1871) L.R. 12 Eq. 18.
[67] 87 L.T. 736.
[68] L.R. 2 Eq. 358. See ante, Chap. 12, p. 676.

But as a general rule the builder cannot restrain the employer from forfeiting the contract, while the employer can restrain the builder from interfering with his taking the works out of the builder's hands, subject to an undertaking in damages if the court requires it.

ILLUSTRATION

R. contracted to construct a bridge for the C. corporation. The contract contained a condition that if, in the opinion of the engineer, R. was not making due progress, the corporation might enter and complete.   Under this condition the corporation gave notice to R. of their intention to enter.   R. refused to give up the works.   The corporation brought an action against R. and applied for an interlocutory injunction to restrain R. from preventing the corporation from taking up and completing the works.   *Held*, that the injunction should be granted on the corporation's undertaking in damages: *Cork Corporation* v. *Rooney* (1881).[69]

---

[69] 7 L.R.Ir. 191.

Chapter 14

ASSIGNMENT

(1) Generally

Assignment, in its strict sense, means the transfer of contractual rights to a stranger to the original contract, whether by operation of law or by an act of the person originally entitled to those rights, so as to enable the transferee to sue upon the contract himself. In considering this subject, it is essential to distinguish between contractual rights and liabilities, or, in other language which is sometimes used, between the benefit and burden of the contract.

In a building contract, speaking generally, the liability of the builder is to do work and supply materials, and of the employer to make due payment for them. The correlative rights of the parties are, on the part of the builder, to receive payment, and, on the part of the employer, to have the work done in accordance with the contract. Much of the difficulty of the law of assignment is due to the fact that the rules governing the subject have been evolved from comparatively simple contracts, such as money debts and contracts of sale, and the convenient dichotomy of benefit and burden and rights and liabilities is not so easy to observe in the case of more complicated contracts, of which not the least are building contracts.

English law does not recognise or permit the assignment of contractual *liabilities*, so as to extinguish the liability of the assignor, without the consent of the other party to the contract. Thus in *Tolhurst* v. *Associated Portland Cement Manufacturers* (1903) [1] Collins M.R. said [2]: " It is, I think, quite clear that neither at law nor in equity could the burden of a contract be shifted off the shoulders of a contractor onto those of another without the consent of the contractee. A debtor cannot relieve himself of his liability to his creditor by assigning the burden of the obligation to somebody else; this can only be brought about by the consent of all three, and involves the release of the original debtor."

[1] [1903] 2 K.B. 660.
[2] At p. 668.

So, in building contracts the employer cannot divest himself of the liability to pay for the work, or the builder of his responsibility for duly completing it, in the absence of a novation (that is to say, an agreement with the third party supported by consideration to which the other party to the original contract is also a party), or some act or conduct on his part acquiescing in the new arrangement.[3]

This is well illustrated by the case of *Young* v. *Kitchin* (1878),[4] where a builder validly assigned his right to payment under the contract, and his assignee sued upon the contract. The building owner was permitted to set off damages due to delay by the builder to the extent of the assignee's claim as an equitable set-off (or defence), but not to recover any excess, for which the builder-assignor remained liable.

Contracts of Novation (under which the rights and liabilities of one of the original contracting parties are extinguished altogether) require to be distinguished from contracts of guarantee or indemnity, where the original parties remain bound.[4a] Contracts of guarantee are dealt with *post* Chapter 17.

(2) Vicarious Performance of Contractual Liabilities

The above rule does not, however, prevent *vicarious performance* of contractual liabilities in the great majority of cases, so that a party to a contract may adequately discharge his obligations by arranging for performance by a third person. This is what happens every time a main contractor arranges, privately or by way of nomination, for any part of the work to be sub-contracted. This is not a case of assignment, even if it arises as an incident of a purported assignment of the contract, since the third person cannot be sued, and the assignor's rights and liabilities will remain unaffected. Thus in *Nokes* v. *Doncaster Amalgamated Collieries Ltd.* (1940)[5] Viscount Simon said [6]: " The rules of law restricting the assignability of contracts are, however, by no means limited to contracts of personal service. In the case of contracts for the sale of goods, for example (unless the contract expressly or by implication covers the purchaser and his assigns), the seller is entitled to rely on the credit of the purchaser and to refuse to recognise any substitute. Similarly, the purchaser is entitled to rely upon the seller and to hold him responsible for due performance. I may add that a possible confusion may arise from the use of

[3] See *e.g. Jaegers etc. Ltd.* v. *Walker* (1897) 77 L.T. 180.
[4] (1878) 3 Ex.D. 127, *infra*, Section 2.
[4a] See also *infra*, pp. 725–726.
[5] [1940] A.C. 1014.   [6] At p. 1019.

the word ' assignability ' in discussing some of the cases usually cited on this subject. Thus in *British Waggon Co.* v. *Lea* (1880), the real point of the decision was that the contract which the company had made with Lea for the repair of certain wagons did not call for the repairs being necessarily effected by the company itself, but could be adequately performed by the company arranging with the British Waggon Co. that the latter should execute the repairs. Such a result does not depend on assignment of contract at all. It depends on the view that the contract of repair was duly discharged by the Parkgate company by getting the repairs satisfactorily effected by a third party. In other words, the contract bound the Parkgate company to produce a result, not necessarily by its own efforts, but, if it preferred, by vicarious performance through a sub-contractor or otherwise."

In general, the law permits the vicarious performance of contractual liabilities except in the case of personal contracts where the personal skill, financial credit, or other characteristics of the contracting party, are regarded as of the essence of the contract.[7] Thus in *British Waggon Co.* v. *Lea* (1880) [8] Cockburn C.J. said: " Where a person contracts with another to do work or perform service, and it can be inferred that the person employed has been selected with reference to his individual skill, competency, or other personal qualification, the inability or unwillingness of the party so employed to execute the work or perform the service is a sufficient answer to any demand by a stranger to the original contract for the performance of it by the other party, and entitles the latter to treat the contract as at an end, notwithstanding that the person tendered to take the place of the contracting party may be equally well qualified to do the service."

Modern forms of building contract contain explicit provisions authorising or forbidding sub-contracts, and also providing for the selection or nomination of sub-contractors by the employer.[9] But in the absence of express provisions, the principle is that vicarious performance will not be permitted if the result will be to alter or prejudice the obligations or rights of the other party to the contract. Judged by this test, it is obvious that vicarious performance of the employer's liability to pay in building contracts cannot be objected to. On the other hand, though there is not a great deal of authority upon the point, it is suggested that the builder's general obligations in the more substantial building contract may be personal in this sense, and any

---

[7] As *e.g.*, the contract of employment of an architect or engineer—see Chap. 16 pp. 793–794 *post.*
[8] 5 Q.B.D. at p. 153.   [9] See *post*, Chap. 15, Sub-contractors, pp. 740 *et seq.*

attempt to transfer performance of these particular obligations would be a breach of contract. A distinction ought, it is suggested, to be made between a builder's general obligations—*e.g.* to control and supervise the site organisation and labour force, and co-ordinate the works generally—and his obligation to complete the whole of the work in detail. In normal building work certain parts of the work, such as plumbing and plastering, are nearly always carried out by sub-contractors, and it is clear, it is submitted, that vicarious performance of these parts of the works would not be objectionable. Thus in *British Waggon Co.* v. *Lea* (1880) the court said [10]: " Much work is contracted for, which it is known can only be executed by means of sub-contracts; much is contracted for as to which it is indifferent to the party for whom it is to be done, whether it is done by the immediate party to the contract, or by someone on his behalf."

While, therefore, it is submitted that a considerable degree of sub-contracting is permissible, and that this will include parts of the work billed to be carried out by the builder—*e.g.* bricklaying or plastering—there may be obligations, particularly in larger contracts, which a builder cannot transfer, depending on the circumstances surrounding the selection of the builder and the particular contract in question. If this view is correct, then a trustee in bankruptcy or liquidator of a sub-contractor for the whole of the work will not be able to complete a contract of this kind without the consent of the building owner.[11] This must, however, be regarded as a very difficult question which has not yet been fully considered by the courts, and though it frequently arises in cases of bankruptcy or insolvency, is unlikely to arise in practice in other cases if a standard form of contract is employed, since these contain express prohibitions on " assigning " or " sub-letting " without consent which, while not very precisely worded in legal terms, appear to be aimed at preventing vicarious performance rather than true assignment.[12] The reason why there is a dearth of authority in cases of insolvency is probably that the financial consequences to an employer of a contract abandoned in " mid-stream ", with only an insolvent debtor to look to for reparation, are so serious that an election by the trustee or liquidator to continue with the contract is financially so attractive that it is unlikely to be resisted.

[10] At p. 154.

[11] See *post*, Chap. 16, Bankruptcy and Liquidation, p. 775, and see *Knight* v. *Burgess* illustrated *infra*.

[12] Clause 17, 1963 R.I.B.A. forms, clause 3, 1955 I.C.E. form. See also *infra*, Section 5 (6), pp. 734–735.

ILLUSTRATIONS

(1) R., a coachmaker, contracted to let D. a carriage for five years and keep it in repair and to paint it once during that term. At the time S. was an undisclosed partner with R., but D. only knew of and contracted with R. Three years afterwards D. was informed that R. had retired from business, and that S., his successor, would do the repairs in future. D. refused to deal with anyone but R., and returned the carriage. *Held*, that he was entitled to do so: *Robson* v. *Drummond* (1831).[13]

(2) A contractor commenced and partially completed a chapel which he had undertaken to build. The contract contained a power of determination in the event of his default. The contractor became financially embarrassed, and discharged his workmen, and, two days after notice had been given under the determination clause, assigned all his assets to trustees for the benefit of his creditors. The trustees corresponded with his employers, who eventually insisted on the forfeiture. The trustees asked for a declaration that they were entitled to the benefit of the contract and to complete the work themselves, and for an injunction against the employers. *Held*, the contract was personal to the contractor and the trustees could not be substituted for him by any assignment, voluntary or otherwise. *Per* Stuart V.-C.: " What is to be considered here is the right of those who are called ' the contractors ' and who have now wholly disappeared from the scene to appoint . . . any other person to set out the work and perform all those personal obligations which they have undertaken ": *Knight* v. *Burgess* (1864).[14]

(3) The plaintiff and another were joint sub-contractors under the defendant to " clean up " certain timber land, *i.e.* remove trees. The other joint sub-contractor assigned to the plaintiff, who completed the work, and sued the defendant for the price. The defendant pleaded that he had not assented to the assignment. *Held*, that there was no reason making it necessary that he should assent, and that he was liable whether he had assented or not: *Smith* v. *Mayberry* (1878).[15]

(4) A wagon company let to the defendant a number of railway wagons for a term of years, and agreed to keep them in repair. The company was dissolved and the contract assigned to another wagon company, who were ready and willing to repair the wagons. The repairs were, *per* Cockburn C.J., " a rough description of work, which ordinary workmen conversant with the business would be perfectly able to execute," and the defendant, in entering into the contract, could not be supposed to have " attached any importance as to whether the works were done by the company or by anyone with whom the company might enter into a sub-contract to do the work." *Held*, that the repair of the wagons by the company to whom the contract was assigned was a sufficient performance by the plaintiffs of their agreement to repair: *British Waggon Co.* v. *Lea* (1880).[16]

[13] 2 B. & Ad. 303.
[14] 33 L.J.Ch. 727.
[15] 13 Nev. 427.
[16] 5 Q.B.D. 149.

(5) J. contracted to supply to R. iron plates of a certain quality. J. was a manufacturer of, and not a dealer in, the iron plates. J. closed his works and tendered to R. iron plates of the specified quality, but made by another maker. R. rejected them, on which J. brought an action for breach of contract. *Held*, (1) that evidence was admissible of a custom that where a customer ordered iron plates from a manufacturer, he was entitled to reject plates not of the manufacturer's own make; (2) that even without such evidence the contract implied that the plates supplied should be of J.'s own make: *Johnson* v. *Raylton* (1881).[17]

(6) The defendants contracted to supply a coal merchant with 10,000 tons of coal extending over a period of two years. The coal merchant's business, which he had been carrying on for some years, consisted in carting coals from the defendants' depots and selling it in small quantities to the working-classes in the district. The coal merchant assigned the contract to the plaintiff, who had no experience of the coal trade. *Held*, that there was that degree of difference between the coal merchant's and the plaintiff's knowledge of the business which constituted an element of confidence personal to the coal merchant, and which rendered the contract unassignable: *Cooper* v. *Micklefield Coal and Lime Co.* (1912).[18]

(7) A contractor undertook to pave certain streets and maintain the surface in good condition for ten years. *Held*, the contract was not personal and could be assigned: *Asphaltic Limestone Co.* v. *Glasgow Corporation* (1907).[19]

SECTION 2. ASSIGNMENT OF CONTRACTUAL RIGHTS

(1) Generally

English law at first refused to permit the assignment of contractual *rights*, but drastic inroads upon this restriction were made, first by the Courts of Equity, and secondly, by statute.[20]

Contractual rights under building contracts are legal, as opposed to equitable, in character. An assignment of these rights may be " absolute," that is to say, the assignor may have transferred all his rights under the contract without qualification. This will include an assignment with an express or implied proviso for reassignment to the assignor upon repayment by the assignor of a loan, or some other event.[21] On the other hand, the assignment may be " conditional," in that the assignment may be expressed to come to an end (or,

---

[17] 7 Q.B.D. 438 (C.A.).
[18] 107 L.T. 457.
[19] 1907 S.C. 463.
[20] For a full history and analysis of the present law, see Cheshire and Fifoot, *Law of Contract*, 4th ed., Part VI, Chap. 3.
[21] *Tancred* v. *Delagoa Bay & East Africa Ry.* (1889) 23 Q.B.D. 239; *Hughes* v. *Pump House Hotel Co.* [1902] 2 K.B. 190 (*infra*).

indeed, to come into existence) automatically upon some future event without any further act of assignment or reassignment by the parties. The procedural importance of this distinction is explained *infra*, subsection (2), and its substantive importance in the *Durham Brothers* case illustrated *infra*.

ILLUSTRATIONS

(1) T. was a creditor of the defendants for work done and plant and materials supplied to an amount which was, subsequent to the assignment, but previous to the action, ascertained under an award as £31,109. By an indenture between G. and T., reciting the contract with the defendants, a previous advance by G., an agreement to advance £5,000 more, and a further sum not exceeding £10,000, T., after covenanting to repay with interest such advances, assigned to G. all sums of money due or to become due to him, T., from the defendants, subject to a proviso for redemption on re-payment of all moneys due. G. was held entitled to sue the defendants on this assignment: *Tancred* v. *Delagoa Bay etc. Railway* (1889).[22]

(2) A firm of builders delivered a document to the plaintiffs as follows: " In consideration of money advanced from time to time we hereby charge the sum of £1,086, which will become due to us from . . . Robertson on the completion of the above buildings as security for the advances, and we hereby assign our interest in the above-mentioned sum *until the money with added interest be repaid to you.*" The plaintiffs gave notice to Robertson and sued for the sums due. *Held*, following *Tancred* v. *Delagoa etc. Railway*,[23] that while an assignment under a mortgage with an express proviso for reassignment on redemption was an absolute assignment, as the mortgagor-assignor would have to give notice on the reassignment to the original debtor and the latter would know with certainty in whom the legal right was vested, and while that principle ought not to be confined to cases where there was an express provision for reassignment, the present assignment was nevertheless conditional because of the use of the words " until the money . . . be repaid," which limited the assurance to Robertson, and consequently the plaintiffs, having sued alone, could not succeed: *Durham Brothers* v. *Robertson* (1898).[24]

(3) A building contractor, in consideration of an overdraft from his bankers, executed an instrument by way of continuing security to them for all money due or falling due or to become due under his building contracts, and empowering them to settle all accounts in connection with the works and to give receipts for the moneys assigned, and to sue for and take any steps necessary to enforce payment. Notice in writing was given to the building owners. *Held*, following the reasoning in *Durham Brothers* v. *Robertson*,[25] that the principle relating to mortgages was not confined

---

[22] 23 Q.B.D. 239.
[23] *Supra*.
[24] [1898] 1 Q.B. 765.
[25] *Supra*.

to cases where there was an express proviso for reassignment, and the assignment was absolute: *Hughes* v. *Pump House Hotel Co.* (1902).[26]

An assignment may also be by way of charge only, in which case the right or fund in question is never actually transferred, but the chargee is given a right to payment out of that right or fund. An assignment may also be of part only of the rights or sum due under the contract. And, finally, an assignment may relate only to a future contractual right—*e.g.* a builder may assign rights under any contracts to be undertaken by him in the future—which, however expressed, can only operate as an agreement to assign. On the other hand, an assignment of rights not yet accrued under an existing contract is valid.[27]

(2) Statutory Assignments

The importance of distinguishing absolute assignments is that only these can qualify as *statutory* assignments under section 136 of the Law of Property Act 1925. This section provides that absolute assignments in writing of any debt or other legal thing in action of which express notice in writing is given to the debtor or other person from whom the assignor would have been entitled to claim are effective to transfer the legal right as from the date of the notice. The effect of this section is procedural, and means that, as from the date of *receipt* of the notice,[28] the assignee may sue upon the contract *in his own name*, without joining the assignor in the proceedings, and may give a good discharge for the contractual obligation involved without the consent of the debtor. No consideration is necessary to support such an assignment.[29] But the notice must be accurate in all substantial respects, so that if, for instance, it mis-states the date of the assignment, it will be invalid as a statutory assignment.[30]

In building contracts it is not unusual to find that a builder in financial difficulties will assign moneys due or to become due under a contract,[31] and an assignment of the retention moneys alone is also not uncommon in practice. An assignment of the latter kind was held to qualify as a valid statutory assignment in *G. & T. Earle Ltd.* v. *Hemsworth R.D.C.* (1928),[32] but in view of the later decision in

---

[26] [1902] 2 K.B. 190.
[27] See Section 5 (2) *infra*.
[28] *Holt* v. *Heatherfield Trust Ltd.* [1942] 2 K.B. 1.
[29] *Re Westerton* [1919] 2 Ch. 104.
[30] *W. F. Harrison & Co. Ltd.* v. *Burke* [1956] 1 W.L.R. 419 (or if the amount of the debt is wrongly stated, *per* Denning L.J., *ibid.*).
[31] See Section 5, *infra*.
[32] 44 T.L.R. 758, *infra*, p. 729.

Williams v. *Atlantic Assurance* (1933),[33] that an assignment of part only of a debt cannot qualify as a statutory assignment, it is suggested that an assignment of the retention moneys only, and not of all sums due, may not so qualify.[34]

(3) Equitable Assignments

Even if an assignment cannot qualify as a *statutory* assignment, either because it is not in writing, or because notice is not given, or because it is conditional, or by way of charge only, or of part only of the debt, it may nevertheless be a valid *equitable* assignment. An equitable assignment may be perfectly effective despite its being by word of mouth only, and equally need not be supported by consideration,[35] though the completed transfer of the right in question must be plainly evinced. Nor need notice to the debtor be given, though this is highly desirable from the assignee's point of view, since by doing so priority against any other assignee will be obtained, and the risk of the debtor's obligation being discharged by payment to the assignor avoided.

The procedural effect of an equitable assignment is that the assignee cannot sue in his own name alone, but must join the assignor as co-plaintiff or, if he will not agree, as co-defendant.[36] The necessity of this in all cases of non-absolute assignment is obvious, since the court and the debtor will be concerned with the state of accounts as between the assignor and assignee.[37] For the same reason, an assignor under an equitable assignment may not sue alone, at any rate once notice of the assignment has been given.[38]

ILLUSTRATION

Plastering sub-contractors claimed that £1,808 was due to them by the main contractors. The sub-contractors had entered into an arrangement with their own suppliers and with the main contractors whereby the latter were given an irrevocable authority to pay £1,558 to the suppliers as a good and sufficient discharge of the money due for the plastering work to the extent of the sum so paid. *Held,* the arrangement amounted to an assignment to the suppliers by way of charge of part of the alleged debt due to the plastering sub-contractors, who could not sue for the work done without joining the suppliers: *Walter & Sullivan Ltd.* v. *J. Murphy & Sons Ltd.* (1955).[39]

[33] [1933] 1 K.B. 81.
[34] Both the above decisions are Court of Appeal decisions. The assignment would, of course, be perfectly valid as an equitable assignment: see *e.g. Ex p. Moss, re Toward* (1884) 14 Q.B.D. 310, *post,* Chap. 16, p. 794.
[35] *Holt* v. *Heatherfield Trust Ltd.* [1942] 2 K.B. 1.
[36] *Bowden's Patent Syndicate Ltd.* v. *Herbert Smith & Co.* [1904] 2 Ch. 86.
[37] See the *Durham Brothers* case, *supra.*
[38] See *e.g. Re Steel Wing Co. Ltd.* [1921] 1 Ch. 349 (assignment of part of the debt).
[39] [1955] 2 Q.B. 584.

(4) Assignment of Personal Contracts

It has already been pointed out, in relation to the vicarious performance of contractual liabilities, that vicarious performance will
not be permitted in so-called " personal contracts " where this would
prejudice the position of the other party to the contract. This principle is in fact of wider application—for instance, it will prevent an
undisclosed principal from suing on such a contract where the agent
has expressly described himself as principal,[40] and it will also prevent
the assignment of contractual rights in such a case.

By the nature of building contracts, it is not likely that an assignment of the parties' *rights*, whether of the builder to receive the price
or of the employer to have the work done according to the contract,
can prejudice the other party to the contract. In certain very special
cases, it is conceivable that an assignment by the employer in a contract where the work was not very clearly defined, or to a large extent
provisional, and wide powers to order variations were available,
might prejudice the builder, depending upon the requirements or
standing of the proposed assignee. But usually this will not be so.
The following illustrations are not, it will be noted, building cases.

ILLUSTRATIONS

(1) Owners of chalk pits contracted to supply all the chalk
requirements for fifty years of a company operating a cement
works. The cement manufacturers assigned their whole undertaking, including the benefit of their various contracts. *Held*, the
chalk pit owners were bound to continue to supply the requirements of the works for the new company: *Tolhurst* v. *Associated
Portland Cement* (1903).[41]

(2) A provision merchant agreed to supply a cake manufacturer
with all the eggs he should require for his business for one year,
the manufacturer undertaking not to purchase eggs elsewhere
during that period provided the merchant was able to supply them.
During the year the manufacturer transferred his business to a bakery
company with branches all over the country, whereas the manufacturer had only three places of business. *Held*, distinguishing
Tolhurst's case, *supra*, on the ground that the contract there was to
supply the needs of a particular place (the cement works), that the
contract was personal and could not be assigned: *Kemp* v. *Baersel-
man* (1906).[42]

(5) Notice

As already stated, notice of an assignment to the debtor or party
liable is procedurally essential for a statutory assignment, and while

---

[40] See *Humble* v. *Hunter* (1848) 12 Q.B. 310.
[41] [1903] A.C. 414.
[42] [1906] 2 K.B. 604.

not essential in the case of equitable assignments, is highly desirable from the point of view of the assignee, in preventing the obligation being discharged by payment or performance of the obligation by the other party to the contract to the assignor, and in securing priority as against other possible assignees. Only the statutory notice need be in writing (except in the case of equitable interests in land or personalty, under section 137 (3) of the Law of Property Act 1925, but this is not likely to arise in building contracts). No particular form is required, but the notice must be clear and unambiguous. The fact of assignment should be stated, and the debtor informed that the assignee is by virtue of the assignment entitled to payment or performance of the obligation. A mere indication that payment may be made to a third party as agent for the creditor is insufficient.[43]

(6) Assignee takes Subject to Equities

Assignees, whether under statutory or equitable assignments, take subject to all defences available against the assignor, including equitable set-offs (*i.e.* counter-claims for damages arising out of the same contract or transaction which rank as a defence up to but not exceeding the amount of the claim. The excess thereafter represents a true counter-claim and not a set-off).

ILLUSTRATION

A builder assigned to the plaintiff money due from the defendant building owner on completion of the building. *Held*, the defendant might set-off any damages caused by delay of the builder to the extent of the claim, but might not recover damages in excess of the claim against the plaintiff: *Young* v. *Kitchin* (1878).[44]

SECTION 3. NEW CONTRACT WITH THIRD PERSON

This may either take the form of a novation, in which, under a tripartite agreement the original contractor is released from, and the third party assumes, his obligations, or of a simple agreement between the third party and the employer whereby the employer undertakes to pay the third party, usually in consideration of the third party assuming the responsibilities of the original contractor.

These are not cases of assignment at all, but bring a new contract into existence on which either party can sue. The substitution may be

---

[43] See *Percival* v. *Dunn* (1885) 29 Ch.D. 128 (*infra*), Section 5 (4) p. 731.
[44] 3 Ex.D. 137. (This subject is further discussed in detail, *infra*, Section 5, pp. 731 *et seq*.)

by express agreement, or it may be implied from the conduct of the
parties, though such an implication will be comparatively rare.[45]

In arrangements of this kind, it is important for the parties to
define clearly what responsibilities or liabilities of the original contractor are being assumed by his substitute—for instance, the liability
for liquidated damages for delay.[46]

SECTION 4.   UNASSIGNABLE RIGHTS

(1) Bare Right of Litigation

Certain rights are by reason of their nature not permitted to be
assigned.   Thus an assignment of a bare right of litigation offends
against the principles of the tort of maintenance, and will not be
permitted,[47] unless the right to sue is ancillary to a right of property,
as in the case of a dilapidations claim under a lease.[48] Applying this
principle to building contracts, an assignment by the employer of
the right to have the work done would probably come within the
exception above stated, since such an assignment would usually
accompany an assignment of the land on which the building was being
erected, and the assignee could accordingly sue for damages under
the building contract. On the other hand such an assignment after
the building was completed, or an assignment by the builder of a right
to damages, as opposed to moneys due, would offend against the
principle, and the assignee would be unable in either case to sue.[49]

(2) Rights of Seizure and Forfeiture

Certain rights under a contract otherwise assignable may also be so
personal in nature as not to pass upon an assignment of the benefit
of the contract. Thus in hire-purchase agreements, the right of the
owner to enter and seize in default of payment has been held to be a
right personal to the original owner, and hence not to pass on an
assignment of the benefit of the agreement.[50] Despite the closeness of
the analogy, there can be little doubt that this will not apply to an

---

[45] See *Re European Assurance Association, Conquest's Case* (1875) 1 Ch.D. 334; *Scarf* v. *Jardine* (1882) 7 App.Cas. 345 and *Head* v. *Head* [1894] 2 Ch. 236.
[46] See *Re Yeadon Waterworks Co. & Wright* (1895) 72 L.T. 832, *ante*, Chap. 11, p. 634.
[47] *Prosser* v. *Edmonds* (1835) 1 Y. & C.(Ex.) 481; *Glegg* v. *Bromley* [1912] 3 K.B. 474.
[48] See *Ellis* v. *Torrington* [1920] 1 K.B. 399.
[49] See, however, the Scottish case of *Constant* v. *Kincaid* (1902) 4 F. (Ct. of Sess.) 901, where a bankrupt shipbuilder was permitted to assign to the shipowner a right of action for damages against a sub-contractor.
[50] *Ex p. Rawlings, re Davis* (1888) 22 Q.B.D. 193 applying *Brown* v. *Metropolitan Counties Life Assurance Society* (1859) 28 L.J.Q.B. 236.

assignment by a building owner of his rights under a building contract, since in most cases any right of determination or forfeiture in
the contract is exercisable by the architect rather than the owner himself, and in any event it is illogical and impractical so to emasculate
the rights of the employer upon an assignment. The hire-purchase
cases can be treated as depending on the highly personal nature of
the right to enter the home of another and seize his chattels, and is,
it is submitted, easily distinguishable from the employer's right to
re-enter his own land when faced with a recalcitrant builder.

(3) Arbitration Clauses

An example of the difficulties that may arise where isolated rights of
this kind are held to be personal upon an assignment of a complicated contract such as a building contract is to be found in relation
to the arbitration clause. Thus an assignment of " all moneys due
or to become due under the contract " by a builder was held not to
pass the right to arbitration, and consequently an arbitrator had
jurisdiction to entertain a claim by the builder, but, his right to the
moneys having been assigned, was bound to find against him: *Cottage
Club Estates Ltd.* v. *Woodside Estates Co. Ltd.*[51] Wright J. in that
case stated that the benefit of an arbitration clause was personal and
could not be assigned, but this view is inconsistent with section 4 (1)
of the Act of 1950, and was rejected in *Aspell* v. *Seymour* (1929),[52]
where an assignee of all the builder's rights sued in his own name,
and a stay was ordered on the application of the building owner, and
in *Shayler* v. *Woolf* (1946).[53] It is submitted that Wright J.'s decision
cannot really be upheld on principle. An assignment confers a right
to sue. The contract provides that a method of suing available to the
parties is arbitration. The assignee has the benefit of this clause, and
it seems inconceivable that the other party can lose the right to go to
arbitration merely because there has been an assignment of the
benefit of the contract. Nor is it clear how an assignee being given
the right to arbitrate (as opposed to suing in the courts) can possibly
prejudice the other party who has signed a contract referring disputes
to arbitration. Other considerations might just possibly apply to a
submission of a specific dispute to arbitration (as opposed to the
general submission of future disputes, which is the essential feature
of arbitration clauses) but it is submitted that the decision cannot be
supported in regard to ordinary arbitration clauses.

[51] [1928] 2 K.B. 463.   [52] [1929] W.N. 152.
[53] [1946] Ch. 320 (*per* Morton L.J. at p. 323).

An assignee should nevertheless make certain that the wording of an assignment is sufficient to pass the right to arbitrate.

SECTION 5.   ASSIGNMENT OF MONEYS DUE

(1) Generally

The foregoing sections of this chapter have dealt with the more general aspects of the law of assignment, but in practice the commonest examples of assignment in connection with building contracts are assignments by the builder of moneys due or to become due under the contract, usually in consideration of the provision of credit facilities or other financial accommodation by the assignee.[54]   It is proposed in this section to examine the practical effect of the foregoing rules on transactions of this kind.

(2) Moneys not yet Due

It is no objection to an assignment that the moneys assigned are not yet due, and when the expectancy falls into possession the assignment will operate effectively and bind the subject-matter of the agreement to assign.   A future debt of this kind is within the requirements of section 136 of the Law of Property Act 1925.[55]

ILLUSTRATIONS

(1) A bill of sale assigned to the mortgagee all book debts due and owing or which might during the continuance of the security become due and owing to the mortgagor.   *Held*, a subsequent assignee of the mortgagee received a good title to a debt accruing due after the bill of sale, and notice having been served on the debtor prior to the mortgagor's bankruptcy, his title defeated the trustee in bankruptcy: *Tailby* v. *Official Receiver* (1888).[56]

(2) G. contracted to build a ship for the defendant for £1,375, £900 to be paid in various instalments according as the work progressed, and the residue on the certificate of completion.   G. being in difficulties, the defendant, in order that the ship might be finished, advanced him from time to time sums amounting on October 27, 1876 to £1,015, which was in excess of the amount then due, or, it would seem, earned, since the last instalment did not become due till November 23, 1876, and the residue not till February 11, 1877.   On October 27, G. borrowed £100 from the plaintiff, and assigned to him £100 out of moneys " to become due " from the defendant.   The defendant had due notice of this, but, notwithstanding, subsequently advanced money to an amount

---

[54] Examples of this have already been seen in the illustrations in Section 2, *supra*.
[55] *Holroyd* v. *Marshall* (1862) 10 H.L.C. 191; *G. & T. Earle Ltd.* v. *Hemsworth R.D.C.* (1928) 44 T.L.R. 758.   [56] 13 App.Cas. 523.

greatly exceeding £100 to G. *Held*, by Bramwell L.J. and Cotton L.J. (Brett L.J. dissenting), that the defendant was liable to pay the £100 to the plaintiff, the assignment being a good and equitable one, and that the right of the plaintiff could not be defeated by a voluntary payment by the defendant to G., or by any subsequent equity: *Brice* v. *Bannister* (1878).[57]

(3) A building contract provided for interim payment and for 10 per cent. retention. The builders assigned to certain suppliers " all moneys now or hereafter to become due to us . . . for retention moneys." Notice in writing was given at once to the employers. Later the employers paid the retention moneys to the receiver for debenture holders of the builders. The suppliers brought an action against the employers, who raised no question of priorities, but pleaded that the builders as assignors should have been joined. *Held*, the retention money, though not becoming payable till after the assignment, was a debt or legal thing in action which could be assigned within the terms of the Law of Property Act, and could be sued for without joining the assignors as parties: *G. & T. Earle Ltd.* v. *Hemsworth R.D.C.* (1928).[58]

[Note: Where a conflict arises between the interest of an assignee and a trustee or liquidator, an assignment of moneys to become due will be valid against the trustee only if the moneys have been earned at the date of the bankruptcy, even if not actually due or payable.[59]]

(4) Clause 11 (*h*) of the standard F.A.S.S. form of sub-contract provided that, to the extent that the amount retained by the employer under the main contract included any retention money under the sub-contract, the main contractor's interest in the money was fiduciary as trustee for the sub-contractor. The main contractor went into voluntary liquidation after completion of the work but before the expiry of the maintenance period. *Held*, the provision effected a valid equitable assignment of the relevant part of the retention moneys in favour of the sub-contractor, who was accordingly entitled to them whether in the hands of the employer or of the liquidator: *Re Tout and Finch* (1954).[60]

The last of the above decisions is now of increased importance, since similar wording has been inserted in the post-1963 standard R.I.B.A. forms of contract in relation to retention moneys *of the main contractor* so as to create a trust in favour of the main contractor binding on the employer and, on the authority of the above case, on the latter's assignees, trustee or liquidator.[61] It does not, however, appear to have been appreciated that retention moneys for the main

[57] 3 Q.B.D. 569 (C.A.). (And see *May* v. *Lane* (1894) 64 L.J.Q.B. 236; *Western Waggon and Property Co.* v. *West* [1892] 1 Ch. 271.)

[58] 44 T.L.R. 758. (But see *Williams* v. *Atlantic Assurance* [1933] 1 K.B. 81, where the Court of Appeal held that an assignment of part of a debt could not qualify as a statutory assignment.)

[59] See *Ex p. Nicholls*, *re Jones* (1883) 22 Ch.D. 782, as explained in *Ex p. Moss*, *re Toward* (1884) 14 Q.B.D. 310, and the cases cited, *post*, Chap. 16, Bankruptcy and Liquidation, pp. 794–796.

[60] [1954] 1 W.L.R. 178.   [61] Clause 30 (4) (*a*).

contractor are never likely to be an identifiable fund in the hands of an employer to which the trust could attach, and in the absence of such a fund the provision amounts to little more than an attempt to obtain a preferential debt for the main contractor which, it is submitted, would fail. In a case like *Re Tout and Finch* (1954) the provision can often be effective because in such cases the money may be available and identifiable in the hands of a third party, the employer, at the time the sub-contractor wishes to assert his claim, and in any case can rank as an equitable assignment apart from any question of a trust being created. Even in the case of sub-contractor's retention moneys, however, should the retention moneys have been paid to the main contractor prior to his insolvency, the provision, in the absence of the possibility of tracing the funds in question, or of notice given to the employer, is also likely to fail, it is submitted, particularly since in such a situation the moneys, even if traceable, are likely to come into the hands of a purchaser for value without notice, such as the contractor's overdrawn bank account (where the bank will have the prior claim).[62]

(3) Notice to Building Owner

This is strongly advisable from the assignee's point of view for a number of reasons. First, provided the assignment is in writing and not conditional, or by way of charge only, or of part of the debt only (*e.g.* of retention moneys only and not other sums due under the contract) the fact of notice will entitle it to rank as a statutory assignment, and hence enable the assignee to sue in his own name without the expense of joining the assignor in the proceedings.

Secondly, the building owner who disregards the notice and pays the contractor and not the assignee will do so at his peril, and be liable to pay twice over.[63]

Thirdly, the assignee will thereby gain priority over any other assignees there may be who have not already given notice.[64] Even if no notice is given, however, an assignee for value takes priority over a subsequent garnishee, since the latter can only take under his order what could properly and without violation of the rights of others be dealt with by the judgment debtor.[65]

---

[62] See *Thompson* v. *Clydesdale Bank* [1893] A.C. 282.

[63] *Brice* v. *Bannister* (1878) 3 Q.B.D. 569.

[64] *Ward* v. *Duncombe* [1893] A.C. 369.

[65] *Pickering* v. *Ilfracombe Ry.* (1868) L.R. 3 C.P. 235; *Badely* v. *Consolidated Bank* (1888) 38 Ch.D. 238, and *Davis* v. *Freethy* (1890) 24 Q.B.D. 519; *Evans Coleman & Co.* v. *Nelson Construction* (1958) 16 D.L.R. (2d) 123 and see *post*, pp. 735 *et seq.*

(4) Form of Assignment

The assignment (which often may only be clearly evidenced by the terms of the notice to the debtor) must be intended to operate as an actual transfer of the right, and must specify the right or fund in question. A mere authority to the employer to pay someone as the agent of the builder will not operate as an assignment or a notice of the assignment.

ILLUSTRATIONS

(1) A railway contractor gave his bankers a letter directing the railway company to pass the cheques which might become due to him " to his account to the bank." *Held*, that this was not an equitable assignment, as it would have been if it had directed that the cheques should be passed to the credit of the bank: *Bell* v. *London & North Western Ry.* (1852).[66]

(2) The defendant, Dunn, being the agent for the owner of the Park Estate at Tottenham, let part of the estate to Davis under a building agreement, and agreed to make him advances from time to time as the buildings were erected. Davis being indebted to Percival, the plaintiff, a builder and brickmaker, for goods supplied for building, handed him the following order: " Dear Sir, please pay Percival the amount of his account and oblige, £42 14s. 6d. for goods delivered at Park. W. Davis. To J. Dunn." Money was then and subsequently due from Dunn to Davis, and notice was given of the above order. *Held*, by Bacon V.-C., that the defendant was not liable on this, as it was not an equitable assignment, but a mere polite note by one person asking some other person to pay his debt, and that it imposed no obligation upon that other person to pay the debt: *Percival* v. *Dunn* (1885).[67]

Provided, however, that the intention is clear, the language used is not important. Thus, speaking of an equitable assignment, Lord Macnaghten [68] said: " It may be addressed to the debtor. It may be couched in the language of command. It may be a courteous request. It may assume the form of mere permission. The language is immaterial if the meaning is plain."

There is no special requirement as to the person who should give the notice, and it would not seem to matter by whom it is given. Nor is there any limit of time for giving it (subject to the risk of other assignees acquiring priority).

(5) Equities

It has already been stated that the assignee, whether statutory or equitable, takes subject to equities, and that this includes claims for

[66] 15 Beav. 548.
[67] 29 Ch.D. 128.
[68] *Brandt's Sons & Co.* v. *Dunlop Rubber Co.* [1905] A.C. 454 at p. 462.

damages arising out of the same contract.[69] The effect of this upon an assignee's right to moneys due under a building contract may well be catastrophic, since despite the fact that substantial sums may have been earned and retained at the time of the assignment, the right to these may disappear upon some subsequent default of the builder, either by reason of a set-off by the employer, or because of the exercise of a power of forfeiture by the employer, which might, depending on the terms of the contract, prevent the retention moneys, or indeed any other sums, from becoming payable.

ILLUSTRATION

A contract provided for 25 per cent. retention. There was a power for the employer to employ another builder in the event of non-completion by a certain date. During the course of the work, the builder assigned to the plaintiff £200 out of moneys to accrue due under the contract. The builder went bankrupt after the completion date when the work was still unfinished. The employer wrote to the trustee indicating his intention to forfeit the contract. Later the trustee by agreement with the employer completed the work. *Held*, the trustee had not completed under the contract, but under a new agreement, and consequently the plaintiff could not claim the £200 as against the trustee: *Tooth* v. *Hallett* (1869).[70]

[Note: In so far as this case may suggest that an assignment of future payments is invalid against the trustee, it has been distinguished and explained in *Drew* v. *Josolyne* (1887).[71] As between a prior assignee of moneys to become due and the trustee in bankruptcy, the test is whether, at the date of the bankruptcy, the money had been earned by the work being done.[72] Normally, however, completion of the work by a trustee in bankruptcy will be a completion under the contract, and strong evidence that no power of forfeiture has in fact been exercised by the employer.[73]]

In the case of *Young* v. *Kitchin* (1878),[74] the right to the set-off in question existed at the date of the assignment, but equities subsequently arising under the contract are equally valid against the assignee.

ILLUSTRATION

A company agreed in 1881 with the Government of Newfoundland to construct 340 miles of railway from S. to H. by 1886, in consideration of grants of land and an annual subsidy, " to attach

[69] *Young* v. *Kitchin* (1878) 3 Ex.D. 127, *supra.* See also *Hanak* v. *Green* [1958] 2 Q.B. 9.
[70] L.R. 4 Ch.App. 242. (And see *Young* v. *Kitchin, supra,* p. 725.)
[71] (1887) 18 Q.B.D. 590. Illustrated, *post*, Chap. 16, Section 7, p. 795.
[72] See *post*, Chap. 16, Bankruptcy and Liquidation, pp. 794–796.
[73] See *Drew* v. *Josolyne* (1887) 18 Q.B.D. 590, illustrated on this point *ante*, p. 688, but see *Re Asphaltic Wood Pavement Co.* (1885) 30 Ch.D. 216, Chap. 16, *post*, pp. 776–777 (right to damages not affected).
[74] *Supra*, p. 725.

in proportionate parts . . . as and when each five mile section is completed and operated." In 1882 the company assigned a portion of its property and the subsidy to trustees for the bondholders. In 1886 only eighty-five miles were completed, and there was no probability of anything more being constructed. *Held*, that a proportionate part of the subsidies was payable for the specified term on the completion of each section. It was further held by the Judicial Committee that as against the assignee trustees the Government had a right to set off, against such proportionate payment of the subsidies for the eighty-five miles, a claim of damages for non-completion of the whole railway: *Newfoundland Government* v. *Newfoundland Railway* (1888).[75]

But set-offs arising from matters unconnected with the debt or contract assigned, or purely personal to the assignor, or not existing at the date of notice of the assignment, may not be raised against the assignee by the debtor. This class of case is not always easy to define.

ILLUSTRATION

One Price induced the defendant by fraudulent misrepresentations to purchase a newspaper, and assigned the unpaid balance of the purchase money to the plaintiff. Notice of the assignment was given, and the plaintiff sued the defendant for the money. The defendant took no steps to have the contract of sale rescinded, but brought in Price as a defendant to his counterclaim, and obtained judgment against him for damages for fraudulent misrepresentations. *Held*, that he could not set off those damages against the debt: *Stoddard* v. *Union Trusts Ltd.* (1912).[76]

On the other hand, the fact that a certificate of an architect has been given fraudulently and in collusion with the builder, in order to give him a title to receive money, may be set up by the employer as a defence to an action by the assignee of the builder. This is, of course, a breach of a term of the contract by the builder,[77] and not a mere representation inducing the contract as in *Stoddard's* case.

ILLUSTRATION

T. agreed, in 1874, to construct a reservoir for a local board for £3,983, to be paid for on certificates of an engineer, L., the last of which was given on February 15, 1876. This certificate was not paid because the reservoir would not hold water, and T. sued the board for £1,067 11s. 6d. as the balance certified to be due. This action was compromised by an agreement dated February 13, 1877, whereby the local board consented to pay T. £800 on

[75] 13 App.Cas. 199.
[76] [1912] 1 K.B. 181. (See also *Re Pinto Leite & Nephews, ex p. Des Olivaes* [1929] 1 Ch. 221.)
[77] (Of an implied term not to interfere with the certifier, see *ante*, Chap. 7, Section 5 (4) p. 458.)

August 12, 1877, and to take over the works. On February 24,
1877, T. assigned this £800 to the plaintiffs, who gave notice of
the assignment to the board. The board had the reservoir examined
in February, 1878, and it was proved in evidence that it was not
merely improperly, but fraudulently, constructed, and that L. and
T. had conspired together to defraud the board by false certificates
given by L. and presented by T. The board did not inform the
plaintiffs of the fraud, although they had been in correspondence,
till 1879. *Held*, by the Court of Appeal, that this defence being good
as against the assignor, the assignees could get no better title; that
the board were not bound by acquiescence and delay, and that the
plaintiffs could not recover: *Wakefield and Barnsley Banking Co.* v.
Normanton Local Board (1881).[78]

An equity does not cease to be an equity for this purpose if it is
prosecuted to judgment. So an assignee of a contract under which
the debtor has already obtained judgment for damages against the
creditor will be held bound to allow the amount of the judgment to
be set off against his claim.[79] Furthermore, the assignee will be bound
by all the conditions as to payment binding the assignor—*e.g.* the
necessity of obtaining a certificate.[80]

The building owner who has been notified of an assignment must
be careful to avoid any mitigation of the terms of the contract in
favour of the builder which may prejudice the position of the assignee,
for example by making advances to the builder, or he may have to
pay twice over.[81]

(6) Provisions against Assignment

Whether a stipulation in a contract prohibiting assignment of contractual *rights* (*e.g.* by the builder of moneys due or to become due)
is valid or not is open to doubt.[82]

In building contracts there is frequently a provision prohibiting
" assignment " of the contract or " sub-letting " of a portion of the
works by the builder without the consent of the building owner.[83]
In nearly all cases, such provisions on examination appear to be
aimed at prohibiting assignment of *liabilities* rather than rights, and
since the law does not in any event permit the assignment of liabilities,

---

[78] 44 L.T. 697 (C.A.); strictly, the fraud in this case was a defence to the action on the
compromise, it would seem. *Cf.* the case of a surety for due performance of a
contract where there has been fraud in obtaining the certificate, *ante,* Chap. 7, p.
457; *post,* Chap. 17, pp. 807–808.

[79] *Lawrence* v. *Hayes* [1927] 2 K.B. 111.

[80] See *per* Lord Blackburn in *Lewis* v. *Hoare* (1881) 44 L.T. 66.

[81] *Brice* v. *Bannister* (1878) 3 Q.B.D. 569, *supra.*

[82] See *Re Turcan* (1888) 40 Ch.D. 5, and *Re Griffin* (1898) 79 L.T. 442.

[83] *Cf.* clause 19 of the 1963 R.I.B.A. forms of contract, and clause 3 of the 1955 I.C.E.
form. This is not a fundamental term justifying rescission if broken.

it is in most cases also fairly clear that what is being sought to be prohibited is *vicarious performance* of the liabilities rather than their actual assignment.[84]

(7) Attachment of Moneys Due

Attachment is a form of execution available to a judgment creditor who, in his search for assets of the debtor against which to execute, discovers that some third person owes money to the judgment debtor. Such a debt can be attached by what is known to lawyers as a garnishee order, and once the order has been made absolute, the third party debtor (or garnishee) must discharge his liability by payment to the judgment creditor (or garnishor) and not to his original creditor (the judgment debtor). The whole transaction therefore has many similarities to an assignment of the third person's debt by the judgment debtor to the judgment creditor, but there are some important differences. Thus while debts arising in the future may be validly assigned, the power of attachment of debts is more limited, and an order of the court attaching a debt will only be valid if at the date of the order the debt was an existing debt, even though not then ascertained or ascertainable.[85] The attachment of debts earned or existing but not yet due or payable is however valid.[86] The application of these fine distinctions to building contracts has not surprisingly given rise to difficulty.[87]

ILLUSTRATIONS

(1) Judgment creditors of a nominated sub-contractor sought to garnish the moneys owing to him by the main contractor after the sub-contract work was complete but before any certificate relating to it had been issued under the main contract, which was in the pre-1963 R.I.B.A. form, and which by clause 24 provided that payments for nominated sub-contractors' work should not be due till issue of the architect's certificate. (This latter clause was held to have been incorporated in the sub-contract.) The main contractors had obtained all certificates except the final certificate, for which they had applied. *Held*, by the Court of Appeal, that there was no debt capable of being garnished by the judgment creditors: *Dunlop & Ranken Ltd.* v. *Hendall Steel Structures* (1957).[88]

(2) A sub-contract order form provided: " The amount certified by the Architect to be due in respect of the sub-contract work and

---

[84] See Section 1, *supra*.
[85] *O'Driscoll* v. *Manchester Insurance Committee* [1915] 3 K.B. 499.
[86] *Tapp* v. *Jones* (1875) L.R. 10 Q.B. 591.
[87] See also the closely analogous situation of assignment of such debts as between assignee and trustee or liquidator of the assignor, *post*, pp. 794 *et seq*.
[88] [1957] 1 W.L.R. 1102. See the comment on this rather difficult case *ante*, Chap. 7, p. 496, and the further comment *infra*.

any authorised variation thereof shall not become payable until
fourteen days after the receipt by the contractor of the appropriate
Architect's certificate and remittance from the employer." A judgment creditor of the sub-contractor garnished the main contractor's
debt at a time when the work was complete and when it was admitted
by the main contractor that some moneys would be due after certain
contra-accounts and claims, but before any architect's certificate
or remittance by the employer had been received. *Held*, by the
Supreme Court of Alberta, Appellate Division, following *O'Driscoll*
v. *Manchester Insurance Committee* (1915) [89] and not following *Dunlop
& Ranken Ltd.* v. *Hendall Steel Structures*,[90] that there was a debt,
though not yet payable, and it could accordingly be garnished by
the judgment creditor: *Sandy* v. *Yukon Construction Co. Ltd.* (1961).[91]

(3) Local authority employers terminated a contract under
clause 19 of the pre-1963 R.I.B.A. form of contract. At the time
there was some £1,700 of retention money in the council's hands.
On the following day judgment creditors of the contractor issued
a garnishee summons. *Held*, by the Court of Appeal, the retention
moneys were not yet due, and further by clause 19 no further moneys
were payable until completion of the work by the council and certification of their expenses. Accordingly there was no debt capable
of being garnished: *Grant Plant Hire* v. *Trickey* (1961).[92]

O'Driscoll's case, referred to in *Sandy* v. *Yukon Construction Co.
Ltd.*, was a case where a medical practitioner, by serving for a period
of time, had earned a right to be paid out of a pool a share which, at
the time of the garnishee order, could not yet be finally ascertained.
It does not appear from the report whether in the court's view an
action of some sort to recover the share could have been maintained.
It would seem clear on any view that a debt must be capable of being
attached if at the time of attachment an action can be brought for the
money concerned, even though the court may have to order an
inquiry as to the moneys due.[93]

In *Tapp* v. *Jones* (1875),[94] however, attachment was permitted of
a debt repayable by instalments not yet due at the time of attachment,
and this principle was approved in the judgments in the *O'Driscoll*
case.[95] Applying this reasoning to building cases, it would seem
strongly arguable, where work has been done but the price is not
yet payable by reason of the necessary certificate not having been
issued, or because the date for payment has not yet arrived (as in the

[89] [1915] 3 K.B. 499.
[90] *Supra*.
[91] 26 D.L.R. (2d) 254 (Canada).
[92] 105 S.J. 255.
[93] See *Olds Discount Ltd.* v. *Alldred*. (In chambers, March 1952; unreported, but
noted in the *Supreme Court Practice* under R.S.C., Ord. 49, r. 1.)
[94] (1875) L.R. 10 Q.B. 591.
[95] [1915] 3 K.B. 499. See also R.S.C., Ord. 49, r. 1, and notes thereunder.

case of retention moneys), that there is an existing debt though not yet payable. Thus Lord Blackburn, in a case involving the construction of a guarantee for the completion of building work, said of a clause in the usual form for payment upon a certificate of completion: " Upon the completion of the building there would be a debt due to Thick, but not payable until Griffith had certified the fact of completion." [96] This view appears to have been accepted in Canada in *Sandy* v. *Yukon Construction Co. Ltd.* (1961)[97] but rejected in the *Dunlop & Ranken* (1957) [97] and *Grant Plant Hire* [97] cases. There is much to commend the view of the Canadian court, and it is suggested that the matter requires reconsideration by the English courts.

There is a further separate ground for criticism of the *Dunlop & Ranken* case, since it appears that the main contractor, who had applied for a final certificate, might well have been in a position to arbitrate his claim under the arbitration clause (or, failing arbitration, to sue).[98] If so, it is difficult to believe that the terms of incorporation of the main contract into the sub-contract would not equally have permitted the sub-contractor, his own work being completed and the maintenance period (presumably) having expired, to arbitrate his claim or sue notwithstanding the absence of a certificate. From the report it does not appear that this aspect of the matter was considered by the Court of Appeal.

It should also be remembered that modern arbitration clauses in the United Kingdom appear to permit arbitration during the carrying out of the works of disputes over interim payment under the contract,[99] so that despite the absence of an interim certificate such claims can be pressed by arbitration, or, failing arbitration, in the courts.[1] In such cases it is clear, it is submitted, that when the date or other event on which interim certification depends has arrived, there is a debt not only existing but due and payable for the sums which should have been certified under the contract, and such a debt would, it is submitted, be attachable notwithstanding the absence or refusal of a certificate.

It has already been pointed out [2] that as between a garnishee and a prior assignee for value of a debt the latter's claim will prevail,

[96] *Lewis* v. *Hoare* (1881) 44 L.T. 66 at p. 67.
[97] *Supra.* This decision was, however, clearly right by virtue of the express provisions of clause 19 of the contract.
[98] See *ante*, Chap. 7, pp. 447, 494–496; Chap. 9, p. 574.
[99] See the case of *Farr* v. *Ministry of Transport* [1960] 1 W.L.R. 956, and the discussion *ante*, Chap. 7, pp. 494–496 and Chap. 9, p. 575.
[1] See *ante*, Chap. 7, Section 4, p. 447.
[2] *Supra*, subsection (3), p. 730.

contrary to the general rule, notwithstanding that notice to the debtor has not been given.

SECTION 6.   ASSIGNMENT BY OPERATION OF LAW

(1) Generally

Assignment of contractual rights can often arise by statute, *e.g.* a statute setting up a statutory corporation to take over the rights and liabilities of other persons. But the commonest examples in practice arise upon bankruptcy or liquidation, or upon the death of a contracting party.[3]

(2) Death

Upon the death of a contracting party, his rights and liabilities on non-personal contracts vest in his executors or administrators, and, to this extent, the liability of his estate is an exception to the general rule of law which prevents the assignment of contractual liabilities.[4] But the distinction between " personal " and other contracts remains of vital importance, since the former become void upon death and can have no future effect thereafter, though rights accrued at the date of death will be enforced.

ILLUSTRATION

S. was appointed, on December 5, 1865, as consulting engineer, to complete the construction of works on a railway line, to be completed in fifteen months, and his fee was £500 in five equal payments. He commenced, and received £100 in March 1866. He continued two quarters more, and soon after the end of the third quarter and before any payment beyond the £100 had been made, died intestate. Less than three-fifths of the whole work had been performed, but no default of the deceased was proved. *Held,* that notwithstanding that the contract was one of personal confidence, and therefore dissolved by death, and null for the future, the administrator might recover for the money due for work actually done, *i.e.* the £200 for the two quarters, and was not thrown back on *quantum meruit*: *Stubbs* v. *Holywell Railway* (1867).[5]

In such cases, the estate will not be liable for any damage arising from the death itself.[6]

On the other hand, where there is no personal element, both the burden and the benefit of the contract pass on the death, and

---

[3] The subject of bankruptcy and liquidation is dealt with, *post*, Chap. 16.
[4] See Section 1, *supra*. See also the discussion of death and illness of a contracting party, *ante*, pp. 360–361.
[5] L.R. 2 Ex. 311.
[6] See *e.g. per* Pollock C.B. in *Hall* v. *Wright* (1859) E.B. & E. at p. 793.

the same result will occur in a personal contract if the death is that of
the party whose personality is not material.

ILLUSTRATIONS

(1) The defendant employed the testator to erect a temporary
gallery and other woodwork for the purpose of a public dinner,
and shortly after the order was given, and before it was begun,
the testator died, and the plaintiffs, as executors, performed
the work, using the materials of the testator. *Held*, the executors
might recover for work done and materials supplied: *Marshall* v.
Broadhurst (1831).[7]

(2) W. engaged D. as a civil engineer in connection with certain
harbour works. W. covenanted for himself and his executors to
employ D. at a fixed salary for six years. W. raised D.'s salary,
and subsequently died. W.'s executors again raised D's salary but
dismissed him before the expiration of the term. *Held*, that the
agreement bound W.'s executors: *Davison* v. *Reeves* (1892).[8]

(3) The plaintiffs, a troupe of music-hall performers, contracted
with a partnership, consisting of the defendants and another person,
to give certain performances at a music-hall. The other member
of the partnership died before the contract was performed. The
plaintiffs had no knowledge of who composed the partnership.
Held, that the contract was not of such a personal character on the
part of the partnership as to be put an end to by the death of the
deceased partner: *Phillips* v. *Alhambra Palace Company* (1901).[9]

[7] 1 Cr. & J. 403.
[8] 8 T.L.R. 391.
[9] [1901] 1 K.B. 59.

CHAPTER 15

SUB-CONTRACTS

SECTION 1. GENERALLY

As has already been pointed out,[1] while there may be some doubt in
the case of the contractor's general obligations, *e.g.* to control and
supervise the site and labour-force, there is usually no objection to
vicarious performance of much of the work itself, in the absence of
contractual provisions to the contrary.

Such vicarious performance will in practice be secured by the
contractor entering into sub-contracts, some of which may be merely
sub-purchases of materials or fittings, from merchants and others,
some sub-purchases of what is in reality building work carried on off
the site in factory or workshop conditions, such as pre-cast concrete
units or joinery items, while others may be for the doing of work only
(that is to say, on the site), or for the supply of labour only, or for the
doing of work in connection and together with the supply of goods or
fittings, such as the work of erection or installation on the site of the
goods or fittings supplied. Furthermore, the growth of specialisation
in the building industry has led to the widespread use of substantial
sub-contracts involving not only the supply of materials and the
doing of work, but also responsibility for design by the sub-contractor [2]—examples are the structural steel or reinforced or precast
concrete frame of a large modern building, specialist piling and
foundation work, heating and ventilation, specialist roofing and
floors, metal windows, electrical work, and so on. Much of this latter
specialist work is placed with sub-contractors selected by the employer under a power reserved to him in the main contract.

Nominated sub-contracts of this kind can give rise to the most
serious anomalies and difficult legal problems for the building owner,
since when such a sub-contractor defaults in any way, the employer
will require to have a suitable remedy to recover his loss against either
the main contractor or the sub-contractor, and if the main contract
documents are not suitably drafted, may find himself without any
remedy at all, since in general he will have no direct right against the

[1] *Ante*, Chap. 14, Assignment, pp. 716 *et seq.*, 734–735.
[2] See the considerable discussion of this topic and of the abuses to which it is subject,
ante, Chap. 2, pp. 98, 129–131 and Chap. 5, pp. 277–278, 281–282, 294–304, 323–324.

sub-contractor, not being in contractual relations with him, and if the main contract is not explicit on the point, may not be able to show, under the scheme of nomination used in most modern contracts, any sufficiently explicit express or implied term of the main contract in relation to the sub-contract work.[3] Those concerned with drafting main contracts should therefore be particularly careful to fix the main contractor with the fullest responsibility in every respect for the work of nominated or selected sub-contractors. There is no hardship in this, since the main contractor, who under most modern forms of contract has wide powers to reject selected sub-contractors who will not enter into a suitable sub-contract (and who, it is submitted, has an implied right in any event to refuse such nominations[4]), or for any other good reason, can, when sued or suffering deduction at the hands of the employer, recover damages to an equivalent amount under the sub-contract against the sub-contractor. Any provision in or interpretation of the main contract absolving the main contractor from responsibility for acts or defaults of a nominated sub-contractor[5] is open to the serious objection that it prevents the employer from recovering his loss from either party.

Draftsmen have traditionally sought to assert the undiminished responsibility of the main contractor for the nominated sub-contractor's work by the use of some such expression as " such persons are hereby declared to be sub-contractors employed by the contractor " or " shall be deemed to be sub-contractors of the contractor." This phrasing was adopted because certain decisions of the courts prior to the First World War had held that the contractor was entering into these sub-contracts as agent for the employer.[6] The expression has been most successful in its aims for a period of fifty years, but since the last edition of this book two recent decisions in the House of Lords[7] have thrown considerable doubt on the entire edifice and effectiveness of the system of nomination as it has hitherto been provided for in English contracts. It has already been submitted that of the many possible interpretations of the *Gloucestershire County Council* case, only the most limited of all should be accepted,[8] and

---

[3] For the scheme of nomination, see *infra*, Section 3.

[4] *Ante*, Chap. 5, pp. 301–302, 329 *et seq.*; *infra*, p. 764.

[5] See, for instance, the right of the main contractor to an extension of time for sub-contractor's delays in clause 23 (*g*) of the 1963 R.I.B.A. standard forms, and the stinging criticisms of this provision by Salmon L.J. in *Jarvis Ltd.* v. *Westminster Corporation*, cited *ante*, Chap. 11, pp. 650–652.

[6] See *infra*, pp. 751–753, 754–755.

[7] *Gloucestershire C.C.* v. *Richardson* [1969] A.C. 480; *Bickerton* v. *N.W. Metropolitan Hospital Board* [1970] 1 W.L.R. 607.

[8] *Ante*, Chap. 5, p. 304.

the consequences of the *Bickerton* case which held that there was a
duty on the employer to renominate a second sub-contractor whenever the original nominee repudiated his sub-contract obligations, and
which has already been fully considered,[8a] can confidently be pre-
dicted to occupy the time of the English courts for many years in an
effort to control and regulate the difficulties and anomalies to which
it must inevitably give rise. The whole of the remainder of this
chapter may need to be reconsidered in the light of that decision, the
full consequences of which it is too early to assess. It is suggested
that only compelling contractual wording and the most careful consideration of the consequences should permit the case to be followed
outside England.

In the case of ordinary sub-contractors not selected by the employer, no special legal difficulty arises, since their work is for all
legal purposes the work of the main contractor and is accordingly
covered by the detailed descriptions of the work and the express or
implied obligations of the main contractor contained in the main
contract.

SECTION 2. POSITION BETWEEN BUILDING OWNER AND
SUB-CONTRACTOR

It cannot be over-emphasised that no privity of contract between the
employer and the sub-contractor can arise out of a sub-contract concluded between the main contractor and the sub-contractor. Attempts
have been made from time to time to argue that the main contractor
or architect on the facts contracted as agent for the employer, and at
one time this view appears to have prevailed in the courts, at least in
relation to nominated or selected sub-contractors,[9] but it is clear that
only the most special and unusual facts, showing that the employer
expressly or by his conduct authorised the main contractor or the
architects so to contract, could justify such a finding, which is contrary to the sense of the usual main contract and the almost universal
practice in the building industry.[10]

The history of the cases in which the courts finally (and rightly)
rejected the notion of privity between the building owner and the
selected sub-contractor is shown in the cases illustrated at pp. 749–
754, *infra*, but under the present system of nomination, which is

---

[8a] *Ante*, Chap. 5, pp. 333 *et seq.*
[9] See *Crittall Manufacturing Co.* v. *London County Council* (1910) 75 J.P. 203 and
illustrations, *infra*.
[10] See *Hampton* v. *Glamorgan C.C.* [1917] A.C. 13, *infra*.

widely used and understood in the industry, it can often happen that architects will have to obtain quotations from and negotiate with tendering sub-contractors (particularly those whose work or products are subject to long delivery dates) during the planning stage of a project when the identity of the ultimately successful tendering main contractor is still unknown. In such cases it is generally well understood by the parties that the sub-contractor will in due course be required to enter into a sub-contract with the successful main contractor. Sub-contractors, however, even after accepting an order from the main contractor, sometimes seek to rebut the usual inference of privity with the main contractor if the main contractor becomes financially embarrassed, in an endeavour to charge the building owner for their work; and it is easier to advance such an argument in cases where their original pre-contract negotiations have taken place with the architect. The two modern cases now illustrated are examples of this type of situation.

ILLUSTRATIONS

(1) An architect, prior to letting the main contract, which was in the 1948 R.I.B.A. form, arranged with a nominated supplier of facing bricks for stocks to be held available for delivery by certain dates. In due course the main contractor placed his order, having been informed by the architect of the delivery arrangement. The supplier defaulted on his promised dates, and the architect authorised certain changes in the work to assist the contractors in the resultant shortage of bricks. The builders claimed extra payment on the ground that the arrangements for delivery and subsequent later changes in the work amounted to architect's instructions involving a variation. *Held,* by Sellers J., following *Leslie v. Metropolitan Asylums District,*[11] the delivery arrangements were part of the nomination, the main contractor was bound to supply the bricks by the stipulated dates, and the change in the work being authorised to assist him in a matter which was primarily his liability, no variation was involved: *Kirk & Kirk Ltd. v. Croydon Corporation* (1956).[12]

(2) A contract in South Africa contained a clause for the nomination of suppliers for all practical purposes identical with that in the R.I.B.A. standard forms. Reinforcement steel was billed as a P.C. item.[13] At an interview at which was present a representative of the employer, the architect, the main contractor and the supplier, the latter was asked by the architect to reduce his prices but refused to do so. The supplier stated he would require a deposit of £3,000 and complained about the main contractor being a slow payer, but was reassured by the employer's representative, who said that a substantial loan had been arranged and that the supplier would be paid monthly on the certificates issued to the main contractor by

---

[11] Illustrated *infra*, pp. 750–751. For the changes in the work, see the case illustrated *ante*, Chap. 8, p. 526.   [12] [1956] J.P.L. 585.

[13] *i.e.* it was to be supplied by a nominated sub-contractor—see *infra*, Section 3.

the architect. Later that day the architect wrote a letter to the supplier as follows: " On behalf of our clients (the employers) we accept your tender. . . . The sum of £3,000 to be paid by S. Keidan & Co. (the builders) on acceptance of this order by you . . . ," to which the supplier replied by letter making various stipulations including " the sum of £3,000 to be paid as mentioned above " and ending " Our acceptance of your order is hereby confirmed." The main contractor the same day wrote to the employer authorising him to pay the £3,000 and debit the main contractor's account. It was not clear whether the architect had sent the main contractor copies of his letter to the suppliers and their reply, but the main contractor was at all times aware of the arrangements being made. *Held,* by the South African Court of Appeal, following *Hampton* v. *Glamorgan C.C.*[14] and *Leslie* v. *Metropolitan Asylums District,*[15] that the language of the main contract virtually permitted the architect, who was the agent of the building owner, to conclude a contract between the contractor and the sub-contractor, and that bearing this in mind the correct inference on the facts, in spite of the correspondence, was that the contract had been made between the main contractor and the supplier and not with the employers: *Concrete Construction Ltd.* v. *Keidan & Co. Ltd.* (1955).[16]

The second of the above cases is a typical example of the vagueness of the contractual arrangements with nominated sub-contractors often encountered in practice, and the South African Court of Appeal is to be congratulated on making a correct analysis of the practice of the industry and the real intention of the parties in the face of difficult and inaccurate documentation of their arrangements made by the parties themselves. The reference to the architect contracting as agent for the contractor is not, as the court itself recognised, to be taken literally; but the point of the case is that, if the architect is in these negotiations with sub-contractors acting for anybody, it is for the main contractor rather than the employer, since it is with the main contractor that the sub-contractor will have to contract, though he has implied or ostensible authority to contract for neither party in the full sense.[17]

ILLUSTRATION

An architect informed a sub-contractor that his tender was accepted and that in due course an order would be placed by the main contractor. The main contractor's order introduced a new term (no payment of sub-contractor till main contractor was himself paid). The sub-contractor started work. *Held,* by Blain J., no contract had been concluded with the architect, and the sub-contractor

---

[14] *Infra,* p. 753.
[15] *Infra,* pp. 750–751.
[16] 1955 (4) S.A. 315 (South Africa).
[17] *Ante,* Chap. 2, pp. 108 *et seq.* (See, however, an exception in the case of local authority officers, *ante,* Chap. 2, pp. 110–111.)

had accepted the main contractor's terms by starting work without protest: *Davies Shopfitters Ltd.* v. *William Old* (1969).[18]

In cases where work has to be put in hand before the main contractor has been selected, however, there is, no doubt, a contingent liability of the employer to the sub-contractor, in the event that no main contractor materialises ready and willing to place the necessary order.[18a] The nature of this liability will depend on the exact course of the negotiations between the employer and the sub-contractor. It should be remembered in this context that an architect cannot, without express authority, bind his employer in contract,[17] so that it is not impossible that if unauthorised negotiations have taken place between the architect and the sub-contractor and the latter has commenced work, the architect will find himself personally liable for breach of warranty.

Another situation in which, despite the general rule of lack of privity, the employer and sub-contractor may establish a direct legal relationship can arise if during the course of negotiations warranties are given or representations made by the supplier or sub-contractor on the faith of which the employer instructs the main contractor to place his order with the sub-contractor.

ILLUSTRATIONS

(1) The director of a paint firm interviewed the managing director of pier-owners and later their architect, and made representations as to the suitability of his company's products for the protection of the pier from corrosion, as a result of which the main contractors were required to order the firm's paint. On the paint proving defective, the pier owners sued the paint manufacturers, alleging that the representations were warranties as to the suitability of the paint given in consideration of the pier-owners causing their contractors to order the paint. *Held*, by McNair J., that the contention was correct and the manufacturers were liable to the pier-owners in damages: *Shanklin Pier Co. Ltd.* v. *Detel Products* (1951).[19]

(2) The nursery manager of the plaintiffs, who were chrysanthemum growers, visited the defendants, who were sand suppliers, looking for a fine sand suitable for propagating the plants. The defendants suggested a particular sand, and produced an analysis of it showing a very low iron content. An assurance was also given that deliveries would conform to the sample. The defendants quoted a price " *ex pit* " but said it might be cheaper for the growers to provide their own transport. Apart from one delivery, the plaintiffs did not buy the sand directly from the defendants, but placed orders for it with a firm specialising in the transport of building materials, which itself obtained the sand from the defendants' pits. The

---

[18] (1969) 113 S.J. 262.
[18a] Compare the analogous contingent liability of the employer for quantity surveyor's fees under the old practice, *ante*, Chap. 2, pp. 194–195.   [19] [1951] 2 K.B. 854.

plaintiffs were in fact induced to buy the sand by the defendants' representations, which were incorrect but innocent, as the iron content was far higher than that indicated, so that the plants were damaged. *Held*, by Edmund Davies J. the statements were not mere representations, but were warranties forming part of a collateral contract, and were enforceable notwithstanding that no specific main contract was discussed at the time they were given. Two ingredients only were needed, (1) a promise or assertion as to the nature, quality or quantity of the goods which might reasonably be regarded as made with an intention to create legal relations and (2) acquisition of the goods in reliance on the promise or assertion: *Wells* v. *Buckland Sand Ltd.* (1964).[20]

The first of the above cases turned on rather special facts, and in practice statements made in brochures or at meetings with architects might, depending on the circumstances, be held to amount to mere representations,[21] and, further, the rather special consideration necessary in this type of case might be absent, or not actually expressed in so many words by the parties. The second case, however, shows that Edmund Davies L.J. was prepared to adopt a welcome approach based on the underlying commercial realities rather than an insistence on verbal or written warranties spelling out the consideration in precise terms.[22] It has already been suggested that a liability in tort for such statements might also arise in certain circumstances under the principle of the case of *Hedley Byrne* v. *Heller*.[23] (The distinction between the two above situations and that in the *Hedley Byrne* case is that in the former the representors had a commercial interest in securing sales of their goods, which was the essence of the consideration present, whereas in the *Hedley Byrne* case the representor derived no advantage from the situation, so that no consideration was present and a liability in tort had to be evolved if there was to be any liability at all.)

The reason why, even in the case of sub-contractors selected by the employer, a contractual relationship with the employer will not be inferred (for instance, by holding that the main contractor or architect contracted with the sub-contractor as agent for the employer), is that an employer wishing to have a building erected or works carried out wishes and intends to contract, as a general rule, with one contractor for the performance of the whole work. By this means he obtains one price for the whole work, avoids a multiplicity

---

[20] [1965] 2 Q.B. 170.
[21] For the distinction between representations and warranties, see *ante*, Chap. 1, p. 41.
[22] See also K. W. Wedderburn [1959] C.L.J. 58; Halsbury *Laws*, Vol. 34, pp. 51–55, and *Brown* v. *Sheen* [1950] 1 All E.R. 1102; and *Andrews* v. *Hopkinson* [1957] 1 Q.B. 229.
[23] Discussed *ante*, Chap. 1, pp. 64 *et seq.*

of contracts and liabilities, and the complicated problems of delay
and interference which would certainly arise if the works were to be
carried out by various contractors and their workmen, each separately
employed by him to perform various parts of the work on the same
site, though dependent on each other for speedy and economical
progress. In such a situation the ultimate financial responsibility for
co-ordinating the work of the various sub-contractors would fall on
the employer, who would become in effect his own main contractor.
The intention is not negatived by the fact that in the standard forms
of contract the employer may retain the right to employ other contractors on the site himself,[24] since without such a right the main
contractor could object that he was not being given free and unfettered possession of the site [25] even though the other work was not
closely connected with his own either in point of time or location.

In re-stating the general inference that privity of contract between
employer and sub-contractor does not exist, it is quite irrelevant that
the sub-contract may in its terms follow closely those of the main
contract; for instance, by provisions making the sub-contractor's
payment dependent upon the certificates or satisfaction of the architect under the main contract, or empowering the architect under the
main contract to order extras or variations from the sub-contractors.[26]
Usually such provisions only have the effect, as between the main
contractor and the sub-contractor, of constituting the architect the
main contractor's agent in the same sense that he is the employer's
agent under the main contract.[27]   Nor is it relevant that the sub-
contractor will normally be conferring a benefit upon the employer by
doing the work, which he cannot retrieve, as he could in the case of a
chattel, by virtue of the work being attached to the employer's land.[28]
An important consequence of this lack of privity between employer
and sub-contractor is that, in the event of default by the sub-
contractor, while the main contractors can of course sue for breach
of contract, in such a case he can only recover to the extent of his own
damage, not the employer's, and the two types of damage will

[24] Clause 29, 1963 R.I.B.A. forms; clause 31, 1955 I.C.E. form.
[25] As to which right see *ante*, Chap. 5, p. 317.
[26] Where there is no such power, the architect, by ordering variations from a sub-
contractor, may render the employer liable for them. See illustrations, *infra*.
[27] See *e.g. Geary, Walker & Co. Ltd.* v. *Lawrence* (1906) Hudson's B.C., 4th ed., Vol. 2,
p. 382, illustrated *infra*, p. 768. (The interpretation of sub-contracts which
purport to incorporate all or some provisions of the main contract, often in informal
terms, frequently gives rise to difficulties due to lack of precision or forethought
when providing for the incorporation in vague and general terms. See Section 4,
infra.)
[28] See *ante*, Chap. 6, pp. 376, 377 *et seq.*

usually differ very considerably. Where the sub-contract work and the nature of any express or implied warranties relating to it are clearly set out in or to be inferred from the main contract (as in the case of all " privately " sub-contracted work where the work will, of course, be described in the contract as part of the main contractor's obligations) no difficulty will arise and the main contractor's claim against the sub-contractor will (unless he has failed to obtain a satisfactorily worded sub-contract) include any item of loss, such as liquidated damages for delay, which he may have suffered as a result of claims made against him by the employer. Where, however, the work is not carefully described (as in the case of much nominated specialist work, which under the normal scheme of nomination in modern contracts is described in the abbreviated form of P.C. or provisional sum items in the bills of quantities or specification) [29] and where the extent of any warranties or implied terms in the main contract relating to the work may be doubtful (as, for instance, an implied term that the main contractor should assume responsibility for the quality of the work of selected specialists)[30] the contractor's damage may be limited to the effect on the profitability of his own work of the sub-contractor's breaches, if he is not himself legally liable to the employer in any way. It has already been pointed out that the R.I.B.A. standard forms in effect protect defaulting sub-contractors from meeting the employer's losses on a delayed contract by expressly giving the main contractor a right to an extension of time for nominated sub-contractor's delays,[31] and a remarkable result of this is seen in the *Jarvis* v. *Westminster Corporation* case,[32] where a sub-contractor (with a neutral main contractor not taking part in the argument though a party to the proceedings) was actually (though in the end unsuccessfully) asking the court to accept that delay to the works *had* been caused by his own default within the terms of clause 23 (*g*), so as to avoid his own liability to pay the employer's liquidated damages to the main contractor for onward transmission to the

---

[29] As to which see *infra*, Section 3.

[30] Compare the *Gloucestershire County Council* case, *ante*, Chap. 5, pp. 298–300.

[31] (While at the same time taking explicit pains to see that any damages recovered from a sub-contractor shall be the property of the contractor and not the employer— clause 30 (5) (*c*) proviso—and while attempting to make specific provision to assist in the recovery of liquidated damages *for the contractor* from the sub-contractor— clause 27 (*a*) (vi), 1963 forms.) See Chap. 11, Section 5, pp. 650–652, and the out-spoken criticism of this provision by Salmon and Davies L.JJ. in *Jarvis Ltd.* v. *Westminster Corporation* [1969] 1 W.L.R. 1448, there illustrated. See also *infra*, p. 766 where this provision is further criticised in a passage cited by Edmund Davies L.J. in the same case.

[32] [1970] 1 W.L.R. 637 (H.L.), *ante*, Chap. 11, p. 652.

employer. Nor can difficulties of this kind be overcome by an assignment of the main contractor's rights under the sub-contract to the employer, even if the assignment is not invalidated as being an assignment of a bare right to sue.[33] Such an assignment could only pass the same rights as those enjoyed by the main contractor.[34]

The only way to overcome such difficulties is to ensure by express provision in the main contract that the work of selected sub-contractors is described in sufficient detail, that any desired warranties as to the quality, design or suitability of the sub-contracted work are set out in the main contract, and that express provisions absolving the main contractor from responsibility for selected sub-contractor's work should be rigorously avoided. It is, however, submitted [35] that under the scheme of nomination adopted in modern contracts any express or implied warranties given by specialist sub-contractors do in fact enure for the benefit of the main contractor ultimately placing an order with them, and do form part of the obligations of the main contractor to his employer, but until the case of *Gloucestershire County Council* v. *Richardson*[36] has elicited further consideration and explanation by the courts the matter will be surrounded by far more doubt than appeared to exist at the time this same submission was made in the Ninth Edition.

The following cases illustrate the somewhat difficult stages by which the courts came to recognise the underlying reality of the contractual relationships arising out of the sub-contracting of building and civil engineering work, and the later, more sophisticated arrangements under which employers expressly retained the right to nominate or select sub-contractors and suppliers.[37]

ILLUSTRATIONS

(1) A. contracted with B. for certain works on A.'s house. C. supplied goods to B. for use in such works. *Held*, that A. was not liable to C. for their price: *Bramah* v. *Abingdon* (*Lord*) cited in *Paterson* v. *Gandasequi* (1812).[38]

---

[33] See *ante*, Chap. 14, Assignment, p. 726, but see *Constant* v. *Kincaid* (1902) 4 F. (Ct. of Sess.) 901 there referred to.

[34] For a full discussion of the difficulties, see Section 3, *infra*, Building Owner and Contractor.

[35] *Infra*, Section 3.

[36] [1969] A.C. 480, *ante*, Chap. 5, pp. 298–301.

[37] In addition to the cases illustrated below, see *Pritchett & Gold* v. *Currie* [1916] 2 Ch. 515, illustrated *ante*, Chap. 12, p. 657 (though not on this point) where money paid into court by a building owner was held not to be due to sub-contractors of a bankrupt main contractor who had delivered goods to the site.

[38] 15 East 66.

(2) S. employed T. to do certain work. E., who was a sub-contractor under T., did certain work, which E. alleged was outside the contract, and sued S. for the price of it. *Held,* that E. must prove a distinct contract between S. and himself: *Eccles* v. *Southern* (1861).[39]

(3) During the progress of building works, the architect, *in the presence of the building owner,* requested a plastering sub-contractor to gauge the plasterwork, which was a more expensive process than that specified, and told him he would be paid extra. The sub-contractor sued the employer for the extra cost. *Held,* there was evidence to go to a jury that the architect was to this extent authorised to contract on behalf of the building owner: *Wallis* v. *Robinson* (1862).[40]

(4) A building contract made with the plaintiffs as main con-tractors provided that the employers " reserved to themselves the right to employ other parties to execute the works for which pro-visions are made, and to deduct the full provided amount (*i.e.* the prime cost plus 10 per cent.) thereon from the contract sum. In such cases the contractors are to allow such parties every facility for the execution of their several works simultaneously with their own. The managers are to be at liberty to omit any provisional sums or quantities. The contractors are to pay the sub-contractors the amount provided in the contract for such purpose, or less or more, as may be certified, and the payments thus made will be considered as work done by the contractors, and will be included in the certificate to the contractors next following such payment. No payment is to be made to such sub-contractors, except upon the architect's certificate. The contractors are to pay such amount as may be certified from time to time within seven days from the date of the certificate, and should the contractors neglect or refuse to make such payment within the said period, the managers shall be at liberty to pay the amount thereof to such sub-contractors, and to deduct from the contract sum the gross amount which the contractors have included in their estimate in respect of such work and their profit thereon, the amount so to be deducted not being less in any case than such amount so certified." Chimney stacks and heating apparatus were to be provided by specialists. Specialists were appointed to execute this work by the architect, who made terms with them. The plaintiffs were instructed by the architect to give the orders and did so, and the work was executed. The main con-tractors sued the employers for damages for delay caused by the specialists. *Held,* although the contract empowered the employers to contract direct with the specialists, the specialists had in fact been employed by the contractors, and the architect's negotiations had in fact been on behalf of the contractors,[41] who consequently could not recover damages from the employers: *Leslie & Co. Ltd.* v. *The Managers of the Metropolitan Asylums District* (1901).[42]

---

[39] 3 F. & F. 142.
[40] 3 F. & F. 307.
[41] Compare the language in *Concrete Construction Ltd.* v. *Keidan, supra,* pp. 743–744.
[42] (1901) 68 J.P. 86.

[Note: This case was expressly approved by Bankes L.J. in the Court of Appeal in *Hampton* v. *Glamorgan C.C.*[43] and it and that case in the Court of Appeal (rather than in the House of Lords where the judgments are somewhat generalised) represent, it is submitted, the two cases of greatest authority in this field.]

(5) Clause 28 of the 1909 R.I.B.A. form of contract provided that the provisional sums mentioned in the specification for materials to be supplied or work to be performed by special artists or tradesmen should be paid and expended at such times and in such amounts and in favour of such persons as the architect should direct and the sums so payable should be payable by the contractor without discount or deduction *or by the employer* to the said artists or tradesmen. At the settlement of accounts the amount paid by the contractor to the said artists or tradesmen should be set off against all such provisional sums and the balance added to or deducted from the contract sum. The architect ordered a sub-contractor to supply certain metalwork, which was delivered, invoiced and debited to the contractor. The architect certified the sum due to the sub-contractor, and sent the certificate *direct to the building owner.* The sub-contractor sued the building owner *on the certificate. Held,* clause 28 contemplated payment either by the main contractor or the employer. The proper inference on the facts was that the contractor was acting as agent for the employer, in such circumstances that while the contractor might himself be liable to the sub-contractor, he nevertheless also rendered his principal liable: *Hobbs* v. *Turner* (1902).[44]

[Note: In *Milestone & Sons* v. *Yates Brewery* (1938) [45] Singleton J., in a case where the same form of contract was used, doubted if clause 28 by itself could effect privity between the employer and sub-contractor and clearly regarded the case as turning upon the certificate being issued to the employer. See also the comments of Lord Haldane L.C. in *Hampton's* case.]

(6) The plaintiff contracted to do certain works for the defendants for a lump sum. The contract provided that the engineering and other specialist work was to be done by named firms, who were to be paid by the plaintiff. The plaintiff was not to be liable for delay caused by the specialists or for defective plant supplied by them unless he was guilty of contributory negligence. The specialists caused delay in the execution of the works which caused damage to the plaintiff. The plaintiff sued the defendants for this damage alleging that there was an implied promise by the defendants that the delivery of the machinery should not be unreasonably delayed or that the delivery and fixing should be made and done at such reasonable times during the erection of the buildings as would enable the plaintiff to complete the same within the time fixed by the contract or within a reasonable time thereafter. *Held,* following *Leslie's* case, there was no such implied promise and there being no contract between the defendants and the specialists the defendants were not liable for the delay: *Mitchell* v. *Guildford Union* (1903).[46]

[43] (1915) 84 L.J.K.B. 1306.
[44] (1902) 18 T.L.R. 235.
[45] [1938] 2 All E.R. 439, illustrated *infra*, p. 771.
[46] 68 J.P. 84.

(7) The L.C.C. employed L. & Co. to erect a building. The contract provided that casements should be ordered from specialists. The architect to the council invited the plaintiffs to quote for these casements, saying that the accepted quotation would be inserted in L. & Co.'s contract as a P.C. item; that the plaintiffs should enter into an agreement with L. & Co. to complete the casements to time under a penalty; that the council's architect should have power to vary the work, and that payment should only be made upon the certificate of the council's architect. The plaintiffs quoted a price, and then the council requested L. & Co. to order the work. L. & Co. informed the plaintiffs that they were requested by the council to accept the quotation. The plaintiffs sued the council for the price of the work. *Held*, that while the contract for the casements was prima facie between L. & Co. and the plaintiffs, it was also a contract by L. & Co. as agents for the council, because it was to procure something for their benefit, and because in contracts made to procure work, which is the subject of a provisional sum of prime cost item, the building owner is the real principal, and because the price was quoted to the building owner and not to the contractors: *Crittall Manufacturing Co.* v. *London County Council* (1910).[47]

[Note: The reasoning of Channell J. summarised in the above case was expressly disapproved by all three judges in the Court of Appeal [48] in *Hampton* v. *Glamorgan County Council, infra* (see [1917] A.C. at pp. 16 and 17] and by Lord Shaw of Dunfermline, *ibid.* at p. 22, and it is clear that this case, and the case of *Young & Co.* v. *White* (1912) 28 T.L.R. 87, *infra*, must be regarded as overruled.]

(8) W. who was erecting a building, engaged N. to carry out the work. The contract with N. provided that " all specialists executing any work or supplying any goods for which prime cost prices or provisional sums are included in the specification who may at any time be nominated, selected or approved by the architect are hereby declared to be sub-contractors employed by the contractor." [49] The specification referred to in the contract with N. said that " the architects reserve the right in all items of P.C. and provisional amounts to employ the contractor or such other person as they may think fit to execute them." The plaintiffs were specialists in steelwork, and the architects sent to the plaintiffs drawings, inviting a tender for the steelwork contained in the contract, as the subject of a provisional sum. The plaintiffs did not then know who the builder was, nor what the terms of the building contract were. They sent a tender to the architects at the request of the architects, and the architects wrote saying that N. was the builder and that they had instructed him to order the work. The plaintiffs wrote to N. asking for the order accordingly. N. tried to extract terms as to discounts, and the plaintiffs wrote to the architects asking them to instruct N. to give them the order as agreed. The order was given on the terms of the estimate. The architects certified for payment to N. an amount which they stated included a sum for the plaintiffs. N. went bankrupt without having paid the

---

[47] 75 J.P. 203; approving *Hobbs* v. *Turner* (1900) 18 T.L.R. 235.
[48] (1915) 84 L.J.K.B. 1306.
[49] (The formula used in the present-day R.I.B.A. forms, see *post*, p. 756.)

plaintiffs, who sued W. *Held*, that the contract with the plaintiffs had been made by his agents on W.'s behalf: *Young & Co.* v. *White* (1912).[50]

[Note: This case was expressly disapproved by the Court of Appeal in *Hampton's* case—see *e.g. per* Buckley L.J.]

(9) The respondents contracted to erect a picture theatre for a company. The contract was in the R.I.B.A. form, and provided that " all specialists, merchants, tradesmen or others executing any work or supplying any goods, for which prime cost prices or provisional sums are included in the specification, who may at any time be nominated, selected or approved by the architect are hereby declared to be sub-contractors employed by the contractor." The appellants were employed by the architect as specialists to supply fittings, which were the subject of a prime cost item in the contract with the respondents. The architect, before delivery of the fittings, informed the builders that these fittings were being supplied by the appellants. The builders used the fittings in carrying out their contract. *Held*, that the delivery of the goods at the theatre and their use by the builders implied a contract by the builders to pay for them: *Ramsden and Carr* v. *Chessum & Sons* (1913).[51]

(10) A builder contracted with the defendants to build a school in accordance with the specifications and directions of the Council's architect for a lump sum. The specification contained the following provisional item: " Provide the sum of £450 for a low pressure heating apparatus." There was no provision expressly referring to the carrying out of such work by sub-contractors, nominated or otherwise. The plaintiff, a water engineer, submitted a scheme to the architect for the heating apparatus for £391, and upon the instructions of the architect this offer was accepted by the builder. During the progress of the work the builder paid to the plaintiff £200 on account, but was unable to pay the balance. The plaintiff sued the defendants for the balance. *Held*, by the House of Lords, that the builder's overall obligation to complete the school included the obligation to provide the heating apparatus within the provisional sum, and that the builder, in employing the plaintiff to install the heating apparatus, was acting as a principal and not as the agent of the defendants, and the plaintiff's action failed: *Hampton* v. *Glamorgan County Council* (1917).[52]

(11) Under the 1931 R.I.B.A. form of contract there was power to pay sub-contractors direct on default by the builder. Sub-contractors tendered for the work of flooring, and the tender was accepted in June 1938. Early in June the contractors went into liquidation, and on June 9 the architect, with the acquiescence of the building owner, arranged with a director of the contractors that the latter should take over the contract. The architect sent to the employer, for signature by her, a mandate to the bank from which she had borrowed money on the security of the building advising them of the director's substitution for the company, and authorising payment to him or such nominated sub-contractors as might appear in future certificates. This was sent to the bank. Subsequently, the

---

[50] 28 T.L.R. 87.   [51] 78 J.P. 49 (H.L.).
[52] [1917] A.C. 13. See also the judgments in the Court of Appeal (1915) 84 L.J.K.B. 1306.

architect gave the flooring sub-contractors instructions to lay the floors and purported to pledge the employer's credit for that purpose. *Held*, the intention of the main contract was that there should be no privity between the employer and sub-contractors. The architect had no authority to contract on behalf of the building owner under the original contract, nor under the substituted contract. The reference in the mandate to the bank to payment of sub-contractors was referable only to the contractual right to pay direct, and the employer had done nothing to ratify the pledging of her credit, and was accordingly not liable to the sub-contractors: *Vigers Sons & Co. Ltd.* v. *Swindell* (1939).[53]

It may be worth noting that the words " are hereby declared to be sub-contractors . . . " (compare " shall be deemed to be sub-contractors " in the I.C.E. Conditions[54]) seem to have come into use shortly after 1900. Prior to that it was quite common (as *e.g.* in *Hampton's* case) to have no special provision about the exact status of the specialist, and merely to have provisional (or rather provided[55]) sums for the work in question. The judgments show that it was the *fact* of a sub-contract rather than the exact wording used which ultimately weighed most with the courts.[56]

The earlier cases illustrated above undoubtedly reveal a serious judicial conflict, but this may now be regarded as resolved. In the light of the subsequent cases, and in particular of the judgments of the Court of Appeal in the *Hampton* case, the *Crittall* and *Young* cases [57] can only be regarded as wrongly decided, and the source of error in these cases is to be found in the special wording of clause 28 and the issue of a certificate direct to the employer in *Hobbs* v. *Turner* (1900),[58] a decision which was carried too far by the two later cases.[59] In addition to the cases cited above, reference should also be made to the two more modern cases of *Kirk and Kirk Ltd.* v. *Croydon Corporation* (1956) and *Concrete Construction Ltd.* v. *Keidan & Co. Ltd.* (1955).[60] The latter decision of the South African Court of Appeal is in many ways the clearest and most satisfactory example of the correct principle applied to a most difficult set of facts of a type very frequently encountered in practice, but *Kirk and Kirk*, in which Sellers J. followed *Leslie's* case, also faced very difficult and compli-

---

[53] [1939] 3 All E.R. 590.
[54] See *infra*, Section 3 (1) for the two current provisions.
[55] See *infra*, Section 3 (2).
[56] See the *Hampton* and *Leslie* cases.
[57] *Supra.*   [58] *Supra.*
[59] See *per* Lord Shaw at p. 22 in *Hampton* v. *Glamorgan County Council supra.*
[60] Both illustrated, *supra*, pp. 743–744.

cated facts in which it might easily have been possible to lose sight of the no-privity principle.

No discussion of the no-privity principle can be concluded at the present day without indicating that in *Gloucestershire County Council* v. *Richardson*[61] the House of Lords held that a main contractor was not, under the 1957 (revised) R.I.B.A. form of contract, in breach of contract himself in respect of concrete columns which had cracked owing to poor workmanship during their manufacture by a nominated supplier, where the terms of the supplier's contract limited his liability to replacement of defective columns; and that in *Bickerton* v. *N.W. Metropolitan Hospital Board*[62] the House of Lords held that upon a repudiation by a nominated sub-contractor the employer under the post-1963 R.I.B.A. forms of contract was contractually bound to nominate a successor sub-contractor. The implications of the *Gloucester* case and of the *Bickerton* case[62a] are, as already stated, likely to be of the most profound character, and will inevitably lead to further attempts to qualify or invade the principle still further, unless the standard forms are revised.

Even where, however, the employer is in direct contractual relations with a supplier or sub-contractor, it does not follow in every case that, *ipso facto*, the employer will be liable to the main contractor for default by the supplier. This will depend on the circumstances in which the contract was made, or upon the construction of the main contract, which may contemplate such a direct relationship without imposing any liability on the employer.

ILLUSTRATION

A main contract for the construction of two lodges and a back entrance provided that the employer should pay the stone supplier direct and deduct the sum from the contract price. With the consent of the main contractor, the employers negotiated with the suppliers and fixed the quantity and price of the stone to be supplied. The suppliers delayed delivery of the stone, and in consequence the contractors sued the employers for the additional cost occasioned by the delay. *Held*, there was no implied obligation on the employers to supply the stone. At the highest, they were only obliged to hold the benefit of the contract with the suppliers for the contractors, and accordingly were not liable to the contractors: *Gaze (W. H.) & Sons Ltd.* v. *Port Talbot Corpn.* (1929).[63]

[61] [1969] A.C. 480, *ante*, Chap. 5, pp. 298–301; Chap. 8, pp. 527–528.
[62] [1970] 1 W.L.R. 607, *ante*, Chap. 5, pp. 333–334.
[62a] Both fully discussed, *ante*, Chap. 5, pp. 301 *et seq.* and 334 *et seq.*
[63] 93 J.P. 89.

SECTION 3. BUILDING OWNER AND CONTRACTOR

(1) Nomination of Sub-Contractors

Nearly all modern forms of contract contain provisions enabling the employer or his architect to select sub-contractors. In the R.I.B.A. forms [64] this is (presumably) achieved by the following difficult wording:

" Where prime cost sums are included in the contract bills [or specification] or arise as a result of [sic] architect's instructions given in regard to the expenditure of provisional sums [(clause 27) in respect of persons to be nominated by the architect to . . . execute work] [(clause 28) in respect of materials or goods to be fixed by the contractor], such sums shall be expended in favour of such persons as the architect shall instruct, and all specialists merchants tradesmen or others who are nominated by the architect . . . are hereby declared to be [(clause 27) sub-contractors employed by the contractor . . . referred to as ' nominated sub-contractors '] [(clause 28) suppliers to the contractor . . . referred to . . . as ' nominated suppliers ']."[64a] Further the contract provides that nothing in the conditions should render the employer in any way liable to a nominated sub-contractor,[65] and that in the settlement of accounts any sums paid or allowed to the contractor by the sub-contractor or supplier as damages shall be the property of the contractor and not of the employer.[66]

In the I.C.E. form [67] more direct wording is used: " All specialists merchants and others executing any work or supplying any goods for which provisional or prime cost sums are included in the bill of quantities who may have been or be nominated or selected or approved by the employer or the engineer and all persons to whom by virtue of the provisions of the bill of quantities or specification the contractor is required to sub-let any work shall in the execution of such work or the supply of such goods be deemed to be sub-contractors employed by the contractor and are herein referred to as ' nominated sub-contractors.' "

The intention of such provisions when first used shortly after 1900 [68] was to establish beyond doubt the absence of privity between the employer and the selected sub-contractor, and, it is submitted (*pace*

[64] Clauses 27 and 28, 1963 ed.
[64a] See the criticism of the R.I.B.A. wording by Danckwerts L.J. in *Bickerton* v. *N.W. Metropolitan Hospital Board* [1969] 1 All E.R. at p. 996.
[65] Clause 27 (*f*).
[66] Clause 30 (5) (*c*) (proviso).
[67] Clause 59 (1).   [68] See *supra*, Section 2, pp. 751 *et seq.*

the *Gloucester* and *Bickerton* cases), makes clear that the contractual responsibility in relation to the sub-contract work is that of the main contractor and no one else, in accordance with the reasoning in the cases of *Hampton* v. *Glamorgan County Council* (1917) and *Leslie & Co. Ltd.* v. *Metropolitan Asylums District* (1901) illustrated in Section 2, *supra*. The only doubt relates to the strange expression " nominated suppliers " in clause 28 of the R.I.B.A. forms, which by itself has, of course, no legal significance and is nowhere further defined or explained in the contract; nor is any indication given of its legal consequences other than in the purely accounting provisions of the contract,[69] but its effect appears to be identical in fixing the main contractor with liability for the nominated supplier.[70]

It is widely thought, particularly by lawyers and, it would seem, the draftsmen of building contracts, that the system of nomination of specialists springs from the employer's desire or need to control the *quality* of specialist work. In fact this is frequently not the case and, on analysis, the system really springs from the employer's need to secure a *competitive price* for such work as is not normally carried out by main contractors or is outside the more familiar building processes. An ordinary main contractor will generally find difficulty in tendering a keen price for such specialist work without himself first obtaining a competitive tender from a specialist. This would mean that all the tendering main contractors would have to make numerous enquiries and obtain sub-tenders from specialists, often involving much duplication of effort, before being able to tender themselves, and the cost of and time needed for main-contract tendering would be materially increased. By removing such unusual work from the main contractor's area of pricing, in the form of a P.C. or provisional sum common to all the tendering main contractors, and by retaining the right to select, the employer retains control over the price competition for the sub-contracted work, which he would lose if the right to select the specialist in question was to be exercised by the main contractor. It is vital to an understanding of the system of nomination to appreciate this, and it seems likely that many of the modern decisions[70a] and some contractual provisions which have had the effect of modifying the no-privity principle have been based on the assumption that control over the personality, rather than the price, of the sub-contractor is the principal object of the system. The true view

---

[69] See clause 30 (5) (*c*), 1963 forms.
[70] See *per* Lord Pearson in the *Gloucestershire* case [1969] A.C. 480 at p. 512, quoted *ante*, Chap. 5, p. 282.
[70a] See the comment on the *Bickerton* case, *ante*, Chap. 5, pp. 334 *et seq.*

in the majority of cases is that control over the personality is only necessary machinery in order to achieve the principal object, which is control over the price.

(2) Provisional and P.C. Sum Items

One of the peculiar characteristics of the traditional nomination draftsmanship (which as has been seen actually preceded in point of time provisions spelling out the nomination procedure in detail) is the procedural technique, as can be seen from the wording of the above clauses, whereby nearly all work intended to be sub-contracted by selected specialists is designated in specifications or bills of quantities either as a prime cost or provisional sum or item.[70b] Though these terms are in virtually universal use in the building industry, no clear and authoritative definition of their meaning has emerged from the cases dealing with sub-contracts,[71] but it is not difficult to see how the terms came into use.

The explanation of the words " provisional sum " emerges clearly from the judgment of Romer L.J. in *Leslie's* case,[72] which points out that these items in Victorian specifications usually commenced with the words " Provide the sum of £—," and were frequently referred to as " provisions." The word " provisional " was a corruption, meaning no more than " provided," and did not connote " provisional " in its correct sense of " contingent." The expression " P.C.," standing for prime cost, was an alternative method of describing such work, since it indicated that on this work the builder would be paid on the basis of actual cost to himself (that is to say, the actual amount of the sub-contractor's account) as opposed to his being required to tender a price for it.

Over the years, however, the origin of " provision " became forgotten, and a tendency for it to be applied to *contingent* work seems to have developed, particularly since the lump-sum device in the specification or bills was used for such work, even if it was main contractor's work. The expressions were undoubtedly, however, freely interchangeable for a long period of time, and certainly lack any real precision at the present day in the absence of a clear-cut definition in the contract documents, which is almost always lacking.

[70b] See, in addition to the present discussion, *ante*, Chap. 3, pp. 204–205.

[71] The definitions boldly hazarded by Channell J. in *Crittall Manufacturing Co.* v. *L.C.C.* (1910) 75 J.P. 203 and by Coleridge J. in *Young & Co.* v. *White* (1912) 28 T.L.R. 87 were expressly disapproved by the Court of Appeal in *Hampton* v. *Glamorgan C.C.* [1917] A.C. 13.

[72] *Leslie* v. *Metropolitan Asylums District* (1901) 68 J.P. 86. See also in *Hampton's* case, *per* Lord Haldane. Compare the wording in *Leslie's* case, *supra*, p. 750.

In the last edition of this book it was suggested that the term " provisional sum " is apt to describe work the extent of which is indeterminate at the time of letting the contract, while the term " P.C. " is usually applied to items which are determinable, but whose price is uncertain, usually by reason of an element of choice on the part of the building owner. Thus normally provisional sums would apply to work alone or work and materials, while P.C. items would usually apply to materials or fittings only, though there was no hard-and-fast rule. The contractual effect to be attached to the terms in practice always appears to be identical, though the terms by themselves have no contractual implication without some provision in the contract governing their effect. Now by the latest standard method of measurement of building works,[73] in accordance with which the bills of quantities in contracts using the R.I.B.A. standard forms are deemed to have been prepared,[74] " provisional sums " are to mean sums provided for work or for costs which cannot be entirely foreseen, defined or detailed at the time of issuing tender documents, and " prime cost sums " mean sums provided for work or services to be executed by a nominated sub-contractor or for materials or goods to be obtained from a nominated supplier. It is doubtful to what extent this definition has been incorporated into the contract conditions in the standard R.I.B.A. forms of contract [75] however, and the definition is not only not referred to in any way in the forms without quantities (which of course will need to use the expressions in the specification), but none of the R.I.B.A. forms in fact expressly condescend to any definition of the terms, other than the oblique reference, in the case of the bill forms only, to preparation of the bills in accordance with the standard method. In *Bickerton's* case,[76] the Court of Appeal were of the clear opinion that the definition was not incorporated by the conditions of contract, but in that case there was a sufficiently clear express provision in the bills of quantities themselves.

In nearly all modern contracts, these provisional sums and P.C. items are the subject of provisions requiring an adjustment of the contract sum, according to whether the work is wholly or partially executed or omitted, and whether the sub-contractor's accounts eventually exceed or are less than the sums or items. Where the addition or deduction has to be made on the basis of cost it appears clear,

[73] 5th ed., 1963, p. 2, para. A7.
[74] See Clause 12 of the 1963 forms with quantities.
[75] See the last three lines of Clause 12 (1) of the 1963 forms with quantities for example.
[76] *Bickerton* v. *N.W. Metropolitan Hospital Board* [1969] 1 All E.R. 977.

unless there is some special provision to the contrary, that cost means actual cost, and the contractor is not entitled to retain any trade discounts, nor, except under special circumstances such as those in *London School Board* v. *Northcroft* (1889),[77] would he be entitled to any discount for cash.

ILLUSTRATION

Where auctioneers were to be paid a lump sum as commission and " all out-of-pocket expenses." *Held*, that they were not entitled to retain trade discounts in respect of printing and advertising, although no such discount would have been allowed to their client if he had dealt direct: *Hippisley* v. *Knee Brothers* (1905).[78]

In fact the so-called " cash-discounts " under the R.I.B.A. forms are an elaborate misnomer, and represent pure profit to the builder, since under the terms of these contracts the builder is not required to pay the sub-contractor before, in effect, he is paid himself by the employer, yet the contract specifically allows him the " discount," which is a vitally important element in the profitability of, and tendering for, major contracts, where the total of nominated work may exceed 50 per cent of the contract price, and where a profit of $2\frac{1}{2}$ or 5 per cent. on *turnover* may represent a profit of many tens per cent. per annum on *capital employed*.[79]

All the standard forms contain express provisions regulating the method of adjustment of the contract price in respect of P.C. or provisional sums. It has been suggested elsewhere [80] that in the absence of express provision a usage to adjust the contract price may now be capable of proof where these expressions are used, but as yet the matter has not come before the courts. As stated, the standard R.I.B.A. forms permit the contractor to retain certain " cash " (but not trade) discounts upon nominated work, but the I.C.E. form only permits the retention of a cash discount in certain special (and in practice, rare) circumstances where the contractor has paid the sub-contractor before receiving payment from the employer,[81] though this provision seems to be more honoured in the breach than in the observance by many engineers, who appear to allow such discounts freely to contractors.

[77] Hudson's B.C., 4th ed., Vol. 2, p. 147, *ante*, Chap. 2, p. 192.
[78] [1905] 1 K.B. 1.
[79] Clauses 27 (*b*), 28 (*b*) (iv) and 30 (i) of the post-1963 forms. See also *ante*, Chap. 9, Section 2, pp. 597 *et seq.*, for discussion of the economics of building contracts.
[80] See *ante*, Chap. 1, p. 55, Chap. 3, p. 205.
[81] Clause 58 (5), 1955 form.

(3) Main Contractor's Responsibility for Nominated Sub-Contractor's Work

One unfortunate result of the use of the P.C. and provisional sum item procedure is that in many cases the main contract documents contain no detailed description of the work to be carried out or goods to be supplied by the nominated sub-contractor. All that is to be seen in the contract documents is some such item as " Structural Steelwork. P.C. Sum £4,000." The detailed description of the work can often only be found in the quotations of the sub-contractor upon which the main contractor is required to order, and the full contractual extent of the sub-contractor's obligations is generally only to be found in the quotations and correspondence, often passing between the sub-contractor and the architect in the first place, and any subsequent correspondence passing between him and the main contractor at the time of placing the order. Even where a formal sub-contract in the F.A.S.S. form is used, it is quite usual for the schedule describing the work to consist merely of attached copies of the original quotations and acceptance.

There are two main difficulties, in the absence of a sufficiently precise main contract, in determining the exact extent of the main contractor's obligation to the employer for the work of nominated sub-contractors. It is reasonably clear that the *express* specification or description of the sub-contracted work is contained in the sub-contract documents, whatever they may be, and it is submitted that there is no difficulty in the way of the employer suing the main contractor for, or calling for remedy of, any breach of such express provisions by the sub-contractor.[82] But if there is no such breach of an express term, and it is some *implied* term as to workmanship or suitability upon which the employer wishes to rely, there is clearly a superficial difficulty at least, since it is necessary to imply *in the main contract* a term that the work will be carried out with (in many cases) the degree of skill to be expected from a specialist. The difficulty is heightened in those very frequent cases where, if the sub-contractor was contracting directly with the employer, the facts and circumstances would show that both architect and employer were, to the sub-contractor's knowledge, relying on the latter's skill and judgment in relation (*inter alia*) to design services which the sub-contractor was

---

[82] See, however, the *Gloucestershire County Council* case, *ante*, pp. 298–301, which while it was concerned with breach of an implied term, may lend support to the view that breaches of express terms might in similar circumstances not be a breach of the main contract.

being required to provide, and for which he was undoubtedly charg-
ing in his overall price. An illustration of the difficulty, in a field
quite different from building and engineering contracts, is to be found
in the case of *Stewart* v. *Reavell's Garage* (1952),[83] where, in a motor
repairing case, Sellers J. held that a repairer was liable for defective
work on the part of his sub-contractor, even if the customer consented to the work being done by that particular sub-contractor,
*unless the customer, without placing reliance on the skill and judgment
of the repairer, selected a particular sub-contractor by whom the work
was to be done.*

The second difficulty arises because, apart from any implied
obligations of this kind, it is very usual in practice for sub-contractors
to give oral warranties and undertakings as to the suitability of their
work during the negotiating stage with either the architect or the
employer which, if the contract was made between them and the
employer, would undoubtedly have contractual force. When this
occurs, can such undertakings or statements be imported into the
contractual relationship between the main contractor and the sub-
contractor?[84]

These two sources of difficulty are of the greatest practical
importance and occur frequently, but there is as yet no reported case
upon the matter. It is obviously in the highest degree desirable that
specialist sub-contractors should not be enabled to escape the normal
contractual consequences which would follow if they were contracting directly with the employer merely because of the accident of the
procedure of nomination and of the employer's requirement, known
to all parties from the beginning, that the contract should eventually
be placed with the main contractor and not with himself.

It is submitted that, in a case where the parties are aware (as in
the United Kingdom is now almost invariably the case in such situations) that the object of all negotiations correspondence and other
dealings is to enable a contract eventually to be placed by the main
contractor, whether or not already chosen, with the sub-contractor
or, in cases where this prior awareness does not already exist, where
the sub-contractor later agrees to accept the main contractor's order,

---

[83] [1952] 2 Q.B. 545, illustrated and explained, *ante*, Chap. 5, pp. 285–286.
[84] *Cf.* the facts in the case of *Shanklin Pier Co. Ltd.* v. *Detel Products* [1951] 2 K.B.
854 illustrated *supra*, p. 745. As already pointed out, the reasoning of this case,
which depended on rather strong facts, could not always be applied so as to bring
about a direct contractual relationship between the employer and sub-contractor
where such statements are made during the negotiating period, though *Wells* v.
Buckland Sand Ltd., *supra*, pp. 745–746, undoubtedly shows a common-sense approach which will frequently result in liability being established.

the effect must be that he thereby agrees that his full contractual liabilities, express or implied, together with any oral warranties given, shall be imported into the contract with the main contractor. This view, it is suggested, is strongly reinforced by the reasoning in the cases of *Leslie & Co. Ltd.* v. *Metropolitan Asylums District* (1901) [85] and *Concrete Construction Ltd.* v. *Keidan & Co. Ltd.* (1955)[86] which held (it is submitted entirely correctly) that, during such negotiations, the architect is for all practical purposes the agent of the main contractor. So too, it is submitted, oral representations or implied undertakings would enure for the benefit of the main contractor even if, for instance, the representations were made to the employer rather than his architect.

On this view the main contractor is entitled to sue the sub-contractor for breach of any express or implied obligations as to the suitability, design, or specialist standards of workmanship of the sub-contracted works, whether arising out of his own dealings with the sub-contractor or those of the employer or his architect. Once this position is reached, the provisions of the main contract clearly, it is submitted, require the contractor to carry out, by the selected sub-contractor, whatever work and attendant obligations the sub-contractor has assumed when the main contractor has, on the architect's or employer's instructions, concluded the sub-contract with the sub-contractor. As a result, the employer will have his full remedies in regard to the sub-contracted work, and any damages recovered or moneys deducted by him can be recovered by the main contractor from the sub-contractor. It has already been pointed out,[87] that even where an architect is employed by the building owner, a contractor may incur obligations as to design and suitability if the circumstances of the contract warrant it. This is particularly true, it is submitted, of specialist sub-contractors, who, in many cases, possess in their own particular fields a degree of skill and experience greater, or at least as great, as any independent consultants available to the employer, and certainly greater than that of the ordinary skilled architect in private practice. It is to this very fact that these specialists or their products frequently owe the nominations which they obtain in building and engineering contracts, and any legal decision which, in the absence of explicit wording excluding liability, sought to cut down these specialists' legal responsibility for, in appropriate cases, the design suitability or specialist quality of their work, either because of the presence of an architect or consulting

---

[85] Illustrated *supra*, pp. 750–751.   [86] Illustrated *supra*, pp. 743–744.
[87] *Ante*, Chap. 5, pp. 273 *et seq.*

engineer advising the employer, or because of the accident of the system of nomination, would not be in touch with the reality of the commercial relationships between such parties in the United Kingdom at the present day.

The preceding pages of this sub-section, which are as in the Ninth Edition, have received considerable support, in regard to the implied terms of good quality, from the decision of the House of Lords in *Young and Marten* v. *McManus Childs*,[88] perhaps the most important case in this field for a quarter of a century. Unfortunately, as explained *ante*, Chapter 5, in their very next decision in the *Gloucestershire County Council* case,[89] certain dicta in the House of Lords, if accepted as the true basis of the decision, would mean that the essential protection of the implied terms would be absent in all cases where an express right to reject a nomination was not given in the main contract. It has been submitted[90] that this is not in fact the true basis of the decision, which should be interpreted as narrowly as possible. In regard to warranties or representations made by subcontractors during early negotiations with the architect, there is as yet no authority, and it may be supposed that in such cases employers will be more likely to consider proceeding directly against the subcontractor, as in *Wells* v. *Buckland Ltd.*[91] rather than indirectly via the main contractor on what is at present an uncharted sea. Where the greatest difficulty is likely to be encountered, however, is in the case of express or implied design or suitability obligations where the design would normally be the responsibility of the architect. It seems very arguable that an architect could not in such a case use the nomination procedure, under the terms of most contracts, to shift the responsibility from his own (or the employer's) shoulders to those of the main contractor.[92]

In the absence of clear authority, however, those advising employers in the preparation of contracts should endeavour to see that the required warranties from specialist sub-contractors are clearly expressed, not only in the sub-contract documents, but also, wherever pre-planning or the timing of early negotiations and quotations permit, in the main contract documents as well. A full list of what it is submitted must now be the architect's duties in this regard are set out *ante*, Chapter 2, Section 6 (2) (d).

---

[88] [1969] A.C. 454, *ante*, Chap. 5, p. 298.
[89] [1969] A.C. 480, *ante*, Chap. 5, pp. 298–301.
[90] *Ante*, Chap. 5, p. 304.
[91] *Supra*, pp. 745–746.
[92] See *ante*, Chap. 2, pp. 129–131 and Chap. 5, pp. 277–278, 281–282, 323–324, and the case of *Moresk* v. *Hicks* illustrated at p. 131.

(4) Defects of the Modern System of Nomination

The system of nomination adopted by English contracts contains some defects at the present day. There is little doubt that the draftsmanship and scheme now used was originally evolved primarily to enable an employer to select goods and fittings at a relatively late stage of the traditional building work when the carcass was complete and finishing trades were beginning their work. This need to select was most understandable, and would involve, for instance, the quality texture or colour of facing bricks or tiles, the choice of panelling decorations and sanitary fittings, and the installation of heating systems and electricity. Even in civil engineering works, the need for specialised supplies (*e.g.* machinery, piping, dock-gates, pumps, turbines etc.) at a later stage was common. Under the early standard forms, these matters were dealt with by provisions permitting selection *after the main contract was let.* Unfortunately, the system has not been changed, while with the growth of specialisation a great increase in work so dealt with has taken place, much of it important structural work taking place at an early stage, or even prior to the main contractor's own work, and often requiring the original sub-orders to be placed earlier in point of time than the main contract itself. Thus piling, steel frames, reinforced or precast concrete frames, precast structural units, and special external cladding work, is frequently let in this way, and, in engineering and some building work, specialised processes such as cementation, soil stabilisation, piling and de-watering may also be done by nominated sub-contractors. This overall tendency is not discouraged by main contractors, since the method of payment for this work is such that all pricing risks are removed and a highly satisfactory profit calculated on turnover (representing many times the stated percentage on real capital employed) is assured[92a]; it is also not discouraged by professional advisers because the amount of initial preparatory work in the early stages is reduced (including, in particular, of course, the amount of work necessary to prepare bills of quantities and the number of drawings and specifications which the quantity surveyor will require). Furthermore, although all the structural and earlier work previously mentioned by its nature calls for pre-planning as intensive as the work of the contractor himself, it is in fact nominally governed by a system of post-contract nomination in which the work is treated as if it was provisional in character at the time of contracting, when in fact it

---

[92a] See *supra*, p. 760.

was nothing of the sort (and, as has already been pointed out,[92b] is more often than not concerned with obtaining the most competitive price for specialist work rather than with any other consideration). In other words, while there is no reason in logic why work which is to be carried out by selected sub-contractors should be any more pro-visional in character than that of the main contractor, it is in appear-ance[92c] treated as such in the contract documents, which therefore themselves tend to militate against pre-planning of the contract work as a whole. This is unfortunate since, under the current R.I.B.A. forms in particular, the contractor is given substantial rights and pro-tection in regard to such work, which are difficult to justify, except in relation to sub-contractors whose identity is unknown at the date of the contract (and on the basis that their identity, rather than their price, is the primary purpose of the nomination). Thus the main contractor is entitled to an extension of time for delays by nominated sub-contractors,[93] and under the pre-1963 forms was even entitled to determine the contract if the works were delayed for one month due to this cause.[94] The effect of such clauses does not appear to have been properly considered, since they merely have the effect of reduc-ing the liability of defaulting sub-contractors to the advantage of no one else, as in the event of the employer being entitled, for instance, to liquidated damages for such delays, the main contractor would otherwise recover the amount as damages from the sub-contractor and not be out of pocket himself.[95]

Apart from the purely legal anomalies (now increased in potential scope by the *Gloucestershire County Council* and *Bickerton* decisions) the following further abuses of the system may be noted:

(a) No proper description of the sub-contract work exists or is necessary for inclusion in the main contract at the time of signature.[96] This militates against proper pre-planning, and permits the placing of main contracts without the employer being aware of the unplanned state of the project, or enables employers to obtain budgetary support which is only avail-able on an annual basis notwithstanding its unplanned state.

(b) It seems impossible to educate architects and others on the

[92b] See *supra*, p. 757.
[92c] See *e.g.* the confusion in the origin of the word " provisional," *supra*, p. 758.
[93] Clause 23 (*g*), 1963 R.I.B.A. forms, commented on *ante*, Chap. 11, pp. 650 *et seq.*
[94] Clause 20 (1), pre-1963 R.I.B.A. forms.
[95] This last sentence was cited by Edmund Davies L.J. in *Jarvis* v. *Westminster Corporation* [1969] 1 W.L.R. 1448, illustrated *ante*, Chap. 11, p. 652.
[96] See *supra*, p. 761.

necessity for obtaining proper contractual protection for the employer either (i) in the main contract documents or (ii) in the sub-contract documents or (iii) by way of direct warranty from the sub-contractor to the employer, or by a combination of all these.[97]

(c) Particularly serious legal anomalies with the main con-tractor, and a basic clash of commercial interest between sub-contractor and employer, will arise if the nomination includes a design service provided by the sub-contractor.[98]

(d) The transfer of design work from architect to others is often effectively concealed from the employer, who will be effec-tively paying increased fees in the belief that the architect is designing the work.

(e) If design work is transferred, it becomes impossible to obtain really competitive tenders from sub-contractors in cases where a pre-tender design is needed, since one of them has to be selected to do the design on which the others are required to tender.

SECTION 4.   INCORPORATION OF TERMS OF MAIN CONTRACTS

It frequently happens that sub-contracts purport to incorporate the terms of the main contract, or some of the terms. This can give rise to considerable difficulties, since the incorporation is often loosely expressed in the most general words and without any precise or careful consideration of the consequences. Each case must be separately considered to determine exactly to what extent the term or terms of the main contract are incorporated. It follows from the absence of privity between the employer and the sub-contractor that, without incorporation, the terms of the main contract cannot bind the sub-contractor.[99]

ILLUSTRATIONS

(1) A sub-contractor undertook to carry out work in accordance with certain specifications in the main contract. One of these pro-vided for disputes to be settled by arbitration. The sub-contractor sued for his work, and the contractor pleaded that the matter was covered by the arbitration clause. *Held*, the arbitration clause was incorporated only to the extent of making the arbitrator's decisions

---

[97] See the suggested duties, *ante*, Chap. 2, Section 6 (2) (d), pp. 141–142.

[98] See *ante*, Chap. 2, pp. 129–131, and Chap. 5, pp. 277–278, 281–282, 323–324, and the case of *Moresk* v. *Hicks* there illustrated and referred to.

[99] See also as to this *supra*, Section 2, p. 747.

binding on matters of dispute between the main contractor and his employer, and was not incorporated as regards matters between the contractor and sub-contractor: *Goodwins, Jardine & Co.* v. *Brand* (1905).[1]

(2) A sub-contract provided " the terms of payment shall be exactly the same as . . . clause 30 " of the main contract. Clause 30 provided for interim payments on certificates of the architect at the rate of 80 per cent. of work done, and for the usual payments on completion as certified by the architect. The architect refused to certify for certain of the sub-contractor's work on the ground that it was defective. *Held*, the contractor had a good defence to the sub-contractor's claim: *Geary Walker & Co. Ltd.* v. *Lawrence & Son* (1906).[2]

(3) A sub-contract contained many provisions in similar terms to those in the head contract, but none referring to or incorporating a power in the main contract of the engineers to require the removal of a sub-contractor with whom they were dissatisfied. The sub-contractor was delayed by lack of funds, and the engineers served a notice under the main contract. *Held*, (a) the parties had the main contract before them when the sub-contract was concluded, and must be taken to have contemplated this possibility, and no term could be implied in the sub-contract giving the main contractor power to determine the sub-contract upon the engineer's notice being given, and (b) a recital that the sub-contractor had agreed to carry out the work in accordance with the terms of the main contract did not, where other clauses were expressly included, incorporate the clause in question: *Chandler Bros. Ltd.* v. *Boswell* (1936).[3]

(4) Tunnelling sub-contractors undertook for the main contractor " the execution of the work . . . according to the dimensions and specifications as set forth in the contract between (the main contractors and the employers)." Clause 318 of the general specifications provided " The City also reserves the right for the engineer to stop the excavation or any other portion of the work and to require the contractor to complete the sewer and backfilling up to such point as the engineer may direct before proceeding further with the excavation, and the contractor shall not thereby become entitled to demand or recover any allowance or compensation other than an extension of the contract time." This power was exercised, and the sub-contractor sued the main contractor for damages. *Held* by Schroeder J., in the High Court of Ontario, that, following *Chandler* v. *Boswell*, clause 318 was not incorporated into the sub-contract: *Smith & Montgomery* v. *Johnson Bros.* (1954).[4]

(5) The main contractor's order to a nominated sub-contractor contained two provisions: firstly " The party to whom this order is given shall observe and perform the conditions contained in the contract

---

[1] 7 F. (Ct. of Sess.) 995. See also *The Portsmouth* [1912] A.C. 1.

[2] Hudson's B.C., 4th ed., Vol. 2, p. 382.

[3] [1936] 3 All E.R. 179. (*Cf. Osborn* v. *Leggett* (1930) S.A.S.R. 346 (Australia).)

[4] [1954] D.L.R. 392 (Canada). See also the case of *Croft Construction Co.* v. *Terminal Construction Co.* (1960) 20 D.L.R. (2d) 247, illustrated, *ante*, Chap. 7, p. 424. (Not, perhaps, strictly a case of incorporation.)

held by (the main contractor) (which can be inspected at their office) and this order shall be deemed to be supplemental thereto "; and secondly—" Payment for this order is to be made (a) as to the amount if any provided . . . in (the main contractor's) said contract for the works in this order; in accordance with the certificates and the terms provided in the said contract." The main contract (in the then R.I.B.A. form) provided by clause 21 (3) (a) that payment in respect of any work comprised in a nominated sub-contract would not be due until receipt by the main contractor of the architect's certificate relating to the work. *Held*, by the Court of Appeal, that the second provision (but not the first) had the effect of incorporating, as between the main contractor and the sub-contractor, the provisions of the clause 21 (3) (a): *Dunlop & Ranken Ltd* v. *Hendall Steel Structures* (1957).[5]

It is submitted that there is usually little difficulty in giving effect to loose or generalised incorporations where what is referred to is the contract description of the work in question in the main contract (as *e.g.* in the drawings, specification or bills of that contract) and that in cases of doubt it is this part of the main contract which is intended, rather than the detailed application of contractual provisions as to liability, indemnities, or special claims for additional payment. On examination, these are almost always impossible to apply with any precision to the very different relationship between main contractor and sub-contractor.

SECTION 5.   PAYMENT OF SUB-CONTRACTOR DIRECT

Architects not infrequently indicate in their certificates for payment to the contractor what proportion of the sums certified is payable to specialists. This is done with a view to assisting them to obtain payment from the contractor and to prevent the latter from contending, as an excuse for delay in payment, that he has not been paid for the work. This practice occurs even in those cases where there is no power in the main contract so to certify, and arises from the natural anxiety of the architect on behalf of the employer to avoid disturbance of the contract programme.

Unless, however, there is an express power in the main contract for the employer to pay a sub-contractor directly and deduct the sums so paid from moneys due to the main contractor, an employer who actually pays a sub-contractor places himself in peril, since he will nevertheless remain liable to the builder for the same work.

[5] [1957] 1 W.L.R. 1102.

ILLUSTRATION

H. contracted to do certain work for S. By the contract H. was to pay M. £95 net for certain fittings. The architect increased this sum to £137. H. ordered the goods from M. in his own name. H. became bankrupt. The architect deducted £95 from the sum payable to H., and S. paid the £95 to M. under an indemnity. H.'s trustee applied to the county court judge for an order directing the architect to certify that £137 was due from S. to H.'s estate. *Held*, that the judge had jurisdiction to make the order, and that he should have exercised it: *Re Holt, ex p. Gray* (1888).[6]

Though there is no authority on the point, it is submitted that in such a case the employer, if he was acting under the necessity to get the work completed, might have a right to sue or counterclaim against the builder in quasi-contract for money paid to the defendants' use,[7] and that if a payment of this kind took place before the bankruptcy or liquidation and without notice of any act of insolvency, it would be a defence to a claim by the liquidator or trustee under the mutual credit and dealing clause.[8] If the payment was made (as usually it would be in practice) after notice of an act of bankruptcy, however, it would probably not rank as an equitable set-off,[9] with the result that the building owner would have to pay in full and prove in the bankruptcy or liquidation. But it seems clear that if the payment is gratuitous and not made under any compulsion,[10] there could be no relief of any kind against the main contractor and the employer would in fact find himself liable to pay twice for the same work, without even a right to prove in the contractor's liquidation or bankruptcy.

Where, however, an express power does exist, the employer may pay direct, provided the conditions stipulated for the exercise of the power have been strictly observed, and such payment will be valid against the builder's trustee or liquidator. It should be appreciated that if, as is almost invariably the case, the power to pay direct is conditioned upon a failure of the main contractor to pay sums previously certified over to the sub-contractor in question, the essence of the employer's power is to pay twice over for the work in question, and subsequently to recoup from the contractor one of the payments.

ILLUSTRATIONS

(1) W. contracted to construct certain sewerage works for an urban district council. The contract provided (clause 54) that " if

---

[6] 58 L.J.Q.B. 5. See *post*, pp. 777–778, where this case is more fully illustrated.
[7] See Halsbury's *Laws of England*, Vol. 8, pp. 227–229.
[8] *Post*, Chap. 16, p. 781.
[9] *Ante*, Chap. 14, Sections 2 (6) and 5 (5), pp. 725 and 731–734.
[10] Halsbury's *Laws of England*, Vol. 8, p. 231.

the engineer shall have reasonable cause to believe that the contractor is unduly delaying proper payment to the firms supplying
the machinery, he shall have power if he thinks fit to order direct
payment to them." Another clause (129) provided for the supply
of machinery and plant by certain specified firms. Clause 7 provided for the retention of 10 per cent. of the value of the work
executed for six months after completion. On October 12, 1904,
W. was adjudicated bankrupt. At this date W. owed £368 8s. 9d.
to the specialists. £1,349 17s. 8d. was owing under the contract,
but was retention money, and £224 18s. 2d. was payable on the
next certificate of the engineer. On February 7, 1905, the engineer,
after stating that he had reasonable cause to believe that W. was
unduly delaying payment to the specialists, ordered direct payment
to them of sums proportionate to the £224 18s. 2d. On April 5,
he made a similar order directing payment to the specialists of
£611 10s. 7d., the balance of their accounts. On April 24, the
engineer gave his final certificate that W. was entitled to be paid
£738 7s. 1d., which, together with the £611 10s. 7d., so paid to the
specialists made up the retention money. *Held*, that W. had " unduly
delayed proper payment of the specialists." *Held*, also, that the power
conferred by clause 54 on the engineer was not annulled or revoked
by the bankruptcy of W., and that the specialists were entitled to be
paid according to the orders of the engineer in priority to W.'s trustee
in bankruptcy: *Re Wilkinson, ex p. Fowler* (1905).[11]

(2) The 1909 edition of the R.I.B.A. form of contract, identical
to that set out in *Hobbs* v. *Turner* (1902),[12] provided by clause 28
that provisional sums should be paid to such persons as the architect
might direct, and the sums so expended should be payable by the
contractor without discount or deduction *or by the employer* to the
tradesmen. The architect certified in favour of the contractor for
certain sub-contracted work, which he set out in the certificate. The
contractors went into liquidation, and the employers claimed as
against the liquidator to be entitled to pay the sub-contractors upon
certain certificates issued subsequently by the architect in favour of
the sub-contractors. *Held*, clause 28 did empower the architect to
certify direct payment. But, following Maugham J. in the unreported
case of *British S.S. Investment Trust Ltd.* v. *Foundation Co. Ltd.*[13]
the power to pay direct must be strictly construed, and under this
form of contract the architect had no power to issue a certificate in
favour of sub-contractors once he had issued a certificate in favour
of the main contractor in respect of the same work: *Milestone &
Sons Ltd.* v. *Yates Brewery* (1938).[14]

(3) Under clause 21 (*c*) of the then current R.I.B.A. form of
contract, the employer was given power to pay a nominated sub-
contractor direct if, before " any certificate " was issued to the contractor, the latter could not prove that the nominated sub-contractor's
accounts included in previous certificates had been duly discharged.
Held, by Wynn-Parry J., that the power under clause 21 (*c*) could be
exercised prior to the final certificate after the work was complete and

[11] [1905] 2 K.B. 713.
[12] *Supra*, p. 751.
[13] (1930) December 15.
[14] [1938] 2 All E.R. 439.

was not limited to occasions when an interim certificate was due: *Re Tout & Finch Ltd.* (1954).[15]

A word of caution should perhaps be inserted here drawing attention to the complicated conditions which have to be satisfied under the provisions for payment direct in the current R.I.B.A. and I.C.E. forms of contract.[16] There is an important distinction between the two, because whereas under R.I.B.A. forms the power can be exercised at any time when a further certificate to the main contractor is due, the I.C.E. power can only be exercised when a further certificate is due to the main contractor *in respect of the sub-contractor's work.* This means that under the I.C.E. conditions the engineer, if he suspects he may wish to certify payment direct in respect of current work of a sub-contractor, must ensure that there will be some further sum remaining to be certified in a later certificate if he is to be able to do so. It also means that under the I.C.E. conditions a sub-contractor whose work is completed in one month can never be paid direct if the engineer certifies the whole sum in that month. Apart from such complications, the employer must ensure that the ultimate state of accounts between the main contractor and himself will be in his own favour (a) as a matter of commercial prudence, since otherwise he will only be able to prove in the bankruptcy or liquidation for the payment direct and (b) because most provisions of this nature only give a right to deduct, not to sue, following the direct payment. In any event, an employer should never pay direct without obtaining an indemnity from the sub-contractor to cover the eventuality of the payment being successfully challenged. In addition to the power to pay direct conditioned on failure of the main contractor to pay the sub-contractor, the determination clause in the R.I.B.A. standard forms of contract contains the widest powers to take an assignment of any sub-contract and a far wider power to pay direct any sub-contractor or supplier, nominated or otherwise, of the main contractor once a determination has been effected.[17]

In so far as such a determination may be based on the bankruptcy or liquidation of the contractor, however, these powers are almost certainly invalid as offending against the policy of the bankruptcy laws.[18]

---

[15] [1954] 1 W.L.R. 178.
[16] See clause 27 (*c*), 1963 forms and clause 59 (2), 1955 I.C.E. forms.
[17] Clause 25 (3) (*b*), 1963 forms.
[18] See *post*, Chap. 16, pp. 784 *et seq.*

SECTION 6.   SUB-CONTRACTOR'S LIEN AND PROPERTY

In the absence of any provision to the contrary in the sub-contract, a sub-contractor retains the property in materials until they are built into the contract works.[19]

Normally, if the contractor becomes insolvent, the sub-contractor cannot claim any lien or charge on money due to the contractor in respect of the sub-contract work.[20] But a sub-contract can be so framed as to impress retention or other moneys received by the main contractor for sub-contracted work with a trust in favour of the sub-contractor, and this will bind the builder's trustee or liquidator.[21]

SECTION 7.   PERFORMANCE OF SUB-CONTRACTS

In Chapter 5 of this book an attempt has been made to set out the basic general obligations and rights of the parties to a building or engineering contract. It was possible to do this, notwithstanding that under the law of contract everything must naturally yield to the expressed intention of the parties, because the main requirements of such contracts are generally similar in character, and are consequently either left for implication or generally expressed in broadly similar terms. It was thus possible to deal in a general way with questions such as the right of the contractor to possession, the time for giving information to him, and his duty to proceed with due diligence and many other more detailed matters.

Such generalisations are neither possible nor useful in relation to sub-contracts. Thus one type of sub-contract may require a series of visits to the site, often after relatively short notice (as by a plasterer where a number of buildings or a large number of rooms are involved in one contract), whereas another may require a single unbroken period of working (as in the case of a sub-contractor for the structural steel frame of a building). Again, one type of sub-contractor may require physically undisturbed possession of the site as a whole (as for instance an excavation-only or structural steel sub-contractor) whereas another must of necessity work with and in dependence upon

---

[19] See the discussion and cases, *ante*, Chap. 12, pp. 656 *et seq.*

[20] *Pritchett and Gold and Electric Power Storage Co.* v. *Currie* [1916] 2 Ch. 515 (see *ante*, p. 679).

[21] For a discussion of this subject and the important practical limitations upon it, see *ante*, pp. 729–730, and the case of *Re Tout & Finch* [1954] 1 All E.R. 127 there illustrated. For the position of the sub-contractor in the builder's bankruptcy, see *post*, Chap. 16, Bankruptcy and Liquidation, pp. 791–793.

others (as for instance in the case of concreting, shuttering and steel-fixing or in the case, very often, of plasterers and painters). Every such contract must turn on its special facts, and in many cases it would be an almost superhuman task for the draftsman to express with any precision the obligations and rights of the parties as to time for performance and possession of the site in sub-contracted work of this kind. In practice this kind of work is usually let under condensed and loosely phrased documents such as quotations and orders, although very large sums of money may be involved, and if disputes arise it will only be by the implication of terms that the rights of the parties can be established. The terms to be implied will be largely governed by the nature of the work carried out by both the employing contractor and the sub-contractor, the contract programme of the former, and the known size and capacity of the sub-contractor's organisation.

Examples of the difficult problems of fact likely to arise in such cases are to be found in the Canadian cases illustrated in Chapter 5 of *Smith & Montgomery* v. *Johnson Bros.* (1954),[22] *Pigott Construction Ltd.* v. *W. J. Crowe Ltd.* (1961),[23] and *Swanson Construction* v. *Government of Manitoba* (1963).[24]

[22] 1 D.L.R. (2d) 392, illustrated *ante*, p. 351.
[23] 27 D.L.R. (2d) 258, illustrated *ante*, pp. 338–339.
[24] 40 D.L.R. (2d) 162, illustrated *ante*, pp. 339, 358.

CHAPTER 16

BANKRUPTCY AND LIQUIDATION

SECTION 1. GENERAL EFFECT OF BANKRUPTCY AND
WINDING UP

SEPARATE codes govern the law of insolvency, depending upon whether the insolvent person is an individual or a company. The law relating to individuals is substantially governed by the provisions of the Bankruptcy Act 1914; that relating to companies, by the provisions of Part V of the Companies Act of 1948. While the broad effect of the two codes is similar, there are important differences of detail and an attempt will be made to indicate these in the course of this chapter, in so far as they are relevant to building contracts.

The effect of a winding up is to bring all the assets of a company, including its current contracts, into the custody and control of the liquidator as from the date of the winding-up order.

The effect of bankruptcy is actually to vest the property of the bankrupt, including both the benefit and burden of his contracts, in the trustee, except those contracts of the debtor which are of a personal character and are still uncompleted at the date of the bankruptcy—i.e. where the personal skill of the bankrupt is of the essence of the contract, so that the other party is entitled to refuse to accept vicarious performance of the contract by the trustee.[1] Even in such a case, however, if the bankrupt is willing to complete the contract he may sue the other party on the contract or for breach of it, subject to any right the trustee may have to intervene and claim the proceeds of the action.[2]

The extent to which building contracts are personal in this sense is a matter of some difficulty, and has been discussed *ante*, Chapter 14, and there is an absence of modern authority on the matter. It has been suggested [3] that a distinction may need to be drawn in some contracts between a builder's general obligations to supervise and co-ordinate the work and his obligation to carry out the work in

---

[1] *Knight* v. *Burgess* (1864) 33 L.J.Ch. 727, *ante*, p. 719. (This may include some building contracts, see *ante*, Chap. 14, pp. 717 *et seq.* and p. 724, where this is discussed.)

[2] *Bailey* v. *Thurston & Co. Ltd.* [1903] 1 K.B. 137.

[3] See *ante*, Chap. 14, Assignment, pp. 717–718. See also pp. 719–720, 724, and 738–739.

detail, and that, at any rate in substantial building work, the personality of the builder in the former case may be essential. There is, however, little doubt that contracts between employers and their architects, engineers or surveyors would in most cases not vest in the trustee of the professional men concerned.[4]

In bankruptcy the effective date for the vesting of property is not the date of adjudication, but the commencement of the bankruptcy, which by section 37 of the Act of 1914 occurs at the time of commission of the act of bankruptcy to which the receiving order relates, or, if more than one, to the first act occurring within three months preceding the presentation of the petition. This doctrine of " relation back " is, however, considerably mitigated by section 45 of the Act of 1914, which protects all " transactions " made with the bankrupt for valuable consideration prior to receiving order and without notice of an act of bankruptcy. This provision is of great importance in relation to the exercise of powers of forfeiture after the bankruptcy since the " transaction " for this purpose is the original contract under which the powers are conferred, and consequently a power of forfeiture or other contractual right can be validly exercised after the bankruptcy provided the contract itself was entered into prior to the receiving order without notice of an act of bankruptcy.[5]

Unlike death or illness, therefore, the bankruptcy or liquidation of a party to a contract does not by itself have the effect of terminating the contract or constitute a breach of it, since both liquidator and trustee have the power, after obtaining leave, to carry on the business of the debtor so far as may be necessary for its beneficial winding up,[6] and can therefore in appropriate cases carry on and complete any contracts of the debtor. However, contracts under which the debtor has assumed long-term obligations in the future will be treated as impossible for the trustee or liquidator to perform, and in such a case the other party can prove at once for damages even though the trustee or liquidator purports to carry out the contract.

ILLUSTRATION

A company agreed with Commissioners to pave a street with wood and, if required, to keep it in repair for fifteen years at a specified price. When the work of paving was partly done the company went into liquidation, but the liquidator completed the paving. Upon the facts it was held that the covenant to repair

---

[4] See infra, Bankruptcy of Architect or Engineer at pp. 793–794. See also Stubbs v. Holywell Ry., ante, Chap. 14, p. 738.

[5] See infra. Section 5, subs. (1).   [6] Act of 1914, s. 56; Act of 1948, s. 48.

for fifteen years was broken and rendered impossible, and that the Commissioners could prove in the liquidation for unliquidated damages for breach of contract: *Re Asphaltic Wood Pavement Co. ex p. Lee & Chapman* (1885).[7]

Furthermore, a right exists for any person who is, as against the trustee or liquidator, entitled to the benefit or subject to the burden of a contract made with the debtor, to apply for an order rescinding the contract on such terms as to payment of damages for non-performance of the contract or otherwise as the court may consider equitable.[8]

In addition it is, of course, the case that many forms of building contract contain express provisions against assignment, or enabling the employer and the contractor to terminate the contract on, amongst other things, the bankruptcy or liquidation of the other party. Although the matter is not entirely free from doubt, it is submitted that such a clause is in fact void against the trustee or liquidator if exercised on the ground of bankruptcy or liquidation alone,[9] but where valid when exercised on other grounds the effect of such a clause obviously imposes a drastic limitation on the power of the trustee or liquidator to elect to complete the contract, should the other party decide to exercise his contractual rights under the clause.

One further remedy should be mentioned which is available to a builder's trustee under section 105 of the Act of 1914. In those cases where an insolvent builder's remuneration depends upon an architect's certificate and the builder has clearly earned the right to payment, it has been held that the architect can be ordered to grant the certificate, independently of any contractual right, under section 105 (1) of the Act of 1914. This section provides in wide terms that the court shall have full power to decide all questions of priorities and all other questions whatsoever, whether of law or fact, which may arise in any case of bankruptcy or which it may be necessary to decide for the purpose of doing complete justice or making a complete distribution of property.

ILLUSTRATION

H., a builder, contracted to perform joiner's work. Payment was to be on architect's certificate. Certain stable fittings were the subject of a provisional sum for £95, and were to be procured from M. & Co. By the architect's direction this sum was increased

---

[7] 30 Ch.D. 216 (C.A.). See also the comment on this case *infra*, pp. 781–782.
[8] Act of 1914, s. 54 (5); Act of 1948, s. 323 (5).
[9] See *infra*, pp. 784 *et seq.*

to £137, and fittings to this value were duly installed. On H.'s bankruptcy, M. & Co. had not been paid, and applied to the employers for payment direct. On receipt of an indemnity the employers paid £95 to M. & Co. direct. H.'s trustee applied to the architect for a certificate for £137, but the architect refused to certify more than £42, namely, £137 less the sum of £95 paid direct by the employer to M. & Co. *Held*, that under section 102 (1) of the Bankruptcy Act 1883,[10] the bankruptcy court had jurisdiction to order the issue of the certificate for payment of the full sum to the trustee. The architect was attempting to interfere with the bankruptcy laws, which required M. & Co. to prove in the bankruptcy for the sum owing to them: *Re Holt, ex p. Gray* (1888).[11]

Such a power would not appear to exist in the case of a winding up, where the liquidator would probably be limited to bringing an action on the contract, as it seems unlikely that this provision is applied to winding up by section 317 of the Act of 1948.[12] But there would be no defence (apart from the absence of any certificate required by the contract) to such a claim by the liquidator, and the fact of payment direct would afford no answer to the claim.

Section 2.   Disclaimer and Adoption

(1) Disclaimer

As the natural corollary of their obligation only to carry on the business of the debtor so far as may be necessary for its beneficial winding up, both trustee and liquidator have power within twelve months of appointment to disclaim unprofitable contracts which are still uncompleted at the commencement of bankruptcy or liquidation.[13] Since uncertainty for such a long period could be gravely prejudicial to the other party to the contract, both trustee and liquidator are, however, compelled to give notice of their intention to disclaim within twenty-eight days (or such extension as the court may allow) on application in writing being made by any person interested requiring a decision. In the event of the trustee or liquidator taking no action within this period, the trustee or *the company* (not the liquidator, who is not usually personally liable in the same way as a trustee in bankruptcy), as the case may be, will be deemed

---

[10] Re-enacted by s. 105 (1) of the Act of 1914.

[11] 58 L.J.Q.B. 5.

[12] Modern contracts, however, frequently contain clauses empowering employers to pay sub-contractors direct. See *infra*, pp. 791 *et seq.* and *ante*, Chap. 15, p. 769.

[13] Act of 1914, s. 54; Act of 1948, s. 323.

to have adopted the contract.[14] Should the building owner wish for an even speedier decision, he can apply to the court for rescission under section 54 (5) of the Act of 1914, or section 323 (5) of the Act of 1948.

The effect of the disclaimer is to discharge the trustee from all personal liability as from the date when the contract vested in him (*i.e.* upon his appointment) and, as from the date of disclaimer, to terminate all the rights, interests and liabilities of the bankrupt in the disclaimed contract.[15] In the case of a company, the liquidator is never personally liable, but disclaimer has a similar effect on the *company's* rights, interests and liabilities as it has on the bankrupt's [16] (*i.e.* from the date of disclaimer). Thus in both cases disclaimer puts an end to the contract, and in the case of a building contractor becoming bankrupt, for instance, it will leave the building owner with the right to prove for damages for what he has lost by the disclaimer.[17] In the absence of any authority, it is not clear to what extent he may forfeit materials or exercise other specific powers conferred on him by the contract after the disclaimer. Where the property in materials or right to their possession and user has already passed under a vesting or seizure clause, it seems clear that disclaimer would make no difference. In *Re Fussell, ex p. Allen,*[18] it was held that a trustee could not disclaim a lease under which both chattels and land had been leased to the debtor, and at the same time claim the chattels under the doctrine of reputed ownership.[19] The cases on disclaimer of leases do show that, even on disclaimer, the trustee may be subject to certain rights of the landlord. But the question remains to what extent the trustee or liquidator of a builder remains liable on disclaimer to powers or provisions reserved in the contract to the owner in the event of the builder's default. On principle, it would seem that disclaimer operates on the state of affairs as at the time of the disclaimer, when there may have been no default or no valid seizure or passing of property, leaving the other party to prove in damages. If this is correct, the trustee would be entitled to remove property not yet seized, and the employer prevented from exercising any further rights over them based upon the hypothesis that the contract was still in being. On the other

---

[14] Act of 1914, s. 54 (4); Act of 1948, s. 323 (4).

[15] Act of 1914, s. 54 (2).

[16] Act of 1948, s. 232 (2).

[17] s. 54 (7) of the Act of 1914; s. 323 (8) of the Act of 1948.

[18] (1882) 20 Ch.D. 341.

[19] As to which, see *infra,* p. 788.

hand, disclaimer in such a case deprives the builder of all those clauses in the contract which are for his benefit, so that a builder's trustee may be unable to recover the retention moneys, and the clauses as to certificates will probably be inoperative. In effect, therefore, disclaimer operates as a repudiation of the contract which the other party must accept, subject to his right to prove for damages. Despite the apparent period of twelve months allowed to the trustee or liquidator by the Acts to elect between disclaimer and adoption, this will not override provisions in the contract empowering the owner to terminate on default or enter and complete himself, provided he can establish the facts upon which the power of determination is conditioned.[20]

(2) Adoption of the Contract

Adoption of the contract has a slightly different effect as between trustee and liquidator. Once a trustee adopts a contract, he does so subject to all its terms and becomes personally liable for all breaches as from the date of his appointment, though with a right to recoupment out of the estate.[21] It has, however, been suggested [22] that the effect of section 54 (4) of the Act of 1914 is to limit his liability to the extent of the assets of the estate in a case where he is deemed to have adopted the contract under that section (*i.e.* by failing to give a decision within the twenty-eight-day period). On the other hand a liquidator is never personally liable, since the company's property does not automatically vest in him, and even if a vesting order is obtained it vests the property in him in his official and not his personal capacity.[23] The practical effect of adoption of a contract by the liquidator is therefore to enable the other party to the contract to have recourse to the company's assets in priority to ordinary creditors in the winding up, should he have a claim under the contract. Obviously, this may be a less effective protection than the trustee's personal liability in bankruptcy [24] (and is no doubt the reason for the special rules under section 447 of the Companies Acts whereby security for costs of litigation can be obtained in the case of companies in liquidation). In a case where the liquidator fails to give a decision within twenty-eight days when required to do so and, in

---

[20] See *e.g. Re Waugh, ex p. Dicken* (1876) 4 Ch.D. 524; *Re Garrud, ex p. Newitt* (1881) 16 Ch.D. 522; *Re Keen, ex p. Collins* [1902] 1 K.B. 555; *supra*, pp. 777–778.

[21] *Titterton* v. *Cooper* (1882) 9 Q.B.D. 473 (C.A.).

[22] *Williams on Bankruptcy*, 17th ed. at p. 408.

[23] See *Buckley on Companies*, 12th ed., pp. 514–516.

[24] But see the possible additional protection under the rule in *Re Sneezum, infra*, Section 4, p. 782.

the words of section 323 (4) of the Act of 1948 " the company shall be deemed to have adopted " the contract, the same result follows, though the wording of the section, which contemplates adoption by a company of its own contracts and is clearly based on the provisions of section 54 of the Act of 1914 relating to disclaimer by a trustee, is not very happy. Where, however, a liquidator enters into a fresh contract after the winding up, he would appear to be personally liable.[25] In both cases, once there has been adoption the contract may be terminated by the other party for any cause—e.g. delay— which might have given a right of termination as against the debtor.[26]

If a trustee or liquidator completes a contract, questions of priority may arise between him and prior assignees, e.g. of moneys due or to become due under the contract.[27]

A trustee who has adopted is entitled to the benefit of any arbitration clause (Arbitration Act 1950, s. 3 (1)).

SECTION 3.   RIGHT OF SET-OFF UNDER MUTUAL CREDIT
AND DEALING CLAUSE

By section 31 of the Act of 1914 (applied to winding up by section 317 of the Act of 1948), it is provided that where there have been mutual credits, mutual debts, or other mutual dealings between a debtor and any person proving a debt, an account shall be taken of what is due from the one party to the other in respect of mutual dealings and the balance of the account and no more shall be claimed or paid on either side respectively. This is obviously a necessary and important advantage to the solvent person, since he will not have to pay one debt in full to the bankrupt while being limited to a dividend only when pursuing his other claim against the bankrupt. The section applies to persons having no notice of an act of bankruptcy on the part of the debtor, and is a provision of great practical importance in building contracts, since claims by a building owner for breach of contract actual or prospective [28] can be set off against moneys claimed by a trustee or liquidator in all cases, whether the contract has been adopted or disclaimed—see e.g. Re Asphaltic Wood Pavement Co.,

[25] Burt, Boulton & Hayward v. Bull [1895] 1 Q.B. 276 (a case on receivers and managers appointed by the court).
[26] Supra, p. 776.
[27] This subject is dealt with in Section 7, post, pp. 794 et seq. See also ante, Chap. 14, p. 729.
[28] (And perhaps in quasi-contract, e.g. for direct payment of sub-contractors—see Chap. 15, p. 770.)

ex p. Lee & Chapman,[29] where it was further held that under section 39 of the Bankruptcy Act 1869 (which corresponds to section 31 of the Act of 1914) the damages could be set off by the Commissioners against the payments and retention moneys due to the company on the completion of the paving. Conversely, in an employer's bankruptcy a builder proving for his remuneration could set off any moneys owed by him under the contract—*e.g.* liquidated damages for delay in completion—and prove only for the balance owing to him. But the rights in question must arise under the contract. So, where an employer has a right to detain and use plant until completion of the contract (but not to sell and dispose of it), he cannot by virtue of this section deduct the value of the plant after completion from sums due to him from the contractor under this section, there being no contractual provision or rule of law entitling him to do so.[30]

SECTION 4.   INSOLVENCY OF EMPLOYER

Many building contracts may involve the giving of credit to the employer by the builder, either in respect of goods and materials supplied or work and labour being done, whether by way of work done prior to entitlement to interim payment, or of retention money or otherwise. Since a builder has no lien on his finished work for the price,[31] the employer's insolvency may place him in a position of some difficulty, at any rate until adoption of the contract by the trustee; and if the employer is a company even adoption by the liquidator might not be an adequate protection if the assets of the company appear inadequate. In cases relating to the sale of goods where the contract provided for delivery of goods on credit, or for payment by instalments, it has been held that the seller need not deliver after the bankruptcy until he has been paid,[32] and in *Re Sneezum* (1876),[33] Mellish L.J. suggested this would apply also to contracts of employment. It is submitted that this modification of the liability of the solvent party to the contract must properly be extended to building contracts in appropriate cases, and that the

[29] (1885) 30 Ch.D. 216 (C.A.), *supra*, pp. 776–777.
[30] *Re Winter, ex p. Bolland* (1878) 8 Ch.D. 225, *ante*, Chap. 12, pp. 665–666. See also *ante*, Chap. 12, pp. 678–679 for a full discussion of the special considerations relating to clauses governing materials and plant.
[31] See Chap. 12, pp. 612 *et seq.*
[32] *Ex p. Chalmers* (1873) 42 L.J.Eq. 37, and see *Ex p. Carnforth, etc. Co.* (1876) 4 Ch.D. 108.
[33] 3 Ch.D. at p. 473.

builder will in such a case be entitled to refuse to continue work unless the cost of doing so is secured to him.[34]

A further protection for the contractor in the event of the employer's insolvency has now been sought to be conferred by the 1963 standard R.I.B.A. forms of contract, under which the contractors, following the example of the provision in the F.A.S.S. form of sub-contract imposing a trust in favour of the sub-contractor on the retention moneys relating to sub-contracted work, have secured a similar provision [35] affecting the retention moneys under the main contract. In the case of the F.A.S.S. sub-contract, the validity of the trust so created in favour of the sub-contractor, and the fact that it bound the trustee or liquidator or other assignee of the main contractor, was upheld by Wynn-Parry J. in the case of *Re Tout and Finch* (1954),[36] and there is no reason to suppose that the validity, as against the employer's trustee or liquidator in favour of the main contractor, of the new provision in the 1963 R.I.B.A. form will not be similarly upheld. The practical difficulties in the way of giving effect to such a provision, (a) because there is not likely to be any ascertainable or traceable fund of money to which the trust can be attached, and (b) because of the virtual certainty that such funds as are available will be in the hands of purchasers for value without notice, may, however, reduce its practical value to negligible proportions.[37]

SECTION 5.   INSOLVENCY OF BUILDER

Under this heading it is proposed to deal with such provisions of the usual forms of building contract as are particularly affected by, or contemplate, the insolvency of the builder. There are three main kinds, namely, provisions for forfeiture, vesting provisions, and provisions for the direct payment of sub-contractors by the employer.

(1) Forfeiture

As has been seen, forfeiture in the context of building contracts is a somewhat loose expression. In other branches of the law, *e.g.* of leases or contracts for the sale of land, it has a well-defined meaning, the nearest analogy to which in a building contract would be a simple

---

[34] See in particular *Bellamy* v. *Davey* [1891] 3 Ch. 540, illustrated *ante*, Chap. 12, Section 1, p. 657, and commented on p. 679.

[35] Clause 30 (4) (*a*).

[36] [1954] 1 W.L.R. 178, *ante*, Chap. 14, Section 5 (2), p. 729.

[37] See *ante*, Chap. 14, p. 730 where the subject is discussed.

right to determine the contract itself or treat it as at an end in certain events, which is also the right of any party to a contract where a fundamental term has been broken by the other. Such a provision is, in fact, comparatively rare in building contracts. It is more usual to find somewhat elaborate provisions whereby, in certain events, the employer is empowered to enter into possession and complete himself, or appoint others to do so, seizing and using plant and materials for the purpose and regulating the state of accounts between the parties. Each such clause must be considered separately, and in some cases at least the clause cannot be satisfactorily invoked if the employer does not wish to complete the works, as a simple clause for forfeiture or termination could.[38]

For the purpose of this chapter, which is concerned with the interrelation of the law of bankruptcy with the provisions of building contracts, the term " forfeiture clause " will be treated as comprehending a clause permitting the employer to terminate the contract *simpliciter*, or a clause for entry into possession and completion by the employer, or a clause empowering the employer merely to detain, or to have a lien upon, or to seize and use, or to seize and obtain ownership of, plant materials or other property (including the benefit of sub-contracts) of the builder, or a clause automatically transferring to or vesting such property in the employer, or any combination of such clauses.[39]

This broad category follows the reasoning and language of the courts, who in formulating the principles of bankruptcy affecting clauses of these various kinds, all of which in a greater or lesser degree pass rights of property, however limited, from the builder to the employer, do not appear to have made any clear distinction between them. It is submitted, in fact, that the same principles apply to them all, though there is an absence of clear authority in the case of forfeiture of the contract as a whole.

It is submitted that the correct view in relation to a clause of any of these kinds is that, if it is expressed to arise or take effect upon the bankruptcy or liquidation of the builder, *and is in fact invoked upon that ground*, then, while perfectly valid between the parties themselves, it will be void against the trustee or liquidator.

As regards determination, this may not be entirely free from doubt, since, in the case of leases, provisions for forfeiture of the entire lease in the event of the lessee's bankruptcy or liquidation are

---

[38] A full discussion of this subject is to be found in Chap. 13, Forfeiture, *ante*.

[39] For the construction of these latter clauses, see *ante*, Chap. 12, Vesting of Materials and Plant, pp. 661 *et seq*.

undoubtedly valid against the trustee.[40] This is probably, it is suggested, because a lease is looked on as a grant rather than a contract for this purpose, and it has long been settled law that a person alienating an interest to another can impose a condition limiting or controlling the interest in the event of the other's bankruptcy. There seems no doubt, however, in the case of lesser rights.

The reason for the rule in building cases was stated by Fry L.J. in *Ex p. Barter, re Walker* (1884).[41] " But in our opinion, a power upon bankruptcy to control the user after bankruptcy of property vested in the bankrupt at the date of the bankruptcy is invalid. The general rule on this subject was thus expressed many years ago by Mr. Swanston in language which was adopted as accurate by Lord Hatherley in *Whitmore* v. *Mason*: ' The general distinction seems to be that the owner of property may, on alienation, qualify the interest of his alienee by a condition to take effect on bankruptcy; but cannot, by contract or otherwise, qualify his own interest by a like condition, determining or controlling it in the event of his own bankruptcy, to the disappointment or delay of his creditors. . . .' It was strenuously argued before us that the clause in question is clearly for the benefit and not for the detriment of the creditors because, it is said, the completion of the ship will lessen the amount for which the [shipowner] might otherwise prove against the bankrupt's estate. But this argument appears to us fallacious because, in the absence of the clause in question the trustee in bankruptcy would have had the election to complete the ship or not as might seem best for the creditors, but the presence of this clause has transferred that election to the buyers. . . . "

ILLUSTRATIONS

(1) Under a building contract, the owners were empowered to take possession of work already done by the builder, subject to paying a fair proportion of the contract price, in the event of his bankruptcy. Certain sash frames had been delivered to the site for approval by the clerk of works and, after approval, returned to the builder's workshop to be fitted with iron pulleys. Three days after an act of bankruptcy they were re-delivered to the site. The builder went bankrupt, and had in fact been substantially overpaid. The trustee claimed the frames or their value. *Held*, the frames were not " work already done," not having been incorporated in the work, and could not be taken by the owners under their power, but even if they were work done, the bankrupt had no power to make a contract which, after his bankruptcy, would vest in other

---

[40] See *e.g. Smith* v. *Gronow* [1891] 2 Q.B. 394 and *Civil Service Co-operative Society* v. *McGrigor's Trustee* [1923] 2 Ch. 347.

[41] (1884) 26 Ch.D. 510 at p. 519.

persons the property which would otherwise vest in his trustee: *Tripp* v. *Armitage* (1839).[42]

(2) A building lease agreement provided that in the event of certain defaults or bankruptcy of the builder all improvements materials and effects on the land should become absolutely forfeited to the landlord, and the landlord was to be at liberty to re-enter and take possession of the ground, premises, chattels, and effects and to relet the same as if the agreement had never been made. The builder became bankrupt and the landlord went into possession. Up to the time of entry there had been no default, so the lessor could base his forfeiture only on the bankruptcy. *Held*, the provision for forfeiture of materials to the landlord on the bankruptcy of the builder was void, as contrary to the policy of the bankruptcy law. *Per* Cotton L.J.: " Here the forfeiture is to take place on the happening of either of two events, which were (1) default in the performance of certain stipulations and (2) bankruptcy or insolvency. . . . One of the two events is not hit by the decided cases. But as to the other, though the contract is good as between the parties to it, it is on principle void in the event of the builder's bankruptcy ": *Ex p. Jay, re Harrison* (1880).[43]

[Note: This was a building lease agreement, and at the time of bankruptcy no lease had been executed. The lessor's re-entry itself was not in dispute between the parties, and in fact the trustee had disclaimed the agreement at a later stage. It is just possible that in the case of a building lease agreement, re-entry on bankruptcy might be upheld on the analogy of the law relating to leases, though the close connection between this right and the associated rights of seizing materials, etc. might create considerable difficulties.]

(3) A vesting clause in a shipbuilding agreement effectively vested in the purchaser a ship and her engines and everything " bought or ordered " for them. A seizure clause, expressed to arise on default or bankruptcy, provided that it should be " lawful for the buyer to cause the ship to be completed by any person he might see fit to employ, or to contract with some other person for the completion of the work agreed to be done by the builder, and to employ such materials belonging to the builder as should then be on his premises." The buyers took formal possession on the bankruptcy, but allowed the trustee to continue the work until he suspended it, when the buyers finished the ship using the materials. *Held*, the use of the materials bought or ordered for the ship was not a conversion, as they already belonged to the buyer, but so far as the remaining materials were concerned, the clause was void as against the trustee as being an attempt to control the user after bankruptcy of the bankrupt's property, and as depriving him of the right of election, and the buyers were liable for their value. Nor could the seizure be supported because, subsequent to the seizure, work had been suspended: *Ex p. Barter, re Walker* (1884).[44]

[Note: Again, the entry into possession was not in dispute between the parties, and the trustee eventually suspended work himself. It can

[42] 4 M. & W. 687 (*per* Abinger C.B. at p. 699).
[43] 14 Ch.D. 19 (C.A.).
[44] 26 Ch.D. 510.

be argued that the right to determine the contract on the ground
of insolvency is not, just as in the case of leases, bad in principle,
and that the right is only invalidated if accompanied by some provision forfeiting materials, goods or other physical property of the
debtor in the event of his insolvency. But it is submitted that the
language of Fry L.J. in this case in referring to the trustee's right of
election makes it clear that, where a trustee elected to complete,
the entry into possession and expulsion of the builder would be
invalid in the same way as the right to use materials.]

Where, however, a clause of this kind is expressed to depend
upon bankruptcy or upon some other event or events, it will be valid
as against the trustee or liquidator if in fact invoked upon another
ground.[45] On the other hand, once invoked on the ground of
bankruptcy, such a clause cannot be supported because subsequently the other events occur upon which the clause could have
been validly invoked.[46]

It has been argued on numerous occasions that where a power of
this kind (whether exercisable on bankruptcy or not) has been
exercised with notice of an act of bankruptcy, or after the receiving
order, the doctrine of relation back prevents the power being validly
exercised against the trustee. This argument has been consistently
rejected by the courts, who have held that a power of forfeiture
exercised under a building contract is a protected transaction under
(now) section 45 of the Act of 1914, and that, in effect, the transaction for the purpose of the section is the original contract, so that,
provided the contract itself was entered into before a receiving order
and without notice of an act of bankruptcy, the powers under it can
be exercised at any time and independently of notice.[47]

ILLUSTRATIONS

(1) A building contract contained a provision that, in the event
of default or bankruptcy, the architect might, on two days' notice,
appoint other persons to complete the work, and seize plant and
materials.[48] On May 30 the builder filed his petition (an act of
bankruptcy) and on June 2 the employers gave notice for default,
and then entered and seized. *Held,* the evidence as to whether the
employers had notice of the filing of the petition when they gave
notice under the contract was obscure, but that did not matter,
because the transaction for the purpose of section 94 of the Act of
1869 really took place at the date of the contract. *Per* Bacon C.J.:

---

[45] See, *e.g. Re Waugh, ex p. Dicken* (1876) 4 Ch.D. 524, *infra,* and *per* Cotton L.J. in
ex p. Jay, re Harrison (1880) 14 Ch.D. 19, *supra.*
[46] *Ex p. Barter, re Walker, supra.*
[47] In addition to the cases illustrated below, see *Re Wilkinson, ex p. Fowler* [1905]
2 K.B. 713, illustrated *ante,* Chap. 15, pp. 770–771.
[48] For the clause in full, see Chap. 12, p. 664, *supra.*

" If that was a valid contract, and if the licence there granted was unimpeachable, it does not signify to what time the trustee's title related back ": *Re Waugh, ex p. Dicken* (1876).[49]

(2) A building lease agreement contained a clause empowering the lessor, on default only, to re-enter, repossess and expel the lessee as if the agreement had not been made, and on such re-entry all buildings, erections, materials and things in and about the premises were to be forfeited and become the property of the lessor as and for liquidated damages. The lessor re-entered under the clause after the lessee had filed his petition. *Held*, the re-entry and seizure of materials was valid against the trustee. *Per* James L.J.: "Another point taken before us was . . . that the seizure was not made in sufficient time, that it was not made before the filing of the liquidation petition. To my mind it is immaterial at what particular moment the seizure was made. The broad general principle is that the trustee in bankruptcy takes all the bankrupt's property, but subject to all liabilities which affected it on the bankrupt's lands, unless the property which he takes as the . . . representative of the bankrupt is added to by some express provision of the bankruptcy law ": *Ex p. Newitt, re Garrud* (1881).[50]

(3) A building contract provided that, in the event of delay by the builder, the employer might serve notice, and on non-compliance with the notice, no further sums should be paid on account of the contract by the employer, and all plant and materials should be forfeited to him, and in such event it should be lawful for him to enter and take possession of the works and employ any other person to carry on and complete them. After the builder filed his petition, the employer gave notice to the builder and the receiver, and then entered and seized under the clause. *Held*, the contract was a protected transaction, and under it the builder's title to the goods was a defeasible title, and the trustee could have no better title: *Re Keen, ex p. Collins* (1902).[51]

(2) " Vesting " Clauses, and the Doctrine of Reputed Ownership

These clauses have been fully examined in Chapter 12, Vesting of Materials and Plant, and the distinction between them and " seizure " clauses considered and analysed. Obviously, such clauses can only assist the employer in the event of the builder's bankruptcy or insolvency if they have the effect of transferring ownership or a right to possession of the contractor's materials or plant before the bankruptcy, or of enabling the employer to seize or acquire them afterwards, and whether or not this is effected under a vesting or seizure clause is immaterial. The classical type of vesting clause, which transfers full ownership upon delivery to the site, is not affected by

[49] L.R. 4 Ch.D. 524 (following *Krehl* v. *Great Central Gas Co.* (1870) L.R. 5 Ex. 289).
[50] 16 Ch.D. 522.
[51] [1902] 1 K.B. 555.

the rules described under " forfeiture " above, because it does not take effect upon the bankruptcy of the builder, and it may well save an employer whose seizure on bankruptcy has been invalidated, where both " seizure " and " vesting " clauses exist side by side in the same contract. Thus in *Ex p. Barter, re Walker* (1884)[52] the existence of a separate vesting clause in addition to the seizure clause was held sufficient to protect the shipowner where the subject-matter of the seizure was already his property under the vesting clause.

But the effectiveness as a protection and security of any clause passing full ownership of materials or plant to the employer (including typical vesting clauses) is, however, subject to major qualifications, one legal and one practical. In the first place, under the doctrine of reputed ownership (which applies only in personal bankruptcies and not in company liquidations), which is governed by section 38 of the Act of 1914 (sometimes known as the " order or disposition " section), there are vested in the trustee " all goods being, at the commencement of the bankruptcy, in the possession, order or disposition of the bankrupt, in his trade or business, by the consent and permission of the true owner, under such circumstances that he is the reputed owner thereof." This means that the employer's right to goods as against the trustee may, paradoxically enough, be defeated if, at the date of the bankruptcy, he has already acquired ownership of the goods under some clause in the contract, but has allowed them to remain in the possession or control of the builder. Nearly always, of course, this will have occurred under some kind of vesting clause, since seized goods will not generally remain in the bankrupt's possession.

Whether or not, however, the circumstances are such that the builder is the " reputed owner " so that the trustee's title will prevail, is, of course, a matter of inference from the facts, and clearly with the passage of time and changed circumstances in the building industry, different inferences can be drawn from similar facts. It is now clear that materials on a building site (as opposed to plant or equipment of the builder) will not be in the reputed ownership of the builder.

ILLUSTRATIONS

(1) A building agreement provided that all loose materials and plant brought upon the premises should " be deemed to be annexed to the freehold." There was also a seizure clause. *Held,* that the vesting clause operated to transfer ownership to the landlord " in a general sense " prior to the bankruptcy, and that consequently the

---

[52] *Supra*, p. 786.

requirements of the reputed ownership provisions were satisfied and the goods vested in the trustee: *Re Weibking, ex p. Ward* (1902).[53]

(2) Clause 11 of the pre-1963 R.I.B.A. form of contract provided that " unfixed materials and goods intended for and placed on or adjacent to the works," the value of which had been included in any interim certificate under clause 24, became the property of the employer.[54] The builder's trustee in bankruptcy claimed three categories of goods, which had been paid for by the employer, as being in the reputed ownership of the builder. These were (a) certain materials provided by the builder which, because of congestion on the site, had by permission of the architects been left in the builder's yard, (b) certain materials provided by the builder lying loose on the site and (c) certain loose materials provided not by the builder but by a sub-contractor on terms that they remained the sub-contractor's property until incorporation in the work. *Held*, by the Court of Appeal, (1) that the goods in category (a), being in the builder's yard, were in his reputed ownership and vested in the trustee, but (2), distinguishing *Re Weibking, ex p. Ward* on the ground that in that case from rather incomplete facts it seemed that the builder was a speculative builder on his own account, neither of the other two categories were in the builder's reputed ownership, because a hypothetical enquirer seeing goods on a building site where the contractor was building for someone else and not on his own account would know that ownership of materials on site would depend on the terms of the building contract, and that they might or might not be the property of the builder: *Re Fox, ex p. Oundle & Thrapston R.D.C.* v. *The Trustee* (1948).[55]

The doctrine will only apply, however, where full ownership, as opposed to a lesser right, has been transferred at the relevant date. If only a lesser right has passed at the commencement of the bankruptcy, then a subsequent lawful seizure of the property under the contract will bind the trustee. On the other hand, if the property has passed, a subsequent seizure will be of no effect against the trustee.

ILLUSTRATION

A building contract provided that " all plant and materials brought to and left upon the ground shall be considered to be the property of the Board, and shall not on any account be removed without the express licence of the architect." There were other clauses, including a forfeiture clause, not wholly consistent with a passing of property under this clause.[56] *Held*, on the true construction of the contract as a whole, the vesting clause did not pass the property, but only a right to detain and use the plant and materials. Consequently a seizure under the forfeiture clause validly exercised on the ground of delay subsequent to the commencement of the bankruptcy could not be defeated by the trustee, who contended that at

---

[53] [1902] 1 K.B. 713.
[54] For the necessary limitation even on this right, see *ante*, Chap. 12, pp. 662, 670–671.
[55] [1948] Ch. 407.
[56] For the forfeiture clause, see *ante*, Chap. 12, p. 667.

the relevant date they were goods of the employer in the reputed
ownership of the builder: *Re Keen, ex p. Collins* (1902).[57]

However, the doctrine of reputed ownership, as stated, does not
apply to liquidations, since it has been held that section 317 of the
Act of 1948 does not introduce the rules as to reputed ownership into
the winding-up rules,[58] and it also might not apply in bankruptcies if
the inference of reputed ownership was destroyed by notice—*e.g.*
plant being marked with the name of the employer, as in large contracts occasionally happens—or by proof of a custom, though a
custom would require, however, to be known in business generally,
and not in a particular market or locality.[59] Such a custom has been
held to exist in shipbuilding contracts.[60]

The second qualification on the effectiveness, from the employer's
point of view, of clauses transferring ownership (and indeed lesser
rights as well) arises from the fact that many types of plant are
seldom in practice owned by the builder, but are usually hired.
Even when it is not hired by the builder, in the case of large public
companies the ownership of plant is often vested in a subsidiary
company.   In these circumstances, no provision in the contract
between the parties can be of assistance as against the true owner,
unless perhaps the main contractor can be regarded as contracting
as agent on behalf of his subsidiary company in agreeing to the
employer's rights over the plant, or on the other hand the subsidiary
can be regarded as the *alter ego* of the parent.[61] This will only very
rarely be the case, however.

(3) Payment of Sub-contractors Direct

Many building contracts contain provisions designed to enable the
employer to effect direct payment of sub-contractors and suppliers
where the builder fails to make payment, and to deduct the sums
so paid from the builder's remuneration.[62] Without some such provision the employer, whose interest lies in the speedy completion of
the contract, may be in serious difficulty, since any payment made

---

[57] [1902] 1 K.B. 555, more fully illustrated and explained, *ante*, pp. 666–667.
[58] *Re Crumlin Viaduct Works* (1879) 11 Ch.D. 755.
[59] *Re Goetz, ex p. the Trustee* [1898] 1 Q.B. 787.
[60] *Clarke* v. *Spence* (1836) 4 A. & E. 448 at p. 472, but *cf.* the current R.I.B.A. form
   of contract, which has no vesting clause in relation to plant, though materials will
   be paid for on monthly certificate.
[61] See *Smith, Stone & Knight* v. *City of Birmingham* [1939] 4 All E.R. 116, *Gramophone
   & Typewriters Ltd.* v. *Stanley* [1908] 2 K.B. 89 and *Re Apthorpe* (1899) 4 Tax Cas.
   41. See also *ante*, Chap. 12, p. 678.
[62] This subject is more fully discussed, *ante*, Chap. 15, pp. 769 *et seq.*

by him direct to a supplier or sub-contractor with a view to ensuring their continuing their services will not avail him when the main contractor requires payment under the contract for the same services.[63] Accordingly, in most contracts the contingency upon which the employer is empowered to pay direct is undue delay by the main contractor in making payment to a sub-contractor or supplier.

Such a provision, in accordance with the general principle that the trustee or liquidator takes the bankrupt's property subject to liabilities which affected it in the bankrupt's hands,[64] is binding on the trustee or liquidator,[65] and the fact of bankruptcy usually has the practical result of delaying payment sufficiently to enable the clause to be operated.

It should be emphasised, however, that, in order to have a good defence to a claim by a trustee or liquidator, the employer must be careful to comply exactly with the terms of the contract empowering him to make direct payments, and that the right to deduct moneys so paid from the builder's remuneration will be lost, with a corresponding liability to pay twice for the same work,[66] unless the terms of the contract empowering direct payment are strictly observed.

Certain forms of sub-contract[67] also contain provisions constituting the main contractor trustee for the sub-contractor of any rights of the main contractor under his contract with the employer to retention money in respect of the sub-contracted work. The validity of such provisions was also upheld in *Re Tout & Finch* (1954),[68] with the result that the liquidator or trustee is bound to pay such sums over in full to the sub-contractor in preference to the claims of other creditors. The 1963 R.I.B.A. forms of contract now contain a similar provision imposing a trust in the main contractor's favour on the main contract retention moneys.[70]

The R.I.B.A. forms also contain far wider powers to pay direct any sub-contractor or supplier, nominated or otherwise, in the event of a determination by the employer.[71] However, such a clause offends

---

[63] *Re Holt, ex p. Gray* (1888) 58 L.J.Q.B. 5, *supra*, Section 1, pp. 777–778.
[64] See *Ex p. Newitt, re Garrud, supra*.
[65] See *Re Wilkinson, ex p. Fowler* [1905] 2 K.B. 713 and *Re Tout & Finch* [1954] 1 W.L.R. 178 illustrated *ante*, Chap. 15, pp. 770–771, 771–772.
[66] For a full discussion of this, and of the best courses of action for the employer, see *ante*, Chap. 15, Section 5, pp. 769 *et seq*.
[67] *e.g.* the F.A.S.S. form, 1963 ed., clause 11 (*h*).
[68] Illustrated on this *ante*, Chap. 14, Section 5, p. 729.
[70] Clause 30 (4) (*a*). See *supra*, Section 4, and *ante*, Chap. 14, Section 5.
[71] Clause 25 (3) (*b*). See also clause 59 (2), 1955 I.C.E. form.

against the principles of the bankruptcy laws set out in Section 5 (1), *supra*, if exercised upon the ground of bankruptcy or liquidation alone and will not, it is submitted, be effective to validate such payments as between the employer and the builder's trustee or liquidator, though it will be perfectly valid if exercised on any other ground than insolvency.

SECTION 6.	BANKRUPTCY OF ARCHITECT OR ENGINEER

The employment of an architect or engineer to supervise a building contract clearly involves his personal skill and labour, and accordingly such a contract will not, on the principles already set out,[72] vest in his trustee if it is still uncompleted, since in order to sue on such a contract the trustee would have to allege that the bankrupt was ready and willing to complete it, without being able to compel such co-operation. The trustee may, however, sue for moneys due and owing or for breach of the contract if the debt or breach occurred prior to the bankruptcy.[73]

But the fact that the trustee does not join in the action or intervene in an action by a bankrupt on a personal contract will not be any defence to the claim.[74]

While it is a general rule in bankruptcy that the earnings of the bankrupt during the bankruptcy do not pass to the trustee, so far as they are reasonably necessary for the support of the bankrupt and his family, this rule has been strictly applied to cases where the earnings are of an exclusively personal character, and it has been held that an architect's earnings are not exclusively personal in this sense, so that upon an architect suing for fees earned during the bankruptcy the trustee has a right to intervene and claim the proceeds of the action.[75] It has also been suggested that whenever earnings accrue under a partnership agreement they will become the property of the trustee.[76]

An architect's earnings by way of fees from private practice are not " salary or income " within section 51 of the Act of 1914, and

---

[72] See pp. 775–776, *supra*, and *ante*, Chap. 14, pp. 717–720, 724, 738–739. It may be a question, however, whether a contract with a firm of architects or engineers is personal in this sense, though it is suggested that even in the case of a firm the reputation and standing of the partners is essential to the performance of the contract—see *ante*, pp. 719–720, 738–739.

[73] *Bailey* v. *Thurston* [1903] 1 K.B. 137.

[74] *Ibid.*

[75] *Emden* v. *Carte* (1881) 17 Ch.D. 169, 768.

[76] *Re Rogers, ex p. Collins* [1894] 1 Q.B. 425 at p. 431.

consequently an order cannot be obtained under that section for payment direct to the trustee. The section only applies to remuneration in the nature of fixed income.

The general effect of the architect's bankruptcy upon a building contract will therefore be slight. The employer will be adequately safeguarded if, after notice of presentation of a petition or a receiving order, he pays all further fees due to the bankrupt either to or in accordance with the directions of the receiver or trustee.

SECTION 7.   PRIORITY BETWEEN TRUSTEE AND OTHER
INTERESTS

It frequently happens upon a builder's bankruptcy that he will have assigned moneys due or to become due under the contract to some other person prior to the bankruptcy. Assuming notice to have been given to the building owner, the assignment will be valid as against the trustee to the extent that money has actually been earned by the work being done at the relevant date, even if the money is not yet payable under the contract at that date. So the right to all retention moneys and the value of work done up to the date of the bankruptcy or liquidation will effectively pass to an assignee for value as against the trustee.[77]

ILLUSTRATIONS

(1) Lessees of the Alexandra Palace assigned the right to future receipts of admission money to a railway company. The lessees subsequently went into liquidation. *Held*, the company was entitled to the receipts till the date of liquidation, but the trustee was entitled to receipts after that date: *Ex p. Nichols, re Jones* (1883).[78]

(2) A shipbuilder charged future instalments due to him under a contract. At the time, he had done 6/7ths of the work but been paid only 2/7ths of the price. He went bankrupt and the ship was completed by the trustee. *Held*, explaining *Ex p. Nichols*, the charge was upon the margin between the work done and paid for and was good against the trustee in bankruptcy. *Per* Matthew J.: " It was admitted in the course of argument that if the margin had been created in the way in which a margin sometimes comes into existence under a building contract, *viz.* by the reservation of a certain percentage of each instalment, if such a reservation had been made and the sum so reserved was not to be payable until some time after the completion of the work, it could not be questioned that a valid charge might be made upon that margin as a subject of property ": *Ex p. Moss, re Toward* (1884).[79]

---

[77] See also the discussion and cases *ante*, Chap. 14, Section 5 (2), pp. 728–730, and the closely analogous situation of attachment of debts (Section 5 (7), pp. 735–738).
[78] 27 Ch.D. 782.   [79] 14 Q.B.D. 310.

(3) Builders under a contract which provided for 20 per cent. retention, payable on completion, assigned a part of the retention moneys due or which might become due as security for a debt. They filed their petition at a time when the work was approximately 3/4ths complete, but the retention moneys exceeded the amounts assigned. The trustee completed at a cost of approximately £4,000, to pay for which there were no assets available except the retention moneys. *Held*, distinguishing *Tooth* v. *Hallett* (1869),[80] the assignment was good against the trustee: *Drew* v. *Josolyne* (1887).[81]

These cases illustrate the rule that while an assignment of future debts or receipts is valid as between the assignor, the assignee and the debtor, and any other assignees,[82] it will not avail against a trustee or liquidator of the assignor in respect of debts or receipts arising from work done or the carrying on of business after the bankruptcy.[83]

Furthermore, it should not be forgotten that an assignee takes subject to equities, so that if the employer validly exercises a right to terminate the contract on the failure of the builder, the completion of the work by a third person will not perfect the assignee's right to the retention or other moneys, as would a completion under the contract. Thus in *Tooth* v. *Hallett* (1869),[80] it was held that a prior assignee could not intervene to prevent payment of the builder's trustee by the building owner, the reason being that, though the contract had been completed by the trustee, it had already been lawfully terminated, and the trustee's completion was referable to a new agreement with the employer. Normally, however, completion by the trustee would be under the contract and strong presumptive evidence of the non-exercise of any power of forfeiture,[84] so that the prior assignee, provided the sums claimed by him related to work done before the bankruptcy, would to that extent defeat the trustee's title to the payments made by the employer.[85] Furthermore, completion by a building owner may, under the terms of the contract, result in a final balance due to the contractor or his trustee. On analysis,

---

[80] (1869) L.R. 4 Ch. 242, *ante*, p. 732, where the case is illustrated and explained.

[81] 18 Q.B.D. 590. (See also *Re Tout and Finch* [1954] 1 W.L.R. 178, *ante*, Chap. 14, p. 729; *Re Asphaltic Paving* (1885) 30 Ch.D. 216, *supra*, pp. 776–777, and *Ex p. Rawlings, re Davis* (1888) 22 Q.B.D. 193.)

[82] See *ante*, Chap. 14, Assignment, pp. 728–729.

[83] *Cf. Re de Marney* [1943] Ch. 126 (professional earnings), *Re Trytel etc.* v. *Performing Right Society* [1952] 2 T.L.R. 32 (royalties), and *Re Tout & Finch* [1954] 1 W.L.R. 178 (assignment of retention moneys to sub-contractor).

[84] *Drew* v. *Josolyne, supra.* For a fuller discussion of this aspect of the subject, see Chap. 13, Forfeiture, *ante*, pp. 687–690.

[85] See *ante*, Chap. 14, Section 5 (2), pp. 728–730, and *Drew* v. *Josolyne, supra.*

such a payment would only result from the pre-determination work of the contractor (and in most cases, therefore, of pre-bankruptcy work) so that usually the assignee would in such circumstances take in priority to the trustee.

Chapter 17

GUARANTEE AND SURETIES

Building and engineering contracts sometimes require, or if not the employers may independently require, the contractor to find sureties who, by bond or simple contract of guarantee, will make themselves responsible for due performance by the contractor of the work undertaken. Generally, local authorities insist on such security being given, as the Model Standing Orders issued by the Ministry of Housing and Local Government provided for the taking of sufficient security for the due performance of every contract in excess of a specified value, and for the execution of works or the supply of goods or materials otherwise than at one time.

As this chapter shows, many of the events (such as the making of changes in the nature of the work or the method of construction to be employed), which are regarded as common incidents in the course of the performance of any large-scale contract, and are, as such, envisaged by the contract, are sufficient to render ineffective a bond in its simplest form. It is, therefore, essential that the bond should be carefully drawn, so as to cover the completion of the undertaking as provided for in the contract. In early editions of this book this point required to be very clearly stressed, as the majority of bonds encountered in practice were in the archaic legal form appropriate only to the discharge of some comparatively simple obligation, such as the payment of a debt. Nowadays, however, partly no doubt as a result of this insistence, the common forms of bond are usually so drafted as to make the instrument an effective and comprehensive document.

Apart from being required to provide sureties for the due performance of his contract, the contractor may be required to find sureties to guarantee his banking account or other liabilities which he may incur. On the other hand, though more rarely, the employer may provide sureties to guarantee payment of the contractor.

Where a contract requires the finding of sureties, it is a question of construction whether the actual provision of sureties is a condition precedent. It may, moreover, be expressly agreed that the formation of the contract itself shall be dependent upon the provision of the required security.[1] Generally speaking, the provision of a bond required by the contract will be regarded at the very least as a fundamental term or condition of the contract.

ILLUSTRATIONS

(1) Two parties contracted, the one to procure a ship and the other to have telegraphic cable ready to put on board her. The contract (*inter alia*) provided that " for the due performance of the covenants hereinbefore contained " each party should give to the other a bond with two sureties, for £5,000. *Held*, that the giving of the bond was a condition precedent to the right to sue for breach of contract: *Roberts* v. *Brett* (1865).[2]

(2) A contractor was expressly required by the contract documents " forthwith on the acceptance of his tender " to provide a surety bond for the due and punctual fulfilment of his obligations. *Held*, that the provision of security was a vital matter in a building contract, and failure to do so was a breach of a fundamental term justifying the other party in treating the contract as repudiated: *Swartz & Son (Ppty.) Ltd.* v. *Wolmaranstadt Town Council* (1960).[3]

The rule for construing guarantees was laid down by Bovill C.J. in *Coles* v. *Pack* (1869) [4] in these terms: " The document in question, like every other guarantee, must be construed according to the intention of the parties as expressed by the language they have employed, understanding it fairly in the sense it is used; and this intention is best ascertained by looking to the relative position of the parties at the time when the instrument is written."

SECTION 2.   ESSENTIAL REQUIREMENTS AND DURATION

(1) Contract must be in Writing

The contract of suretyship is one to answer for the debt, default or miscarriage of another, *i.e.* his failure to discharge some obligation which he has already taken upon himself or contemplates incurring.[5]

Suretyship is a collateral agreement, that is to say, it is subsidiary or accessory to some other undertaking in which the surety undertakes no obligations, and the surety is only liable if the principal debtor defaults.

---

[1] For a discussion of the general principles, see also *ante*, Chap. 3, pp. 217 *et seq.*
[2] 11 H.L.Cas. 337.
[3] 1960 (2) S.A. 1 (South Africa).
[4] (1869) L.R. 5 C.P. 65 at p. 70.
[5] See *Lakeman* v. *Mountstephen* (1874) L.R. 7 H.L. 17.

By section 4 of the Statute of Frauds a contract to answer for the debt, default or miscarriage of another must, to be enforceable, be in writing; but the consideration need not be stated. As this particular provision of the Statute of Frauds was not repealed by the Law Reform (Enforcement of Contracts) Act 1954, it remains one of the few surviving types of contract required to be in writing.

A question often arises whether a particular contract amounts to an original contract or a contract of indemnity, in both of which cases it need not be in writing, or to a guarantee. The question turns upon whether the words used amount to an acceptance of the whole liability in any event or only to an undertaking to be responsible if the person originally liable fails to discharge his obligation. The distinction drawn by the cases is somewhat fine, and was designed to whittle away the effect of the statute.[6]

When the result of the agreement is to substitute one debtor for another who is thereby released, the case is one not of suretyship, but of assignment (in which case it will be ineffective unless it is also a novation).[7]

The following rather old cases are of relevance only if an oral promise in the way of a guarantee or indemnity is sought to be relied upon, since if an oral promise is held to be a guarantee it will be unenforceable.

ILLUSTRATIONS

(1) W. undertook to complete the carpenter's work in H.'s house and find the materials. W., being delayed for want of credit or funds to procure the timber, it was supplied by M. on H.'s signing the following undertaking: "I agree to pay M. for timber to house in A.C. out of the money that I have to pay to W., provided W.'s work is completed." *Held*, that this was not a guarantee to pay if W. should fail to pay, but a contract to pay M. out of a certain fund upon completion of the work: *Dixon* v. *Hatfield* (1825).[8]

(2) H. was employed to do work on certain houses, and S. was employed as surveyor of the work and to receive moneys to be paid to H. for the work. In consideration of A. providing H. with the necessary materials, S. promised to pay A. out of so much of the moneys received by him as should become due to H. for the work, if H. should give him an order for the purpose. H. gave the order, but S. refused to pay on it. *Held*, that this was not a suretyship contract, as there was nothing to show any contract under which H. was ever liable to A., and that the facts set up only showed a

---

[6] See *Sutton* v. *Grey* [1894] 1 Q.B. 285, *Guild* v. *Conrad* [1894] 1 Q.B. 885, *Harburg Indiarubber Comb Co.* v. *Martin* [1902] 1 K.B. 778 and *Davys* v. *Buswell* [1913] 2 K.B. 47.

[7] *Commercial Bank of Tasmania* v. *Jones* [1893] A.C. 313. See *ante*, Chap. 14, for the assignment of liabilities.

[8] 2 Bing. 439.

prospective or equitable assignment of funds of H.'s to come into
S.'s hands: *Andrews* v. *Smith* (1835).[9]

(3) C., being desirous of obtaining on credit certain plates which
M. had contracted to supply for cash on each delivery, B., who was
interested in the work for which the plates were to be used, verbally
agreed that, if M. would deliver the remainder of the goods at one
month's credit, and would allow B. 3 per cent. upon the amount
of the invoices, he would cash for him the acceptances of C. for the
price of the goods to be delivered, and protect M. from default on the
bills when they became due. *Held*, that the engagement was substantially not a purchase of the bills, but an engagement by the defendant
to answer for the debt and default of C., and by section 4 of the Statute
of Frauds required to be in writing: *Mallett* v. *Bateman* (1865).[10]

(4) M. contracted to do certain drainage work for a local board.
The board gave notice to certain persons to make connections
with the drain. These persons disregarded the notice. I., the
chairman of the board, said to M.: " Go on and do the work, and
I will see you paid." *Held*, that L.'s words were evidence to sustain
a claim against him personally, and that they did not constitute a
promise to pay the debt of another so as to come within the operation of the Statute of Frauds: *Lakeman* v. *Mountstephen* (1874).[11]

(5) A. contracted to build houses for T., and sublet the plastering
to P. P. began the work, but refused to go on without security.
A. gave a written order to the architect to give P. certificates for the
plastering as the work proceeded. P. was paid on these certificates
without reference to A. A. failed and P. stopped working. T. then
told P. to go on, saying that T. knew that it was all right. P. then
completed the work. *Held*, that there was no substitution of T. for
A., and that T.'s promise, being collateral and verbal, was unenforceable under the Statute of Frauds: *Poucher* v. *Treahey* (1875).[12]

(6) C. was employed by the defendant to erect a house for him.
and employed the plaintiff and others as plasterers and plumbers.
The defendant, finding that C. was in arrears, dismissed him and
began to complete the work himself, and subsequently, on C.'s advice,
verbally agreed with the plaintiff that if they would fulfil their contracts with C. he would see them paid. *Held*, that as the original
contract between C. and defendant was put an end to and not assigned,
there was a new and distinct contract by the defendant with the
plaintiffs on which they could sue him: *Petrie* v. *Hunter* (1882).[13]

(2) Consideration

Unlike most other commercial transactions, consideration may not
always be present as between surety and principal creditor to support
a promise to guarantee a contractual obligation; frequently, indeed,
such consideration as exists is between surety and principal debtor.

[9] 2 Cr. M. & R. 627.
[10] L.R. 1 C.P. 163.
[11] L.R. 7 H.L. 17.
[12] Up.Can.Q.B. 367. This case was distinguished in *Petrie* v. *Hunter, supra.*
[13] 2 Ont.Rep. 233.

It is for this reason that the bond, being a document under seal not requiring consideration, is so frequently employed for important contracts of suretyship, since on general principles, every agreement of suretyship, unless it be under seal (*i.e.* usually by bond), will be void unless it can be shown that it was entered into for valuable and legal consideration, which must be concurrent with the execution of the guarantee, and not a mere past consideration. Section 3 of the Mercantile Law Amendment Act 1856 provides, however, that the consideration need not be expressed in the suretyship contract itself. The consideration need not be any benefit obtained by the surety; it is sufficient that some detriment or inconvenience should be suffered by the party for whose benefit such obligations are to be performed, *e.g.* abstention from enforcing a right of forfeiture by the principal creditor.

(3) Duration of Guarantee

A guarantee may be a guarantee of the performance of one or more acts of a defined nature, or it may be a continuing guarantee of the performance of all such acts. For example, a person may guarantee the payment of a merchant for so many thousands of bricks to be supplied to a builder, or he may guarantee the builder's account with the brick merchant, either at large or with the restriction that credit beyond a specified amount at any one time shall not be given. Whether a guarantee is continuing or not is a question of construction in each case. Thus a surety under a " bid-bond " that a tenderer whose bid is accepted will execute a binding agreement, does not become liable if the tender is validly withdrawn before a contractually binding acceptance has been given.[14]

SECTION 3.   DISCHARGE OF SURETY

(1) Generally

The kind of conduct on the part of the employer which will generally discharge anyone guaranteeing performance by the builder was described by Lord Loughborough in *Rees* v. *Berrington* (1795) [15] as follows: " It amounts to this, that there shall be no transaction with the principal debtor without acquainting the person who has a great interest in it. The surety only engages to make good the deficiency.

[14] *Hamilton Board of Education* v. *U.S.F.G.* [1960] O.R. 594 (Canada).
[15] 2 Ves.Jun. 543.

It is the clearest and most evident equity not to carry on any transaction without the privity of him who must necessarily have a concern in every transaction with the principal debtor. You cannot keep him bound and transact his affairs (for they are as much his as your own) without consulting him. You must let him judge whether he will give that indulgence contrary to the nature of his engagement."

However, as has already been said, many of the acts which would otherwise discharge the surety are nowadays expressly provided for by the contract or guarantee, or bond, as the case may be. Nevertheless, it is important to know the contingencies which may, in the absence of specific provision, result in a discharge of the surety. There are, further, certain events, such as the termination of the obligation guaranteed, which will inevitably result in the discharge of the guarantor.

(2) Completion of Obligation

When the obligation guaranteed has come to an end the surety is under no further obligation under this guarantee.

ILLUSTRATION

B was surety for a debt due to a bank by A. The bank released A and accepted D as debtor in his stead. B agreed to give a guarantee for D and to continue his previous guarantee until he did so. B died without having given the guarantee for D. *Held*, that the debt which B had guaranteed being gone, the remedy against B had gone also: *Commercial Bank of Tasmania* v. *Jones* (1893).[16]

The surety for due performance of a building contract by the contractor is discharged on completion of the work, if completion of the work is the subject of the guarantee. But questions may arise whether completion in such case means completion in fact or completion to the satisfaction of the architect. This is a matter of construction.

ILLUSTRATION

H. advanced money to R. on a guarantee by L., a building owner, that it should be repaid on the completion of six houses in accordance with a contract between himself and T. One of the terms of that contract was that the houses were to be built to the satisfaction of a surveyor, and payment made on his certificate. In an action on the guarantee the jury held that the houses were, in fact, completed, though no certificate of completion had been obtained. *Held*, that completion in the guarantee meant completion in fact, and that L. was accordingly liable on the guarantee: *Lewis* v. *Hoare* (1881).[17]

[16] [1893] A.C. 313.   [17] 44 L.T. 66 (H.L.).

If a certificate of completion is expressly required, a certificate obtained by the fraud or collusion of the builder and the surety, or by the fraud of the builder only, will not serve to discharge the surety.

ILLUSTRATION

A contract was entered into by sureties that a contractor would well and truly execute his contract. The contractor's contract provided for retention of part of the contract price until a final certificate should be given by the engineer six months after completion. The contractor did defective work, and concealed it from discovery until after the final certificate, and the retention money was paid. *Held*, that the mere giving of the certificate did not alter the position of the sureties, and that as both certificate and retention money were dishonestly obtained, the sureties were liable on their guarantee: *Kingston-upon-Hull Corporation* v. *Harding* (1892).[18]

So if the performance of the obligation guaranteed is such that it can be set aside by process of law, it will not serve to discharge the surety, *e.g.* a surety for payment is not discharged by such a payment as can be and is set aside under the bankruptcy law.

ILLUSTRATION

S. and C. made a joint promissory note, C. being surety for S. for the payment of money due from S. to P. S. paid to P. the amount of the note, but was at the time of such payment insolvent, and so paid in expectation of bankruptcy, although C. was ignorant of this fact. S. then went bankrupt, and his trustee claimed the sum so paid as being a fraudulent preference, and P. paid it over to him. *Held*, that C. was not discharged from his liability as surety by reason of this payment by S.: *Petty* v. *Cooke* (1871).[19]

On the other hand, where a payment is guaranteed, the creditor must do everything necessary to entitle him to payment, and there will be no disposition, it would seem, to construe the contract of suretyship as subject to the doctrine of substantial performance,[20] whatever might be the position under the building contract itself.

ILLUSTRATION

A surety guaranteed payment under a building contract, which was to be in four instalments of £375 on named dates " subject to the works being duly executed." The first instalment was not paid, and the Official Referee gave judgment against the surety for £375 less a sum of £88 which was necessary to complete the work in accordance with the contract. *Held*, by the Divisional Court and the Court of Appeal, that whether or not the contractor could maintain an action

---

[18] [1892] 2 Q.B. 494. Further illustrated *infra* pp. 807–808.
[19] L.R. 6 Q.B. 790.
[20] *Ante*, Chap. 5, pp. 245 *et seq.*

for the instalment less the set-off of £88 under the doctrine of substantial performance, the liability of the surety only arose when the
work done to earn the instalment had been fully completed: *Eshelby*
v. *Federated European Bank Ltd.* (1932).[21]

Where what is guaranteed is due performance by the builder
the builder's obligation, for example in regard to defective work,
may continue after completion or a final certificate for the full
period of limitation—or even longer if the builder becomes liable
to the employer, for example, under a contractual obligation such
as an indemnity clause. In such a case the surety's obligation may
also continue long after completion of the work. This depends on
the exact nature of the obligation which is the subject of the
guarantee or bond.

(3) Change in the Law

In the case of the guarantee of the performance of a building contract, if the work is legal when the contract is entered into, but
subsequently becomes illegal, both principal and surety are discharged.[22] However, on general principles if a contract is capable of
being operated by the parties so as to avoid an illegality, neither the
original contract nor a contract of suretyship dependent upon it will
be avoided. So a building contract was held valid notwithstanding
that the original contract drawings, (which were also annexed to the
surety's bond) contravened the by-laws due to an error of design,
since the terms of the contract permitted the work to be altered so as
to comply with the by-law.[23] Furthermore, a guarantee by a director
of a company of a loan to the company was held valid and enforceable notwithstanding that the loan was *ultra vires* the powers of the
company and hence not recoverable from the company itself.[24]

Moreover, the surety cannot be compelled to accept any modification of the plans or the scheme of the work, consequent upon
the change of the law, unless the contract of suretyship expressly
binds him to do so.

Where the guarantee is against the debt, default or miscarriage of
the engineer, architect or surveyor of a public body, any statutory
alteration of his liabilities and duties may discharge his sureties.[25]

---

[21] [1932] 1 K.B. 254 and 423.
[22] As to illegality, see *ante*, Chap. 5, pp. 361 *et seq.*
[23] See *One Hundred Simcoe Street Ltd.* v. *Frank Burger Contractors Ltd.* [1968] 1 Ont.
L.R. 452 (Canada), illustrated *ante*, Chap. 5, Section 3 (5), p. 367.
[24] *Yorkshire Railway Wagon Co.* v. *Maclure* (1881) 19 Ch.D. 478.
[25] See *e.g. R.* v. *Herron and Montgomery* (1903) 2 Ir.R. 474; *cf. Oswald* v. *Berwick-
upon-Tweed Corporation* (1856) 5 H.L.C. 856.

However, a surety may be liable on a bond for the due performance of duties when the duties have been added to and the duties so added are capable of separation from the duties guaranteed.[26]

(4) Acts to the Prejudice of the Surety

Where building contracts are guaranteed the surety usually covenants that the builder will satisfactorily perform and complete the contract subject to all the terms of the principal contract as to time, instalments, certificates, extras and the like, in which case the terms are to be treated as imported into the suretyship contract.

Generally, the building owner must not act, in dealing with the contractor, or in any connection where the surety's interest is affected, in a manner inconsistent with the suretyship contract, or do anything to prejudice the right of sureties to contribution or indemnity. If he does, the sureties will be released either wholly or *pro tanto*.[27]

These rules arise from the anxiety of the courts to recognise in favour of a surety every equity arising upon a contract of so onerous and thankless a character.[28]

Stipulations as to things which the building owner must or must not do are sometimes inserted, by way of conditions precedent, in the bond, *e.g.* a provision that the surety must be notified if the contractor fails to start work on a certain date. Failure to comply with such stipulations will discharge the surety.[29]

Generally speaking, acts to the prejudice of the surety fall under three heads:

(1) Fraud and Concealment;
(2) Laches;
(3) Material variation of the terms of the principal contract without the consent of the surety (including making advances of money not authorised by the contract).

(a) Fraud or concealment

Guarantees are not, like contracts of insurance, contracts *uberrimae fidei*.[30] There is not, therefore, a universal obligation to

---

[26] See *e.g. Skillett* v. *Fletcher* (1866) L.R. 1 C.P. 217.
[27] *Re Wolmershausen* (1890) 62 L.T. 541.
[28] See *per* Selborne L.C. in *Re Sherry* (1884) 25 Ch.D. 692 at p. 703.
[29] *Clydebank and District Water Trustees* v. *Fidelity and Deposit Co. of Maryland*, 1916 S.C.(H.L.) 69.
[30] See *per* Shee J. in *Lee* v. *Jones* (1863) 17 C.B.(N.S.) 482 at p. 495; *Davies* v. *London and Provincial Marine Insurance Co.* (1878) 8 Ch.D. 469; *per* Romer L.J. in *Seaton* v. *Heath* [1899] 1 Q.B. 782 at p. 792.

make disclosure of everything affecting the liability to be undertaken by the surety.[31]   But concealment of material facts may vitiate the contract, and the courts have held that the person to whom the security is given must disclose anything altering in any unexpected way the relation which the surety might naturally believe to exist between the parties,[32] *e.g.* the fact that the person guaranteed is already in debt to the creditor.[33]

If any part of the burden upon the principal is not disclosed to the surety, so that he is not aware of the full extent of his undertaking, he will not be bound.

ILLUSTRATIONS

(1) H. agreed to execute sewerage works for the defendants, to be paid for by instalments on the certificates of the defendants' surveyor. By a bond of even date, the plaintiff and another bound themselves as sureties, and H. bound himself as principal, under penalties, to finish the work by a day named. Before the contract with H., it was alleged that the defendants had agreed with a local landowner that the works should be executed at their joint expense and under the joint supervision of his and their surveyor. This was not disclosed to the plaintiff. H. failed to complete his contract and the work was placed in the hands of the landowner. The defendants then commenced an action to enforce the penalty under the bond. The plaintiff sought, and obtained, an injunction, restraining the defendants from prosecuting their action, on the ground that the concealment exonerated the surety. *Held*, on appeal, that the concealment could be raised as a defence, but the injunction must be discharged: *Stiff* v. *Eastbourne Local Board* (1868).[34]

(2) After acceptance of his tender, a contractor wrote saying that he had made a mistake in his tender (which totalled $88,500) overlooking two items of $6,000 and $7,000, and asking to be released. The employers refused, and the contractor decided to go on. The sureties were not informed of this at a time when they were required to and did give a different and wider bond than one already given by them to the owners. *Held*, by the Supreme Court of Canada, the sureties were entitled to be discharged: *Doe* v. *Canadian Surety Co.* (1937).[35]

(b) Laches

Laches, in the context of contracts of suretyship, means: " Omission to do something which the employer has contracted with the

---

[31] *Railton* v. *Matthews* (1844) 10 Cl. & F. 934.

[32] *Hamilton* v. *Watson* (1845) 12 Cl. & F. 109; *Cooper* v. *National Provincial Bank Ltd.* [1946] K.B. 1.

[33] *Lee* v. *Jones* (1863) 17 C.B.(N.S.) 495, where such non-disclosure was treated as evidence of fraud to go to the jury. As to what is a " material fact," which must be disclosed, see *London General Omnibus Co.* v. *Holloway* [1912] 2 K.B. 77; *Trade Indemnity Co.* v. *Workington Harbour and Dock Board* [1937] A.C. 1.

[34] 20 L.T. 339.

[35] [1937] S.C.R. 1 (Canada) illustrated further on another point, *infra*, p. 810.

surety to do, or to preserve some security, to the benefit of which the surety is entitled. There the omission would be one inconsistent with the relation between the surety and the person with whom he has contracted to be surety." [36]   Thus, where the employer " shall and may " insure the works at the contractor's expense, failure to do so will release the surety.

ILLUSTRATION

H. agreed with the plaintiff to complete fittings for a warehouse for £3,450, to be paid by instalments during the progress of the work. The contract contained a stipulation that " the plaintiff shall and may insure the fittings from destruction by fire at such time and for such amount as the architects may consider necessary, and deduct the costs of such insurance for the time during which such works are unfinished, from the amount of the contract." The defendant, by an agreement reciting the building agreement, guaranteed the due performance of the works by H. The plaintiff advanced £1,800 during the progress of the works, after which the fittings, to the value of £2,300, were destroyed by fire in H.'s workshop. H. became insolvent, and never repaid the £1,800. The plaintiff had to pay £340 over the original contract price to complete the work. *Held*, that the plaintiff was bound to insure, and that this omission discharged the surety *in toto: Watts* v. *Shuttleworth* (1861).[37]

The mere passive inactivity of the employer in neglecting to call the builder to account in a reasonable time, or to enforce proper performance by him, does not operate to release the surety. The rule, both at law and in equity, is that in order that the surety may be released, there must be some act or omission by the employer to the positive prejudice of the surety, or such degree of negligence on the part of the employer as to imply connivance with the builder, and amount to fraud.[38]   So, mere failure of the employers to exercise their powers of superintendence under a building contract does not amount to laches. Nor would omission to dismiss a contractor for delay in performance, it is submitted, discharge the surety.

ILLUSTRATION

A jury found that there had been a failure properly to supervise a contract, with the result that deliberate scamping of the work took place. The contract (*inter alia*) provided that all work was to be

---

[36] *Per* Bowen L.J. in *Kingston-upon-Hull Corporation* v. *Harding* [1892] 2 Q.B. 494 at p. 508.

[37] 7 H. & N. 353.

[38] *Madden* v. *M'Mullen* (1852) 13 Ir.C.L.R. 305; *Strong* v. *Foster* (1855) 17 C.B. 201; *Black* v. *Ottoman Bank* (1862) 15 Moo.P.C. 472; *Durham Corporation* v. *Fowler, infra*; approved in *Kingston-upon-Hull Corporation* v. *Harding* [1892] 2 Q.B. 494 at p. 508.

executed under the superintendence and to the satisfaction of the engineer, whose decision as to the manner of working was to be conclusive and final. *Held*, by the Court of Appeal, the provisions imposed no duty, but only conferred a right or option to supervise, and failure to do so could not release the sureties: *Kingston-upon-Hull Corporation* v. *Harding* (1892).[39]

The clause in a building contract conferring powers to dismiss the contractor in such circumstances is almost invariably a mere option in favour of the employer, who is perfectly entitled not to enforce strictly the conditions of the contract. In effect, he is giving an indulgence to the sureties as well as the principal.[40]

ILLUSTRATION

The plaintiffs entered into a sub-contract with one B., a government contractor, to supply him with certain articles within the period stipulated in the main government contract, in which (but not in the sub-contract) there were penalties and deductions for delay in delivery. The defendant guaranteed the plaintiffs " the payment of the value " of the articles thus to be supplied by the plaintiffs to the government contractor so soon as he should have received payment from the Government. There was delay in the delivery under both contracts, but the Government did not exact any penalties, and paid their contractor the full contract price. *Held*, that the contractor was liable to pay the plaintiffs the full contract price under their contract with him, and that, therefore, the defendant was liable on his guarantee to the same amount: *Oastler* v. *Round* (1863).[41]

Omission to preserve a collateral security against the builder, however, will release the surety.[42]

Omission to dismiss an engineer, or architect, or surveyor, where his fidelity is guaranteed, stands on a different footing. It is submitted that if he can be lawfully dismissed for anything which forms part of the subject of the guarantee (*e.g.* embezzlement), he should be at once dismissed or suspended, unless the surety after full disclosure agrees to the contrary.[43]

Where there is an agreement that there shall be two or more co-sureties, and one or more of them execute the bond on the faith that the others will do so in due course, the bond only becomes

[39] [1892] 2 Q.B. 494 illustrated *supra*, p. 803, on the effect of the final certificate not releasing the sureties.
[40] *Bell* v. *Banks* (1841) 3 Scott N.R. 497.
[41] 11 W.R. 518.
[42] *Kingston-upon-Hull Corporation* v. *Harding* [1892] 2 Q.B. 494, 508; *General Steam Navigation Co.* v. *Rolt* (1858) 6 C.B.(N.S.) 550.
[43] See *e.g. Phillips* v. *Foxall* (1872) L.R. 7 Q.B. 666.

effective when so signed by all. It is the creditor's duty to see that the bond is executed by all the necessary parties.[44]

(c) Alteration of the contract obligations of the debtor

(i) **Alteration in contractual arrangements.** Any alteration in the form of the agreement between the principals, or any alteration of any provision thereof (as distinct from a variation of the work the making of which is provided for by the original contract and contemplated by the contract of guarantee), will discharge the surety, unless it is self-evident that such alteration cannot prejudice him. Short of such certainty, the surety himself is the judge of the materiality of the alteration.[45]

ILLUSTRATIONS

(1) M. contracted to build a ship for the plaintiff at a given sum, to be paid by instalments as the work reached certain stages, and R. became surety for due performance by M. The plaintiff allowed M. to anticipate the last two instalments; M. became bankrupt before the ship was finished, and the plaintiff was compelled to spend more than the unpaid portion of the purchase-money in completing her. In an action by the plaintiff against R. to recover the excess and damages for delay, R. pleaded that the payments were made to M. without his knowledge or consent, and that by making such payments without his consent the plaintiff had materially prejudiced and altered R.'s position. The plaintiff replied that such payment was made with the knowledge, authority and consent of R., and at his request, or for his use and benefit or on his account. *Held*, that R.'s plea afforded a prima facie answer to the action, and that the onus lay upon the plaintiff to prove that the advances were made with the knowledge and assent, and at the request of R.: *General Steam Navigation Co.* v. *Rolt* (1858).[46]

(2) The plaintiffs, who were ship chandlers and ship smiths, agreed with L. & Co. to do all the woodwork on an iron ship which L. & Co. were building for M. & Co. A clause in the contract provided " any important work not mentioned in this tender that may be required to be done by the owners, to be paid for by them in addition to the amount hereinafter specified." The plaintiffs undertook the work on the faith of a guarantee by E., whereby E. guaranteed payment to the plaintiffs according to the contract. The word " important " in the contract was inserted by the plaintiffs, with the consent of L. & Co. after signature of the guarantee by E. *Held*, that the surety was not discharged from his liability: *Andrews* v. *Laurence* (1865).[47]

---

[44] *Fitzgerald* v. *M'Cowan* (1898) 2 Ir.R. 1; see also *Evans* v. *Bremridge* (1855) 25 L.J. Ch. 102 and 334; and *Ward* v. *National Bank of New Zealand* (1883) 8 App.Cas. 775 (P.C.).

[45] *Whitcher* v. *Hall* (1827) 8 D. & R. 22; *Holme* v. *Brunskill* (1877) 3 Q.B.D. 495 (C.A.).

[46] 6 C.B.(N.S.) 550, 584, Ex.Ch.　　　　　　[47] 19 C.B.(N.S.) 768, Ex.Ch.

(3) At the end of a contract, rain was leaking into the building, which the owner blamed on workmanship and the contractor on design. A number of sub-contractors were unpaid. The owners agreed with the builder that he would be given his final certificate for the balance, which would be paid by the employers direct to the the sub-contractors, in return for his undertaking to repair the defects (on terms which left the question of payment for the repairs open). The surety was not informed. *Held*, by the Supreme Court of Canada, that the surety was entitled to be discharged: *Doe* v. *Canadian Surety Co.* (1937).[48]

(ii) Alteration in the physical work. Where, however, the surety guarantees performance of a contract in terms which recognise in advance that the work under the contract may be varied (as is the case in most surety bonds for building contracts drafted at the present day), the surety is not discharged from his obligation on the ground of absence of notice of the variation, unless the party claiming under the bond had reason to believe that the adoption of the alterations would involve harmful results to the surety.[49] So, the surety will be released if the plans are materially altered, unless power to alter them is expressly reserved in the building contract, and the mode of determining the alteration prescribed by the contract is substantially followed.

ILLUSTRATION

A contract provided that changes might be made in the plans and specification by written agreement of the parties. *Held*, that a surety for the performance of the contract was not discharged by changes in the plans and specifications, which were not so extensive as radically to change the contract and substitute a different one: *United States* v. *Walsh* (1902).[50]

(iii) Alteration of submission to arbitration. Where the condition of the bond given by the sureties is that the contractor will perform and keep all the terms and conditions in the contract between the building owner and the contractor, and one of those terms is a submission to arbitration to a named arbitrator, the substitution by consent of the contractor and building owner of another arbitrator, under a new and different submission, may have the effect of releasing the sureties from liability to pay the costs of the reference under the new submission.

ILLUSTRATION

A contractor agreed with the plaintiff council to carry out certain sewerage works; the arbitration clause in the contract was

---

[48] [1937] S.C.R. 1 (Canada).
[49] *Hayes* v. *City of Regina* (1960) 20 D.L.R. 586 (Canada).
[50] 115 Fed.Rep. 697.

very wide and provided that any dispute or difference between the
contractor and the council should be referred to the surveyor to
the council, whose decision was to be final and conclusive. The
defendants, as sureties, gave to the plaintiffs a bond in the sum
of £500, the condition of the bond being that the contractor " shall
well and truly perform, fulfil and keep all and every the clauses, terms,
conditions and stipulations in the said recited contract." Disputes
arose between the contractor and the council, and the contractor
brought an action against the council claiming that a sum of money
was due to him. The council applied under section 4 of the Arbitration Act 1889 to stay the action, intimating that they had a
counterclaim against the contractor, and upon that application an
order was made by the district registrar by consent that the whole
of the cause be tried before a named arbitrator. The arbitrator awarded
the council £177, on balance, and costs, which were taxed at £398,
and the council sued the defendants to recover the £500 secured
by the bond. The defendants admitted liability to pay the £177
but denied liability for the costs. *Held* (Bailhache J.), that as the
liability to pay the costs arose not under the contract but under
the judgment upon the award the defendants were not liable.

Held, in the Court of Appeal (without giving any decision upon
the point of law decided by Bailhache J.), that the plaintiffs by
agreeing to the reference in place of that provided by the arbitration
clause in the contract had, without the knowledge or consent of the
defendants, entered into a new agreement of reference, probably
a longer and more expensive reference, which was a departure
from the terms of the contract, and was therefore not covered by the
defendant's bond, and that the plaintiffs were not entitled to recover
from the defendants the costs of the reference: *Hoole Urban District
Council* v. *Fidelity and Deposit Co. of Maryland* (1916).[51]

[Note: This decision seems to carry solicitude for the surety to
remarkable lengths. A change from an arbitrator in the pay of the
employer to one who was fully independent would seem, prima facie,
incapable of prejudicing and, on the contrary, likely to advantage the
debtor.]

(iv) Extending or giving time. A binding agreement to extend the
builder's time for completion without the assent of the surety will,
it seems, release the latter, unless provision to the contrary is made
in the contract of guarantee, or unless the extension is made under
the provisions of the principal contract guaranteed (which in building contracts will usually be the case).[52] The surety will also be
released where the time for completion has been shortened without
his consent.

ILLUSTRATION

S. agreed to buy the ship *D.* from H. for a sum down and the
transfer of the ship *L.* H. agreed to lend S. £46,000 on the *L.*, and
S. agreed to repair her and the *D.* in the manner, to the extent, and

[51] [1916] 2 K.B. 568.
[52] See *Rouse* v. *Bradford Banking Co.* [1894] A.C. 586.

within a time, specified. The defendant became surety by bond for the performance of this agreement. H. and S. afterwards, without the defendant's knowledge, extended the amount of repairs to be done to the D. and the time for completing them. *Held*, that the conditions in the bond as to the two ships were distinct, and that the defendant was released as to the *D.* by the variation of the principal contract: *Harrison* v. *Seymour* (1866).[53]

The defence that the employer has given time will not, however, avail the surety unless the employer has placed himself under some binding obligation to the principal debtor to extend the time.[54]

ILLUSTRATION

The obligee of a bond placed himself in such a position that he could not demand payment of the debt until an agreement with third parties had been carried into effect. *Held*, that this was such a giving of time as discharged a surety for payment of the debt: *Cross* v. *Sprigg* (1850).[55]

Thus an extension of time to the principal debtor in consideration of an increase in the debt of £2,500 discharged the surety.[56] But a binding agreement, for good consideration, made between the creditor and a stranger to give time to the principal debtor does not operate to discharge the surety for the principal debtor.[57] If assent is required to the giving of time to the builder, and there is more than one surety, the assent of all must be separately obtained, and the assent of one will not bind the others, and any who have not assented will be discharged.[58] Where the contract of suretyship is to secure the payment of monthly instalments or the like, and the contract is separable, giving time as to one instalment will release the surety as to that instalment, but will not release him as to subsequent instalments.[59] But where the liability for payments is one and indivisible, the surety will, in similar circumstances, be discharged.[60]

(v) By overpayment. In the absence of a provision to the contrary it would seem that, if the building owner knowingly advances to the builder more than he is, prima facie, entitled to under the contract, then the builder's surety will be released. The making of such advances may amount to a variation of the contract between the

[53] L.R. 1 C.P. 518.
[54] *Philpot* v. *Briant* (1828) 17 C.B. 201; *Fraser* v. *Jordan* (1857) 8 E. & B. 303.
[55] 2 Mac. & G. 113.
[56] *Bell* v. *National Forest Products* (1964) 45 D.L.R. (2d) 249.
[57] *Fraser* v. *Jordan, supra.*
[58] *Clarke* v. *Birley* (1889) 41 Ch.D. 422.
[59] See *e.g. Croydon Gas Co.* v. *Dickenson* (1876) 2 C.P.D. 46.
[60] *Midland Motor Showrooms Ltd.* v. *Newman* [1929] 2 K.B. 256.

principals without the consent of the surety; but another reason given for the discharge of the surety by over-advances is that the employers, by anticipatory payment to the builder, have " thereby prejudiced the position of the surety, who loses, by that anticipatory payment to the principal, the strong inducement which otherwise would have operated on his (the principal's) mind to induce him to finish the work in due time." [61]

ILLUSTRATIONS

(1) S. agreed with the plaintiff to construct an entrance to a dock. S. was to receive payment of three-fourths of the price by instalments during the progress of the work, and the remaining fourth a month after completion. The agreement contained power to employ others to perform the contract if S. failed to complete and to deduct the expenses thereof from the contract price. The defendant, by bond, guaranteed due performance. The plaintiff, at the request of S., and on new security given, had advanced more than the cost of the work done, but less than the whole contract price. S., after part performance, abandoned the contract. On the abandonment the plaintiff had the work completed at an expense which, added to the cost of the work actually done by S. was less than the contract price but which, added to the sum actually advanced to S. exceeded the contract price. *Held,* that as against the defendant the plaintiff was entitled only to nominal damages for the breach, inasmuch as the loss arose from the overpayment of S. by the plaintiff, and not from non-performance by S., and the advances were not under the terms of the contract: *Warre* v. *Calvert* (1837).[62]

(2) S. entered into a contract with the treasurer of a dock company to execute certain works for the company for £52,200, payable by instalments. W. and L. were sureties to the company for the due performance by S. of his engagement. The company advanced sums to S., without the knowledge or consent of W. and L., in excess of what they were bound to pay. *Held,* that the sureties were thereby released, and that proceedings to enforce the guarantee should be stayed: *Calvert* v. *London Dock Co.* (1838).[63]

If the language in the old case of *Warre* v. *Calvert, supra,* is accepted at its face value, it would mean that all overpayments, whether negligent or deliberate, would discharge a surety. It is submitted that in principle this should not be so, and only if the overpayments were so gross and careless as to amount to a reckless disregard of the contractual provisions for interim payment on account would the surety be discharged. The matter appears not to be covered by authority, however, and modern bonds usually make express provision for the possibility of overpayment.

[61] *General Steam Navigation Co.* v. *Rolt* (1858) 6 C.B.(N.S.) at p. 595, illustrated *supra,* p. 809. See, however, *Trade Indemnity* v. *Workington* [1937] A.C. 1.
[62] 7 A. & E. 143.
[63] 7 L.J.Ch. 90.

(5) Release of Principal or Co-Sureties

If the building owner releases the principal from his contractual obligation, it follows that he releases the surety. Further, if he releases one of several sureties, who have bound themselves jointly and severally, he releases them all; otherwise he would be free to deprive a surety of the right to contribution, which is incidental to all guarantees.[64]

A surety is not, however, discharged by the release of the principal if he has expressly bound himself by the terms of the contract of suretyship to remain liable in such an event.[65]

(6) Death of the Surety

Although an authority is revoked by death, a contract is not, if from its own nature it may continue, and hence the executors of a guarantor may be liable on a continuing guarantee entered into by the deceased. The mere fact of death will not revoke a continuing guarantee.[66]

And where the consideration for the guarantee is given once for all, the guarantee is not revocable by the guarantor, and does not determine on his death. Such a guarantee differs from the case of guarantees for repayment of future advances, which the creditor is not bound to make. In *Coulthart* v. *Clementson* (1879),[67] Bowen J. decided that, in the absence of express provision, a continuing guarantee was revoked, as to subsequent advances, by the death of the guarantor; but in *Re Silvester, Midland Railway* v. *Silvester* (1895),[68] Romer J. held that mere notice of the death by the executor was insufficient to determine a guarantee in a case where a continuing guarantee was made determinable by a month's written notice from a guarantor or his representatives. The death of one surety does not put an end to the liabilities of the surviving sureties.[69]

(7) Death or Illness of the Contractor

The death or illness of the contractor will not ordinarily determine the contract of guarantee, or release the sureties.

---

[64] *Ward* v. *National Bank of New Zealand* (1883) 8 App.Cas. 755 at p. 764; *Commercial Bank of Tasmania* v. *Jones* [1893] A.C. 313.
[65] *Perry* v. *National Provincial Bank* [1910] 1 Ch. 464.
[66] *Bradbury* v. *Morgan* (1862) 1 H. & C. 249; *Lloyds* v. *Harper* (1880) 16 Ch.D. 290.
[67] 5 Q.B.D. 42.
[68] [1895] 1 Ch. 573.
[69] *Beckett* v. *Addyman* (1882) 9 Q.B.D. 783.

(1) If one be bound to another that I.S. shall make him a house by such a day or else pay him £20 by such a day, it is no plea for him to say that I.S. was dead before the day, for that another might have made it: 31 Hen. 6; Fitz. tit. Bar, pl. 59, cited in *Quick* v. *Ludburrow* (1616).[70]

(2) A. contracted to perform work for a local authority, but became insane, and was incapacitated from performing the work personally. *Held*, that his sureties for the due performance of the contract were entitled to complete the contract: *Tracey* v. *McCabe* (1892).[71]

SECTION 4.   REMEDIES

(1) Of the Principal Creditor or Obligee

A judgment in an action against the principal debtor, or an award in an arbitration against such debtor, is not binding on the debtor's surety, nor is it evidence against him in an action against him by the creditor of the principal debtor, unless the surety shall in the clearest terms have agreed to be bound by such judgment or award. In any other case his liability must be proved in the same way as it would have to be proved against the principal debtor.[72] But an account delivered by the principal debtor showing any sum to be due from himself may be evidence against the surety.[73] It may consequently be unwise to sue the principal debtor alone, except in cases where the contract of guarantee requires that the principal debtor shall be first sued, or provides that judgment against the principal shall bind the surety. Conversely, it follows that the creditor is not, in the absence of express provisions, bound to pursue his remedies against the principal debtor upon the latter's default.

The surety may be sued alone, or principal and surety may be sued together, and if a surety is sued alone, he can bring in his co-sureties for contribution, and his principal debtor for indemnity, under the usual Third Party procedure of the High Court.

The plaintiff sued the defendants for preventing the plaintiff from completing certain work according to a contract with the defendants. The defendants set up a forfeiture clause whereby on the failure by the plaintiff to proceed with requisite expedition

---

[70] 3 Bulstr. 29 at p. 30.
[71] 32 L.R.Ir.R. 21.
[72] *Ex p. Young*, *re Kitchin* (1881) 17 Ch.D. 668 (C.A.).
[73] *Lysaght* v. *Walker* (1831) 5 Bligh (N.S.) 1; *Abbeyleix Guardians* v. *Sutcliffe* (1890) 26 L.R.Ir.R. 332.

the defendants might enter; and pleaded that the plaintiff did so fail, and that the defendants entered and completed, and counter-claimed that owing to the plaintiff's breach of contract they had been obliged to spend £850 in completing the work, being £256 in excess of the cost thereof if the plaintiff had fulfilled his agreement. The counterclaim also set out a bond, executed by R., in which he had bound himself to be answerable to the defendants to the extent of £200 for the proper execution of the contract by the plaintiff to the entire satisfaction of the defendants' engineer. The defendants, by the counterclaim, sought to recover £256 from the plaintiff and £200 from R., and served R. with a third party notice. *Held*, that notwithstanding that R.'s bond was separate and his liability several, he could be brought in as a third party: *Turner* v. *Hednesford Gas Co.* (1878).[74]

(2) Of the Surety

The surety is entitled to prove in the bankruptcy of the principal debtor, or of a co-surety, for indemnity or contribution, or to make the principal creditor prove, and the liability of a bankrupt co-surety to contribution, even though it is not ascertained at the date of the bankruptcy, is provable in the bankruptcy.[75]

The person secured is not entitled as of right to the benefit of any counter-securities given by the principal debtor to his sureties.

ILLUSTRATION

A testator guaranteed the current account of S. with the plaintiffs, and took mortgages by way of a counter-security from S. S. failed, and the plaintiffs claimed an exclusive right to the proceeds of the counter-security. *Held*, that the claim could not be sustained: *Re Walker, Sheffield Banking Co.* v. *Clayton* (1892).[76]

Sureties are entitled to contribution *inter se*.[77] And a surety who has been sued to judgment by the principal creditor can maintain an action for contribution or indemnity without paying to the principal creditor the whole judgment debt.[78]

Any security held by any surety from the principal must be brought into hotchpot for the benefit of his co-sureties even if he only undertook the suretyship upon the terms of having such security, and if the co-sureties, when they became sureties, were unaware of his agreement for security.[79]

---

[74] 3 Ex.D. 145.
[75] *Wolmershausen* v. *Gullick* [1893] 2 Ch. 514.
[76] [1892] 1 Ch. 621.
[77] *Davies* v. *Humphreys* (1840) 6 M. & W. 153; *Ex p. Snowden* (1881) 17 Ch.D. 44 (C.A.); and see *Stirling* v. *Burdett* [1911] 2 Ch. 418.
[78] *Wolmershausen* v. *Gullick* [1893] 2 Ch. 514.
[79] *Steel* v. *Dixon* (1881) 17 Ch.D. 825.

Where co-sureties have bound themselves in varying amounts they are only liable to contribute in proportion to those amounts to the limits of their respective liabilities, and not in equal proportions.[80]

For the purpose of assessing the proportion to be contributed by each surety, insolvent sureties and those from whom no payment can be recovered are not reckoned.[81]

Where, however, the sureties have contracted severally and not jointly no absolute right to contribution exists.[82]

(3) Statute of Limitations

The Limitation Act 1939 runs in favour of the surety from the date when the cause of action arises, *i.e.* from the date when the principal creditor could first have sued the surety.[83]

The period does not, therefore, begin to run on the promise of a surety to pay the principal debt on demand, until the demand is made.[84]

Nor does it run as between co-sureties until the liability of the surety is ascertained, nor until the claim of the principal creditor has been established, even though the action for contribution is not brought till after the remedy of the principal creditor against the co-surety is statute-barred.[85]

---

[80] *Ellesmere Brewery Co.* v. *Cooper* [1896] 1 Q.B. 75.
[81] *Lowe* v. *Dixon* (1885) 16 Q.B.D. 455; *Peter* v. *Rich* (1830) 1 Ch.Rep. 19.
[82] *Cf. Smith* v. *Cock* [1911] A.C. 317 (P.C.).
[83] *Reeves* v. *Butcher* [1891] 2 Q.B. 509; *Henton* v. *Paddison* (1893) 9 T.L.R. 333.
[84] *Re Browne's Estate* [1893] 2 Ch. 300.
[85] *Wolmershausen* v. *Gullick* [1893] 2 Ch. 514.

CHAPTER 18

ARBITRATION

SECTION 1. WHAT IS AN ARBITRATION AGREEMENT

THE following chapter is written with two main ends in view, namely, on the one hand to assist the parties to building contracts and their advisers to understand when and to what extent the process of arbitration may be available to them to resolve a dispute which has arisen, and the reasons and considerations which should govern the choice of arbitration rather than the courts as the appropriate tribunal for a dispute, and on the other hand to assist arbitrators in the just and efficient conduct of the arbitrations before them. Other matters, such as the revocation of arbitrators' appointments and setting aside of awards, are only incidentally noticed.

(1) The Arbitration Agreement Generally

Once the parties enter into an arbitration agreement in writing the provisions of the Arbitration Act 1950 apply; but not all agreements to have a dispute decided by a third person are arbitration agreements, in particular in building cases where references of matters in dispute to the decision of certifiers are frequently provided for,[1] and it is sometimes necessary to consider if such an agreement is in fact an arbitration agreement in order to ascertain whether the 1950 Act is applicable. The need for an arbitration agreement to be in writing is in practice overwhelming, since otherwise it is revocable by either party at will at any time before the making of the award.

Section 32 of the Arbitration Act 1950 defines an arbitration agreement as meaning " a written agreement to submit present or future differences to arbitration, whether an arbitrator is named therein or not." Thus an arbitration agreement, in order to receive the important protection of the Act in regard to irrevocability, and to attract the numerous powers of the High Court which are available to assist the proper conduct of the arbitration, must be in writing. There is some doubt, however, as to whether the agreement must also be signed by the parties. If the agreement is such as to fall

---

[1] See *ante*, Chap. 7, pp. 402, 416–418, 435–437, 450, for the distinction as well as subs. (2) *infra*.

within section 40 of the Law of Property Act 1925, then it must be signed by the party to be charged.[2] Except in this case, however, there seems no reason why the arbitration agreement should be signed.[3]

The necessary agreement may be made by duly authorised agents, and an endorsement on counsel's brief has been held to be a good agreement.[4]

Where arbitration agreements relate to a present existing dispute, they usually recite the nature of the dispute which has arisen, and then state that the parties have agreed to refer the matter to a named arbitrator for decision in accordance with the Arbitration Acts. Such specific agreements to refer an existing dispute are sometimes termed " submissions," in contradistinction to " agreements to refer," which deal with any disputes which may arise in the future between the parties; though the term " submission " is frequently used in a sense wide enough to include both. In building and engineering contracts the vast majority of arbitrations come about as a result of the " agreements to refer " any future disputes, which are to be found in the contract documents themselves in the form usually known as an arbitration clause. Examples of clauses governing future disputes included in a contract between the parties are to be found in the R.I.B.A. form of contract [5] and the I.C.E. form of contract.[6] In some arbitration clauses (e.g. that in the I.C.E. form of contract) there is a requirement that a dispute or difference shall first be referred to the architect or engineer for his decision. In some cases it may be a very difficult question whether such preliminary references are themselves arbitration agreements, or merely a first step in invoking the right to arbitration. Sometimes, also, the arbitration clause requires that notice of arbitration shall be given within a fixed period after receiving the architect's or engineer's preliminary decision. Failure to give notice within this fixed period may act (depending on the words of the provision) as a bar to any further proceedings, but the High Court has power under section 27 of the Act to extend this fixed period if it is of opinion that undue hardship might be caused, notwithstanding that notice has not been given within the

---

[2] *Walters* v. *Morgan* (1792) 2 Cox Ch.Cas. 369.
[3] *Baker* v. *Yorkshire Assurance Co.* [1892] 1 Q.B. 144; *Hickman* v. *Kent and Romney Marsh Sheepbreeders' Association* [1915] 1 Ch. 881; but see the doubts expressed in *Russell*, 18th ed., pp. 44–45.
[4] *Aitken* v. *Batchelor* (1893) 62 L.J.Q.B. 193.
[5] Clause 35, 1963 ed.
[6] Clause 66, 1955 ed.

time fixed. The following decision is on the very difficult clause 66
of the I.C.E. conditions.

ILLUSTRATION

Clause 66 of the I.C.E. standard form of contract provided that
if any dispute should arise between the employer or engineer and the
contractor, it should be referred to and settled by the engineer
who should state his decision in writing. If either party was dissatisfied with the decision, then either party, within three calendar months
of receiving notice of the decision, might require the matter to be
referred to an arbitrator. By April 11, 1960, certain claims had
been put forward by the contractor and had been disputed by the
engineer in correspondence, and the contractor wrote on that date:
" Our claims are now well in course of preparation and will be submitted to you with our Semi-Final Certificate. Upon receipt of
the claims you can, of course, give your decision under the relevant
clauses of the contract and we in due course will have to notify you
of our intention to go to arbitration." On March 8, 1961, the contractor wrote enclosing eleven claims, some of which were new and
some of which had been previously advanced but rejected. The
engineer replied by letter, enclosing " my observations and comments
on your claims," and at the end of his detailed comments on each
claim, wrote " I cannot agree with or consider this claim." The
contractor failed to give notice of arbitration within three months of
this letter.

Held, by Mocatta J.[7] (after deciding that there was no valid
ground for extending time under section 27 of the Act) (1) Clause 66
expressly made the engineer's decision final unless notice requiring
arbitration was given within the requisite period; and once he had
made his decision, no action or arbitration could be brought, failing
such notice. (2) Before the engineer could give a decision having
this effect under clause 66, there must be a dispute, that is to say,
a rejection by the engineer or the employer of the claim in question.
(3) No special words were necessary for the statement of the decision,
which need not specifically purport to be a decision. (4) In so far
as he was dealing with claims previously rejected by him, the engineer
in his final letter had given his decision and the right to litigate those
claims had been lost. _Held_, by the Court of Appeal, the statement
must make it quite clear that it was intended as a decision under the
clause. There was no express reference to a decision under the terms
of the clause in the letter, and no distinction between the wording
used on claims previously rejected and those being received for the
first time. On the facts the letter was not a decision under the clause
on any of the claims. _Per_ Harman L.J., words of this kind needed to
be construed strictly since they could have the effect of shutting out
the right to go to the courts. _Per_ Winn L.J., the second limb of clause
66 pays close attention to the manner of the submission. It was
possibly realised that the engineer under the first part would not be
strictly an arbitrator as he would often be personally involved.
Monmouth C.C. v. _Costelloe & Kemple Ltd._ (1965).[8]

[7] (1964) 63 L.G.R. 131.
[8] (1965) 63 L.G.R. 429.

The exact status of the engineer on this preliminary reference which, as the above case shows, gives a conditional finality to the engineer's preliminary decision, is by no means clear, but it is submitted that it is identical with that of the certifier, which in appropriate cases, it has been suggested, involves a duty to receive representations from the parties before finally reaching a decision.[9] The following case does not seem in line with the dicta on the subject in the English cases, and its reasoning does not, with respect, appear entirely satisfactory.

ILLUSTRATION

An arbitration clause in a South African engineering contract provided that if any disputes should arise between the employers, or the engineer on their behalf, and the contractor, the engineer should determine the dispute by a written decision given to the contractor. This decision was to be final and binding unless *the contractor* should dispute it within fourteen days of receipt of the decision, in which event either party could require it to be referred to arbitration. The contractor did not complete his work properly and ignored notices requiring him to do so, and finally the employers employed another contractor to do so under a power in the contract. The cost of this was claimed from the contractor, who disputed his liability to pay. The engineer, without informing the contractor beforehand of his intentions, forwarded a written decision to the contractor that he was liable for the sum in question unless he disputed the decision within fourteen days of its receipt. The contractor failed to do so, whereupon the employer proceeded in the courts to recover the sum in question. The contractor contended that the decision had no force or effect as he had not been afforded an opportunity of being heard on the merits. *Held*, by the Appellate Division of the Supreme Court of South Africa, overruling Banks J. and the Full Court of the Cape Provincial Division, that as the engineer would be a party to the dispute under the clause, and as his decision was not final so far as the contractor was concerned, and as the contractor on his argument would be entitled to two full-scale arbitrations, it was not necessary to require the engineer to act as an arbitrator, *nor could his functions be regarded as quasi-arbitral in character*: Kollberg v. Cape Town Municipality (1967).[10]

[Note: Much of the above reasoning seems open to doubt. Clearly the engineer's decision did have a high degree of conditional finality (and was binding on the employer in any event unless disputed by the contractor), and in any case it has been suggested, and there are decisions and dicta to the contrary, that whether or not it is finally binding is irrelevant.[11] The engineer was no more likely to be involved in the dispute than any other certifier, and the contractor would not need to ask for a full hearing—merely that his representations

[9] See *ante*, Chap. 2, Section 6 (3) and 6 (4), pp. 159 *et seq.*; Chap. 7, Section 5, pp. 463–465, Section 9, pp. 499–502.
[10] 1967 (3) S.A. 472 (South Africa).
[11] *Ante*, Chap. 2, Section 6 (4), p. 167.

or comments should be received before the decision.[12] It is submitted that the comment of Harman L.J. in the *Monmouth* case, *supra*, about shutting out the right of the parties to go to the courts is applicable, and it is difficult not to approve the judgment of Banks J.[13] as a correct statement of the law in England.]

Under the pre-1963 R.I.B.A. standard forms the reference was to " the arbitration and final decision of—, and in the event of his death or unwillingness or inability to act to a person to be appointed by the President of the R.I.B.A." Failure to insert a name or to delete the words after the blank space rendered the arbitration clause, it was suggested in the previous edition of this book, too uncertain to have any effect. But in a case where a schedule modifying or deleting several of the other provisions of the R.I.B.A. conditions (but not the arbitration clause) formed part of the contract documents, the Court of Appeal held that there was a clear intention to arbitrate, and that the words following the blank space could be ignored as being ineffective.[14] The 1963 forms are worded so as to avoid this problem, however.

Arbitration agreements may be implied in certain cases, as where, after the original agreement containing an arbitration clause has expired, parties have gone on dealing on the same terms [15]; or where a contract was intended to be construed with and as supplemental to a previous contract containing an agreement for arbitration,[16] or where an arbitration clause in another document is incorporated by reference.[17]

ILLUSTRATIONS

(1) A railway construction contract contained a clause naming an arbiter for the settlement of disputes. After part of the work was executed an Act was passed for the deviation of the line. The contractor completed the line as deviated. *Held*, that the arbitration clause in the original contract remained effectual in reference to the making of the deviated line as well as the other portions of the railway: *Barr* v. *Dunfermline Railway* (1855).[18]

(2) A and B continued to deal upon the terms of an expired agreement which contained an arbitration clause. *Held*, that under section 11 of the Common Law Procedure Act 1854, an order could

---

[12] See *ante*, Chap. 7, Section 9, pp. 499 *et seq.*
[13] 1966 (3) S.A. 471. This judgment makes a careful and full review of the authorities.
[14] *Davies Middleton & Davies Ltd.* v. *Cardiff Corporation* (1964) 108 S.J. 74.
[15] *Gillett* v. *Thornton* (1875) L.R. 19 Eq. 599, *infra.*
[16] *Wade-Gery* v. *Morrison* (1877) 37 L.T. 270. This case is explained and distinguished in *Turnock* v. *Sartoris* (1889) 43 Ch.D. 150 at 155, illustrated *infra*, p. 837. See also *Goodwins, Jardine & Co.* v. *Brand* (1905) 7 F. (Ct. of Sess.) 995, illustrated *ante*, Chap. 15, pp. 767–768.
[17] See *ante*, Chap. 15, Section 4, for example.
[18] 17 D. (Ct. of Sess.) 582.

be made staying litigation pending arbitration: *Hattersley* v. *Hatton* (1862).[19]

(3) Articles for a partnership for one year contained an arbitration clause. The partnership was continued beyond the year. *Held*, that the arbitration clause remained in force after the year: *Gillett* v. *Thornton* (1875).[20]

An agreement to submit to three arbitrators, one to be appointed by each party and the third by the two chosen, is an arbitration agreement.[21] Such an agreement will now have effect as if it provided for an umpire and not for the appointment of a third arbitrator by the two arbitrators appointed by the parties.[22] If the agreement simply provides for three arbitrators to be appointed, an award of any two of those arbitrators is binding.[23] This latter arrangement is in fact preferable to having an umpire, which involves serious procedural disadvantages. An umpire's jurisdiction generally only arises if the two arbitrators disagree—this means that, unless he is present at the hearing before the arbitrators, the umpire has to hold a rehearing; and even if he is present at the original hearing he has no power to intervene or control the proceedings, or to consult with the two arbitrators. The clumsy expedient of formally notifying disagreement to the umpire before the hearing is sometimes resorted to to avoid these difficulties, but it seems of doubtful validity and effectively results in a single arbitrator with two advocates of questionable status.

In very large and complicated arbitrations it is greatly preferable to appoint one arbitrator and for the parties to agree, if it is thought he should have further assistance, that he should sit with one or more assessors, or alternatively to appoint three arbitrators, one to be chairman, and to provide for majority decision. Umpires should only be appointed if a genuine two-stage arbitration is desired in the event of the first stage leading to disagreement, but it is difficult to believe that this arrangement could be suitable for the complicated and expensive disputes involved in building and engineering arbitrations.

Arbitrations, whether under a specific submission or an agreement to refer, are regarded as initiated by a notice of arbitration, as

---

[19] 3 F. & F. 116.

[20] L.R. 19 Eq. 599.

[21] *Manchester Ship Canal* v. *Pearson* [1900] 2 Q.B. 606.

[22] s. 9 (1) of the Arbitration Act 1950; but this latter subsection does not apply if the agreement merely gives the two arbitrators power to appoint a third arbitrator: *British Metal Corporation Ltd.* v. *Ludlow Brothers Ltd.* [1938] 1 All E.R. 135.

[23] s. 9 (2) of the Arbitration Act 1950.

to which there is no special form, though it must essentially require the dispute in question to be referred to arbitration. By virtue of section 27 (3) of the Limitation Act 1939 and section 29 (2) of the Arbitration Act 1950, this is the date equivalent to a writ in High Court proceedings for the purpose of determining whether any relevant period of limitation has expired.

Where there is an agreement to submit to the jurisdiction of a foreign court, the High Court will stay any action brought in contravention of that agreement: *Austrian-Lloyd Steamship Co.* v. *Gresham Life Assurance Co.* (1903).[24] In this latter case, the action was stayed on the basis that section 4 of the Arbitration Act 1889 was applicable, but it may be that the basis is the court's inherent power to prevent abuse of its process.[25] An agreement providing for arbitration out of the jurisdiction and before a foreign arbitrator is an agreement within the Arbitration Act 1950, and an award obtained from a foreign arbitrator can be enforced in the English courts.[26]

However, the whole subject of arbitrations in the field of private international law is, unfortunately, extremely obscure. In particular, it is by no means clear which of the rights conferred by the Act of 1950—*e.g* the case-stated procedure—are to be regarded as procedural or substantive. This may be vitally important if an arbitration is held outside England, because in the absence of stipulation to the contrary it would seem that questions of *procedure* are held to be governed by the *lex fori*, at least if the arbitration agreement stipulates the country where the arbitration is to take place.[27] The proper law of the contract itself is frequently, in foreign contracts, expressly stated to be that of the foreign employer, but an arbitration clause may expressly require the arbitration to be held in England, which is the above situation in reverse. Questions of the proper law of a contract, where there is an arbitration clause requiring arbitration in a jurisdiction different from what would otherwise be the proper law, can also be very difficult. Generally the English courts will, if there is a reference to arbitration in England by the arbitration clause, hold that the proper law is English even though the surrounding facts would otherwise point to a different conclusion,[28] but this will yield to language in the contract

24 [1903] 1 K.B. 249.
25 *Racecourse Betting Control Board* v. *Secretary for Air* [1944] Ch. 114.
26 *Norske Atlas Insurance Company* v. *London General Insurance Company* (1927) 43 T.L.R. 541.
27 Dicey and Morris, *Conflict of Laws*, 8th ed., pp. 1047–1048.
28 *Tzortzis* v. *Monark Line A/B* [1968] 1 W.L.R. 406.

indicating the contrary, either expressly,[29] or impliedly.[30]   Thus the use of the ordinary English R.I.B.A. form by the parties is likely to govern the proper law of the contract, though it will not necessarily govern the procedural law of the arbitration.

ILLUSTRATION

A Scottish contractor undertook to construct a factory in Scotland for an English employer.   The contract was in the post-1963 R.I.B.A. standard form available immediately prior to the 1965 version (which latter form contained express alternative provisions for Scottish contracts).   The architect was English, but the agreement was made in Scotland.   A Scottish arbitrator had commenced an arbitration, but refused to state a case for the opinion of the English courts, being of opinion that Scottish law governed the procedure of the arbitration.   He had himself been appointed by the President of the R.I.B.A. following the commencement of proceedings in the English courts by the Scottish contractor, and the granting of a stay by those courts on the application of the English employer.   The Scottish contractor had then applied to the President of the R.I.B.A. for the appointment of an arbitrator, specifically mentioning the Act of 1950.   *Held,* by the Court of Appeal and by a majority of the House of Lords, that while the general facts of the contract might point to Scottish law as the proper law of the contract, the use of the English R.I.B.A. form of contract, with its many references to and dependency on English substantive and procedural law, pointed to a contrary intention, which was reinforced by the subsequent conduct of the parties.   But *held* by the House of Lords, over-ruling the Court of Appeal, that the procedural law could be different from the proper law, and that the conduct of the parties after the appointment, notwithstanding the contractor's reference to the Act of 1950 in his letter asking for the appointment, showed acceptance that the proceedings should be governed by the law of Scotland, and consequently the arbitrator's award was final: *James Miller & Partners* v. *Whitworth Street Estates* (1970).[31]

This case is of great practical importance, since building and engineering arbitrations are frequently held in foreign countries in order, for example, to be near the site of the works or the technical witnesses.   It shows that the parties should be careful to agree expressly on the procedural law of the arbitration beforehand, however clear the contract may be as to the proper law of the contract.

(2) Arbitration Agreements Distinguished from Agreements for Valuation or Certification

It is important to distinguish between arbitrations, on the one hand, and valuations, appraisements and certificates, on the other, since in

---

[29] *Compagnie Tunisienne* v. *Compagnie d'Armement* [1969] 1 W.L.R. 449.
[30] See the case illustrated.   [31] [1970] 2 W.L.R. 728.

the latter cases the provisions of the Arbitration Acts are not applicable.[32]

If a person is appointed, owing to his skill and knowledge of the particular subject, to decide any questions, whether of fact or of value, by the use of his skill and knowledge and without taking any evidence or hearing the parties, he is not, prima facie, an arbitrator.

" It has been held that if a man is, on account of his skill in such matters, appointed to make a valuation, in such manner that in making it he may, in accordance with the appointment, decide solely by the use of his eyes, his knowledge and his skill, he is not acting judicially: he is using the skill of a valuer, not of a judge. In the same way, if two persons are appointed for a similar purpose, they are not arbitrators but only valuers. They have to determine the matter by using solely their own eyes and knowledge and skill." [33]

If, on the other hand, a person is appointed with the intention that he should hear the parties and their evidence and decide in a judicial manner, then he is an arbitrator, though a mere absence of a hearing, provided it does not result in any unfairness to the parties, will not necessarily invalidate an award.[34] Obviously this must depend on the subject-matter of the dispute and the terms of any written pleadings or submissions to the arbitrator.

Lord Esher M.R., in *Re Carus-Wilson and Greene* (1886),[35] defined the position as follows: " If it appears, from the terms of the agreement by which a matter is submitted to a person's decision, that the intention of the parties was that he should hold an inquiry in the nature of a judicial inquiry, and hear the respective cases of the parties, and decide upon evidence laid before him, then the case is one of arbitration. The intention in such cases is that there shall be a judicial inquiry worked out in a judicial manner. On the other hand there are cases in which a person is appointed to ascertain some matter for the purpose of preventing differences from arising, not of settling them when they have arisen, and where the case is not one of arbitration but of a mere valuation. There may be cases of an intermediate kind [35a] where, though a person is appointed to settle disputes that have arisen, still it is not intended that he shall be bound to hear evidence and arguments."

This passage refers primarily to the certifier (treated in the judgments as identical with a valuer), who is of course commonly

---

[32] *Collins* v. *Collins* (1858) 26 Beav. 306.
[33] Per Lord Esher M.R. in *Re Dawdy & Hartcup* (1885) 15 Q.B.D. 426.
[34] *Star International* v. *Bergbau-Handel* [1966] 2 Lloyd's Rep. 16. [35] 18 Q.B.D. 7.
[35a] *Cf.* the engineer under the I.C.E. arbitration clause, and clause in *Pierce, infra*, p. 830.

found in building contracts.[36] A certifier's decisions may be binding upon the parties, yet he will not be an arbitrator in the full sense, or subject to the control of the Arbitration Acts. Consequently, his decisions cannot be set aside or remitted,[37] or his appointment revoked, as in the case of an arbitrator, nor can he be required to state a case on a point of law for the opinion of the High Court. Paradoxically, therefore, the lesser status of the certifier or valuer may result in his decisions being more difficult to circumvent.[38] It may therefore be of considerable practical importance to determine whether a particular clause confers the jurisdiction of a true arbitrator, on the one hand, or a valuer or certifier, on the other, on the person named in the clause. In imprecisely drafted contracts this can give rise to considerable difficulty, particularly as in some cases both may be provided for, with consequential overlapping or conflict of jurisdictions.[39] It has already been seen [40] that in the I.C.E. form of contract the engineer's decision under clause 66 is a necessary preliminary to arbitration, but his function in this respect is clearly not that of an arbitrator, though his decision is binding on the parties if arbitration is not invoked within a certain period. It was submitted in the Ninth Edition that his function was that in the last category mentioned in the passage from Lord Esher's judgment cited above (*i.e.* that of a certifier or quasi-arbitrator) and it is still so submitted notwithstanding the lesser status apparently accorded him by the Appellate Division of the Supreme Court of South Africa in a case using a rather similar form of arbitration clause.[41]

ILLUSTRATIONS

(1) H. agreed to purchase from L. certain property at a price to be determined, and L. demanded the price from H., but H. refused to pay. The agreement had been made a rule of court. *Held,* that this was not a reference to arbitration within the statute 9 & 10 Will. 3, c. 15: *Re Lee and Hemingway* (1834).[42]

(2) An adjudication under a clause that upon certain defaults the builder would pay the employer such sums " as the said J. E. or other the engineer for the time being of the employer shall, in

[36] His position and status are dealt with fully, *ante*, pp. 402, 416–418, 435–437, 450–451, 499–504.
[37] The grounds upon which a certifier's decisions can be disregarded or invalidated are discussed fully, *ante*, Chap. 7, Section 5.
[38] Unless overridden by the arbitration clause itself—see *ante*, Chap. 7, Section 4.
[39] See also Chap. 7, *ante*, pp. 438–444, and the cases there cited, in particular *Lloyd Bros.* v. *Milward* (1895) Hudson's B.C., 4th ed., Vol. 2, p. 262 and *Clemence* v. *Clark* (1880), 4th ed., Vol. 2, p. 54, and also *ante*, pp. 503–504.
[40] *Supra*, p. 820.
[41] See *Kollberg* v. *Cape Town Municipality*, illustrated and doubted *supra*, p. 821, and *ante*, pp. 464, 502.   [42] 3 Nev. & M. 860.

his opinion, adjudge to be reasonable and proper to be paid for
such default " is an appraisement, not an award: *Northampton
Gas Light Co.* v. *Parnell* (1855).[43]

(3) Contracts for making waterworks for the city of Liverpool
contained a clause giving power of forfeiture for default, which
provided that on such termination of the contract " the engineer
shall fix and determine what amount, if any, is then reasonably
earned by the contractor in respect of work actually done, and
in respect to the value of any materials, implements, or tools provided by the contractor and taken by the corporation . . . and
the said engineer shall be at liberty to authorise by his certificate
the said corporation to deduct the damages, losses, costs, charges
and expenses in his opinion incurred by them in consequence of
the premises, or to which they may be put or liable, together with
the forfeiture, if any, incurred by the said contractor, from any sum
which would become due to the said contractor." *Held*, on appeal,
that this was not a provision for an arbitration: *Scott* v. *Liverpool
Corporation* (1858).[44]

(4) An agreement for the sale of land provided that compensation
was in certain events to be given, to be settled by two referees,
one to be appointed by either party, or an umpire. The events
happened, and the defendants having failed to appoint a referee,
the plaintiffs, acting under the provisions of the Common Law Procedure Act 1854, s. 13, appointed their referee to act as sole arbitrator, and a sum of money was awarded by him to them by way
of compensation. *Held*, following *Collins* v. *Collins* (1858),[45] that
the agreement was not a reference to arbitration of an existing or
future difference within the meaning of the Common Law Procedure
Act 1854, s. 11, and that the plaintiffs had therefore no power
under section 13 of that Act to appoint their referee as sole arbitrator: *Bos* v. *Helsham* (1866).[46]

(5) A lease of a farm stipulated that, in the event of a sale of the
premises during the term, the tenant, upon notice, should quit,
and that in such case each party should appoint a valuer to estimate
the compensation to be given to the tenant for so quitting. The
premises having been sold, the amount of compensation to be paid
to the tenant was, by deed between the parties, submitted to the
award of A and B, or such third person as they should appoint as
umpire under their hands, to be endorsed on the submission before
proceeding to value, with power to examine witnesses, etc. *Held*,
that the reference was not merely to ascertain the amount of compensation or value to be paid to the tenant in the nature of an
appraisement, but was an arbitration within section 17 of the
Common Law Procedure Act 1854: *Re Hopper* (1867).[47]

(6) A contract for the sale of land contained a stipulation that
each party should appoint a valuer, and give notice thereof by
writing to the other party within fourteen days from the date of the

[43] 24 L.J.C.P. 60.
[44] 28 L.J.Ch. 230; distinguishing (at p. 237) *Scott* v. *Avery* (1856) 5 H.L.C. 811.
[45] 28 L.J.Ch. 184; 26 Beav. 306.
[46] L.R. 2 Ex. 72.
[47] L.R. 2 Q.B. 367.

sale, and that the valuers thus appointed should, before they proceeded to act, appoint an umpire in writing, and that the two valuers, or, if they disagreed, their umpire, should make the valuation. The valuers disagreed and the umpire made the valuation. *Held*, that this was not a provision for arbitration: *Re Carus-Wilson and Greene* (1886).[48]

(7) Where by the terms of a contract it was provided that the engineer " shall be the exclusive judge upon all matters relating to the construction, incidents and consequences of these presents, and of the tender, specifications, schedule and drawings of the contract, and in regard to the execution of the works or otherwise arising out of or in connection with the contract, and also as regards all matters of account, including the final balance payable to the contractor, and the certificate of the engineer for the time being, given under his hand, shall be binding and conclusive on both parties ": *Held*, that such clause was not an arbitration clause, and that the duties of the engineer were administrative and not judicial: *Kennedy Ltd.* v. *Barrow-in-Furness (Mayor of)* (1909).[49]

(8) W. undertook to pay to a railway company the cost of labour and interest on the value of materials employed upon the construction of work. By the contract, the engineer of the company had to fix the amount of the cost and value. *Held*, that he was to do this as a skilled person, and could arrive at this determination as he chose and need not hear the parties or take evidence: *North British Railway* v. *Wilson* (1911).[50]

(9) A building contract provided for payments on account of the price of the works during their progress, and for payment of the balance after their completion, upon certificates of the architect, and that a certificate of the architect, showing the final balance due to the contractor, should be conclusive evidence of the works having been duly completed and that the contractor was entitled to receive payment of the final balance. The Court of Appeal (Romer L.J. dissenting) held that the architect, in ascertaining the amount due to the contractor, and certifying the same under the contract, occupied a position similar to that of an arbitrator and could not be sued for negligence in certifying: *Chambers* v. *Goldthorpe* (1901).[51]

(10) The plaintiff contracted to build a house for the defendant, for which he was to be paid by instalments when a certificate was given by the architect. By clause 8 of the contract, in case of dispute arising out of the contract, the decision of the architect was to be binding upon the parties. The Court of Appeal in this case based their judgment on the fact that the architect by clause 8 was an arbitrator in regard to disputes arising from his own certificates: *Neale* v. *Richardson* (1938).[52]

---

[48] 18 Q.B.D. 7.

[49] Hudson's B.C., 4th ed., Vol. 2, p. 411 (*cf.* the very similar wording in *Hickman* v. *Roberts* [1913] A.C. 229 quoted, *infra*).

[50] 1911 S.C. 738.

[51] [1901] 1 K.B. 624. This case did not decide that he was an arbitrator in the full sense. See the discussion *ante*, Chap. 2, pp. 164 *et seq.* as to its exact effect, and also *ante*, pp. 504–505. See also *Boynton* v. *Richardson* [1924] W.N. 262.

[52] [1938] 1 All E.R. 753. Illustrated more fully *ante*, Chap. 7, p. 441.

(11) A clause provided "If . . . any dispute shall arise . . . as to whether the works have been properly executed or completed or as to delay in such completion or as to extras to or deviations from the works either the owner or the builder may apply to X to appoint an architect to decide the same and such architect *after such investigations as he may consider proper* may by his certificate in writing decide such dispute and declare what payment or deduction is to be made . . . and such decision and declaration shall be conclusive and binding on both the owner and contractor." *Held*, following *Jowett* v. *Neath R.D.C.* (1916) [53] that as there was no indication of a judicial hearing or inquiry this was not an arbitration clause: *Pierce* v. *Dyke* (1952).[54]

The passage from Lord Esher M.R.'s judgment in *Re Carus-Wilson and Greene* (1886) [55] makes plain one common difference between a certifier and an arbitrator, namely, that the former's function is administrative and arises independently of any dispute between the parties, and indeed may be regarded as intended to prevent disputes arising, whereas the latter's function can only arise after a dispute, when his duty is to hear the parties' contentions and determine the dispute in a judicial manner. This is not to say that a certifier may not be required to exercise his function after a dispute has arisen, but his doing so is in many cases fortuitous and not the consequence of the dispute. There are, however, cases where disputes are intended to be dealt with by a person who is not a full arbitrator, of which examples are *Pierce* v. *Dyke* (1952), *supra*, and the engineer's power to give decisions as a preliminary to arbitration under clause 66 of the I.C.E. form of contract.[56] In such cases the distinction arises from the sense of the contract which does not contemplate a judicial hearing with legal representation permitted and rights of appeal to the High Court on points of law, and the other attributes of arbitration proper.

As has been pointed out above, this distinction between a certifier's and an arbitrator's functions, while quite plain in principle, can become blurred in some contracts by imprecise language or the draftsman failing to appreciate the distinction, *e.g.* the language of the clause in *Hickman* v. *Roberts* (1913) [57] " the decision of the architect relating to any matters or thing or the goodness or sufficiency of any work or the extent or value of any extra or omitted work shall be final, conclusive and binding on all parties." It is

---

[53] (1916) 80 J.P.J. 207 (a decision on virtually identical wording).
[54] [1952] 2 W.I.R. 30 (Jamaica).
[55] Cited *supra*, p. 826.
[56] See *supra*, pp. 819, 826, note 35a.
[57] [1913] A.C. 229.

submitted, despite the wording of the judgments in this case, that this was not an arbitration clause.[57a] In most modern contracts the arbitration clause is sufficiently widely drafted to give the clause an overriding effect over any clauses conferring finality upon the certifier's decisions, and the modern tendency is to interpret arbitration clauses as widely as possible for this purpose, since an arbitration clause will be largely nugatory if the arbitrator is bound by the certifier's decisions.[58]

In those cases where the certifier's decisions are given binding force by the terms of the contract, the parties are likely to find themselves in even greater difficulties in escaping the consequences of the decision than in the case of a full arbitrator, since no appeal by way of case stated is available, no power of the court to appoint a substitute exists, and it may well be more difficult to establish a sufficient bias or interest to invalidate the decision in the case of a certifier, whose close connection with the employer and interest in the subject-matter of the contract is known to the parties at the time of contracting, and who cannot, like an arbitrator, be removed on the ground of such an interest under section 24 of the Act of 1950.[59]

SECTION 2.   THE EFFECT OF THE ARBITRATION AGREEMENT

(1) Generally

An arbitration agreement does not oust the jurisdiction of the courts. Either party is still at liberty to commence an action in the courts in respect of the dispute covered by the arbitration agreement. But the party against whom an action is started in connection with a dispute covered by an arbitration agreement has a right to apply to the court to have the action stayed, and the court is given a discretion whether or not to stay the action in all such cases by section 4 (1) of the Arbitration Act 1950.

Consequently, where the other party makes no application to stay the action, the arbitration agreement will have no effect (unless it is expressed to be in what is called " *Scott* v. *Avery* " form, that is to say, the contract expressly provides that the obtaining of an award of an arbitrator shall be a condition precedent to bringing an action[60]).

[57a] See also *Chambers* v. *Goldthorpe, supra,* p. 829.
[58] But see now clauses 24 and 26 of the 1957 (revised) and clauses 30 (7) and 35 of the 1963 R.I.B.A. forms of contract commented upon *ante,* Chap. 7, pp. 489–492.
[59] See *ante,* p. 450, and *infra,* pp. 847 *et seq.*
[60] As to which see *infra,* Section 4, pp. 853 *et seq.*

In such circumstances, or where the court refuses to order a stay, the arbitrator no longer has any jurisdiction to determine the matter.

ILLUSTRATION

D. contracted to construct a sewerage works for the defendants. The contract provided that disputes should be referred to the defendants' engineer, who should be competent to enter upon the subject-matter of such disputes with or without formal reference or notice to the parties. D. sued the defendants for money alleged to be due under the contract and for damages for wrongful determination of the côntract. The defendants did not apply for a stay of proceedings. After action brought, the engineer, without the knowledge or consent of D., made an award, and the defendants pleaded the award as a bar to D.'s claim. *Held* (reversing the decision of Scrutton J.), by Fletcher Moulton L.J. and Farwell L.J. (Vaughan Williams L.J. dissenting), that it was not competent for the engineer to determine the matters in question pending the action, and that the award was not a bar to D.'s claim: *Doleman* v. *Ossett Corporation* (1912).[61]

Where an action is not stayed for one reason or another, any specific powers conferred on the arbitrator by the arbitration clause will, it is submitted, and notwithstanding certain *obiter dicta* to the contrary in the House of Lords,[62] also be available to the courts—the commonest example is the express or implied power under many modern arbitration clauses to disregard or revise decisions or certificates of the certifier. The basis for this, it is suggested, is that the courts will not permit the parties to confer wider powers on an arbitrator than on the courts in settling disputes—to do so would be partially to oust the jurisdiction of the courts. Further, the practical anomalies and difficulties to which any other view would give rise are so serious that the courts should hesitate long, it is submitted, before giving effect to any such presumed intention of the parties, who would not be likely to intend that one kind of tribunal, but not another, should have power to override the certifier.[63]

(2) Refusal of Stay

(a) Dispute within jurisdiction of arbitrator

The courts are only able to exercise their discretion to stay an action when the requirements of section 4 (1) of the 1950 Act have been met. This subsection provides:

---

[61] [1912] 3 K.B. 257 (C.A.).

[62] See the references to the judgments in *East Ham B.C.* v. *Sunley*, *ante*, Chap. 7, p. 447.

[63] See *ante*, Chap. 7, Section 4, pp. 446–448 for a full discussion.

" If any party to an arbitration agreement, or any person claiming through or under him, commences any legal proceedings in any court against any other party to the agreement, or any person claiming through or under him, in respect of any matter agreed to be referred, any party to those legal proceedings may at any time after appearance, and before delivering any pleadings or taking any other steps in the proceedings, apply to that court to stay the proceedings, and that court or a judge thereof, if satisfied that there is no sufficient reason why the matter should not be referred in accordance with the agreement, and that the applicant was, at the time when the proceedings were commenced, and still remains, ready and willing to do all things necessary to the proper conduct of the arbitration, may make an order staying the proceedings."

In order for the section to apply, there must be a valid written agreement between the parties to submit present or future differences to arbitration.

It was decided in *Shayler* v. *Woolf* (1946)[64] that an arbitration clause is assignable. Consequently an assignee can claim arbitration through a party to an arbitration agreement. Where, however, a debt arises out of a contract containing an arbitration agreement and that debt (as distinct from the contract) is assigned, it has been held that the benefit of the arbitration agreement will not pass to the assignee.[65]

Further, by section 2 (1) of the 1950 Act an arbitration agreement is enforceable by or against the personal representatives of a party to that agreement, and by section 3 (1), if a trustee in bankruptcy adopts a contract, any arbitration provision in that contract is enforceable by or against the trustee.

In order to obtain a stay there must be a dispute in fact, that is to say, there must be some issue joined between the parties which the arbitrator will have to try. The effect of there being a dispute between the parties, but not one within an arbitration agreement, is, of course, that the court has no power to stay an action.[66] Furthermore, if a trader persists in not paying for goods delivered to him without disclosing any substantive defence, this is merely a refusal to pay and not a dispute, and an action brought for the money will not be stayed

[64] [1946] Ch. 320. But see *ante*, Chap. 14, pp. 727–728.
[65] *Cottage Club Estates Ltd.* v. *Woodside Estates Co.* (*Amersham*) *Ltd.* [1928] 2 K.B. 463; but that decision has been criticised (see *ante*, Chap. 14, pp. 727–728).
[66] *Monro* v. *Bognor U.D.C.* [1915] 3 K.B. 167.

on account of an arbitration clause.[67] This will be *pro tanto* the case if there is only a dispute as to part of the claim, and judgment can be obtained for the remainder, subject to any available defence or set-off.

In addition, the nature or character of the dispute must be within the jurisdiction of the arbitrator, that is to say, it must be within the terms of the arbitration agreement. In the case of a submission of an existing dispute, difficulties of jurisdiction of this kind are less likely to occur, but in the case of agreements to refer future disputes (as in the case of the classical arbitration clauses in building and engineering contracts) it is obviously essential in order to obtain a stay to show that the dispute comes within the terms of the clause and that the arbitrator accordingly has jurisdiction to deal with the matter. Cases where the arbitrator's jurisdiction is restricted by reason of a conclusive certificate or satisfaction under the contract have already been considered.[68] It is, of course, possible to regard such cases as not involving the jurisdiction of the arbitrator, who technically can be said to have jurisdiction to hear the dispute though bound to give effect to the overriding certificate or satisfaction, but this is only a form of words and the reality is, of course, that the arbitrator is without jurisdiction to hear and determine the merits of the dispute, once he has satisfied himself that a conclusive certificate has been issued. Thus in *Monmouth C.C.* v. *Costelloe & Kemple* (1964),[69] Mocatta J. made a declaration preventing an arbitrator from hearing a claim under clause 12 of the I.C.E. conditions of contract where no proper notice under that clause had been given. In each case it is necessary to consider the exact words of the arbitration clause, which in modern times is generally drafted in the widest terms so as to bring any dispute under the contract within its terms. Thus a dispute involving the allegation that an admitted contract had been terminated by repudiation has been held to be within the wording of a modern clause,[70] as also disputes involving the allegation that the contract has been frustrated, in the one case at a time when the contract remained unperformed and in the other when partly performed.[71] On the other hand, without sufficiently explicit words, a dispute whether or not a contract had been entered into at all would

---

[67] *London and North Western Ry.* v. *Billington* [1899] A.C. 79, *infra*, p. 837. See also *Plucis* v. *Fryer* (1967) 41 A.L.J.R. 192, illustrated *infra*, p. 854.

[68] *Ante*, Chap. 7, Section 4.

[69] Illustrated for this purpose *ante*, Chap. 9, Section 1 (1) (c), p. 570.

[70] *Heyman* v. *Darwins* [1942] A.C. 356, *infra*.

[71] *Kruse* v. *Questier & Co. Ltd.* [1953] 1 Q.B. 669; *Government of Gibraltar* v. *Kenney* [1956] 2 Q.B. 410, both *infra*.

generally not be within the terms of an arbitration clause in the contract, and so, too, disputes involving the allegation that the contract was void for illegality or fundamental mistake,[72] or that it should be rescinded because of a fraudulent misrepresentation in the specification.[73] Nor will some forms of arbitration clause be wide enough to permit the arbitrator to rectify the contract out of which his jurisdiction springs.[74] It is the court which will decide whether or not the dispute falls within the arbitration agreement, as the court will not normally leave a question of jurisdiction to be decided by the arbitrator himself.[75]

ILLUSTRATION

Arbitration under a building contract was not permitted till after completion of the works. *Held*, that an award made by the arbitrator before the works had in fact been completed was bad, since he had no jurisdiction to decide conclusively whether or not the works were complete: *Smith* v. *Martin* (1925).[76]

An arbitration agreement may, however, explicitly empower the arbitrator to decide whether or not a particular dispute is within the arbitration agreement. In such a case the court, subject to its discretion, will, it would seem, stay the action without considering the question of jurisdiction, provided a prima facie case is made out.[77]

The court may refuse to stay an action in cases where a substantial part of the claim does not fall within the agreement and cannot conveniently be separated.[78] But if only a small part of the relief claimed is outside the agreement, the court will normally stay the action.[79] The court may also refuse to stay the action where the arbitrator can only decide the amount due and not the question of liability.[80] A claim arising not out of the contract but out of alleged unfair conduct tending to defeat the contract has also been held not to be within the arbitration clause of the contract.[81]

---

[72] *Heyman* v. *Darwins, infra.*
[73] *Monro* v. *Bognor U.D.C.* [1915] 3 K.B. 167.
[74] *Crane* v. *Hegeman-Harris* [1939] 4 All E.R. 68.
[75] *Heyman* v. *Darwins* [1942] A.C. 356 at p. 393; *Toller* v. *Law Accident Insurance Society Ltd.* [1936] 2 All E.R. 952.
[76] [1925] 1 K.B. 745.
[77] *Heyman* v. *Darwins* [1942] A.C. 356 at pp. 385, 392. See also *Willesford* v. *Watson* (1873) L.R. 8 Ch. 473.
[78] See *e.g. Moyers* v. *Soady* (1886) 18 L.R.Ir. 499 and *Turnock* v. *Sartoris* (1889) 43 Ch.D. 150 illustrated, *infra.*
[79] *Ives & Barker* v. *Willans* [1894] 2 Ch. 478. See also *Re Donkin and Leeds and Liverpool Canal Co.*, Hudson's B.C., 4th ed., Vol. 2, p. 239, where revocation of the submission was refused on a similar ground.
[80] *O'Connor* v. *Norwich Union Co.* [1894] 2 Ir.R. 723.
[81] *Nobel Bros.* v. *Stewart* (1890) 6 T.L.R. 378.

ILLUSTRATIONS

(1) A partnership deed provided for the reference of disputes to arbitration, " so that every such reference shall be made within forty days next after such dispute, doubt, or question shall arise." Disputes arose, but the time for referring expired, except as to an isolated dispute arising in the course of the other differences. *Held*, that the court would not stay an action pending arbitration: *Young* v. *Buckett* (1882).[82]

[Note: This case was distinguished in *Bruce* v. *Strong* (1951) [83] where the clause was in a " *Scott* v. *Avery* " form [84] and to refuse a stay might accordingly deprive the party desiring arbitration of all remedy.]

(2) There was an implied term in a dredging contract that the removal of certain staging by the Local Board would not be unreasonably delayed. There was also a provision: " if any difference shall arise between the Local Board and the contractor concerning the work hereby contracted for, or any part thereof, or concerning anything in connection with this contract, such difference shall be referred to the engineer and his decision shall be final and binding on the Local Board and the contractor." The implied term was broken and the engineer certified a sum " in full satisfaction of all the contractor's claims on the Local Board for work executed pursuant to the contract and in connection therewith." *Held*, the measure of damages payable for breach of the implied term was not a difference concerning a matter in connection with the contract: *Lawson* v. *Wallasey Local Board* (1883).[85]

[Note: There were other independent reasons for the actual decision in this case (including a finding that there never had been an arbitration held by the engineer) and it must, it is submitted, be regarded as out of line with modern authority.[86]]

(3) Under a building contract containing an arbitration clause, the plaintiffs (the contractors) sued at law, alleging that the commissioners (the employers) had directed some of the work to be suspended, and had directed additional work, not provided for by the contract, to be executed, and claimed (1) £1,112 10s. damages for the suspension; (2) £3,658 8s. 6d. for materials and labour in the additional works; (3) £370 10s. 2d. for furniture supplied to the commissioners at their request; (4) £66 15s. 4d. for interest on these sums. The defendants applied to have the action stayed. Dowse B. refused to stay the action, because, it being admitted that claim (1) was not within the arbitration clause, " it would be highly inconvenient to stay the proceedings as to one part of the cause of action and to allow the other part to go on before a jury. The whole case is so inextricably'intertwined in all its parts that full justice could not be done to all the parties unless the entire case was heard before the same tribunal ": *Moyers* v. *Soady* (1886).[87]

---

[82] 51 L.J.Ch. 504.
[84] See *post*, Section 4.
[86] The case is further criticised *ante*, Chap. 7, pp. 408–409. The C.A. upheld this decision but expressed no opinion on the question whether or not the action could have been stayed.
[87] 18 L.R.Ir. 499.

[83] [1951] 2 K.B. 447.
[85] 11 Q.B.D. 229.

(4) A lessor covenanted to supply the lessee with a certain quantity of water per day. The lease contained a clause providing that if any difference should arise between the parties touching the lease, or anything therein contained, or the construction thereof, or in any way connected with the lease or the operation thereof, it should be referred to arbitration. Some years afterwards, disputes having arisen between the parties as to the water supply, a written agreement was entered into binding the lessor to take certain steps with a view to securing a better supply, and in some points varying the rights of the lessee as to the supply. Afterwards the lessee commenced an action, alleging that the lessor had not supplied the stipulated quantity of water, and claimed an inquiry as to the damages sustained by the plaintiff by reason of the matters aforesaid. The defendant moved to stay proceedings and have them referred to arbitration. The Court of Appeal, after deciding that the arbitration clause did not apply to all the matters that might arise under the subsequent agreement, refused to stay the proceedings: *Turnock* v. *Sartoris* (1889).[88]

(5) A fire policy contained a condition that if any difference arose in the adjustment of a loss, the amount to be paid should be submitted to arbitration, and that the insured should not be entitled to commence or maintain any action upon the policy until the amount of the loss has been so ascertained. There was a loss admittedly in excess of the amount of the policy, the only matter of dispute being whether the insured had violated another condition of the policy. In an application to stay an action on the policy: *Held*, that no difference in the adjustment of the loss having arisen, a stay must be refused: *O'Connor* v. *Norwich Union Insurance Society* (1894).[89]

(6) A railway Act empowered the company to charge a reasonable sum for certain services rendered to a trader, and enacted that " any difference arising under this section shall be determined by an arbitrator to be appointed by the Board of Trade." The company sued a trader for services rendered under the section. The defendant applied for a stay pending arbitration. *Held*, that as there was no difference existing between the parties before action brought, the arbitrator had not, and the court had, jurisdiction: *London & North Western Railway* v. *Billington* (1899).[90]

(7) A lease contained a proviso that any dispute, difference, or question touching the construction, meaning or effect of the lease, or the right of the parties under or in relation to the lease, should be referred. The lessors brought an action against the lessees claiming rectification of the lease and damages for breach of covenant and the lessees moved to have the action stayed and the matters referred. *Held*, that the claim for rectification was not within the arbitration clause, and the action, in so far as it claimed rectification, must proceed; the claim for damages being stood over: *Printing Machinery Co.* v. *Linotype and Machinery Ltd.* (1912).[91]

[88] 43 Ch.D. 150 (C.A.)
[89] [1894] 2 Ir.R. 723.
[90] [1899] A.C. 79; and see *London & North Western Ry.* v. *Jones* [1915] 2 K.B. 35.
[91] [1912] 1 Ch. 566.

[Note. This case is sometimes cited as authority for the proposition that an arbitrator has no jurisdiction to rectify the contract out of which his jurisdiction arises. The language of the judgment, however, which was approved in *Crane* v. *Hegeman-Harris Co. Inc.*,[92] shows that it proceeds on the basis that the language of the particular submission before the court was not sufficiently wide to enable the arbitrator to consider anything but the contract referred to in the submission in its unrectified form.[93] In some forms of contract the arbitrator's jurisdiction is expressed to cover not merely matters " arising out of the contract " (which on the authority of the above cases might not include the contract as rectified), but also matters arising, " out of the carrying out of the works " [94] and it is submitted that this wording will be sufficient to enable an arbitrator to rectify the contract if necessary. Under the standard R.I.B.A. forms there is an express power [95] to rectify errors in the bills of quantities or the contract drawings and specifications, but this is merely a use of language and has nothing to do with the legal remedy of rectification.] [96]

(8) A contractor alleged fraudulent misrepresentation in the specification as to the nature of the sub-soil. *Held*, by the Court of Appeal, this dispute did not " arise upon or in relation to or in connection with the contract ": *Monro* v. *Bognor U.D.C.* (1915).[97]

(9) An arbitration submission referred all disputes between an architect and his employer " arising out of or relating to the said agreement (of employment of the architect) or the subject-matter thereof or as to the rights duties or liabilities of either of the parties in connection with the premises " to a named arbitrator. An arbitration was held as to the construction of part of the contract. The unsuccessful party, having unsuccessfully pursued his remedy by way of case stated on a point of law, finally resisted enforcement of the award by applying to the court for rectification of the agreement. It was objected that the court should not entertain the claim for rectification, since this might have been raised before the arbitrator in the first instance. *Held*, that the arbitrator would have had no jurisdiction under such a submission to rectify the agreement, so that rectification could be granted by the court: *Crane* v. *Hegeman-Harris Inc.* (1939).[98]

[Note: The word " premises " above appears to be used in the legal and not the physical sense. It does not appear to have been argued in this case that the words " arising out of or relating to . . . the subject-matter thereof " might be wider in this context than the words " arising out of or relating to the said agreement." It is submitted that on wording of this kind the matter is not free from doubt.]

(10) An arbitration clause referred future disputes " in respect of this agreement or any of the provisions herein contained or anything

[92] [1939] 4 All E.R. 68, *infra*.
[93] See *per* Lord Greene M.R. [1939] 4 All E.R. 68 at p. 72.
[94] See clause 66, 1955 I.C.E. form.
[95] In clause 12 of the post-1963 forms.
[96] For rectification generally, see *ante*, Chap. 1, pp. 32 *et seq*.
[97] [1915] 3 K.B. 167.
[98] [1939] 4 All E.R. 68.

arising hereout " to arbitration. *Held,* by the House of Lords, an arbitrator appointed under the clause had jurisdiction to determine whether the agreement had been repudiated by one of the parties to it: *Heyman* v. *Darwins Ltd.* (1942).[99]

(11) An arbitration clause referred to arbitration " all disputes from time to time arising under this contract." *Held,* by Pilcher J., that an arbitrator appointed under the clause had jurisdiction to decide a dispute as to whether or not the contract had been frustrated by a supervening event while still unperformed: *Kruse* v. *Questier & Co. Ltd.* (1953).[1]

(12) An arbitration clause referred to arbitration disputes " in relation to any thing or matter arising out of or under this agreement." *Held,* by Sellers J., that an arbitrator appointed under the clause had jurisdiction to decide a dispute as to whether the contract had been frustrated by supervening events during the performance of the contract: *Government of Gibraltar* v. *Kenney* (1956).[2]

For further decisions on the factors affecting the discretion of the court in deciding whether or not to grant a stay, see paragraph (c) *infra.*

(b) No step in proceedings

The application for a stay may be made by any party to the legal proceedings. Thus, when there is more than one defendant, any defendant may make the application, even though other defendants may not be willing to have the proceedings stayed.[3]

The applicant for a stay of proceedings must have taken no step in those proceedings. " The authorities show that a step in the proceedings means something in the nature of an application to the court and not mere talk between solicitors and solicitors' clerks nor the writing of letters, but the taking of some step such as taking out a summons, which is, in a technical sense, a step in the proceedings."[4]

ILLUSTRATION

In an action for a sum of money due on an architect's certificates under a building contract, which included an arbitration clause to be operative on either party giving to the other notice of any dispute or difference, the plaintiffs took out a summons for judgment under Order XIV. The defendants filed an affidavit claiming that they had a defence to the action but the Master gave the plaintiffs leave to sign final judgment, and on the appeal by the defendants coming before the judge in chambers they were granted

---

[99] [1942] A.C. 356.
[1] [1953] 1 Q.B. 669.
[2] [1956] 2 Q.B. 410.
[3] *Willesford* v. *Watson* (1873) L.R. 8 Ch. 473.
[4] *Per* Lindley L.J. in *Ives & Barker* v. *Willans* [1894] 2 Ch. at p. 484. As to what does or does not constitute a step in the proceedings, see Russell, 17th ed., pp. 73–75.

an adjournment to enable them to take out a summons to determine whether they were entitled to a stay of proceedings. At the hearing a stay was refused but leave was given to defend the action. *Held,* by the Court of Appeal, that the defendants had taken a step in the action within the meaning of section 4, when they appeared before the Master and asked for leave to defend the action: *Pitchers Ltd.* v. *Plaza (Queensbury) Ltd.* (1940).[5]

The applicant for a stay of proceedings must show that he is, both at the time of his application and at the commencement of proceedings, ready and willing to do everything necessary for the proper conduct of the arbitration. The fact that the defendant proposes to argue that under the terms of the contract the plaintiff has lost the right to any remedy is not a ground for refusing a stay.

So, where the arbitration clause lays down a time limit within which an arbitration must be commenced [6] a party may still plead that the arbitration is out of time and yet be ready and willing to do everything necessary for the proper conduct of the arbitration.[7] (The High Court does, however, have power under section 27 of the Act of 1950 to extend any time limit within which arbitration proceedings must be begun.) On the other hand, if the person asking for a stay is at the same time denying the existence of the contract in which the provision appears, no stay will be granted.[8] The same would be the case if fundamental mistake or illegality were alleged, and these were not within the arbitrator's jurisdiction.[9]

(c) General discretion to refuse stay

Quite apart from questions of jurisdiction, the court has a discretion as to whether or not it will stay an action. It will generally refuse a stay where any stipulated time for referring the dispute has expired [10] (but not where the clause is in " *Scott* v. *Avery* " form,[11] that is to say, where an award of the arbitrator is expressed to be a condition precedent to a party's right to sue [12]) or when the appropriate remedy is an injunction [13] (or presumably, any other remedy which an arbitrator could not give).

---

[5] [1940] 1 All E.R. 151.
[6] *e.g.* the standard form issued by the Institute of Civil Engineers, see *Monmouth C.C.* v. *Costelloe & Kemple, supra,* p. 820.
[7] *Bruce* v. *Strong* [1951] 2 K.B. 447.
[8] *Toller* v. *Law Accident Insurance Society Ltd.* [1936] 2 All E.R. 952.
[9] See the judgments in *Heyman* v. *Darwins Ltd.* [1942] A.C. 356.
[10] *Young* v. *Buckett* (1882) 51 L.J. Ch. 504, *supra.*
[11] *Bruce* v. *Strong* [1951] 2 K.B. 447.
[12] See Section 4, *post.*
[13] *Law* v. *Garrett* (1878) 8 Ch.D. 26; *Kirchner & Co.* v. *Gruban* [1909] 1 Ch. 413 and see *Marchon Products Ltd.* v. *Thornes,* (unreported; Danckwerts J., Chancery Division) April 27, 1954; 71 R.P.C. 445.

" There is no limitation as to the cases in which a judge may exercise his discretion by refusing to stay." [14]

ILLUSTRATION

A contract for the execution of works gave by its fifteenth clause power to the employers' engineer in certain events to determine the contract, and stipulated that in such events the employers might complete the contract, and that if they did so their engineer should, within a certain time, settle and certify the amount earned by the contractors for work actually done by them, and the value of materials forwarded which were then on the ground. The contract also contained an arbitration clause. After the works were more than half finished the employers exercised their powers under clause 15, and proceeded with the works themselves, but did not finish for nearly three years. Their engineer, though often required by the contractors to do so, never made a valuation under clause 15, or gave any final certificate. The contractors sued for an account of what was due, or to have the contract specifically performed. An application by the employers to stay the action was refused on the ground that the dispute was due to the gross default of the employers and their engineer, and that it could not have been intended to substitute an arbitrator for the ordinary tribunals when through the wilful default of the employers and their engineer the plaintiffs could not get a proper certificate: *Swiney* v. *Ballymena Commissioners* (1888).[15]

Once an applicant has established that a dispute falls within an arbitration clause, the modern tendency of the courts is undoubtedly to stay the action unless the party opposing the stay can show cause to the contrary.[16]   Further, where the arbitration clause is in the " *Scott* v. *Avery* " form,[17] the courts will be even more reluctant to refuse a stay, since by doing so they may deprive a party of his substantive rights altogether.[18] The following subsections describe circumstances in which the courts may refuse to stay actions. It should be remembered that very different considerations of discretion are likely to arise where a specific submission has been made, as opposed to general agreements to refer future disputes.

(i) **Where fraud or charges of a personal character are alleged.** Where a dispute arises as to whether either party has been guilty of fraud, the High Court has express statutory power to order that the

---

[14] *Per* Vaughan Williams L.J. in *Kennedy Ltd.* v. *Barrow-in-Furness* (1909) Hudson's B.C., 4th ed., Vol. 2, p. 411 at p. 414.

[15] 23 L.R.Ir. 122.

[16] *Heyman* v. *Darwins Ltd.* [1942] A.C. 356 at p. 388.

[17] See *infra*, Section 4, p. 853.

[18] See *per* Phillimore L.J. in *Smith, Coney & Barratt* v. *Becker, Gray & Co.* [1916] 2 Ch. 86 at p. 101, and *per* Somervell L.J. in *Bruce* v. *Strong* [1951] 2 K.B. at p. 453.

agreement shall cease to have effect, and to revoke the authority of the arbitrator or umpire appointed by virtue of the agreement.[19]

In the event of fraud being charged and the person charged with fraud objecting to arbitration, arbitration will seldom be enforced [20]; a stay of proceedings is usually refused if the charge is substantial. But at least a prima facie case of fraud must be made out, and a mere general charge unsupported by definite particulars will not prevent the action being stayed.[21]

In such a case any difficulty caused by a " Scott v. Avery " clause can be avoided, because by section 25 of the Act of 1950 the court has power to order that such a clause should have no effect in any case where it has power to order the revocation of an arbitrator's authority or his removal, or where charges of fraud are involved.

In the event of there being an express stipulation in an arbitration agreement that questions involving fraud of the parties should be submitted to arbitration, the court will probably not refuse to stay the action,[22] a fortiori, of course, where the dispute in question has been specifically agreed to be referred.

When substantial personal charges other than fraud are alleged, the court will normally allow the party against whom they are made to have them investigated in open court, but the mere fact that a dispute will involve questions of credit is not sufficient.[23]   The principle would appear to be that the court will hesitate before depriving a party against whom serious personal charges are made of his right of appeal upon questions of fact.[24]   But where the arbitration agreement clearly contemplates the type of dispute in question (as will always be the case, of course, where a dispute is the subject of a specific submission, and will often be the case, for instance, where professional negligence is alleged even where there is only an agreement to refer) there would seem to be no justification in principle for refusing a stay.

[19] Section 24 (2) of the Act of 1950.
[20] Per Jessel M.R. in Russell v. Russell (1880) 14 Ch.D. 471 observing on Wickens V.-C.'s remarks in Willesford v. Watson (1873) L.R. 14 Eq. 572 at p. 578 (affirmed L.R. 8 Ch. 473, but without referring to those remarks of the Vice-Chancellor).
[21] Wallis v. Hirsch (1856) 1 C.B.(N.S.) 316; Russell v. Russell (1880) 14 Ch.D. 471.
[22] Heyman v. Darwins Ltd. [1942] A.C. 356 at p. 392.
[23] Minifie v. Railway Passengers Assurance Co. (1881) 44 L.T. 552.
[24] Cf. Charles Osenton and Co. v. Johnston [1942] A.C. 130, a decision as to referring cases of professional negligence to official referees. But see now Ord. 58, r. 5, and e.g. Scarborough R.D.C. v. Moore (1968) 112 S.J. 986, referred to ante, Chap. 2, Section 6, pp. 126–127.

(ii) Where questions of law are involved. If the contract expressly refers questions of law to the arbitrator (this would include, of course, specific submissions), a stay will usually be granted.[25] So, too, when the point of law is one of a class which is constantly dealt with by arbitrators,[26] or where the question of law is intermingled with questions of fact.

ILLUSTRATION

A contract for engineering works provided that any disputes arising should be referred to an arbitrator who was to be an engineer. One of the parties to the contract took out a summons for the consideration of a clause in the contract. It appeared that evidence would be needed both as to custom in such matters and as to the meaning of technical terms used before the clause could be construed. *Held*, by the Court of Appeal (overruling the judge below) that the proceedings should be stayed: *Metropolitan Tunnel etc. Ltd.* v. *London Electric Railway* (1926).[27]

There has, however, been a tendency in the past when the dispute involved a pure question of law and the matter was not expressly referred to arbitration to refuse a stay of any court proceedings brought to try that point of law, at any rate where the clause was not in the " *Scott* v. *Avery* " form.

" Where in such a document as a building contract or a partnership agreement you have an all-embracing arbitration clause, it may often be bad practice to permit matters of law or construction to go to arbitration for, though such matters are strictly covered by the agreement, they are questions not appropriate to be dealt with by arbitration and it may be futile to allow them so to be." [28]

Again in *Bristol Corporation* v. *John Aird Ltd.* (1913) [29] Lord Parker said: " Everybody knows that with regard to the construction of an agreement it is absolutely useless to stay the action because it will only come back to the court on a case stated."

This last statement must, however, be read in the light of the comments of the law lords, and in particular Lord Wright, in *Heyman* v. *Darwins Ltd.* (1942),[30] which suggest a change in the judicial attitude on this point.[31] The modern tendency in England

---

[25] *Absalom Ltd.* v. *Great Western Garden Village Society Ltd.* [1933] A.C. 592 at pp. 607–608.

[26] *Heyman* v. *Darwins Ltd.* [1942] A.C. 356 at p. 369.

[27] [1926] Ch. 371.

[28] *Per* Evershed M.R. in *Martin* v. *Selsdon* (*No.* 2) (1950) 67 R.P.C. 64 at p. 69.

[29] [1913] A.C. 241, 261.

[30] [1942] A.C. 356, see *e.g.* at pp. 388–389.

[31] See, however, the unreported decision of Danckwerts J. in *Marchon Products Ltd.* v. *Thornes*, Ch.D., April 27, 1954; (1954) 71 R.P.C. 445, and Lord Evershed's remarks in *Martin* v. *Selsdon* cited *supra*.

is undoubtedly against refusing a stay, and the onus will be on the party opposing the stay to show, for example, that the point is of such substance that it must inevitably come to the courts whatever the arbitrator decides.[32]

(iii) Convenience. If it is more practical or convenient for a dispute to be dealt with in the courts, the courts can take this into account in exercising their discretion whether or not to stay. This was clearly the basis of the decisions referred to in the preceding subsection of this book where applications to stay have been refused on the ground that only a point of law was involved in the dispute.

One of the gravest inconveniences of arbitration, which arises frequently in practice in building and engineering disputes, is that there are often more than two parties involved. Thus a building owner might wish to proceed against the contractor, or failing a successful result against him, the architect, or vice versa. A contractor when sued might wish to seek a remedy, if liable, against a sub-contractor. An employer, if sued by the contractor, might wish, if liable, to seek a remedy against his architect. In addition, if the principle in *Hedley Byrne* v. *Heller* (1964) [33] is further developed by the courts, employers might in certain special circumstances wish to proceed in tort against sub-contractors, and contractors against architects.

In the courts procedural techniques, such as suing two defendants, or joining third parties or co-defendants, are available to the parties, which have the advantage of finally resolving the position of all parties at one hearing, avoiding any possibility of conflicting decisions of fact by different tribunals and the inevitable consequential injustices and anomalies, and also reducing the gross total of costs involved.

The perennial difficulty facing litigants and their advisers in this field is that only very rarely are arbitration clauses present in all the contracts between the various parties and, even if they are, they are never couched in a form which enables the parties as of right to require the same arbitrator to determine such multiple disputes, let alone at one hearing. There is no doubt that this procedural difficulty is often exploited by defendants or third parties so as to impose additional delay and expense on plaintiffs or defendants wishing to press their claims against another defendant or third party.

---

[32] Compare, in New Zealand, *Goodwin Ltd.* v. *Stephenson and Watt* [1967] 2 N.S.W.R. 637.

[33] *Ante*, Chap. 1, p. 64.

It might have been thought that the courts would not have been slow to appreciate this, and in exercising their discretion would have lent support to the swiftest and most convenient way of settling such disputes, but in *Bruce* v. *Strong* (1951),[34] which would seem to be a very strong case from this point of view, the Court of Appeal over-ruled Parker J. (as he then was) and ordered a stay where a dispute arose as to the quality of goods, and an arbitration clause existed only between the fourth and fifth parties, notwithstanding that this broke the chain of liability in the courts between earlier and later parties. It would be tempting to think that the *ratio decidendi* of that case was that the arbitration clause was in the " *Scott* v. *Avery* " form and a contrary decision might have deprived the fourth party of his rights and broken the chain of liability altogether, but Somervell L.J. said [35]: " In my view, without laying down an absolute rule, for there must be a discretion to look at all the circumstances of the case, prima facie all these matters are *res inter alios acta* and irrelevant to the consideration of the issue raised as between these two parties who agreed to this arbitration procedure. . . ." This reasoning was not, however, adopted by McNair J., who in a later case [36] involving ship-owners, charterers and owners of cargo in a claim for general average adjustment, said: " A serious risk would be run that our whole judicial procedure, at any rate in relation to this claim, would be brought into disrepute if . . . you get conflicting questions of fact decided by two different tribunals."

Happily these difficulties have been partly at least mitigated by the decision of the Court of Appeal in *Taunton-Collins* v. *Cromie* (1964),[37] where a building owner sued his architect in the courts for negligent design and supervision and, on the architect blaming the contractor, sought to join the latter as co-defendant, but the latter applied for a stay. The Court of Appeal, approving The " *Pine Hill* " (1958) and declining to follow *Bruce* v. *Strong* (1951), refused a stay, Lord Denning M.R. on the ground that the possibility of inconsistent findings of facts should be avoided, and Pearson L.J. on the ground of the undesirability of a multiplicity of proceedings.

The decision in the *Taunton-Collins* case does much to assist plaintiffs to obtain agreement upon one tribunal in a multiple dispute, either by commencing an action in the courts and objecting to a stay, or by offering to agree to a stay on condition that all parties involved

[34] [1951] 2 K.B. 447.
[35] At p. 453.
[36] *The " Pine Hill "* [1958] 2 Lloyd's Rep. 146.
[37] [1964] 1 W.L.R. 633.

agree in the appointment of a single arbitrator with power to decide all disputes at one hearing. The value of the case is, however, limited, (a) because in the last resort the party seeking to obtain a single tribunal can only obtain such a tribunal in the High Court, notwithstanding that all parties may have signed contracts with arbitration clauses, and that arbitration before a technical arbitrator may be particularly appropriate to the dispute, and (b) because if an arbitration is once started between some of the parties before he commences proceedings in the courts, it is impossible for him to bring that arbitration to an end while, if he himself is a party to the arbitration, he will have to seek to revoke the appointment of the arbitrator before he can institute High Court proceedings which will embrace all parties. Though logically it would seem that the courts should apply the same principles in deciding whether to revoke an arbitrator's appointment on the ground of convenience as in a case where the question is whether or not to grant a stay, it is obvious that any such discretion would need to be exercised with more care once regularly constituted arbitration proceedings had begun and costs been incurred. But in fact in *City Centre Properties* v. *Matthew Hall* (1969) [38] the Court of Appeal (in particular Harman L.J.) suggested that, in the absence of misconduct of some kind by the arbitrator, there was no jurisdiction to revoke an arbitrator's authority on grounds of convenience. If this were so, it would mean that the value of the *Taunton-Collins* decision would be largely emasculated, since any party anxious to avoid a single tribunal dealing with all the issues and parties could initiate arbitration proceedings, albeit unilaterally and prematurely, purely for this reason. It is submitted that the *City Centre* case (or rather the reasoning on which it was based) may need reconsideration, and that in appropriate cases revocation on the ground of convenience should be permitted, but it may be conceded that to allow it freely in such circumstances would be to deprive many arbitration agreements of the greater part of their effect, since in many industries such as the building and civil engineering industries, tripartite or quadripartite disputes are the rule rather than the exception. There is arguably a lacuna in the Arbitration Acts, which might be amended so as to permit multipartite arbitrations to be ordered by the courts in appropriate cases, with the arbitrator enjoying the same powers as those of a judge under the High Court procedures for trying such disputes.

[38] [1969] 1 W.L.R. 772.

SECTION 3.   DISQUALIFICATION OF ARBITRATORS

(1) Generally

Interest, misconduct or bias of an arbitrator are grounds for refusing a stay, for revoking an arbitrator's appointment if he has already taken up his duties, or for setting aside or remitting his award if he has already made it. The court has wide powers under the Act for removing arbitrators, setting aside or remitting their awards, appointing new arbitrators in substitution for arbitrators who have died or misconducted themselves, or refuse or are unable to act, or are guilty of unreasonable delay, or where the parties cannot agree upon an arbitrator. Consideration of most of these subjects is outside the scope of this chapter, which is primarily concerned with giving guidance to the parties to building and engineering contracts, and architects and arbitrators, as to the interpretation of arbitration clauses, the results of going to arbitration, and as to the conduct of and procedure in arbitrations. But some discussion of the type of conduct or interest which will disqualify an arbitrator may be useful, particularly as a guide to arbitrators, in addition to the earlier discussion in this book relating to the disqualification of certifiers.[39]

(2) Interest, Misconduct or Bias

Interest, misconduct or bias is a ground for refusing a stay or, once appointed, for revoking the arbitrator's authority and removing him under section 23 of the Act of 1950, though in such circumstances the court has power to appoint a new arbitrator under section 25 of the Act, or on the other hand to order that the arbitration agreement should no longer have effect. But an interest which was known to the parties at the time of the submission as existing, or likely in the ordinary course of business to exist, did not in the past disqualify an arbitrator.[40] This was a serious difficulty in the contracts commonly found in the past where the architect or engineer of the employer was appointed as arbitrator. In such a case it was necessary to show actual bias, not the potential bias arising from the position of the arbitrator as the employer's architect or engineer, which was known to the parties at the time of contracting.[41]

---

[39] *Ante*, Chap. 7, pp. 449–451, 451 *et seq.*, 471–472, 473–474, 499 *et seq.*

[40] For a further discussion of this subject in relation to certifiers, see *ante*, Chap. 7, pp. 451 *et seq.*

[41] See *e.g. Eckersley* v. *Mersey Docks & Harbour Board* [1894] 2 Q.B. 667, and *Bright* v. *River Plate Construction Co.* [1900] 2 Ch. 835.

But now by section 24 (1) of the Arbitration Act 1950,[42] " where an agreement between any parties provides that disputes which may arise in the future between them shall be referred to an arbitrator named or designated in the agreement, and after a dispute has arisen any party applies, on the ground that the arbitrator so named or designated is not or may not be impartial, for leave to revoke the authority of the arbitrator or for an injunction to restrain any other party or the arbitrator from proceeding with the arbitration, it shall not be a ground for refusing the application that the party at the time when he made the agreement knew, or ought to have known, that the arbitrator by reason of his relation towards any other party to the agreement or of his connection with the subject referred, might not be capable of impartiality." In such a case the court may also refuse to stay any action which may be brought,[43] but, again, there is power to appoint a substitute under section 25.

It is important to emphasise that section 24 does not apply to certifiers, but only to a true arbitrator.[44] The appearance of this section does much to explain the comparative rarity in modern times in England of clauses appointing the employer's architect or engineer as arbitrator, since the section makes possible an application for his removal on the ground of the fact of his employment alone.

Apart, however, from the effect of the above section, it has been held that an arbitrator is disqualified where there is a bona fide dispute as to whether the engineer or architect, himself the arbitrator, has or has not performed some act which is a condition precedent to the right of the contractor to be paid [45]; or a bona fide allegation that such engineer or architect, in his capacity of servant to the employer, has acted unfairly to the contractor [46]; or reason to believe that, without the necessity of any allegation of moral turpitude in the nature of fraud or collusion with the employer, the engineer or architect has so far mistaken his position as to be incapable of a judicial attitude [47]; or where the dispute is such that there probably will arise a conflict of evidence between the engineer or architect and the contractor, in which the engineer or architect would necessarily be placed in the position of both witness and judge.[48]

---

[42] Reproducing s. 14 of the Act of 1934.
[43] s. 24 (3) of the 1950 Act.
[44] See Chap. 7, p. 450, *ante*, Recovery Without a Certificate, and Section 1, *supra*.
[45] *Freeman* v. *Chester Rural District Council* [1911] 1 K.B. 783.
[46] *Blackwell* v. *Derby Corporation* (1909) Hudson's B.C., 4th ed., Vol. 2, p. 401.
[47] *Hickman & Co.* v. *Roberts* [1913] A.C. 229.
[48] *Bristol Corporation* v. *Aird* [1913] A.C. 241, illustrated *infra*, p. 852.

The following are illustrations of cases on disqualification prior to the passing of section 14 of the Act of 1934,[49] and it is clear that in many of the cases disqualification was negatived on the ground that the general nature of the interest or bias was or should have been known at the time of the arbitration agreement or submission to arbitration. It must be assumed that disqualification will now be much more readily conceded in appropriate cases, in view of the new provision which appears to have been specifically aimed at building and engineering or comparable contracts under which the employer's or purchaser's agent is constituted arbitrator.[50] The decision of the House of Lords in *Bristol Corporation* v. *Aird* (1913) [51] shows, however, that even prior to the 1934 Act a change of opinion seems to have taken place.

ILLUSTRATIONS

(1) An arbitrator was held not to be disqualified by being owed or paid money by one of the parties in the ordinary course of business, such as the debt due from an employer to the architect: *Morgan* v. *Morgan* (1832).[52]

(2) The circumstances of the engineer who was arbitrator under a contract for constructing a railway subsequently being appointed manager of the company was held not to be, *per se*, a sufficient ground to disqualify him from acting as such arbitrator: *Phipps* v. *Edinburgh, etc., Railway* (1843).[53]

(3) A. acted as agent for the S. Railway Company, and as such made an offer to E. of a price for a certain piece of land which the company wished to purchase under their compulsory powers. The company and E. not agreeing, the price was to be settled by arbitration. The company appointed A. as their arbitrator: E. appointed B. as his arbitrator; and an umpire, C., was chosen by B. from a list supplied to him by A. B. was, unknown to E., a surveyor of, and a shareholder in the G. Company, who were interested in the success of the undertaking of the S. Company. C. was also, unknown to E., a surveyor employed by the G. Company. *Held*, that E. by appointing his own arbitrator had waived any objection to the appointment of A., and that the facts as to B. and C. did not afford any judicial grounds for setting aside the award: *Re Elliott, ex p. South Devon Railway* (1848).[54]

(4) An engineer was held not to be disqualified from acting as arbitrator under a railway building contract from the personal

---

[49] Now s. 24 of the 1950 Act.
[50] For disqualification of certifiers, and further discussion of this subject, see *ante*, Chap. 7, Section 5, pp. 450 *et seq.*, and Section 9, p. 499.
[51] Illustrated *infra*, p. 852.
[52] 2 L.J.Ex. 56: see also *Stevenson* v. *Watson* (1879) 4 C.P.D. 148, *ante*, pp. 422–423.
[53] 5 D. (Ct. of Sess.) 1025.
[54] 12 Jur.(o.s.) 445.

interest natural to his position, nor by holding shares in the company for which he was acting: *Ranger* v. *G. W. Railway* (1854).[55]

(5) A., one party to an arbitration, before final award raised an action to declare the arbitrator disqualified, because he had been connected with P., the other party, as his law agent, and because he had a personal interest in P.'s solvency. *Held*, that these averments were not relevant to support an action, which was not to set aside an award, but to stop the proceedings under the submission: *Drew* v. *Drew* (1855).[56]

(6) Accepting hospitality from a party was held to be an improper act on the part of an arbitrator, but unless it could be shown that he had been influenced thereby, his award should not be set aside: *Re Hopper* (1867).[57]

(7) If in the course of an arbitration the arbitrator is found to have a large interest in the award, a party may move to have him removed, and an injunction may issue: *Beddow* v. *Beddow* (1878).[58]

(8) Complaints by the engineer of the employer of the way in which the work is done by the contractor under the contract, in which the engineer is arbitrator, will not disqualify him from acting as arbitrator: *Scott* v. *Carluke Local Authority* (1879).[59]

(9) M. contracted to do engineering work for the B. Parochial Board. All matters, claims, and obligations whatever arising out of the contract were to be referred to A., who was, in fact, the engineer of the board. A. had, as engineer, complained of some of M.'s work, and had measured the work and brought out as due to M. less than he claimed. *Held*, that A. was not disqualified from acting as arbitrator: *Mackay* v. *Barry Parochial Board* (1883).[60]

(10) An arbitrator was held not to be disqualified by the fact of his having previously made a valuation for third persons for a mortgage of the property, the building of which was the subject of the arbitration: *Botterill* v. *Ware Guardians* (1886).[61]

(11) The arbitration clause in a contract for making a railway provided that the arbitrator should not be disqualified from acting by being or becoming consulting engineer to the railway company. *Held*, that he was not barred from acting as arbitrator by the fact that he had revised the specifications and schedules upon which the work which formed the subject of the arbitration was performed: *Adams* v. *Great N. of Scotland Railway* (1889).[62]

(12) An award was set aside on discovery that the plaintiff had assigned to his arbitrator for value his claim under a fire policy, the subject of the dispute: *Blanchard* v. *Sun Fire Office* (1890).[63]

(13) Where a dispute arose as to timbering a trench, because the contractors wished to leave the timber *in situ*, and contended

[55] 5 H.L.Cas. 72. But see the explanation of this case, Chap. 7, p. 453, *ante*.
[56] 14 D. (Ct. of Sess.) 559; affirmed by (H.L.), *The Times*, March 12, 1855.
[57] L.R. 2 Q.B. 367.
[58] 9 Ch.D. 89.
[59] 6 R. (Ct. of Sess.) 616.
[60] 10 R. (Ct. of Sess.) 1046.
[61] 2 T.L.R. 621 (C.A.); where *Kemp* v. *Rose* (1858) 1 Giff. 258 was distinguished.
[62] 26 S.L.R. 765 at p. 772; [1891] A.C. 31.
[63] 6 T.L.R. 365.

that it would not be safe to remove it, and the engineer ordered its removal and refused to certify for payment for it if left: *Held*, that the contractors must not be compelled to submit to the arbitrament of the engineer, whose professional capacity and reputation were at stake: *Nuttall* v. *Manchester Corporation* (1892).[64]

(14) By an engineering contract disputes were to be referred to the engineer as arbitrator. A dispute arose as to whether a certain work was an extra. The dispute was then referred to the engineer. After the reference, and on the day for which the first appointment had been made, the engineer wrote to the contractor repeating his former view. *Held*, that as the engineer must necessarily, in his position as agent of the company, have already expressed his opinion on the point in dispute, his repeating that opinion after the arbitration had commenced did not disqualify him unless, on the fair construction of the letter, it appeared that he had so made up his mind as not to be open to change it upon argument: *Jackson* v. *Barry Railway* (1893).[65]

(15) Disputes under an engineering contract were by its terms referred to the engineer. At the end of the work the contractor put in claims, of which somewhat less than half involved the allegation that there had been radical and extensive alterations, and that there had been delay in supplying the plans. He further complained that some items of the other claims had been disallowed at this time without any reasons being given. The employers required the contractor's claims to be referred to the engineer under the arbitration clause, whereupon the contractor applied to revoke the submission to the arbitrator. *Held*, the allegation of delay when carefully examined did not show any misconduct or negligence by the engineer as in *Nuttall's* case, but only an allegation of delay arising from the necessity to alter the work. Consequently the appointment would not be revoked: *Re Donkin and Leeds and Liverpool Canal Co.* (1893).[66]

(16) An arbitrator, after the close of the hearing but before making his award, asked the solicitor for a company, one of the parties, whether the company would not undertake to take up the award in any event; to this an affirmative answer was given. It was suggested that an undertaking by a solvent company to take up the award amounted practically to the same thing as payment of money, and was a ground for setting aside the award for misconduct of the arbitrator. *Held*, that the award must be upheld, and that there was no misconduct on the part of the arbitrator: *Re Kenworthy and Queen Insurance Co.* (1893).[67]

(17) The fact that one of the main questions in dispute was as to the care and competence and skill of the arbitrator's son, who had acted as assistant engineer, and might hope to succeed to his father's position, was held not to be a sufficient ground for refusing to enforce the arbitration clause: *Eckersley* v. *Mersey Docks and Harbour Board* (1894).[68]

[64] Hudson's B.C., 4th ed., Vol. 2, p. 203.
[65] [1893] 1 Ch. 238.
[66] Hudson's B.C., 4th ed., Vol. 2, p. 239.
[67] 9 T.L.R. 181.
[68] [1894] 2 Q.B. 667 (C.A.).

(18) A building contract contained an arbitration clause referring disputes in the widest possible terms to the engineer. The contractors brought an action involving first, the proper construction of a verbal contract made with the engineer, and secondly, whether certain varied work was ordered as a concession to the contractors, or to remedy a deficiency in the engineer's design. *Held*, by the House of Lords, that where a dispute involved a probable conflict of evidence between the contractor and the engineer, the fact that the engineer, without any fault of his own, must necessarily be placed in the position of judge and witness was a sufficient reason why the matter should not be referred: *Bristol Corporation* v. *Aird* (1913).[69]

(19) A county court judge in an industrial accident case inspected the place of work and saw a demonstration of the system of working. By a mistake the plaintiff workman was not informed of the appointment and was not present, though the defendants' representatives were. *Held*, whether or not an inspection amounted to receiving evidence (*per* Denning L.J. it did, *per* Hodson L.J. it did not) a new trial before a different judge should be ordered: *Goold* v. *Evans & Co.* (1951).[70]

(20) An arbitrator appointed under statute to determine the amount of compensation for works executed by a local authority under certain land informed the parties at the end of the hearing that he would view the land himself. Unknown to the landowner, he in fact viewed the land in the company of the local authority's engineer. *Held*, by the Irish Supreme Court, that while accepting the arbitrator's statement that nothing relating to the case was discussed, and whether or not the view amounted to receiving evidence in the technical sense, the arbitrator's award should be set aside on the ground of misconduct, since justice must not only be done but be seen to be done: *The State* v. *Winters* (1953).[71]

(3) Power of Court to Appoint Arbitrator

Apart from its power under section 25 to appoint an arbitrator in those cases of disqualification or misconduct where the court has exercised its power to revoke the authority of or remove an arbitrator, the court also has power under section 10 of the Act to do so where an arbitrator dies or refuses to act, or where one party to an arbitration agreement refuses to concur in the appointment of an arbitrator. For this latter purpose, a written notice to concur in the appointment of an arbitrator without naming a particular person is sufficient.[72] Where the conditions specified in section 10 (*b*) of the Act of 1950 (that is to say, the arbitrator refuses to act, is incapable of acting, or dies, and the arbitration agreement does not show that it was intended that the vacancy should not be supplied) have

[69] [1913] A.C. 241.
[70] [1951] 2 T.L.R. 1189.
[71] (1953) 92 I.L.T.R. 66.
[72] *Re Eyre and Leicester Corporation* [1892] 1 Q.B. 136.

been fulfilled and there are no other facts to influence the decision of the court, the court will exercise its power by appointing an arbitrator; it is the duty of the court to give effect to the contract between the parties where there is no material on which it can refuse to do so.[73]

In contracts where the architect or engineer " for the time being " of the employer is constituted arbitrator, an arbitrator to whom a dispute has been referred cannot, in the event of his refusal to act, be replaced by the employer purporting to appoint a new architect. In such an event, the new arbitrator must be appointed by the parties, or, failing agreement, under the Act.[74] " For the time being " refers, it is suggested, to the date of the reference and not to any subsequent date.

SECTION 4.   ARBITRATION CONDITION PRECEDENT TO ACTION

The parties to a submission cannot agree that the courts shall have no jurisdiction whatsoever.[75] They can, however, agree that no right of action shall accrue in respect of any disputes between them until after those disputes have been decided upon by an arbitrator. Such provisions are sometimes termed " *Scott* v. *Avery* " clauses, after the case referred to in the first of the following illustrations. It will be seen that their provisions need to be considered in the greatest detail in order to ascertain their exact legal effect, should one of the parties decide to bring proceedings without first obtaining an award.

ILLUSTRATIONS

(1) An insurance company inserted in all its policies a condition that, when a loss occurred, the suffering member should give in his claim and prove his loss before a committee of members appointed to settle the amount, that if a difference thereon arose between the committee and the suffering member the matter should be referred to arbitration, and that no action should be brought except on the award of the arbitrators.   *Held*, that this condition was not illegal as ousting the jurisdiction of the courts: *Scott* v. *Avery* (1856).[76]

(2) A fire policy contained a condition that, if any difference should arise in the adjustment of a loss, the amount to be paid should be submitted to arbitration, and that the insured should not be entitled to commence or maintain an action upon the policy until the amount of the loss should have been so determined, and

---

[73] *Per* Warrington L.J. in *Re Bjornstad and the Ouse Shipping Co.* [1924] 2 K.B. 673.
[74] *Strachan* v. *Cambrian Ry.* (1905) Hudson's B.C., 4th ed., Vol. 2, p. 374.
[75] *Caledonian Ry.* v. *Greenock Ry.* (1874) L.R. 2 H.L.Sc. 347.
[76] 5 H.L.C. 811.

then only for the amount so determined. In an action by the insured on the policy, the insurer pleaded that a difference had arisen, and that the amount of the loss had not been determined by arbitration. *Held*, that the determination of the amount by arbitration was a condition precedent to the right to recover on the policy, and that the defence was an answer to the action: *Viney* v. *Bignold* (1888).[77]

(3) An arbitration clause provided that if any dispute should arise the dissatisfied party should give the architect seven days' notice requiring the matter to be referred to arbitration. Neither party was to be entitled to commence an action upon such matter in dispute until determined by arbitration, etc. The builder sued upon an interim certificate, and the employer counterclaimed for defective work. The employer pleaded as a defence that disputes had arisen and that the builder could not sue without an award. The builder replied that if there was a dispute as to the interim certificate, the employer was the dissatisfied party, and that failing steps by the employer to refer the matter to arbitration, the builder was entitled to recover. On the employer's counterclaim the builder similarly pleaded that the employer was the dissatisfied party, and in the absence of an award could not prosecute it. *Held*, by the High Court of Australia (Latham C.J. and McTiernan C.J. dissenting) that the builder could recover on the interim certificate, and by the whole court that the employer could not pursue his cross-action: *John Grant & Sons Ltd.* v. *Trocadero Building Ltd.* (1938).[78]

(4) An arbitration clause required notice of a dispute to be served and reference to arbitration within seven days thereafter, and that " neither party shall be entitled to commence or maintain any action upon any such dispute or difference until such matter shall have been referred or determined. . . ." *Held*, distinguishing *Grant* v. *Trocadero* (1938), while mere refusal to pay an unchallenged interim certificate was not a dispute, once a dispute was in existence under the contract the clause operated automatically and without notice to inhibit the commencement of an action: *Plucis* v. *Fryer* (1967).[79]

[Note: For what is a dispute, see further the case of *Monmouth C.C.* v. *Costelloe & Kemple Ltd.* (1965).[79a]]

So where the parties make arbitration followed by an award a condition of any legal right of recovery under the contract, the courts will give effect to the condition unless the condition has been waived, or the party seeking to set it up has somehow disentitled himself from doing so.[80]

It has already been seen [81] that in the case of *certificates* which are a condition precedent to a right of action, improper pressure on

---

[77] 20 Q.B.D. 172.
[78] (1938) 60 C.L.R. 1. (Australia).
[79] (1967) 41 A.L.J.R. 192.
[79a] Illustrated *supra*, p. 820. See also Section 2 (2), p. 834, *supra*.
[80] See *per* Lord Wright in *Heyman* v. *Darwins Ltd.* [1942] A.C. 356 at 377.
[81] *Ante*, Chap. 7, Section 5.

the certifier,[82] or a refusal for wrong reasons by the certifier to act,[83] enable the certificate to be dispensed with. Similar principles no doubt apply to arbitrations proper,[84] but the extent to which a party should, before suing without the award, pursue remedies such as case stated or an application for removal of the arbitrator, or the appointment of a new arbitrator (none of which is, of course, available in the case of mere certifiers), does not appear to have been considered by the courts as yet.

The Act does, however, contain a specific provision [85] that, wherever the court has power to order that an arbitration agreement shall cease to have effect in relation to a dispute, it may also order that any " Scott v. Avery " clause in force shall likewise cease to have effect. Broadly speaking, this applies in every case where there is power to revoke an arbitrator's authority, or to remove the arbitrator, or where the dispute involves charges of fraud. Furthermore, as already stated, wherever notice of arbitration within a stipulated period is necessary if the remedy is not to be lost, the court has power under section 27 of the Act to extend the period.[86]

Section 5. Procedure in Arbitrations

(1) Generally

Undoubtedly the main reason for the popularity of arbitration is the fact that the parties have greater confidence in a tribunal, when the subject-matter of the dispute is almost entirely technical, if the tribunal itself is technically qualified and experienced in the same field. There is no doubt that the fact that the tribunal is so qualified restrains the exuberance of the parties and their experts and induces a degree of caution in their evidence not always so apparent in ordinary legal proceedings. In addition, in building and engineering disputes where the dispute is one of fact the documentation can sometimes be extremely heavy and the relative informality of arbitration proceedings can reduce the expense of copying and preparing documentary

---

[82] *Hickman* v. *Roberts* [1913] A.C. 229. (Clause 17 of the contract in this case, notwithstanding the wording of the judgments and Lord Thankerton's observations in *Panamena etc.* v. *Leyland* [1947] A.C. 428 at p. 438, clearly constituted the architect a certifier rather than an arbitrator, it is submitted.) See the very similar wording in *Kennedy Ltd.* v. *Barrow-in-Furness (Mayor of)*, illustrated *supra*, p. 829.

[83] *Panamena* v. *Leyland* [1947] A.C. 428, *ante*, Chap. 7, p. 468.

[84] See *e.g. Neale* v. *Richardson* [1938] 1 All E.R. 753, *ante*, p. 441.

[85] See clause 25 (4). For a discussion of this power and of the circumstances in which it may be exercised, see the judgments in *Bruce* v. *Strong* [1951] 2 K.B. 447.

[86] For the principles, see *Liberian Shipping Corporation* v. *King* [1967] 2 Q.B. 86.

evidence in the form usually required in the courts. On the other hand, the inexperience of arbitrators in sifting and weighing evidence can be a more serious disadvantage, even in reaching findings of fact, than laymen usually realise, and, in the absence of a high degree of restraint and fairness by the parties' legal representatives, a lay arbitrator can be placed in a most difficult position if the rules of evidence or procedure are ignored by the parties during the hearing, since he is usually in no position to judge the validity of legal sub-missions or objections in procedural matters, and may be quite unaware of the failure or inability of a party to comply with proper evidentiary or procedural requirements, or of the inferences of fact or credit to be drawn therefrom. Arbitrators of great note in their own field can also have understandable difficulty analysing the underlying reasons for rules of substantive or procedural law, and can give way to impulses of sympathy or compromise producing anomalous and sometimes startling results. This instinct for compromise, and of reluctance to hold a claim wholly valid or invalid, is perhaps the most serious fault of non-legal arbitrators; it can work great injustice, and is perhaps the greatest single factor encouraging unrealistic tendering to secure the contract coupled with the presentation of unmerited claims.[86a] On the other hand, arbitration proceedings have what is sometimes the extremely important advantage, from the point of view of one or other party, of privacy, and also a fair degree of finality after any award is made by an arbitrator, as it is relatively difficult to upset such an award once it has been made, since an appeal is by way of case stated upon a point of law only. It should be borne in mind, however, that, owing to the practice prevalent in the High Court of referring nearly all building and engineering disputes, how-ever important they may be, to an official referee for trial, the official referees have themselves acquired a considerable knowledge of building and engineering problems and practice. Moreover, trial by an official referee is usually a somewhat cheaper means of settling disputes than are arbitration proceedings (since the arbitrator's fees have to be paid for and accommodation rented for the arbitration) and, as in the case of arbitrations, the only appeal allowed is upon a point of law, except in cases of fraud or professional negligence.[87] It is also possible for the parties to an arbitration agreement to refer the dispute between them to an official referee, who then sits not as a judge but as an arbitrator.[88]

[86a] An increasingly common feature of the civil engineering industry in England. Compare *ante*, p. 569, attitude of some engineering arbitrators to clause 12 claims.
[87] R.S.C., Ord. 58, r. 5.   [88] Arbitration Act 1950, s. 11.

(2) Institution of Proceedings

For the purposes of the Limitation Acts, an arbitration commences when a party to an arbitration agreement serves on the other notice requiring the appointment of an arbitrator, or the submission of the dispute to the arbitrator designated in the agreement.[89] As already mentioned, machinery exists for the appointment of an arbitrator by the court if the other party refuses to co-operate.[90] Once appointed, the arbitrator has power to call on the parties to attend before him so that he may give directions. Prior to this, the arbitrator will be well advised to consider the terms of the arbitration agreement or of the submission, so as to ascertain whether it contains any limits on his jurisdiction to hear the dispute. Frequently where there is an arbitration clause in the widest terms, the parties purport to describe their dispute in fairly narrow terms when making an agreed submission (which in view of the clause is not, of course, strictly necessary). If so, the arbitrator should obtain the parties' confirmation that he is to act under the clause and that there is no intention to restrict its scope. On the other hand, the widest clause or submission inevitably contains important restrictions when defining the disputes which are or may be referred. In addition, there may of course be provisions in the contract outside the arbitration clause which, while not going to jurisdiction, effectively limit or reduce the arbitrator's powers. For instance, the R.I.B.A. 1963 standard forms make very considerable inroads on the arbitrator's effective powers, if notice of arbitration has not been given before the final certificate by the employer or within fourteen days thereafter by the contractor.[91] An important but most obscurely worded restriction on jurisdiction (albeit of a temporary nature) arises under both the building and engineering standard forms, which prohibit the " opening " of an arbitration without consent until after completion of the work (presumably this wording refers to the actual hearing, and to alleged or substantial completion, although there is no authority on the point), except in defined circumstances.

ILLUSTRATION

The arbitration clause in the standard I.C.E. form of contract [92] provided that references to arbitration should not be opened without consent until after completion of the work " except references as to

[89] Limitation Act 1939, s. 27 (3).
[90] *Supra*, Section 3 (3), pp. 852–853.
[91] See the criticism of this policy *ante*, Chap. 7, pp. 489–492.
[92] Clause 66, 1955 form.

the withholding by the engineer of any certificate or the withholding of any portion of the retention money under Clause 60 hereof to which the contractor claims to be entitled." In Clause 60, which provided for interim payments, there were, as it happened, express powers to withhold certificates and also the second half of the retention money in certain events which did not, in the event, occur. The contractor contended on interim measurement that, as a matter of construction of the contract, he was entitled to certain additional payments for working space outside the actual retaining walls of the tunnel he was constructing. The engineer certified the work done at the billed rates but refused to include any such additional payments in the interim certificates. *Held*, by Buckley J., (a) that the exception applied to any certificate of any kind withheld by the engineer, and not merely the particular withholding of a certificate referred to in Clause 60 and (*obiter*) (b) that while a simple difference on valuation or measurement on interim certificate would not constitute a " withholding of the certificate to which the contractor claimed to be entitled," an adverse decision on a matter of principle, which, if incorrect, would mean that the contractor was clearly entitled to an additional payment, did amount to a withholding of a certificate, and (c) that consequently the arbitration could be held before completion of the works: *Farr* v. *Ministry of Transport* (1960).[93]

(3) Preparation for Hearing

The general purpose of the preliminary meeting before the arbitrator is equivalent to that of proceedings on a summons for directions in the High Court. It is a curiosity of the Act that no specific reference to written pleadings is made, but section 12 (1) requires the parties to " do all other things which, during the proceedings or the reference, the arbitrator may require," and arbitrators in practice in cases of any substance or complexity almost invariably order delivery of pleadings in the same way as the High Court. There is no doubt that, once the parties have delivered pleadings, the arbitrator has power to allow amendments and control them in the same way as the courts.[94] Arbitrators, unless they are given express power by the terms of their submission to dispense with the procedural techniques of the courts, should endeavour to model their control of the proceedings at the interlocutory stage, as it is called in the courts, and indeed at all stages, as closely as possible upon the correct legal procedure and rules as to pleadings, which, while refined in detail, are in the last analysis based on principles of natural justice designed to give parties adequate warning of the case they will have to meet, and to assist in securing all available evidence for that purpose. If

---

[93] [1960] 1 W.L.R. 956. The second *obiter* finding above is discussed fully *ante*, Chap. 7, pp. 495–496. See also the discussion *ante*, Chap. 9, pp. 573–574. For reference to the corresponding R.I.B.A. provision, see *ante*, p. 495.

[94] *Re Crichton* v. *Law Car & General Insurance Corporation Ltd.* [1910] 2 K.B. 738.

necessary, arbitrators should not hesitate to take legal advice when in doubt. That they are expected so to control their proceedings is a fair inference from the terms of section 12 of the Act, in particular clause 12 (6), which places the High Court at the parties' disposal for the provision of nearly all of the important procedural remedies associated with High Court procedure, such as security for costs,[95] discovery of documents, interrogatories, inspection, interim injunctions, and so on.

An important variant of formal pleadings evolved by the High Court for cases where there are large numbers of items in dispute is the " Scott Schedule " or, more correctly, Official Referee's Schedule. This is a document which, while there is no rigid rule as to its make-up, conveniently summarises the parties' contentions in columns opposite the listed and numbered items of the claim. A typical Schedule will have columns, reading from left to right, containing item number, the sum claimed, the claimant's reasons for claiming, the respondent's reasons for disputing the claim, the sum allowed by the respondent, if any, possibly the claimant's reply to the respondent, and (depending on circumstances) columns for the arbitrator's decisions and for any notes he may wish to make. The exact make-up of the document will vary with the nature of the dispute between the parties, and the parties may be ordered to plead in this form at any convenient stage of the proceedings. It is particularly suitable where a large number of relatively minor items, but with differing bases of legal liability or defence, are in issue between the parties.

The arbitrator also has express power [96] to order discovery of documents himself. The necessity for and extent of this remedy frequently appear to take laymen by surprise, and contractor claimants in particular appear to have difficulty in appreciating that, in nearly all cases, their internal documents, and in particular the documents showing the make-up of their tender prices, are relevant and require to be disclosed. " Relevancy " in this context is given the widest scope, and is not dependent on admissibility of the documents in question, or limited to documents of probative effect, the test being whether the document " contains information which may (not must) either directly or indirectly enable the party [applying for discovery] either to advance his own case or to damage that of his adversary, or if it is a document which may fairly lead him to a train of enquiry,

---

[95] See *Bilcon* v. *Fegmay Investments* [1966] 2 Q.B. 221.
[96] s. 12 (1).

which may have either of these two consequences." [97] In building
and engineering cases, particularly those where disturbance of the
contractor's programme is alleged, every contemporary document
on the contract files of each party relating to the work, or the ordering of materials for it, has the potential quality referred to, and any
person seeking to exclude a document from discovery in such a case
on the ground of irrelevancy would be assuming a very heavy burden
indeed. It is a commonplace in building and engineering arbitrations
that documents thought to be wholly unnecessary from the evidentiary
point of view and not worth copying for the purpose of the hearing
may by the end of the evidence assume a crucial importance in
supporting or rebutting the parties' contentions of fact.

During the ensuing period between his order for directions and
the hearing, and while the parties are preparing for trial, they are at
liberty to apply to the arbitrator for further directions, *e.g.* for an
order for further and better particulars of a pleading, or for an
interim award, *e.g.* where some sum is admitted as due upon the
pleadings, or in regard to other interlocutory matters.

While the preliminary meeting before the arbitrator is analogous
to a summons for directions in the High Court, it differs in one very
important respect, namely, that in the High Court the summons is
heard when pleadings are closed, whereas pleadings have not yet
been delivered when parties come before an arbitrator for the first
time. Arbitrators nevertheless frequently endeavour to fix a date for
the hearing at this first meeting, and, even if they do not, often seek
to do so at a later stage, sometimes even against the wishes of the
parties. Recently they may have been influenced in this regard by
publicity given in the United Kingdom to the strong views expressed
by the Court of Appeal from time to time (nearly always in personal
injuries cases) as to delay by legal advisers in pursuing their clients'
claims, and the greater readiness of that court to dismiss actions for
want of prosecution. [98] There is in fact little or no connection between delays of this kind and the time needed to pursue building and
civil engineering litigation. Arbitrators should realise that pleadings
are of the greatest importance in narrowing the issues between the
parties and reducing ultimate cost, and in building and engineering
disputes the time needed for completing the pleadings is often far
greater than in ordinary litigation, by reason of the multiplicity of

---

[97] *Per* Lord Esher M.R., *Compagnie Financière* v. *Peruvian Guano Co.* (1882) 11 Q.B.D.
at p. 63.
[98] See *e.g. Allen* v. *Sir Alfred McAlpine Ltd.* [1968] 2 Q.B. 229.

issues and the necessity of obtaining instructions in detail from professional and technical witnesses who have many other commitments, and will in many cases have been dispersed throughout the United Kingdom or even abroad after a building or engineering project is completed. The sheer bulk of the pleadings and documents, and the frequent multiplicity of issues, also mean that the periods of time provisionally allowed in the High Court for the pleading stages of ordinary litigation are wholly inappropriate. In fact, even with punctilious attention and immediate availability by all concerned, pleadings in a complicated building or engineering matter can rarely take less than twelve to eighteen months, and frequently more than that. The parties who are most vociferous in complaining of and seeking to shorten the time available to their opponents are frequently those whose pleadings are the most defective and lacking in precision. Arbitrators should appreciate that none of this delay, and the great expense of such interlocutory work, is wasted, since building and engineering litigation is concerned with a careful assessment of the monetary value of claims. Very frequently it is not till the parties reach their legal advisers that this type of assessment even begins to be made, and the course of patient and thorough investigation of all aspects of claim and defence during the pleading stages will in many cases produce a different attitude and will enhance the likelihood of a settlement before the hearing takes place. Arbitrators should remember that a weak or unjustified claim can be put forward in a comparatively short time but its rebuttal may require long and careful preparation and patient probing in the form of requests for particulars. A premature hearing date in disputes of this kind may result in a confused presentation of the facts and documentary chaos, which may benefit the weaker case at the expense of the stronger, and will reduce the chances of an accurate and satisfactory resolution of the dispute before the hearing. It can also lead to cases which should never be fought being pursued to a conclusion at a cost in time and money out of all sensible proportion to the real issues involved. The only proper justification for fixing an early date or pressing for early delivery of pleadings against the wish of one or other of the parties is that the facts show a desire to obtain delay by an impecunious respondent. In nearly all other cases the arbitrator's power to award interest [99] is a sufficient protection to the claimant.

[99] *Ante*, Chap. 9, pp. 575–577.

(4) Sealed Offers

One serious gap in the procedural sections of the Act of 1950 is that
no provision is made for payment into court, a device of the greatest
importance by which a defendant in the courts can place the plaintiff
in peril as to all subsequent costs if the amount so paid exceeds the
amount finally awarded against the defendant. This in fact is a
device almost unique to English procedure and of the greatest
value in protecting defendants from undue prosecution of a claim
by a plaintiff, and is doubly important because of the unsympathetic
attitude for some reason shown in other respects by the courts and
the rules to successful parties in litigation, as evidenced by the
difference between actual and taxed costs and the frequent inadequacy
of awards of interest. It is surprising that this most serious omission
has not been remedied by legislation, in particular because some
judges in the courts affect to treat with suspicion, if not levity, the
very sensible practice evolved by legal practitioners in the field of
arbitration which is designed to remedy this omission, and which
rests for its effectiveness upon the consent and good sense of the
parties, their legal advisers and arbitrators. The value of a payment into court can, of course, be sensibly diminished if the fact and,
in particular, the amount of the offer are known to the tribunal before
its decision is reached.[1] Since an offer which is made " without
prejudice " (*i.e.* an offer made in the course of negotiations to settle
or compromise, which is not permitted to be revealed without the
consent of the party making it) cannot be relied upon by either party
even on questions of costs,[2] any offer made for this purpose in an
arbitration must be contained in what is technically an " open "
letter (that is to say, one which *can* be adduced in evidence). Further,
as arbitrators traditionally have been permitted by the parties to
make and publish their awards on the question of costs at the same
time as their substantive award,[3] there is no means, where this is so,
of concealing the fact of the offer from the arbitrator before he makes
his substantive award. (As explained *infra*, subsection (7), this latter
difficulty can be and now is increasingly frequently avoided by separating the substantive award and the award as to costs in point of time.)

The older practice is for the party making the offer to do so in an
open letter, offering a certain sum plus costs incurred to date in
settlement of the claim, and to state that it is not intended to place

---

[1] This is expressly prevented from happening under the High Court rules, of course.
[2] *Walker* v. *Wilsher* (1889) 23 Q.B.D. 335.
[3] The undesirability of this practice is explained *infra*, subsection (7).

the letter in the agreed bundle of correspondence before the arbitrator, but to hand the letter to him in a sealed envelope at the conclusion of counsel's closing speech at the end of the arbitration, with the request that the arbitrator consider its contents after making his decision as to the amount of his substantive award, but before addressing his mind to the question of costs.

This procedure is, of course, obviously imperfect, since the arbitrator knows the fact, and, if he wishes, also the amount, of the offer before making his substantive award, but if the procedure outlined in subsection (7), *infra*, is followed, the arbitrator does not need to be informed on the matter of the offer until after his substantive award has been made, in the same way as a judge. There is in fact nothing but the integrity and good sense of the claimant's advisers to prevent the offer being tendered in evidence as an admission.

All arbitrators should, it is submitted, treat such offers as the equivalent of a payment into court, and, in making their awards as to costs, follow the practice of the courts, as to which they should, if necessary, take legal advice.

(5) The Hearing

Although an arbitrator undoubtedly has a wide discretion as to how he should control the proceedings before him [5] the wisest course, in the absence of the consent of the parties, is to see that the conduct of any arbitration where the parties appear by solicitors or counsel should follow as nearly as possible the procedural rules of the High Court, since these are not based on any technicalities or historical anomalies, but are grounded on long experience of the fairest and most accurate way of enabling the parties' cases to be presented, and so may be accepted as a model about which no possible complaint can be made. The claimants' representative addresses the arbitrator and calls his witnesses, each of whom is examined, cross-examined, re-examined and, if desired, questioned by the arbitrator. The respondent then has a similar right. In those cases where the items in dispute are numerous, and of their nature are likely to stand or fall on their own, it is often more convenient to deal with the evidence on each side item by item, a useful practice not infrequently adopted by official referees in the High Court; but where this method is adopted no final decision should be reached on any disputed item until the speeches are concluded. The reason for this is that in a lengthy case

---

[5] See *e.g.* the case of *Star International* v. *Bergbau-Handel* [1966] 2 Lloyd's Rep. 16, referred to *supra*, Section 1 (2), p. 826.

the examination and cross-examination of opposing witnesses on the same item may not be heard for weeks, and this may impose a considerable strain on the memory of the court and witnesses, and an unnecessary degree of note-taking, as well as preventing some matter which could be cleared up or conceded or compromised at once from being removed from the area of dispute at the earliest possible stage. After the evidence is complete the respondent's representative addresses the arbitrator, followed by the claimants' representative. During such addresses it is quite usual for the arbitrator to discuss any matters upon which he wishes further guidance, although it is not permissible at this stage to hear further evidence without the consent of both parties. An arbitrator should be careful to avoid reaching or indicating a decision on any of the disputes before him until the speeches are over and the hearing concluded, though there is no objection, and indeed sometimes every advantage, to his indicating the way his mind is working, provided that he makes it plain that he has not made up his mind and has no intention of doing so till the end of the hearing, since this will enable the advocates to assist him at once by way of explanation or concession, and avoids misunderstandings.

(6) Statement of Special Case for Court

Should either party require him to do so, the arbitrator may, and, if he refuses, can, in a proper case, be compelled by the court to make his award, or any part of it, in the form of a special case for the opinion of the court upon a point of law.[6] A case so stated must contain all the facts showing how the point arises and necessary for its determination, and formulate the questions of law for decision by the court. The question may relate to a point arising on an interim award, or an interlocutory matter in the course of the reference, as well as upon a matter relevant to the making of the arbitrator's final award. But since an arbitrator is *functus officio* once he has made his final award, the case must be requested and stated either before or as part of the final award. If an arbitrator ignored a request and issued a final award without giving the party concerned an opportunity to apply to the court for an order compelling the arbitrator to state the case, he would be guilty of misconduct. An arbitrator should be careful to see that the question for the decision of the court is formulated in the exact terms used by the party requesting the case to be stated. The only situation in which a party might not be entitled

---

[6] Arbitration Act 1950, s. 21.

to a case stated, apart from the *de minimis* rule, would appear to be in a case where the original dispute referred to an arbitrator was limited to a pure point of law on which he was subsequently required to state a case,[7] but it is possible to conceive of many such situations where the court would, nevertheless, order a case stated, particularly if the reference was under an agreement to refer future disputes and not a specific submission.

There are in fact three types of possible case stated, namely, a final award so stated (where the arbitrator by the form he uses exhausts his duties, so that when the courts have determined the legal consequences of the facts there is nothing more for him to do), an interim award so stated under section 21 (2) of the Act of 1950 (where the arbitrator finds the necessary facts to enable a decision on the point to be reached without further recourse to himself, but where there will still remain other matters to be decided by him) and a consultative case under section 21 (1) (*a*) of the Act of 1950 where the opinion of the court is sought before the arbitrator reaches his own decision. The distinction between the last two can be important, because a decision on an interim award will be final and binding once the court has given its opinion, and a party will not be allowed to raise new reasons or arguments for disputing the interim award.

ILLUSTRATION

Shipowner claimants claimed demurrage from charterers. The respondent charterers alleged an exclusion clause applied, and the claimants replied that if it did, it had been waived by the respondents. The arbitrator stated a case at the request of the charterers awarding demurrage if the court agreed with his view that the exclusion clause did not apply, and asking for the case to be remitted for reconsideration of his award if the court did not agree with his view. The waiver point, which had been argued before him, was not dealt with in the case, nor had the shipowners asked that it should be. The court ruled that the exclusion clause did apply, and remitted to the arbitrator, before whom the shipowners now sought to raise the question of waiver. *Held*, by the Court of Appeal, overruling Mocatta J., that the award was an interim award and not a consultative case, and that since the shipowners could have but did not raise the waiver point on the interim award, they were now seeking to obtain a reversal of the court's determination of the issue which was the subject of the interim award: *Fidelitas Shipping Ltd.* v. *V/O Exportchleb* (1965).[8]

In practice, counsel on both sides should, failing agreement, inform the arbitrator of the matters on which they will require a finding of fact, and this is often best done in practice by supplying

[7] See *e.g. Re Canadian Line Materials etc.* (1960) 22 D.L.R. (2d) 741.
[8] [1966] 1 Q.B. 630.

the arbitrator with a written statement of the facts which each side wish him to find. In addition, the arbitrator should formulate the questions of law as requested by one or both sides. If the case is to be stated as part of the final award, the most convenient practice is for the arbitrator to make awards in alternative form, depending on the answers to the questions formulated, and stating expressly that, failing the setting down of the case for hearing by the court by either party within a stipulated time, one or other of his alternative awards is to be his final award. The advantage of this course is that, if cases are stated in this way, the necessity for remitting the case to the arbitrator in the event of the court coming to a different view from him is avoided.

(7) Conclusion of Hearing and Award

At the conclusion of the hearing, the arbitrator usually indicates that he will, in due course, make his award, which (unless a case is to be stated) is usually in a form that A do pay B a certain sum (or that nothing is due from A to B). If the award is to be in the form of a case stated, the parties' advisers usually supply him then or at a later stage with a draft of the case, or at least of the questions to be formulated and facts desired to be found. But, apart from this, no further hearing is usually contemplated, though no doubt the arbitrator is bound to hear applications by either side until, by making his final award, he is *functus officio*, and no further hearing of any kind is possible. There are two serious practical anomalies to which this practice gives rise.

In the first place, if adopted, this practice means that counsel must address the arbitrator at the conclusion of their speeches on the question of costs while still quite unaware of what the arbitrator's award will be. In simple, straightforward cases this may not give rise to undue difficulty, but building and engineering disputes are usually complicated and involve many issues on which the parties may win or lose, and on which careful submissions may be necessary. In the High Court, judges are not, of course, addressed on the question of costs, and make no order as to costs, until after judgment, which is often given some time after the hearing is concluded, as in the case of all arbitrations, since even if he has made up his mind the arbitrator has to draw up and publish his award.

In the second place, where a party decides to protect his position in law by asking for a case to be stated, it by no means follows that his opponent wishes, in the event of losing before the arbitrator upon the question of law, to take the matter further himself. Consequently, in the event of the arbitrator's decision being in favour of the party requesting a case, no application to the court will be made. But, if the practice of no further hearing before the award is adopted, the expense and trouble has to be incurred of preparing and stating a case which, in the event, may never be taken up.

A useful solution to both these difficulties is for the parties to request the arbitrator, at the conclusion of the hearing where a point of law may be involved, not to issue his award in final form, but only in draft form, and to give the parties a fixed period of notice before publishing his award in final form to enable them to decide whether or not to ask for a case. Where no point of law is involved, the arbitrator can be asked at the conclusion of the hearing merely to make his substantive award, but not any award as to costs, and to give the parties an opportunity either of addressing him at a subsequent hearing or of submitting written submissions on costs within a fixed period after his substantive award is known. This procedure has the added advantage that the arbitrator need not be informed of the existence of any sealed offer [9] until after his substantive award is known. There is no reason why this procedure, which accords far more closely with the procedure of the courts (where, it should also be noted, a judgment is not final until it has been drawn up), should depend on any request of or consent by the parties, since arbitrators have full power to control the proceedings before them and there is no special legal validity in the practice here criticised. It is to be hoped that arbitrators will increasingly make use of the procedure here recommended, which is both convenient and just to the parties, as part of their normal practice and not as an exceptional measure when requested to do so. This procedure has been approved by the courts.

ILLUSTRATION

An arbitrator was asked by the parties at the conclusion of the hearing (a) to issue his award in relation to a specified number of items only in draft form, so that the parties might consider whether or not to ask for a case stated, and (b) to make no award as to costs until the parties had had time to consider the remainder of his award and had made submissions to him at a further hearing. By inadvertence, the arbitrator issued his award in final form as to a number of the specified items, and purported to make an award as to costs. *Held*, by Wynn J., that the arbitrator was guilty of misconduct and that the award should be set aside and remitted to the arbitrator so that

---

[9] Which under the older conventional method cannot be avoided, see *supra*, pp. 862–863.

he might comply with the parties' request: *Marples Ridgeway & Partners Ltd.* v. *C.E.G.B.* (1964).[10]

(8) Appeal from Arbitrator

Once an award has been made, judgment can be obtained upon it—usually, of course, in summary proceedings under Order 14—by suing upon the award in the High Court, unless, in the case of an award in the form of a special case (as to which see *supra*, subsection (6)) the dissatisfied party has exercised his right under section 21 of the Act of 1950 to apply for a decision of the court upon the case stated by the arbitrator, or, in an appropriate case, has applied to remit or set aside the award.[11]

No appeal can be made from an award except under the case stated procedure under section 21 or, where no case has been requested or stated, where the award discloses an error upon its face. To avoid this latter possibility, awards are usually kept as short as possible and, if finality is desired, it is undesirable for an arbitrator to state his reasons for making his award. There is no hardship to the parties in this, since prior to the award the case stated procedure was available to them if they wished to preserve their position.

Some arbitrators appear to resent the existence of the case stated procedure. They should realise that, not only can the procedure be of the greatest assistance to them in reaching a correct decision, but also that the last reason why parties choose to go to arbitration is likely to be a desire to substitute the arbitrator's instinct for compromise or his personal views as to what is fair or just in exchange for their full legal rights under the contract they have signed. Arbitrators should, therefore, welcome the fact that, in the field in which they cannot profess skill, their decisions are subject to review and will not bind the parties.

Until recently there was a serious gap in the otherwise satisfactory system of review available under the case stated procedure, and this related to arbitrators' decisions as to costs. In no direction, in practice, do arbitrators' awards tend to stray more frequently from proper legal principles than in this particular field. In the High Court, if a judge makes what is, prima facie, an unusual order as to costs, he will almost invariably state his reasons for doing so, and if he has applied a wrong principle his order on costs will be reviewed

---

[10] [1964] Q.B.D. (Special Paper), unreported.

[11] For the various grounds on which such an application can be made, see Russell, *Arbitration*, 18th ed., Chap. 21.

and, if necessary, upset on appeal. Notwithstanding the most understandable view expressed by Goddard L.C.J., in *Lewis* v. *Haverfordwest R.D.C.* (1953) [12] that in such a case the courts have power to
require an arbitrator to state his reasons for his order as to costs,
this view appeared to have been overruled by the Court of Appeal in
Perry v. *Stopher* (1959),[13] following the reasoning of Diplock J. in
Heaven & Kesterton v. *Sven Widaeus* (1958),[14] which held that only
if the award itself, or the arbitrator on some other occasion (for
instance, on affidavit), gave invalid reasons for the award, could the
award be set aside. Thus, in the case of *Lashmar* v. *Phillips & Cooper
Ltd.* (1960) [15] Diplock J., refused to intervene in a case where, notwithstanding that the respondent in an arbitration had been wholly
successful, the arbitrator awarded that each side should bear its own
costs. This state of the law fully justified the following statement by
Megaw J.: " The parties should realise that if they adopt the procedure of arbitration they will find that, if an arbitrator makes an award
as to costs which they regard as unjust or unfair, the possibility of
their being able to procure a review and a remedy for that in the
courts is very limited almost to the point of non-existence unless the
arbitrator sees fit, when the exercise of his discretion is challenged, to
state what were the reasons, so that the court can see whether the
reasons were sound in principle."[16]

This state of the law was severely criticised in the Ninth Edition
of this book, which pointed out that those who sought to justify such
anomalies by suggesting that parties who choose to go to arbitration
have only themselves to blame for the consequences, appeared to
overlook the fact that very few parties choosing arbitration, in the
knowledge that a comprehensive system of review and control by the
courts exists on all points of law, could be presumed to be aware that
no such review was possible on questions of costs, however perverse
the finding of the arbitrator, or however wrong in principle.

It is pleasing to record that this no longer appears to be the law,
or that the earlier cases were not properly understood.

ILLUSTRATION

A builder, sued for about £75 worth of defects, pleaded in his
defence (a) lateness of a notice under the defects clause, (b) his
agreement to make good the defects, but the owner's refusal to

[12] [1953] 1 W.L.R. 1486.
[13] [1959] 1 W.L.R. 415.
[14] [1958] 1 W.L.R. 248.
[15] April 5, 1960, Q.B.D. Special Paper, unreported.
[16] *Matheson* v. *A. Tabah & Sons* [1963] 2 Lloyd's Rep. 270.

allow remedial work when a workman attended, (c) later dates for access offered by the owner which gave too short notice or were not practicable, (d) refusal of the owner to suggest later dates for access, and (e) his own readiness at all material times to remedy the defects. He denied the owner's entitlement to an award of damages and specifically asked for his own costs to be paid by the owner. The arbitrator awarded £45, but costs against the owner. *Held,* by the Court of Appeal, after reading the correspondence between the parties and the affidavits of the solicitor advocates (a) that there is a settled practice of the courts that in the absence of special circumstances a successful litigant should receive his costs, (b) that it was for the party seeking to justify an order which departed from this principle to show that there was material justifying such a departure, (c) on the facts no such material existed in the present case. Dictum of Lord Goddard C.J. in *Lewis* v. *Haverfordwest R.D.C.* (1953) [17] (to the effect that it is necessary to show grounds why an order of this kind should be made) approved, and of Diplock J. in *Heaven & Kesterton Ltd.* v. *Sven Widaeus* (1958) [18] (to the effect that unless reasons were given interference with the award was not possible) disapproved, and (d) that the award should be set aside and the builder ordered to pay the owner's costs: *Dineen* v. *Walpole* (1969).[19]

Arbitrators approaching their duties in a judicial spirit should therefore, not hesitate to state their reasons for their orders as to costs if asked to do so by either party, or if they intend to depart from the usual rule that costs should follow the event.

It should be remembered that in building and engineering cases the issue between the parties is almost invariably financial, and that the machinery of the sealed offer is available to protect the position on costs. Though there may be many issues, in legal pleading terms, of claim, set-off, and counterclaim, the parties' eyes will always have been fixed on the final balance owing one way or another. Whoever secures or avoids paying that balance in effect has won. Only in the case of wildly exaggerated claims, or separate and costly issues on which the successful party has failed and which it was wholly unreasonable for him to raise, can there be, it is submitted, any justification for departing from the rule that the party ultimately successful on a final balance of claim and counterclaim should be paid his costs. There are cases in other situations where separate orders for costs on claim and counterclaim are appropriate, but counterclaims on building and engineering contracts arise out of the same transaction and are equitable set-offs,[20] and the basic commercial realities, in the vast majority of cases argue very strongly,

---

[17] [1953] 1 W.L.R. 1486 at p. 1487.
[18] [1958] 1 W.L.R. 248 at p. 253.
[19] [1969] 1 Llovds' Rep. 261.
[20] See *ante,* Chap. 14, pp. 725–731–734.

it is submitted, for a single award of costs in favour of the party ultimately successful on balance, unless the balance is so small as to justify the view that a party responsible for initiating the litigation and obtaining such a balance can be regarded as having been effectively unsuccessful.

INDEX

INTEREST,
concealed from employer, liability of architect for, 175–177
disqualifying,
arbitrator, 451–458, 847–853
certifier, 451–458, 471–472
See also BRIBES AND SECRET COMMISSIONS.

INTEREST ON MONEY OWING, 575–577
arbitrator, awarded by, 575
fraud, when money obtained by, 575
Law Reform Act, 1934, awarded under, 575–576
rate of, 576–577

INTERFERENCE,
certifier, with, 458–465, 472–473, 474–475
employer, by, by carrying out works, 326–329, 339–340, 755
other contractors, by, employer's liability for, 316–320, 337–339, 532–533, 755
sub-contractors or suppliers, by, 316–320, 329–340, 755
third parties, by, whether employer liable for, 327–329
variations, by timing of, 322–326
See also PREVENTION.

INTERIM CERTIFICATES, 492–497, 573–575
arbitration concerning, 494–496
binding effect of, 382, 492
condition precedent, whether, 494
defective work, no bar to claim for, 381
function of, 492–494
liquidated damages, effect of payment under, 634–635
nature of, 492–494
negligence in issuing, 161–169
orders in writing for variations, whether, 536, 538–539
payment on, 494–497
without deduction, effect on liquidated damages, 634–635
subsequent sanctions of variations, as, 536, 538–539
" value," meaning of, in, 494
variations, constituting, 536, 538–539
See also generally CERTIFICATES.

INTERIM PAYMENT. *See* PAYMENT BY INSTALMENTS.

INTERNATIONAL LAW,
arbitrations in the field of, 823–824

INVENTIONS. *See* NOVEL METHODS.

INVITATION TO TENDER. *See under* TENDER.

JUDGMENT,
assignment, as equity on, 734
attachment of moneys due under, 238, 730, 735–738

JUDGMENT—*cont.*
interest or debt on, 575–577
principal, against, surety not bound by, 815–816

JURISDICTION,
arbitrator's, 832–839
certifier's, 406–411, 446–449, 476–478
mistake as to, effect of, 467–468, 476–478
courts, of,
arbitration does not oust, 831–832
powers of review, 159–160, 447–448, 832
injunction, arbitrator can not grant, 840
rectification, as to, of arbitrator, 38, 835–839
See also ARBITRATION, CERTIFIER, COURT, DAMAGES, INJUNCTION *and* RECTIFICATION.

LABOUR,
fluctuations clauses covering, 566–567
holidays with pay, " wages " of, 566
National Joint Council of the Building Industry, wages decided by, 567
shortage of, no excuse, 353
sufficiency of, how far contractor warrants, 614–615

LACHES. *See* GUARANTEE AND SURETIES.

LAND,
employer's interest in, relevance of, 1, 655–658
fixing of materials or plant, effect of, 654–660. *See also* VESTING AND SEIZURE.
occupation of, not acceptance of work, 377–379
sale of,
contractor's liability for house on, 71–81, 281–291
effect on assignment of rights under building contract, 726–727
when time of essence, 608–612
specific performance of building contract on sale of, 371–375
with house,
completed, 71–81
in course of erection, 281–291
See also HOUSE.

LAW,
ignorance of, certifier not liable for, 159
knowledge of, required of architect, 142–144
mistake as to, 25

LEASE,
building. *See* BUILDING LEASE.
disclaimer of, in bankruptcy, 779
forfeiture of, on bankruptcy, 784–785

PERFORMANCE—*cont.*
  employer, by—*cont.*
    co-ordination of own work with
      contractor's, 337–339
    instructions as to execution of
      work, 135–141, 322–326
      sub-contracts, as to, 138–139,
        329–337
    interfere, not to, 326–329
    nomination of sub-contractors, 329–
      337
      non-completion by sub-contrac-
        tor, 332–333
      renomination, duty of, 333–337
    omission of work, 339–340, 532–
      533
    other contractors, by, 337–339
    payment, on, 315
    site,
      possession of, 317–320
      state of, 316–317
  entire contracts, of, 243–262
    interim payment under,
      express terms for, 257–260
      implied terms for, 260–262
    nature of, 243–245
    severable contracts, as distinguished
      from, 247–249
    substantial completion, doctrine of,
      245–247, 249–254
    substantially complete, failure to,
      254–255
  illegality in manner of, 362–363
  impossibility of. *See* FRUSTRATION.
  interim payment,
    express terms for,
      effect of, 255–257
      entire contracts, as to, 257–260
    implied terms for, 260–262
  part. *See* PART PERFORMANCE.
  prevention of. *See* PREVENTION.
  specific. *See* SPECIFIC PERFORMANCE.
  substantial, doctrine of, 245–247, 249–
    254
    abandonment, and, 250
    acceptance of work, and, 376–377
    damages, effect on, 581–582
    substantially complete, failure to,
      254–255
  time for, 604–616
  vicarious, distinguished from assign-
    ment, 716–720

PERSONAL CONTRACTS,
  architects' are, 82–84, 104–105, 361,
    716–717, 738–739, 793–794
  assignment of, 717–718, 738–739
  bankruptcy, effect on, 104–105, 718,
    738–739, 775–776
  building contracts, how far, 104–105,
    360–361, 717–720, 724, 738–739,
    775–776
  death, effect of, 104–105, 360–361,
    738–739
  illness or insanity, effect of, 104–105,
    360–361, 814–815

PERSONAL CONTRACTS—*cont.*
  partnership of architects, how far,
    104–105, 793 (n.)
  specific performance of, 371
  vicarious performance of, 716–720

PLANS,
  alteration without power discharges
    guarantee, 809–810
  architect's right to retain, 189
  copyright in, 190–191
  employer's liability to pay for even
    if not used, 7, 181–182
  guarantee discharged by alteration if
    no power to vary, 809–810
  lien on, of architect, 189
  ownership of, 189–190
  retain, architect's right to, 189

PLANT,
  See under FORFEITURE, BANKRUPTCY
    AND LIQUIDATION *and* VESTING AND
    SEIZURE.

POSSESSION. *See generally* SITE.

PRELIMINARY ITEMS,
  bills of quantities, in, 169–171, 203,
    555 (n. 44)
  description of, 169–171, 203
  failure to price, effect of, 203
  variations, effect of on valuation of,
    555 (n. 44)

PRE-PLANNING,
  architect, effect on duties, 125, 132–
    141, 322–326
  drawings and instructions, effect on
    time for, 135–141, 322–326
  lack of, 125, 132–134, 199, 210–211,
    225, 564
  not possible, form of contract when,
    210–211
  specification or bills concealing lack
    of, 199

PREVENTION,
  architect, by failure to appoint, 135–
    141, 320–322, 474–475, 485–487
  bonus for expedition, of, 647–648
  certificate, how affected by employ-
    er's, 320–322, 406–411, 458–470,
    472–475
  certifier, by dismissal of, 135–141,
    320–322, 474–475, 485–487
  employer, by, effect on liquidated
    damages, 624–633
  forfeiture, how affected by em-
    ployer's, 700, 708–710
  liquidated damages released by
    employer's, 624–633
  principle of, 340–347, 700, 708–710
  See also BREACH OF CONTRACT.

PRICE, 563–578
  adjustment of,
    architect's implied power of, 484,
      515–520
    arithmetical errors, as to, 35–36.
      38, 515–521, 564–566

TORT—*cont.*
building operations,
architect's liability arising out of, 68–71
contractor's liability arising out of, 68
employer's liability arising out of, 68
claims by employer in, 80–81
completed buildings, liability arising out of, 71–72
contractor's liability in, 67–81, 592–593
dangerous or defective work, liabiility for, 71–81
employer,
claims by, in, 80–81
liability for contractor's, 68
fraud. *See* FRAUD.
limitation of action in, 370
nature of, 63–64
negligence. *See* NEGLIGENCE.
nuisance, contractor's liability for, 68
Occupier's Liability Act 1957, liability under, 75–80
sub-contractor's liability in, 66–67
third persons, liability towards, 63–81
trespass, contractor liable for, 68
See also FRAUD *and* NEGLIGENCE.

TRADE USAGE,
standard forms of contract distinguished from, 54
See generally CUSTOM.

TRADING CORPORATIONS, CONTRACTS OF, 239–240

TRUSTEE IN BANKRUPTCY. *See under* BANKRUPTCY AND LIQUIDATION.

ULTRA VIRES,
corporations, contracts of, 236
doctrine of, 236
trading corporations, contracts of, 239–240

USAGE. *See* CUSTOM.

USER. *See* VESTING AND SEIZURE.

VALUATION,
arbitration, distinguished from, 825–831
architect's duties as to, 156–159
certificate, when binding as to, 481–483, 489–494
certification, 435–449, 499–505, 825–831
final certificate, when binding as to, 489–492
interim certificate, in, 492–494
omissions, of, 557
quantity surveyor's employment for, 116–119
R.I.B.A. contract, by architect under, 489–492

VALUATION—*cont.*
skill required in, degree of, 150, 156–157
substitution of, for P.C. and provisional sums, 205
variations, of, 555–558
contra items, 557
items included in, 555–557
omissions, 557
quantity surveyor, employment of, 116–119
quantum meruit, 558
schedule rates, at, 558
See also CERTIFICATES, CERTIFIER, ESTIMATE OF COST *and* MEASUREMENT.

VARIATION OF PRICE CLAUSE. *See* FLUCTUATIONS CLAUSE.

VARIATIONS,
additional expense caused by, 327
valuation of, 555–558
additional work, contractor's right to do, 532–533
add or omit, construction of clause giving power to, 531
alteration to work not necessarily, 545–546
architect,
authority of, implied,
measure, to, 118–119
order, to, 108–110, 534
authority of, to order, 533–534
implied, 108–110, 534
duty to employer with regard to, 155, 322–326
refusal to order in writing, 541–543
appropriation of payments to, 559–562
assistance to contractor, distinguished from, 524–529
bills of quantities,
actual quantities differing from, 509–515
standard method, failure to follow, 515–520, 565–566
valuation at rates in, 555–557, 558
work not mentioned in, 515–520
bonus provisions, effect on, 578
certificate binding as to, where, 401, 553–555
completion, effect on time for, 606–608, 624–633
concession to contractor, distinguished from, 524–529, 545–546
confirmation of, 538–539
consideration for, 19, 523–524
construction of clauses for, 531
contract for, separate, 506, 543–546
contract, of, 22–24
contract work,
contractor's right to do, 532-533
extra to, items, not ordered in writing, 548–553